Nineteenth-Century Literature Criticism

Guide to Gale Literary Criticism Series

For criticism on	Consult these Gale series
Authors now living or who died after December 31, 1959	***CONTEMPORARY LITERARY CRITICISM (CLC)***
Authors who died between 1900 and 1959	***TWENTIETH-CENTURY LITERARY CRITICISM (TCLC)***
Authors who died between 1800 and 1899	***NINETEENTH-CENTURY LITERATURE CRITICISM (NCLC)***
Authors who died between 1400 and 1799	***LITERATURE CRITICISM FROM 1400 TO 1800 (LC)*** ***SHAKESPEAREAN CRITICISM (SC)***
Authors who died before 1400	***CLASSICAL AND MEDIEVAL LITERATURE CRITICISM (CMLC)***
Authors of books for children and young adults	***CHILDREN'S LITERATURE REVIEW (CLR)***
Dramatists	***DRAMA CRITICISM (DC)***
Poets	***POETRY CRITICISM (PC)***
Short story writers	***SHORT STORY CRITICISM (SSC)***
Black writers of the past two hundred years	***BLACK LITERATURE CRITICISM (BLC)***
Hispanic writers of the late nineteenth and twentieth centuries	***HISPANIC LITERATURE CRITICISM (HLC)***
Native North American writers and orators of the eighteenth, nineteenth, and twentieth centuries	***NATIVE NORTH AMERICAN LITERATURE (NNAL)***
Major authors from the Renaissance to the present	***WORLD LITERATURE CRITICISM, 1500 TO THE PRESENT (WLC)***

ISSN 0732-1864

Volume 77

Nineteenth-Century Literature Criticism

Excerpts from Criticism of the Works of Novelists, Poets, Playwrights, Short Story Writers, Philosophers, and Other Creative Writers Who Died between 1800 and 1899, from the First Published Critical Appraisals to Current Evaluations

Suzanne Dewsbury
Editor

Detroit
San Francisco
London
Boston
Woodbridge, CT

STAFF

Suzanne Dewsbury, *Editor*
Gianna Barberi, *Associate Editor*
Janet Witalec, *Managing Editor*

Maria L. Franklin, *Permissions Manager*
Kimberly F. Smilay, *Permissions Specialist*
Kelly A. Quin, *Permissions Associate*
Erin Bealmear, Sandra K. Gore, *Permissions Assistants*

Victoria B. Cariappa, *Research Manager*
Cheryl Warnock, *Research Specialist*
Patricia T. Ballard, Wendy Festerling, Tracie A. Richardson,
Corrine Boland, *Research Associates*
Timothy Lehnerer, *Research Assistant*

Dorothy Maki, *Manufacturing Manager*
Cindy Range, *Buyer*

Gary Leach, *Graphic Artist*
Randy Bassett, *Image Database Supervisor*
Robert Duncan, Michael Logusz, *Imaging Specialists*
Pamela A. Reed, *Imaging Coordinator*

This book is printed on acid-free paper that meets the minimum requirements of American National Standard for Information Sciences—Permanence Paper for Printed Library Materials, ANSI Z39.48-1984.

Library of Congress Catalog Card Number 84-643008
ISBN 0-7876-1671-0
ISSN 0732-1864
Printed in the United States of America

10 9 8 7 6 5 4 3 2 1

Contents

Preface

Since its inception in 1981, *Nineteenth-Century Literature Criticism* has been a valuable resource for students and librarians seeking critical commentary on writers of this transitional period in world history. Designated an "Outstanding Reference Source" by the American Library Association with the publication of its first volume, *NCLC* has since been purchased by over 6,000 school, public, and university libraries. The series has covered more than 300 authors representing 29 nationalities and over 17,000 titles. No other reference source has surveyed the critical reaction to nineteenth-century authors and literature as thoroughly as *NCLC*.

Scope of the Series

NCLC is designed to introduce students and advanced readers to the authors of the nineteenth century, and to the most significant interpretations of these authors' works. The great poets, novelists, short story writers, playwrights, and philosophers of this period are frequently studied in high school and college literature courses. By organizing and reprinting commentary written on these authors, *NCLC* helps students develop valuable insight into literary history, promotes a better understanding of the texts, and sparks ideas for papers and assignments. Each entry in *NCLC* presents a comprehensive survey of an author's career or an individual work of literature and provides the user with a multiplicity of interpretations and assessments. Such variety allows students to pursue their own interests; furthermore, it fosters an awareness that literature is dynamic and responsive to many different opinions.

Every fourth volume of *NCLC* is devoted to literary topics that cannot be covered under the author approach used in the rest of the series. Such topics include literary movements, prominent themes in nineteenth-century literature, literary reaction to political and historical events, significant eras in literary history, prominent literary anniversaries, and the literatures of cultures that are often overlooked by English-speaking readers.

NCLC continues the survey of criticism of world literature begun by Gale's *Contemporary Literary Criticism (CLC)* and *Twentieth-Century Literary Criticism (TCLC),* both of which excerpt and reprint commentary on authors of the twentieth century. For additional information about *TCLC, CLC,* and Gale's other criticism series, users should consult the Guide to Gale Literary Criticism Series preceding the title page in this volume.

Coverage

Each volume of *NCLC* is carefully compiled to present:

- criticism of authors, or literary topics, representing a variety of genres and nationalities
- both major and lesser-known writers and literary works of the period
- 4-8 authors or 4-6 topics per volume
- individual entries that survey critical response to an author's work or a topic in literary history, including early criticism to reflect initial reactions, later criticism to represent any rise or decline in reputation, and current retrospective analyses.

Organization

An author entry consists of the following elements: author heading, biographical and critical introduction, list of principal works, excerpts of criticism (each preceded by a bibliographic citation and an annotation), and a bibliography of further reading.

- The **Author Heading** consists of the name under which the author most commonly wrote, followed by birth and death dates. If an author wrote consistently under a pseudonym, the pseudonym will be listed in the author heading and the real name given in parentheses on the first line of the biographical and critical introduction. Also located at the beginning of the introduction to the author entry are any name variations under which an author wrote, including transliterated forms for an author whose language uses a nonroman alphabet.

- The **Biographical and Critical Introduction** outlines the author's life and career, as well as the critical issues surrounding his or her work. References are provided to past volumes of *NCLC* in which further information about the author may be found.

- Most *NCLC* entries include a **Portrait** of the author. Many entries also contain reproductions of materials pertinent to an author's career, including manuscript pages, title pages, dust jackets, letters, and drawings, as well as photographs of important people, places, and events in an author's life.

- The list of **Principal Works** is chronological by date of first publication and identifies the genre of each work. In the case of foreign authors with both foreign-language publications and English translations, the English-language version is given in brackets. Unless otherwise indicated, dramas are dated by first performance, not first publication.

- **Criticism** in each author entry is arranged chronologically to provide a perspective on changes in critical evaluation over the years. All titles of works by the author featured in the entry are printed in boldface type to enable the user to easily locate discussion of particular works. Also for purposes of easier identification, the critic's name and the publication date of the essay are given at the beginning of each piece of criticism. Unsigned criticism is preceded by the title of the journal in which it appeared. Publication information (such as publisher names and book prices) and some parenthetical numerical references (such as page and line references to specific editions of works) have been deleted at the editors' discretion to provide smoother reading of the text. Footnotes that appear with previously published pieces of criticism are reprinted at the end of each essay or excerpt. In the case of excerpted criticism, only those footnotes that pertain to the excerpted text are included.

- A complete **Bibliographic Citation** provides original publication information for each piece of criticism.

- Critical excerpts are prefaced by **Annotations** providing the reader with a summary of the critical intent of the piece. Also included, when appropriate, is information about the critic's reputation, individual approach to literary criticism, and particular expertise in an author's works, as well as information about the relative importance of the critical excerpt. In some cases, the annotations cross-reference excerpts by critics who discuss each other's commentary.

- An annotated list of **Further Reading** appearing at the end of each entry suggests secondary sources on the author. In some cases it includes essays for which the editors could not obtain reprint rights.

Cumulative Indexes

- Each volume of *NCLC* contains a cumulative **Author Index** listing all authors who have appeared in Gale's Literary Criticism Series, along with cross-references to such biographical series as *Contemporary Authors* and *Dictionary of Literary Biography.* Useful for locating authors within the various series, this index is particularly valuable for those authors who are identified with a certain period but who, because of their death dates, are placed in another, or for those authors whose careers span two periods. For example, Fyodor Dostoevsky is found in *NCLC,* yet Leo Tolstoy, another major nineteenth-century Russian novelist, is found in *TCLC* because he died after 1899.

- Each *NCLC* volume includes a cumulative **Nationality Index** which lists all authors who have appeared in *NCLC*, arranged alphabetically under their respective nationalities.

- Each new volume in Gale's Literary Criticism Series includes a cumulative **Topic Index**, which lists all literary topics treated in *NCLC, TCLC, LC 1400-1800*, and the *CLC* Yearbook.

- Each new volume of *NCLC*, with the exception of the Topics volumes, contains a **Title Index** listing the titles of all literary works discussed in the volume. In response to numerous suggestions from librarians, Gale has also produced a **Special Paperbound Edition** of the *NCLC* title index. This annual cumulation lists all titles discussed in the series since its inception. Additional copies of the index are available on request. Librarians and patrons have welcomed this separate index: it saves shelf space, is easy to use, and is recyclable upon receipt of the following year's cumulation. Titles discussed in the Topics volume entries are not included in the *NCLC* cumulative index.

Citing *Nineteenth-Century Literature Criticism*

When writing papers, students who quote directly from any volume in Gale's Literary Criticism Series may use the following general forms to footnote reprinted criticism. The first example pertains to material drawn from periodicals, the second to material reprinted from books:

[1]Kim McQuaid, "William Apes, Pequot: An Indian Reformer in the Jackson Era," *The New England Quarterly*, 50 (December 1977), 605-25; excerpted and reprinted in *Nineteenth-Century Literature Criticism,* Vol. 73, ed. Janet Witalec (Farmington Hills, Mich.: The Gale Group, 1999), pp. 3-4.

[2]Richard Harter Fogle, *The Imagery of Keats and Shelley: A Comparative Study* (Archon Books, 1949); excerpted and reprinted in *Nineteenth-Century Literary Criticism,* Vol. 73, ed. Janet Witalec (Farmington Hills, Mich.: The Gale Group, 1999), pp. 157-69.

Suggestions Are Welcome

In response to suggestions, several features have been added to *NCLC* since the series began, including annotations to excerpted criticism, a cumulative index to authors in all Gale literary criticism series, entries devoted to criticism on a single work by a major author, more illustrations, and a title index listing all literary works discussed in the series.

Readers who wish to suggest authors, single works, or topics to appear in future volumes, or who have other suggestions, are cordially invited to write: The Editors, *Nineteenth-Century Literature Criticism,* The Gale Group, 27500 Drake Rd., Farmington Hills, MI 48331-3535; call toll-free at 1-800-347-GALE.

Acknowledgments

The editors wish to thank the copyright holders of the excerpted criticism included in this volume and the permissions managers of many book and magazine publishing companies for assisting us in securing reproduction rights. We are also grateful to the staffs of the Detroit Public Library, the Library of Congress, the University of Detroit Mercy Library, Wayne State University Purdy/Kresge Library Complex, and the University of Michigan Libraries for making their resources available to us. Following is a list of the copyright holders who have granted us permission to reproduce material in this volume of *NCLC*. Every effort has been made to trace copyright, but if omissions have been made, please let us know.

COPYRIGHTED MATERIALS IN *NCLC*, VOLUME 77, WERE REPRODUCED FROM THE FOLLOWING PERIODICALS:

American Literature, v. 32, January, 1961; v. 60, March, 1988; v. 60, December, 1988. Copyright © 1961, 1988 Duke University Press, Durham, NC. All reproduced by permission.—***American Transcendental Quarterly***, v. 1, September, 1987. Copyright 1987 by Kenneth Walter Cameron. Reproduced by permission.—***Dickinson Studies***, v. 77, 1st half, 1991, for "Dickinson and the Process of Death" by Paula Hendrickson. Reproduced by permission.—***ESQ: A Journal of The American Renaissance***, v. 34, 1988, for "Welcome and Beware: The Reader and Emily Dickinson's Figurative Language," by Karen Oakes Kilcup; v. 40, 1994, for "'He Asked If I Was His': The Seductions of Emily Dickinson," by R. McClure Smith. Both reproduced by permission of the publisher and the respective authors.—***Journal of the Folklore Institute***, v. 1, December, 1964. Reproduced by permission.—***New German Critique***, v. 9, Fall, 1982, © New German Critique, Inc. All rights reserved. Reproduced by permission.—***New York Folklore Quarterly***, v. 27, March, 1971 for "Richard Harris Barham and His Use of Folklore," by David J. Winslow. Reproduced by permission of the publisher and author.—***Nineteenth-Century Fiction***, v. 10, September, 1955. © 1955, renewed 1983 by The Regents of the University of California. Reproduced by permission of the Regents.—***Papers on Language & Literature***, Vol. 23, No. 3, 1987. Copyright © 1987 by The Board of Trustees, Southern Illinois University. Reprinted by permission.—***Parnassus: Poetry in Review***, v. 15, 1989 for "Her Moment of Brocade: The Reconstruction of Emily Dickinson." © 1989 Alice Fulton. All rights reserved. Reproduced by permission of the author.—***Social Research***, v. 35, Autumn, 1968. Copyright 1968 by New School for Social Research. Reproduced by permission of the publisher.—***University of Dayton Review***, v. 19, Winter 1987-1988. Reproduced by permission.—***The Victorian Newsletter***, 1990 for "Behind Golden Barriers: Framing and Taming the Blessed Damozel" by Andrew Leng. Reproduced by permission of publisher and the author.—***Victorian Poetry***, v.V, Spring, 1967 for "Rossetti's A Last Confession: A Dramatic Monologue" Ronnalie Roper Howard; v. 17, Autumn, 1979 for "Political Themes in the Work of Dante Gabriel Rossetti" by D.M.R. Bentley; v. 20, Autumn-Winter, 1982 for "The Blessed Damozel: A Young Man's Fantasy," by D.M.R. Bentley; v. 22, Summer, 1984 for "D.G. Rossetti's Jenny: Sex, Money, and the Interior Monologue" by Daniel A. Harris; v. 26, Winter, 1988 for "Dante Gabriel Rossetti and the Betrayal of Truth" by Jerome McGann; v. 29, Winter, 1991 for "The Mirror's Secret: Dante Gabriel Rossetti's Double Work of Art" by J. Hillis Miller; v. 30, Summer, 1992 for "Rossetti's On the field of Waterloo: An Intertextual Reading" by Ernest Fontana. © West Virginia University, 1967, 1979, 1982, 1984, 1988, 1991, 1992. Reproduced by permission of respective authors.

COPYRIGHTED MATERIALS IN *NCLC*, VOLUME 77, WERE REPRODUCED FROM THE FOLLOWING BOOKS:

Bann, Stephen. From ***The Clothing of Clio: A Study of Representation of History in Nineteenth-Century Britain and France***. Cambridge University Press, 1984. Reproduced with the permission of Cambridge University Press and the author.—Bennett, Paula. From "The Pea That Duty Locks: Lesbian and Feminist-Heterosexual Readings of Emily Dickinson's Poetry" in ***Lesbian Texts and Contexts: Radical Revisions***. Edited by Karla Jay and Joanne Glasgow. New York University Press, 1990. © 1990 by Karla Jay and Joanne Glasgow. All rights reserved. Reproduced by permission of Karla Jay.—Buckingham, Willis. From "Poetry Readers and Reading in the 1890's: Emily Dickinson's First Reception" in ***Readers in History: Nineteenth-Century American Literature and the Contexts of Response***. Edited by James L. Machor. Johns Hopkins University Press, 1993. © 1993 The Johns Hopkins University Press. All rights reserved. Reproduced by permission of The Johns Hopkins University Press.—Eberwein, Jane Donahue. From ***Dickinson: Strategies of Limitation***. Amherst: University of Massachusetts Press, 1985. © 1985 by the University of Massachusetts Press. All rights reserved. Reproduced by permission.—Ellis, John M. From ***One Fairy Story Too Many: The Brothers Grimm and Their Tales***. University of Chicago Press, 1983. © 1983 by the University of Chicago Press. All rights reserved. Reproduced by permission.—Haase, Donald. From "Response and Responsibility in Reading Grimms' Fairy Tales" in ***The Reception of Grimms' Fairy Tales: Responses, Reactions, Revisions***. Edited by Donald Haase. Wayne State University Press. © 1993 by Wayne State University Press, Detroit, Michigan 48202. All rights reserved. Reproduced by permission of the publisher and the author.—Harrison, Anthony H. From ***Victorian Poets and Romantic Poems: Intertextuality and Ideology***. University Press of Virginia, 1990. © 1990 by the Rector and Visitors of the University of Virginia. Reproduced by permission.—Kamenetsky, Christa. From ***The Brothers Grimm and Their Critics***. Ohio University Press, 1992. © 1992 by Christa Kamenetsky. Reproduced by permission.—Lane, William G. From ***Richard Harris Barham***. University of Missouri Press, 1967. © 1967 by The Curators of the University of Missouri. Reproduced by permission.—Maria M. Tatar. From "Born Yesterday: Heroes in the Grimms' Fairy Tales" in ***Fairy Tales and Society: Illusion, Allusion, and Paradigm***. Edited by Ruth B. Bottigheimer. University of Pennsylvania Press, 1986. © 1986 by the University of Pennsylvania Press. All rights reserved. Reproduced by permission.—McGowan, John P. From "The Bitterness of Things Occult: D.G. Rossetti's Search for the Real" in ***Critical Essays on Dante Gabriel Rossetti***. Edited by Zack Bowen. G. K. Hall & Co., 1992. © 1992 by David G. Riede. All rights reserved. Reproduced by permission.—Miller, Christanne. From ***Emily Dickinson: A Poet's Grammar***. Harvard University Press, 1987. © 1987 by the President and Fellows of Harvard College. All rights reserved. Reproduced by permission.—Snyder, Louis L. From ***Roots of German Nationalism***. Indiana University Press, 1978. © 1978 Louis L. Snyder. Reproduced by permission.—Walker, Cheryl. From "Locating a Feminist Critical Practice: Between the Kingdom and the Glory," in ***Emily Dickinson: A Celebration for Readers***. Edited by Suzanne Juhasz and Cristanne Miller. Gordon and Breach, 1989. © 1989 by Gordon and Breach, Science Publishers, Inc. and Gordon and Breach Science Publishers S.A. All rights reserved. Reproduced by permission.—Zipes, Jack. From ***Fairy Tales and the Art of Subversion: The Classical Genre for Children and the Process of Civilization***. Heinemann Educational Books Ltd, 1983. © Jack Zipes 1983. Reproduced by permission.

PHOTOGRAPHS AND ILLUSTRATIONS APPEARING IN *NCLC,* VOLUME 77, WERE RECEIVED FROM THE FOLLOWING SOURCES:

Dickinson, Emily, photograph of a painting. The Library of Congress.—Grimm, Wilhelm and Jacob, photograph. The Library of Congress.—Heinze, Mitchell, illustrator. From a cover of *Selected Poems of Emily Dickinson*, by Emily Dickinson. Tor Books, 1993. Reproduced by permission.—A title page for *The Ingoldsby Legends* by Thomas Ingoldsby, 1919 edition, photograph. The Department of Rare Books and Special Collections, The University of Michigan Library. Reproduced by permission.—Richard Harris Barham (1788-1845), engraving. Archive Photos. Reproduced by permission —Rossetti, Dante G., photograph. The Bettmann Archives, Inc.. Reproduced by permission.—"Snow White" (holding poison apple), in the animated film *Snow White and the Seven Dwarfs*, 1937, photograph. The Kobal Collection. Reproduced by permission.

Richard Harris Barham

1788-1845

English novelist and humorist.

INTRODUCTION

An English writer and cleric, Barham is known primarily for his ghost stories and tales of the supernatural collectively entitled *Ingoldsby Legends.* Written in skillful, lively rhyming verse, the stories have delighted generations of English school children, as well as adults, many of whom committed the comical and gruesome tales to memory. Although the stories began to fall out of favor by the 1920s, Barham is considered one of the most inventive and witty authors of light, humorous rhyme of the Victorian age.

Biography

Barham was born December 6, 1788, in Canterbury to Richard Harris Barham, a country squire, and Elizabeth Fox, his housekeeper. When Barham was a boy his father died, leaving him the heir to the family home. Under his guardians' care, Barham was well educated, first at St. Paul's in London, where he befriended Richard Bentley and, later, at Oxford, where he met Thomas Hook. At the age of fourteen, Barham was severely injured in a stagecoach accident and never regained complete use of one arm. After earning a Bachelor's Degree at Brasenose College, Barham decided to pursue Holy Orders and in March, 1813, he was established in his first church in Kent. A year later he moved to Westwell Parish where he met and wed Caroline Smart, with whom he would have several children. Three years later the family moved to Snargate in Romney Marsh where the family remained until they moved to London in April, 1821. Barham was injured again in an accident and, while recovering, wrote his first novel, *Baldwin; or, a Miser's Heir* (1820), and started on his second, *Some Account of My Cousin Nicholas; To Which Is Added, The Rubber of Life* (1841.) Neither novel was successful. After moving to London, Barham secured a minor canonry at St. Paul's and, in his spare time, entered the literary world, reacquainting himself with Bentley and Hook and meeting Charles Dickens and Sidney Smith. Almost immediately, Barham began to contribute reviews and then stories to various publications. In October, 1822, the *London Chronicle* serialized his story "The Ghost" the first of his Ingoldsby Legends. In February, 1837, Barham published "The Spectre of Tappington," using the pseudonym "Thomas Ingoldsby" for the first time. The tales became popular, contributing to the success of the journal *Bentley's Miscellaneous* in which most were published. Two collected volumes of the tales entitled *The Ingoldsby Legends* were printed in 1840 and 1842. All the while, Barham performed his duties within the Church of England successfully and was well liked by his parishioners. He advanced in the Church, rising to Vicar of St. Augustine and St. Faith Parish in London in 1842 and serving as president of Sion College, an institution for Anglican clergy. After a prolonged illness, Barham died on June 17, 1845. His son published a third volume of *Ingoldsby Legends* after his father's death.

Major Works

Although Barham published two novels and many reviews, he is known primarily for his *Ingoldsby Legends,* a series of ghost stories which are loosely bound by a common setting and family. Most, although not all, of the approximately seventy stories are written in rhyming verse and many are set at Tappington Everend, based on Barham's family home. In these stories, the characters commit crimes such as murder, adultery, abuse, and dismemberment, and they are punished for the crimes in grisly ways. They, as well as more innocent characters, encounter ghosts, are buried alive, mystified, tormented, and terrified. However, Barham infused the tales with humor and even the concluding moral tales seem to be in jest. Barham based many of the stories on folktales imparted to him by Mary Ann Hughes, who maintained an extensive correspondence with many people, including Sir Walter Scott. Barham based other tales on folklore and medieval history which he encountered in his reading. Among his best known stories are: "The Grey Dolphin," "The Spectre of Tappington," and "Legend of Hamilton Tighe."

Critical Reception

Despite the popularity of the *Ingoldsby Legends,* Barham has not elicited much critical attention. The greatest controversy surrounding his work occurred in 1844 when Richard Hengist Horne published a series of essays entitled *A New Spirit of the Age.* In one of these essays, Horne criticized Barham's tales, claiming they appealed to the baser side of human nature, relied upon cheap wit and slang, and were a bad influence on youth. Critics of the day rallied to Barham's aid, defending the stories for their humor and entertainment. Since Barham's death, critics have been interested in the author's skill at turning folktales into humourous, popular stories. David J. Winslow claims, "all Barham needed was the germ of an idea or story . . . to set in motion his genius and to bring laughter by his artistic remodeling and imaginative treatment of the original." Winslow compares Barham's skill at transforming folktales to that of Alfred, Lord Tennyson, Edmund Spenser, and Nathaniel Hawthorne. Finally, critics note the skill with which Barham employed rhyme and humor in his stories. William Lane states that Barham's position "as a delightful humorist appeared incontrovertible," and that the author continues to entertain readers more than a century after his death. Wendell V. Harris credits Barham with being "the first consistent English writer of the true short story."

PRINCIPAL WORKS

Baldwin; or, a Miser's Heir (novel) 1820
The Ingoldsby Legends, or Mirth and Marvels (prose poem) 1840
Some Account of My Cousin Nicholas; To Which Is Added the Rubber of Life (novel) 1841
The Ingoldsby Legends: Second Series (prose poem) 1842
The Ingoldsby Legends: Third Series (prose poem) 1847

CRITICISM

Malcolm Elwin (essay date 1934)

SOURCE: "Wallflower the Third: 'Ingoldsby,' " in *Victorian Wallflowers,* Kennikat Press, 1934, reissued 1966, pp. 128-53.

[*In the essay that follows, Elwin places Barham's work within the context of Victorian literature.*]

When, following the foundation of *Fraser,* Thomas Campbell and Cyrus Redding shook the dust of Colburn's office from their shoes, they soon afterwards undertook the editorial of a new magazine, the *Metropolitan,* issued by a publisher named Cochrane. Campbell was an instance of a writer who succeeded early in building a high reputation, which he failed to consolidate because he feared that, by writing below his own standard, he might pull himself down from his own pedestall. As Scott remarked in 1826, 'he wants audacity, fears the public, and what is worse, fears the shadow of his own reputation'. Describing him as 'an idle man—an abstracted man', Redding recognized that he was 'not the man to lead in anything bold or novel, either in literary or political writing'; Talfourd, another colleague, considered him, for the editorial function, 'the most unfit person who could be found in the wide world of letters'; Maginn shrewdly put into his mouth the editorial dictum of 'never let anything go into your Magazine that has the least chance of being displeasing to anyone whatever'.[1] He finally retired from journalism when Cochrane, tiring much more quickly than Colburn of his timidity and pusillanimity, sold the *Metropolitan,* after eighteen months, to Captain Marryatt.

The *Metropolitan* never entered upon serious competition with the brilliant and militant *Fraser,* Marryatt using it merely as a vehicle of publicity for his own writings. Its importance in journalistic history rests on the fact that it was the first magazine to rely for its circulation on the work and reputation of a single individual writer. Marryatt, in fact, revolutionized magazine policy by promoting the serial story, which had been hitherto sparingly exploited both in *Blackwood* and *Fraser,* to the position of being the main feature of interest and attraction. A quarter of a century later, George Smith founded the *Cornhill* with the primary idea of similarly exploiting Thackeray's work and reputation, and Colburn was influenced by Marryatt's example when, in 1836, he appointed Theodore Hook as editor of the *New Monthly.*

Hook was now at the height of his reputation; it was at this time that Thackeray knew him and derived the impressions crystallized in 'Mr. Wagg'. Regarded as the brightest wit of the age, his broad, humorous, red face and proportionately broad white waistcoat were familiar sights in every club and fashionable assembly. He had now considerable reputation as a popular novelist, as well as for his social wit and humorous writings, and Colburn, having allowed his magazine to jog along in humdrum mediocrity under the direction of Samuel Carter Hall since Bulwer's resignation, now hoped to renew its vitality with the lustre of Hook's reputation and by featuring his novels as serials. Quite content to be boosted by his publisher in return for the advertisement of his name, Hook, like Campbell before him, left the real work of editing the magazine to a subordinate. Hall, resentful of being superseded for the second time, having resigned, the energetic John Forster undertook the business of management; as Thackeray relates, 'Mr. Bole' was 'the real editor of the magazine of which Mr. Wagg was the nominal chief'.

As Colburn was the original Mr. Bacon of *Pendennis,* the prototype of his rival, Mr. Bungay, was Richard Bentley. In 1829, Colburn took Bentley into partnership and soon afterwards sold his flourishing business to him. Here Thackeray utilizes the novelist's licence to lend romantic colour to their relations, the breaking of the partnership between Bacon and Bungay being ascribed to the strife between their wives, each having married the other's sister. Nevertheless, there was definitely rancour in the rivalry between the erstwhile partners when they became competitors. Bentley, a hard bargainer and an adept in drawing up contracts profitable to himself,[1] obtained in the deed of purchase a promise from Colburn that he would not recommence the business of publishing in London. But, like an old soldier, the elder publisher yearned in retirement for the familiar smell of powder and soon reopened business in opposition to Bentley.

The character of their competition is not exaggerated by Thackeray.

> 'Since they have separated, it is a furious war between the two publishers; and no sooner does one bring out a book of travels, or poems, a magazine or periodical, quarterly, or monthly, or weekly, or annual, but the rival is in the field with something similar. I have heard poor Shandon tell with great glee how he made Bungay give a grand dinner at Blackwall to all his writers, by saying that Bacon had invited his corps to an entertainment at Greenwich. When Bungay engaged your celebrated friend Mr. Wagg to edit the *Londoner,* Bacon straightaway rushed off and secured Mr. Grindle to give his name to the *Westminster Magazine.* When Bacon brought out his comic Irish novel of "Barney Brallagan", off went Bungay to Dublin, and produced his rollicking Hibernian story of "Looney Mac Twolter". When Doctor Hicks brought out his "Wanderings in Mesopotamia" under Bacon's auspices, Bungay produced Professor Sandiman's "Researches in Zahara"; and Bungay is publishing his *Pall Mall Gazette* as a counterpoise to Bacon's *Whitehall Review.*'

So when Colburn secured Hook's services for the *New Monthly,* Bentley immediately conceived the ambition of starting a magazine in opposition. Though Colburn commanded the biggest guns among the novelists—Bulwer, Marryatt, Disraeli, Hook, Horace Smith, and G. P. R. James—Bentley published the earliest successes of Harrison Ainsworth, Dickens, and Lover, and he shrewdly decided to recruit his magazine team from promising new writers on the threshold of their reputations. He evinced enterprise and astute judgment in engaging as editor, in August 1836, Charles Dickens, whose *Pickwick Papers,* still in their early numbers, were just taking hold of the public and about to lift their author from obscurity to fame. Dickens accepted his offer of twenty pounds a month to edit the magazine, and agreed to supply two serial stories at £500 each. The first of these was *Oliver Twist,* which, following upon the success of *Pickwick,* procured for the magazine such popularity that the publisher gladly increased his editor's salary to thirty pounds a month and the price of the serials to £750 each. Even so, by the time *Oliver Twist* had run its course and Dickens had become the best-selling novelist of his day, such payment was utterly indequate, and Bentley was compelled to offer four thousand pounds for the second serial, *Barnaby Rudge.* Hard pressed by work and reluctant to risk injury to his reputation by hasty writing, Dickens requested a respite of six months before commencing publication of the new story. To this Bentley refused to agree as, without the star attraction of Dickens's serial, the sales of the magazine must have shown a serious decline, and Dickens thereupon resigned the editorship, in which he was succeeded by Harrison Ainsworth.

Ainsworth, who had become a best-selling novelist with *Rookwood* in 1834, was among the earliest contributors to the magazine. As publisher of their novels, Bentley naturally relied upon his allegiance and that of Samuel Lover, and he successfully poached upon the preserves of *Fraser* and the *New Monthly* by securing as contributors Maginn and 'Father Prout' from the former, and no less a person than Hook, the editor himself, from the other. It was probably Hook of whom Cruikshank relates that, on receiving from Bentley the confidence that he had changed his original idea of calling the magazine *The Wits' Miscellany,* owing to the invidiousness of the title, and decided to follow the example of *Fraser* and *Blackwood* by prefacing his own name, he replied, 'Yes, there was good reason why you should not call it *The Wits' Miscellany,* but why go to the *opposite extreme?'*

It is interesting to compare the opening number of *Bentley's Miscellany,* which appeared in January 1837, with the first of *Fraser,* issued seven years earlier. At a first glance, *Bentley* appears to be directing its appeal to a lower class of readers. Apart from Maginn's 'Prologue', the most serious article is Hook's reminiscences of the dramatist, George Colman, and the only verse is the light, humorous stuff of 'Father Prout'. With the first instalment of Lover's *Handy Andy,* which ran concurrently with *Oliver Twist,* the latter beginning in the second number, and short stories by Thomas Love Peacock, Fenimore Cooper, Marryatt, and 'Boz', the prevalence of fiction is the most arresting feature, while a glance at *Fraser* reveals as equally remarkable the absence of provocative reviewing. The difference signifies the change of taste and fashion. Henceforth, fiction and 'light reading' comprised the province of the magazine, and reviewers like Lockhart and Maginn were compelled to seek a market mainly in the more serious literary and political weekly journals.

The success of *Blackwood* and *Fraser* had been due to the sensationalism of satiric lampooning, the vigorous style of reviewing, and the originality of political, literary, and social comment. The success of *Bentley's Miscellany* was mainly owed to the serial publication of several brilliantly successful novels. After *Oliver Twist* and *Handy Andy,* followed Ainsworth's *Jack Sheppard* and *Guy Fawkes,* Henry Cockton's *Stanley Thorn,* and Albert Smith's *Adventures of Mr. Ledbury* and *Fortunes of the Scattergood Family.* Apart from novels and stories, the illustrations of Cruikshank, Crowquill, and Leech, and a few poems by Longfellow, the only other popular contributions were the humorous and satirical verse of 'Father Prout', such as he had formerly written for *Fraser,* and the ***Ingoldsby Legends.***

'Family Stories, by Thomas Ingoldsby' began in the second number with ***The Spectre of Tappington,*** which was followed by the ***Legend of Hamilton Tighe, Grey Dolphin, The Squire's Story, The Execution,*** and others, continuing over a period of years. Even Dickens was at first unaware of the identity of his contributor, for as late as the end of April 1837, the author told a friend that to 'that very funny fellow' Boz, 'I am only known as a veritable Mr. Ingoldsby'. Bentley, of course, knew the secret, though by special arrangement, as the author declared, his copy 'goes at once from me to the printer, and is returned in proof to him without any intermediate channel'. But, as Ingoldsby's biographer[2] relates, the popularity of the legends 'rendered the pseudonym he had for obvious reasons assumed a very insufficient disguise, and, though he never entirely abandoned it, he was soon pretty generally known to be their author'. So the secret was out, and the inquisitive reading public, hoping for a sensational disclosure as dramatic as in the case of the author of *Waverley,* doubtless felt only a curious interest and considerable disappointment on learning that Ingoldsby was merely a minor canon of St. Paul's Cathedral. Quiet and unobtrusive, he made no figure in the fashionable literary world of Ainsworth and Bulwer. The manner in which he began to be noticed is instanced by an entry in the diary of Thomas Moore after he had attended a dinner at Bentley's house in New Burlington Street, where the publisher gave literary parties such as that of Mr. Bungay's attended by Pendennis.

> 'November 21st, 1838. Dined at Bentley's: the company all the very *haut ton* of the literature of the day. First (to begin *low* in the scale) myself, then Mr. Jerdan of *The Literary Gazette,* then Mr. Ainsworth, then Mr. Lover, then Luttrell, and lastly "Boz" (Dickens) and Campbell . . . Our host very courteous and modest, and the conversation rather agreeable. Lover sang . . . Forgot, by the bye, one of the cleverest fellows, Barham, the Minor Canon. . . . '

The Rev. Richard Harris Barham had been in London some sixteen years, and during all that time, he had been in the habit of making occasional contributions to journalism. He had done nothing of note, however, and before the appearance of the legends, his most ambitious work had been a serial tale in *Blackwood's Magazine.* His life, indeed, had been that of a fashionable clergyman, with a taste for literature and the conversation of literary men; he loved the anecdotes of the dinner-table, told over the consumption of excellent port, and liked to call on his friends and, finding them out, to leave little messages in doggerel verse improvised on the spur of the moment. Eagerly he took advantage of the social avenues opened to him by his professional position: he enjoyed good wine and gossip—not scandal, but the rumours and news of the world of letters. Preferring mythology to theology and a squib to a sermon, he fulfilled his official functions competently and conscientiously, preserving a more truly Christian spirit than many an enthusiastic ecclesiastic. With a strong sense of humour, tolerant, witty, and amusing, he was a congenial companion and a good friend.

Born December 6th, 1788, of good old Kentish stock, at Canterbury, he was the only son of an old-fashioned country squire, who, though of superior intellectual equipment to the standard of his class, preferred his port to activity, either mental or physical, and achieved the enormous weight of twenty-seven stone before his fiftieth year. Probably this abnormal obesity hastened his end, for he died when his son was seven, leaving him the 'moderate estate, somewhat encumbered', of Tappington Everard. We are warned by Barham's biographer to dismiss as 'pardonable myths' the 'shaded avenue, terminating in a lodge, whose gates support the Ingoldsby device', together with Mrs. Botherby and the secret passage, but the Tappington Everard of fact was indeed the 'antiquated but commodious manor-house' of fiction, with a variety of archaeological interest and legendary history. In this environment, calculated to impress the imagination of a lonely and rather studious boy, young Barham spent his childhood, and cultivated that insatiable appetite for ghost-stories and 'old wives' tales', which characterized his tastes throughout his life.

At the age of nine, he was sent to St. Paul's School, where 'he made rapid progress in the classics', though 'for mathematics he had no taste'. It was when proceeding from Tappington to town by the Dover mail that the coach overturned, and he sustained an injury to his arm, which partially crippled the limb. He was fourteen at the time. From St. Paul's he went up to Oxford, where he was a contemporary, though much the junior, of De Quincey and 'Christopher North'. At Brasenose, his career was remarkable only for a passion for the drama—if the O.U.D.S. had existed in his day, he would probably have been a president—and there was never a suggestion of his becoming a parson until he himself conceived the idea during 'the course of a short and severe illness'. Accordingly, in March, 1813, he was appointed to the curacy of Ashford, in Kent, where he remained about a year before removing to the small neighbouring parish of Westwell. On going to Westwell, he married Miss Caroline Smart, daughter of a captain in the Royal Engineers. Three years later, he received the rectory of Snargate in Romney Marsh, where he remained until, in April 1821, he was appointed to the vacant minor canonry at St. Paul's. During his sojourn at Snargate occurred only one incident of importance, which he recorded with almost comical terseness in a pocket-book:

> '*May 13, 1819.* Drove William and Dick into Ashford—overturned the gig—broke my right leg and sprained my left ankle. Mary Anne came back in the chaise with me.'

During the convalescence succeeding this injury, he wrote his first novel, called ***Baldwin,*** for which he was paid twenty pounds by the Minerva Press, which, by all accounts, made no profit by the transaction.

Having settled himself and his growing family in a house in Great Queen Street, Barham decided to increase his income—a necessary procedure in view of the expense of living in town—by essaying literary journalism. Like many literary beginners of that time, he was taken into the warm bosom of William Jerdan, the editor of the *Literary Gazette,* and also contributed to *John Bull* and the *Globe and Traveller.* These contributions consisted, except for an occasional review, entirely of verse, and cannot have supplied that addition to his income which he desired. Very soon, however, he obtained the more profitable but laborious privilege of editing the *London Chronicle,* a position he held until, a year or two later, the journal was amalgamated with the *St. James's Chronicle.* Referring to this connection in his journal, Barham remarked: 'Of this journal Dr. Johnson was the first editor, and I the last. The causes of its decline may be inferred. Colonel Torrens, the proprietor, sold it to Mr. C. Baldwin for £300'. On its ruins Baldwin founded the *Standard,* which Giffard edited with Maginn's assistance.

His most enduring literary connection before the advent of Ingoldsby was with *Blackwood's Magazine,* to which he was probably introduced by Maginn. In the summer of 1826, ***The Ghost, a Canterbury Tale,*** which had previously appeared by instalments in the *London Chronicle,* was published in that famous periodical, and for several years afterwards, Barham not only contributed short stories of a similar type, but supplied old 'Ebony' with a certain amount of hack-work. He noted in his diary about this time:

> 'My wife goes to bed at ten, to rise at eight, and look after the children and other matrimonial duties. I sit up till three in the morning, working at rubbish for *Blackwood.* She is the slave of the ring and I of the lamp.'

So he worked for a decade, during which he suffered domestic afflictions—he had a large family, of which five failed to survive childhood—with a sturdy fortitude, and never lost his cheerful outlook on life. Rarely has a man left behind him letters and a journal so uniformly genial and benevolent in tone, so utterly destitute of malice and petty irritation, so genuinely ingenuous and unassuming. There is no acidity in the taste of his life. When he came into contact with suffering, he did not assume a heavy professional air of sanctimonious sophistry, but spoke simply and sincerely from a philosophical and delicate understanding. Speaking of the insanity of Southey's wife in a letter to his consistent correspondent, Mrs. Hughes, grandmother of the author of *Tom Brown,* he says:

> 'A heart like his does not the less speak because a strong sense of religious duty induces him to attempt to silence it. Let us hope he will be spared the additional affliction which you appear to anticipate. I should be the most ungrateful of beings if I did not sympathise with one to whom I am indebted for more comfort and resignation under calamity than to any other source save one.'

Mrs. Hughes had, it appears, shown Barham, when recently bereaved of one of his children, a letter from Southey, as is explained in an extract from one of the latter's letters to Henry Taylor late in 1834:

> 'Mrs. Hughes thought it would gratify me to peruse a letter which she had just received from one of her friends, a clergyman, who had recently suffered some domestic affliction. He said that his greatest consolation had been derived from a letter of mine which she had allowed him to transcribe some years ago, and which he verily believed had at that time saved his heart from bursting. The letter must have been written upon my dear Isabel's death . . . This made me reflect upon the difference between religious resignation and that which is generally mistaken for it, and, for immediate purpose, in no slight degree supplies its place.'

His charity was likewise truly Christian—not that which is generally mistaken for it. His biographer quotes a memorandum of 1831 showing that, when a parishioner was convicted of murder and the more fashionable of the flock immediately visited the onus of his crime upon the criminal's widow, Barham instituted a systematic defence of her character and added his own personal assurance in vindication. Such a course in the teeth of parochial opinion bespoke considerable moral courage in those days.

Barham was acquainted with most of literary London during the 'thirties. With Theodore Hook he formed a close friendship and, like many contemporaries, he recounted continually in his letters and journal the public and private 'sayings and doings' of that inimitable wit. When Hook died, writing to Bentley of that 'public calamity', he said:

> 'For myself the shadow of a shade never intervened during our long intercourse to cloud our friendship for a moment. I have seen him at times irritable, and sometimes, though rarely and only when other circumstances had combined to ruffle him, disposed to take offence with others; with myself *never!* and it is a source of sincere satisfaction to me at this moment that I cannot recall even an expression of momentary petulance that ever escaped either to the other.'

Another intimate friend was Sydney Smith, who became his colleague on his appointment to a canonry in 1831. At first, Barham, who was a Tory, 'looked upon the introduction of the great Whig wit into the chapter with some feeling of misgiving', but he soon came to appreciate his attractive personality and enjoyed many a pleasant dinner at Smith's house. Of William Jerdan, the industrious editor of the *Literary Gazette,* he always speaks with respectful regard—another evidence of his independent honesty, for men like Macready and Carlyle are too frequently found admiring private virtue only in men of manifest genius and almost entirely ignoring such as were unlikely to 'do them good'. Jerdan, like Barham, was an original member of the Garrick Club, 'a society in which actors and men of education and refinement might meet on equal and independent terms', for the opening dinner of which 'Ingoldsby' composed these lines, which were set to music as a glee and sung on the occasion:

> Let poets of superior parts
>   Consign to deathless fame
> The larceny of the Knave of Hearts,
>   Who spoiled his Royal Dame.
>
> Alack! my timid muse would quail
>   Before such thievish cubs,
> But plumes a joyous wing to hail
>   Thy birth, fair Queen of Clubs!

For ten years, Barham spent many pleasant evenings at the club with Hook, Fladgate, Lockhart, James Smith of *Rejected Addresses,* Crofton Croker, John Murray, and others, until, on Hook's death, he wrote:

> 'Mathews, Frank Bacon, poor Power, Tom Hill, and James Smith—and now Hook!—he who flung his life and spirit into the rest . . . I doubt if I shall have the courage now to enter the Garrick Club again.'

Meanwhile, Barham was writing for *Blackwood* and other less celebrated periodicals. One of his most interesting squibs, from a literary point of view, was ***The Wondrous Tale of Ikey Solomons,*** a notorious receiver of stolen goods, which was intended to parody Disraeli's *Alroy,* published in 1832. He was always collecting anecdotes of antiquarian interest and was an enthusiastic student of Sir Walter Scott's works. The author of *Waverley* he never met, though he was acquainted with Lockhart soon after the latter came to London to edit the *Quarterly;* Scott would have liked him, for they had many tastes in common. In *Blackwood* during 1834 appeared his second novel, ***My Cousin Nicholas;*** which he had begun fourteen years before, after the completion of *Baldwin,* and which he resumed at the suggestion of his correspondent, Mrs. Hughes. To the same magazine, he contributed various short stories and verses, some of which, like ***The Sheriff's Ball, Nursery Reminiscences,*** and ***The Country Seat,*** were afterwards included in the collected edition of ***The Ingoldsby Legends.*** These writings were of sufficient interest to suggest that their author was a decidedly useful magazine writer, and accordingly Bentley, when pursuing the project of his *Miscellany,* applied to Barham for a promise of his assistance. The result of the application was the invention of 'Thomas Ingoldsby' and the contribution of the legends.

The idea of 'Ingoldsby' was no premeditated and carefully elaborated project; it arose simply out of Barham's desire to oblige Bentley and his keen interest in the new magazine. He exerted such influence as he possessed to procure the right sort of support for the venture, and writing to Bentley to tell him that he has hopes that the poet Moore may write something for him, he supplies the key to the manner in which 'Ingoldsby' came into being.

> 'A scheme has come into my head, which I will mention to you when we meet! . . . I hope you will come out strong this time, as in my mind all depends on it; but I do not know of a single article but my own, which to whatever other faults it may possess will, I fear, add that of being too long. Indeed, I was afraid of that before, and did cut it as much as I could to leave it intelligible. If it tells, I have a plan for the rest, by means of making *Tom Ingoldsby,* your correspondent, and some of the other characters, actors in the by-play, serve as pegs on which to hang the stories. If it is a miss, I shall drop the whole party. I am the more doubtful, as it is my *coup d'essai* in this style, but they tell me it will pass muster.'

The article of 'my own' was, of course, ***The Spectre of Tappington,*** which is the subject of another note to Bentley:

> 'I send you the whole of the ***Tappington Spectre,*** the last page or two is rough, for I am really too unwell to make a fair copy, and, as the month is running out, it is better to let you have it so than to wait another day. It is all right in essentials, though a sentence or two may be better turned in the proofs. Let me have them as soon as you can . . . I have got a very good link to keep the stories together, and, as you will see, throw out a hint there anent in the close of the narrative.'

The success of the legends was instantaneous and did much to establish the prosperity of the magazine. They were eagerly and greedily read; the identity of 'Ingoldsby' was the burning question of the day.

But Barham's head was not turned. He was now too old to be easily intoxicated by the noise of applause. Probably his sense of humour would in any event have prevented any assumption of pretentious vanity, but his native modesty definitely did so. In a postscript to Bentley, he says of ***The Witches' Frolic:***

> 'I am glad the ***Frolic*** pleases you. I have certainly heard, in two or three quarters, where nothing is known about the author, that it tells; but Cruikshank's illustrations would make a worse thing go down.'

He appears to have taken as much pride in the progress of the periodical as in his own personal success, and he did not relax his efforts to secure the services of celebrated writers—possibly potential rivals for his own popularity—for his publisher. There is an abundance of evidence, including a letter of Harrison Ainsworth's, written at the time of the difference between himself and Bentley which ended in his resignation of the editorship, that Barham acted as a literary adviser as far as the *Miscellany* was concerned. His own letters are full of criticisms and suggestions which, when writing to Bentley, he often promises to expound at length when they meet at the Garrick Club. Warning Bentley that he has taken 'a plunge in *Joe Grimaldi's Life* at the outset', he points out that 'Boz' had declared 'Old Grimaldi came to England with Queen Charlotte as her dentist, in 1760!—Why the play-bills at the Garrick will tell you that he played in the farce of *The Miller* in 1753. Joe the Second's mother, too, was not Mrs. Grimaldi, but Miss Brooker, the dancer—*Tant pis!'* He pronounced the *Secret History of the Court of England,* published in 1832 as the work of Lady Anne Hamilton and immediately suppressed, 'the most impudent forgery that I ever saw', and produced circumstantial evidence to prove that the perpetrator was 'the notorious Jack Mitford'. Bentley evidently made a practice of sending prospective publications for his opinion, and it was doubtless in accordance with this custom that Barham came to read Ainsworth's *Jack Sheppard* in proof. In view of the execration lavished upon the moral tendencies of this amazingly successful novel by such writers as John Forster and R. H. Horne, the opinion of one who was a clergyman by profession, as well as a writer, is of important interest. Ainsworth had set scriptural texts as mottoes at the head of each section of the story, and Barham, with an almost prophetic foresight, begged him to cancel them, as 'mixing up sacred texts with a work of fancy will revolt many persons who would otherwise read it with pleasure, and will afford your enemies such a handle as they will not fail to use powerfully'. Otherwise he liked the book, telling Mrs. Hughes that 'I think you will be pleased with *Jack*' and Ainsworth himself that he was looking forward 'with great eagerness' to seeing the next set of proofs.

During 1841, when Thackeray was known merely as the 'Michael Angelo Titmarsh' of *Fraser,* Barham informed Bentley in a note principally written in reference to the publication of Hook's unfinished *Peregrine Bunce:*

> 'Thackeray called here yesterday; wants to be busy, so I recommended him to treat with you for a three vol. historical novel, which he is very well inclined to do. From his reading I think he would succeed, especially if, as I suggested, it were of the Queen-Hoo Hall style, illustrated by his own woodcuts of costume, caricature, etc., in the livelier parts. Turn this over in your mind.'

Evidently the publisher did not favour the proposition, but Barham's suggestion provided the germ of *Denis Duval,* which Thackeray began, cast aside, resumed more than twenty years later, and left unfinished at his death. On another occasion, Barham supplied the inspiration for two separate works of fiction, one of which acquired extraordinary celebrity. Near the end of 1838, he projected a picaresque novel to be written by himself in collaboration with three others and called the *Modern Rake's Progress;* he was to conduct the hero from birth through early boyhood, John Hughes to describe his life at a public school, Barham's son, Dalton Barham, to carry him through Oxford, and Lord William Lennox to introduce him to the Guards and to Crockford's. The design fell through, but young Leech, who had already executed some of the illustrations, completed the series and published it in *Bell's Life,* while the idea was delivered for what it was worth to Henry Cockton, and adapted by him in *Stanley Thorn* for the *Miscellany.* Dalton Barham records that John Hughes, approaching his part of the task with a conscientious attention to local colour, applied for assistance to one of his sons, then at Rugby, and received thence a rough draft 'of remarkable quality'. The name of the son is not mentioned, but Thomas Hughes, then about sixteen, was at Rugby, and it is reasonable to suppose that Barham's plan for a composite novel supplied the suggestion for *Tom Brown's Schooldays.*

The business connection with Bentley eventually ended in 1843, though its cessation was the occasion of no friction or ill-feeling, and their personal relations continued to be cordial. He wrote thus to Mrs. Hughes in May:

> 'It was from the first understood between Bentley and myself that our arrangements were to continue only so long as they should be thought mutually advantageous, and that if ever a contrary opinion should arise in the mind of either, they should be dissolved. It is our business tie alone that is severed, and we continue just as good friends as ever. Whether I shall form any other periodical liaison I am as yet undetermined. I have had three separate proposals made to me from three separate publishers, none of them inferior in point of emolument or respectability to the one I have given up.'

One of these offers came from Colburn to continue the ***Legends*** in the *New Monthly Magazine,* where the rest of them duly appeared, and went on appearing after Colburn parted with the proprietorship to Harrison Ainsworth in 1845. Ainsworth, indeed, was one of the most intimate of a new circle of literary friends with which Barham came to be surrounded after Hook's death in 1841 removed the last of an older generation, except Sydney Smith and Talfourd. He dined frequently with Dickens and Forster, where Maclise and Albany Fonblanque were usually of the party, and on one occasion at the house of the former, in December, 1843, the company included, besides himself and this quartette, Sydney Smith, Talfourd, and old Samuel Rogers, thus containing a curious link between the generations of Coleridge, Lamb, and Hazlitt, and another which knew men like Meredith and Swinburne. He was often accompanied to these dinners by his daughter, Lady Bond, who has entertained many men yet living with her lively reminiscences of those who knew the London of Dr. Johnson and remembered the *Edinburgh Review*—so lately, alas, deceased at the age of a hundred and twenty-seven years!—as a vigorous bantling, offending the conventions and shocking the sensibilities of elders with its pugnacious individuality and its ruthless iconoclasm.

But the end was near for this genial clergyman, so recently sprung into prominence after long years of literary obscurity, and yet far short of sixty years of age. In the winter of 1844-45, he contracted one chill upon another, thereby accentuating an affliction of the throat which had apparently been a source of weakness for some years. In the new year, he went down to Bath for a rest and a respite from his various engagements, but a meeting of the newly-founded Archaeological Association, of which he was a zealous member, for the settlement of a wrangle which threatened to imperil the society's existence, occasioned his premature return to town. The playwright Planché, who was also a prominent member of the society, expressed his opinion that this journey was the cause of Barham's death. Indirectly, it was so, for he made a prolonged speech at the meeting, so imposing a strain upon his throat, against which he had been particularly warned. But the real trouble was that he remained in town to attend to his affairs and contracted another chill. He records the calamity with a characteristic entry in his diary:

> '*April 19.* Called on the Dean; To Vestry meeting at St. Paul's; caught cold: relapse.'

He died two months later, on June 17, in his fifty-seventh year.

As Richard Garnett remarked, Barham 'owes his honourable rank among English humorists to his having done one thing supremely well'. Hood was immeasurably more of a poet and Hook infinitely more of a natural genius; the former was as far superior to him in the refined, Meredithian kind of humour, as was the latter in the riotous, Smollettian sort. But neither enjoyed an inspired period of production like Barham. Both were professional writers, their productivity of necessity prolific, and their lives lacking the leisure almost invariably preliminary to original inspiration. Barham, it is true, was a journalist, and his masterpiece was a contribution to the periodical press, but his living was not dependent upon his pen, his regular routine was occupied in other functions, and his writing was in a measure a recreation. He had the time to contemplate and ruminate, to indulge his hobbies, to 'stand and stare'. His career may be compared in a figurative sense with that of another literary cleric—with Sterne. He settled regularly to literature late in life and, like Sterne, produced his masterpiece when his sand was short in the glass. His native humour, too, resembled Sterne's—a love of the ludicrous in the bizarre, a delight in the mingling of the ridiculous with the revolting, an irresistible inclination to ambiguous inference and innuendo. Intellectually, both were instinctively Rabelaisian, Barham as much as, if not more so, than Sterne, for the difference between them in this respect was moral, not intellectual—relatively a physical difference, Barham being a decent creature, clean in body and mind, Sterne a lecherous reprobate. But, like Sterne, he had a taste for ribaldry and bawdy; he liked none the less a dinner-table story if it had a fulsome flavour, and relished a pot of porter the better if it was brought by a buxom wench like his own 'Nell Cook'. A robust appetite cannot be concealed by a cassock.

His poetical pedigree is rather obscure; the ***Legends*** can scarcely be described as the legitimate offspring of any influences. But they might be inscribed without inaccuracy in stud-book jargon as by Chaucer, out of Theodore Hook, by Sir Walter Scott and Mrs. Radcliffe. The parodies of Chaucer are readily apparent. ***Nell Cook*** is described in a sub-title as **'The King's Scholar's Story',** and deals with the adventures of the heroine, 'a comely lass', her master, a portly canon, who, though 'of Latin and Greek learned lore, he had good store', was short, sleek, and possessed of 'a merry eye', and a certain 'Lady gay', who stayed in the canonical abode as her host's niece, and yet had so little concern for her comfort that she allowed the poker and tongs to remain in her bed 'full six weeks and a day'. ***The Lay of St. Gengulphus*** and ***The Lord of Thoulouse*** are likewise Chaucerian, to name only two more, and the plan by which the tales are connected owes its origin to the Canterbury pilgrims. Likewise the Marmion vein of Scott is tapped in pieces like ***Netley Abbey*** and ***The Lay of St. Cuthbert,*** though to the author of *Waverley,* the debt is deeper than that of a parodist, for Barham was a voracious reader of his works and delighted to follow up Scott's antiquarian footnotes with his own research, a hobby in which he had indulged for years before he conceived the idea of utilizing the data he had collected for original composition.

These traits, however, are external, and manifest to the most casual reader of the ***Legends,*** as are the deliberate parodies of Hood in ***Aunt Fanny*** and the ***Nursery Reminiscences.***

> 'I remember, I remember,
> When I was a little Boy,
> One fine morning in September
> Uncle brought me home a toy.'

But there are others of a less palpable derivation at first sight. For instance, ***Bloudie Jacke of Shrewsberrie, The Witches Frolic,*** and ***The Hand of Glory:***

> 'On the lone bleak moor, At the midnight hour,
> Beneath the Gallows Tree,
> Hand in hand the Murderers stand
> By one, by two, by three!'

This is neither Chaucerian nor Scotian, in rhyme or scene! Its derivation is 'extensive and peculiar', going back on the one side by Lamb's *Specimens* to Dekker and Webster, on the other by Harrison Ainsworth to Horace Walpole and Mrs. Radcliffe. Parody, it may be said, is a nineteenth-century product. James and Horace Smith, both friends of Barham's, produced their *Rejected Addresses* as far back as 1812, but from that date to the advent of ***Ingoldsby*** no great example of the art had been perpetrated, and the *Bon Gaultier Ballads* of Aytoun and Martin were not forthcoming for another five years. But, in the meantime, Theodore Hook was scattering skits and squibs about the body of the periodical press, and both he and James Smith set a fashion for dinner-table doggerel and impromptu burlesques. To pass for a wit in Congreve's day, the ticket was neat and polished epigram; in Hook's, the pun was the vogue. Hook was the prince of punsters, but he was more than that—he was a skilful parodist, and nothing was safe from his mischievous wit. Proofs of his powers are amply provided, not only in his published writings, but by all the letter-writers of the time, including Barham, who, as an intimate of Hook's for about fourteen years, practically acquired the rhyming habit from him. From Hook he learned his business.

To turn to Harrison Ainsworth's influence, self-acknowledged by Barham in ***The Hand of Glory***—.

> 'For another receipt the same charm to prepare,
> Consult Mr. Ainsworth and *Petit Albert.*'

Ainsworth, when writing his romance of *Rookwood* in 1834, had planned his tale as an Anglo-Saxonized version of Mrs. Radcliffe's once popular thrillers. He assimilated the same melodramatic atmosphere, into which he introduced appropriate ballads, charged with archaic slang picked up from his studies of the Elizabethan dramatists, to which he had been attracted by a youthful infatuation for Lamb's *Specimens.* When the first ***Ingoldsby Legend*** was written, Ainsworth was running a neck-and-neck race with Dickens for the title of the best-selling novelist, his novels were read by everybody, and his fashion for 'criminal' fiction was being followed by his rival in *Oliver Twist.* It was no wonder that Barham, in search of popular themes, seized eagerly upon the eerie atmosphere of Rookwood Hall, with its superstitions, its gruesome history, and its spectral surroundings, and imitated some of Dick Turpin's songs, which were set to music and sung at all the cheap theatres, in certain of the ***Legends.***

Thus, from Mrs. Radcliffe, *via* Ainsworth, came such of the ***Legends*** as ***The Spectre of Tappington,*** which, with Mrs. Botherby as a substitute for old Alan Rookwood and 'bad Sir Giles' for the wicked Sir Reginald, is a very neat skit on Ainsworth's first successful romance. Another topical note is sounded in the opening lines of ***The Ingoldsby Penance:***

'Out and spake Sir Ingoldsby Bray,
A Stalwart Knight, I ween, was he,
"Come east, come west, Come lance in rest
Come falchion in hand, I'll tickle the best
Of all the Soldan's Chivalrie!" '

Macaulay published *The Lays of Ancient Rome* during 1842. No doubt when ***Ingoldsby,*** along with other contemporaries, becomes a subject for the same diligent research as the light literature of the previous century, a mass of evidence 'internal' and 'external', will be collected to show that in every legend Barham was parodizing something or somebody. We shall then witness a revival of interest in ***Ingoldsby,*** whose animal attractions have been allowed to languish a little of late.

Not that Barham has not received his dues as an author. His popularity was such that Horne considered ***Ingoldsby*** qualified as an example of *The New Spirit of the Age*—no great compliment perhaps, since Horne's selection was not distinguished by much discernment—and, though he subjected the ***Legends*** to a severity of censure which now seems so excessive as to be absurd, he admitted that they stood 'quite alone' and even prophesied that 'they always will stand quite alone'. For Barham possessed a knack for narrative clearly amounting to genius. According to his own avowal, he was lacking in invention: 'Give me a story to tell,' he said, 'and I can tell it, in my own way; but I can't invent one!' It is because he told his tales in his own way that he achieved greatness. He was not a fine prose-writer and there are no purple passages ready to hand for quotation; his charm as a story-teller lies in the colloquial manner of relation. He is essentially fireside reading for wintry evenings: with ***Ingoldsby*** in hand, one's wish is a parody of old Sarah Battle's, 'a clear fire, a clean earth, and the vigour of the muse'. His verse is even better than his prose, even Horne, an avowed enemy, remarking that 'in freedom and melody of comic versification, and in the originality of compound rhymes, the ***Ingoldsby Legends*** surpass everything of the kind that has since appeared since the days of Hudibras and Peter Pindar'. The opening stanzas of ***The Knight and the Lady*** illustrate the truth of Horne's statement:

'The Lady Jane was tall and slim,
The Lady Jane was fair,
And Sir Thomas, her Lord, was stout of limb,
But his cough was short, and his eyes were dim,
And he wore green "specs", with a tortoiseshell rim,
And his hat was remarkably broad in the brim,
And she was uncommonly fond of him,
And they were a loving pair!
And the name and the fame
Of the Knight and his Dame
Were ev'rywhere hail'd with the loudest acclaim;
And wherever they went, or wherever they came,
Far and wide, The people cried,
"Huzzah! for the Lord of this noble domain,
Huzzah! huzzah! huzzah!—once again!—
Encore! Encore! One cheer more!
All sorts of pleasure, and no sort of pain,
To Sir Thomas the Good, and the Fair Lady Jane!"

'Now Sir Thomas the Good, Be it well understood,
Was a man of a very contemplative mood,
He would pore by the hour O'er a weed or a flower,
Or the slugs that come crawling out after a shower;
Black beetles, and Bumble-bees,—Blue-bottle flies,
And Moths were of no small account in his eyes;
An "Industrious Flea" he'd by no means despise,
While an "Old Daddy-long-legs', whose 'long legs" and thighs
Pass'd the common in shape, or in colour, or size,
He was wont to consider an absolute prize,
Nay, a hornet or wasp he could scarce 'keep his paws off'
—he
Gave up, in short, Both business and sport,
And abandon'd himself *tout entier,* to Philosophy.

'Now, as Lady Jane was tall and slim,
And Lady Jane was fair,
And a good many years the junior of him,
And as he, All agree,
Look'd less like her *Mari,*
As he walk'd by her side, than her *Père,*
There are some might be found, entertaining a notion
That such an entire and exclusive devotion
To that part of science folks style Entomology,
Was a positive shame, And, to such a fair Dame,

Really demanded some sort of apology:
—No doubt it would vex One half of the sex
To see their own husband in horrid green "specs,"
Instead of enjoying a sociable chat,
Still poking his nose into this and to that,
At a gnat, or a bat, or a cat, or a rat,
Or great ugly things, All legs and wings,
With nasty long tails, arm'd with nasty long stings . . . '

No poet from Byron to Mr. Alfred Noyes had a more delicate ear for verbal melody than Barham; the rollicking rhythm of his verses bubbles as merrily, musically, and inevitably, as a stream over stones.

In our time, ***Ingoldsby*** is a favourite Christmas present, for he is delightfully suitable for both children and adults, and can, moreover, be obtained in all sorts and sizes of bindings, illustrated or unillustrated, expensive or inexpensive. But he is not a book to buy for the beauty of a binding and to be admired upon a shelf; he should be loved and cherished as a convivial companion.

Notes

[1] *Vide Charles Reade: A Biography,* London, 1931. Bentley was Reade's first publisher, and after Reade had become a best seller by means of *It is Never Too Late to Mend,* he issued cheap reprints of his earlier books which the novelist considered likely to be detrimental to his reputation, while of insignificant profit to himself. He filed an injunction to restrain Bentley from issuing his works, and the subsequent action of Reade *v.* Bentley, which remains a classic authority for the relations between author and publisher, discloses the unfairness of the profit-sharing agreement then in vogue and did much to establish the royalty system now generally used.

[2] *Life and Letters of the Rev. Richard Harris Barham,* by his son, London, 2 vols., 1870. This son, the Rev. R. H. Dalton Barham, also compiled *The Life and Remains of Theodore Edward Hook,* issued in two volumes by Bentley, 1849.

William G. Lane (essay date 1955)

SOURCE: "R. H. Barham and Dickens's Clergyman of *Oliver Twist,*" *Nineteenth-Century Fiction,* Vol. 10, No. 2, September, 1955, pp. 159-62.

[In the following essay, Lane refutes the theory that Barham was the model for Dickens's cleric in Oliver Twist.*]*

In an article occasioned by the centenary of the first issue of *Bentley's Miscellany,* Miss L. M. Littlewood makes a connection between the clergyman of *Oliver Twist* and Richard Harris Barham ("Thomas Ingoldsby").

> "Boz," all the world knows, was a sensitive man [she writes] and, in this case, there is ground for supposing that he resented Barham's friendship with Bentley, with whom he was becoming dissatisfied, and also the power of gentle satire possessed by the Minor Canon. He was a Tory and a cleric, and Dickens, at that time, had no use for either. The irreverent clergyman in Chapter V of *Oliver Twist* may have originated in this underlying resentment.[1]

Mr. Edgar Johnson's fine study[2] of the novelist helps bring into clearer focus the long and bitter Bentley-Dickens dispute. Until now, most accounts have pitted Boz's undeniable sensitivity against Bentley's alleged selfishness; of Bentley's sensitivity and Dickens's selfishness little has been said. In the battle of epithets the publisher has come off a poor second best: few writers have excelled Dickens's capability of invective, and some measure of his skill has been demonstrated by subsequent prejudiced commentators—Dame Una Pope-Hennessy, for example.[3] Mr. Johnson does not succumb to this temptation, but his work has already been called "patently unfair" to Bentley and others who incurred Dickens's displeasure.[4]

Miss Littlewood does not take a definite position regarding the controversy; the scope of her article may have precluded her doing so. Her suggestions, however, that Dickens resented Barham's friendship with Bentley, and, what is more strange, that he resented Barham's power of gentle satire at the time she specifies are difficult to accept.

The chronology of events is as follows: E. S. Morgan, Bentley's confidant, says[5] that in October, 1836, he recommended the promising young writer Boz as editor of the publisher's projected magazine. Bentley accepted the suggestion, and on November 4 an agreement[6] was signed whereby Dickens would receive twenty pounds monthly as editor and an additional twenty guineas for a monthly article. On January 2, 1837, appeared the first issue of *Bentley's Miscellany; Oliver Twist* began in the February issue, and chapter v of that novel was included in the April number.

Barham had published anonymously from 1826 onward in *Fraser's* and *Blackwood's* several of the pieces later incorporated in the collected ***Ingoldsby Legends.*** By April, four of the legends had appeared in the *Miscellany;*[7] in the second of these he originated his pseudonym "Thomas Ingoldsby."

Barham first met Bentley when they were schoolboys at St. Paul's.[8] Upon leaving there Barham went on to

Oxford, and Bentley entered the publishing firm of his father and his uncle, John Nichols. When Barham came up to London from Kent in 1821 to become a minor canon at St. Paul's, the men renewed their long-standing friendship. When the publisher undertook his new magazine, he called upon his friend for help as proof-reader, literary adviser, and contributor. Barham gave valuable service in all three capacities. So matters stood when the *Miscellany* got underway.

The "Wits of Bentley's" gathered from time to time at the publishing house in Burlington Street to correct proofs and to enjoy "bibaceous evenings," and Barham, perhaps from the first, attended these meetings. Why he was so late in meeting the new editor is not clear. But on April 29, 1837, he wrote his good friend Mrs. Hughes[9] that, although he had remonstrated with Bentley about some forthcoming articles for the magazine, to Boz he could say nothing, "never having as yet seen that very funny fellow, to whom I am only known as a veritable Mr. Ingoldsby."[10] The statement is important not only as showing that as yet Barham did not know Dickens, but as emphasizing the fact that Bentley, who had insisted upon veto power over all articles submitted for the magazine, made decisions in which his editor took no part. Here was the root of the trouble between Dickens and Bentley.

Certainly there is nothing in the four pieces Barham had contributed to the magazine to raise Dickens's ire against him, although Barham was a stanch Tory and a cleric. Moreover, as an enthusiastic and conscientious editor, as it is clear Dickens was at the outset, he would welcome having these highly successful and immediately popular items in the magazine. It seems highly unlikely that "Boz" resented "Ingoldsby" professionally.

Dickens's idea of a clergyman had doubtless crystallized long before he met the "cordial"[11] minor canon of St. Paul's who was soon to be his friend and one of the mediators in his relentless struggle to "burst the Bentleian bonds." But the two men were not yet acquainted in April, 1837.

No reader would have seen in the wretched clergyman of *Oliver Twist,* chapter v, the kindly and conscientious minor canon of St. Paul's. Dickens did not deal in ineffectual half measures: when in time he came to resent Bentley and expressed his dissatisfaction, it was not through an attack on a third person, however close, but directly against the inaptly named "Brigand of Burlington Street" himself.

Notes

[1] "A Victorian Magazine," *Contemporary Review,* CLI (1937), 335.

[2] *Charles Dickens: His Tragedy and Triumph* (2 vols., New York, 1952).

[3] She attributes major responsibility for the breach to Bentley, whom she describes as being "purblind and mean of soul" (*Charles Dickens* [New York, 1946], p. 83).

[4] Gordon N. Ray, "Seeing Dickens Plain," *Virginia Quarterly Review,* XXIX (1953), 301.

[5] *Brief Retrospect* (London, 1873). Quoted in Gordon N. Ray, "The Bentley Papers," *Library,* Fifth Series, VII (1952), 181.

[6] The full agreement is published in the *Dickensian,* XXXI (1935), 246-247.

[7] "The Monstre Balloon," "The Spectre of Tappington," "Hamilton Tighe," and "Grey Dolphin." The most celebrated of Barham's legends, "The Jackdaw of Rheims," appeared the following month.

[8] They were not, as Mr. Johnson says (I, 246), "old college friends," but friends from childhood.

[9] Mrs. Hughes was the wife of the Rev. Thomas Hughes, a canon of St. Paul's, and grandmother of Thomas Hughes, author of *Tom Brown's Schooldays.* Among her literary friends were Ainsworth, Southey, and Scott.

[10] R. H. Dalton Barham, *The Life and Letters of the Rev. Richard Harris Barham* (2 vol., London, 1870), II, 20.

[11] John Forster refers thus to Barham (*Life of Charles Dickens,* ed. J. W. T. Ley [London, 1928], p. 531).

Royal A. Gettmann (essay date 1957)

SOURCE: "Barham and Bentley," *The Journal of English and Germanic Philology,* Vol. LVI, No. 3, July, 1957, pp. 337-46.

[*In the essay that follows, Gettmann describes the working relationship and friendship between Barham and publisher Richard Bentley.*]

The story of the relations between R. H. Barham and Richard Bentley will throw some light upon mid-nineteenth-century publishing and especially on the financial aspects of a best seller, ***The Ingoldsby Legends.*** Barham became associated with the House of Bentley in 1837 when, according to his son, the publisher sought the "auxiliar services" of his father for the *Miscellany.* Bentley himself said that it was in November, 1839, that Barham offered to replace

Charles Ollier whose engagement as literary adviser with the firm ceased at that time.[1] The two men had been friends since their schooldays at St. Paul's, and their letters show that Bentley was asking advice of Barham as early as 1837. It may be that Bentley had in mind the date on which Barham's name was added to the regular payroll of the firm.

There is not much specific information as to Barham's actual influence in the acceptance or rejection of manuscripts. In a letter of October 20, 1840, he informed a correspondent: "Bentley is a man who will see with his own eyes and hear with his own ears, and thinks the former piercing enough, and the latter sufficiently long to enable him to judge for himself in all matters of literary taste. All I can do is to transmit the MS. with a recommendation to him to read."[2] But there were occasions when Barham spoke with decisiveness as, for example, in a letter of March 23, 1837, regarding a manuscript of Thomas Chandler Haliburton. "Lose no time but get it into type *at once,*" he urged, "& if that cant be done immediately, *have it transcribed forthwith.* . . . Print it at once if possible."[3] Bentley promptly acted on Barham's advice, he actually published *The Clockmaker* four days later, March 27. On the other hand Barham could disapprove of a work with equal firmness: "The Graduate MS won't do at all."[4]

Barham also served Bentley by revising manuscripts and supervising their progress through the press. Indeed the sentence, "I suppose Mr. Barham is to see it through the press," appears more than once in the official correspondence of the firm. In a letter of June 21, 1840, he wrote: "I spend almost all my time here on the sea-beach working at Bentley's proofs."[5] One of his duties was to discover and to expurgate or tone down questionable passages. By temperament and position he was well suited for his assignment. His sense of humor and his social experience made him responsive to and tolerant of robust fun; yet he could discriminate, thanks to his own good taste and to his awareness of the proprieties. Both qualities come out in the following appraisal of a manuscript: "The Casti [?] is extremely well done and very comical but I doubt from the *nature of the subject matter* whether it *could* be sobered down enough without emasculating it of all its vigour."[6] Barham must have been warned to keep an eye on the manuscripts of Mrs. Trollope, for he assured Bentley: "I have looked over the two chapters of the Widow Barnaby and like the opening very much there is nothing objectionable as yet save one word which is not English & which I have corrected."[7] But Mrs. Trollope's next novel, *The Vicar of Wrexhall,* required some censorship, and in sending the corrections for the second volume Barham explained: "You will find that all the revolting expressions are changed and taken out at the same time the *cant* is as strong as ever. The other parts to which you alluded are almost entirely in the third volume and that I am going to attack forthwith."[8] In this instance Barham was obviously following suggestions which had been made by his chief, but there were times when he himself insisted upon expurgation: "Look to the excisions I have made about Dimond they *must* come out or the book cannot lie on any decent table."[9]

One interesting case suggests that as censor Barham was quite willing to do a considerable amount of rewriting. In a letter postmarked December 6, 1839, he wrote to Bentley as follows: "I return the last proof of Acte [deprived?] of one most disgusting scene and otherwise corrected but the most fearful part is I suspect behind. The introduction of St. Paul and other sacred persons into a novel would damn it and I think deservedly. A little management however may do away with all this still I should like to see the *whole* before I venture to change the identity of the personages. When the whole is before me it will be easy to do away with all that is offensive yet keep the spirit of the story."[10] This novel, then, was in proof in 1839, but, after what must be the longest delay in the history of publishing, it appeared on April 2, 1890. Without commenting on this curious circumstance, the *List,* a year-by-year record of the books issued by the firm, describes it as a "spiritual" novel set in the time of Nero and notes that it went into a second edition on June 25. The reason for Barham's reservations about *Acte* is clear: he simply objected to the introduction of "sacred persons" into a work of fiction. The circumstances behind the publication of this novel after a postponement of over fifty years are a mystery, but in any case, whatever editing Barham may have given the book, he did not remove St. Paul. The *Athenaeum* (May 24, 1890) praised the spirit and cleverness of the novel but demurred at the depiction of St. Paul as "a mild old revivalist gentleman of the evangelical school."

If Barham did not revise *Acte,* there were numerous other books which he scrutinized and reworked. One of these was *Memoirs of Charles Mathews, Comedian* (1838). On the advice of Theodore Hook, Bentley had paid the actor's son £500 for this work, but Hook had been too indolent to read it. Upon examination it was found not only to be wretched in quality but short as to quantity. Bentley asked Barham to persuade Hook to rewrite the *Memoirs* for the handsome sum of £500. But Hook must have done the work carelessly, for Barham went through the manuscript removing unimportant matter, passages in poor taste, and some "twaddle about the purity of actresses."[11] Another task which Barham undertook was the preparation of works for the Standard Novels. For example he pruned Cooper's *Homeward Bound* and grafted upon it the relevant portions of the sequel, *Eve Effingham.* In order to bring the work within the allotted 405 pages he reduced the original three volumes of the later novel to 130 pages, and he was satisfied that *Homeward Bound* was "a much better and more readable book in its present than in its former shape."[12] He also compressed—and in his opinion improved—Fanny Burney's *Camilla* into one volume for the Standard Novels, but in this instance his work came to nothing, for the book was never published. On his own initiative Barham suggested that *Three Brothers,* a Gothic tale by Joshua Pickersgill, published in 1803, be included in the Standards, and he added that "with the proper puffs it would be popular."[13] He later reported that it was full of objectionable matter and written in a strange, affected idiom. Although he was quite willing to rewrite the novel, nothing came of this project.[14]

A further aspect of Barham's "auxiliar services" was to seek out authors for the Bentley imprint. In this respect he should have been well served by his wide social contacts and his capacity for friendship: he was a long-time intimate of men so different as Theodore Hook and Sydney Smith. In his search for talent Barham was obviously sensitive to the social position of writers. Rehearsing an interview he had had with a Miss Sparkes about a work in progress, he dwelt upon the young lady's exceedingly good connections, and he concluded: "She can *ensure* three, perhaps four hundred subscribers."[15] Nothing, however, came of this effort at recruitment. On another occasion Barham was pleased to report that he had talked with Lord William Lennox who had just completed a novel of fashionable life originally intended for Colburn. Lord William had no objection to publishing over his own name, and he had consented to take a "quiet chop" with Barham. As a further inducement Barham offered to correct proofs for his lordship. Barham's strategy was eventually successful, for on March 15, 1841, Bentley published *Compton Audley.* The novel, alas, proved to be a failure in every way. To cite another instance: on April 10, 1839, Barham wrote that Dr. Taylor had agreed to give Bentley the first chance at his translation of Count Gustave de Beaumont's *Ireland.*[16] Bentley did publish it in August, but, though highly praised in the *Athenaeum* on its publication in Paris, the book did not bring profit or prestige to New Burlington Street. In the later months of the following year Barham narrowly missed the opportunity of launching a great Victorian on his career as novelist. "Thackeray called here yesterday," Barham reported to Bentley, "wants to be busy so I recommended him to treat with you for a 3 vol *historical* novel which he is very well inclined to do. From his reading I think he would succeed especially if as I suggested it were of the Queenhoo Hall style illustrated by his own woodcuts & caricatures & to the livelier parts of it—Turn this over in your mind."[17] That both Bentley and Thackeray looked favorably upon the projected book is indicated by the fact that the latter shortly turned to "reading widely in the chroniclers of the period."[18] But the tragic situation in his household compelled Thackeray to return to the writing of short pieces which would yield immediate money.

It would appear, then, that except for the case of Haliburton, Barham was something less than successful in his efforts to bring new writers to Bentley's imprint. But he must have been most serviceable in the task of keeping happy the authors who were already on Bentley's roster. The correspondence provides numerous glimpses of Barham unraveling the knots in which the publisher and his writers entangled themselves. In one letter Barham bluntly asked "What the deuce" Bentley had done to Reynolds. "I had smoothed everything," Barham continued, "only to have Reynolds report that 'you had got him into a row with somebody.' What does this mean?"[19] In a second letter touching upon this difficulty Barham complained that Bentley did not answer Reynolds' letters: "You are invisible as well as incomprehensible."

Barham's gifts as conciliator also came into play during the altercation over Dickens' abandonment of the editorship of the *Miscellany.* Angered by Dickens' abdication and by his determination to name Ainsworth as his successor, Bentley called upon Barham to parley with his adversary. After a long interview with Dickens and Ainsworth, Barham wrote in great detail to Bentley and recommended that Ainsworth be made editor.[20] The high regard which Ainsworth developed for Barham comes out in a statement to Bentley: "I mentioned to [?] Barham your intention of inviting him to dinner tomorrow, and I trust I shall have the pleasure of meeting him. I look upon the acquisition of his friendship as quite equal in value to the Editorship of the Miscellany, and I do not (as you may suppose) underrate the latter."[21] And a short time later, when Ainsworth wished to discuss "a few matters" with Bentley, he brought Barham with him. Barham's talent as conciliator was soon needed, for a feeling of distrust developed between publisher and editor. It flared up in connection with a misunderstanding about the correction of the proofs of *Jack Sheppard.* In September Ainsworth, in a too peremptory tone, warned Bentley that the first two volumes of the novel were not to be sent to the printers until he had thoroughly revised them. Despite Ainsworth's confident assertion that the book would be ready for publication on October 15, the anniversary of Sheppard's great escape—as in fact it was—and that it was sure "to reach the Oliver Twist mark," Bentley feared a conspiracy. And he had reason to do so, for he had been outwitted by Dickens and he suspected that Ainsworth was a tool of Dickens. Bentley construed Ainsworth's letter as a threat to postpone or withhold the novel, and he composed what must have been a censorious reply. He enclosed this in a letter to Barham and asked his advice about sending the rebuke. He then continued: "I really do not know how to

The INGOLDSBY LEGENDS OR
MIRTH & MARVELS
BY THOMAS INGOLDSBY
Esqre
ILLUSTRATED BY
ARTHUR RACKHAM. A.R.W.S.
WILLIAM HEINEMANN.
•1919•

thank you sufficiently for the many good offices you do me. . . . At this critical moment it is in your power to set our friend Mr. Ainsworth right. He thinks that he has become necessary to me. I *know* he is not. Do not let him throw away at the end of the present year the position and Emolument of Editor. If he is trickey, that must inevitably follow."[22] And once more Barham served as a patient though bewildered intermediary. He deplored the feeling of mutual distrust between the two men, but he somehow managed to put out the flames.

Barham's greatest service to Bentley was of course the composition of ***The Ingoldsby Legends,*** the first series of which was published on January 30, 1840. It is not strictly accurate to say that Richard Bentley was the begetter of these verses, for two of the pieces appeared in *Blackwood's* prior to Ingoldsby's debut in the *Miscellany,* January, 1837. Nevertheless the fact that eighteen of the twenty-two poems were published in that periodical, together with the fact that the prefaces were addressed to Bentley, led to the association in the public mind of Richard Barham and Richard Bentley. The second series was published on December 30, 1842, and the third on December 26, 1846. These three volumes, priced at 10/6 each, started slowly but sold steadily, reaching a total of 20,750 copies by 1856. In 1857 the three series were combined for the first time, and between that date and 1894 ***The Ingoldsby Legends*** went through seventy-seven further editions or printings for a total of about 425,000 copies.[23] Of the more than fifteen named editions some particulars may be given for the following examples: during the period 1857-77 the Five Shilling edition went through thirty-four printings and reached a total of 87,500 copies; the Carmine, which sold at 10/6 was printed nine times (14,750 copies) from 1865 to 1887; the Quarto, priced at a guinea, was printed six times during the years 1863-77 for a total of 16,500 copies; and the People's, appropriately selling at sixpence, was twice printed in 1881-82 to the extent of 140,000 copies.

Such sales as these arouse curiosity as to the profit which ***The Ingoldsby Legends*** brought into New Burlington Street. Making use of the available ledgers I have reckoned the total profit for the years 1862-77 to be £14,345. 3. 2. This sum does not include the yield from the 35,700 copies printed before 1861, the income from American sales, and the sharply diminished receipts after the expiration of the copyright in 1888.[24] Perhaps the clearest evidence of the financial importance of the ***Legends*** is George Bentley's declaration on February 14, 1879, that *Temple Bar* and Ingoldsby were his two most valuable properties—thirty-nine years after the first publication.[25]

What of Barham's share in the earnings of ***The Ingoldsby Legends***? He received one guinea a page for the pieces as they appeared in the *Miscellany,*[26] and he must have got some kind of payment when they were gathered into book form. The only definite information I have uncovered is that on January 16, 1840, a fortnight before the publication of the first series, Barham assigned the entire remaining interest in ***The Ingoldsby Legends*** to Richard Bentley for "the sum of £100 this day received."[27] What arrangements were made for the second and third series I do not know, but presumably Barham got similar sums for those copyrights. The fact that he received no further payments on the first does not detract from the good name of Bentley, for it must be remembered that the outright sale of copyright was a regular kind of agreement and that ***The Ingoldsby Legends*** did not sell briskly at the outset. (The first two printings, 1,500 copies, were not exhausted at the time of the publication of the second series.) And finally it must be remembered that Barham's death occurred before the appearance of the third series.

Even so, it is puzzling to scan the hundreds of pages which carry the accounts of ***The Ingoldsby Legends*** and to see profits recorded which mount well upwards of £15,000 with not a single entry of a payment to the author. When one notices that a single edition of 5,000 copies of an illustrated ***Ingoldsby*** resulted in payments of £180. 4. 6. to Tenniel, £153. 4. 6 to Cruikshank, and £40. 4. 6 to Leech, and a profit of more than one thousand pounds to the House of Bentley, then one sees the fateful unfairness of the outright sale of copyright and the difficulty of devising a just mode of remuneration in the publication of best-sellers.

In view of the prolonged and profitable life of ***The Ingoldsby Legends*** it was ironical that in 1843, in an effort to economize, Richard Bentley partially broke off his association with Barham. On May 11 of that year he wrote a letter to his old friend which he began by declaring that as a "matter of duty" he had to set himself to open a subject which was to him "most unpalatable." He went on to explain that at a time when business was prosperous he had entered into an agreement with Barham which he had trusted might be long continued. Now, however, business had taken a downward turn, and the sale of the *Miscellany* had fallen to one-third of what it was in 1839. In sum Bentley said that it was impossible to continue their "arrangement."[28] On the following day Barham, apparently unruffled, acknowledged the letter by saying that Bentley was quite right and that "in thus terminating our connexion as author and publisher I hope to retain that of a friend." In a brief note (May 16) Bentley declared that Barham had misconstrued the letter. The next day Barham expressed his puzzlement and rehearsed what he took to be the terms of the arrangement: his stipend was £10 a month and one guinea a page for contributions to the *Miscellany;* he was to help in any way possible with the revising and adapting of works for the Standard Novels; he was to act in any dispute that arose between Bentley and any third party; and finally, Bentley had the right to dissolve the agreement at any time. Barham was unable to see how he had misunderstood the recent letter, and he once more assured Bentley that his termination of the agreement was quite in order. The following day (May 18) Bentley explained that the relation between them had rested on two separate parts and that Barham's work as literary adviser was entirely apart from his contributions to the *Miscellany*. In short, Bentley wished to save £10 a month, but he had no intention of breaking with Ingoldsby—that is, of losing future ***Legends*** for the periodical. Barham's response (May 19) was that he did not understand Bentley's explanation. He said that he had been offered double and more than double a guinea a page by other magazines and that he had always declined such offers as a point of honor. In other words he had always acted on the assumption that his arrangement with Bentley was a single one, not "a sort of Siamese twin." Barham then pointedly asked how long Bentley would have continued paying him the £10 a month for advising if Barham had sold his writings to other publishers. And with a touch of tartness Barham concluded: "I have followed your lead and thrown up the other part." Despite his son's declaration that the business separation did not touch the friendship between the two men, it is very likely that Barham's feelings were bruised. After May, 1843, Thomas Ingoldsby did not appear in the pages of the *Miscellany* for a period of over two years. Then, in the issue of August, 1845, by "the express wish" of Barham the last lines he ever wrote, **"As I laye a-thinkynge,"** were published in the *Miscellany* so that "Thomas Ingoldsby might close his career where he had commenced it."[29]

There is no reason to doubt this account of the final affection and harmony between the two men, and one could wish that this was the end of the story. But many years later a discordant postscript appeared in the pages of *Society*. In the issue of August 25, 1883, the editor of that journal, in his column "My View of Things," asserted that the relationship between publisher and author must inevitably be one of distrust and even animosity. In support of his contention he wrote: "William Carleton, the Irish novelist, once astonished a party of literary friends by proposing to drink in solemn silence the memory of Napoleon. Tears were shed when the *convives* asked why this thusness. 'He once shot a publisher,' was the grim rejoinder, alluding to the Frankfort episode of Ullman. Byron girded even at John Murray, and chaffed him in the memorable Bible with the changed passage, 'Now Barrabas was a *publisher,*' whilst the hatred 'Ingoldsby' Barham had to Bentley was truly Christian." Naturally enough, George Bentley resented this charge and vigorously denied it in a letter which the editor, along with an apologetic note, published in the next number of *Society*. The denial read in part: "Mr. Barham and my father were Paulines together, and a long and close friendship subsisted between them, well known to literary men of the time. Barham dedicated his famous Legends to my father, and a day or two before his death he desired that his last legend **'As I laye a-thinking,'** shou'd be 'carried to Bentley.'

"I avail myself of this opportunity to express a conviction, founded upon some experience, namely, that the relations of author and publisher are much more pleasant than some gentlemen of the Press seem rather glad to describe them to be."

There was at one time, as we have seen, a break in the connection between Barham and Bentley, but in view of the strains in the publishing trade—the difficulty of appraising a manuscript, unpredictable fluctuations in the circulation of a periodical, the unforeseen rise in the popularity of a book, the inadequacy of the existing commercial arrangements for literary properties, and the unevenness of rewards—we may accept as true George Bentley's summary of the relations between the two men.

Notes

[1] R. H. D. Barham, *The Life and Letters of the Rev. Richard Harris Barham* (London, 1880), p. 231, and the Letterbook of the publishing firm (BM Add. MSS 46, 639).

[2] *Life and Letters,* p. 325.

[3] This letter and the other letters from Barham to Bentley are in the Henry W. and Albert A. Berg Collection of the New York Public Library. For permission to use them I am grateful to Dr. John Gordan, Curator of the Collection, and Mr. Paul North Rice, Chief of the Reference Department.

[4] From an undated letter, probably late 1839 (Berg Collection).

[5] *Life and Letters,* p. 316.

[6] Undated letter, but early 1837 (Berg Collection).

[7] Letter of November 26, 1838 (Berg Collection).

[8] Letter postmarked November 27, 1839 (Berg Collection).

[9] Letter of May 1[?], 1840 (Berg Collection). I have not been able to identify the book.

[10] Berg Collection.

[11] Letter from Morgan to Bentley, August 1, 1837 (Illinois Collection). Undated letter from Barham to Bentley (Berg Collection).

[12] Letter to Bentley, August 25, 1842 (Berg Collection).

[13] Letter to Bentley, April 27, [1842?] (Berg Collection). Barham was more than willing to write puffs. Referring to an American novel, *Rob of the Bowl,* he informed Bentley that through his connections with journalism he could push this book, as well as others, in the *Torch* and in the *Globe* (undated letter, Berg Collection). On another occasion Barham supplied Morgan, Bentley's chief clerk, with a review of Jesse's *Memoirs of the Court of England during the Reign of the Stuarts.* After the review appeared in the *Times,* Morgan used it as a puff in the *Miscellany.* Morgan's letters to Bentley, August 18 and 27, 1840 (Illinois Collection).

[14] Letter to Bentley, October 7, 1842 (Berg Collection).

[15] Letter to Bentley, September 10, [1837?] (Berg Collection).

[16] Berg Collection.

[17] Undated letter (Berg Collection).

[18] Gordon N. Ray, *Thackeray: The Uses of Adversity* (New York, 1955), p. 268.

[19] Letter of February 23, 1837 (Berg Collection).

[20] Edgar Johnson, *Charles Dickens: His Tragedy and Triumph* (New York, 1952), p. 249.

[21] Letter to Bentley, February 8, 1839 (Illinois Collection).

[22] Letter of September 24, 1839 (Letterbook, BM Add. MSS 46, 640). As a matter of fact John Forster, who had almost certainly fanned the flames of Dickens' resentment against Bentley, warned Ainsworth against the publisher in such strong terms as these: "Remember what I told you yesterday—that you are now in a better position than Bentley. *You can get all you wish from him, and hold a superiority over him,* if you do not wilfully and willingly put yourself beneath his feet." See S. M. Ellis, *Harrison Ainsworth and His Friends* (London, 1911), 1, 387-88.

[23] The *List* (January 30, 1840) estimates that with "overflows" taken into account, the total may be taken "as close upon 450,000 copies."

[24] Furthermore there are gaps in the Ledgers. For example, the account for the Five Shilling edition does not cover the years 1871-77 during which, according to the *List,* two printings totalling 3,000 copies were run off.

[25] BM Add. MSS 46, 644. In 1877 *Temple Bar* was showing a profit of about £115 a month. See BM Add. MSS 46, 598.

[26] In 1839 when the *Miscellany* was flourishing, the attitude of both men in respect to money matters was free-hearted. For example, in thanking Bentley for payment of a legend Barham remarked that the check was for a rather larger sum than Ingoldsby was entitled to. He added: " . . . if you have given him the turn of the market this time you must take it yourself the next" (letter of October 23, 1839, Berg Collection).

[27] BM Add. MSS 46, 613.

[28] This letter and the ones that follow are in the Letterbook, BM Add. MSS. 46, 639.

[29] R. H. D. Barham, *op. cit.,* p. 365.

William G. Lane (essay date 1958)

SOURCE: "The Primitive Muse of Thomas Ingoldsby," *Harvard Library Bulletin,* Vol. XII, 1958, pp. 220-41.

[*In the following excerpt, Lane examines the critical reception of Barham's work.*]

. . . Barham's pseudonym quickly became established in the mind of the reading public, but the name did not then, as it does not now, carry with it the picture of the conscientious clergyman of St Paul's. The 'secular signature' was known widely, that of the minor canon to a much smaller group. The reputation of the clergyman was impeccable, and to all who knew him in this capacity the memory of his name must have remained green as long as they lived. His many services to his parishioners, his real concern and activity in behalf of those in need of charity, whom he supported freely, but with discretion, his readiness to lend an ear to others in trouble and to counsel them wisely—these are matters of record.[68] John Hughes has well summarized the matter: 'To do everything for everybody was his nature, and I doubt if he could have helped it.'[69] And Dr W. C. Taylor, writing in the *Miscellany* upon the occasion of the appearance of the Third Series of the ***Legends,*** expressed what many others say in different terms: 'To be acquainted with him, was to admire him;—to know him, was to love him.'[70] But Dr Taylor realized that Ingoldsby, not Barham, would be known to succeeding generations.

From the first appearance of the Legends, Ingoldsby was said to be 'a most pleasant fellow in his mirthful mood' (**'The Monstre Balloon'** or **'The Coronation'**) and, in a different manner, 'when making the flesh creep with terror in some old ghastly goblin legend.'[71] One might hesitate to believe that these ghastly goblin Legends were ever capable of having quite so strong an effect upon listeners were there not supplementary evidence. John Hughes, writing a few years later, assures us that it was so: 'Suffice it to state, what my friend Miss Mitford can confirm, that the simple recitation of **"Hamilton Tighe"** has actually made persons start and turn pale, and complain of nervous excitement.'[72] This 'Victorian' reaction to only one of several such stories may go far to explain the initial appeal of the collected tales.

Like John Hughes and Miss Mitford, 'Dr. Pangloss,' writing in the *Miscellany* of the Legends and safe in the assumption that all readers of that periodical would know the poetical vagaries of Ingoldsby, recognizes the 'ghastly horror in his **"Legend of Hamilton Tighe,"** which even Coleridge has scarcely surpassed.'[73] But especial praise is given to the 'rich and racy quality' of Ingoldsby humor and the 'meteoric play of his fancy.' His drollery, 'like Falstaff's chuckling laugh, breathes the very spirit of good fellowship'; it is broad, subtle, fantastic, extravagant as occasion requires. In this respect, as in its 'strong catholic tendency even in its wildest freaks,' it is 'thoroughly Rabelaisian.' This is the first, I think, of many comparisons of Barham to Rabelais. Noteworthy also is the fact that Ingoldsby's 'spirit of good fellowship' was easily discerned and early praised.

It was well that there were friends to support Ingoldsby, for not long afterwards he was subjected to the 'virtuous' attack from R. H. Horne (1803-1884) already mentioned.

Horne, whose active career included a term as midshipman in the Mexican navy and as Commander of the Gold Escort in Australia, was a onetime editor of the *Monthly Repository* and the author of plays about Marlowe and Gregory VII and a history of Napoleon. His principal work, *Orion,* an epic poem, appeared in 1843. With so much literary experience behind him, he felt capable of emulating Hazlitt in delineating *A New Spirit of the Age* (1844). The third piece in this collection of twenty-five critical essays is devoted to Ingoldsby and rubricked 'Poison in Jest.' It is an egregious and highly opinionated attack in the most extravagant language that anyone has used about the ***Legends.*** Horne is forced by the extensive sale and extensive popularity of the work to condemn its 'hideous levity,' constructed upon an 'outrageous principle.' He objects violently to Ingoldsby's **'Gengulphus'** chiefly because of the comparison of the dismembering of the husband by the young clerk and the wife to the manner in which 'the late Mr. Greenacre served Mrs. Brown.' (Greenacre, a notorious criminal, was executed on 10 May 1837.) Here, exclaims Horne, is just the point: the direct comparison with an actual horror!

Not all of Horne's essay is condemnatory, however. With all his objections on moral grounds, he recognizes that Ingoldsby is a master of comic versification. Indeed, because the Legends show the possibilities of the English language for true rhyme, that is, rhyme depending solely on ear and not limited by the eye, they are in this respect 'philological studies, indisputable theoretically, and as novel as they are amusing.' Perfect rhymes—simple, double, and triple—are abundant, he finds, and he gives many illustrations of Ingoldsby's astonishing ability.

Horne concludes by reminding the reader that he has objected to the Legends solely on 'the abstract grounds of Literature and Art': he has excluded religious grounds, conventional morality, and personalities. But he felt that he must condemn these licentious works unredeemed by any one sincere passion—and therefore a bad influence on the rising generation, which is bad enough without such assistance. 'Wherefore an iron hand is now laid upon the shoulder of Thomas Ingoldsby, and a voice murmurs in his ear, "Brother!—no more of this!" '

Objections to Horne's book came from all quarters, some of which did not mention the chapter on Ingoldsby, although the consensus was that he, more than any other writer, had been maligned. The *Athenaeum,*[74] taking a fairly temperate view, observed that the selection savored too much of literary *coterie*—'a peculiar view of a peculiar set of minds'—but still found much to amuse, as well as to suggest thought. The attack on Ingoldsby was termed a 'slaughter,' nevertheless; and though Ingoldsby's banter was 'reckless,' Horne dealt with it 'somewhat too savagely.'

The *Literary Gazette*[75] was stronger on both counts. While finding Horne's opinions not always lacking in acumen, it objected to his critical jargon (that of a new school of 'highly clouded, mystical, and metaphysical pretenders'), and to his total failure to perceive, or have power over, the humorous. It found him sadly inadequate on Dickens, the most popular man of the time, and then turned to Ingoldsby, 'one of the most original and entertaining writers, and one of the most curious as well as tuneful versifiers of the day (in the former equal to Butler, in the latter to Pope).' But in dismissing the follies exposed by Ingoldsby as those solely of another age, the *Gazette* itself was pretty far from understanding his real motives.

Samuel Laman Blanchard, then sub-editor of *Ainsworth's Magazine,* leveled the batteries of that periodical on the *New Spirit* and its author with an article entitled 'The New Gull's Horne-Book.'[76] After explaining at some length how far short of Hazlitt's example the new work fell and objecting that it was simply a book on literature alone, not on the spirit of the age, Blanchard proceeded to lay down a counter-barrage for Ingoldsby.

Horne had spoken of the lack of refinement and ideality in the ***Legends*** and had used fairy tales as an example of what he thought the Legends should have been. 'Alas, for fairy-tale and legend,' said Blanchard, 'for now they have fallen under the iron hand of a merciless moralist.' 'Knowing of what the hand consists, it would be pleasant to know of what metal the face that belongs to it is made.' In explicating the concluding sentence of Horne's essay, he asks what sin the ***Legends*** committed: 'Alas, [he answers] the worst of sins—it has made men laugh; it has incurred the deadly, the inexpiable guilt of popularity!' And replying to Horne's charge that the principle on which the Legends are constructed is unsound, Blanchard writes that, hitherto delighting in 'the wild and original pleasantries' of Ingoldsby, the reader

> has yet to learn that in every smooth but tortuous line of the many-winding legend, there lurks a snake—it hisses in the melody, and stings in the moral. Where he has laughed, he should have trembled and shuddered. When he has been shaking his sides, he should have shaken his head—shed iron tears, and stretched forth the iron hand. Any objection that may have been made heretofore, has been a shallow, undiscerning, insufficient objection, and now for the first time has a discovery been made—that what our good spirits have fed upon so merrily, was either "poison" or "twaddle."

Blanchard concludes sarcastically: 'Some say that the spirit of the age is quackery; only grant that, and then the projectors of this design become its fair and legitimate representatives."

This level of calumny—so it was considered by Horne—was not reached even by the *New Monthly,*[77] to whose pages Barham was then a contributor. That he should be strongly defended by his own journal was of course natural. Horne's book, declared the reviewer, stands in a very unhappy predicament. 'It has had the effect of sorely puzzling some people—of offending others—of satisfying none.' Even those praised therein were made uneasy under its approbation. The reviewer denounced Horne's book on several counts, but he found strangest of all the chapter on Ingoldsby.

The real difficulty, he says, is that Horne simply does not know what to make of Ingoldsby. He is pretty sure that Ingoldsby is a comic poet, but if so, then unlike all others. And quoting Horne's comments on the passage from **'Gengulphus'** he exclaims in feigned surprise at the astuteness of the critic:

> It never occurred to this sincere wiseacre, that there was something else to ridicule besides the diseased appetite for horrors—namely, *the diseased food by which it is nourished.* He sees plainly enough that Ingoldsby indulges in a jocose use of horrors, and he takes his stand upon that. If he had looked an inch further he must have discovered that all this raw-head and cross-bones whimsicality is the vent, not of a scoffing spirit, but of a strong wit lashing with matchless ridicule the ribald and profane narratives of horror, which daily solicit the morbid sympathies of the public in an endless variety of shapes. . . . Thomas Ingoldsby has scourged the brutal taste in a way not likely to be forgotten. He has heaped overwhelming satire upon that minute style of delineating crime, which might be said to have created the passion upon whose indulgence it subsisted; and he has given such an effectually ludicrous turn to the genius for the horrible, that the whole school of penny-a-line pathos may be fairly said to shudder through his verses and expire in their echoes.

I have given this reviewer's remarks at some length, not only because they are an effective rebuttal of Horne, but, more importantly, because they explain the editorial policy behind the publication of the Legends in the *New Monthly.* They show conclusively that the Legends were not taken merely as a rush of fun thrown out by a facile rhymer.

In this same connection the marginal note written by Leigh Hunt at the end of the chapter on Ingoldsby in Horne's personal copy of *A New Spirit* is of particular interest: 'May not Ingoldsby have intended to bring into popular contempt the morbid tendency to crime itself? to make Greenacres, for instance, ashamed and disgusted at the idea of becoming Greenacres?' To this has been appended Horne's reply: '*No*—R. H. H.'[78] This suggestion of Hunt's, found also in various reviews of Horne's book, doubtless prompted the insertion of the following paragraph in a second edition, published later the same year:

> Those who endeavour to justify this writer by the sudden discovery of a moral aim in his ridiculing real horrors (in order to teach the vulgar to laugh at them) say not one syllable of the gross licentiousness of these tales! There *is* nothing to say for them.[79]

The critical reaction was so preponderantly pro-Ingoldsby that Horne felt it necessary to reply at some length in the 'Introductory Comments' to this second edition, despite Elizabeth Barrett's admonition: 'Let them rave! That the book does not deserve their abuse we know as well as they themselves do—and there is no need to know better. What turns *against* it is simply the worm—or the friend of the worm, wormy, and right wormily!'[80] But in replying, Horne refused to be drawn into a controversy with the reviewers. 'I receive their shots, and pass on my way. I presume a period will some day arrive when Thomas Ingoldsby may consider himself sufficiently avenged by eight or ten attacks in return for my one.'[81] That day was not long in coming. While it is true that Horne's replies to his critics were 'mere foil-play,' as Walter Jerrold says,[82] they are ample evidence of the general popularity and success of the Legends.

If Elizabeth Barrett's remark was intended to equate Ingoldsby with the 'worm'—and if so, it is the only comment on Barham by either of the Brownings that I have been able to discover—then one 'friend of the worm' was Thackeray. In the *Morning Chronicle,* 2 April 1844, Titmarsh wrote that Horne's 'easy candour' ought to lead people to deal sincerely with him. Most of his views were commonplace, said Thackeray; only in the matter of commenting on Barham did he show 'spleen,' and even that had a sort of 'clumsy sincerity.' These strictures upon Horne's intellectual scope, compiled with remarks concerning his style of dress, provoked appropriate rejoinder in the second edition of *A New Spirit.* Horne objected to Thackeray's abuse of 'so important a position of influence on the public mind, by inserting his "good fun" in the leading liberal morning paper.' 'Besides,' he went on, 'the book was open enough on literary grounds for sharp handling, and [Thackeray] might have found ample grounds, either to advocate the cause of comic poetry, or to assist his friend Ingoldsby, the "amusing poet," with the "harmless phantasies." '

In one phase of this minor literary turmoil a point claimed by Horne redounds to his credit. Addressing himself to Ingoldsby in the introduction to the second edition he remarks that 'in dealing with his "Legends," which I conceived it a duty to treat unsparingly, I yet exercised the utmost forbearance towards himself personally—a forbearance which has not been exercised by his friends who have attacked me, but which I have not resented upon him, nor intend.' Horne could well have taken satisfaction from his stand, for in less than a year—on 17 June 1845—Ingoldsby died.

The appearance of the Third Series in December, 1846, drew notices in the book columns of periodicals, and in the *Miscellany* and *New Monthly* it was of course given special attention. Ingoldsby's fame was still spreading at home and abroad. During the fifties and sixties the better pieces began to find their way into anthologies. For example, James Parton's *Humorous Poetry of the English Language* (New York, 1856), containing many of Ingoldsby's tales, went into a sixth edition before the end of the following year. As a rhymer, Ingoldsby was held by Parton to have but one equal in English literature—Byron.[83]

Between 1857 and the end of 1864 some 56,250 authorized copies of the ***Legends*** were printed in twenty-three different editions.[84] Up to that time, it may be noted, the text was all-important, for the majority of the illustrations, which have undoubtedly counted in the work's subsequent fame, had not been added. These came in the thirty-second (1864) edition and were by George Cruikshank (who had illustrated a few of the pieces upon their initial appearances in the *Miscellany*), John Leech, Du Maurier, and John Tenniel.[85] The notices of the edition of 1864, while shorter than earlier ones, leave no doubt of Ingoldsby's then firmly established reputation. As one reviewer said: 'His name is duly inscribed on the long role of English Humourists.'[86] That name had been made 'a household word.'

Such statements attest the popularity of the ***Legends*** during the sixties. The next three decades, roughly, witnessed the apogee of Ingoldsby's fame. Within that period appeared the two most comprehensive editions of the ***Legends*** (1870, 1894), the two versions of the ***Life*** (1870, 1880), the ***Ingoldsby Lyrics*** (1881), and the most extensive reviews devoted to Ingoldsby, occasioned by the appearances of these works.[87] It marked the culmination of the efforts by the illustrators, anthologists, parodists,[88] elocutionists,[89] and musicians. With Ingoldsby's tide at the full, the reviewer in *Fraser's Magazine* in 1871 was led to say of him: 'We own we expect to see fresh Tennysons, fresh Thackerays, and fresh Lyttons, before we again fall in with that peculiar combination of qualities required for the production of the ***Ingoldsby Legends.***'[90]

Richard Bentley must be given principal credit for keeping Ingoldsby's work before the public and in favor. Some critics, indeed, say that much of its popularity was due to that publisher's refurbishing the ***Legends*** from time to time and putting them out in every conceivable kind of edition—in brief, exploiting them to the full. Now it need not be denied that Bentley did something of this sort, but to charge him with unscrupulousness or in any sense with unfairness would, I think, be unjustifiable. The ***Legends*** was one of the most popular works published by the Bentley firm during its entire existence. The printing history bears testimony to its popularity: approximately 450,000 authorized copies of the work were in print by 1895. As the price of the work dropped, the circulation naturally spread among new groups of readers. The success of an edition aimed to catch the widest possible audience serves to indicate not only the book's continuing success, but the acumen of the Bentley firm. An edition of 1881, the 'People's Edition,' selling for sixpence, had a printing of 100,000 copies, and 60,513 of these were sold on the day of publication.[91]

But toward the end of the same period a notable ground swell of dissent became evident. The burden of this opinion was that the ***Legends*** were passé, a relic of humor of the past, a delight only to a former generation but now something to be looked upon with mingled affection and disbelief, like an outmoded suit of clothes belonging to one's grandfather.[92]

Walter Whyte, who wrote the commentary on Barham for Miles's *Poets and Poetry* (1894), found that Ingoldsby's great popularity had declined somewhat but seemed little likely to expire. But while recognizing the popularity and the merits of Ingoldsby's Legends, Whyte asks if they are not somewhat overrated. 'When two or three of them are read consecutively, does not the cleverness become a trifle irksome? Does not the dead rattle of the rhyme begin to jar on the ear? Does not one grow weary before long of that gluttonous, bibulous, amorous crew of burlesque monks, and churchmen, and saints, and devils, and frail fair ladies?'[93] And further on he says that after Praed's verses Ingoldsby's rhymes 'sound like the clatter of castenets after a chime of silver bells.'

Other critics during the late nineties found Ingoldsby wanting in delicacy of wit and melody of verse when compared to Hood and Praed; and by then it was possible to compare him also with Calverley and Lewis Carroll, to his disadvantage.

It was at this time, however, that George Saintsbury, whose work on minor literary figures of the nineteenth century is yet recognized by such critics as Edmund Wilson as among the best, called the ***Legends*** 'immortal' and 'the most popular book of light verse that ever issued from the press.'[94] Gathering up several aspects of Ingoldsby's reputation, he says:

> Very recently they [the Legends] have met with a little priggish depreciation, the natural and indeed inevitable result, first of a certain change in speech and manners, and then of their long and vast popularity. Nor would any one contend that they are exactly great literature. But for inexhaustible fun that never gets flat and scarcely ever simply uproarious, for a facility and felicity in rhyme and rhythm which is almost miraculous, and for a blending of the grotesque and the terrible which, if less *fine* than Praed's or Hood's, is only inferior to theirs—no one competent to judge and enjoy will ever go to Barham in vain.

Only 'bad prigs' and persons of 'undue natural density,' he claims elsewhere, could fail to be delighted with reading these pieces 'at fourteen and at forty-eight.' As for himself, Saintsbury thought he could repeat half the Legends—he was sure he could with only an occasional cue.[95]

To realize that men of such disparate tastes as Charles Roach Smith, John Ruskin, and George Saintsbury were so fond of these tales that they memorized large numbers of them is to realize something of their widespread appeal. The remarks of these men help us, also, to understand something more of what constituted the basis for this appeal.

Yet another attraction was recognized by writers of the century's end. H. Morse Stephens first pointed out to readers Barham's 'extraordinary skill' in weaving his Legends about actual Kentish localities.[96] To visit the Ingoldsby County, one's open copy of the ***Legends*** in hand, became an exciting sport for confirmed Barhamites. There was Tappington to be visited, and from there the trails led one to Canterbury, to Thanington, or down to Dover. And not long afterword, in 1903, J. B. Atlay's edition of the tales first gave some indication of the surprising range of social history covered by the Legends. All subsequent writers have remarked upon these features of the work.

We may bring to a close the kind of criticism detailed in the foregoing pages, with a commentary that, because of its authoritative source, in 1915 set a seal of approval on Ingoldsby. *The Cambridge History of English Literature* says of him:

> High-principled but feeble-minded persons actually regarded the ***Legends*** at the time, and have regarded them since, as an infamous attempt to undermine the high church movement by ridicule; as a defiling of romance; as a prostitution of art; as a glorification of horse play and brutality; as a perilous palliation of drunkenness, irreverence, loose and improper conduct of all sorts. With quite infinitely less than the provocation of Rabelais, allegations and insinuations of faults not much less heinous than those charged by anti-Pantagruelists were raised, while, for a decade or two, more recently, has been added the sneer of the superior person at 'fun out of fashion.' On the other hand, it is a simple fact that not a few fervent high-churchmen, medievalists, men zealous for religion and devotees of romance, have been among ***Ingoldsby's*** most faithful lovers. For they have seen that 'Love me and laugh at me' is a motto not in the least self-contradictory, and that the highest kind of laughter is impossible without at least a little love, and a very high kind of love compatible with at least a grain of laughter.[97]

The chief attacks on Ingoldsby had for the time spent themselves. His niche—if only that—in English literature seemed henceforth assured, and while only an occasional strongly prejudiced supporter made extravagant claims to greatness, Ingoldsby's rooted stand as a delightful humorist appeared incontrovertible.

From 1916 to the present, Ingoldsby's work has continued slowly to decline in popularity and to lose favor with critics, though there are notable rear-guard activities by writers such as Stewart M. Ellis, the Reverend Arthur W. Fox, Sir Henry Newbolt, and Malcolm

Elwin. Ellis added to our knowledge of Barham's biography, and served to remind us that by 1917 Ingoldsby's lines had long been familiar and had 'become colloquial and as much a part of allusive and familiar English as the most inspired quotations from the national classics.'[98] Whatever may be the reaction of modern readers to Fox's sentimentalized account of Ingoldsby as 'perhaps the merriest companion of the soothing pipe within the varied range of English literature,' it is not without significance as a reflection of the wide appeal still exerted by the ***Legends*** upon one kind of reader.[99] Newbolt made a belated defense of Ingoldsby against those who denied literary merit to the ***Legends.*** When a writer has had 'the consideration of reasonably qualified contemporaries,' whose taste he has expressed or influenced, he may not thereafter be overlooked.[100] Newbolt reiterates Ingoldsby's claim for assessment in the long line of comic writers. Elwin is more valuable in showing Barham's literary relations than he is as a critic of the ***Legends.*** But his concluding remarks[101] are also evidence that not all of the affection for the man behind the Legends and the impact of his personality on readers like Fox have disappeared.

During the same period, Lionel Stevenson in America weighed Ingoldsby's claim to consideration along with other members of 'the irresponsible decade,' and found that he had 'followed his indomitably frivolous comrades into the Limbo of the superseded' even at the time of Horne's anguished denunciation of the ***Legends.***[102] The evidence I have cited may suggest that, if nothing more, the time factor is in error.[103] Newbolt, too, agreed in 1926 that Hook, Cannon, and Mathews had disappeared; but Barham, he said, 'still sits and laughs with us in a very substantial form.'

The centennial of the first appearance of the ***Legends*** in the *Miscellany* was noticed in the *Times Literary Supplement.* The article reveals much enthusiasm for 'that unique repertory of laughs, shudders, goblinry, and freshly minted *loci classici,*'[104] the ***Ingoldsby Legends.*** It finds Barham to have been 'the only genuine Early Victorian medievalist' and at the same time the most contemporary of commentators. Others at that period who were 'hankering after the Middle Ages' were either too insincere, too awkward, too pious, or too artificial. And Barham's 'lusty cry' was all the more unexpected for emanating from under the dome of St Paul's. But with the appearance of his work the Middle Ages themselves awoke:

> All over the country the gargoyles began to grin again, the imps and apes sprang off the carved misericords, marble saints and prelates sat up on their tombs and wagged reproving fingers as they had been wont to do in their days of flesh and blood, the witches muttered their spells afresh in every village, the ghost walked once more in every manor house—and the whole of England, which had watched with mistrust the medievalism of "stained-glass attitudes," gave a shout of hilarity and recognized its own self.

Barham's own 'clear and healing laugh,' still sounding in the ears of readers more than a century after his death, is the aspect of his fame that he himself would most cherish. For, loving his fellow men and giving himself unsparingly to their service, he found humor to be the great regulating force in the sane conduct of human affairs.[105]

Notes

68 See, for example, the *Illustrated London News,* 28 June 1845, p. 416; *Bentley's Miscellany,* XXI (1847), 104; and, for the details of Barham's aid through the Literary Fund to Hood and the latter's widow, K. J. Fielding's 'The Misfortunes of Hood,' *Notes and Queries,* CXCVIII (December 1953), 534-536.

69 *New Monthly Magazine,* LXXIV (1845), 528.

70 *Miscellany,* XXI (1847), 103.

71 *Athenaeum,* No. 643 (22 February 1840), p. 154.

72 *New Monthly Magazine,* LXXIV (1845), 529. I do not know a specific reference to Barham or the *Legends* in Miss Mitford's own writings.

73 'Notes on Some New Novels,' *Miscellany,* IX (1841), 528.

74 No. 856 (23 March 1844), pp. 263-265.

75 XXVIII (16 March 1844), 169-171.

76 *Ainsworth's Magazine,* V (1844), 317-325.

77 LXXI (1844), 129-136.

78 Horne's own copy of *A New Spirit,* extended from two to four volumes by the insertion of a large number of autograph letters from various literary figures of the day (including three by Barham), is in HCL. It contains annotations identified by Horne as being 'by my friend Leigh Hunt, to whom I lent these vols.'

79 *A New Spirit of the Age,* 2nd ed. (London, 1844), I, 147.

80 *Letters of Elizabeth Barrett Browning, Addressed to Richard Hengist Horne,* ed. Richard Henry Stoddard (New York, 1877), I, 227-228. Ingoldsby's influence on Robert Browning is apparent in such poems as 'The Pied Piper.'

[81] In dealing with both the *New Monthly* and *Ainsworth's* he was brief. Of the former he expressed incredulity that it should have stooped to attack him on personal grounds, though he realized that in taking a firm position against 'its principal contributor' he was in a vulnerable position. As to the latter, he was indeed surprised to find the 'gallant Editor' so implacably virulent in resorting to puns and personalities, and surprised also that Ainsworth did not add his own name to the piece.

[82] *A New Spirit of the Age,* ed. Walter Jerrold (London, 1907), p. xv.

[83] *Humorous Poetry,* p. 669.

In 1860 William Allingham, the Irish poet and friend of the Pre-Raphaelites, edited an anthology of verse entitled *Nightingale Valley.* He included Barham's 'graver verses,' 'As I Laye A-Thynkynge,' which met his rigid criterion ('nothing below a pure and loving loyalty to the Muse'), but rejected the other Legends as work in which 'great cleverness is but poorly employed.'

[84] Bibliographical information about the *Legends* is taken from the Bentley Private Catalogue, *A List of the Principal Publications Issued from New Burlington Street during the Year 1840* (London, 1895), compiled by Richard Bentley the younger and his assistant F. E. Williams. Only fifty copies of this work were printed, and much of the information it contains is not available elsewhere. (I have used the copy in the University of Illinois Library.) Michael Sadleir's *XIX-Century Fiction* (1951) should be consulted for bibliographical descriptions of the first editions of the Three Series and his discussion of the complexities surrounding the determination of the proper order of issue. Brief comments on the principal editions may be found in an appendix to Mrs Bond's edition of the *Legends* (1894). For further details about the financial aspects of the *Legends* as a Victorian best seller, see Royal A. Gettmann, 'Barham and Bentley,' *Journal of English and Germanic Philology,* LVI (1957), 337-346.

[85] For a description of a special copy of the 1864 edition at Harvard see Appendix I. Later noteworthy illustrations are those by Arthur Rackham (1898, revised and enlarged edition 1907), by Herbert Cole (1903), and by H. G. Theaker (1911).

[86] *Notes and Queries,* 3rd ser., VI (1864), 504.

[87] The review of the *Life* in *Temple Bar,* XXXI (1870/71), 66, provides information that an Ingoldsby Club, 'with literary tastes like his own,' had been formed sometime prior to December 1870 and held its meetings at the Freemasons' Tavern, near Great Queen Street, where the earliest Legends were written. One of the club members was James Alberry, a writer of such comedies as 'The Two Roses.'

The highly complimentary review of the *Life* in *Fraser's Magazine,* LXXXIII (1871), 302-316, makes an amusing apology for Barham's associates like Edward Cannon, Theodore Hook, and the members of the Garrick Club, finding it to Barham's credit that he 'mixed familiarly with such a set without compromising his calling.' The fallacy of the proffered excuse—that Ingoldsby was 'reading mankind, as others read books, with the view to the collection of hints and materials'—will be recognized at once by anyone who reads Barham's notebooks and letters.

A third article, reviewing both the *Legends* and the *Life,* in the *British Quarterly Review,* LIII (1871), 391-408, is substantial and informative.

[88] For some of the many parodies of Ingoldsby see Walter Hamilton, comp., *Parodies of the Works of English & American Authors* (London, 1884-89), V, 293-311.

[89] The recitations and 'penny readings' of the time usually included selections from *Pickwick* or from the *Legends.* Sam Weller, Tiger Tim, and the Jackdaw of Rheims became especial favorites. 'The Jackdaw' was part of the repertoire of the Webling sisters, Josephine and Peggy, famous 'readers' of the day. Evidence of their reputation and the fame of the Legend is to be found in a letter of 16 February 1880 from John Ruskin to their father: 'I also know the "Jackdaw of Rheims" pretty nearly by heart; but I would gladly come to London straightway, had I the time, to hear Miss Peggy speak it again' (*The Works of John Ruskin,* ed. Edward T. Cook and Alexander Wedderburn, London, 1903-12, XXXIV, 546). Ruskin had commented before on Barham: see *Works,* XXXIV, 103-104. William Henry Harrison, Ruskin's first editor, included a brief sketch of Barham, his former friend, in his 'Notes and Reminiscences' published in the *Dublin University Magazine,* XCII (1878), 66-67, recalling after more than thirty years that Barham was 'as witty and entertaining in his conversation as in his celebrated "Legends." '

Barham met Charles Roach Smith through their common interest in archaeology (see the letter's *Retrospections, Social and Archaeological,* London, 1883-91, I, 13-15). But also, Smith gave recitations; nor was he at all modest about this claim to fame. He gives an inadvertently amusing account of one of these readings 'before a large and first-class audience at Lewes' at which he proposed to follow excerpts from *Lear* with 'The Execution.' He was asked to replace the offending Legend ('there were full twenty clergymen in the audience'), which he did, but read it the next night to many of the same group with outstanding success.

[90] LXXXIII, 304.

[91] *Legends* (1894), III, 277.

[92] See, for example, a piece headed 'Ingoldsby' and signed 'K.' in the *Academy,* LV (1898), 340-341. A second article, unsigned, 'The Tedium of Irreverence,' *Academy,* LXI (1901), 569-570, occasioned by publication of the Legends in Grant Richards' World's Classics series, is more specific: the writer castigates Ingoldsby's want of reverence and lawlessness of form.

[93] Alfred H. Miles, ed., *The Poets and the Poetry of the Century* (London, 1891-94), IX, 200. E. C. Stedman in the mid-seventies had tried to dismiss Ingoldsby's tales as 'jingling trifles' (*Victorian Poets,* Boston, 1876, p. 238)—but he found it desirable to include 'The Jackdaw' and 'The Coronation' in his *Victorian Anthology 1837-1895* (Boston, 1895). With Hugh Walker's disparaging judgment in *The Literature of the Victorian Era* (Cambridge, 1910), p. 331, compare S. G. Tallentyre's favorable one in 'The Parson-Poets,' *North American Review,* CXCV (1912), 92-93.

[94] *A History of Nineteenth Century Literature (1780-1895)* (New York, 1896), pp. 209-210. Of Peacock, Crabbe, Borrow, Hogg, Praed, and Barham, Edmund Wilson says: 'It is impossible to take care of these writers by subsuming them under some bigger name. Each is unlike anyone else, unique and fully developed; each has to be explored for his own sake' (*Classics and Commercials,* New York, 1950, pp. 308-309).

[95] *Essays in English Literature 1780-1860, Second Series* (London, 1895), pp. 290-291.

[96] 'With Thomas Ingoldsby in Kent,' *Temple Bar,* CVI (1895), 89-98. This new element of criticism reached its culmination in Charles G. Harper's *The Ingoldsby Country* (London, 1904).

[97] XII (Cambridge, 1915), 123 (in chapter by Saintsbury on 'Lesser Poets, 1790-1837').

[98] Stewart M. Ellis, 'Richard Harris Barham—"Thomas Ingoldsby," ' *Bookman,* LI (1916/17), 112-118; reprinted with additions in *Mainly Victorian* (London, 1925), p. 30. Ellis does not specify lines of Ingoldsby's verse that became popular quotations, but at least one couplet, from 'The Lay of St. Odille,' suggests itself:

> For this you've my word, and I never yet
> broke it,
> So put that in your pipe, my Lord Otto, and
> smoke it!—

[99] 'Puffs from My Pipe. V. Thomas Ingoldsby,' *Papers of the Manchester Literary Club,* XLV (1919), 184.

[100] 'The Ingoldsby Legends,' *Studies Green and Gray* (London, 1926), p. 289. The extent of Barham's influence has not yet been determined. For evidence of his probable influence on an American author, see W. B. Stein, 'A Possible Source of Hawthorne's English Romance,' *Modern Language Notes,* LXVII (1952), 52-55, where the relation of 'The Spectre of Tappington' to *Doctor Grimshawe's Secret* is discussed.

[101] *Wallflowers,* p. 153.

[102] 'Barham and the Irresponsible Decade,' *University of California Chronicle,* XXVIII (1926), 400-418. Other articles of similar purport, though not specifically concerned with Barham, are Stevenson's 'Romanticism Run to Seed,' *Virginia Quarterly Review,* IX (1933), 510-525, and Agnes Repplier's 'The Laugh That Failed,' *Atlantic Monthly,* CLVIII (1936), 210-216. Mr Stevenson's first article is especially valuable in its delineation of the paradoxes that made up Barham's type of mind.

[103] There is no adequate bibliography of Barham. The various articles I have cited, taken together, comprise the fullest checklist available.

[104] 'The Ingoldsby Legends: "Mirth and Marvels" from St. Paul's,' *TLS,* 26 December 1936, p. 1057; this article is also quoted in note 49, above. See also 'Mirth and Marvels: Ingoldsby after a Hundred Years,' *TLS,* 16 June 1945, p. 282, published for the hundredth anniversary of Barham's death.

[105] I am indebted to the Research Council of Duke University for a grant that enabled me to complete my article. It is a pleasure to acknowledge the aid given and kindness shown me by Professor Hyder E. Rollins and Mr G. W. Cottrell, Jr.

William G. Lane (essay date 1967)

SOURCE: "Ingoldsby's Fame: Contemporary and Posthumous," in *Richard Harris Barham,* University of Missouri Press, 1967, pp. 206-22.

[*In the following essay, Lane discusses the critical and popular reception of Barham's* The Ingoldsby Legends.]

> We own we expect to see fresh Tennysons, fresh Thackerays, and fresh Lyttons, before we again fall in with that peculiar combination of qualities required for the production of the ***Ingoldsby Legends.***
>
> FRASER'S MAGAZINE, LXXXII (1871), 304

From the first appearance of the Legends, Ingoldsby was said to be "a most pleasant fellow in his mirthful mood" (**"The 'Monstre' Balloon"** or **"The Coronation"**) and, in a different manner, "when making the flesh creep with terror in some old ghastly goblin legend."[1] One might hesitate to believe that these ghastly goblin Legends were ever capable of having quite so strong an effect upon listeners were there not supplementary evidence. John Hughes's writings of a few years later assure us that it was so: "Suffice it to state, what my friend Miss Mitford can confirm, that the simple recitation of **'Hamilton Tighe'** has actually made persons start and turn pale, and complain of nervous excitement."[2] This "Victorian" reaction to only one of several such stories may go far to explain the initial appeal of the collected tales.

With John Hughes and Miss Mitford, "Dr. Pangloss," who wrote in the *Miscellany* of the Legends, safe in the assumption that all readers of that periodical would know the poetical vagaries of Ingoldsby, recognized the "ghastly horror in his **'Legend of Hamilton Tighe,'** which even Coleridge has scarcely surpassed."[3] But especial praise is given to the "rich and racy quality" of Ingoldsby humor and the "meteoric play of his fancy." His drollery, "like Falstaff's chuckling laugh, breathes the very spirit of good fellowship"; it is broad, subtle, fantastic, extravagant, as occasion requires. In this respect, as in its "strong catholic tendency even in its wildest freaks," it is "thoroughly Rabelaisian." This is the first, I think, of many comparisons of Barham to Rabelais. Noteworthy also is the fact that Ingoldsby's "spirit of good fellowship" was easily discerned and early praised.

It was well that there were friends to support Ingoldsby, for not long afterwards he was subjected to the "virtuous" attack from R. H. Horne (1803-1884) already mentioned. Horne, whose active career included a term as midshipman in the Mexican Navy and as Commander of the Gold Escort in Australia, was a onetime editor of the *Monthly Repository* and the author of plays about Marlowe and Gregory VII and of a history of Napoleon. His principal work, *Orion,* an epic poem, appeared in 1843. With so much literary experience behind him, he felt capable of emulating Hazlitt in delineating *A New Spirit of the Age* (1844). The third piece in this collection of twenty-five critical essays is devoted to Ingoldsby and entitled "Poison in Jest." It is an egregious and highly opinionated attack in the most extravagant language that anyone has used about the Legends. Horne was forced by the extensive sale and widespread popularity of the work to condemn its "hideous levity," constructed upon an "outrageous principle." He objected violently to Ingoldsby's **"Gengulphus,"** chiefly because of the comparison of the dismembering of the husband by the young clerk and the wife to the manner in which "the late Mr. Greenacre served Mrs. Brown." (Greenacre, a notorious criminal, was executed on 10 May 1837.) Here, exclaimed Horne, is just the point: the direct comparison with an actual horror!

Not all of Horne's essay is condemnatory, however. With all his objections on moral grounds, he recognized that Ingoldsby was a master of comic versification. Indeed, because the Legends show the possibilities of the English language for true rhyme, that is, rhyme depending solely on ear and not limited by the eye, they are in this respect "philological studies, indisputable theoretically, and as novel as they are amusing." Perfect rhymes—single, double, and triple syllabic—he found abundant in the Legends, and he cited many illustrations of Ingoldsby's astonishing ability. Horne concluded by reminding the reader that he objected to the Legends solely on "the abstract grounds of Literature and Art": he excluded religious grounds, conventional morality, and personalities. He felt it necessary to condemn these licentious works that are unredeemed by any one sincere passion—and therefore a bad influence on the rising generation, which was bad enough without such assistance. "Wherefore an iron hand is now laid upon the shoulder of Thomas Ingoldsby, and a voice murmurs in his ear, 'Brother!—no more of this!' "

Objections to Horne's book came from all quarters, some of which did not mention the chapter on Ingoldsby, although the consensus was that he, more than any other writer, had been maligned. *The Athenaeum,*[4] taking a fairly temperate view, observed that the selection savored too much of literary coterie—"a peculiar view of a peculiar set of minds"—but still found much to amuse as well as to suggest thought. The attack on Ingoldsby was termed a "slaughter," nevertheless; though Ingoldsby's banter was "reckless," Horne had dealt with it "somewhat too savagely."

The *Literary Gazette*[5] was stronger on both counts. While finding Horne's opinions not entirely lacking in acumen, it objected to his critical jargon (that of a new school of "highly clouded, mystical, and metaphysical pretenders") and to his total failure to perceive or to have power over the humorous. It found him sadly inadequate on Dickens, the most popular writer of the time, and then turned to his treatment of Ingoldsby, "one of the most original and entertaining writers, and one of the most curious as well as tuneful versifiers of the day (in the former equal to Butler, in the latter to Pope)." In dismissing the follies exposed by Ingoldsby as those solely of another age, however, the *Gazette* itself was rather far from understanding his real motives.

Samuel Laman Blanchard, then subeditor of *Ainsworth's Magazine,* leveled the batteries of that periodical on the *New Spirit* and its author with an article entitled "The New Gull's Horne-Book."[6] After explaining at some length how far short of Hazlitt's example the new work fell and after objecting that it was solely a book on literature and not on the spirit of the age, Blanchard proceeded to lay down a counter-barrage for Ingoldsby.

Horne had spoken of the lack of refinement and ideality in the Legends and had used fairy tales as an example of what he thought they should have been. "Alas, for fairy-tale and legend," wrote Blanchard, "for now they have fallen under the iron hand of a merciless moralist. . . . Knowing of what the hand consists, it would be pleasant to know of what metal the face that belongs to it is made." In explicating the concluding sentence of Horne's essay, he asked what sin the Legends committed; then answered: "Alas, the worst of sins—it has made men laugh; it has incurred the deadly, the inexpiable guilt of popularity!" Replying to Horne's charge that the principle on which the Legends were constructed was unsound, Blanchard warned that, hitherto delighting in "the wild and original pleasantries" of Ingoldsby, the reader

> has yet to learn that in every smooth but tortuous line of the many-winding legend, there lurks a snake—it hisses in the melody, and stings in the moral. Where he has laughed, he should have trembled and shuddered. When he has been shaking his sides, he should have shaken his head—shed iron tears, and stretched forth the iron hand. Any objection that may have been made heretofore, has been a shallow, undiscerning, insufficient objection, and now for the first time has a discovery been made—that what our good spirits have fed upon so merrily, was either "poison" or "twaddle."

Blanchard concluded sarcastically: "Some say that the spirit of the age is quackery; only grant that, and then the projectors of this design become its fair and legitimate representatives."

This level of calumny—so it was considered by Horne—was not reached even by the *New Monthly,*[7] to whose pages Barham was then a contributor. That he should be strongly defended in his own journal was of course natural. Horne's book, declared the reviewer, stood in a very unhappy predicament. "It has had the effect of sorely puzzling some people—of offending others—of satisfying none." Even those praised therein were made uneasy under its approbation. The reviewer denounced Horne's book on several counts, but he found strangest of all the chapter on Ingoldsby.

The real difficulty, according to the reviewer, was that Horne simply did not know what to make of Ingoldsby. He was fairly sure that Ingoldsby was a comic poet, but if so, then unlike all others. Quoting Horne's comments on the passage from **"Gengulphus,"** the reviewer exclaimed in feigned surprise at the astuteness of the critic:

> It never occurred to this sincere wiseacre, that there was something else to ridicule besides the diseased appetite for horrors—namely, *the diseased food by which it is nourished.* He sees plainly enough that Ingoldsby indulges in a jocose use of horrors, and he takes his stand upon that. If he had looked an inch further he must have discovered that all this raw-head and cross-bones whimsicality is the vent, not of a scoffing spirit, but of a strong wit lashing with matchless ridicule the ribald and profane narratives of horror, which daily solicit the morbid sympathies of the public in an endless variety of shapes. . . . Thomas Ingoldsby has scourged the brutal taste in a way not likely to be forgotten. He has heaped overwhelming satire upon that minute style of delineating crime, which might be said to have created the passion upon whose indulgence it subsisted; and he has given such an effectually ludicrous turn to the genius for the horrible, that the whole school of penny-a-line pathos may be fairly said to shudder through his verses and expire in their echoes.

I have given this reviewer's remarks at some length, not only because they are an effective rebuttal of Horne but, more importantly, because they explain the editorial policy behind the publication of the Legends in the *New Monthly.* They show conclusively that the Legends were not taken merely as a rush of fun thrown out by a facile rhymer.

In this connection the marginal note written by Leigh Hunt at the end of the chapter on Ingoldsby in Horne's personal copy of *A New Spirit* is of particular interest: "May not Ingoldsby have intended to bring into popular contempt the morbid tendency to crime itself? to make Greenacres, for instance, ashamed and disgusted at the idea of becoming Greenacres?" To this has been appended Horne's reply: "*No*—R. H. H."[8] This suggestion of Hunt's, found also in various reviews of Horne's book, doubtless prompted the insertion of the following paragraph in a second edition, published later the same year:

> Those who endeavour to justify this writer by the sudden discovery of a moral aim in his ridiculing real horrors (in order to teach the vulgar to laugh at them) say not one syllable of the gross licentiousness of these tales! There *is* nothing to say for them.[9]

The critical reaction was so preponderantly pro-Ingoldsby that Horne felt it necessary to reply at some length in the Introductory Comments to this second edition, despite Elizabeth Barrett's admonition, "Let them rave! That the book does not deserve their abuse we know as well as they themselves do—and there is no need to know better. What turns *against* it is simply the worm—or the friend of the worm, wormy and right wormily!"[10] In replying, Horne refused to be drawn into a controversy with the reviewers: "I receive their shots, and pass on my way. I presume a period will some day arrive when Thomas Ingoldsby may consider himself sufficiently avenged by eight or ten attacks in return for my one."[11]

That day was not long in coming. While it is true that Horne's replies to his critics were "mere foil-play," as Walter Jerrold remarked,[12] they are ample evidence of the general popularity and success of the Legends.

If Elizabeth Barrett's remark was intended to equate Ingoldsby with the "worm"—and if so, it is the only comment on Barham by either of the Brownings that I have been able to discover—then one "friend of the worm" was Thackeray. In the *Morning Chronicle,* 2 April 1844, Titmarsh wrote that Horne's "easy candour" ought to lead people to deal sincerely with him. Most of his views were commonplace, wrote Thackeray; only in the matter of commenting on Barham did he show "spleen," and even that had a sort of "clumsy sincerity." These strictures upon Horne's intellectual scope, coupled with remarks concerning his style of dress, provoked appropriate rejoinder in the second edition of *A New Spirit.* Horne objected to Thackeray's abuse of "so important a position of influence on the public mind, by inserting his 'good fun' in the leading liberal morning paper. . . . Besides," he went on, "the book was open enough on literary grounds for sharp handling, and [Thackeray] might have found ample grounds, either to advocate the cause of comic poetry, or to assist his friend Ingoldsby, the 'amusing poet,' with the 'harmless phantasies.' "

In one phase of this minor literary turmoil a point claimed by Horne redounds to his credit. Addressing himself to Ingoldsby in the Introduction to the second edition he remarked that "in dealing with his **'Legends,'** which I conceived it a duty to treat unsparingly, I yet exercised the utmost forbearance towards himself personally—a forbearance which has not been exercised by his friends who have attacked me, but which I have not resented upon him, nor intend." Horne could well have taken satisfaction from his stand, for in less than a year—on 17 June 1845—Ingoldsby died.

The appearance of the Third Series in December, 1846, drew notices in the book columns of periodicals, and in the *Miscellany* and *New Monthly* it was of course given special attention. Ingoldsby's fame was continuing to spread at home and abroad. During the fifties and sixties the better pieces began to be included in anthologies. For example, James Parton's *Humorous Poetry of the English Language* (New York, 1856), containing many of Ingoldsby's tales, went into a sixth edition before the end of the following year. As a rhymer, Ingoldsby was held by Parton to have but one equal in English literature—Byron.[13]

Between 1857 and the end of 1864 some 56,250 authorized copies of the ***Legends*** were printed in twenty-three different editions.[14] Up to that time, it may be noted, the text was all-important, for the majority of the illustrations, which have undoubtedly counted in the work's subsequent fame, had not been added. These enhanced the thirty-second (1864) edition and were by George Cruikshank (who had illustrated a few of the pieces upon their initial appearances in the *Miscellany*), John Leech, Du Maurier, and John Tenniel.[15] The notices of the edition of 1864, while shorter than earlier ones, leave no doubt of Ingoldsby's then firmly established reputation. As one reviewer said: "His name is duly inscribed on the long role of English Humourists."[16] That name had been made "a household word."

Such statements attest the popularity of the ***Legends*** during the sixties. The next three decades, roughly, witnessed the apogee of Ingoldsby's fame. Within that period appeared the two most comprehensive editions of the ***Legends*** (1870, 1894), the two versions of the ***Life*** (1870, 1880), the ***Ingoldsby Lyrics*** (1881), and the most extensive reviews devoted to Ingoldsby, occasioned by the appearances of these works.[17] It marked the culmination of the efforts by the illustrators, anthologists, parodists,[18] elocutionists,[19] and musicians. With Ingoldsby's tide at the full, the reviewer in *Fraser's Magazine* in 1871 was led to say of him: "We own we expect to see fresh Tennysons, fresh Thackerays, and fresh Lyttons, before we again fall in with that peculiar combination of qualities required for the production of the ***Ingoldsby Legends.***"[20]

Richard Bentley must be given principal credit for keeping Ingoldsby's work before the public and in favor. Some critics, indeed, say that much of its popularity was due to that publisher's refurbishing the ***Legends*** from time to time and putting them out in every conceivable kind of edition—in brief, exploiting them to the full. Now it need not be denied that Bentley did something of this sort, but to charge him with unscrupulousness or in any sense with unfairness would, I think, be unjustifiable. The ***Legends*** was one of the most popular works published by the Bentley firm during its entire existence. The printing history bears testimony to its popularity: Approximately 450,000 authorized copies of the work were in print by 1895. As the price of the work dropped, the circulation naturally spread among new groups of readers. The success of an edition aimed to catch the widest possible audience serves to indicate not only the book's continuing success but also the acumen of the Bentley firm. An edition of 1881, the "People's Edition," selling for sixpence, had a printing of 100,000 copies, and 60,513 of these were sold on the day of publication.[21]

Toward the end of the same period a notable ground swell of dissent became evident. The burden of this opinion was that the Legends were passé, a relic of humor of the past, a delight only to a former generation but now something to be looked upon with mingled affection and disbelief, like an outmoded suit of clothes belonging to one's grandfather.[22]

Walter Whyte, who wrote the commentary on Barham for Miles's *Poets and Poetry* (1894), found that Ingoldsby's great popularity had declined somewhat but was unlikely to expire. While recognizing the popularity and the merits of Ingoldsby's Legends, Whyte asked if they are not somewhat overrated. "When two or three of them are read consecutively, does not the cleverness become a trifle irksome? Does not the dead rattle of the rhyme begin to jar on the ear? Does not one grow weary before long of that gluttonous, bibulous, amorous crew of burlesque monks, and churchmen, and saints, and devils, and frail fair ladies?"[23] He suggested that, after Praed's verses, Ingoldsby's rhymes "sound like the clatter of castanets after a chime of silver bells." Other critics during the late nineties found Ingoldsby wanting in delicacy of wit and in melody of verse when compared to Hood and Praed, and by then it was customary to compare him also with Calverley and Lewis Carroll, sometimes to his disadvantage.

It was at this point, however, that George Saintsbury, whose work on minor literary figures of the nineteenth century is yet recognized by such critics as Edmund Wilson as among the best, called the ***Legends*** "immortal" and "the most popular book of light verse that ever issued from the press."[24] Gathering up several aspects of Ingoldsby's reputation, he remarked:

> Very recently they [the Legends] have met with a little priggish depreciation, the natural and indeed inevitable result, first of a certain change in speech and manners, and then of their long and vast popularity. Nor would any one contend that they are exactly great literature. But for inexhaustible fun that never gets flat and scarcely ever simply uproarious, for a facility and felicity in rhyme and rhythm which is almost miraculous, and for a blending of the grotesque and the terrible which, if less *fine* than Praed's or Hood's, is only inferior to theirs—no one competent to judge and enjoy will ever go to Barham in vain.

Only "bad prigs" and persons of "undue natural density," he asserted elsewhere, could fail to be delighted with reading these pieces "at fourteen and at forty-eight." As for himself, Saintsbury thought he could repeat half the Legends—he was sure he could with only an occasional cue.[25]

To realize that men of such disparate tastes as Charles Roach Smith, John Ruskin, and George Saintsbury were so fond of these tales that they memorized large numbers of them is to realize something of their widespread appeal. The remarks of these men help us, also, to understand something more of what constituted the basis for this appeal.

Yet another attraction was recognized by writers at the century's end. H. Morse Stephens first pointed out to readers Barham's "extraordinary skill" in weaving his Legends about actual Kentish localities.[26] To visit the Ingoldsby Country, one's open copy of the ***Legends*** in hand, became an exciting sport for confirmed Barhamites. There was Tappington to be visited, and from there the trails led one to Canterbury, to Thanington, or down to Dover. And not long afterward, in 1903, J. B. Atlay's edition of the tales first gave some indication of the surprising range of social history covered by the Legends. All subsequent writers have remarked upon these features of the work.

We may bring to a close the kind of criticism detailed in the foregoing pages with a commentary that, because of its authoritative source, in 1915 set a seal of approval on Ingoldsby. *The Cambridge History of English Literature* says of him:

> High-principled but feeble-minded persons actually regarded the *Legends* at the time, and have regarded them since, as an infamous attempt to undermine the high church movement by ridicule; as a defiling of romance; as a prostitution of art; as a glorification of horse play and brutality; as a perilous palliation of drunkenness, irreverence, loose and improper conduct of all sorts. With quite infinitely less than the provocation of Rabelais, allegations and insinuations of faults not much less heinous than those charged by anti-Pantagruelists were raised, while, for a decade or two, more recently, has been added the sneer of the superior person at "fun out of fashion." On the other hand, it is a simple fact that not a few fervent high-churchmen, medievalists, men zealous for religion and devotees of romance, have been among ***Ingoldsby's*** most faithful lovers. For they have seen that "Love me and laugh at me" is a motto not in the least self-contradictory, and that the highest kind of laughter is impossible without at least a little love, and a very high kind of love compatible with at least a grain of laughter.[27]

The chief attacks on Ingoldsby had spent themselves. His place in English literature is now assured, and while only an occasional strongly prejudiced supporter would make extravagant claims to greatness, Ingoldsby's rooted stand as a delightful humorist appears incontrovertible.

From 1916 to the present, Ingoldsby's work has occasionally, after unfavorable criticism, been defended, notably by writers such as Stewart M. Ellis, the Reverend Arthur W. Fox, Sir Henry Newbolt, and Malcolm Elwin. Ellis added to our knowledge of Barham's biography, and his book serves to remind us that by 1917 Ingoldsby's lines had long been familiar and had "become colloquial and as much a part of allusive and familiar English as the most inspired quotations from the national classics."[28] Whatever may be the reaction of modern readers to Fox's sentimentalized account of Ingoldsby as "perhaps the merriest companion of the soothing pipe within the varied range of English literature," it is not without significance as a reflection of the wide appeal still exerted by the Legends upon one kind of reader.[29] Newbolt made a strong defense of Ingoldsby against those who denied literary merit to the Legends. When a writer has had "the consideration of reasonably qualified contemporaries," whose taste he has expressed or influenced, he may not thereafter be overlooked.[30] Newbolt reiterated Ingoldsby's claim for assessment in the long line of comic writers. Elwin's work is more valuable in showing Barham's literary relations than as a criticism of the Legends. His concluding remarks[31] are evidence, however, that there persists much affection for the man behind the Legends and that the impact of his personality on readers like Fox is still strong.

During the same period, Lionel Stevenson in America weighed Ingoldsby's claim to consideration along with other members of "the irresponsible decade" and found that he had "followed his indomitably frivolous comrades into the Limbo of the superseded" even at the time of Horne's impassioned denunciation of the Legends.[32] The evidence I have cited may suggest that, if nothing more, the time factor is in error. Newbolt, too, agreed in 1926 that Hook, Cannon, and Mathews had disappeared, but Barham, he said, "still sits and laughs with us in a very substantial form."

The centennial of the first appearance of the Legends in the *Miscellany* was noticed in the *Times Literary Supplement*. The article reveals much enthusiasm for "that unique repertory of laughs, shudders, goblinry, and freshly minted *loci classici*,"[33] the ***Ingoldsby Legends.*** It finds Barham to have been "the only genuine Early Victorian medievalist" and at the same time the most contemporary of commentators. Other writers in that period who were "hankering after the Middle Ages" were either too insincere, too awkward, too pious, or too artificial. Furthermore, Barham's "lusty cry" was all the more unexpected for emanating from under the dome of St. Paul's. With the appearance of his work the Middle Ages awoke:

> All over the country the gargoyles began to grin again, the imps and apes sprang off the carved misericords, marble saints and prelates sat up on their tombs and wagged reproving fingers as they had been wont to do in their days of flesh and blood, the witches muttered their spells afresh in every village, the ghost walked once more in every manor house—and the whole of England, which had watched with mistrust the medievalism of "stained-glass attitudes," gave a shout of hilarity and recognized its own self.

Barham's own "clear and healing laugh," still sounding in the ears of readers more than a century after his death, is the aspect of his fame that he himself would most cherish. For, loving his fellow men and giving himself unsparingly to their service, he found humor to be the great regulating force in the sane conduct of human affairs.

Notes

[1] *The Athenaeum,* No. 643 (22 February 1840), p. 154.

[2] John Hughes, "Sketches of the Late Rev. R. H. Barham, with a few lines to his Memory," *New Monthly Magazine,* LXXIV (1845), 529. I do not know a specific reference to Barham or to the *Legends* in Miss Mitford's writings.

[3] Dr. Pangloss, "Notes on Some New Novels," *Miscellany,* IX (1841), 528.

[4] No. 856 (23 March 1844), 263-65.

[5] XXVIII (16 March 1844), 169-71.

[6] Samuel L. Blanchard, "The New Gull's Horne-Book," *Ainsworth's Magazine,* V (1844), 317-25.

[7] LXXI (1844), 129-36.

[8] Horne's copy of *A New Spirit,* extended from two to four volumes by the insertion of a large number of autograph letters from various literary figures of the day (including three by Barham), is in Harvard College Library. It contains annotations identified by Horne as being "by my friend Leigh Hunt, to whom I lent these vols."

[9] Richard H. Horne, *A New Spirit of the Age,* 2d ed., I, 147.

[10] *Letters of Elizabeth Barrett Browning, Addressed to Richard Hengist Horne,* Richard Henry Stoddard, ed., I, 227-28. Ingoldsby's influence on Robert Browning is apparent in such poems as "The Pied Piper."

[11] In dealing with both the *New Monthly* and *Ainsworth's* he was brief. Of the former he expressed incredulity that it should have stooped to attack him on personal grounds, though he realized that in taking a firm position against "its principal contributor" he was in a vulnerable position. As to the latter, he was indeed surprised to find the "gallant Editor" so implacably virulent in resorting to puns and personalities and was surprised also that Ainsworth did not add his own name to the piece.

[12] Richard H. Horne, *A New Spirit of the Age,* Walter Jerrold, ed., p. xv.

[13] James Parton, *Humorous Poetry of the English Language from Chaucer to Saxe,* p. 669. In 1860 William Allingham, the Irish poet and friend of the Pre-Raphaelites, edited an anthology of verse entitled *Nightingale Valley.* He included Barham's "graver verses," "As I Laye A-Thynkynge," which met his rigid criterion ("nothing below a pure and loving loyalty to the Muse"), but rejected the other Legends as work in which "great cleverness is but poorly employed."

[14] Bibliographical information about the *Legends* is taken from the Bentley Private Catalogue, *A List of the Principal Publications Issued from New Burlington Street during the Year 1840,* compiled by Richard Bentley the younger and his assistant F. E. Williams. Only fifty copies of this work were printed, and much of the information it contains is not available elsewhere. Sadleir's *XIX Century Fiction* may be consulted for bibliographical descriptions of the first editions of the three series and for his discussion of the complexities surrounding the determination of the proper order of issue. Brief comments on the principal editions may be found in an appendix to Mrs. Bond's edition of the *Legends* (1894). For further details about the financial aspects of the *Legends* as a Victorian best seller, see Royal A. Gettmann, "Barham and Bentley," *The Journal of English and Germanic Philology,* LVI (1957), 337-46.

[15] Later noteworthy illustrations are those by Arthur Rackham (1898, revised and enlarged edition 1907), by Herbert Cole (1903), and H. G. Theaker (1911).

[16] *Notes and Queries,* 3d Series, VI (1864), 504.

[17] The review of the *Life* in *Temple Bar,* XXXI (1870/71), 66, provides information that an Ingoldsby Club, "with literary tastes like his own," had been formed some time prior to December 1870 and held its meetings at the Freemasons' Tavern, near Great Queen Street, where the earliest Legends were written. One of the club members was James Alberry, a writer of such comedies as "The Two Roses."

The highly complimentary review of the *Life* in *Fraser's Magazine,* LXXXIII (1871), 302-16, makes an amusing apology for Barham's associates like Edward Cannon, Theodore Hook, and the members of the Garrick Club, finding it to Barham's credit that he "mixed familiarly with such a set without compromising his calling." The fallacy of the proffered excuse—that Ingoldsby was "reading mankind, as others read books, with the view to the collection of hints and materials"—will be recognized at once by anyone who reads Barham's notebooks and letters.

A third article, reviewing both the *Legends* and the *Life,* in the *British Quarterly Review,* LIII (1871), 391-408, is substantial and informative.

[18] For some of the many parodies of Ingoldsby, see *Parodies of the Works of English & American Authors,* Walter Hamilton, ed., V, 293-311.

[19] The recitations and "penny readings" of the time usually included selections from *Pickwick* or from the *Legends.* Sam Weller, Tiger Tim, and the Jackdaw of Rheims became especial favorites. "The Jackdaw" was part of the repertoire of the Webling sisters, Josephine and Peggy, famous "readers" of the day. Evidence of their reputation and the fame of the Legend is to be found in a letter of 16 February 1880 from John Ruskin to their father: "I also know the 'Jackdaw of Rheims' pretty nearly by heart; but I would gladly come to London straightway, had I the time, to hear Miss Peggy speak it again" (*The Works of John Ruskin,* Edward T. Cook and Alexander Wedderburn, eds., XXXIV, 546). Ruskin had commented before on Barham: see *Works,* XXXIV, 103-4. William Henry Harrison, Ruskin's first editor, included a brief sketch of Barham, his former friend, in his "Notes and Reminiscenes," published in the *Dublin University Magazine,* XCII (1878), 66-67, recalling after more than thirty years that Barham was "as witty and entertaining in his conversation as in his celebrated 'Legends.' "

Barham met Charles Roach Smith through their common interest in archaeology (see the latter's *Retrospections, Social and Archaeological,* I, 13-15). But also, Smith gave recitations; nor was he at all modest about this claim to fame. He wrote an inadvertently amusing account of one of these readings "before a large and first-class audience at Lewes" at which he proposed to follow excerpts from *Lear* with "The Execution." He was asked to replace the offending Legend ("there were full twenty clergymen in the audience"), which he did, but read it the next night to many of the same group, with outstanding success.

[20] LXXXIII, 304.

[21] *Legends* (1894), III, 277.

[22] See, for example, a piece headed "Ingoldsby" and signed "K." in the *Academy,* LV (1898), 340-41. A second article, unsigned, "The Tedium of Irreverence," *Academy,* LXI (1901), 569-70, occasioned by publication of the *Legends* in Grant Richards' World's Classics series, is more specific: The writer castigates Ingoldsby's want of reverence and his lawlessness of form.

[23] *The Poets and the Poetry of the Century,* Alfred H. Miles, ed., IX, 200. E. C. Stedman in the mid-seventies had tried to dismiss Ingoldsby's tales as "jingling trifles" (*Victorian Poets* [Boston, 1876], p. 238), but he found it desirable to include "The Jackdaw" and "The Coronation" in his *Victorian Anthology 1837-1895* (Boston, 1895). With Hugh Walker's disparaging judgment in

The Literature of the Victorian Era (Cambridge, 1910), p. 331, compare S. G. Tallentyre's favorable comment in "Parson-Poets," *North American Review,* CXCV (1912), 92-93.

[24] George Saintsbury, *A History of Nineteenth Century Literature 1780-1895,* pp. 209-10. Of Peacock, Crabbe, Borrow, Hogg, Praed, and Barham, Edmund Wilson wrote: "It is impossible to take care of these writers by subsuming them under some bigger name. Each is unlike anyone else, unique and fully developed; each has to be explored for his own sake" (*Classics and Commercials,* pp. 308-9).

[25] George Saintsbury, "Three Humourists," in *Essays in English Literature 1780-1860,* Second Series, pp. 290-91.

[26] H. Morse Stephens, "With Thomas Ingoldsby in Kent," *Temple Bar,* CVI (1895), 89-98. This new element of criticism reached its culmination in Charles G. Harper's *The Ingoldsby Country.*

[27] XII (Cambridge, 1915), 123 (in chapter by Saintsbury on "Lesser Poets, 1790-1837").

[28] Stewart M. Ellis, "Richard Harris Barham—'Thomas Ingoldsby,' " *Bookman,* LI (1916/17), 112-18; reprinted with additions in *Mainly Victorian,* p. 30. Ellis did not specify lines of Ingoldsby's verse that became popular quotations, but at least one couplet, from "The Lay of St. Odille," suggests itself:

> For this you've my word, and I never yet
>   broke it,
> So put that in your pipe, my Lord Otto, and
>   smoke it!—

[29] Arthur W. Fox, "Puffs from My Pipe. V, Thomas Ingoldsby," *Papers of the Manchester Literary Club,* LXV (1919), 184.

[30] Sir Henry John Newbolt, "The Ingoldsby Legends," *Studies Green and Gray,* p. 289. The extent of Barham's influence has not yet been determined. For evidence of his probable influence on an American author, see W. B. Stein, "A Possible Source of Hawthorne's English Romance," *Modern Language Notes,* LXVII (1952), 52-55, where the relation of "The Spectre of Tappington" to *Doctor Grimshawe's Secret* is discussed.

[31] Malcolm Elwin, *Victorian Wallflowers,* p. 153.

[32] Lionel Stevenson, "Barham and the Irresponsible Decade," *University of California Chronicle,* XXVIII (1926), 400-418. Other articles of similar purport, though not specifically concerned with Barham, are Stevenson's "Romanticism Run to Seed," *Virginia Quarterly Review,* IX (1933), 510-25, and Agnes Repplier's "The Laugh That Failed," *Atlantic Monthly,* CLVIII (1936), 210-16. Mr. Stevenson's first article is especially valuable in its delineation of the paradoxes that made up Barham's type of mind.

[33] "The Ingoldsby Legends: 'Mirth and Marvels' from St. Paul's," *TLS,* 26 December 1936, p. 1057. See also "Mirth and Marvels: Ingoldsby after a Hundred Years," *TLS,* 16 June 1945, p. 282, published for the hundredth anniversary of Barham's death.

David J. Winslow (essay date 1971)

SOURCE: "Richard Harris Barham and His Use of Folklore," *New York Folklore Quarterly,* Vol. 27, March, 1971, pp. 370-84.

[*In the following essay, Winslow examines the English folklore that formed the basis for much of Barham's poetry.*]

Richard Harris Barham, Victorian poet and humorist, provides an interesting subject for the analysis of the use of folklore in literature. Wit, clergyman, antiquarian, and poet, Barham managed to assemble, transform, and stamp with roguish humor a wide array of authentic folklore material, although he himself was far removed from the folk in mind, manner, and milieu. Traditional oral prose narratives, in particular legends, tales, and anecdotes, along with superstitions, were eagerly seized by Barham from oral and literary sources and became the fabric for his major work, ***The Ingoldsby Legends.*** Neither Barham nor any other author have written folklore, but many have embellished, juxtaposed, and re-worked this material in the alchemy of literature. An analysis of the relation between oral, literary, and historical sources to Barham's skillfully conceived poetical product, is the goal of this essay.

Barham was born in Canterbury on December 6, 1788, and he claimed descent from the brother of the notorious historical personage Reginald Fitzurse and the Irish Macmahons, although this impressive genealogy has been questioned.[1] However, the old Kentish landowning stock from which he descended served him well as a basis for ***The Ingoldsby Legends.*** Barham's home in historic Canterbury and his later home, Tappington, were influences strongly reflected in his literary works. Tappington, a small picturesque building of timber and brick with latticed windows and a covering of vines, was to become in later years the focal point of ***The Ingoldsby Legends.*** Here Barham placed the dwelling of the Ingoldsby family, compounded of imagination and some family tradition. Of course, he greatly idealised and enlarged the place of his literary descriptions, a hoax which delighted him and which he elaborated by appending to the collected editions of ***The Legends*** a woodcut of his imaginary Tappington Hall. In reality, according to S. M. Ellis, "His own little farmstead was no stately Manor House with avenue guarded by heraldic lodge gates. The real Tappington Hall was Broome Hall near by, on the way to Canterbury, beneath Barham Downs—that bleak elevated land so impregnated with Roman and Saxon remains, and the actual Tappington Moor of **'The Hand of Glory.'** "[2] Barham was graduated from Brasenose College, Oxford, where he became acquainted with Theodore Hook, another Victorian humorist, who was to become his lifelong friend. In 1813 Barham was severely injured in a stage-coach accident, resulting in his abdication of a convivial life and the decision to become a clergyman, his first curacy being at Ashford, Kent, from which he moved on to other country parishes. It is highly probable that his experiences in this role with country folk and their superstitions left their impact on his mind, which already had an antiquarian bent. His son wrote, "Among my father's memoranda I find an account, abridged from Scott's curious work, of a case of witchcraft which occurred in this village of Westwell in the reign of Queen Elizabeth."[3] In 1817 he became rector of Snargate and curate of Warehorne, situated in the drear, lonely region of Romney Marsh, said to be "magic-ridden country."[3] Snargate, its damp church and unhealthy parsonage hemmed in by trees, was the most dismal of villages; and Warehorne was not much better off in the midst of the weird, mist-drenched marshland. And yet "this recondite region," as Barham characterized it in **"The Leech of Folkestone,"** has its own peculiar grim fascination, like the fens of East Anglia and Chat Moss in Lancashire, for those such as Barham, with an imaginative mind and a flair for the supernatural: these vast flat expanses are full of suggestion, aided by the mystery of the mist, and atmospheric effects, and fen lights at night. Barham's parishioners were illiterate folk, avowed smugglers, but were civil to him as long as he overlooked their illicit trade. Once, however, they commandeered his belfry at Snargate as a place to conceal contraband tobacco. In 1821 Barham was transferred to London.

Barham's Church of England, nepotistic and pluralistic, coddled clergymen who, besides tending their flocks, enjoyed their bottle, their game of cards, and their sport. In these days, too, there was a deep longing for the Middle Ages, which is reflected in the subjects of many of Barham's poems and prose works. He was no exception to the spirit of the times, as he was preoccupied with the supernatural and with antiquarian activities. He was one of the founders of The Archaelogical Association, and with other clergymen, somewhat in the manner of Mr. Pickwick, made forays into the countryside questing for relics of England's noble past. But one of the most interesting challenges of the folklorist is the quest for sources, original versions, and prototypes of folklore materials used by literary artists such as Barham. "The complex interrelation of oral and literary tradition is one of the most baffling problems the folklore scholar encounters,"[4] Stith Thompson has written. Too often, this statement is indeed very true. However, when dealing with ***The Ingoldsby Legends,*** the researcher is on somewhat firmer footing than he would be when trying to discover the sources, either literary or oral, of most other writers. One of the sources for ***The Ingoldsby Legends*** was Mrs. Hughes, the wife of Dr. Hughes, the latter an intimate friend of Barham in London. When Barham was introduced to her, she was quite elderly but still had an unusually sharp memory and possessed much knowledge of local history. Actually, she was a rather widely known informant:[5]

> She is mentioned by Lockhart as the frequent correspondent of Sir Walter Scott and Southey, and for nearly a quarter of a century she kept up a regular interchange of letters with Barham, besides numerous face to face visits. To her he was indebted not only for a large proportion of the legendary lore which forms the groundwork of ***The Ingoldsby Legends,*** but also for the application of a stimulus that induced him to complete many papers which he had left unfinished.

"The Nurse's Story," subtitled **"The Hand of Glory,"** is one of the most interesting of the series of poems, which first appeared in *Bentley's Miscellany,* edited by Charles Dickens, in 1837. The version which provided the background for Barham's interpretation owes its origin to a conversation at the house of Mrs. Hughes, who narrated the story.[6] In this poem, the scene opens on a "bleak moor, at the midnight hour," with three murderers standing under a gallows, upon which another murderer recently has been hanged. The old woman, who we know immediately is a witch, instructs the three men to cut off the dead man's hand and also pluck five locks of his hair. She is to make a charm of the hand:

> The dead shrivell'd hand, as she clasps it with glee!—
> And now, with care, The five locks of hair
> From the skull of the gentlemen dangling there,
> With the grease and the fat O a black Tom cat
> She hastens to mix, And to twist into wicks,
> And one on the thumb, And each finger to fix.—
> (For another receipt the same charm to prepare,
> Consult Mr. Ainsworth and *Petit Albert.*)

This charm, as will be seen in the next stanza, will cause the door to open and the victim to fall asleep.

All then is silent around Tappington Hall, save in the narrow casement where an old miser is counting his money. The spell is articulated by the miscreants:

> Open lock To the dead man's knock!
> Fly bolt, bar and band!
> Nor move, nor swerve Joint, muscle or nerve,
> At the spell of the dead man's hand!
> Sleep all who sleep!—Wake all who wake!—
> But be as the dead for the dead man's sake!

They enter the chamber with the dead man's hand lighting the way. The murder is done, the gold taken. A hue and cry is raised, and the culprits are arrested and summarily hanged. The witch, with the dead man's hand and a dead Tom cat tied to her neck, toes and thumbs tied together, is thrown into the water for the traditional "swimming" of an accused witch. If she floats or swims, she is guilty; if she sinks she is innocent. She swims, revealing her guilt, but before she can be disposed of, Satan, appearing as a man attired in black,[7] astride a horse, snatches her from an angry mob and carries her off: "And she scream'd so, and cried, We may fairly decide / That the old woman did not much relish her ride!" Then, as was Barham's custom at the end of every poem or tale, a moral is attached. This one advises that murder will out, and that even witchcraft and sorcery will not protect the guilty. The final line ends in a pun, a frequent device used by Barham to transform folklore to verbal humor: "He'll be sure to be caught by a Hugh and a cry." The previous description of the witch not relishing her ride is a visually produced incongruity, providing humor as the reader conjures up this image in his mind. Illustrations corresponding to important scenes in the narratives appear in most editions of ***The Ingoldsby Legends,*** and provide the element of graphic humor, an integral part of so much Victorian humor.

The superstition that the hand of a dead man can be used as a charm is known in most parts of the Western world, and it was particularly strong in England. There are records of its use in France, Germany, Spain, Ireland, and even the United States. In France, for example:[8]

> The Hand of Glory is the hand of a man who has been hung, and is prepared in the following manner. Wrap the hand in a piece of winding-sheet, drawing it tight so as to squeeze out the little blood which may remain; then place it in an earthernware vessel with saltpetre, salt, and long pepper, all carefully and thoroughly powdered. Let it remain a fortnight in this pickle till it is well dried, then expose it to the sun in the dog-days till it is completely parched, or, if the sun be not powerful enough, dry it in a oven heated with vervain and fern. Next make a candle with the fat of a hung man, virgin wax, and Lapland seasame. The Hand of Glory is used to hold this candle when it is lighted. Wherever one goes with this contrivance, those it approaches are rendered incapable of motion as though they were dead.

It also has been asserted that monks used The Hand of Glory as a spell to conceal treasure. In *Thalaba the Destroyer,* Southey places it in the hands of the enchanter-king Mohareb, when he would lull to sleep Yohak, the giant keeper of the caves. So in this poem we find Barham taking a piece of genuine folklore, gathered from oral tradition, and giving it an imaginative yet faithful treatment. He indicated that the story is being told by an old nurse, a likely narrator, for such persons were among the major folk tradition bearers.

Barham's awareness of authentic folk contexts is further demonstrated by the fact that he has a milkmaid for the narrator of **"Look at the Clock."** This air of authenticity is supported by our knowledge that such girls were bearers of such traditions until recent years. A folk informant recalled in 1940 that:[9]

> We heard from the milkmaids strange legends of our country [Ireland], of saints, kings and queens, witches, banshees, merrows, leprechauns, pucas, monsters, serpents, and great wurr'ms imprisoned in deep lakes. To hear these entrancing stories we had to follow the narrator as she went about her work, perching on the edge of a table, wash-tub, or an inverted bucket.

As with the previous tale, we know something about this one's genealogy. Barham obtained a version of **"Look at the Clock"** from Mrs. Hughes, who had heard the tale from Lady Eleanor Butler, who recounted it as "a whimsical Welsh legend."[10] This lady was one of the celebrated ladies of Llangollen, and said that it occurred during her residence at Llangollen and in its immediate neighborhood. This is a typical claim of many folk informants and demonstrates the tendency of folklore to become personalized and localized. While in **"The Hand of Glory"** the humor is largely verbal, there is more humor, both verbal and pictorial (as the reader envisions the scenes), in this poem, and typifies Barham's ability to transform grotesque folk material into humorous literature. The story involves two country folk, David Pryce and his nagging wife, Winifred. In the opening stanza Barham's use of the dialect transformation of "v" to "w", recalling the speech of Sam Weller, elicits humor at the start: "'Look at the clock!' quoth Winifred Pryce, / As she opened the door to her husband's knock, / She paused to give him a piece of advice, / 'You nasty Warmint, look at the clock!' "In a typically shrewish manner she nags him, as she has in the past, about coming home late from the tavern, shouting, "Look at the clock!" As she bellows, she points to her grandmother's clock, a family heirloom of which she was very proud. This night, in a fit of rage, David clubbed Winifred over the head with a stick and, whether intentional or not, she died from the blow. A jury found him innocent of murder, however, with the verdict: "We find, Sarve her right!" Soon David went courting another woman over the mountain but, when he goes to propose marriage to her, he is overtaken on the bleak mountain by an apparition of the infamous clock:

'Twas the very same Head, and the very same Case
And nothing was altered at all—but the face!
In that he perceived, with no little surprise,
The two little winder holes turned into eyes
Blazing with ire, Like two coals of fire;
And the 'Name of the Maker' was changed to a lip,
And the hands to a nose with a very red tip.
No!—he could not mistake it, 'twas she to the life!
The identical face of his poor defunct wife.

He fled from the revenant in clock form to the home of his beloved, only to be rebuffed, and then to return to the village, where ever after he was a model of behavior. He shunned ale, and whenever at the Goat and Boots Tavern, he announced at 10 o'clock, "Gentlemen, Look at the clock!" All Barham needed was the germ of an idea or story, in this case an orally related tale, to set in motion his genius and to bring laughter by his artistic remodeling and imaginative treatment of the criginal. In folklore he found the necessary stimulus for this creative act. "He was accustomed to assert that he was lacking the power of literary invention. " 'Give me a story to tell,' he said, 'and I can tell it in my own way; but I can't invent one.' "[11]

In **"The Spectre of Tappington"** Barham draws on more general ghost legend motifs, rather than on any one particular legend. In this ludicrous treatment of the supernatural, Sir Charles Seaforth and his faithful servant, Barney Maguire, are guests of Tom Ingoldsby at Tappington Hall. Sir Charles is plagued by the loss of various pairs of breeches on successive nights, after the skeletal shade of old Sir Giles appeared before him in search of such garments. After several humorous scenes, it is revealed that Sir Charles is the victim of somnambulism and has indeed been burying these garments. The climax occurs when Sir Charles is bending over the hole in the ground containing the breeches, and is clouted from the rear by Tom Ingoldsby. In essence, Barham is poking fun at the whole idea of ghosts in this prose tale, but in others he suggests that he might be a half-believer. In commenting on this piece, one critic has suggested that:[12]

> **'The Spectre of Tappington'** is an unconscious parable of the author's own divided personality. Barham walked in his sleep and made himself into the ghost that the repressed part of his nature craved. Like many others who have believed that they have outgrown the mysteries, miracles, and apparitions of institutionalized religion, he went peeping under a light cloak of mockery down the by-ways of belief.

The British folklorist Christina Hole has written that, "Rumors of haunting often spring up when death by murder or suicide is known to have occurred or is strongly suspected. . . . There is an ancient belief that the violently slain cannot rest until they are avenged."[13] Illustrative of this point is Barham's poem **"The Dead Drummer Boy,"** based on the legend of the ghost of a murdered drummer boy. Barham creates visual humor in the opening of the poem, which portrays two sailors lost in a storm on Salisbury Plain, the bleak area of Stonehenge. Much humor is derived from his description of stereotyped British tars, their gait, and conversation. Also, he provides verbal humor by such bizarre rhymes as: "Two nautical terms which, I'll wager a guinea, are / Meant to imply What you, Reader, and I / Would call going zig-zag, and not rectilinear." During the thunder and lightning, one of the sailors is confronted by the ghost of a dead drummer boy who was killed, so it turns out, by the sailor when he was a soldier earlier in life, the penalty for which the sailor had been attempting to evade for several years. However, the ghost had been relentless in pursuit and Harry Waters confesses the murder, saying, "Vex'd Spirit, rest!—'twill soon be o'r,— / Thy blood shall cry to Heav'n no more!" The murderer is hanged and the corbies pick his bones. This murder of a drummer boy is a historical fact, attested to by a contemporary pamphlet entitled *A Narrative of the Life, Confession, and Dying Speech of Jarvis Matchan,*[14] signed by the Rev. J. Nicholson who attended him as minister. The murder, however, was committed not on Salisbury Plain, but in the vicinity of Alconbury, in Huntingdonshire, and the culprit was executed by hanging. This rare pamphlet contains the story of Matchan's (Barham changed the name to Matcham) escape to the sea and the appearance of the apparition before him on Salisbury Plain, the latter experience frightening him into a confession of the murder. Although part of the tale differs slightly from Barham's version, details of the murder are related in great detail, and the supernatural phenomena closely parallel Barham's rendition. At the time Barham wrote the poem, it is highly unlikely that he had ever examined this rare pamphlet. He obtained his version of the tale orally from Mrs. Hughes,[15] and this may explain the reason he had the murder occur on Salisbury Plain. Here again we have an example of the tendency of folklore to become localized as it enters the stream of oral tradition.

Although some have suggested that **"The Leech of Folkestone"** is based on a tale Barham heard while at

Romney Marsh, possibly because he had the tale set there, it is more probable that he based his tale on a literary version. In the *Gesta Romanorum,*[16] an early collection of exampla, there is a story of a certain knight from Rome, who when on his way to the Holy Land, was cuckolded by his wife in an intrigue with a clerk skilled in *nigromancia.* The wife asked the clerk to murder her husband so that he, the clerk, could marry her. A waxen image of the knight was made by the evil *nigromancer,* and the image was given the knight's name and placed on the wall. Later another magician confronted the knight as the latter was strolling through a public square in Rome, and warned him of his wife's plot to kill him. This magician now offered his help to the knight, who was directed to climb into a bath and to look into a specially prepared polished mirror. In this magic mirror he viewed a surprising sight: his own room with the clerk preparing to shoot an arrow into the image. The magician then ordered the knight to quickly duck under the water when the arrow was released from the bow. The first shot missed; so, too, the second. Then the clerk was confounded, for he said that if he missed the image on the third shot, he would lose his own life. His third arrow was no truer than the others and it returned to kill him. The knight was a witness to all of this as he looked in the mirror.

Barham's version opens with a paragraph filled with examples of ways to tell if one has been bewitched, and then continues:

> The world, according to the best geographers, is divided into Europe, Asia, Africa, America, and Romney Marsh. In this last-named, and fifth quarter of the globe, a witch may still be occasionally discovered in favourable, *i.e.,* stormy seasons, weathering Dungeness Point in an eggshell, or careering on her broomstick over Dymchurch wall. A cow may yet be sometimes seen galloping like mad, with tail erect, and an old pair of Breeches on her horns, an unerring guide to the door of a crone whose magic arts have drained her udder.

The story concerns Thomas Marsh of Marston Hall, who, when the story opens, is sitting at his table over a flagon of "hummingbub," which, according to Barham, really is "ale strong enough to blow a man's beaver off." Marsh is being cockolded by his wife and the leech, the latter pretending to be treating him for an unknown ailment, which in actuality is being caused by the two plotters who have made a waxen image of Marsh, and pierced it with long hat pins.

Marsh loses faith in the leech and all physicians, complaining: "Doctor Phiz says it is wind,—Doctor Fuz says it is water,—and Doctor Buz says it is something between wind and water." He goes to the wizard Aldrovando, who reveals the cause of the former's malady. Aldrovando's magic arts are pitted against those of the leech, climaxing in a hilarious scene of the leech and Mrs. Marsh, furious at their inability to puncture the wax doll, attempting to destroy the doll, and hopefully Marsh himself, by a blast from an overloaded shotgun, which bursts and kills the leech. Marsh is the victor and his wife absconds.

In this tale Barham is in top form in the creation of both pictorial and verbal humor. His alchemy transforms the magical skills of the leech and Aldrovando into comedy, but all based on a sound knowledge of the folk belief in sympathetic magic. Although Barham probably based this tale on a literary source, the belief in the practice of image magic is universal and doubtlessly was known by the rural folk of Romney Marsh. Of this practice Kittredge has written:[17]

> From remote periods of history in Egypt, Assyria, Babylonia, and India, from classic times and lands, from the middle ages, and so on down to the present, the practice of image magic has been prevalent, and is still common the world over, among savage men and civilized. It depends, of course, on the doctrine of sympathy. An effigy of wax, clay, wood, metal, or almost any substance, is pierced with nails, pins, or thorns, and burned or roasted slowly.

Also, the motif of a contest between two powerful magicians is often found in folklore, the ballad "The Twa Magicians," being one example.

Several other pieces in ***The Ingoldsby Legends*** are worthy of mention in connection with Barham's use of folklore and his sources. The **"Legend of Hamilton Tighe"** deals with the familiar folklore motif of the headless revenant.[18] The original ghost story, according to Mrs. Hughes who related it to Barham, was said to have originated with the family of Henry James Pye, the poet laureate of England from 1790-1813, who was a neighbor of the maternal grandmother of Mr. Hughes. **"Nell Cook," "Grey Dolphin," "The Ghost,"** and **"Smuggler's Leap"** seem to be related to traditions of Kent, but are so far removed from authenticity that the precise sources probably never will be discovered. In **"The Old Woman Clothed in Grey"** Barham took great liberties with the original tale, because the original was a well-disposed ghost, despite evidences to the contrary in Barham's version. The original of this ghost was said to have haunted an old rectory within a few miles of Cambridge.[19] It is told that it was her custom to wander about the house at the dead of night with a bag of money in her hand, offering it to whoever she happened to meet; no one, however, seems to have been bold enough to accept the gift, because it was considered bad luck to accept gifts from witches or ghosts. The **"Singular Passage in the Life of the late Dr. Harris"** has been traced to a communication to Barham from a young lady on her sick bed. Again we have a tale based on black magic, sympathetic magic. Barham was begged by the young lady to notify the police of her suspicions that a young man was working diabolical spells on her.[20]

Sixteen of ***The Ingoldsby Legends,*** those medieval ecclesiastical or saint's legends, have caused some dispute. In connection with these pieces, we know that Barham's major source was the *Legenda Aurea,* the most important compendium of saint's legends, written by Jacobus a Voragine, and which has appeared in many editions. Here he is not really handling viable folklore, but is adapting material from a literary source which long ago had been the oral property of the folk. Barham's humorous treatments brought charges of irreverence because he was poking fun at holy things. Others thought it was downright wicked of him to have such high jinks with the devil. He was found by some to be "a coarse and slanderous Protestant,"[21] while others indicated that he wrote such things to expose the errors of the Church of Rome, for he laughs at mortification, purgatory, and holy water. Evidence to support the latter theory is apparent at the opening of **"Netley Abbey."** However, the general tone and style of these so-called "lays" are the most powerful arguments against those who have found a didactic purpose in them. Furthermore, if Barham's purpose were didactic, he took a strange tack, because the saint always wins, a situation unlikely to persuade anyone against offering an invocation to a saint. **"The Jackdaw of Rheims"** is the first of these "lays," and doubtlessly brought chuckles of approval to those early readers who could appreciate that "When at the end of the cardinal's curse, / Nobody seemed one penny the worse." But the cardinal himself was the worse, so it turns out, and was saved only by restitution, repentance, and reform. Barham said that the source for this "lay" was a "High Dutch author," and that if he had more time he would have grafted on it a story about a magpie which had been told to him by Canon Hughes.[22]

In conclusion it appears that Barham made a very conscious and selective use of folklore gleaned from both literary and oral sources, and used it largely as a stepping stone or foundation for his own artistic creation, much like Tennyson, Spenser, and Hawthorne. His was not a natural and integrated use of folklore received firsthand from the folk, like that of Hardy or Synge, neither was it an exploitation and commercialization. Barham was a wit, and his initial success was won by his startling originality. His blending of saints and demons, ghosts and abbots, monkish legend and romance, antiquarian lore and classic knowledge, murder and crime, with his own freakish and whimsical sense of humor, his lightning leaps from grave to gay, his quaint verbal quips, his wealth of topical allusion and bizarre rhymes—all combined to secure for him a firm niche in the Victorian hall of humor.

Notes

[1] George Saintsbury, "Three Humorists: Hook, Barham, and Maginn," in *The Collected Papers of George Saintsbury 1875-1920,* II (London, n.d.), 151-176.

[2] S. M. Ellis, "Richard Harris Barham—'Thomas Ingoldsby,' " *The Bookman,* LI (January 1917), 112-118.

[3] Richard Church, *Kent* (London, 1948), p. 199.

[4] Stith Thompson, *The Folktale* (New York, 1951), p. 5. Cf. Albert Wesselski, *Marchen des Mittelalters* (Berlin, 1925), *passim.*

[5] R. H. D. Barham, *The Life and Letters of Rev. Richard Harris Barham* (London, 1870), I, 144.

[6] *Ibid.,* II, 4.

[7] Motif G 303.5.1, *Motif-Index of Folk Literature,* Ed. Stith Thompson (Bloomington, 1966).

[8] William Henderson, *Notes on the Folklore of the Northern Counties of England and the Borders* (London, 1866), pp. 200-201.

[9] Mary Carbery, *The Farm by Lough Gur* (London, 1940), p. 46.

[10] Barham, II, 2.

[11] Ellis, p. 115.

[12] *London Times,* December 26, 1936, p. 1057.

[13] Christina Hole, *Haunted England—A Survey of English Ghost Lore* (London, 1940), p. 96. Cf. Motif E 231.1.

[14] Alconbury, 1819.

[15] Barham, II, 3.

[16] *Gesta Romanorum,* ed. Charles Swan, trans. Wynnard Harper (London, 1877), pp. 187-190.

[17] George Lyman Kittredge, *Witchcraft in Old and New England* (Cambridge, 1929), p. 73.

[18] Motif E 422.1.1.

[19] C. G. Harper, *The Ingoldsby Country* (London, 1919), p. 80.

[20] Barham, II, 5.

[21] M. Sadlier, "*Ingoldsby Legends* 100 Years After," *London Times Literary Supplement* (June 10, 1945), p. 282.

[22] Barham, II, 21.

Stephen Bann (essay date 1984)

SOURCE: "Defences against Irony: Barham, Ruskin, Fox Talbot," in *The Clothing of Clio: A Study of the Representation of History in Nineteenth-Century Britain and France,* Cambridge University Press, 1984, pp. 112-23.

[*In the following excerpt, Bann traces the evolution of literary irony by comparing the works of Barham and Sir Walter Scott.*]

In 1856 the child Henry James was 'thrilled' by the French painter Delaroche's 'reconstitution of far-off history', which his elder brother William regarded as being of little interest. The anecdote reminds us that by this stage (and for a decade or so before that date), the freshness and evocative power of the historical recreations of the 1820s and 1830s were tempered by familiarity. As the novel and popular works of the earlier period progressively lost favour with the sophisticated, they were in the same process reclassified as appropriate material for the entertainment of the immature, the young and the simple. Even in the case of Scott, this process is undeniable, though it takes place over a long period, perhaps culminating at the stage when Scott is omitted from Dr Leavis's 'Great Tradition', well over a century after the first appearance of the Waverley Novels. In the case of a historian like Barante, the transformation takes place with bewildering rapidity. During the late 1820s the *Ducs de Bourgogne* had gained the respect and enthusiasm of such high authorities as Stendhal, Guizot and Villemain. When Barante finally died in 1866, the anonymous obituarist in the *Journal de Bruxelles* thought it most apt to celebrate his galvanising effect on an audience of adolescents:

> When I was pursuing my studies in a provincial college which had kept the old traditions, I recollect having heard the twelve volumes of this work being read from beginning to end, at mealtimes. A pupil ascended, at the beginning of dinner, to a raised platform at the end of the refectory, and from there, in a loud and slow voice, he tried to dominate the terrible noise of clattering dishes which arose from all the tables. At the end of the a month, when we were used to it, we ended up by not losing a word, while carrying on with munching and swallowing our food.[1]

The meals so graphically described in this passage probably took place in the 1830s or early 1840s. From the same period (recollected towards the end of the century) comes Anatole France's account of the avidity with which he and his school-fellows devoured Barante's text. He adds, however, an important rider: 'As for the *History of the Dukes of Burgundy,* I have not re-read it. But I have read Froissart.'[2] Barante had evidently succeeded in creating, for his contemporaries, a 'chronicle effect'. But such an effect was radically undercut when readers acquired the opportunity of comparing the text with the authentic material which it was designed to simulate. Once that comparison could be made, the ersatz authenticity of the *Ducs de Bourgogne* became, in Michelet's cutting phrase, 'nothingness'. When the real Froissart beckoned, only the immature would continue to enjoy the substitute.

But it would be foolish to imply that mid-nineteenth-century adult readers were all qualified to make the leap, with Anatole France, from Barante to Froissart. For the more popular taste, an intermediate stage existed. This is well demonstrated by the appearance in 1843 of a collection like Barry St Leger's *Stories from Froissart.* No less than Barante, St Leger is obliged to rely for much of his material on the *Memoirs* of Commines. But whereas Barante contrasted the qualities of the two choniclers very much to the advantage of Froissart's 'naiveté', St Leger rather surprisingly gives the benefit of his arbitration to Commines. Froissart is termed 'the butterfly only of the court . . . contented with its externals'; Commines, by comparison, is credited with having 'with the industry of a bee, studied the main-spring of diplomatic machinery', and with being 'contented only with the treasures of truth'.[3] Such a preference, which squares oddly with the title of the collection, involves St Leger in precisely that discrediting of his main source which Barante had hoped to eliminate from the historical narrative. Froissart, for all his vivid presentation, is arraigned in footnotes for treating 'the insurgent people as mere swine'. The reader is treated to sudden spasms of protest like: 'Thank heaven! this, among other opinions of the 14th century, is obsolete.'[4] St Leger's reformist conscience keeps him constantly on guard against the seductions of Froissart's prose.

Of course St Leger knows perfectly well that there is some ambivalence in his attitude to his main source. He takes advantage of a 'Prefatory Essay' to develop the whole issue of the relation between credulity and scepticism in the study of the past. Here his chief explanatory tool is an extended analogy with the cycle of the individual life, from youth to age, which fits well with the argument that we have begun to develop in this chapter:

> It has been observed that the latter part, or, rather, the more advanced periods of life, are spent in

> unlearning a great deal of that which has been acquired at its commencement. Sentiments and thoughts are engendered by early reading, which are destined to be changed by experience; the ardours of boyhood are quenched by the coldness of that maturity by which they are considered follies; and the dreams of youth are dispelled by the dull realities of manhood. Romance is succeeded by reason, and the illusions of our early sentiments and opinions vanish before the touchstone of our maturer judgment. The destruction of these early illusions is painful, but it is unfortunately in the natural course of events in the history of the human mind. In youth we *read* for entertainment, and without analysing what we read; but at a more advanced age we *think* for instruction, and look with very different eyes upon what had formerly conferred pleasure and excited admiration. As one prominent illustration of this change of feeling, who is there, that in his early readings and conversation, has not learned to boast of what are called the 'golden days of good queen Bess', and looked back at that monarch as the honour of our country, and considered her as a model fit for the imitation of any future sovereign? And who is there that, on a cool and dispassionate perusal of the times of Elizabeth, in the days of his maturer judgment, has not pronounced her to have been little else than a capricious tyrant—her reign characterised by her own favouritism and cruelty, and by the cupidity and exactions of her ministers?[5]

It is interesting that St Leger does not acknowledge the fatal flaw in this analogy. If 'reason' follows 'romance' as maturity follows youth, then how can he explain the cultural morphology of his own period? The fact that an age of Romance, or Romanticism, succeeded an Age of Reason squares oddly with such a naively developmental attitude to history. But if St Leger's analogy fails to explain an earlier generation's fascination with Froissart, it compels attention as a rhetorical figure. And it can be used to suggest, not only that we abandon naive credulity as we (and the human race) grow up, but that 'illusions' and maturer 'judgment' are inextricably bound up with one another. Just as we preserve within our own past the youth who '*read* for entertainment', so we cannot entirely blot out our vision of the 'golden days of good queen Bess' and replace it with 'a cool and dispassionate perusal'. De Quincey, writing on Michelet's 'Joan of Arc' in 1847, uses a similar, though less ambiguous figure when he frankly confesses that credulity and scepticism follow one another as day follows night: the gloomier the night, the less the temptation to remain sceptical:

> I believe Charlemagne knighted the stag . . . Observe, I don't absolutely vouch for all these things: my own opinion varies. On a fine breezy forenoon I am audaciously sceptical; but as twilight sets in, my credulity grows steadily, till it becomes equal to anything that could be desired. And I have heard candid sportsmen declare that, outside of these very forests, they laughed loudly at all the dim tales connected with their haunted solitudes; but, on reaching the spot notoriously eighteen miles deep within them, they agreed with Sir Roger de Coverly, that a good deal might be said on both sides.[6]

With De Quincey's remarks, we are of course in the province of irony. His statement about the relativity of credulity and scepticism itself invites a somewhat sceptical reading. But if De Quincey suggests an ironic attitude to history, this is not to be confused with the more integral irony of an eighteenth-century historian like Gibbon. As Lionel Gossman has persuasively demonstrated, irony in Gibbon is a means of vindicating, through particular linguistic forms, 'the value of urbanity, of cool and imperturbable detachment, and of deliberate, controlled, timeless elegance of form, against the ugly formlessness of uncontrolled passion and disorderly content'.[7] For De Quincey, irony consists in retaining and exploiting a kind of existential ambiguity. Its purpose is not to affirm values, but to insist upon the absolute relativity of the positions alternately adopted.

Irony should be seen in this context as much more than a stylistic effect. It is a method of vindicating, through style, a cultural stance—of responding in the appropriate way to a cultural predicament. For Gibbon, in the eighteenth century, it had been a question of establishing urbane values, and sharing them with the elite which was alone qualified to appreciate them. For the men of the 1840s, it was a matter of counteracting the unprecedented and perhaps excessive faith in historical recreation which had characterised the immediately previous period. Such a reaction might take the form of Barry St Leger's editorial petulance. The naive source was hedged about with intrusive annotations, which held up to ridicule the hollowness of so-called chivalric values. But it is clear that such sniping from the side-lines risked creating incoherence and confusion, and contributed little to forming a revised and revitalised image of the past. Now that historical recreation had inevitably entered its Mannerist phase, a more vivid imagination and a more resourceful poetic talent were needed to mark the distance travelled from the earlier period. In England, these qualities combined triumphantly in the unique figure of the Rev. Richard Barham, author of the ***Ingoldsby Legends.*** Scott had been the commanding presence of the first phase of historical rediscovery. Barham was to be his epigone, mimicking but also subverting the poetic modes which Scott had developed and popularised.

It is neither possible, nor necessary for the purposes of this argument, to establish a direct and documented relationship between Scott and Barham. To Scott, at the end of his life, the name 'Barham' would have meant above all the English frigate in which he embarked for the Mediterranean in 1831—an enterprise which was to be doomed to a sad ending, since he had hardly arrived at his destination when a premonition assailed him, and he hurried back overland to Scotland in unceremonious haste, reaching Abbotsford and dying there shortly afterwards in the early autumn of 1832. The future author of the ***Ingoldsby Legends*** had been born a generation after Scott, in 1788, and as a young man he was close to (though by no means familiar with) Scott's circle. An entry for his diary in 1827 records, if not a meeting, at least a near miss: 'Sir Walter Scott had been there the day before.'[8] Of more significance than these jottings, perhaps, is Barham's well-attested friendship with Mrs Hughes, the wife of a Canon of St Paul's, who was also a close friend and correspondent of Scott. Barham's biographer indeed cites Mrs Hughes as the origin of 'a large proportion of the legendary lore which forms the groundwork of the "Ingoldsby" effusions' and quotes the dedication to the lady in her presentation copy of the ***Legends:***

To Mrs. Hughes who *made* me do 'em,
Quod placeo est—si placeo—tuum.[9]

Yet this connection weighs little beside the very striking symbolic parallels which can be drawn between the careers of Scott and Barham. If they imply the existence in the younger poet of some considerable 'anxiety of influence', then it is hardly surprising that Barham should have made so little explicit reference to his interest in, or knowledge of, the work of Scott.

The symbolic parallels can be demonstrated best if we refer to the previous chapter, and particularly to Maynard Mack's suggestive use of the notion of 'composition of place'. In the earlier argument, I contrasted the ironic, fragmentary treatment of Newstead Abbey in Byron's poetry with the constructive procedures (both poetic and real) which Scott employed to build Abbotsford. I also suggested that the profound psychological effect of Scott's 'loss' of Dryburgh was a contributory factor in his zeal for the building of Abbotsford. Deprived of Dryburgh (the authentic medieval building which would, but for a senseless economic transaction, have devolved upon his father and then upon himself), Scott used the substantial resources of his purse and his imagination to construct a surrogate.

Richard Barham's construction of place, by comparison, arose from an even more pressing menace of disinheritance. Succeeding to his father's property in the vicinity of Canterbury in 1795 (when he was still a child), Barham was almost killed as a result of a carriage accident in 1802. Indeed his over-hasty executors had already taken steps to send their surveyor to look over the Manor of Tappington Everard, with a view to establishing its value and selling it. Barham recovered, and the property was not sold. He therefore escaped Scott's compulsion of having to create a new, substitute inheritance in another place. But the very possibility of loss seems to have stimulated his poetic capacities in a similar direction. If Scott palliated a *real* loss with a *real* construction, Barham was to offset the threatened loss with a new, but totally fictional, construction. His poetic strategy was to build, upon the very modest foundations of the Kentish manor-house which he hardly ever occupied, the legendary house of Ingoldsby with its ancestral crusading connections, its comic spectres and its skeletons in the cupboard. To quote Barham's son and biographer once again: 'the description of the mansion therein given is rather of what it might, could, would, or should be, than of what it actually and truly is . . . '.[10]

A strange logic, or morphology, seems to be at work in the cycle which leads from Byron and Scott to Barham. With Byron, first of all, the ironic text is used to register the anomalies of the 'Mix'd Gothic' building, and to stigmatise Newstead as:

Monastic dome! condemn'd to uses vile!

But Newstead remains what it was: to its many other vestiges and associations, it simply adds the mythic presence of the Romantic poet. In the case of Scott, by contrast, the building which was created in an attempt to realise a personal vision of the medieval past becomes above all a monument to the creative genius of the author of Waverley. By the time of Scott's death (it would appear), Abbotsford had become known throughout Europe through the medium of cheap prints—the master himself had to decline an example offered to him in June 1832 by a Frankfurt bookseller with the testy remark: 'I know that already, Sir.'[11]

In both these cases, the 'place' exists independently of the poet, despite the mythic connections between the two. In Barham's case, however, the real Tappington Everard is hardly an adequate reference point for the very much more splendid and richly historical 'place' which is built upon its name. This is not to say that the point of reference is entirely unnecessary. For Barham's ***Ingoldsby Legends*** engage in a systematic exploration of the areas of Kent which form the geographical context of the paternal manor. But it does mean that the relationship between text and 'place' has been significantly changed. The gap between the modest farm of Tappington and the proliferating poetic construction is as wide as the gap between fact and fantasy. The Manor which we discover exists, and can only exist, in the form of a book.

A parallel could be drawn with the strategy of a much greater Romantic figure, who nevertheless shared Barham's experience of coming slightly too late, as a young man, to the banquet of European Romanticism. Victor Hugo puts into the mouth of one of the characters in *Notre Dame de Paris* (the priest Claude Frollo) the suggestive prediction: 'Le livre tuera l'édifice.' 'The book will kill the building.'[12] This remark could be explained, in its primary sense, as a comment on the development of European history from the Middle Ages to the Renaissance, at which time the construction of cathedrals did indeed decline whilst the first printed books were being published and disseminated. But Hugo's dictum also (as has been pointed out by Jeffrey Mehlman) applies to his own fictional achievements. *Notre Dame de Paris,* the novel which takes for its title the name of a great cathedral, can be regarded as an attempt to measure up to the highly diversified symbolic achievement of the medieval architect, through the imaginative potentiality of the fictional text. But at the same time it is the index of a kind of struggle between medieval and modern creativity; in a sense, Hugo seeks to cover the pre-existent building with his text, to make the proliferating channels of his fiction a substitute for the manifold passages and stairways of Notre Dame. An extended comparison between Hugo and Barham would rapidly fall into incongruity. But it is worth retaining at least this notion of the building—the historical building—as, one might say, the *pretext.* The secret stairway which Barham discloses as his solution to the enigma of **'The Spectre of Tappington'** is no more than a fictional device, which permits an unexpected resolution to a carefully developed plot. To this extent it has blatantly left behind, or passed beyond, its supposed location in the actual manor-house of Tappington.

The mention of Victor Hugo prompts one further comment, if only to underline once again the crucial difference between the epitome of French Romanticism and Richard Barham. The relatively late flowering of Romanticism in France, which was due in part to the artificial effects of Napoleonic censorship but also to the persistence of the classicising Academy, gave Hugo his opportunity to become the most comprehensive of all French Romantic authors—both a poet and a novelist, as Scott had been. For Barham, on the other hand, the sense of late-coming must have been an omnipresent one. Signs abound throughout the ***Ingoldsby Legends*** of the awareness that we are no longer in the infancy of the Romantic movement. If Ossian is referred to, his name is glossed with the ironic comment '(or Macpherson for him)'.[13] Where Scott is invoked, it is in order to bring out the utter incongruity of the reference, as in **'The Witches' Frolic',** which quotes without acknowledgment the well-known line from 'Young Lochinvar'—applied to a rather different type of ceremony:

> Now tread we a measure, said she.[14]

As if the incongruity of the reference were not absolutely patent, we are obliged to suffer it again, at a later stage in the poem, when Berham makes a mock acknowledgment to his source in the manner of Bello's *Cautionary Tales:*

> One touch to his hand, and one word to his
> ear,—
> (That's a line that I've stolen from Sir Walter,
> I fear,)[15]

Of course, it is not only Scott, but the whole range of contemporary historical representation that Barham includes within his repertoire of reference. In **'A Lay of St Dunstan',** he cites a well-known historical painting in the following terms:

> You must not be plagued with the same story
> twice,
> And perhaps have seen this one, by W. DYCE,
> At the Royal Academy, very well done,
> And marked in the catalogue Four, seven,
> one.[16]

As this quotation makes clear, the problem of belatedness aquires a particularly acute form where the representation of history is concerned. For the historical poet, novelist or painter is—whether actually or notionally—telling a story for the second time: he works on the basis of the real or supposed text which is the primary source. Barham, in making ironic references of this kind, proclaims himself to be even later in the field. He tells his own 'Lay' or story with acknowledgment to his immediate predecessor—who has himself made use of an original story, or history, of the period in question. Clearly, at this remove from the supposed events, the audience's credulity is bound to be tested severely. But the question of credulity can also be seen from the other side. This is how we might interpret the apparently casual anecdote which Barham records in his diary for 8 December 1828.

The subject, indeed the hero, of this uproarious anecdote is Barham's great friend, Theodore Hook, who was said to rival the Rev. Sidney Smith as one of the most noted wits of his period. As Hook relates (in Barham's account), the scene is the trial of Lord Melville in the House of Lords. Hook is asked for information on the processions, as they enter the House, by 'a country-looking lady' from Rye, and succeeds in fobbing her off with solemnly delivered, but cumulatively outrageous, falsehoods. First of all, he maintains that the Bishops, in their elaborate state dress, are 'not gentlemen', but 'ladies, elderly ladies—the Dowager Peeresses in their own right'. The information is accepted and conveyed to the county-looking lady's offspring. But more is to come:

> All went smoothly, till the Speaker of the House of Commons attracted her attention by the rich embroidery of his robes.

'Pray, Sir,' said she, 'and who is that fine-looking person opposite?'

'That, Madam,' was the answer, 'is Cardinal Wolsey!'

'No, sir!' cried the lady, drawing herself up, and casting her informant a look of angry disdain, 'we knows a little better than that; Cardinal Wolsey has been dead many a good year!'

'No such thing, my dear Madam, I assure you,' replied Hook, with a gravity that must have been almost preternatural, 'it has been I know so reported in the country, but without the least foundation in fact; those rascally newspapers will say anything.'[17]

The little scene is instructive, as well as being extremely funny. For it cannot have escaped Barham's biographer that his own subject behaves with the same scant regard for historical fact as his friend, Theodore Hook. After all, Hook is playing a game with his interlocutor's credulity. He initially gives correct information, and then is tempted into the minor falsehood of proclaiming the Bishops to be Peeresses—a statement that is apparently not contradicted by the evidence of the 'country-looking lady's' eyes. But his master stroke is a projection into the past, when he asserts the presence of a celebrated historical figure, and maintains his ground, with 'preternatural' gravity and against all reason. Obviously Hook's harmless joke takes for granted the context of a decade in which even the 'country' public were witnessing the imaginative recreation of Richard Coeur de Lion, Louis XI of France, James I, and a host of other historical figures, in the pages of Scott and his successors. His ploy is a *reductio ad absurdum* of the notion of historical resurrection. But if this must be conceded, then Barham must be acknowledged to be closer to Hook than to Scott, in the way in which he cites and introduces his historical characters. When Barham gives us a **'Lay of St Dunstan'**, it is not simply that we disbelieve the events attributed to the Saint's agency. The text systematically subverts every expectation that we might have of a standard of fidelity to the past. Where the achievement of Scott was to stimulate credulity and so to provide a new wealth of iconic references for the imaginative recreation of the past, that of Barham is to manipulate incredulity. We are continually made aware of the artificial, and indeed grotesquely contrived, devices through which past events are purportedly evoked.

The **'Lay of St Dunstan'** illustrates this distinction effectively as the following extract will show:

The monks repair
To their frugal fare,
A snug little supper of something light
And digestible, ere they retire for the night.
For, in Saxon times, in respect to their cheer,
St. Austin's rule was by no means severe,
But allow'd, from the Beverley Roll 'twould appear,
Bread and cheese, and spring onions, and sound table-beer,
And even green peas, when they were not too dear;
Not like the rule of La Trappe, whose chief merit is
Said to consist in its greater austerities;
And whose monks, if I rightly remember their laws,
Ne'er are suffer'd to speak
Think only in Greek,
And subsist as the Bears do, by sucking their paws.[18]

Up to a point, and especially in the first few lines, Barham's verse mimes the process of offering correct historical information. There are indeed such institutions as the rules of St Austin and La Trappe, and the latter is certainly more austere than the former. The phrase 'in Saxon times', and the shift in tenses from present to past historic, prepare us for the itemisation of the monks' diet: 'bread and cheese, and spring onions'. Since there is a fair degree of plausibility in the catalogue, we are inclined to accept its minute detail as a 'reality effect'. But (as with Theodore Hook) our credulity is then tested, step by step, until it reaches breaking point. The 'green peas' (with their suspicious qualifications) are already questionable. The statement about the rule of La Trappe, though veracious, is partly undercut by the whimsical rhyming of 'merit is' and 'austerities'. By the end of the extract, the information strikes us, of course, as completely wortheless, and our attention is transferred to the outrageous vagaries of the rhyming scheme—which, capitalising on the presence of 'Bears', produces a delightful anomaly only a few lines later by rhyming Reginald Heber (the eminent divine) with 'She-bear'.

This extract puts us in mind of the fact that Barham's 'historical' evocations are mostly in verse. This fact alone would not, of course, suffice to account for their distinctiveness. Sir Walter himself was universally known as a writer of historically evocative ballads before he was unveiled as the author of Waverley. But there is a blatant difference between a poem like the **'Lay of St Dunstan'** and one like the 'Lay of the Last Minstrel'. Where Scott maintains an equilibrium between narrative function and metric pattern, never inhibiting the former for the sake of the latter, Barham continually interrupts the narrative, digresses and dilates, while at the same time drawing our attention to metre and rhyming scheme. In Jakobson's terms, he foregrounds the 'poetic' at the expense of the 'referential' function.

The infallible sign of this practice is, of course, his cult of the pun. An illuminating comparison might be made with Daumier's contemporary series of satricial prints, the *Histoire ancienne,* whose irreverent portrayal of classical subjects was much appreciated by Baudelaire.[19] When Daumier gives us his 'Oedipus and the Sphinx', he treats the famous riddle as a ridiculous pun: 'Why can't you count on the pyramids?'—'C'est qu'ils sont près Caire ('by Cairo' being in French the homophone of 'precarious'). In any form of realist or would-be realist discourse, the pun is bound to be anathema, since it violates the distinction between *signifier* and *signified.* Through combining two distinct *signifieds* (Heber/She-bear; 'Près Caire'/ précaire) in one *signifier,* it implicitly raises the problem of the transparency of discourse to reality. Both for Barham and for Daumier, therefore, the insistence upon the pun is an anti-realist tactic, which successfully subverts the conventions of historical discourse.

One could in fact go further in Barham's case, and conclude that his verse forms are selected deliberately for their disjunctive and mechanistic effects; not only the obtrusive rhyming scheme and the urge to digress, but almost every aspect of Barham's prosody works against the principle of narrative 'flow', challenging the natural assumption that we have to do with a representation of past events. And this effect is accentuated by the design, or rather lack of design, in the ***Ingoldsby Legends*** as a whole. Barham's biographer recorded after his death: 'He intended, had he been spared, to have thrown together the *disjecta membra* of his design into a more systematic form, and to have rendered it more perfect and compact.'[20] But, despite the pious claim, it is unthinkable that so ragged a bunch of yarns could have been, to any noticeable extent, systematised.

In fact, we can single out the significant phrase 'disjecta membra' (disjointed limbs) not only as an apt characterisation of the structure of the ***Ingoldsby Legends*** as they now appear, but also as further index of the opposition between Barham's discursive procedures and those of Scott. I suggested in the earlier chapter on 'Abbotsford and Newstead Abbey' that Scott's originality can be detected in his shift from a strategy of metonymic reduction (whole to part) to one of synecdochic integration (part to whole); the case of the 'antique little lion' from Melrose aptly summed up this shift, which was also epitomised in the theme of the 'Talisman'. By comparison Barham certainly tries to mimic—at innumerable stages in his work—the process of integration by synecdoche. But because he treats the process ironically, he actually succeeds in inverting the effect: a reductive process of metonymy is uncovered beneath synecdoche, and his apparently organicist strategy revealed as mere mechanism. The opposition may seem unduly schematic. But a few verses from the **'Lay of St Gengulphus'** will demonstrate the point. The saint has, by this stage, been dismembered. But he does not stay so for long:

Kicking open the casement, to each one's
amazement,
Straight a right leg steps in, all impediment
scorns,
And near the head stopping, a left follows
hopping
Behind,—for the left leg was troubled with
corns.

Next, before the beholders, two great brawny
shoulders,
And arms on their bent elbows dance
through the throng,
While two hands assist, though nipp'd off at
the wrist,
The said shoulders in bearing a body along.

They march up to the head, not one syllable
said,
For the thirty guests all stare in wonder and
doubt,
As the limbs in their sight arrange and unite,
Till Gengulphus, though dead, looks as
sound as a trout.[21]

It is difficult to miss the pathological element in this description, as in so many others by Barham which re-enact the fantasy of dismemberment and rehabilitation. Probably a psychoanalytic interpretation of his work would make much of the details of his accident as a child, which involved the mutilation of his right arm. But such an explanation (if it can be classed as an explanation) in no way accounts for (or diminishes the relevance of Barham's work to) the 'ironic' stage of historical discourse which is being described here. If, in the 1820s, historiography was able to draw sustenance from and contribute to the new ideal of 'life-like' representation, this was because it was one aspect of a wide-spread cultural reorientation which was organicist in character, and synecdochic in its poetic procedures. Barham signals the belated stage at which those procedures have themselves become a vehicle for ironic play: St Gengulphus is rehabilitated, limb by limb, before the assembled audience. But even after he has been restored to wholeness—'sound as a trout'—there is a troublesome remainder, his beard, which determines to adhere to the wicked wife who chopped him up in the first place. As Barham's verse records, she is punished for her own reductive activities by becoming a walking *catachresis:*

She shriek'd with the pain, but all efforts
were vain;

In vain did they strain every sinew and
muscle,—
The cushion stuck fast!—From that hour to
her last
She could never get rid of that comfortless
'Bustle'![22]

There is no need to multiply the examples from **'A Legend of Sheppey'**, **'The Jackdaw of Reims'** and many more *disjecta membra* of the ***Legends***—to show that Barham's ironic discourse, however light-weight we may find it, is organised with a purpose in mind. Instead of following Barry St Leger's system of juxtaposing the 'naive' source with an 'ironic' modern commentary, Barham invents a distinctive form of doggerel which very frequently (though not exclusively) uses historical material, but subverts its own claim to authenticity through the pervasive use of ironic devices. If Scott's achievement was that of a historical discourse more comprehensively *integrative* than that of his predecessors, Barham responded to the challenge of a *dispersive* historical discourse, which took for granted the antecedent coding and contrived to rearrange some of its central elements in an original and subversive way. In a sense, Barham had simply inherited Scott's public at a later stage in the cycle of taste; the ***Ingoldsby Legends*** were to have a popularity in the 1840s which could reasonably be compared with that of the Waverley Novels in the 1810s and 1820s. But where Scott's achievement was orderly and coherent—an almost unique example of a creative *persona* imposing its new rhetoric upon the European mind—Barham's offered the timely relief of disorder and incoherence. His first preface uses the authority of Shakespeare to proclaim:

The Devil take all order!!—I'll to the throng!

No doubt the best way of characterising, in two images, the difference between Scott and Barham is to compare the sedulous medieval recreation of the entrance hall at Abbotsford (still garnished today with its suits of armour, niches, weapons and coats of arms) with the title-page of the ***Ingoldsby Legends***—furnished in a very similar manner, but in such a style as to turn the references to ridicule. With Scott, the decor of the entrance hall partakes of the utter seriousness of his engagement with the past, an engagement which characterised not only his literary production but also his building of Abbotsford. In the case of Barham, Gwilt's lively design—with its supporting comic bears punning upon the origin of the author's name—is a farrago of false medievalism. The Jackdaw of Reims stands perched upon the highest pinnacle of the uncertain structure, as if to say: 'Abandon credulity, all ye who enter here!'

I have spent some time on the ***Ingoldsby Legends*** because of their amusing and intriguing historical flavour. But it must be admitted that Barham only accentuates (and carries to an excessive degree) the ironic features which are already becoming perceptible in more traditional forms of historical representation. The publishing of the ***Legends*** took place between 1840 (the date of the preface to the first edition of the First Series) and 1847, when Barham's son provided the preface for the Third and last series. Barry St Leger's *Stories from Froissart,* with their ineffectual mixture of credulity and criticism, appeared in 1843. I have already mentioned, in connection with Barham, Daumier's splendid series of lithographs, *Histoire ancienne,* which Baudelaire saw as a response to the ironic question: 'Qui nous délivrera des Grecs et des Romains?'—'Who will deliver us from the Greeks and Romans?'[23] This series of fifty plates appeared in *Le Charivari* between December 1841 and January 1843, to be followed in 1851-52 by an English equivalent in Leech's uproarious *Comic History of the Romans.* Nor should the diagnosis of the onset of irony be confined simply to these parodic forms, in which historical representation is undisguisedly satirical or ironic.

I argued earlier, when discussing the histories of Barante and Thierry, that there is a crucial shift when illustrative material ceases to be metonymic (a simple adjunct to historical recreation), and becomes metaphoric, capable of substituting for an action related in the text. This change takes place (in the case of Thierry's *Histoire de la Conquête*) in the edition of 1838, and (for the *Ducs de Bourgogne*) in 1842. Though there is no particular reason to suppose that these new full-page illustrations to such well-known historical works were taken as anomalous or absurd, there can be little doubt that they established an alternative system to the pure order of narrative. The texts of Barante and Thierry were juxtaposed with the vivid and dramatic evocations of contemporary French painters like Deveria and Ary Schefer, who had learned from the evolution of Salon art over the previous twenty years. Even if there is no necessary anomaly, there is certainly the 'double vision' of irony which threatens to be involved here. Historical representation registers the effects of a prodigious extension and development from the 1820s onwards, which has marked a great variety of different fields. But when such diverse models are placed in confrontation with one another, the conventional nature of the strategies of representation threatens to come into view. It is difficult to imagine what Thierry's readers made of the illustration which was unmasked in an adjacent note as being 'not historical' but 'taken inadvertently by the draughtsman from a legend that is cited as being a mere fable'.[24] But such a lapse must surely have raised doubts about the degree of credence that could be accorded to the other plates, or indeed to the work as a whole. . . .

Notes

[1] Extract from *Journal de Bruxelles* (undated), preserved in black box labelled 'Brochures diverses de

Prosper de Barante', No. 1516, Archives of the Château de Barante, near Thiers, Puy-de-Dôme, France.

[2] Anatole France, 'La jeunesse de M. de Barante', in *La vie littéraire,* vol. IV (Paris, 1897), p. 28.

[3] Barry St Leger, *Stories from Froissart* (London, 1834), vol. I, p. viii.

[4] *Ibid.,* p. 84.

[5] *Ibid.,* pp. xxi-xxii.

[6] Thomas de Quincey, *The English Mail Coach and other essays,* p. 143.

[7] Lionel Gossman, *.The Empire Unpossess'd* (Cambridge, 1981), p. 74.

[8] (Richard Barham), *The Ingoldsby Legends or Mirth and Marvels by Thomas Ingoldsby Esquire* (Third Series, second edition, London, 1847), p. 40.

[9] *Ibid.,* p. 73.

[10] *Ibid.,* pp. 3-4. A notable point in common between the real and the fantastic Tappington is the 'blood-stained stair, the scene of the remarkable fratricide, which is a genuine tradition, and the sanguinary evidence of which is pointed out with enviable faith by the present tenants' (*ibid.*). Tappington Farm can still be seen to the right of the Canterbury-Folkestone road, a little to the south of the village of Denton.

[11] J. G. Lockhart, *The Life of Sir Walter Scott,* abridged version (London, 1912), p. 767.

[12] Victor Hugo, *Oeuvres complètes* (Paris, 1967), vol. IV, p. 135: quoted in Jeffrey Mehlman's highly stimulating study, *Revolution and Repetition—Marx, Hugo, Balzac* (Berkeley and London, 1977), pp. 72-3.

[13] *The Ingoldsby Legends* (Second Series, second edition, 1842). p. 110; cf. also *The Ingoldsby Legends* (First Series, second edition, 1843), p. 334.

[14] *Ibid.,* p. 167; young Lochinvar also comes in useful later in the same collection, in the 'Lay of St. Odile' (p. 252).

[15] *Ibid.,* p. 178.

[16] *Ibid.,* p. 224.

[17] *The Ingoldsby Legends,* Third Series, p. 71.

[18] *The Ingoldsby Legends,* First Series, p. 229.

[19] Cf. 'Some French Caricaturists', translated in Charles Baudelaire, *The Painter of Modern Life and other essays* (London, 1964), pp. 166-86.

[20] *The Ingoldsby Legends,* Third Series, p. 139.

[21] *The Ingoldsby Legends,* First Series, p. 242.

[22] *Ibid.,* p. 248.

[23] Baudelaire, *The Painter of Modern Life,* p. 178; Baudelaire is quoting from the first line of a satire by Joseph Berchoux.

[24] Thierry, *Histoire de la Conquête* (fifth edition, Paris, 1838), vol. III, p. 79 (plate 22). Cf. p. 43.

FURTHER READING

"Thomas Ingoldsby (Barham)." *Fraser's Magazine* III n.s., No. XV (March 1871): 302-16.

Considers the people in Barham's life who most influenced his writings.

Horne, Richard Hengist. "Thomas Ingoldsby." In *A New Spirit of the Age,* edited by Richard Hengist Horne, pp. 91-106. Oxford University Press, 1907.

Famed, scathing critique of *The Ingoldsby Legends.*

Hughes, John. "Sketch of the Late Rev. R. H. Barham, with a Few Lines to His Memory." *The New Monthly Magazine* (1845): 526-32.

Argues that Barham's mother provided him with the plots to several of his stories.

Saintsbury, George. "Three Humourists: Hook, Barham, Maginn." *Macmillan's Magazine* (December 1893): 105-15.

Defends *The Ingoldsby Legends.*

Emily (Elizabeth) Dickinson

1830-1886

American poet. For additional information on the life and works of Emily Dickinson, see *NCLC*, Volume 21.

INTRODUCTION

Although only seven of Dickinson's poems were published during her lifetime—all anonymously and some apparently without her consent—Dickinson is considered a premier American poet. Choosing the lyric as her form, Dickinson wrote on a variety of subjects, including nature, love, death, and immortality. As she honed the lyric format, Dickinson developed a unique style, characterized by compressed expression, the use of enjambment, and an exploration of the possibilities of language. In 1955 the publication of Thomas H. Johnson's edition of Dickinson's complete poems prompted renewed scholarly interest in her work. Modern criticism has focused on Dickinson's style, structure, use of language, and the various themes found in her poetry. Some critics have examined these same issues from a feminist viewpoint. Regardless of the critical angle, most modern scholars incorporate some discussion of Dickinson's life experiences into their examinations of her work.

Biographical Information

Critical and popular interest in Dickinson's life has been fueled by the mythology that has grown up around the limited factual knowledge available. Dickinson was born in Amherst, Massachusetts, in 1830. The daughter of a prosperous lawyer and an invalid mother, Dickinson's schoolwork was often interrupted by time spent at home learning domestic chores. Beginning in 1835, she spent four years at a primary school and then attended Amherst Academy from 1840 to 1847. From there, Dickinson advanced to Mount Holyoke Female Seminary for one year, where her studies were influenced by New England Puritanism. This, together with Dickinson's Unitarian upbringing, heavily influenced her poetry's structure—the lyric form she used was a revision of the hymn quatrain—as well as its content—religious themes are the focus of many of her poems. Despite these influences on her work, though, personal faith eluded her and she remained an agnostic throughout her life.

After her year at Mount Holyoke, Dickinson returned to her family's home where she remained almost exclusively for the rest of her life. From 1851 to 1855, she made a few brief visits to Boston, Washington, D.C., and Philadelphia. Biographers speculate that on one trip to Philadelphia, Dickinson fell in love with a married minister, the Reverend Charles Wadsworth, and that her disappointment from this affair triggered her subsequent withdrawal from society. This, and other rumors of romantic entanglements, are largely conjecture; however, it is known that her reclusiveness intensified over the years. Her personal habits—always wearing white, never leaving her home, refusing to receive visitors—earned her a reputation for eccentricity. In 1874, Dickinson's father died unexpectedly, leaving her to care for her invalid mother, who died in 1882. Dickinson died in 1886 after being diagnosed with Bright's disease, a kidney disorder.

Major Works

Over the course of her writing career, Dickinson composed nearly eighteen hundred poems, all in the form of brief lyrics. She explored a variety of subjects: the austerity and beauty of nature, experiences of love and loss, and her own skeptical attitude toward religion and immortality, as well as her fascination with death. Drawing heavily from biblical sources and influenced by such poets as George Herbert, Shakespeare, and John Keats, Dickinson developed a highly personal system of symbol and allusion, assigning complex meanings to colors, places, times, and seasons. She experimented with compression, enjambment, and unusual rhyme schemes, and also employed an idiosyncratic use of capitalization and punctuation, thereby creating a poetic style that further distinguished her verse from contemporary American poetry.

Critical Reception

Initial criticism of Dickinson's work, following the 1890 publication of *Poems of Emily Dickinson*, was largely unfavorable, yet her work received widespread popular acclaim. Willis Buckingham has noted that readers in the 1890s often praised Dickinson's "inspired" thoughts and emotions rather than her poetic technique. Modern critics, though, have come to appreciate Dickinson's accomplishments in language and poetic structure. Margaret Dickie has challenged critics who have attempted to provide a narrative analysis of Dickinson's work by studying her poetry as a whole. Dickie maintains that the poems were written as lyrics, and should be examined as such. Karen Oakes has explored Dickinson's use of metonymy to establish an intimate, feminine discourse with her readers. Other critics, such as Judy Jo Small and Timothy Morris, have analyzed Dickinson's rhyme structure, Small noting the acoustical effects of this structure, and Morris observing how Dickinson's patterns of rhyme and enjambment developed over time.

Many critics have also explored the various themes of Dickinson's poetry against the backdrop of events in her personal life. Among these are Jane Donahue Eberwein, who has studied the poems concerning love and its redemption, and Nadean Bishop, who has focused on Dickinson's spirituality, specifically the poems that seem to indicate the poet's rejection of religious dogma in favor of a private version of God and heaven. Paula Hendrickson, who has examined Dickinson's poems that focus on the precise moment of death, notes that these poems are typically treated as a subcategory of the death poem genre and are rarely treated individually.

Power is another of Dickinson's themes that has received a great deal of critical attention. R. McClure Smith has examined how Dickinson uses the trope of seduction to explore her relationship to patriarchal power. Feminist critics have also found the issue of power of great significance in Dickinson's work. Cheryl Walker maintains that while many feminist critics try to assert that Dickinson's life was "a model of successful feminist manipulation of circumstances," in fact, the poet was attracted to masculine forms of power. Paula Bennett, on the other hand, has contended that Dickinson's relationships with women were more significant than her struggles with men, male power, or male tradition. Bennett argues that Dickinson's relationship with women provided her with the comfort and safety necessary for the poet to explore her own sexuality. This contention, Bennett states, is supported by a reading of Dickinson's poems that recognizes their homoeroticism and use of clitoral imagery.

The enigmatic details surrounding Dickinson's life continue to fascinate readers and critics alike. Yet it is the technical originality of her poetry, the variety of themes she addressed, and the range and depth of intellectual and emotional experience she explored that have established Dickinson's esteemed reputation as an American poet.

PRINCIPAL WORKS

Poems by Emily Dickinson (poetry) 1890
Poems by Emily Dickinson, second series (poetry) 1891
Letters of Emily Dickinson. 2 vols. (letters) 1894
Poems by Emily Dickinson, third series (poetry) 1896
The Single Hound: Poems of a Lifetime (poetry) 1914
Further Poems of Emily Dickinson (poetry) 1929
Unpublished Poems of Emily Dickinson (poetry) 1935
Bolts of Melody: New Poems of Emily Dickinson (poetry) 1945
The Poems of Emily Dickinson. 3 vols. (poetry) 1955
The Letters of Emily Dickinson. 3 vols. (letters) 1958

CRITICISM

John Crowe Ransom (essay date 1956)

SOURCE: "Emily Dickinson: A Poet Restored," in *Emily Dickinson: A Collection of Critical Essays*, edited by Richard B. Sewell, Prentice Hall, 1963, pp. 88-100.

[*In the following essay, originally published in 1956, Ransom provides a general overview of twentieth-century criticism of Dickinson's poetry, noting in particular the impact of Thomas H. Johnson's 1955 edition of Dickinson's verse, as well as the characteristics and major themes of her poetry.*]

We would have to go a good way back into the present century to find the peak of that furious energy which produced our biggest and most whirling flood of verse in this country. So it is not too foolhardy to make a proposal to the literary historian: Will he not see if the principal literary event of these last twenty years or so has not been the restoration just now of an old poet? Emily Dickinson's life was spanned by the years 1830-86, and in most ways she was surely not one of our "moderns."

But I will anticipate the historian's reservation. There is one kind of literary event which we think of as primary, and it occurs when a new poet comes decisively into his powers and starts upon his unique career. But often this event occurs obscurely, and receives only a small public notice. I am sure I do not know if a poet of Emily Dickinson's stature has launched himself in these late years, as she did about a century ago. Evidently it may be much later before the full notice is ready to be taken, and when this happens it will seem only a secondary event, to that romantic conviction in us which would rate importances intrinsically and instantly, as do the judgments of Heaven. Nevertheless it is a first-rate event for our practical or civic way of thinking.

In the autumn of 1955 appeared ***The Poems of Emily Dickinson,*** a complete variorum edition in three volumes, in which are arranged according to a rough but ingenious chronology all the poems which survived her, reaching to a number of 1,775 precisely. The editor was Thomas H. Johnson, and the Harvard University Press, acting through its new subsidiary the Belknap Press, was the publisher. The event is having its proper effect at once; already obsolete are all those scattered books which appeared one by one in the fifty or more years following the poet's death, and gave us the only version of the poems which we could have.

This was a poet who in her whole lifetime saw only seven of her poems in print, and wanted to see no more; so graceless was the editorial touch which altered her originals. After her death the manuscripts fell into various hands, and their possession was contested; the public critic was very bold if he cared to offer much comment on the published verse when he could not know if the lines as they were printed were the lines as they had been written. The scandal lasted too long even for a community of untidy literary habits. But now it is as if suddenly, say about ten years ago, there had arisen a shamed sense of literary honor, of an obligation overdue to the public domain; and with it a burst of philanthropic action all round. The Dickinson Collection is now housed forever in Harvard's library, and Mr. Johnson was ready at the earliest possible moment to go to work on it, along with a troop of willing helpers. The Collection is complete except for one considerable set of manuscripts, and that too was made available for his edition.

Many editors and critics will follow up Mr. Johnson's sound labors. For example, the Dickinson reader is not going to repair to the Harvard library, nor even as a rule possess himself of Mr. Johnson's three volumes, but will require a Dickinson Anthology, or Selected Poems Edition; and he will probably get more than one. Shall we say that the poems which are destined to become a common public property might be in the proportion of one out of seventeen of the 1,775? They will hardly be more. But it will take time to tell.

And even when the poems are selected there will be hundreds of times when the editors will have to make hard decisions about straightening out some of those informalities in the manuscripts. Emily Dickinson was a little home-keeping person, and while she had a proper notion of the final destiny of her poems she was not one of those poets who had advanced to that late stage of operations where manuscripts are prepared for the printer, and the poet's diction has to make concessions to the publisher's style-book. She never found reason to abandon her habit of capitalizing her key-words, but her editor will have to reckon with certain conventions. He will respect those capitalizations, I think, even while he is removing them. They are honorable, and in their intention they are professional, and even the poet who does not practice them must have wanted to; as a way of conferring dignity upon his poetic objects, or as a mythopoetic device, to push them a little further into the fertile domain of myth. The editor will also feel obliged to substitute some degree of formal punctuation for the cryptic dashes which are sprinkled over the poet's lines; but again reluctantly, because he will know that the poet expected the sharp phrases to fall into their logical places for any reader who might be really capable of the quick intuitional processes of verse.

Since I have intimated so strong a sense of the event, I must not wait a moment longer to exhibit some of the characteristic poems, in order that my reader and I may have exactly the same poet before us. I give the poems not quite as they were written, but altered with all possible forbearance. For in none of the poems in its manuscript form has there been so much as a single line wasted on a title, and I shall identify ours by the serial numbers and the dates which Mr. Johnson has assigned to them.

And since this was a strange poet, I shall begin with two of the stranger poems; they deal with Death, but they are not from the elegiac poems about suffering the death of others, they are previsions of her own death. In neither does Death present himself as absolute in some brutal majesty, nor in the role of God's dreadful minister. The transaction is homely and easy, for the poet has complete sophistication in these matters, having attended upon deathbeds, and knowing that the terror of the event is mostly for the observers. In the first poem a sort of comic or Gothic relief interposes, by one of those homely inconsequences which may be observed in fact to attend even upon desperate human occasions.

465 (1862)

I heard a fly buzz when I died.
The stillness in the room
Was like the stillness in the air
Between the heaves of storm.

The eyes around had rung them dry,
And breaths were gathering firm
For that last onset when the King
Be witnessed in the room.

I willed my keepsakes, signed away
What portion of me be
Assignable, and then it was
There interposed a fly,

With blue, uncertain, stumbling buzz
Between the light and me;
And then the windows failed, and then
I could not see to see.

The other poem is a more imaginative creation. It is a single sustained metaphor, all of it analogue or "vehicle" as we call it nowadays, though the character called Death in the vehicle would have borne the same name in the real situation or "tenor." Death's victim now is the shy spinster, so he presents himself as a decent civil functionary making a call upon a lady to take her for a drive.

712 (1863)

Because I could not stop for Death,
He kindly stopped for me;
The carriage held but just ourselves,
And Immortality.

We slowly drove, He knew no haste,
And I had put away
My labor and my leisure too,
For His civility.

We passed the school, where children strove
At recess, in the ring.
We passed the fields of gazing grain,
We passed the Setting Sun.

Or rather, He passed us;
The dews drew quivering and chill,
For only gossamer my gown,
My tippet only tulle.

We paused before a House that seemed
A swelling of the ground;
The roof was scarcely visible,
The cornice in the ground.

Since then 'tis centuries, and yet
Feels shorter than the day
I first surmised the horses' heads
Were toward Eternity.

Next, two little extravagances or fantasies. The first is like a Mother Goose rhyme, with a riddle which it takes a moment to interpret:

1032 (1865)

Who is the East?
The Yellow Man
Who may be Purple if he can
That carries in the Sun.

Who is the West?
The Purple Man
Who may be Yellow if he can
That lets Him out again.

The other exhibits an action such as would be commonplace for the Portrait of the Artist as a Kind Maternal Woman, but that the setting could only have existed in her exotic imagination:

566 (1862)

A Dying Tiger moaned for drink;
I hunted all the sand,
I caught the dripping of a rock
And bore it in my hand.

His mighty balls in death were thick,
But searching I could see
A vision on the retina
Of water, and of me.

'Twas not my blame, who sped too slow;
'Twas not his blame, who died
While I was reaching him; but 'twas—
The fact that he was dead.

The concluding line is flat, like some ironic line by Hardy. Its blankness cancels out the expostulation we had expected, and pure contingency replaces the vicious agent we would have blamed, and there is nothing rational to be said. Who is going to blame a fact?

And of course there must be some poems about nature. It is still true that the spontaneous expression of our metaphysical moods—that consciousness whose objects are emphatically *not* those given to the senses—is to be found in the incessant and spacious drama of the natural world. Poets are much more concerned with earth than with Heaven. And why not? Natural events have visibility, and audibility too; yet they seem touched with Heavenly influences, and, if you like, they are sufficiently mysterious. But it is common belief among readers (among men readers at least) that the woman poet as a type is only too familiar with this philosophy, and makes flights into nature rather too easily and upon errands which do not have metaphysical importance enough to justify so radical a strategy. And they might want to cite many poems by Emily Dickinson, concerning her bees and butterflies perhaps. But see the following:

1084 (1866)

At half past three, a single bird
Unto a silent sky
Propounded but a single term
Of cautious melody.

At half past four, experiment
Had subjugated test,
And lo, Her silver Principle
Supplanted all the rest.

At half past seven, Element
Nor implement was seen,
And Place was where the Presence was,
Circumference between.

The times are half past three and half past four in the morning and half past seven in the evening of a summer's day. Where has the music gone, the silver Principle, when it grows dark? To some far corner of Circumference, the poet says, and that is a term she is fond of using. Perhaps it means: the World of all the Mysteries, where Principles have not necessarily perished when they have vanished. There is great metaphysical weight in that Circumference—as there is in Principle and Element, or in Immortality and Eternity in the second Death poem above. I suggest that there is a special Americanism here. It has been remarked how much of our political feeling has turned on abstract key-words like Democracy and Equality and Federal Principle and Constitution, and even now perhaps turns on new ones like United Nations and Conference at the Summit. These are resonant words, and the clang of them is Latinical and stylistically exact yet provocative. Our poet had a feeling for the metaphysical associations of her Latinities, and almost always invoked them when she dealt with ultimate or theological topics: the topics of the Soul. But here is a small nature poem which is of a more conventional order:

757 (1863)

The Mountains grow unnoticed;
Their purple figures rise
Without attempt, Exhaustion,
Assistance, or Applause.

In Their Eternal Faces
The Sun with just delight
Looks along, and last, and golden,
For fellowship at night.

And finally, a group of personal poems. These will be from the large category of Emily Dickinson's love poems. They begin in 1861, when the poet has turned thirty, and now she professes experiences which become decisive upon the direction of her poetry. These crucial poems often have an erotic tone which is unmistakable. The dates assigned to these as to all poems are based on the handwriting, which changes perceptibly from one period to another. It changed most of all in 1861. The strokes became bold and long and uneven, tending toward the separation of the characters, and registering, for Mr. Johnson's expert staff, strong emotional disturbance. The boldness persisted into other years, of course, but the unevenness subsided, as if to witness a gradually achieved serenity. The first of our poems testifies to a mutual flame that has been fully acknowledged and enacted, and this is the time of that despair which comes after its denial.

293 (1861)

I got so I could hear his name
Without—tremendous gain—
That stop-sensation on my Soul,
And thunder in the room.

I got so I could walk across
That angle in the floor,
Where he turned so, and I turned how,
And all our sinew tore.

I got so I could stir the box
In which his letters grew,
Without that forcing, in my breath,
As staples driven through;

Could dimly recollect a Grace
(I think they call it "God")
Renowned to ease extremity,
When formula had failed;

And shape my hands, petition's way,
Tho' ignorant of a word
That Ordination utters;
My business with the Cloud;

If any Power behind it be
Not subject to Despair,
It cares in some remoter way
For so minute affair

As Misery—: Itself too great
For interrupting more.

(*Further Poems of Emily Dickinson.* Copyright 1929 by Martha Dickinson Bianchi.)

And the next poem is dated in the following year, and continues a little more resignedly in that same stage after first love when it is enough to receive new letters from the beloved.

636 (1862)

The way I read a letter's this:
'Tis first I lock the door,
And push it with my fingers next,
My transport to make sure;

And then I go the furthest off
To counteract a knock,
Then draw my little letter forth
And slowly pick the lock;

Then glancing narrow at the wall,
And narrow at the floor
For firm conviction of a mouse
Not exorcised before,

Peruse how infinite I am
To no one that you know,
And sigh for lack of Heaven, but not
The Heaven God bestow.

But now we come to the famous poem which displays the image of the Soul electing her lover to be now her one "Society," her communing Fellow Soul even though physically absent. Renunciation has succeeded upon Despair; it has its own happiness and even an arrogance befitting a Soul assured by Heaven.

303 (1862)

The Soul selects her own Society,
Then shuts the Door;
To her divine Majority
Present no more.

Unmoved she notes the Chariots pausing
At her low gate;
Unmoved though Emperor be kneeling
Upon her Mat.

I've known her from an ample nation
Choose One,
Then close the valves of her attention
Like Stone.

Our final poem stands only three poems later than this, in Mr. Johnson's arrangement. If that is approximately correct, the speaker has learned her lesson fast, almost too fast for the human drama becoming to her situation. She is talking now about those Superior Instants when the Soul's Society is God, and all that is of earth, including the beloved, is withdrawn. This is a Platonic or a Christian climax, and the last fruits of renunciation. I cannot think it represents a moment quite characteristic of this poet, or of poets generically. She indicates in many poems her acceptance of the saying that in Heaven there is no marrying nor giving in marriage. But the Colossal Substance of existence there is made magnificent by the flood of Latinities, which appear to render their objects with technical precision, and yet really point to objects that are ineffable.

306 (but undated)

The Soul's Superior instants
Occur to Her alone,
When friend and earth's occasion
Have infinite withdrawn,

Or She Herself ascended
To too remote a Height
For lower recognition
Than Her Omnipotent.

This Mortal Abolition
Is seldom, but as fair
As Apparition, subject
To Autocratic Air;

Eternity's disclosure
To favorites, a few,
Of the Colossal Substance
Of Immortality.

(*The Single Hound.* Copyright 1914 by Martha Dickinson Bianchi.)

Emily Dickinson is one of those poets who make almost constant use of the first person singular. If the poems are not autobiographical in the usual sense of following actual experience—and it is not likely that they do, inasmuch as the poetic imagination is scarcely going to consent to be held captive to historical fact, and prevented from its own free flight—then they are autobiographical in the special sense of being true to an imagined experience, and that will be according to the dominant or total image which the artist proposes to make up for herself. I suppose it is the common understanding that a poem records an experience which is at least possible, and we enter into it, by and large, because it is better than our actual experience; it does us good, and it gratifies those extravagant aspirations which we cherish secretly though proudly for ourselves. And as Emily Dickinson went from poem to poem, I must suppose that she was systematically adapting her own experience, which by common standards was a humdrum affair of little distinction, into the magnificent image of her Soul which she has created in the poems. It may have been imaginary in the first instance, but it becomes more and more actual as she finds the courage to live by it.

There was another public event associated with the definitive edition: in the appearance of *Emily Dickinson; An Interpretive Biography,* written by Mr. Johnson himself, and published at the same time as the poems and by the same house. I have a good deal of confidence in Mr. Johnson's setting out of both the primary or original image of Emily Dickinson as an actual person and the later and greater image of her literary personality. It is a good book, though far too short and lacking in documentation to be a definitive one; sometimes Mr. Johnson tells his findings without taking his readers into his confidence by showing them his evidences. But as compared with earlier biographers he is superior indeed.

It is the love poems which are decisive for the literary personality of Emily Dickinson. Most probably the poems would not have amounted to much if the author had not finally had her own romance, enabling her to fulfill herself like any other woman. She always had quick and warm affections for people, and she loved nature spontaneously with what Wordsworth might almost have called a passion. But here are the love poems, with their erotic strain. Now it happens that the god was in this instance again a blind god, or perhaps we should allow also for the possibility that the style of the romance fitted exactly into a secret intention of her own—at any rate it still appears to be the fact, for Mr. Johnson confirms it, that her grand attachment was directed to the person of a blameless clergyman who was already married. She could never have him. We know next to nothing as to what passed between them, for his letters to her have all been destroyed, except apparently for one letter, pastoral but friendly in its tone. And what becomes of the experience asserted so decently yet passionately in the poems? That was all imaginary, says Mr. Johnson roundly, if I follow him; and does not even add that it was necessary to the effectiveness of the poems. It would seem very likely that he is right about the fact; it is so much "in character," insofar as we are able to understand herself and her situation. Mr. Johnson is himself a native and a historian of her region, the valley of the Connecticut at Amherst, where in her time the life and the metaphysics were still in the old Puritan tradition, being almost boastfully remote from what went on across the state in Boston. In her Protestant community the gentle spinsters had their assured and useful place in the family circle, they had what was virtually a vocation. In a Roman community they might have taken the veil. But Emily Dickinson elected a third vocation, which was the vocation of poet. And the point is that we cannot say she deviated in life from her honest status of spinster, and did not remain true to the vows of this estate, so to speak, as did the innumerable company of her sisters. But it was otherwise for the literary personality which she now projected.

We can put this most topically nowadays, perhaps, if we say that about 1861, when Emily Dickinson had come into her thirties, she assumed in all seriousness her vocation of poet and therefore, and also, what William Butler Yeats would have called her poet's mask: the personality which was antithetical to her natural character and identical with her desire. By nature gentle but indecisive, plain in looks, almost anonymous in her want of any memorable history, she chose as an artist to claim a heroic history which exhibited first a great passion, then renunciation and honor, and a passage into the high experiences of a purified Soul. That is the way it would seem to figure out. And we have an interesting literary parallel if we think in these terms about the poetry of her contemporary, Walt Whitman. A good deal of notice has been paid lately to Whitman by way of pointing out that he was an impostor, because the aggressive masculinity which he asserted so blatantly in the poems was only assumed. But that would be Walt Whitman's mask. Whitman and Emily Dickinson were surely the greatest forces of American poetry in the nineteenth century, and both had found their proper masks. (Poe would be the third force, I think; just as original, but not a poetic force that was at the same time a moral force.)

But in Emily Dickinson's own time and place she could not but be regarded as an unusually ineffective instance of the weaker sex. She was a spinster, becoming more and more confirmed in that character. And not a useful spinster, but a recluse, refusing to enter into the world. Next, an eccentric; keeping to her room, absenting herself even from household and kitchen affairs. Perhaps a sort of poet, but what of that? The town of Amherst knew she could make verses for Saint Valentine's Day, and was always ready to send somebody a poem to accompany a flower, or a poem to turn a compliment or a condolence; once in a long while it was known that a poem got into print; but it scarcely mattered. It is a great joke now, though not at her expense, to discover with Mr. Johnson that the poems sent out on these occasions were often from her very finest store.

The slighting of the professional poet in her life-time is made up for in our time by especial gallantries on her behalf and an exquisite hatred for those who neglected her. Perhaps the most satisfying image of her, from this perspective, would now see Emily Dickinson as a kind of Cinderella, in a variant version of the story with a different moral. The original story surely sprang from man's complacent image of woman. The Ur-Cinderella scrubbed away at her pots and pans and never stopped until the kind Prince came by and took her away to his palace, where virtue had its reward. Our own Cinderella could do without the Prince; she preferred her clergyman, and he did not take her anywhere. She proceeded to take her own self upstairs, where she lived, happy ever after with her memories, her images, and her metaphysics.

She busied herself with writing, revising, and sometimes fabulously perfecting those slight but intense pieces; for the eye of the future. When there were enough of them she would stitch them down the sides together into a packet, like a little book, and put it into the cherry bureau drawer. We may suppose that she did not fail to wonder sometimes, in that ironical wisdom which steadied and protected her: What if her little packets might never catch the great public eye? But this was not her responsibility.

Among her most literate acquaintances it is scarcely possible that there was one (or more than one, says Mr. Johnson) who would not have told her, had it not been too cruel, that if she was clever enough to know the accomplishments it took to make a real poet, she would be clever enough to know better than try to be one. Consider her disabilities. She had a good school education which gave her some Latin, but after a year in Miss Lyon's advanced school for young ladies at Mount Holyoke she did not return, and we cannot quite resolve the ambiguity of whether this was due to her wish or to her poor health. She read well but not widely; the literature which gave her most was the hymnbook. And she was amazed when she was asked why she did not travel; was there not enough of the world where she was already? When she made her decision to be a poet, it is true that she sent some poems to a man of letters, and wanted to know if she should continue. The gentleman answered kindly, and entered into a lifelong correspondence with her, but did not fail to put matters on a proper footing by giving her early to understand that she might as well not seek to publish her verse. And she made little effort to find another counsellor. Perhaps it seemed to her that there was no particular correlation between being a poet and having the literary companionship of one's peers.

Of course all her disabilities worked to her advantage. Let us have a look at that hymnbook. She had at hand, to be specific, a household book which was well known in her period and culture, Watts' *Christian Psalmody.* (Her father's copy is still to be seen.) In it are named, and illustrated with the musical notations, the Common Meter, the Long, the Short, and a dozen variations which had been meticulously carried out in the church music of her New England. Her own poems used these forms with great accuracy, unless sometimes she chose to set up variations of her own, or to relax and loosen the rules. Since she was perfect in her command of these meters, they gave her a formal mastery over the substantive passions of the verse. But since these meters excluded all others, their effect was limiting. Her meters are all based upon Folk Line, the popular form of verse, and the oldest in our language. I have been used to saying that the great classics of this meter are the English Ballads and Mother Goose, both very fine, and certainly finer than most of the derivative verse done by our poets since the middle of the eighteenth century. Hereafter I must remember to add another to these classics: the Protestant hymnbooks, but especially the poetry of Emily Dickinson, which is their derivative. Folk Line is disadvantageous if it is used on the wrong poetic occasion, or if it denies to the poet the use of English Pentameter when that would be more suitable. Pentameter is the staple of what we may call the studied or "university" poetry, and it is capable of containing and formalizing many kinds of substantive content which would be too complex for Folk Line. Emily Dickinson appears never to have tried it.

The final disability which I have to mention, and which for me is the most moving, has been most emphatically confirmed in Mr. Johnson's book. Her sensibility was so acute that it made her excessively vulnerable to personal contacts. Intense feeling would rush out as soon as sensibility apprehended the object, and flood her consciousness to the point of helplessness. When visitors called upon the family, she might address them from an inner door and then hide herself; but if deep affection was involved she was likely to send word that she must be excused altogether, and post a charming note of apology later. She kept up her relations with many friends, but they were conducted more and more by correspondence; and in that informal genre she was of the best performers of the century. The happy encounter was as painful as the grievous one. But we need not distress ourselves too sorely over this disability when we observe the sequel. It made her practice a kind of art on all the social occasions; conducting herself beautifully though rather theatrically in the oral exchanges, and writing her notes in language styled and rhythmed remarkably like her poetry.

It was even better than that. The poet's Soul, she might have said, must have its housekeeping, its economy, and that must be severe in proportion as the profuse sensibility, which is the poet's primary gift, tends to dissipate and paralyze its force; till nothing remains but a kind of exclamatory gaping. The Soul must learn frugality, that is, how to do with a little of the world, and make the most of it; how to concentrate, and focus, and come remorseless and speedy to the point. That is a kind of renunciation; all good poets are familiar with it. And critics, too, I believe. Do we not all profess a faith in the kind of art which looks coolly upon the turgid deliverance of sensibility and disciplines it into beauty?

David J. M. Higgins (essay date 1961)

SOURCE: "Emily Dickinson's Prose," in *Emily Dickinson: A Collection of Critical Essays, edited by Richard B. Sewell,* Prentice Hall, 1963, pp. 162-77.

[*In the following essay, originally part of a 1961 doctoral dissertation, Higgins studies Dickinson's letters, observing that in both prose and poetry Dickinson reduced thoughts and ideas to their essences, Higgins discusses the method by which Dickinson composed her letters and her habit of combining poetry with her prose.*]

> An earnest letter is or should be a life-warrant or death-warrant, for what is each instant but a gun, harmless because "unloaded," but that touched "goes off?"
>
> —Emily Dickinson

"Last night the Warings had their novel wedding festival." T. W. Higginson wrote to his sister in 1876. "The Woolseys were bright as usual & wrote some funny things for different guests—one imaginary letter to me from my partially cracked poetess at Amherst, who writes to me & signs 'Your scholar'" (II, 570).[1]

The partially cracked poetess, Emily Dickinson, had no idea her letters were shown to strangers or parodied, but she knew they were unusual. A few days before Higginson enjoyed the Woolseys' imitation of her style, Emily had sent his wife Emerson's *Representative Men* as "a little Granite Book you can lean upon." In lieu of a signature she had written, "I am whom you infer—" (II, 569).

Mrs. Higginson had no trouble inferring. The prose of Emily Dickinson was as unmistakable as her poetry. In both she tried to condense thought to its essence in epigram, trusting her reader to solve the puzzling paradoxes and puns and ambiguities along the way. While her contemporaries gushed pages of nature description, Emily achieved single sentences like "The lawn is full of south and the odors tangle, and I hear today for the first the river in the tree" (II, 452). Such impressionism, for all its economy and beauty, must have sounded strange to mid-Victorian ears. Prose, especially in letters, was supposed to be prosaic. Emily was aware of this: about 1865 she parodied the flatness of most correspondence by writing a poem in the form of a letter:

> Bee! I'm expecting you!
> Was saying Yesterday
> To Somebody you know
> That you were due—
>
> The Frogs got Home last Week—
> Are settled, and at work—
> Birds, mostly back—
> The Clover warm and thick—
>
> You'll get my Letter by
> The seventeenth; Reply
> Or better, be with me—
> Yours, Fly.[2]

If Emily Dickinson's letters did not sound like Fly's, it was because the subtlety and surprise of her thoughts required subtle and surprising words.

A biographical portrait of Emily Dickinson is necessarily the portrait of a letter-writer. Emily's physical existence in the Dickinson homestead was merely a round of household chores, aside from her writing. Her poems, except for those sent to friends as messages, are doubtful sources of fact. There are few accounts of her conversation because she preferred to write to her friends rather than see them. Indeed, some of her most intimate friendships were conducted almost entirely by mail. When, in her early thirties, she decided against publishing her poems, letters became the sole vehicles for her poetry. Her eventual publication and her present rank as a world poet depend to a great extent on the letters she wrote to Colonel Higginson and Mabel Loomis Todd, her posthumous editors. Higginson visited Emily only twice; Mrs. Todd talked with her between rooms and around corners but never met her face to face.

It is not a great exaggeration, then, to say that Emily Dickinson lived through the mail. Such a life is a hindrance to biography: the usual travels, public appearances, meetings with other poets, criticism by contemporaries, and so on, all are lacking. On the other hand, her very remoteness from her neighbors gives her posthumous audience an advantage. Today's reader of Emily's letters can know her almost as well as the friends who received the letters nearly a century ago. In fact, the modern reader may know her better than the correspondents who neither met her nor had access to her letters to others. For Emily Dickinson was audience-conscious; she carefully adapted each correspondence to her estimate of the reader's capacities. Today it is possible to compare letters and to see that Emily sent her most prosaic messages to dull friends, her most striking, oblique flashes of thought to those who would grasp them.

Sometimes she misjudged. She thought Helen Hunt Jackson, for instance, acute enough to understand the most esoteric letters. Though Mrs. Jackson was the only contemporary to call Emily Dickinson a great poet, she could not measure up to Emily's pronouncement, "Helen of Troy will die, but Helen of Colorado, never" (III, 889). In October 1875 Emily sent the following wedding congratulation to Helen Jackson:

Have I a word but Joy?

E. Dickinson.
Who fleeing from the Spring
The Spring avenging fling
To Dooms of Balm—

(II, 544)

Mrs. Jackson returned the note, asking for an explanation. Emily did not reply, of course. To do so would have been like explaining a joke.

Whatever the disadvantages of society-by-mail, there were rewards as well. Emily Dickinson lived deliberately and preferred to present herself to the world only by deliberate art. On the rare occasions when Emily met her friends, she made almost theatrical entrances, dressed completely in white and carrying flowers. Her conversations at such times are said to have been brilliant, but a conversation can have no second draft. Letters, however, can be deliberate creations from salutation to signature, and the letters of Emily Dickinson show a great deal of "stage presence."

Emily's creation of a letter might begin years before she mailed the final draft. Among her papers at the time of her death were hundreds of scraps and drafts of her writing. Some were torn corners of envelopes or backs of grocery lists; others were fair copies ready for mailing, or letters marred by corrections. The collection included poetry and prose in all stages of composition. It was the scrapbasket of Emily's workshop and she kept it as other New England women saved string and wrapping paper and ribbon, against a future need.

The greater part of the scrapbasket collection is poetry, but there is much prose, almost entirely in the handwriting of Emily's last ten years, 1876-86. Certainly she made earlier collections: phrases and whole sentences were repeated in letters written years apart. Probably she systematically destroyed all but the last group.

Emily jotted sentences as they occurred to her while she worked in the kitchen or garden. The roughest of the scraps were penciled scrawls, almost illegible, on any handy bit of paper. Later, in her room, she added them to her workshop collection. When she wrote letters she chose appropriate fragments and worked them into her prose. Sometimes the letter as a whole would pass through two or more drafts before it satisfied her. Meantime she would have chosen poems from the scrapbasket or from her "packets"[3] and fitted them also into her letter. The final writing—the letter her correspondent actually received—might look spontaneous, but it was the last of several creative stages.

An illustration of Emily's method of composition is a letter of 1885 to Helen Hunt Jackson. The message Emily mailed is missing, but all the preliminary drafts remain. On February 3, 1885, Mrs. Jackson wrote to Emily from California. She described her convalescence from a badly broken leg, and the natural beauty of Santa Monica:

> —As I write—(in bed, before breakfast,) I am looking straight off toward Japan—over a silver sea—my foreground is a strip of high grass, and mallows, with a row of Eucalyptus trees sixty or seventy feet high:—and there is a positive cackle of linnets.
>
> Searching, here, for Indian relics, especially the mortars or bowls hollowed out of stone, . . . I have found two Mexican women called *Ramona,* from whom I have bought the Indian mortars.—
>
> I hope you are well—and at work—I wish I knew what your portfolios, by this time, hold. (III, 869)

The "portfolios" Mrs. Jackson wondered about contained, among other things, the following prose fragments: "Strength to perish is sometimes withheld" and "Afternoon and the West and the gorgeous nothings which compose the sunset keep their high Appointment Clogged only with Music like the Wheels of Birds" (III, 868). The final phrase appeared in another fragment somewhat altered: "It is very still in the world now—Thronged only with Music like the Decks of Birds and the Seasons take their hushed places like figures in a Dream—" (III, 868).

Early in March, Emily composed her reply to Mrs. Jackson. Her first draft included the first two fragments, as well as a poem which Emily had used in a letter to Eben J. Loomis the previous January:

> Dear friend—
>
> To reproach my own Foot in behalf of your's, is involuntary, and finding myself, no solace in "whom he loveth he chasteneth" your Valor astounds me. It was only a small Wasp, said the French physician, repairing the sting, but the strength to perish is sometimes withheld, though who but you could tell a Foot.
>
> Take all away from me, but leave me Ecstasy
> And I am richer then, than all my Fellow
> Men.
>
> Is it becoming me to dwell so wealthily
> When at my very Door are those possessing
> more,
> In abject poverty?

> That you compass "Japan" before you breakfast, not in the least surprises me, clogged only with the Music, like the Wheels of Birds.
>
> Thank you for hoping I am well. Who could be ill in March, that Month of proclamation? Sleigh Bells and Jays contend in my Matinee, and the North surrenders, instead of the South, a reverse of Bugles.
>
> Pity me, however, I have finished Ramona.
>
> Would that like Shakespere, it were just published! Knew I how to pray, to intercede for your Foot were intuitive—but I am but a Pagan.
>
> Of God we ask one favor,
> That we may be forgiven—
>
> (III, 866)

At this point the draft ends. The second draft continues to the end of the poem, adding, "May I know once more, and that you are saved?" It is signed, "Your Dickinson."

The greater part of the letter, answering Mrs. Jackson's, occurred to Emily as she wrote her first draft. The changes from one draft to the next are minor, but they are an artist's changes. The separate origin of the prose fragments seems to have caused most difficulty. Emily was dissatisfied with the words which introduced "Take all away from me. . . . " She cut out portions of the second draft and rearranged them, in effect creating a third draft. "But the strength to perish is sometimes withheld" finally became a separate sentence at the end of the poem. The second fragment was replaced by the third, its alternate form: "That you glance at Japan as you breakfast, not in the least surprises me, thronged only with Music, like the Decks of Birds" (III, 867).

Emily's fragmentary prose could serve more than one purpose. Another 1885 letter adapts the last quoted scrap to the memory of Judge Otis Lord: "He did not tell me he 'sang' to you, though to sing in his presence was involuntary, thronged only with Music, like the Decks of Birds" (III, 861).

The exact point at which Emily Dickinson became conscious of prose style remains obscure, but it certainly was early. In the first months of 1850, when she was nineteen, she wrote several letters in an exaggerated rhetoric which was nearly metrical. To her uncle Joel Norcross, who had failed to write to her after promising to do so, Emily depicted a light-hearted apocalyptic vision:

> And I dreamed—and beheld a company whom no man may number—all men in their youth—all strong and stout-hearted—nor feeling their burdens for strength—nor waxing faint—nor weary. Some tended their flocks—and some sailed on the sea—and yet others kept gay stores, and deceived the foolish who came to buy. They made life one summer day—they danced to the sound of the lute—they sang old snatches of song—and they quaffed the rosy wine—One promised to love his friend and one vowed to defraud no poor—and *one* man told a lie to his niece—they all did sinfully—and their lives were not yet taken.

The letter went on to picture the forgetful uncle in hell and to deliver a series of curses: "You villain without rival—unparalleled [sic] doer of crimes—scoundrel unheard of before—disturber of public peace—'creation's blot and blank'—state's prison filler—*magnum bonum* promise maker—harum scarum promise breaker—" (I. 78). The final rhyme undoubtedly was intentional. A valentine letter of the following month, published in the Amherst College *Indicator* (and incidentally the only prose of Emily Dickinson known to have been published in her lifetime) contains three pieces of verse written as prose. The longest, with its typically Dickinsonian off-rhymes, can be read as four long lines or eight short ones: "Our friendship sir, shall endure till sun and moon shall wane no more, till stars shall set, and victims rise to grace the final sacrifice" (I, 92).

The first hints of Emily's later prose came in letters of 1854 to an Amherst College student, Henry Vaughan Emmons. Among the long-winded sentimental letters Emily was writing to others appear messages like this:

> Friend.
> I look in my casket and miss a pearl—I fear you intend to defraud me.
> Please not forget your promise to pay "mine own, with usury."
> I thank you for Hypatia, and ask you what it means?
>
> (I, 294)

Emily exchanged poems with Emmons and they discussed books. The tone of her letters to him became the one she adopted when writing to men of letters—especially Thomas Wentworth Higginson—a few years later. Eventually it spread to almost all her correspondence.

Letters of the mid-'fifties suggest the existence of a prose scrapbasket. In January 1855 Emily wrote to her brother's fiancée Susan Gilbert, "I fall asleep in tears, for your dear face, yet not one word comes back to me from that silent West. If it is finished, tell me, and I will raise the lid to my box of Phantoms, and lay one more love in . . ." (II, 315). The next year Emily used the final sentence again, altering it to fit the departure of her cousin John Graves: "Ah John—*Gone?* Then I lift the lid to my box of Phantoms, and lay another in, unto the Resurrection—" (II, 330). In 1859 she wrote to Mrs. Joseph Haven, "Thank you for recollecting me in the sweet moss—which with your memory, I have lain in a little box, unto the Resurrection" (II, 357).

During the 1860's Emily seems to have repeated herself very little. Perhaps she was more inventive than before or after; more likely, though, she was conducting her correspondences so individually that few sentences appropriate to one could be used in another. The letters to Colonel Higginson, for example, were far more mannered than those to her cousins Louisa[4] and Frances Norcross or her friend Mrs. J. G. Holland, far less ardent and frightened than those to Samuel Bowles. It was only after her father's death in 1874 that the several variant styles began to approach a single manner. In her last years only a few of her most intimate correspondents—the Norcrosses, Judge Lord, and Mrs. Holland—received letters distinctly separate from a general style.

The legendary Emily Dickinson—the one about whom a number of novels and plays and pseudo-biographies have been written—is a romantic figure. She is imagined as completely remote from the life of her generation, a classic artist-in-a-garret (in all but the standard poverty), unknown, unrecognized by her contemporaries. She writes because of a hopeless love and for the same reason becomes a total recluse at an early age.

The real Emily was just enough like the mythical to keep the legend alive. In the last fifteen years of her life (she was fifty-five when she died) she secluded herself from all but children, servants, doctors, immediate family, and a few friends. But her way of life was as deliberate as her poems and letters. Though she avoided physical contact with most of her friends, they remained vivid envoys of the daily world, and, more important, of the world of arts.

For a shy spinster in a small town, Emily Dickinson knew a surprising number of notable contemporaries. Her regular correspondents, all but a few, were known to the public of the day. Among her closest friends were the Reverend Charles Wadsworth, sometimes considered second only to Henry Ward Beecher (himself a friend of the family) as a pulpit orator; Samuel Bowles, whose *Springfield Republican* had gained a national reputation; T. W. Higginson, a leading man of letters and reformer; Helen Hunt Jackson, author of *Ramona* and (in Emerson's opinion) the best poet of her time; and Josiah G. Holland, editor of *Scribner's Monthly Magazine* and best-selling novelist. The one man who indisputably returned Emily's love was Judge Otis P. Lord of the Massachusetts Supreme Court.

Many of Emily's friendships came about through the social standing of her father and brother in Amherst and the Connecticut Valley. Emily, as her sister Vinnie said, "was always watching for the rewarding person to come."[5] When one did, famous or obscure, Emily began another correspondence.

At a certain level of New England society everyone knew everyone else. So it seems, at least, to the modern student of any nineteenth-century New England writer. Among Samuel Bowles's writings one finds mention of almost all of Emily's close friends. Helen Hunt Jackson, whom Emily had first known as a child, was a protégée of Higginson, a regular writer for Holland's magazine, and a friend of Bowles.

Those correspondents who were not well-known themselves were usually close to the New England Olympus. Maria Whitney, a relative of Mrs. Samuel Bowles, was the sister of three notable men—one of them the Yale philologist William Dwight Whitney, another the geologist for whom Mount Whitney, in California, was named. Emily's aunt Catherine Sweetser had received love letters from Beecher.[6] Franklin B. Sanborn was a friend and biographer of Thoreau. Higginson's first wife was closely related to Ellery and William Ellery Channing. Mrs. Lucius Boltwood was a cousin of Emerson. Mabel Loomis Todd corresponded with Howells and the Thoreau family; her father, Eben J. Loomis (to whom Emily wrote several notes), had been a companion of Thoreau, Whitman, and Asa Gray. Emily's girlhood friend Emily Fowler was a granddaughter of Noah Webster. Even the thoroughly commonplace cousins Fanny and Louisa Norcross were friends of the sculptor Daniel Chester French, whom Emily had known slightly when he lived in Amherst.

The foregoing list (by no means complete) suggests how close even a recluse might be to the intellectual currents of her time. It explains how she could write to Higginson, "You ask me if I see any one—Judge Lord was with me a week in October, and I talked . . . once with Mr. Bowles" (II, 548). There was no need to tell which Judge Lord, which Mr. Bowles she meant. Higginson would know.

Emily Dickinson's correspondents were the only readers of the poetry she refused to publish, but she could hardly have found a more perceptive audience. Higginson and Helen Jackson shared with each other the poems and letters Emily sent them. In 1875 Higginson read and discussed some of Emily's poems in a Boston lecture on unknown poets. Mrs. Jackson memorized poems and copied them into a commonplace book. She even mentioned them to her publisher, Thomas Niles of Roberts Brothers, who wrote to Emily in 1882, "'H. H.' once told me that she wished you could be induced to publish a volume of poems. I should not want to say how highly she praised them, but to such an extent that I wish also that you could" (III, 726).

The survival of a handful of letters written to Emily Dickinson by Niles, Higginson, and Mrs. Jackson—most of them praising her poetry and asking her to publish—is still a mystery. In 1872 Emily told Louisa Norcross how she disposed of such requests: "Of Miss P—[perhaps Elizabeth Stuart Phelps, an editor of *The Woman's Journal*] I know but this, dear. She wrote me in October, requesting me to aid the world by my chirrup more. Perhaps she stated it as my duty, I don't distinctly remember, and always burn such letters, so I cannot obtain now. I replied declining" (II, 500). Just before she died, Emily asked Lavinia to burn all correspondence. Vinnie, when she carried out her sister's wish, did not read or set aside any of the letters Emily had received.[7] But on March 3, 1891, Mabel Loomis Todd wrote in her diary that Vinnie had found "a lot of letters from Col. Higginson and Helen Hunt to Emily—thank Heaven!"[8]

Probably Emily herself separated these letters from the others she had received. Since she did not order Vinnie to destroy her poems, she may have hoped that letters praising them would aid in their eventual publication. Posthumous publicity would not compromise her objection to it during her lifetime. "If fame belonged to me, I could not escape her," Emily wrote to Higginson in 1862 (II, 408). Publication then was out of the question. Editors, Emily had found, tried to smooth her off-rhymes and variable metres. She even declined to answer Helen Hunt Jackson's request to be her literary executor. That request, however, was among the letters Vinnie discovered in 1891. Perhaps, at the last, Emily tried to make sure that fame would not escape her.

In a way, her own letters were guarantees of recognition. Emily often wrote in aphorisms which transcended the daily events she was describing. The sense of royalty which she cultivated in her poems was frequent in her prose. These timeless elements have helped to keep the letters from oblivion. Even when Emily's inward royalty carried her to the brink of rudeness, her phrasing redeemed her. Mrs. Holland once made the mistake of addressing a letter to both Emily and Vinnie, and received this reply:

> A mutual plum is not a plum. I was too respectful to take the pulp and do not like a stone.
>
> Send no union letters. The soul must go by Death alone, so, it must by life, if it is a soul.
>
> If a committee—no matter. (II, 455)

The overstatement, understatement, and paradox which characterized Emily's poetry became part of her prose. Sometimes wit, sometimes pathos was conveyed by turning a thought inside out. In December 1881, two months after J. G. Holland died, his daughter Annie was married. Emily wrote to Mrs. Holland with paradoxical optimism, "Few daughters have the immortality of a Father for a bridal gift" (III, 720). A distraught 1861 letter to the man Emily called "Master"—probably Samuel Bowles—was an attempt to convince him of her love and pain. She began,

> Master—
>
> If you saw a bullet hit a Bird—and he told you he wasn't shot—you might weep at his courtesy, but you would certainly doubt his word.
>
> One more drop from the gash that stains your Daisy's bosom—then would you *believe?* Thomas' faith in anatomy was stronger than his faith in faith. (II, 373)

Emily's anguish was genuine, but she could not resist a *bon mot.*

One of her favorite devices was the inclusion of poetry in the body of a letter, either in stanza form or disguised as prose. Not that all poems sent to her correspondents were made parts of the letters: the greater number of poems she gave to Higginson and to her sister-in-law Sue were enclosures on separate sheets of paper. Often, though, Emily led up to a stanza or a complete poem with a prose introduction. A love poem could become a praise of spring, for instance, by a sentence or two of preface:

> Infinite March is here, and I "hered" a bluebird! Of course I am standing on my head!
>
> Go slow, my soul, to feed thyself
> Upon his rare approach.
> Go rapid, lest competing death
> Prevail upon the coach.
> Go timid, should his testing eye
> Determine thee amiss,
> Go boldly, for thou paidst the price,
> Redemption for a kiss.
>
> (II, 523)

The final stanza of another love poem, **"There came a day at summer's full,"** took on a new meaning when adapted to the memory of a friend, Mrs. Edward Dwight, whose picture Emily had just received from the bereaved husband:

> Again—I thank you for the face—her memory did not need—
>
> Sufficient troth—that she will rise—
> Deposed—at last—the Grave—
> To that new fondness—Justified
> by Calvaries of love—
>
> (II, 389-90)

Sometimes the prose of a letter becomes merely a setting for poetry. The rough draft of an October 1870 letter to Colonel Higginson shows how much verse Emily could crowd into a single letter:

> The Riddle that we guess
> We speedily despise—
> Not anything is stale so long
> As Yesterday's Surprise—
>
> The risks of Immortality are perhaps it's charm—A secure Delight suffers in enchantment—
>
> The larger Haunted House it seems, of maturer Childhood—distant, an alarm—entered intimate at last as a neighbor's Cottage—
>
> The Spirit said unto the Dust
> Old Friend, thou knewest me
> And Time went out to tell the news
> Unto Eternity—
>
> Those of that renown personally precious harrow like a Sunset, proved but not obtained—
>
> Tennyson knew this, "Ah Christ—if it be possible" and even in Our Lord's "that they be with me where I am," I taste interrogation.
>
> Experiment escorts us last—
> His pungent company
> Will not allow an Axiom
> An Opportunity—
>
> You speak of "tameless tastes"—A Beggar came last week—I gave him Food and Fire and as he went, "Where do you go,"
>
> "In all the directions"—
>
> That was what you meant
>
> Too happy Time dissolves itself
> And leaves no remnant by—
> 'Tis Anguish not a Feather hath
> Or too much weight to fly—
>
> (II, 480-81)

Emily's handwriting, in her last years, was childlike and resembled widely-spaced printing rather than longhand. She wrote only two or three words to a line, so the poems she put into her letters were difficult to distinguish from her prose. Realizing this, she wrote messages which might be either. The following note, sent to Mary Warner Crowell in March 1885 as a *bon voyage* message, is a four-line stanza plus a line of prose, but the first line of the poem is separated from the others to seem a prose introduction:

> Is it too late to touch you, Dear?
>
> We this moment know—
> Love Marine and Love terrene—
> Love celestial too—
>
> I give his Angels charge—
> Emily—
>
> (III, 865)

George F. Whicher described such letters as Emily's game of "Guess what I am thinking."[9] There can be no doubt that she liked to mystify her correspondents. The number of puzzles depended upon the abilities of the recipient, as Emily judged them. There are few enigmas in the letters to Loo and Fanny Norcross, but a great many in messages to Higginson and Samuel Bowles.

One of Emily's strangest patterns of speech, her use of personal pronouns, seems less intentional. "Would it teach me now?" she asked Higginson in 1867 as if the Colonel were inanimate. There is the remote chance that this was the effect she intended, in order to show respect for her "preceptor," but more probably she began to write "it" or "they" instead of "you" and "he" for the sake of privacy. The first friend so impersonalized was "Master." Emily's use of this name, coupled with "Daisy" (herself), appears in the 1859 poems of Packet 1. In the same packet is this poem:

> My friend must be a Bird—
> Because it flies!
> Mortal, my friend must be,
> Because it dies!
> Barbs has it, like a Bee!
> Ah, curious friend!
> Thou puzzlest me![10]

Not a good poem, but well enough disguised. If someone in the Dickinson household had come upon the poems of Packet 1 he would have found nothing that clearly specified a man who interested Emily.

The last of three surviving letter-drafts to "Master" (with deleted words and phrases in parentheses) begins, "Oh, did I offend it—(Did'nt it want me to tell it the truth) Daisy—Daisy—offend it—who bends her smaller life to his (it's) meeker every day—who only asks—a task—(who) something to do for love of it—some little way she cannot guess to make that master glad—" (II, 391). The letter dates from about 1862, and 1862 poems also make the master impersonal. But in both poetry and prose, Emily usually slipped back into the personal before she was finished. A letter-poem to Samuel Bowles, written in 1863 or 1864, begins,

> If it had no pencil
> Would it try mine—

Worn—now—and *dull*—sweet,
Writing much to thee.[11]

Another poem (of about 1862) is an enigmatic mixture of personal and impersonal pronouns:

Why make it doubt—it hurts it so—
So sick—to guess—
So strong—to know—
So brave—upon it's little Bed
To tell the very last They said
Unto Itself—and smile—and shake—
For that dear—distant—dangerous—Sake—
But—the Instead—the Pinching fear
That Something—it did do—or dare—
Offend the Vision—and it flee
And They no more remember me—
Nor ever turn to tell me why—
Oh, Master. This is Misery—[12]

In this case Emily is "it," the master "They." A substitution of pronouns makes the meaning clear:

Why make me doubt? It hurts me so—
So sick to guess—
So strong to know—
So brave, upon my little bed,
To tell the very last you said
Unto myself, and smile and shake
For that dear, distant, dangerous sake.
But the Instead—the pinching fear
That something I did do or dare
Offend the vision, and it flee
And you no more remember me,
Nor ever turn to tell me why—
Oh, Master, this is misery!

Emily was aware of the strange effect she was creating in such poems. An 1862 poem begins, in its draft form,

While "it" is alive—
Until Death—touches it—
While "it" and I—lap one—Air—[13]

as if the poet could not decide whether to set off the unusual pronoun by quotation marks. In the final copy of the poem there are none.

Many of Emily Dickinson's 1862-64 poems employ "it" or "this" to refer to death, perhaps as an extension of the theme of death which runs through so many poems about the dangerously ill "Master." After 1864 the peculiar pronouns diminished. Emily called Colonel Higginson "it" in 1867, but did not repeat the word in a personal sense until December 1878, when she congratulated him on his engagement to Mary P. Thacher: "Till it has loved—no man or woman can become itself—" (II, 628). Here the problem seems to be grammatical. The construction demanded the singular pronoun, but "he" or "she," "himself" or "herself" would have been inappropriate.

Meanwhile another circumlocution had appeared in Emily's letters. She was peculiarly sensitive to the words "wife" and "husband," and often found ways to avoid them. The series of marriage poems she wrote between 1860 and 1863 establish the special meaning of the words:

I'm "wife"—I've finished that—
That other state—
I'm Czar—I'm "Woman" Now— . . . [14]

"My Husband"—women say—
Stroking the melody— . . .

(II, 758)

Emily began to avoid the words when she spoke of others' marriages. Like her impersonal pronouns, her oblique references to marriage were sporadic. When she spoke of the first Mrs. Higginson in the letters of 1876-78 she sometimes wrote "Mrs. Higginson," sometimes "your friend." In November 1878 she was able to write, "I had a sweet Forenoon with Mrs. Jackson recently, who brought her Husband to me for the first time— . . ." (II, 627), but Mr. Jackson was not always so described. Helen Hunt Jackson quoted one of the circumlocutions in an 1879 letter to Emily: "'The man I live with' (I suppose you recollect designating my husband by that curiously direct phrase) is in New York— . . ." (II, 639).

Colonel Higginson and Mrs. Jackson were amused by such oddities of speech. Yet obliquities also occur in Lavinia Dickinson's letters. When Mabel Loomis Todd was away from Amherst in the spring of 1883, Vinnie wrote to her about Professor Todd: "I've seen your companion once. I should be glad to lessen his loneliness in any way in my power."[15] Either the sisters habitually avoided speaking directly of marriage, or Emily's substitute words crept into Vinnie's vocabulary.

Other oddities of the Dickinson prose style include archaisms and localisms. Emily's capitalization of words within the sentence may be called archaic, but it is not a problem of style, nor (usually) are the short dashes she used as a rhythmic device or in lieu of punctuation. More fundamental are her Elizabethan turns of speech, probably gained through her intimate knowledge of the King James Bible and Shakespeare. When Emily writes "What Miracles the News is!" (II, 483) one is reminded of Shakespearean constructions like "All is but toys."[16] There is the flavor of Shakespeare, too, in a comment on a dead child: "The little Furniture of Loss has Lips of Dirks to stab us" (III, 679).

Emily's subjunctive was another archaism. Coupled with the New England colloquial substitution of "be" for "is," it appeared often in her poetry, occasionally in her prose. When the old-fashioned form appears in a letter, there is a good chance that a poem is present, disguised as prose. "That you be with me annuls fear" (II, 482) is strictly prose, but the following sentences makes a poem: "Too few the mornings be, too scant the nights. No lodging can be had for the delights that come to earth to stay, but no apartment find and ride away" (II, 488).

Regionalisms are most frequent in Emily's girlhood letters,[17] though she wrote "a'nt" (for "isn't"), "he don't," and "eno'" when she was mature. Like her subjunctives, most of her localisms made her writing terser. One of the few exceptions is the added "that" in "because that you were coming" (II, 402) or "because that he would die" (II, 431). Occasionally Emily's expressions may mislead the modern reader. For instance, a poem sent to the Bowleses after the birth of a son in 1861 hopes that when the baby begins to talk, his scriptural "Forbid us not—" will sound "Some like 'Emily'": *somewhat* like "Emily."[18] The conditional "did you not" for "if you did not" has misled many editors of "The Snake."

The uniqueness of Emily Dickinson's prose style does not depend on these minor oddities of diction. Rather, it lies in her originality of thought and her ability to set down her ideas in prose almost as compact and dramatic as her poetry. Emily pared all that seemed superfluous, even usual connectives, from the essence of her thought.

The letters Emily wrote were part of her art, but the life she chose made them also her conversation and autobiography. Her prose tells a great deal about her poetry, simply because the same mind conceived both in much the same way. The letters point the way toward art before Emily wrote a line of passable verse, and the last words she wrote were those of a letter. Now that more than a thousand of her letters are in print it is possible to follow with some accuracy the course of Emily's life in her prose expressions of it, and in the letter-poems she sent to friends. There are still gaps—some as long as a year—but the real Emily Dickinson, far more interesting than the legendary one, has begun to emerge from generations of myth and misconception.

Notes

[1] Thomas H. Johnson and Theodora V. W. Ward, eds., *The Letters of Emily Dickinson* (Cambridge, Mass.: The Belknap Press of Harvard University Press, 1958), II, 570. References to this edition (hereafter called *Letters*) will be indicated in the text by volume and page number only, in parentheses.

[2] Thomas H. Johnson, ed. *The Poems of Emily Dickinson* (Cambridge: The Belknap Press of Harvard University Press, 1955), II, 734-35. This edition hereafter will be referred to as *Poems.*

[3] "Packet" does not accurately describe the booklet grouping into which Emily Dickinson gathered hundreds of poems. Each booklet is made up of several sheets of paper, lightly sewn together along the left margin. I use the word "packet" because it is used throughout *Poems.* Emily Dickinson's word for the booklets is not known; Lavinia Dickinson called them "volumes," Millicent Todd Bingham, "fascicles."

[4] In *Letters* the name is given as Louise; Miss Norcross signed letters thus in her later years. The Dickinsons, however, knew her as Louisa. Letters of Edward Dickinson which speak of "Louisa" are printed in Millicent Todd Bingham's *Emily Dickinson's Home* (New York: Harper & Row, Publishers, 1955), pp. 464, 469. Mabel Loomis Todd, who discussed Loo with Austin and Lavinia Dickinson, and even with Frances Norcross, used only the name Louisa. See *Letters of Emily Dickinson,* edited by Mabel Loomis Todd (New York: Harper & Row, Publishers, 1931), pp. 214-15. (This edition will be referred to as *Letters* [1931].)

[5] Bingham, *Emily Dickinson's Home,* p. 413.

[6] Paxton Hibben, *Henry Ward Beecher: an American Portrait* (New York: The Heritage Press, 1942), pp. 57-58.

[7] Millicent Todd Bingham, *Ancestors' Brocades: the Literary Debut of Emily Dickinson* (New York: Harper & Row, Publishers, 1945), pp. 26-27.

[8] *Ibid.,* p. 152.

[9] George F. Whicher, *This Was a Poet: a Critical Biography of Emily Dickinson* (New York: Charles Scribner's Sons, 1938), p. 147.

[10] *Poems,* I, 73.

[11] *Ibid.,* II, 673. The catalogue of manuscripts in the Millicent Todd Bingham Collection, in the Amherst College Library, lists Bowles as the recipient of this poem.

[12] *Ibid.,* I, 356-57.

[13] *Ibid.,* I, 374.

[14] *Ibid.,* I, 142.

[15] Bingham, *Ancestors' Brocades,* p. 8.

[16] *Macbeth,* II, 99.

[17] See Whicher, *This Was a Poet,* p. 232.

[18] *Poems,* III, 875.

Jane Donahue Eberwein (essay date 1985)

SOURCE: "'The Wildest Word': The Habit of Renunciation," in *Dickinson: Strategies of Limitation*, University of Massachusetts Press, 1985, pp. 21-46.

[*In the following essay, Eberwein examines the theme of renunciation in Dickinson's love poems, suggesting the possible correlation between certain life experiences and Dickinson's verse.*]

"Dont you know you are happiest while I withhold and not confer—dont you know that 'No' is the wildest word we consign to Language?" (L 562). Dickinson posed these questions in an 1878 letter to Judge Otis Phillips Lord at an early stage in her autumnal romance with the widowed Salem jurist, her father's friend and ally in Massachusetts Whig politics. They exemplify a pattern of thinking that had come to characterize her over the years: a habit of renunciation, an excitement in denial, a preference for restrictions. Notions about Emily Dickinson's pitifully deprived life originated in her biography itself; the deprivation was there (mostly of her own choosing) though the pity is misplaced if it presumes her preference for normal domestic routine over an artistically chiseled existence. In a comment to Higginson that accompanied a memoir of George Eliot, the poet clearly recognized the chasm between life as written and life as lived: "Biography first convinces us of the fleeing of the Biographied—" (L 972). But it is inevitable that her readers take the same sort of personal interest in her that she took in Eliot and the Brownings and natural that we should look to biography for insight into the metaphorical design that governed her writing. The well-circulated myths about Emily Dickinson that originated in Amherst and the relatively prosaic facts of her existence as detailed by scholarly biographers display a pattern of constriction within her life (a tendency to intensify every limiting factor she confronted) and a habit of exploiting those constrictions for artistic growth.

The romantic myths started early and provide the most imaginative examples of this pattern. Best of all, in terms of comprehensiveness, is the story published by Genevieve Taggard in *The Life and Mind of Emily Dickinson* (1930); the tale reached Taggard through Mary Lee Hall, who got it from Mrs. Aurelia Hinsdale Davis, who may have picked it up from Lavinia Dickinson in her old age.[1] Quite probably, this is a version of the legend Mrs. Todd began to hear when she and her husband reached Amherst in 1881. The story is that Emily Dickinson, recently returned from Mount Holyoke, fell in love with George Gould, who was Austin's fraternity brother and Amherst College classmate. Gould was a prominent member of the class of 1850: an oratorical star and editor of a new literary journal, the *Indicator.* Their courtship, however, proved ill-fated, running afoul of Edward Dickinson's judgment of the suitor, who, as a ministerial candidate, might never be able to support Edward's daughter adequately. He forbade Gould further access to their home and required that Emily give him up. On the evening of commencement exercises, following the annual reception given by Mr. Dickinson as treasurer of the college, Emily is said to have met Gould on her father's lawn, dressed all in white, to pledge filial obedience and renounce her lover. She is said to have told him "that love was too vital a flower to be crushed so cruelly" and to have signified her stifled will by withdrawing into spinsterish seclusion and wearing nothing but white. This makes a good story in that it offers a complete (if hackneyed) narrative with a touching climax, character conflict, and foreshadowing. But there seems to be no substance to the report.

Certainly Dickinson's 1850 prose valentine to Gould, which he published in the February *Indicator,* shows little sign of serious commitment—especially in view of the verse valentine she dispatched a few weeks later to her father's law partner, Elbridge Bowdoin (P **I**). The missive to Gould, a tour de force of sprightly wit that begins "Magnum bonum, 'harum scarum,' zounds et zounds, et war alarum, man reformam, life perfectum, mundum changum, all things flarum?" hardly reads like one of Dickinson's eventual love poems.[2]

Nor was Gould denied access to Edward Dickinson's home, which he visited occasionally after his graduation before undertaking his ministerial career. Nor did Emily retreat to her father's house for over a decade, nor bleach her dresses. Still, it is a good story in the sentimental vein and most likely quite typical of what her neighbors whispered.

The family's retaliation for such talk about patriarchal cruelty came in another story, promulgated by Mrs. Bianchi to explain how her aunt had reached "the end of peace" during her 1855 visit to her father, then a congressman in Washington.[3] While visiting friends in Philadelphia, Dickinson "met the fate she had instinctively shunned" and which she supposedly confided during her lifetime only to "Sister Sue." Bianchi describes the crisis with the most tactful suggestiveness: "Certainly in that first witchery of an undreamed Southern springtime Emily was overtaken—doomed once and forever by her own heart. It was instantaneous, overwhelming, impossible. There is no doubt that two predestined souls were kept apart only by her high sense of duty, and the necessity for preserving love untarnished by the inevitable destruction of another woman's life." The Yankee heroine fled to her home for refuge, only to be pursued there within days by the impassioned lover. Bianchi narrates how Lavinia raced to Susan Gilbert, crying "Sue, come! That man is here!—Father and Mother are away, and I am afraid Emily will go away with him!" But, of course, Emily held fast to duty and another woman's right. Her disappointed lover left his profession and home, withdrawing "to a remote city, a continent's width remote," and died prematurely, "the spell unbroken," while "Emily went on alone in the old house under the pines." This, too, makes a touching sentimental tale, paralleling the Hall story in its theme of love, renunciation, and enduring sorrow. The main distinction, however, is that Dickinson herself emerges as the focal will of this narrative and the source of renunciation. She seems a stronger though sadder figure, in charge of her own tragic destiny.

Again, it proves difficult to confirm this tale by recourse to poems, since Dickinson's 1855 visit to Washington and Philadelphia preceded the love poems by at least three years, generally six or seven. Yet the lyrics themselves seem to preserve moments in a narrative that follows the same curve of passion, renunciation, and elegiac remembrance evident in both the Hall and Bianchi stories. Poems of 1861 and 1862, in particular, offer a compelling if shadowy impression of disappointed love. If one reads them autobiographically (often a misleading approach to Dickinson's work but always tempting), one can discover an intense commitment to one man as the central figure of the poet's universe, a competitor with God for her devotion. She avows that she has elected one "Atom" from among "all the Souls that stand create" as an object of adoration (P **664**). Yet the reader finds no promise of beholding this fascinating atom until eternity brings its revelation. Speculation naturally ensues. The lover remains a faceless figure in the poems, with no distinguishing characteristics to help biographers choose from among the names (Wadsworth, Bowles, Lord, or Mr. X) they want to offer as "That portion of the Vision / The Word applied to fill" (P **1126**).

This romance, whether real or imaginary, had its passionate moments and climaxed in an encounter such as Hall and Bianchi fantasized. The most famous poem commemorating this communion of loving souls moves from a sense of elated possession through acceptance of parting to a hope of celestial marriage.

> There came a Day at Summer's full,
> Entirely for me—
> I thought that such were for the Saints,
> Where Resurrections—be—
>
> The Sun, as common, went abroad,
> The flowers, accustomed, blew,
> As if no soul the solstice passed
> That maketh all things new—
>
> The time was scarce profaned, by speech—
> The symbol of a word
> Was needless, as at Sacrament,
> The Wardrobe—of our Lord—
>
> Each was to each The Sealed Church,
> Permitted to commune this—time—
> Lest we too awkward show
> At Supper of the Lamb.
>
> The Hours slid fast—as Hours will,
> Clutched tight, by greedy hands—
> So faces on two Decks, look back,
> Bound to opposing lands—
>
> And so when all the time had leaked,
> Without external sound
> Each bound the Other's Crucifix—
> We gave no other Bond—
>
> Sufficient troth, that we shall rise—
> Deposed—at length, the Grave—
> To that new Marriage,
> Justified—through Calvaries of Love—
>
> (P **322**)

The darkening tone of this initially jubilant poem reflects the general pattern of romance within Dickinson's work. The pledge of love and mutual commitment occurs in an hour, creating an anniversary to be recalled through life and a point from which subsequent change is measured.

Such an anniversary sets the occasion for **"One Year ago—jots what?"** (P **296**) in which the speaker recalls the "Glory" of the previous year, whose "Anniversary shall be—/ Sometimes—not often—in Eternity." She says she tasted the "Wine" of this private communion "careless—then—," ignorant that it "Came once a World" and wondering whether the lover—larger and older—had recognized the uniqueness of that day. In the intervening year, however, she feels herself to have grown. He had spoken then of her "Acorn's Breast" and claimed greater capacity for fondness in his "Shaggier Vest" of mature masculinity. But her suffering has developed the acorn and aged the young sweetheart so that she claims to be "As old as thee" now through experience of pain. This passionate love that cannot be expressed except in a memorable hour turns out to be one of those limitations fostering growth—one of the circumstances that allow the wren to soar, if the lover chooses, to be "Great" or "Small" at his behest (P **738**). Clearly the speaker of this and similar poems responds appreciatively to the enhanced self-image bestowed by her lover, by the sense of infinite possibility he conveys to her, even though the greatness arises from pain.

The aftermath of romantic ecstasy is misery and a desperate attempt to recover self-possession without the lover's continued presence to sustain her.

I got so I could hear his name—
Without—Tremendous gain—
That Stop-sensation—on my Soul—
And Thunder—in the Room—

I got so I could walk across
That Angle in the floor,
Where he turned so, and I turned—how—
And all our Sinew tore—

I got so I could stir the Box—
In which his letters grew
Without that forcing, in my breath—
As Staples—driven through—

Could dimly recollect a Grace—
I think, they call it "God"—
Renowned to ease Extremity—
When Formula, had failed—

And shape my Hands—
Petition's way,
Tho' ignorant of a word
That Ordination—utters—

My Business, with the Cloud,
If any Power behind it, be,
Not subject to Despair—
It care, in some remoter way,
For so minute affair
As Misery—
Itself, too great, for interrupting—more—

(P **293**)

The tight parallel organization with which this agonized poem begins breaks down in syntactic confusion. The speaker can neither voice a prayer when unsure whether any person or power will hear it nor completely articulate even to herself her own final sentence, in which the subordinate "if" clause dangles helplessly to express her stammering and skeptical wishfulness.

Occasionally Dickinson refers to the nature of this union as a kind of implicit marriage, recognized as binding by the lovers but not to be revealed until heaven (should there turn out to be marriage or giving in marriage above for earth's hopeless lovers). With its humble, reverent expression of gratitude for the hidden gift of the lover's name, "The World—stands—solemner—to me—" (P **493**) articulates the complexity of her response. The "Dream" of the lovers' mutual choice proves here "Too beautiful—for Shape to prove—," and Dickinson's longest poem mourns the frustration of one who can live neither with nor without her lover: who can neither die with him nor rise with him for fear "Your Face / Would put out Jesus'—" yet who yearns to be with him for eternity, whether in heaven or hell (P **640**). She concludes by describing their apparently fixed earthly situation.

So We must meet apart—
You there—I—here—
With just the Door ajar
That Oceans are—and Prayer—
And that White Sustenance—
Despair—

In "**The face I carry with me—last—**" (P **336**), the speaker looks for heavenly coronation "As one that bore her Master's name—/ Sufficient Royalty!" On earth, however, this love story ends in renunciation. She writes elsewhere that she must be content with honor foregone "With one long 'Nay'—/ Bliss' early shape / Deforming—Dwindling—Gulphing up—/ Time's possibility" (P **349**). This "one long 'Nay'" of inevitable renunciation may be "the wildest word we consign to Language," but it hurts her nonetheless. "Renunciation," she found through this implicit story underlying her romantic poems, "is a piercing Virtue—" (P **745**).

If Emily Dickinson's love lyrics assume any narrative shape, this is its design: mutually avowed passionate love climaxed in one or perhaps two brief, intense, profoundly troubled meetings; a commitment amounting to secret marriage; a lifetime's renunciation; a resultant yearning for recognition of this love (perhaps even its consummation) in an afterlife beyond the circumference of this. This narrative clearly reflects a reader's ordering of the lyrics, chiefly those Johnson dates to 1861 and 1862, and presumes that the poems express their author directly rather than one of the imagined persons discernible in many other poems. Quite probably no such specific sequence occurred in Dickinson's own life; yet it is fair to say that this pattern of avowal, renunciation, and expectancy existed within her imagination and shaped her perception of such courtship as required "No" to be "the wildest word." Her readers and biographers have displayed remarkable ingenuity in their efforts to name the lover whom the poet identified only as "Master" and "Sir," making the strongest arguments for the Reverend Charles Wadsworth,[4] Samuel Bowles,[5] and Otis Lord.[6] The biographical narratives her readers have constructed to account for her relationships with Wadsworth and Bowles (both of them married) follow the design articulated above, with passion leading to inevitable renunciation. The eventual courtship with her father's widowed friend (better documented than the others though far too late in life to account for the love poems discussed above) traced a somewhat different curve toward a similar result.

As Mary Lee Hall cautioned Mrs. Todd, however, "The poems cannot be interpreted solely by Emily's love affairs, the *shadows* drove her into herself. She found much elation in the men who came into her horizon, and they seemed to be the matches that ignited her mental oil tanks."[7] The oil was already there, ready to explode. Neither Lavinia nor Austin believed there had been any one great love of their sister's life. As Lavinia put it, Emily "was always watching for the rewarding person to come,"[8] and the reward she derived from her friendships was largely an artistic one. She relished friendships while they stayed strong (sometimes defeating them herself by the sheer force of her possessive passion, as seems to have happened with school friends) but discovered early the fragility of love. In January of 1855, she wrote first to Susan Gilbert (then engaged to Austin) and later to her cousin, John L. Graves, essentially the same statement of habitual renunciation: "If it is finished, tell me, and I will raise the lid to my box of Phantoms, and lay one more love in" (L 177; 186). Certainly, she held onto the box of outgrown love and relied on its contents, hidden in her drawer, as a precious emotional investment (P **887**). Recognizing limitation even to the force of love, Dickinson intensified that limitation by restricting her affection to fewer and fewer people and renouncing all but epistolary involvement even with most of the chosen. Still, the phantoms in her box and the lost loves in her drawer took on new life in poems that bespeak a depth of passion she probably never experienced directly and derive a startlingly universal insight into human emotions from drastically limited resources.

This tendency to devote herself to unreachable men whom she idealized and to court romantic disaster, if only unconsciously, for the sake of renunciation and its fruits naturally militated against the romantic and even marital attachments Dickinson could have formed in a college town with its annual influx of bachelors and in a family headed by lawyers who introduced her to young men of their profession. Although most of Dickinson's friends married, she cultivated instead a habit of exclusion in emotionally vulnerable relationships. From textual evidence, it would be hard to prove that she ever wished marriage, as distinct from love and the sense of being chosen. Her few fantasies of this sort appear in "**Forever at His side to walk—**" (P **246**) and "**Although I put away his life—**" (P **366**), the latter spoken from the perspective of a woman who has already renounced the lover but fantasizes the comforts she might have brought him: gardening for him, nursing him, clearing "the pebble from his path," playing for him on her lute, doing his errands, eagerly performing his "weariest Commandment," and carrying sticks to light the fire in his cottage. Inspected closely, this love-in-a-cottage picture seems to scream slavery! Why would Emily Dickinson have chosen marriage, anyway? For loving companionship of the sort she could depend upon at home? For the economic support and community status that her father provided, even posthumously? For motherhood, one of the few female roles she never played in her poetic fantasies?[9] For romantic love, which seems never adequately to have been offered her—her standards being high and Robert Browning unique? For social engagements, when she increasingly craved solitude? Her brother's unhappy marriage and the troubles she sensed in other families (including Mary Bowles's jealous dependence on her husband) demonstrated the fragility of marital peace even among persons she idealized. To imagine that Emily Dickinson would ever have chosen the public responsibilities and private obligations of a minister's, lawyer's, or editor's wife in small-town New England is to capitulate entirely to the conventions of sentimental domestic fiction.

Directly or indirectly, Dickinson chose spinsterhood, which her neighbors regarded as a slightly unnatural condition unless the unclaimed jewel attracted sympathy with a sad story of disappointed love, like the Gould and Wadsworth legends the town fabricated on her behalf. The spinster's role in society was one of charitable service, an option that irritated the poet, prompting this youthful explosion to Jane Humphrey: "work makes one strong, and cheerful—and as for society what neighborhood so full as my own? The halt—the lame—and the blind—the old—the infirm—the bed-ridden—and superannuated—the ugly, and disagreeable—the perfectly hateful to me—all *these* to see—and be seen by—an opportunity rare for cultivating meekness—and patience—and submission—and for turning my back to this very sinful, and wicked world. Somehow or other I incline to other things—and Satan covers them up with flowers, and I reach out to pick them" (L 30). In her maturity, the flowers Satan scattered were few; she seemed to renounce temptation with other things. And her letters show her as a kindly, comforting neighbor—so long as she neither had to see the objects of her charity nor, still worse, be seen by them. Her solution, characteristically, was to choose the most constricted option available to a woman of her class—turning her back more fully to the sinful and wicked world than the teachers she mimicked in this letter ever imagined and settling for the inviolate privacy of an aristocratic New England recluse, responsible only to herself and God.

Not even to her family did she ever fully communicate her vocation as a poet or the achievement represented by the drawerful of manuscript that Lavinia discovered on her death. Yet hiding her light beneath the proverbial bushel barrel, Dickinson made sure the smoldering flame would eventually ignite its container. She used her apparently unproductive seclusion for astonishing artistic ends and drew lifelong artistic benefits from the isolation that afforded her privacy for artistic craftsmanship while shielding her hypersensitive emotional nature from sensory overload.

As the Gould and Wadsworth legends demonstrate, Dickinson's neighbors instinctively attributed the young woman's withdrawal to her supposedly broken heart rather than to her judgment "of the hollowness & awfulness of the *world,*" which Austin noticed forming as early as 1851 when his sisters visited him in Boston.[10] By 1863, Samuel Bowles was referring to his friend as "the Queen Recluse," inquiring with amusement in a letter to Austin about the musical entertainments his sister enjoyed in heaven and expressing sympathy for her achievement in overcoming the world.[11] She replied with a squib, "I could'nt let Austin's note go—without a word—,"[12] and a poem reminding him that experiences are discovered by their opposites: fire from ice, red from white, paralysis from vitality, and (presumably) society from solitude and the universe from her chamber (P **689**).

Dickinson probably liked Bowles's queen image—one of a constellation of royal terms she tended to employ in interchanges with him. Often she combined it with shrinking, humble metaphors that also reflected aspects of her expanding and contracting self-image. One poem, **"A Mien to move a Queen"** (P **283**), alternates her characteristic images of limitation (references to the wren, a tear, tiny hands, and a soft voice) with those of empowerment (queen, duke, realm, diadem). The strength comes from chosen patterns of behavior, such as adopting a haughty mien or speaking in a commanding voice. The smallness prevents men from fearing this aristocratic mite, and distance, while cutting short opportunities for affection, precludes contempt. "And so Men Compromise—/ And just—revere—." They honor what they might otherwise disdain because distance makes the regal performance more convincing.

The regal aspect of Dickinson's withdrawal came from her habit of exclusion. "The Soul," she said in one of her most famous poems, "selects her own Society—/ Then—shuts the Door—" (P **303**). Lavinia tried to defend her sister from charges of snobbishness by arguing that "she was not withdrawn or exclusive really. She was always watching for the rewarding person to come, but she was a very busy person herself. She had to think—she was the only one of us who had that to do."[13] Evidently, Dickinson found most persons unrewarding and easily expelled them from her self-selected society. Her comments to Higginson on the persons without thoughts whom she noticed parading by her window demonstrate that she would look for no help in her thinking from most of her neighbors (L 342a).

There can be no question that her isolation intensified neurotic tendencies in Emily Dickinson and allowed for the flowering of eccentric behavior that contributed nothing to her happiness or anyone else's. Yet the Reverend E. Winchester Donald, Austin's friend and a frequent summer visitor to Amherst, was one of the first to recognize the benefit she may have drawn as an artist from the penalties she paid as a woman when he asked Mrs. Todd on receipt of the 1890 ***Poems,*** "One other thing: was the inexorable cost of all this illumination her seclusion renunciation & ache? Would John Baptist be forerunner without the years in the desert, the locusts and all that? Is the nun's self-effacement, her veil and her virginity, the explanation of her unquestioned power? We cannot wear lace and pearls—go often to town & the play, be experts in salads beers and truffles, know what to do with our hands—and expect either to see heaven or to have anyone believe we have seen it."[14] So much for Bowles's taunting questions to his "Queen Recluse": "Is it really true that they ring 'Old Hundred' & 'Aleluia' perpetually, in heaven—ask her; and are dandelions, asphodels, & Maiden's [*vows?*] the standard flowers of the ethereal?"[15] Yet even in her fantasies of celestial bliss, Dickinson retained her habit of limitation in writing: "I went to Heaven / 'Twas a small Town—" where she could be "Almost—/ contented—" (P **374**).

Emily Dickinson's reclusive situation resulted from her own choice. Even if her father had wanted to keep his daughters home (an assertion apparently based on Lavinia's late-life tales but not otherwise substantiated), he never confined Emily to the house and, in fact, counteracted her tendencies toward seclusion by sending her away to school, inviting her to Washington, contriving opportunities for her to go to Boston, and finally requiring her to participate in his commencement receptions. It was her own choice not to "cross my Father's ground to any House or town" (L 330). And there were odd behavior choices she made within his house that carried to an eccentric extreme her habit of limitation. It must be borne in mind that these quirks developed only gradually and that the legendary spinster of the 1880s is a later and somewhat distorted development of the poet of the 1860s. When she wrote most of her poems in that brilliantly productive Civil War period, Dickinson was still making periodic medical jaunts to Cambridge, still visiting at her brother's house, and still receiving visitors even though the very pressure of composing and recording so much poetry (apparently about a poem a day in 1862) must itself have restricted her social involvement. Nor is there any evidence that withdrawal or any other eccentricity proved a recoil from disappointed love. It seems more probable that the romantic renunciations emerged from the same deep-seated need to explore and exploit limitations as did the domestic behavior patterns. So did the poetry.

Perhaps the strangest of her eccentricities was her secretive artistic life. Granted, family members, friends, and neighbors all knew that Emily Dickinson wrote, but apparently none of them suspected either the quantity or quality of her poems; and her habit of attaching bits of verse to letters or gifts actually helped to promote the notion of her versifying as a decorative feminine accomplishment. So, perhaps, did her refusal to let Helen Hunt Jackson (another Amherst native, by then a nationally famous author) publish any of her poems despite the other's decisive moral argument that "You are a great poet—and it is a wrong to the day you live in, that you will not sing aloud. When you are what men call dead, you will be sorry you were so stingy" (L 444a).

Other behavior patterns seem decidedly eccentric. Innate shyness, for example, which always made her ill at ease with crowds or strangers, developed with time into almost total seclusion except for her dizzyingly extensive correspondence. Clearly, Dickinson took an intense interest in people she cared about, and her heart ranged widely—happily opening itself to friends of friends and survivors of acquaintances. Yet she refused almost all visitors, including some she had directly invited to call upon her. To soften the blow of her refusals, she developed charming habits like that of sending to a friend kept waiting in the garden a servant with a silver tray bearing a flower or glass of wine and a cryptic note or verse.[16] She gave herself the benefit of visitation without exposing herself to discovery by having a family friend like Mrs. Todd play the piano and sing for her while she enjoyed the performance from a distant part of the house, signifying her pleasure by faint applause and little gifts.[17] The exclusion was selective, however. She was more open to persons she regarded as unthreatening: children, servants, an Indian squaw selling baskets. Her brother's children and their little friends enjoyed her secretive play with them—the mysteries she contrived and surprises she planned.[18] Even these involvements could be strangely distant, as when she lowered baskets of gingerbread from her bedroom window to her nephew's friends below. Dickinson even planned the details of her own funeral in a way that excluded the town, leaving orders that her body (enclosed in a white casket) be carried by family servants out the backdoor, across the garden, through the barn, and over the fields to the grave—wholly evading the usual public procession along Amherst streets.[19]

The white casket, like the white dress in which Dickinson chose to be buried, calls to mind that other idiosyncrasy her neighbors attributed to romantic disaster: her habit of dressing in white. Just when this pattern developed is hard to tell. Sewall traces the tendency to the mid-1860s but doubts that the habit became fixed before her father's death in 1874.[20] When Higginson met the poet in 1870, he found her costumed in a white dress and blue shawl (L 342a). Interpretations of her action vary almost as dramatically as the symbolism spun from Moby Dick's pallor. White is the bride's color, hence Dickinson's choice to signify the mystic marriage with her lover to be revealed in heaven. And it is the color of the shroud and of ghosts, representative of death. It can be found in gothic novels as well as Revelation. This "colorless all-color" of Ishmael's meditation leads Dickinson's critics, like Melville's, to the heart of ambiguity.[21]

If we turn to **"Mine—by the Right of the White Election!"** (P **528**) to resolve this puzzle, we can recognize the tone of triumphant entitlement ringing through one of Dickinson's most joyful lyrics, but we are at a loss to identify the occasion that evoked it, whether mystical marriage, spiritual election, or discovery of herself as a great poet. Some of the poems she grouped with it in fascicle 20 suggest her association of whiteness with frigidity or death. Her juxtaposition of **"I think the Hemlock likes to stand"** (P **525**) with "**Dare you see a Soul *at the White Heat?***" (P **365**) offers a sharp contrast. The hemlock—black, massive, nobly drooping tree that she identifies with northern climates and races (such as her own)—finds the complement of its dark power in the snow because, she says, it satisfies "An instinct for the Hoar, the Bald." In some moods, anyway, Dickinson too shared this craving that satisfied her awe with its austerity; and she may have complemented the blackness of her tragic moods with Lapland's chill pallor. Yet "**Dare you see a Soul *at the White Heat?***" immediately counters the iciness of snow with the contradictory colorless light of "unannointed Blaze"—far more searing than the red flame of ordinary passion. The soul, which has "vanquished Flame's conditions," threatens destruction to the body ("Forge") that still tries to contain it. "Some say the world will end in fire," wrote Robert Frost, "some say in ice"; Dickinson could signify either one by her ambiguous whiteness, which could include the desire and hatred of his quatrain as well as her "White Sustenance—/Despair—" (P **640**).[22]

Another poem, **"A solemn thing—it was—I said—"** (P **271**), links the white costume more directly to the themes of smallness and renunciation that characterized her personal mythology of growth. Here Dickinson directly associates the choice of white costume with a God-given vocation that involved dropping her life into the mystic (or "purple") well of disappearance from the world until new revelation in eternity. She meditates the "bliss" that might accompany such apparently total self-abnegation and proudly recognizes the growth, the disproval of smallness, the push toward circumference, that would be the paradoxical reward of elected self-denial. That Mrs. Todd entitled the poem "Wedded" in the 1896 ***Poems*** demonstrates the possibility of reading it as a marriage poem and using it as evidence to support the bridal theory of Dickinson's white costume. The imagery makes more sense, however, in terms of the poet's distinctive metaphor of growth through pressing upon limits—especially when she concludes "And I sneered—softly—'small'!"

In the poem immediately following, the speaker makes no reference to clothes but may already be vested in a shroud. She has died but retained the appearance of breathing so that touch rather than vision confirms the numb coolness of the corpse (P **272**). Associations between whiteness and both death and emotional extremes emerge more strongly in this sequence than the bridal motif and sustain the impression that the poet's distinctive costume represented the loss of one kind of life and the assumption of a new one. The "mute Pomp" and "pleading Pageantry—" (P **582**) of this private symbol suggest that the glorious entitlement of her **"White Election"** came at considerable cost, involving renunciation and vicarious experience of that incommunicable **"White Exploit"** (P **922**) of dying.

This lexicon-loving writer occasionally characterized profound change in other people's lives with the word *translation,* which offers further insight into the kind of change her costume signified. In 1852 she reported to Austin on *Dream Life* by Ik Marvel, pleasant reading but inferior to the sketches that had earlier enchanted her, with the comment, "I cant help wishing all the time, that he had been *translated* like Enoch of old, after his Bachelors Reverie, and the 'chariot of fire, and the horses thereof,' were all that was seen of him, after that exquisite writing" (L 75). A little over a year later, she reflected to Emily Fowler on her impressions of this friend's marriage to Gordon Lester Ford: "when it came, and hidden by your veil you stood before us all and made those promises, and when we kissed you, all, and went back to our homes, it seemed to me translation, not any earthly thing, and if a little after you'd ridden on the wind, it would not have surprised me" (L 146). Both Mrs. Ford and Mr. Marvel, of course, remained disappointingly earthbound—neither of them was "translated" or carried across the circumference between this life and a better by the power of either love or artistic creation. But a decade later Dickinson may herself have felt afloat on the wind by virtue of her own poetry (more soaring art than Marvel's essays) and may have considered herself to have transcended her original identity and attained a kind of heaven by God's lifting her in imagination over the barrier of death without her directly experiencing it.[23] In a poem of 1862, at any rate, she used this distinctive word to claim a supernaturally exhilarating aesthetic experience such as the saints might enjoy: "Better—than Music! For I—who heard it—/ I was used—to the Birds—before—/ This—was different—'Twas Translation—/ Of all tunes I knew—and more—" (P **503**). This sound carried the poet retrospectively to legends of "a better—/ Melody—" in Eden and projected her, humming in "faint Rehearsal," toward the celestial singers "around the Throne—." Only religion provided imagery adequate to the experience.

Translation was a biblical concept, as Dickinson's epistolary examples demonstrate with their easy mingling of scriptural texts that fuse the stories of Enoch and Elijah, each drawn miraculously to heaven without experiencing death. The word *translation* itself would have been familiar to the poet from Paul's Epistle to the Hebrews, where she read: "By faith Enoch was translated that he should not see death; and was not found, because God had translated him: for before his translation he had this testimony, that he pleased God" (Hebrews 11:5). In this passage Paul worked out the theology of translation, identifying this experience as one initiated by God and accomplished through the power of faith as a reward to the prophet for pleasing God. But the colorful aspects of Dickinson's version come not from Hebrews or even from the comparatively flat narrative of Enoch's translation in Genesis (5:24).[24] They came from the story in 2 Kings of Elijah's comparable translation: "And it came to pass, as they [Elijah and Elisha] still went on, and talked, that, behold, there appeared a chariot of fire, and horses of fire, and parted them both asunder; and Elijah went up by a whirlwind into heaven" (2 Kings 2:11). This was a story that fascinated Dickinson and that she celebrated in several poems, most notably **"Elijah's Wagon knew no thill"** (P **1254**). God alone could portray the details of this miraculous journey, but its destination was clearly heaven—reached by dramatic ascension rather than through the routine tunneling of the grave.

Without dying, Elijah rose—to be seen again at Christ's Transfiguration, when he and Moses appeared to the Apostles as walking and talking with Jesus, who was himself dazzling like a translated saint: "his face did shine as the sun, and his raiment was white as the light" (Matthew 17:2-3). The Transfiguration itself anticipated the most wonderful example of translation, Christ's rising from the dead and ascension into heaven; and the behavior of the risen Christ exemplified the qualities of the person so favored by God. Like Enoch, Elijah, and Jesus, the translated saint would disappear from the ordinary world, leaving worshipers in wonder. He or she would resemble the risen Christ—visible to close friends, fleshless but powerful, already living in the glory that Christian iconography traditionally represents by shining garments. This, I believe, is the state Emily Dickinson signified by her white clothing. As her epistolary examples of Marvel and Mrs. Ford indicate, it was a state she thought possible for persons of her time, though a rare reward for pleasing God—an exceptional heightening of election. It was a particularly appropriate glory for her, whose poetry probed the awesome circumference of death and tried to penetrate its barrier by imaginative strategies if not by faith. Like Jesus, she dressed in white; like Elijah, she saw herself as the center of a superb adventure; like Enoch, she was not found by those who looked for her.

Yet again, renunciation for Dickinson proved the secret of power and withdrawal from the world—virtual denial of her continuing identity—became the symbol that she had penetrated (at least through imagination) the circumference of ordinary human limitation. If her neighbors chose to think of her as a Miss Havisham rather than an Enoch, she left them to their speculation—discovering that her austere wardrobe and reticent habits evoked pity, which she never wanted, while securing a privacy that liberated her for the artistic work to which she felt called.[25] Her eccentric habits even provided an untroublesome sort of notoriety, itself a small-scale assault on personal annihilation. As a child, Emily was quoted as saying, "I have a horror of death; the dead are so soon forgotten. But when I die, they'll have to remember me."[26] By dying to Amherst for at least the last decade of her life, she cultivated a reputation for exclusion that left people eager for any glimpse into her private mystery and provided herself with an initial audience for the poems that justified her translation.

Reinforcing these rather stylized renunciations that Emily Dickinson herself directly chose to build her metaphorical life action, there were other, less picturesque, limitations that also circumscribed her opportunities. Some derived from her small-town Connecticut Valley environment, some from the Victorian era, some from her femaleness. Yet the consistent pattern that emerges from comparing Dickinson's personal experience with those culturally imposed limitations is one of supplemental personal choice. Her background almost never exemplified these limiting factors to an extreme degree; indeed, she had noticeable advantages over many women of her culture even though sexual and social constraints were always present. What happened, however, is that Dickinson herself tightened the screws on each restriction. By her own choices, she immured herself within the magic prison that paradoxically liberated her art.

The first limitation, one that Dickinson shared with most American contemporaries, was that of small-town provincialism. Amherst's population was small and, except for Irish and black workers, heterogeneously Yankee. Its citizens all knew each other and each other's business. Although Jay Leyda has chronicled how Amherst acquainted even its most retiring daughter with the dread realities of "the violent deaths, suicides, lynch mobs, abortions, dishonesties that are the normal portion of village life," even *The Years and Hours of Emily Dickinson* shows the town to have been a quiet place on the whole and respectable in the Victorian manner.[27] Always more concerned with beauty than morality, Dickinson seems to have taken less interest than many others in her neighbors' sins but must still have felt the lack of cultural resources in a town that, like most others across the United States, offered its citizens few opportunities to appreciate artistic excellence. Yet Amherst was not a backwater. It had a college, literary societies, and a lecture series. The combination of cultural appetite with artistic privation forced this community toward language for expression and enjoyment. Lecturers could be hired and books sent for. For Dickinson in Amherst, as for Hawthorne in Salem and Thoreau in Concord, literature was the only art form familiar enough to be understood, imitated, and eventually created.

That Dickinson turned inward toward books and eventually substituted written correspondence for almost every other kind of communication was, then, only her intensification of a general cultural pattern. If books opened to her a world more exciting than Amherst, she was prepared to renounce the town. Luckily, when she withdrew from lectures, concerts, and tableaux, she had adequate literary resources to make up the loss: a steady supply of reading matter, including popular novels and magazines; correspondents who appreciated her allusive habits; and the good taste to winnow ordinary writing from great literature. She told Higginson that "After long disuse of her eyes she read Shakespeare & thought why is any other book needed" (L 342b). When her preceptor invited her to join his Boston salon of artistic ladies, she chose to stay in Amherst.

Throughout the Connecticut Valley, in South Hadley even more insistently than in Amherst, Dickinson encountered yet another reminder of her finitude in the omnipresent atmosphere of Calvinist piety. But even in religion she was spared the extremes of evangelical fire-and-brimstone terror on the one hand and broad-minded intellectual vapidity on the other. At home, in church, and at school, young Emily confronted the awesome contrast between human weakness and divine omnipotence; she knew her radical insufficiency—her presumably depraved natural condition. She felt great pressure from those who loved her to accept Jesus as her savior, although she knew she must wait for conversion and cipher at its signs. Dickinson's friends Abiah Root and Abby Wood found themselves converted in adolescence, as did Lavinia, who—with Edward Dickinson—formally joined the church during the revival of 1850. Austin joined just before his marriage, leaving Emily the sole outsider within the family. At least in adolescence, her letters showed a somewhat envious awareness of the peace these Christians claimed to enjoy (L 10; 39), but she never formally recognized herself as converted and referred to herself in later years as "but a Pagan—" (L 976).

When Edward Dickinson summoned his minister to examine his daughter spiritually, Mr. Jenkins declared her "sound," but the religion she substituted for her family's Congregationalism imposed radical limitations on normal religious practice.[28] Susan Dickinson's obituary for her independent sister-in-law established a parallel between her literary and spiritual selectivity. Just as "she sifted libraries to Shakespeare and Browning," she stripped devotion of all excess: "To her life was rich, and all aglow with God and immortality. With no creed, no formulated faith, hardly knowing the names of dogmas, she walked this life with the gentleness and reverence of old saints, with the firm step of martyrs who sing while they suffer."[29] Keeping her Sabbath by staying home in her garden, professing disregard for doctrine, refusing to judge behavior in moralistic terms, she responded with her "wildest word" to most of what her neighbors valued as religion.

Nonetheless, it is futile to treat Dickinson as other than a religious poet. She divorced herself from the visible signs of religion in her community to distill its essence, focusing intense spiritual passion on the intimate encounter between herself and God—an interchange in which she hoped to smash circumference and snatch the prize of immortality. The encounter was not always a loving one—often painful and terrible—but it was the central action of her life, to which she applied all the resources she had learned for exploiting her finitude. "God was penurious with me," she asserted, "which makes me shrewd with Him" (L 207). The strategies she developed were poetic ones to bridge the chasm between the finite and the infinite, the mortal and the immortal—a process that is simultaneously the essence of religion and the definition of her quest.

A third overwhelming cultural limitation on Dickinson's growth was the sexual stereotyping of the Victorian era that accorded a decorative and subordinate role to her presumably fragile sex and especially to its genteel representatives within her social class. Physiology joined with social convention to confine women within the home.[30] Discrimination took its intellectual toll as well as an emotional one. Partly as a consequence of adolescent illness and even more because of restrictive notions about feminine needs, most girls of Emily Dickinson's generation were educated less rigorously than their brothers. Even people who thought girls might have adequate intelligence for formal education worried about the physical strain of schooling and questioned the usefulness of a masculine curriculum for young ladies. (Higginson himself, champion of Radcliffe College, failed to complete his daughter's education.) Few girls attended school beyond the primary grades, undertook higher education, or studied the classical languages and mathematics that would equip them for the learned professions they were unwelcome to enter in any event. Domestic skills, the social graces, religious principles, and superficial artistic accomplishments prepared a lady to ornament her husband's home. "How invaluable to be ignorant," Dickinson responded, "for by that means one has all in reserve and it is such an Economical Ecstasy."[31]

Yet she was hardly ignorant, being provided with an education far superior to the norm. At Amherst Academy and Mount Holyoke she studied science, philosophy, Euclid, and Latin—much the same curriculum Austin faced—and endured similar rigors of public examinations. Under the governance of Mary Lyon, the female seminary set high academic standards in order to prepare its graduates for lives of competence and service—preferably in the missions. But Dickinson spent only one year at South Hadley, and even that period (like her previous Academy experiences) was interrupted by parentally mandated intervals at home for rest and domestic training. The contrast between Austin's Amherst College and Harvard Law privileges with his role as paternal delegate in snatching his tearful sister home from Mount Holyoke is a painful one, illustrative of that greater respect for his only son's mind that Mr. Dickinson increasingly displayed (L 23).[32] Still, the elder daughter pursued her education independently. First with Benjamin Newton as tutor, then with Higginson as preceptor, she concentrated her extraordinary intellectual and volitional force on her poetic growth.

Both at school and at home, a young woman of Dickinson's class could exercise her mind in comparative safety by reading imaginative literature, and Dickinson's letters reveal the eagerness with which she seized upon fiction and poetry to counteract educational deprivation. She seems to have read almost anything recommended by her like-minded friends: Shakespeare, of course, and Emerson, Thoreau, Hawthorne, the Brontës, and the Brownings—but also Longfellow, Ik Marvel, and a host of popular writers.[33] It was the current sentimentalism that dominated her early letters, probably because society approved such reading for young ladies—if indulged in moderately so as not to round the shoulders or erode good sense. The popular fiction reinforced values to which the society conditioned its girls.[34] It accorded kind attention to women, both as characters and authors, even as it narrowed their aspirations.

By fixing attention on domestic life and locating heroism in meek acceptance of suffering, sentimental literature exalted women in their capacities as dutiful daughters, sacrificing mothers, and model Christians. It presented life as sadly beautiful without examining the economic or political bases for the sorrow—preferring to justify all crises as moral tests. . . . some of the stock situations of this literature are discoverable even in her poetry, as are the compassionate, benevolent feelings that sentimental literature evokes. Yet lyric poetry distills images and feelings at the expense of narrative, and the only way to impose outright sentimental fictions on her work is to spin a narrative that binds the lyrics somewhat arbitrarily, as I have done in reorganizing her love poems to suggest a story—a distinctly sentimental tale like most of those that readers generate in the hope of restoring plot, character, and situation to these imaginatively compelling lyrics. Dickinson exploited even the conventions of sentimental literature to create her poems and call forth her audience.

Sentimental writing, which implicitly honored the restrictions of genteel Christian womanhood, promoted the reputations of writers as diverse as Harriet Beecher Stowe, Lydia Sigourney, Lucy Larcom, and Frances Osgood.[35] Women demonstrated in Dickinson's day that they could turn a profit out of their ostensibly timid calls upon public attention, and they established their own magazines to publish the edifying fiction for which the public appetite appeared insatiable. But Dickinson—always an elitist—refused to superimpose ordinary, culturally acceptable meanings on the amazing sense of her poetry, and she never availed herself of the feminine literary marketplace to which both male and female literati willingly consigned all the sweet singers with whom they would have classified her.

Denial of publication to this astonishingly gifted poet is the limitation within her life that rankles most sharply today. Dickinson, who described her verse as "my letter to the World" (P **441**), must have wished an audience. The few poems that reached print anonymously and in corrupted texts reveal an initial willingness to publish, although her reaction against editorial blunders shows an aversion to compromise not possible for more professional-minded poets (L 316). Perhaps she hoped for a while that Bowles, Holland, and Higginson would help her to publish in well-read, respectable journals. When they failed her, she characteristically refrained from offering her verses to the plethora of literary magazines that might have printed some. It was hardly impossible for women poets to publish in nineteenth-century America (though difficult to make a living), but those who succeeded often did so, like their male counterparts, by pandering to conventional tastes and commercial pressures. Too proud to join Hawthorne's "d———d mob of scribbling women," Dickinson stitched her own little "volumes" (Lavinia's word) and tucked them in drawers to await their resurrection.

In **"Publication—is the Auction / Of the Mind of Man—"** (P **709**), Dickinson expressed her contempt for commercial composition. To read this poem only as an ironic attempt at disguising authorial pain is to miss the genteel Yankee pride that spits out the key word, "Auction." Recall Thoreau's sneers at auctions in *Walden,* the associations he draws between bodily death and material accumulation; and remember Frost's New England reversal of consumerist values: "The having anything to sell is what / Is the disgrace in man or state or nation." Edward Taylor had suspected that his Connecticut Valley neighbors would reject salvation itself if allowed to haggle over its cost.[36] Dickinson, a lady comfortably provided for, had nothing to sell in the garage sale of imagination. She substituted the concept of stewardship for that of property in the statement "Thought belong to Him who gave it—/ Then—to Him Who bear / It's Corporeal illustration—" and refused to reduce her proud spirit "To Disgrace of Price—." If her talent belonged to God, he would somehow get the value of it and she perhaps the fame. References to whiteness here link her translated self to her Creator, by whom her "Snow," artistically fashioned, would be validly appraised.

It is amusing that Emily Dickinson's very reserve about publication, coupled with her incremental release of sample verses in multitudinous messages of friendship or consolation, eventually resulted in a local reputation for literary performance. The *Springfield Daily Republican* (which itself had printed several of her poems anonymously), the *Record,* and the *Union* all fostered conjecture that an Amherst lady named Dickinson was the author of Helen Hunt Jackson's unacknowledged Saxe Holm stories. As early as 1878, then, Dickinson could have read ascriptions of her authorship in the newspaper with reviewers finding the same characteristics in another woman's prose that their successors would find in her poetry come 1890.[37] Dickinson made no money from her writing and probably never wanted to. She seldom saw her name in print (never with a poem) and most likely gave thanks for the privacy. She did, nevertheless, find a few appreciative readers. Her correspondence with Susan Gilbert Dickinson on **"Safe in their Alabaster Chambers—"** (P **216**) reveals a more sensitive editor next door than in the offices of the *Springfield Daily Republican* or *Atlantic Monthly* (L 238). The eventual editing history of Dickinson's poems, especially the contributions of Mabel Loomis Todd, demonstrates that the poet had access to responsive, critical readers—most of them women. The enthusiasm for literature of all sorts among middle-class American ladies resulted in the emergence of a reading audience capable of artistic discrimination beyond the level the commercial marketplace assumed, capable of welcoming Emily Dickinson's poems as soon as they appeared.[38] Not only Dickinson, then, but others as well managed to transcend the stultifying limits of Victorian feminine culture, although her admirers quickly capitulated to that culture by fashioning a sentimental myth around "Emily" herself.

Genteel nineteenth-century American society limited women in their power to make significant choices, encouraging men to think of active decisions and women of passive ones. A woman should wait for a man to choose her in marriage, should learn to subordinate her will to her father's or husband's. She should look for signs of God's approval. Yet to emphasize such constraints on female choices is to exaggerate the problem. Women did have important areas of freedom, particularly with regard to religion.[39] Within the home, also, a woman could exercise a great many choices about furniture, clothing, and medical treatment. Although some women used their privileges to acquire fashionable property, defining themselves by possessions, the Yankee women of Dickinson's time were more likely to use freedom in making negative choices. They demonstrated thrift and prudence by showing what they could do without; taste defined itself by discriminations. Mocking this tendency in her youth, Dickinson amused herself in several letters with references to a neighbor's potentially fatal fastidiousness: "Mrs. Skeeter' is very feeble, 'cant bear Allopathic treatment. cant have Homeopathic'—dont want Hydropathic—Oh what a pickle she is in—should'nt think she would deign to *live*—it is so decidedly vulgar!" (L 82). Yet this woman, who would eventually require her own doctor to diagnose her from a distance as she paced back and forth in an adjoining room, lived to carry to extremes this habit of selecting, discriminating, excluding.[40]

In subject matter, Dickinson's poems stress both sides of a woman's situation. She could express delight at being chosen—the passive beneficiary of a more powerful being's option, but she also communicated the painful power of making exclusions. At her most ebullient, describing herself as self-sufficient, self-defined, she claimed the right even to positive choice: characteristically a grand one. "With Will to choose, or to reject," she chose, "just a Crown—" (P **508**). Yet even this coronation came by a process of negative choices, rejection of the name and roles her family had assigned her.

I'm ceded—I've stopped being Their's—
The Name They dropped upon my face
With water, in the country church
Is finished using, now,
And They can put it with my Dolls,
My childhood, and the string of spools,
I've finished threading—too—

She asserted her right to do without most of the satisfactions she had been taught she needed.

In her life, as in her poems, Dickinson exploited the opportunity to make negative choices, recognizing that her tendency to deny opportunities marked her off as eccentric and exclusive while exposing her to pain. "Odd, that I, who say 'no' so much, cannot bear it from others," she wrote to Louise Norcross, "Odd, that I, who run from so many, cannot brook that one turn from me" (L 245). Wanting to be chosen by important others, she habitually abstained from positive choices herself: "With one long 'Nay'—/ Bliss' early shape / Deforming—Dwindling—/ Gulphing up—/ Time's possibility" (P **349**). Emily Dickinson shaped her life, by a startlingly consistent pattern of negative choices, in a way that intensified every limitation upon her, exaggerated every barrier. And she did so consciously, not in order to punish herself or court discomfort, but to promote reflexive inward growth. If "No" was "the wildest word we consign to Language," it could somehow liberate other words—including those she would select to formulate the literature of limitation and rejection that initiated her metaphysical quest for circumference.

Notes

[1] Leyda, *Years and Hours,* I:177-178. Sewall also presents this story, with reasons for doubting it, in *The Life,* II:419-422. A variant appears in Leyda, *Years and Hours,* II:478-479.

[2] Leyda, *Years and Hours,* I:168.

[3] Bianchi, *Life and Letters,* pp. 43-51; *Emily Dickinson Face to Face,* pp. 51-53.

[4] Johnson, *Emily Dickinson: An Interpretive Biography* (Cambridge, Mass.: Harvard University Press, Belknap Press, 1955), pp. 76-84; George Frisbie Whicher, *This Was a Poet: A Critical Biography of Emily Dickinson* (1938; reprint ed., Ann Arbor: University of Michigan Press, 1957), pp. 99-112. See also Sewall, *The Life,* II: chap. 20; William R. Sherwood, *Circumference and Circumstance: Stages in the Mind and Art of Emily Dickinson* (New York and London: Columbia University Press, 1968), chap. 3; William H. Shurr, *The Marriage of Emily Dickinson: A Study of the Fascicles* (Lexington: University Press of Kentucky, 1983); and John Crowe Ransom, "Emily Dickinson: A Poet Restored," *Perspectives USA* (1956), reprinted in Sewall, ed., *Emily Dickinson: A Collection,* p. 98.

[5] Ruth Miller, *The Poetry of Emily Dickinson* (Middletown, Conn.: Wesleyan University Press, 1968), esp. chaps. 5-7; David Higgins, *Portrait of Emily Dickinson: The Poet and Her Prose* (New Brunswick, N.J.: Rutgers University Press, 1967), chap. 4; and Sewall, *The Life,* II: chaps. 21-22.

[6] Millicent Todd Bingham, *Emily Dickinson: A Revelation* (New York: Harper and Brothers, 1954). For reservations about the authenticity of documents published by Bingham, consult Anna Mary Wells, "ED Forgeries," *Dickinson Studies* 35 (1979): 12-16. Further attention to this relationship may be found in John Evangelist Walsh, *The Hidden Life of Emily Dickinson* (New York: Simon and Schuster, 1971).

[7] Sewall, *The Life,* I:255.

[8] Bingham, *Emily Dickinson's Home,* p. 413.

[9] An early letter to Abiah Root makes sportive reference to maternity: "Twin loaves of bread have just been born into the world under my auspices—fine children—the image of their *mother*—and *here* my dear friend is the *glory*" (L 36).

[10] Leyda, *Years and Hours,* I:213.

[11] Ibid., II:76.

[12] Ibid., 77.

[13] Bingham, *Emily Dickinson's Home.* pp. 413-414.

[14] Bingham, *Ancestors' Brocades,* p. 77.

[15] Leyda, *Years and Hours,* II:76.

[16] Accounts of such experiences appear in memoirs by MacGregor Jenkins, Gertrude Montague Graves, and an unidentified Amherst correspondent quoted in Leyda, *Years and Hours,* II:482-484.

[17] Ibid., 357. See also Bingham, *Ancestors' Brocades,* p. 12, and Bianchi, *Emily Dickinson Face to Face,* pp. 34-35.

[18] Bianchi, *Emily Dickinson Face to Face,* chap. I, and MacGregor Jenkins, *Emily Dickinson: Friend and Neighbor* (Boston, Mass.: Little, Brown, 1930).

[19] Leyda, *Years and Hours,* II:474-476; Sewall, *The Life,* II:610.

[20] Sewall, *The Life,* II:448.

[21] Consider, for example, Austin Warren, "Emily Dickinson," in Sewall, ed., *Emily Dickinson: A Collection,* pp. 113-115; Sherwood, *Circumference and Circumstance,* p. 152; and Gilbert and Gubar, *The Madwoman in the Attic,* pp. 613-621.

[22] "Fire and Ice," in *The Poetry of Robert Frost* (New York: Holt, Rinehart and Winston, 1969), p. 220.

[23] Noah Webster's *An American Dictionary of the English Language* (Springfield, Mass.: George and Charles Merriam, 1849) encouraged this use of the word *translation* by offering as the third of five meanings "the removal of a person to heaven without subjecting him to death" and by citing Hebrews 16 as an example of the verb *translate:* "By faith Enoch was *translated,* that he should not see death."

[24] Genesis 5:24: "And Enoch walked with God: and he was not; for God took him." Dickinson focused attention on this text in poem 1342, thought by Johnson to be an elegy for her father.

[25] Commenting on local gossip by "women who wore sensible stuff dresses" about her aunt's white costume, Bianchi concludes, "And the only person who never thought of it as a mystery was Emily herself, as she moved about her father's house and garden. They could no more approach her than they could make the moon come down and sit on their parlor sofas!" *Emily Dickinson Face to Face,* p. 37.

[26] Leyda, *Years and Hours,* II:480-481.

[27] Leyda, "Introduction," in *Years and Hours,* I:xxi.

[28] The Reverend Jonathan L. Jenkins, in his memorial sermon for Edward Dickinson, suggested a close relationship between her father's religious views and ED's: "He had no great faith in ceremonies, in formulas of doctrine. He was free in his speech about religion, most unconventional in his practices. His religion was however most excellent and genuine." Sewall, *The Life,* I:68.

[29] Leyda, *Years and Hours,* II:473.

[30] Barbara Welter, *Dimity Convictions: The American Woman in the Nineteenth Century* (Athens: Ohio University Press, 1976).

[31] L, III, PF 36.

[32] See Barbara J. Williams, "A Room of Her Own: Emily Dickinson as Woman Artist," in Cheryl L. Brown and Karen Olson, eds., *Feminist Criticism: Essays on Theory, Poetry, and Prose* (Metuchen, N.J.: Scarecrow Press, 1978), pp. 69-91.

[33] Jack L. Capps, *Emily Dickinson's Reading: 1836-1886* (Cambridge, Mass.: Harvard University Press, 1966). The clearest perspective on her literary habits, including her disposition to read "competitively and for companionship," may be found in Sewall, "Books and Reading," in *The Life:* II: chap. 28.

[34] Ann Douglas, *The Feminization of American Culture* (New York: Alfred A. Knopf, 1977).

[35] Emily Stipes Watts, *The Poetry of American Women from 1632 to 1945* (Austin: University of Texas Press, 1977), chaps. 3-5.

[36] *Walden* may well be the closest parallel in American literature to Dickinson's assessment of values, and it resembles her work in its paradoxical application of Yankee economics to spiritual growth. "When a man dies he kicks the dust," Thoreau wrote in his chapter "Economy," and his neighbors buy the dust (even a dried tapeworm) at auctions. The Frost excerpt comes from "New Hampshire," which contrasts New England pride in scarcity with a national zeal for surplus. Tay-

lor had speculated in "Gods Selecting Love in the Decree" that colonial Yankees would have admired God's coach sent to carry the saints to heaven but would have rejected it as too expensive.

[37] A 25 July 1878 editorial in the *Republican* suggested one of Helen Hunt Jackson's Amherst neighbors as Saxe Holm on the basis of subtle mystical questions found in the stories, morbidity, ideality, weirdness, interpolated poems "like strains of solemn music floating at night from some way-side church" with each thought "complete and rare, solemn with the solemnity of intense conviction." The domestic scenery to which the tales were limited, the smallness of the episodes, and the writer's humorlessness were all felt to point away from Mrs. Jackson as author and toward some reclusive woman whom the editorialist envisaged as "robed in white" like Hawthorne's Hilda. A later editorial note in the 3 August 1878 *Republican* terminated speculation with fact: "we happen to *know* that no person by the name of Dickinson is in any way responsible for the Saxe Holm stories." Leyda, *Years and Hours,* II:295-297.

[38] Reviews of the *Poems* (1890) were mixed but surprisingly plentiful, as Klaus Lubbers demonstrates in *Emily Dickinson: The Critical Revolution* (Ann Arbor: University of Michigan Press, 1968), chap. 2. Reader response may be estimated by the rapid appearance of new printings—five editions between 12 November 1890 and February 1891, with a second volume in preparation.

[39] Douglas, *The Feminization of American Culture.*

[40] Leyda, *Years and Hours,* I:xxix-xxx.

Douglas Leonard (essay date 1987)

SOURCE: "'Chastisement of Beauty': A Mode of the Religious Sublime in Dickinson's Poetry," in *American Transcendental Quarterly*, University of Rhode Island, Vol. 1, No. 3, September, 1987, pp. 247-56.

[*In the following essay, Leonard considers Dickinson as a Romantic poet, arguing that her emphasis on emotion in her poetry (like that of other Romantic poets) is rooted in the eighteenth-century notion of the sublime.*]

Emily Dickinson shared with other Romantic poets, American and European, the intuition that the age of reason had run its course and had failed to bring the hoped-for illumination and order. In the new century, as the focus turned toward the self, the feelings of the individual tended to replace authority and schema in the measure of truth and beauty. From the beginning, Dickinson's poetry reflects the poet's awareness that emotional sensations occur in various dimensions within the consciousness, so that joy and grief, for example, or exultation and fear, may combine in single complex reactions. The most intense emotions, in fact, are frequently the most paradoxical. The combination of emotional opposites would become characteristic in Dickinson's poetry, and it is in fact the indivisible unity of terror and ecstasy which constituted what Dickinson considered the most intense emotion of all, what she called "awe."

Dickinson's expression of emotion, like that of other Romantics, has its roots in the eighteenth-century aesthetic of the sublime. There is no doubt that Dickinson was aware of the tradition, even if we cannot be certain whether she had studied Edmund Burke's influential *Enquiry into the Sublime and the Beautiful* or Kant's *Critique of Judgement* (Gelpi, 124-125). At least two of Dickinson's Mount Holyoke textbooks summarize the sublime aesthetic: Samuel P. Newman's *Practical System of Rhetoric* and Thomas C. Upham's *Elements of Mental Philosophy* (Newman, 42-47; Upham, 300-309). Newman relates the sublime to his discussion of literary taste and style, citing examples; and Upham, following Burke, more lengthily explains characteristics which evoke sublime emotions: expanse, height, depth, color, light, darkness, sound, motion, and power. An immediate relevance can be seen in the passage in which Upham contemplates the sublimity of the sea.

> In regard to the ocean, one of the most sublime objects which the human mind can contemplate, it cannot be doubted that one element of its sublimity is the unlimited expanse which it presents. . . . The sailor on the wide ocean, when, in the solitary watches of the night, he casts his eye upward to the lofty, illuminated sky, has a sublime emotion; and he feels the same strong sentiment striving within him when, a moment afterward, he thinks of the vast unfathomable abyss beneath him, over which he is suspended by the frail plank of his vessel. (302-303)

Upham's description of sea travel seems to underlie the sublime expression in this familiar early Dickinson poem **(76).**

> Exultation is the going
> Of an inland soul to sea,
> Past the houses—past the headlands—
> Into deep Eternity—
>
> Bred as we, among the mountains,
> Can the sailor understand
> The divine intoxication
> Of the first league out from land?[1]

Whether the sea represents passionate love, life, art, "circumference," or, as the words "eternity" and "divine" seem to suggest, mystical union with God, the specific reference of the poem is not material for the present purpose (Sewall, 2:522; Miller, 66-67, 155-156; Cody, 304; Ward, 42). The quality of the emotion is the poet's first concern. Dickinson calls going out into "deep Eternity" "exultation," an emotion usually considered unadulterated bliss. But for Dickinson as for Upham, the "divine intoxication" of the adventurer is composed of dread as well as exultation. Dickinson's own contribution to the sublime aesthetic in "**Exultation is the going**" is that her "going to sea" is symbolic of an inner voyaging.

In 1848, Austin Dickinson presented a translation entitled "From Longinus on the Sublime" at the Spring Exhibition of Amherst College (Leyda, 1:142). Although there is no direct evidence that Emily and Austin shared their knowledge of the sublime, it is probable that they did since the two corresponded frequently into the mid-fifties. Until Austin married Susan Gilbert in 1856, he was Emily's closest intellectual companion. We know further that around the same time Austin sent her a book of poetry by Alexander Smith, a leader of the so-called "Spasmodic School" of poets who during the 1850s practiced an extreme form of sublime expression. Dickinson replied in a letter to her brother that she enjoyed Smith's "exquisite frensy" (Anderson, 68; ***Letters*** 1:256).[2]

Dickinson's reading of James Thomson and Ralph Waldo Emerson would also have made her familiar with the aesthetic of the sublime. Thomson's *The Seasons,* cited as an example of the sublime poetic technique in Dickinson's college rhetoric, was also in the Dickinson's family library. She quoted from Thomson's verse on at least two occasions (Capps, 75, 111, 187; ***Poems*** 131). In addition, Dickinson certainly knew Emerson's essay "The Oversoul," which consciously employs the sublime in a way Dickinson would follow, if not precisely imitate. "The influx of the Divine mind into our minds," Emerson writes, "agitates men with awe and delight" (Emerson, 223).

Although the external evidence that Dickinson understood the concepts of the sublime is persuasive, the evidence within the poems is compelling.[3] A poem of 1862 **(582)** demonstrates especially well Dickinson's use of Burkean elements of the sublime.

Inconceivably solemn!
Things so gay
Pierce—by the very Press
Of Imagery—

Their far Parades—order on the eye
With a mute Pomp—
A pleading Pageantry—

Flags, are a brave sight—
But no true Eye
Ever went by One—
Steadily—

Music's triumphant—
But the fine Ear
Winces with delight
Are drums too near—

The poem's subject is the emotional response of consciousness to a "Parade" of imagery in the natural world, and Dickinson here identifies a number of aspects of the sublime: color, brightness, intensity, arrangement, motion, and loudness. Bright "imagery" is piercing; its arrangement viewed from afar affects one like "Pomp" and "Pageantry"; flags are so "brave" that a "true Eye" cannot steadily look at one; and triumphant music makes the "fine Ear" wince with "delight." *Dickinson* seems to echo Burke in her reference to a "true Eye" and "fine Ear," for Burke states that sublime perception requires "finer and more delicate organs, on which, and by which, the imagination and perhaps the other mental powers act" (135).

Such examples of Dickinson's sublime response to things in the natural world could be multiplied, but I want to concern myself especially with her use of an inner sublime. As in "**Exultation is the going,**" Dickinson often evokes the sublime to describe the internal landscape of her own consciousness. The vastness, loudness, power, suddenness, brightness, obscurity, difficulty, and infinity of the consciousness elicit the delightful terror which constitutes the sublime. In **"It's Hour with itself" (1225),** written about 1872, Dickinson looks into the interior sublime.

It's Hour with itself
The Spirit never shows.
What Terror would enthrall the Street
Could Countenance disclose
The Subterranean Freight
The cellars of the Soul—
Thank God the loudest Place he made
Is licensed to be still.

The isolated self-scrutiny of consciousness is represented as sublime by use of the metaphor of a gothic cellar. The terror must remain a secret because it would "enthrall"—either in the sense of delight or enchant—any who discovered it. Yet this "loudest place" is also simultaneously "still."

Another poem depicting the interior sublime, "**'Tis so appalling—it exhilirates** [sic]" **(281)** is exactly the kind of Dickinson poem which is condemned by some critics as being too vague, meaninglessly obscure.

'Tis so appalling—it exhilirates—
So over Horror, it half Captivates—

The Soul stares after it, secure—
To know the worst, leaves no dread more—

To scan a Ghost, is faint—
But grappling, conquers it—
How easy, Torment, now—
Suspense kept sawing so—

The Truth, is Bald, and Cold—
But that will hold—
If any are not sure—
We show them—prayer—
But we, who know,
Stop hoping, now—

Looking at Death, is Dying—
Just let go the Breath—
And not the pillow at your cheek
So Slumbereth—

Others, Can wrestle—
Your's, is done—
And so of Wo, bleak dreaded—come,
It sets the Fright at liberty—
And Terror's free—
Gay, Ghastly, Holiday!

Some attempt to "salvage" this "obscure" poem by interpreting it by Dickinson's life. Richard B. Sewall, for example, considers the poem the "obverse" of **"I felt a funeral in my brain" (280)** in that it is a healthier response to the departure of her alleged would-be lover, Samuel Bowles. "In the therapeutic view," Sewall explains, "she has come near mastering her affliction and is on the way to health. . . . The Truth of the third stanza is her failure to elicit response from Bowles (or whomever or whatever); the Death of the fourth stanza is the death of her hopes" (2:503). Instead, what really creates unity and coherence in **"'Tis so appalling—it exhilirates"** is its steady concern with describing the emotive consciousness facing the prospect of death. Prayer, suspense, torment, dying, a ghost, and "Wo"—none of these things is the true subject of the poem; they are metaphors for sublime emotions evoked by the contemplation of death.

"He fumbles at your Soul" (315) is a description of spiritual intercourse between the persona and God, and Dickinson makes full use of sexual imagery to convey the emotional intensity of the relationship, its extremes of pleasure and pain.[4] At the same time, besides further amplifying the intensity of the sensations, Dickinson's use of the sublime serves to indicate the persona's profound ambivalence in response to the experience of intimacy between the self and God.

He fumbles at your Soul
As Players at the Keys
Before they drop full Music on—
He stuns you by degrees—
Prepares your brittle Nature
For the Etherial Blow
By fainter Hammers—further heard—
Then nearer—Then so slow
Your Breath has time to straighten—
Your Brain—to bubble Cool—
Deals—One—imperial—Thunderbolt—
That scalps your naked Soul—
When Winds takes Forests in their Paws—
The Universe—is—still—

The metaphoric fabric of this unusual sonnet is richly interwoven from the first line. The word "fumbles" suggests an ineptitude of overly-eager passion on the part of God, but of course it is the soul, not the body, which is here being "undressed." Immediately, though, the sexual metaphor is set aside temporarily in favor of a musical one. But the players' "fumbling" at the keys implies not clumsiness so much as the gentle fluttering of skillful hands as they play very softly in that moment just before the abruptly "drop" the "full music on."[5] The musical metaphor is also temporarily suspended as Dickinson now compares the increasing intensity of the spiritual encounter with a physical attack. God "stuns" the soul "by degrees," in order to prepare it for the "etherial blow." The soul is "brittle" because it is mortal, limited, and fallen, and therefore needs to be "prepared" for intimacy with the divine. So God approaches the soul gradually, like the "fainter Hammers" of the piano heard from a distance. At the same time, the "Hammers" God wields associate him with Thor in violence, even while their far away music suggests his gentleness.

Now the sublime suspense builds as the music approaches nearer and then slows so that the persona's breathing returns to normal and her temperature cools. These physical references set up the climax of the spiritual experience, which is again described in sexual terms. God, like Thor or Zeus, now "Deals—One—imperial—Thunderbolt," which "scalps" the "naked Soul." Surely Dickinson was not unaware of the sexual connotations of her imagery or of her references to the lustful gods of mythology. Thus Dickinson's poem reaches a terrible climax of violence, a climax all the more shocking because it is the objective correlative of the spiritual union between God and the soul.

The final two lines are set apart from the rest of the sonnet to indicate the stillness which follows the boom of the thunder. Here Dickinson employs another metaphor from nature to convey this peaceful aftermath: "When Winds take Forests in their Paws—/The Universe—is—still—." This image is difficult, but it follows that the "Winds" refer to the spirit of God, while the "Forests," as they are material, refer to the human being who has been visited by God. The "Paws" of the wind, like a cat's, can be gentle as well as violent. At the end the "Universe" of the persona's consciousness is stilled, both because it is enervated after its painfully intense communion with God, and because God himself has fulfilled and quieted the soul in visiting it.

In sum, **"He fumbles at your Soul,"** in order to convey the complex nature of spiritual intimacy between the soul and God, compares God successively with a lover, a musician, the music itself, a scalping attacker, a wielder of thunderbolts, the wind, and a cat. To do this in fourteen lines while maintaining unity is an astonishing achievement. This rare sonnet expresses the ambivalance of the soul's response to communion with God. Consciousness plainly desires that communion as the body desires sexual love, and the soul enjoys communion with God as one's aesthetic sensibility enjoys music. Both experiences combine gentleness and violence. At the same time, because of its "brittle Nature," its humanness, consciousness fears and resists being "violated" by the sovereign will of the divine spirit. What is finite cannot contain the infinite, yet the soul can receive God. It is not appropriate, then, to read "**He fumbles at your Soul**" as an explicit or even "sublimated" rape fantasy, just as it is not appropriate to dismiss the mystical experience of Teresa of Avila, for example, as a rape fantasy.[6] Have critics accused John Donne of indulging in rape fantasy in his Holy Sonnet 14 because he asks God to "take," "enthrall," and "ravish" him? Dickinson, like Donne, has simply put to use a number of things from the natural world, including human sexuality, in order to communicate a supernatural experience which is both anguish and bliss.

Whenever Dickinson desired to characterize the most intense emotions—sexual, aesthetic, or spiritual—she usually did so in terms of the sublime. In Burke's phrase, the sublime is "productive of the strongest emotion which the mind is capable of feeling" (39). A final poem will take us the last step in Dickinson's emotional consciousness. She considered awe the highest of all emotions, and in fact the essence of the sublime response is awe. **"My period had come for Prayer" (564)** also treats the sublime experience of the soul encountering God, but this time the metaphor is a cosmic quest, in which the persona now becomes the aggressive partner in the relationship.

> My period had come for Prayer—
> No other Art—would do—
> My Tactics missed a rudiment—
> Creator—Was it you?
>
> God grows above—so those who pray
> Horizons—must ascend—
> And so I stepped upon the North
> To see this Curious Friend—
>
> His House was not—no sign had He—
> By Chimney—not by Door
> Could I infer his Residence—
> Vast Prairies of Air
>
> Unbroken by a Settler—
> Were all that I could see—
> Infinitude—Had'st Thou no Face
> That I might look on Thee?
>
> The Silence condescended—
> Creation stopped—for Me—
> But awed beyond my errand—
> I worshipped—did not "pray"—

Here Dickinson presents prayer as a difficult journey through the cosmos into God's presence. The childlike persona travels beyond the physical horizon of the "North" to seek the "house" of the Creator, and finds only "vast Prairies of Air," or what Inder Nath Kher has called "the landscape of absence." The infinitude of space, itself a sublime image, is extended in its sublime quality by the suggestion of the persona's solitude and lostness. Finally, when she has cried out to God in desperation, "the Silence condescended." As in the poem which begins **"I know that He exists" (338),** God is here described as removed, dwelling in "Silence," until suddenly he "surprises" the seeker with bliss.[7] This supernatural visitation is the most sublime experience of all, again because it involves the union of the human with the divine, the finite with the infinite, and the personal with the universal. The persona, now no longer a child, is "awed" by the experience. No longer interested in addressing God in petitionary prayer, she simply worships. After all, what most she sought from God was communion with himself.

"My period had come for Prayer," though not, I think, a great poem, shows the primacy of awe in Dickinson's consciousness. Awe was her consummate emotion, combining qualities like beauty and terror, faith and doubt, into a sublime whole. In a poem of 1874, **"Wonder is not precisely Knowing" (1331),** Dickinson calls the paradoxical sensation of awe "a beautiful but bleak condition," as the consciousness, which sees and believes but is never certain, experiences a fundamental suspense at once both "delightful" and "mangling."

A year before her death, in thanking an unknown correspondent for the gift of a book (presumably a Bible), Dickinson expanded on the paradoxical character of awe.

> I thank you with wonder—Should you ask me my comprehension of a starlight Night, Awe were my only reply, and so of the mighty Book—It stills, incites, infatuates—blesses and blames in one. Like Human Affection, we dare not touch it, yet flee,

> what else remains? . . . How vast is the chastisement of Beauty, given us by our Maker! A Word is inundation, when it comes from the Sea—Peter took the Marine Walk at great risk. (***Letters*** 3:858)

This passage, as it reveals how Dickinson associated awe and the sublime, also manifests the convergence in Dickinson's thinking of things awe-inspiring. These things had become as one in her consciousness: the infinity of the night sky, beauty, the Bible, human love, the ocean of divine love, and the walk of faith. Dickinson's poems frequently express an awareness of the multifold miracle of existence, and her own circumscribing consciousness of it all was itself both part and whole of the awful miracle. Manifestly, Dickinson considered the ecstatic terror of such consciousness the appropriate subject for a great many poems. In her emphasis and insights she was well ahead of her time, while also conscious of the long tradition of mystical poetry behind her.

Notes

[1] Reprinted by permission of the publishers and the Trustees of Amherst College from *The Poems of Emily Dickinson,* edited by Thomas H. Johnson, Cambridge, Massachusetts: The Belknap Press of Harvard University Press. Copyright 1951, 1955, 1979, 1983 by The President and Fellows of Harvard College. All quotations from Dickinson's poems and identifying numbers are from this edition. Poems 281, 564, 582, and 1225 are from the *Complete Poems of Emily Dickinson,* edited by Thomas H. Johnson. Copyright 1929, 1935 by Martha Dickinson Bianchi. Copyright renewed 1957, 1963 by Mary L. Hampson. By permission of Little, Brown and Company.

[2] An obscure comment in a letter to T. W. Higginson might lead to a speculation that he had suggested to Dickinson that her verse savored too much of the "spasmodic school," but Dickinson's opaque reference to his supposed suggestion cannot be offered as a firm proof: "You think my gait 'spasmodic'—I am in danger—sir—You think me 'uncontrolled'—I have no tribunal" (*Letters* 2:409). The letter from Higginson is missing.

[3] Gelpi (192 n. 55) lists some poems he classifies as "natural sublime": 1609, 210, 1171, 1677, 1678, 1419, 1217, 1486.

[4] "He fumbles at your Soul," has a confused history of explication. George F. Whicher, 101, started it by saying that the "he" in the poem is the preacher Wadsworth, the alleged lover of Dickinson. Anderson, 17, agrees "he" is a preacher, but a "hell-fire preacher," not Wadsworth. Chase, 204-205, thinks "he" is a lover like Wadsworth and that Dickinson's ambiguity is "bad" or vague. Johnson, in *Emily Dickinson: An Interpretative Biography,* 237, restricts his interpretation of "he" in the poem to Wadsworth. William R. Sherwood, who makes reference to all the readings above in 108-109 and 255, notes 116-118, thinks Dickinson's "he" is God, as do Cleanth Brooks, R. W. B. Lewis, and Robert Penn Warren, II, 1238. Sewall, II, 451, note 703, argues that the "he" is *not* Wadsworth.

[5] Music is sublime for Dickinson. See *Letters,* Letter 390, II, 507, in which Dickinson says to her cousin Frances Norcross: "Glad you heard Rubinstein. . . . He makes me think of polar nights Captain Hall could tell! Going from ice to ice! What an exchange of awe!"

[6] St. Teresa's account of her famous "ecstasy": "Besides me, on the left hand, appeared an angel in bodily form, such as I am not in the habit of seeing except very rarely. Though I often have visions of angels, I do not see them. . . . But it was our Lord's will that I should see this angel in the following way. He was not tall but short, and very beautiful; and his face was so aflame to be all on fire. They must be of the kind called cherubim, but they do not tell me their names. . . . In his hands I saw a great golden spear, and at the iron tip there appeared to be a point of fire. This he plunged into my heart several times so that it penetrated my entrails. When he pulled it out, I felt that he took them with it, and left me utterly consumed by the love of God. The pain was so severe that it made me utter several moans. The sweetness caused by this intense pain is so extreme that one cannot possibly wish it to cease, nor is one's soul content with anything but God. This is not a physical, but a spiritual pain, though the body has some share in it—even a considerable share. So gentle is this wooing which takes place between God and the soul that if anyone thinks I am lying, I pray God in His goodness, to grant him some experience of it" (Teresa 210 and *passim*).

[7] The awful "silence" dominates more ambiguously in "I felt a funeral in my brain" (280), where the persona ends her cosmic voyage of consciousness "wrecked, solitary" with her companion a personified "silence."

Works Cited

Anderson, Charles R. *Emily Dickinson's Poetry, Stairway of Surprise.* New York: Holt Rinehart and Winston, 1960.

Brooks, Cleanth, R. W. B. Lewis, and Robert Penn Warren. *American Literature: The Makers and the Making.* 2 vols. New York: St. Martin's Press, 1973.

Burke, Edmund. *A Philosophical Enquiry into the Origin of our Ideas of the Sublime and the Beautiful.* New York: Columbia University Press, 1958.

Capps, Jack L. *Emily Dickinson's Reading.* Cambridge, Massachusetts: Harvard University Press, 1966.

Chase Richard. *Emily Dickinson.* New York: William Sloane Associates, 1951.

Cody, John. *After Great Pain: The Inner Life of Emily Dickinson.* Cambridge, Massachusetts: Belknap Press of Harvard University Press, 1971.

Dickinson, Emily. *The Poems of Emily Dickinson.* Ed. Thomas H. Johnson. 3 vols. Cambridge, Massachusetts: Belknap Press of Harvard University Press, 1955.

———. *The Letters of Emily Dickinson.* Eds. Thomas H. Johnson and Theodora Ward. 3 vols. Cambridge, Massachusetts: Harvard University Press, 1958.

Emerson, Ralph Waldo. "The Oversoul." *Essays: First Series.* Boston and New York: Houghton, Mifflin and Company, 1895.

Gelpi, Albert J. *Emily Dickinson: The Mind of the Poet.* Cambridge, Massachusetts: Harvard University Press, 1975.

Johnson, Thomas H. *Emily Dickinson: An Interpretative Biography.* Cambridge, Massachusetts: Belknap Press of Harvard University Press, 1955.

Kher, Inder Nath. *The Landscape of Absence: Emily Dickinson's Poetry.* New Haven: Yale University Press, 1974.

Leyda, Jay. *The Years and Hours of Emily Dickinson.* New Haven: Yale University Press, 1960.

Miller, Ruth E. *The Poetry of Emily Dickinson.* Middletown, Connecticut: Wesleyan University Press, 1968.

Newman, Samuel P. *A Practical System of Rhetoric.* 20th ed. New York: Mark H. Newman, 1846.

Sewall, Richard B. *The Life of Emily Dickinson.* 2 vols. New York: Farrar, Strauss and Giroux, 1974.

Sherwood, William R. *Circumference and Circumstance: Stages in the Mind and Act of Emily Dickinson.* New York: Columbia University Press, 1968.

Teresa, of Avila, Saint. *The Life of St. Teresa.* J. M. Cohen, tr. Harmondsworth: Penguin, 1957.

Upham, Thomas C. *Elements of Mental Philosophy.* New York: Harper and Brothers, 1850.

Ward, Theodora. *The Capsule of the Mind, Chapters in the Life of Emily Dickinson.* Cambridge, Massachusetts: Harvard University Press, 1961.

Whicher, George F. *This Was a Poet: A Critical Biography of Emily Dickinson.* New York: Charles Scribner's Sons, 1938.

Nadean Bishop (essay date 1987)

SOURCE: "Queen of Calvary: Spirituality in Emily Dickinson," in *University of Dayton Review*, Vol. 19, No. 1, Winter, 1987-1988, pp. 49-60.

[*In the following essay, Bishop asserts that the spirituality so central to Dickinson's poetry is characterized by the poet's dismissal of contemporary religious dogma as well as by her decision, "based on Self-Reliance," to envision her own version of God and heaven.*]

Many books and essays on Emily Dickinson's poetry have appeared in the last five years, and each approaches the question of spirituality divergently depending on the author's dominant focus. Barbara Mossberg deals with Dickinson as dutiful and rebellious daughter; Jane Eberwein concentrates on strategies of limitation; Sandra Gilbert rehabilitates domesticity; and Vivian R. Pollak analyzes the anxiety of gender. The critics agree, however, that spirituality holds a central place in Dickinson's poetry.

Charles Anderson concludes his essay, "Grief," in Harold Bloom's 1985 collection on Dickinson by saying: "She dedicated herself to creating the one thing of absolute value that, in her view, the human being is capable of. It goes under the rather inadequate name of religion, or art, the vision that comes with human's utmost reach towards truth and beauty. (Anderson, 35) Jane Eberwein asserts: "God was the most important person in Emily Dickinson's life. Her relationship with him excelled all others in endurance and intensity. . . . God was awe; he was also love. Infinite and immortal, he transcended all human imagination. . . . She was drawn to the power and safety God manifested. She reverenced awe. . . . She felt free to quarrel with the jealous, angry, cruel figment of other people's imaginations because that figure was not the divinity she never stopped worshipping." (Eberwein, *Strategies,* 244-245)

> Who was the divinity Emily Dickinson worshipped?
>
> What is the "heaven of her own" that she created?
>
> How does her love of Nature feed her spirituality?

Too often in the past, critics have taken Emily Dickinson's Mount Holyoke rejection of the God of the revival meeting as her final word on divinity. In writing girlhood friends who accepted the vengeful Yahweh God, she did often put herself in the opposite camp with some regret:

> I think of the perfect happiness I experienced while I felt I was an heir of heaven as of a delightful dream, out of which the Evil one bid me wake & again return to the world & its pleasures. Would that I had not listened to his winning words! . . . I determined to devote my whole life to [God's] service & desired that all might taste of the stream of living water from which I cooled my thirst. But the world allured me & in an unguarded moment I listened to her syren voice. (L 11)

Yet as Margaret Homans documents so fully in "Emily Dickinson and Poetic Identity," "When she writes to her more religious friends, her apparently genuine self-depreciation may be as fictive as the most extravagant of her announced fantasies." (Homan, 133)

Much of what we know about Emily Dickinson's spirituality can be summarized by quoting a stanza from Harold Bloom's favorite Dickinson poem, chosen because it is such a strong "work of un-naming, a profound and shockingly original cognitive act of negation." (Bloom, 5)

> The Tint I cannot take—is best—
>
> The Moments of Dominion
> That happen on the Soul
> And leave it with a Discontent
> Too exquisite—to tell—
>
> (P **627**)

Bloom exults: "It is rugged and complete, a poetics, and a manifesto of Self-Reliance." (Bloom, 6)

I will argue that Emily Dickinson's spirituality is also marked by negation of the existing religious dogmas and a decision based on Self-Reliance to remake God and to create her own Heaven. This process is parallel to that undertaken during this decade by a dozen prominent theologians, who, like Carter Heyward in *The Redemption of God: A Theology of Mutual Relation,* describe a deity, no longer Omnipotent, Invisible, Only Wise, but a God constantly in process, interacting lovingly with suffering humankind.

As Barbara Mossberg so carefully documents in *Emily Dickinson: When a Writer Is a Daughter,* the God of the Calvinist religion of Dickinson's day was an "Awful Father of Love" whom Emily came to see as like her own father:

> An analysis of the representation of the Deity in Dickinson's poems confirms the parental archetype: rejecting, absent, absent-minded, careless, businesslike, incompetent, contradictory, and pernicious. Edward Dickinson came first: God is simply a blown-up version, a ballooned Edward Dickinson on a string whom the daughter addressed as "Father in Heaven." (Mossberg, *Daughter,* 115)

Emily Dickinson shows how often this "Burglar! Banker—Father!" God of "I never lost as much but twice" (P **49**) uses punishment and repression to gain obedience. The ultimate threat is "Judgment Day," which provides a corrective to the young child's impulse to "run away/ From Him—and Holy Ghost—and All—."

> I never felt at Home—Below—
> And in the Handsome Skies
> I shall not feel at Home—I know—
> I don't like Paradise—
>
> Because it's Sunday—all the time—
> And Recess—never comes—
> And Eden'll be so lonesome
> Bright Wednesday Afternoons—
>
> If God could make a visit—
> Or ever took a Nap—
> So not to see us—but they say
> Himself—a Telescope
>
> Perennial beholds us—
> Myself would run away
> From Him—and Holy Ghost—and All—
> But there's the "Judgment Day"!
>
> (P **413**)

This "Papa Above" is unresponsive and distant:

> Of Course—I prayed—
> And did God Care?
> He cared as much as on the Air
> A Bird—had stamped her foot—
> And cried "Give Me"—
>
> (from P **376**)

In poem after poem the poet is conciliatory and patient in the face of an Adamant God who is begged to be "sweet," challenged to "drop down":

> Just Once! Oh least Request!
> Could Adamant refuse
> So small a Grace
> So scanty put,
> Such agonizing terms?
> Would not a God of Flint
> Be conscious of a sigh
> As down His Heaven dropt remote
> "Just Once" Sweet Deity?
>
> (P **1076**)

Dickinson discusses at length the reasons for rejecting "the Father and the Son" of her childhood:

> Who were "the Father and the Son"
> We pondered when a child,
> And what had they to do with us
> And when portentous told
>
> With inference appalling
> By Childhood fortified
> We thought, at least they are no worse
> Than they have been described.
>
> Who are "the Father and the Son"
> Did we demand Today
> "The Father and the Son" himself
> Would doubtless specify—
>
> But had they the felicity
> When we desired to know,
> We better Friends had been, perhaps,
> Than time ensue to be—
>
> We start—to learn that we believe
> But once—entirely—
> Belief, it does not fit so well
> When altered frequently—
>
> We blush, that Heaven if we achieve—
> Event ineffable—
> We shall have shunned until ashamed
> To own the Miracle—
>
> (P **1258**)

Contemporary women theologians have taken up the cry against the gods of patriarchy, particularly for the concept of God as Father. Union Theological Seminary Hebrew scholar Phyllis Trible wrote as early as 1973: "Israel repudiated the idea of sexuality in God. Unlike fertility gods, Yahweh is neither male nor female, neither he nor she . . . As Creator and Lord, Yahweh embraces and transcends both sexes. To translate for our immediate concerns: the nature of the God of Israel defies sexism." (Trible, "Depatriarchialism," 34) Mary Daly in *Beyond God the Father* exclaims: "If God is male, then male is God!" (Daly, 19)

Systematic Theologian Rosemary Radford Ruether argues for Mother-Father God as imagery of the rootedness and groundedness in the universe but delineates a weakness in the whole conceptualization of the parent image for God:

> God becomes a neurotic parent who does not want us to grow up. To become autonomous and responsible for our lives is the gravest sin against God. Patriarchal theology uses the parent image for God to prolong spiritual infantilism as virtue and to make autonomy and assertion of free will a sin . . . We need to start with language for the Divine as redeemer, as liberator, as one who fosters full personhood and, in that context, speak of God/ess as creator, as source of being. (Ruether, 69-70)

Dickinson gives us dozens of examples of this little girl persona, but as Mossberg illustrates, she uses it to play along with society's view of her insignificance and turn it to her own advantage: "Her creation and obsessive use of the little girl persona appears to be a brilliant but inevitable metaphor for her experience as a woman poet in her culture, reflecting and resolving her 'small size'—the lack of society's esteem for and encouragement of her mental abilities. . . . Seeing her as a child could be a way to neutralize her, neuter her, keep her well-behaved, as if against her will—to shut her up." (Mossberg, *Nursery,* 47)

> They shut me up in Prose—
> As when a little Girl
> They put me in the Closet—
> Because they liked me "still"—
>
> Still! Could themself have peeped—
> And seen my Brain—go round—
> They might as wise have lodged a Bird
> For Treason—in the Pound—
>
> (from P **613**)

Through her disguise as "a little ninny, a little pussy cat, a little Red Riding Hood" (L I, 117), Emily kept peace with the men in her household and with their mirrored images in heaven. She used her extraordinary poetic talent to escape the Pound, the cage of patriarchal repression employed in that era to keep women "still." But most women of her era and many of our own have been silenced, neutered, oppressed through the image of the Father God who keeps us in infantilism.

Calvinism applauded self-abnegation. Sin was defined as self-aggrandizement and love by contrast as "unconditional forgiveness . . . the concrete relatedness of an I to a Thou, in which the I casts aside all its particularities, all its self-affirmations, everything which separates it from the Thou." (Saiving, 27) Thus this theology condemned autocrats like Edward Dickinson but allowed them power; it applauded sacrifice like that of Emily Dickinson, but made powerlessness its reward.

Delivering the Dudleian lectures at Harvard in 1960, Valerie Saiving challenged these traditional definitions and showed that for women, socialized to be the little girl in Dickinson's poems or the selfless mother of Victorian "angel-in-the-house," for idealism was actually socialized into sin of an opposite nature from that of men. The sins which the church

Fathers castigate are "pride, will-to-power, exploitation, self-assertiveness, and the treatment of others as objects." (Saiving, 35) As Saiving delineates them, women's sins are better suggested by such terms as "triviality, distractibility, and diffuseness; lack of an organizing center or focus; dependence on others for one's own self-definition; tolerance at the expense of standards of excellence . . . in short, underdevelopment or negation of the self." (Saiving, 37) Thus the temptation to remain a child, to be locked in perpetual Pounds, to be subordinate to the Imperial godhead, creates those sins which lead a woman to loss of self. Dickinson's cheeky rebelliousness that Mossberg captures with such glee indicates one strategy for thwarting the autocrats in her household, but she became able to refuse to make such self-abnegating concessions to the Divine.

What she gained by putting on the little girl persona in the Dickinson household was protection. As she wrote to Mrs. Holland soon after her father's death: "Thank you for the Affection. It helps me up the Stairs at Night, where as I passed my Father's Door—I used to think was safety." (L 432) As Jane Eberwein tells us: "If God the Father offered similar protection, she might feel indebted to him. Yet flawed teaching in childhood had undermined her confidence in a way that fastened upon her memory." (Eberwein, *Limitations,* 242) Thus she shapes her address to God the Father with an irony felt by many contemporary women so trapped in misapprehensions about the godhead:

"Heavenly Father"—take to thee
The supreme iniquity
Fashioned by thy candid Hand
In a moment contraband—
Though to trust us—seem to us
More respectful—"We are Dust"—
We apologize to thee
For thine own Duplicity—

(P **1461**)

Process theology portrays a God who is not autocratic, who does not act arrogantly without consultation with the human beings whose lives are being affected, and who rewards collaborative effort over individualism. Carter Heyward and John Cobb give extensive evidence from scripture and human history for demolishing the duplicitous "Papa Above" and forming communities where God acts in a trusting way toward interactive humans working to bring the Kingdom on earth. Men as well as women today find the Calvinistic God of Edward Dickinson unacceptable.

We are not surprised to see Dickinson rejecting the God of her Father. Jane Eberwein summarizes: "Dickinson's father-master-lover figure elicits awe, terror, even rage. She finds him fascinating but cruel and knows that she must somehow evade his dominance that reduces her to a condition of feminine victimization even as she gathers to herself his power." (Eberwein, 123) Her response to "the Son" is quite altered from that of the Father, but sometimes even Jesus appears to be not loving but punishing as in "**He strained my faith**."

He strained my faith—
Did he find it supple?
Shook my strong trust—
Did it then—yield?

Hurled my belief—
But—did he shatter—it?
Racked—with suspense—
Not a nerve failed!

Wrung me—with Anguish—
But I never doubted him—
'Tho' for what wrong
He did never say—

Stabbed—while I sued
His sweet forgiveness—
Jesus—it's your little "John"!
Don't you know—me?

(P **497**)

Dickinson here places in the character of John, the beloved disciple, those attributes which she might wish could be found reciprocally in the godhead: thoroughgoing faithfulness, strong trust, willingness to forgive. The contrast between the expectation of infinite love and ultimate protection and the reality of anguish combined with guilt for who knows what wrong creates a natural rebelliousness.

"The Son" who is simply a replica of the Father holds no appeal. But the loving Jesus came to be cherished by Dickinson because of his suffering. As she told a neighbor toward the end of her life: "When Jesus tells us about his Father, we distrust him. When he shows us his Home, we turn away, but when he confides to us that he is 'acquainted with Grief,' we listen, for that also is an Acquaintance of our own." (L 932) The Jesus whom Dickinson loved and listened to was the co-suffering God of Liberation Theology.

Jon Sobrino, speaking of Theology in the Americas of the martyrdom of many in El Salvador because of their solidarity with rebel priests, was asked, "Don't the people of El Salvador shake their fists at heaven and ask God, 'Why are you doing this to us?'" He looked incredulous for a moment and then said, "That's not the God we worship in El Salvador. Our God is constantly with us in our terror and bereavement, bringing solace and healing when tyranny robs us of our sons and daughters." The God of Liberation Theology is no longer the All Powerful God of Calvinism, but God is instead the comforting loving one whom Dickinson seems constantly to seek: "Don't you know—me?" Far from the alienation of the punishing Father in the sky, this God kneels like the Good Samaritan over the battered body of the faithful to do "all that is needful" to bring healing.

Dickinson honors the Christ of the Crucifixion but includes that among many other human traumas in **"One Crucifixion is recorded—only."**

One Crucifixion is recorded—only—
How many be
Is not affirmed of Mathematics—
Or History—

One Calvary—exhibited to Stranger—
As many be
As persons—or Peninsulas—
Gethsemane—

Is but a Province—in the Being's Centre—
Judea—
For Journey—or Crusade's Achieving—
Too near—

Our Lord—indeed—made Compound
Witness—
And yet—
There's newer—nearer Crucifixion
Than That—

(P **553**)

Emily Dickinson continually returned to the portrait of Jesus in the gospel of John and saw not only the suffering servant so clearly delineated there but also the much more mystical personification of the Greek concept of Logos. Elisabeth Schussler Fiorenza, in her thoroughly documented study of the Jesus Movement called *In Memory of Her,* shows how closely John's portrait of the Logos parallels the Hebrew figure of Wisdom, Sophia. Greek women worshippers who feared the "merciless powers" in the worship of Isis, much as Dickinson rejects the approving God who decapitates the flowers, were attracted to Jesus. They saw him as "Jesus Christ the Sophia of God who appeared on earth and is now exalted as the Lord of the whole cosmos." (Florenza, 190) This cosmic Wisdom inspired acts of gentleness and kindness in egalitarian gatherings in the house churches in contrast to the hierarchical worship of the heathen cults. Priscilla is credited with teaching this concept in the church at Corinth, so that after the resurrection Jesus is understood by many as "cosmic Lord and life-giving Spirit-Sophia." Believers then participate in the power and energy of Christ-Sophia. (Fiorenza, 189-190)

John's community viewed themselves as living in this kind of universe, permeated by the power of the risen Christ. The Gospel of John presents eschatological acts such as "the coming of the Messiah, resurrection, judgment, eternal life," as "already present for the believer in the encounter with Jesus." (Perrin, 344) Their response was to act in harmony with Nature to promote the flow of healing energy.

Emily Dickinson, after rejecting the autocratic God of patriarchy, longs for the gentle and generous God and writes of a female deity who does exude this loving spirit:

Mama never forgets her birds,
Though in another tree—
She looks down just as often
And just as tenderly
As when her little mortal nest
With cunning care she wove—
If either of her "sparrows fall,"
She "notices," above.

(P **164**)

Adelaide Morris reconstructs the spiritual world Dickinson created in letters to her closest women friends—her sister Lavinia, Kate Scott Turner Anthon, Mrs. Holland, and the Norcross sisters—when she dared suggest "the possibility of constituting the world differently." (Morris, 111) "As Dickinson's imagery of female governance reveals, authority in this world belongs to female rulers. . . . The poems to Sue present queens without kings, reigning monarchs who across some distance salute each other's splendor and sovereignty." (Morris, 110) Often this imagery includes the weightiest theological concepts encapsulated in such phrases as "Queen of Calvary."

The formerly self-deprecating little girl can achieve the ultimate in self-affirmation in the context of this world which is constituted differently.

Mine—by the Right of the White Election!
Mine—by the Royal Seal!
Mine—by the Sign in the Scarlet prison—
Bars—cannot conceal!

Mine—here—in Vision—and in Veto!
Mine—by the Grave's Repeal—
Titled—Confirmed—
Delirious Charter!
Mine—long as Ages steal!

(P **528**)

Citing the "deft fusion of the language of love with the vocabulary of Christianity," by this woman whom Sandra Gilbert terms "this self-mythologizing New England nun," Gilbert goes on to focus on the daily "mysteries of domesticity." Dickinson's world is shown to be a world of Nature, a world of process and ritual:

> This priestess of the daily, after all, continually meditated upon the extraordinary possibilities implicit in the ordinary flowerings of the natural world. In her "real" life as the "Myth of Amherst," she created a conservatory and a herbarium; in the supposed life of her poetry, she saw through surfaces to the "white foot" **(302)** of the lily, to the "mystic green" **(24)** where "Nicodemus' Mystery / Receives its annual reply" **(140),** to the time of "Ecstasy—and Dell" **(392)** and to the time when "the Landscape listens" **(258).** . . . For hers was a world of process in which everything was always turning into everything else, a world in which her own, and Nature's, "cocoon" continually tightened, and colors "teased," and, awakening into metamorphosis, she struggled to take "the clue Divine" **(1099).** (Gilbert, 41)

The poem from which Sandra Gilbert drew her title, "The Wayward Nun beneath the Hill," shows clearly Dickinson's devotion to Nature and her identification as one "Whose service—is to You—," one dwelling within those "Sweet Mountains," "My Strong Madonnas."

> Sweet Mountains—Ye tell Me no lie—
> Never deny Me—Never fly—
> Those same unvarying Eyes
> Turn on Me—when I fail—or feign,
> Or take the Royal names in vain—
> Their far—slow—Violet Gaze—
>
> My Strong Madonnas—Cherish still—
> The Wayward Nun—beneath the Hill—
> Whose service—is to You—
> Her latest Worship—When the Day
> Fades from the Firmament away—
> To lift Her Brows on You—
>
> (P **722**)

Embracing Nature as the universe in which our deepest spiritual quests find fulfillment, we may learn to see God and World as co-extensive as Beatrice Bruteau does:

> As a consequence of this union and mutual indwelling there is no sense of opposition between God and the World. The life of the Deity pours continuously and unconditionally into the beings of the world, which develop not as a response to the Lord but as a spontaneous unfolding and blooming of the Divine Life which they themselves are in finite form. The life-energy circulates among the beings of the world, being communicated by each to all within the comprehensive oneness of the Divine Being . . . Love which is the Life of God . . . pours through us, radiating out from us to all other individuals, and reaching by means of us to newness of being in the finite realm. (Bruteau, 110)

Dickinson never forgot that the love which Jesus modeled in his suffering and which she experienced in the natural world must be expressed by human beings in very concrete ways. She constantly projects her hopes for deeper love and community and intimacy beyond the grave, but she also enacts them in her daily life. Her many charitable actions, the consoling poem and bouquet from her garden, the loving encouragement of the sick, all speak of her desire to make Love the equivalent of Life. Her letter of consolation to Higginson when his wife died is typical of dozens which promise the healing power of Love channeled from the Divine: "Do not try to be saved—but let Redemption find you—as it certainly will—Love is its own resuce, for we—at our supremest, are but its trembling Emblems." (L 522)

In the context of sharing compassionate healing energy with others so that life's anguish can become the basis for intimacy and the preparation for future joy, **"I should have been too glad, I see—"** can be read in a new way.

> Earth would have been too much—I see—
> And Heaven—not enough for me—
> I should have had the Joy
> Without the Fear—to justify—
>
> (from P. **313**)

Mortal experience, lived in mutuality, is not simply the contrastive bleakness to Heaven's grandeur but is most of all a training ground for the new Circumference. "The homelier time behind" prepares the faithful for the Victory. Christian concepts of Crucifixion are always tied to Resurrection; having practiced "Sabachthini" and gracious comforting of the bereaved in the manner of Jesus, she can anticipate acceptance into the Banquet on the "Shore beyond."

The poems of Emily Dickinson do indeed as Jane Eberwein reminds us:

> testify to a lifelong process of religious search and communicate a grateful, loving adoration she found it impossible to express adequately in the language her Calvinist culture gave her. God reached her indirectly through everything that she loved, and she responded indirectly through the magical associations of language. As she told Judge Lord, "It may surprise you I speak of God—I know him but a little, but Cupid taught Jehovah to many an untutored Mind—Witchcraft is wiser than we—" (L 562) (Eberwein, 259)

Works Cited

Anderson, Charles R. "Despair," in *Emily Dickinson,* ed. Harold Bloom. New York: Chelsea House, 1985.

Bloom, Harold, ed. *Emily Dickinson.* New York: Chelsea House, 1985.

Bruteau, Beatrice. "Nature and the Virgin Mary," in *Womanspirit Rising,* ed. Carol P. Christ and Judith Plaskow. New York: Harper & Row, 1979.

Christ, Carol P., and Judith Plaskow, eds. *Womanspirit Rising: A Feminist Reader in Religion.* New York: Harper & Row, 1979.

Cobb, John B., Jr. *The Structure of Christian Existence,* New York: Seabury, 1979. New York: Seabury, 1979.

Daly, Mary. *Beyond God the Father: Toward Philosophy of Women's Liberation.* Boston: Beacon, 1973.

Dickinson, Emily. *The Complete Poems of Emily Dickinson.* ed. Thomas H. Johnson. Boston: Little Brown and Co., 1960.

———. *The Letters of Emily Dickinson.* ed. Thomas H. Johnson and Theodora Ward. 3 vols. Cambridge, Mass: Harvard University Press, 1958.

Eberwein, Jane Donahue. *Dickinson: Strategies of Limitation.* Amherst: University of Massachusetts Press, 1985.

Fiorenza, Elisabeth Schussler. *In Memory of Her: A Feminist Theological Reconstruction of Christian Origins.* New York: Crossroads, 1983.

Gelpi, Albert J. *Emily Dickinson: The Mind of the Poet.* Cambridge, Mass.: Harvard University Press, 1965.

Gilbert, Sandra M. "The Wayward Nun beneath the Hill: Emily Dickinson and the Mysteries of Womanhood," in *Feminist Critics Read Emily Dickinson,* ed. Suzanne Juhasz. Bloomington: Indiana University Press, 1983.

Heyward, Carter. *The Redemption of God: A Theology of Mutual Relation,* Washington, D.C.: University Press of America, 1982.

Homans, Margaret. "Emily Dickinson and Poetic Identity," in *Emily Dickinson,* ed. Harold Bloom. New York: Chelsea House, 1985.

———. "'Oh, Vision of Language!': Dickinson's Poems of Love and Death," in *Feminist Critics Read Emily Dickinson,* ed. Suzanne Juhasz. Bloomington: Indiana University Press, 1983.

———. *Women Writers and Poetic Identity.* Princeton: Princeton University Press, 1964.

Juhasz, Suzanne. *Feminist Critics Read Emily Dickinson.* Bloomington: Indiana University Press, 1983.

Morris, Adalaide. "'The Love of Thee—a Prism Be': Men and Women in the Love Poetry of Emily Dickinson," in Suzanne Juhasz, ed., *Feminist Critics Read Emily Dickinson.* Bloomington: Indiana University Press, 1983.

Mossberg, Barbara Antonina Clarke. "Emily Dickinson's Nursery Rhymes," in Suzanne Juhasz, ed., *Feminist Critics Read Emily Dickinson.* Bloomington: Indiana University Press, 1983.

———. *Emily Dickinson: When a Writer is a Daughter.* Bloomington: Indiana University Press, 1982.

Perrin, Norman, and Dennis Duling. *The New Testament: An Introduction.* New York: Crossroads, 1982.

Pollak, Vivian R. *Dickinson: The Anxiety of Gender,* Ithaca: Cornell University Press, 1984.

Rich, Adrienne. "Vesuvius at Home: The Power of Emily Dickinson," in *On Lies, Secrets, and Silence,* New York: Norton, 1979.

Ruether, Rosemary Radford. *Sexism and God-Talk: Toward a Feminist Theology.* Boston: Beacon, 1983.

Saiving, Valerie. "The Human Situation: A Feminine View," in *Womanspirit Rising,* ed. Carol P. Christ and Judith Plaskow. San Francisco: Harper & Row, 1979.

Seager Baddeley, Laura, and Nadean Bishop. "Perpetual Noon: The Mystic Experience in the Poetry of Emily Dickinson," *Studia Mystica,* Spring, 1984.

Shurr, Samuel H. *The Marriage of Emily Dickinson: A Study of the Fascicles.* Lexington: University of Kentucky Press, 1983.

Trible, Phyllis. "Depatriarchialism in Biblical Interpretation," *Journal of the American Academy of Religion,* 41 (1973): 34.

———. *God and the Rhetoric of Sexuality,* Philadelphia: Fortress, 1978.

Cristanne Miller (essay date 1987)

SOURCE: "Names and Verbs: Influences on the Poet's Language," in *Emily Dickinson: A Poet's Grammar,* Harvard University Press, 1987, pp. 131-203.

[*In the following essay, Miller investigates the various works and authors who influenced the style, theories, and themes of Dickinson's poetry. Miller contends that perhaps the greatest influence on Dickinson was the Bible, which served as a model for Dickinson's use of several techniques, including compression, parataxis, and disjunction.*]

> Books are the best things, well used; abused, among the worst. What is the right use? . . . They are for nothing but to inspire. I had better never see a book than to be warped by its attraction clean out of my own orbit, and made a satellite instead of a system . . . One must be an inventor to read well.

Ralph Waldo Emerson, "The American Scholar"

. . . I present a case for various stylistic, theoretical, and thematic influences on Dickinson's writing, examining probable models or sources for the most striking of her language techniques and ideas. Dickinson read widely and passionately. By the number of her references to books and quotations from them, it is evident that the Bible was her best known text—although, like Melville, she seems to have regarded it more as a "lexicon" of "certain phenomenal men" and mysteries than as an orthodox spiritual guide.[1]

Biblical style, in its King James version and as modified by seventeenth-century writers and Americans generally, provided a model for the extreme compression, parataxis, and disjunction of Dickinson's style. Contrary to the assumptions generally underlying scripturalism, however, Dickinson believes both that language is essentially fictitious or arbitrary and that language's potential for meaning exceeds the individual's control of it and its application to any single circumstance. For her, language is simultaneously inadequate and too powerful. It is, therefore, primarily a tool for delineating moments of epiphany or change, not the tool of Adamic naming or for inscribing commandments in stone; it does not reveal eternal truth. This belief and its concomitant linguistic tendencies toward fragmentation and emphasis on the verb rather than the noun find partial support in the work of two New Englanders, Emerson and Noah Webster. In her fifth letter to Higginson, the poet claims "[I] never consciously touch a paint, mixed by another person—" (L 271). Like every poet Dickinson helps herself to colors, but the mix is unmistakably her own.

The Language of the Bible

To be familiar with the Bible was as unquestioned a part of nineteenth-century New England life as eating, and in some minds as necessary a part. The Bible was a primary text in schools, including Amherst Academy and Mount Holyoke Female Seminary, where Dickinson studied, respectively, from the ages of 9 through 16 and for ten months of her seventeenth year (two terms). Written into the Academy by-laws was the stipulation that "the instructors should be persons of good moral character . . . firmly established in the faith of the Christian religion, the doctrines and duties of which they shall inculcate as well by example as precept . . . The Preceptor shall open and close the school each day with prayer. All the students shall uniformly attend upon the public worship of God on the sabbath."[2] Mount Holyoke prided itself on its piety and its conversion of non-believers, and the Bible heads the list of textbooks circulated by its principal (*Life* II, 362, n. 19). Thus Dickinson was under considerable pressure to convert while at Mount Holyoke, and this caused her some concern. There were other students who, like her, refused to "give up and become a Christian" (L 23), but she felt herself to be in the erring minority.[3] Waves of religious revivalism swept New England and Amherst during Dickinson's girlhood and youth, and all her family and close friends eventually joined the church. Scripture was common idiom among them. At the age of 14, for example, in a playful letter informing her friend Abiah Root that she is not at school this term and is about to learn to make bread, Dickinson writes (L 8; September 1845):

> So you may imagine me with my sleeves rolled up, mixing flour, milk, salaratus, etc., with a deal of grace. I advise you if you don't know how to make the staff of life to learn with dispatch. I think I could keep house very comfortably if I knew how to cook. But as long as I don't, my knowledge of housekeeping is about of as much use as faith without works, which you know we are told is dead. Excuse my quoting from the Scripture, dear Abiah, for it was so handy in this case I couldn't get along very well without it.

Writers of popular and scholarly literature also apparently "couldn't get along very well without" quoting or paraphrasing the always "handy" Bible. For cultural and familial reasons, then, as well as for her own spiritual and aesthetic ones, Dickinson knew her Bible well.

Although critics frequently refer to the Bible as Dickinson's primary literary source, discussion has focused on her use of particular biblical passages, ideas, and myths. Even Johnson's extreme claim that the poet's "words and phrases . . . are absorbed from the Bible" and "have passed through the alembic of the King James version of biblical utterance" retreats at once to note which books the poet quotes most frequently.[4] Yet the stylistic correspondences of Dickinson's language to the Bible's are easily isolated and identified.

The language of the Bible is characteristically conjunctive, highly economical, and often organized in parallel sets or binary pairs, variously thematic, syntactic, and lexical. James Kugel describes the biblical sentence as "highly parallelistic . . . usually consisting of two clauses, each clause stripped to a minimum of three or four major words."[5] For example, the following lines from Dickinson's favorite gospel author move in terse, heavily conjunctive syntax organized in repeating sequences and pairs:

> And in them is fulfilled the prophecy of Esaias, which saith, By hearing ye shall hear, and shall not understand; and seeing ye shall see, and shall not perceive: For this people's heart is waxed gross, and *their* ears are dull of hearing, and their eyes they have closed; lest at any time they should see with *their* eyes, and hear with *their* ears, and should understand with *their* heart, and should be converted, and I should heal them. But blessed *are* your eyes, for they see: and your ears, for they hear. (Matthew 13:14-16)[6]

The passage begins with balanced pairs of affirmation and denial: ye shall hear and not understand, and shall see and not perceive. The sequence then becomes longer, at first through plain addition of evidence: hearts are gross, and ears are dull, and eyes are closed. The *ands* here are symmetrical; the order of the phrases may be changed without altering the meaning of any unit. In the clause beginning "lest at any time they should . . ." the first *and* (linking *see* with *hear*) is simply conjunctive, but the sequence then becomes asymmetrical and misleadingly simple: the *ands* preceding *understand* and *heal* substitute for what should logically be a subordinating conjunction or conjunctive phrase. In rough paraphrase, the sentence might run: "this people's heart, ears, and eyes are closed lest they should see and hear, *which would lead them to* understand, and *which would make it possible that* I heal them." The work of the reader in following this sentence consists in filling in the blanks created by these *ands*. To interpret "and I should heal them," the reader must construct a phrase to replace *and*. Particularly in "and I should heal them," *and* is more disjunctive than conjunctive; it does not belong in the same sequence as "see . . . and hear . . . and understand." Because the parallel sequence of verbs allows the repeated subject *(they)* to be omitted, "should heal" appears parallel to "should understand" and the other verbs preceding it; however, "heal" has a different agent of action (*they* see, *I* heal). The unexpected and syntactically disguised move from *they* to *I* creates a masterful rhetorical effect: Jesus' healing seems as inevitable a result of opening one's eyes as actual seeing is.

The conjunctive parataxis of this passage is complex in its intent and effect.[7] It creates suspense and builds to a surprising but apparently inevitable climax—the perfect combination for representing the simple effectiveness of God's grace if you but "see and hear" it. At its conclusion the passage returns to what Kugel calls the most characteristic biblical mode, the parallel double clause, here repeated so that its figure is doubled twice: in the deleted repetition "but blessed are your eyes . . . and [blessed are] your ears . . ." and within each clause: "your eyes, for they see . . . your ears, for they hear . . ." The extreme compression of Dickinson's poems and that of biblical text are strikingly similar. In both cases the compression stems from frequent use of ellipsis, parallel and short syntactic structures linked paratactically or by simple conjunction, and apposition.

Compact and conjunctive or paratactic syntax occurs in biblical passages less artful than the one just quoted. In Genesis, for example, the story of Babel begins:

> And the whole earth was of one language, and of one speech. And it came to pass, as they journeyed from the east, that they found a plain in the land of Shinar; and they dwelt there. And they said one to another, Go to, let us make brick, and burn them thoroughly. And they had brick for stone, and slime had they for mortar. And they said, Go to, let us build us a city and a tower, whose top *may reach* unto heaven; and let us make us a name, lest we be scattered abroad upon the face of the whole earth. (Genesis 11:1-4)

At the conclusion of a psalm from which Dickinson quotes in a letter, we find:

> Keep back thy servant also from presumptuous *sins;* let them not have dominion over me: then shall I be upright, and I shall be innocent from the great transgression. Let the words of my mouth, and the meditation of my heart, be acceptable in thy sight, O Lord, my strength, and my redeemer. (Psalm 19:13-14)

First Corinthians contains the more extreme but not atypical passage:

> Therefore let no man glory in men. For all things are yours; Whether Paul, or Apollos, or Cephas, or the world, or life, or death, or things present, or things to come; all are yours; And ye are Christ's; and Christ *is* God's. (I Corinthians 3:21-23)

In each of these passages there is a rhythmical sameness of tone. Sentences or clauses are short, and connections between them are coordinate rather than subordinate, the most frequently used being *and.* Often there is no linking conjunction or adverb, which causes a momentary lapse in the reader's progress forward. In the lines "Keep back thy servant also from presumptuous *sins;* let them not have dominion over me," for example, the antecedent for "them" is not immediately clear, nor is the role fearfully ascribed to *sins* in the servant's life. "Dominion" in the second clause thematically echoes the opening clause's possessive "*thy* servant" to mark the difference between welcome and unwelcome servitude. But the two are not given equal syntactic weight: God's dominion is presumed and receives merely the possessive "thy"; sin's dominion is feared and can only with God's help be avoided. Linking the sequence of pleas "Keep back thy servant . . . let them not" is the unarticulated assumption that God controls all, but also that any contact with "presumptuous sins" would give them "dominion" over even God's servant. The second clause explains why the plea of the first clause is necessary. As in so many of Dickinson's poems, the logical connecting work of the syntax is left to the reader and is only clear on repeated readings.

Kugel, too, concludes that the point of biblical parallelism is to make the reader discover the connection between "two apparently unrelated parallel utterances."[8] "A is so and B is so" or "A is so and B is not" will make sense as a complete statement only when we understand A and B in relation to each other. We see the similarity between the Bible's and Dickinson's suggestive use of paratactic juxtaposition most clearly in comparing its proverbs to her aphorisms. For example, the proverb "A good name *is* better than precious ointment; and the day of death than the day of one's birth" (Ecclesiastes 7:1) may be interpreted multiply. The reader must imagine and order the array of possible relations between its halves, between ointment and birth, and a good name and death. Remember the similar gap between subjects at the end of Dickinson's poem **"He fumbles at your Soul":** "Deals—One—imperial—Thunderbolt / That scalps your naked Soul—/ When Winds take Forests in their Paws—/ The Universe—is still—." Like the thematic lapses created by parataxis in Dickinson's poems, the blank space (or the space filled with a coordinate conjunction) in biblical texts becomes a focal point of meaning; the text is transparent only when a sentence or clause is isolated, and then the transparency is misleading. The Bible's word, like the New Testament's Word incarnate, carries the greatest meaning when it links apparently discontinuous or separate realms: the literal and the figurative, the personal and the universal, earth and heaven.

Dickinson uses parataxis, repeated conjunctions, and parallel syntax less frequently than the Bible does. Even poems as markedly paratactic and conjunctive, respectively, as **"It was not Death"** and **"My Life had stood"** appear sparing in their juxtapositions in comparison with the biblical passages just quoted. Recall the opening lines of the former poem:

It was not Death, for I stood up,
And all the Dead, lie down—
It was not Night, for all the Bells
Put out their Tongues, for Noon.

It was not Frost, for on my Flesh
I felt Siroccos—crawl—
Nor Fire—for just my Marble feet
Could keep a Chancel, cool—

And yet, it tasted, like them all . . .

(510)

In these lines we hear biblical sparseness and see an overlapping balanced effect in the repeated "It was not . . . for" clauses and in the qualifying coordinate clauses "for I . . . And all . . ." of lines 1 and 2. Dickinson, however, repeats few besides function words, and her syntax is generally less repetitive than the Bible's: here she repeats the initial structure of balancing clauses only in the first two stanzas, and with considerable variation.[9]

In both biblical prose and Dickinson's verse, the short clauses and rapid progression from one unit to the next give a feeling of inevitability to the narrative's progression. The paratactic linking of phrases "And now we roam . . . And now we hunt . . . And do I smile" of **"My Life had stood—a Loaded Gun,"** like Paul's "All is yours, and ye are Christ's, and Christ is God's," collapses hierarchies of importance and precedence at the same time that it builds toward a climax. Individually every action or conclusion—like every soul or "sparrow" in New Testament theology—holds equal weight, yet all gain their importance from their existence within the whole, be it Dickinson's poem or the Christian God. When the linked actions form a sequence, it seems equally inevitable. In a poem about what the heart asks, Dickinson's speaker seems to move from childhood to old age, although the process of decreasing demands could as easily happen in a single night as in the course of a lifetime:

The Heart asks Pleasure—first—
And then—Excuse from Pain—
And then—those little Anodynes
That deaden suffering—

And then—to go to sleep—
And then—if it should be
The will of it's Inquisitor
The privilege to die—

(536)

Regardless of which time scheme is primary, the sequence (combined with the poem's opening definite article—*The* Heart) implies that no heart continues to ask for pleasure and that every heart will eventually have received enough pain to desire its own death.

Seventeenth-Century Stylists

Compression, (disjunctively) conjunctive syntax, and parallelism characterize other modern writing besides Dickinson's—much of it, like hers, influenced by biblical style. Morris Croll describes "baroque" or early to mid-seventeenth-century prose in terms easily convertible to both Dickinson's and the Bible's language. The similarities have a logical basis on both sides: Montaigne, Burton, Pascal, Sir Thomas Browne—Croll's major examples of baroque stylists—were extremely familiar with the Bible and biblical texts, and

Browne and George Herbert were among Dickinson's favorite writers. In fact, the resemblance between Dickinson's and Herbert's poetry was so strong that Millicent Todd Bingham published two stanzas of his "Matin Hymn" that Dickinson had copied out and stored with her verses as Dickinson's own.[10] The seventeenth-century sentence, Croll tells us, is "exploded." It uses either loose coordinating conjunctions, or has "no syntactic connectives . . . In fact, it has the appearance of having been disrupted by an explosion within" (209). In both its "loose" and "curt" forms, this style portrays "not a thought, but a mind thinking" (210); the sentence's movement is spiral, not "logical" or straight. Rather than adopting the Bible's balanced parallelism, this style tends to be asymmetrical, to break a parallelism as soon as it has been established: " . . . out of the struggle between a fixed pattern and an energetic forward movement" the baroque style creates its "strong and expressive disproportions" (226).

According to Croll, "curt" baroque prose tends to begin with a complete statement of its idea, much like a proverb in style and tone; the rest of the paragraph or section (or poem) provides new apprehensions or varying imaginative aspects of that logically exhaustive initial statement. Abrupt changes in subject and changes from one mode or style to another (from literal to metaphoric, or from concrete to abstract form) characterize the following imaginative exploration of the kernel idea. Croll gives an example from Browne's *Religio Medici* (which Dickinson owned):

> To see ourselves again, we need not look for Plato's year: every man is not only himself; there have been many Diogenes, and as many Timons, though but few of that name; men are lived over again; the world is now as it was in ages past; there was none then, but there hath been some one since, that parallels him, and is, as it were, his revived self. (218)

Browne's prose anticipates, and Croll's anatomy describes, the progress of several Dickinson poems: first the aphoristic statement of the theme, then brief varying elaborations of its idea. "Essential Oils—are wrung" announces its theme immediately. Other poems begin: "Life—is what we make it" **(698);** "Impossibility, like Wine / Exhilarates the Man / Who tastes it; . . ." **(838);** "Perception of an object costs / Precise the Object's loss—" **(1071);** "To disappear enhances" **(1209);** "The Rat is the concisest Tenant" **(1356).** An even more extreme example of curt baroque prose is Herbert's "Prayer, I," which consists of numerous fragmentary representations of prayer, beginning:

> Prayer, the Church's banquet, Angel's age,
> God's breath in man returning to his birth,
> The soul in paraphrase . . .

and ending:

> Church-bells beyond the stars heart, the soul's
> blood,
> The land of spices, something understood.

The poem contains no complete predicate. Much of Dickinson's poetry, like baroque poetry and prose, moves by a sequence of "'points' and paradoxes reveal[ing] the energy of a single apprehension in the writer's mind" (218-219).

"Loose" baroque style, usually intermingled with the "curt" style, differs only in its greater use of participals and subordinate conjunctions, according to Croll. Its subordinate conjunctions, however, are used so loosely as to have the effect of coordinate conjunctions: individual clauses maintain great autonomy, and there is no tightly logical or single means of advance from one member to the next. Look, for example, at the Herbert stanzas that Dickinson copied out (stanzas 2 and 3 of Herbert's "Matin Hymn"):

> My God, what is a heart?
> Silver, or gold, or precious stone,
> Or star, or rainbow, or a part
> Of all these things, or all of them in one?
>
> My God, what is a heart,
> That thou shouldst it so eye, and woo,
> Pouring upon it all thy art,
> As if that thou hadst nothing else to do?

Although the second of these stanzas is considerably less paratactic than the first, its connectives remain loose. "That" refers back to the preceding (repeated) question "What is a heart," and thus carries the weight of the whole preceding stanza. *Eye, woo,* and *pour* (thy art) may present the same action of God with increasing specificity, or "pouring . . ." may be a less direct, more general action, as its less active (participal) form suggests. Herbert's descriptions of God's actions overlap one another, as do his speculations about the substance of the heart in the previous stanza. Each embedded or branching clause repeats part of a previous idea and leads in a new direction; the progress of the sentence continues to seem spontaneous and to offer multiple directions for interpretation.

Because Dickinson's poetic mode anticipates that of twentieth-century poets, particularly the Modernists with their revived interest in the metaphysical poets, her poetry sounds less strange to the twentieth-century ear than it did to her century's. A glance at Longfellow's verse, which Dickinson greatly admired and referred to frequently, illuminates the gulf she created between her own and her contemporaries' work. This does not mean there were no similarities between her poetry and, for example, Longfellow's; like Dickinson, Longfellow experimented with rhyme, meter, and the rhythms and diction of speech. In "The Jewish Cemetery at Newport" his language is colloquial: he uses relatively simple syntax, leaves sentences incomplete, and uses frequent exclamations and colloquial phrases ("all this moving"). Yet the long lines, the repetitive, highly adjectival phrasing, the heavily right-branching parallel syntax, and the lack of metaphorical complexity give this poem an entirely different character from Dickinson's poetry. The first stanza runs:

How strange it seems! These Hebrews in their graves,
Close by the street of this fair seaport town,
Silent beside the never-silent waves,
At rest in all this moving up and down!

In "My Lost Youth" Longfellow writes in shorter, rhythmically and syntactically looser lines, but the contrast with Dickinson's economy and ellipsis is still striking. The last stanza of this poem follows:

And Deering's Woods are fresh and fair,
And with joy that is almost pain
My heart goes back to wander there,
And among the dreams of the days that were,
I find my lost youth again.
And the strange and beautiful song,
The groves are repeating it still:
"A boy's will is the wind's will,
And the thoughts of youth are long, long thoughts."

Longfellow's poems are readily accessible on the levels of narrative and intent as neither Herbert's nor Dickinson's are. His verse, and most nineteenth-century American verse, works through extension and repetition, whereas Dickinson's works through compression and juxtaposition.

The Hymns of Isaac Watts

From the Bible and from Herbert's poems and Browne's prose, Dickinson would be familiar with tersely conjunctive syntax, sentences that progress asymmetrically or through apposition and paradox, and paradoxical or cryptically metaphorical rather than extended logical developments of an idea. Closer to home, the psalms and hymns of Isaac Watts, as familiar to many New Englanders as the Bible itself, offered her these same characteristics in a meter she adopted for almost all her poems. Emily's mother, Lavinia Norcross Dickinson, owned *Watts' Hymns,* and the family library housed copies of his *Church Psalmody* and *Psalms, Hymns, and Spiritual Songs of the Reverend Isaac Watts.*[11] Although the poet does not mention Watts by name, she was undoubtedly familiar with several of his hymns, and she quotes from one of them.[12] Her use of hymn meter (often called the common meter) for all but a few metrically experimental poems is widely attributed to her reading, and singing, of Watts.

In addition to being part of the common New England vocabulary of rhythm and verse, Watts may have held special attraction for Dickinson because of his frequent use of irregular rhymes and harsh-sounding phrases (usually involving vocabulary considered neither poetic nor religious), and because of the extraordinary variety of sounds and themes he used within a simple rhythmical frame.[13] Watts's hymn 632, for example, uses a common conjunctive parallelism and irregular rhyme in stanza 5:

And must my body faint and die?
And must this soul remove?
O, for some guardian angel nigh,
To bear it safe above!

Watts rhymes *men* with *vain, fell* with *miracle, haste* with *test, throne* with *down* (hymns 347, 438, 632, 648), or, in hymn 352 alone, *lies* with *ice, stood* with *God, sea* with *away.* In lines unusually vivid and metaphorical, Watts's hymn 630 uses the polysyllabic "abominable" with an art anticipating Dickinson's. It begins: "My thoughts on awful subjects roll, / Damnation and the dead," then recounts the "horrors" a "guilty soul" imagines on her deathbed:

Then, swift and dreadful, she descends
Down to the fiery coast,
Among abominable fiends,
Herself a frighted ghost.

There endless crowds of sinners lie,
And darkness makes their chains;
Tortured with keen despair, they cry,
Yet wait for fiercer pains.

A darkness so tangible it "makes" chains; a soul in herself "dreadful" or in "dreadful" flight; sinners keenly despairing "Yet" waiting for "fiercer pains": these images and ambiguities would appeal to Dickinson's imagination.

Dickinson's own rhythms, loose rhymes, and abbreviated (therefore often cryptic) metaphors of description sound less unusual when placed beside Watts's hymns than when compared with the work of her contemporaries. Listen, for example, to the similarities in meter, rhyme, use of polysyllables to fill a line (her "possibility" and "Cordiality," like Watts's "abominable"), and vivid substantiation of the insubstantial between Watts and Dickinson in a poem she writes on the soul's near escape from death:

That after Horror—that 'twas *us*—
That passed the mouldering Pier—

Just as the Granite Crumb let go—
Our Savior, by a Hair—

A second more, had dropped too deep
For Fisherman to plumb—
The very profile of the Thought
Puts Recollection numb—
The possibility—to pass
Without a Moment's Bell—
Into Conjecture's presence—
Is like a Face of Steel—
That suddenly looks into our's
With a metallic grin—
The Cordiality of Death—
Who drills his Welcome in—

(286)

Like Watts, Dickinson uses common meter here; lines coincide with clause or phrase boundaries, and stanzas form complete syntactic and metaphorical units; abstractions gain concrete properties (his darkness forms chains; her thought has a profile); and rhyme is consistent but not perfect (note her *Pier* with *Hair, Bell* with *Steel*). Dickinson's poem compacts more metaphors, and her primary metaphor for the soul's meeting with death is far more chilling than Watts's, but her familiarity with his dramatic and loosely irregular verse may have cleared a way for Dickinson to her own extraordinary poems.

The American Plain Style

In a still broader sense of influence, the American idiom itself, in both its literary and daily forms, may have contributed to Dickinson's use of a style that is biblical in origin.[14] By the mid-nineteenth century Puritan "plain style" had become the language of self-expression, the trusted idiom in America, although—or perhaps because—it had lost its bolstering doctrinal and political contexts. According to Perry Miller's "An American Language," the plain style's demand that one speak from personal knowledge and as comprehensibly as possible made it the natural mode of discourse for a people living "in the wilderness" and, by the late eighteenth century, attempting to form a democracy.[15] All American writers, he claims, have had to deal with the consequences of this wholesale adoption of the principles and techniques of plain style (214). Because of its pervasiveness, Dickinson would inevitably have used language to some extent within its dictates. For epistemological reasons also, Dickinson may have felt some affinity for this style. Miller describes the plain style as inherently "defiant"—a style that both proclaims authority for the word and places the word's authority in individuals' articulate examinations of the truth; the style encourages practical discourse on theoretical or spiritual truths. Hence, it can as easily be turned against the idea of an authoritative God as it can be used to support that idea. Authority of language lies with the "plainest" (that is, apparently most artless yet still most commanding) speaker. The Puritans kept the style's implicit defiance in check by subordinating their word to God's Word; the latter was the law which theirs attempted to interpret and reflect. Emerson, Miller claims, partially maintained this check on defiance through his romantic belief in Nature as the origin of language, while Thoreau released the defiance of this style in his prose, "glory[ing] in his participation in the community of sin" (226).

More covertly than Thoreau, Dickinson does the same. Her very disguise of defiance, however, may also stem in part from inherent characteristics of the plain style, which demands the simplicity reflected in its name but paradoxically also a kind of reticence that may prevent its complete message from being articulated. Ideally, the plain speaker "convey[s] the emphasis, the hesitancies, the searchings of language as it is spoken" (232); plainness lies in the apparent artlessness of the speaker's or writer's use of the word. Partly as a consequence, writers in the plain style leave much unsaid, and they claim that their discourse says even less than it does. Using words sparingly leaves much to implication, and making modest claims for a text may disguise the authority its author in fact feels. Thus the plain style frequently underplays its own importance and seriousness;[16] even when it most anarchically expresses the perception of the individual, it maintains the guise of saying little, and that only matter-of-factly. Hence, while speaking "plain" truth, an individual may confound every doctrine that the Puritans held true and believed the plain style must express. As Miller puts it: "The forthright method [plain style] proved to be . . . the most subversive power that the wicked could invoke against those generalities it had, long ago, been designed to protect" (220). Through reticence, indirection, and disguised claims for the authority of her word, Dickinson manipulates characteristics of the plain use of language in poetry that contradict Puritan convictions about the individual's relation to God and His Word. The style that affirms God's truth for the Puritans, and denies that God's power is the only good (while still celebrating it) for Thoreau, becomes ironic with Dickinson: while appearing to affirm or naively question, she denies the trustworthiness of any superhuman power.

Although biblical style, particularly in its King James translation, has been widely influential, the Bible has influenced ideas of language at least as profoundly as it has actual language use. In the Bible, language is authority: "And God said, Let there be light: and there was light" (Genesis 1:3); or as John redescribes this moment: "In the beginning was the Word, and the Word was with God, and the Word was God" (John 1:1). Adam's name giving is a second creation; he brings into the human world of language what God's Word has made. For Moses, the word is law to be preserved in stone. Language in all these cases is transparent; it has an immediate relation to things and principles and reflects their essential nature. By knowing the proper names, one may know the world. For American Puritans, this idea of language led to the belief that an individual's power to articulate depended on his or her spiritual condition. Those who had been converted were expected to manifest their condition of grace and to demonstrate their obedience to God through the quality of their understanding as represented in their use of words. What one knew one could, and must, express.

This notion of language depended on the inherent "truth" of the word; no word could be ambiguous or ironic and still manifest the essential truth of God. By the same logic, lying—that is, abusing the word by distorting or obscuring its meaning—diminished a person's ability to know the world and, through it, God. Hence, lying was a grave sin. William Ames preached that "the frequent use of obscene speeches seemeth to be more hurtful to piety, than the simple act of fornication," while proper or "plainly" eloquent speech ideally would be so powerful "that an unbeliever comming into the Congregation of the faithful . . . ought to be affected, and as it were digged through with the very hearing of the Word, that he may give glory to God."[17] According to this philosophy, the most economical style is also the most efficacious. Regardless of the speaker's immediate audience, all language is directed ultimately to God, and "God's Altar needs not our pollishings," as the compilers of the 1639 preface to the *Bay Psalm Book* proclaim. Flourishes at worst confuse meaning, but even at best they hinder a statement's force: "The efficacy of the Holy Spirit doth more clearly appeare in a naked simplicity of words, then in elegance and neatness . . . So much affectation as appeares, so much efficacy and authority is lost."[18] Authority and utility are the twin supports of this system.

The idea that language should adequately define and name things had a broad secular base as well in nineteenth-century America. In his essays "On Candor" and "On Language," James Fenimore Cooper lists an increasing lack of directness in expression as one of the greatest flaws of American English.[19] Fearful of the vulgarizing effect of democracy even while he extols its virtues, Cooper laments that Americans pervert the significance of words by using them inappropriately and inexactly. The original meaning of a word is its proper meaning; to transfer its use to a different context or to use it more broadly constitutes a misuse of the word, not to mention a "misapprehension of the real circumstances under which we live" (112). Believing that a word may be misused and thus cause a "misapprehension of the real circumstances" of life presupposes that the proper use of language leads to accurate or proper apprehension of the world. Language delineates and labels the facts of nature. The word Cooper chooses as an example reveals the social roots of his anxiety about language change: the broadening misuse of the word "gentleman" does not make a tramp into a gentleman, he insists; it only weakens the proper meaning of the word and confuses the "natural" distinctions between types of men. Without saying so explicitly, and like the Puritans, Cooper would have language be unironical, immediately and unambiguously connected to the equally "plain" facts of the world.

It is in her attitude toward language and toward communication itself as much as in her characteristic manipulations of the word that Dickinson differs from her contemporaries and predecessors who wrote in plain style. Like them, she emphasizes the bare force of the word, eschewing elaborate syntax, modifiers, and extended conceits. Like them, she tends to stress the word's direct mediation between the individual and the world (for them, God). Like them, but to an unusual extreme, she makes small claims for her writing: her poems are "a letter to the World"; she is often a girl, or (like) a daisy, bird, spider, or gnat. Even when she has volcanic power, she generally appears harmless and unimportant: "A meditative spot—/ An acre for a Bird to choose / Would be the General thought—" **(1677).** Dickinson, however, senses a different need for both plainness and reticence from those who believe in a natural or divine law of language. The word has two faces for her. Its effect may be epiphanic and it may come to her as a "gift," revealing "That portion of the Vision" she could not find without the help of "Cherubim" **(1126).** This is the language of poetry, of pure communication, "Like signal esoteric sips / Of the communion Wine" **(1452),** or a "word of Gold" **(430).** At other times the word is all but meaningless—an "Opinion" **(797),** an empty term. In a letter to Bowles she writes: "The old words are *numb*—and there *a'nt* any *new* ones—Brooks—are useless—in *Freshettime*—" (L 252). Her trick as poet is to make the old words new. To do this, she trusts "Philology," not God or Nature, and when she succeeds in doing this she feels that she has been lucky.

To Dickinson's mind, success in speaking plainly, in creating a word "that breathes" **(1651),** does not prove spiritual salvation or make her a candidate for fame, partly because her sense of moral superiority depends on overthrowing the notion that God or the world can save her. The economical use of the words of ordinary life gives language its power. Speaking indirectly or subversively disguises the poet's usurpation of moral judgment from divine or human law, and thus saves her to speak again. As Perry Miller suggests, in Dickinson's poetry the pull between plainness and reticence subverts the whole idea of plainness. Because her meanings are not plain, they cannot be expressed plainly despite her use of simple words; her plainest speech *is* that of indirection.

As this conception of language implies, for Dickinson there is no stable relation between spiritual truth, the facts of existence, and the terms of language. Names are not adequate to things, and the function of language is not primarily to name. Things are perceived and understood through their relations to the rest of the world and by the process of cumulative, even contradictory, definition rather than by categorization or labeling. Dickinson has greater affinity with the lexicographer, the scientist of language seeking to clarify each word's various meanings, than she does with the Romantic *Ur*-poet Adam. Her language stresses the relation between object and its effects or relations in an active world; meaning, for her, is not fixed by rules or even by her own previous perception of the world. The principles of Dickinson's world do not have to do with immutable properties and distinctions.

Dickinson manifests her belief in the flux or instability of relationship in the narratives of her poems more obviously than in her use of language. For example, the figures of her poems often change positions relative to each other, or prove to be undifferentiable rather than separate identities. In **"The Moon is distant from the Sea,"** first "She" is the moon and "He" the water, then she becomes "the distant Sea—" and his are the ordering "Amber Hands—" of light **(429);** the "single Hound" attending the Soul proves to be "It's own identity." **(822);** in an early poem, she and her playmate Tim turn out to be "I—'Tim'—and—Me!" **(196).** In a late poem, desired object, self, and "Messenger" are indistinguishable in both their presence and their absence; in a mockery of simplicity, all have the same name:

We send the Wave to find the Wave—
An Errand so divine,
The Messenger enamored too,
Forgetting to return,
We make the wise distinction still,
Soever made in vain,
The sagest time to dam the sea is when the
sea is gone—

(1604)

Although this poem may be read as an elaboration of a truism—that one must give to receive, or that some losses cannot be prevented—it also ironically suggests that distinguishing present and absent sea (loved "Wave" from our own) is "vain." The "wise distinction" persists in failing to recognize the absurdity of damming what is not there and cannot be kept anyway. We attempt to conserve only what we have already lost.

Similarly, in **"The Sea said 'Come' to the Brook" (1210),** the grown Brook takes the same form and title as the Sea that wanted to keep it small, as if to prove that the existence of one sea does not prevent the growth of innumerable physically indistinguishable others. In the last stanza it is not immediately clear which "Sea" is which:[20]

The Sea said "Go" to the Sea—
The Sea said "I am he
You cherished"—"Learned Waters—
Wisdom is stale—to Me"

In countless other poems, unspecified and multiply referential "it" or "this" is as meaningful a subject for speculation as any clearly delineated event or object. Metaphor serves as the primary tool of definition and explanation because it allows for the greatest flexibility in its reference to fact.

Emerson's Theories of Language

To the extent that language does reflect the world for Dickinson, her conception of language is closer to Emerson's than to the Puritans'. The Amherst poet was familiar with the Concord poet's works from at least 1850 on. In that year, she received "a beautiful copy" of Emerson's 1847 *Poems* (L 30). In 1857 Emerson lectured in Amherst, eating and sleeping at the Evergreens, where Emily may have joined Austin and Sue in entertaining him. She told Sue that he seemed "as if he had come from where dreams are born" (*Life* II, 468). In 1876 the poet gave Mrs. Higginson a copy of *Representative Men*—"a little Granite Book you can lean upon" (L 481). She also quotes or paraphrases five of Emerson's poems in her letters and poems, most notably his "Bacchus" in her **"I taste a liquor never brewed" (214)** and "The Snow Storm" in her **"It sifts from Leaden Sieves" (311).**[21]

Emerson writes at length of language as an ideal system of meaning in his essays "Nature" and "The Poet." His use of language in his own prose, however, contradicts his theories. In theory, Emerson's notion of language stems from Puritan ideas of the word as an extension of the Oversoul, or God. For him, as for the Puritans, language in its pristine or original state is transparent: "Words are signs of natural facts."[22] Similarly, for Emerson, speech that derives from an accurate perception of nature "is at once a commanding certificate that he who employs it is a man in alliance with truth and God" (*Works* I, 36). In its ideal form, language translates and interprets spiritual truths as for the Puritans, but now through the mediation of nature. Because of this mediation, at its plainest and most authoritative language is "picturesque"; it is "poetry." Words stand for (name, signify) facts of nature, which are in turn "emblematic" of spiritual facts. Language, then, is both referential (transparently reflective of nature) and metaphorical.

Human language derives from nature, which is in turn "the organ through which the universal spirit speaks to the individual" (*Works* I, 66). Ideally there would be a one-to-one correspondence between the facts of nature, the words of speech, and the facts of the spirit; that is, human language would exactly reproduce the language of the universe.

Because of its base in nature, according to Emerson, language is also both fixed or universal and constantly undergoing change. The laws of the spirit or Oversoul, the ultimate referent of language, do not change, but their forms in nature may. Natural objects "furnish man with the dictionary and grammar of his municipal speech" (*Works* I, 37); when these objects are altered so are the meanings of our language. Each age requires its own interpreter or poet to keep language true to nature (and to read nature's new forms), but each interpreter expresses the same truths, albeit in different forms. Because the laws of nature are fixed, the primary act of language making is naming and the principle word is the noun. Emerson traces the development of language through that of the individual: "Children and savages use only nouns or names of things, which they convert into verbs and apply to analogous mental acts"—a necessary stage in language making, he implies, but a departure from language as pure poetry (*Works* I, 32). Verbs provide, as it were, the transitional form in the desired transformation of language from directly referential (noun to fact) to symbolic (noun to spiritual fact). Language translates perceived nature into human speech and thereby assists in the transformation of nature into spirit. It is not itself stable, but it leads from the world of nameable things to the sphere of immutable spirit.

Emerson never develops the implications of this philosophy for the use of a particular syntax or parts of speech. Were he to do so, the poet or premier language user would logically be Adamic, a pronouncer of names. The ceaseless contradictions and qualifications of Emerson's prose, however, suggest otherwise. Although he preaches about natural laws, he sees nothing but change, and he bases all knowledge and all language on what may be seen (the inner eye interpreting through the outer). While at one minute in "Self-Reliance" he commandingly and absolutely propounds: "Trust thyself: every heart vibrates to that iron string" or "Whoso would be a man must be a nonconformist," in the next he questions: "Suppose you should contradict yourself; what then?" (*Works* I, 47, 50). In a longer passage from the same essay, Emerson characteristically combines highly embedded syntax replete with parallel modifiers and self-referring phrases with paratactically juxtaposed aphorisms as pithy as any that Dickinson coins: "In this pleasing contrite wood-life which God allows me, let me record day by day my honest thought without prospect or retrospect, and, I cannot doubt, it will be found symmetrical though I mean it not and see it not. My book should smell of pines and resound with the hum of insects. The swallow over my window should interweave that thread or straw he carries in his bill into my web also. We pass for what we are. Character teaches above our wills" (*Works* I, 58). Emerson's essays move by associative elaboration of a central idea—often first presented in metaphorical form—not by formal, logical stages or steps. He uses language as if its meaning were less certain or clear than he describes it as being.

Certainly Dickinson recreates the full force of Emerson's perception that all nature, and thus all language, is in constant "flux" in her definition of nouns. Recall, for example, her use of repeated verbs and restrictive clauses in her definition poems: "Revolution is the Pod / Systems rattle from / When the Winds of Will are stirred" **(1082);** "Escape" is "the Basket / In which the Heart is caught / When down some awful Battlement / The rest of Life is dropt—" **(1347);** or "Bloom—is Result—" of a process requiring some thing or someone "To pack the Bud—oppose the Worm—/ Obtain it's right of Dew—/ Adjust the Heat—elude the Wind—/ Escape the prowling Bee / [and] Great Nature not to disappoint . . ." **(1058).** To repeat earlier and more extreme examples, the love "diviner" than that "a Life can show Below" can only be defined by its cumulative acts and effects. In this poem's final stanza, the subject-noun is almost lost in the barrage of its verbs:

> 'Tis this—invites—appalls—endows—
> Flits—glimmers—proves—dissolves—
> Returns—suggests—convicts—enchants—
> Then—flings in Paradise—
>
> **(673)**

Similarly, Dickinson defines the nominalized verb "saved" by its relation to the act or art of saving: "The Province of the Saved / Should be the Art—To save—" **(539).** An abstraction, like an object, stems from or stimulates action, and hence it can be known. Ernest Fenollosa, a later pupil of Emerson's, articulates the philosophy that seems to underlie Dickinson's definitions: "Fancy picking up a man and telling him that he is a noun, a dead thing rather than a bundle of functions! A 'part of speech' is what it does . . . one part of speech acts for another . . . 'Farmer' and 'rice' are mere hard terms which define the extremes of the pounding. But in themselves, apart from this sentence-function, they are naturally verbs. The farmer is one who tills the ground, and the rice is a plant which grows in a special way . . . a noun is originally 'that which does something,' that which performs the verbal action."[23] By Fenollosa's logic, land apart from their "sentence-function," Dickinson's action-oriented nouns are "naturally verbs."

Dickinson's poems typically conceptualize action instead of presenting it, or they make the action itself conceptual, epistemological. Even in poems about action or change in nature **("A Route of Evanescence"** or **"Further in Summer than the Birds"),** the poet emphasizes process, causality, and relationship more than temporal acts; the flight of her hummingbird receives its effect from reflected light and the bush it touches. The poem is full of action, but there is only one verb *(Adjusts):*

A Route of Evanescence
With a revolving Wheel—
A Resonance of Emerald—
A Rush of Cochineal—
And every Blossom on the Bush
Adjusts it's tumbled Head—
The mail from Tunis, probably,
An easy Morning's Ride—

(1463)

Revolving, Resonance, Rush, tumbled, and *Ride* refer to aspects of the bird's movement but do not present it. The poet's use of nouns and participial adjectives suggests that the bird flies so fast and so effortlessly that the act itself cannot be perceived; we know the act by what it touches and by what we can surmise ("the mail from Tunis").

For Emerson, the whole end of nature is to be interpreted; things are "characters" to be read, and "every object rightly seen, unlocks a new faculty of the soul"; language and the world and language and the soul are one (*Words* I, 31, 36, 41). For Dickinson, nature is not transparent and language is not an organic adjunct (or reflected image) of its processes. We "consign" words to language instead of allegorically perceiving them in nature's great poem. As though in response to Emerson's maxim that "Words are signs of natural fact," Dickinson finds language's greatest power in abstraction, in what cannot be found in nature. "Dont you know that 'No' is the wildest word we consign to Language?" (L 562), she questions; and her "Essential Oils" of meaning are "wrung," "not expressed by Suns—alone—". To enliven language, this poet makes it less instead of more natural; she distorts grammar, inverts syntax, and represents words as produced or conventional units which she can reproduce for her own purposes. Powerful words are blades, swords, and distilled attar—things created by human civilization for human use. In their less powerful aspect, words are arbitrary labels and may be tossed aside: "If the Bird and the Farmer—deem it [a tree] a 'Pine'—/ The Opinion will do—for them—" **(797).**

Emerson expresses the idea that language is inadequate and primarily conventional (not organic) in the ceaseless reexaminations and shifting balances of his prose and in his numerous references to the fallen state of humanity and language in the contemporary world. Dickinson holds the same belief but does not find it a reason to despair. The impermanence of meaning and language liberates her to speak as she might not otherwise dare. Emerson's search for meaning is directed toward nature: his poet is always in part the scribe of what he sees. Dickinson's search most often occurs within "Philosophy" **(1126, 1651),** not nature. Her dictionary is her "companion," and she ranges freely in her explorations of meaning there.

Noah Webster and Lexicography

Dickinson may have found support for her semantic emphasis on the verb or change and for her belief in the constant changes of language in her family dictionary. Temperamentally and philosophically, she was suited to lexicography. Unlike understanding that stems from archetypes or symbols, lexical understanding works from context and always provides alternative shades or directions of meaning. Lexicography encouraged both Dickinson's scientific and her fanciful tendencies: speculating on the connections of a word's various definitions or possible etymologies might lead to the profound, or it might lead to the ludicrous.

Dickinson may also have felt a special affinity for the lexicographer Noah Webster. In opposition to almost all grammarians and philologists of his day, Webster was convinced that language stems etymologically from verbs, not from nouns. In an introductory essay to his 1841 *American Dictionary of the English Language,* Webster theorizes that the "ordinary sense" of all words in any language may be expressed by thirty or forty verbs and that these radical verbs originate as modifications of the primary sense "to move."[24] These verbs are then modified into the "appropriate" or "customary" significations that we now recognize as entries in our modern dictionaries. The "principal radix" of a family of words may be a noun or an adjective instead of a verb (as *just* is the radix of *justice* and *justly*); that primary word, however, would always theoretically be traceable back to a verb (as Webster traces *just* back to "setting, erecting" and the adjective *warm* to Latin *ferveo*—"I boil"). Webster states in another essay: "Motion, action, is, beyond all controversy, the principal source of words."[25]

Given Dickinson's interest in language and in her dictionary (an 1844 reprint of Webster's 1841 edition), there can be little doubt that she read Webster's introductory essay. In 1862 she wrote Higginson that "for several years, my Lexicon—was my only companion—" (L 261), and she speaks in a poem of "Easing my famine / At my Lexicon—" **(728).** Even taking hyperbolic self-posing into account, we can assume that the young poet spent a lot of time reading her dictionary. A family connection between the Dickinsons and the

Websters may also have encouraged her interest in the family dictionary. Webster lived in Amherst from 1812 to 1822 and served with the poet's grandfather on the first Board of Trustees for Amherst Academy; Emily Dickinson later attended the Academy with the lexicographer's granddaughter, Emily Fowler. Although she may not have been influenced by Webster's theory, Dickinson would at least have found scholarly support there for her own probably unarticulated interest in the verb's role in meaning.

Nineteenth-Century Women Writers

Dickinson was influenced in establishing the techniques of her style by writing which states or implies both that language is primarily an instrument of naming and that language primarily expresses the boundaries of motion, of interactive meaning. Although it is not the focus of this study, Dickinson's use of narrative is also an element of her style. The poet tends to tell a story in her poems, to present ideas or feeling through a plot. The Bible's use of parables—in fact, the Bible itself as an encyclopedia of stories—may have encouraged her propensity to write in tales. Her plots, however, resemble those of popular writers of the period, particularly women writers, suggesting that they may well have influenced this aspect of her style. Certainly Dickinson's most common plot closely resembles the base plot of several women writers.

The Dickinson family subscribed to *The Atlantic Monthly, Harper's New Monthly Magazine,* and *Scribner's Monthly* along with *The Springfield Republican* and two other newspapers—all of which published at least occasional current fiction, poetry, or literary criticism. Emily, Lavinia, Austin, Sue and their friends also bought books on a regular basis and exchanged them with one another. The poet's letters are full of references to what recently published story or book she is reading or that someone has recommended that she read. Although the most frequently repeated references are to authors famous at the time and now (Emerson, Longfellow, both the Brownings, Eliot, and so on), the poet also speaks highly of a number of American women writers, mostly less well known at present: among others, these include Helen Hunt Jackson, Harriet Beecher Stowe, Rebecca Harding Davis, Francis Prescott Spofford, Elizabeth Stuart Phelps, and Marcella Bute Smedley. In a letter of her early twenties (L 85; 1852), for example, Dickinson writes Sue how "small" her "catalogue" of reading has been of late and then goes on:

> I have just read three little books, not great, not thrilling—but sweet and true. "The Light in the Valley" [a memorial of Mary Elizabeth Stirling, who died a few months previously], "Only" [by Matilda Anne Mackarness] and A "House upon a Rock" [also by Mackarness]—I know you would love them all—yet they dont *bewitch* me any. There are no walks in the wood—no low and earnest voices, no moonlight, nor stolen love, but pure little lives, loving God, and their parents, and obeying the laws of the land; . . . I have the promise of "Alton Lock" [by Charles Kingsley]—a certain book, called "Olive," [by Dinah Maria Craik] and the "Head of a Family," [also by Craik] which was what Mattie named to you.

Dickinson's debt to British women authors as role models is much greater than her debt to Americans, but in terms of plot her response to the two groups is largely indistinguishable. Gilbert and Gubar attribute not only her primary romantic plot but also the forms of her daily life to Dickinson's familiarity with the plots of British and American women's novels and poetry: "The fictional shape Dickinson gave her life was a gothic and romantic one, not just (or even primarily) because of the family 'rhetoric' of exaggeration but because the gothic/romantic mode was so frequently employed by all the women writers whom this poet admired more than almost any other literary artists." In her poems, they argue, she articulates variously the details of the plot she has constructed for her reclusive and eccentric life.[26]

The most common plot of Dickinson's poems involves a speaker who is the victim of some monstrous power, usually ambiguously sexual or romantic and usually specifically male. Several poems involve courtship (about which the speaker is ambivalent). For example, death is a courteous gentleman who "kindly stopped for me—" **(712)** or "the supple Suitor / That wins at last—", bearing his bride away to "Kinsmen as divulgeless / As throngs of Down—" or, in another variant, "as responsive / As Porcelain." **(1445).** A bee and rose act out the drama of courtship in a number of poems; for example, in **"A Bee his burnished Carriage / Drove boldly to a Rose—"**, she "received his visit / With frank tranquility" and then, as he flees, "Remained for her—of rapture / But the humility." **(1339).** Another poem **(239)** seems to give the withholding lover both feminine and (implicitly) masculine roles; in the middle of the poem, "Heaven" is first a seductress but then a Conjuror—a term usually reserved for male magicians:

> Her teasing Purples—Afternoons—
> The credulous—decoy—
> Enamored—of the Conjuror—
> That spurned us—Yesterday!

Heaven teases without giving what she promises and, in what Dickinson usually makes the masculine role, spurns the already enamored. **"I cannot live with You" (640),** like any number of poems written to "you" or "him," rests on the same premise as **"'Heaven'—is what I cannot reach!" (239):** relationship here is impossible (except in the cases where it is not desired, as with death) and so the speaker is left with "that White Sustenance—/ Despair—".

Haunted houses or ghosts appear in several poems, the most famous of which are well known: **"One need not be a Chamber—to be Haunted,"** with its gothic chase through an "Abbey" and with "Assassin hid in our Apartment" **(670)**; and **"The Soul has Bandaged moments,"** where a "ghastly Fright come[s] up / And stop[s] to look at her—" **(512).** Ghosts appear as everything from "Eternity's Acquaintances" **(892)** to the "Emerald Ghost—" of a storm that cannot be shut out in **"There came a Wind like a Bugle" (1593),** and figures in these and other poems are frequently haunted.[27] Dickinson once wrote to Higginson that "Nature is a Haunted House—but Art—a House that tries to be haunted" (L 459a). Gilbert and Gubar claim that this comment's "frank admission of dependence upon [gothic] metaphors . . . tells us that the self-hauntings of (female) gothic fiction are in Dickinson's view essential to (female) art."[28] At the very least, the metaphor shows Dickinson's conscious and theatrical use of popular gothic and domestic metaphor.

In most of Dickinson's plots the speaker feels herself besieged or unjustly tormented. One might speculate, of course, that Dickinson writes of suitors, unrequited love, and goblins or specters because these are her primary day-to-day concerns, but this seems unlikely. What we know of her life suggests rather that these story elements are a literary coin she trades in to give her thoughts currency and drama. The poet's twisting and even mockery of the stock gothic plot in several poems (for example, where ghosts are not the "superior spectre" one need fear; **670**) also suggest its distance from the larger concerns of her life. She does not live as a heroine and probably does not believe that heroines as such exist, but she knows how to dress her speakers, and to some extent her public self, in that garb.

In her study of nineteenth-century American women poets, Cheryl Walker accumulates evidence that the commonly held nineteenth-century stereotype of the poetess also provided material for Dickinson's themes and plots and may have contributed to the molding of her life (especially her reclusiveness, dressing in white, and repeated assertion of extreme sensitivity). Focusing on the expressions of feeling that the pose of poetess invites, Walker sees less irony in Dickinson's manipulation of that common plot than I do. The poet assumed a role in and out of her poems, Walker argues, partly for convenience, as protective camouflage, but partly because the role fit, and perhaps also because the paucity of roles for a woman poet left her relatively little choice: "Sometimes it is hard to distinguish the true feelings of these women poets from those dictated by the role they assumed to satisfy public expectations. For a woman like Dickinson the sense of difference from others, the intense feelings, were certainly real. But it is also important to remember that one's self-conception is determined in part by the social vocabulary of one's culture. Still, the poetess was more than a social norm. She was an accessible image for a literary self." According to Walker, Dickinson's frequent reference to or use in her poems of "intense feeling, the ambivalence toward power, the fascination with death, the forbidden lover and secret sorrow"—all major features of expression and plot in the "women's tradition" in poetry—mark her familiarity with this tradition if not its influence on her. Although her language itself (and thus ultimately the poetry) is at great variance from that of her contemporary female and male poets—Walker herself admits that the poet "certainly . . . ignored [this tradition's] stylistic conventions"—Dickinson's topics and sentiments are often indistinguishable from those of her sister poets.[29]

Judging by a contemporary writer's characterization of typical feminine and masculine styles, Dickinson shares more with the latter than with the former. Mary Abigail Dodge, whose sketches Dickinson almost certainly read in the *Atlantic Monthly* in the late 1850s and 1860s and who chose her pen name "Gail Hamilton" because it allowed her to write with a "sexually indeterminate pen," brags of her ability to keep her gender unknown by demonstrating her mastery of both masculine and feminine styles:

> I inform you that I could easily deceive you, if I chose. There is about my serious style a vigor of thought, a comprehensiveness of view, a closeness of logic, and a terseness of diction, commonly supposed to pertain only to the stronger sex. Not wanting in a certain fanciful sprightliness which is the peculiar grace of woman, it possesses also, in large measure, that concentrativeness which is deemed the peculiar strength of man. Where an ordinary woman will leave the beaten track, wandering in a thousand little by-ways of her own,—flowery and beautiful, it is true, and leading her airy feet to "sunny spots of greenery" and the gleam of golden apples, but keeping her not less surely from the goal,—I march straight on, turning neither to the right hand nor to the left, beguiled into no side-issues, discussing no collateral question, but with keen eye and strong hand aiming right at the heart of my theme. Judge thus of the stern severity of my virtue.[30]

When writing of women's digressiveness, Hamilton's prose becomes every bit as "flowery" and "airy" as that of the writers she describes. This sentence uses embedded and parallel descriptive clauses, repeated right-branching constructions, and a profusion of adjectives. The style of the "stronger sex," in contrast, is to the point, as typified by the first two and last sentences above. More than Hamilton, Dickinson writes with what might in her age be called a "masculine" "terseness of diction" and "concentrativeness." Although the speech of the poems may resemble women's more than men's speech, the poems' language does not for the most part resemble nineteenth-century women's written language, especially prose. Hamilton openly disproves the accuracy of her stereotypes of masculine and feminine writing by combining what she considers the best features of both in her own prose. Nonetheless, the stereotypes basically hold as descriptions of nineteenth-century prose. American women's writing did tend to be more adjectival, "flowery," and digressive than men's writing—although a twentieth-century reader of popular nineteenth-century men's writing might well describe it using the same adjectives. What Dickinson takes from this writing is its indirection (leaving the straight "beaten track" for a more ambiguous goal), its primary story elements, and its feeling—not its form.

The claims of influence on the work of any writer must be tenuous. My purpose here has not been to argue that Dickinson writes as she does *because* of her familiarity with the Bible, or with Emerson's writing and philosophy, or with Webster's theory of the origins of language, or because of any other sources. Rather, I present this . . . evidence as a way of reiterating that all language has a supporting context. The syntactic, structural, semantic, and narrative aspects of Dickinson's poems echo writers and texts the poet knew well. She did not manufacture her style out of thin air any more than she lifted it full blown from other writers' pages. Her seclusion from the world was not, in short, a seclusion from language. In delineating stylistic similarities, I have described some of the affinities between Dickinson and the writers who provide the closest models for her language use. . . .

Notes

[1] Herman Melville, *Billy Budd, Sailor (An Inside Narrative),* ed. Harrison Hayford and Merton M. Sealts, Jr. (Chicago: University of Chicago Press, 1962), 75.

[2] Frederick Tuckerman, *Amherst Academy: A New England School of the Past* (Amherst, Mass., 1926), 97.

[3] Sewall refutes the myth that Dickinson was isolated socially and spiritually at Mount Holyoke because she did not convert (*Life* II, 362-364). It is also important to note in this age of greater religious variety that one could be a regular churchgoer and generally adhere to the principles of Christianity without being "a Christian." The poet's letters contain several references to sermons and ministers that she heard until she became completely reclusive in her early thirties.

[4] Thomas H. Johnson, *Emily Dickinson: An Interpretive Biography* (Cambridge, Mass.: Harvard University Press, 1955), 151.

[5] James R. Kugel, *The Idea of Biblical Poetry: Parallelism and Its History* (New Haven, Conn.: Yale University Press, 1981), 300.

[6] Dickinson alludes to the gospel of Matthew seventy-four times in her poems and letters, more than twice as often as to any other book of the Bible. Jack L. Capps, *Emily Dickinson's Reading, 1836-1886* (Cambridge, Mass.: Harvard University Press, 1966), 40-41, 192.

[7] One of the primary initial arguments of Mueller's *The Native Tongue and the Word: Developments in English Prose Style 1380-1580* (Chicago: University of Chicago Press, 1984) has to do with the complexity and effectiveness of a conjunctive and paratactic style. Mueller notes that the shift of subject (here from third to first person) occurs frequently in scripturalism and in spoken language; it also occurs frequently in Dickinson's poetry.

[8] Kugel, *The Idea of Biblical Poetry,* 10.

[9] There are more extreme examples of Dickinson's repetition, but they follow the same pattern of functional repetition and semantic variation. For example, in "Mine—by the Right of the White Election!" (528), six of the poem's nine lines begin "Mine—" and four begin "Mine—by the . . ." Like "It was not Death," this poem never identifies its subject, what the speaker insists is "Mine."

[10] Morris Croll, "The Baroque Style in Prose," ed. John M. Wallace, in *Style, Rhetoric, and Rhythm: Essays by Morris Croll* (Princeton, N.J.: Princeton University Press, 1966), 207-237 (originally published in 1929). Subsequent citations of Croll in the text will be indicated by giving page numbers in parentheses. Croll speaks only of biblical prose, but Kugel argues at length that the lack of meter in Hebrew makes the Romance language distinction between poetry and prose meaningless. At its most "poetic," biblical language employs the greatest number of "heightening features" to create the greatest intensity (*The Idea of Biblical Poetry,* 85-86).

Dickinson wrote to Higginson: "For Prose [I have]—Mr Ruskin—Sir Thomas Browne—and the Revelations." "For Poets," she names only Keats and the Brownings (L 261). Millicent Todd Bingham and Mabel Loomis Todd published Herbert's stanzas as Dickinson's in the first edition of *Bolts of Melody: New Poems of Emily Dickinson* (New York: Harper and Brothers, 1945).

[11] James Davidson ("Emily Dickinson and Isaac Watts," *Boston Public Library Quarterly,* 6, 1954, 141-149)

mentions the former two books. Capps mentions only the latter, stating that it belonged to the poet's father (*Emily Dickinson's Reading,* 187). All three were enormously popular in the nineteenth century.

[12] Watts concludes his hymn "There is a land of pure delight" (626) with the stanza: "Could we but climb where Moses stood, / And view the landscape o'er; / Not Jordan's stream, nor death's cold flood / Should fright us from the shore." Dickinson parodies this vision of heaven in "Where bells no more affright the morn" with her wish for a "town" (or "Heaven") where "very nimble Gentlemen" can no longer wake sleeping children. Her poem concludes: "Oh could we climb where Moses stood, / And view the Landscape o'er' / Not Father's bells—nor Factories, / Could scare us any more!" (112). Watts's hymn is in his *Psalms, Hymns, and Spiritual Songs* (Boston: Crocker and Brewster, 1834).

[13] According to Davidson, Watts's psalms and hymns were frequently smoothed out by editors because of this irregularity and harshness. *Church Psalmody,* however, one of the Watts books belonging to the Dickinsons, was virtually unchanged by editors ("Emily Dickinson and Isaac Watts," 143).

[14] Mueller argues that modern English as a whole has been deeply influenced by scripturalism, primarily through translations of the Bible preceding the King James version *(The Native Tongue and the Word).* American adoption of some characteristics of biblical style seems to be more specific and more closely tied to biblical authority than were the earlier British borrowings from scripturalism.

[15] Perry Miller, "An American Language," in *Nature's Nation* (Cambridge, Mass.: Harvard University Press, 1967), 208-240. Subsequent page references to this essay will appear in parentheses in the text.

[16] Think of the inevitable opening apologia in Puritan writing, from Bunyan's *Pilgrim's Progress* to the "foolish, broken, blemished Muse" that Anne Bradstreet claims for herself in her "Prologue."

[17] William Ames was the most articulate proponent of the plain style. The passages quoted in the text are from his "Conscience with the Power and Cases Thereof" (1643) and *The Marrow of Sacred Divinity* (1643) as cited respectively in Larzer Ziff's *Puritanism in America* (New York: Viking Press, 1973), 14, and Perry Miller's *The New England Mind: The Seventeenth Century* (Boston: Beacon Press, 1939), 301.

[18] From Ames's *Marrow of Sacred Divinity,* quoted in Miller, "An American Language," 219.

[19] In *The American Democrat* (New York: Alfred A. Knopf, 1931; a reprint of the 1838 edition), 108-116.

[20] Given the context of the poem, it must be the old Sea that says "Go" to the new or "Brook"-Sea. The Brook-Sea speaks last, addressing the older "Waters."

[21] Capps, *Emily Dickinson's Reading,* 173-174.

[22] Ralph Waldo Emerson, *Complete Works,* 12 vols. (Cambridge, Mass.: Riverside Press, 1883). This quote is taken from vol. I, 31. Subsequent quotations from Emerson will be cited in the text as *Works,* with volume and page number.

[23] Ernest Fenollosa, *The Chinese Written Character as a Medium for Poetry,* ed. Ezra Pound (San Francisco: City Light Books, 1969), 20-21, 23; originally published in 1936.

[24] "An Introductory Dissertation on the Origin, History and Connection of the Languages of Western Asia and Europe, with an Explanation of the Principles on which Language are Formed," ix-lxxi. It is possible that Webster's interest in etymological derivations in this essay and throughout his dictionary influenced Dickinson's similar interest, but there is no special reason to assume this connection. More likely, Webster's derivations provided empirical support for an interest and habit the poet had already developed on her own.

[25] Webster, "State of English Philology," in *A Collection of Papers on Political, Literary and Moral Subjects* (New York, 1843), 365.

[26] Sandra Gilbert and Susan Gubar, *The Madwoman in the Attic: The Woman Writer and the Nineteenth-Century Literary Imagination* (New Haven, Conn.: Yale University Press, 1979), 584.

[27] See, for example, poems 75, 184, 274, 281, 311, 413, 670, 817, 1181, and 1400 for ghosts and 167, 195, 253, 472, 788, 841, 938, and 1004 for haunting.

[28] Gilbert and Gubar, *Madwoman in the Attic,* 585-586.

[29] Cheryl Walker, *The Nightingale's Burden: Women Poets in America, 1630-1900* (Bloomington, Ind.: Indiana University Press, 1982), 88, 116, 87.

[30] Mary Abigail Dodge, from "My Garden," *Atlantic Monthly,* 1862. Reprinted in *Provisions: A Reader of Nineteenth-Century American Women,* ed. Judith Fetterley (Bloomington, Ind.: Indiana University Press, 1985), 421-445.

Margaret Dickie (essay date 1988)

SOURCE: "Dickinson's Discontinuous Lyric Self," in *American Literature*, Vol. 60, No. 4, December, 1988, pp. 537-53.

[*In the following essay, Dickie maintains that Dickinson's poems should be analyzed not as pieces of a narrative, but as lyric poems in which the qualities of brevity, repetition, and figuration are the most pertinent and the most telling. Dickie stresses that such an analysis reveals a sense of self that is "particular, discontinuous, limited, private, hidden," and that this conclusion challenges those reached by feminist and psychoanalytic narrative character analyses.*]

It is the habit of our times to read poetry as if it were prose perhaps because recent strategies for reading derive from and are most easily applied to prose. Psychoanalytic, Marxist, feminist models for reading all depend to one extent or another upon a plot, upon character, and upon extended development. When these models are applied to a form such as a lyric poem that is brief, repetitive, and figurative, they fit uneasily and most usefully only when the lyric form itself is neglected in favor of the narrative that can be derived from joining together a number of poems. It must be admitted that the brevity of the lyric poses an obstacle to a critical argument because it is equally difficult to make a compelling point on the basis of a single brief lyric and, for different reasons, to discuss a series of poems as one continuous work. Perhaps then what is needed is a critical argument that will start by noticing that the properties of the lyric—its brevity, its repetition, its figuration—obstruct readings that are determined by a socially limited understanding of the self or the subject, by a view of character as expressed in a cause and effect logic, by an insistence that the poet can be understood by certain representative attitudes. The lyric poem resists the totalizing ambition of such readings.

In trying to formulate a new model for reading the lyric poem, Emily Dickinson's poetry may be instructive especially because it has been given a recent and vigorous reading by American feminist critics who have been reading it for plot, character, and the extended argument of the work.[1] For example, Alicia Ostriker has commented: "Dickinson genuinely despises publicity and power, prefers the private and powerless life—and the reverse is equally true. We may say the same about many of her poems in praise of deprivation: they reject what they commend, commend what they reject. Their delight, their strength derives from their doubleness" (p. 41). Power and deprivation are themes that interest Ostriker, issues central to feminist criticism; but Ostriker's own claims would suggest that they are not issues equally central or politically determined to Dickinson.

The brevity with which the lyric "I" is presented in Dickinson's poems should suggest that that "I" is not to be known in terms such as publicity and power that might define a character in a novel.[2] The longer life of an individual in the novel, and especially in the nineteenth-century novel, tends inevitably toward steadfastness of character. Even an effort such as Edgar Allan Poe's to undermine the stalwartness of fictional characters by the use of unreliable narrators relies upon a consistency of representation that is foreign to the lyric "I." In a lyric poem, the "I" is known only in limited detail. For a lyric poet of consistent productivity such as Dickinson, this limitation is a deliberate choice of self-presentation, expressive of a particular sense of the self (of herself or a self) as shifting, changing, reforming. Such a self will be distorted in being described in terms appropriate for either a real-life or novelistic character.

But what terms can be used then? Brevity, repetition, and figuration, I repeat. These qualities articulate a sense of the self as particular, discontinuous, limited, private, hidden. Such a concept of self directly subverts the idea that the self is a publicly knowable, organized, single entity. Thus, it challenges all kinds of narrative explanations of character, not only the feminist and psychoanalytic reading of Dickinson's work but the dominant ideology of self-reliance expressed in the prose of nineteenth-century American culture.[3] Dickinson's poetry has been read typically as an expression of that ideology when actually it is far more revolutionary in its understanding of the self. Its chief means of revolt is its choice of the publicly degraded lyric form.

Only in America, where there was no great lyric tradition and thus no great tradition of reading the lyric, would this easily conventionalized genre be available for subversive expression. Despite Poe's claim for its importance, the lyric was a woman's form, considered insufficient to express the grandness of America and the American individual, the central mission of the nineteenth-century American literary establishment. This insufficiency of form was coextensive with the insufficiency of a self conceived as incomplete, unsure, recalcitrant, and—it must be admitted—female. The precariousness of identity, the unmappable privacy, and the unacknowledged limitations of individuality could be suggested, evoked, tentatively recognized in the lyric form which shared the very qualities it was called upon to express. Furthermore, the lyric was uniquely available for self-expression in a society where other literary forms for such expression (the diary, the letter, for example) had been conventionalized and absorbed by the cultural imperatives of the Puritan tradition.

Dickinson's exclusive choice of the lyric genre separated her from Emerson and Thoreau, but she was also distanced from them in time. She wrote the bulk of her poems in the early years of the Civil War at the very juncture when the ideology of individualism established by its links to an American destiny was beginning to reveal the limits not of its optimism, which was much later in developing, but of its comprehensiveness. The individualism of Emerson and Thoreau was male, white, middle class, and Protestant. It did not extend to the work of a woman. It is no surprise then that in this woman writer, individualism as a concept gave way to the expression of individuality.

The two are not commensurate as we know from reading Emerson, but it is perhaps Nietzsche who most fully articulates the idea that the word individuality is always spoken with a forked tongue. The concept of individuality with its sense of commonality threatens the claims to individuality. Discussing Nietzsche, Werner Hamacher argues:

> Individuality is so fully determined as incommensurability that no individual could correspond to its concept if it were at one with and equal to itself, if it were a thoroughly determined, whole form. *Human, All Too Human* proposes, in the interests of knowledge, that one not uniformize oneself into rigidity of bearing and that one not treat oneself "like a stiff steadfast, *single* individual." Only the individual's nonidentity with itself can constitute its individuality. Measured against itself as concept, bearing, and function, the individual proves to be other, to be more—or less—than itself. Its individuality is always only what reaches out beyond its empirical appearance, its social and psychological identities, and its logical form. Individuality is unaccountable surplus.[4]

This unaccountable surplus is what cannot be made uniform, .narrated, and organized into a single individual. It is best expressed not in prose but in lyric poetry where a brief and repeated form depends upon the exposure of particularity and peculiarity. Such limited details rather than extended narrative development will provide relief from the self-defeating ambitions of a coherent and definitive presentation of the self. The lyric poem does not mythologize the individual as a readable organization, making coherence out of isolated moments and fragmentary experience as the novel does; rather the lyric makes isolated moments out of coherence and restores with words the contingency of the self that has been lost to experience.[5] Unlike the novel, the lyric's "significant form" does not signify social viability.[6]

The brevity of the lyric focuses the sharp edges of details that will be necessarily scant. But the pressure of the brief form also attenuates the detail until it changes under scrutiny. Thus, the lyric's brevity enlarges rather than contracts the possibility of the details. Such presentation relies on the profligacy of details rather than on their coherence.

The value of profligacy is the subject of **Poem 634** where Dickinson represents not a human being but a bird. A riddle or more accurately a quasi-riddle since it is evident from the start that the subject is a bird, the poem demonstrates the way in which the lyric strains the techniques of representation by rendering clear details opaque and then creating out of that opacity the central clarity. The poem's riddling quality is an important element of its representation because it allows Dickinson to present one thing in terms of another as an image and in the instability of the image to suggest thereby the paradox of identity.[7] What we see best, we see least well; what we cannot see or refuse to see becomes clearest evidence. Offering instruction on how to know a bird, Dickinson provides too an inquiry into self-representation.

She starts with alarming confidence in the brief detail: "You'll know Her—by Her Foot." And that particularity presents itself as immediately obstructive since to know *her* by her foot is to know nothing of the conventional feminine beauty of her face or figure. Nor is it to know much by symbolic extension. The foot, unlike the hand or the heart, does not stand for anything except standing. But, curiously, the first stanza insists on its own particular way of knowing by metaphorical extension, developing in apposition:

> You'll know Her—by Her Foot—
> The smallest Gamboge Hand
> With Fingers—where the Toes should be—
> Would more affront the Sand—

No poet could make these connections without thinking of how she herself is known by her poetic foot, and in the apposition of the foot/hand Dickinson makes a whimsical connection between bird and poet, hand writing and poetic foot, which will be developed in the final stanza where she meditates on an idea close to the Nietzschean surplus in individuality.

Before that, however, the poem appears to be a detailed taxonomy of the bird, identified by particular details—her foot, her vest, her cap. But these typical parts lose their immediate force in the poet's efforts to maintain the metaphor of bird and woman. The bird's foot described as "this Quaint Creature's Boot" is rendered unknowable as either foot or boot when the speaker says it is "Without a Button—I could vouch." That testimony guarantees enigma. Without a button, it is not a boot, and so the vouching undoes the knowledge it would confirm. The excursion seems merely decorative, as does the admission that inside her tight-fitting vest she wore a duller jacket when she was born. This wandering bird-knowledge appears inappropriately applied to a figure described as small, snug, tightly encased, finely plumed.

Like Nietzsche's individual, this bird is something other than its type. Its foot is a boot but not a boot; its orange-brown vest is the opposite of its original jacket; its cap appears from a distance no cap at all and then closer up proves to be a cap that is no cap since it has no band or brim. By the sixth stanza, Dickinson has demonstrated convincingly the extent to which details do not represent the whole, and concomitantly the uncertainty of ever knowing the whole either by knowledge of parts as in synecdoche, by knowledge derived from identifying one thing in terms of another or relating the familiar to the unfamiliar as in metaphor, or by personal testimony or by precise description and careful distinction. Even in combination, such ways do not lead to a satisfactory representation of the whole. But the poem does not end with this conclusion toward which it appears to be drawing. Rather, it presents the bird presenting herself:

> You'll know Her—by her Voice—
> At first—a doubtful Tone—
> A sweet endeavor—but as March
> To April—hurries on—
>
> She squanders on your Ear
> Such Arguments of Pearl—
> You beg the Robin in your Brain
> To keep the other—still—

The "doubtful Tone" that turns into "Arguments of Pearl" is an excessive presentation. And it is perhaps the excess from which the poet imagines the recipient retreating, preferring the idea to this reality.

Such self-presentation as the bird's is always more than enough. It must be excessive if it is to be the expression of an individual, of the "unaccountable surplus" of individuality. This bird of doubtful tone exemplifies Hamacher's description of the Nietzschean individual: "The individual does not live. It outlives. Its being is being out and being over, an insubstantial remainder and excess beyond every determinable form of human life. Instead of being a social or psychic form of human existence, the individual—the self surpassing of type, or genius—is the announcement of what, generally translated as 'superman' or 'overman,' is best translated in this context as 'outman'" (p. 119).

Leaving aside for the moment the absurdity of considering Dickinson's bird an "outman," I draw attention to the way in which the poet presents a bird by brief details and then obliterates these details in the verb "Squanders" where the bird surpasses the type. Thus, the bird is profligate in Nietzschean terms. And the poet behind the bird knows too that, in its squandering, it is casting pearls before swine, claiming individuality in a world that prefers types.

Thus, the brevity of the lyric allows a certain kind of knowing. It demands the excessive patience and attention that only a poet would possess, and it requires an indulgence that Dickinson had every reason to believe her readers would lack. To know by the foot is not a simple knowledge nor is it a different way of knowing something that exists outside the poem; it is rather a form of knowing by excesses only available in brief and metrical form.

Such excesses figure in the brevity of lyric representation by distorting syntax and sense. Knowing by the foot means fitting language to form as in the lines, "Nor is it Clasped unto of Band—/ Nor held upon—of Brim." Extracted from the poem, these lines fail to signify anything; they can signify only in an arrangement of language that prizes apposition, parallel structures, or periphrasis, in short, that prizes excessive statement. Or, another example, the opening quatrain with its comparison of foot to a hand that "Would more affront the Sand" is a deictic chaos, made necessary and then managed by the only full rhyme in the poem—"Sand" holds "hand" in place. Here, Dickinson seems to be underscoring the whimsy of knowing in rhyme and rhythm. Like the bird, the poet too is a squanderer and, like the bird's, her squandering is permitted and limited by brief form and the formal repetition it requires.

The lyric's repetition derives from its brevity, but repetition is curiously essential both *to* and *in* the lyric poem. As a way of representation, repetition brought Dickinson's lyrics into conflict with Romantic conceptions of form and subject in nineteenth-century America. A form that depends upon the repetition of its formal elements will not be free nor will it necessarily grow by the principle of organic form. Moreover, the subject presented in repetitive images will not be original and new. It will always be a copy and a copy of a copy.

The vulnerability of the lyric to conventional form and subject is well documented in the history of literature. But for Dickinson, it posed a particular problem. She shared with her fellow Romantics a suspicion of convention. She knew, as they did, the limits of the self that was made and the character that was formed in large and in little by repeating familiar patterns of behavior, by repeated professions of faith, by copying over moral precepts both in school books and in embroidery lessons at home, by duties performed and performed again. She resisted in her own life these means through which one generation inculcated into the next its values, its identity, its way of life, and forced the self through repetition to grow into a presentable self. It was this self that Thoreau hoped to wash off each morning in his dips into Walden Pond. It was this self that Emerson intended to escape by writing "Whim" on his lintel post and departing from family and friends for a day. And it was this self that Dickinson drew and satirized in several poems. But while Thoreau believed in the natural man beyond the social man and Emerson relied on the genius within, Dickinson as a lyric poet had no access to these plots of redemption.

Rather, she was tied by the repetition in and of the lyric to use repetition as the constituent of character. Again, the limits of the genre enlarged her understanding, and when in **Poem 443,** for example, she takes repetition as her subject she uses it to express ranges of experience inaccessible to narrative organization. The poem has been enforced into such organization by Barbara Mossberg, who reads it as evidence of the duplicity imposed upon women by the dominant patriarchal culture (p. 197). The repetitive language and strategies of the poem reveal, however, a miserable lack of duplicity or division between inner and outer actions.

The repetition in the verb tense—"I tie my Hat," "I crease my Shawl," "I put new Blossoms in the Glass," "I push a petal from my Gown," "I have so much to do"—describes particular habits by which the lyric "I" prepares herself and her house for presentation to the world. Yet they are not aids in self-making so much as subterfuges behind which she hides both from the world and from herself. More crucially, the theatricality of these acts is doubled by the theatricality within; the outer self acting is in danger at every point of being upstaged by the dramatic, even melodramatic, inner self who "got a Bomb—/ And held it in our Bosom." By this convergence of outer show and inner show, Dickinson calls into question the nature of identity. What is real? What is cover-up? Or, more to the point, do these questions even apply? Is the self only show?

The repetitive gestures of putting on hats and taking off shawls may be obsessive acts, but no more so than the "stinging work—/ To cover what we are," the effort of holding a bomb in the bosom. The speaker justifies her "life's labor" by claiming that it holds "our Senses—on." But on to what? What is the center? What is the periphery here? The speaker's sense that she must "simulate" is, as it must be in the lyric, unexplained. Her boast that she only trembles at the bomb that would make others start suggests a fondness for her own dilemma. She is holding on to "Miles on Miles of Nought" by the same effort of will that nullified the self. Both her inner and her outer life reflect a willingness to act as if "the very least / Were infinite—to me."

Often accused of speaking from beyond the grave, here Dickinson brings the grave into the center of life. This is not a poem in which life as disruption of stasis "seems like an outbreak around which control keeps trying, unsuccessfully, to close" or where "meaning disrupts both vacuous action and the sententia in which such action takes refuge," as Sharon Cameron would have it.[8] It is rather a poem about a life in which control is the only meaning and meaning the only control.

In this poem where the inner self is fashioned by the same patterns of repetition that fashion the outer self, the collapse of the division between inner and outer in the speaker makes it possible to collapse the division between self and other. "I" becomes "we" at the very point in mid-poem where the speaker turns from her daily duties to announce the unique errand that should have distinguished her from all others. It is not that the catastrophe deprives her of individuality but that she divests herself of her individuality by surrendering to this single event. "*We* came to flesh" and "*we* got a Bomb," the speaker boasts, as if she were somehow made more grand, indeed "completed," by this dwindling of life into a single purpose which it is now her duty to memorialize.

In life lived as a duty, there can be no difference between private and public. The repetitive strategies of the lyric are used here to express the dilemma of the self ensnared in its own trap of meaning. The clotting of the lines with internal rhymes, assonance, consonance, alliteration, anaphora, and phrases in apposition suggests the way in which language can be used to impede change, to repeat sameness, even as it seems to press forward.

"I tie my Hat" is not about loss but about the refusal to give up loss. The speaker in this poem wants to account for the unaccountable surplus of individuality, to explain it in terms of a single completed "errand." But insofar as that "errand" appears undetailed and only abstractly named, it will require endless repetition.

The "Bomb" in the bosom that somehow mysteriously never goes off, that is paradoxically "calm," is pure melodrama, an image that loses its power the second it fixes itself in the imagination or should lose its power. In fact, in critical commentary, it has not. The restitution of order around the bomb evident in the persistent present of the verb "we do life's labor" has come to signify the speaker's martyrdom for critics who want to see in the poem a cause and effect explanation of character, a narrative that will contrast the liveliness of the bomb to the deadliness of routine existence (Mossberg, p. 197). But such a reading provides a plot where plot has been deliberately suppressed by repetitive action; it finds biography where Dickinson has placed only habit.

Dickinson's poems have been particularly vulnerable to narrative explanation, specifically to biographical explication. Vivian R. Pollak justifies this practice by arguing that Dickinson's art of self-display and self-advertisement draws attention to the person behind the poems and so calls for an examination of biographical relationships.[9] What Pollak terms self-display and self-advertisement could as easily be called repression as in **"I tie my Hat,"** where the staged performance of daily duties is an evasion of self-knowledge and even the inner faithfulness to the bomb in the bosom has its element of ritual—a display perhaps, but not of the bared self.

The relationship of poet to speaker is not a simple equation; it is always mediated through and suppressed by the lyric's figurative language. Dickinson wrote to Thomas Wentworth Higginson, the editor who advised her against publishing, "When I state myself, as the Representative of the Verse—it does not mean—me—but a supposed person" (II, 412). In these terms, she points us in a different direction to ask questions that lead away from biography and toward figuration and supposition or, as in **Poem 505,** the person supposing. Dickinson's art of self-presentation depends on supposition in "I would not paint—a picture."

The relationship of speaker to Dickinson is intricate and inadequately understood in Adrienne Rich's powerful reading of the poem that identifies Dickinson with the speaker and with the fear of her poetic power.[10] All that is known about the actual person who wrote this poem, about her difficulties in reaching the kind of appreciative audience she imagines in this speaker, about the doubts that she might have entertained over the breathlessness of this speaker, about her attitude toward art in general and her own poetry in particular, all this information must be added to the poem when it is read as a political and social tract. But if such reading seems reductive in its extraneousness, equally reductive is the view of the speaker here as purified of contingency by the lyric. It is a poet, after all, who is writing "Nor would I be a Poet" and imagining what the dower of art would be. Hers is a mixed voice, contaminated by its source and, as we shall see, easily blending into its circumstances.

The speaker of this poem is a person supposing, dwelling in supposition, and, as such, she moves in and out of identities. She figures, refigures, and figures again. Now audience, now artist, she is a creature without a core, free to dwell on and in the creator's feelings and the feelings that creation inspires, as open to elevation as to fixity, both impotent and privileged. The speaker is all feeling here, and her feeling is dependent on what will arouse it. But it is a productive and willing dependency that drives her to superfluous denials and extravagant affirmations. "I would not paint," "I would not talk" are excessive protestations. Denying herself what she most wants, the speaker intensifies its pleasures by doubling them in creating the occasion for the poem. Sweet torment and sumptuous despair are moods of desire prolonged and longingly anticipated, not evidence of Dickinson's passivity as Rich has argued. The speaker's relishing of her own relishing cannot fit into Rich's narrative of female repression because it is perversely an unrepressed narrative—a desire that is always for something else, always reaching out toward something, never satisfying itself except in its repetition and perpetuation. The poet is not frustrated in her desire to be a painter but rather thrilled by the desire to feel what the painter feels. She is not denied art; she has after all "fingers" of her own which stir, as we read, evoking both in the writer and in the reader their own sweet torment.

Again, in the second stanza, the speaker repeats her rapture. Just as in the first stanza where there was an odd disproportion between the "bright impossibility" of paintings and the "fingers" of the painter, so here the speaker as "endued Balloon" launched by "a lip of Metal" presents herself as soaring high from rather low inspiration. The talk of cornets is banal by comparison to the speaker's elevation through "Villages of Ether." The transport of art and the ability to be transported by art thrill the speaker who marvels at her own powers to be moved by "*but* a lip." The cornet player is a performer, not a creator, and his performance is rendered remarkable by the response of the "One / Raised softly to the Ceilings." She, too, is a performer—and on a higher wire.

The final stanza narrows the gap between creator/performer and audience/performer by endowing the speaker with the "Ear" *for* the poet and *of* the poet. Identities blur. The ear of the poet as of her audience is "Enamored—impotent—content," a passive receiver and willing receptacle. It is through the ear that both will be inspired and stunned by "Bolts of Melody." The separate identities of the creator and the reverent appreciator of poetry compose a fantasy that had started disingenuously in the speaker's wondering how the painter's fingers feel and how the musician's lips could inspire her, but it is a fantasy of self-empowerment, not self-diminishment. The speaker also has fingers, also has lips, even as she has "the Ear." "What would the Dower be, / Had I the Art to Stun myself," she speculates, but only after she has presented herself as stunned and stunnable. She has the "Art."

The supposed person that Dickinson might have called the representative of this verse is less a person than the power of supposition. Drawing up a *dramatis personae* for the poem or outlining a narrative continuity of envy and renunciation both diminishes and mislocates the power which names itself only in repetition. "I would not paint," "I would not talk," "Nor would I be a Poet" are repeated affirmations of the always unsatisfied, always to be satisfied desire to create. They celebrate themselves in prolonging the moment of desire just before it is satisfied. If a narrative of sexual longing and consummation cannot be easily generated from these unanchored images, the eroticism of the language here has its oddity.

The description of a painter creating a picture by the "rare—celestial—stir" of fingers is not mimetic. The words move from perceiver to perceived, from effect to affect, along a wayward path that zigzags between sound and sense. Sound alone seems to require the preposterous metaphor "Pontoon" for the self. And finally the wish to know what the dower would be if one could electrify oneself seems willful semantic wandering.

The excess in this language cannot do more than point to the excessiveness in the speaker's fantasy of self. She would be *sweetly* tormented, *sumptuously* despaired, raised and endued, awed and stunned, moved beyond sense. In her state of elevated and extravagant longing, the speaker is wanton with language, disposing lines with abandon as if they were impediments to rather than expressions of anticipated ecstasy. If language cannot speak itself, it must appropriate a channel for its transmission. The channel in lyric poetry need not be a fully developed character defined by birth and death dates, by family and a maturation plot; it can be, as here, a voice that speaks from shifting perspectives, that inhabits various frequencies, that has no center but rather many circumferences.

From the robin to the woman of melodramatic routine to this disembodied power of supposition, the examples I have chosen appear—when placed together—random, discontinuous, and uncentered. They are intentionally so because I want to suggest something of Dickinson's profligacy. It is possible to set the poem about the robin in the context of Dickinson's riddles or of her bird poems and to discuss **Poem 505** with other poems in which Dickinson sets out her poetics. Or all three poems could be adapted to one or more narratives of social repression, artistic restriction, romantic deprivation. But although such order and explanation might justify critical discourse, even my own, it would have to be superimposed and designed to suppress or ignore the fact that the poems are discrete forms, perhaps part of a larger whole that is the poet's imaginative world but deliberately brief, separate, disconnected units of expression.

Even as I insist on that aspect of the work, I am aware of the misfit between the brevity of the lyric and the length of my own commentary. Little can be concluded from one brief lyric or three. Only the fact that Dickinson chose this form consistently makes it possible to argue that the form itself is an important confirmation or creation of her sense of self. Thus, I return once more to consider the properties of the lyric: brevity, repetition, and figuration.

The brevity of the lyrics she wrote is a form of artistic restraint that relies paradoxically on excess. In an age of sprawling masterpieces that followed the laws of nature, chapters proliferating as branches grow from trunks, in Melville's terms, the brevity, compactness, and convention of the lyric form appear unnecessarily restrictive. Yet Dickinson could use the brevity of the lyric to suggest even more freely than Melville the unaccountability of individuality. Although the lyric speaker can be conventionalized by the form itself, insofar as she is imaged in details rather than as a whole, particularized rather than totalized, she appears not conventional at all.

Such a speaker presents herself partially, not fully; her whole existence is, for us, partial. Measured against Ahab, for example, the lyric speaker suggests a sense of self that is certainly limited and yet remains paradoxically free from the restraints of social viability that will be exerted on the novelistic character. The partial may be, if not all there is, more than we realize. Brevity, then, may be the soul of character.

The brevity of the lyric form enforces its repetition. It encourages a refiguration of the already figured, and so it permits a concept of the self not only as partial but as excessive. In composing over a hundred poems that start with "I," Dickinson could create and recreate a supposed person supposing one way and then another. No single "errand" for her, the lyric speaker is singular, unique, isolated, changeable, not to be made into one composite person by joining poems together. The lyric "I" is not the real-life poet or even part of her because she will not share her beginning or her end, her history. She is not a copy of that original either because she is always and conventionally partial.

Formally, repetition encourages a predictability that nonetheless permits disruption and gaps. Dickinson establishes a repetitive rhythm or rhyme scheme or organizing grammar and then breaks it, as she does in "I tie my Hat" when she breaks the rhythm with "Stopped—struck—my ticking—through" and the rhyme in "Too Telescopic Eyes / To bear on us unshaded—/ For their—sake—not for Ours" and the grammar in "But since we got a Bomb—/ And held it in our Bosom." The disruption, only made possible by the expectations of repetitive form, allows the brief lyric to expand its space, to incorporate blanks, to open indeterminately.

Repetition in the lyric as, for example, in the anaphora of "I would not paint—a picture—" becomes a means of obstructing narrative explanation. It also precludes the organization of events in a causal series. And it leaves open the question of what is original, what copy, as, for example, in **"I tie my Hat"** in which the repetitive routine gestures of the speaker may imitate a deadened inner life or may be themselves the originator of that life.[11]

Finally, the figurative language of a lyric poem represses one term under another and suggests again the profligacy of such repression. The self is not exposed in figurative language but hidden and shielded and thus freed from social definition. Such freedom allows for the whimsy always available in self-presentation. The lyric character may be called "Pontoon" perhaps only to rhyme with "Balloon" or stuck in the improbable pose of holding a bomb in the bosom or singing not a tune but a "tone." The lyric "I" is free because its relationship to even the "I" of a supposed person is of copy to copy. It can proliferate endlessly. Although Dickinson describes one speaker acting "With scrupulous exactness—/ To hold our Senses—on," she actually calls into question the center around which such exactness would accrue both in that particular poem and in a lifetime's accumulation of such poems.

In concentrating on the brevity, the repetition, and the figuration of the lyric form, I have attempted to read Dickinson's poems by the qualities they possess. These terms may only be useful for Dickinson's work; they will not all serve Wordsworth's lyrics or Milton's or Shakespeare's, for example. Thus, they cannot be worked into a model for reading all lyric poetry. But they are important here because they point to the essential qualities of Dickinson's work: its interest in the unaccountable surplus of individuality, in repetition as constituent of character, and in figurative excess as essential to self-presentation.

The problems of interpretation that Dickinson's poetry poses are essentially problems of narrative readability which have usually been resolved by the imposition of a master narrative on the work and the life. Feminist critics of Dickinson who have brought so much new energy to the reading of her poetry are only the latest version of this tendency; they have been preceded by psychoanalytic critics, biographers, and cultural historians. Dickinson's work evades them because it represents a much more radical understanding of the self than American feminists, tied as they are to a social explanation of character, can allow. Dickinson's lyric speakers have no narrative continuity, no social viability, no steadfast identity.[4] In their squandering, melodrama, and excesses, they express an individuality that resists final representation and the control that signifies. Yet Dickinson's lyric presentation of a self that obstructs narrative reading because it is discontinuous, profligate, and excessive may be the nineteenth century's most revolutionary expression of individuality. Thus, it may offer not only a new model for reading the lyric but a new and perhaps persuasively feminist model of self-presentation.

Notes

[1] It is not only the feminists who have read for the plot. Early and late, narrativizing critics have worked on Dickinson. See for example Clark Griffith's *The Long Shadow: Emily Dickinson's Tragic Poetry* (Princeton: Princeton Univ. Press, 1964) which traces her traumatic relationship with her father as the source of her tragic poetry or John Cody's *After Great Pain: The Inner Life of Emily Dickinson* (Cambridge: Harvard Univ. Press, 1971) which uses the poetry as a psychoanalytic case study. Among representative feminist readings of Dickinson are Margaret Homans, *Women Writers and Poetic Identity* (Princeton: Princeton Univ. Press, 1980), Joanne Feit Diehl, *Dickinson and the Romantic Imagination* (Princeton: Princeton Univ. Press, 1981), Barbara Antonina Clarke Mossberg, *Emily Dickinson: When a Writer Is a Daughter* (Bloomington: Indiana Univ. Press, 1982), Sandra M. Gilbert and Susan Gubar, *The Madwoman in the Attic* (New Haven: Yale Univ. Press, 1979), and Alicia Suskin Ostriker, *Stealing the Language: The Emergence of Women's Poetry in America* (Boston: Beacon, 1986). Based on a model of binary opposition, these varied readings of Dickinson stress the extent to which she was different because she was made to be by a society that restricted or repressed women's expression. Sacvan Bercovitch in *The Puritan Origins of the American Self* (New Haven: Yale Univ. Press, 1975) explores the strain on the individual from the demands of American individualism in terms that explain some of the difficulties of reading Dickinson's poetry.

References to Dickinson's work are to *The Complete Poems of Emily Dickinson,* ed. Thomas H. Johnson (Boston: Little, Brown, 1957), and *The Letters of Emily Dickinson,* ed. Thomas H. Johnson and Theodora Ward, 3 vols. (Cambridge: Harvard Univ. Press, 1958). References will appear in the text in parentheses.

[2] In talking about the brevity of Dickinson's poems, I mean only to suggest a general characteristic of all lyric poems and not to stress the particular ways in which Dickinson exploited brevity or limitation as a theme. For such treatment, see Jane Donahue Eberwein's *Dickinson: Strategies of Limitation* (Amherst: Univ. of Massachusetts Press, 1985).

[3] See Sacvan Bercovitch's discussion of Emerson for a complete treatment of his sense of the public self. The whole question of privacy is a central concern of Dickinson. For example, in Poem 1385, she deals directly with the impossibility of publishing the private, making public the secret. Dickinson's privacy is an issue of some debate among her critics. She is charged with being too private by Elinor Wilnor, "The Poetics of Emily Dickinson," *ELH,* 38 (1971), 126-54, and David Porter, *Dickinson: The Modern Idiom* (Cambridge: Harvard Univ. Press, 1981). Robert Weisbuch has defended her habit of privacy in *Emily Dickinson's Poetry* (Chicago: Univ. of Chicago Press, 1975). More recently, Christopher E. G. Benfey has discussed the issue of privacy and secrecy as a longing for invisibility in *Emily Dickinson and the Problem of Others* (Amherst: Univ. of Massachusetts Press, 1984).

[4] "'Disintegration of the Will': Nietzsche on the Individual and Individuality," in *Reconstructing Individualism: Autonomy, Individuality, and the Self in West-*

ern Thought, ed. Thomas C. Heller et al. (Stanford: Stanford Univ. Press, 1986), p. 110.

[5] For more on Nietzsche, the self, and contingency, see Richard Rorty, "The Contingency of Self," *London Review of Books*, 8 (8 May 1986), 11-15.

[6] I am indebted here to the arguments of Leo Bersani in *The Freudian Body: Psychoanalysis and Art* (New York: Columbia Univ. Press, 1986), pp. 82-83.

[7] I rely here on Andrew Welsh's discussion of riddle in *Roots of Lyric: Primitive Poetry and Modern Poetics* (Princeton: Princeton Univ. Press, 1978), p. 30.

[8] "'A Loaded Gun': Dickinson and the Dialectic of Rage," *PMLA*, 93 (1978), 431.

[9] *Dickinson: The Anxiety of Gender* (Ithaca: Cornell Univ. Press, 1984), pp. 18-19.

[10] "Vesuvius at Home: The Power of Emily Dickinson," in *On Lies, Secrets, and Silence: Selected Prose 1966—1978* (New York: Norton, 1979), p. 169. Rich gives this much repeated reading its most palatable form because she does understand that for Dickinson there is no split between masculine creativity and feminine receptivity. Other feminists have taken up the split that Rich identifies and then denies and have made much of it. See Diehl, pp. 19-20.

[11] I am indebted here to Gilles Deleuze's discussion of repetition in *Différence et Répétition* (Paris: Presses Universitaires de France, 1968), pp. 96-168.

Karen Oakes (Kilcup) (essay date 1988)

SOURCE: "Welcome and Beware: The Reader and Emily Dickinson's Figurative Language," in *ESQ*, Vol. 34, No. 3, 1988, pp. 181-206.

[*In the following essay, Oakes argues that Dickinson uses metonymy to develop a "culturally feminine" discursive intimacy with her readers.*]

"Much Madness is divinest Sense—/ To a discerning Eye," affirms Emily Dickinson: how one "reads" depends on the quality of the reader's lens, the "I." Dickinson muses often, directly and indirectly, about reading. Poetry stuns with **"Bolts of Melody"**; from **"A Word dropped careless on a Page,"** the reader may "inhale" "Infection," "Despair," "Malaria."[1] To Higginson, she insists, "If I read a book [and] it makes my whole body so cold no fire ever can warm me I know *that* is poetry. If I feel physically as if the top of my head were taken off, I know *that* is poetry. These are the only way I know it. Is there any other way" (Letter 342a). But how does poetry engage or threaten a reader? What or who is Dickinson's reader?

I will argue that the poet's vivid sense of participation in the reading process, based in her feminine psychology, informs how she imagines her strongest relationship with her own reader. Specifically, I will argue that Dickinson uses metonymy, and, in particular, the implied or stated "you," to seek a culturally feminine (that is, not merely female) discourse which establishes or presumes a process of intimacy with a reader.[2] Her attitude toward this intimacy ranges from anxiety and hostility to hospitality. As a preliminary, I will outline Dickinson's version of the poet-reader drama and compare it to some contemporary perspectives on reading; then I will discuss those poems which imagine a masculine reader; finally, I will engage poems that, because they invite and require of the reader a role beyond interpreter, test more vividly and kinetically the balance of intimacy between a feminine self and other.

Feminist psychological theory suggests that the feminine self is more fluid than the autonomous, individuated masculine self. Nancy Chodorow argues that the "basic feminine sense of self is connected to the world, the basic masculine sense of self is separate," and that "feminine personality comes to include a fundamental definition of self in relationship." Jean Baker Miller observes that "for many women the threat of disruption of an affiliation is perceived not as just a loss of a relationship but as something closer to a total loss of self." Finally, Carol Gilligan emphasizes that "The conflict between self and other . . . constitutes the central moral problem for women, posing a dilemma whose resolution requires a reconciliation between femininity and adulthood." In a culture which defines adulthood as independence and care of the self—that is, in masculine terms—and femininity as connection with and care of others, the adult female faces chronic conflict and loss of authenticity.[3]

Dickinson enacts this conflict in all aspects of her life. Cynthia Griffin Wolff describes the poet's fears of losing Austin and Lavinia in terms that echo Miller and Gilligan: "'Childhood' was that time when the three Dickinson children had all been together and Emily had experienced the deep, intuitive understanding that her nature craved; 'adulthood' entailed the possibility of prolonged, perhaps permanent loneliness—and it was a threat not merely to her happiness, but to the integrity of her very self." Wolff concludes, "Emily Dickinson consistently construed separation as a kind of 'death'—death of the beloved friend or disintegration of her own sense of coherent identity." Often requiring separation from beloved others, "adulthood" remained at best an ambivalent goal.[4]

Being a poet exacerbates this dilemma of femininity. As Lionel Trilling describes "normal" artist-audience relations in *Sincerity and Authenticity,* over the past two centuries the writer has increasingly come to define himself as privileged, autonomous and even hostile to his audience. Similarly, Sandra Gilbert and Susan Gubar emphasize the poet's essential separateness: "the poet, even when writing in the third person, says 'I.'" At best, these concepts of the poet suggest his remoteness or detachment from the reader.[5] Trilling, in particular, suggests the psychologically masculine, hierarchical terms in which the poet perceives his reader, for if he conceives himself as unitary and independent, then readers, while necessary for fulfillment of the poetic project, seem invasive, even inimical.

Does Dickinson's story of reading reflect the potential indifference or hostility of masculine writers, or her own predilections as a feminine reader? Discussing the reading process in ways which elucidate the poet's experience, Judith Kegan Gardiner and Patrocinio Schweickart argue that women read with more involvement than men; both suggest that for feminine selves, reading involves process, temporality. Gardiner emphasizes the proximity and interaction between women writers, women characters, and women readers: "The implied relationship between the self and what one reads and writes is personal and intense."[6] Schweickart extends Gardiner's observation, proposing that the female reader and writer share a "dialogic" relationship, noteworthy as an "intersubjective encounter." "The reader encounters not simply a text, but a 'subjectified object': the 'heart and mind' of another woman. She comes into close contact with an interiority—a power, a creativity, a suffering, a vision—that is *not* identical with her own."[7] In terms which echo Gilligan's conflict between (normative, masculine) adulthood and femininity, Schweickart argues that the dilemma for feminine writer and reader is balancing the claims of other and self, "of managing the contradictory implications of the desire for relationship (one must maintain a minimal distance from the other) and the desire for intimacy," up to and including a symbiotic merger with the other (p. 55).

Dickinson's work explores and underscores the difficulties of achieving this balance. For several reasons, metonymy offers an appropriate means by which to engage the poems. First, as a figure of proximity and linking, connection with the other, metonymy offers a cultural and psychological metaphor for the feminine.[8] Second, it involves the "you," and while the mere presence of "you" in a poem does not suggest a rapprochement with the reader (nor does its absence signal our exclusion), focus on the second person provides a potential means of access to the reader.[9] Third, linked with narrative and chronology, metonymy emphasizes process, which Gardiner and Schweickart identify as a feminine concern and which the idea of reading as interactive suggests.[10] The intensity and immediacy which the second person enhances often intrigues Dickinson, who suggests the idea of poetic "experience"—knowing rather than knowledge—in her comments to Higginson. Finally, metonymy occupies the feminine position in poetry, for as Jakobson points out, interpreters have consistently devalued it in contrast to metaphor, assigning it "prosaic" status, in part because of the shared metalinguistic function of metaphor and interpretation.[11]

In two essays which investigate how Dickinson uses metonymy, Margaret Homans explores not only the hierarchy in metaphor's dominance of poetry, but that within the figure itself. In the first, she cites French feminist critic Luce Irigaray, underlining metaphor's concern with power relationships: "one term claims the authority to define the other term—or, in its implications for the personal, one person claims the authority to define another person."[12] Homans parallels the hierarchy of metaphor to the romantic coupling of male and female; and while she investigates metonymy in Dickinson as the figure for relationships among equals—women—she argues that the poet rejects as "stasis" the proximity and connection which this figure comprehends. In this first essay, Homans regards metonymy more as figure and less as gesture toward the reader.

In her more recent study, Homans shows the potential of metonymy to undermine metaphor's hierarchy. Using the same theoretical framework, she suggests that metaphor is the figure of choice for the male subject pursuing and desiring the unavailable or distant female object within a masculine sexual economy founded in specular self-definition. Because female sexuality is "invisible," it defies representation by a (metaphoric) figurative structure based on resemblance, or "looking" ("'Syllables,'" pp. 570ff.). Homans argues that Dickinson substitutes for this economy a feminine perspective which values a nonhierarchical "pleasure" over appropriative "desire," and "a female sexuality (privileging touch) that is also a female textuality (privileging metonymy)" over a visual, metaphoric male sexuality/textuality (pp. 580, 579). This substitution is a happy one: "in a relation that lacks the distinction between subject and object and that therefore lacks the motive for metaphor, the motive for desire, the painful plot of desire is replaced by a plotless and joyous intersubjectivity" (p. 583).

Although she does not focus directly on the "you," Homans speaks most to the present study when she turns her attention to reader relations. In discussing one poem **(Poem 334),** Homans argues that in the "undecidability of the referentiality" offered by metonymy, Dickinson emphasizes the reader's equal importance in lyric: "Reading is equivalent to writing or speaking, and these communciations are equivalent to sexual communion . . ." (p. 584). Furthermore, the poem's interchangeable pronoun references underline how "speaker and reader have become interchangeable (as interchangeable as sexual partners, especially of the same sex) . . ." (pp. 584-585). The poem empowers the reader by refusing to be referential, metaphorical—by refusing to subordinate ground to figure. Three aspects of Homans' argument seem useful here: her emphasis on Dickinson's indeterminacy, which she suggests emphasizes the reader's role in the production of meaning; her notion of sexual intimacy with the reader; and her description of reading as a process rather than a search for a product.[13]

In extending Homans' argument, we need to examine in more detail the nature and effects of this intimacy and Dickinson's attitude toward it. To what degree does she perform or rewrite the masculine concept of the poet as autonomous, distinct from the reader, and hence potentially threatened by that reader? How does the implied gender of the reader affect the poet-reader relationship? What are the consequences when a poet imagines herself and her reader as essentially feminine? Metonymy is not necessarily non-hierarchical and feminine, linking self and other on equal terms in what Homans calls "a plotless and joyous intersubjectivity" (p. 583); rather, Dickinson's feminine discourse dramatizes a dialogical tension between self and other, "I" and "you." From one perspective in particular, Dickinson suggests the potential violence inherent in the coupling of reader and poem, perhaps because that joining may echo the romantic, masculine sexual economy which Homans describes. In this version of Dickinson's drama, the masculine reader desires the poet.

I

Dickinson and the Masculine Reader

In her comments to Higginson about reading, Dickinson emphasizes her visceral involvement and personal danger; nevertheless, poetry compels by virtue of its power and immediacy. Cognitive engagement alone does not satisfy her, but affective engagement must parallel or even supercede it.[14] Physical, transformative, mimicking death, reading becomes interactive, even sexual, according with Homans' view of the sexual and kinetic aspect of reading and writing. In **Poem 1247,** Dickinson makes the link between poetry, love, and death more explicit:

To pile like Thunder to it's close
Then crumble grand away
While Everything created hid
This—would be Poetry—

Or Love—the two coeval come—
We both and neither prove—
Experience either and consume—
For None see God and live—

Emphatically kinetic, the reading process, figured by the verb "Experience," which suggests a kind of "knowing," offers a dramatic and climactic sexual coupling of reader and poet, of reader and poem. What kind of "Love" does she envision? If she imagines the reader as masculine, that is, as autonomous, remote, and hence potentially judgmental, Dickinson approaches him in at least three ways: first, detached, objective, and noncommittal; second, childlike, and hence sexually and romantically unavailable; and third, adversarial and preemptive.

Intercourse or dialogue is difficult to achieve with a certain kind of reader. In a poem about a bird singing **(Poem 526),** Dickinson's prototypical metaphor for poetry, she emphasizes the disparity between speaker and reader. The poem begins:

To hear an Oriole sing
May be a common thing—
Or only a divine.

It is not of the Bird
Who sings the same, unheard,
As unto Crowd—

The Fashion of the Ear
Attireth that it hear
In Dun, or fair—

So whether it be Rune
Or whether it be none
Is of within.

Whether they regard the song as "Dun" or "fair," "common" or "divine," its auditors "fashion" it as much as its singer does. Associated with femininity, "Fashion" suggests the ephemeral nature of interpretation, perhaps reassuring the singer that recognition or oblivion depends not solely on merit. But Dickinson has in mind a particular kind of interpreter:

The "Tune is in the Tree—"
The Skeptic—showeth me—
"No Sir! In Thee!"

She portrays the listener as a specifically male "Skeptic"; and she gestures toward her comment to Higginson that "All men say 'What' to me, but I thought it a fashion—" (Letter 271). As much a gender term as a generic one, "men" seem to be the primary readers in this scene; she knows that "Sir," as embodied by Dickinson's "Preceptor," hears certain voices with neither perceptiveness nor originality. Yet the terms of her criticism suggest that she attacks cultural gender identity rather than biological gender. Intersubjectivity, and sometimes even communication, are problematic, in part because of the masculine reader's perspective of detachment, polarity, and judgment, which she underlines in her specious "conversation" with the "Skeptic."

The speaker's stance here answers her reader's: apparently "objective," analytical, non-narrative, and metaphoric, with the "Oriole" representing a poet. But if the bird's song figures poetry, it represents an incomplete version of the poet, signaling only a part of the whole bird whom the masculine listener erases. Similarly, Dickinson embeds metonymy in the striking image, "Fashion of the Ear," which reduces the interpreter to a mere physical organ, suggesting the limitation of his apprehension, a limitation she underlines with the irony of "only a divine." Detaching and distinguishing herself from him while she echoes his voice, she addresses the poem's "you" to him, only indirectly, at the end.

If the workings of this interpreter appear mysterious, concealed, "of within," they also appear potentially hostile, transforming at whim an initially value-free song into ho-hum dailiness or transcendent meaning. Dickinson envisions a similarly vulnerable but more childlike speaker in **Poem 441:**

This is my letter to the World
That never wrote to Me—
The simple News that Nature told—
With tender Majesty

Her Message is committed
To Hands I cannot see—
For love of Her—Sweet—countrymen—
Judge tenderly—of Me

In spite of its stick-out-the-tongue opening lines, what strikes me most forcibly is the speaker's sense of remoteness from her readers, whom she reduces, metonymically, to "Hands," capable of applauding or tearing apart, caressing or spanking. As in "**To hear an Oriole sing**," the workings of the reader are invisible; as in that poem, she assigns to the reader the role of remote, hence masculine "Judge," not participant. Given his detachment, the speaker hesitates to attribute her words to herself; instead, she is the purveyor of Nature's "Message," just as in **Poem 526,** she becomes an "Oriole." These speakers imagine readers capable of harm who necessitate her withdrawal or concealment, even though the notion of poem as "Letter" suggests, if not an intimate relationship with the reader, at least one with prior boundaries, context, and history.[15]

Dickinson's "real" letters were an important resource of proximity, capable of healing broken connection, and (as we shall see later in more detail) equally capable of the kind of excess rhetoricity and distance that we normally associate with poems. In **Poem 441,** she foresees and tries to fend off potential hostility from an adversarial other, while she expresses it covertly in the sulky, defiant first stanza. Metonymy, specifically the "you" implied in the "countrymen," underlines the distance between speaker and reader. The end of this pseudo-letter parodies the intimacy of real letters, for the vulnerable and receding inscriber addresses it to "Occupant": "Sweet—countrymen."

In **Poem 416,** which suggests a similar childlike perspective, Dickinson enacts the conflict between femininity and adulthood. It opens with an apparently contextless narration:

A Murmur in the Trees—to note—
Not loud enough—for Wind—
A Star—not far enough to seek—
Nor near enough—to find—

A long—long Yellow—on the Lawn—
A Hubbub—as of feet—
Not audible—as Our's—to Us—
But dapperer—More Sweet—

A Hurrying Home of little Men
To Houses unperceived—

As if writing a letter to a familiar other, the speaker begins with the recreation of a shared scene—we know what "Trees" and "Lawn" she's talking about—and she invites the reader/listener to recall an imaginative perspective capable of "recognizing" the unspecified "Murmur," the "Star," and the "long Yellow." The conflation of "you" and "I" into "Our's" suggests their metonymic connectedness; interestingly, the terms of perception are those of "**To hear an Oriole sing**," for speaker and reader share less a way of seeing than a way of hearing. What they hear is somehow secret or private, for their object is the childlike world of elves or dolls, "little Men."

Her recollection of the phallic and ostensibly metaphoric "little Men," however, seems to inspire withdrawal, and she underscores the disparity of imagination between herself and her auditor:

All this—and more—if I should tell—
Would never be believed—

Of Robins in the Trundle bed
How many I espy
Whose Nightgowns could not hide the
  Wings—
Although I heard them try—

But then I promised ne'er to tell—
How could I break My Word?
So go your Way—and I'll go Mine—
No fear you'll miss the Road.

The speaker detaches herself from the shared perspective of "Our's" and emphasizes her own "childish" vision and speech: the comic, even ridiculous figure of "Nightgown[ed]" "Robins in the Trundle bed" will "never be believed" by the "you" the speaker imagines in the last stanza. Imagining that we fail because we evade full participation in the role of playmate which she invokes at the beginning, the speaker dramatizes her separation from the reader with the ironic last line, in which "the Road" suggests a narrow and unimaginative "adult" perspective.

The obverse of this failure is our exclusion—the speaker sets herself apart from her listener, whom she teasingly and ironically "tell[s]" and refuses to tell. If we wonder to whom she has given her "Word" to be silent, then we become the outsider whom she imagines; at the same time, she gives us her "Word," in the form of the poem itself. Telling and not telling, invoking metonymic proximity and metaphoric distance, she underlines her ambivalence about relationships which involve secrets and intimacy. Withdrawing into the world of children, where potent adults can be reduced to "little Men," she screens herself from invasion by a foreign consciousness. She throws the judgmental deaf adult, the masculine reader, out of her dollhouse.

Dickinson rehearses the theme of intimacy again in a poem which indicates more shockingly her attitude toward the masculine reader. **Poem 577** begins:

> If I may have it, when it's dead,
> I'll be contented—so—
> If just as soon as Breath is out
> It shall belong to me—
>
> Until they lock it in the Grave,
> 'Tis Bliss I cannot weigh—
> For tho' they lock Thee in the Grave,
> Myself—can own the key—
>
> Think of it Lover! I and Thee
> Permitted—face to face to be—
> After a Life—a Death—We'll say—
> For Death was That—
> And This—is Thee—

Enticing us with its quiet informality, the speaker's proleptic perspective evinces a peculiar combination of courtesy and shocking casualness about her lover's dead body. Her desire for the corpse appears particularly macabre and demented in relation to her lucid, courteous language; parodying elegiac convention and the nineteenth-century female's pre-occupation with death, this speaker expresses not a lament for death but her "contented" state, her "Bliss."[16] By beginning in an elliptical manner, she assumes that we are familiar with her context and situation; with her confidential tone addressed to "Thee" and with the imperative, Dickinson assumes the most personal of relationships, internal to the poem, between the "I" and the "you," who is eventually defined as a "Lover." By withholding his identity, she entices us to become the "Lover," the poem's intimate other.[17]

In the next stanza she concedes that "our" death has given her pain, and she goes on to confess that pain gives way to numbness and to a kind of sign-language that seems to recover the relationship after the death of both lovers:

> Then how the Grief got sleepy—some—
> As if my Soul were deaf and dumb—
> Just making signs—across—to Thee—
> That this way—thou could'st notice me—
>
> I'll tell you how I tried to keep
> A smile, to show you, when this Deep
> All Waded—We look back for Play,
> At those Old Times—in Calvary.

"Play" reminds us of the childish speakers in the two previous poems, and it suggests the possibility of shared delight. Homans claims that the post-mortem realm offers a non-hierarchical because non-verbal context for relationship.[18] But Dickinson transforms the game into a very serious sexual drama in which the masculine lover/reader must silence his desire for her and become the object of her desire, because the narrator has assumed his traditional power as speaking subject:

> Forgive me, if the Grave come slow—
> For Coveting to look at Thee—
> Forgive me, if to stroke thy frost
> Outvisions Paradise!

Although in the penultimate stanza the speaker imagines her own death, she ultimately refuses to relinquish her vision of the lover, making the reader-lover the poem's victim, placing him uncompromisingly in the position of the silent corpse. Such a relationship, however "intimate," is unequal and dangerous.[19] If the imagination of loss enables the speaker to construct an Edenic future for herself, it is based on the lover-reader's exclusion: she prefers "strok[ing] thy frost," caressing him verbally, to "Paradise." The speaker's "Play" is not mere playfulness with the "Lover," but a veiled drama of murder and detachment from him. We learn from this speaker that reading as a masculine, desiring other can result in death.[20]

II

The Lover and the Sororal Drama

Does Dickinson view "Love" as necessarily destructive, aimed with sinister intention at a hapless victim? The answer rests in part on how she conceives the reader; "intimacy" assumes many forms, for she attracts, frustrates, and endangers a participant, affective reader whom she imagines as feminine.[21] These dramas share a concern for self-preservation and for dialogue, and they locate meaning less in the residue of ideas with which we conclude a reading, in the script, and more in the performer and performance. A portion of an early letter to her friend Sue Gilbert illuminates the complexity of close personal relationships for the poet, as she regards and enacts both romantic and sororal connections:

> Those unions, my dear Susie, by which two lives are one, this sweet and strange adoption wherein we can but look, and are not yet admitted, how it can fill the heart, and make it gang wildly beating, how it will take *us* one day, and make us all it's own, and we shall not run from it, but lie still and be happy! (Letter 93)

Dickinson's attitude toward the romantic relationship of husband and wife emerges vividly in her images: the lover-husband simultaneously attracts and repels, inspires awe and fear. The tension between excitement and fear culminates in her ambiguous assertion that "we shall . . . lie still and be happy!"

As striking as the subject matter of the letter is its style, for it makes a gesture toward the reader which exceeds the demands of a private and anxious letter about marriage—it has an excess rhetoricity which reaches beyond the boundaries of the particular situation.[22] Although Dickinson's letter addresses a friend to whom she may (presumably) say almost anything, her language is curiously restrained and artificial. At the same time, the structure and movement of this paragraph, as well as its conjunctive style and address to the intimate "you," invite the reader's participation in a reenactment of the process she describes. The climactic moment in this process occurs when we perceive the "[heart] gang wildly beating." With its association of blood and passion, this synecdoche intimates the fearful and exciting sexuality of "[t]hose unions," which the rhythm of the paragraph mimics, as she encloses each phrase with commas. She invites the reader to become equally "possessed," an invitation which suggests her ambivalence about the "you."

The second section of the letter performs a similar process of increasing involvement and intensity:

> You and I have been strangely silent upon this subject, Susie, we have often touched upon it, and as quickly fled away, as children shut their eyes when the sun is too bright for them. . . . How dull our lives must seem to the bride, and the plighted maiden, whose days are fed with gold, and who gathers pearls every evening; but to the *wife,* Susie, sometimes the *wife forgotten,* our lives perhaps seem dearer than all others in the world; you have seen flowers at morning, *satisfied* with the dew, and those same sweet flowers at noon with their heads bowed in anguish before the mighty sun; think you these thirsty blossoms will *now* need naught but—*dew?* No, they will cry for sunlight, and pine for the burning noon, tho' it scorches them, scathes them; they have got through with peace—they know that the man of noon, is *mightier* than the morning and their life is henceforth to him. Oh, Susie, it is dangerous, and it is all to dear, these simple trusting spirits, and the spirits mightier, which we cannot resist! It does so rend me, Susie, the thought of it when it comes, that I tremble lest at sometime I, too, am yielded up.

Although the experience centers on a metaphor, the striking "man of noon," Dickinson uses metonymy both to detach herself and Susan and to participate vicariously in the risk and excitement which such a relationship entails. Removing herself and her friend from the hierarchical social realm, describing "their" "lives" as distinct from "our lives," the poet reenacts the appropriation of the feminine other, stylistically as well as semantically. The wavelike, sexual tension of the passage gathers, as she accretes image after image, separated by semicolons, and it climaxes with the rhetorical question—will *"dew"* now suffice for these "blossoms"—whose only possible response is "No."

If the poet eludes the appropriative masculine figure, however, the reader's role is far less certain. With Susan, we may only partially share the safe space she creates for herself with the "you," because the letter works not merely as message but also as process; in its rhythms and pauses, its emphases, it recreates (or we recreate as we read), even on a physiological level, the self-erasure which is its subject. In our own way, we too are "yielded up," and relief arrives only with the poet's retrospective and ironic comment on her extravagance (and her freedom): "Susie, you will forgive me my amatory strain—it has been a very long one, and if this saucy page did not here bind and fetter me, I might have had no end." This remark foregrounds her "artificial" relationship to her audience, both contemporary and present. Dickinson makes demands upon her reader, exploring not only social connections but also conventions of written intercourse. This letter illustrates Dickinson's ambivalent, feminine concern with relationship, and it provides us with an example of the reader as intimate feminine other. The poet offers us, with Susan, the chance to rehearse being "yielded up"—not merely to the "man of noon" but also to the rhetorical cavern of the poet's metonymy.

Many of Dickinson's other poems include a gesture to the "you" imagined as a permutation of a feminine other, involving the reader not as a "Skeptic," "Judge," or even "Lover," but as a playmate, friend, and intimate. Like the speakers of **Poem 441** and **Poem 416,** the speaker of **Poem 288** assumes the role of a child.

This poem, however, even more explicitly scripts an interaction between reader and speaker, underlining the process of reading.

> I'm Nobody! Who are you?
> Are you—Nobody—too?
> Then there's a pair of us!
> Dont tell! they'd banish us—you know!
>
> How dreary—to be—Somebody!
> How public—like a Frog—
> To tell your name—the livelong June—
> To an admiring Bog!

The speaker invites our participation by asking questions, by defining us as her equal; the only person capable of hearing her or of being hospitable to her is another "Nobody." To be a "Nobody" is to be at once an individual, different from the crowd, the "Bog," and in some respects banished as outsider and Other, but also to have a subversive private dialogue with those able to share the joke. Like Odysseus in the Cyclops' cave, the narrator at once proclaims her name and triumphantly recedes behind it. Unlike him, she shares her triumph with her auditor.

The potential publicity of being "Somebody" carries a specifically sexual threat. In the cycle of seasons, the "Frog" announces himself in order to find a mate; here, ironically, the speaker finds a "mate," the other member of a "pair," in the reader, but they share an unavailability to the sexual egress of the fairytale frog-prince, whom the speaker fends off with her childlike persona ("Dont tell!" she urges). To participate, we must become playmates engaged in intercourse. The metonymy of the "you," aimed at the reader, overcomes the metaphoric, romantic economy of the larger world of the "Bog." Homans' observation that the interaction between the speaker and reader occurs most efficiently between members of the same sex seems accurate here; however, the relationship Dickinson depicts is relentlessly pre-sexual, recalling once again Gilligan's argument that in the feminine self, desire for relationship clashes with an adult self-definition. The poet's feminine discourse insists that the reader-other in the poem must choose between two roles, that of "public" masculine frog or "private" feminine playmate. While emphasizing the process of relationship, Dickinson resolves her conflict by refusing adult sexuality.

In **Poem 188,** the auditor is a friend with a different role:

> Make me a picture of the sun—
> So I can hang it in my room—
> And make believe I'm getting warm
> When others call it "Day"!

Apparently genderless, the vulnerable speaker recalls Gilligan's definition of women's dilemma in choosing between femininity and adulthood; this observation suggests that there is a sense in which all child-voices are feminine. Less with command than with request or plea, this speaker attracts us, though she does not welcome us, into her domain. The auditor seems to have some privilege, for she has had experience, if not contact, with the "sun," the center of the world outside of the speaker's "room"; at the same time, she shares the knowledge of the speaker's desires and fears. The sun's value is problematic, for though the narrator desires it, its image alone fails to keep her "warm," and she will have to "make believe," to play a game. Like children playing with fingerpaints, the speaker asks her friend to recreate (at a safe distance, in the haven of her room/womb) the adult world of the sun, the desirable and fearful "man of noon." She questions his image's ability to "warm" her: to sustain her and, perhaps, to excite her sexually. In contrast, "others" excluded from this privileged pairing seem deluded by such representations—or they may partake of a kind of freedom, outside the narrator's confinement.

Her relationship to her auditor-reader is troubled, for she simultaneously invites and distances, asks for help and insists on her separation. Stanza two reenacts a similar conflict between closeness and distance, freedom and circumscription:

> Draw me a Robin—on a stem—
> So I am hearing him, I'll dream,
> And when the Orchards stop their tune—
> Put my pretense—away—

Like the picture of the sun, the representation of the "Robin" enables a moment of "pretense," of dubious "make believe," but this moment cannot adequately replace reality, concrete presence. Like Dickinson speaking to Susan, the narrator intimates her frightful desire for the world outside. Claiming to be a listener rather than a singer, the speaker ironically performs a process of reaching out, of trying to communicate without the screen of language; the sun and robin become a backdrop in the mime show between speaker, listener, and the absent-but-present "man of noon."

In the final stanza, the speaker asks not for a depiction, but for a verbal, perhaps even specifically oral representation of the "outside":

> Say if it's really—warm at noon—
> Whether it's Buttercups—that "skim"—
> Or Butterflies—that "bloom"?
> Then—skip—the frost—upon the lea—
> And skip the Russet—on the tree—
> Let's play those—never come!

"*Say* if it's *really*—warm at *noon,*" she insists (my italics). Her self-imposed distance from the outside world of "others" and of adulthood engenders confusion, and the listener shares this confusion; language in a vacuum becomes transposed, as "Buttercups" "skim" and "Butterflies" "bloom." The last stanza suggests not an exclamation but a plea for help. Because we can have no ready answers, her final gesture is one of doubt. She underlines our role as playmate, but this connection is a subtly desperate one, for she frustrates our ability to change the terms of her perception of the world. Confronted by her request to outline the realities of noon—which must include a depiction of the adult woman's "confinement," especially when pregnant or "creative"—the feminine reader must be mute, choosing instead to share with her the child's confusion, her uncertainty about language and the drama it clothes, and her own circumscription. The poet's performance in the "man of noon" letter, with its enactment of desire (and its pleasure and confinement) and detachment (and its freedom and loss) echoes the conflict and ambivalence here. In both instances, we should not be surprised that she prefers the child's domain.

At its most extreme, the metonymic "you" does even more than gesture toward the poem as process, for it effectively prevents "meaning" as we ordinarily construe it. This process-oriented, anti-interpretive stance differs from that assumed by art which invites multiple interpretations, and it does not imply that her poems are hostile to the reader; rather, they are hospitable in the stringent demands they place upon us. A poem that Dickinson actually sent to Susan reveals the intensity and potential pain of the demands which a dialogical relationship between reader and speaker imposes:

He fumbles at your Soul
As Players at the Keys
Before they drop full Music on—
He stuns you by degrees—
Prepares your brittle Nature
For the Etherial Blow
By fainter Hammers—further heard—
Then nearer—Then so slow
Your Breath has time to straighten—
Your Brain—to bubble Cool—
Deals—One—imperial—Thunderbolt—
That scalps your naked Soul—

When Winds take Forests in their Paws—
The Universe—is still—

(Poem 315)

Line one introduces an unspecified masculine force. By not "identifying" him, however, the speaker in effect assumes that like Susan, her intimate other, we already "know" him. As Dickinson does in the "man of noon" letter, this speaker goes on to include us in a recreation of the protagonist's devastating violence, but here we are even more the object of this violence. If we choose to perceive the poem as an artifact, and to identify our task as providing a coherent and detached "interpretation," we falsify the very concrete and painful *process*—apparent particularly in line eleven, with its explosive dashes—in which we participate as we read; we normalize the poem's most troubling and most original quality.

This sense of poetry's danger and pain, a constant theme of Dickinson's, emerges vividly and concretely for the reader in an even less "accessible" poem which appears to enact the culturally-excluded experience of madness:[23]

'Twas like a Maelstrom, with a notch,
That nearer, every Day,
Kept narrowing it's boiling Wheel
Until the Agony

Toyed coolly with the final inch
Of your delirious Hem—
And you dropt, lost,
When something broke—
And let you from a Dream—

As if a Goblin with a Guage—
Kept measuring the Hours—
Until you felt your Second
Weigh, helpless, in his Paws—

And not a Sinew—stirred—could help,
And sense was setting numb—
When God—remembered—and the Fiend
Let go, then, Overcome—

As if your Sentence stood—pronounced—
And you were frozen led
From Dungeon's luxury of Doubt
To Gibbets, and the Dead—

And when the Film had stitched your eyes
A Creature gasped "Repreive"!
Which Anguish was the utterest—then—
To perish, or to live?

(Poem 414)

In **"'Twas like a Maelstrom,"** Dickinson recreates the intensity of her own reading experience—here, indeed, is a poem capable of making its auditor feel frozen or sweltering. She invites, even requires, our complicity for its comprehension, and both her subject and her rhetoric contribute to the drama. The subject, ostensibly an experience of pain verging on madness, is one she might recount only to the closest of friends; like a letter to an intimate other, the poem-drama assumes a previously-established context within which speech can occur. We begin in the middle of things with the auditor's implied question in a dialogue: "What was it like?" Not only does the speaker omit the tenor of the metaphor, she compresses even a reference to it: "'Twas."

Furthermore, her ellipsis, and in particular her refusal to ground the metaphor, destabilizes the referential duality of metaphor and hence thrusts the responsibility of "meaning" toward the "you." She frees the "Maelstrom" (male storm?) to become a multiple and more terrifying figure, as it announces only intensity and process. Similarly, though "Agony" is one obvious association we might make with the maelstrom and the "boiling Wheel," we can't say whether it is identical to either one, or whether it results from their activity. The narrator underlines the immediacy of reading in her use of the imperfect tense ("Kept narrowing," "Kept measuring"), of the adverbs "Until" and "When," and of the narrative, conjunctive, metonymic "And."[24] As the poem proceeds, our inability to synthesize, to abstract meaning and to "pronounce" a "Sentence"—to judge the poem—becomes even more painfully apparent.[25]

The poem resists an interpretation which gives it an extractable meaning because from a metonymic perspective, it doesn't "develop," it only includes, signaling pure context; and its principle of "coherence" is the intimate, troubling speaker-audience connection. Focusing on minutiae such as "with a notch" and "the final inch," it challenges our ability to synthesize them into a system of metaphor initiated by the "Maelstrom." Parodying "development," the speaker's language, not her status, is all that changes. Frustrating our desire to judge, to distance ourselves from the drama, the poem couples with us, but refuses to let us go, performing a frustrating and painful process of meaning. As with so many Dickinson poems, the ending suggests a brief sigh, an expiration of breath preceding an inevitable return to beginning again.[26]

Confronting the tendency to detach ourselves from the poetic experience, to define ourselves as "objective" outsiders, Dickinson also attempts to disable the artist's assumptions about a reader's role which may provoke this posture: that is, she transforms the traditionally feminine, passive, and inferior role which Trilling's masculine artist characteristically assigns to the reader. Refusing to regard us as inferior "others," she imagines an equality which enables and encourages the play of our imagination in the recreation of a poem-as-process.[27] Readers' active role in the recreation of the poem endangers their self-integration and autonomy, for, no longer detached, judgmental, we may suffer and we may partake of the irrational. Dickinson echoes and enacts this danger in her own role as reader-victim. Feminine discourse—speech which invites and engages the other on equal terms—remains a balancing act for the feminine poet, who fears obliteration while she seeks interaction and closeness. "'**Twas like a Maelstrom**" expresses the poet's ambivalence because it welcomes and cautions the reader: it welcomes us to share an important experience; it urges us to beware the consequences of that sharing. Finally, it enacts the potential loss of selfhood which ensues for the feminine speaker if the other either comes too close or disappears, as it treads the margin between fear and need.

Intercourse with a reader, masculine or feminine, troubles and excites Dickinson. A letter to Dr. and Mrs. Holland expresses her dilemma clearly. Telling them a story of herself and a bird she has seen outside her window, she affirms, "*My* business is to love. . . . '*My* business is to *sing*'" (Letter 269). Sometimes she evades the conflict between the traditional poetic self and femininity, becoming a child instead of an invaded adult female; sometimes she parodies the language of desire; sometimes she invites intimacy, imagining her listener as friend or confidante. Whatever perspective she chooses to assume, Dickinson imagines the reader-speaker relationship less often as Homans' "plotless and joyous intersubjectivity" and more often as a drama of complex and conflicting emotions whose climax is uncertain at best and potentially destructive at worst: "for none see God and live."

If we risk self-obliteration, Dickinson's feminine discourse offers a potential compensation: we enter the poem as creators, assigning a "meaning" which is located in a shared experience. The "loss" of selfhood entailed by this discourse affirms a kind of "transcendence."[28] The poet accomplishes this affirmation, not by enabling us to "get outside of" or to "escape" a self conceived of as autonomous and separate—to enter a "higher" and more "spiritual" realm—but, rather, by encouraging us to engage in the feminine process of expanding the boundaries of the self, of empathizing, of participating in Otherness. Dickinson explored this domain by writing her original and dangerous poems, and she invites us, with many cautions, to join her.

Notes

[1] Dickinson's poems are identified according to the numbering in *The Poems of Emily Dickinson,* ed. Thomas H. Johnson, 3 vols. (Cambridge: Belknap of Harvard Univ. Press, 1955), here poems 435, 505, 1261; her letters are cited according to the numbering in *The Letters of Emily Dickinson,* ed. Thomas H. Johnson and Theodora Ward, 3 vols. (Cambridge: Belknap of Harvard Univ. Press, 1958).

[2] For a definition of metonymy, see C. Carroll Hollis, *Language and Style in "Leaves of Grass"* (Baton Rouge: Louisiana State Univ. Press, 1983), pp. 158, 177-178, 184, 189. I do not think that Dickinson's

"you" is limited to a specific, literal "lover," the addressee of the "Master Letters." Nevertheless, in trying to specify the "you" in this way, William Shurr underlines what I call the characteristically intimate tone of the poems; *The Marriage of Emily Dickinson* (Lexington: Univ. of Kentucky Press, 1983), pp. 6ff., passim. On metonymy and intimacy, see Karen Kilcup Oakes, "Reading the Feminine: Gender Gestures in Poetic Voice," PhD. diss., Brandeis University, 1986. As implied by my claim of "intimacy," I imagine Dickinson's reader as singular (not collective). For a different view of audience, see Walter J. Ong, "The Writer's Audience is Always a Fiction," *PMLA*, 90 (1975), 9-21. Dickinson's "you" poems are not the only ones which encourage intimacy, but they highlight this connection; less explicit connections with the reader are the subject of another essay.

[3] Nancy Chodorow, *The Reproduction of Mothering: Psychoanalysis and the Sociology of Gender* (Berkeley: Univ. of California Press, 1978), p. 169; Jean Baker Miller, *Toward a New Psychology of Women* (Boston: Beacon, 1976), p. 83; Carol Gilligan, *In a Different Voice: Psychological Theory and Women's Development* (Cambridge: Harvard Univ. Press, 1982), pp. 70-71. Miller, Chodorow, and Gilligan emphasize the cultural foundations of their accounts of "feminine" and "masculine," and I would argue that these terms are not limited by the sex of the poet. Since the feminist psychologists' work focuses primarily if not exclusively on white, middle-class (and perhaps heterosexual) women, the interpretive theory which rests on such a foundation must be correspondingly limited.

[4] Cynthia Griffin Wolff, *Emily Dickinson* (New York: Knopf, 1986), p. 111. Wolff emphasizes Dickinson's search for "autonomy" (p. 127), as does Paula Bennett, who argues that the poet empowers her voice by ultimately rejecting her self-definition as child, choosing instead to be a self-authorized "bride," an adult woman who has the privilege without the sacrifice of marriage. Bennett's argument, which addresses itself to the work of Gilligan, Miller, and Chodorow, suggests a psychologically masculine construction of the poet and her development; Bennett, *My Life a Loaded Gun: Female Creativity and Feminist Poetics* (Boston: Beacon Press, 1986), pp. 81, 94, and passim.

[5] Lionel Trilling, *Sincerity and Authenticity* (Cambridge: Harvard Univ. Press, 1972), pp. 97-102; Sandra M. Gilbert and Susan Gubar, *The Madwoman in the Attic: The Woman Writer and the Nineteenth-Century Literary Imagination* (New Haven: Yale Univ. Press, 1979), pp. 548; 539-549, Chs. 1-2. See also Margaret Homans, *Women Writers and Poetic Identity: Dorothy Wordsworth, Emily Brontë, and Emily Dickinson* (Princeton: Princeton Univ. Press, 1980), Chs. 1-2; Sharon Cameron, *Lyric Time: Dickinson and the Limits of Genre* (Baltimore: Johns Hopkins Univ. Press, 1979), pp. 23, 54, 135, 205; T. S. Eliot, "The Three Voices of Poetry," *On Poetry and Poets* (London: Faber and Faber, 1957), pp. 89-102; David Bleich, "Gender Interests in Reading and Language," in *Gender and Reading: Essays on Readers, Texts, and Contexts*, ed. Elizabeth A. Flynn and Patrocinio P. Schweickart (Baltimore: Johns Hopkins Univ. Press, 1986), p. 262; Bennett, *My Life a Loaded Gun*, p. 3.

[6] Judith Kegan Gardiner, "On Female Identity and Writing by Women," in *Writing and Sexual Difference*, ed. Elizabeth Abel (Chicago: Univ. of Chicago Press, 1982), p. 185. Gardiner comments on the "processual" nature of female identity (pp. 179ff). The primary difficulty with Gardiner's theory is that it enforces sex, not gender difference; see Carolyn G. Heilbrun, "A Response to 'Writing and Sexual Difference,'" in *Writing and Sexual Difference*, pp. 295-296.

[7] Patrocinio Schweickart, "Reading Ourselves: Toward a Feminist Theory of Reading," in *Gender and Reading*, p. 52. Schweickart contrasts this interaction with male readers' concern with "control" (pp. 36-37).

[8] Homans, "'Oh Vision of Language!': Dickinson's Poems of Love and Death," in *Feminist Critics Read Emily Dickinson*, ed. Suzanne Juhasz (Bloomington: Indiana Univ. Press, 1983), pp. 121, 124; "'Syllables of Velvet': Dickinson, Rossetti, and the Rhetorics of Sexuality" *Feminist Studies*, 11 (1985), 579-580. Homans sees the cultural basis of "feminine" and "masculine."

[9] Hollis identifies the second person as metonymic (*Language and Style*, pp. 158, 164ff.). The degree of intimacy with the reader which a poetic speaker assumes depends upon how s/he defines both the "you" and the "I"; see Jonathan Culler, "Apostrophe," in *The Pursuit of Signs: Semiotics, Literature, Deconstruction* (Ithaca: Cornell Univ. Press, 1981), pp. 135-154.

[10] Gardiner, "On Female Identity," p. 179; Schweickart, "Reading Ourselves," pp. 45, 49, 51. Since feminine and masculine, metonymy and metaphor occupy a continuum, they may mesh or overlap.

Emile Benveniste suggests that while the third person refers to "an 'objective' situation," "you" resides solely in "a reality of discourse," and it "has no value except in the instance in which it is produced." In other words, the second person pronoun engenders immediacy and process. Benveniste, "The Nature of Pronouns," *Problems in General Linguistics*, trans. Mary Elizabeth Meek (Coral Gables: Univ. of Miami Press, 1971), pp. 221, 218. Interestingly, Benveniste points to the potential for the speaker's manipulation of the reader, his or her "appropriation." For an account of the relationship between narrative, chronology, and metonymy, see Roman Jakobson "Two Aspects of Language and Two Types of Aphasic Disturbances," *Selected Writings* (The Hague: Mouton, 1971), II, 254-259.

[11] On the relative privilege of metaphor, see Jakobson, *Selected Writings*, pp. 258-259; Jonathan Culler, "The Turns of Metaphor," in *Pursuit*, pp. 188-209; Culler, "Reading as a Woman," in *On Deconstruction: Theory and Criticism after Structuralism* (Ithaca: Cornell Univ. Press, 1982), 43-64; David Lodge, *The Modes of Modern Writing* (Ithaca: Cornell Univ. Press, 1977), 110-111, 118, 214; Gerard Genette, "Rhetoric Restrained" in *Figures of Literary Discourse*, trans. Alan Sheridan (New York: Columbia Univ. Press, 1982), pp. 103-126; Hollis, *Language and Style*, pp. 202-203; Hugh Bredin, "Metonymy," *Poetics Today*, 5 (1984), 45-58; Barbara Johnson, "Metaphor, Metonymy, and Voice in *Their Eyes Were Watching God*," in *A World of Difference* (Baltimore: Johns Hopkins Univ. Press, 1987), pp. 157-158. While many of these writers debate the definition of metonymy, I am concerned with its effects. I do, however, assume with Jakobson that synecdoche is a form of metonymy; *Selected Writings*, pp. 255ff.

[12] "'Oh Vision,'" p. 116. On Dickinson's metonymy, see also Cameron, *Lyric Time*, pp. 32-34; Agnieszka Salska, *Walt Whitman and Emily Dickinson: Poetry of the Central Consciousness* (Philadelphia: Univ. of Pennsylvania Press, 1985), p. 189. On the potential intimacy of metaphor, see Ted Cohen, "Metaphor and the Cultivation of Intimacy," in *On Metaphor*, ed. Sheldon Sacks (Chicago: Univ. of Chicago Press, 1979), pp. 1-10.

[13] Roland Hagenbüchle also emphasizes the role of metonymy in Dickinson's indeterminacy, while William Doreski emphasizes the poet's metaphoricity and the irrelevance of gender to her poetic project. Hagenbüchle, "Precision and Indeterminacy in the Poetry of Emily Dickinson," *ESQ: A Journal of the American Renaissance*, 20 (1974), 36, 47; Doreski, "'An Exchange of Territory': Dickinson's Fascicle 27," *ESQ: A Journal of the American Renaissance*, 32 (1986), 55-56.

[14] Schweickart, "Introduction" to *Gender and Reading*, ix-xii.

[15] Cameron, *Lyric Time*, p. 188. Although Cameron distinguishes between letters and poems, arguing that the former have a prior context and the latter create a context, I am arguing that many of Dickinson's poems conjure a context which suggests this priority.

[16] Dickinson's older contemporary, Lydia Sigourney, provides an interesting contrast; see Ann Douglas, *The Feminization of American Culture* (New York: Discus-Avon, 1977), p. 247.

[17] Dickinson's ellipsis is not an extraordinary gesture for love poetry; what distinguishes her work is its fairly constant ambivalence, her desire and rejection of desire; she not only inverts but deconstructs the architecture of desire as Homans describes it. See "'Syllables,'" pp. 571ff. See also Poems 461, 640, 663, 1072.

[18] "'Oh Vision,'" pp. 125-127. Bennett notes the connection between love and death in Dickinson, *My Life*, pp. 90-91.

[19] In suggesting her own superiority, the speaker subverts an important poetic convention which Ellen Moers identifies: "In women's love poetry, just as in men's, the convention holds that the beloved must be placed high above the lover, a divine or royal object on a superior plane"; Moers, *Literary Women: The Great Writers* (Garden City, NY: Doubleday, 1976), p. 169. Moers also notes that women more often write "I-You" poetry, while she implies that men write "I-She" poetry pp. 167-168).

[20] Poem 611 may represent a more positive view of the relationship after death or it may be another version of Poem 577.

[21] Although she does not address the issue of reader-speaker relations directly, Adelaide Morris argues that Dickinson uses the same language to speak to lovers of both genders, but that she refers to different structures of love: with males, love is defined by "difference and hierarchy" and with females, it is defined by "similarity and equality" and "reciprocity"; Morris, "'The Love of Thee—a Prism Be': Men and Women in the Love Poetry of Emily Dickinson," in Juhasz, ed. *Feminist Critics*, pp. 102, 103.

[22] See also Letters 31, 35, 45, 49, 173, 868—not to mention the "Master Letters."

[23] See also Poems 264, 281, 286, 410, 806. Clearly, I'm not saying that all poems which we cannot understand are good on the basis of the "emotion" they convey; but I am saying that some poems are "good" in ways that are difficult to understand from an analytical perspective.

[24] Hollis identifies "and" (parataxis) as a metonymic strategy (*Language and Style*, p. 159).

[25] Karl Keller points out that Dickinson uses oxymoron to foreground and to question the reading process; Keller, *The Only Kangaroo Among the Beauty: Emily Dickinson and America* (Baltimore: Johns Hopkins Univ. Press, 1979) pp. 129-130. Roy Harvey Pearce notes the creative role Dickinson demands of her reader;

Pearce, *The Continuity of American Poetry* (Princeton: Princeton Univ. Press, 1961), p. 175, n. 18.

[26] For the simultaneous closural and anti-closural effects of the concluding or rhetorical question, see Barbara Herrnstein Smith, *Poetic Closure: A Study of How Poems End* (Chicago: Univ. of Chicago Press, 1968), pp. 247-250; Paul de Man, *Allegories of Reading* (New Haven: Yale Univ. Press, 1979), pp. 9-13.

[27] Robert Langbaum suggests that this mode of response is characteristic of the dramatic monologue. The difference between Langbaum's account and mine is that ultimately his reader makes a judgment, while Dickinson's often cannot; Langbaum, *The Poetry of Experience* (New York: Random House, 1957), pp. 94, 104ff., 204ff.

[28] In contrast to Homans' Romantic transcendence; see *Women Writers,* p. 4.

Timothy Morris (essay date 1988)

SOURCE: "The Development of Dickinson's Style," in *On Dickinson: The Best from American Literature*, edited by Edwin H. Cady and Louis J. Budd, Duke University Press, Vol. 60, No. 1, 1990, pp. 157-72.

[*In the following essay, originally published in 1988, Morris contends that, contrary to the opinion of many critics, Dickinson's style did change and develop over time. Morris maintains that by measuring the rhyme and enjambment patterns of Dickinson's poetry, one can see that the "formal contours of her verse" evolved throughout her writing career.*]

It has become a given of Dickinson criticism that the poet's style never changed. A recent study begins: "As more than one critic has observed, Emily Dickinson's poetry reaches its maturity almost immediately. Beginning with the verse valentine of 1850 **(P-1),** she is in full possession of the technical and thematic powers that distinguish her finest lyrics."[1] Most critics in the last twenty years have accepted this view; several of the most distinguished writers on Dickinson agree that her style was unchanging, including Barbara Antonina Clarke Mossberg, David Porter, and Robert Weisbuch.[2] The thesis that Dickinson's style never developed owes a great deal to Charles R. Anderson. In 1960 Anderson wrote: "The chronological arrangement of the new edition [Thomas H. Johnson's 1955 variorum] has been useful in minor ways, but not for selecting or ordering the poems. There are no marked periods in her career, no significant curve of development in her artistic powers, such as might furnish the central plan for a book on Milton or Yeats."[3] Hence, Anderson arranged his readings by theme, an approach that has been followed by many of Dickinson's interpreters.

The thematic reading of Dickinson's poetry has produced a great deal of valuable and provocative criticism; it is not my purpose to argue with the fine readings of Mossberg and Weisbuch, or to undermine the method that led to those readings. But the development of Dickinson's style deserves more critical attention.

By measuring Dickinson's patterns of rhyme and enjambment, we can see that these formal contours of her verse changed over time, especially from 1858 to 1865. As Dickinson refined her verse technique, her approach to the subjects of her poems changed as well. But her poetry did not develop in the ways we are accustomed to see with poets whose work is published during their lifetimes and subjected to criticism and editorial advice.

Dickinson's poetic development consists mainly of two achievements that mark her work as unique and have established her as a great and difficult poet. First, she revised the hymn quatrain and made of it a more purely literary genre than it had ever been before. By "literary genre" I mean one where the work is intended to exist on the page alone and to be read silently. Dickinson's quatrain poems go even farther beyond the musical hymn of Isaac Watts than the literary ballad of Cowper, Coleridge and others goes beyond the sung ballad. Far from being constrained by her form or immured within the tradition of the hymn, she escaped that tradition completely, to the point where most of her poems no longer bear even a parodic or contrasting relationship to hymns.

Dickinson's second achievement is even more radical. In moving to her late manner she commented on her own texts, producing poems that were adaptations of earlier texts in her growing collection of manuscript fascicles. Having created a genre unique to her own work, she spent her career exploring and redefining that genre. Her reworkings of the subjects of her earlier poems show her concern with the interrelations between texts and with the effects of her own characteristic diction on her subjects. Her use of later poems to comment on earlier ones gives rise to those problems of interpretation that confront any reader of reworked material—except that here the poet is not adapting another's work but her own.

The most striking thing about Dickinson's work is that it is not directed outward. Although her letters teem with references to and talk about literature, there are hardly any uses in her poetry of the language of other poets. Even her few allusions to Shakespeare are mostly character names, except for **"Mail from Tunis"** in **1463,** used for an impossibly long haul, as in *The Tempest.*[4] One of her poems, **960—"Lay this Laurel on the One"**—is an adaptation of T. W. Higginson's "Decoration." There is one possible use of Emerson

(214), one of Percy Shelley **(1620)**. Her only use of the language of Elizabeth Barrett Browning is in **449, "I died for Beauty—"**; and it is a commonplace equation of Beauty and Truth which obviously owes at least as much to Keats, or to dozens of other poets.[5] Criticism has traced powerful undercurrents of the influence of Dickinson's wide reading on her poetry, and of the implicit relation of her style to that of her precursors.[6] But in the language of her poems, Dickinson never appropriated the language of another poet and never used the characteristic diction of a school or movement.

The state of Dickinson's surviving manuscripts confirms this picture of her as an inward-directed artist. There are no prose jottings on the construction of poems, no notebooks on art. We have no idea what her philosophy of composition was. We know that she revised carefully, sometimes taking great pains to find the right word.[7] But she left no explicit clue to her crêative process. Her fair copies, bound into fascicles, are a vast and enigmatic book that has evoked many competing interpretations. But that book is not externally a record of artistic experiment. Aside from changes in handwriting over the years, the fascicles are uniform in presentation. They are featureless aside from the texts of the poems and variant readings recorded, without comment, by the poet herself.

But of course this very featurelessness of the fascicles is silent testimony to Dickinson's concern with the status of her texts. Many of the fair copies contain text alone. But the fair copies that contain variant readings are problematic. Johnson considers these manuscripts to be poems in "the semifinal stage"; the variants, carefully written at the end of each poem and keyed to crosses over the words in the poem's text, seemed to him to be suggested changes.[8] This may be true; but it may just as well be true that Dickinson was preserving not future possibilities but stages in the composition of the poem, recording alternatives she had considered but rejected. Most semifinal drafts of a poet's work contain crossings-out and lists of alternatives; many of Dickinson's manuscripts are in this state. But the variants in the meticulously transcribed fair copies do not seem like intermediate draft alternatives but like part of the poet's attempt to preserve her own handwritten variorum edition. It is possible that the careful preservation of variants indicates great attention by Dickinson to versions of her poems and to the consequent refinements in diction that different versions entail.

The manuscript books offer a blank face in terms of the poet's own discussion of her poetics; but they do allow for the establishment of a chronology of Dickinson's poems from 1858 to 1865 (nearly all the fascicles are from these years). The chronology, in turn, can be used to show how Dickinson's use of rhyme and enjambment developed over time. The efforts of Johnson, Theodora Ward, and R. W. Franklin have established a sound, approximate dating of the fascicle poems.[9]

Table 1 presents this chronology. Only the years 1850-1865, the crucial ones for Dickinson's poetic development, are included.

Table 1
Chronology of Dickinson's Poems

1850-54	1-5
1858	6-57, 323, 1729-1730
1859	58-151, 216
1860	152-215, 318, 324
1861	217-298, 317, 319, 322, 325, 330, 687, 1737
1862	299-316, 320-321, 326-329, 332-432, 434-608, 610-664, 678, 683, 688, 712-717, 759-770, 1053, 1072, 1076, 1181, 1710, 1712, 1725, 1727, 1739
1863	665-677, 679-682, 684-686, 689-711, 718-758,771-807
1864	808-981, 1114
1865	433, 982-991, 993-1052, 1054-1066, 1070, 1073, 1177, 1540

The analysis of Dickinson's rhymes is made straightforward by the conventionality of her poems in terms of meter and rhyme-scheme. She did write a small number of poems in a "free-rhyming" verse that rhymes erratically, with no regular meter or rhyme-scheme, and I have excluded those poems from this analysis.[10] And of course some of her poems are fragmentary or in very rough drafts; these have also been excluded. But apart from these exceptions, all of her poems are in hymn stanzas and rhyme in one of the basic hymn rhyme-schemes: *aab ccb* or *xaxa*. Nearly all the places where rhyme would be expected in these poems have some type of rhyme; Dickinson wrote very little unrhymed or free verse (she approaches free verse only in **690** and in parts of **252**, **253**, **352**, and **1720**).

Eighty-eight percent of Dickinson's rhymes are of three phonetic types: exact, consonantal, and vowel rhymes.[11] Exact rhyme is the most common type, as in **67**:

> Success is counted sweetest
> By those who ne'er *succeed.*
> To comprehend a nectar
> Requires sorest *need.* (Italics mine here
> and in the next two examples.)

Nearly as common is consonantal rhyme, where the final consonants, but not the preceding vowels, are identical:

One dignity delays for all—
One mitred After*noon*—
None can avoid this purple—
None evade this *Crown!*

(98)

Dickinson also frequently uses vowel rhyme, where any vowel rhymes with any other:

I stepped from Plank to Plank
A slow and cautious *way*
The Stars about my Head I felt
About my Feet the *Sea.*

(875)

Table 2
Dickinson's Rhymes by Year and Rhyme-Type

	Exact	Consonantal	Vowel
1850-54	80.4	10.7	—
1858	68.1	14.4	7.5
1859	57.7	19.1	10.0
1860	45.5	25.8	13.4
1861	40.0	34.6	13.1
1862	34.5	33.8	17.2
1863	30.5	36.1	18.8
1864	28.3	35.5	17.5
1865	29.9	36.5	16.8

(The percentages given are of *all* rhymes in a given sample, and exclude less common types of rhyme, so totals are less than 100%.)[12]

Table 2 shows the development of Dickinson's technique in terms of rhyme. For each year, the percentage of all rhymes is given for each of the three most common phonetic types. In her earliest surviving poems (**1-5,** from 1850-54) Dickinson uses mainly exact rhymes; the poems are Valentines, or bits of verse incorporated into letters, and are highly conventional in diction. By the time when she was first binding poems into fascicles, in 1858-59, she had developed a much less conventional rhyming technique. Unfortunately, we have no evidence about how she created these early fascicle poems; none of her manuscripts from the years 1855-57 survive. We see her now in the manuscripts, after four years of silence, as a poet who had broken with the conventional rhyming of her earliest verse.

After 1865, Dickinson wrote so little poetry that analysis of trends is not reliable. There are few fascicles from 1866 and after; most of the later poems survive in isolated copies and transcripts. Dickinson stopped her great outpouring of poetry in 1866, and the technique she had developed through so many hundreds of poems shows no strong growth in any direction thereafter.

Even more than her rhyme, Dickinson's characteristic enjambment is probably the one formal element that makes her quatrains sound so distinctive. Hymn quatrains are always end-stopped. The hymns of Watts, though they employ inexact rhyme, are entirely unenjambed. In performance, it would be intolerable for a syntactic phrase to be broken at the end of one stanza and picked up at the beginning of the next after an instrumental passage or chorus. But the quatrains of purely literary poems that are meant to be read silently or recited in a speaking voice need not be end-stopped. And in Dickinson's hands, the quatrain became a form meant to be read silently, similar in diction to that of the unenjambed couplets of Keats (as in "Sleep and Poetry") or Browning (*Sordello* or "My Last Duchess"). With their frequent inexact rhyme and their true syntactic verse paragraphs, Dickinson's quatrains are a new genre, one unique to her own poetry.

Table 3 shows how Dickinson's use of enjambment developed from her earliest verse until 1865. (The final quatrains of poems are not included, as it makes no sense to speak of them as being enjambed or not.)

Table 3
Dickinson's Enjambment

	percentage of enjambed quatrains
1850-54	5.6
1858	16.7
1859	14.6
1860	15.4
1861	20.4
1862	29.8
1863	27.1
1864	34.1
1865	36.7

Dickinson began by using conventional hymn-like end-stopping. Her earliest poems are heavily end-stopped, and the first fascicle poems, in 1858-59, show only infrequent enjambment. But from 1860 to 1865, the amount of enjambment in her poetry grows steadily. By 1864, more than one-third of her quatrains are enjambed.

Dickinson used her later style, enjambed and using frequent inexact rhyme, to write adaptations of her earlier poems. The themes and subjects of these earlier poems reappear in the late style, but Dickinson adapts them by compressing or expanding the diction, changing the amount and nature of subordinate detail, and shifting—or often suppressing—key symbolic references.

Several readers have noticed compression in Dickinson's later poetry. George Frisbie Whicher discusses the condensation of the hummingbird poem **"Within my Garden, rides a Bird"** (**500,** dated 1862) into the famous **"A Route of Evanescence"** (**1463,** dated 1879).[13] Richard B. Sewall notes the impact of the boiling-down of the nine-stanza **"I watched the Moon around the House"** (**629,** dated 1862) into the two-stanza **"The Moon upon her fluent Route"** (**1528,** dated 1881).[14] The ultimate of this compressing process is what Gérard Genette calls *haïkaïsation.*[15] No matter how far haïkaïsation goes, the central referent of the original text (hummingbird, moon) remains present in the rewritten text. And so, the essential element of what Genette calls the "hypotext," the original version, is still present in the "hypertext," the revised version.

But Dickinson did not always condense; she often chose more complex ways of adapting her earlier work. Particularly problematic is the kind of hypertext produced by what Genette calls demotivation.[16] In this type of adaptation, the presence of the hypotext is absolutely necessary for the reading of the hypertext. There is no sense in which otiose material has been removed from the hypotext; or rather, the otiose and the essential are both removed, or essential material is replaced by new otiose material. In Flaubert's tale "Hérodias," Genette explains, the author retells the Biblical story. But he omits a vital part of the story, the crucial act of Hérodias that dooms John the Baptist. When adapting a Biblical story, Flaubert takes advantage of the fact that every reader knows the hypotext. But it is entirely possible for an author to practice demotivation of a text that is not well known, or that is unknown to every reader but herself; and this is what Dickinson does in reworking **72, "Glowing is her Bonnet"** (about 1859), into **978, "It bloomed and dropt, a Single Noon—"** (about 1864). Here is the earlier poem:

Glowing is her Bonnet,
Glowing is her Cheek,
Glowing is her Kirtle,
Yet she cannot speak.

Better as the Daisy
From the Summer hill
Vanish unrecorded
Save by tearful rill—

Save by loving sunrise
Looking for her face.
Save by feet unnumbered
Pausing at the place.

These quatrains are typical in form for an early Dickinson poem. They rhyme exactly, and the only enjambment comes between the second and third stanzas, at a break between paratactic phrases.

The first stanza establishes that someone is dead. It does so indirectly; but the central referent is clear. The following two stanzas express a preference for the way flowers die. The diction of the poem is characteristically Dickinson's, especially in its terse obliqueness; many of her early poems are terse and telegraphic in a similar way.

This early poem is marked strongly by the absence of tension. The poem, with its stock metrical phrases—"tearful rill," "loving sunrise"—and its conventional meter, rhyme, and end-stopping, is a metaphoric cliché. This is true despite Dickinson's metonymic evasiveness, her reluctance to name the central referents. And it is also clear that no amount of compression could complicate the poem much. In fact, not much compression is possible, given the poem's already small bounds.

In reworking the material of this poem, then, Dickinson elaborated rather than compressed it. But as she elaborated the detail and the rhetorical structure of the poem (by adding "I," in this case), and as she loosened the prosody by means of inexact rhyme and enjambment, she also removed the initial reference to a human death that motivates the consideration of the flower. The result is the demotivated text of **978.**

It bloomed and dropt, a Single Noon—
The Flower—distinct and Red—
I, passing, thought another Noon
Another in its stead

Will equal glow, and thought no More
But came another Day
To find the Species disappeared—
The Same Locality—

The Sun in place—no other fraud
On Nature's perfect Sum—
Had I but lingered Yesterday—
Was my retrieveless blame—

Much Flowers of this and further Zones
Have perished in my Hands
For seeking its Resemblance—
But unapproached it stands—

The single Flower of the Earth
That I, in passing by
Unconscious was—Great Nature's Face
Passed infinite by Me—

In contrast to **72, 978** contains all the features of Dickinson's later style. In the variation of rhyme and enjambment and in its verse-paragraphing, the poem avoids the stock phrases that fill out **72.**

Poem **72** compares a human death and the death of a flower; **978** expands on the death of the flower and removes the human death altogether. Dickinson expands the terseness of the narrative detail in the earlier poem; "Vanish unrecorded" becomes "came another Day / To find the Species disappeared—/ The Same Locality—/ The Sun in place—no other fraud / On Nature's perfect Sum—." But no similar refinement is applied to the first stanza of **72.** It is simply dropped. The result of this demotivation is to throw great emphasis on the disappearance of the flower, and to demand a symbolic referent for it. But the poem refuses to associate the flower with anything else. The extremity of the speaker's emotions becomes extremely puzzling: "retrieveless blame" and "Great Nature's Face / Passed infinite by me" suggest a psychological depth that the literal situation doesn't call for. The reader is left wondering what so extreme an emotion could be evoked by, and what the hidden connection between the flower and the unknown symbolic referent could be. One is led, when reading such a poem, to a state of *presque vu* about the poet's intentions and private associations. The powerful suggestiveness of the poem results from its being a demotivation of a hypotext that was more explicit about these associations.

Over the course of Dickinson's career, she returned again and again to the basic themes that figure in her early poems—hence the observation by many critics that her subject matter remained static. But while the early poems tend to be simply descriptive or to present stock conclusions (even when they are paradoxical or ironic stock conclusions), the later poems employ compression, or demotivation, or a shift in symbolic direction, to cause problems of interpretation. Dickinson's later style demands that the intricacy of her early hymn-like poems be doubled back on itself to produce a problem of interpretation every time the poem is read. The style in itself becomes the argument. This pattern can be observed in the large clusters of poems on death, marriage, loneliness, and other subjects; one small cluster of poems that shows it well is on Indian Summer, the period of warm weather after the first frost. Dickinson's first Indian Summer poem is **130:**

> These are the days when Birds come back—
> A very few—a Bird or two—
> To take a backward look.
>
> These are the days when skies resume
> The old—old sophistries of June—
> A blue and gold mistake.
>
> Oh fraud that cannot cheat the Bee—
> Almost thy plausibility
> Induces my belief.
>
> Till ranks of seeds their witness bear—
> And softly thro' the altered air
> Hurries a timid leaf.
>
> Oh Sacrament of summer days,
> Oh Last Communion in the Haze—
> Permit a child to join.
>
> The sacred emblems to partake—
> Thy consecrated bread to take
> And thine immortal wine!

The poem is far from being a simple appreciation of the season. Even though the final stanza seems like an ecstatic acceptance of Indian Summer, the poem is, centrally, ambiguous. Indian Summer is a "Sacrament," but it is also a "fraud" and a "mistake": it is a repetition of the "sophistries of June." And if June itself, the real summer, is full of sophistries, a false June must be even falser. The speaker seems weary of the summer itself, because it is necessarily transient, and even wearier of the final deceit of the Indian Summer.

And yet, paradoxically, the speaker regains her faith at the very moment when she is made certain that the false summer is false: when "ranks of seeds their witness bear." Now that the season has stopped pretending to be anything other than summer's last gasp, she is ready to participate, and the poem slips into the devotional language of the last two stanzas. Or maybe it doesn't; maybe the last two stanzas are a satire on a type of attitude toward faith that embraces faith despite a deep-rooted skepticism. This satiric logic is papered over by the end-stopped hymn stanzas and the light tone. The satirical level is there, but it remains smirking, not serious; mock-devotional, not anti-devotional. Above all, the poem does not confront the problem of faith. It poses outside the problem, and we can either appreciate or reject that pose, but not engage it in an argument.

Poem **130** was written about 1859. Five years later, Dickinson returned to the theme of Indian Summer to write a more problematic poem, **930:**

> There is a June when Corn is cut
> And Roses in the Seed—
> A Summer briefer than the first
> But tenderer indeed
>
> As should a Face supposed the Grave's
> Emerge a single Noon
> In the Vermillion that it wore
> Affect us, and return—
>
> Two Seasons, it is said, exist—
> The Summer of the Just,
> And this of Ours, diversified
> With Prospect, and with Frost—
>
> May not our Second with its First
> So infinite compare
> That We but recollect the one
> The other to prefer?

The problems of interpretation in this poem come from its piling up of comparisons, comparisons that at each level embody paradoxes. The enjambment from the first stanza to the second makes the first comparison, between Indian Summer and the brief reappearance of someone buried. Indian Summer itself is presented paradoxically, as a "June when Corn is cut," instead of simply as "the days when Birds come back." And the season is not merely accused of sophistry, as in **130;** it is directly compared to an experience that is impossible: someone coming back from the dead not as a ghost but "in the Vermillion," in the flesh. Most similes present the unfamiliar in terms of the familiar, but this one presents the familiar in terms of the impossible. In the third stanza, Indian Summer, in its impossible beauty, is compared to the bliss of heaven, the "Summer of the Just." Which is better? The fourth stanza should tell us, but it doesn't quite manage to; its syntax is as baffling as anything Dickinson ever wrote. "Our Second" is Indian Summer, and "its First" is heaven, but which of these is "the other" that we have recollected "the one" to prefer?

The answer, I think, lies not in any internal evidence, but in an echo of **130** that the whole situation of **930** brings to mind. Remember that both June and Indian Summer in the earlier poem are accused of "sophistries," in an offhand way that the speaker does not elaborate. The speaker instead drifts into a formulaic appreciation of the season she has accused. Here in **930,** though, the sophistry is examined and explained. The reappearance of someone buried in the second stanza is, of course, only humanly impossible; there is a notable example of it, beyond human power, in the Resurrection. And we are certainly reminded of the Resurrection in the second stanza, because the very impossibility of the simile demands it. After the end-stopping at the end of the second stanza, the poem picks up the same comparison that it made in that second stanza, because the Resurrection and the "Summer of the Just" are, after all, identical. The Resurrection defeated death and made this summer that is not "diversified" possible.

So when we "recollect the one," we are recollecting that Resurrection and its promise of eternal summer. But we are preferring "the other," the Indian Summer that so paradoxically can only be appreciated because it is false—palpably, not metaphysically, false. Poem **930,** welded together out of a tremendous tension of style and symbol, is a rejection of the whole mystery of immortality in favor of a confidence trick by Nature that seems honest in comparison. But the poet is not merely expounding a position here; she is arriving at it by the process of adapting an earlier text. In another poem or set of poems she may very well—she certainly did—arrive at other conclusions about Christ and about immortality. But here, she takes what is only hinted at in the contradictions of **130,** and by pressing those contradictions to their limit, she arrives at the agonizing puzzle of **930.**

Dickinson continued to rework the theme of Indian Summer, and her **1364,** written about 1876, is a late haïkaïsation of the subject. As in many of these extremely compressed poems, the central term has become enigmatic:

> How know it from a Summer's Day?
> Its Fervors are as firm—
> And nothing in its Countenance
> But scintillates the same—
> Yet Birds examine it and flee—
> And Vans without a name
> Inspect the Admonition
> And sunder as they came—

The first five lines of the poem are a simple compression of Dickinson's earlier descriptions of Indian Summer. The speaker knows that it is not summer; the only difficulty is in proving it, and this is accomplished by noting that the birds aren't fooled. (In **130,** the proof was the "ranks of seeds." Also in that poem, it was the bees, not the birds, that couldn't be fooled; but bees actually are very active on warm autumn days, perhaps leading Dickinson to drop that element of the treatment.) The problem of the poem lies in lines 6-8. "Vans without a name" is an impossibly obscure phrase, and deliberately so. These Vans are only named by their lack of a name, and their only action in the poem is to refuse to appear in it. They might be insects; the vaguely visual evocation of them makes them "look" like insects; but why would insects lack a name when birds are given one? As they appear, nameless, almost in the poem, they are spiritual presences of some sort, hovering on the edge of the poem's consciousness. Their sundering, in the last line, is a melting into silence of all the sarcasm and anguish that surrounded Indian Summer in **130** and **930,** and **1364** is eerier and more cryptic than either of its predecessors.

The Indian Summer poems chart, in miniature, the development of Dickinson's style, from something resembling a hymn, at least in formal outline, to a far more individual treatment of the same subjects, made possible by inexact rhyme, enjambment, verse-paragraphing, haïkaïsation, demotivation—in general, by a ceaseless reworking of the one book that meant more to Dickinson than any other, even the Bible: the book of her own poetry. R. P. Blackmur accused Dickinson of "revolving in a vacuum" when she wrote her unconventional verse, and the accusation is true.[17] She never adopted conventional technique, but started very early with something idiosyncratic and then revised her own idiosyncrasies. Probably it is fortunate that she did, as she was led to complicate rather than to polish her early work. An editor would have noted very early on that she had gotten the bees and birds mixed up in **130,** and while she was smoothing that out, she might never have composed **930.**

Picasso is supposed to have said that he didn't care who influenced him, so long as he didn't influence himself. Dickinson proceeded oppositely; she was vigorously anti-eclectic. This leads to the difficulty of considering her work as a single integrated corpus. In the Indian Summer poems, Dickinson certainly has her earlier poems—carefully preserved in the fascicles—in mind as a context for the later ones. But for other sequences of poems, such as the many that affirm faith and immortality, her manuscript books provide different contexts. It is customary to think of lyric poems as being strictly independent utterances, or as being elements in a narrative or meditative sequence. But Dickinson's fascicles are neither. The logic of clusters on different themes—or even, sometimes, of different poems within a cluster on the same theme—develops in different directions. When interpreters attempt to capture her thought on a given subject by referring to poems written over a twenty-five-year period, they are not proceeding incorrectly—very often there is no other way to proceed if we want to make sense of Dickinson—but they are compiling provisional indexes to what was still, in its final "edition," very much a work in progress.

So was *Leaves of Grass,* of course, but the difference is that Dickinson was not making a book for anyone but herself. Her work is inward-directed to a unique extent, and not just in its lack of appropriation of the language of others and in her lack of interest in publication. The most distinctive thing about her poetry is, finally, the intensely problematic nature of her painstaking and often enigmatic adaptation of her private texts.

Notes

[1] Douglas Anderson, "Presence and Place in Emily Dickinson's Poetry," *New England Quarterly,* 57 (1984), 205.

[2] See Mossberg, *Emily Dickinson: When a Writer Is a Daughter* (Bloomington: Indiana Univ. Press, 1982); Porter, *Dickinson: The Modern Idiom* (Cambridge: Harvard Univ. Press, 1981); Weisbuch, *Emily Dickinson's Poetry* (Chicago: Univ. of Chicago Press, 1975).

[3] *Emily Dickinson's Poetry: Stairway of Surprise* (New York: Holt, Rinehart, and Winston, 1960), p. xii.

[4] All quotations from Dickinson's poetry are from *The Poems of Emily Dickinson,* ed. Thomas H. Johnson (Cambridge: Harvard Univ. Press, 1955). They are referred to by the numbers given them in that edition.

[5] See Jack L. Capps, *Emily Dickinson's Reading: 1836-1886* (Cambridge: Harvard Univ. Press, 1966), pp. 147-88.

[6] See Joanne Feit Diehl, *Dickinson and the Romantic Imagination* (Princeton: Princeton Univ. Press, 1981), which treats Dickinson's responses to her major Romantic precursors; Susan Howe, *My Emily Dickinson* (Berkeley, Cal.: North Atlantic Press, 1985), which examines far-reaching networks of associations between Dickinson's reading and her poetry; A. R. C. Finch, "Dickinson and Patriarchal Meter: A Theory of Metrical Codes," *PMLA,* 102 (1987), 166-76, looks at Dickinson's choice of the quartrain in relation to the tradition of pentameter in English verse.

[7] See *Poems,* I, xxxiii-xxxviii.

[8] *Poems,* I, xxxiii.

[9] The chronology of Dickinson's poems is from *Poems* with corrections from *The Manuscript Books of Emily Dickinson,* ed. R. W. Franklin (Cambridge: Harvard Univ. Press, 1981).

[10] See Timothy Morris, "The Free-Rhyming Poetry of Emerson and Dickinson," *Essays in Literature,* 12 (1985), 225-40.

[11] Of 4,840 rhymes in Dickinson's poems, 2,006 (41.4%) are exact (of the type see/me, 1732); 167 (3.5%) pair a vowel with a reduced version of itself (me/immortality, 712); 80 (1.6%) are assonantal (breath/quench, 422); 731 (15.1%) are vowel (blew/sky, 354); 1,535 (31.7%) are consonantal (mean/sun, 411); 164 (3.4%) pair a consonant with a cluster containing that consonant (night/erect, 419); 23 pair a cluster with another cluster that shares one consonant with it (disclosed/blind, 761); 2 rhyme a cluster with the same cluster reversed (used/birds, 430); 84 (1.7%) rhyme one nasal consonant with another (thing/begun, 565); 20 rhyme one fricative with another (breeze/divorce, 896); 2 rhyme one voiced stop with another (sob/wood, 45); 5 rhyme one unvoiced stop with another (frock/night, 584); 21 rhyme-positions show less close approximations to exact rhyme, and cannot be considered rhyme at all (for instance, blaze/forge in 365).

[12] I have not found it worthwhile to give a fascicle-by-fascicle analysis of Dickinson's rhymes. The broad trends of the change in her style do show, of course, in such an analysis: for example, she uses 78.1% exact rhyme in Fascicle 1 and only 24.3% exact rhyme in Fascicle 24. But the trend would only be obscured by noting the very small variations from fascicle to fascicle. The dating of the fascicles can never be precise enough to permit statements about development over very brief intervals of time anyway; the year-by-year

dating shows Dickinson's stylistic development in general terms, which is my aim here.

[13] *This Was a Poet* (New York: Scribners, 1939), p. 262.

[14] *The Life of Emily Dickinson* (New York: Farrar, Straus, and Giroux, 1974), I, 240-43.

[15] *Palimpsestes* (Paris: Seuil, 1982), chap. 9.

[16] "Demotivation in *Hérodias*," in *Flaubert and Postmodernism*, ed. Naomi Sekori and Henry F. Majewski (Lincoln: Univ. of Nebraska Press, 1984), pp. 192-201. Trans. Marlena Corcoran.

[17] "Emily Dickinson: Notes on Prejudice and Fact," *Southern Review*, 3 (1937), 323-47.

Alice Fulton (essay date 1989)

SOURCE: "Her Moment of Brocade: The Reconstruction of Emily Dickinson," in *Parnassus: Poetry in Review*, Vol. 15, No. 1, 1989, pp. 9-44.

[*In the following essay, Fulton contends that while Dickinson is acknowledged as a premier American poet, there remains a resistance among critics to a "Dickinsonian tradition in American letters." Fulton explores the possible reasons for this resistance and notes that when Dickinson is judged by the criteria derived from the work of other major poets and movements, her unique accomplishments, particularly in the area of language, are overlooked.*]

The way Hope builds his House
It is not with a sill—
Nor Rafter—has Mars—
But only Pinnacle—

(**1481**, variant version)

The following bit of apocryphal gossip made the rounds of writers' conferences last summer: Two well-known poets stand at a podium, both of them in their fifties. One waits to read her poems; the other to introduce her. The poet who'll read wears a fifties circle skirt to which a large felt poodle is appliquéd. Her introducer, a short heavy woman, is dressed in paisley jodhpurs and a jeweled sweater. In the audience an up-and-coming man poet[1] of a younger generation shifts restlessly in his chair. (The fashion report on him is never given.) Leaning toward the man beside him, he whispers "Debutantes from Mars." Hearing this story, I imagined a third figure flickering behind the lectern: a middle-aged woman in a long, button-fronted, kick-pleated white shift resembling a nightgown. If the audience could see this specter, they'd recognize the template of the female poet as alien invader: Emily Dickinson. Would a poet of her genius and gender receive more respectful attention today than the two women of my anecdote? Moreover, might this snippet, with its emphasis on couture, girlishness, Otherness, illuminate the resistance to a Dickinsonian tradition in American letters?

Of course, Dickinson is a canonical writer. Among scholars and general readers, her eminence is taken for granted. But who among contemporary poets has been placed within a Dickinsonian context? Where are her heirs? Essays and reviews of twentieth-century poets frequently point to Whitman as influence or forebear. The Beat poets, among others, are construed as *his* descendants. Yet it's hard to think of any criticism that places a man poet within a primarily Dickinsonian orbit, although she's often mentioned in passing. (The problems for female poets are different, and I'll come to them.) Perhaps the resistance to a Dickinsonian linkage or lineage has its basis in the patriarchal assumptions and cultural insecurities surrounding gender. Americans tend to view poetry writing as an unmanly or "feminine" vocation. That "feminine" has associations of weakness or unworthiness in the common mind says a great deal about this culture's unspoken assumptions. In her perceptive book *Made in America: Science, Technology, and American Modernist Poets,* Lisa M. Steinman quotes Williams in 1949 as saying "We seldom think of . . . poetic structure, as we do of engineering: a field of action worthy of masculine attack." Note the martial language with which he describes his ideal enterprise. It implies that poetry, properly regarded, is a combative activity. This attitude is with us still. How could the women of my opening anecdote, those flaky fluttery Others, endow literary kin with a seminal aura "worthy of masculine attack"? If literature is warfare, men need robust father figures to defend, shield, authorize, and sequester their enterprise. Although *female* poets are sometimes compared to Dickinson, the comparison serves to underscore eccentricity rather than brilliance.

I said that Dickinson's eminence is taken for granted. I must add that her status is also resented. As part of a recent symposium in *The Texas Review*[2] called "Nominations for Oblivion," novelist Robert Bausch wrote, "No imagination could possibly wish to construct so many silly rhymes with the *same* rhythmical pattern except one that has been stilted by some sort of oddly imposed and intractable virginity. The only reason people are forced to study Emily Dickinson in American universities is that she is female and in these days of socially relevant education teachers *have* to include a woman somewhere. Imagine how disappointed everybody's going to be when critics and scholars return to their senses and discover that Emily Dickinson's poetry is nothing less than something less than nothing at all. . . . It leaves me feeling as though I have been trampled by a McDonald's advertisement." I'm glad that Bausch published the above sentiment because most Dickinson-bashing takes place in private conversations. Since the symposium is presented as "satire, intended for fun," one is asked to believe that Bausch's comment (I've quoted only a fraction of his spleen-venting) has no meaning, subtext, or effect. Like the "Debutantes from Mars" anecdote, Bausch's words hide damaging premises behind a pretense of wit and ask for our laughing complicity. Anyone who detects hostility in such "fun" is a spoilsport. I'm not saying we can't have Dickinson jokes, but we have to acknowledge that humor has latent meanings and that those meanings can be sexist, racist, or just plain dumb.

Bausch's mention of "intractable virginity" shows that his knowledge of Dickinson begins and ends in superficial stereotypes. Such mythology began to take shape within Dickinson's lifetime, and there's been an undue emphasis on her biography ever since. The legend no doubt helps explain why students, writers, and readers often speak of "Emily" as if they held frequent tête-à-têtes with her. Perhaps the spurious intimacy she evokes encourages this fatuous address. But the poetry and biography of Keats provide equally fertile ground for identification and empathy. And who ever thinks of him as John? Referring to writers by their first names signals familiarity, and we know what that breeds; it also undermines the writer's authority. Ultimately it's a reductive address, a means of conferring minion status upon one who would be Queen. With this in mind, I'll refer to "Emily" only when discussing her within the context of her family, those other Dickinsons.

The Dickinson of popular mythology is an ingenuous sufferer whose lonely life of seclusion results from a mysterious unrequited love (hence her "intractable virginity"). She is a naive folk artist lacking an ars poetica or tradition, which of itself consigns her to eccentricity. Her genius, when conceded, is said to be anomalous: She will have no literary heirs because her accomplishment is too wayward for assimilation. Recent studies of Dickinson work against some of these tired notions. One can't, however, dismantle clichés so firmly entrenched in the collective imagination by publishing scholarly books. And in trying to dismantle The Myth, scholarship has produced new, sometimes more fantastic legends. The recombinant Emily Dickinson who emerges from these disparate opinions resembles Joanne Woodward playing *The Three Faces of Eve*. She is the nun; the heretic; the psychotic; the anorexic; the agoraphobe; even the unwed mother. In trying to counteract a phallocentric bias, feminist readings have turned the simpering flower into Fury; the jilted spinster into thwarted lesbian. Even those who knew Emily Dickinson were often mystified or fooled. According to Austin, his sister posed in her letters to Higginson. And she must have stayed in character for their single face-to-face meeting, a coming-out party for the interplanetary ingenue, if we can believe Higginson's description of a whispery, intense, "half-cracked poetess." Given all this, it's tempting to view the poet as an actress, her lyric "I" a form of dramatic monologue. Whitman's self-descriptive lines apply: She is large. She contains multitudes.

In fact, Dickinson's current standing has nothing to do with her education (which was rigorous and wide-ranging), her own influences (which were diverse), her absence of an aesthetics (available in her poetry and letters as surely as in those of Keats), her method (again comparable to Keats), or her writing (which is anomalous only in its extraordinary achievement). The historical Dickinson is irretrievable. We are left with our fantasies, which say as much about us as her. In poem **526** she reminds us of our intractable subjectivity:

> To hear an Oriole sing
> May be a common thing—
> Or only a divine.
>
> It is not of the Bird
> Who sings the same, unheard,
> As unto Crowd—
>
> The Fashion of the Ear
> Attireth that it hear
> In Dun, or fair—
>
> So whether it be Rune,
> Or whether it be none
> Is of within.
>
> The "Tune is in the Tree—"
> The Skeptic—showeth me—
> "No Sir! In Thee!"

The observer alters what's observed; a poet's reception depends upon "The Fashion of the Ear." The listener (reader) determines whether poetry is magical script ("Rune"), failure (ruin), or "none." The last fate is reserved for work that remains unread, consigned to absence. We, the current audience, create and alter a poet's standing. The Martha Graham Dance Company, in their recent production of "Letter to the World," cast the glamorous Kathleen Turner as Dickinson. Why do we insist upon her being Belle of Amherst? Perhaps it's because a nubile woman who writes poetry is a pretty concept. She may adore her older male teachers and pose no threat. But what if she continues to develop as an artist, devoting the main portion of her life and energies to her writing? What happens to the female poet too mature to be called "promising," too well known to be "emerging?" There's a good chance she'll become an object of scorn, the butt of jokes like the one at the beginning of this essay. Little will be written about her work. Her poems may go out of print, as Marianne Moore's did during the seventies. Whenever older female poets read for my classes, students are surprised that women their mother's age can write about ideas, including sexuality and politics, without trotting out tuna-casserole platitudes. Some of the young men seem amazed that such women can think at all! Their reports dwell upon the poet's matronly appearance that belies (to their minds) the shocking (to their minds) content of the poems. "I'd expected a much younger woman," they write. In contrast, men poets of comparable age are said to be "distinguished," as if they embodied the debonair charm of aging movie stars.

Of course, some brilliant men poets also suffer neglect.[3] But so few women have been accorded major status that one must connect their gender with their disenfranchisement. Most significant awards still go to men. Whether the recipients of the accolades are more deserving, more gifted, than their less fortunate *brothers* isn't the point. Their sisters aren't in the running at all. "What about Adrienne Rich, Rita Dove?" Lest we confuse tokenism with equity, consider the following facts: MacArthur Fellowships have been awarded to sixteen poets, one of whom is female. The Literature Department of the American Academy of Arts and Letters includes approximately thirty poets, six of them women. Seven members of the Academy are poets, none of them women. The twelve-member board of Chancellors of The Academy of American Poets includes two women. Either there are very few significant female poets, or else such poets suffer discrimination. One must remind oneself that women are not a minority. On the contrary, women's writing is majority writing, both in the sense of numbers and in coming of age. Yet the evidence suggests that most people still want their great poets to be men. Such a cultural climate affects the reception of Dickinson's work as surely as it does that of contemporary poets. She worried that her poetry would be seen as "the only Kangaroo among the Beauty." "It afflicts me," she wrote Higginson. And how do we see her? As a wonderful yet anomalous presence, given to unexpected leaps, equipped with bizarre pockets, comic as a cartoon, powerful as a boxer—great, yes, but aberrant, Other: kangarooish!

Ironically, it was patriarchy that afforded Dickinson the time to write and think. Male dominance as practiced in Victorian Amherst became for her both enablement and disablement, protection and prison. The word *patriarchy* provokes extreme reactions, perhaps because people are unsure what's meant by the term. I offer *Webster's* definition: "a: social organization marked by the supremacy of the father in the clan or the family in both domestic and religious functions, the legal dependence of wife or wives and children, and the reckoning of descent and inheritance in the male line. b: a society so organized." In nineteenth-century Amherst, females of Dickinson's economic class were not expected to be self-supporting. Her father's social standing and wealth saved her from the grim jobs available to women: factory work or the middle-class option of teaching school. There's little doubt that Edward Dickinson ruled supreme within his family, and his possessiveness is said to have discouraged his daughters' suitors. If so, this might have been a disguised blessing for Emily. In the 1800s, women married for financial security (which she already had), companionship (which she found in Austin and Lavinia), and children (although many women did not regard pregnancy as a desirable aspect of matrimony).

A little reading on the development of obstetrics convinces one—and it is an astounding knowledge—of the overwhelming dread with which women historically viewed childbirth. The silence and neglect surrounding this formidably central province of human experience encourages us to misunderstand any American women born before 1930—including Emily Dickinson. We have forgotten that until recently childbirth was woman's heroic sphere. As such, it provided a more frequent and dependably excruciating trial than man's transcendent analogue of war. Contraception was limited and seldom practiced; anaesthetics (chloroform and laudanum) were unreliable and sometimes unavailable; doctors were just beginning to attend births, and their lack of experience and ignorance of bacteria made their presence more risk than boon. Judith Leavitt, in *Brought to Bed,* writes, "Women knew that if procreation did not kill them, it could maim them for life." Children aside, a married woman of Dickinson's social standing was expected to oversee the details of an elaborate household and play hostess to her husband's business associates, tasks that would leave little time for the writing of 1775 poems. All in all, the realities of marriage might have seemed less attractive to Dickinson than the relationships she inhabited through writing.

Of all the forms of male dominance, perhaps the most evident to Dickinson was patrilineage, "the reckoning of descent and inheritance in the male line." Her domineering father accorded Austin, his son and heir, immense respect as his birthright. Dickinson undoubtedly loved her brother. Yet she might have felt some chagrin at hearing their father declare Austin's letters "altogether before Shakespeare" while her own great talents went unremarked. Indeed, Mr. Dickinson was so taken by his son's letters that he wished "to have them published to put in our library." Here's how Emily reacted to the family's designated genius in 1853: "And Austin is a Poet, Austin writes a psalm. Out of the way, Pegasus, Olympus enough 'to him,' and just say to those 'nine muses' that we have done with them! Raised a living muse ourselves, worth the whole nine of them. . . . Now, Brother Pegasus, I'll tell you what it is—I've been in the habit *myself* of writing some few things, and it rather appears to me that you're getting away my patent, so you'd better be somewhat careful. . . . " By 1866, her sense of poetic mastery extended beyond the household competition. In a letter describing the March weather she wrote, "Here is the 'light' the Stranger said 'was not on land or sea.' Myself could arrest it but we'll not chagrin Him." The quote is from Wordsworth's *Elegiac Stanzas.*

As a cultural norm, patrilineage is responsible for the most destructive prejudice surrounding Emily Dickinson: the view that she is a curiosity of American literature. Patrilineage means all children must receive their father's surname as a means of creating identity, order, legacy, and connection. A child who receives a mother's name is a bastard. The pervasiveness of this view makes it difficult for us to imagine women as creators of dynasties—be they familial, financial, or literary. Since lineage must pass from father to son, Dickinson cannot offer legitimacy to her successors. Unable to envision her as progenitor, critics and scholars regard her work as too eccentric to exert broad influence. The same prejudices apply to Marianne Moore, Elizabeth Bishop, and all poets who are women. They are our perennial spinsters, deprived of issue and succession.

In fact, Dickinson is not without her descendants, but they are the heirs unapparent: favored sons who have been awarded steadier pedigrees, or orphaned females sans geneology. A. R. Ammons, for example, should be recognized as a great scion of Dickinson. Ammons's pervasively used colon is analogous to the Dickinsonian dash; his subjects are hers; his abstract vocabulary draws upon her matrix—from sphere to difference. His process of writing is comparable, as is the sheer amount of poetry he has produced. Yet the comment accompanying his National Book Critics Circle Award in 1981 summarizes the way his work has been read: "He is a poet of the American Sublime . . . standing in the tradition of Wordsworth, Emerson, and Whitman." Apparently Dickinson is not part of "the American Sublime." Although Ammons studied with the late Josephine Miles, her possible influence upon his work is never mentioned. Being female, she is unable to confer legitimacy. Miles herself shows a Dickinsonian influence in the ontological questioning, colloquial ease, and abstract vocabulary of many poems.

Dickinson's influence makes itself felt in the stropped language of Robert Creeley; the head-spinning intelligence and atomized linguistic sparks of Heather McHugh; the wickedly unconventional wit, philosophical teasing, and subtle explorations of gender perfected by Phyllis Janowitz; the delight in formal experiment, passion for the natural world, and vernacular charm of May Swenson; the religious sensibility of Denise Levertov. The work of Charles Simic, with its spacious leaps, honed syntax, and decocted folklore is also kin. When I mentioned this consanguinity, Mr. Simic wrote, "Dickinson is the poet who means more and more to me as the years pass. . . . Her poems think as they unfold—that's my dream! My hope is to understand her great art before I die." When I jokingly suggested that his line stemmed from "the seldom-mentioned Serbian side" of her family, Simic offered the following geneology: "I believe they were Russian. Came out of Dostoyevsky's rooming house for poor students. A family of anarchists who kept their children out of school. Taught them themselves. They read so much they all wore thick glasses by the time they were four years old. When they came to America they opened a delicatessen in Springfield, Massachusetts. Miss Emily used to go there on the q.t. for gherkins. She thought she was pregnant. She was! With theology, poetry, and philosophy." Simic's imagined history places the poet within a context of intelligent rebellion (anarchists, thick glasses) while affectionately crediting her creative fertility.

For myself, I continue to learn from Dickinson's genius with abstraction; the manyness rather than singleness of her imagery; the pronouns enlarged by slippery antecedents; the variety one can achieve in prosody. In this age of conservative formalism, when every other poem one reads is in the C major of blank verse, Dickinson reminds me of the countless tones and keys at my disposal. Her poems show the heady brilliance of successful experiment. They convince me of the value and possibility of delineating inner states so subtle as to be almost subconscious. The volume and quality of her accomplishment instill a faith that language is both unbounded and mine: an infinite resource, limited only by my limitations. Her life teaches American poets to keep their eyes on the luminous, infinite sphere of language rather than the bouncing ball of regular iambs or the gold ring of poe-biz acclaim. Her poems prove that one can embrace complication without forfeiting the reader's pleasure.

Dickinson's fame began in 1890 with the publication of ***Bolts of Melody.*** The public adored the book, which went into multiple printings. Mabel Loomis Todd (with the help of Thomas Higginson) took on the monumental task of selection and editing. Their attempts to normalize meter, rhyme, and punctuation, along with their choice of the more conventional poems, made Dickinson palatable at a time when her experiments would have met with befuddlement. Although her work found a popular audience, serious acclaim was slow to come. *The Atlantic Monthly* stated that "an eccentric, dreamy, half-educated recluse in an out-of-the-way New England village—or anywhere else—cannot with impunity set at defiance the laws of gravitation and grammar. . . . Oblivion lingers in the immediate neighborhood." The adjectives in that first sentence live on in Dickinson mythology, along with the tendency to anthologize her least ambitious work.

Given its high degree of indeterminacy and plurality, Dickinson's most complex poetry is best suited to a postmodernist age. New literary theories and contemporary science offer ways of constructing reality that help us appreciate poems previously consigned to the periphery. Yet in trying to represent Dickinson's essential canon, *The Norton Anthology of Poetry* (third edition) prizes the simple, the plain, the ecstatic, the erotic, the natural, and the macabre, all traits of a romantic disposition. More cerebral, disjunctive, and ambiguous poems are excluded. Of course, many of the anthology chestnuts number among Dickinson's great works. But poem **449,** for example, expresses conventional nineteenth-century sentiments in fairly conventional style. It comes as close to being a set piece as anything Dickinson ever wrote.

I died for Beauty—but was scarce
Adjusted in the Tomb
When One who died for Truth was lain
In an adjoining Room—

He questioned softly "Why I failed?"
"For Beauty," I replied—
"And I—for Truth—Themself are One—
We Brethren, are," He said—

And so, as Kinsmen, met a Night—
We talked between the Rooms—
Until the Moss had reached our lips—
And covered up—our names—

This poem owes so much to Keats's Grecian Urn that I can never read it without envisioning him as the One interred beside the speaker. At least the poem contains a few Dickinsonian grace notes. The extra comma in line eight ("'We Brethren, are,' He said—"); the coupling of singular and plural within one noun ("Themself" rather than the "Themselves" in line seven); and the hypotaxic syntax (three of the last six lines begin with "And") distinguish it, though marginally, from brand *X* Victorian verse. **"The Bustle in a House" (1078),** another favorite of anthologists, voices its platitudes in unremarkable language:

The Bustle in a House
The Morning after Death
Is solemnest of industries
Enacted upon Earth—

The Sweeping up the Heart
And putting Love away
We shall not want to use again
Until Eternity.

The pun on morning, the deletion of function words in lines three and five, and the metrical stress that underscores and isolates each syllable of the final word, "Eternity"—such stylistic oddities are Dickinson's signature. But these devices appear throughout her work. This poem differs from hundreds of other Dickinson poems in three ways: It is plainer in style, it is simpler in syntax, and it draws upon one central metaphor (housewifery) rather than melding two or more images into one new emotional nexus. As a result, it's an easy poem to grasp on a first reading. In fact, many of Dickinson's anthology poems seem to be chosen for their clarity, rather than their intellectual or stylistic richness. I suppose editors might make these selections with student readers in mind. Yet the same editors never omit "The Waste Land" in favor of "easier" Eliot poems. As for students, I've heard them say they thought Dickinson a bees-in-her-bonnet versifier with an elfin range, the Beatrix Potter of American Literature, until they read her complex, lesser-known work.

Those anthology favorites **"A narrow Fellow in the Grass" (986)** and **"I like to see it lap the Miles—" (585)** are more contiguous than disjunctive in metaphor and syntax. They select their object—a snake or a train—and stare it down. They don't begin by focusing on a boxcar and in stanza two shift their gaze to wayward phenomena—volcanoes, India, or bodices—as a means of enriching the brew. Concrete rather than abstract in language, their imagery tends to be singular rather than multiple; their structure and success rest upon all they choose to exclude, rather than all they manage to embrace.

I like to see it lap the Miles—
And lick the Valleys up—
And stop to feed itself at Tanks—
And then—prodigious step

Around a pile of Mountains—
And supercilious peer
In Shanties—by the sides of Roads—
And then a Quarry pare

To fit its Ribs
And crawl between
Complaining all the while
In horrid—hooting stanza—
Then chase itself down Hill—

And neigh like Boanerges—
Then—punctual as a Star
Stop—docile and omnipotent
At its own stable door—

The train/horse metaphor extends throughout, with only a few mischievous imaginings from farther afield (the "hooting stanza" of its voice, for instance). Like many Dickinson poems, this one is a riddle. The little mystery is what sort of animal we have here—dragon, lion?—and that question isn't resolved until the final stanza's allusion to Boanerges. It is a delightful description, and one is charmed by Dickinson, the nature poet, taking on the technology of her day. Reading it, I wonder what use she would have made of automobiles, computers, or fast food had she been born a century later. Although the poem exemplifies one way in which Dickinson succeeds, it shouldn't be mistaken for the only way. In valuing imagistic, nondiscursive poems over more linguistically myriad work, we are applying the standards of contemporary poetry workshops to Emily Dickinson, rather than enlarging our scope to encompass one whose "splendors are Menagerie."

The term "workshop poetry" is too often used as a convenient catch-all for whatever someone wants to bemoan in American poetry. Here are a few shopworn maxims that seem to have had an effect upon contemporary verse: *The language should be as much like everyday speech as possible: It must not draw attention to itself. A good poem sticks to the same tone: it does not mix levels of diction. If metered, the prosody should be fairly regular (blank verse is encouraged). Metaphors and imagery are to be added like salt and pepper—not too many, not too few. The imagery should all be drawn from the same group—that is, don't compare something to a football field in one line and a coal mine in the next.* It is perhaps true that only a few Dickinson poems feature smooth prosody, a central governing metaphor, and pronouns with clear antecedents. Those who judge poetry's value by these lights will prize poems in which the language is most normalized. If we limit Dickinson's canon to "well-crafted" verse and work that can be understood within the romantic tradition, we overlook poems whose success rests upon breaches of syntax and plurality of subject. By reading Dickinson according to standards derived from other major poets and movements, we blind ourselves to what she, and she alone, accomplished with language. It's as if all other poems are trees and her poems are birds. Given arboreal expectations, we admire hers most when they sit on the ground. "I don't like the way it keeps flitting around," we complain.

Dickinson is primarily an ontological poet with a unique ability to forge inner landscapes from abstract, rather than concrete, language and to express ideas—states of being, if you will—without resorting to an objective correlative. Her most characteristic use of language reverses Williams's famous credo, "No ideas but in things," to "No Things within Ideas." The reversal of synecdoche is another signature technique. "You will perceive that the whole stands for a part in this place—" she wrote at the age of twenty (Letter 29). In her poetry an abstract whole such as Difference or Circumference elicits particular and partial examples in the reader's mind.

Poem **1046,** for example, uses a high proportion of abstract language to describe a terrifying state of suspended animation, neither fully alive nor fully dead.

I've dropped my Brain—My Soul is numb—
The Veins that used to run
Stop palsied—'tis Paralysis
Done perfecter on stone

Vitality is Carved and cool.
My nerve in Marble lies—
A Breathing Woman
Yesterday—Endowed with Paradise.

Not dumb—I had a sort that moved—
A Sense that smote and stirred—
Instincts for Dance—a caper part—
An Aptitude for Bird—

Who wrought Carrara in me
And chiselled all my tune
Were it a Witchcraft—were it Death—
I've still a chance to strain

To Being, somewhere—Motion—Breath—
Though Centuries beyond,
And every limit a Decade—
I'll shiver, satisfied.

The speaker's inner being has ossified, although she was "A Breathing Woman / Yesterday—Endowed with Paradise." She was, however, "Not dumb—," and the figures used to describe her lost legacy, dance and birds, are among Dickinson's favored metaphors for poetry. The poem implies that the ability to smite and stir, the narrator's power, is linked to her disinheritance. For a woman to speak her mind is dangerous: "I think Carlo would please you—," Dickinson wrote to Higginson in Letter 271. "He is dumb and brave. . . . " Carlo was her dog. The persona's creative life is changed from active force to tombstone engraving: "Who wrought Carrara in me / And chiselled all my tune," she asks. If this petrifaction is a result of witchcraft or death, the speaker still may "strain / To Being, somewhere—Motion—Breath—/ Though Centuries beyond. . . . " The lines imply that there is a deadlier abnegation than that of mortality: the silencing of one's creative futurity. In the case of women, patrilineage leads to the loss of rightful endowment, an eternal silencing. If, however, the speaker's ossification is due to those lesser forces, Witchcraft or Death, she plans to sprint through the Centuries until she finds that Utopian "somewhere—," a world in which she will be allowed to sing.

Poem **326 ("I cannot dance upon my Toes—")** finds the narrator transforming such disinheritance into private enablement. Her poetry, she implies, is freakish because "No Man instructed me—." Indeed, if she had "Ballet knowledge" she could "blanch a Troupe—/ Or lay a Prima, mad." Here Dickinson describes the professional, published poet as engaged in an outlandish performance that passes for dance. Such poeticians hop "to Audiences—like Birds, / One Claw upon the Air," more grasping than graceful. Rather than engaging in such ignominious public display, her Art plays to the audience of herself, a gathering "full as Opera."

Whether she's protesting her pure, unpublished state or feeling obscurity as deadening force, such poems underscore Dickinson's ambivalence toward fame. I think she liked to imagine herself as a renowned writer. "I play at Riches—to appease / The Clamoring for Gold—," she wrote **(801).** As long as she was able to envision herself as a powerful literary presence, she could live with her effacement. The act of imagining herself to be both woman and acknowledged sovereign writer, a Queen, keeps her from the "Sin" of becoming "that easy Thing / an independent Man—." She is comforted to know that should she "in the long—uneven term" be declared a winner, she'll be fitter for her experience of Want. Poem **486** undermines the act of publication by means of puns: "I was the slightest in the House—" (publishing house); "I never spoke—unless addressed—" recalls Dickinson's habit of enclosing poems in letters to friends. "I could not bear to live—aloud—/ The Racket shamed me so—," she says, and The Racket refers as much to the life of a public poet as to any audible sound. Although the poem equates obscurity with integrity, in the last stanza the speaker realizes that because of her awkward ethics she might have no posthumous literary existence: "—I had often thought / How noteless—I could die—."

On the other hand, the voice of poem **612** is far less content with her small lot and furious to think suicide would lead to hereafter rather than to an appealing obliteration of consciousness.

It would have starved a Gnat—
To live so small as I—
And yet I was a living Child—
With Food's necessity

Upon me—like a Claw—
I could no more remove
Than I could coax a Leech away—
Or make a Dragon—move—

Nor like the Gnat—had I—
The privilege to fly
And seek a Dinner for myself—
How mightier He—than I

Nor like Himself—the Art
Upon the Window Pane
To gad my little Being out—
And not begin—again—

Here, as in other poems, Dickinson defines subtle states by saying what they are *not,* possibly because no word exists for the emotional realm she's creating. She describes what she can't do as a means of evoking her obscured achievement (as in poem **486**) or her entrapment (as in poem **612**). The speaker of **"It would have starved a Gnat—"** can't remove the Claw of need; she can neither fly away to independence nor kill herself. Such negative locutions might well be influenced by gender. Women are defined in terms of what they are not (not man, not central; the Other, the peripheral, the distaff) and constructed according to what they lack rather than what they have. The female self is seen as the negative space that allows the positive pattern to emerge. Dickinson created a language embedded with this gendered attrition, a world in which What-Is-Not is something in itself. The voice of poem **646** uses negative definition to imagine a fuller life than the one currently known. In this poem, once again, the speaker and her work are stymied, lacking the power to live and the power to die.

I think to Live—may be a Bliss
To those who dare to try—
Beyond my limit to conceive—
My lip—to testify—

I think the Heart I former wore
Could widen—till to me
The Other, like the little Bank
Appear—unto the Sea—

I think the Days—could every one
In Ordination stand—
And Majesty—be easier—
Than an inferior kind—

No numb alarm—lest Difference come—
No Goblin—on the Bloom—
No start in Apprehension's Ear,
No Bankruptcy—no Doom—

But Certainties of Sun—
Midsummer—in the Mind—
A steadfast South—upon the Soul—
Her Polar time—behind—

The Vision—pondered long—
So plausible becomes
That I esteem the fiction—real—
The Real—fictitious seems—

How bountiful the Dream—
What Plenty—it would be

Had all my Life but been Mistake
Just rectified—in Thee

In stanza two, the speaker's self (the Heart of being) widens to oceanic size, a feat that necessarily removes her from a tangential position. When placed beside this expanded self, the not-me or Other takes on a new scale: ratioed as "the little Bank" is to the Sea. The speaker's wishful vision includes days that stand "In Ordination," a time when Majesty is easier to achieve than inferiority. To ordain is to canonize, in both literary and religious senses. In Dickinson's day, as now, the highest religious and political offices were held by men. For those whose religion is literature, the poet must be priest and prophet. It's difficult to envision a woman in this sphere when actual religions restrict her, at best, to the role of nun, sibyl, or handmaiden to men of the cloth. Thus, the role of poet/priest is seldom accorded a female writer, as it is an Emerson, Thoreau, or Whitman. In this poem, the speaker imagines an impossible utopia or "Bliss" in which her life, her "Days," would be officially invested (ordained) with literary or religious authority. This condition is so hard to describe—because it has never existed—that in stanza four Dickinson resorts to negative definition. She creates the ideal, enfranchised state by saying all it is not. The fullest realization of life is achieved only when one manages to be unafraid of "Difference," possibly because, as stanza two suggests, the Difference has been eradicated: One is no longer in a position of gendered Otherness. Instead of "Bankruptcy," the fully alive woman enjoys "Certainties of Sun—" (Son). Her world of negative definition is replaced by the sure singular faith experienced by Sons, the birthright of those who are culturally central, rather than "Polar." The last two stanzas find the poet utterly convinced by the fantasy she's concocted.

In poem after poem Dickinson defies notions of Otherness by reminding us that all components are mutually dependent and equally important to the whole. The second stanza of **1754** asks us to consider the unseen depths that support the ocean:

To lose thee—sweeter than to gain
All other hearts I knew.
'Tis true the drought is destitute,
But then, I had the dew!

The Caspian has its realms of sand,
Its other realm of sea.
Without the sterile perquisite,
No Caspian could be.

The sandy ocean floor is Other to the ocean's dominant One. Its position, like woman's, is that of "sterile perquisite" or unfruitful privilege. Yet without such a hidden pedestal the sea's visible aspect could not exist.

Poem **584** views women as agents in their own curtailment: The speaker's Grief is likened to the needles "ladies softly press" in pincushions "To keep their place." And the state of numbed, emotional abeyance that appalls in other poems is welcomed as a release from this Anguish.

It ceased to hurt me, though so slow
I could not feel the Anguish go—
But only knew by looking back—
That something—had benumbed the Track—

Nor when it altered, I could say,
For I had worn it, every day,
As constant as the Childish frock—
I hung upon the Peg, at night.

But not the Grief—that nestled close
As needles—ladies softly press
To Cushions Cheeks—
To keep their place—

Nor what consoled it, I could trace—
Except, whereas 'twas Wilderness—
It's better—almost Peace—

In this reversal of synecdoche, "It," "the Anguish," is an immense whole standing for whatever part the reader cares to inscribe. The specifics of "It" could include a failed love affair, the death of a loved one, or the knowledge of creative abnegation. The poem draws upon the same matrix of imagery—the frock upon the Peg, the Cheeks, Wilderness—as **430,** another great poem, which I will analyze in depth.

It would never be Common—more—I said—
Difference—had begun—
Many a bitterness—had been—
But that old sort—was done.—

Or—if it sometime—showed—as 'twill
Upon the Downiest—Morn—
Such bliss—had I—for all the years—
'Twould give an Easier—pain—

I'd so much joy—I told it—Red—
Upon my simple Cheek—
I felt it publish—in my Eye—
'Twas needless—any speak—

I walked—as wings—my body bore—
The feet—I former used—
Unnecessary—now to me—
As boots—would be—to Birds—

I put my pleasure all abroad—
I dealt a word of Gold
To every Creature—that I met—
And Dowered—all the World—

When—suddenly—my Riches shrank—
A Goblin—drank my Dew—
My Palaces—dropped tenantless—
Myself—was beggared—too—

I clutched at sounds—
I groped at shapes—
I touched the tops of Films—
I felt the Wilderness roll back
Along my Golden lines—

The Sackcloth—hangs upon the nail—
The Frock I used to wear—
But where my moment of Brocade—
My—drop—of India?

Syntactical deletion, compression, and blurred pronouns create a degree of profusion extreme even for Dickinson. Almost every line can be reconstructed in several ways, allowing for many variant meanings and a high level of reader involvement. Of course, all literary texts require imagination and reconstruction from a reader. In Dickinson this process is exaggerated as the reader's decisions create one of many possible narratives. If asked to describe the poem's meaning in the simplest terms, we might say it tells a story of gain followed by loss. But what the speaker has won and forfeited is not revealed. The poem's first word, that expansive "It," enforces multiple interpretations by refusing to be pinned to a definite antecedent. Rather than creating an annoying vagueness, as might be expected, Dickinson's unspecified catalysts allow for a greater degree of reader engagement. One notices, too, that this poem does not settle on a single image to describe the inner domain, the way housekeeping represents grief in **"The Bustle in a House."**

Dickinson's signature dashes and her technique of capitalization satisfy our preference for physicality without sacrificing conceptual thought. We linger on "Common" (line one) because of the capital C: Our minds give the abstract word a solidity equal to its typographic weight. In stanza two, line four, "'Twould give an Easier—pain—," the adjective "Easier" precedes the pause of the dash, momentarily taking the syntactical place of the direct object. Since the object of a sentence is frequently a noun, and nouns are often concrete words, "Easier" borrows a nounlike substance before our eyes move on to the syntactically normal direct object, "pain." The potential melodrama of the latter word is undercut by the absence of capitalization, and the lowercase p throws "Easier" into high relief.

Quantum physics, the representative science of our age, offers not one but many ways in which the world might be constructed. One popular theory holds that reality is created by the observer. That is, phenomena such as the moon or trees do not exist until they are observed. This belief is akin to idealism in philosophy, which holds that the world is nothing but mind, and to reception theory in literary criticism, which stresses that readers create a text by connecting and interpreting a series of "gaps" between words and phrases. In an early letter (#32), Dickinson replaced the entire salutation with a dash, explaining "That is'nt [sic] an *empty* blank where I began—it is so full of affection that you cant see any—that's all." Dickinson's dashes underscore the high proportion of such resonant gaps in her poetry. In *Physics and Philosophy,* Heisenberg says that the elementary particles " . . . form a world of potentialities or possibilities rather than one of things or facts. . . . The probability wave . . . means a tendency for something. It's a quantitative version of the old concept of *potentia* in Aristotle's philosophy. It introduces something standing in the middle between the idea of an event and the actual event, a strange kind of physical reality just in the middle between possibility and reality." Dickinson's dashes are a linguistic analogue of probability waves. Moreover, many of her poems are marked with tiny crosses directing us to alternate word choices in the margins. Scholars cannot determine which of these possible words she finally privileged since various drafts make various selections, and other options are never ruled out. One must either allow the poem to be a palimpsest of multiple inscriptions or else participate in the composition by choosing the best word.

One of the more outrageous claims made by some physicists is that reality consists of a steadily increasing number of parallel universes. To quote Nick Herbert's *Quantum Reality,* "For any situation in which several different outcomes are possible (flipping a coin, for instance) some physicists believe that *all outcomes actually occur.*" Just as a flipped coin can show both heads and tails in Heisenberg's world, in the kingdom of Dickinson contradictory events occur simultaneously. Her poetry affords such pleasure in part because it allows us to eat many cakes and have them all. In real life, taking one path usually means forsaking all others. A Dickinson poem, in contrast, allows us to experience many outcomes, some of them conflicting. "I dwell in Possibility—," she wrote. Her poems prolong the intoxicating moment before choice when all options are potentially ours. The loss implicit in any decision is permanently forestalled.

The first line of **430,** for example, can be reconstructed in the following ways:

It [my life] would never be Common
[ordinary, taken for granted]—[what's]
more—I said—

It [my purpose] would never be Common
[known to all, as in common
knowledge or held in common]—[it would
be] more—I said—

It [your love for me] would never be Common [something that occurs
frequently]—[so give me] more—I said—

All these narrative catalysts can be extended throughout the poem. And as we read on, additional narratives spring up to accommodate the connotations of new words, syntax, and context. The poem becomes more myriad with each line, as possible meanings mutate and increase. Hence my reading of **430** doesn't pretend to be the one "right" interpretation or the meaning Dickinson intended. Rather, I offer it as an approach that allows us to appreciate the text's expansive quality.

It's possible to read **430** as a poem in which a woman confronts literary effacement. There are two revelatory moments, the first an experience of empowerment, the second of divestment, as the speaker realizes that lineage and legitimacy must pass from father to son, that she is a Commoner rather than a ruling Queen whose descendants will assume the throne. The narrative progresses from the speaker's recognition of her gift and her ensuing euphoria to her attempts to "dower" or bequeath her poetic legacy. The temerity of this action leads to her sudden downfall and an awareness of her "beggared" state. The languages of royalty, fabric and fashion, publishing and the writer's trade, spatial abstraction, architecture, geometry, and gambling create a bouquet of meaning different from the one that would be achieved by extending a single metaphor throughout.

As the poem begins, the speaker has just become aware of her extraordinary poetic gift. She speaks confidently, in the first flush of accomplishment.

It would never be Common—more—I said—
Difference—had begun—
Many a bitterness—had been—
But that old sort—was done—

This is the moment of triumph all artists know upon achieving work that pleases the inner critic: It [my poetry] would never be Common [plebeian as opposed to royal]—[any] more—I said—/ [My awareness of] Difference—[from other writers] had begun—. Difference entails Otherness; the speaker recognizes herself as alien, "from Mars," if you will. This line also implies that Difference in the sense of argument had begun. The speaker's quarrel is with her peers and with those writers who preceded, indeed overshadowed her. Another reconstruction is: It [my poetry] would never be Common—[any] more—/ [*because*] Difference—had begun—. Hence, the reason for my newly royal status *is* this Difference, this Otherness, this argument. Many a bitterness—had been—[as a result of my Difference] / But that old sort—[of bitterness] was done—[once I saw my Difference as a strength.]

Or—if it sometime—showed—as 'twill
Upon the Downiest—Morn—
Such bliss—had I—for all the years—
'Twould give an Easier—pain—

The indeterminate "it" in the first line harks back to "bitterness" in stanza one as the closest antecedent. But since we've already defined "It" as the speaker's poetry, that meaning must be allowed as well. The open pronoun also might refer to "Difference." The last word in this line, "'twill," is a pun, a figure of speech seldom found in romantic literature but occurring frequently in the metaphysical poets and Shakespeare, which is where Dickinson might have schooled her usage. Readers first recognize "'twill" as an archaic contraction of "It will." But it is also "a basic textile weave producing an allover surface pattern of fine diagonal lines or ribs . . . made by floating weft or warp threads over groups of two or more threads and staggering these floats regularly or irregularly to form a slanting line." (*Webster's Third New International Dictionary,* my source for all the definitions that follow.) "Tell all the truth but tell it slant," Dickinson wrote. The definition of "twill" reads like a marvelous description of her verse, with its surface pattern of narrative lines advancing on their parallel (diagonal) tracks, its regular or irregular meter, and its "slanting line." The concept of floating, staggering threads also contains seeds of the spatial imagery developed in lines to come. Lest this seem farfetched, remember we're reading a poet who claimed her lexicon as her only companion. Surely the definition of *twill,* a stout, old-fashioned gabardine, can't have changed much over the years.

In the stanza's second line, we first hear the preposition "Upon" as meaning "on the occasion of." However, it also introduces the poem's spatial metaphor. When empowered, the speaker is able to view the world from above; her vantage point is akin to a bird's freewheeling prospect or a Queen's enthroned pinnacle. She's on top of things, in the colloquial sense. A bitterness, the firm "twill" of her writing, and/or her Difference—any of these possible subjects might show Upon [on the occasion of, or resting on top of] the Downiest—Morn—. In its noun form, *down* is a covering of soft fluffy feathers that *clothes* young birds before they acquire true feathers; it's used for pillow stuffing because of its light weight and good insulating quality. In Dickinson's poem, "Downiest," most simply, is a vivid descriptor of the *ne plus ultra* in feathery, woolly morning clouds. But it also suggests a costume of false protection or insulation.

The obvious reconstruction of the second stanza is this: Or—if it [the old bitterness] sometime—showed [permitted itself to be seen]—as 'twill [as it will, as it is certain to]—/ Upon [on the occasion of] the Downiest [most insulated, soothing]—Morn—/ Such bliss—had

I—for [in spite of] all the years—/ 'Twould [the bitterness would] give an Easier—pain—. However, the lines take on another dimension when read this way: Or—if it [my poetry] sometime—showed [proved itself]—as 'twill [to be like twill, that firm fabric of slanting lines] / Upon [resting on top of] the Downiest—[most insubstantial] Morn—/ Such bliss—had I—[enough] for all the years—/ 'Twould [the bliss would] give an Easier—pain [than the bitterness I'd had before]. In this reading, the speaker's writing shows itself to be a firm fabric above a more insubstantial, adolescent stuff: down, the false feathers shed by young birds as they mature. Thus, the narrator's art might occasionally achieve an uncommon quality, which gives her infinite joy. Such extreme bliss is painful in itself, but it's an "easier" pain than "that old sort" of bitterness.

I'd so much joy—I told it—Red—
Upon my simple Cheek—
I felt it publish—in my Eye—
'Twas needless—any speak—

The punning Red/read and the verb "publish" work as slant allusions to writing; "Upon" appears again, suggesting spatial hierarchies. But in this context, "Upon" also can mean "against in vengeance or punishment" (wage war upon); very soon after; in answer to; or by means of. "Simple" is a surprisingly rich choice, with its denotations of artless, common, credulous, naive, and "lacking admixture or qualification." Shakespeare used the word to mean feeble or insignificant, as Dickinson surely knew. In addition to the anatomical meaning, "Cheek" is both insolence and "a lateral side of any mass, structure, or opening as . . . either of the side posts of a door or gate." Thus, stanza three can be rendered as follows: I'd so much joy—[that] I [had] told it [my poetry]—Red [Read! I am read]—/ Upon [by means of] my simple [unqualified] Cheek [boldness]—/ I felt it [my poetry] publish—[therefore] in my Eye [Eyes]—'Twas needless—any [other] speak [on my behalf]—. Or alternately, I felt it [my poetry] publish—in my Eye [in my "I," within myself]—/ [therefore] 'Twas needless—[that] any [of my poetry] speak [aloud or publicly]—. Yet another reading suggests the speaker wore her jewel-bright words (Red) like a vivid brocade atop her previously simple (dull, untutored) cheek (face). As in stanza two, when her writing floated a firm warp and weft over less substantial material, in the latter reading her poetry rests atop inferior stuff.

The poem at midpoint finds the narrator held aloft like a bird by her uncommon powers. From this prospect, the meter (feet) she once used moves with a heavy-booted tread.

I walked—as wings—my body bore—
The feet—I former used—
Unnecessary—now to me—
As boots—would be—to Birds—

One of the meanings of "wings" is "a turned back or extended edge on an article of clothing," as in a woman's spreading collar with pointed corners. Dickinson's famous white gown sported just such wings. Of course, wing collars are at the top of a garment, unlike lowly boots, affirming the speaker's taste for what is up rather than "down." Reading "wings" in the most obvious sense, the speaker is a mature bird, unlike those downy creatures flapping in the subtext without the power of flight. In addition, a wing is "either of the parts of a double door or screen," which makes it very like an architectural cheek. It's also a part of a building subordinate to the main or central part and an outlying region or district. By using these senses, Dickinson again locates empowerment in Difference and periphery. Her wings are built on the Circumference of central structures. They project from, are different from, the central part, and therein lies their value. Although we first hear the word "bore" (line one) as the past participle of the verb "to bear," it also means to "pierce . . . make a cylindrical opening in or through by removal of material." With this in mind, the stanza's first lines can mean: I walked—as [the way] wings [walk]—[which is to say, I flew]. My body [of work] bore [opened and deleted] / The [poetic] feet—I former used—/ [which are] Unnecessary—now to me / As boots—would be—to Birds—." Heard in the above sense, "bore" lets us see the speaker's new prosody removing cylinders from the "old sort" of meter. The old "common" meter is riddled with holes, round absences. The speaker's wings are also part of the circular imagery, since a wing can be the arc-shaped piece of a pair of wing compasses that permits the legs (feet) to be fixed at a desired angle. Dickinson very likely knew Donne's "A Valediction: Forbidding Mourning," with its extraordinary comparison of lovers to "stiff twin compasses." Drawing upon the same imagery, she invests her speaker with wings, each one an arc or partial circle. It is their partial quality, their deletions, that make them wings at all and enable navigation. Just as the wings of a compass permit the legs to be fixed at a desired angle, so Dickinson's wings enable her to angle her poetic feet on the slant.

I put my pleasure all abroad—
I dealt a word of Gold
To every Creature—that I met—
And Dowered—all the World—

Here the winged speaker goes public with her powers, endowing the World with portions of her royal estate: Readers probably first understand the verb "put" (line one) as *put forth:* make public. If the speaker's "pleasure" is her writing, then she is making a public assertion of her talent. To *put* also means to express or state, and one's *pleasure* can be one's dearest purpose or inclination. So the regal speaker is proclaiming her desire as well as sharing her wealth. The first meaning of *put* is "to send (as a weapon or missile) into or through something: thrust" (put a bullet through). Thus, the speaker's pleasure/poetry bores through the World "abroad," endowing her literary heirs with deletions, absences identical to the holes she drilled into her own work in stanza four: I put [drilled] my pleasure [through what was] all abroad—. Dickinson's legacy, a paradoxical aesthetic of expansion by deletion, is both eccentric and dangerous. To be *abroad* is to be away from one's home, out in the open. Thus far, Dickinson has stressed the value of what is neither common nor simple, but royal and exotic. Here her persona ventures forth from ordinary life at home into a wider sphere. As a preposition, *abroad* means "throughout, over," and the *Webster's* example is taken from another Dickinson poem: "and then abroad the world he goes." Clearly, "abroad" had connotations of height in her mind. The poem's speaker is aloft, calling the shots from on high. Yet *abroad* can also mean wide of the mark: astray. In this sense, she could be succumbing to a confusion of purpose in sending her creative riches into the public forum: I put [put to use, employed] my pleasure [writing] all abroad [astray]—. If we read *put* as *supposed* ("put the absurd, impossible case for once—"—Robert Browning) or *wagered,* the speaker is allowing publication to determine her pleasure/writing. She is supposing all her riches lay "abroad," rather than within herself; she is basing her pleasure/writing upon a public opinion; and she is gambling by allowing her writing to be published.

She then becomes a linguistic croupier, dealing her "word of Gold." Just as gold can be woven into cloth, her elemental words form an extraordinary twill: malleable, occurring "chiefly in the free state. . . . " One remembers, too, that gold is hardened or changed in color for commercial use by alloying with less precious metals. " . . . Bullion is better than minted things, for it has no alloy," she wrote (Letter 889). If strewing her words abroad is a commercial gesture, the words are devalued in the process. *To deal* is to bestow a fair share, hence the speaker's stance is expansively democratic: She will apportion her wealth widely and equitably. However, dealing "a word of Gold," a metallic command rather than a downy poeticism, is also akin to dealing a blow. The targets of such words are "every Creature." The darker denotations of "Creature"—instrument, minion; "one whose will is not free" (creature of habit)—suggest the speaker as imperialist or emancipator, using her "word of Gold" to dominate or to empower.

In the stanza's last line, she bequeaths the lines/lineage of her poetry to all circumference, all posterity. The verb *dower* means "dare to give," as well as to endow. *Dowry,* the noun form, is not only the gift given to one's spouse at marriage, but also a sum required of postulants by some religious communities. By dowering the world, the poem's persona enacted two roles forbidden women under patriarchy: She dared to bequeath her poems (synonymous with her mind and name) to her literary heirs, and she offered her work as religious dues, a dowry to secure her status as poet/priest. "When a little Girl," she wrote in Letter 330, "I remember hearing that remarkable passage and preferring the 'Power,' not knowing at the time that 'Kingdom' and 'Glory' were included."

> When—suddenly—my Riches shrank—
> A Goblin—drank my Dew—
> My Palaces—dropped tenantless—
> Myself—was beggared—too—

The narrator's sudden divestment is the predictable outcome of her temerity. Her formerly wide prospect shrinks like unsized cloth; her futurity, the amorphous Creatures she hoped to endow, clarify into monsters: "A Goblin—drank my Dew—." The portion of fame the speaker justifiably expects, her due, is consumed by the Goblin posterity. Whereas once her resources were wide enough to encompass an immense sphere (the World), they are now tiny globes of Dew: "small deposits of water . . . produced . . . in the free atmosphere." Her creative Riches become a condensation of vapor directly from the ground, insubstantial and lowly as Down.

"My Palaces—dropped tenantless—," she notes, and one can envision those residences of sovereign and bishop raining down in tiny dew-shaped pieces. Such watery bullets are unable to drill or "bore" enabling deletions in their targets. Of course, a thing has to be highly placed in order to drop. If her lofty Palace was a large public building, "as for . . . superior court," then we see her case dismissed to a lawless inferior realm. But if her Palace was "a gaudy establishment fitted up as a place of public resort," its fall could signal entry into an unsullied, noncommercial realm. If we read "dropped" as a descent "from one line or level to another," the speaker's Palaces, her verbal architecture, are descendants but not progenitors. ("For the Voice is the Palace of all of us. . . . "—Letter 438) She who wished to endow the World is patronized instead: My Palaces [writing]—dropped [descended to me from on high] tenantless [without a legal occupant]. To drop is also to give birth (as in "she dropped her foal"). The speaker's Palaces bear nothingness: They drop (give birth) "tenantless," with nothing to bring forth. And since *to drop* often means "to die," her Palaces perish without issue. Gamblers know that *to drop* is to withdraw from a poker pot by discarding one's hand. In this sense the speaker is choosing to withdraw from competition: My Palaces [my writing]—[I] dropped [withdrew] tenantless [from occupation by others]—. Moreover, *drop* is used to describe a card that must be played because of the obligation to follow suit (as when the queen drops under the ace). The poem's protagonist, formerly a dealer, now finds herself aced, her hand forced by conventional, arbitrary rules. The last line goes out of its way to equate disenfranchisement of work with impoverishment of being. Now that the persona is "beggared," her inner life (Myself) and the eternal life of her work (My Palaces) depend on the largesse of others.

This poem is composed entirely of quatrains until its penultimate stanza, which has one extra line. As the speaker's patterned, hierarchical spheres dissolve into entropic Wilderness, the breaking of stanzaic form enacts her loss of control.

> I clutched at sounds—
> I groped at shapes—
> I touched the tops of Films—
> I felt the Wilderness roll back
> Along my Golden lines—

The syntax of the first two lines is simple and declarative. The protagonist's voice takes on optimum directness, as if she can't afford more complex formulations. This is the only stanza with no midline dashes, since hesitant caesuras would brake the urgency. I noted earlier that Dickinson's abstractions frequently have a concrete quality. In this extremity, her persona views abstract sounds and shapes as physical solids able to support her. She who relied upon the marvelous "twill" of her poems, a cloth of gold suspending her above "the Downiest—Morn," now finds herself supported by "the tops of Films," a veil of fabric flimsy as down. "Films" also suggests blindness: "a pathological growth on or in the eye." One recalls Dickinson's eye problems—serious enough to call for prolonged treatment in Boston.

Once a wanderer in the realms of Gold, she now flounders in a filmy Wilderness like the downy, indeterminate cloudscape of stanza two. In contrast to her former fertility, a *wilderness* is a barren and remote expanse; a confusing multitude or mass. The speaker saw herself as Bird. Now this role is appropriated by the Wilderness, which rolls or trills back at her in a mockery of applause. Viewed as landscape, a rolling Wilderness has an undulating contour—much like downs. A composite of high and low, it rebuts the speaker's firm spatial hierarchies. In fact, the motion of this Wilderness is frighteningly hard to predict. Is it the Common, old sort of bitterness returning, closing over the Golden lines of her poetry like a rolltop desk? Or does it coil backwards, winding itself up like a gauzy roller bandage, in accordance with the speaker's directions (Along her Golden lines)? Rather than settling such questions, Dickinson's syntax and vocabulary allow us to locate agency in either Wilderness or speaker. Whereas once the protagonist roamed freely, now the Wilderness extends in abundance: wallowing, rolling. However, the speaker's Golden lines may be pipes or reins to channel its expansive force. One can imagine the Wilderness as an immense steamroller, leveling the irregular pattern of the poetic line. Or one can read *roll* as "to make (a stereotype matrix) or mold (a form) in a mangle" and envision the Wilderness molding both itself and the lines back into a Common, stereotypical form: I felt the Wilderness roll [itself] back [up] / Along [with] my Golden lines [of poetry]—. The Wilderness becomes a giant metronome enforcing regular prosody when *roll* is percussive: I felt the Wilderness roll [drum] back [in response] / Along [over the length of] my Golden lines—. Thus, the enabling holes the speaker drilled in meter return in this monstrous, whirling Wilderness capable of obliterating her language entirely. Dickinson's fascicles come to mind when we learn that *along* means "for the whole length . . . specif: with the thread stitches of a book passed direct from two opposed kettle stitches—used with *all* (to handsew a book or section all along)." One envisions a Wilderness of literary obscurity wheeling all along the orderly books she stitched with lines of thread. *Rolled gold* is a base metal sheathed in a thin plate of gold. Here, however, the values are reversed as a brass Wilderness plates 24-karat lines. But all of these readings are undermined when we realize a *line* is also a length of material used in measuring and leveling. One can use such lines to regularize foundations—or chaos.

The speaker and the Wilderness are engaged in sportive struggle, since *roll* is to throw dice in competition: I felt the Wilderness roll back [take its turn at dice] / Along [alongside] my Golden lines (*lines* can be "a strip on a craps layout on which are placed side bets to the effect that the caster of dice will pass")—. *Lines* are also the means of defense or control that present a front to the enemy; they are threads of a spider's web; ropes attached to whaling harpoons; the four imaginary areas on a fencer's body when confronting an opponent; or snares for fish—all meanings that suggest battle. The twill of this poetry is spun from long fibers of flax known as *lines;* and the word also describes the style or cut of the speaker's winged garment. Most importantly, *lines* means a person's ancestors and descendants, as in bloodlines. Thus the Wilderness, in rolling back along the speaker's lines or descendants, obliterates her literary issue. If, on the other hand, a *line* is a leash, the Wilderness is rolling over like a trained puppy on a Golden lead.

Most of these reconstructions take "Golden lines" as a sincere reference to high-quality verse. However, the phrase may be an ironic, self-mocking comment on language ordered like a merchant's line of goods, with salability and public demand in mind. Earlier the poem equated entry into the public sphere with confusion of purpose. Now the speaker may recognize that the act of putting her "pleasure all abroad" changed her "word of Gold" into fool's Gold. Such Golden lines are like an actor's golden-tongued utterances: a glib means of persuasion and manipulation.

By the last stanza, the narrator's golden lines have been woven into a garment of mourning and placed on high, in the honorific realm where she had flown.

> The Sackcloth—hangs upon the nail—
> The Frock I used to wear—
> But where my moment of Brocade—
> My—drop—of India?

But sackcloth can also signal protest. A symbol of repentance or rebellion, it hangs in abeyance beside the Frock she wore in the Common days, before the "difference" of poetry. In stanza five, the narrator tried to "dower" all the World with poems, as if they were the dues paid by a religious postulant. However, rather than being canonized, she finds herself defrocked. In addition to its religious denotation, a frock is "an outer garment worn chiefly by men"; "a coat of mail"; "a workman's outer shirt"; "a military coat"; "a woman's dress"; and "a dress . . . formerly worn by both boys and girls." Thus deprived of religious, combative, plebeian, protective, androgynous costumes, what role is left her? If frock and sackcloth are the same garment, as the syntax can suggest, the roles associated with "Frock" are also forms of mourning or protest. Even if the narrator willingly discarded these possible states—from Commoner to priest—what sphere now remains for her?

These questions are among many clustered in the poem's last two lines. Brocade, a rich oriental silk fabric with raised patterns embroidered in gold and silver threads, is a royal twill indeed. Readers probably hear "moment of Brocade" as the speaker's instant of empowerment. The final line "My—drop—of India?" most obviously refers to her minute part of an exotic public domain. If, however, we define *moment* as "an essential or constituent element," we hear her wonder what's become of the elemental Gold thread in her impoverished Brocade. That this fabric had connotations of legacy, firmness, and solitude to Dickinson is clear from her letters. To Samuel Bowles (Letter 277) she wrote of " . . . your memory that can stand alone, like the best Brocade." And in letter 368, to Higginson, she said "—But truth like Ancestor's Brocades can stand alone—." Since George Eliot was one of Dickinson's enthusiasms, the notion of Brocade as a coat of arms was probably suggested by this passage from *The Mill on the Floss:* "Mrs. Glegg . . . had inherited from her grandmother . . . a brocaded gown that would stand up empty, like a suit of armour. . . . " And *drop* means "a small pear-shaped figure occasionally borne as a heraldic charge." In this poem, the speaker has lost her "drop—of India," the tiny woman-shape that served as emblem of her feminine yet royal lineage. Heraldry, however, is based on patrilineage; hence the narrator's attempt to forge a heraldic device of her own, in the India ink drops of her poems, is an impossible task. Dickinson uses the verb *to drop* in the sixth stanza ("My Palaces—dropped tenantless—") to show a grand verbal structure giving birth to nothingness. In this conclusion, we hear her persona wondering what has become of her progeny: [Where is] My—drop [the act of giving birth or the young so born]—of India [ink]? A *drop* is also the space through which an unrestrained escape wheel moves while disengaged from the pallets. Thus the space of poetry might provide an escape from the rolling Wilderness of stanza seven: But where my moment [impetus] of Brocade [poems]—/ [which was] My—drop [escape route]—of India [ink]? And since *drop* is a pendant jewel or ornament, the last line oscillates between ideas of words as gems and words as baubles: But where my moment [essential element] of Brocade [language]—/ [which is] My—drop [jewel or bauble]—of India [ink]?"

Thinking of *moment* as consequence, and recalling Dickinson's eye troubles, one sees the lines this way: But where [is] my moment [effect, consequence] of Brocade [verb: "to weave patterns into"]—/ [Where is] My—drop [eyedrop]—of India [ink]? *Drop* is "a solution for dilating the pupil of the eye." One takes in too much through such an open gaze; the expanded pupil winces at the gemmy glittering world it must admit. But where is the influence I should exert having written brilliant poems? she asks. And where are the poems that enlarged my vision? Those drops of India ink afforded protection and identification, as well as a dazzling expansion.

We've noticed the speaker's ambivalence toward publication or putting her "pleasure all abroad." That vacillation continues if *drop* is read as "a decline in quality." And Dickinson might have known an obscure meaning of *moment* from Shakespeare, who used the word to mean a cause or motive of action ("I have seen her die twenty times upon far poorer moment"). Just as "to embroider" is a gentle way of saying "to lie," the verb *brocade* connotes a language of false, decorative overlays. In light of this, the last lines might be rendered: But where my moment [motivation] of Brocade [verb: to embroider, falsify]—/ [which was] My—drop [deterioration]—of India [ink]? Having lost the impulse to "brocade" her poems, the narrator is in a state of indeterminate purity: neither high nor low, royal nor common. Her relinquishment of fame signals her ordainment as poet rather than poetician.

The Newtonian definitions of *moment* also were available to Dickinson, who was well educated in the science of her day. These meanings speak to the poem's large tropes of center and periphery, public and private spheres. Scientifically speaking, a *moment* is the tendency to produce motion, especially about a point or axis. When applied to "moment of Brocade" we see the gorgeous raised patterns of the narrator's poetry creating a stir on the periphery of a literary center. *Moment* is also "the product of quantity (as a force) and the distance to a particular axis or point," as in moment of a couple, moment of a force, moment of inertia, or "moment of Brocade." In Dickinson's poem, *moment* results when her genius (force) is multiplied by her distance from a literary axis. Thus in the last lines, the speaker has lost the problem of genius times distance that resulted in the "product" of her poems. But she is unable to lose or "drop" her longing for a public domain: "But where [is] my moment [product] of Brocade [poems]—/ [And where] My—drop [relinquishment]—of India [the foreign sphere she wished to enter]? The speaker's Otherness, her aberrant quality, is prized if "moment" is read as " . . . some power of the deviations of the elements of a frequency distribution from a specified norm. syn: importance." In *Emily Dickinson, A Poet's Grammar,* Cristanne Miller writes, "In poetry, meaning may lie as much in the interaction of semantic content and form as in a message that can be isolated from the poem. The more a poem calls attention to its formal elements by various foregrounding techniques, the more the reader is likely to learn about its meaning from them. If we assume as a norm language that calls no attention to its formal properties by deviating from the conventions of standard communication (that is, an utterance intended solely to communicate a message), then Dickinson's poetry is richly deviant." Thus, her Brocade's importance is equal to its degree of deviation from the norms of language: But where my moment [important deviance] of Brocade [foregrounded difference in language]—?

A Poet's Grammar provides a fascinating analysis of Dickinson's syntactical strategies. The book also will interest all who enjoy thinking about the formal aspects of language, since Miller's tools and methods can be applied with profit to any poet's work. While considering the distance between biographical mythology and Miller's brilliant formalist approach, I was tempted to call this essay "A Poet's Glamour." In the Middle Ages, those who had "grammar" or knowledge seemed to possess magical occult powers. Eventually the Scots substituted an *l,* making "glamour" the etymological daughter of "grammar." In like fashion, Dickinson's glamour is the corrupt form of her grammar. Her poetry has been diluted and her readers deluded by fanciful images of the poet—from debutante to Dragon Lady. It's time we turned our attention to her grammar in the ancient sense: that enchanting, learned language she inexplicably magicked from hymns, trash, canon, culture, and self.

I think Emily Dickinson believed herself a great poet. She needed that faith in order to make poetry central to her life. By choosing to be a recluse and refusing publication, she protected herself from the world's opinion of her talent, which might have destroyed her as an artist. Helen Hunt Jackson, a highly successful poet herself, pressed Dickinson to publish, and could have helped her had she shown any interest. But it was as if she intuited (perhaps from her correspondence with Higginson) that publication would diminish her. Indeed, had she read the scathing *Atlantic* review of her debut, it would have been much harder to regard herself as Queen of language. Only full enfranchisement, the recognition of her stature as a mature woman genius, would suffice. "Queen" appears in nineteen of her poems; "princess" in none.

Although Dickinson went to great lengths to protect her gift, at times the world's disregard must have impinged. Like **430** ("It would never be Common—more—I said—"), the following poem **(458)** can be read as a female writer's awakening to disenfranchisement. In this case, the persona addresses either her own reflection or an imagined literary daughter. The speaker may be regarding herself and considering the same question posed in another poem: "What would the Dower be / Had I the Art to stun myself / With Bolts of Melody!" **(505)** As a woman, however, she is incapable of endowing herself or her descendants with any illuminating lineage. As in **430,** the speaker's slant vision, her culturally defined Otherness, is recognized as the source of both her creative power and her historical effacement. Having said this, I must add that I offer such suggestions only as an invitation. I hope readers will stitch shimmering absences and orchestrate bountiful options to arrive at their own versions of the poem.

Like Eyes that looked on Wastes—
Incredulous of Ought
But Blank—and steady Wilderness—
Diversified by Night—

Just Infinites of Nought—
As far as it could see—
So looked the face I looked upon—
So looked itself—on Me—

I offered it no Help—
Because the Cause was Mine—
The Misery a Compact
As hopeless—as divine—

Neither—would be absolved—
Neither would be a Queen
Without the Other—Therefore—
We perish—tho' We reign—

Notes

[1] Women who write poetry are commonly called "women poets"; men who write poetry are commonly called "poets." I use "man poet" here because the term establishes linguistic parity and questions the implications of singling out women for difference. When "female poet" replaces "woman poet" as the popular term, it will be fair to say "male poet" rather than "man poet."

[2] Spring/Summer 1988.

[3] This paragraph seems to belong in the early seventies, when the practical aspects of women's status underwent much investigation. Yet despite the many resultant changes in our lives, the statistics I cite prove that there has been little sharing of power or esteem within the higher echelons of poetry. Rather than being self-evident, this state of affairs is willfully ignored. Hence I offer these facts, though in doing so I feel I'm reinventing the wheel.

Cheryl Walker (essay date 1989)

SOURCE: "Locating a Feminist Critical Practice: Between the Kingdom and the Glory," in *Emily Dickinson: a Celebration for Readers,* edited by Suzanne Juhasz and Cristanne Miller, Gordon and Breach, 1989, pp. 9-19.

[*In the following essay, Walker analyzes the way in which Dickinson's views and portrayals of power relationships were influenced "by her experience of gender." Walker maintains that while some feminist examinations of Dickinson have painted her life as a "model of a successful feminist manipulation of circumstances," this view is inaccurate, given Dickinson's fascination with male power.*]

In three different letters, numbered by Johnson and Ward 292, 330, and 583, Emily Dickinson uses a passage from the Sermon on the Mount (Matthew 6:13) to privilege power as a category surpassing or incorporating kingdom and glory. One such passage reads: "When I was a little Girl I remember hearing that remarkable passage and preferring the 'Power,' not knowing at the time that 'Kingdom' and 'Glory' were included" (L 330).

As a feminist critic I am concerned with power: both the power language confers and the power relations which affect language use itself. Dickinson was first taken up in a major way by the New Critics who preferred what I would call the glory aspect of power in its synchronic dimensions. This was an era in which the "universality" of Dickinson's poems, particularly those about God, love and death, was applauded along with her linguistic originality. Dickinson herself called glory "that bright tragic thing/ That for an instant/ Means Dominion" in poem # **1660.** The "instant" seems to lie outside of time though it might also be said to "remember" time which gives it the aura of tragic limitation.

Kingdom, on the other hand, is a signalling word frequently used to differentiate different forms of time, as in **#721 ("Behind me dips Eternity")** or forms of power. As a Janus-faced image, the kingdom may look toward heaven or toward earth, but when the word appears, we are usually reminded that on earth the Soul is exposed to time, to history, and to the power relations which may inhibit her, especially if she is a woman. The poems I am most interested in seem to emerge at the crux, or crossing, of kingdom and glory, in the nexus of power. Holding kingdom and glory in tension, these poems provide a discourse about power which says a great deal about one version of the nineteenth-century female imagination.

Interpreting the poems, however, involves locating one's critical practice itself within the nexus of power. As a feminist critic, I must evaluate a number of critical strategies already in place. If New Criticism tended to prefer the glory of Dickinson's work, feminist criticism inevitably concerns itself with the kingdom, with patriarchy, and with the power relations which affect language use itself.

A recent fashion in feminist criticism is to tell success stories. Having passed beyond telling the stories of women as victims, we now celebrate the way women writers remained undefeated and managed to subvert oppressive male power structures embodied in both social and literary conventions. The virtues of this criticism are often its courage, imagination, and gusto. However, my problem with it is that it seems at times to lack fidelity and sensitivity to the past. Also, by emphasizing transcendence, it minimizes the effects of patriarchy and thus subtly reinforces its hold over our past and our present.

Let me be more specific in respect to the case of Emily Dickinson. It is now fashionable to celebrate Dickinson's withdrawal from the world, to acknowledge her cleverness in avoiding various forms of social oppression many nineteenth-century women who led more normal lives had to contend with. It is also fashionable for feminist critics to feel that they can find ample evidence for Dickinson's essential sympathies with feminism in her poems and letters. Certain facts about Dickinson's life and art provide at least a degree of friction against such theories, however.

Her fearfulness and dependency upon others late into her life, her choice of conservative Judge Lord as a lover, her dismissal of most women and admiration of powerful men, her mental breakdowns: all suggest that Dickinson's life is not quite the model of a successful feminist manipulation of circumstances we sometimes wish it to be.

Furthermore, Dickinson was not unusually concerned about being "a *woman* poet." At least her *conscious* dedication to gender-neutral philosophical issues in a great many poems distinguishes her from most other nineteenth-century American women poets and has led us as feminist critics to return again and again to the same comparatively small number of poems and letters which do address gender in some overt way.

In the space I have left I would like to consider a different way of reading Dickinson historically. The *modus operandi* I wish to adopt, which might loosely be called a form of post-structuralism, is in no sense unique to my reading of Dickinson. In fact, I wish only to confirm a set of strategies used occasionally and with varying degrees of success by many critics. Though not nearly as often situating herself in a gender-specific context as many of her female contemporary writers, Dickinson is more directly conscious of allying herself with power than they were. Her poems and letters are liberally sprinkled with references to power and certainly her language use exhibits a desire to equate poetry not with release of feeling, as many nineteenth-century poetesses did, but with the assumption of power and the defiance of tradition. One way of reading her historically is to consider the way her representation of power relations might have been affected by her experience of gender. Dickinson clearly admired power but her orientation to it was highly ambivalent and as such it both unites her to other women poets and reflects her position in a power structure which allies power with masculinity.

Susan Gilbert Dickinson was rare among her associates in being a woman who inspired Dickinson with a sense of earthly ascendancy. Even to miss her was power, as she says in letter #364, and from early to late Susan brings the word *power* to Emily Dickinson's mind. As late as 1882 she is writing to Susan: "Thank her dear power for having come, an Avalanche of Sun!" (L755).

It is usually men, however, who represent power in Dickinson's imagination. Higginson is a figure of power who often evokes the poet's most timid self. In the letter with which I began this essay, in addition to reflecting on the relationship between kingdom, power and glory, Dickinson compliments Higginson's letter for a "a spectral power in thought that walks alone," adding: "I would like to thank you for your great kindness but never try to lift the words which I cannot hold" (L 330). (Apparently he has been criticizing her diction.) She also poses as comparatively insignificant in a letter to Samuel Bowles. After her tribute to his influence in the lives of "so many," she confesses that she has no such range of impact. However, she further muses, "How extraordinary that Life's large Population contain so few of power to us" (L 275). In this reflection, she characteristically turns the tables. Though her power over others is limited, the power of most people to affect her is also limited. These two letters suggest two typical modes Dickinson employed in dealing with male power figures.

Clearly, Dickinson was attracted to masculine forms of power. She writes approvingly of a portrait of Tommaso Salvini in 1884 in terms that bring to mind her feelings about her father: "The brow is that of Deity—the eyes, those of the lost, but the power lies in the *Throat*—pleading, sovereign, savage—the panther and the dove!" (L 948). Her admiration for her father and the Master letters further confirm their attraction to stimulating versions of male force. And we must remember her involvement with the intimidating Judge Lord. She describes his face in these terms in 1885: "Had I not loved it, I had feared it, the Face had such ascension" (L967).

Even Dickinson's definitions of poetry are clothed in the rhetoric of power. "If I read a book [and] it makes my whole body so cold no fire ever can warm me, I know *that* is poetry. If I feel physically as if the top of my head were taken off, I know *that* is poetry. These are the only way I know it" (L342a). *Art* and *power* are sometimes used interchangeably.

But the synthesis power effects in Dickinson is always decaying into antithesis, into powerlessness, and that too is a fundamental property of her imagination and an indication of her shared relation to a gender-differentiated power structure. In order to explore why that might have been characteristic of her, it is helpful to look a little outside the usual critical structure and to bring to bear on Dickinson's work some of the insights of recent French feminist theory.

Helene Cixous begins her strange, provocative essay "Sorties" in *The Newly-Born Woman* with the following set of reflections:

> Where is she?
> Activity/Passivity
> Sun/Moon
> Culture/Nature
> Day/Night
>
> Father/Mother
> Head/Heart
> Intelligible/Palpable
> Logos/Pathos

> Form, convex, step, advance, semen, progress
> Matter, concave, ground—where steps are taken, holding-and dumping ground.
> Man
> ———
> Woman
>
> Always the same metaphor: we follow it, it carries us, beneath all its figures, wherever discourse is organized. If we read or speak, the same thread or double braid is leading us throughout literature, philosophy, criticism, centuries of representation and reflection.
>
> Thought has always worked through opposition,
> Speaking/Writing
> Parole/Ecriture
> High/Low
>
> Through dual, hierarchical oppositions. Superior/Inferior, Myths, legends, books. Philosophical systems. Everywhere (where) ordering intervenes, where a law organizes what is thinkable by oppositions (dual, irreconcilable; or sublatable, dialectical). All these pairs of oppositions are *couples*. Does that mean something? Is the fact that Logocentrism subjects thought—all concepts, codes and values—to a binary system, related to "the" couple, man/woman? (63-63)

Cixous' provocative suggestion that we read a binary opposition between man and woman as the basis of many other paired oppositions in philosophical discourse is at the heart of my argument for a historical and gendered reading of Dickinson. We can, of course, search the poems for places where Dickinson consciously and directly reflects upon gender. If we are cultural critics, we can look for direct references to historical persons and events. However, we do not need to proceed in this way in order to find the impact of patriarchy on the poet's work. As a poet whose work is necessarily inscribed within the codes of nineteenth-century American bourgeois culture, Emily Dickinson could not fail to reproduce in part the structure of power relations in which she was enmeshed.

No cultural hegemony is absolute, however. Consider, for instance, this pair of statements about women and power made by two men of Dickinson's time and milieu. In his novel *Miss Gilbert's Career,* Josiah Holland, Dickinson's friend, congratulates his heroine for giving up her literary career in exchange for a career of marriage and self-sacrifice. Her need for power is re-routed so that it is no longer her own "imperious will" which she seeks to gratify. Holland writes: "She learned that a woman's truest career is lived in love's serene retirement—lived in feeding the native forces of her other self—lived in the career of her husband" (466). Here we have the common and recognizable version of true womanhood's relation to power: indirect, self-effacing, domestic, and predicated on the virtues of heart and hearth.

Austin Dickinson's description of the impact of women on some aspects of nineteenth-century culture is quite different, however. His opinion is that "the women count in our modern census. They have appeared above the surface in the last generation, and become a power, nowhere more than in parish affairs, where they have found a congenial field for their activities . . . They are hardly longer the power behind the throne; they are a good part of the throne itself" (Sewall, *The Life,* 121-22).

Leaving aside here the complex issues of biographical origins, of sincerity and authenticity raised by these quotations, let us acknowledge that they do point to a situation first experienced by middle-class American women in the nineteenth century: the situation of finding themselves able to operate in a public arena in *relatively* large numbers while they were at the same time deeply afflicted with a sense of guilt for betraying the ethical code of femininity and the domestic sphere. This is the double bind nimbly captured in Mary Kelley's title, *Private Woman, Public Stage.*

It is not enough to say that women were in many ways effectively powerless in nineteenth-century American bourgeois culture. We must also acknowledge that in parish activities, in education, in certain political causes, and *as writers,* middle-class women had more public influence than ever before. Many nineteenth-century women writers supported whole families with the proceeds of their writing. Lydia Sigourney could command $100 for four poems and $500 from *Godey's Lady's Book* for the use of her name on its title page. However, the cost of playing on the public stage, or entering the market, could be great as well. In the nineteenth century we see the first major alliance between creative women and madness.

Catherine Clement in her disquisition on "the hysteric" in *The Newly-Born Woman* gives us a set of highly-charged statements applicable to many guilt-ridden nineteenth-century women writers. Clement, in the essay called "The Guilty One," writes:

> That is the easiest solution: keeping oneself in a state of permanent guilt is to constitute oneself as a subject. Caught up in themes which are not hers, repeating her cues, always somewhere between sleep and wakefulness, between a hypnotic and an excited state, she is not she, but through the play of identifications, she is successively each one of the others. They are going to help her become a subject: they are going to make her guilty. (46)

This is the way Clement describes the simultaneous attraction and threat represented by the powerful male intermediary to the talented but conflicted woman.

These interventions in the on-going discussion about women and power must serve as an introduction to my reading of two poems about power in Emily Dickinson's canon: **"My life had stood a loaded gun"** and **"Behind me dips eternity."** Both of these poems have been extensively discussed by others; few critics, however, have attempted to talk about the loaded gun poem as a particularly historical document.

The poem really clicks into place when we consider it as one written by a certain kind of woman in nineteenth-century America.

Let's look at the poem in more detail:

> My Life had stood—a Loaded Gun—
> In Corners—till a Day
> The Owner passed—identified—
> And carried Me away—
>
> And now We roam in Sovreign Woods—
> And now We hunt the Doe—
> And every time I speak for Him—
> The Mountains straight reply—
>
> And do I smile, such cordial light
> Upon the Valley glow—
> It is as a Vesuvian face
> Had let it's pleasure through—
>
> And when at Night—Our good Day done—
> I guard My Master's Head—
> 'Tis better than the Eider-Duck's
> Deep Pillow—to have shared—
>
> To foe of His—I'm deadly foe—
> None stir the second time—
> On whom I lay a Yellow Eye—
> Or an emphatic Thumb—
>
> Though I than He—may longer live
> He longer must—than I—
> For I have but the power to kill,
> Without—the power to die—

Written about 1863, this poem examines the effects of assuming certain kinds of power. A moral focus is conspicuously absent as a divining rod until the last stanza where the speaker with only "the power to kill" reveals her morally compromised position. The poem does a double take, strangely, in that last stanza. Up until this point, the reader is invited to see the speaker's newly assumed identity as beneficial and even heroic. The Wordsworthian mountains echo her speech, the day done has been a "good day," a strenuous day more satisfying than sleeping on a downy pillow. Only the third stanza with its "Vesuvian face" throws an eerie light over this whole proceeding. It's worth remembering that Mount Vesuvius erupted a number of times during the 1850s climaxing with a particularly fearsome and destructive eruption in 1861. Should we ignore the threat implied in a volcanic eruption? Up until the final stanza the poet seems peculiarly unwilling to judge negatively this assumption of destructive force. A variant for "None stir the second time" is "None *harm* the second time," again suggesting that the gun's destructive force is not morally suspect since it is used defensively.

However, the final stanza clearly introduces a new emotion into the poem. The emotion is guilt. I agree with Barbara Clarke Mossberg that this poem represents "an array of conflicting attitudes toward art and the self, which result in severe identity conflict" (23). The poem is hysterical in certain ways and that hysteria must be understood in the historical context of a continent and a century in which women were invited to assume certain sorts of power while at the same time subtly tortured for their desires to do so.

Let us go back to Catherine Clement's description of the hysterical woman as "the guilty one": she has been possessed by her doctors. They have offered her the chance to become a subject. "Caught up in themes which are not hers, repeating her cues, always somewhere between sleep and wakefulness, between a hypnotic and an excited state, she is not she, but through the play of identifications, she is successively each one of the others. They are going to help her become a subject: they are going to make her guilty." This is the position described by the female gun self.

From my point of view, this poem is not a confession of the poet's personal misery, however. Richard Sewall provides a helpful reminder in his biography that the *Springfield Republican* used the eider-duck image in an 1860 article discouraging women poets from writing "the literature of misery." The speaker here rejects the eider duck's deep pillow. Instead of being a confessional poem, this work is closer to a definitional exploration of a certain kind of power.

My intuition is that Dickinson began this poem with the intention of writing another celebration of her relation to the Master Force. This would connect the first stanza, at least, to other works like **"I'm ceded, I've stopped being theirs," "He put the belt around my life,"** and **"A wife at daybreak I shall be."** There is a sense of strain in the poem, however, as though as she went along—at first admiring the power conferred upon the speaker by her relation to the Owner—another set of issues presented itself in her mind. What does it mean for a woman to subsume herself so totally in the life of a masculine presence? The metatext begins to unravel the text by suggesting the destructiveness of a pure instrumentality. Negative associations with power lurch through the backcountry of the poetic landscape.

Without the owner, the speaker cannot speak at all. She cannot roam in "Sovreign Woods," that is, in the forest protected for the king's own hunting, the forest of patriarchal power. However, the cost of accepting this empowerment is hunting the doe, killing off her linkage to female life, and surrendering a maternal, nurturing influence like that of the eider duck (known to cushion her babies by feathering her nest with down plucked from her own breast). Though we cannot help feeling the emphatic thumb of the poet's conscious attempt to make us admire this power through most of the poem, we also cannot ignore the accumulation of underground hints of guilt.

At the end, the speaker seems to throw up her hands in horror at the satanic bargain she has made. As a ventriloquist's dummy, as a pure instrument of another's force, she has surrendered her status as a subject. Power can only be understood as part of an oppositional pair in juxtaposition with powerlessness as life can only be lived fully with the knowledge of death as its terminus. Having agreed to speak only for him, the gun seals *his* immortality while at the same time accepting the status of non-being for herself. The power to kill involves the preliminary death of the self recorded in the gun's admission that she no longer has the power to die. She is already dead. The speaker has become not a self, as she had hoped, but a mouthpiece.

As we watch the sovereign female self assume the mantle of power in the poem only to turn that mantle inside out at the end in a confession of guilt and powerlessness, we witness a ritual performed again and again in the nineteenth century by creative women, for whom power, once admired, turns ugly and self-destructive. Toward the end of the century, Ella Wheeler Wilcox summed it up in *Men, Women and Emotions* (1893): "Seen from a distance, fame may seem to a woman like a sea bathed in tropical suns, wherein she longs to sail. Let fame once be hers, she finds it a prairie fire consuming or scorching all that is dearest in life to her. Be careful before you light these fires with your own hands" (291). As in so many statements of its kind, for the more narrow instance of fame, we might very well substitute the broader, more threatening term: power.

Another poem in which fears for a female self emerge is **"Behind me dips eternity"** (# **721**).

Behind Me—dips Eternity—
Before Me—Immortality—
Myself—the Term between—
Death but the Drift of Eastern Gray,

Dissolving into Dawn away,
Before the West begin—

'Tis Kingdoms—afterward—they say—
In perfect—pauseless Monarchy—
Whose Prince—is Son of None—
Himself—His Dateless Dynasty—
Himself—Himself diversify—
In Duplicate divine—

'Tis Miracle before Me—then—
'Tis Miracle behind—between—
A Crescent in the Sea—
With Midnight to the North of Her—
and Midnight to the South of Her—
And Maelstrom—in the Sky—

Reading this poem in a gendered historical context, I am particularly struck by the speaker's positioning of herself in terms of these two axes: An east-west metaphysics rendered male and a north-south temporal realm rendered female. In a century which at least paid considerable lip service to the notion of separate spheres of gender, in a country in which those spheres have paradigms in Puritan gender divisions predicated on Adam and Eve, the poet seems both to invoke and to revoke conventional mappings of power. This poem can be read as the poet's self-insertion of the female into history: "Myself—the Term between." *His* power, from this point of view, looks comparatively lifeless. As under the aegis of the patriarchal god, patriarchal authority clones itself repeatedly in what Cixous might call a "repetition of the same," the speaker understands her position as not merely personal (an *I*'s position) but generic (a *Her*'s position). "With Midnight to the North of Her-/ And Midnight to the South of Her," she has no points of reference to determine her own power, however. Might not this "Maelstrom in the Sky" suggest a whirlpool of male force threatening to derange her "crescent in the sea"? It will take a miracle of a different kind to preserve her from harm.

My intention in this brief textual discussion has been to make an argument not only for the plausibility of historical, gender-sensitive criticism but for its continuing exfoliation. To the extent that we can find new ways of decoding the power relations which operate both behind and within literature we open up new ways of seeing our own linguistic situations in the present. As Toril Moi puts it in *Sexual/Textual Politics,* "It is necessary to deconstruct the opposition between traditionally 'masculine' and traditionally 'feminine' values *and* to confront the full political force and reality of such categories" (160). This means locating a feminist critical practice along two axes, ignoring neither the kingdom which circumscribed an Emily Dickinson nor the glory which she learned to appropriate for her art.

Works Cited

All references to the poems and letters of Emily Dickinson are taken from the following sources and reflect the numbering system used in these sources: *The Letters of Emily Dickinson,* 3 vols. Edited by Thomas H. Johnson and Theodora Ward. Cambridge, Mass: Harvard UP, 1955; *The Poems of Emily Dickinson.* 3 vols. Edited by Thomas H. Johnson. Cambridge, Mass.: 1958.

Cameron, Sharon. *Lyric Time: Dickinson and the Limits of Genre.* Baltimore: Johns Hopkins UP, 1979.

Cixous, Helene and Catherine Clement. *The Newly Born Woman.* Minneapolis: U of Minnesota P, 1986.

Holland, Josiah Gilbert. *Miss Gilbert's Career.* New York: Scribner's, 1860.

Kelley, Mary. *Private Woman, Public Stage.* New York: Oxford UP, 1984.

Moi, Toril. *Sexual/Textual Politics.* New York: Methuen, 1985.

Mossberg, Barbara Antonina Clarke. *Emily Dickinson: When a Writer is a Daughter.* Bloomington: Indiana UP, 1982.

Sewall, Richard B. *The Life of Emily Dickinson.* 2 vols. New York: Farrar, Straus, 1974.

Wilcox, Ella Wheeler. *Men, Women, and Emotions.* Chicago: Mirrill, Higgins, 1893.

Paula Bennett (essay date 1990)

SOURCE: "The Pea That Duty Locks: Lesbian and Feminist-Heterosexual Readings of Emily Dickinson's Poetry," in *Lesbian Texts and Contexts: Radical Revisions*, edited by Karla Jay and Joanne Glasgow, New York University Press, 1990, pp. 104-25.

[*In the following essay, Bennett challenges feminist critics who study Dickinson "as a woman poet" but within the context of Dickinson's "relationship to the male tradition." Bennett asserts that Dickinson's erotic poetry suggests that the poet viewed her relationships with women as safe and protected, and that these relationships allowed Dickinson to explore her sexuality.*]

> [The clitoris] is endowed with the most intense erotic sensibility, and is probably the prime seat of that peculiar life power, although not the sole one.
>
> —Charles D. Meigs, *Woman: Her Diseases and Remedies,* 1851

> One would have to dig down very deep indeed to discover . . . some clue to woman's sexuality. That extremely ancient civilization would undoubtedly have a different alphabet, a different language. . . . Woman's desire would not be expected to speak the same language as man's.
>
> —Luce Irigaray, *This Sex Which is Not One,* 1985

In a 1985 essay in *Feminist Studies,* Margaret Homans brilliantly analyzes Emily Dickinson's use of vaginal imagery ("lips") as a multivalent figure for female sexual and poetic power ("'Syllables'" 583-86, 591). Homans quite rightly identifies Dickinson's concept of the volcanic "lips that never lie" in **"A still—Volcano—Life"** (***The Poems* 461**)[1] with the genital/lingual lips from which the hummingbird sucks in **"All the letters I can write"**:

> All the letters I can write
> Are not fair as this—
> Syllables of Velvet—
> Sentences of Plush,
> Depths of Ruby, undrained,
> Hid, Lip, for Thee—

Play it were a Humming Bird—
And just sipped—me—

(#**334**)

Less happily, Homans treats Dickinson's use of genital imagery entirely within the context of the (male) tradition of the romantic love lyric (that is, as a "subversion" of the "scopic" economy, or visual orientation, of masculinist love poetry). Not only does she fail to discuss the poem's homoerotic or lesbian possibilities, she barely notes them—this despite the fact that the poem's only known variant was originally sent—with a flower—to a woman, Dickinson's cousin, Eudocia (Converse) Flynt, of Monson, Massachusetts. For Homans, text—not sex—is the issue.

As in **"A still—Volcano—Life,"** the imagery in **"All the letters I can write"** is undoubtedly (if not necessarily, consciously) sexual. The reader-lover-bird is told to sip from the well-hidden "depths" of the poet-vagina-flower: "lip" to lips. But the form of sexual congress which the poet fantasizes in this poem is—as Homans fails to specify—oral; and the sex of the beloved-reader-bird is left deliberately (though, for Dickinson, not atypically), vague. He/she/you is referred to as "it." If this poem overturns the scopic conventions of the male-dominated romantic love lyric, it does so not to critique male "gaze," but to celebrate a kind of sexuality the poet refuses, or is unable, to name.

Because of her ambiguity, which makes variant readings such as the above not only possible but inevitable, Dickinson has become a preeminent example of the splitting of feminist criticism along sexual orientation lines. To those critics who read the poet heterosexually, the central narrative of Dickinson's career is her struggle with the male tradition—whether this tradition is seen as embodied in her lover, father, God, muse, or merely her precursor poets. Critics writing from this perspective (which represents, in effect, a feminist retelling of traditional mainstream narratives of the poet's career) include, in chronological order, Gilbert and Gubar, Margaret Homans, Joanne Feit Diehl, Barbara Antonina Clarke Mossberg, Suzanne Juhasz, Vivian Pollak, Jane Donahue Eberwein, Helen McNeil, Alicia Ostriker, and, most recently, Cynthia Griffin Wolff. Although all of these critics are deeply committed to understanding Dickinson as a woman poet, the framework for their discussion is the poet's relationship to the male tradition. Their concern is with "woman's place in man's world," even when, as in Homans's case, they acknowledge the presence of homoerotic strands in the poet's life and work.

In contrast to these critics are those like Rebecca Patterson, Lillian Faderman, Adalaide Morris, Judy Grahn, Martha Nell Smith, Toni McNaron and myself, who believe that Dickinson's relationships with women are of greater significance than her struggles with men or with the male tradition. While lesbian critics do not necessarily deny the prominence of certain male figures in Dickinson's life, they have dug beneath the more mythic aspects of the poet's heterosexuality (in particular, her supposed "love affair" with a "Master") to uncover the ways in which Dickinson used her relationships to the female and to individual women such as her sister-in-law Susan Gilbert Dickinson to empower herself as a woman and poet. To these critics, the central struggle in Dickinson's career is not, as Joanne Feit Diehl puts it, "to wrest an independent vision" *from* the male ("Reply" 196),[2] but to find a way to identify and utilize specifically female power in her work.

While both heterosexual and lesbian/feminist readings of Dickinson exemplify what Elaine Showalter calls "gynocritisicm" (128), that is, both focus on the woman as writer, the difference between these two approaches to the poet—one privileging the male, the other the female—results in remarkably different presentations of Dickinson's biography and art. In this essay, I will discuss what happens to our reading of Dickinson's poetry when we give priority to her homoeroticism—and what happens when we do not. In particular, I will focus on the ways in which the privileging of homoeroticism affects our interpretation of Dickinson's erotic poetry as this poetry projects Dickinson's sense of self as a woman and as a woman poet (the two issues raised by Homans's essay).

For "straight" readers of Dickinson's texts, the poet's struggle with the tradition is mediated through her relationship with a man whom history has come to call the "Master," since his biographical identity (if any) has yet to be confirmed. Whoever or whatever this man was to the poet—whether lover, father, God, or muse—Dickinson's relationship to him is, according to this view of her texts, fundamental to her poetic development—the means by which she came to define herself. In response to critiques by Lillian Faderman and Louise Bernikow of her theory of a male muse in Dickinson's poetry, Joanne Feit Diehl articulates the underlying assumptions governing the feminist-heterosexual approach to the Master Phenomenon in Dickinson's work:

> Bernikow's and Faderman's remarks offer nothing that would cause me to change my assertion that Dickinson found herself by confronting a male-dominated tradition. My essay acknowledges that she sought inspiration and courage from women poets engaged in similar struggles toward self-definition; however, hundreds of poems attest that her primary confrontations are with the male self. Furthermore, it is Dickinson who enables later women poets to trace a more exclusively female lineage. Refusing to ignore the tradition Bernikow

and Faderman would deny her, Dickinson confronts her masculine precursors to wrest an independent vision. No woman poet need ever feel so alone again. ("Reply" 196)

The key word here is "alone." Like a latter-day feminist confronting a totally male-dominated environment (whether home, office, or academic department), Dickinson struggles in isolation to "wrest" vision from a male figure (or "tradition") infinitely more powerful than herself, a figure whom she wishes both to seduce and to defy. Because her Master is superior to her—and, perhaps, because she *does* love him—the form her struggle takes is (as Alicia Ostriker puts it), "subversive" not rebellious (39). Dickinson's tools are traditional female weapons, the "weapons" of those who are subordinate and isolated: play, parody, duplicity, evasion, illogic, silence, role-playing, and renunciation. As Ostriker says of the first five, they are strategies "still practiced by women poets today" (43).

For this particular interpretation of the poet and her plight, **"The Daisy follows soft the Sun"** has, not surprisingly, become the signature poem, mentioned or analyzed in a striking number of feminist-heterosexual readings:[3]

The Daisy follows soft the Sun—
And when his golden walk is done—
Sits shily at his feet—
He—waking—finds the flower there—
Wherefore—Maurauder—art thou here?
Because, Sir, love is sweet!

We are the Flower—Thou the Sun!
Forgive us, if as days decline—
We nearer steal to Thee!
Enamored of the parting West—
The peace—the flight—the Amethyst—
Night's possibility!

(**#106**)

In light of the above discussion, the reason for this poem's appeal to feminist-heterosexual readers should be obvious. Duplicity and subversion are the Daisy's essence. Cloaking herself in a veil of modesty (sitting "shily" at her Master's "feet"), the speaker claims to "follow" the Sun all simplicity and adoration, when in fact her real aim is to "steal" from him at night what he will not allow her to have by day: call it love, poetry, or power. The Daisy's reverence for her Master may be sincere, but it is also a cloak for highly disobedient ("Marauder"-like) ambitions, ambitions which only "Night's possibility"—and the Sun's "decline"—can fulfill.

I have no quarrel with this reading of the poem or those like it on which it is based. As Diehl's "hundreds of poems" testify, Dickinson was both attracted to and jealous of male power (from her brother's to God's), and she sought a variety of ways, including duplicity and subversion, seduction and evasion, and maybe even fantasies of madness and necrophilia, to compensate for—or to change the conditions of—her unwanted subordination. Indeed, the poet's need to claim power equal to the male's is the primary theme of most of her heterosexual love poetry. His is the "Shaggier Vest" against which she asserts her smaller "Acorn" size (**"One Year ago—jots what?" #296**). His is the "crown" or "name" she wants to bear (**"The face I carry with me—last," #336**), even if she—and he—must die in order for her to have it:

Think of it Lover! I and Thee
Permitted—face to face to be—
After a Life—a Death—We'll say—
For Death was That—
And This—is Thee—

. . . . .

Forgive me, if the Grave come slow—
For Coveting to look at Thee—
Forgive me, if to stroke thy frost
Outvisions Paradise!

(from **#577**)

When writing heterosexually, Dickinson apparently could not imagine achieving equality in any other way. Men had the power. For her to have power equal to her male lover's, she had to take, steal, or seduce it from him—or they both had to be dead. Given nineteenth-century gender arrangements (including the arrangements within the Dickinson household), it is not surprising that the poet thought of heterosexual relationships in this way. But this is not the only kind of "love" poem that Dickinson wrote, nor is this the only kind of love story (or story about power) her poems tell.

As research by feminist historians Carroll Smith-Rosenberg and Lillian Faderman suggests, the rigid separation of the sexes produced by nineteenth-century American gender arrangements did not totally disadvantage women (Smith-Rosenberg 53-76, Faderman, *Surpassing,* 147-230). True, women spoke of themselves typically as "low" or "inferior" in respect to men. These are terms Dickinson herself uses in variants to a poem on Elizabeth Barrett Browning (**#593**). But nineteenth-century women were not solely reliant on their relationships with men for their sense of personal or sexual power (as heterosexual woman in our society tend to be today). On the contrary, one of the ironies of the doctrine of separate spheres was that it encouraged women to form close affectional bonds with each other. Within these bonds, women were able to affirm themselves and their female power despite their presumably inferior state.

Dickinson's letters and poems indicate that she participated in such relationships with women throughout her life and, as I have discussed elsewhere (*My Life a Loaded Gun* 27-37, 55-63), she drew an enormous amount of comfort, both emotional and sexual, from them. Indeed, a study of Dickinson's erotic poetry suggests that it was precisely the safety and protection offered by her relationships with women—that is, by relationships in which sameness not difference was the dominant factor (Morris in Juhasz 103 and *passim*)—that allowed her full access to her sexual feelings. Unlike unambiguously heterosexual poets such as Plath, Wakoski, and Olds, Dickinson did not find male difference exciting. She was awed, frightened, and, finally, repelled by it. In her often-quoted "man of noon" letter, sent to Susan Gilbert prior to the latter's engagement to Austin, the poet's brother, Dickinson compares male love to a sun that "scorches" and "scathes" women (*The Letters* 210). And in her poetry, she exhibits similar anxieties. Thus, for example, in **"In Winter in my Room,"** she depicts male sexuality as a snake "ringed with Power" from whom her speaker flees in terror:

I shrank—"How fair you are"!
Propitiation's claw—
"Afraid he hissed
Of me"?

. . . . .

That time I flew
Both eyes his way
Lest he pursue

(from #**1670**)

And this same response of mingled awe and repulsion is repeated more subtly in other poems as well: **"I started Early—Took my Dog,"** (#**520**) for instance, and **"I had been hungry, all the Years"** (#**579**). In each of these poems, the poet's fear of male sexuality—not the arousal of her desire—is the operative emotion. If she cannot find some way to reduce male power, to bring it under control, then she either loses her appetite for it (as in **"I had been hungry, all the Years"**) or else she pulls back before she is engulfed (as in **"I started Early—Took my Dog"**). As she says in the latter poem, she feared male desire "would eat me up" (#**520**).

When relating to women, on the other hand, or when describing female sexuality (her own included), Dickinson's poetry could not be more open, eager, and lush. Permeated with images of beauty, nurturance, and protectiveness, and typically oral in emphasis, this poetry bespeaks the poet's overwhelming physical attraction to her own sex, and her faith in the power of her own sexuality even when, as in the following poem, Dickinson is presumably writing from a heterosexual point of view:

I tend my flowers for thee—
Bright Absentee!
My Fuschzia's Coral Seams
Rip—while the Sower—dreams—
Geraniums—tint—and spot—
Low Daisies—dot—
My Cactus—splits her Beard
To show her throat—

Carnations—tip their spice—
And Bees—pick up—
A Hyacinth—I hid—
Puts out a Ruffled head—
And odors fall
From flasks—so small—
You marvel how they held—

Globe Roses—break their satin flake—
Upon my Garden floor—

(from #**339**)

At the conclusion of this poem, the speaker vows to "dwell in Calyx—Gray," modestly draping herself while "Her Lord" is away, but the damage, so-to-speak, has already been done. The entire emphasis in the poem lies in the speaker's riotous delight in the sensual joys that female sexuality has to offer. Like a painting by Georgia O'Keeffe or Judy Chicago, "I tend my flowers" takes us into the very heart of the flower: its sight, smell, taste, and feel. It is all coral and satin, spice and rose. In its image of the budding hyacinth coming into bloom, it could well be orgasmic.

As in **"The Daisy follows soft the Sun,"** Dickinson employs a heterosexual context in "**I tend my flowers**" in order to assert female sexuality subversively, but her focus is obviously on female sexuality itself. It is this (not the charms of her absent male lover) that evokes the poet's intensely colored verse, her sensual reveries. When writing outside a specifically heterosexual context, as in the following poems, Dickinson is able to revel in female sexuality's Edenic pleasures without apology or restraint:

Come slowly—Eden!
Lips unused to Thee—
Bashful—sip thy Jessamines—
As the fainting Bee—

Reaching late his flower,
Round her chamber hums—

Counts his nectars—
Enters—and is lost in Balms.

(#**211**)

Wild Nights—Wild Nights!
Were I with thee
Wild Nights should be
Our luxury!

. . . . .

Rowing in Eden—
Ah, the Sea!
Might I but moor—Tonight—
In Thee!

(from #**249**)

Within that little Hive
Such Hints of Honey lay
As made Reality a Dream
And Dreams, Reality—

(#**1607**)

As Lillian Faderman first observed of **"Wild Nights"** ("Homoerotic Poetry" 20), these poems are all written from what we would normally think of as a male perspective. That is, they are written from the perspective of one who enters, not one who is entered. Because of this ambiguity, they effectively exclude the male. ("He" is at most a male bee, and hence, being small and round, equivocally, as we shall see, a female symbol.) The poems focus on female sexuality instead. "At sea" with this sexuality, Dickinson's speaker bathes in bliss and moors herself in wonder, eats hidden honey, adds up her nectars and is "lost in balms." The undisguised lushness of the imagery, especially when compared to Dickinson's poems on male sexuality, speaks for itself. For Dickinson, the dangerous aspects of sexual power lay with the male—the power to devour, scorch, and awe. The sweetness and balm (the healing) of sexuality, as well as its abundant pleasures, lay in women. And it was within this basically homoerotic context (a context created and sustained by nineteenth-century female bonding) that Dickinson defines her own desire.

As I discuss in *Emily Dickinson: Woman Poet,* in the poetry in which Dickinson privileges the clitoris even more than in the poetry in which she extols the delights of vaginal entry, she puts into words her subjective awareness of this desire and its paradoxical "little-big" nature. In this poetry, a poetry characterized by images drawn from the "neighboring life"—dews, crumbs, berries, and peas—Dickinson (in Irigaray's words) digs beneath the layers of male civilization to recover the ancient language of female sexuality itself (25). As Dickinson says in a poem sent to Susan Gilbert Dickinson in 1858, it is a language that sings a "different tune":

She did not sing as we did—
It was a different tune—
Herself to her a music
As Bumble bee of June

. . . . .

I split the dew—
But took the morn—
I chose this single star
From out the wide night's numbers—
Sue—forevermore!

(from #**14**)

In *Literary Women* Ellen Moers observes that women writers—including Dickinson—have a predilection for metaphors of smallness which Moers relates to their small physical size. "Littleness," she writes, "is inescapably associated with the female body, and as long as writers describe women they will all make use of the diminutive in language and the miniature in imagery" (244). Even though Moers summarizes these metaphors suggestively as "the little hard nut, the living stone, something precious . . . to be fondled with the hand or cast away in wrath" (244), she does not identify such images as clitoral. However, I believe that we should. Indeed, I believe that we must if we are to understand how a great many women—not just Dickinson—have traditionally (if, perhaps, unconsciously) chosen to represent their difference to themselves.

As nineteenth-century gynecologists such as Charles D. Meigs recognized over a hundred and forty years ago (a recognition "lost" later in the century), the clitoris is the "prime seat" of erotic sensibility in woman just as its homologue, the penis, is the prime seat in man (130).[4] It is reasonable to assume, therefore, that the clitoris's size, shape, and function contribute as much to a woman's sense of self—her inner perception of her power—as does her vagina or womb—the sexual organs on which psychoanalytic critics since Freud have chosen to concentrate.[5] Images of smallness in women's writing unquestionably relate to woman's body size and to her social position. But like phallic images (which also serve these other purposes), such images have a sexual base, and so does the power women so paradoxically attribute to them. In identifying their "little hard nut[s]" with "something precious," women are expressing through their symbolism their body's subjective consciousness of itself. That is, they are expressing their conscious or unconscious awareness of the organic foundation of their (oxymoronic) sexual power.

The existence of a pattern of imagery involving small, round objects in Dickinson's writing cannot be disputed. Whether identified as male or female, bees alone appear 125 times in her poetry. Dews, crumbs, pearls, and berries occur 111 times, and with peas, pebbles, pellets, beads, and nuts, the total number of such images comes to 261. In the context of the poems in which they appear, many of these images are neutral, that is, they seem to have no sexual significance. But their repetitiveness is another matter. So is the way in which they are given primacy in many poems. Analysis of the latter suggests that on the deepest psychological level, these images represented to the poet her subjective awareness of her female sexual self, both its "littleness" (when compared to male sex) and the tremendous force nevertheless contained within it. In privileging this imagery, consciously or unconsciously, Dickinson was replacing the hierarchies of male-dominated heterosexual discourse—hierarchies that disempowered her as woman and poet—with a (paradoxical) clitorocentrism of her own, affirming her specifically female power.

Over and over clitoral images appear in Dickinson's poetry as symbols of an indeterminate good in which she delights, yet which she views as contradictory in one way or another. It is small yet great, modest yet vain, not enough yet all she needs. The following poem brings together many of these motifs:

God gave a Loaf to every Bird—
But just a Crumb—to Me—
I dare not eat it—tho' I starve—
My poignant luxury—

To own it—touch it—
Prove the feat—that made the Pellet mine—
Too happy—for my Sparrow's chance—
For Ampler Coveting—
It might be Famine—all around—
I could not miss an Ear—
Such Plenty smiles upon my Board—
My Garner shows so fair—

I wonder how the Rich—may feel—
An Indiaman—An Earl—
I deem that I—with but a Crumb—
Am Sovreign of them all—

(#791)

There are a number of things to note here. First, the poet is undecided whether the crumb in her possession satisfies her physical or her material appetite. In the first three stanzas it takes care of her hunger (albeit, by touching). In the fourth stanza it makes her wealthy, an "Indiaman" or "Earl." She also cannot decide whether she is starving or not. For while she can touch and feel the crumb, she cannot eat it. Owning it is, therefore, a paradoxical business. It is a "poignant luxury," that is, a deeply affecting, possibly hurtful, sumptuousness that has archaic overtones of lust. Finally, poor though she is, the crumb makes this sparrow a "Sovreign," that is, it gives her power. She prefers it to "an Ear," presumably an ear of corn, and hence, given the poem's erotic suggestiveness, a phallus.

From one point of view, this poem is, obviously, a stunning example of Dickinson's ambiguity. Despite the many terms whose status as erotic signifiers can be established by reference to passages elsewhere in her work (loaf, bird, eat, luxury, sparrow, famine, plenty, Indiaman, earl, sovereign), there is no way to "know" what the poem is about. Not only do masturbation and cunnilingus fit but so do having a male or female lover, having some other unnamed good instead, sharing communion with God, and being content with her small/great lot as poet.

But whatever reading one adopts, what matters is that Dickinson has used imagery based upon her body as the primary vehicle through which to make her point. Whether or not she intended this poem to be about the clitoris, the clitoris is the one physical item in a woman's possession that pulls together the poem's disparate and conflicting parts. What other *single* crumb satisfies a woman's appetite even though she cannot eat it, and gives her the power of a "Sovreign" (potent male) whoever she is? In trying to represent her sense of self and the paradoxes of her female situation, consciously or unconsciously, Dickinson was drawn to what she loved most: the body she inhabited, the body she shared with other women. And it is the specific and extraordinary power of this body, its sovereign littleness, that she celebrates in this poem. As she says in another poem, this was the "crumb" for which she sang. As figure and fact, it was the source, motivation, and substance of her song:

The Robin for the Crumb
Returns no syllable
But long records the Lady's name
In Silver Chronicle.

(#864)

By giving primacy to a clitoral image in this poem, Dickinson is asserting a form of female textuality and female sexuality that falls explicitly *outside* the male tradition. The song this "Robin" sings is "Silver," not golden like the sun/son. It is a "chronicle" that records "the Lady's," not her Master's, "name." And because it is female, it is written in different "syllables" from those of male verse, syllables drawn from the backyard life to which Dickinson's "lot" as a woman had consigned her—the life of robins, bees, and, above all, *crumbs*. From this life comes the "alphabet" in which female desire is reco(r)ded, an alphabet suited to the very different "Pleasure" loving women (as opposed to loving men) gives rise:

There is an arid Pleasure—
As different from Joy—
As Frost is different from Dew—
Like element—are they—

Yet one—rejoices Flowers—
And one—the Flowers abhor—
The finest Honey—curdled—
Is worthless—to the Bee—

(#**782**)[6]

For Dickinson, devoting oneself to this homoerotic pleasure inevitably meant writing a different kind of verse:

As the Starved Maelstrom laps the Navies
As the Vulture teazed
Forces the Broods in lonely Valleys
As the Tiger eased

By but a Crumb of Blood, fasts Scarlet
Till he meet a Man
Dainty adorned with Veins and Tissues
And partakes—his Tongue

Cooled by the Morsel for a moment
Grows a fiercer thing
Till he esteem his Dates and Cocoa
A Nutrition mean

I, of a finer Famine
Deem my Supper dry
For but a Berry of Domingo
And a Torrid Eye.

(#**872**)

In the first three stanzas of this poem, Dickinson compares the "malestorm"[7] created by male appetite sequentially—and hyperbolically—to a whirlpool, a vulture, and a man-eating tiger. In the final stanza, she celebrates her own "finer Famine," satisfied with "a Berry of Domingo/And a Torrid Eye." The theater of blood and lust which Dickinson depicts in the first three stanzas of this poem is so blatantly exaggerated it seems meant to be humorous. Male appetite is so voracious, the speaker claims, it will consume anything, including, finally, itself. (I read both "Crumb of Blood" and "Dates and Cocoa" as references to women.) In the final stanza, the speaker proudly asserts her own "limited" appetite by way of comparison. It is this appetite which defines her, making her the woman and poet she is: "I, of a finer Famine."

For Dickinson this "finer Famine" was a "sumptuous Destitution" (#/**1382**), a paradoxical source of power and poetry, that nourished her throughout her life. In 1864, the same year in which she wrote **"As the Starved Maelstrom laps the Navies,"** she sent Susan the following poem.

The luxury to apprehend
The luxury 'twould be
To look at Thee a single time
An Epicure of Me
In whatsoever Presence makes
Till for a further food
I scarcely recollect to starve
So first am I supplied—
The luxury to meditate
The luxury it was
To banquet on the Countenance
A Sumptuousness bestows
On plainer Days,
Whose Table, far
As Certainty—can see—
Is laden with a single Crumb—
The Consciousness of Thee.

(#**815** Version to Sue)

And in a letter written to Susan in 1883, she declared: "To be Susan is Imagination,/To have been Susan, a Dream—/What depths of Domingo in that torrid Spirit!" (*The Letters* 791). Over the twenty years that intervened between these poems and this letter, Dickinson's patterns of female sexual imagery and the homoerotic values these patterns encoded did not substantially change. Taken together, they were the "berries," "crumbs," and "dews" that—in imagination and in reality—nourished and sustained her as male love (and the male literary tradition) never could.

The importance of Dickinson's commitment to a woman-centered sexuality and textuality seems hard to dispute. But why then have so many feminist critics found it difficult to acknowledge the centrality of Dickinson's homoeroticism to her writing? Put another way, why have so many of them insisted on depicting her, in Diehl's terms, as "alone," even when (given her bonds to other women), she was not? What follows is not meant as a personal attack on these critics, but rather as an exploration of what I believe to be one of the most difficult issues confronting feminist-heterosexual women today—an issue whose political and sexual nature Dickinson was not only aware of but which she addressed in her poetry.

In *This Sex Which Is Not One,* Luce Irigaray makes the following comments on the (heterosexual) woman's place in the "dominant phallic economy," that is, in male-dominated culture:

Woman, in this sexual imaginary, is only a more or less obliging prop for the enactment of man's

> fantasies. That she may find pleasure there in that role, by proxy, is possible, even certain. But such pleasure is above all a masochistic prostitution of her body to a desire that is not her own, and it leaves her in a familiar state of dependency upon man. Not knowing what she wants, ready for anything, even asking for more, so long as he will "take" her as his "object" when he seeks his own pleasure. (25).

Women, Irigaray argues, have been "enveloped in the needs/desires/fantasies of . . . men" (134). As such, they have been cut off from their own sexuality. In Irigaray's terms, they have learned to "masquerade" (133-34), assuming the sexual roles men have imposed upon them, while devaluing their own capacity for autonomous sexual response. As "conceptualized" within the phallic economy, Irigaray writes, "woman's erogenous zones never amount to anything but a clitoris-sex that is not comparable to the noble phallic organ, or a hole-envelope that serves to sheathe and massage the penis in intercourse: a non-sex . . ." (23). That women can be sexually equal to men (agents, as it were, of their own desire) is an idea both men and (many) women resist.

The historical appropriation and devaluation of female sexuality by men is hardly news; women in the nineteenth century were also aware of it. But in **"The Malay—took the Pearl,"** Dickinson gives this perception a twist by addressing it from a homoerotic perspective, that is, from a perspective shaped by the poet's (homoerotic) awareness of the role the clitoris plays in autonomous woman-centered sex:

> The Malay—took the Pearl—
> Not—I—the Earl—
> I—feared the Sea—too much
> Unsanctified—to touch—
>
> Praying that I might be
> Worthy—the Destiny—
> The Swarthy fellow swam—
> And bore my Jewel—Home—
>
> Home to the Hut! What lot
> Had I—the Jewel—got—
> Borne on a Dusky Breast—
> I had not a deemed Vest
> Of Amber—fit—
>
> The Negro never knew
> I—wooed it—too
> To gain, or be undone—
> Alike to Him—One—
>
> (#**452**)

Whether the "Pearl" in this poem stands synecdochically for the woman Dickinson loved or metonymically for the sexual and poetic powers which the poet believed were hers,[8] or, as is probable, for both, the poem's main point is clear. The "Jewel" that the Malay takes and then devalues (brings "Home" to his "hut") is an object of desire not just for the man but the speaker also. Indeed, the speaker (presumably a woman even though she cross-dresses as an "Earl") has far more title to the pearl than the Malay since she appreciates its true worth whereas he does not. (He wears it on a "Dusky," sun-darkened, "Breast" where she would not deem a "Vest/Of Amber—fit" to bear it.) Nevertheless, she feels she has no right to this prize. She "fears" to touch the sea.

In cross-dressing her speaker in this poem, Dickinson may be expressing some of the awkwardness or perhaps even "unnaturalness" she felt in attributing (active) sexual desire to herself as a woman. As a young woman, Dickinson's problem—as she states in **"The Malay—took the Pearl"**—had been to gather the courage to appropriate female power for herself, to see herself as equally "sanctified"—and sanctioned—to "dive" (or "climb") into forbidden territories, whether erotic or poetic. In maturity, she lashes out again and again at the damage done women psychologically by such self-serving (masculine) prohibitions, prohibitions that not only prevent women from maturing fully, but turn them into the passive objects of male desire (and male art). Not permitted to act on their own needs or in their own stead, women inevitably become the victims of the men who "envelop" them (or eat them up):

> Over the fence—
> Strawberries—grow—
> Over the fence—
> I could climb—if I tried, I know—
> Berries are nice!
>
> But—if I stained my Apron
> God would certainly scold!
> Oh, dear,—I guess if He were a Boy—
> He'd—climb—if He could!
>
> (#**251**)

The little girl voice Dickinson adopts in this poem is deliberate and calculated. Boys have a right to "forbidden" fruits, but women (those whose sexual maturation is tied to—and "tied down" by—apron strings) do not. Yet, as this poem's symbolism makes clear, it is precisely women who are the "Berries" that boys so eagerly pick. Hence men's desire to guard their access to this fruit by divine interdiction. The God men worship (or create) protects male right.

What Dickinson is alluding to in this poem is—and has historically been—the paradox (and tragedy) of female sexuality: that its power is something women themselves have been forbidden to enjoy. It is a paradox Dickinson gives brilliant expression to in one of her most teasing yet trenchant epigrams:

> Forbidden Fruit a flavor has
> That lawful Orchards mocks—
> How luscious lies within the Pod
> The Pea that Duty locks—
>
> (#**1377**)

Whether this poem is about cunnilingus, masturbation, or something else altogether, the sexual implications of its final line are hard to evade. "Duty," that is, women's sense of obligation to a male-dominated culture's self-serving prohibitions, has made women's sexuality inaccessible to them. Women's loss of their sexuality occurred literally during the nineteenth century as they were propagandized to believe that they did not have orgasms. As we now know, in the space of less than fifty years, the physiological importance of the clitoris was expunged from the record and apparently from many women's conscious awareness as well (Laqueur 1-41).

Symbolically, this silencing of female sexual power continues to occur today in the writing of those critics, including those feminist critics, who ignore the significance of the homoerotic (and autoerotic) elements in poetry like Dickinson's. Indeed, feminist-heterosexual interpretations of Dickinson's poetry testify all too vividly to the degree to which, as Irigaray says, female sexuality remains "enveloped" in the needs and desires of men, despite the woman-centeredness of feminist vision. Committed to a heterosexual perspective (a perspective that makes women sexually as well as emotionally and intellectually dependent on men, no matter how much they may compete with them for power), these critics cannot see the centrality of Dickinson's homoeroticism even when—as in her clitoral poetry—it is obviously there. They cannot decode the "alphabet" in which these poems are written. Dickinson's relationship to the Master (a paradigm, perhaps, for these critics' own relationship to what Diehl calls "the male self") overwhelms ("envelopes") their eyes.

No one understood the magnitude of the task involved in women's reappropriation of their sexual power better than Dickinson and there were times when she questioned whether her "Pebble" was adequate to the task. It was a struggle of epic proportion in which she was David (indeed, less than David) to her culture's Goliath:

> I took my Power in my Hand—
> And went against the World—
> 'Twas not so much as David—had—
> But I—was twice as bold—
>
> I aimed my Pebble—but Myself
> Was all the one that fell—
> Was it Goliath—was too large—
> Or was myself—too small?
>
> (from #**540**)

But there were other times when she was able to assert without reservation her absolute right to the "Crown" she knew was hers:

> I'm ceded—I've stopped being Their's—
> The name They dropped upon my face
> With water, in the country church
> Is finished using, now . . .
>
> My second Rank—too small the first—
> Crowned—Crowing—on my Father's breast—
> A half unconscious Queen—
> But this time—Adequate—Erect,
> With Will to choose, or to reject,
> And I choose, just a Crown
>
> (from #**508**)

The full impact of these lines can only be appreciated when they are read against those poems in which the speaker yearns pathetically for her Master's "Crown." In this poem, she stands masculinely "Erect" and crowns herself. Doing so, she takes back the symbol of her womanhood that men have usurped. In baptizing their daughters (as in wedding their wives), men give their names to women, making them "half unconscious Queens"—Queens who are not in full possession of their power (their "Crown"). In "**I'm ceded**," these rights (and rites) of male possession come to an end. The woman's vagina-ring-crown is hers. So presumably is the personal (creative) power—the "crumb"—that goes with it.

As I have asserted in *Emily Dickinson: Woman Poet,* Dickinson's ability to pose female sexuality and textuality as valid, autonomous *alternatives* to male sexuality and textuality derives from her romantic commitment to women and from her willingness to see in women sources of love, power, and pleasure independent of what Mary Lyon calls "the other sex" (Quoted by Hitchcock, 301). Her use of female sexual imagery suggests, therefore, not the "subversion" of an existing male tradition—but rather the assertion of a concept of female sexuality and female textuality that renders male sexuality and the poetic discourse around male sexuality irrelevant. In privileging the clitoris over the vagina, Dickinson privileged the female sexual organ whose pleasure was clearly independent of the male. She also privileged the sole organ in either sex whose *only* function is pleasure. For Dickinson, her "crumb" was "small" but it was also "plenty." It was "enough."

Notes

This essay deals with issues which troubled me during the writing of *Emily Dickinson: Woman Poet.* In the book, I argue the case for Dickinson's homoeroticism (and autoeroticism) much more fully. Here I wish to look at what feminist-heterosexual critics have—or, rather, have not—made of this material—and why.

[1] All subsequent citations to Dickinson's poems will appear parenthetically in the text as the # symbol, followed by the Johnson number of the poem. In quoting from Dickinson's poetry and letters, I have retained her idiosyncratic spelling and punctuation.

[2] Diehl's original essay has been republished in her *Dickinson and the Romantic Imagination* (13-33).

[3] Analyses of "The Daisy follows soft the Sun" may be found in Gilbert and Gubar (600-601), Homans (203-4), and the essays by Gilbert, Keller, Mossberg, Morris, Homans, and Miller published in *Feminist Critics Read Emily Dickinson,* edited by Suzanne Juhasz.

[4] The knowledge which Meigs states so definitively was "lost" in the course of the nineteenth century as part of a general (politically motivated) redefining of female sexuality. See Laqueur (1-41).

[5] Naomi Schor is the only critic with whom I am familiar who has treated the subject of clitoral imagery and she discusses it only in relation to the use of synecdoche (detail) in male writing ("Female Paranoia" 204-19). In her full-length study of detail in male writing *(Reading in Detail: Aesthetics and the Feminine),* she drops the idea altogether.

The *locus classicus* for a discussion of uterine imagery in women's "art" is Erik Erikson's influential essay "Womanhood and the Inner Space" (Erikson 261-94). In *Through the Flower,* Judy Chicago discusses her development of vaginal imagery and the empowering effect working with this imagery had on her (especially 51-58).

[6] Dickinson identifies two kinds of sexual pleasure in this poem: one that gives the flowers joy and one that dries up *or* freezes them ("arid," "Frost"). If my reading is correct, this latter "pleasure" is the product of male sexuality which Dickinson depicts in some poems as a "sun," and in others as "frost." See for example, "A Visitor in Marl" (#391), and "The Frost of Death was on the Pane" (#1136). In either case, of course, male sexuality's ultimate effect on the women-flowers is the same: death.

[7] I am indebted to Ms. Deborah Pfeiffer for calling my attention to this anagram.

[8] I have discussed the biographical elements of this poem in *My Life a Loaded Gun* (52-53).

Works Cited

Bennett, Paula. *Emily Dickinson.* London: Harvester, 1990.

———. *My Life a Loaded Gun: Female Creativity and Feminist Poetics.* Boston: Beacon, 1986.

Chicago, Judy. *Through the Flower: My Struggle as a Woman Artist.* 1975. Garden City, N.Y.: Anchor-Doubleday, 1982.

Dickinson, Emily. *The Letters of Emily Dickinson.* Ed. Thomas H. Johnson and Theodora Ward. 3 vols. Cambridge, Mass.: Belknap Press of Harvard Univ. Press, 1958.

———. *The Poems of Emily Dickinson.* Ed. Thomas H. Johnson. 3 vols. Cambridge, Mass.: Belknap Press of Harvard Univ. Press, 1958.

Diehl, Joanne Feit. *Dickinson and the Romantic Imagination.* Princeton: Princeton Univ. Press, 1981.

———. "Reply to Faderman and Bernikow." *Signs* 4 (1978): 196.

Erikson, Erik. *Identity: Youth and Crisis.* New York: Norton, 1968.

Faderman, Lillian. "Emily Dickinson's Homoerotic Poetry." *Higginson Journal* 18 (1978): 19-27.

———. *Surpassing the Love of Men: Romantic Friendship and Love between Women from the Renaissance to the Present.* New York: Morrow, 1981.

Gilbert, Sandra M., and Susan Gubar. *The Madwoman in the Attic: The Woman Writer and the Nineteenth-Century Literary Imagination.* New Haven: Yale Univ. Press, 1979.

Hitchcock, Edward, ed., *The Power of Christian Benevolence Illustrated in the Life and Labors of Mary Lyon.* Northampton, Mass.: Hopkins, Bridgman, 1852.

Homans, Margaret. "'Syllables of Velvet': Dickinson, Rossetti, and the Rhetoric of Sexuality." *Feminist Studies* II (1985): 569-93.

———. *Women Writers and Poetic Identity: Dorothy Wordsworth, Emily Brontë, and Emily Dickinson.* Princeton: Princeton Univ. Press, 1980.

Irigaray, Luce. *This Sex Which Is Not One.* Trans. Catherine Porter. Ithaca: Cornell Univ. Press, 1985.

Juhasz, Suzanne, ed. *Feminist Critics Read Emily Dickinson*. Bloomington: Indiana Univ. Press, 1983.

Laqueur, Thomas. "Orgasm, Generation, and the Politics of Reproductive Biology." In *The Making of the Modern Body: Sexuality and Society in the Nineteenth Century*. Ed. Catherine Gallagher and Thomas Laqueur. Berkeley: Univ. of California Press, 1988. 1-41.

Meigs, Charles D. *Woman: Her Diseases and Remedies*. Philadelphia: Lea and Blanchard, 1851.

Moers, Ellen. *Literary Women: The Great Writers*. 1976. Rpt. New York: Oxford Univ. Press, 1985.

Ostriker, Alicia Suskind. *Stealing the Language: The Emergence of Women's Poetry in America*. Boston: Beacon, 1986.

Schor, Naomi. "Female Paranoia: The Case for Psychoanalytical Criticism." *Yale French Studies* 62 (1981):204-19.

———. *Reading in Detail: Aesthetics and the Feminine*. New York: Methuen, 1987.

Showalter, Elaine. "Toward a Feminist Poetics." In *The New Feminist Criticism: Essays on Women, Literature, and Theory*. Ed. Elaine Showalter. New York: Pantheon 1985. 125-43.

Smith-Rosenberg, Carroll. *Disorderly Conduct: Visions of Gender in Victorian America*. New York: Knopf, 1985.

Judith Banzer Farr (essay date 1990)

SOURCE: "'Compound Manner': Emily Dickinson and the Metaphysical Poets," in *On Dickinson: The Best from American Literature*, edited by Edwin H. Cady and Louis J. Budd, Duke University Press, 1990, pp. 52-68.

[*In the following essay, Farr traces the influence of seventeenth-century metaphysical poets, such as John Donne and George Herbert, on Dickinson's verse.*]

The habit of Emily Dickinson's mind led her, like George Herbert, to construct a "Double Estate" in which this world was "furnished with the Infinite," in which God was her "Old Neighbor," and death, agony, and grace were fleshly companions. The discipline that wrought many of her poems was the metaphysical one of a "Compound Vision" by which the eternal is argued from the transient, the foreign explained by the familiar, and fact illumined by mystery. She could speak of "Infinite March," of Calvary as another Amherst, of the "Diagram—of Rapture" because she practiced the metaphysical awareness of the unity of experience. Reared in the sternly religious society of the Connecticut Valley and in the rigorous atmosphere of the Dickinson household, she learned early to meditate upon essentials: mortality, the temporal presence of God, man's relationship with God and with creation. The acute sensibility that prompted the remark of the girl of twenty-one: "I think of the grave very often" shaped the witty double consciousness of the mature poet who saw, like Vaughan, "through all this fleshly dress/Bright shootes of everlastingnesse." Sharing the prime concerns of the seventeenth century, Emily Dickinson felt also its passionate interest in the microcosm of the self whose "polar privacy" was peopled with thoughts and emotions which supplied the data of existence and the stuff of art. Since that self was poised between scepticism and faith, desire and renunciation, optimism and despair, the artist, like Donne, sought release in a poetry of paradox, argument, and unifying conceits: "Much Madness is divinest Sense—"; "I cannot live with You—/It would be Life—"; "[A Pine is] Just a Sea—with a Stem." The Dickinson poems are the record of an imagination which kept "fundamental" both in substance and technique, recreating experience as it conceived it in terms of multiple connections and infinite semblances, often conveying its highly personal and analytic vision in the arresting manner of the metaphysical.

In comparing the matter and style of Emily Dickinson's verse with that of Donne or Herbert, one finds parallels which do not seem accidental. They suggest that her perspective was tempered and her craft confirmed from contact with the tradition of seventeenth-century poetry in England.

Almost certainly, Emily's reading was the cause of contact. She had easy access to metaphysical poetry in books owned by herself or her family and in periodicals which quoted or discussed it at length. What seem to be her pencil-markings of several poems argue close attention to their vision and technique. Emily Dickinson's poetry, however, creates a related idiom which is the crucial argument for her knowledge of Donne or Herbert; and this argument should be sifted first.

I

It is not difficult to find similarities between the insights and techniques of John Donne and Emily. Like her, he relished the divided joys of earth and spirit. Like hers, his poetry attempts, with frequent success, to fuse them. She refrained from professing Christ because it was "hard for [her] to give up the world"; he hesitated to take Holy Orders because he delighted in the pleasures of the questioning intellect and of the senses. Both enjoyed their disbelief for the aesthetic stimulus it supplied. Donne advised "doubt wisely";

Emily never relinquished her "old Codicil of Doubt." Yet each addressed God familiarly with petulance, awe, and passion as a divine lover. His orthodoxy hard-won, a middle-aged Donne demanded of God both intellectual rest and emotional satisfaction:

> Divorce mee, 'untie, or breake that knot
> againe,
> Take mee to you, imprison mee, for I
> Except you' enthrall mee, never shall be free,
> Nor ever chast, except you ravish mee.

Emily's faith was heterodox, her attitude towards God highly ambivalent. He was the central Idea to question, to attack or embrace in verse. Yet at the same age and with the same thirst for definition, she begged to be "Immured in Heaven," to be "ravished" by Love's "Bondage," insisting that Deity "Tie the strings to [her] life" and show her Himself. This quest for God, for permanence, was the generative impulse of visions alike evolved by the "columnar self" as it scrutinized values which transcended change. The reality of spirit and the chemistry of physical dissolution, the ecstasy of love and the pain of betrayal, the beauty of the mysterious, and the glamour of hard fact became, for Donne and Emily, firm truths in a world of motion and coexisted "in Being's center." Highly conscious of the supreme activity of the soul, both believed that "the body in his booke"; that

> The Music in the Violin
> Does not emerge alone
> But Arm in Arm with Touch, yet Touch
> Alone—is not a Tune—
> The Spirit lurks within the Flesh
> Like Tides within the Sea
> That make the Water live, estranged
> What would the Either be?

Therefore, they explained their sense of the communion of mystic with material in language drawn from both worlds. Donne compared love's increase with "new taxes" or spoke of Change as "the nursery/Of music," while Emily wrote of "the Grave's Repeal" and pronounced Doom "the House without the Door—." This locative language worked within poems of a subtle, all-encompassing framework; poems like mental theaters in which the scene, a garden or bedroom, a tomb or Gethsemane, was presented vividly and in which an aspect of the poet was chief actor, inviting us to transcend the limits of our experience and imagine "The Habit of a Foreign Sky" or the way in which Christ, a young woman, or the poet himself died. The persuasiveness of that invitation is apparent in dynamic first lines like "I'll tell thee now (deare Love) what thou shalt doe" or "I'll tell you how the Sun rose—." They are lines which convey a brilliant colloquial voice inflecting many moods, asserting the self that is its subject. This keen personal consciousness which analyzed its every awareness and most sharply, its sense of God, love, and death chose similar expression in the work of both poets. The most crucial techniques of Donne and Emily Dickinson are akin: the use of Anglo-Saxon and Latinate words as double witnesses of one truth in one phrase; the abortion of regular metrics to assist the immediacy of the speaking voice; the development of a poem according to the thesis of its opening line or by the elaboration of a radiant conceit like that of "The Flea" or of **"He put the Belt around my life"**; the use of religious phraseology to express profane love as in "The Funerall" or **"There came a day at summer's full"**; a fondness for paradoxical arguments like the following:

> Thou canst not every day give mee they heart,
> If thou canst give it, then thou never gavest it;
> Love riddles are, that though thy heart depart
> It stayes at home, and thou with losing savest
> it.

> A Death blow is a Life blow to Some
> Who till they died, did not alive become—
> Who had they lived, had died but when
> They died, Vitality begun.

Donne, who required the honest, original force of words like "itchy" and "snorted" in his most elegant poems, would have understood Emily's use of the provincialism "heft" to describe the solemn tenor of church music. An extraordinary number of poems like "The Legacie" or **"I heard a Fly buzz—when I died—"** demonstrate the delight each took in probing the sensation of death in shockingly intimate accents. Both crowded their lines with verbal excitement, as if in excess of athletic apprehension: "let/Mee travel, sojourne, snatch, plot, have, forget"; "'Tis this invites, appals, endows,/Flits, glimmers, proves, dissolves." Both enjoyed a pun and the poetry of each occasionally displays the unconciliating quality of the overly ingenious metaphysical wit:

> She guilded us: But you are gold, and Shee;
> Us she inform'd but transubstantiates you;
> Soft dispositions which ductile bee,
> Elixarlike, she makes not cleane, but new.

> Enchantment's Perihelion
> Mistaken oft has been
> For the Authentic orbit
> Of it's Anterior Sun.

Yet their central relationship is one which ordered these incidental ones: the participation in what Louis L. Martz in his study, *The Poetry of Meditation* (Yale University Press, 1954) has defined as the "meditative" vision. Donne, practicing its three-fold mode of divine communion and Emily, moved by her theocratic environment to the constant contemplation of Essence, shared a conviction of the oneness of being. This produced in their poetry the continual creation of an explorative and unifying self. Eccentric imagery, syntax, metrics, the denomination of her freckled person as "Empress of Calvary," her shrewd colloquies with God, a bee, or the spirit of a word, demonstrate in Emily's verse the same sense of the drama of the "I" with which his meditative exercises informed the poetry of Donne.

George Herbert's verse functions within this vision also, and with him, Emily claims a distinct relationship. Herbert asserts, like Emily, that "There's newer—nearer Crucifixion" than the Biblical one and contemplates his intimacy with his divine lover in the virile assents of the speaking voice. He, too, expresses his confidence in the unity of being by describing the transcendent in material conceits of orderliness and neat symmetry.

The Temple, like Emily's lyrics, abounds in homely images of safe enclosure. For Herbert, Heaven is a "manour," furnished with "glorious household-stuffe"; the Trinity is a "statelie cabinet"; the soul, "a poor cabinet of bone" with rooms and a latchkey; Man is a "house" whose thoughts are walls and earth is his "cupboard of food" or, as his sepulchre, "God's ebony box." Emily used enclosure images similarly to capture an exquisitely-felt tension between body and spirit. In her "Ablative Estate," the soul has cellars and caverns which it roves or tries to shatter; the mind is a planked cell and gives banquets; the brain is furnished with mighty rooms and windy chambers wherein funerals, rejoicings, and visions occur; Heaven is the "house of supposition"; the sky is an "Astral Hall," swept by housewives like Herbert's Reason. Both poets devise poems in which enclosure is violated by the "marauding Hand" of God or a keen emotion; thus, Herbert's "Confession" or Emily's **"The Soul should always stand ajar":** poems which reverse the conceit of the opened door as Herbert attempts to shut out "cunning" grief, and Emily to let in "accomplished" Heaven. Herbert describes his apprehension of the divine in terms of habitation: he "dwells" in prayer, in peace, in sacred music; equally, he invites God in "The Banquet," "A Parodie," and "The Glimpse" to live in his soul's "brave . . . palace" as in the days when he "didst lodge with Lot." Emily, too, speaks of her communion with God as that of host with Visitor:

The Soul that hath a Guest
Doth seldom go abroad—
Diviner Crowd at Home—
Obliterate the need—

And Courtesy forbid
A Host's departure when
Upon Himself be visiting
The Emperor of Men—

Both poets compare the perfecting or sensitive development of a soul to the erection of a building: thus, "The World" or "The Props assist the House." Even as Herbert called his sacred verse his "best room," Emily described the departure of inspiration from her soul's "unfurnished Rooms," expressing her aesthetic mission by means of an architectural conceit:

I dwell in Possibility—
A fairer House than Prose—
More numerous of Windows—
Superior—for Doors—

Of Chambers as the Cedars—
Impregnable of Eye—
And for an Everlasting Roof
The Gambrels of the Sky—

Of Visitors—the fairest—
For Occupation—This—
The spreading wide my narrow Hands
To gather Paradise—

Enclosure imagery functions here, as in Herbert's poems, to create a sense of freedom and union. Possibility, both the lively receptiveness of the poetic mind and Poetry itself, is as reliable as a house. It is fairer than the insular home of Prose because its many apertures withhold the cursory glance, admitting supreme callers and thoughts divinely positive as sun's rays. Like the house of man's soul, it is firm because it lacks limits.

The reflective practices which put Herbert forever in the divine presence and Emily's habit of strolling with Eternity prompted the signal similar movement in the work of both poets: one by which, ardently or childishly, they asked God's lasting interview, requiring him to yield their vision fullness:

Come, Lord, my head doth burn, my heart is
  sick,
 While Thou dost ever, ever stay;
Thy long deferrings wound me to the quick,
 My spirit gaspeth night and day.
 O, show Thyself to me,
 Or take me up to Thee!

At least—to pray—is left—is left—
Oh Jesus—in the Air—
I know not which thy chamber is—
I'm knocking—everywhere—

Thou settest Earthquake in the South—
And Maelstrom in the Sea—
Say, Jesus Christ of Nazareth—
Hast thou no Arm for Me?

The tradition that lives in Herbert's Sidneyesque, in Emily's urgent, tones is that which disposed their use of empiric conceit, their description of Shame as a wine or a pink shawl, their building of poems around Biblical theses, their discussions with Death or Passion, their domestication of mystery and soberly playful references to the "handkerchief" of Christ's "grave clothes" or to the "fashions—of the Cross—." It is the custom of seeing "Comparatively," of fitting all experience, sublime or ordinary, into one plane and finding it the haunted "Ground Floor" of a familiar Infinite. Emily Dickinson's exotic symbols: Cashmere, Domingo, Vera Cruz, "fairer—for the farness—/ And for the foreignhood," merged in her awareness with the homely beauty of the Pelham hills to make a mental Eden round which Eternity swept "like a Sea." While Herbert praised Sunday as a

> day most calm, most bright,
> The fruit of this, the next world's bud,
> Th' indorsement of supreme delight,
> Writ by a friend; and with His bloud

she could rhapsodize the "General Rose" which those beneath her window augured and speak of a June when all corn will be cut, for which "Our Lord—thought no/Extravagance/To pay—a Cross—." Like Herbert, she found it an "Estate perpetual" to "entertain" her own sensations, discovering that Grief, like his Affliction, had "size"; like him, she used techniques which emphasized a personal and cohesive vision: forthright syntax and economical metaphor; litany-like exclamation and meters derived from hymns; the binding melody of the tercet and, in poems like "Publication—is the Auction/Of the Mind of Man," the framework of thesis, deliberation, directive that shapes his lyrics.

Emily's kinship with the metaphysical poets is remarkable. One suspects that it developed not simply through a creativity led by instinct and by Puritan and Transcendental forces to elect a meditative mode, but from a familiarity with that mode in the work of Donne, Marvell, and the rest. Her letters and poems provide slim support for this conclusion. She writes once of Vaughan to T. W. Higginson in 1880, spelling his name "Vaughn" and misquoting his line "My days, which are best but dull and hoary" as "My Days that are at best but dim and hoary." Emily spelled casually, as did her associates: a certain engaging cotton farmer was spoken of on three occasions in the 1863 *Springfield Republican* as Mr. "Vaughan," "Vaughn," and "Vaughne." Her substitution of "dim" for "dull" was perhaps due to a recollection of "glimmering" in the poem's next line. Her mistake argues an acquaintance with "They are all gone into the world of light!" But this is her sole allusion to Vaughan, although the following poem, with its interesting implication in the word "enables," suggests that, by 1863,[1] she knew his verse, as she did Thomas Browne's prose, intimately:

> Strong draughts of Their Refreshing Minds
> To drink—enables Mine
> Through Desert or the Wilderness
> As bore it Sealed Wine
>
> To go elastic—Or as One
> The Camel's trait—attained
> How powerful the Stimulus
> Of an Hermetic Mind

That she tasted Herbert's "Sealed Wine" is deduced from her transcription of the middle stanzas of "Mattens."[2] Her poem **"I've heard an Organ talk sometimes"** suggests that she knew the basic meditative tradition as it appeared in the devotional mysticism of St. Bernard of Clairvaux. Describing her wordless rapture at hearing church music, she says that she had "risen up," afterwards, and "gone away/ A more Bernardine Girl—." She makes no reference to Donne; none to Marvell, whose equations of the soul with a garden resemble hers; none to Crashaw, Cowley, or King, some of whose insights and conceits are like her own.

II

It is highly likely, however, that Emily read metaphysical verse in her favorite newspapers and magazines and in books which she owned or borrowed. She would have done so because this poetry was available; because she read omnivorously; because critics, poets, and friends she admired praised it.

Samuel Bowles was a friend of the Dickinsons and a frequent correspondent of Emily's. His newspaper, the *Springfield Republican,* evinced the active spirit and wide tastes of its editor, becoming "a sovereign authority in Amherst" and "next in importance to the Bible in determining the mental climate of Emily Dickinson's formative years."[3] Emily's letters indicated its importance to her not only as a link with the busy world of politics and friends' lives but as a literary guide. In the "vital times" when Bowles "bore the Republican," aided by his associate editor, Emily's friend Dr. Holland, the paper reviewed reissued classics like Jeremy Taylor's *Holy Living and Dying* or rebuked new volumes like *Dramatis Personae.* It carried critical articles by Frank B. Sanborn, Emerson's biographer, which ranged from scathing accounts of the recent numbers of the *Atlantic Monthly* and estimations of the poems of Whitman and Joaquin Miller to affectionate praise of Spenser's *Shepherd's Calendar,* Marlowe's plays, and Drayton's sonnets. Alongside lines from *Beppo,* advertising Hostetter's Stomach Bitters, were printed selections from Francis Bacon and *Paradise Lost.* On May 20, 1863, an extract from the *Providence Journal* anticipated Emily's decision that "Bees are Black, with Gilt Surcingles—/Bucaneers of Buzz": "A bee buzzed in at our window yesterday. He was dressed like a colonel of cavalry, in a dark suit, with yellow trimmings." The metaphysical school was not neglected. Marvell's "Bermudas" and Herbert's "Money" were reprinted at least three and four times respectively between 1858 and 1863, while "Dr. Donne's *Holy Sonnets* and the devotional poems of "holy Herbert" were applauded for their intent and reproved for "fantastic conceits" in 1863. In the same year, the following article appeared. It was probably written by Sanborn, who was then supplying critical articles to the Boston *Transcript* and *Traveller* as well as to the *Republican* and with whom Emily had corresponded in 1871, thanking him for literary advice. The article compliments Vaughan for the very economy that Bowles demanded of his reporters and that Higginson had required of his "Young Contributor."

(*The Springfield Daily Republican*, February 14, 1863)

BOOKS, AUTHORS, AND ART

Henry Vaughan and His Poems

We notice, in one of our exchanges, a poem entitled 'Dew and Frost,' credited to George Herbert. It is not, however, his, but was written by Henry Vaughan, and with additional verses forms the poem called in the collection of that author's works, 'LOVE AND DISCIPLINE.' It is sweet and suggestive; we give it entire, below. The mistake which attributed it to Herbert, had it occurred during the life time and within the notice of Vaughan, would have afforded him the greatest pleasure, as indicating a similarity between his own compositions and those of one whom he delighted to call his master. A few specimens of Vaughan's poetry may not be uninteresting to those of our readers who are not familiar with it. Amid the quaint conceits and profuse imagery which characterize his poetry, (though in a less degree than that of most authors of his age,) there sparkles the true radiance of genius. Here and there you find thoughts simply, strongly, tenderly expressed; a volume in a line; a nineteenth century essay in three words. And over all shines the hallowing lustre of a truly Christian spirit. As he himself says: "He that desires to excel in this kind of hagiography, or holy writing, must strive by all means for perfection and true holiness; that a door may be opened to him in heaven, and then he will be able to write with Hierotheus and holy Herbert, 'a true hymn.'"

Henry Vaughan was born A.D. 1621, and died A.D. 1695. The selections which follow are taken from a volume entitled 'SILEX SCINTILLA[N]S,' and published in London in 1655.

The article then quotes "Love and Discipline" and "The Evening-watch" in their entirety. They are followed by this comment on "Rules and Lessons" and an extract central to Emily Dickinson's creed:

'RULES AND LESSONS' is one of Vaughan's most characteristic poems. Though less pleasing in diction than some others, it is full of just and beautiful thought. We have space but for one verse:—

Seek not the same steps with the crowd; stick
  thou
 To thy sure trot; a constant, humble mind
Is both his own joy and his Maker's too;
 Let folly dust it on, or lag behind,—
A sweet self—privacy in a right soul
Outruns the earth, and lines the utmost pole.

The first six stanzas of "Cock-crowing" are quoted as exemplary of "Vaughan's sympathy with nature." The article then concludes with lines 25 to 50 of "The Seed growing secretly."

Emily Dickinson, who told the Hollands in a letter of autumn, 1853, that she "read in [the *Springfield Republican*] every night," probably saw this article. She might have been impressed with Vaughan's use of "Essential Oils" and she would have liked his lines "*A sweet self-privacy in a right soul*/Outruns the earth, and lines the utmost pole"; for she herself, in 1863, had commended the "solitary prowess/Of a Silent Life—" and written:

Suffice Us—for a Crowd—
Ourself—and Rectitude—
And that Assembly—not far off
From furthest Spirit—God—

It was the kernel of her life and art.

That frequent criticisms of metaphysical verse appeared in the *Republican* during Emily's most creative years is important. That they appeared under Bowles's aegis is also significant. He, like Emerson—himself a lover of Donne and Herbert—, was an occasional caller at Austin's villa, bringing books for Susan Dickinson and her "Sister" across the lawn. One of these was Charles A. Dana's *Household Book of Poetry*, published in 1860, and reviewed in 1864 by the *Republican*. In 1950, the book was presented to Harvard University by Gilbert Montague and is now preserved in Harvard's Houghton Library. A letter from Bowles, still in it, suggests that the volume was given to the Dickinsons shortly after its arrival in 1862 at the Boston publishers, Ticknor & Fields. The book contained a small selection of metaphysical verse. There were Marvell's "On A drop of Dew," "The Mower to the Glow-Worms," the "Horatian Ode," and "Bermudas." Herbert was represented by "The Call," "Complaining," "The Flower," and "Virtue." Of Vaughan, there were "Peace," "The Bee," "The Feast," the famous "They are all gone into the world of light!," and the important meditative poem, "Rules and Lessons." Crashaw's "On a Prayer Book Sent to Mrs. M. R.," his Italianate song "To thy Lover," and "Temperance: or the Cheap Physician" were included with scores of Herrick's lyrics including his "Litany to the Holy Spirit" and many of Carew's less "metaphysical" pieces. Emily, who was, as her letter demonstrates, a constant borrower of Sue's books, could have read these poems; but they would have been slender diet. Bowles's letter to Sue, however, had called the book the "complement to your collection of poets"; for the Dickinson libraries, both Austin's and Emily's, were replete with anthologies and volumes of verse.

One of the most interesting of these for our purposes is *The Sacred Poets of England and America,* edited by Rufus Griswold and published by D. Appleton & Co. in 1849. Like other books I shall discuss, it, too, was presented to Harvard in 1950 on the premise that it had been in the Dickinson family during Emily's lifetime. This last seems certain: it is inscribed to Susan by members of the Utica Female Academy, "Dec. 22, 1848." It contains a generous selection of metaphysical poetry. Donne is represented by Holy Sonnets I, VI, VII, and X, and by his hymns "To Christ at the Authors last going into Germany" and "To God, my God, in my sicknesse." Herbert's "The Collar," "The Quip," "Virtue," "Business," "Peace," and "Grace" appear, followed by Vaughan's "The Pursuite," "The World," "The Bee," "The Shepherds," "The Garland," "The Dwelling-place," "The Wreath," "Son-dayes," "The Retreate," "Childe-hood," "Peace," "Looking back," and "They are all gone into the world of light!" Marvell's "On a Drop of Dew" and "Bermudas" are printed, together with Crashaw's "The Martyr," "Dies Irae Dies Illa," and the "Full Chorus" from "In the Holy Nativity." There were Cowley's "The Garden" and "The Ecstasy" besides eight poems by William Drummond; several, including "The Anniversary" and "The Dirge," by Bishop King; many from Herrick's *Noble Numbers* and from Quarles's *Emblems* and several poems by Baxter and Habington. It is unthinkable that Emily, who was with difficulty kept from reading even Motherwell, overlooked this volume. Vaughan's poems are those which best convey the mystic insight she shared and the lines like "Eternity/In time" which she approximates. Donne's poems and sonnets, with the grand "death, thou shalt die," resemble many of hers in technique and in her affirmations that "Death [is] dead." Marvell's "On a Drop of Dew," with its delicate meditative structure, and Crashaw's "Full Chorus" would have appealed to her in substance and style, as would Cowley's "The Garden" or Herbert's "The Collar," which, like his "Love," her own poem **"'Unto me'? I do not know you"** closely resembles.

But Emily did not require this volume to read Herbert. Her sister-in-law owned an 1857 edition of *The Temple.* Whether it was Susan's or Emily's is a nice question. The autograph signature on the flyleaf is "S. H. Dickinson." This suggests that it was signed by Sue shortly after her marriage in 1856, since her signature in the period of the seventies was "Mrs. Wm. A. Dickinson." In the latter fifties and early sixties, when she and Emily were reading *Aurora Leigh* and *Sordello,* her autograph on the flyleaves of those and other books bore the middle initial she had used as Susan Huntington Gilbert. Edward Dickinson, whose reading was "lonely and rigorous," may not have bought a Herbert for Emily; but, like Sue's Coventry Patmore, commended by Bowles, it doubtless crossed the lawn, remaining there, with Sue's copies of Theodore Parker's *Prayers* and Carlyle's essays, for the principal use of her sister-in-law. The Houghton Library catalogue describes the volume as "bearing pencil marks—probably by Emily." The conjecture is valid; for the markings in *The Temple,* as in other books I shall discuss, follow a pattern. This pattern is accompanied in other volumes by critical comments in what seems Emily's hand of the early sixties.[4] The major indication that the markings are Emily's is, in every case, what is marked or the nature of the comment. The hand that scored *The Temple* used the same light, single stroke to the right of the page as the one that scored the following passage in De Quincey's *Essays on the Poets:* "the literature of power builds nests in aerial altitudes of temples sacred from violation, or of forests inaccessible to fraud." Alongside the passage, in Emily's hand, is the note "View Mrs. Browning's *Essays on the Greek Poets.*" Throughout the Dickinson books are such markings, surmised to be Emily's, which are applied to passages that recall her poems. Thus, line 861 in "The Book and the Ring," "Art may tell a truth/Obliquely," resembles the notion conveyed in **"Tell all the truth but tell it slant—"**; while a line marked in Emerson's *Compensation,* "There is a deeper fact in the soul than compensation, to wit, its own nature," expresses Emily's belief in the value of the independent spirit. Whoever made these markings knew the mind of the poet as well as she herself. That they were made by Susan is unlikely: as Vinnie Dickinson said, "to think" was Emily's job; Susan was a busy hostess to Austin's many friends; and those few of her books which she marked—*Palgrave's Treasury* (1877) for example—are underlined or crossed in ink: a different system entirely. The marked passages in Herbert's *Temple* voice concepts crucial to Emily's creed. The following lines from "The Church-Porch," "A verse may finde him who a sermon flies,/ And turn delight into a sacrifice," assert Emily's conviction that a poet was the "Merchant—of the Heavenly Grace" whose creative activities were his form of worship; while others, like "Dare to look in thy chest; for 'tis thine own;/ And tumble up and down what thou find'st there" declare the principle of self-analysis that supports all Emily's verse.

Edward Dickinson owned Robert Chambers's *Cyclopedia of English Literature,* in an edition published in 1847 by the Boston firm of Gould & Kendall. It contained metaphysical poems and criticisms of the poets. Sue Dickinson had an Edinburgh, 1844, edition of the same book. On its flyleaf, she records that it was purchased in 1856, before her marriage. It is possible that Emily received her volume after admiring Sue's. In Edward Dickinson's copy, the Vaughan section, like that of Crashaw, is well-thumbed and creased from right to left. It comprised "The Rainbow," "Timber," and "Rules and Lessons." The fourth stanza of the latter bears a thin line at right. The stanza alludes to Jacob wrestling with the Angel, a Biblical example of perseverance frequently cited by Emily in letters and in poems like **"A little East of Jordan."** The *Cyclopedia* also contained selections from Donne, pronounced—with some qualification—"real poetry, and . . . of a high order," including his "Valediction—forbidding mourning," "The Will," and "Satyre IV" from line 17b. "The Broken Heart," often compared with Emily's **"My Life had stood—a Loaded Gun—"** was criticized for its use of "mere conceit." Cowley's poems included "On the Death of Mr. Crashaw," "The Wish," "The Epicure," and others, along with two poems whose imagery is similar to Emily Dickinson's. In "Upon the shortness of Man's Life," human life is compared with an arrow; in **"A Day! Help! Help! Another Day!",** Emily had said, "my soul: What issues/Upon thine arrow hang!" Cowley's "Description of Heaven" contains the couplet, "Nothing is there To come, and nothing Past,/ But an Eternal Now does always last"; Emily affirms "Forever is composed of Nows—/'Tis not a different Time." Crashaw, praised for his "mystical style of thought," was represented by "Wishes to a Supposed Mistress," "Music's Duel," "Temperance," and the "Hymn to the Name of Jesus," one of the finest examples of his peculiar meditative technique. Marvell's "the Nymph complaining," "The Garden," and his satire on Holland were included, together with Herbert's "Mattens," "The Pulley," and other poems. There were several selections from Wither, Davies, and Southwell.

The Dickinsons also owned a volume called *Hymns of the Ages,* subtitled "Selections from Wither, Crashaw, Southwell, Habington, and other Sources," published in Boston by Ticknor & Fields in 1861 and favorably reviewed by the *Republican* on December 7, 1864. As the book truthfully claimed, it contained "large selections" of the "tender and earnest numbers of Southwell and Crashaw and Habington, the gentle symphonies of Vaughan, the rugged verse of Donne . . . and the voluminous "Halleujah" of Wither, which touched with a poetic glow each object of daily life." The volume is neither autographed nor marked and carries no acquisition date. Emily Dickinson rarely autographed her own books: Martin Tupper's *Proverbial Philosophy* is one of the few which bear her own signature. Others, like *The Imitation of Christ* were marked "Emily Dickinson" by Sue or the giver. That this book is not autographed, unlike each of Sue's volumes, suggests that it may have been the poet's.

Selections and criticisms of metaphysical verse were available to Emily in magazines; in the Amherst College Library, of which Austin was trustee; in friends' libraries. She subscribed to the *Atlantic Monthly* and probably saw reviews of George Duyckinck's *Life of Herbert* in the June, 1859, issue and articles like E. P. Whipple's on John Donne and the "Minor Elizabethan Poets" in the July, 1868, issue. Copies of each issue are preserved with the Dickinson books. That Emily borrowed volumes from the college shelves is indicated by a letter, written in 1858, to the wife of Joseph Haven, professor of metaphysics at Amherst: "Have you . . . in [your] Library, either *Klosterheim* or the *Confessions of an Opium Eater* by De Quincey? I have sent to Northampton, but cannot get them there; and they are missing just now from the College Library." Unfortunately, the present Converse Library of Amherst College lacks check-out lists from Emily's time. But, through Austin, who was purchasing the library's books in the early sixties, she could have borrowed copies of *The British Poets* series of the works of Donne, Crashaw, and Davies, published in 1855 by Little, Brown & Co. and popularized by the *Republican.*

Emily's favorite authors praised and quoted metaphysical verse. This alone would have piqued the Dickinson curiosity. Higginson commended the "vital vigor" of Andrew Marvell's poems to his "Young Contributor." Emerson, in "The Oversoul," employed Emily's Dionysian conception of art to distinguish between the poetry of "accomplished talkers" like Pope and that of a "fervent mystic" like Herbert, "prophesying half insane under the infinitude of his thought." Browning invoked the "revered and magisterial Donne" in "The Two Poets of Croisic," and George Eliot quoted three stanzas of "The undertaking" and one of "The good-morrow" in Chapters XXXIX and LXXXIII of *Middlemarch.*

Emily Dickinson's control of her inmost thoughts in lean, colloquial, incandescent verse; her conviction that "Drama's Vitallest Expression is the Common Day" with its rare vibrations; her simultaneous analysis of earth and eternity compose the "Compound Manner" that commits her to the metaphysical tradition. From the poets of this tradition she doubtless sought imaginative stimulus and an occasional technical lesson. Her genius and her poetry are unique, but her inner vision and unifying style link her with Donne, Marvell, Vaughan, and Herbert, poets who argued the community of all "that which God doth touch and own."

Notes

[1] If we accept Thomas H. Johnson's dating in his *Poems of Emily Dickinson* (Cambridge, Mass., 1955), II, 545.

I am grateful to Charles R. Green of the Jones Library, Amherst, for advice and for access to Dickinson material; to William A. Jackson of the Houghton Library, Harvard, for permission to use Harvard's Dickinson collection; and to Mrs. Alfred Leete Hampson for allowing me to see Dickinson books still at Evergreens.

[2] See *Bolts of Melody,* ed. Millicent Todd Bingham, with Mabel Loomis Todd (New York, 1945), p. 125.

[3] Van Wyck Brooks, *New England: Indian Summer* (New York, 1940), p. 317; George F. Whicher, *This Was a Poet* (New York, 1938), p. 170.

[4] This conclusion was reached after a comparison of the comments with specimens of Emily's writing given by Theodora Ward in the introductory chapter to Johnson's *Poems.* It is, of course, a layman's attempt to identify the writing chronologically.

Paula Hendrickson (essay date 1991)

SOURCE: "Dickinson and the Process of Death," in *Dickinson Studies*, Vol. 77, 1st Half, 1991, pp. 33-43.

[*In the following essay, Hendrickson studies the poems of Dickinson which refer to the precise moment of death, stating that these poems are often grouped as a subcategory of Dickinson's death poems and are rarely studied individually. Hendrickson analyzes in particular the imagery and themes specific to these poems.*]

While many books and articles have been written on the topic of Emily Dickinson's death poems, virtually nothing has been published about her moment of death poems. On rare occasions, scholars have mentioned the moment of death poems as a sub-catagory of her death poems. In researching this paper, I found nothing which dealt with this topic any further. This is unfortunate, because the most fascinating of ED [Emily Dickinson]'s death poems involve the description of the very moment of death. Some of these poems are seen thru the eyes of a bystander, and some are seen thru the eyes of the person who is dying. It has been documented by Dickinson in her own letters that she held a certain fascination about the process of dying. She had even been known to write letters to the bereaved, asking for the details of the deceased's final moments. Characteristically, this near-obsession with the process of dying found its way into her poetry. Perhaps the clearest example of her morbid curiosity is **"To know just how He suffered—would be dear" (622).** This poem is virtually a series of questions asking about a man's death. The speaker asks if the man's eyes sought out a particular person; if he had any last words; if he was patient; if dying was as he imagined it would be; if he was thinking about any singular thing; if he had any last wishes; if he was frightened; if he was conscious; and if it was "a pleasant day to die." These questions, and others, are addressed in Dickinson's process of death poems. This particular genre of poems has many references to vision, and to the eyes. Many of these poems also discuss the anesthetic power of death, with sleep acting as a metaphor for death. There are many other elements which emerge from the topic of dying, including the enigma of dying, and the bodily reactions to death (thirist, loss of senses, coldness). On the whole, all of these concerns help to portray death as an easy process, much like sleep, in which the victim gradually grows weak and weary.

One of her definitions of death is found in **"I like a look of Agony" (241).** Here it says that "The eyes glaze once—and that is Death." Eyes do play an important role in the moment of death poems. In the majority of these poems, the speaker, usually a bystander, reflects upon the actual appearance of the dying person's eyes. In **"She bore it till the simple veins/ Traced azure on her hand" (144),** the dying woman's eyes are described as "quiet," "pleading," surrounding by "purple Crayons." These latter could either refer to dark circles under the eyes, or to bloodshot eyes. In either case, the reader's attention is firmly fixed upon those dying, pleading eyes. The dying person's eyes in **"'Twas warm—at first—like Us" (519)** are called "busy." Following the thought of similar Dickinsonian poems, these eyes are busy seeking out some unknown object—God, Death, or perhaps an escort to the afterlife—an object which could be termed an enigma of death. These "busy eyes" are said to have congealed with the coldness of death. **"A Dying Tiger moaned for Drink" (566)** describes the dead tiger's eyes as having "A Vision on the Retina/Of Water—and of me." In **"To know just how He suffered—Would be dear" (622),** the speaker wonders what the dying man, presumably Christ, last saw before viewing Paradise. The poem **"He scanned it—staggered—/ Dropped the Loop" (1962)** says the suicidal man felt "as if/His Mind were going blind" only moments before killing himself. His motive, or at least one of his motives, for suicide is the belief that his soul has died (his mind is blind) and his body must follow suit. The actions of a dying person's eyes are most vividly described in **"I've seen a Dying Eye" (547).** This brief poem tells of the final movements of the eyes as they seem to search for, and locate, that elusive, enigmatic object of death.

"I've seen a Dying Eye" (547) also deals with the gradual obscurement of a dying person's vision. Words such as "Cloudier" and "Fog" help to emphasize the encroaching blindness of impending death. After being clouded with fog, the eyes seal shut in death. Not fog, but a fly obscures the dying person's vision in **"I heard a Fly buzz—when I died" (465).** Here the fly can be construed as Death itself, for only seconds before the speaker dies, the fly "interposes" itself "Between the light' and me." In obscuring the dying person's vision, the fly's actions become the catalyst of the actual moment of death, when, "I could not see to see." **"The Sun kept setting—setting—still" (692)** combines the use of light and dark imagery with the fading eyesight of the dying person. The speaker believes it is dusk, when in reality it is noon. In the lines "It's only fainter—by degrees—/And then it's out of sight," from **"To die—takes just a little while" (255),** the theme of fading, or a gradual obscurement of vision is used to compare death to falling asleep. Death and sleep are both . . . gradual processes resulting in total oblivion.

The anesthetic power of death can be found in many of Dickinson's death poems. "To die—takes just a little while—/They say it doesn't hurt" **(255)** clearly refers to the anesthetic power of death by stating that dying is painless, as if the person's body has grown numb. The closing two lines of this poem say that death was as if he "Had gone to sleep—that soundest time—? Without the weariness." **"The Heart asks Pleasure—first" (536)** is more explicit in comparing death to sleep. This poem mentions a pain-killing drug, Anodyne, deadening the pain of dying while causing the sufferer to fall asleep in death. Another poem, **"I've dropped my Brain—My Soul is numb" (1046),** describes a paralyzed woman as being a "Breathing Woman" trapped inside of a dead, lifeless body. The coldness, numbness, and paralysis mentioned in the first stanza strengthen the anesthetic references. **"'Twas Warm—at first—like Us" (519)** also contains the theme of the anesthetic power of death. In the first stanza, the word "Chill" reminds the reader of the chilling numbness associated with anesthetics and painkillers such as Novacaine. Again, the coldness and numbness are brought up in the lines "The Fingers grew too cold/To ache." A handful of other moment of death poems use words such as "drowsing" and "drowsiest" to suggest the sleep-inducing qualities of death.

Dickinson's moment of death poems question, but seldom answer, the enigma of what lies ahead after death. However, some of her death poems (in particular, **"One dignity delays for all" (98), "Death is the supple Suitor" (1445),** and **"Because I could not stop for Death" (712)** suggest an after-life to which one is escorted by attendants or coachmen. By acknowledging this frequently recurring theme, the reader can assume that the fly in **"I heard a Fly buzz—when I died" (465)** is either an escort or Death itself. It then can also be supposed that the dying eye in **"I've seen a Dying Eye" (547)** is searching for God or an escort to Paradise, visible only to the dying person. A more difficult puzzle is what "the Light" mentioned towards the end of **"The Sun kept setting—setting—still" (692)** represents. The first two lines of the final stanza can be read as if the dying person can see "the light at the end of the tunnel," so to speak. Here it is also revealed that the speaker knows she is dying and is not afraid. So, it is also possible that here "Light" actually means death. Death need not be portrayed with dark imagery because the speaker has no fear of death. In creating such enigmas, she allows her readers to arrive at their own, independent conclusions.

The number of times sight is mentioned in Dickinson's moment of death poems far out-numbers the number of times all other senses together are brought up. The only one of the five senses not addressed in her moment of death poems is the sense of smell. In most cases, the dying person experiences a gradual loss of feeling. The best example of the diminishing sense of feeling is seen in **"'Twas warm—at first—like Us" (519)** as the victim grows cold and numb. Rarely mentioned in her moment of death poems is the sense of sound. **"The Sun kept setting—setting—still" (692)** raises the question, "Yet why so little sound—Myself/Unto my Seeming make?" These lines suggest that along with fading vision and physical numbness, the dying person also suffers a hearing loss. The senses of taste and touch are addressed in **"The World—feels Dusty/When We stop to Die" (715).** The opening stanza contains the lines, "We want the Dew—then—/Honors—taste dry." Here the dying person is so thirsty, so parched, for water and for salvation that the events and honors of his life seem meaningless in comparison. The final stanza completes the thought by referring to death as "Thirst." The speaker essentially says that when her loved one is dying, it will be her job to quench his thirst with "Hybla Balms," and "Dews of Thessaly." In death, even animals grow thirsty, as in **"A Dying Tyger—moaned for Drink" (566).** Of course, this thirst is very obvious in the **"The Dying need but little, Dear, / A Glass of Water's all" (1026).**

In Dickinson's poems, death is not a swift occurrence, but a gradual process. In **"She bore it till the simple veins / Traced azure on her hand" (144),** Dickinson portrays the complexity of death by connecting various stages of death with the phrase "and then." In this poem, this phrase is used in the lines, "And then she ceased to bear it—/And with the Saints sat down." While, the title may be slightly misleading, **"To die—takes just a little while" (255)** describes death as a gradual process. Again, using the phrase "and then," this poem sums up the process of death in two lines, "It's only fainter—by degrees—/And then—it's out of sight." **"I heard a Fly buzz—when I died" (465)** uses "and then" three times, each time introducing a new stage of death. First, the fly blocks the speaker's vision, next, "the Windows failed," and lastly, "I could not see to see." This same process is detailed in **"I've seen a Dying Eye" (547)** as the eyes seek out an unknown object, then are obscured by fog, then are soldered shut. Here the phrase "and then" is used twice. Without the use of "and then," the poem **"'Twas warm at first—like us" (519)** follows the process of death from a growing chill to the final breath of life. The different stages of dying are arranged into four separate stanzas in **"The Sun kept setting—setting—still" (692).** At first, the speaker is slightly confused, feeling as if it is dusk, yet knowing it is noon. The sensations endured by the speaker eventually convince her that she is indeed dying. The most times "and then" is used in a single moment of death poem is four. This occurs in **"The Heart asks Pleasure—first" (536),** a poem of just eight lines. Here the dying person drifts into sleep, and from sleep, falls into death. With or without the phrase "and then," these poems manage to convey the idea that death is a gradual, natural, process.

In writing her moment of death poems, ED may have drawn her images from hearsay about the final stages of death. More likely, tho, she gathered her ideas thru more systematic means. She was apparently not timid about inquiring as to the particulars of a person's death. She avidly pursued questioning anyone she knew who had witnessed a death. Her letters reflect her interest in even the smallest details of death. ED would not be pleased with a reply that the deceased died quietly. She would desire to know if he moved, blinked, spoke, or smiled. She seemed to be searching for even the faintest clue to the enigma of death. Her curiosity about the afterlife is evident even in letters written when she was quite young.

Dickinson's earliest surviving letter probing for information about a friend's death was written in early 1854, when she was just 23. She wrote to Reverend Edward Everett Hale asking about the death of her friend Benjamin F. Newton, "I often have hoped to know if his last hours were cheerful, and if he was willing to die. . . . You may think my desire strange, Sir, but the Dead was dear to me, and I would love to know that he sleeps peacefully" (Johnson 1:282). In another example, from 1862, she asked her cousin, Louise Norcross, to tell her how Louise's aunt Myra died. She wrote, "You must tell us all you know about dear Myra's going. . . . Was Myra willing to leave us all? I want so much to know if it was hard, husband and babies and big life and sweet home by the sea. I should think she would rather have stayed . . ." (2:406-7).

1881 marked a point when ED's letters about death became more frequent. In October of that year, Dr. Holland, the husband of one of her closest friends, died. When inquiring about Dr. Holland's death, she wrote, "I am yearning to know if he knew he was fleeing—if he spoke to you. Dare I ask if he suffered?" James Clark, a man with whom ED had occasionally corresponded, died in 1883. To his brother Charles, she wrote:

> I never had met your brother but once . . . An unforgotten once. . . . I hope he was able to speak with you in his closing moment. . . . I am eager to know all you may tell me of those final Days. (3:778)

After the death of her treasured friend, H.H. Jackson, Dickinson wrote to the widower:

> . . . I. . . . express my sympathy for my grieved friend, and to ask him [sic] when sorrow will allow, if he will tell me a very little of her life's close? She said in a note of a few months since, "I am absolutely well."
>
> I next knew of her death. Excuse me for disturbing you in so deep an hour.
>
> Bereavement is my only plea.
>
> Sorrowfully,
>
> E. Dickinson. (3:885).

Dickinson also wrote to a clergyman, Forrest F. Emerson, asking about Mrs. Jackson's death. Dickinson claimed that her sister Lavinia "Vinnie" desired the information:

> . . . Vinnie hoped, too, to speak with you of Helen of Colorado, whom she understood you to have a friend, a friend also of hers.
>
> Should she know any circumstances of her life's close, would she perhaps lend it to you, that you might lend it to me? (3:890).

That Dickinson would go as far as asking a friend of Mrs. Jackson for details of the death suggests the increasing importance such matters held.

Just as she expected from others, Dickinson included in her own letters detailed accounts of the deaths of her loved ones. When her father died in 1874, Dickinson's letters contained no specific information as to his death, but when her mother died in 1882, her letters were very specific. She wrote to Mrs. Holland:

> She seemed entirely better the last Day of her Life and took Lemonade—Beef Tea and Custard with a pretty ravenousness that delighted us. After a restless Night, complaining of great weariness, she was lifted earlier than usual from her Bed to her Chair, when a few quick breaths and a "Don't leave me, Vinnie" and her sweet being closed—That the one we have cherished so softly so long,

> should be in that great Eternity without our simple Counsels, seems frightened and foreign, but we hope that Our Sparrow has ceased to fall, though at first we believe nothing—(3:746).

Similar details are mentioned in letters to Mrs. Howard Smith (3:748) and Louise and Frances Norcross (3: 749-50). Dickinson was deeply grieved by the death of her eight year old nephew Gilbert in 1883. She wrote about his death to Mrs. Holland:

> "Open the door, open the door, they are waiting for me," was Gilbert's sweet command in delirium. *Who* were waiting for him, all we possess we would gladly give to know—Anguish at last opened it, and he ran to the little Grave at his grandparent's feet—(3:803)

Here Dickinson's fascination and frustration with the enigma of death are more strongly expressed than at any other time of her life. It seems that most of her thoughts about dying came to fruition in her own death. After being bed-ridden for the better part of six months, ED sank into a coma on May 13, 1886. Two days later she died at home. Dickinson's own death seems to prove that death *is* a gradual process much like falling asleep. She appears to have resolved the enigma of death for herself, because in what is believed to be her final letter (to Louise and Frances Norcross) she wrote:

> Little Cousins,
> Called back.
> Emily.
>
> (3:906).

Source Cited

Johnson, Thomas H., ed. *The Letters of ED.* 3 vol. Cambridge, Mass: The Belknap Press of Harvard UP, 1958.

Willis Buckingham (essay date 1993)

SOURCE: "Poetry Readers and Reading in the 1890's: Emily Dickinson's First Reception," in *Readers in History: Nineteenth-Century American Literature and the Contexts of Response*, edited by James L. Machor, Johns Hopkins University Press, 1993, pp. 164-79.

[*In the following essay, Buckingham reviews the reception of Dickinson's poetry by readers in the 1890s, stating that they praised her inspirational thoughts and feelings more than they respected her poetic technique.*]

When Emily Dickinson's ***Poems*** first appeared in 1890, her reluctant Boston publisher, Thomas Niles of Roberts Brothers, wondered whether his firm could afford to underwrite even a small edition of 500 copies.[1] Within three months the book had elicited well over 100 reviews, and Roberts Brothers was shipping its sixth printing. By decade's end, sales of that first volume alone had reached 10,000; two additional collections of poems and one of letters accounted for another 10,000 books sold. The 600 notices her books received are recently collected in my *Emily Dickinson's Reception in the 1890s: A Documentary History.*[2] These reviews demonstrate that Dickinson's ***Poems*** occasioned an immediate and remarkable response from magazinists and journalists of the day. During that first decade of publication the Amherst poet was brought and held in prominence by a community of some 500 commentators who contributed reviews, book trade news, and literary gossip to papers and journals throughout the country. Hers was distinctly a "reviewers' book," a case of readers dictating to the book trade led by professional readers.[3]

Having the early reviews in hand corrects the long-standing belief that Dickinson could not find an appreciative audience until the twentieth century.[4] These readers' reports also tell us how end-of-the-century reviewers formulate norms of valuation and define poet-reader relations. In so doing, they illuminate the readership to which Dickinson herself belonged. Those who write about her in the nineties are only, on average, about fifteen years her junior. Nor are the reviewers all male; forty percent of the signed reviews are by women, a percentage that probably held overall.

The focus of this study is not on ways Dickinson was first taught or studied or on how these documents reveal schools of criticism. Rather, in drawing on all known writing about the poet from the decade, it seeks what is common among poetry audiences as their fulfillment conditions for the reading of verse. The attention here is to Dickinson's first reviewers less in their roles as arbiters than as describers (and interpreters) of the social experience of poetry available to readers of their time. In their extent and diversity, these documents provide a broadly based perspective on nineties' poetry users and their shared interests and satisfactions.

More particularly, this essay highlights an often unrecognized feature of nineteenth-century literary activity: the way in which poetry reading, though taking place in solitude, joined itself to other social activities, especially communion between like-minded persons. According to the interpretive logic of these documents, poetry reading at its best creates an intimacy between the reader and the poet, a sacramentalized society of two. Verse reading also defines (and in the eyes of some reviewers, may slightly redefine) a larger community: those persons already loosely bounded as the "poetry lovers" for whom the reviewers speak. Nineties' descriptions of these dynamics between reader and writer and among readers underscore the processes by which literature enters people's lives and by which reading communities and their values are shaped with the help of texts.[5]

It is not as easy as it might seem, a century later, to give these voices from the nineties a well-considered hearing. Their statements have long struck modern readers as quaint critical baby-talk, threaded through with analytically useless terms like "genius" and "sympathy." As Joyce Carol Oates observes, we are more profoundly separated from the Victorians than from earlier literary communities. This disjunction, she notes, is especially acute in language: "We presumably share a common language with our [Victorian] ancestors but much of our vocabulary—such words as 'soul,' 'eternity,' 'subservience,' 'dependence'—even 'lady'—even 'sin'—is irrevocably altered."[6] Opaque as "genius" and "sympathy" seem today, they encode the normative satisfactions of a historically distinct and influential group of professional poetry readers.[7] By means of such terms as these, nineties commentators intend to reveal and shape the poetry desires of their generation.[8]

"Genius" and "sympathy" are the two most frequent and powerful words in Dickinson's first readers' vocabulary of praise. They refer to the mind and to the heart, the centers of enjoyment most often referenced in these documents. Reviewers also prominently mention aesthetic pleasure. But their admiration for technique is only as an adjunct to inspired thought and feeling. The true poet, says the Springfield (Mass.) *Sunday Republican,* will use a technical device such as rhythm "as an instrument and not as an object of attainment" (178).[9] The desired poetical goals remain thought and feeling, to the poetic expression of which some critics believe song and sound are indispensable. Indeed, when Dickinson is faulted, it is almost always for her technical irregularities.[10] However, form for her reviewers is ancillary satisfaction, of mind and heart, rather than a sufficient pleasure in itself.

Interest in "affect" holds as true for those critics praising Dickinson's "genius" as for those commending her "sympathy." "Genius" occurs in nearly one hundred notices, often in their first paragraph. The *Boston Saturday Evening Gazette* writes of Dickinson's verses that they "are the outcome of the genius of an accomplished woman" (33). Phrases suggestive of originality and enthrallment accompany the appearance of this word: "witchery of genius," "rare and original genius," "so singular a genius," "the erratic and unconfinable genius," "wonderful and strange genius," "the surprises of genius," and a genius whose trait is that "startling abruptness of the seer." For one writer she has "too much genius and too little flesh and blood," and to another she is a "genius without talent," but on no characterization of the new poet is there greater accord than on this. And in Dickinson's case "genius" is not a term reviewers wait for her second or third book to validate, for the word appears with equal frequency throughout the decade. With her first slim book she skips *cum* and *magna* and goes right to *summa.*[11]

T. W. Higginson, throughout the nineties, praises Dickinson above all for her "high thoughts." Many follow his lead but not in the sense of ideas as arguable propositions or mere opinion. As Arlo Bates says, "Her theology is of a sort to puzzle metaphysicians, and yet one finds it often most suggestive and stimulating" (32). It is a "high sort of seeing" and contains elements of excitement, risk, surprise, intensity, awe, and even suggestions of the occult. For nineties reviewers, Dickinson's ideas are fresh, original, intense, condensed, oracular, and unhackneyed.[12] Innumerable references to "power" appear in this context, as do indicators of strangeness and suddenness ("barbaric," "startling,") and words that combine the two in ignition imagery: the "fire" and "sparks" of genius (243, 391).

This sense of "truth" as "superb surprise" parallels Dickinson's own delight in poetic discourse as revelation "at a slant" and tallies with her description of poetry as untranslatable experience, as "Sumptuous destitution," and as those moments "when abroad seems close." It derives from Transcendentalist ideas of genius and theories of inspiration. The proof of genius is that suggestive, even extravagant statement can occasion illumination and profound inner affect. Nineties reviewers steadily apply this model to Dickinson, describing her poems ballistically as the "swift revelations" of "lyrical projectiles" (348, 336), frequently comparing her to other American sages and seers: to Thoreau in fourteen notices, to Whitman in twenty, and to Emerson in fifty-six. The *Boston Sunday Herald* begins its review, "Madder rhymes one has seldom seen—scornful disregard of poetic technique could hardly go farther—and yet there is about the book a fascination, a power, a vision that enthralls you, and draws you back to it again and again" (34).

Startling originality, strangeness, and vision are some of the reviewers' most frequent terms for Dickinson's attractiveness to them. A related cluster contains words associated with masculinity: strength, power, vigor, and magnetism. In her study of antebellum fiction reviewing, Nina Baym remarks that on the subject of style.

> the most common word of praise was "vigorous," and along with it came such related terms as animated, powerful, terse, bold, nervous, vivid, vivacious, spirited, warm, elastic, impassioned, salient, racy, energetic, original, direct, expressive, sprightly. The second most common operative concept was most often expressed by the word

"graceful," along with its relatives: melodious, fluent, flowing, harmonious, sweet, cadenced.

She points out that "vigor in style was associated with the masculine, grace with the feminine" and that when fiction reviewers had to choose between the two they preferred vigor.[13] Nineties reviewers are intensely aware of Dickinson writing as a woman, yet most of the adjectives of praise for her thought and oracular manner suggest that the poet's genius has masculine components. As the *Philadelphia Evening Bulletin* put it, "Her verse . . . was epigrammatic in quality and almost masculine in the vigor of its underlying thought" (385).

Not surprisingly, critics relate the other central interest of Dickinson's poems, their emotional expressiveness, to her womanhood. "They are the poems," said the *Christian Inquirer,* "of a woman, in that their inspiration is that of subtle feeling rather than philosophic thought." Especially disclosing Dickinson's heart is her "comprehending sympathy" (127, 128). "Sympathy" is a frequent word in reviews of the nineties, one fundamental to the friendship ethos of nineteenth-century literary culture. It reflects a deep sense of bonding, of inner sharing, and of spiritual knowing and kindredness discovered with nature, between persons, and as between friends, between author and reader.

When the nineties reviewers give so much attention to their subject author's personal traits, as they do with Dickinson's sympathy, they are not substituting shallow filiopietism for the critic's job of work. They are sketching the poet's implied character, and in so doing they are talking about their experience of intimacy with the speaker of the poems and the "best self" in themselves that that experience brings forth. When reviewers remark on the Amherst poet's "sympathy," whether the immediate context is her empathy with nature or with those who suffer, the implied larger reference is to readers' pleasure in like responding to like, their spirits vibrating with the soul of the writer.

In other words, reviewers feel themselves "supposed." Dickinson evokes for them pleasures similar to those produced by delineation of character in nineteenth-century fiction with its demand for psychological characterization wherein "human passions respond to their own description." "For every man recognizing in himself the elements of character delineated," *Harper's* had declared in 1860, "recognizes also the fidelity of the picture of their inevitable operation in life—sees himself openly revealed—his secret sympathies, impulses, ambitions—his vices, his virtues, his temptations; and follows with terrible fascination the course of his undeveloped future—passes thoughtful and alarmed, and hangs back upon the very edge of sorrow and destruction."[14] Dickinson's "very great power," reports the Chicago *Figaro,* "thus concentrated, has laid bare many emotions that we all hide deep down in our hearts, thoughts . . . we hardly are conscious of thinking until these vivid words light up with flashes here and there that deep, dark undercurrent of life from which arise, almost unbidden, the best and the worst that is in us" (118).

In associating poetry that "breathes" with human presence, these Dickinson readers mirror the affectivist aesthetic of Matthew Arnold, who valued poetry because of its direct appeal, in his words, "to the great primary human affections: to those elementary feelings which subsist permanently in the race, and which are independent of time."[15] These responses also reflect one of the chief pleasures associated with novel reading, in which "deep emotion called up on another's behalf was morally uplifting."[16]

At least provisionally, Dickinson's reviewers tend to keep mental and emotional responses to poetry distinct, as if they are separate poles of experience, as different as male and female. Thus, the issue of Dickinson's femininity is never far from their minds. Reviewers are sure Dickinson is a genius, and there is no doubt about her womanliness, yet with many models of male genius they had but few of undoubted female genius. They had Sappho, but among modern examples there were George Sand, George Eliot, Harriet Beecher Stowe, and Charlotte Brontë, all of whom were strong in thought and all of whose work was regarded as thematically unfeminine. Poetry commentators of the 1890s speak of Dickinson as fiction reviewers had of George Sand in the 1840s: "Next to the pleasure of talking about one's-self to a sympathizing listener, is the expression of one's secret thoughts by another and a superior mind."[17] The omnipresence of words of power and their contiguity with the word "genius" suggest that the stunning epigrammatic force of Dickinson's thought fits easily into the male model of genius foremost in readers' minds. The *Figaro*'s review of the first volume begins: "Strange product of heredity, environment and climate are these profound, far-reaching, often unmusical 'poems' of Emily Dickinson's. They are instinct with a woman's sensitiveness, and yet are strong with the fearlessness of a man. With sudden flashes of genius," it continues, "she touches the very heart of things" (118).

If these readers enjoy the almost masculine flash and force of her thought, Dickinson also provokes in them constantly heightening sympathies, leading to uplifting communion with her. Realizing Dickinson spiritually is indistinct from appreciating what they believe her presence is founded in, her female "nature." Her poems, they readily admit, lack feminine grace and finish in their forms of expression. But everywhere they have womanly feeling, as the *Independent* claims about her poem on her second baptism into maturity, "I'm ceded, I stopped being theirs" (53). *Godey's Magazine* notes that the poems are not only womanly and feminine;

they have "housewifeliness" (502). This strong sense of gender derives partly from Dickinson's focus on themes common to female verse, such as womanhood, home, human relationships, melancholy, and death. For this community of readers, she is the very model of retiring womanhood, strong in endurance and fortitude, capable of intense feeling for nature, able to discriminate among and tellingly render the various states of the human soul. With the precision of a woman genius (ten critics compare her to Emily Brontë in this respect), her poetry expresses, at its best, what the nineties assume is a characteristically feminine sensitivity to human feeling.

Some reviewers also respond to her as a "type" of woman in a more restricted sense. William Dean Howells's influential nineties review describes the new poet in terms of local color portraiture: her native themes and her "heart of full womanhood" derive from "tendencies inherent in the New England, or the Puritan, spirit" (77, 74).[18] Henry Lyman Koopman, writing for the magazine of Brown University, argues that qualities that appear now as only idiosyncratic to Dickinson will, as the race advances, emerge as general characteristics of womankind. Dickinson prefigures, Koopman continues, what women in literature would soon make plainer: "Woman is at once more conservative and more lawless than man; more abandoned both to love and to hate; more intense in imagination and sympathy, but narrower; capable of an apparently intellectual enthusiasm that really springs from the affections" (512).

Others find Dickinson hauntingly expressive of feminine repression. The New York *Commercial Advertiser* attributes her poems' "strange visions" and their "extreme hunger" for "human companionship" to "her woman nature" (85). Gertrude Meredith, writing a poem in tribute, confesses:

I hold her volume in my hand,
With half my mind I snatch its words:
(The other half enough affords
For listening and answer bland).

She was a woman, too, it seems,
Whom life not wholly satisfied;
She loved: more heartily, she died;
To die's the keener in her dreams.

And I, who flagged, my zeal renew:
The trivial's phantom-terrors flee
This witness of reality.
I can live more since death's so true.

(129)

Caroline Healey Dall, prominent in the women's rights movement, is among a dozen nineties reviewers who connect Dickinson with Marie Bashkirtseff, a cosmopolitan Russian painter whose posthumous diary had just been published, candidly revealing her experience of gender repression. Bashkirtseff's *Journal,* the moment-to-moment record of feelings and impulses, read like a novel and (according to its 1890 translator) described a woman "at odds with destiny, as such a soul must needs be, when endowed with great powers and possibilities . . . continually thwarted by the impediments and restrictions of sex."[19] "Quite as remarkable a revelation" as Bashkirtseff's, writes Caroline Dall, "is to be found in the poems of Emily Dickinson." Like Gertrude Meredith, Dall finds Dickinson a catalyst for thinking about women's roles and women's fate. It is necessary to know more "of the poet's history," she says in her review, because "face to face with life and love, but above all with death and disappointment has this woman come. Nothing of human experience has she scorned, nothing evaded, and so critically has she tested what she has endured that few people will understand what they find in her alembic. Every line challenges much thinking. . . . The women who have this book in their hands have a good deal to think of" (121, 122).

This reading of the new poet as specifically revelatory for women unites admiration for both emotional and intellectual—and what corresponded in the logic of the period to female and male—sources of power. There is no question to reviewers that Dickinson speaks as a woman—in her style, which had reserve and (some dared to maintain) inner harmony; in her subjects, the domestic and the private; and in her tone, exalted, piquant, and pure. She also has spontaneity, "the birthright gift," according to the New York *Critic,* "of the lyric poet and of woman" (416). She has, above all, a woman's passions and sensitivity. But her words also carry rough, stunning, epigrammatic directness, just as her thought has the attraction, freshness, intelligence, and orphic force of assured genius.[20]

By the nineties, in other words, whatever strengths poets draw from, whether those of mind or heart, their office is to exert affective force. Poetry is a "hotted up" medium; when it works, something within reels and stumbles. As Dickinson herself puts it, describing the mysterious power of honest passionate language:

By homely gift and hindered Words
The human heart is told
Of Nothing—
"Nothing" is the force
That renovates the World.[21]

For her first commentators as well, even at its most visionary and cerebral, poetic expression remains ontologically separate from textuality, from words as impersonal objects. Arlo Bates describes the Amherst poet's "high muse" as an ability to express, androgynously, "real emotional thought" (29). Delineation of affect, not meaning, is her reviewers' goal.[22] When both genius and sympathy are affectively felt, reading becomes a series of pleasing aftermaths: on the genius side, a kinetic push of forceful mental presence; on the sympathy side, a warmth or bonding response to personal presence. Writing as a craft can be studied and criticized, but these professional readers place distinctively literary experience, with poetry as it highest form, well beyond scientific analysis; one cannot parse while reeling from a blow or opening to love.

These nineties readers also isolate poetry from science by insisting on its mysteriousness. Dickinson's "high sort of seeing" contains elements of excitement, risk, surprise, intensity, awe, all with suggestions of the occult. Lilian Whiting, a frequent reviewer of Dickinson and a woman with a lifelong interest in spiritualism, remarks on mediumship when she finds the poems "profound in thought and full of almost startling divination and insight" (26). There is in Dickinson's poems, says the *Boston Evening Transcript,* "a strange magic of meaning so ethereal that one must apprehend rather than comprehend it" (61). Her poems seem an enactment of breathed-forth fervor and passion within the affiliatory presence of moved spectators. For H. P. Schauffler in the *Amherst Literary Monthly,* it is not insights but "hope, remorse, anger, patriotism; these all seem to live and breathe out their various lights and shadows under the guiding influence of her magnetic touch" (226). This prospect of achieving "inner room" companionship with the poet is similarly imagined by the *Boston Transcript:* "Having been allowed by Mrs. Todd to enter into the outer chambers of knowledge of this poet in the first and second volumes, the door is opened in the third into an inner, a sacred room, whose air is the very breath of a human spirit" (458). The vestal, temple imagery elsewhere associated with her oracular thought here expresses expectations for personalized devotional experience, yearnings for deepened human relationships, modeled on that between Christ and the individual.[23] The reader and poet become secret friends. Louise Chandler Moulton confesses to her *Boston Herald* readers, "With every page I turn and return I grow more and more in love" (37).

Reflecting this intimate friendship ethos, Dickinson's publisher, Roberts Brothers, regularly issued her 1890 ***Poems*** in delicate gift-book bindings. By sacramentalizing poetry reading (the best selves of "devoted" readers enjoying heart-to-heart communication with nearly divine poet-friends and preceptors), reviewers situate the reading experience at the farthest remove from rational explanation. This extreme subjectivizing of imaginative experience claims for poetry reading a world apart from Darwin and Spencer. Facing the supposedly superior objectivity of science and its increasing demands for objectivity and verifiability, critics move poetry to the sanctuary, hoping the temple doors will close behind them. Dickinson's gnomic accents accord well with this need to mystify the office of poetry. It is with the free spirits—the brilliant, untrammeled, and the enigmatical, like Blake and Emerson, Whitman and Browning—that the strength and originality of her thought reminds her first readers.[24] She is a refreshingly aboriginal presence in a literary world that already has as many "excellent formalists" as it needs (182). The *Christian Register,* which begins its review comparing Dickinson to an Aeolian harp, concludes that just as Browning and Emerson finally elude us, so "we cannot parse or analyze [her poems]." They "usher us into the deeper mysteries" (134, 135).

This strategy for dealing with the threat of science italicizes an ambivalence implicit in these reviews: that poetry, in a democratic age, is increasingly an elitist diversion. In terms of readership percentages, poetry during the century had steadily given way to fiction. But the review columns show little egalitarian interest in teaching poetry appreciation. As the poetry-reading life becomes increasingly personalized and sacralized, the less amenable to direct instruction (through explication) it becomes. The ability to take poetic pleasures becomes an unearned grace; one has it or does not. Though Dickinson's "odd" life draws attention, her typical notice primarily delineates the responses of the reviewer as a qualified reader. Reviews consist of brief excerpts from poems, each tagged with such impressionistic comment as "noble and inspiring" (107). Readers learn not how to read but whether they belong among "poetry Lovers." When their responses tally with the reviewers', they are confirmed as sensitive readers. The *Amherst Literary Monthly* is typical in phrasing its remarks as polite exclamations: "Note the dainty touch" and "Mark the power of naturalness both in thought and expression. Why you feel perfectly at home when that thought, clad in its simple, unadorned attire, greets your mind" (150). The way to write a review in the nineties is to identify the various affects a new volume of verse evokes, illustrating each through brief quotation.

Literary litmus tests cannot enlarge poetry's potential audience; they serve, rather, to confirm the reading fitness and practice of those who consult reviews, a community already presumably experienced and confident as readers of verse. Reviewers assume alliance with their readers on the basis of mutual love of good poetry, and almost none of them, at the outset of Dickinson's debut, predict a wide readership for the new poet. Her intellect seems too bold and sibylline and her sentiments too rare and delicate ("too little flesh and blood") to attract the common reader. When, to everyone's surprise, she achieves popularity, many express relief, as if her booming sales are unlooked for but welcome evidence that poetry still functions in an egalitarian culture. The democratic ethos apparent here also finds expression in her reviewers' disinclination, overtly at least, to base their judgments on learning and taste. But as Dickinson's reception develops, her popularity begins to be held against her, especially by the most influential high-culture arbiters.[25] Critics express their impressions as if certain of their universality, but their exclusive reliance on subjectivity demonstrates little confidence that her poetry can appeal to those outside the steadily decreasing circle of persons like themselves. The *Boston Transcript*'s insistence (noted earlier) that Dickinson must be apprehended, not comprehended, implies a self-selected community of qualified readers who, in perusing reviews, expect the pleasures of self-confirmation and the "social" reward (union with the reviewer) of sharing "high-minded" and like-minded felicities. Reading poems and reading reviews have much in common. "Those who are fit," says the *Springfield Republican* of Dickinson, "will read and know themselves divined" (21).

Taken as a whole, these notices demonstrate how social constructions of femininity and masculinity worked on Dickinson's behalf when her first book entered the literary marketplace. As reading expectations for fiction and especially for poetry moved toward increased intimacy, mystery, and sacred personalism, her voice and the way it constructed the writer-reader relationship ("These are my letters to the world") found ready acceptance. Dickinson, herself an avid fiction reader, reflected that crossover of sacred tears from fiction to poetry when she exclaimed to Susan Gilbert in the fifties: "I would paint a portrait which would bring the tears, had I canvass for it, and the scene should be—*solitude,* and the figures—solitude—and the lights and shades, each a solitude. I could fill a chamber with landscapes so lone, men should pause and weep there."[26]

In fiction of worth, said the *Christian Examiner* in the same decade (when the poet was in her twenties), there must be "some ingenuity of contrivance to keep the mind of the reader suspended and engaged, and swept forward, while it is swayed to and fro, by curiosity and emotion, and a constantly heightening sympathy."[27] Nineties readers respond to Dickinson (as the poet did to her favorite authors) as a friend and correspondent, bold, brilliant, attractive, and passionate, a loved presence evoking uplifting feelings. For her first reviewers, Dickinson's half-veiled verses have the power to engage and sweep them forward, in comprehending sympathy. When fulfilled, these expectations constitute poetry's special exhilaration and expanse. But it is an expanse perceived only by a coterie of knowing respondents, whose sympathies testify to the mysterious power of poetry even as their reading strategies rarefy that power.

Notes

This essay is dedicated to David Porter, organizer of the Emily Dickinson International Conference entitled "Emily Dickinson in Public," held in Amherst, Mass., October 27-28, 1989, at which an earlier version of this paper was presented.

1 Before publication Niles confessed, "It has always seemed to me that it would be unwise to perpetuate Miss Dickinson's poems" (quoted in Millicent Todd Bingham, *Ancestors' Brocades: The Literary Debut of Emily Dickinson* [New York: Harper's, 1945] 53).

2 Willis Buckingham, ed., *Emily Dickinson's Reception in the 1890s: A Documentary History* (Pittsburgh: Pittsburgh UP, 1989). An appendix summarizes sales records, printing by printing, of each Dickinson volume published in the nineties (557-58). All page references in the text are to reviews collected in this volume. In subsequent note references this volume is cited as *EDR.*

3 The writers largely responsible for Dickinson's emergence, especially during the first weeks, were contributors to dailies and weeklies in New England. She was a "Boston fad" before the national monthlies had a chance to comment. On the phenomenon of the "reviewers' book" see Cathy N. Davidson, "Toward a History of Books and Readers," in *Reading in America: Literature and Social History,* ed. Cathy N. Davidson (Baltimore: Johns Hopkins UP, 1989) 20-21.

4 It has been a commonplace of twentieth-century Dickinson scholarship that the poet was poorly received and understood when first published. A "war-of-the-critics" approach to her reception caused this impression in part; by treating opposed views equally, this method overrepresented the handful of critics who cleverly savaged Dickinson's verse. For example, Caesar R. Blake and Carlton J. Wells reprinted sixteen 1890s reviews in their *Recognition of Emily Dickinson* (Ann Arbor: U of Michigan P, 1964) 3-68. Among them, six were strongly positive, three ambivalent, and seven strongly negative. The 600 items assembled in *EDR* indicate a largely favorable early response.

5 Of course, using reviews as cultural evidence is itself an interpretive act and does not substitute for reading the reviews themselves.

6 Oates continues: "We can analyze our [Victorian] ancestors' stated beliefs, and the philosophical, sociological, political, and psychological foundations of those beliefs, but it is virtually impossible for us to believe: we read their musical notations but we can't hear them. . . . Hamlet is our contemporary, Emma Bovary is our contemporary, even Swift's Gulliver is our contemporary, but what of the numberless hero-

ines of the best-selling novels of 1850-1950?" ("Pleasure, Duty, Redemption Then and Now: Susan Warner's *Diana,*" *American Literature* 59 [1987]: 423). Fred Kaplan makes a similar point in *Sacred Tears: Sentimentality in Victorian Literature* (Princeton: Princeton UP, 1987) 4-5.

[7] Among nineties reviewers different and overlapping subgroups can be identified—principally by the specific readerships they implicitly and explicitly address: well- or less-educated readers, regional audiences, college students, housewives, those interested in book trade news or literary gossip, those choosing books as special occasion gifts, etc. Nevertheless, nineties commentators seldom show interest, on the surface at least, in identifying themselves as a special kind of poetry reader, nor do they reflect differences among their presumed auditors, except when they comment on the difficulty of Dickinson's poetry and its accessibility to the general as opposed to the "discerning" reader. Some of those who stress the poet's thought are concerned, especially in the first weeks and months of her reception, that her work is too oracular to appeal to the common reader. Those who respond primarily to Dickinson's power of character usually have no such worries; they assume that the force of her personal presence will be transparent to all.

[8] The intended audience of these professional reviewers, of course, consists of persons curious about new poetry books, a "literary class" of readers. However, professional critics and journalists may constitute a "high culture" community, or they may reflect what they believe their readers *ought* to appreciate rather than what they honestly enjoy themselves. *EDR,* attempting as it does to collect all known comment on the poet, includes representation from the humbler magazines and papers (such as religious and home weeklies and smaller city dailies). Even so, we need to be aware of an unvoiced readership in the nineties, just as today inexpensive editions in bookstores and cardshops testify to a Dickinson constituency not represented in the academic community.

[9] Dickinson's poems occasioned fierce debate between those who believed poetry could dispense with traditional form and finish and those who believed it could not. For example, T. W. Higginson claimed on the poet's behalf that "when a thought takes one's breath away, a lesson on grammar seems an impertinence" (*EDR* 14). T. B. Aldrich countered: "But an ungrammatical thought does not, as a general thing, take one's breath away, except in a sense the reverse of flattering" (284).

[10] A surprising number of nineties reviewers, admitting the absence of conventional metrics in Dickinson, nevertheless rejoiced in her "wilding" music; see *EDR* items 27, 44, 51, 64, 135, 145, 263, 334, 419, 441, 495, 557. For a recent study of the poet's sound as it relates to meaning, see Judy Jo Small, *Positive as Sound: Emily Dickinson's Rhyme* (Athens: U of Georgia P, 1990).

[11] Interestingly, neither Mabel Loomis Todd nor Thomas Wentworth Higginson, co-editors of the 1890 *Poems,* used "genius" in their prepublication promotional articles on the new poet. However, they were quick to use the term once others had applied it.

[12] The nineties reception reinforces a model of reading which is active and engaged rather than merely passive. See Cathy N. Davidson's discussion of Rolf Engelsing's theory that as books became mass-produced, readers read extensively rather than intensively ("Towards a History of Books and Readers" 14-18).

[13] Nina Baym, *Novels, Readers, and Reviewers: Responses to Fiction in Antebellum America* (Ithaca: Cornell UP, 1984) 131.

[14] Ibid. 107, 55; *Harper's* quoted in ibid. 55.

[15] *The Complete Prose Works of Matthew Arnold,* ed. R. H. Super (Ann Arbor: U of Michigan P, 1960) 1:4.

[16] Baym, *Novels, Readers, and Reviewers* 141.

[17] Quoted in ibid. 52. Higginson once wrote to Dickinson, "It is hard to understand how you can live so alone, with thoughts of such a quality coming up in you" (quoted in Thomas H. Johnson, ed., *The Letters of Emily Dickinson* [Cambridge: Harvard UP, 1958] 2:461).

[18] Howells's "Editor's Study" review drew notice because of his fame and the literary heft of *Harper's Monthly.* His essay resonated as late as 1896, when the *Boston Transcript* observed, "This New England woman was a type of her race" (*EDR* 505). Howells's comments may also have been notable to *Harper's* subscribers because his "Editor's Study" infrequently devoted itself to poetry, especially to new poets; see James W. Simpson, ed., Introduction, *Editor's Study by William Dean Howells* (Troy: Whitston, 1983) xxxviii.

[19] Mathilde Blind, trans., Introduction, *The Journal of Marie Bashkirtseff* (London: Cassell, 1890) 1:[vii]-viii.

[20] In her study of antebellum fiction reviewing, Nina Baym stresses the tendency of critics to place restrictions on individuality for female characters and for women authors. Though many of those writing about Dickinson in the nineties enjoy her feminine presence, in general she is admired for some "womanly virtues" (freshness, charm, naturalness) more than others Baym mentions (unselfishness, inexperience, grace). The poet's most appealing personal quality

for both male and female critics appears to be the freedom and individuality (at the level of genius) which Baym feels was specifically denied women novelists before the war: "Where the novel, generally speaking, was defined as a field for the expression of the individual author, possibly rising to genius, it was defined in the case of the woman author as a field for the expression of the sex, in which case genius in the large sense is out of the question, since the most she can do is lose herself in gender and hence sacrifice the individuality that is the foundation of genius" (*Novels, Readers, and Reviewers* 103, 257).

[21] *The Poems of Emily Dickinson,* ed. Thomas H. Johnson (Cambridge: Harvard UP, 1955) 3:1077 (as numbered in this edition, poem 1563).

[22] See Jane P. Tompkins's discussion of the importance of personal experience in nineteenth- and twentieth-century literary interpretation, "The Reader in History," in *Reader-Response Criticism: From Formalism to Post-Structuralism,* ed. Jane P. Tompkins (Baltimore: Johns Hopkins UP, 1980) esp. 216-19, 224-26.

[23] See Richard Rabinowitz, *The Spiritual Self in Everyday Life: The Transformation of Personal Religious Experience in Nineteenth-Century New England* (Boston: Northeastern UP, 1989) 180.

[24] For nineties comparisons of Dickinson to particular authors and artists see "Index and Finding List," *EDR.*

[25] See Introduction, *EDR* xviii-xix.

[26] Johnson, *Letters* 1:310. Barton St. Armand finds parallels between Dickinson's vision here and "nineteenth-century emblem books and other folk works, especially popular 'sandpaper' drawings" (*Emily Dickinson and Her Culture: The Soul's Society* [Cambridge: Cambridge UP, 1984] 222).

[27] Quoted in Baym, *Novels, Readers, and Reviewers* 78.

R. McClure Smith (essay date 1994)

SOURCE: "'He Asked If I Was His': The Seductions of Emily Dickinson," in *ESQ*, Vol. 40, No. 1, 1994, pp. 27-65.

[*In the following essay, Smith traces the influence of Dickinson's relationship to the "disciplinary power of her patriarchal culture," arguing that this power struggle is portrayed in Dickinson's use of the "trope of seduction."*]

The poetry of Emily Dickinson is a superb testing ground for any literary analysis that emphasizes historical considerations. Indeed, while recent critical studies that attempt to "relate" Dickinson to her contemporary culture are interesting and informative, it would be more difficult to argue that any are particularly revelatory. I would suggest that the affinities such studies trace between the poet's culture and her text are of limited validity due to the implicit determinism of their method.[1] The central problem with these critical texts (and, to a degree, also their merit) is their monologic ambition. Each assumes that literary text and history can be distinguished as foreground and background and that the devices through which the text refracts or reflects that contextual background are therefore easily observable for the critical analyst. As a result, these critical studies go on to find (by partially constructing) a series of historical master narratives that demonstrate how Dickinson's poetry was unequivocally *determined* by the culture within which it was embedded.

While every expressive act is certainly embedded in a network of material practices, literary and nonliterary texts circulate inseparably in such a way that observing the intermingling of cultural and social events proves more problematic than a deterministic historical approach would allow. Therefore, this study pursues decidedly more limited, essentially local ambitions: it traces one particular negotiation or exchange between the social and cultural fields of antebellum New England by examining how a particular discursive field may have influenced (as opposed to determined) Dickinson's literary and linguistic imagination. From the outset, however, I want to acknowledge the necessary partiality of my own historical reading. My suggestion that Dickinson's self and text were defined by her relationship to the disciplinary power of her patriarchal culture—a power perfectly figured and dissolved in the trope of seduction—is decidedly partial both in the sense of being incomplete (as one discursive field among many) and in being a critically constructed narrative (one to which I have myself clearly become partial). My own analysis, therefore, should be regarded as a "negotiation" between Dickinson's poetic text and the critical approach of new historicism or cultural poetics that, in its own attempt at critical mastery, seeks to "seduce" that text.

1

Critics of Dickinson's poetry have often been intrigued by what Joanne Dobson characterizes as a "particularly intense constellation of images, situations, and statement in her poetry [that] reveals an intriguing preoccupation with masculinity, and, more particularly, with a facet of masculinity that is perceived as simultaneously omnipotent, fascinating, and deadly."[2] Indeed, this obvious preoccupation led Clark Griffith to suggest that Dickinson "stood in dread of everything masculine, so that one of the bogies she fled from was nothing less than the awful and the implacable idea of *him*."[3] Griffith correctly points out that although Dickinson's poetic victims and victimizers take many forms, the former are usually feminine figures and the latter invariably masculine: the female child is molested by a male sea or equally tormented by a male God;[4] female flowers are blasted by a male frost **(391),** while the female morning is betrayed by an uncaring male sun **(232);** the female narrator is sent scurrying by a male snake **(986)** or driven to eternity by a ghostly coachman **(712)**—all apparent evidence that Dickinson came to regard "cosmic depredations as depredations practiced by one sex upon the other." Griffith observes that "[f]ar too often to be either chance or coincidence, the 'loved one' arrives on the scene to alarm as well as to delight; his actions threaten even as they gratify; and the possibilities he extends are always somehow double-edged, so that love shades off into pursuit, betrothal can easily become seduction."[5] Certainly, in Dickinson's poetry the reader frequently finds a female speaker whose narrative emphasizes her own passivity, weakness, and insignificance. That speaker is locationally dwarfed by proximity to the powerful presence of a clearly superior masculine force. When that force is personified and directly addressed as God, Lover, Father, King, Emperor, Lord, or Master, the speaker's relative powerlessness invariably defines the relationship. Within such a system of established hierarchy, the speaker often characterizes herself as the tiny "Daisy" juxtaposed to the "Immortal Alps" **(124)** and the "Himmaleh" **(481)** or unflatteringly paired with the "Great Caesar!" **(102)** who is her "Her Lord" **(339).**

Dickinson's experience of antebellum culture must have provided ample evidence of the ways male power had been codified not only in patriarchal religion and the institution of marriage but also in an essentially masculine poetic tradition. The exercise of power, whether social, religious, or aesthetic, and the assertion of masculinity were virtually simultaneous activities. Given that fact, Dobson has chosen to interpret the masculine figure in Dickinson's poetry as a composite image of appropriated power: the poet's desire for a power that she inevitably associated with the masculine impelled her to reconstruct a male archetype that could effectively symbolize that power. Readers of the poetry, according to Dobson, witness a complex figuration of Dickinson's imagined relationship to a male muse, or Jungian animus, a relationship she often regarded as one of potential threat and probable subordination. Dobson's conclusion parallels that reached by a number of her critical predecessors—most obviously, Adrienne Rich, Joanne Feit Diehl, and Albert Gelpi—who have variously asserted that the hierarchical relationship between Dickinson's poetic narrators and a variety of male others does not necessarily express or examine a relationship between individuals but instead meditates in quintessentially romantic fashion on the relationship between the poet and her creative imagination.[6]

Though interesting, this critical perspective is distinctly limited in its ability to recognize any more overt social critique. Most obviously, confining the male/female relationship figured within the poems to an internal agon of the female psyche presumes the poet's relative disinterest in the more significant external power dynamics that contributed to her particular aesthetic problem. It is both more interesting *and* more plausible to argue that while the male figure in the poems is indeed a "composite figure" of power, he is also a recognizable derivation of a more specific and identifiable sociohistorical "character." In fact, Dobson suggests as much herself, albeit inadvertently, when she asserts that "[t]he Death as Lover configuration that is such an inextricable part of Dickinson's mythos of masculinity is vitally relevant to the understanding of this *seductive* aspect of her negative animus," and that **"Because I could not stop for Death" (712)** and **"Death is the supple Suitor" (1445)** are "explicit in their assignment of this characteristic of the *masterful seducer* to the death figure."[7] Dobson is perfectly correct (as was Griffith) in characterizing the composite male figure as seductive, not least because he derives in large part from the cultural image of the "masterful seducer" so common in the discourse of antebellum women.

In August 1847, the sixteen-year-old Emily Dickinson was preparing to begin her first (and only) year as a student at Mount Holyoke Female Seminary at South Hadley. When on 13 August the *Hampshire and Franklin Express* published an article on the tenth anniversary commencement of that "flourishing institution," it would therefore have been of considerable interest to the young student. In that article, the correspondent declares himself most impressed by the graduating class, particularly by their public display of knowledge; he observes that during the pupils' public examinations "the questions were promptly and adequately answered and distinctly expressed, evincing a thorough discipline to render them so familiar with their subjects," and that their performance as singers "gave a gratifying proof of their proficiency in music, and showed how many had cultivated it, and with what success." The commencement examinations proved to be a fine advertisement for Principal Mary Lyon's educational establishment.

As Dickinson would have expected to participate in a similar ceremony, this report might interest a scholar who chose to argue that the poet's year at Mount Holyoke was particularly significant. For example, the fact that the graduating class "were all plainly attired in white, without any artificial ornaments," might have some relevance to the poet's later choice of a plain white dress as her idiosyncratic personal signature; that dress, it could be argued, was an eccentrically personal compensation for the college graduation she never had, or perhaps the sign of her individual *poetic* graduation, a surprising "collegially" conceived cosmic white election. Equally suggestive might be the four major compositions written by the students that year: the "beautifully written" "Coronation and the Execution"; the satirical "Fashion"; the cryptic "Earth had but Two—and one she gave to Fame, and one to God"; and "The Two Friends" (a piece that makes particular reference to two Mount Holyoke pupils who had died during the course of the school year). The thematic grounding of much of the Dickinson poetic canon seems to parallel the content of those student essays, suggesting that the poet's interests in crowning and transcendence, temporality and satire, renunciation and election, and death and the memory of the departed were far from peculiar to her. Clearly, the details of the *Express* report on the graduation ceremony could be used to argue that the ambience of Mount Holyoke College under Lyon had an even more formative influence on Dickinson's thought than has previously been suggested.

The newspaper column that contains the report of the Mount Holyoke commencement is placed (not surprisingly) beside those for Amherst Academy and Amherst College. But it has a more striking adjacency with a parallel column that contains a rather different narrative, a narrative that is only in the most oblique sense of the word "educational." This article, captioned in bold type "THE LATE SEDUCTION CASE IN NEW YORK," describes in detail the arrest of one Michael Hare, a married man of twenty-eight, who had eloped with the fifteen-year-old daughter of his employer, a Mr. Fox of New York City. Since his arrest, Hare had proven himself an early adept at the technique of blaming the victim, accusing the unfortunate Miss Fox of seducing him. The *Hampshire and Franklin Express* was suitably outraged by this behavior and quoted approvingly, and at length, from the previous week's *New York Tribune,* which had extended its report on the affair into a full scale editorial declaration.[8] It is worth quoting the reprinted excerpt from the *Tribune* editorial in full:

> But the practical question in the business is this: *Shall anything be DONE to subject such villains to the wholesome discipline of Law?* Hare is now in custody, and in this city, *but seduction is not reckoned as a crime by our laws!* Attempts will be made to bring him to justice on a charge of bigamy (he having, it is said, got some sort of a marriage with his victim) or on that of larceny, in taking away the clothes of the girl. But the essential and horrible crime of violating his marriage vows, deserting her he had ever sworn to love and cherish, and seducing his childish prey from her home of innocence and love to the haunts of pollution and shame is not at all forbidden by the laws of New York. Shall this continue? We do not remember that one of the journals now vociferous against Hare ever aided to arouse the public mind to the necessity of providing legal penalties for crimes like this. Will they *now* take hold? Will the press generally speak out on this subject? Had any hungry wretch stolen from Mr. Fox a few spoons worth twenty dollars, the law directs that the culprit shall be punished therefore by several years' imprisonment at hard labor in the State Prison; but for the most perjured and base Seduction it has no penalty whatever! Why is this? Can it be deemed uncharitable if we say it is because our law-makers are seldom thieves, in the legal sense, but *are* too generally libertines? Why else is the most flagrant crime next to murder left unpunished while minor and even venial offences are visited with merciless severity? Why is it? Why?

Like the Mount Holyoke commencement report, this editorial is suggestive material for a Dickinson scholar, providing an arresting narrative—an antebellum fable of the Fox and the Hare—that could facilitate the historical setting of a *critical* narrative. For example, the angry polemic of the editorial (of which I shall say more later), though more usually confined to local political discourse, is not at all unusual in the *Express.* That diatribe suggests that while the refined delicacy of sentimentalism had a major place in the Hampden County press of 1847, it was not necessarily the predominant tone. The *Express*'s use of the *Tribune* editorial might serve as a critical corrective, conveniently reminding Dickinson's twentieth-century readers that her hometown was a place where political, religious, and personal passions had been known to run high and that the occasional anger in her poetic voice might be as much an expression of her culture as is her periodic indulgence in maudlin sentiment. And beyond the tone of the report, the space assigned to it vividly demonstrates that the local Amherst newspapers were not averse to printing sensationalistic and not particularly edifying news. Such a brief perusal of the local press could modify the contemporary reader's assumption—an assumption based on the apparent thematic concerns of Dickinson's poetry—that antebellum Amherst was a repressive enclave of survivalist puritanism.

Clearly, a little critical prestidigitation of the details in these two articles could construct a rereading of Dickinson's cultural milieu that could, in turn, be connected to her later poetic strategies. While tempted by that smoke and mirrors approach to history, I have chosen a different route of access to those poetic strategies, one not quite so dependent on the dangerously assumed principle of causality. Instead, I would suggest that what can be learned from the narrative content of the two articles is not nearly as interesting as the questions provoked by their parallel placement on the page. Was it simply an editorial lapse that led to their striking adjacency? How would the antebellum Amherst reader have dealt with that strange juxtaposition of commencement and seduction narratives on the same page? Even more interestingly, how would the sixteen-year-old female reader have reacted? Would she have interpreted the adjacent columns as separate and distinct paths, as possible alternative futures for herself, as diametrically opposed fates that could befall her?

In fact, the antebellum reader would not have recognized the juxtaposition as jarring because the same cultural discourse that produced the editorial diatribe provoked by the Fox seduction informed the education of the 1847 Mount Holyoke graduating class. Briefly, I want to return to that class and focus on one particularly rigorous examination that graduating students were expected to undergo. On the Wednesday of commencement week, the major examination of the graduating class concerned Milton's *Paradise Lost.* The details were not reported in the newspaper, but presumably this was the same examination that had been in place for the previous four years. For example, an *Express* reporter writing about the 8 August 1845 commencement describes "an examination of nearly or quite the entire graduating class in *Paradise Lost,* under the direction of Miss Lyon," during which "the poem was analyzed, some of its more striking beauties pointed out, and its agreement with scripture shown by reference to lines and texts." The reporter observes that "it must have been a thorough discipline to render the class so familiar with its structures." The commencement report for the following year, printed in the 14 August 1846 edition of the *Express,* usefully goes into more detail about what was required of that graduating class's hermeneutic skills as they were applied to Milton's text:

> The analysis of the "Argument" was full and discriminating. It comprised a sketch of the ends designed by the Poet, and the means used to reach them, the characters that figure and the parts they act. On the learned allusions of the text, the Encyclopedia had been patiently consulted. And from the Scriptures, passages were read elucidating the theology of the classic. Evidently the young ladies had forgiven the severity of the poet to his daughters.

The would-be graduate of Mount Holyoke apparently was expected to leave with as thorough a knowledge of *Paradise Lost* as she had of the King James Bible.

Paradise Lost is the quintessential narrative of seduction. In Milton's epic, as in Genesis, Satan is the first tempter of woman into sin, the first successful seducer. It is Satan's subtle persuasion of Eve, his rhetorical seduction, that introduces into the discourse of humanity the possibility of using linguistic signs to deceive. And it is precisely that initial satanic cunning, the playing on a feminine vulnerability to flattery and verbal wile, that deprives the Christian search for redemption of its ultimate reliability, leaving it instead to construct a massive metaphorical and typological apparatus that can cope with the semantics of deceit initiated by the Edenic interloper. Ironically, therefore, it is also that satanic cunning, that awareness of the deceptively seductive powers of rhetoric, that first makes poetry possible. If living in a Christian dispensation of necessity requires an awareness of the dangerous power of satanic seduction, then living in a poetic dispensation requires the simultaneous awareness of the attractiveness of that seduction.

In some ways, however, Satan's rhetorical seduction of Eve is a decidedly ambiguous affair, especially when the Genesis narrative of the Fall is read through the reinterpretive lens of *Paradise Lost.* The Miltonic narrative of the Fall of Man subtly implicates Eve herself as a candidate for the first successful seducer. The pivotal point of this interpretation is the moment when Satan, stunned into immobility, unobtrusively observes the beauty of Eve and is *tempted* to be her seducer. It is eminently possible to view Satan as a tempter tempted. Indeed, it might well be argued that from *Paradise Lost* onward, the literary representation of woman predetermines (or perhaps overdetermines) her as the agent of sin through the desire she inspires rather than through any desire she herself experiences. After her encounter with Satan, Eve seduces Adam through the medium of her own double allure, her physical and verbal charms working in irresistible tandem. As every subsequent literary seduction scene can be read as an allegory of the Fall, we must be alert to the ambiguities implicit in these first seductions. In particular, the Edenic seductions of *Paradise Lost* suggest the "victim's" culpability, since she appears to be susceptible to the straying. What makes Eve such a fascinating character is her paradoxical doubleness: she is the seductive seducee. Whatever Milton's narrative intention, his representation of an Eve who, even in her passivity, powerfully controls male figures might be far from negative for a woman reader. Indeed, the figure of a latently subversive Eve, the first "fallen woman," proved particularly useful to the antebellum woman writer seeking a suitable model of empowerment. After all, Eve's disobedience is the first challenge to patriarchal authority: a direct challenge to God and man. Feminist critics propose that Victorian novels by women are subtle rewritings of the Fall myth that conflate women's sexuality, power, and hunger in a new literary order of transgression. In general, the notion of trespass comes to represent a significant source of power for the woman writer. More specifically, Eve's desire, or perhaps more accurately her desirability, comes to represent that decentering power. Of course, the appropriation and rewriting of the Fall myth was especially necessary for women poets of the era, who had to confront Milton's "bogey," the most dangerous of poetic precursors, as a more direct threat.[9]

In the Miltonic universe of *Paradise Lost,* the Fall has major consequences not only for the users of language but also for language itself. In order to effect any physical seduction, the would-be seducer must first "produce felicitous language."[10] In other words, the seducer must be an exemplary rhetorician. Indeed, a rhetorician might well be defined as a seducer of language, for in the etymological sense of "seduction" *(seducere),* the rhetorician purposely leads language astray. Throughout *Paradise Lost,* Satan is an exceptional rhetorician, an exemplary seducer, a prototypical poet. Similarly, as the fallen Adam and Eve soon learn, the immediate consequences of eating from the Tree of Knowledge are the death of humankind *and* the birth of rhetoric. Milton's Fall is therefore also metaphorical to the degree that it signifies a fall *into* metaphor. What enters the lapsarian world with death is the deviation of language into a series of seductive possibilities: language as an unnecessary but delicious ornament; language as the means to covert insinuation; language as the means to use and manipulate others; language as rhetoric pure and simple. For Milton, language determined by rhetorical intention is corrupt because rhetoric deviates words from their originally perfect correspondence with nature into a misleading, intrinsically evil entity.

The attitude of Milton, the religious poet who found the uses of rhetoric intrinsically satanic, toward his own poetry is therefore distinctly paradoxical. That paradox is implicit in *Paradise Lost,* which often seems to be the epic narrative of its author's regret that poetry is possible. While Milton's doubled attitude toward rhetoric can easily be overlooked by the reader predisposed to religious orthodoxy, it was blatantly apparent to the later romantic poets who, more committed to problems of art than problems of faith, would willfully misread the epic poem as Milton's troubled satanic manifesto. This might lead one to expect that a young quasi-romantic poet, herself a distinctly unorthodox Christian who was probably quite familiar with the text of *Paradise Lost* and its deviations from the original Genesis text, would read the poem in a similarly critical light.

And Dickinson appears to have done just that. During her year at Mount Holyoke the significance of the text might well have been instilled in her. Certainly, there was a copy of *Paradise Lost* in the Dickinson family library from which the poet directly quoted in a number of letters. As Jack Capps observes, "On two separate occasions [in Letter 304] she refers to Eve's reluctant departure from Eden, and both instances seem closer to Milton's description of the expulsion than the concluding verses of the third chapter of Genesis."[11] It is likely that Dickinson did just what a Mount Holyoke student was expected to do: reinterpret the King James Bible through the filter of its Miltonic rewriting.

What Dickinson seems to have derived most from Milton is a paradoxical attitude toward her own art, a sense that her calling as a poet was simultaneously an invitation to sin. This paradoxical attitude is most evident in her frequently troubled identification with the figure of Eve. Of course, it was in a distinctly playful vein that Dickinson confided in an early letter, "I have lately come to the conclusion that I am Eve, alias Mrs. Adam. You know there is no account of her death in the Bible, and why am I not Eve?" (9). But the recurrence of Eve imagery elsewhere makes it one of her most significant tropes,[12] particularly when connected with her early tendency to associate her "calling" to poetry with a dangerous external temptation and her later resistance to that temptation. This is a heretical Dickinson who remarks, "I dont wonder that good angels weep—and bad ones sing songs," and who famously comments on what we may well assume is her poetic vocation, "I have dared to do strange things—bold things, and have asked no advice from any—I have heeded beautiful tempters, yet do not think I am wrong" (Letters 30 and 35). The explication of "beautiful tempters" is perhaps self-evident, but if not, it is succinctly explained in other vivid exploratory letters of her late adolescence:

> I think of the perfect happiness I experienced while I felt I was an heir of heaven as of a delightful dream, out of which the Evil one bid me wake & again return to the world & its pleasures. Would that I had not listened to his winning words! . . . But the world allured me & in an unguarded moment I listened to her syren voice. From that moment I seemed to lose my interest in heavenly things by degrees. (11)

Here Dickinson imagines herself a type of the tempted Eve, an identification repeated in a letter to her friend Jane Humphries: while charitable works, she writes, may provide the opportunity "for turning my back to this very sinful, and wicked world[, s]omehow or other I incline to other things—and Satan covers them up with flowers, and I reach out to pick them. The path of duty looks very ugly indeed—and the place where *I* want to go more amiable—a great deal—it is so much easier to do wrong than right—so much pleasanter to be evil than good" (30). This is an Eve susceptible to the direct seductions of rhetorical possibility, the latent poet surrendering to her daemon. Moreover, she seems virtually incapable of resisting the seductive temptations of the world. Even when she does succeed, the victory is, to say the least, ambiguous:

> [A] friend I love *so* dearly came and asked me to ride in the woods, the sweet-still woods, and I wanted to exceedingly—I told him I could not go, and he said he was disappointed—he wanted me very much—then the tears came into my eyes, tho' I tried to choke them back, and he said I *could,* and *should* go, and it seemed to me unjust. Oh I struggled with great temptation, and it cost me much of denial, but I think in the end I conquered, not a glorious victory Abiah. . . . I had read of Christ's temptations, and how they were like our own, only he did'nt sin; I wondered if *one* was like mine, and whether it made him angry—I couldnt make up my mind; do you think he ever did? (Letter 36)

In the same letter, a Dickinson deadly serious in her playfulness asks her correspondent: "Where do you think I've strayed, and from what new errand returned? I have come from '*to* and *fro,* and walking up, and down' the same place that Satan hailed from, when God asked him where he'd been, but not to illustrate further I tell you I have been dreaming, dreaming a *golden* dream, with eyes all the while wide open." Interestingly, she chooses to analyze her reprobate condition in the terms of an interpretive problem that she cannot solve and that leaves her "one of the lingering *bad* ones." She continues, "[S]o do *I* slink away, and pause, and ponder, and ponder, and pause, and do work without knowing why . . . and I ask what this message *means* that they ask for so very eagerly, *you* know of this depth, and fulness, will you *try* to tell me about it?" This process of continual pausing and pondering, of asking what the message means, seems not unlike the process that the poet requires her readers to pursue. But what makes Dickinson's association in this letter between the inability to interpret and her satanic persona so fascinating is its recurrence in other letters of the same apprentice period. In another letter to Abiah Root, Dickinson engages in a poetic whimsy and then says, defensively: "Now my dear friend, let me tell you that these last thoughts are fictions—vain imaginations to lead astray foolish young women. They are flowers of speech, they both *make,* and *tell* deliberate falsehoods, avoid them as the snake, and turn aside as from the *Bottle* snake, and I dont *think* you will be harmed" (31). In the course of discussing her various "mistakes" and her tendency to "sin," Dickinson essentially demands that Abiah, in turn, play the role of Eve to her own female Satan, whose final signature will be, appropriately, "Your very sincere, and *wicked* friend." There is an assumption of complicity here—an assumption that the initially tempted can and has duly become the tempter of another. In a letter written in approximately the same week, Dickinson emphasizes the contagion of her art to another correspondent: "[Y]ou are out of the way of temptation—and out of the way of the tempter—I did'nt mean to make you wicked—but I was—and am—and shall be—and I was with you so much that I could'nt help contaminate." At the same time, she emphasizes the sheer inevitability of her surrender to the process: "Is it wicked to talk so Jane—what *can* I say that isn't? Out of a wicked heart cometh wicked words" (30).

In many of these early letters, as Margaret Homans has observed, Dickinson moves easily between Eve and Satan as equivalent metaphorical figures. The assumption is that Eve is Satan's accomplice and therefore a tempter in her own right—in short, the tempted temptress. As such, she is a significantly doubled figure, an affirmatively subversive presence, and perhaps attractive to the woman poet for precisely that reason. The attractiveness of the Eve figure to the woman poet is that her seductiveness, while potentially her undoing, is simultaneously the means to an equally powerful seduction of her own. At the heart of her apparent powerlessness, at her weakest point of surrender, is a significant generator of power. And the passive power of luring, delighting, pleasing, need not signify weakness if it eventually confers the power to persuade actively. This entire scenario, of course, also offers a significant commentary on the possibilities of language. According to Homans's analysis of the Fall myth in Dickinson: "Adam becomes the traditional symbol for literal language in which words are synonymous with meaning, but Eve is the first to question that synonymity, the first critic, the mother of irony. It is in this sense that she is similar to Satan, and in making tempter and tempted synonymous Dickinson is recognizing this aspect of her inheritance from Eve."[13]

What emerges from that early Dickinson correspondence concerned with her poetic vocation is an almost Miltonic association of poetry, or of rhetoric in general, with intrinsic evil. Since the motor of poetry, metaphor, is the giving to an object a name that belongs to something else, the art of poetry is the art of the lie. In any Christian dispensation, "beautiful tempters" must be the offspring of Satan, the Father of Lies. In choosing to be a poet, Dickinson comes to view herself as a Mother of Lies, a necessary return to Eve. This is a consistent Dickinson, the same who enjoys reporting a nephew who "tells that the Clock purrs and the Kitten ticks" because "[h]e inherits his Uncle Emily's ardor for the lie" (Letter 315), and who delights in the successful dupings of the commercial world; commenting on her father's suspicion that he has been defrauded by the local steel market, she says, "I cannot stop smiling, though it is hours since, that even our steelyard will not tell the truth" (Letter 311). Perhaps this celebration of the lie is what gives such resonance to the story Dickinson told T. W. Higginson of her brother concealing Longfellow's *Kavanagh* under the piano cover for her in order to deceive their father (Letter 342B). It seems such a characteristic, appropriate gesture that it is not difficult to imagine the poet reveling in such a deception. Indeed, either way her narrative is one of deception: if the story is true then her father was her dupe, if not, then the dupe is Higginson. We would do well to remember, as readers of Dickinson, that the enjoyment of deception is prerequisite not merely for the poet but also for the love of poetry. And most frequently that deception is seduction. More specifically, a rhetorical seduction that is, I would suggest, firmly grounded in antebellum culture.

2

In her analysis of the postrevolutionary American novel, Cathy N. Davidson notes the particular significance of the printer's advertising technique for William Hill Brown's early novel *The Power of Sympathy*:

> [E]ven a casual glance at the Thomas's typography . . . registers the prominent placement of the word "SEDUCTION." This key word is centered in the middle of the page; occupies an entire line; and is written in the darkest, clearest, boldest type on the page. Even the spacing between each letter gives further prominence to the word. What we have here is another graphic illustration (literally and figuratively) of the role of the printer in the creation of the American novel and in the "seduction" of the American reading public.[14]

But "seduction" is not merely a "key word" that helps us understand the techniques of commercial printing and advertising in the "selling" of the postrevolutionary novel; it is also the essential keyword toward any comprehension of the major fictional strategies of women writers from the postrevolutionary through the antebellum period. Seduction became the focal point of so many early American sentimental novels because it was a succinct metaphor for the gendered power inequalities of contemporary society. As Davidson neatly puts it:

> Seduction spun so many of these sentimental plots precisely because seduction set forth and summed up crucial aspects of the society—the author's, the characters', the contemporary readers' (especially if they were women)—that did not have to be delineated beyond the bare facts of the seduction itself. Seduction thereby becomes a metonymic reduction of the whole world in which women operated and were operated upon.[15]

Postrevolutionary literature offers myriad examples of a female character whose reputation is ruined by a villainous male the characterization of whom, over time, assumes stereotypical proportions—the Lovelace of Samuel Richardson's *Clarissa* perpetually recontextualized. However, the fictional portrayal of sentimental seduction, almost always represented as the temptation of the central female character, with narrative suspense generated by the threat of her succumbing to the charms of that predatory male, is never merely a sexual interaction. A primary economic component is also implied in the fictional seduction: the eventual success of the seducer depends upon his superior social status, and therefore upon the greater economic and educational prospects of the middle-class American male. The scene of seduction is invariably a scene of inequality, and its fictional portrayal implicitly critiques the distribution of power and evaluation of worth in that society.

The social critique implicit in the novel of seduction produces fundamental ambiguities in the reader's response to the genre—not least because the central female character (in postrevolutionary sentimental fiction often a representation of irresistible innocence, in later antebellum sensationalism more likely a model of unfathomable deviousness) inevitably sets up a field of fatal attraction not only for the novel's male characters but also for the female reader. This raises the interesting question of who is being seduced by whom and points to a complex ambiguity at the heart of any sentimental novel that turns on the plot mechanism of seduction: to maintain the sympathy of the reader, the victim of the attempted seduction has to be "seductively" attractive to that reader. This leaves the reader uncomfortably occupying an extratextual location that duplicates the seducer's position within the text. The ambiguous position of the reader vis-à-vis such a text, empathizing with the powerless while participating in an exercise of power, permits the novel of seduction its subversive subtext, its suggestive critique of *social* hierarchies. The subtext of the sentimental novel subtly questions the societal rules that are textually affirmed by the fall of a woman character. Not only is there an implicit critique of a generalized cultural misogyny, there is also the suggestion of possible reform; such inequalities could be rectified by legally enforceable punishment of the seducer and by superior education for women.

The basic ambiguities implicit in literary seduction would become explicit in the antebellum period. Such early American novels as *The Power of Sympathy* (1789) and its best-selling successors Susanna Rowson's *Charlotte Temple* (1791) and Hannah Webster Foster's *The Coquette* (1797), which particularly center on the possible seduction of a female character, were superseded by a stream of more sensational literature whose agendas included nothing remotely covert. While the seduction plot virtually disappeared from sentimental fiction by 1818, its basic concerns survived in the later sensational design that informs novels like Alice Cary's *Hagar: A Story of Today* (1852) and *Married, Not Mated* (1859). Meanwhile, the latent agenda of many early novels of seduction (that the seducee could become a potent seducer in her own right) was realized in later novels such as Lillie Devereux Blake's *Southwold* (1859), whose heroine, Medora Fielding, attracts men in order to destroy them, and Louisa May Alcott's *Behind a Mask; or, A Woman's Power* (1866), whose heroine, Jean Muir, wreaks vengeance on the male sex after first attracting them with her seeming innocence. David Reynolds notes that in many sensational novels of the period, "the fallen woman became a fantasy figure of vindictive violence and unrestrained sexuality. It was taken for granted that woman, once seduced and released from the constrictions of female propriety, was capable of becoming more ferocious and more sexually aggressive than man."[16] In these novels we can glimpse a recurring paradigm: the assumption that seduction, far from being an incontrovertible disaster for the female victim, could in fact be a highly ambigious boon insofar as the surrender of a false, socially legislated vulnerability could release untapped power from within the central female character.

The scene of seduction was therefore double-edged. Seduction, conventionally the representation of female weakness before rapacious male sexuality, could simultaneously be associated, through a subtext reinforced by the reading experience, with the exercise of female power. If seduction "served as both metaphor and metonymy in summing up the society's contradictory views of women,"[17] then those contradictory views, inevitably internalized by the middle-class female reader, found an expressive outlet in the paradoxical scene of fictional seduction, a male/female power interaction of fundamental ambiguity. The social ambiguities of the scene of seduction were probably heightened for nineteenth-century women writers because of their increased awareness of the fluid connections and strange parallels between the "real" and "fictional" rhetorics of their society—as in the overlapping of the "novel of seduction" and the moral-reform movement.[18]

In many ways, society and the socioliterary had established a certain equilibrium in the antebellum period. Society was effectively represented in a sentimental literature that, through its pervasive commercial appeal, came to influence the social structures that initially inspired it.[19] The line between fiction and reality was especially transitive as regards seduction; if the fictional seductions of the sentimental novel were primarily a metaphor for larger power inequalities in postrevolutionary society, then the moral-reform movement, for example, suggests the active reemergence or effective literalization of that fictional rhetoric into the discourse of antebellum society. Of course, the similarity between the goals of the moral reformers and the concerns of a spectrum of women novelists before and during the antebellum period is scarcely coincidental. They shared an interest not only in the social inequalities figured in the scene of seduction but also in the potential rearrangement of the power dynamic that seduction offered.

The moral-reform movement was most active in the period from 1830 to 1860 and primarily aimed to eliminate seduction from contemporary society. This aim required that the movement focus on a double target, as there were clearly two subjects in need of moral "reforming": the actual or potential female victim and the actual or potential male seducer. To that end, the movement advocated not only the abolition of prostitution, which was regarded, somewhat naively, as purely a consequence of seduction, but also the exposure of male seducers who were viewed as the root cause of myriad social ills.[20] The voice of the Female Moral Reform Society can be heard most clearly in its journal, *The Advocate of Moral Reform,* which by 1837 was publishing 20,000 copies semimonthly. That relatively large readership was neither disinterested nor passive, but a primarily female audience that responded enthusiastically to the journal's appeal for correspondence that would recount specific instances of seduction and name the male seducers involved. This strategy influenced the popular press of the day. For example, the *Hampshire Gazette* reports the case of a hysterical young woman found wandering the streets of Williamstown and notes that "the unfortunate heroine of the mysterious affair . . . is probably another of the thousand victims of seduction." The following week's issue follows up the story by observing that "the Pittsfield papers state that the betrayer of the artless girl is Edward Bulger. As no statute law can probably reach him, it is proper that the public press should herald his infamy, the whole length and breadth of the land."[21] In so doing, the Hampshire County press not only reproduced the cause of the moral-reform movement but also assumed the typical rhetorical flourishes of that movement's mouthpiece.[22]

By studying the causes and effects of prostitution in urban areas, the female moral reformers came to recognize the working-class prostitute as the embodiment of a double standard that pervaded all social classes. The prostitute thus served as a convenient symbol of a general subjugation of women, and prostitution, signifying both sexual victimization and female powerlessness, as a convenient representation of the antebellum female condition. The moral-reform movement's straightforward commitment to eliminating the sexual double standard (the assumption that men could be promiscuous while women had to remain chaste or face the direst of consequences) hid a larger unwritten agenda of equality for women. Even though seduction implies a degree of mutuality, notions of choice are complicated when power centrally defines the relationship between the participants (many of the sexual encounters that nineteenth-century reformers considered "seduction" would today be categorized as rape). Only through exposure could the male seducer be placed on the same level as his victim. That subtle emphasis on leveling and equality explains how so many suffragists began in the ranks of the moral-reform movement.

The rhetoric of moral reform was the verbal manifestation of a widespread, if latent, female anger at social powerlessness, and it directly addressed the existing power dynamic. For while the *narratives* of the movement represented women as passive victims of male lust, the *language* of moral reform evoked the possibility of women's power: a power to avenge seduction (by publishing the name of the male responsible); a power to control the consequences of seduction (by treating the victim as precisely that, with no stigma of blame); and a power to reform the basic cause of seduction itself (by creating a more equitable society that would circumvent the power hierarchies that facilitate its operation). Thus, while "seduction" came to function for the moral-reform movement as a complex metaphor representing the gender power inequities that supported antebellum society, the actual scene of seduction, activating as it did those inequities, could be transformed into an assertion of female power; the message of the moral-reform movement, and its own literal example, was that a powerful female voice could make itself heard, even from the depths of male-instituted corruption. It was the recognition that at the ultimate limit of female powerlessness lay a reservoir of energy that could be tapped and expressed as female power. Of course, the submission of the self to a superior force as a preliminary to vital self-assertion is an essentially Christian message. The moral-reform movement reproduced that message but rewrote it more politically as a morally secular aesthetic of assertion, combining the vocabulary of religious conversion and the scene of seduction in a potent fusion of powerful intent.

3

Of course, it would be erroneous to assert that Emily Dickinson was in any way directly influenced by the *cause* of moral reform. Indeed, it might be more plausible to make the case that her poetry was sometimes a reaction to contemporary reform movements for which she often expressed nothing but disdain. The fact that her father was the respected Amherst executive officer of the Hampshire County Temperance Union in the 1850s probably only exacerbated a more general cynicism obvious in the gleeful sarcasm of her personal correspondence:

> The Sewing Society has commenced again—and held its first meeting last week—now all the poor will be helped—the cold warmed—the warm cooled—the hungry fed—the thirsty attended to—the ragged clothed—and this suffering—tumbled down world will be helped to it's feet again—which will be quite pleasant to all. I dont attend—notwithstanding my high approbation—which must puzzle the public exceedingly. (30)

The same tone comes through more interestingly in her poetry, most memorably in **Poem 401:**

> What Soft—Cherubic Creatures—
> These Gentlewomen are—
> One would as soon assault a Plush—
> Or violate a Star—
>
> Such Dimity Convictions—
> A Horror so refined
> Of freckled Human Nature—
> Of Deity—ashamed—
>
> It's such a common—Glory—
> A Fisherman's—Degree—
> Redemption—Brittle Lady—
> Be so—ashamed of Thee—

Indeed, this poem's attack on the "Dimity Convictions" of the atypical woman reformer might well be targeted precisely at moral reformers and their particular concern with the "assault" and "violation" of young, innocent women. Part of the effectiveness of Dickinson's irony in this poem is her insinuation of the substantial distance between the reformers and the objects of their reforms. To put it bluntly, Dickinson seems to suggest that the women concerned need not worry that the circumstances affecting other members of their sex will directly affect them in any more vividly personal way; that they, in effect, scarcely merit the attention of any seducer.

Another poem that can be read as an oblique critique of moral reform is the often-discussed **Poem 315:**

> He fumbles at your Soul
> As Players at the Keys
> Before they drop full Music on—
> He stuns you by degrees—
> Prepares your brittle Nature
> For the Etherial Blow
> By fainter Hammers—further heard—
> Then nearer—Then so slow
> Your Breath has time to straighten—
> Your Brain—to bubble Cool—
> Deals—One—imperial—Thunderbolt—
> That scalps your naked Soul—
>
> When Winds take Forests in their Paws—
> The Universe—is still—

Critics have often pointed out that this representation of a particularly effective preacher of the latter-day hellfire school is couched in terms of physical violence and sexual violation.[23] This is the type of minister who attempts to ravish his congregation into heaven. One of the most effective contemporary critiques of the earlier male moral reformers was that they implicated themselves in the same sins that they condemned, wallowing in the very iniquity that they sought to correct. In this poem, the viciously violating power of the preacher's rhetoric may well be subverting the content of his address, ironically unraveling the power of its moral message.

The influence of the actual cause and agitations of the moral-reform movement on the poetry of Dickinson is therefore negligible. Any traces of possible influence are negative ones; the cause of moral reform provided simply another occasion for Dickinson's perpetual irony, the possibility of another studiously satirical exercise. Yet the hyperbolic rhetoric of the moral-reform movement was a pervasive part of the discourse of antebellum Amherst, a discourse within which Dickinson, for all her protested renunciation of society, was inescapably embedded.

To establish moral-reform rhetoric as part of the discourse of antebellum Amherst, I might begin by referring the reader back to the Fox seduction case of 1847. The editorial jeremiad excerpted from the *New York Tribune* is a classic example of the power and strategies of moral-reform rhetoric. What begins as a selected exposure of the conduct of an individual seducer builds to a broad attack on the hypocrisy of the entire male political establishment and its corrupt system. Of course, it might well be argued that the Fox case is primarily an example of New York moral-reform agitation and therefore, despite its appearance in a local newspaper, of limited applicability to Amherst. But that particular example is only one among many. The "seducer," a stock figure of the larger antebellum cultural imagination, was often conveniently localized in the Hampshire County press. A particularly popular narrative, periodically visited by the Amherst press, concerned the temptation of some "guileless girl" by a more experienced male concealing villainous intent. During the 1840s and 1850s, this seduction narrative was strikingly popular and always newsworthy. Tales of elopements and the designing and deserting villains responsible for them were part of the fabric of such local newspapers as the *Springfield Republican,* the *Hampshire and Franklin Express,* and the *Hampshire Gazette.*[24]

For example, in September 1845 an itinerant shoe salesman named Ransom Guillow, who had previously eloped with a young resident of Amherst (a "guileless girl"), was ambushed by a mob of angry townspeople. They tarred him, rode him on a rail, and made him promise never to show his face in town again. The *Gazette* reported, "[T]he whole transaction is causing considerable excitement in Amherst."[25] Guillow, in effect, lost his individuality, subsumed beneath the convenient cloak of an antebellum archetype: the figure of "the seducer" was literalized momentarily by the unfortunate inter(e)loper. Small wonder the residents of Amherst were excited. Over the next four months, the subscriber to the *Gazette* could read of the substantial damages awarded a plaintiff whose daughter was the victim of an "aggravated case of seduction," or of the conviction at Dedham of one John Cook for "abducting an unmarried woman with purposes of seduction."[26] In the years that followed, that same reader would learn the precise nature of the damages awarded; if, in May 1849, one Lawrence Boxer recovered $1000 from Phillip W. Ingalls for "seducing" his daughter, and then, by November of that year, Daniel S. Dickerman went to New Bedford court to recover $2800 in damages from Samuel W. Graves for the "seducing and debauching" of his wife, an inflationary spiral of sorts seemed to be pushing up the price of practicing seduction.[27] While the costs of his action to the convicted seducer could usually be measured in financial terms, the costs to the seducee tended to inscribe themselves on her body more directly. A typical portrayal of the seducee's sad fate appears in an 1849 article entitled "The Prostitute's End—Crime and Remorse," a bleak narrative that begins: "Two young and beautiful women whose beauty had made them a mark for the seducer, were suddenly stricken with death yesterday afternoon. An elder sister decoy'd them from their home and made them prostitutes." Interestingly, the actual cause of the deaths in this case is never specified.[28] Presumably, it did not have to be; the expected premature end of the seducer's "mark" could be left to the reader's imagination.

My own favorite example of this particular newspaper genre is from the *Hampshire Gazette* of 7 April 1846:

> About a year since, a young man named Warren D. Tobey, came to Northfield with high recommendations from the Seminary at Wilbraham as a Methodist preacher, and was stationed at the Methodist Church in Northfield. He became attached to a worthy young lady of that church, by the name of Stratton, and their affection for each other soon apparently ripened into love. Under protestations of the most ardent affection for her, and with assurances that they were already married in the sight of heaven, the confiding girl yielded to the wiles of the seducer. Having accomplished his iniquitous purposes, he left Northfield.

What is so striking about this particular tale of seduction is the extent to which it mirrors many of the narratives imposed upon the life of Dickinson by her later critical readers.[29] I have come to think this hardly coincidental.

Dickinson was still a teenager in the mid 1840s, and it might plausibly be argued that she was too young to be directly affected by such tales of seduction. However, as Dickinson matured there was virtually no way for her to escape the local newspaper fixation on the contemporary seduction of naive young women. For example, even some twenty-five years later Amherst exhibited "considerable excitement" about a case that, in many of its details, paralleled the Guillow affair. Indeed, the affair of 1871 very nearly had the same conclusion with, at one juncture, an irate uncle threatening to raise a mob of 250 students to tar and feather the villain who intended to marry his niece without the consent of her family. Amherst's excitement exploded in gossip that ran through all social strata. In a February 1871 letter to his wife about what had come to be known as the "Count Mitiewicz/Miss Lester affair," J. Leander Skinner noted that "Amherst was never so much excited, from the President to the sots, nothing else has been talked of or thought of for several days."[30]

The general interest in the case noted by Skinner is borne out by the considerable coverage and commentary received in the local press. The *Amherst Record* of 9 February 1871 characterized the incident as a "first class sensation," observing, "We do not remember ever seeing so many of our citizens so excited by any local occurrence as during the past week." The *Hampshire Gazette,* under the caption heading "Great Excitement over a Love Romance," also observed that Amherst had been "very much excited for ten days past." Meanwhile, the *Springfield Republican* reported in detail on "facts exciting enough to set romantic hearts palpitating and excite the distrust and anxiety, if not the indignation, of all sober minded and respectable people."[31] "Excitement" was clearly the adjective of choice, just as in 1845.

The facts in the case seem relatively straightforward. Carrie Lester, the niece of a Professor Tyler of Amherst College, had fallen in love with Eugene Mitiewicz. The latter claimed to be a Russian count, although his lineage was apparently closer to the Polish peasantry than the Russian nobility. What Mitiewicz could claim to be with some justification was an adept confidence man. There was already substantial evidence that he had financially cheated a number of gullible individuals (often women whose affections he cultivated) in other locales, and that he had spent time in prison, both in America and England, as a result. The fact that the art of the confidence man worked so well in Amherst exasperated the *Amherst Record,* which observed that the "utter lack of decorum and good manners" displayed by Mitiewicz "in all his performances here shows not only that some people like to be gulled, but also that some people do not know when they are gulled."

The behavior of Carrie Lester provoked similar exasperation. The *Hampshire Gazette* confined its comments to the observation that "the love of the young lady is simply a case of infatuation, for she knows all the previous facts about his previous love and criminal life, and yet seems to love him more than he does her, and will insist on throwing herself away upon him," and the *Amherst Record* judged simply that she was "under a sort of infatuation which she seemed as powerless to resist as a bird under the charms of a basilisk." The *Springfield Republican,* however, used her infatuation as the basis for a more general comment on the vagaries of the female sex: "It is distressingly discouraging to those who want to believe in the right and capacity of woman to take care of herself, when an intelligent and well bred American girl gives herself so unreservedly, and against the advice of all her best friends, to a man so unworthy."[32] The newspapers did reach consensus on one matter: as the *Hampshire Gazette* remarked, while marriage "would be the proper and regular termination of the affair in a novel . . . facts are sometimes dreadfully unromantic." That disparity between fact and fiction led the local press to hope earnestly that "the dreadful calamity—which to any well ordered family would be darker than death—may in some way be averted."[33] But despite the general disapproval of the print media, the marriage eventually did take place in Amherst in May 1872. The church was filled to capacity in only ten minutes, which, since none of the bride's family were present, further reflects the continued excitement in Amherst about the affair, an excitement sustained for more than a year.

The contemporary fascination with the affair seems primarily focused on the character of "the count," an individual generally recognized as "a man of decidedly doubtful character."[34] The precise nature of that fascination is evident in a narration borrowed by the *Amherst Record* from a New York newspaper. It describes the count's typical technique as practiced in his previous charming of another young woman, which also permitted him to appropriate her diamond ring (he later pawned it): "[A]rtistically twirling the ring in the sunbeams, with an apologetic air, the nobleman placed it on his little finger. . . . He was good looking. He was fashionably dressed. He was fascinating. He was deferentially affectionate."[35] While this media portrait casts the "count" as the "confidence man" so fascinating to the American public of the time, it also recalls the earlier antebellum seducer, a prior version of the charming individual who led young women astray in order to appropriate their most valuable possession—be it their diamond ring or their virginity. The fact that traits of an earlier seducer persona cluster around the figure of the "count" suggests their continuing appeal to a later audience.

Between 1845 and 1871 there does appear to have been a declining interest in the seducer as an individual phenomenon. The local newspapers, for example, reported considerably fewer tales of seduction after the Civil War. But perhaps that apparent decline is partially explicable by taking into account how the art of seduction was subtly recontextualized: the seducer took on a different form, the form of the confidence man as exemplified in the person and techniques of the "count," who was simply a stylistic variation on the earlier seducer. At the same time, the media treatment of Carrie Lester would suggest that society recognized that the woman of the 1870s wielded more power over her choices, whether those choices were ultimately for good or ill. This would imply a subtly different attitude toward the probable seducee, too: she was held more accountable for her actions than was her antebellum predecessor. Therefore, the most important evidence provided by the Mitiewitcz/Lester case is that the basic "seduction" formula, structurally updated and adapted, had not only survived but maintained its appeal: the fine art of "seduction" still had the same capacity to generate "considerable excitement" in Amherst that it had a generation before.

Less plausible is the argument that the newspaper treatment of the Mitiewicz/Lester case shows how seduction, reported as a matter of life and death in the 1840s and 1850s, had become more a passing amusement, a media circus, in the 1870s and 1880s. Evidence that public concern and outrage had not dissipated into public entertainment is provided by the *Springfield Republican*. One month after the newspaper reported the dénouement of the Mitiewicz/Lester affair, it (deliberately?) offered a bizarre alternative coda to the scene of seduction. In June 1872, the *Republican*, under the capitalized caption heading "SAD AFFAIR AT AMHERST," noted:

> A young woman at Amherst, of good family and of gay, vivacious and impulsive disposition, fell a victim some while since to the wiles of a seducer. A few weeks ago she gave birth to a child, and the feeling that she had brought disgrace upon her family preyed upon her to such an extent that she lapsed into periods of deep melancholy. . . . [S]he managed in some way to get possession of a small quantity of strychnine, and swallowing it was soon a corpse.

Significantly, this young woman of Amherst fell prey to the same "wiles of the seducer" that were the downfall of Miss Stratton some twenty-five years before. What this series of newsworthy stories reveals is another narrative of exceptional relevance to the antebellum period, one that clearly lingered after the Civil War. That narrative concerns the activities of the seducer, a figure who stalked the young women of Amherst for those twenty-five years in a variety of guises. Less a reality than an effect of the cultural imagination, catered to by the salacious tendency of the local media, the character of the seducer was realized by, or perhaps draped upon the shoulders of, such (un)worthy locals as Guillow and Mitiewicz. In reality, however, such a role could perhaps only be played to clinical perfection by that unnamed seducer whose successful seduction took the equally anonymous young woman's life.

It should by now be evident that many of the surprisingly sensational narrative scenes that critical analysts can plausibly extract from Dickinson's poetry—the seductions, the elopements, the corruptions of young women, the suicides that follow abandonment—were not necessarily gleaned by her from reading available literary texts but were actualized in her own local newspaper sources. Of course, whether Dickinson actually did or did not read, or even have access to, the *Hampshire Gazette* and *Springfield Republican* on certain days is not critical. Given the fact that Amherst was small enough for gossip to spread like wildfire and that Dickinson showed no disinclination toward sharing gossip with her closest female confidantes (indeed, much of her correspondence with Mrs. Holland assumes a mutual and thorough knowledge of that particular week's *Springfield Republican*), she herself may well have been familiar with the content of the news stories from other sources. What clearly is important is that there was considerable local public interest in the figure of the seducer as a regional phenomenon. Dickinson would not have needed to hear of specific seductions for the scene of seduction to form an integral part of her psyche when, through the popular cultural imagination of Amherst, for a period of some twenty-five years, strolled the wily figure of the seducer of guileless young women, a very plausible bogeyman for the adolescent female, or a suitably nightmarish familiar.

That familiar seducer is a fixture of Dickinson's poetry. **Poem 1053** offers a paradigmatic demonstration of his technique:

> It was a quiet way—
> He asked if I was his—
> I made no answer of the Tongue
> But answer of the Eyes—
> And then He bore me on
> Before this mortal noise
> With swiftness, as of Chariots
> And distance, as of Wheels.
> This World did drop away
> As Acres from the feet
> Of one that leaneth from Balloon
> Upon an Ether street.
> The Gulf behind was not,
> The Continents were new—
> Eternity it was before
> Eternity was due.
> No Seasons were to us—
> It was not Night nor Morn—
> But Sunrise stopped upon the place
> And fastened it in Dawn.

This poem, like so many of Dickinson's that feature an unspecified male figure, has a potentially significant double reference. That vague pronoun "He" clearly refers to some male force that could completely efface the world as it was previously known to the speaker. The pronoun could therefore quite plausibly signify yet another of Dickinson's personifications of Death as cosmic travel courier. Similarly, "He" might be the

God who requires a Christian, especially as one of the Calvinist elect, to turn away from mundane earthly concerns. However, the poem resonates with the possibility of a secular equivalent, an earthly transformation of a woman speaker by a male figure that is of sufficient magnitude to ensure that "Eternity it was before / Eternity was due." This figure takes her not "Be*yond* this mortal noise" but "Be*fore* this mortal noise," a significant difference. Establishing the seductive aspect of the deathlike masculine figure who strikes the speaker dumb when "asked if [she] was his" is therefore of particular importance. It is worth recalling that the antebellum woman who succumbed to the wiles of the seducer would, in a real sense, have comprehensively destroyed her world. That destruction went considerably beyond social ostracizement and isolation: the succumbing to the seducer, at least in its fictional representation, was inevitably considered a prefiguring of the seducee's death. Therefore, it was not only God whom none could see and live; for an antebellum woman, the same was often true of the seducer.

Similarly, Dickinson's personification of the frost in **Poem 391** develops a further resonance that hardly needs explication:

> A Visitor in Marl—
> Who influences Flowers—
> Till they are orderly as Busts—
> And Elegant—as Glass—
>
> Who visits in the Night—
> And just before the Sun—
> Concludes his glistening interview—
> Caresses—and is gone—
>
> But whom his fingers touched—
> And where his feet have run—
> And whatsoever Mouth he kissed—
> Is as it had not been—

The fact that Dickinson tended to represent not just frost but also God, Christ, and Death as seductive male figures who demand of her narrators the willing surrender of their entire being is not likely to be coincidental. Indeed, that fact might remind us of the extent to which the social ramifications of seduction were presumably more significant determinants of the Dickinson psyche than was her fearful approach toward the symbolization of a Jungian animus. The unspecified "He" whom the reader of Dickinson's poetry can variously find fumbling at the victim's soul before scalping her **(315)**, snapping the belt around her life preliminary to folding her up **(273)**, finding, setting up, and adjusting her being **(603)**, touching her in particularly memorable ways **(506)**, and in general, living a life of ambush in anticipation of her passing **(1525)** is, I would suggest, somewhat more than an all-purpose, protean "Burglar! Banker—Father!" male figure **(49)**. While *sometimes* "He" may be identifiable as God or Death or Lover or Father, what can *always* be said with some certainty is that his typical actions and strategies are those of a first-rate seducer.

4

I would argue that seduction rhetoric influenced Dickinson's poetics by making available to her certain rhetorical structures. The pervasiveness of such rhetorical structures helped create an antebellum milieu in which seduction was a prevalent thematic center, not simply as a narrative subject but also as a linguistic, rhetorical category. For ninteenth-century women, the act of seduction, whether fictional or real, came to be a metaphoric and metonymic representation of their subject position in society—a "structure of feeling," in Raymond Williams's felicitous phrase.[36] For any woman writer who began writing in the 1850s (as Dickinson almost certainly did), this cultural rhetorical code was available; for a writer with the courage to adopt a more liminal position within that culture, it was adaptable. Moreover, essentially reflective of the power dynamic operative in antebellum society, it was particularly attractive, as a *rewritable* discursive formation, to the woman writer who sought to rechannel linguistic power.

Cheryl Walker has shown how many Dickinson poems are subtle rewritings of the paradigmatic structures that inform an antebellum women's poetics. She identifies three thematic stances for the woman poet: "identifications with power, identifications with powerlessness, and reconciling poems that attempt to establish a ground for power in the midst of powerlessness itself."[37] Dickinson, an avid reader of sentimental fiction, a skeptic only too aware of the masks worn by the orthodox, and a radically unorthodox Christian herself, was perfectly situated at the juncture of many of the major cultural manifestations of seduction rhetoric. Given her liminal positioning, she could restructure that rhetoric, particularly within the grounds of the "reconciling poem" concerned with establishing power at the heart of powerlessness. Thus, while Dickinson's contemporaries, the literary domestics, were continually re-adapting the seduction theme as a cultural given, part of an inherited discourse, essentially treating it as a textual element that could be integrated into their fictional content,[38] Dickinson absorbed it into her poetics, the code at once becoming part of the form and inhering in the very structure of her poetry. Rewritten, the code became a new rhetoric, a new poetics of power.

Dickinson's new poetics of power often begins with the creation of narrative scenarios of seduction. Of course, if the scenario Dickinson's female speaker establishes within the poem is a scene of seduction, then she herself has assumed the parallel role of antebellum seducee. But as we have seen, the *role* of antebellum seducee was not without its possibilities when deliberately and consciously assumed. In the antebellum period, the scene of seduction had become for women the convenient representation of the existing gender hierarchy and the act of seduction the effective symbol of their own relative powerlessness. However, the fictional or rhetorical rendering of a scene of seduction by a woman writer offered the potential both to address and to directly expose that hierarchy. The recreation of that power structure in writing—which amounted to the fictional representation of a relationship that already represented a larger social structure—could be the means of access to a power grid that potentially could be rerouted. When the female speaker of a Dickinson poem appears to set up and validate a traditional male/female hierarchy within the scene of seduction, she is simultaneously engaged in a subtle questioning and sometimes an inversion of the very same power coordinates that support that hierarchy. Indeed, this subversive process occurs frequently enough to suggest that the examination and dismantling of the power dynamic between the speaker and her male addressee is the primary theme of the poems.

The typical strategy of seduction in such a poem is figured in the apparently submissive female speaker's address to a significantly more powerful male reader/addressee. In the course of that address, however, it is precisely the relative power of the two subjects that is increasingly called into question. Frequently within Dickinson's poems, the establishment of a scene of seduction between a powerful male and a powerless female is the preliminary to its inversion; the would-be seducer becomes the seduced and the great Caesar is himself the greatly seized.[39] In effecting that seizure, both of the male addressee and of the reader who momentarily occupies the addressee's position, Dickinson italicizes an existing rhetoric of seduction in order to venture an ironic commentary on male power and on the gender hierarchies instituted by the society within which her poetics took shape.[40] Her poetry therefore often provides a consummate demonstration of how the powerful male can have both his role and his power usurped by the submissive female, or more precisely, of how the seducer can so easily be seduced through rhetoric by the intended object of his seduction. I would argue that this dynamic has also had significant ramifications for the critical dialectic, for the ways in which Dickinson has been interpreted. Contemporary scholars have frequent recourse to "seduction" as a critical trope of varying application: John Cody sees Dickinson as "repeatedly seducing" Higginson "into submitting his self-important and inept literary advice"; Suzanne Juhasz argues that Dickinson's letters practice a "seduction carried out by flattery, so that the compliment serves as the essential rhetorical act"; Karl Keller views Dickinson both as a "crude seductress" *and* as a "daring virgin inviting seduction, foreplay and penetration"; and William Shurr reinstates "the theory that Dickinson was seduced and abandoned, and that such an event had something to do with her poetry."[41] In so doing, these critics have perhaps identified the antebellum dialectic implicit in Dickinson's rhetorical approach to readers, but they have also foregrounded the evidence of their own ahistorical seduction.

Notes

[1] Recent studies that are guilty of varying degrees of historical determinism but that also make invaluable contributions to Dickinson scholarship include Joanne Dobson's *Dickinson and the Strategies of Reticence: The Woman Writer in Nineteenth-Century America* (Bloomington: Indiana Univ. Press, 1989); Barton Levi St. Armand's *Emily Dickinson and Her Culture: The Soul's Society* (Cambridge: Cambridge Univ. Press, 1984); and David S. Reynolds's *Beneath the American Renaissance: The Subversive Imagination in the Age of Emerson and Melville* (Cambridge: Harvard Univ. Press, 1988).

[2] Joanne Dobson, "'Oh, Susie, it is dangerous': Emily Dickinson and the Archetype of the Masculine," in *Feminist Critics Read Emily Dickinson,* ed. Suzanne Juhasz (Bloomington: Indiana Univ. Press, 1983), 80.

[3] Clark Griffith, *The Long Shadow: Emily Dickinson's Tragic Poetry* (Princeton: Princeton Univ. Press, 1964), 166.

[4] See Poems 520 and 476 in *The Poems of Emily Dickinson,* ed. Thomas H. Johnson, 3 vols. (Cambridge: Harvard Univ. Press, Belknap Press, 1955); hereafter cited by poem number only. Dickinson's letters are cited according to the numbering in *The Letters of Emily Dickinson,* ed. Thomas H. Johnson and Theodora Ward, 3 vols. (Cambridge: Harvard Univ. Press, Belknap Press, 1958).

[5] Griffith, *Long Shadow,* 171, 164.

[6] Adrienne Rich makes the case that the male figure is Dickinson's figuration of her poetic imagination ("Vesuvius at Home: The Power of Emily Dickinson," *Parnassus* 5 [Fall-Winter 1976]: 49-74); Joanne Feit Diehl uses the "influence" theory of Harold Bloom to reinterpret the figure as a composite precursor-muse (*Dickinson and the Romantic Imagination* [Princeton: Princeton Univ. Press, 1981], 13-33); and Albert Gelpi develops the idea that the figure is a Jungian animus ("Emily Dickinson and the Deerslayer: The Dilemma of the Woman Poet in America," in *Shakespeare's*

Sisters: Feminist Essays on Women Poets, ed. Sandra M. Gilbert and Susan Gubar [Bloomington: Indiana Univ. Press, 1979], 122-34).

[7] Dobson, "Archetype of the Masculine," 90 (emphasis added).

[8] The *Hampshire and Franklin Express* article contains an interesting copy-reading error. Its introductory summation of the case states that the seducer's name is Michael Kane, even though the editorial quoted from the *New York Tribune* twice asserts that the seducer's name is Hare (the *Tribune* is unsure of the first name, using both Michael and Martin, but certainly not the surname). The altered surname unfortunately destroys the allegorical, animal fable symmetry of the Fox/Hare case. The *Express*'s confusion of two similar Irish surnames is probably an example of the paper's more general tendency toward negative stereotyping of the new and growing Irish community. However, I also like to think that the biblical resonance of the surname, and its connotation of sinner, may have had something to do with the slip.

[9] For a discussion of transgression in Victorian novels by women, see Sandra M. Gilbert and Susan Gubar, *The Madwoman in the Attic: The Woman Writer and the Nineteenth-Century Literary Imagination* (New Haven: Yale Univ. Press, 1979). On the issue of women readers' responses to the Miltonic tradition, see Gilbert's "Patriarchal Poetry and Women Readers: Reflections on Milton's Bogey," *PMLA* 93 (1978): 368-82.

[10] This is Shoshana Felman's characterization of seduction (*The Literary Speech Act: Don Juan with J. L. Austin, or Seduction in Two Languages* [Ithaca: Cornell Univ. Press, 1983], 28).

[11] Jack Lee Capps, *Emily Dickinson's Reading, 1836-1886* (Cambridge: Harvard Univ. Press, 1966), 71.

[12] One of the most significant recurrences is surely Dickinson's hermetic assertion that "[i]n all the circumference of Expression, those guileless words of Adam and Eve never were surpassed, 'I was afraid and hid myself'" (Letter 946).

[13] Margaret Homans, *Women Writers and Poetic Identity: Dorothy Wordsworth, Emily Brontë, and Emily Dickinson* (Princeton: Princeton Univ. Press, 1980), 171.

[14] Cathy N. Davidson, *Resolution and the Word: The Rise of the Novel in America* (New York: Oxford Univ. Press, 1986), 91.

[15] Davidson, *Revolution and the Word,* 106.

[16] Reynolds, *Beneath the American Renaissance,* 363.

[17] Davidson, *Revolution and the Word,* 110.

[18] Two critics particularly interested in Dickinson's relation to her culture have somewhat surprisingly chosen not to analyze the potential influence of reform movements on her rhetorical strategies. St. Armand correctly asserts that "only by charting Dickinson's debt to her own time can we truly be sure how she may have anticipated current aesthetic and philosophical concerns," and he examines the ways she "italicized" aspects of the contemporary dogmas and cults of Calvinism, transcendentalism, Gothicism, occultism, and Ruskinism through "a process of personalization, internalization, exaggeration, and inversion" (*Dickinson and Her Culture,* 11, 73). However, St. Armand does not pursue that process of Dickinsonian *bricolage* to consider her use of the vocabulary provided by contemporary reform movements. On the other hand, while Reynolds states that "moral reform literature offered a wealth of imagery and themes" and assumes that there was a Bakhtinian "stylization" of reform devices by antebellum writers who took the reform impulse and reform imagery as rhetorical materials for their own art, and while he elsewhere discusses contemporary female influences on the poetry of Dickinson, he does not connect the two by discussing the possible influence of female moral-reform rhetoric on Dickinson (*Beneath the American Renaissance,* 54-56, esp. 55).

[19] The transitive line between fiction and reality in the antebellum period is brilliantly explored by Karen Haltunnen in *Confidence Men and Painted Women: A Study of Middle-Class Culture in America, 1830-70* (New Haven and London: Yale Univ. Press, 1982).

[20] My interpretation of the significance of the moral-reform movement is heavily indebted to the argument of Carroll Smith-Rosenberg's study "Beauty, the Beast, and the Militant Woman: A Case Study in Sex Roles and Social Stress in Jacksonian America," in *Disorderly Conduct: Visions of Gender in Victorian America* (New York: Albert A. Knopf, 1985), 109-28; first published in *American Quarterly* 23 (1971): 562-84. My own argument is particularly indebted to her suggestion that "some nineteenth-century women channeled their frustration with women's restricted roles combined with a sense of superior righteousness legitimized by the Cult of True Womanhood into the reform movements of the first half of the nineteenth century; and in the controversial moral-reform crusade such motivations seem particularly apparent" (109). See also Barbara J. Berg, *The Remembered Gate: Origins of American Feminism—The Woman and the City, 1800-1860* (New York: Oxford Univ. Press, 1978).

[21] *Hampshire Gazette,* 26 December 1848; 2 January 1849.

[22] See also the *Hampshire and Franklin Express* of 8 September 1848, which concludes yet another tale of seduction with this pointed rejoinder: "When we last heard of the scoundrel he was living in Boston, Mass., where he may have the pleasure of reading this story for his villainy. And if he feels any uncertainty at his own identity, let him go to the town of Orono, Maine, or to the recorder of the United States Court, and enquire for the name of Mr Woods, who figured conspicuously some ten or twelve years ago, as a thief, mail robber, convict, seducer and ingrate." Such public exposure was clearly not exceptional.

[23] At the same time, of course, it is one of Dickinson's most effective representations of a seducer in action. In that context, see the recent workshop discussion of this poem as power play between Robin Riley Fast, Suzanne Juhasz, and Ellin Ringler-Henderson in *Emily Dickinson: A Celebration for Readers,* ed. Suzanne Juhasz and Cristanne Miller (New York: Gordon and Breach, 1989), 53-84.

[24] The Dickinson family directly subscribed to the *Springfield Republican* and the *Hampshire and Franklin Express* (later to become the *Amherst Record*). Other newspapers, such as the *Hampshire Gazette,* would have been available locally, and there is evidence that Dickinson had access to the *Gazette* in particular. For example, the poem "The Life Clock," a probable model for her own "A Clock stopped" (287), first appeared in that newspaper.

[25] See *Hampshire Gazette,* 9 September 1845.

[26] *Hampshire Gazette,* 25 November 1845; 6 January 1846.

[27] *Hampshire Gazette,* 1 May and 27 November 1849.

[28] See *Hampshire Gazette,* 28 August 1849.

[29] I am referring, of course, to those Dickinson readers who have assumed the possibility of a seduction of sorts by the Reverend Charles Wadsworth. This scenario was revisited in the 1980s by William H. Shurr in *The Marriage of Emily Dickinson: A Study of the Fascicles* (Lexington: Univ. Press of Kentucky, 1983).

[30] Qtd. in Jay Leyda, *The Years and Hours of Emily Dickinson* (New Haven: Yale Univ. Press, 1960), 2:168.

[31] *Amherst Record,* 9 February 1871; *Hampshire Gazette,* 14 February 1871; *Springfield Republican,* 8 February 1871.

[32] *Hampshire Gazette,* 30 April 1872; *Amherst Record,* 9 February 1871; *Springfield Republican,* 7 February 1871.

[33] *Hampshire Gazette,* 30 April 1872; *Amherst Record,* 9 February 1871.

[34] *Springfield Republican,* 8 February 1871.

[35] *Amherst Record,* 9 February 1871.

[36] See, for example, Raymond Williams, *The Long Revolution* (Harmondsworth: Penguin, 1965), 65.

[37] Cheryl Walker, *The Nightingale's Burden: Women Poets and American Culture before 1900* (Bloomington: Indiana Univ. Press, 1982), 38.

[38] For a discussion of the "double bind" that the so-called "literary domestics" had to confront, see Mary Kelley, *Private Woman, Public Stage: Literary Domesticity in Nineteenth-Century America* (New York: Oxford Univ. Press, 1984).

[39] For examples of this hierarchy-inverting process, see Cristanne Miller, "How 'Low Feet' Stagger: Disruptions of Language in Dickinson's Poetry"; and Margaret Homans, "'Oh, Vision of Language!': Dickinson's Poems of Love and Death," in *Feminist Critics Read Emily Dickinson,* 134-55 and 114-33.

[40] Fredric Jameson's suggestion that a literary text is also an intrinsically symbolic act, that the text presents a symbolic resolution to a problematic contradiction within the particular society in which it is written, might be particularly useful for explicating a more "political" mediation between Dickinson's poetic text and the "text" of antebellum culture. See *The Political Unconscious: Narrative as a Socially Symbolic Act* (Ithaca, NY: Cornell Univ. Press, 1981), 80-83. While Dickinson's poetry does not symbolically resolve a contradiction in the larger patriarchal society, it attempts instead to resolve a contradiction at the level of the early and inadequate prefeminist response to the problem of women's role in antebellum society, a response prefigured in a rhetorical trope of seduction.

[41] John Cody, *After Great Pain: The Inner Life of Emily Dickinson* (Cambridge: Harvard Univ. Press, Belknap Press, 1971), 433; Suzanne Juhasz, "Reading Emily Dickinson's Letters," *ESQ: A Journal of the American Renaissance* 30 (1984): 171; Karl Keller, *The Only Kangaroo among the Beauty: Emily Dickinson and America* (Baltimore and London: Johns Hopkins Univ. Press, 1979), 25-26; Shurr, *Marriage of Emily Dickinson,* 189.

FURTHER READING

Barker, Wendy. *Lunacy of Light: Emily Dickinson and the Experience of Metaphor.* Ad Feminam: Women and Literature, edited by Sandra M. Gilbert. Carbondale: Southern Illinois University Press, 1987, 214 p.

Provides a feminist analysis of the light and dark imagery in Dickinson's poems.

Bennett, Paula. "Beyond the Dip of Bell." In her *Emily Dickinson: Woman Poet.* Key Women Writers, series edited by Sue Roe, pp. 24-50. New York: Harvester Wheatsheaf, 1990.

Studies Dickinson's apparent desire to exceed the conventional limits of poetry and language.

Bloom, Harold, ed. *Emily Dickinson.* Modern Critical Views. New York: Chelsea House Publishers, 1985, 204 p.

Provides a collection of previously published essays on Dickinson. The essays focus on such issues as Dickinson's cultural and literary influences, and her poetic style, themes, and techniques.

Bray, Paul. "Emily Dickinson as Visionary." *Raritan* 12, No. 1 (Summer 1992): 113-37.

Maintains that Dickinson experienced an "abnormally heightened mental or spiritual" awareness and examines the way she used her poetry to control this excess.

Cody, John. "A Plank In Reason." In *Critical Essays on Emily Dickinson*, edited by Paul J. Ferlazzo, pp. 147-67. Boston: G. K. Hall & Co., 1984. Reprinted from *After Great Pain: The Inner Life of Emily Dickinson*, Cambridge, Mass.: The Belknap Press, 1971, pp. 291-315.

Offers a psychoanalytic approach to Dickinson's life and works.

Dobson, Joanne. *Dickinson and the Strategies of Reticence: The Woman Writer in Nineteenth-Century America.* Bloomington: Indiana University Press, 1989, 160 p.

Analyzes Dickinson's verse within the context of nineteenth-century American women's literature, observing that during this time period women writers were consumed by frustration with the cultural proscription against addressing their personal experiences, especially in the areas of "sexuality, ambition, and anger. . . ."

Juhasz, Suzanne. "Writing Doubly: Emily Dickinson and Female Experience." *Legacy* 3, No. 1 (Spring 1986): 5-15.

Examines the "doubleness" present in Dickinson's poetry, identifying this as an indication "of the ontological situation of women in patriarchal culture."

Kirkby, Joan. *Women Writers: Emily Dickinson.* New York: Saint Martin's Press, 1991, 163 p.

Offers a book-length study of Dickinson's life and work, focusing on gender issues, the Gothic influence in Dickinson's poetry, and the poems dealing with nature.

Knapp, Bettina L. *Emily Dickinson.* New York: Continuum, 1989, 204 p.

Examines Dickinson's life and poetry, maintaining that Dickinson produced "a poetry for all time," not to be understood simply within the context of the poet's immediate background.

Loeffelholz, Mary. "Violence and the Other(s) of Identity." In her *Dickinson and the Boundaries of Feminist Theory*, pp. 81-115. Urbana: University of Illinois Press, 1991.

Studies the conflict between the feminist and psychoanalytic approaches to Dickinson's poetry.

Leder, Sharon, with Andrea Abbott. *The Language of Exclusion: The Poetry of Emily Dickinson and Christina Rossetti.* New York: Greenwood Press, 1987, 238 p.

Compares Dickinson's and Rossetti's poetry, focusing on gender issues, particularly the exclusion of women from full participation in nineteenth-century society.

Small, Judy Jo. "Experiments in Sound," in her *Positive as Sound: Emily Dickinson's Rhyme*, pp. 117-39. Athens, Ga.: University of Georgia Press, 1990.

Analyzes the acoustical effects of Dickinson's rhyme structure.

Ward, R. Bruce. "Center." In his *The Gift of Screws: The Poetic Strategies of Emily Dickinson*, pp. 74-108. Troy, N.Y.: The Whitston Publishing Company, 1994.

Argues that Dickinson's "creative center" is revealed in her poetry and may be studied without psychological speculation.

Additional coverage of Dickinson's life and career is contained in the following sources published by The Gale Group: *Dictionary of Literary Biography*, Vol. 1, and *Poetry Criticism*, Vol. 1.

Jakob Ludwig Karl Grimm

1785-1863

Wilhelm Karl Grimm

1786-1859

German philologists and collectors of folktales. The following entry presents criticism of their *Kinder- und Hausmärchen, Gesammelt Odurch die Brüder Grimm* (1812-15; *Children's and Household Fairy Tales, Collected by the Brothers Grimm*; generally known as *Grimm's Fairy Tales*). For a discussion of the complete careers of the Grimm brothers, see *NCLC*, Volume 3.

INTRODUCTION

The fairy tales of brothers Jakob and Wilhelm Grimm are among the most widely read and beloved works of literature in the world. The result of the Grimms' extensive studies in German folklore and philology, their *Kinder- und Hausmärchen* has gone through numerous German editions, including seven that were extensively revised or edited by the Grimms themselves, and has been translated into several foreign languages—a testament to the tales' longevity and universal appeal. Although the violence of some stories and the German nationalism of the Grimm brothers has given some readers pause, *Kinder- und Hausmärchen* has endured both early critical indifference and modern skepticism to become part of the Western collective consciousness.

Biographical Information

Scholarly partners all their lives, Jakob and Wilhelm Grimm shared an interest in Germanic languages and literature and particularly in the preservation of their native culture. Both brothers studied at the Cassel lyceum beginning in the late 1790s, and a few years thereafter began collecting from friends and acquaintances the stories that would make up *Kinder- und Hausmärchen*. The Grimms then moved on to Marburg University to study law, although both were distracted from their studies by their interest in medieval German literature. The brothers studied closely with Roman law scholar Friedrich Karl von Savigny, from whom they learned the value of the historic method for their literary studies. It was as a guest in Savigny's home that Jakob became interested in a collection of the songs of German minnesingers; Jakob later reflected that this discovery would significantly influence the direction of his scholarly career. Although Wilhelm remained in Cassel to finish his law degree, Jakob left with Savigny in 1805 to conduct research in Paris, then returned to work in the War Office, and in 1808, after the French occupation of German territory, in the library of the newly established king of Westphalia, Napoleon's brother Jerome Bonaparte. The humiliation of the French occupation gave the Grimms further impetus to collect stories of the German nation, and Jakob's position in the library offered him the opportunity and resources to do so. According to many critics, the Grimms hoped that the publication of the German tales would prove to be a unifying force among the German people and ignite in them feelings of national autonomy. Both Jakob and Wilhelm contributed materials to Achim von Arnim and Clemens Brentano's journal *Zeitung für Einsiedler*; other materials collected at this time eventually became part of *Kinder- und Hausmärchen*, the first volume of which was published in 1812. The brothers continued working together, publishing additional works on German folklore and philology and the folktales of other nations, but as early as 1815 they began taking separate scholarly directions. Following the withdrawal of the French from German territory in 1813, Jakob was named legation secretary for Hessian diplomats in France, and Wilhelm took a position as assistant librarian in the electoral library back at Cassel. Although the second volume of *Kinder- und Hausmärchen* (1815) was attributed to both brothers, Wilhelm was the primary editor of that volume and most later editions; in fact, many scholars have found that, as evidenced in the many successive editions of the fairy tales, Wilhelm became an expert at polishing and altering text. Both brothers continued to have very successful and prominent scholarly careers after the publication of their most famous work, and became hallowed national figures due to the immense contribution to German culture contained in their collection of folktales.

Textual History

Until fairly recently, it was believed that the stories in *Kinder- und Hausmärchen* were collected primarily from the oral tradition of German peasants, mainly in Hesse and in the Main and Kinzig regions in the county of Hansau. However, according to many modern critics, including folktale scholar Jack Zipes, most of the tales were collected not from illiterate peasants and simple townspeople, but from educated members of the bourgeoisie. Moreover, the reported primary source for the majority of tales in the second volume—a peasant woman named Frau Katherina Viehmännin—was later revealed not as a peasant but as the poor widow of a tailor. Although the brothers originally offered the tales as an accurate reproduction of authentic German folklore, the revisions the stories underwent over time—including substantial changes in plot and character—suggest that they are not as close to their originals as is often believed. Scholars have found evidence, too, of the Grimms' tendency to combine different versions of a story in order to produce the "best" account. The first seven editions of *Kinder- und Hausmärchen* are each textually significant, bearing the stamp of their editor, Wilhelm Grimm, and reflecting both the Grimms' intent in publishing the tales and the reception the tales received. The first edition was criticized, even by the Grimms' friends, as too accurate; Brentano complained that it was "on account of its fidelity exceedingly negligent and slovenly." Both the second (1819) and third (1837) editions contain significant changes provided by Wilhelm that appear to address that problem; more poetic descriptions are added, and in a few cases previously unnamed characters are given monikers. The seventh edition, called "Grosse Ausgabe" (definitive edition), was published in 1857. A planned third volume of tales never materialized.

Plot and Major Characters

The great variety of stories and characters contained within *Kinder- und Hausmärchen* is immense and almost impossible to survey fully. Among the best known and best loved of the 211 tales are "Cinderella," "Little Red Riding-Hood," "The Bremen-Town Musicians," "Snow White," "Hansel and Gretel," "Rumpelstiltskin," and "Sleeping Beauty." The stories are populated not so much by fairies and elves, as their names might suggest, as by foolish younger brothers, wicked witches, beautiful and virtuous maidens, stolid kings, vain queens, and anthropomorphized roosters, mice, frogs, geese, and cats. Many of the tales feature trickster figures who embody at once both evil and the path to wisdom; heroes and heroines very often must solve a puzzle or trick the trickster in order to fulfill their destinies. The stories were not intended specifically for children, however; the Grimms intended their work as a cultural archive of German philology and mythology, and hoped sincerely that the work would serve as a resource for the study of German literature and history.

Major Themes

Many of the tales in *Kinder- und Hausmärchen* are coming-of-age stories: young girls must grow up and leave their parents behind for their husbands, young boys must prove themselves against the forces of nature or their overbearing older siblings. Often the stories suggest some notion of how a proper lady or gentleman should behave, emphasizing decorum, responsibility, and—especially—respect for and obedience to superiors. Closely related to the motif of obedience are the themes of love and reverence for the king and the honor and glory connected with serving him in the military. Loyalty to one's ruler and protection of one's community is also played out in the many stories stressing fear of the outsider, with the stranger representative of a force dangerous to the nationalistic spirit. Class separations are very distinct in the tales: although many heroes are of seemingly low social status, either they only interact with their own class or, on occasion, they turn out to be royalty after all. Compassion for the less fortunate is also a common theme, however; very often a foolish character who slights a poor old woman finds himself the victim of a debilitating magic spell, while the gentle hero who assists a wounded animal or an old hag finds himself rewarded with treasure or a beautiful bride. According to many critics, the Grimms themselves wanted their tales to serve as a moral education for children, demonstrating that virtue is rewarded while sin is punished.

Critical Reception

Among modern critics of *Kinder- und Hausmärchen*, a major theme of scholarship is the extent to which the Grimms altered their source material and the effect of these editorial alterations. Early scholarship generally accepted the Grimms' claim in their first edition that "we have endeavored to present these *Märchen* as exactly as possible . . . no detail is added or embellished and changed." Noting that in the first edition the Grimms claimed they were collectors, not writers, John M. Ellis has argued against this claim, contending that the changes made by the Grimms reflect their conscious efforts to promote German nationalism. Echoing this prominent thought in contemporary Grimm scholarship, Louis L. Snyder has asserted that the tales have become part of the German national tradition, displaying a genuine German spirit and marking a critical stage in the development of German romantic-nationalism. Other scholars have focused on the social messages implicit in the plots, often finding the brothers to be socially conservative and advocates of traditional class and gender hierarchies. Ruth B. Bottigheimer, for instance, has focused on the task of spinning and has found two separate attitudes toward the task—one describing it as a mean and harsh station in life, while the other heralding it as a vocation that leads to riches. Other scholars have looked at various literary aspects of the tales. Taking a thematic approach, Henry Carsch, for example, has studied the figure of the devil in the tales, claiming that the devil serves as a sort of "collective motivation" for readers who waver between morality and evil. Studying the characterization, Maria M. Tatar has focused on male heroes in particular, observing that though most of them are cowardly or "dull-witted," many of them do share the redeeming qualities of compassion and humility. And, exploring the tales as works of romantic literature, Alfred and Mary Elizabeth David have studied how the Grimms incorporated theories of art and nature into the tales.

CRITICISM

Alfred and Mary Elizabeth David (essay date 1964)

SOURCE: "A Literary Approach to the Brothers Grimm," in *Journal of the Folklore Institute,* Vol. 1, No. 3, December, 1964, pp. 180-96.

[*In the following essay, the Davids advocate approaching the tales as imaginative literature rather than as folklore. Examining the Grimms' approach to nature and art, the critics consider the tales in the context of the Romantic movement of the nineteenth century.*]

Upon the hundredth anniversary of the death of Jacob Grimm, folklorists the world over have united to pay tribute to the memory of the Brothers Grimm. The Institute for Central European Folklife Research at Marburg has brought out a memorial volume of essays entitled *Brüder Grimm Gedenken 1963*[1]—a reminder not simply of the closeness of the brothers but of the ideals of brotherhood that their lives represent and that their works have done much to promote. The astonishing thing about Jacob and Wilhelm Grimm is the sweep of their learning in many related fields. Although they made enormous contributions to the study of folklore, philology, and literary history, they transcend the boundaries of academic disciplines. "To see European literature as a whole," wrote Ernst Curtius, another great German scholar on the model of the Grimms, "is possible only after one has acquired citizenship in every period from Homer to Goethe."[2] The brothers achieved this difficult citizenship and a view of European literature as a whole that has left its mark on all of their achievements. It is fitting, then, to approach the most universal of their works—the ***Kinder- und Hausmärchen***—as a great monument of European literature.

When the Grimms entitled their collection of folktales ***Kinder- und Hausmärchen,*** they did not mean to imply that they had compiled a volume of stories for the nursery. It was in part their purpose that, as has actually happened, generations of children should read their book and that it should become a household work. But the title implies primarily an idea of the fairy tale, not an audience for which fairy tales are destined. For the Grimms it meant that the stories preserved the simplicity and innocence that their generation—the first generation of romantic writers—associated with childhood and the family hearth. In the foreword to the first volume Wilhelm Grimm wrote: "These stories are pervaded by the same purity that makes children appear so marvelous and blessed to us."[3] In other words, it is not that the stories are primarily *for* children (though most children enjoy them), but the stories are *like* children, have lived *among* children, and have been treasured and preserved within the family.

This childlike sense of wonder and the moral simplicity that the Grimms saw in fairy tales were also qualities that they attributed to the earlier literature of the Germanic peoples, and it was primarily for what remained in them of the spiritual heritage of the past that the Grimms collected folktales. In the study and preservation of the literature of the past the Grimms had a cultural and moral aim: they were striving to make their own generation and future generations conscious of the national soul that, so they believed, had lived on subconsciously in the traditional stories of the folk.

The Grimms came to folklore through literature, specifically through the literature of the Middle Ages.

Before they had published their first volume of fairy tales in 1812, the brothers had already brought out, individually or together, ***Über den altdeutschen Meistergesang*** (1811), ***Altdänische Heldenlieder, Balladen und Märchen*** (1811), and an edition of the Old High German ***Hildebrandtslied*** (1812). Their interest was drawn to folk literature by the poets Achim von Arnim and Clemens Brentano with whom they collaborated on the third volume of ***Des Knaben Wunderhorn*** (1808). In the course of this collaboration and in their subsequent correspondence with von Arnim[4] they began to develop their own ideas about folk literature, which differed essentially from those of Brentano and von Arnim, who looked upon folk songs and ballads chiefly as raw material for original poetry.

The Grimms' interest in fairy tales was, therefore, literary and historical and was just one aspect of their broader interest in ancient Germanic languages and literature. In order to understand why they began collecting folktales and how they went about recording and, in many instances, reworking the stories they had collected, it is necessary to see the *märchen* as part of their life work—the restoration of the German literary past.

Although the Grimms were the first to collect folktales at all systematically and to make some effort to preserve the stories in their oral form, they also reworked their material considerably. The final result is a subtle blending of folklore and literary craftsmanship, and it is of interest both to the folklorist and to the student of literary history to obtain some insight into the growth and development of the ***Kinder- und Hausmärchen*** into their present form.[5]

The Grimms published seven major editions in their lifetime. The first edition consists of two volumes (1812 and 1815), each with a short foreword by Wilhelm Grimm. These were revised and combined as the foreword to the second edition (1819), which also contains two longer essays, **"Über das Wesen der Märchen"** and **"Kinderwesen und Kindersitten."** All but the last of these contain important statements about the Grimms' concept of the folktale and all, with the exception of the revised 1819 foreword, are reprinted in Wilhelm Grimm's ***Kleinere Schriften.*** The 1819 foreword is available in most modern editions of the so-called ***Grosse Ausgabe;***[6] and it is from this that Margaret Hunt translated several excerpts in the preface to her translation of 1884.[7] Unfortunately these excerpts, unless they are read very carefully, are apt to give a misleading impression of the Grimms' method of collecting. They would seem to have misled Mrs. Hunt, for she comments:

> They wrote down every story exactly as they heard it, and if some of its details chanced to be somewhat worse, or if sacred persons were occasionally introduced with a daring familiarity, which to us seems almost to amount to profanity, they did not soften or omit these passages, for with them fidelity to tradition was a duty which admitted no compromise—they were not providing amusement for children, but storing up material for students of folklore.[8]

This statement contains a half-truth and does not really represent what the Grimms themselves said they were doing. It is perfectly evident that in fact the Grimms changed and added a great deal—how much one comes to realize only after comparing the various editions and the few manuscripts that have survived.

Margaret Hunt certainly did not mean to misrepresent the Grimms. She seems to have sincerely believed that, wherever possible, they had taken down their stories almost word for word. The misunderstanding is possible because the true picture is very much confused for a number of reasons. For one thing, the Grimms' attitude toward the tales and their methods of recording them developed gradually over a period of years, and they have left behind a number of statements, written at different times and on different occasions, that do not always seem consistent. The brothers themselves differed about method, at times even heatedly; Jacob, as one would expect, was the more scholarly and more insistent upon faithfulness to oral tradition. Finally, there is the prose style of Wilhelm's prefaces. They are written in a lyrical and highly metaphorical language, as obscure and as intricate as only German romantic prose can be. All the same, a more or less coherent theory does emerge from the various forewords and statements, which goes far to explain the Grimms' method of collecting and the changes they made in their material. The theory is not argued with scientific consistency, but it can be extracted, much in the same way that Coleridge's critical doctrines may be extracted from his scattered writings.

All the labors of the Grimms, whether in philology or in folklore, stem from a basic premise that they share with most of the major figures of the romantic movement: there is a spiritual force in nature that finds expression in literature. Nature means not only external nature—mountains, forests, lakes—but human nature which responds to these things. One may call this force God, or the Immanent Will, or the Over-Soul. Wordsworth captures the essence of the faith when he writes in "Tintern Abbey" of

> A presence that disturbs me with the joy
> Of elevated thoughts; a sense sublime
> Of something far more deeply interfused,
> Whose dwelling is the light of setting suns,
> And the round ocean and the living air,
> And the blue sky, and in the mind of man;

> A motion and a spirit, that impels
> All thinking things, all objects of all thought,
> And rolls through all things.

The ancient poets, the Grimms and their fellow romantics felt, had lived closer to nature, and their works were therefore imbued with fundamental truths and values. These truths and values had been given their noblest embodiment in the ancient epic poetry, much of it lost, but they still survived in the humbler form of the folktale. Wilhelm Grimm compares the old poetry to a field of grain that has been beaten down by a storm; in a few sheltered places, by shrubs and hedges, isolated ears have remained standing; these continue to grow, solitary and unnoticed; and at harvest time they are gathered by the pious hands of poor gleaners to provide nourishment for the winter and seed for the future harvest.[9] (The image itself is characteristically romantic.) The folktales are of course the solitary ears of grain; the pious hands are those of collectors like the Brothers Grimm; the future harvest is no doubt the future greatness of German literature that they foresaw springing from the native soil. Ideas such as these are recurrent themes in the forewords. In justifying the time and labor they bestowed on these simple stories, Wilhelm Grimm wrote in the foreword to the 1812 volume:

> . . . their very existence is sufficient to defend them. Something that has pleased, moved, and instructed in such variety and with perpetual freshness contains within itself the necessity for its being and surely comes from that eternal fountain that quickens all living things with its dew, even if it be but a single drop, clinging to a small tightly-folded leaf, sparkling, nevertheless, in the first light of the dawn.[10]

Translation cannot render the double sense of "first" in this sentence. The drop of dew not only sparkles in the *early* light of the dawn, but it still reflects the glory of the *first* dawn, that primal creative dawn in which the older literature had flourished.

The "eternal fountain" was for the Grimms the mystical power of nature, the source of all good. Anything partaking of nature must be good, and so the Grimms saw a natural morality in stories that told of "faithful servants and honest craftsmen, . . . fishermen, millers, charcoal burners, and shepherds who live close to nature."[11] One is again reminded of Wordsworth who in the Preface to *Lyrical Ballads* declared that he had chosen "incidents and situations from common life" because "in that condition the passions of men are incorporated with the beautiful and permanent forms of nature."

In fairy tales the cycle of human life is intimately related to the cycle of nature, as in the beautiful passage at the beginning of **"The Juniper Tree"** where the mother's pregnancy is described in terms of the fruitfulness of nature, specifically of the juniper itself:

> In front of the house was a yard in which there stood a juniper tree. Once in wintertime the woman was standing under it peeling an apple, and as she was peeling the apple, she cut her finger, and the blood fell upon the snow. "Oh," said the woman, sighing from the bottom of her heart, and she looked at the blood in front of her and was very sad. "If only I had a child as red as blood and as white as snow." And as she said this, she felt quite cheerful; she had a feeling that something would come of it.
>
> She went back into the house, and a month passed and the snow melted; and two months, and things were green; and three months, and the flowers came out of the ground; and four months, and all the trees in the wood put out leaves and their green branches became entangled with each other—there the little birds sang so that the whole wood echoed and the blossoms fell from the trees. Then the fifth month was gone, and she stood under the juniper tree, which smelled so sweet, and her heart leaped and she fell on her knees and was carried away by joy. And when the sixth month had passed, the fruit got thick and heavy, and she became completely calm. And the seventh month, and she snatched at the juniper berries and ate them very greedily, and she became sad and sick. Then the eighth month passed, and she called her husband and wept and said, "If I should die, bury me under the juniper tree." Then she was consoled and was glad until the ninth month had passed; then she bore a child as white as snow and as red as blood; and when she saw it she was so happy that she died.[12]

In both **"The Juniper Tree"** and **"Cinderella"** the guardian spirit of the dead mother passes into a tree that magically protects her children. In **"Briar Rose"** the briar hedge is the symbol of nature guarding her rose: the princess who sleeps inside the castle. When the right prince comes along, the briars turn into flowers that separate of their own accord to let him pass. On the other hand, nature punishes whatever is unnatural and evil. The doves who help Cinderella, peck out the eyes of her wicked sisters, and the two older brothers in **"The Water of Life"** are imprisoned by the mountains, as hard and unyielding as their own pride.

In the many parallels between the fairy tales and Germanic mythology and legend the Grimms thought that they detected the traces of a primitive natural religion. The sleeping Briar Rose surrounded by the hedge of thorns is like the sleeping Brunhild surrounded by the ring of flames; the three spinners are the Norns; the boy who goes to Hell to bring back the Devil's three golden hairs is like all the legendary heroes who travel to the Underworld. Even ostensibly Christian figures like God and Saint Peter wander over the earth as Odin did. Such parallels suggested to the Grimms that the fairy tales were not merely delightful stories but had a deeper religious significance:

> They preserve thoughts about the divine and spiritual in life: ancient beliefs and doctrine are submerged and given living substance in the epic element, which develops along with the history of a people.[13]

Thus the Grimms applied romantic theories of nature and art to the folktale. Wilhelm's prefaces reflect a strain of romantic primitivism that has been attributed to Rousseau. Although the Grimms themselves did not point this out, the folktales are a perfect example of "naive" poetry, in the sense of Schiller's essay *On Naive and Sentimental Poetry;* they are the unreflecting art of men moved directly by nature itself instead of self-conscious contemplation of nature. The folktale might well be added to the list of things in nature that Schiller, at the beginning of the essay, says have a power to move us in a particular way:

> There are moments in our lives when we respond to nature—in plants, minerals, animals, and landscapes, as well as in human nature, in children and in the customs of country folk and primitive peoples—with a kind of love and affectionate regard, not because it pleases our senses, nor because it satisfies our reason or our taste . . . but simply because it is nature.

In such a view, folklore, the literature of "common folk" and "primitive peoples," appeared as something that had been produced, as it were, by nature itself working through human instruments, and romantic writers everywhere turned eagerly to folk literature for inspiration. Moreover, the emergent sense of nationalism gave men a further reason to cherish not only what grew from the soil but especially what grew from the soil of their native land. Thus Sir Walter Scott collected the ballads of the *Minstrelsy of the Scottish Border,* and in America Washington Irving attempted to celebrate the legendary past of a country that had barely had time to acquire one.

The Grimms, then, shared a widespread interest in the preservation and use of native culture. The originality of their contribution lay in the care with which they collected folk materials and in their respect for oral tradition. Collections of folktales had been made before, but the earlier collectors had relied primarily on literary sources and had not scrupled to change the stories in whatever manner suited their fancy. The Grimms, too, occasionally went back to literary versions, but it was their aim to preserve the *märchen,* as far as possible, in the form in which they were still being told in the German provinces.

But exactly what does this mean in 1812 when it comes to the actual matter of preparing stories received from oral tradition for publication? It may be demonstrated that the Grimms' genuine desire to preserve oral tradition was consistent, at least in their eyes, with a considerable amount of changing and adding. It certainly did not mean that they felt obliged to transmit every story word for word. The fact that, as a rule, they did not take the stories down from dictation is evident in the well-known passage describing the exceptional instance when they did. This is the description of their most interesting contributor, Frau Katherina Viehman, the famous Märchenfrau of Niederzwehren. The Grimms had already published their first volume when they discovered Frau Katherina. Wilhelm wrote of her in the foreword to the 1815 volume:

> This woman is still vigorous and not much over fifty . . . she has firm, pleasant features and a clear, sharp expression in her eyes; in her youth she must have been beautiful. She retains these old legends firmly in her memory—a gift that she says is not granted to everyone, for some people cannot remember anything. She tells a story with care, assurance, and extraordinary vividness and with a personal satisfaction—at first with complete spontaneity, but then, if one requests it, a second time, slowly, so that with a little practice one can take down her words.[14]

There is no evidence here that the stories in the 1812 volume, or for that matter the stories of the other contributors to the 1815 volume, were ever recorded in this way; in fact, the implication is strong that they were not.

Unfortunately all but a handful of the manuscripts from which the Grimms worked were lost. But through a lucky accident of literary history we do have a considerable number of the stories that went into the first volume in an *Urfassung* that makes it possible to get some notion of what sort of material the Grimms started with. In 1809 their good friend Clemens Brentano asked the brothers for copies of tales in their collection for use in a volume of fairy tales that Brentano himself was contemplating. They generously made a copy for him of practically everything in their possession at the time. Nothing ever came of Brentano's own project, but the manuscripts sent to him by the Grimms have survived among his literary remains. They are preserved today in a Trappist monastery in Alsace and were brought out in 1927 in a handsome edition by Professor Joseph Lefftz.[15]

The tales in this interesting volume are often little more than plot summaries. Numerous motifs, later to be added, are not yet present. Some of the stories have alternate beginnings and endings. There is no question that any of these stories was a direct transcript from oral delivery. They seem to have been sketched out from memory with the aid of notes. They are clearly meant to be reworked, and this is exactly what Wilhelm Grimm tells us in one of the passages translated by Margaret Hunt, referred to above: "As for our method of collecting, our primary concern has been for accuracy and truth. We have added nothing of our own, nor have we embellished any incident or feature of the tale, but we have rendered the content just as we received it."[16] The key word here is *content.* Wilhelm is careful to distinguish this aspect of the collection from the question of style, and continues:

> That the mode of expression and execution of particular details is in large measure our own is self-evident; nevertheless, we have tried to preserve every characteristic turn that came to our attention, so that in this respect, too, we might let the collection retain the diversified forms of nature. Moreover, anyone who has engaged in similar work will realize that this cannot be regarded as a careless and mechanical sort of collecting; on the contrary, care and discrimination, which can be acquired only with time, are necessary in order to distinguish whatever is simpler, purer, and yet more perfect in itself from that which has been distorted. We have combined different versions as one, wherever they completed each other and where their joining together left no contradictory parts to be cut out; but when they differed from each other and each preserved individual features, we have given preference to the best and have retained the other for the notes.

From this description of their method it can be seen that the Grimms did not make free use of their materials as had been the practice of Brentano and von Arnim in *Des Knaben Wunderhorn.* The Grimms felt that such reworking would destroy not only the historical value of their collection but the inner "truth" of the stories. However, this did not mean that they felt obliged to retell the stories exactly as they had heard them or that they might not combine different versions of a story (or to introduce motifs from other stories) in an attempt to arrive at the "best" form. They consciously strove in their retellings to retain the flavor of oral narrative and, indeed, felt that it was their duty to purify the stories of any corruptions or artificialities that might have crept in in the process of oral transmission. They were thus not inventing details but simply drawing, like the original storytellers, on the vast stockpile of traditional material in an effort to approach the ideal form of a story, a form that might never have existed in fact but that was nonetheless "present and inexhaustible in the soul."[17] This is to say that they had no hope of getting back to some ultimate, uncorrupted *Urform* of a story. Instead they aimed at a version such as might have been told by some gifted storyteller like Frau Katherina, some Homer of the fairy tale. In selecting the best among several variants or in combining details from different sources, the basis of their choice was stylistic. It becomes important, therefore, to establish what they took to be the genuine "folk style"—for the changes they made in the stories are to some extent influenced by their romantic concept of the folk. Their ideas about nature and history turn out to have a direct influence on the literary style of the ***Kinder- und Hausmärchen.***

Wilhelm Grimm had stated that the ability to distinguish the true folk material from the false was a gradually acquired skill, and it was natural that as he heard and recorded more and more stories, especially those told by Frau Katherina, he should have become conscious of a definite fairy-tale style and attempted to imitate it. This style became, especially for Wilhelm, an intrinsic part of the value of the *märchen* and an objective test for what in a story was "true" or "false." This gradually developing sense of style was applied not only to new stories, but many of the older ones, already printed in the first volume, were revised in the light of it. The history of the seven editions of the ***Kinder- und Hausmärchen*** is a constant polishing and refinement of the style.[18] Some of the favorite stories like **"Snow White," "The Wolf and the Seven Kids,"** and **"The Brave Little Tailor,"** were revised in almost every edition. The difference may be seen by comparing any of these tales with a story like **"Jorinda and Joringel,"** which has hardly undergone any change since the 1812 volume and seems mysterious, choppy, incomplete, and yet strangely powerful.

In the first volume the tales had already been polished considerably, but not enough to suit the Grimms' friends von Arnim and Brentano. "If one wants to exhibit a child's garment," Brentano wrote to von Arnim, "it can be done in all honesty without displaying one that has all the buttons missing, that is covered with mud, and that has the shirt sticking out of the breeches."[19] The brothers were deeply concerned about the genuineness of their stories, and Jacob defended their method vigorously in a series of letters to von Arnim.[20] He admitted that some changes were inevitable in printing the tales. However, he drew an analogy between collecting folktales and breaking open an egg. Even if it is done very carefully, some of the white of the egg will run out, but the yolk remains intact; the yolk of the stories, he staunchly maintained, they had preserved.[21] Yet who was to say what in a fairy tale constituted the white and what the yolk? Jacob and Wilhelm themselves differed on this score, and on one occasion Jacob took his brother severely to task for what he regarded as unwarranted changes. Eventually, perhaps realizing more and more the subjective element in their procedure, he abandoned the *märchen* to Wilhelm and concentrated on his philological studies. Von Arnim was much better pleased with the second volume of tales, and he wrote Wilhelm: "You have been fortunate in your collecting, and occasionally you have been quite fortunate in lending a helping hand—naturally you do not tell Jacob about this. You should have done this oftener and many of the endings of the fairy tales would have been more satisfactory."[22] Wilhelm did, in fact, do this oftener. It is obvious today that the style of the Grimm fairy tales is in large measure the creation of Wilhelm Grimm. Even in the ***Urfassung,*** the stories in his handwriting are more finished and literary. If perhaps he has received more than his due as a folklorist, he has never received sufficient recognition as an artist—except for the tribute of being universally read.

For the most part the changes and additions are those that might be made by any good storyteller to make his narrative more coherent, more dramatic, and more vivid. This particular aspect of the *märchen* has been thoroughly treated by Ernest Tonnelat.[23] Tonnelat expressed his admiration for the trouble the Grimms took to polish the style of their narrative, a practice that he noted was not common among their compatriots. He lists some twenty kinds of stylistic changes made in the *märchen,* only a few of which need be mentioned here.

The Grimms supplied motivation where it was lacking. For example, in the first edition of **"Rumpelstiltskin"** the miller simply tells the king that he has a daughter who can spin straw into gold. In the sixth edition we are told that he said it "to give himself an air of importance." In the first edition the king merely summons the girl. In the second we are informed that he loved gold. In the first edition he tells the miller's daughter that he will marry her if she succeeds in spinning the straw into gold. In the second edition he thinks to himself, "I won't find a richer woman in the world." In the final edition he thinks, "Even if she is only a miller's daughter, I won't find a richer woman in the world." As one can see, the king's character is steadily developed.[24]

As in the examples just cited, indirect discourse and statements about what the characters thought and did are replaced by dialogue, and thus the stories acquire a dramatic quality. The character of the wicked queen in **"Snow White"** is made blacker through her reactions when she thinks that she has succeeded in poisoning the heroine. In the ***Urfassung*** her reactions are not even mentioned. In the first edition we are told that she "was satisfied," that "her heart felt light," and that "she was glad." In the final version she gloats, "Now you *were* the most beautiful," "You paragon of beauty . . . now it's all over with you," and the third time, "White as snow, red as blood, black as ebony! This time the dwarfs can't revive you again."[25] Details are made more concrete and vivid, often through the use of simile. **"Snow White"** originally began, "The snow was falling from the sky"; this becomes, "The snowflakes were falling like feathers from the sky."

Many phrases and expressions are added to give the stories a homely, colloquial flavor. When the seven kids are cut out of the wolf's belly, they hop around their mother "like a tailor at his wedding." Rumpelstiltskin's little house stands "where the fox and the hare say goodnight to each other." The father of Hansel and Gretel is forced to abandon his children a second time because "Whoever says 'A' has to say 'B'." Animals are given humorous nicknames; for example, the princess calls the frog king "alter Wasserpatscher."

In the case of these last-mentioned additions, the aim is evidently not just to make a better story but to create the atmosphere of a particular kind of story. Many of the homely touches that charm the reader with the naiveté of these tales were added in a very sophisticated way to have precisely this naive effect. They were put in to suggest the folk origin of the stories. Indeed, some of the characteristics that one would surely expect to have come from oral tradition are often the result of skilful retouching. Asides to the audience, closing formulas, and many of the verses have been inserted. Everyone knows that in fairy tales things happen in threes. So did the Grimms, and if their sources were content with only one or two occurrences from an obvious sequence, they occasionally made up the deficiency.

Thus many of the changes they introduced were meant to make the stories conform more closely to their notion of what a folktale should ideally be like. Their ideas on this subject, as has been said, were influenced by their romantic theories of nature and literature. Tonnelat also calls attention to the place of the Grimms in the Romantic Movement,[26] but he does not show how profoundly romantic theory affected the style of the *märchen.*

The most interesting changes are those in which the Grimms, no doubt quite unconsciously, modified the stories to conform with their idea of nature. Snow White's wicked stepmother was originally her own mother. The Grimms would have felt justified in such a change because of the wicked stepmothers in other stories; in any case, a mother's jealousy of her daughter would have clashed with their romantic belief in the purity of the love that mothers in folk literature ought to show for their own children. (Even the stepmothers love their own daughters!) Similar revisions in other stories have resulted in occasional inconsistencies so that the same character may be called "the mother" on one page and "the stepmother" on another.[27]

Some of the most characteristic changes emphasize the role of nature in the tales. Snow White's coffin was at one time kept in the dwarfs' cottage and lit by candles; later it was transferred to the mountainside where Snow White is mourned by the owl, the raven, and the dove.

The Grimms had a lot of trouble finding a satisfactory ending for **"Snow White."** In the first edition one of the prince's servants, who gets tired of having to carry the coffin around from place to place for the prince, thumps Snow White on the back like a petulant child punishing a doll, and thus the piece of poisoned apple is ejected. The ending is actually comic. In the final version the servants carrying the coffin trip over a bush, almost as if nature itself were taking a hand in restoring Snow White to life and marrying her to the prince. In the manuscript version of **"Briar Rose"** when the princess pricks her finger, we are told that everything went to sleep "down to the flies on the wall." In the first edition the horses go to sleep in the stable, the doves on the roof, the dogs in the courtyard, and even the fire on the hearth. The fourth edition adds the final magic touch: "The wind dropped, and not a leaf stirred on the trees in front of the castle." Thus all of nature is made to fall asleep in sympathy with the sleeping princess.

Family relationships are emphasized everywhere. The opening of **"The Wolf and the Seven Kids"** is an excellent example. In the ***Urfassung*** the tale begins: "Once upon a time there was a goat who had seven kids." The first edition adds: "whom she loved dearly." The second edition makes it: "whom she loved like a mother." In the fifth it reads: "Once upon a time there was an old goat who had seven young kids, and she loved them the way a mother loves her children." One should note, incidentally, the artistic contrast in this last version between the *old* goat and her young kids.

The Grimms believed that the stories contained a natural morality, but they often pointed the moral for the reader. Thus when the queen at last feels at peace after she has poisoned Snow White with the apple, they later added, "so far as a jealous heart can ever be at peace." Because they found deeper spiritual meaning expressed with childlike purity in the fairy tales, they believed that their collection could serve "as a book of education,"[28] a book that would develop the moral character of children. Consequently they were sensitive to objections raised by von Arnim and others against the first volume that certain details and stories were unsuitable for children. To these criticisms Wilhelm replied in the foreword to the second volume with the argument that what was natural could not be harmful. He compared the stories to flowers that might, for exceptional reasons, give offense to a few: such a one "who cannot enjoy their benefit, may pass them by, but he cannot ask that they be given a different color or shape."[29]

Yet the Grimms themselves must have felt a few colors were too strong to be natural. The first volume had contained two stories in which children play "butcher" and one child slaughters another. These tales were suppressed in the second edition. In the original version of **"The Twelve Brothers,"** the brothers actually carry out their vow to kill every girl that they meet, and when their sister comes to the house in the forest, her youngest brother orders her to kneel: "Your red blood must be shed this instant!" It is not that the Grimms objected to the horror of such scenes—there is nothing here to match the horror in **"The Juniper Tree."** But the action of the twelve brothers, who are intimately associated with nature in their forest retreat, would tend to contradict the Grimms' idea of nature whereas **"The Juniper Tree"** perfectly confirms it. The tree is the symbol of nature, and through it the murdered boy is brought back to life and his unnatural stepmother is destroyed. More than any other story, this mysterious and primitive tale reveals the connection that the Grimms perceived between fairy tales and ancient mythology and religion.

Fundamentally the Grimms were right—fairy tales derive from nature, although to a post-Darwinian and post-Freudian generation nature may not always appear as the pure moral force the Grimms thought it to be. The children's "butcher" game may seem more like nature to readers of *The Lord of the Flies* than the affection of Hansel and Gretel for each other did to the Brothers Grimm. We may, if we like, see all of the stepmother figures as symbolic substitutions for the mother figure, as was really the case in **"Snow White."** No doubt there is a symbolic significance that the Grimms failed to recognize in the many situations where a princess is locked in a tower or where the hero must perform impossible tasks to win her from a jealous father or mother. Their own intimacy gave them no reason to suspect that the hatred of older for younger brothers is by no means abnormal.

This is not to say that they were wrong. The truth that they saw in fairy tales is also valid. The mother and stepmother, the good and the wicked brothers in fairy tales are, after all, dual aspects of complex human relationships that *are* made pure and simple in fairy tales where good and evil are given separate identities instead of remaining closely knit parts of a single psyche. What matters is that these stories present recognizable patterns of human behavior. The Grimms' achievement was to present them in such a way that their humanity could be recognized by everyone—by children, by adults, and especially by later writers for whom, as the Grimms had hoped, the *märchen* served as inspiration.

Although with their collection the Grimms made an invaluable contribution to the study of folklore, still their final achievement was in literature. The literary influence of the *märchen* began to be felt almost at once, not only in Germany in writers like E. T. A. Hoffmann, but in other European countries where translations soon began to appear. Andersen is the most brilliant example. In England Dickens, Thackeray, and

Ruskin all tried their hands at writing fairy tales that in their self-consciousness are a far cry from the simplicity and artlessness the Grimms were striving for.

But the influence of the Grimms is perhaps not limited to literary imitations of the *märchen* form. Many nineteenth-century novelists have what may be called a fairy-tale imagination. Objects in the novels of Dickens, like Mrs. Gamp's umbrella, have a life of their own as they do in fairy tales. *Oliver Twist, David Copperfield,* and *Great Expectations* all have typical fairy-tale plots in which an abused child must overcome obstacles in a quest for security. Aunt Betsy Trotwood performs the function of a wise woman who gives good gifts; Abel Magwitch is like the wild Iron Hans, both in his savage nature and in the magical way in which he repays and tests the young hero who has been kind to him. Jane Eyre is both a Cinderella figure and the girl whose love releases a beast-bridegroom from his spell. In the twentieth century the tradition remains vital. James Thurber has written excellent literary fairy tales. F. Scott Fitzgerald created a fairy-tale world in which the kings and princesses are all beautiful but damned.

All this is a way of saying that fairy tales today still speak to us and tell us about ourselves—about our hopes and dreams as well as about our fears and anxieties. They are inspired by nature, then, as the Grimms would have us believe, and they have not lost their power to please, move, and instruct. What Wilhelm Grimm said of them in 1812 can still be said today: their very existence justifies them.

Notes

[1] *Brüder Grimm Gedenken 1963: Gedenkschrift zur hundertsten Wiederkehr des Todestags von Jacob Grimm* (= *Hessische Blätter für Volkskunde,* LIV), ed. Gerhard Heilfurth, Ludwig Denecke, and Ina-Maria Greverus.

[2] *European Literature and the Latin Middle Ages,* tr. Willard Trask (New York, 1953), p. 12.

[3] *Kleinere Schriften,* ed. Gustav Hinrichs (Berlin, 1881), I, 322. Translations of all quotations from German texts are our own unless otherwise indicated.

[4] See Reinhold Steig, *Achim von Arnim und Jacob und Wilhelm Grimm* (Stuttgart and Berlin, 1904), pp. 213-273, *passim.*

[5] The story of the circumstances surrounding the publication of the numerous editions of the *märchen* is told in a series of very informative articles by T. F. Crane, "The External History of the Grimm Fairy Tales," *Modern Philology,* XIV (1917), 577-610, XV (1917), 65-77, 355-383.

[6] See Crane, XIV, 601 and XV, 75. An attractive edition published by Winkler-Verlag (Munich, 1955) contains the 1819 foreword, a memoir by Herman Grimm, drawings by Ludwig Grimm, and an afterword by Herta Klepl.

[7] *Grimm's Household Tales,* tr. and ed. by Margaret Hunt with an introduction by Andrew Lang (London, 1884).

[8] *Ibid.,* I, p. v.

[9] *Kleinere Schriften,* I, 320.

[10] *Ibid.,* pp. 321-322.

[11] *Ibid.,* pp. 322-323.

[12] The translation of this and other passages from the *märchen* is from *The Frog King and Other Tales of the Brothers Grimm.*

[13] *Kleinere Schriften,* I, 338.

[14] *Ibid.,* p. 329.

[15] *Märchen der Brüder Grimm: Urfassung nach der Original-handschrift der Abtei Ölenberg im Elsass* (Heidelberg, 1927).

[16] The translation of this and the passage immediately following is our own, not Mrs. Hunt's. Taken from "Vorrede der Brüder Grimm," *Kinder- und Hausmärchen* (Munich, Winkler-Verlag, 1955), pp. 34-35.

[17] *Kleinere Schriften,* I, 332.

[18] See Kurt Schmidt, *Die Entwicklung der Grimmschen Kinder- und Hausmärchen* (Halle, 1932). Schmidt prints the text of the *Urfassung,* after Lefftz, with all subsequent variants and additions, line by line on top of one another, so that one can follow the process of revision in minute detail over a period of almost fifty years.

[19] Reinhold Steig, *Achim von Arnim und Clemens Brentano* (Stuttgart, 1894), p. 309.

[20] Steig, *Achim von Arnim und Jacob und Wilhelm Grimm,* pp. 213-273, *passim.*

[21] *Ibid.,* p. 255.

[22] *Ibid.,* p. 319.

[23] *Les contes des frères Grimm* (Paris, 1912).

[24] Variants are taken and translated from Schmidt.

[25] Translations of the *Urfassung* and the first edition version of "Snow White" are given in an appendix to *The Frog King.*

[26] *Les frères Grimm, leur œuvre de jeunesse* (Paris, 1912), especially Chapters I, II, and V.

[27] E.g. in "Hansel and Gretel." In "The Twelve Brothers" a wicked mother-in-law turns into a "stepmother."

[28] *Kleinere Schriften,* I, 331.

[29] *Ibid.*

Henry Carsch (essay date 1968)

SOURCE: "The Role of the Devil in Grimms' Tales: An Exploration of the Content and Function of Popular Tales," in *Social Research: An International Quarterly,* Vol. 35, No. 3, Autumn, 1968, pp. 466-99.

[*In the following essay, Carsch considers both implicit and explicit references to the devil in the tales, arguing that the Grimms used the figure as a form of social control to "exemplif[y] the dangers which may accompany the violation of the basic belief system."*]

I

This paper constitutes a part of a comprehensive report dealing with the Grimm Brothers' fairy tales.[1] The Grimms had begun to collect these from a number of informants and literary sources in 1805, when Napoleon had invaded Germany, and when, as a result, a good many Germans had become concerned with problems of national as well as cultural autonomy. It was the explicit intention of the authors to save from extinction part of the German folklore, something they thought to be quintessentially German and which they hoped to forge into an instrument of socialization. The form of nationalism to which they subscribed involved not only the preservation of what they believed to be a valuable part of the cultural heritage, but also, they hoped to manipulate it so as to serve quite specific national purposes. In this they were undoubtedly guided by platonic notions concerning political myths, fables and legends, which, calculated to create a distinctive cosmology in the minds of the citizenry, would serve, it was hoped, to induce the appropriate conduct.[2] " . . . (T)he times of national decline," wrote Herman Grimm, "would have been impossible, had German historical presence and Germanic thinking been made the basis of our popular education."[3] In short, he was thinking of folk literature not so much in terms of its esthetic merits as in terms of the value it might have as an instrument of social control.

Such a stance, of course, closely approximates established positions in the social sciences, for folk tales, the orally transmittable precursors of fairy tales (and other forms of literature including the contemporary screened idioms)[4] are reported to "be present in every known society."[5] Testimony to the importance which is attached to such folk tales is the ritualistic, if not ceremonial, manner, which characterizes their presentation in numerous societies in which tales are told 1) by specially selected raconteurs, 2) at particular times and 3) in specified settings.[6] For instance, Voegelin, writing about such occasions among North American Indian tribes, reports that old men, or sometimes old women, were selected to entertain their fellows with tales from the tribal repertoire in return for small gifts of tobacco. Good raconteurs enlivened the tales with gestures and actions, illustrating and dramatizing certain episodes. Meanwhile, the audience would interrupt recitals with affirmative exclamations to indicate their approval of the style and accuracy of presentation.[7] Similarly, Herskovits, emphasizing the dramatic quality of story-telling practices among African peoples, reports that these occur chiefly at night, sometimes during wakes and again to the accompaniment of audience participation characterized by frequent interpolation of assent.[8] Katherine Luomala found particularly elaborate raconteur behavior to exist in parts of Oceania, where among some people special training of raconteurs was institutionalized and where individuals were expected to specialize in narratives about a single favorite character. Another form of specialization is reported from the Hawaiian courts where raconteurs actually held contests, literary tournaments, as it were, with the lives of the losers at stake. In Samoa, the hallmark of a well-born chief was his ability to indulge in lengthy orations with an abundance of allusions to the established repertoire of folk tales, while in the Marquesas and the Society Islands the dramatic dimension of reconteur styles had been elaborated to the point where narratives were interlaced with chants and dramatic presentations of specific episodes of the tale—such performances being staged in special parts of the villages set aside for the purpose.[9]

This brief survey leaves little doubt about the existence of areas of resemblance if not identities in forms and functions between religious institutions and those connected with the narration of folk tales. With respect to the content of folk tales, both Radcliffe-Brown and Malinowski have stressed their difficulties in distinguishing one tale from another.[10] One notes also how carefully the content of such tales may be controlled in preliterate societies: thus Luomala mentions first of all the institutionalized training of raconteurs in some societies, and secondly, the existence of contests presumably with judges selected on the basis of possessing appropriate attitudes. In the third place, there are situations, mentioned also in Voegelin's and Herskovits' reports, which involve periodic interruptions at given occasions in the narrative, and tend to constrain the narrator's imagination. Riesman has suggested that " . . . for these tribesmen, words are like buckets in a fire brigade, to be handled with full attention, while for us we feel we can afford to be careless with the spoken word, backstopped as we are with the written one . . ."[11] One notes also Riesman's illuminating discussions relating to the coaching of audiences for appropriate responses in modern contexts.[12]

None of this, of course, is to be interpreted as suggesting that folk tales have remained unchanged. Rather, it is to emphasize the probability that changes which did occur were not altogether accidental but served the interests of the narrator, or, perhaps more precisely, those whom he represented.

These processes were greatly simplified by the invention of the printing press and the consequent transition of many orally transmitted folk tales into fairy tales.[13] Editors and perhaps publishers exercised decisive controls, and one reads with interest how the Grimm Brothers quarreled between themselves on this very subject. Thus while the older brother intended to keep the tales intact, the younger brother seems to have desired to give them a more "fairy-tale-like appearance" and seems to have won his point in time for the publication of the second edition in 1819.[14]

Although it has not been possible to ascertain the exact nature of the impact of the Grimms' tales, the mere facts that they appear to have been translated into more than 50 different languages, that they have sold approximately 100,000,000 copies and more than 20,000 editions, lend support to the contention that they may be considered as being of substantial social significance.[15] In addition it may be pointed out that the interest so generated has given rise to the collection of analogous anthologies in many parts of the world as well as to a vast body of research in a variety of disciplines.[16] Despite the indisputable excellence of some of this research it has seemed desirable to add to it from a purely sociological perspective, and in order to obtain a clear understanding of the content of these tales one aspect of the research focused on the roles accorded to the dramatis personae. The assumption was made that the actors are implicated in networks of reciprocally obligatory relations and in this manner stand in analogy to persons in concrete social situations.[17] Agents of the supernatural who were found in each case of presentation to be in interaction with human dramatis personae, were accorded the same treatment. It was possible in this manner to extract from these tales the characteristic manner of interaction for a variety of dramatis personae, to describe their characteristic attributes and the relationship of these to the outcome of interaction. This in turn made it possible to analyze the meanings and values which were ascribed to such attributes and the types of "persons" with whom such attributes were systematically associated. It was hoped in this manner to provide for easy comparability. The following presentation focuses exclusively on the role of the devil: it begins with a description of his visible attributes and proceeds to a further description of the consequences of belief in the devil, while the third section, again descriptive, is devoted to the consequences of the devil's intervention in human affairs. This is followed by analyses of the form and content of the patterns of interaction obtaining between the devil and his alters. The paper concludes with an analysis of some of the functions the devil serves in these tales.

II

A. Visible Attributes of the Devil

The devil is mentioned in twenty-two different tales, in fifteen of which he makes a personal appearance.[18] In eleven of these a more or less detailed description of his physical appearance and behavioral characteristics is provided. Devils may occur singly or in groups. When in groups, they incline to be extremely noisy, while when single, they tend to arrive and depart with the "hissing noise of fermentation" (*Gebraus*) and when asleep, they tend to snore and whistle.

In *puris naturalibus,* devils are black and in some tales they may actually be referred to as "the black one" (*der Schwarze*). The gate to hell is also black, as are the dogs and cats connected with the devil's residence and as are also persons, such as the Princess in one tale, whom the devil transubstantiates. The devil himself, however, may have golden hair as well as horns which appear to be amenable to being retracted or being taken off. Further, devils have goats' eyes which, like the eyes of witches, are red, and in one tale, the devil is referred to as "Master of the Red Feather." It is noteworthy that the color scheme associated with devils is black, red, and gold. Devils' feet are described as "nasty" (*garstig*), and at least one of their feet resembles the hoof of a horse.

Whether appearing alone or in the company of other devils, a devil may assume various disguises and attempt to look like other people; thus, he may arrive on the scene without his horns, as a "little man," as an "old man," or elegantly dressed. In one tale he takes the form of a fiery dragon, and in another he is said to be capable of assuming the form of a goat. Frequently descriptions of his appearance are qualified by the suggestion that he is "unknown" or had not been seen before.

Descriptions of the devil's domestic life are provided in five of these tales: In two tales he lives in hell; in one, in the company of other devils; while in the other he has an impoverished soldier help him stoke the furnaces, and teaches the latter to perform on a musical instrument. In two tales he lives an uneasy and mutually abusive existence with his grandmother in a cave underground, while in the fifth tale he lives on the top floor of a house in which conditions are very strange indeed: fish fry themselves in a pan and the broom is engaged in a feud with a shovel.[19]

B. The Consequences of Belief in the Devil

1) Invocation of the Devil

Just as unanticipated good fortune may be attributed to God, unfortunate happenings may be said to derive from the devil. For instance, in the tale in which the boy who set out to learn to be afraid meets in the church steeple at midnight a tricky sexton disguised as a ghost (who means in this manner to scare the boy), the boy throws the ghostly sexton down the staircase, breaking the latter's leg. The boy's father, who is in league with the sexton, is outraged and interprets this state of affairs as being inspired by the devil: " . . . das muss dir der Böse eingegeben haben . . ." And the evil dwarf, Rumpelstiltsken, on hearing that the poor but beautiful miller's daughter now married to the King has discovered his carefully concealed identity, and that he must consequently forfeit his rights to her first-born child, repeatedly and loudly protests that she obtained the information (i.e., his name) from the devil.

The speakers not only implicate themselves in believing in the devil by attributing these occurrences to him but also, by their further actions, demonstrate this to be true. The boy's father fails to recognize the boy's behavior as bravery (which God rewards), and being ashamed of him, sends him away. (The boy's courage leads him to redeem an enchanted castle and consequently to marriage to a Princess.) Similarly, the miller's daughter, innocent victim of her father, who gave her to the King under the false promise that she could spin straw into gold, is rigorously exploited by the dwarf who does the task for her on three successive nights, demanding in return first her necklace, then her ring, and finally, when she informs him that she has nothing more, that she give him her first-born child. The demands are quite obviously out of proportion to the effort demanded by the services he renders, but she has no alternative, because of the weakness of her position, to acceding to them. Moreover, she discovers the dwarf's name through the efforts of a messenger, and the charge of having used the devil for this purpose is false. Notably, also, in both tales the invocation of the devil then results, or threatens to result, in the separation of parents and children: the brave boy must leave home, as did the miller's daughter—which fact put her into the power of the dwarf to begin with, and in addition the dwarf almost obtains the custody of her first-born child.

Yet, it is to be noted that the speaker, invoking the devil, also loses: thus the father loses his son, and Rumpelstilsken does not obtain the first-born child although he does receive the miller's daughter's ring and necklace as the result of the miller's lack of truthfulness. The fact that those who are believers in the devil ultimately get the worst of things is made particularly clear in the third of these tales in which a father, praying for guidance in the matter of his son's career, is fraudulently led to take him to a witch master to serve an apprenticeship. The sorcerer is to forfeit the apprenticeship fee if the father, on his return after a year, is capable of recognizing his son. When the time comes, a dwarf provides the father with the necessary information and the sorcerer does not receive his fee, and alleges that the father must be in league with the devil.

Willingness to believe others who invoke the devil has similar consequences: Two children of a poor man eat the heart and liver of a "golden bird" caught by the father and, as a result, find each morning a piece of gold under their pillows. The father's brother, envious of this state of affairs, suggests that the children are in league with the devil, that the money should not be taken, and that the children should be led out into the forest and left there. The father follows this advice and leaves his children with a "sad heart."

In the last of these tales a person is actually sent to the devil, i.e., the belief is translated into action. A king attempts to prevent the marriage of his daughter to the son of a poor woman. The marriage takes place nevertheless, and in an attempt to divest himself of his son-in-law, the King sends the boy to hell to bring back three hairs off the devil's head. The boy succeeds and brings back also four donkeys laden with gold; he informs the King that the shores of the underground river, which must be crossed prior to entering hell, are covered with gold rather than sand. The King is so delighted that he sets out for hell and its shores himself, but as he crosses the river the ferryman jumps out of the ferry, leaving the King to row it forever.[20]

It is to be noted that the devil himself appears in none of these tales, but that the mere invocation of his name is closely associated with the separation of parents from their children. In the case of the tale of the King who actually sends his son-in-law to the devil, there occurs the separation of father-in-law and son-in-law as well as the further (temporary) separation of husband and wife.

2) False Perception of the Devil

Belief in the devil may lead to false perceptions, i.e., to mistakenly identifying persons or animals as the devil. For instance, in the well-known tale of the Seven Swabians who set out in quest of adventure and to see the world, a hare, asleep in a field, is so mistaken, giving rise in rhymed form to the following discussion:

. . . *Mike:*	I wouldn't be a bit surprised
	If it's the devil undisguised!
George:	And if it ain't it's his Mum
	Or maybe it's his father's son.[21]

This is but one instance in which ignorance, lack of courage, and unreasonable fear impede the progress of the Swabians.

In this respect the Swabians are not altogether different from the peasant who is a cuckold and who is persuaded to "see" the devil. This tale involves a peasant, en route to the market to sell a cowskin. He finds a crow with a broken wing, takes compassion on the bird and later asks for food and shelter for the night at a mill. The miller is away and his wife, after serving the peasant a cheese sandwich, tells him to sleep on the straw. He has just dozed off when the parson enters and the miller's wife produces wine, cake, a roast, etc., and the two of them make a meal of it. When the husband returns the wife barely has time to hide the victuals and the parson, the latter being put into the closet. The miller requests his dinner, but is given only a cheese sandwich; his wife informs him that this is all the food there is. The miller invites the peasant to partake of the meal and inquires what he is carrying in the cowskin. "A soothsayer," says the peasant. The miller becomes curious and requests the peasant to let it soothsay for him. The peasant squeezes the crow, which gives forth in a hoarse voice. The miller wants to know what it said and the peasant informs him of the presence of the hidden victuals. The miller is incredulous: " . . . das wäre des Kuckucks . . ,"[22] he maintains each time he is informed of the presence of the hidden delicacies. Finally, the peasant demands that the miller pay him 300 thalers for disclosing the last secret, the parson locked in the closet. "The devil," says the peasant, "is hiding in your closet." On hearing this, the parson emerges from his hiding place and, wearing his black clerical dress, runs out of the door while the miller, reassured, comments on the accuracy of the soothsayer: "That's right, I have seen the black fellow with my own eyes . . ."[23]

Ignorance, lack of courage and masculinity then come to be associated with "visions" of the devil in these tales. Finally, in one tale, criminal endeavor is added to these qualities: A lazy, stupid, and possibly psychotic peasant woman gives away her husband's savings to a group of outlaws. When the husband finds out what has happened, he decides to pursue the thieves and retrieve the gold. En route, he becomes hungry and asks his wife to return for some food and to make sure that all the doors of the house are well secured. The wife returns to him carrying some victuals as well as the front door. They eat and decide to spend the night in the forest and climb a tree in order to rest safely. Hardly have they done so when the outlaws arrive and decide to camp underneath the tree. Meanwhile, the door causes the wife a measure of discomfort and she drops it. The outlaws flee, leaving the gold behind and exclaiming: " . . . der Teufel kommt vom Baum herab . . ."[24] The outlaws then tend to attribute unpredictable and unexplainable events to the devil, thereby implicating themselves in "believing" in the devil.

But the story has a sequel: the peasant finally can stand his wife no longer and locks her out of his house. She is supposed to be working in the field but decides to eat and rest before she gets to work. Finally, she wakes up and accidentally disfigures her clothes so that she is no longer sure of her identity. In order to find out whether "she is herself" she runs home and asks Frieder whether she, Catherlieschen, is at home. Frieder replies ironically that she is asleep in her room, whereupon the woman runs away, meeting another band of outlaws whom she joins. However, she soon embarrasses them to the point that they attempt to discontinue the association and they send her to the parson's carrot field to dig carrots at night. She is there observed by the parson and a parishioner who at once take flight, mistaking her for the devil. This identification may not be on the same level of misconception as that of the previous examples, since the woman creates precisely the unpredictable and destructive events which are attributed to the devil.

C. Intervention in Human Affairs: Deception and Trickery

1) The Devil as a Tempter

In this section we shall be concerned with tales in which the devil makes a personal appearance and the manner in which he is related to the people he encounters. In seven of these tales he tempts people, only to deceive them. In the first he is recognized in this role and rejected: thus a man is desperately looking for a godfather for his newborn child, and the devil presents himself with the offer that he will provide his child with his fill of gold and with all the joys of the world. The father rejects him because he "deceives and tempts people." In another tale, in which a man in similar circumstances unwittingly accepts the devil as the godfather of his child, the man is given a bottle of magic water which enables him to cure the sick when Death stands at the foot of the patient's bed. Twice he heals the King's child, but on the third occasion Death is at the head of the bed and he must let the child die. Confused by this, he proceeds to visit the godfather and on finding him to be the devil, he becomes afraid and runs away, presumably leaving the magic water behind.

A somewhat subtler form of deception is practiced by the devil at the expense of a miller and of a merchant. Both had recently lost all of their wealth and the devil appears in disguise promising to restore their lost wealth in return for the first object they encounter on returning home. The miller thinks hopefully that this may be his apple tree and the merchant hopes that it may be his dog, but each finds that it is his child who comes running up to greet him.

In both instances the consequences are severe and lasting. The miller's daughter, living "piously and without sin," is able to defy the devil although her father must hide all water and cut off her hands so that she cannot wash herself. Yet, years later, after she has married a King, the devil, still seeking to exact his price, is able to intercept a letter to the King, who is currently fighting a war, and substitute one of his own in which he withholds the information that the Queen has borne a handsome son; instead the King is informed that she has given birth to a hermaphrodite. The King is saddened by this news and replies that the Queen should be well looked after until his return. The devil once more substitutes his own letter, in which the reply is changed to the command that both the Queen and the child be killed. With the aid of the sympathetic mother of the King the Queen escapes, taking the child with her, and only after seven years are the couple reunited "to celebrate a second wedding."

For the miller's son the consequences are also disastrous. Though he is blessed by a clergyman and stands inside a (magic) circle, he is only partially protected from the devil, who forces his father to set the boy afloat in a small ship on the river. The boat takes him to the shore near an enchanted castle where the boy meets the King's daughter who is transubstantiated into a snake. She at once proposes marriage to him if he can redeem her and her country, for which purpose he must spend three nights in the castle and allow himself to be tortured and decapitated by twelve black men in chains. He proceeds to do this and on the fourth morning the redeemed Princess arrives with a bottle of magic water (*Wasser des Lebens*), magically heals her redeemer, marries him and makes him the King of the "Golden Mountain." However, his troubles are not over. After eight years he desires to visit his father, but the Queen refuses to join him. He forces her to do so, whereupon she abandons him and on his return to the Golden Mountain he finds her celebrating her wedding to another man. The tale ends with the King decapitating his wife, her new suitor, and the entire court.

Thus if the devil does not make a personal appearance after the boy floats off in a boat, his stamp is unmistakably on the remainder of the tale. The absence of the Princess's father, the fact that the castle is enchanted and the Princess transubstantiated into a snake, the name of the kingdom (Golden Mountain), and the presence of the twelve black men in chains who come to torture and decapitate the redeemer, all suggest that the devil has had a hand in the proceedings. The girl's refusal to join her husband on his visit to his father suggests her fear of meeting the father who had, like her own, yielded to the devil's temptation. This may also explain the absence of any mention of the Princess's father, the possibility being that the devil has in fact "got" him. And if the merchant's son remains the King of the Golden Mountain, he does so only after being deprived of both his father and his wife.

The suggestion that the devil may have tempted, deceived, and ultimately "won" another King is repeated in a tale in which the latter is once more suspiciously absent, the castle enchanted, and the King's daughter turned black. The redeemer is a wandering Prince, described as being "afraid of nothing." He is freed from vicarious paternal contamination by the devil, and is able to restore the original white skin color of the Princess by enduring three nights of torture by a number of devils in the enchanted castle. On the fourth morning he has lost consciousness but the redeemed Princess, as in the preceding tale, restores him with her magic water and the wedding takes place immediately.

The reasons which make persons vulnerable to being caught by the devil and the manner in which the devil comes to seize his prey are illustrated in some detail in a tale about a rich but uncharitable peasant. He is described as being hard and parsimonious, unwilling to help the poor in any way, and thoughtful only of the increase of his wealth. In his old age, however, he suddenly becomes generous and strikes a bargain with a poor neighbor: the latter agrees to watch his grave for three nights after his death in return for some farm produce. After the rich peasant dies, the devil arrives at the grave at midnight and only by the combined efforts of the neighbor and a soldier is he tricked out of the rich man's soul.

Alternatively, a person may go to the devil of his own accord and, as in one tale, walk literally into hell. A young man, born with a "lucky skin," (*Glückshaut*) marries the King's daughter against the King's wishes. When the King hears of this he tells his son-in-law that if he wishes to retain his wife he must go to hell and bring back three of the devil's golden hairs. The young husband departs and with the aid of the devil's grandmother succeeds in obtaining the hairs, and on his way back, by means of secrets learned during his sojourn in hell, helps out various people who are in difficulties due to the devil, and obtains as a reward donkeys laden with gold. The avaricious King wants to know how the gold was obtained and his son-in-law informs him that it is to be found on the other side of the river he had to cross to go to hell. The King sets out immediately, but is tricked by the ferryman who jumps off in midstream, leaving the king to work the craft forever.

The devil, therefore, tempts with the promise of more gold relatively rich and powerful persons such as kings, merchants, millers, and rich peasants. The last mentioned tale is particularly revealing for the contrast of the young man who receives "earned" gold, that is, gold that is a reward for the courage he displayed in going to hell and collecting the devil's hair and for helping out people in difficulties, with the old King who wants to collect the gold "off the river bank" without realizing that he is going to hell. The very title of the tale, **"The Devil with the Three Golden Hairs,"** and the plot suggest that gold and the devil are inseparable and that the former invariably leads to the latter. What the King tried to accomplish, of course, was to separate the gold from the devil and to have his son-in-law do it for him. In the process, however, he does not realize that the boy is sending him to the very "source" of the gold, i.e., the bank of the river which flows in hell.

2) The Devil as Deus ex Machina

The devil appears to be particularly interested in those who find themselves in dire distress, and in four of these tales he seeks them out and offers himself as a *deux ex machina.* Thus in one tale, three friends, journeymen, deplore the fact that they have to separate because they are unable to find work in the same town. The devil offers them money under the condition that they restrict their conversation to three phrases. One of the journeymen discovers the devil's cloven hoof and decides to withdraw from the bargain. The devil, however, announces that their souls and salvation will not be in any way impaired and that he means to catch another, who is already half his and who now must be called to account. The three journeymen agree and then go to an inn where, in keeping with the devil's instructions, they restrict their conversation, with the result that the innkeeper and the other guests believe them to be mad. A rich man arrives, is robbed and killed by the innkeeper who, together with the other guests, persuade the judge at the time of the trial that the three journeymen were guilty. The journeymen, courageously keeping their word to the devil, restrict their defense to the three phrases, which seem to prove them guilty. They are sentenced to be hanged but the devil arrives at the last minute, frees them from their oaths, and denounces the innkeeper, who is hanged at once. The devil departs with the innkeeper's soul, and provides unlimited funds for the journeymen.

Similarly, in another tale, the devil rewards an impoverished ex-soldier, waiting for "the war to begin again," with a beautiful wife and unlimited wealth in return for seven years' service. During this time the bride-to-be's elder sisters demonstrate themselves to be malevolent, teasing their younger sister about her fiancé. The latter, while he is in the devil's service, cannot wash or shave, or comb his hair, clip his nails, or pray; he must wear, and sleep in, a bearskin. When the sisters see the ex-soldier at the termination of his seven years' service, he looks so smart ("like a Colonel") that one of them drowns herself in the well and the other hangs herself on a tree out of sheer envy. The devil now has two souls instead of one, and departs commending the soldier for his courage and obedience.

In these tales, then, the devil as *deus ex machina* helps persons of low status and in dire distress, in order to catch the souls of others occupying higher positions in society, such as the dishonest innkeeper and the two malevolent sisters. In two other tales, however, the devil is instrumental in changing the luck of unfortunate persons. In one tale he hopes to trick them and does not anticipate being outmaneuvered; in the other tale his aid is forthcoming without any apparent ulterior motive. In the first of these tales, the devil, flying through the air as a fiery dragon, seeks out three soldiers hiding in a field after deserting for lack of pay. They are starving and their sole alternative at this point is to surrender and face the gallows. The devil proposes a bargain: they are to serve him for seven years, after which time they are to become his unless they can solve a conundrum. The "service" is to consist of using a little whip to beat the ground which thereupon yields unlimited amounts of money. The soldiers, in the absence of reasonable alternatives, accept the bargain, beat the ground with the whip, live "in joy and splendor but without doing evil" until at the end of the allotted time span they become depressed at the prospect of becoming the devil's property. Finally, the third soldier, on the advice of an old woman, goes to the devil's residence, which is a rock looking like a little house in the woods, and conspires with the devil's grandmother to elicit from the devil the solution to the conundrum. The old grandmother transubstantiates him into an ant and when the devil returns home she asks him for the solution to the conundrum. The devil tells her, the "ant" hears the solution, and after being changed back into human form, escapes to tell his friends. When finally the devil appears before them and asks for the solution of the conundrum, they are able to answer correctly. Having no longer any power over them, the devil departs "with a loud scream," while the three soldiers beat the ground for more money.

The last of these tales concerns another impoverished ex-soldier to whom the devil offers unlimited funds if he will enter his service and live in hell, during which time he is not to wash, cut his hair, or clip his nails. At the termination of his service the devil gives him a satchel full of gold, washes him and cuts his hair and nails, and sends him on his way. The soldier comes to a castle, performs on a musical instrument he has learned to play while he was in hell, and thereby pleases the King, who gives him his youngest daughter and whose kingdom he eventually inherits.

3) The Devil as a Trickster

In addition to the instances already described in which the devil attempts to trick persons into selling their souls or in which he tries to use some persons to catch the souls of others, a number of tales deal with miscellaneous cases in which the devil causes a variety of troubles and mischief. An example of this is the tale of the miller's daughter, married to a king, in which the devil exchanges important letters in order to mislead and cause unhappiness to the recipients. In this tale, as has been pointed out, the devil is pursuing the girl who has escaped him because of her piety, cleanliness, and absence of sin. On the other hand, two cases of relatively insignificant mischief are described in another tale in which the devil is responsible for placing a toad at the bottom of a well which causes the well to dry up, and for a mouse which girdles a tree which bears golden apples. The boy with the magic skin overhears the devil telling his grandmother about these acts, and ultimately informs the gatekeepers of the towns which are concerned. He is rewarded with donkeys laden with gold.

4) Deception of the Devil

However, while busy tricking others, the devil sometimes becomes vulnerable to being tricked himself. The goats he creates with "fine long tails" are a nuisance, even after he bites off their tails which cause them to get entangled in thorns and hedges, and they are destructive of "fruitful trees," "noble grapevines," and "tender plants"—so much so that God must send his wolves to tear them apart. But in creating the goats in the first place, the devil has filled a hiatus caused by God's "forgetting" to do so himself. When the devil asks God for reparations for the injuries done by the wolves, God tells him to wait until the oak trees have shed their leaves. The devil returns in late autumn only to be told that one oak remains "in a church in Constantinople" which still has its leaves. The devil departs to examine this tree, but when he returns it is spring and the oak trees are once more in leaf and he must forfeit his damages.

But it is not only God, but also peasants, a soldier, a gambler, and even his own grandmother who play tricks on the devil. Thus a soldier, redeeming an enchanted castle belonging to a nobleman, traps in his magic satchel (a gift from St. Peter), nine of the devils who were running amok in the castle and attempting to torture him. He takes them to the village blacksmith, and beats the satchel containing the devils, killing eight of them in the process.

In some instances the devil's personal appetites render him vulnerable to trickery. Thus in one tale, complaining that he has enough money but that he longs for the fruit of the earth, a devil presents himself to a peasant and demands one half of his produce for two years. The peasant agrees and in return for silver and gold, suggests that the devil take all of that part of next year's harvest that grows above the earth. The devil is pleased, but when he finds that the peasant has sowed carrots he demands that next year he be given that part which grows below the surface. This time the peasant sows oats and, defeated once more, the devil departs in a rage.

The devil loves money, and being afraid of a soldier, seeks to bribe the latter, who is in the company of a peasant, to leave the grave of a rich peasant newly dead so that he can possess his soul. The soldier seemingly agrees, but after the devil has left to get the requisite sum from his friend the moneylender, who lives in a nearby town, the soldier removes part of the sole of his boot which the devil had promised to fill. The devil must therefore take a number of trips to the moneylender, and when he returns from the last trip the sun has risen and the devil must depart without the peasant's soul.

Similarly, a gambler creates so much havoc in hell, by winning money from old Lucifer, that he is expelled and denied readmittance.

Even his own grandmother, as has been shown, will play tricks on the devil when people come to learn some of the devil's secrets. Thus in one tale, the grandmother transubstantiates into an ant the boy who comes to gather three of the devil's hairs and to find out why a well has dried and why an apple tree has ceased to be fertile. After feeding and delousing her grandson she wheedles the secrets and the hairs out of him. Similarly, in the tale of the three deserters, the grandmother hides the soldier who has come to find out the answer to the riddle and questions the devil about it during dinner.

D. Form of Interaction

In the twenty-two tales with which we are here concerned, the devil interacts in one tale with God, in fifteen tales with different men, with two women in two tales, and with four children in four tales. It remains for us to delineate the patterns of interaction.

1) Patterns of Interaction with Human Actors

a) Interaction with Men

Rich Men

The devil in these tales seems to have little interaction with rich men and notably there is no direct interaction with kings. The latter may "believe" in him, as does the king who sends his son-in-law to hell, or they may be absent altogether, as in the case of the tale of the enchanted castle which at night was filled with devils, and the transubstantiated princess who has been turned black; there is no mention of the king, which suggests that he may in fact have gone to the devil. Such a state of affairs is indeed suggested by the tale of the rich peasant, selfish and parsimonious, whom the devil attempts to take immediately after his burial.

On the other hand, the devil actively seeks out and proposes bargains with men who have lost their wealth. But the propositions are made deceptively, so much so that the individuals in question do not realize that they stand to lose in the proposed bargain more (i.e., their children) than they can gain from it (renewed wealth). In fact it would seem to be the devil's aim to deprive the children of such men of the protection and love their parents have for them so that he can obtain power over them.

Poor Men

In these tales the destitute stand in direct analogy to children deprived of their parents. This is rendered explicit by the impoverished father who is looking for a godfather for his thirteenth child. He rejects the devil, it will be recalled, because the latter "deceives and seduces people," and he also rejects God ("not realizing how wisely God distributes wealth and poverty") because he gives to the rich and lets the poor go hungry. Ultimately he has recourse to Death because he renders all equal. The result of the choice becomes apparent when the godchild dies just as he is about to begin to live. The choices, as they are presented by this tale, involve God, Death, and the Devil. But poverty, for this man's child, for six persons making choices in these tales, and for the three destitute journeymen, is the equivalent to choosing death, for they are structurally unemployed and in the absence of skills, unable to fend for themselves. The devil comes to them as *deus ex machina* and at the same time uses them to catch others. Like the child of the second destitute father, the alternative to starvation is to make a temporary deal with the devil, limit their services to a minimum, and attempt not unduly to harm their souls.

It is to be assumed that the devil "knows" this for he approaches characteristically only those who are in distress. It is to be assumed also that the devil is aware that the persons here dealt with would prefer to choose death to giving themselves totally to the devil; for what other reason would he propose a "bargain"? Nor does he seem particularly to "want" the individuals in question; rather, he uses them to catch bigger fry: the two older sisters of the ex-soldier's fiancée, a dishonest innkeeper instead of the three journeymen, and instead of another ex-soldier, etc.

While the devil trades on the rich man's wants and the poor man's needs, his own appetites render him ultimately vulnerable to retributive deception on the part of men—notably poor men, for in these tales no rich men attempt to trick the devil. Thus while he created goats, presented as animals destructive to agriculture, he nevertheless hungers for the "fruit of the earth"; this appetite results in his deception and humiliation by the peasant who rotates his crops. In fact, the devil's delight in food is such that, once dinner is served, his grandmother can easily draw out of him the solution of the riddle by means of which the three soldiers can obtain their freedom—all of this while one of the soldiers is hiding in the cellar, listening to the conversation. Nor does the devil like to be disturbed during his sleep, and when his grandmother pulls out three of his hairs, one after another, rather than being awakened he divulges two important secrets by means of which the Princess's bridegroom sent to hell by his father-in-law can restore a dry well and a sterile apple tree. Keen on gambling and greedy for money, the devil risks losing great sums by gambling with Spielhansel, while his rapacity for souls is such that he is tricked out of vast sums of money by the combined efforts of a poor peasant and a soldier. Finally, as we have noted, eight devils lose their lives for cavorting about in a castle at night, being locked into the magic satchel by a soldier who spends the night in the castle and who has the local blacksmith hammer them to death.

b) Interaction with Women

The devil interacts with women in two tales only. Both deal with his "grandmother" described as a most ancient woman (*eine Steinalte Frau*) who, as has been shown, is not altogether averse to subverting his schemes by helping people to escape from his power. At the same time she keeps house for him, cooks, and, when he so demands, delouses him. On his part, the devil does not seem to be altogether averse to beating her occasionally—at least he threatens to do so in one of these tales after she pulled out two of his hairs while he was sleeping.

c) Interaction with Children

The devil interacts with children in four tales. In each the children are implicated with the devil because of their fathers' transactions with him. The less the need for the father to enter such transactions, the greater the gains he personally receives from them; and the wider the social consequences of such transactions, the greater the vulnerability of the child to the devil and the harder for the child to escape from him.

Thus in the case of the destitute father who unknowingly accepts the devil as godfather for his last-born child, the benefits of the transaction for him are minimal, the more so as the son renounces them as soon as he recognizes the identity of his godfather. In the two tales in which fathers are tricked into selling their children to the devil, the situation is rather more complicated. Both men had just lost their wealth and both promise the devil, in return for the restoration of their wealth, respectively, "that which first contacts the leg" or that "which stands behind the mill," believing that they will encounter respectively the dog and the apple tree. The point is that they did not think of their children and it is the children whom they encounter first. The children themselves do their best to protect themselves from the devil when the time comes for him to fetch them. Although they do not have enough power to escape the devil completely, they are able to win time during which they can prove themselves to be invulnerable to the devil. Thus, at the approach of the devil the merchant's son lets himself be blessed by a clergyman and stands with his father in a circle. When the devil arrives, the son accuses him of deception and after some bargaining the devil does not take him away but agrees to a compromise, in which the son is put out in a little boat and left to the mercy of the river.

The miller's daughter does not fare so well: beautiful and pious, she lives "in fear of God and without sin" for three years while waiting for the devil to return. When finally he arrives, she washes herself thoroughly and makes a "wreath of chalk about herself," as a result of which the devil is unable to come near her; in his rage he instructs the miller to withhold from his daughter the use of water so she cannot wash. The miller obeys but the girl weeps over her hands, to the extent that they remain clean and the devil is frustrated for a second time. Finally, the devil instructs the miller to cut off the girl's hands and, reluctantly and with many apologies to his daughter, the man obeys. But the girl again frustrates the devil by inviting her father to do with her as he pleases and by weeping over the remaining stumps to the point that the devil loses all power over her. He nevertheless follows her and is able later on to effect her separation from her husband for seven years, until in the end God gives her back her hands and reunites the couple.

In the last of these tales the implication of the father with the devil is not rendered explicit. As has been mentioned, the father is absent but his daughter, the Princess, has been turned black, his castle is enchanted, and in it black devils run amok at night. All of this, of course, suggests that the absent King has allowed the devils to take over. The black Princess is totally helpless; she has to accost a stranger, a Prince who happens by, to beg him to redeem her. To do so he must spend three nights with the devils and endure their tortures without any sign of fear. He does so, and later marries the Princess who has turned progressively whiter after each night during which her redeemer endures the devils' tortures.

E. Content of Interaction

These tales, then, provide a consistent image of the devil. However, a distinction has been made between (1) the devil who does not actually exist but who is nevertheless believed in, invoked, and in some tales actually "seen"; (2) devils who appear in groups in castles at night, and (3) the Devil who is presented in various guises and disguises.

All three forms, however, are quite similar in terms of consequence: interaction involves most saliently men who are weak, unmasculine, or greedy, and who, resorting to his aid, lose autonomy, lose control over their families, are separated from their families, and, in the case of Kings, lose their entire influence, as symbolized by enchanted castles in which devils play at night.

And all men seem to be vulnerable to the devil, who knows just how to tempt everyone according to his desires; rich men if they do not share their wealth or if they want to become richer, poor men if they prefer to live rather than starve to death. The case of the poor is of particular significance for, since they have little autonomy or impact on society to begin with, they are of limited interest to the devil. He approaches them in the guise of *deus ex machina* and in return for various and sundry services such as the temporary suspension of cleanliness, piety, etc., he provides food and money and perhaps in the end a Princess, while actually using them for the ulterior motive of extending his influence over more valuable persons. It is made clear, however, that the individuals involved owe their destitution not so much to themselves as to the irresponsibility of powerful persons from whose employ and protection they had been severed for reasons beyond their own control. In contrast to the destitute, young people and children appear to be of great interest to the devil, perhaps because of their longer life expectancy.

By contrast to all of this, there appear to be a number of devices which render persons relatively invulnerable to the devil: Piety, living without sin, frequent washing, unconditional submission to the will of one's father (in the case of girls), courage and, if necessary, opposition to the will of one's father (in the case of boys), bravery in general, awareness, being on guard at all times, and persistent shrewdness prove effective in warding off the devil. On the other hand, the qualities most closely associated with the devil are the tendency to dominate other persons, to deprive them of their autonomy, and to use them for one's own purposes, deceptive promises and fraudulent dealing in financial matters, noisiness, greed, ambition, high-level affectivity (the devil is being taken advantage of while eating and sleeping, he frequently loses his temper when he himself has been tricked, etc.), lack of piety, simplicity and humility.

Symbolically, the role of the devil delineated above would appear to be congruent with that of the "stranger" or "outsider."[25] From the child's perspectives this stranger may be any person, not a member of the nuclear family, who distracts the attention of his parents from him. More importantly, from the point of view of the adult, it is the image of the person whose origins are elsewhere and whose visible differences in dress, etc., may seem to naive provincials a form of disguise. Since the stranger is not enmeshed in the network of locally operative reciprocal relationships, and since the formulation of his attitudes may differ from that institutionalized in the community, his motives may be neither understood nor trusted and may become the objects of projections which may extend to those members of the local community who are involved in transactions with outsiders. Moreover, such outsiders, in the absence of familiarity with locally accepted traditions (especially sacred and semi-sacred traditions) may well appear to be lacking humility and even piety, while similarly there may become apparent disparities in the regulation of affectivity, ambition, and other appetites. Further, it may be a characteristic of outsiders also to appear both stupid and cunning: stupid in the sense that they can easily be out-maneuvered in transactions necessitating an intimate knowledge of various aspects of the local terrain, and cunning or even prescient as a result of their wider ranges of experience.

On the other hand, those devils which appear in groups need not necessarily be symbolically congruent with the marginal stranger described above. Rather, their congruence may involve *dolce vita* activities and orgiastic behavior sometimes associated with courts. The participating courtiers are presented as devils who light fires and proceed to play until they perceive the redeemer, whom they torture for a period of time, after which they are powerless. As soon as the redemption is effected order returns, as symbolized by the conventional (and orderly) celebration of the wedding feast.

III

Folk tales and fairy tales serve as popular vehicles for the articulation of the "belief systems",[26] the "major premises"[27] or the "ideals"[28] which rationalize the mores of a given culture and the symbolic expressions of which make social life possible.[29] This is accomplished by (a) anthropomorphizing the relevant ideas, thus simplifying and concretizing abstract and often complex notions. The "meanings" of such ideas are thus communicable to individuals of widely varying levels of sophistication. (b) Similarly the values which are to be attached to these meanings become amenable to diffusion by involving their anthropomorphized versions in dramatic interaction in which the resultant patterns of interaction terminate in systematic rewards for those acting in the culturally preferred manner, and, conversely, in systematic punishments which are meted out to those whose actions are in opposition to the established cultural patterns.

The following basic premises become apparent as being closely linked with the devil: *a. Lack of truthfulness.* As has been shown, in each of the tales involved the devil somehow deceives his victims and this applies even in those tales in which he presents himself as a *deus ex machina* and in which he uses his victims in order to "catch" more valuable persons. *b. Disruption of family life.* This involves the separation of husbands and wives, parents and children, and is presented as the direct result of the devil's intervention. *c.* Closely allied to this are tales in which the devil is described as being responsible for *loss of fertility. d. Lack of courage, and greed and envy,* in the sense of being unwilling to submit to "fate" (i.e., Divine Providence), and *a belief in the occult arts,* render persons vulnerable to possession by the devil, with the result that such persons lose the ability to perceive reality correctly. But it is not only those who come to be associated with the devil who are punished; the devil himself is the object of punishment and trickery by God, a number of peasants, soldiers and even by his grandmother. The meanings and values which thus become attached to the devil are negative.

The absence of positive attributes from the presentation of the devil recalls Durkheim's juxtaposition of "collective representations"[30] and "representations of a contrary state."[31] These are overdetermined[32] symbols the referents of which involve respectively culturally patterned ideals and those countervailing such ideals. Collective representations remind the group of its ideals, thus not only reinforcing the ideals in question, but also promoting the mutual recognition of the "reality" and potency of the ideas involved, thereby promoting the solidarity of the group. In this manner they give rise to euphoria and feelings of collective strength.[33] Conversely, the appearance of "representations of a contrary state" tends to " . . . set up a resistance to the play of our personal sentiment and *enfeebles* it by directing a great part of our energy in an *opposing* direction . . . that is why a conviction *opposed* to ours cannot manifest itself in our presence without *troubling* us . . ."[34]

The devil as depicted in these tales is a representation of a contrary state, to use Yinger's term, of the contra-culture.[35] In this manner the devil not only defines the contra-culture but in those tales in which he or his followers are dramatically involved in the results of its implementation, he also exemplifies the dangers which may accompany the violation of the basic belief system. The presentation of the devil (and his followers) thus arouses both opposition and a sense of being troubled, while the ultimate defeat restores the feeling that all is well after all.

On the socio-psychological level these processes are amplified and implemented by the facilitating mechanisms of identification or introjection on the one hand, and projection, on the other. Members of the group identify with dramatis personae reflecting the ideals of the culture on the basis of perceptions of a "common quality,"[36] that is, perception of a quality in a character which one believes or hopes oneself to possess. Some or all of the character's behavior may then be introjected, that is, incorporated and perceived to be one's own.[37] The converse of this is the process of projection, that is, the "transfer outwards (of) that which becomes troublesome . . . from within . . ."[38] thus those qualities or aspects of one's behavior which one rejects and detaches from one's own person, but the existence of which one cannot deny, one consequently attributes to others,[39] perhaps because one cannot or does not wish to deny the existence of the phenomena in question. It is suggested that in direct analogy to the processes of identification which are activated by the presence of collective representation, the processes of projection are mobilized by the presence of representations of a contrary state.

The devil as presented in these tales might thus be conceived as serving as an object for the projection of qualities associated with the contra-culture. Conversely, the devil can serve as model for identification for those who are at odds with the salient values of their milieu, or for those who harbor (more or less secret) longings to violate such values.[40] These processes facilitate the vicarious "participation" of the audience in the dramatic presentation.

On the level of analysis which deals with the impact of society on individual personality it is necessary to consider that dimension of personality development which results from the universal dialectic between those levels of the personality which are derived from bio-psychological constants in their relations with the internalized aspects of social control.[41] In the Freudian idiom this problem would be formulated as the relationship between the forces of sexuality and aggression subsumed under the general concept of the id and their relations with the super-ego. It is the function of the ego to mediate the relevant conflicts and it does so by means of the processes of "reality testing," that is, by means of imaginative "feeling-out" of situations so as to predict how much id-derived behavior will be socially tolerable in a given situation. In the dialectic which underlies such behavior the relevant rhetoric is mobilized respectively from "reservoirs" of ideas derived from the super-ego or "conscience" and from an analogous reservoir of feelings derived from the id and translated into form (thoughts, words, actions) by the ego.

The devil, as presented in these tales, can be conceived as an aid to the super-ego in the course of its confrontation with the id, since he presents to the latter the forces emanating from it in a concentrated, palpable, albeit selective form. The selectivity derives from their deprivation of their principal assets, that is, the idea that they lead to tension reduction, gratification and pleasure. In the shape of the devil, however, these feelings acquire a negative connotation in the sense that they may be pleasurable, but that they are ultimately destined to lead to punishment and hence, to pain. This, of course, deprives the ego of some of its "reality testing" activities, for the devil so presented ignores the variabilities of context. In its dialectic with the super-ego, therefore, the id is greatly weakened.

In concrete terms this means that the personality is systematically deprived of exploiting its id-derived capacities in a tension reducing or gratifying manner, perhaps even in a permissible context. The devil constitutes a barrier, as it were, which inhibits in the first place the use of fantasy with respect to the manner in which such capacities may be utilized in a variable manner, while the relevant forces are incorporated in the definition of evil and thus find their expression in the context of forbidden activity, perhaps in conjunction with other forbidden activities.

A question may be raised with respect to the special function of the devil in the general context of the entertainment deriving from these tales (and their analogues). One recalls in this connection Donald Martindale's suggestion that play derives from those excesses of non-committed energies which are liberated, in the sense of evolutionary development from instinctive predetermination:

> . . . [P]layfulness . . . emerges whenever the sphere of instincts is narrowed, but the energy for action remains . . . with each loss of instinctive predetermination, the living creature gains a field of non-committed energy potential. Behavior in this area will . . . be semi-random, experimental, and gradually organized on a foundation of learned habits . . . its peculiar property is availability for variation . . . [42]

However, such variation needs form:

> . . . the essential property of aesthetic sensitivity lies in the capacity to discern the form or pattern in events, in the appreciation of such form or pattern and in the development of preferences of some arrangements over others . . . wherever people are found they enjoy playing with the forms of experience for its own sake. A sense of excitement and satisfaction accompanies the transformation of unordered areas of experience into a unity . . . [43]

Martindale then proceeds to suggest, on the basis of Nietzschean and Freudian formulations, that sublimation respectively of aggressive and sexual drives underlies much of what is conceived of as artistic expression in a given culture. In the course of these processes, the relevant drives are partially abandoned and transformed into culturally acceptable structures.[44]

The image of the devil clearly constitutes a form of such sublimation. However, it would seem apparent that the sublimation is on a low level and far from complete, for the points of departure remain visible, both on the metaphorical and on the literal levels. Again, the devil so presented may constitute a barrier inhibiting the further esthetic exploitation of the relevant materials.

It is apparent that additional "entertainment" functions may be derived from the salient functions listed in the preceding sections. Thus:

a. the presentation of complex and abstract ideas in easily comprehensible forms, perhaps accompanied by humor;

b. the dramatization of the conflict between culturally patterned beliefs and countervailing ideas, with systematic victories for the former;

c. the identification and projection of processes which facilitate the vicarious participation in the relevant drama;

d. The rationalization of the repression of bio-psychological forces and the dramatic presentation of such rationalizations;

e. the sublimation and consequent formulation of esthetically ordered forms of sublimated forces.

It is evident that tales such as these concerned with devils constitute an effective form of social control and that under the aegis of "entertainment" those who are in the position to control the narrative are in a strong position to gain access to various levels of moral consciousness and consequently of collective motivation.

Notes

[1] Henry Carsch, "Dimensions of Meaning and Value in a Sample of Fairy Tales," Doctoral Dissertation, Princeton University Library, 1965.

[2] Plato, *The Republic* (New York: World Publishing Co., 1946), p. 69. Andrew Hacker, *Political Theory* (New York: MacMillan, 1961), p. 44. R. M. MacIver, *The Web of Government* (New York: MacMillan, 1947), pp. 39-54.

[3] J. Grimm, *Deutsche Sagen* (München: Winkler Verlag, 1865), p. 27 (my tr.)

[4] David Riesman, *Abundance for What?* (New York: Doubleday, 1964), pp. 397-402.

[5] G. P. Murdock, "The Common Denominator of Cultures," in R. Linton, *The Science of Man in the World Crisis* (New York: Columbia University Press, 1945), pp. 123-125.

[6] For detailed discussion of the content, form and functions of ritual *cf.*: E. Durkheim, *The Elementary Forms of the Religious Life* (Glencoe: Free Press, 1950), W. Lessa and Evon Z. Vogt, *Reader in Comparative Religion* (New York: Harper and Row, 1965), pp. 142, 144-202.

[7] E. W. Voegelin, "North American Native Literature," in J. T. Shipley (ed.), *The Encyclopedia of Literature* (New York: The Philosophical Library, 1946), pp. 706-721.

[8] M. Herskovits, *The Myth of the Negro Past* (Boston: Beacon Press, 1958), Ch. VII and p. 85, and Herskovits, "African Literature" in Shipley (ed.), *op. cit.*, pp. 3-15..

[9] K. Luomala, "Polynesian Literature" in Shipley (ed.), *op. cit.*, pp. 277-289.

[10] A. Radcliffe-Brown, *The Andaman Islanders* (Glencoe: Free Press, 1958), pp. 330 f.; B. Malinowski, *Argonauts of the Western Pacific* (New York: Dutton, 1961), pp. 299 f.

[11] Riesman, *op. cit.*, p. 401.

[12] Riesman, *Individualism Reconsidered* (Glencoe: Free Press, 1954), pp. 183-201, and Riesman, *The Lonely Crowd* (New Haven: Yale University Press, 1950), pp. 219 f.

[13] M. Luthi, *Märchen* (Stuttgart: Metzler Verlag, 1962), p. 36.

[14] V. v.d. Leyen, *Das Märchen* (Heidelberg: Quelle und Meyer, 1958), p. 8 f. For a more detailed discussion of the modifications which were undertaken *cf.* H. Carsch, "Fairy Tales and Socialization" in R. Endelman (ed.), *Culture and Social Life* (New York: Random House, forthcoming).

[15] G. Kent, "Happily Ever After," *The Readers Digest*, Jan. 1965, p. 167. For a detailed discussion of their popularity in the United States, *cf.*: Wayland Hand, "Die Märchen der Brüder Grimm in den Vereinigten Staaten," in G. Heilfurth (ed.), *Brüder Grimm Gedenken* (Marburg, Elwert Verlag, 1963), pp. 530-534.

[16] L. Dégh, *Märchen, Erzähler und Erzähl-Gemeinschaft* (Berlin: Akademie Verlag, 1962), pp. 47-65, and H. Carsch, *op. cit.*, pp. 6-25.

[17] For further discussions of the concept of role, *cf:* T. Newcomb, *Social Psychology* (New York: Dryden, 1950), pp. 321-332, etc. Also H. Carsch, *op. cit.,* pp. 27-30.

[18] Many of the editions of the tales are illustrated, but the devils which appear in these illustrations do not always look like those described in the tales. The most widely used illustrations are those by Ludwig Richter, originally made for the first edition of Bechstein's *Fairy Tales* in 1853.

[19] In this connection one might note Edward Lear's delightful satire: " . . . O Shovely so lovely!" the Poker he sang, / "You have perfectly conquered my heart. / Ding a dong! if you are pleased with my song I will feed you a cold apple tart. / When you scrape up the coals with a delicate sound / You enrapture my life with delight, / Your nose is so shiny, your head is so round, / And your shape is so slender and bright!" / . . ."Alas Mrs. Broom" sighed the Tongs in his song, / "Oh, is it because I'm so thin, / And my legs are so long—ding a dong, ding a dong! / That you don't care about me a pin? / Ah! fairest of creatures, when sweeping the room, / Ah why don't you heed my complaint? / Must you needs be so cruel, you beautiful Broom, / Because you are covered with paint?" / Mrs. Broom and Miss Shovel together they sang, / "What nonsense you're singing today." / Said the Shovel, "I'll certainly hit you a bang!" / Said the Broom, "And I'll sweep you away!" Edward Lear, *Nonsense Songs* (Mt. Vernon, N.Y.: Peter Pauper) pp. 35-37.

[20] Most probably the devil is the boy's father. The boy, son of a poor woman, is born with a "magic skin" and his marriage to the Princess is prophesied—all circumstances which cast suspicion on the nature of his paternity; his father must have been most unusual for the boy to be born with a magic skin and to have an auspicious marriage prophesied at birth. Moreover, an attempt on the part of the King to drown the boy when a baby failed and a second attempt on the part of the King to have the boy killed is frustrated by a group of outlaws (in league with the devil?) who forge a letter to the Queen arranging for the boy's marriage to the Princess instead of his execution as ordered by the King in the original letter. The helpful assistance of the devil's grandmother is also noteworthy in this connection. This would make the King's demands comprehensive: he wants acknowledgment of paternity and bride price.

[21] *Tales,* pp. 411-415.

. . . *Michel:* "Es wird nit fehle um ei Haar
So ischt es wohl der Teufel gar!"
Jergli: "Ischt er es net so ischt's sei Mudder
Oder des Teufels Stiefbruder."

My translation is somewhat free. In the original German the final alternative is thought to be the devil's stepbrother,—but this could not be made to fit the meter.

[22] *Ibid.,* p. 247. The closest English translation to this German colloquialism would be " . . . the devil there is . . ." (*Teufel auch*) [i.e., wine in the closet, a roast in the oven, etc.] Literally translated, however, his exclamation involves the cuckoo, in folklore often associated with sexual promiscuity: " . . . that would be the cuckoo's . . ." then suggests a high level of irony, the synonym for cuckoo being cuckold and the victuals do indeed belong to the miller and, as will be seen, the parson being indeed misrepresented by the peasant for the credulous miller's benefit as the devil.

[23] For an analysis of the role of the clergy in these tales *cf:* H. Carsch, "The Role of the Clergy in a Sample of Fairy Tales," *Social Compass: Revue Internationale des Etudes Socio-Religieuses* (forthcoming).

[24] *Tales,* pp. 223-28, at p. 227. Tr. " . . . the devil is coming down from the tree . . ."

[25] The tendency to incorporate widely divergent types of "strangers" into a single category is illustrated by a seventeenth century German document in which the author asserts an identity of origin of Jews and Gypsies. *Cf.* J. C. Wagenseil, *Der Meistersinger Holdseligen Kunst,* Mainz (1697).

[26] T. Parsons, *The Social System* (Glencoe: The Free Press, 1951), pp. 249, 328, 332.

[27] P. Sorokin, *Sociological Theories of Today* (New York: Harper & Row, 1966), pp. 23, 24, 245.

[28] E. Durkheim, *The Elementary Forces of the Religious Life* (Glencoe: Free Press, 1947), pp. 230 f.

[29] *Ibid.* For a detailed discussion using a sociological rather than an anthropological idiom *cf.* R. MacIver, *op. cit.,* pp. 4-6, 42, 195.

[30] E. Durkheim, *The Elementary Forms of the Religious Life,* pp. 229 f.

[31] Durkheim, *The Division of Labor* (Glencoe: Free Press, 1947), pp. 96 f.

[32] The term, of course, is Freud's rather than Durkheim's. In Durkheim's idiom such symbols might be referred to as "symbols of symbols." The Freudian idiom, however, appears preferable as overdetermination more readily suggests a plurality of referents. *Cf.* A. A. Brill (ed. and tr.), *The Basic Writings of Sigmund Freud* (New York: The Modern Library, 1938), pp. 330-338.

[33] Durkheim, *The Elementary Forms of the Religious Life,* p. 230.

[34] Durkheim, *The Division of Labor,* p. 96.

[35] M. Yinger, "Contra-Culture and Sub-Culture," *American Sociological Review,* Vol. XXV, No. 5, Oct., 1960, pp. 625-635.

[36] S. Freud, *Group Psychology and the Analysis of the Ego* (London: Hogarth), pp. 60-64.

[37] Brill, (ed. and tr.), *op. cit.,* pp. 224, 597.

[38] Freud, *Collected Papers,* Vol. IV (London: Hogarth), p. 148.

[39] Brill, *op. cit.,* p. 856, and A. Freud, *The Ego and the Mechanisms of Defense* (London: Hogarth, 1947), ch. IX.

[40] For a detailed discussion of the salient aspects of "negative identification" *cf.* E. Erikson, *Childhood and Society* (New York: W. W. Norton, 1950), pp. 36, 215, 266.

[41] *Cf.* also William Lloyd Warner's discussion of "species behavior" in W. L. Warner, *The Living and the Dead,* Vol. V, Yankee Cities Series (New Haven: Yale University Press), pp. 105, 225, 334-335, 444-445, 497-505, *et passim.*

[42] D. Martindale, *Social Life and Cultural Change* (Princeton: Van Nostrand, 1962), pp. 49-50.

[43] *Ibid.,* pp. 50-51.

[44] *Ibid.,* pp. 50 f.

Louis L. Snyder (essay date 1978)

SOURCE: "Cultural Nationalism: The Grimm Brothers' Fairy Tales," in *Roots of German Nationalism,* Indiana University Press, 1978, pp. 35-54.

[*In the following essay, Snyder discusses the* Fairy Tales *in relation to German nationalism and the Romantic movement, focusing on how the tales present positive, praiseworthy traits common to the German people while at the same time promoting the idea of fear of the outsider, personified in the character of the Jew.*]

> All my works relate to the Fatherland, from whose soil they derive their strength.
>
> Jakob Grimm

For generations the Grimm ***Fairy Tales*** have enjoyed international popularity. Children all over the world have been and are still fascinated by the stories of Cinderella, and Hansel and Gretel. Yet, paradoxically, the scholars who collected and refined these tales worked within the framework of that romanticism which became an important element of German nationalism. The Grimms regarded all their work, including the fairy tales, as deriving its strength from the soil of the Fatherland.

When this theme was presented originally, it turned out to be most controversial. It was denounced by defenders of childhood on the ground that no taint of nationalism could possibly exist in stories so popular among the world's children. Among the most vociferous critics were German scholars who had been obliged to leave Hitler's Germany as refugees: to them the idea was exaggerated and unfair. It is, perhaps, an indication of the tenacity of cultural nationalism that even refugee academicians, themselves victims of Nazi irrationalism, should regard this theme as an attack on their old homeland. Somehow, the presentation of nationalistic sentiment in the ***Hausmärchen*** was taken as a reflection upon "the superior cultural standards" of the old but not forgotten *Vaterland.*

It is, therefore, a matter of some satisfaction that distinguished folklorists have come to accept the conclusions presented in this study. Richard M. Dorson, Professor of History and Folklore and Director of the Folklore Institute at Indiana University and general editor of the University of Chicago series, *Folktales of the World,* wrote in the foreword of the eighteenth volume, *Folklore of Germany,* concerning the motivations of the Grimms. In selecting and refining their household stories, Dorson said, the Grimms placed stress on some attitudes as particularly Germanic. In this way they conveyed the impression that their tales reflected praiseworthy national traits of the German people. These included authoritarianism, militarism, violence toward the outsider, and the strict enforcement of discipline. The social classes were set apart: the king, the count, the leader, the hero are glorified, while the lower class, the servants and peasants dependent upon them and obediently executing their commands, is praised. In contrast stand the avaricious, mendacious middle class of merchants and quack doctors and scheming Jews—outsiders who intruded through the dark forest into the orderly system of manor and village. Hence the loathing for outsiders.

Professor Dorson recognized the nexus:

> In the wake of the Grimms, late nineteenth century nationalists extolled the brothers and their ***Märchen*** for helping acquaint Germans with a sense of folk unity and add historical past. Under the Nazis the original edition of the tales with their bloodletting and violence was reintroduced.

> Apart from the distortions by the Nazis, modern German folktale scholarship has largely disavowed the promises and methods of the Grimms. The powerful interest they generated in *Märchensammlung* and *Märchenforschung* has maintained its momentum up to the present time, but with altered directions and revised emphases. [*Folktales of Germany*, ed., Kurt Ranke, tr. Lotte Baumann (Chicago, 1966), pp. xvii-xix. Kurt Ranke is generally regarded as the outstanding folklore scholar in contemporary Germany.]

Nationalism and the Grimm Brothers

"Not a narrow nationalism but the philosophic romanticism of Schelling, Görres, Cruezer and Kanne, the view that the mythos glimpsed more of truth than reason, impelled the brothers Grimm to make such great collections of folk poetry as the ***Kinder- und Hausmärchen.***"[1] And again: "The brothers Grimm had no thought of breeding an overweening nationalism, but rather of paving the way for a profounder comprehension of German character, a national self-knowledge."[2] These two conclusions, reached in 1937 by Rudolf Stadelmann, then of the University of Freiburg i. Br., tend to relieve the famed German philologists, founders of scientific Germanistics, of the onus of "narrow" and "overweening" nationalism that has caused an enormous amount of trouble in recent years. Because nationalism, far from weakening, is growing even stronger as nations everywhere grow more national in thought and in deed, an examination of nationalistic aspects of the work of the two gifted brothers would seem to be in order.

Did nationalism, whether narrow or wide, play a vital rôle in the lives and works of the brothers Grimm? Did they venerate national, indigenous, anonymous folk poetry merely on esthetic grounds or in the belief that it contained primitive folk wisdom which became peculiarly German in character? Is there any evidence to show that the ***Hausmärchen,*** though beloved among many generations of children all over the world, were designed originally to stimulate German national sentiment and to glorify German national traditions?

Die Brüder Grimm, Jakob Ludwig Karl (1785-1863) and Wilhelm Karl (1786-1859), are inseparably linked in the history of German antiquarianism, philology, and folklore. The two were together all their lives. As children they slept in the same bed and worked at the same table, as students they had two beds and tables in the same room. Even after Wilhelm's marriage in 1825, Uncle Jakob shared the house, and they both lived "in such harmony and community that one might almost imagine the two children were common property."[3] The two scholars eventually became leaders of that band of distinguished men who in the nineteenth century devoted themselves to the scientific study of German language and literature and who, at the same time, fashioned the early framework of philology which was used later by some of the linguistic paleontologists in their search for the elusive Aryan by "race."[4] There is versatile genius here, for it is not usual for the same minds to evolve an authoritative grammar and a book of popular fairy tales.[5] Most of the major works of the Grimm brothers stressed national indigenous literature, such as their great collections of folk poetry, as well as their standard works on the history of the Germanic languages, law, folklore, and comparative mythology. The Grimms were certain that every language has its own peculiar spirit standing in mysterious relationship to the national character. They preferred knowledge of native literature to all foreign lore, because "we can grasp nothing else as surely as our innate powers" and because "Nature herself guides us towards the Fatherland."[6] From the beginning they were attracted by all national poetry, either epics, ballads, or popular tales, and they received full satisfaction in the study of the language, traditions, mythology, and laws of their countrymen.

When Jakob in 1805 visited the libraries of Paris, he quickly became homesick and wrote to his brother that he always dreamed of the Fatherland: "At night I am always home in Germany."[7] Four years later he informed Wilhelm that he would not go to a certain vacation resort "because there are too many Frenchmen there."[8] After watching a festival bonfire in 1814, he wrote to Wilhelm: "I wished that a colossal Bonaparte, a *Puppe aus Heu,* be thrown ceremoniously into the fire and burned."[9] When his friend Benecke received a call to Edinburgh in 1821 and asked for his advice, Jakob replied: "I cannot advise you but I can say that, if I were in your place, I would not emigrate. That would be a difficult thing."[10] In his inaugural lecture at Göttingen, Jakob wrote: "The love for the Fatherland is so godlike and so deeply impressed a feeling in every human breast that it is not weakened but rather strengthened by the sorrows and misfortunes that happen to us in the land of our birth."[11] When Bettina in 1838 sought to get the Grimms positions in France after they had been dismissed at Göttingen, Wilhelm Grimm wrote to Dahlmann: "What's the use of doing it? What can become of the matter? All our work would be paralyzed and extinguished in short order if we renounced our Fatherland."[12]

In 1817 the brothers went to Göttingen, where Jakob received an appointment as professor and librarian, Wilhelm as underlibrarian. In 1837 they were among the *"Göttinger Sieben"* who signed a protest against the king of Hanover's abrogation of the constitution. Both were dismissed from their positions and banished from the kingdom of Hanover.[13] On the surface the protest of the Grimms seems to have been motivated by liberal sentiment, but actually they had no extreme faith in parliamentary government. To them constitutions had a negative value—as dikes against a devastating flood, while positive fertility was given by the benevolent grace of a monarch.[14] Wilhelm IV had established a constitution and Ernst had by two successive decrees revoked it. In the sight of the Grimms, Ernst had perjured himself, and it was the duty of *Georgia Augusta,* the University of Göttingen, to protest.[15]

In 1840 Jakob wrote to Lachmann: *"Der Welt bin ich nicht feind und hänge heiss an allem Vaterländischen."*[16] In his dediction to his ***Geschichte der deutschen Sprache,*** Jakob Grimm confessed that his book was meant to be political, since the German people had been responsible for throwing off the Roman yoke, bringing "fresh freedom to the Romans in Gaul, Italy, Spain, and Britain," and with their own strength decided the victory of Christianity "by erecting an unbreakable wall against the constantly pressing Slavs in Europe's middle."[17] "All my works" Jakob wrote later in one of his last essays, "relate to the Fatherland, from whose soil they derive their strength."[18] The distinguished scholar of modern nationalism, Hans Kohn, concluded that "Jakob Grimm, one of the most violent Pan-Germans, expressed his confidence that the peace and salvation of the whole continent will rest upon Germany's strength and freedom."[19]

Romanticism and German Nationalism

From the outset the Grimm brothers took the Romantic position which was closely allied with the rising German nationalism. Following closely upon the lead of the early Romantics—the Schlegel brothers, Ludwig Tieck, Novalis, Herder, Fichte, Schelling, and Schleiermacher, the Grimms in their philological investigations sought to unlock the poetry and the experiences of the German people, which were encased in words and grammatical forms.[20] Many of the German Romantics saw their organic-genetic conception of culture as the expression of the Germanic national soul,[21] which had its beginning in the heroic Middle Ages.[22] Like the Romantics the Grimms issued a plea for the claims of the imagination, of emotion and feeling, of individualism, and above all for a synthetic expression of the national genius in all its manifold aspects of literature, art, religion, and philosophy.[23] But where the Romantics enriched the imagination by presenting the many-colored life of other ages and countries, they remained mostly artists and poets, not scholars, philologists, and historians; the Grimms, on the other hand, functioned in the Romantic circle by giving to it the critical scholarship that hitherto had been lacking.[24] "I strove to penetrate into the wild forests of our ancestors," wrote Wilhelm Grimm, "listening to their whole language, and watching their pure customs."[25] As a group the Romantics profoundly venerated folk poetry and especially the fairy tale.[26] Novalis pronounced the folk tale the primary and highest creation of man.[27] Even the great Schiller had written in extravagant terms:

> Tiefere Bedeutung
> Liegt in dem Märchen meiner Kinderjahre,
> Als in der Wahrheit, die das Leben lehrt.[28]

It was this type of romanticism, stressing folk language, customs, personality, and the idea of *Volksgemeinschaft,* or community of the people, which was an important factor in the historical evolution of modern nationalism.

Planning and Publication of the Fairy Tales

The idea for a collection of children's stories may be traced directly to Herder, who in 1773 aroused immediate attention to folk literature with an essay entitled *Ossian und die Lieder alter Völker.*[29] Such a collection, Herder once remarked, would be a Christmas present for the young people of the future.[30] in 1805 Jakob Grimm was taken to Paris by his teacher, Savigny. "I have been thinking," Wilhelm wrote to Jakob, "that you might look for old German poems among the manuscripts. Perhaps you might find something unknown and important."[31] Soon after Jakob's return the brothers began their laborious collection of German sagas and fairy tales. The work proceeded under difficult conditions, for in 1806 the armies of Napoleon overran Kassel. "Those days," wrote Wilhelm, "of the collapse of all hitherto existing establishments will remain forever before my eyes. . . . The ardor with which the studies in Old German were pursued helped overcome the spiritual depression."[32] Working thus in difficult times but nevertheless hearing "the horns of elfland faintly blowing."[33] the Grimms completed their first volume, which appeared at Christmas, 1812, the winter of Napoleon's retreat from Moscow. It was an immediate success, the masterpiece for which the whole Romantic movement had been waiting.[34]

The name of the Grimms quickly became a household word throughout the Germanies,[35] and eventually it was carried throughout the civilized world in a series of translations. Even the natives of Africa and the South Seas have borrowed tales from the Grimms.[36]

With the publication of the ***Hausmärchen*** the Grimms not only accomplished for the fairy tale what Arnim and Brentano had done for the *Volkslied,*[37] but they also established a universal standard for the telling of fairy tales.[38] The Grimms were ideal interpreters of this literary form. Fascinated by folk-poetry and themselves gifted with a persisting sense of childlike wonder, the dignified scholars at the same time had a rare ability to pass on their own enthusiasm to children. They saw to it that any child could follow the tales.

The youngster loves a beginning, a plot, and an ending, together with a clean-cut moral, and the Grimms gave them all of these. The Grimms recognized that the child loves to know how old people are, what they wear, what they say, and why they say it, details which attract the attention of young minds. That the Grimms knew their way around in the child's world is attested by the simple and subtle humor of the tales. Children love houses built of bread, roofed with cake, and finished with sugar windows. They are delighted to learn that witches have red eyes and cannot see far, that a kettle can be scoured to resemble gold, and that a dwarf fishing can get his beard entangled in his line. They love the little bean who laughed so much that she burst and had to be sewn up with black cotton by a friendly tailor, thus explaining why every bean since that day has a black seam in it.[39]

The Grimms obtained their folk tales from the lips of peasant women, shepherds, waggoners, vagrants, old grannies, and children in Hesse, Hanau, and other areas.[40] Their first concern in collecting the stories was "faithfulness to the truth," and they sought to keep the tales "as clean as possible," adding nothing and changing nothing.[41] Wilhelm Grimm stated explicitly that he and his brother were most careful to avoid embellishing the tales which in themselves were so rich and rewarding.[42] Jackob Grimm, too, was certain that "stories of this kind are sought for with full recognition of their scientific value and with a dread of altering any part of their contents, whereas formerly they were only regarded as worthless fancy-pieces which might be manipulated at will."[43] In their thorough commentary on the stories the Grimms gave painstaking and accurate references to the exact source from which each tale was taken. For example, nineteen of their finest tales were taken from Frau Katerina Viehmann (1755-1815), the wife of a tailor, who lived at Niederzwehrn, a village near Kassel. "Anyone believing that traditional materials are easily falsified and carelessly preserved, and hence cannot survive over a long period, should hear how close she always keeps to her story and how zealous she is for its accuracy."[44]

The fact that the brothers Grimm took down the tales with almost fanatical accuracy does not at all invalidate the thesis that the ***Märchen*** have played a role in the historical evolution of German nationalism. Quite the contrary—the many sentiments typical of German nationalism which are found in the tales, as will be demonstrated, existed among the old peasants, nurses, and workers from whom the Grimms obtained their material. What the anthologists did was to catch the varied strands of German national tradition and weave them into a pattern glorifying German folk stories. Themselves superb patriots who always believed in sanctifying the ancient German tongue,[45] the Grimms, consciously or unconsciously, stressed those peculiar traits which have since come to be known as important elements of the German national character. Moreover, in the very cooperative action by which the tales were written a quality of national validity and individual unity appears.[46]

Analysis of the Tales

The environment of the Grimms' tales was one which reflected similarities of family life in the same culture. The milieu consisted of farmland, villages, towns, and the forest, but the sea was alien. In the village lived the peasant, the tradesman, and the artisan, near the castle of the king and his court. The forest, a dark jewel containing evil spirits and lovely treasures, was a fascinating but frightening unknown, where witches lived in huts and princesses in enchanting castles. The family was a cohesive unit, with the good and able father, respected and obeyed, at its head; its cohesiveness was challenged by such unattractive elements as poverty, the stepmother, and inheritance trouble. There was no primogeniture, hence the Salic law with its cycle of unification, disruption, and unification prevailed.

Society consisted of royalty, the aristocracy, the military, the professionals, merchants, artisans, and peasants. Class distinctions were definite. The upper and lower classes are depicted favorably in the tales, but the middle class, consisting of merchants, innkeepers, doctors, clerics, and Jews, is condemned for its greed and quackery. Virtue is always rewarded and sin punished, though virtue was complicated somewhat by heroes lying, cheating, stealing, and slaying to gain an end.

There is plenty of evidence in the fairy tales to show the existence of what may be called universal factors of personality, qualities which are typical of many peoples from all parts of the world. But at the same time there is also evidence of the existence of such relatively uniform and striking attitudes as respect for order, obedience, discipline, authoritarianism, militarism, glorification of violence, and fear of and contempt for the stranger.

A strong respect for the desirability of order is indicated in the opening paragraph of ***The Sole:***

> The fishes had for a long time been discontented because no order prevailed in their kingdom. None of them turned aside for the others, but all swam to the right or left as they fancied, or darted between those who wanted to stay together, or got into their way; and a strong one gave a weak one a blow with its tail, and drove it away, or else swallowed it up without more ado. "How delightful it would be," said they, "if we had a king who enforced law and justice among us!" and they met together to choose for their ruler the one who would cleave through the water most quickly, and give help to the weak ones.[47]

The concept of obedience is emphasized again and again. A little hare tells a musician: "I will obey you as a scholar obeys his master."[48] When the Devil orders a father to cut off the hands of his own child, the father asks his daughter to understand his predicament. She replies: "Dear father, do with me what you will, I am your child." Whereupon she lays down both her hands, and allows them to be cut off.[49] A king's son, seized with a desire to travel around the world "took no one with him but a faithful servant."[50] When Hans serves his master for seven years, the master gives him as reward "a piece of gold as big as his head."[51] A diligent servant is the first out of bed every monring, the last to go to bed at night, and whenever there was a difficult job to be done, which nobody cared to undertake, he was always the first to set himself to it. Moreover, he never complained, but was contented with everything, and was always merry.[52]

This concept of obedience, together with its corollary—discipline, amounted to something more than mere obedience of the child to its parents. It was closely akin to that type of authoritarianism manifested in attitudes toward the family, society, and the state. The father is head of the home and the ruler of the family; it is wrong and dangerous to challenge his authority. Society itself is static, with definite gradations from top to bottom. The state is supreme and the end of all striving. In the state the king is supreme. His word is law and his orders must be strictly obeyed, even if forfeiture of life be the result. He may on occasion order death or grant wealth at a mere whim.

The nature and personality of the king become dominant themes in the ***Märchen.*** The land of the tales is made up of many small kingdoms, in each of which the king emerges as the strong, all-powerful personality. When a king made a great feast and invited thereto, from far and near, all the young men likely to marry, he marshalled all of them in a row according to their rank and standing: first came the kings, then the grand-dukes, then the princes, the earls, the barons, and the gentry.[53] When Adam and Eve enter Heaven, the Lord saw their pretty children, blessed them, laid his hands on the first, and said, "Thou shalt be a powerful king."[54] When a bird sings well, it is identified as "the king of the birds."[55] It was decided among the birds that he who flew highest should be king.[56] The king is mighty: "such a person arrives in the carriage in full splendor like a mighty king, not like a beggar."[57] The king is wise: "a long time ago there lived a king who was famed for his wisdom through all the land."[58] The verdict always comes before the king.[59] The king is generous: when he hears of a poor peasant's poverty, he presents him with a bit of land.[60] He is handsome: when peasants dress up in splendid garments, and wash, "no king could have looked so handsome."[61] The king is kindly; he always looked kindly at frightened people,[62] and, feeling compassion, raised a poor soldier from poverty.[63] He is a lover of all the better things, including all kinds of fine trees.[64] He is sentimental: "tears rose to the king's eyes."[65] He is omnipresent and omniscient: when a shepherd boy's fame spreads far and wide because of his wise answers, the king naturally hears of it and summons him,[66] when a horn sings by itself "the king understood it all, and caused the ground below the bridge to be dug up, and then the whole skeleton of the murdered man to come to life."[67] Similarly, the various members of the king's family take top rank in the social hierarchy.[68]

The love and reverence for the king, emphasized so strongly in the fairy tales, are a part of a major theme of the stories: the life of the hero. How the hero makes his way through thick, weird forests, how he outwits ferocious animals, and how he wins a propitious marriage, these exert a tremendous appeal to the child's mind. The hero, be he prince, soldier, peasant's son, servant, or tradesman, falls into two categories: he is a cunning, clever fellow, destined from the very beginning to conquer fate by his strength, courage, and brains, or he is slightly stupid and guided in his victorious course by good fairies.[69] In both cases obviousness is the chief characteristic. The clever hero appears less often than the dullard, but his is a glorious life overshadowed by the wings of death. A simpleton son, by a trick of fate, gains his father's inheritance away from his two intelligent, older brothers.[70] In ***The Golden Goose,*** the youngest son, Dummling, attains success and happiness despite his stupidity.[71]

The greatest virtue of either the clever or dullard boy is courage. When Strong Hans beats some robbers, "his mother stood in a corner admiring his bravery and strength."[72] When a young soldier is asked if he is fearless, he replies: "A soldier and fear—how can the two go together"?[73] The cunning little tailor was not frightened by a bear that had never left anyone alive who had fallen into its embraces, but was on the contrary, quite delighted, saying: "Boldly ventured is half-won."[74] When the seven Swabians make up their minds to travel about the world and seek adventures and perform great deeds, they reserve the place of honor at the front for Master Schultz, "the boldest and the bravest."[75] One of the longest of the tales is concerned with a youth who went forth to learn what fear was.[76] Little Thumbling the tiny son of a diminutive tailor, was no bigger than a thumb, "but he had some courage in him."[77]

The virtue of courage is closely associated with another dominant theme of modern nationalism: the veneration of the military spirit. Again and again the tales show that war is good, that fighting gives great moral vigor, that bearing arms is the highest of all possible honors, and that the military instinct is a blessing. There are many great deeds of valor, reminiscent of the *chansons de geste* of the Middle Ages. In ***Iron John,*** a country was overrun by war, whereupon the king gathered together all his people, and did not know whether or not he could offer resistance to the enemy, who was superior in strength. But the gardener's son came to the rescue. "When he got near the battlefield a great part of the king's men had already fallen, and little was wanting to make the rest give way. Then the youth galloped thither with his iron soldiers, broke like a hurricane over the enemy, and beat down all who opposed him. They began to fly, but the youth pursued, and never stopped, until there was not a single man left."[78] A young fellow, who enlists as a soldier, conducts himself bravely, "and was always the foremost when it rained bullets."[79] When three soldiers desert the army, they receive due punishment for it, not by the authorities but by a dragon, who turns out to be the Devil.[80]

The moral is clear: it is not wise nor desirable to desert the army. When the valiant little tailor announces that he is ready to enter the king's service as a soldier, "he was therefore honorably received and a special dwelling assigned to him."[81] "When there is order to be maintained in the kingdom, the king angrily, as is expected, orders a captain to march out with his troops."[82] Even the animals are infected with the war spirit: "when the time came for the war to begin, the willow-wren sent out spies to discover who was the enemy's commander-in-chief"[83] [the spies were gnats, who were the most crafty, and who flew into the forest where the enemy was assembled].[84] Force is accepted as normal and desirable: when a cat jumps upon her friend, the mouse, and swallows her, the story ends: "Verily, that is the way of the world."[85]

Cruelty and violence and atrocity of every kind are characteristic of the fairy tales and myths of all peoples. On a certain level of civilization punishment is meted out without any seeming relation to guilt. Thus Achilles pitilessly drags the corpse of gallant Hector ten times around the walls of Troy, and Ulysses kills his wife's suitors for no greater sin than revelling. These things are common enough. "But typical of the German fairy tale is the juxtaposition of the commonplace and the intimate with the horrors of death and all the tortures of a calculated cruelty."[86] While the king's son is busy putting on his clothes, a giant surprises him, and puts both his eyes out.[87] A king orders a witch cast into the fire and miserably burnt, while her daughter is to be taken to the forest to be torn to death by wild beasts.[88] A wicked stepmother is placed in a barrel filled with boiling oil and venomous snakes.[89] An equally wicked mother-in-law is bound to the stake and burnt to ashes.[90] The two false sisters of Cinderella have their eyes pecked out by pigeons;[91] the cook of a hunter decides to throw Fundevogel into boiling water and eat him;[92] an old woman cuts off the head of her beautiful step-daughter, whereupon drops of blood from the girl's head carry on a conversation.[93]

And so it goes, with Hansel and Gretel shoving the wicked witch into the oven for a merited cremation, bad step-mothers torn to death by wild beasts, others forced to dance in red-hot slippers, and tailors having their eyes gouged out one by one. To find a comparable obsession with vengeance and death it would be necessary to turn to ancient Egypt. But where the Egyptians linked death with elaborate ritual and a traditional piety, the characters in the ***Märchen*** challenge it in a mood of hysterical fear and revenge. Throughout the tales there is a bias toward elementary justice very much like the early Hebrew-Babylonian concept of an eye for an eye.

Much of this, of course, is typical of the primitive instincts of children, which are not very different, in the final analysis, from those of the savage. Dr. Frederic Wertham points out that the lack of respect for human life can begin in childhood in the comparative indifference to torture, mutilation, and death.[94] One of my students, Miss Bertha Pinsky, demonstrated the existence of this callousness to violence in a series of experiments with her own class of six-year-olds. Finding it difficult to maintain order among this group of pupils, she hit upon the expedient of reading the Grimms' fairy tales to them. "I was amazed to discover that I could obtain perfect silence by reading any one of the more violent tales. The children were simply fascinated. The entire class howled with delight when I read to them ***The Jew Among Thorns,*** in which an old Jew is forced to dance among thorns to the tune of a fiddle."

When these primitive sadistic and masochistic social attitudes carry over into the adult years, trouble can be expected. It is to the eternal discredit of the Nazi leaders of Germany that they elevated obscene glorifications of violence and crime into a place of authority. All the cruel pieces of the fairy tales, which had been eliminated under the Weimar Republic, were restored in Hitler's Germany, and the study of folklore was raised to a special place of honor.[95]

Still another obvious theme of the ***Märchen*** was fear of and hatred for the outsider, characteristic of primitive tribalism and modern nationalism. The stepmother is invariably a disgusting old woman who performs evil deeds with inhuman zest and cruelty. She is diabolically cunning in seeking to do away with her stepchildren. If she has any children from her first marriage, she will seek to displace her stepchildren so that her own flesh and blood will acquire the family fortune. In ***Hansel and Gretel,*** the stepmother purposely loses her stepchildren in the forest so that they will no longer be in the family.[96] A king, fearing that the stepmother of his children might not treat them well, and even do them injury, takes them to a lonely castle in the midst of a forest.[97] A little boy takes his younger sister by the hand and proclaims: "Since our mother died we have had no happiness. Our stepmother beats us every day, and if we come near her she kicks us with her foot. God pity us, if our mother only knew."[98] But when a wicked stepmother is taken before a judge, she is placed in a barrel filled with boiling oil and venomous snakes, and dies an evil death.[99] The stepmother's real crime is disruption of the family, the alienation of the children and even the father. She is an alien in the home, an outsider, a foreigner in the state. She must be hated and eliminated because she will throw the accepted order into chaos with her new ideas and foreign attitudes and methods.

The virulent type of anti-Semitism which is a concomitant of German nationalism,[100] appears often in the ***Märchen.*** It was taken as a matter of course that poverty and discontent were directly attributable to the Jew, who was "the unproductive exploiter and employer of other people's labor." The peasant suffers most from the machinations of the Jew.[101] Though the merchant is always a villain, the Jewish merchant is something more—a foreigner, the product of a strange and ancient civilization, who is universally disliked. He is a greedy moneylender who cheats his fellow man, and moreover he is a sycophant and a serio-comic villain. He is always dressed shabbily, has a yellow or gray beard, and it is plainly his fault when some honest person gets into trouble and goes to the gallows.

In ***The Bright Sun Brings it to Life*** a Jew appears as a prophet of death to a hapless tailor.[102] ***The Good Bargain*** is concerned with the struggle between a shrewd peasant and a deceitful Jew, in which the peasant says: "Ah, what a Jew says is always false—no true word ever comes out of his mouth."[103] In ***The Jew Among Thorns*** an honest and clever servant, who played a fiddle, one day meets a Jew with a long goat's beard. When the Jew, who is watching a bird in the thorn bushes, crawls into the bushes to fetch the bird, the good servant's humor leads him to take up his fiddle and play.

> In a moment the Jew's legs began to move, and to jump into the air, and the more the servant fiddled the better went the dance. But the thorns tore his shabby coat from him, combed his beard, and pricked and plucked him all over the body. "Oh, dear," cried the Jew, "what do I want with your fiddling? Leave the fiddle alone master; I do not want to dance."

> But the servant did not listen to him, and thought: "You have fleeced people often enough, now the thorn-bushes shall do the same to you"; and he began to play over again, so that the Jew had to jump higher than ever, and scraps of his coat were left hanging on the thorns.

The story concludes with a courtroom scene, in which the judge "had the Jew taken to the gallows and hanged as a thief."[104]

The effects of such tales upon generations of German youth may well be imagined. In Nazi Germany the unexpurgated fairy tales were read by children and a large part of Nazi literature designed for children was merely a modernized version of the Grimms' tales, with emphasis upon the idealization of fighting, glorification of power, reckless courage, theft, brigandage, and militarism reinforced with mysticism.[105]

It is reasonable to conclude, then, that, with their fairy tales, as well as their dictionary and grammar, the brothers Grimm contributed as much to the German revival and to German nationalism as generals, diplomats, and political figures. The place of the Grimms in the development of German nationalism was recognized a half century ago by Carl Franke:

> To the spirit of German schoolchildren the tales have become what mother's milk is for their bodies—the first nourishment for the spirit and the imagination. How German is Snow White, Little Briar Rose, Little Red Cap, the seven dwarfs! Through such genuine German diet must the language and spirit of the child gradually become more and more German. . . .

> Indeed the brothers Grimm have earned our innermost love and highest admiration as citizens and as men. For they belong doubtlessly in the broadest sense among the founders of the new German Reich. . . . They exhibited all the German virtues: the inner love of family, true friendship, the kindly love for the Hessian homeland, the inspiring love for the Fatherland. . . . With full right they earn therefore a place among Germany's greatest men.[106]

Summary and Conclusions

1. Nationalism played a vital role in the lives and works of the Grimm brothers, who were convinced that all their writings, including the fairy tales, derived their strength "from the soil of the German Fatherland."

2. From the beginning of their work the Grimm brothers took the Romantic position, closely allied with the rising German nationalism, in which they stressed the claims of the imagination, emotions, and feelings.

3. In planning and collecting the fairy tales the Grimms, consciously or unconsciously, were motivated by a desire to glorify German traditions and to stimulate German national sentiment.

4. An analysis of the ***Märchen*** gives ample evidence to show an emphasis upon such social characteristics

as respect for order, belief in the desirability of obedience, subservience to authority, respect for the leader and the hero, veneration of courage and the military spirit, acceptance without protest of cruelty, violence, and atrocity, fear of and hatred for the outsider, and virulent anti-Semitism.

5. The fairy tales thus played a significant role, hitherto little recognized outside of Germany, in the development of modern integral German nationalism. "They have enabled us to understand that we, the German people, bear the power and conditions in ourselves to take up and carry on the civilization of old times, that we are a folk with a high historical mission."[107]

A Question of Authenticity

The ***Hausmärchen*** continue to attract the attention of children everywhere as well as fascinated scholars. Some German folklore specialists are now reluctant to accept the judgment of Hermann Grimm, son of Wilhelm Grimm, that the collection of tales "spring from the soil of Germany." The most recent attempt to purge the tales of what is called romantic politicizing was made in 1976 by Heinz Rölleke, a Wüppertal Professor of German, who for many years was a lecturer at the University of Cologne. Rölleke discovered a manuscript copy of sixty-three of the original tales and compared them with the first edition of 1812.[108] His research led him to question the German origin of some of the tales as well as their very authenticity.

According to Rölleke, the ***Fairy Tales*** are not as German in spirit as has been generally accepted. The Grimm brothers had quoted "elderly peasant women from Hesse" as the main verbal source of their stories. Nineteen of the tales, they noted, came from Frau Katerina Viehmann, the wife of a tailor. "It was one of those pieces of good fortune," Wilhelm Grimm wrote in 1819, "that we got to know an old peasant woman who lived in a small village called Niederzwehrn, near Kassel, and who told us the greatest and best parts of the second volume. She was still hale and hearty, and not much over 50 years old. Her face was firm, pleasant and somehow knowledgeable, and her eyes clear and sharp. She retained the old stories in her head."[109] Further, in 1895 Hermann Grimm told of how an aged woman called "Old Marie" had told his father and uncle most of the remaining stories of the first volume, such as ***Little Red Riding Hood*** and ***The Sleeping Beauty.***

Rölleke's research revealed that Frau Viehmann[110] came from a French Huguenot family, grew up speaking French, and took some of her stories straight from Charles Perrault, a 17th-century French writer. "Old Marie" was a woman named Marie Hassenpflug, also from a Huguenot family; she was brought up in the French tradition and—far from being a peasant woman steeped in German folklore—was the wife of a president of the government. Thus, Rölleke dismisses the traditional explanation that these were genuine "Hesse folk tales" as Wilhelm Grimm had contended but rather the product of comparatively well-educated people from good families in Switzerland or other French-speaking areas. As an example he quotes the story of ***The Sleeping Beauty,*** which hitherto had been held to be particularly German. The story, concerning a princess who was put to sleep for a century by an evil fairy until she was awakened by a kiss from a prince, was told to the Grimms by "Old Marie." Rölleke insists that it is a word-for-word repetition of Perrault's *Histoires ou contes du temps passé,* a collection of French fairy tales which appeared in 1697. He cites other tales as also not reflecting the German folklore language of old peasant women.

Rölleke does not assert that the Grimms were literary swindlers who were aware of the questionable authenticity of the tales. He agrees that they listened to the two old women and that the brothers simply acted within the spirit of the times. Nevertheless, he does conclude that it is an exaggeration to say that the tales were irreproachably German and genuine.

Rölleke deserves much credit for his discovery that Frau Viehmann and "Old Marie" were of French Huguenot background and that several of the tales were French in origin. Yet this does not invalidate the theory of the importance of the tales in the development of German nationalism. Far from it. The methods of the Grimms may well have been faulty, but they endowed their tales with nationalistic bias.

The fact that Frau Viehmann and "Old Marie" were of Huguenot origin does not lessen their role in German cultural life. Historically, many Huguenots or French Protestants who fled from France after the revocation of the Edict of Nantes by Louis XIV in 1685, settled in England, America (the Carolinas, Pennsylvania, and New York), and Germany (especially in Brandenburg and the Rhineland). Of Calvinist persuasion, the Huguenots were skilled as artisans and traders, and wherever they went they constituted one of the most advanced and industrious elements in society. Invariably, they became assimilated in their new homelands, while at the same time retaining many of their old cultural forms. Undoubtedly, they brought with them folklore tales of French origin. But this does not mean that the German folk tales therefore became exclusively French.

Secondly, the Huguenots were but one element among the many ethnic and cultural groups which formed the German nationality. Neither Germans nor any other people are born with a sense of national consciousness: the need for security may be biological but national consciousness is engrained environmentally through family, school, and public life. Because the old women interviewed were of Huguenot origin does not mean that the authenticity of the tales is thereby demolished.

Finally, it is not as much the tales themselves as the *usage* made of them by the Grimms that makes them vital in the development of German romantic-nationalism. As linguistic paleontologists, the Grimms believed that their tales "sprang from the soil of Germany." That was the way they were presented. Perhaps, indeed, some of the tales came not from peasant women but from bourgeois Huguenot families. It may also be true that, despite their denials, the Grimms idealized and stylized the stories. But the two brothers always emphasized the Germanness of their tales. They gave romantic pictures of German medieval life, with its special conglomeration of kings, princes, princesses, peasants, frogs, and pumpkins. Even if Sleeping Beauty were originally French, the Grimms converted her into a fair German maiden. The motivation may well have been unconscious, but it was certainly inspired by the sentiment of nationalism.

The brothers Grimm had no idea that one day their folk tales would become the best-known German book in existence with translations into many languages throughout the world. For them the stories were particularly German and a reflection of true German folkish culture. The elements of loyalty, greed, and cunning may have common international implications, but regarded *in toto,* a special combination of German characteristics, both stereotypes and national, remain in the German versions of the tales.

Notes

[1] R. Stadelmann, "Grimm, Jakob Karl and Wilhelm Karl," in *Encyclopedia of the Social Sciences* (New York, 1937), p. 173.

[2] *Ibid.,* p. 174.

[3] R. Cleasby, *An Icelandic-English Dictionary* (Oxford, 1875), p. lxix.

[4] See Louis L. Snyder, *Race: A History of Modern Ethnic Theories* (New York, 1939), pp. 65-66.

[5] C. Spender, "Grimms' Fairy Tales," *Contemporary Review,* 102 (1912), pp. 673-679.

[6] Stadelmann, *op. cit.,* p. 174.

[7] T. Matthias, *Der deutsche Gedanke bei Jakob Grimm* (Leipzig, 1915), p. 45.

[8] *Ibid.,* p. 52.

[9] *Ibid.,* p. 48.

[10] *Ibid.,* p. 45.

[11] Jakob Grimm, *De desiderio patriae,* in *Göttinger Gelehrte Anzeigen,* November 13, 1830.

[12] Matthias, *op. cit.,* p. 46.

[13] See Veit Valentin, *The German People* (New York, 1945), pp. 407-408; S. H. Steinberg, *A Short History of Germany* (New York, 1946), p. 195; and Matthias, pp. 25-34.

[14] W. P. Ker, *Jakob Grimm* (London, 1915), p. 10.

[15] *Ibid.*

[16] Matthias, *op. cit.,* p. 49.

[17] *Ibid.,* pp. 43-57.

[18] G. P. Gooch, *History and Historians of the Nineteenth Century* 4th ed. (London and New York, 1928), p. 61.

[19] Hans Kohn, *Prophets and Peoples, Studies in Nineteenth Century Nationalism* (New York, 1946), p. 194.

[20] S. Liptzin, *From Novalis to Nietzsche* (New York, 1929), p. 4.

[21] Robert R. Ergang, *Herder and the Foundations of German Nationalism* (New York, 1931), p. 4.

[22] G. Salomon, *Das Mittelalter als Ideal in der Romantik* (Munich, 1922), pp. 46 ff.

[23] See F. Wertham, *The Show of Violence* (New York, 1929).

[24] Gooch, *op. cit.,* p. 54.

[25] J. and W. Grimm, *Fairy Tales* (New York, 1944), p. 943. Hereafter cited as *Fairy Tales.*

[26] H. Hamann, *Die literarischen Vorlagen der Kinder- und Hausmärchen und ihre Bearbeitung durch die Brüder Grimm* (Berlin, 1906), p. 8.

[27] J. Campbell, "The Work of the Grimm Brothers," in *Fairy Tales,* p. 834.

[28] Friedrich von Schiller, *Die Piccolomini,* in *Schillers Werke, herausgegeben von J. J. Fischer* (Stuttgart and Leipzig, n.d.) [The excerpt is from Act III, Scene 4, p. 317.]

[29] E. Lichtenstein, *Die Idee der Naturpoesie bei den Brüdern Grimm und ihr Verhältnis zu Herder, Vierteljahrschrift für Literaturwissenschaft und Geistesgeschichte,* vol. VI (1928), pp. 513-547; E. Laas, *Herders Einwirkung auf die deutsche Lyrik von 1770 bis 1775, Grenzboten* vol. XXX (1871), pp. 581 ff.; W. A. Berendsohn, *Grundformen volkstümlicher Erzählerkunst in der Kinder- und Hausmärchen der Brüder Grimm* (Hamburg, 1921), p. 8; and Ergang, *op. cit.,* pp. 102, 106, 114, 139, 174, 208, 234, 236, 240.

[30] Gooch, *op. cit.,* p. 56.

[31] *Ibid.,* p. 55.

[32] Campbell, *op. cit.,* pp. 835-836.

[33] Spender, *op. cit.,* p. 673.

[34] Campbell, *op. cit.,* p. 838.

[35] Stadelmann, *op. cit.,* p. 173.

[36] Campbell, *op. cit.,* p. 839.

[37] Gooch, *op. cit.,* p. 56.

[38] G. M. Priest, *A Brief History of German Literature* (New York, 1909), p. 253.

[39] Spender, *op. cit.,* pp. 673 ff.

[40] W. School, *Zur Entstehungsgeschichte der Grimm'schen Märchen, Sonderabdruck aus den Hessischen Blättern für Volkskunde,* XIX (Frankfurt am Main, 1931), *passim.* See also R. Steig, *Zur Entstehungsgeschichte der Märchen und Sagen der Brüder Grimm, Archiv für das Studium der neueren Sprachen,* vol. 107 (1901).

[41] Liptzin, *op. cit.,* p. 99.

[42] *Ibid.*

[43] H. B. Paull, *The Grimms' Fairy Tales and Household Stories.* Reviewed in *The Athenaeum,* 3148 (1888), pp. 237-239.

[44] J. Bolte and G. Polivka, *Anmerkungen zu den Kinder- und Hausmärchen der Brüder Grimm* (Leipzig, 1912-1932), vol. IV, pp. 43-44.

[45] J. and W. Grimm, *Deutsches Wörterbuch* (Leipzig, 1854), vol. I, preface.

[46] Campbell, *op. cit.,* p. 848.

[47] *Fairy Tales,* no. 172.

[48] *Ibid.,* no. 8.

[49] *Ibid.,* no. 1.

[50] *Ibid.,* no. 22.

[51] *Ibid.,* no. 83.

[52] *Ibid.,* no. 110.

[53] *Ibid.,* no. 52.

[54] *Ibid.,* no. 180.

[55] *Ibid.,* no. 102.

[56] *Ibid.,* no. 171.

[57] *Ibid.,* no. 54.

[58] *Ibid.,* no. 17.

[59] *Ibid.,* no. 94.

[60] *Ibid.*

[61] *Ibid.,* no. 106.

[62] *Ibid.,* no. 11.

[63] *Ibid.,* no. 146.

[64] *Ibid.,* no. 91.

[65] *Ibid.,* no. 94.

[66] *Ibid.,* no. 152.

[67] *Ibid.,* no. 28.

[68] *Ibid.,* nos. 19, 65, 94, 126, 128, 129, 166.

[69] V. Brun, "The German Fairy Tale," *Menorah Journal,* XXVII, pp. 147-155.

[70] *Fairy Tales,* no. 63.

[71] *Ibid.,* no. 64.

[72] *Ibid.,* no. 166.

[73] *Ibid.,* no. 101.

[74] *Ibid.,* no. 114.

[75] *Ibid.,* no. 119.

[76] *Ibid.,* no. 4.

[77] *Ibid.,* no. 45.

[78] *Ibid.*, no. 136.

[79] *Ibid.*, no. 101.

[80] *Ibid.*, no. 125.

[81] *Ibid.*, no. 20.

[82] *Ibid.*, no. 54.

[83] *Ibid.*, no. 102.

[84] *Ibid.*

[85] *Ibid.*, no. 2.

[86] Brun, *op. cit.*, pp. 153-154.

[87] *Fairy Tales,* no. 121.

[88] *Ibid.*, no. 11.

[89] *Ibid.*, no. 9.

[90] *Ibid.*, no. 49.

[91] *Ibid.*, no. 21.

[92] *Ibid.*, no. 51.

[93] *Ibid.*, no. 56.

[94] Wertham, *op. cit.*, *passim.*

[95] Brun, *op. cit.*, pp. 154-155.

[96] *Fairy Tales,* no. 15.

[97] *Ibid.*, no. 49.

[98] *Ibid.*, no. 11.

[99] *Ibid.*, no. 9.

[100] See I. Cohen, *Anti-Semitism in Germany* (London, 1918), and F. von Hellwald, *"Zur Charakteristik der jüdischen Volk," Das Ausland,* XLV (1872), pp. 951-955.

[101] S. Maccoby, "Modern Anti-Semitism," *Contemporary Review,* CXLVIII (1935), pp. 342-348.

[102] *Fairy Tales,* no. 115.

[103] *Ibid.*, no. 7.

[104] *Ibid.*, no. 110.

[105] V. Petrova and A. Vibakh, "Nazi Literature for Children," *The Living Age,* CCCXLVII (1934), pp. 365-366.

[106] Carl Franke, *Die Brüder Grimm, Ihr Leben und Wirken* (Dresden and Leipzig, 1899), pp. 40, 52, 150-151, 153.

[107] *Ibid.*

[108] This manuscript was originally owned by Clemens Brentano, who acquired it in 1810 because of his active assistance in preparing it. On his death it passed eventually to a Trappist monastery in Alsace, and from there to an auction in New York in 1953, at which time it was acquired by Martin Bodmer, a Swiss national. The Bodmer family passed it on to Rölleke, who used it for his systematic analysis of the tales.

[109] Quoted by Mathias Schreiber in *Kölner Stadt-Anzeiger,* April 17, 1976. Schreiber's article, on which this section is based, gives an excellent résumé of the Rölleke thesis.

[110] Rölleke calls her *Dorothea* instead of *Katerina* Viehmann.

Ruth B. Bottigheimer (essay date 1982)

SOURCE: "Tale Spinners: Submerged Voices in Grimms' Fairy Tales," in *New German Critique,* No. 27, Fall, 1982, pp. 141-50.

[*In the following essay, Bottigheimer, one of the tales' leading modern scholars, examines the role of spinning women in several of the stories, identifying two distinct viewpoints in the tales. According to the critic, one view, expressed by Wilhelm Grimm, extols the virtues of spinning, while the second viewpoint, representative of the original folk material, reveals the harsh and mean realities of the occupation.*]

Each generation approaches old texts with new questions. One text which has shown itself to be a rich site for shifting readership concerns is ***The Household Tales*** (***Kinder -und Hausmärchen*** [hereafter ***KHM.***]) collected by Jacob and Wilhelm Grimm. The evocative power of the collection has been reflected in the changing nature of the assumptions implicit in the criticism and interpretation of these tales over the last 100 years. Beyond their power to delight the young, the tales were perceived in the late 19th century to perform a normative function for its young readers. A generation later the National Socialists found the tales to be archetypically Germanic, and yet another generation later, the neo-Freudian Bruno Bettelheim[1] and the Jungian Hedwig von Beit[2] unearthed a different archetype, that of the lineaments of sexual maturation and psychological world view. In the last decade writers and scholars of a wide variety of social and political persuasions have undertaken revisions of these tales more in accordance with their view of society, a good overview of which can be found in Jack Zipes' "Who's Afraid of the Brothers Grimm? Socialization and Politization Through Fairy Tales."[3]

The tales can also be viewed as documents in themselves. In conjunction with parallel material which can be found above all in the first three volumes of Johannes Bolte and Georg Polivka's continuation and expansion of the Grimms' original notes to the ***KHM,***[4] the folktales—which appeared during the Grimms' lifetime in seven large and twelve small editions from 1812 to 1856—can be seen as a sourcebook for the mentality not only of the 19th century but also of former ages. Investigated in this light, each tale can be seen to consist of interpenetrating layers of narrative. A further level is that evoked in the mind of the reader which arises from the reader's own concerns, which differ again from those of Wilhelm Grimm, who edited the material, from his informants individually and severally, and from their innumerable predecessors in the oral and written tradition. I have chosen to restrict my analysis to the document itself, the tales as published in the final edition of 1856, drawing to a limited extent on variants, where doing so clarifies the thrust of the tale under consideration.

My particular interest here is the work ethic as expressed in a delimited corpus, the spinning tales. I have defined spinning tales as those in which either the act or the implements of spinning form part of the tale. This work ethic is expressed by at least two voices, the first of which is the narrative voice of Wilhelm Grimm, which purports to render faithfully the folk material gathered by himself or by his friends and colleagues. The second voice must be teased out, since it appears to have been overlaid—probably quite unintentionally—by the collating, editing, and refining undertaken by Wilhelm Grimm. Nonetheless, I believe that we can discern faint cries of distress and fatigue from the spinning room—*Spinnstube*—in the centuries preceding the Grimms' work.

The first signal perceived by the reader that the spinning tales differ from other tales in the ***KHM*** lies in the opening phrases of the tales. "Hard by a great forest dwelt a poor wood-cutter with his wife."[5] Thus begins the tale of **"Hansel and Gretel,"** and in a like manner many other tales in the ***KHM.*** There was once a miller, a soldier, a farmer, a king. These phrases are only story initiators, however, for the miller does not grind, nor does the soldier bear arms, nor the farmer plough, nor the king rule. Each of these initiators identifies a character in the tale to follow. Sometimes the story initiator identifies a queen, an old woman, a poor woman, a girl. Yet, among the 200 folk tales, of which approximately thirteen concern spinning directly or indirectly, not a single one begins: "There was once a spinner," although *Spinnerin* occasionally appears in a title. The reason appears to be that the tales grow out of an age and a place in which spinning was yet another task performed by every woman, the task that awaited her when every other household task had been finished. In this context one was not a spinner; one was a girl, a woman, a wife who spun—or who didn't want to spin. And whether or not a woman spun, and spun well, marked her in a particular way.

For the 2,500 years before the 19th century, hand spinning in Western Europe—whether with a drop spindle or with a spinning wheel—had been carried on exclusively by women (with individual exceptions, such as isolated shepherds). Its appearance in association with women is constant in western literature and the visual arts; yet, its specific association with work itself in a collection of tales takes a new tack with Wilhelm Grimm. For instance, Boccaccio did not allow work as such to obtrude in the tales told by his ladies and gentlemen of Florence in the *Decameron.* The same thing is essentially true both of the early 16th-century *Piacevoli Notti* by Straparola, where spinning appears chiefly as a mark of the lowest social level but not as a form of employment *per se,* and of Basile's collection of tales, the *Pentamerone,* produced in 1634, but not published until 1675. This orientation may only reflect the early industrialization of spinning in Italy, which began to take place in the 13th century, so that one may infer that in general in Italy only poor rural women spun, whereas north of the Alps spinning was widespread among both urban and rural women.

In England, France, Switzerland, and the Germanies in the 18th and early 19th centuries different traditions obtained. Women of both the middle and lower economic classes appear to have spun in England and Switzerland, whereas in France it was an occupation for the urban poor and for cottagers, and in the Germanies it appears to have been practiced mainly as a rural occupation. Beyond this difference in geographical and sociological locus, spinning in England, France and Switzerland appears to have been integrated into general family employment, whereas spinning in the Germanies appears to have been characterized as an occupation carried on primarily as a sexually segregated employment.

In the German tradition, Jacob Grimm asserted that "the spindle is an essential characteristic of wise women."[6] The spindle is, as the tales themselves demonstrate, not only the identifying mark of wise women, but of all women, and especially—in the Germanies from the Middle Ages to the 19th century—of diligent, well-ordered womanhood.

Unlike the tales produced for polite society such as *Contes nouvelles ou les Fées á la mode* by Madame d'Aulnoy (1698), German folk tales were assumed to have originated in or to have passed through in many cases the *Spinnstube,* for it was there that women gathered in the evening and told tales to keep themselves and their company awake as they spun. And it was from informants privy to this oral tradition that Wilhelm and Jacob Grimm gathered many of their folk tales. Thus, we can assume a personal relationship between the tales that follow and spinners themselves.

However, two voices seem to be present: one expressing dissatisfaction towards this archetypically female employment, with another voice appearing to affirm and extol spinning as a worthwhile enterprise. The latter voice, I argue, belongs to Wilhelm Grimm, through whom a 19th-century value system and its vocabulary became amalgamated with the tales as we know them today.

"The Three Spinners" exemplifies most completely the characteristics of the spinning tales taken individually or as a group. Spinning itself is the subject of this tale, which is the German expression of a tradition documented from Ireland in the West to Greece in the East and with an ancestry stretching back to the 5th century B.C. Moreover, the continued social relevance of the tales is implied by the modernization of the ancient spindle to the roughly contemporary spinning wheel, the direct agent of the girl's grief.

The tale can be understood as having an ancient lineage from its cast of characters: mother, daughter, queen, three crones, and only peripherally a prince. The prince, however, provides a further modernization in being the agent of the typical 18th-19th century happy ending—poor girl marries prince. Such a cast comes straight from the predominantly female-populated *Spinnstube.* It is related to the oldest level of the German folk tale, in which women were understood as intermediaries between men and natural forces, a theme which is evident in **"The Goosegirl"** and in the figure of **"Mother Holle."** The tale further concerns the spinning of flax, the fiber prepared and worn by the broadest segment of population in Germany.

Specific folk—and fairy—tale elements are basic to this tale. Deceit steers the plot, first when the mother lies to the queen about why her daughter is crying, second when the daughter lies to the queen, and third when the crones imply to the prince that his bride will be transformed into their collective image if she continues to spin.

The number three appears prominently: three chambers full of flax to be spun, three crones who help, three days of futile contemplation of the job, three questions put to the three crones at the wedding feast. And finally there is a promise exacted from the poor girl by the crones, the precise significance of which provides the resolution of the girl's problem at the climax of the tale.

And what does this tale recount? Private preferences and public values. The former is expressed in the opening sentence: "There was a girl who was idle and would not spin." The latter, directly contravening this statement of fact, is a lie; as the mother declares to the queen: "I cannot get her to leave off spinning. She insists on spinning for ever and ever, and I am poor, and cannot procure the flax."

Even in her mother's absence the girl cannot confess the deceit she has been made party to. No threat—as in **"Rumpelstilzchen"**—constrains the girl, for if she doesn't spin, she simply won't marry the prince (whereas the miller's daughter in **"Rumpelstilzchen"** must spin straw to gold—or die).

After the passage of three days in the tale, deliverance is magically provided. Three old women appear, benevolently offering to spin in return for an invitation to her wedding feast, their acceptance of which results in the bride's being released forever from the hated spinning.

Thus, the private preferences of the poor protagonist are recognized, validated, and incorporated into her future by creatures who banish the work ethic publicly espoused by the mother, the queen, and—by his use of the adjective, *faul* (lazy), in the opening sentence—Wilhelm Grimm himself. *Faulheit* (laziness) has triumphed over *unverdrossener Fleiss* (untiring industry), and the *geschickte und fleissige Frau* (clever and industrious wife) is an illusion created by magical forces which free the bride forever from *das böse Flachsspinnen* (the hateful flax-spinning).

Garstig (hateful), which in other tales is applied either to a lazy woman who won't spin or to the flax itself here modifies *Freundschaft* (friendship, friends) in the prince's question: "Wie kommst du zu der garstigen Freundschaft?" Knowing this, the reader first understands that the prince's use of this adjective registers his surprise that his beautiful bride should claim such ugly relatives. But we can also understand the survival of this adjective into the last edition of the ***KHM*** as an implicit commentary by the editor of the effect of the aunts' actions on the entire tale: they've protected and confirmed idleness—*garstig* indeed!

Each of the tales I have defined as a spinning tale can be analyzed similarly, using vocabulary and plot analysis in conjunction with motif and theme. The first—vocabulary analysis—leads us directly into the mental set of the 19th century as exemplified by Wilhelm Grimm, who became more and more identified with the ***KHM*** as Jacob followed other interests in his later life. The second and third directions—plot and motif—take us into the oral tradition which preceded and produced the raw material for the folk tale collection.

In many cases Wilhelm Grimm altered the language of the tales from the source to its first appearance in the ***KHM*** and thereafter from edition to edition. Vocabulary carries it own normative freight, and young readers of these tales could make no mistake about the nature of a girl who took up the work appropriate to her and did it well: she was *geschickt* (clever, skillful), *fleissig* (diligent), *schön* (beautiful), *treu* (loyal), *flink* (nimble), *arbeitsam* (industrious), and *lustig* (jolly). She also took on additional tasks like puffing up her mistress' down comforter, and she was associated with riches in the form of gold.

The two tales, **"King Thrushbeard"** and **"Rumpelstilzchen,"** include young women who would spin if they could, but either the task is impossible or they haven't been bred to it. In this case a slightly different constellation of characteristics appears, mingling those with positive and negative connotations: *schön* (beautiful), *stolz* (proud), *übermutig* (haughty) and riches in the form of gold.

On the other hand the attributes of girls who don't want to spin are an indictment in themselves: *faul, Faulheit, faulenzen* (lazy, idleness, to be lazy), *garstig* (hateful), and *bös* (ugly).

In terms of plot four sub-groups can be distinguished among the spinning tales. In the first, spinning itself is the subject of the tale. In the second, spinning functions as an indicator of the character or characteristics of the female protagonist; while in the third group, spinning as an action serves only to advance the plot. In the last group, spinning symbolizes the female sex and/or onerous tasks.

Where spinning itself is the subject of the tale, the female protagonist is unequivocal in her detestation of spinning, resorting to trickery, deceit, or supernatural powers to avoid it. Parallel tales from nearly every European country warn of the woeful consequences of spinning: hips that become too wide to pass through a doorway, lips licked away from constantly moistening the thread.[7] We are here in a predominantly female circle composed of a mother who wants her lazy daughter to spin; a queen who wants an industrious wife for her son; a daughter who hates spinning; and three wise women who help her and whom she must publicly acknowledge as her relatives (*Basen*) as part of the bargain. We see everything from the woman's point of view, and it declares that flax-spinning is evil, awful (*bös*) and the best one can do is be quit of it!

Like **"The Three Spinners," "The Lazy Spinner"** was one of the earliest tales collected by Wilhelm Grimm. No queen, no prince appears here, just a man and woman. Hard necessity requires the woman to sustain her part of the domestic economy, but she resists. When she claims she can't wind her yarn because she has no reel, her husband goes to the woods to cut her one; but she climbs the tree and—hidden by the foliage—chants down at him: He who cuts wood for reels shall die, And she who winds, shall perish. Such trickery and deception are women's weapons in a generally unyielding environment which is ultimately controlled by men because only they can promise the security which marriage offers, security which nowhere appears attainable outside of marriage.

Among those tales in which spinning functions as a character indicator, four females emerge as diligent and capable, while three are revealed to be either incompetent or lazy. Diligence incarnate doesn't vary much in its appearance, but idleness can take the form of incapacity, sloth, or deceit. For instance, the proud princess in **"King Thrushbeard"** is simply incapable of spinning flax, for her fine hands can't handle the flax fibers; and the industrious maid and her lazy mistress in **"The Hurds"** offer a familiar study in contrasts. On the other hand, the lazy, ugly daughter in **"Frau Holle"** tries to make it appear that she has spun so much that her fingers have bled, whereas in truth she has simply thrust her hand into a thorn hedge in the hope of fooling Frau Holle into believing that she, like her genuinely diligent sister, is worthy of a rich reward. That spinning itself is peripheral to this tale emerges in several ways. Although Frau Holle appears in other contexts as the special protectress of spinners, the original version of this tale in the 1812 edition contains no reference to a bloodied spindle, which derives apparently from a later informant.[8] In addition the main idea of rewarding stepsisters differentially according to their merits also appears in **"The Three Little Men in the Wood,"** which contains reference not to spinning, but to each girl's willingness to share her food with the dwarfs. Functionally, spinning in **"Frau Holle"** stands for female virtues, which are outlined in **"The Three Little Men in the Wood"** as selflessness and/or generosity, traits which in women are also associated with poverty. This complex—selflessness, generosity, women, poverty—is especially clear in **"The Goose-Girl at the Well."** Derived from *Kletke's Almanach* of 1840,[9] it contains many familiar motifs and is more highly structured than the tales rendered by Wilhelm Grimm himself. Here spinning is the symbol for and the visible attribute of the penury and personal degradation into which a princess is plunged when she is deprived of male protection. The same poverty-generosity-spinning complex emerges in **"The Spindle, the Shuttle and the Needle"** with its naive and ingenously moralistic pro-spinning ethic. In this tale, the spinning, weaving, and sewing tools are depicted as operating on their own. "It seemed as if the flax in the room increased of its own accord, and whenever she wove a piece of cloth or carpet, or had made a shirt, she at once found a buyer who paid her amply for it, so that she was in want of nothing, and even had something to share with others." This bourgeois dream of picturesque carefree cottage labor rewarded by rich patrons first appeared in Auerbacher's *Büchlein für die Jugend* in 1834[10] and was taken directly into the next edition of the ***KHM,*** where it remained in subsequent editions as a sentimental evocation of a past age symbolized by the spinning maiden. It is in stark contrast to the actual social condition of spinners in Prussia, whose very occupation made them certifiable mendicants, or in Switzerland and southern Germany, where a day's labor was paid for at a rate which did not even cover the costs of food.

In the next group of tales where spinning serves principally to advance the plot, it is also peripheral to the central theme. A characteristically female occupation—either spinning or sewing—is part of **"Little Briar-Rose"** in all its European and Near Eastern variants: in Catalonia a princess pricks her finger on a flax fiber; in the late French medieval prose novel, *Perceforest,* a tiny splinter in the first fiber pulled from the distaff causes a deep sleep; while in the Arabian story of Sittukan, a flax filament under the heroine's fingernail sends her to sleep. In eastern European variants fibers and spindles as a sleeping agent are replaced by a needle, which characterizes women's occupations much as the spindle does elsewhere. Here spinning represents a neutral value; it is merely a hinge on which the tale turns.

The other tale in this group, **"Rumpelstilzchen,"** represents an amalgamation of several traditions in its historical development into the form in which we know it. Polivka sees a relationship between it and **"The Three Spinners."**[11] "He finds the origin of both (tales) among the Germanic peoples, according to whose beliefs, elves and dwarves spin and weave, which is fostered by Frau Holde and Frikke . . . the Swedish version is the original one, in which the girl receives from the dwarf a pair of gloves with which she can spin straw to gold."[12] If Polivka is correct in this assumption, then one must posit the incorporation of another tradition which appears in many tales: offering help and/or riches in return for something young (**"The Nixie of the Mill-Pond"**), or for the first thing that greets the returning husband or father (**"The Girl Without Hands"**), or for something craved (**"Rapunzel"**). This by no means exhausts the list, but gives an indication of the variety and frequency with which this theme recurs in the ***KHM.*** Even if the historical basis for **"Rumpelstilzchen"** is to be found in the associates of a Frau Holle figure, the antagonistic mien of Rumpelstilzchen to the miller's daughter removes this tale from the tradition of the mild gracious Frau Holle. By the time Wilhelm Grimm collected it from Dortchen Wild in 1811, the plot had changed from the early one in which elves freely offered help to enable a girl to spin straw into gold to a plot in which a girl's father's false pride precipitates her into the greedy hands of a king, from whose threat of death (if she does not spin a roomful of straw into gold) she can be saved only by pledging her firstborn to the dwarf who saves her life. Frau Holle and related figures function quite differently: they reward demonstrated goodwill and diligence, whereas the dwarf, as one of the men who enter or share her life (her father, her sovereign, the dwarf) casts the miller's daughter into a perilous position. It is precisely such shifts in tradition which enable us to make inferences about the way in which minds in another age made sense of the world in which they found themselves. The benevolent assistance of a Frau Holle or of the three crones in the *Spinnstube* in the older tale is here displaced by a fearful tributary relationship to men in general.

In the last group of tales, **"Allerleirauh," "The Water-Nixie," "Tales of the Paddock," "Eve's Various Children,"** and **"The Nixie of the Mill-Pond"** spinning occupies a clearly symbolic position representing either the work appropriate to the female in the tale and/or onerous toil of the captive or poverty-stricken female.

The importance to Wilhelm Grimm of spinning for plot development emerges from a comparison of the Ölenberg MS. of 1810 with the first edition of 1812. In re-working the material for publication, he added spinning as an indication of hardship to several tales. For instance, the princess' sufferings are increased by the addition of spinning in **"King Thrushbeard."** In **"The Water-Nixie,"** the idea of two impossible tasks—filling a leaky waterbucket and hewing a tree with a blunt axe—are amplified by the interpolation in the 1812 edition of spinning flax.[13] Furthermore, although spinning exists in both of the early versions of **"Rumpelstilzchen,"** Wilhelm Grimm changed the entire motivation for the tale between 1810 and 1812. The MS. version begins: "There was once a little girl who was given a hank of flax to spin, but everything she spun was golden thread and not flax at all. She got very sad and sat on the rooftop and started spinning, and for three days she spun nothing but gold. Then a dwarf came along and said: I will help you."[14] The motivation for the entire tale shifts from the girl's being released from spinning gold (1810) to her being forced to spin gold at the risk of her life (1812): "Then the king had the miller's daughter come and commanded her to change the whole room full of straw into gold in one night, and if she couldn't do it, then she'd have to die."[15]

Spinning as an activity is characterized only once in the ***KHM,*** in **"The Three Spinners,"** where spinning is described as *bös* (ugly, awful). In other tales the fibers themselves are represented as *garstig* (hateful), and *hart* (rough, hard).

Throughout the tales the act of spinning emerges as highly undesireable despite the surface message that it will lead to riches. It identifies subjugated womanhood in **"Allerleirauh;"** it is an occupation to be escaped in **"The Lazy Spinner;"** it is also a punishment in **"The Water Nixie,"** a deforming or injurious occupation in **"The Three Spinners," "Mother Holle,"** and **"King Thrushbeard"**; and at its worst an agent of death or a curse in **"Little Briar-Rose."** Although many tales declare that spinning mediates wealth in the form of gold, it is primarily associated with poverty in **"Tales From the Paddock"** and **"The Goose-Girl at the Well."** Above all it is the archetypal employment of domesticated poverty-stricken womanhood in **"Eve's Various Children."** As Louise A. Tilly and Joan W. Scott point out in *Women, Work, and Family,* a poor widow who remarried into an economic situation considerably worse than that which her first husband offered could expect to become an agricultural field laborer or a spinner.[16]

As though to confirm the mean station occupied by spinning women in the Germanies, a Nürnberg woodcut of 1490 adjuring women to stay in their place and spin renders the spinners not in human form at all but as swine.[17] And in a traditional French tale fairies carry two immense boulders, one on their head and one in their apron, while spinning with their free hand. If they didn't have to spin, they say, they could carry four boulders, thus equating the burden of spinning with carrying two immense boulders![18]

Despite the good face that Wilhelm Grimm tried to put on spinning as a pursuit, incontrovertible internal evidence appears to tell us just the opposite. We become aware of the double message of the spinning tales themselves. In plot the tales generally convey the conventional morality of the society which produced them, while on the lexical and thematic level the subjects of these tales themselves communicate with us the reality of their experience.

This mode of articulating the social relevance of the ***Kinder- und Hausmärchen*** offers another interpretive tool in the search for a clearer understanding of the ***KHM.*** In reformulating earlier folk material Wilhelm Grimm—perhaps unwittingly—buried a message within these tales. Uncovering the manner and direction in which the material has been bent reveals not only the social interest and outlook of Wilhelm Grimm, but also of his informants.

Notes

[1] *The Uses of Enchantment* (New York: Alfred Knopf, 1976).

[2] *Die Symbolik des Märchens,* 2nd ed. (Bern: Francke Verlag, 1956-1960).

[3] *The Lion and the Unicorn,* 3 (Winter 1979-1980), pp. 4-56.

[4] *Anmerkungen zu den Kinder- und Hausmärchen der Brüder Grimm,* (1913-32; rpt. Hildesheim: G. Olms Verlag, 1963).

[5] All translations of the tales are taken from *The Complete Grimm's Fairy Tales,* trans. Margaret Flunt and James Stein (New York: Pantheon, 1944).

[6] Bolte-Polivka, I, 440.

[7] Bolte-Polivka, I, 109-114. Quoted from *Die Märchen der Brüder Grimm,* (München: Goldmann Verlag, 1957), whose text reproduces the last edition published by Wilhelm Grimm in 1856.

[8] *Ibid.,* I, p. 207.

[9] *Ibid.,* I, p. 305.

[10] *Ibid.,* III, p. 355.

[11] *Ibid.,* I, p. 437.

[12] *Ibid.,* I, p. 438.

[13] Heinz Röllecke, *Die Älteste Märchensammlung der Brüder Grimm* (Cologny-Genève: Fondation Martin Bodmer, 1975), pp. 118-119, 184-185.

[14] *Ibid.,* p. 238-239.

[15] *Ibid.,* p. 239.

[16] (New York: Holt, Rinehart, and Winston, 1978), p. 52.

[17] *History of Technology,* ed. Charles Singer and others (Oxford: Clarendon Press, 1954-58), II, p. 208.

[18] Jacob Grimm, *Deutsche Mythologie,* 4th ed. (rpt. Graz: Akademische Druck- und Verlagsanstalt, 1953), I, p. 342.

Jack Zipes (essay date 1983)

SOURCE: "Who's Afraid of the Brothers Grimm?: Socialization and Politicization through Fairy Tales," in *Fairy Tales and the Art of Subversion: The Classical Genre for Children and the Process of Civilization,* Heinemann, 1983, pp. 45-70.

[*In the following essay, Zipes examines both the social and political messages of the tales and the attempts of later German writers to adapt them according to their own political agendas. Zipes also compares three versions of such stories as "The Frog Prince" and "Snow White" to demonstrate how the Grimms edited the tales to reflect social norms and beliefs.*]

The wolf, now piously old and good,
When again he met Red Riding Hood
Spoke: 'Incredible, my dear child,
What kinds of stories are spread—they're wild.

As though there were, so the lie is told,
A dark murder affair of old.
The Brothers Grimm are the ones to blame.
Confess! It wasn't half as bad as they claim.'

Little Red Riding Hood saw the wolf's bite
And stammered: 'You're right, quite right.'
Whereupon the wolf, heaving many a sigh,
Gave kind regards to Granny and waved good-bye.

Rudolf Otto Wiemer
The Old Wolf (1976)

Over 170 years ago the Brothers Grimm began collecting original folk tales in Germany and stylized them into potent literary fairy tales. Since then these tales have exercised a profound influence on children and adults alike throughout the western world. Indeed, whatever form fairy tales in general have taken since the original publication of the Grimms' narratives in 1812, the Brothers Grimm have been continually looking over our shoulders and making their presence felt. For most people this has not been so disturbing. However, during the last fifteen years there has been a growing radical trend to overthrow the Grimms' benevolent rule in fairy-tale land by writers who believe that the Grimms' stories contribute to the creation of a false consciousness and reinforce an authoritarian socialization process. This trend has appropriately been set by writers in the very homeland of the Grimms, where literary revolutions have always been more common than real political ones.[1]

West German writers[2] and critics have come to regard the Grimms' fairy tales and those of Andersen, Bechstein, and their imitators as 'secret agents' of an education establishment which indoctrinates children to learn fixed roles and functions within bourgeois society, thus curtailing their free development.[3] This attack on the conservatism of the 'classical' fairy tales was mounted in the 1960s, when numerous writers began using them as models to write innovative, emancipatory tales, more critical of changing conditions in advanced technological societies based on capitalist production and social relations. What became apparent to these writers and critics was that the Grimms' tales, though ingenious and perhaps socially relevant in their own times, contained sexist and racist attitudes and served a socialization process which placed great emphasis on passivity, industry, and self-sacrifice for girls and on activity, competition, and accumulation of wealth for boys. Therefore, contemporary West German writers moved in a different, more progressive direction by parodying and revising the fairy tales of the eighteenth and nineteenth centuries, especially those of the Grimms.

For the most part, the 'classical' fairy tales have been reutilized or what the Germans call *umfunktioniert:* the *function* of the tales has been literally turned around so that the perspective, style, and motifs of the narratives expose contradictions in capitalist society and awaken children to other alternatives for pursuing their goals and developing autonomy. The reutilized tales *function against* conformation to the standard socialization process and are meant to *function for* a different, more emancipatory society which can be gleaned from the redirected socialization process symbolized in the new tales. The quality and radicalism of these new tales vary from author to author.[4] And it may even be that many of the writers are misguided, despite their good intentions. Nevertheless, they have raised questions about the socio-political function of fairy tales, and just this question-raising alone is significant. Essentially they reflect upon and seek to understand how the messages in fairy tales tend to repress and constrain children rather than set them free to make their own choices. They assume that the Grimms' fairy tales have been fully accepted in all western societies and have ostensibly been used or misused in furthering the development of human beings—to make them more functional within the capitalist system and to prescribe choice. If one shares a critique of capitalist society, what then should be changed in the Grimms' tales to suggest other possibilities? What sociogenetic structural process forms the fairy tales and informs the mode by which the human character is socialized in capitalist society?

Before looking at the literary endeavors made by West German writers to answer these questions, it is important to discuss the nature of the Grimms' fairy tales and the notion of socialization through fairy tales. Not only have creative writers been at work to reutilize the fairy tales, but there have been a host of progressive critics who have uncovered important historical data about the Grimms' tales and have explored the role that these stories have played in the socialization process.

I

Until recently it was generally assumed that the Grimm Brothers collected their oral folk tales mainly from peasants and day laborers, that they merely altered and refined the tales while remaining true to their perspective and meaning. Both assumptions have been proven false.[5] The Grimms gathered their tales primarily from petit bourgeois or educated middle-class people, who had already introduced bourgeois notions into their versions. In all cases the Grimms did more than simply change and improve the style of the tales: they expanded them and made substantial changes in characters and meaning. Moreover, they excluded many other well-known tales from their collection, and their entire process of selection reflected the bias of their philosophical and political point of view. Essentially, the Grimm Brothers contributed to the literary 'bourgeoisification' of oral tales which had belonged to the peasantry and lower classes and had been informed by the interests and aspirations of these groups. This is not to say that they purposely sought to betray the heritage of the common people in Germany. On the contrary, their intentions were honorable: they wanted the rich cultural tradition of the common people to be used and accepted by the rising middle classes. It is for this reason that they spent their lives conducting research on myths, customs, and the language of the German people. They wanted to foster the development of a strong national bourgeoisie by unravelling the ties to Germanic traditions and social rites and by drawing on related lore from France and central and northern Europe. Wherever possible, they sought to link the beliefs and behavior of characters in the folk tales to the cultivation of bourgeois norms.

> It was into this nineteenth century where a bourgeois sense for family had been developed that the Grimms' fairy tales made their entrance: as the book read to children by mothers and grandmothers and as reading for the children themselves. The Grimms countered the pedagogical doubts from the beginning with the argument that the fairy-tale book was written both for children and for adults, but not for the badly educated . . . The enormous amount of editions and international circulation of the Grimms' fairy tales as literary fairy tales can also be explained by their bourgeois circle of consumers. Here is where the circle closes. Aside from the questionable nature of the 'ancient Germanic' or even 'pure Hessian' character of the collection, we must consider and admire the genial talents of the Brothers, who were able to fuse random and heterogeneous material transmitted over many years into the harmonious totality of the ***Children and Household Tales.*** They were thus able to bring about a work which was both 'bourgeois' and 'German' and fully corresponded to the scientific temper and emotional taste of their times. The general room for identification provided for the bourgeoisie completely encompassed the virtues of a national way of thinking and German folk spirit, and the Grimms' ***Children and Household Tales*** contained all this in the most superb way. Its success as a book cannot be explained without knowledge of the social history of the nineteenth century.[6]

The sources of the tales were European, old Germanic, and bourgeois. The audience was a growing middle-class one. The Grimms saw a mission in the tales and were bourgeois missionaries. And, although they never preached or sought to convert in a crass manner, they did modify the tales much more than we have been led to believe. Their collection went through seven editions during their own lifetime and was constantly enlarged and revised. Wilhelm Grimm, the more conservative of the two brothers, did most of the revisions, and it is commonly known that he endeavored to clean up the tales and make them more respectable for bourgeois children—even though the original publication was not expressly intended for children. The Grimms collected the tales not only to 'do a service to the history of poetry and mythology,' but their intention was to write a book that could provide pleasure and learning.[7] They called their edition of 1819 an *'Erziehungsbuch'* (an educational book) and discussed the manner in which they made the stories more pure, truthful and just. In the process they carefully eliminated those passages which they thought would be harmful for children's eyes.[8] This became a consistent pattern in the revisions after 1819. Once the tales had seen the light of print, and, once they were deemed appropriate for middle-class audiences, Wilhelm consistently tried to meet audience expectations. And the reading audience of Germany was becoming more *Biedermeier* or Victorian in its morals and ethics. As moral sanitation man, Wilhelm set high standards, and his example has been followed by numerous 'educators,' who have watered down and cleaned up the tales from the nineteenth century up to the present.

Thanks to the 1975 re-publication of the neglected 1810 handwritten manuscript side by side with the published edition of the tales of 1812 by Heinz Rölleke, we can grasp the full import of the sanitation process in relation to socialization. We can see how each and every oral tale was conscientiously and, at times, drastically changed by the Grimms. For our purposes I want to comment on three tales to show how different types of changes relate to gradual shifts in the norms and socialization process reflecting the interests of the bourgeoisie. Let us begin with the opening of **"The Frog Prince"** and compare the 1810 manuscript with the editions of 1812 and 1857.

1810 Manuscript

The king's daughter went into the woods and sat down next to a cool well. Then she took a golden ball and began playing with it until it suddenly rolled down into the well. She watched it fall to the bottom from the edge of the well and was very sad. Suddenly a frog stuck his head out of the water and said: 'Why are you complaining so?' 'Oh, you nasty frog, you can't help me at all. My golden ball has fallen into the well.' Then the frog said: 'If you take me home with you, I'll fetch your golden ball for you.'[9]

1812 Edition

Once upon a time there was a king's daughter who went into the woods and sat down next to a cool well. She had a golden ball with her that was her most cherished toy. She threw it high into the air and caught it and enjoyed this very much. One time the ball went high into the air. She had already stretched out her hand and curled her fingers to catch the ball when it fell by her side onto the ground and rolled and rolled right into the water.

The king's daughter looked at it in horror. The well was so deep that it was impossible to see the bottom. She began to cry miserably and complain: 'Oh! I would give anything if only I could have my ball again! My clothes, my jewels, my pearls and whatever I could find in the world.' While she was complaining, a frog stuck his head out of the water and said: 'Princess, why are you lamenting so pitifully?' 'Oh,' she said, 'you nasty frog, you can't help me! My golden ball has fallen into the well.' The frog said: 'I won't demand your pearls, your jewels, and your clothes, but if you accept me as your companion, and if you let me sit next to you at your table and eat from your golden plate and sleep in your bed, and if you cherish and love me, then I'll fetch your ball for you.'[10]

1857 Edition

In olden times when making wishes still helped, there lived a king whose daughters were all beautiful, but the youngest was so beautiful that the sun itself, who has seen so much, was astonished by her beauty each time it lit upon her face. Near the royal castle there was a great dark wood, and in the wood under an old linden tree there was a well. And when the day was quite hot, the king's daughter would go into the woods and sit by the edge of the cool well. And if she was bored, she would take a golden ball and throw it up and catch it again, and this was the game she liked to play most.

Now it happened one day that the golden ball, instead of falling back into the little hand of the princess when she had tossed it up high, fell to the ground by her side and rolled into the water. The king's daughter followed it with her eyes, but it disappeared. The well was deep, so deep that the bottom could not be seen. Then she began to cry, and she cried louder and louder and could not console herself at all. And as she was lamenting, someone called to her. 'What is disturbing you, princess? Your tears would melt a heart of stone.' And when she looked to see where the voice came from there was nothing but a frog stretching his thick ugly head out of the water. 'Oh, is it you, old waddler?' she said. 'I'm crying because my golden ball has fallen into the well.' 'Be quiet and stop crying,' the frog answered. 'I can help you, but what will you give me if I fetch your ball again?' 'Whatever you like, dear frog,' she said. 'My clothes, my pearls and jewels, and even the golden crown that I'm wearing.' 'I don't like your clothes, your pearls and jewels and your golden crown, but if you love me and let me be your companion and playmate, let me sit at your table next to you, eat from your golden plate and drink from your cup, and sleep in your bed, if you promise me this, then I shall dive down and fetch your golden ball for you again.'[11]

By comparing these three versions we can see how **"The Frog Prince"** became more and more embroidered in a short course of time—and this did not occur merely for stylistic reasons. In the original folk tale of 1810 the setting is simple and totally lacking in frills. There is no castle. The incident appears to take place on a large estate. The king's daughter could well be a peasant's daughter or any girl who goes to a well, finds a ball, loses it, and agrees to take the frog home if he finds the ball for her. He has no other desire but to sleep with her. There is no beating around the bush in the rest of the narrative. It is explicitly sexual and alludes to a universal initiation and marital ritual (derived from primitive matriarchal societies), and in one other version, the princess does not throw the frog against the wall, but kisses it as in the *Beauty and Beast* tales. Mutual sexual recognition and acceptance bring about the prince's salvation. In both the 1812 and 1857 versions the princess provides more of an identification basis for a bourgeois child, for she is unique, somewhat spoiled, and very wealthy. She thinks in terms of monetary payment and basically treats the frog as though he were a member of a lower caste—an attitude not apparent in the original version. The ornate description serves to cover or eliminate the sexual frankness of the original tale. Here the frog wants to be a companion and playmate. Sex must first be sweetened up and made to appear harmless since its true form is repulsive. The girl obeys the father, but like all good bourgeois children she rejects the sexual advances of the frog, and for this she is rewarded. In fact, all three versions suggest a type of patriarchal socialization for young girls that has been severely criticized and questioned by progressive educators today, but the final version is most consistent in its *capacity* to combine feudal folk notions of sexuality, obedience, and sexual roles with bourgeois norms and attirement. The changes in the versions reveal social transitions and class differences which attest to their dependency on the gradual ascendancy of bourgeois codes and tastes.

Even the earlier French *'haute bourgeois'* values had to be altered by the Grimms to fit their more upright, nineteenth-century middle-class perspective and sense of decency. Let us compare the beginning of Perrault's *Le Petit Chaperon Rouge* with the Grimms' 1812 **"Rotkäppchen"** since the French version was their actual source.

Le Petit Chaperon Rouge (1697)

Once upon a time there was a little village girl, the prettiest that was ever seen. Her mother doted on her, and her grandmother doted even more. This good woman made a little red hood for her, and it became the girl so well that everyone called her Little Red Riding Hood.

One day her mother, having baked some biscuits, said to Little Red Riding Hood: 'Go and see how your grandmother is feeling; someone told me that she was ill. Take her some biscuits and this little pot of butter.' Little Red Riding Hood departed immediately for the house of her grandmother, who lived in another village.[12]

"Rotkäppchen" *(1812)*

Once upon a time there was a small sweet maid. Whoever laid eyes on her loved her. But it was her grandmother who loved her most. She never had enough to give the child. One time she gave her a present, a small hood made out of velvet, and since it became her so well, and since she did not want to wear anything but this, she was simply called Little Red Riding Hood. One day her mother said to her: 'Come, Red Riding Hood, take this piece of cake and bottle of wine and bring it to grandmother. She is sick and weak. This will nourish her. Be nice and good and give her my regards. Be orderly on your way and don't veer from the path, otherwise you'll fall and break the glass. Then your sick grandmother will have nothing.'[13]

In a recent article on Perrault's *Little Red Riding Hood,* Carole and D. T. Hanks Jr. have commented on the 'sanitization' process of the Grimms and later editors of this tale. 'Perrault's tale provides a classic example of the bowlderizing which all too often afflicts children's literature. Derived from the German version, **"Rotkäppchen"** (Grimm No. 26), American versions of the tale have been sanitized to the point where the erotic element disappears and the tragic ending becomes comic. This approach emasculates a powerful story, one which unrevised is a metaphor for the maturing process.'[14] The word 'emasculates' is an unfortunate choice to describe what happened to Perrault's tale (and the original folk tales) since it was the rise of authoritarian patriarchal societies that was responsible for fear of sexuality and stringent sexual codes. Secondly, Perrault's tale was not written only for children but also for an educated upperclass audience which included children.[15] The development

A scene from the animated Disney film version of the Grimm Brothers' Snow White and the Seven Dwarfs.

of children's literature, as we know, was late, and it only gradually assumed a vital role in the general socialization process of the eighteenth and nineteenth centuries. Therefore, Perrault's early tale had to be made more suitable for children by the Grimms and had to reinforce a more conservative bourgeois sense of morality. This moralistic impulse is most apparent in the changes the Grimms made at the very beginning of the tale. Little Red Riding Hood is no longer a simple village maid but the epitome of innocence. It is not enough, however, to be innocent. The girl must learn to fear her own curiosity and sensuality. So the narrative purpose corresponds to the socialization for young girls at that time: if you do not walk the straight path through the sensual temptations of the dark forest, if you are not orderly and moral (*sittsam*),[16] then you will be swallowed by the wolf, i.e, the devil or sexually starved males. Typically the savior and rebirth motif is represented by a male hunter, a father figure devoid of sexuality. Here again the revisions in word choice, tone, and content cannot be understood unless one grasps the substance of education and socialization in the first half of the nineteenth century.

Let us take one more example, a short section from the Grimms' 1810 and 1812 versions of **"Snow White."**

1810 Manuscript

When Snow White awoke the next morning, they asked her how she happened to get there. And she told them everything, how her mother the queen had left her alone in the woods and went away. The dwarfs took pity on her and persuaded her to remain with them and do the cooking for them when they went to the mines. However, she was to beware of the queen and not let anyone in the house.[17]

1812 Edition

When Snow White awoke, they asked her who she was and how she happened to get in the house. Then she told them how her mother wanted to have her put to death, but that the hunter spared her life, and how she had run the entire day and finally arrived at their house. So the dwarfs took pity on her and said: 'If you keep our house for us, and cook, sew, make the beds, wash and knit, and keep everything tidy and clean, you may stay with us, and you will have everything you want. In the evening, when we come home, dinner must be ready. During the day we are in the mines and dig for gold, so you will be alone. Beware of the queen and let no one in the house.'[18]

These passages again reveal how the Grimms had an entirely different socialization process in mind when they altered the folk tales. Snow White is given instructions which are more commensurate with the duties of a bourgeois girl, and the tasks which she performs are implicitly part of her moral obligation. Morals are used to justify a division of labor and the separation of the sexes. Here, too, the growing notion that the woman's role was in the home and that the home was a shelter for innocence and children belonged to a conception of women, work, and child-rearing in bourgeois circles more so than to the ideas of the peasantry and aristocracy. Certainly, the growing proletarian class in the nineteenth century could not think of keeping wives and children at home, for they had to work long hours in the factories. Snow White was indeed a new kind of princess in the making and was constantly remade. In the 1810 version the father comes with doctors to save his daughter. Then he arranges a marriage for her daughter and punishes the wicked queen. In the margin of their manuscript, the Grimms remarked: 'This ending is not quite right and is lacking something.'[19] Their own finishing touches could only be topped by the prudish changes made by that twentieth-century sanitation man, Walt Disney.

Aside from situating the compilation of folk tales and grasping the literary transformations within a socio-historical framework, it is even more important to investigate the pervasive influence which the Grimms have had in the socialization process of respective countries. We know that the Grimms' collection (especially the 1857 final edition) has been the second most popular and widely circulated book in Germany for over a century, second only to the Bible. We also know that the tales and similar stories are the cultural bread and basket of most children from infancy until 10 years of age. Studies in Germany show that there is a fairy-tale reading age between 6 and 10.[20] Otherwise the tales have already been read or told to the children by adults before they are 6. Incidentally, this process of transmission means that certain groups of adults are constantly re-reading and re-telling the tales throughout their lives. Ever since the rise of the mass media, the Grimms' tales (generally in their most prudish and prudent version) have been broadcast by radio, filmed, recorded for records, tapes, and video, used as motifs for advertisements, and commercialized in every manner and form imaginable. Depending on the country and relative reception, these particular tales have exercised a grip on our minds and imagination from infancy into adulthood, and, though they cannot be held accountable for negative features in advanced technological societies, it is time—as many West German writers believe—to evaluate how they impart values and norms to children which may actually hinder their growth, rather than help them to come to terms with their existential condition and mature autonomously as Bruno Bettelheim and others maintain.[21]

Here we must consider the socialization of reading fairy tales with the primary focus on those developed by the Brothers Grimm. In discussing socialization I shall be relying on a general notion of culture which is defined by the mode through which human beings objectify themselves, come together, and relate to one another in history and materialize their ideas, intentions, and solutions, in the sense of making them more concrete. By concrete I also mean to imply that there are forms people create and use to make their ideas, intentions and solutions take root in a visible, audible, and generally perceptible manner so that they become an actual part of people's daily lives. Thus, culture is viewed as an historical *process* of human objectification, and the level and quality of a national culture depends on the socialization developed by human beings to integrate young members into the society and to reinforce the norms and values which legitimize the sociopolitical systems and which guarantee some sort of continuity in society.[22]

Reading as internalization, or technically speaking as resubjectification, has always functioned in socialization processes, whether it be the conscious or unconscious 'understanding' of signs, symbols, and letters. In modern times, that is, since the Enlightenment and rise of the bourgeoisie, reading has been the passport into certain brackets of society and the measure by which one functions and maintains a certain place in the hierarchy.[23] The reading of printed fairy tales in the nineteenth century was a socially exclusive process: it was conducted mainly in bourgeois circles and nurseries, and members of the lower classes who learned how to read were not only acquiring a skill, they were acquiring a value system and social status depending on their conformity to norms controlled by bourgeois interests. The social function of reading is not to be understood in a mechanistic or reductive way, i.e., that reading was solely a safeguard for bourgeois hegemony and only allowed for singular interpretations. Certainly the introduction of reading to the lower classes opened up new horizons for them and gave them more power. Also the production of books allowed for a variety of viewpoints often contrary to the ruling forces in society. In some respects reading can function explosively like a dream and serve to challenge socialization and constraints. But, unlike the dream, it is practically impossible to determine what direct effect a fairy tale will have upon an *individual* reader in terms of validating his or her own existence. Still, the tale does provide and reflect upon the cultural boundaries within which the reader measures and validates his or her own identity. We tend to forget the socio-historical frameworks of control when we talk about reading and especially the reading of fairy tales. Both socialization and reading reflect and are informed by power struggles and ideology in a given society or culture. The Grimms' fairy tales were products not only of the struggles of the common people to make themselves heard in oral folk tales—symbolically representing their needs and wishes—but they also became *literary* products of the German bourgeois quest for identity and power. To this extent, the norms and value system which the Grimms cultivated within the tales point to an objectified, standard way of living which was intended and came to legitimate the general bourgeois standard of living and work, not only in Germany but throughout the western world.

In all there were fifty-one tales in the original manuscript of 1810. Some were omitted in the 1812 book publication, and those which were included were all extensively changed and stylized to meet middle-class taste. This process of conscious alteration for social and aesthetic reasons was continued until 1857. The recent findings which have stressed and documented this are not merely significant for what they tell us about the Grimms' method of work or the relation of the tales to late feudal and early bourgeois society in Germany. They have greater ramifications for the development of the literary fairy tales in general, especially in view of socialization through reading.

II

First of all, through understanding the subjective selection process and adaptation methods of the Grimms, we can begin to study other collections of folk tales, which have been published in the nineteenth and twentieth centuries, and analyze similar transcription methods in light of education and socialization. Recent attention has been paid to the role of the narrator of the tales in folklore research, but the role of the collector and transcriber is also significant, for we have seen how consciously and unconsciously the Grimms integrated their world views into the tales and those of their intended audience as well. The relationship of the collector to audience is additionally significant since printed and transcribed folk tales were not meant to be reinserted into circulation as books for the original audience. As Rudolf Schenda has demonstrated in *Volk ohne Buch,*[24] the lower classes did not and could not use books because of their lack of money and training. Their tradition was an oral one. The nineteenth-century and early twentieth-century transcription of folk tales was primarily for the educated classes, young and old. The reception of the tales influenced the purpose and style of the collectors. This remains true up through the present.

As I have noted, psychologists have explored the relationship between dream and fairy-tale production, and moreover they have endeavored to explore the special role which fairy tales have played in socialization. One of the most succinct and sober analyses of why the fairy tale in particular attracts children and functions so well in the socialization process has been made by Emanuel K. Schwartz. He argues that

> the struggle between what is perceived as the 'good parent' and the 'bad parent' is one of the big problems of childhood. In the fairy tale the bad mother is commonly seen as the witch (phallic mother). The great man, the father figure (Oedipus), represents the hero, or the hero-to-be, the prototype, for the young protagonist of the fairy tale. The process of social and psychological change, characteristic of the fairy tale, is childishly pursued, and magic is used to effect changes. On the other hand, experience with having to struggle for the gratification and the fulfillment of wishes results in a social adherence to and the development of an understanding of social norms and social conformities. This does not mean, however, that the reinforcement of an awareness of socialization results in submissiveness; but a certain amount of common sense, which goes into conforming with the social *mores,* is a realistic necessity for children and adults alike.[25]

To a certain extent, Schwartz minimizes the inherent dangers in such narratives as the Grimms' fairy tales which function to legitimize certain repressive standards of action and make them acceptable for children. Reading as a physical and mental process involves identification before an internalization of norms and values can commence, and identification for a child comes easily in a Grimms' fairy tale. There is hardly one that does not announce who the protagonist is, and he or she commands our identification almost immediately by being the youngest, most oppressed, the wronged, the smallest, the most naive, the weakest, the most innocent; etc. Thus, direct identification of a child with the major protagonist begins the process of socialization through reading.

Although it is extremely difficult to determine exactly what a child will absorb on an unconscious level, the patterns of most Grimms' fairy tales draw conscious attention to prescribed values and models. As children read or are read to, they follow a social path, learn role orientation, and acquire norms and values. The pattern of most Grimms' fairy tales involves a struggle for power and autonomy. Though there are marked differences among the tales, it is possible to suggest an overall pattern which will make it clear why and how they become functional in the bourgeois socialization process.

Initially the young protagonist must leave home or the family because power relations have been disturbed. Either the protagonist is wronged, or a change in social relations forces the protagonist to depart from home. A task is imposed, and a hidden command of the tale must be fulfilled. The question which most of the Grimms' tales ask is: how can one learn—what must one do to use one's powers rightly in order to be accepted in society or recreate society in keeping with the norms of the *status quo?* The wandering protagonist always leaves home to reconstitute home. Along the way the male hero learns to be active, competitive, handsome, industrious, cunning, acquisitive. His goal is money, power, and a woman (also associated with chattel). His jurisdiction is the open world. His happiness depends on the just use of power. The female hero learns to be passive, obedient, self-sacrificing, hard-working, patient, and straight-laced. Her goal is wealth, jewels, and a man to protect her property rights. Her jurisdiction is the home or castle. Her happiness depends on conformity to patriarchal rule. Sexual activity is generally postponed until after marriage. Often the tales imply a postponement of gratification until the necessary skills, power, and wealth are acquired.

For a child growing up in a capitalist society in the nineteenth and twentieth centuries, the socialization process carried by the pattern and norms in a Grimms' fairy tale functioned and still functions to make such a society more acceptable to the child. Friction and points of conflict are minimized, for the fairy tale legitimates bourgeois society by seemingly granting upward mobility and the possibility for autonomy. All the Grimms' tales contain an elaborate set of signs and codes. If there is a wrong signaled in a Grimms' fairy tale—and there is always somebody being wronged, or a relation disturbed—then it involves breaking an inviolate code which is the basis of benevolent patriarchal rule. Acceptable norms are constituted by the behavior of a protagonist whose happy end indicates the possibility for resolution of the conflicts according to the code. Even in such tales as **"How Six Travelled through the World," "Bremen Town Musicians," "Clever Gretel,"** and **"The Blue Light,"** in which the downtrodden protagonists overthrow oppressors, the social relations and work ethos are not fundamentally altered but reconstituted in a manner which allows for more latitude in the hierarchical social system—something which was desired incidentally by a German bourgeoisie incapable of making revolutions but most capable of making compromises at the expense of the peasantry. Lower-class members become members of the ruling elite, but this occurs because the ruling classes need such values which were being cultivated by the bourgeoisie—thrift, industry, patience, obedience, etc. Basically, the narrative patterns imply that skills and qualities are to be developed and used so that one can compete for a high place in the hierarchy based on private property, wealth, and power. Both command and report[26] of the Grimms' fairy tales emphasize a *process* of socialization through reading that leads to internalizing the basic nineteenth-century bourgeois norms, values, and power relationships, which take their departure from feudal society.

For example, let us consider **"The Table, the Ass and the Stick"** to see how functional it is in terms of male socialization. It was first incorporated into the expanded edition of the Grimms' tales in 1819, deals mainly with lower middle-class characters, focuses on males, and will be the basis for a discussion about a reutilized tale by F. K. Waechter. All the incidents concern master/slave relationships. Three sons are in charge of a goat, who rebels against them by lying and causing all three to be banished by their father, a tailor. After the banishment of the sons, the tailor discovers that the goat has lied. So he shaves her, and she runs away. In the meantime, each one of the sons works diligently in a petit bourgeois trade as joiner, miller, and turner. They are rewarded with gifts by their masters, but the two eldest have their gifts stolen from them by the landlord of a tavern. They embarrass the father and bring shame on the family when they try to show off their gifts which the landlord had replaced with false ones. It is up to the third son to outsmart the landlord, bring about a family reunion, and restore the good name of the family in the community through exhibiting its wealth and power. The father retires as a wealthy man, and we also learn that the goat has been duly punished by a busy bee.

Though the father 'wrongs' the boys, his authority to rule remains unquestioned throughout the narrative; nor are we to question it. The blame for disturbing the seemingly 'natural' relationship between father and sons is placed on liars and deceivers, the goat and the landlord. They seek power and wealth through devious means. The elaborated code of the tale holds that the only way to acquire wealth and power is through diligence, perseverence, and honesty. The goal of the sons is submission to the father and maintenance of the family's good name. The story enjoins the reader to accept the norms and values of a patriarchal slave/master relationship and private property relations. In general, there is nothing wrong with emphasizing the qualities of 'diligence, perseverence, and honesty' in a socialization process, but we are talking about socialization through a story that upholds patriarchal domination and the accumulation of wealth and power for private benefit as positive goals.

In almost all the Grimms' fairy tales, male domination and master/slave relationships are rationalized so long as the rulers are benevolent and use their power justly. If 'tyrants' and parents are challenged, they relent or are replaced, but the property relationships and patriarchy are not transformed. In **"The Table, the Ass and the Stick"** there is a series of master/slave relationships: father/son, patriarchal family/goat, master/apprentice, landlord/son. The sons and other characters are socialized to please the masters. They work to produce wealth and power for the father, who retires in the end because the sons have accumulated wealth in the proper, diligent fashion according to the Protestant Ethic. The goat and landlord are punished for different reasons: the goat because she resented the master/slave relationship; the landlord because, as false father, he violated the rules of private property. Although this remarkable fairy tale allows for many other interpretations, viewed in light of its function in the bourgeois socialization process, we can begin to understand why numerous West German writers began looking askance at the Brothers Grimm during the rise of the anti-authoritarian movement of the late 1960s.

III

Actually the reutilization and transformation of the Grimms' tales were not the inventions of West German writers, nor were they so new.[27] There was a strong radical tradition of rewriting folk and fairy tales for children which began in the late nineteenth century and blossomed during the Weimar period until the Nazis put an end to such experimentation. This tradition was revived during the 1960s, when such writers as Hermynia Zur Mühlen, Lisa Tetzner, Edwin Hoernle, and Walter Benjamin[28] were rediscovered and when the anti-authoritarian movement and the Left began to focus on children and socialization. One of the results of the general radical critique of capitalism and education in West Germany has been an attempt to build a genuine, non-commercial children's public sphere which might counter the exploitative and legitimizing mechanisms of the dominant bourgeois public sphere. In order to provide cultural tools and means to reutilize the present public sphere for children, groups of people with a progressive bent have tried to offset the racism, sexism, and authoritarian messages in children's books, games, theaters, tv, and schools by creating different kinds of emancipatory messages and cultural objects with and for children.

In children's literature, and specifically in the area of fairy tales, there have been several publishing houses which have played an active role in introducing reutilized fairy tales created to politicize the children's public sphere, where children and adults are to cooperate and conceive more concrete, democratic forms of play and work in keeping with the needs and wishes of a participating community.[29] Obviously the rise of a broad left-oriented audience toward the end of the 1960s encouraged many big publishers to direct their efforts to this market for profit, but not all the books were published by giant companies or solely for profit. And, in 1982, when the so-called New Left is no longer so new nor so vocal as it was during the late 1960s, there are still numerous publishing houses, large and small, which are directing their efforts toward the publication of counter-cultural or reutilized fairy-tale books and children's literature. My discussion will limit itself and focus on the reutilized Grimms' tales published by Rowohlt, Basis, Schlot, and Beltz & Gelberg. In particular I shall endeavor to demonstrate how these fairy tales reflect possibilities for a different socialization process from standard children's books.

In 1972 the large Rowohlt Verlag established a book series for children entitled *'rororo rotfuchs'* under the general editorship of Uwe Wandrey. An impressive series was developed and now contains a wide range of progressive children's stories, histories, autobiographies, handbooks, and fairy tales for young people between the ages of 4 and 18. Here I want to concentrate on two of the earlier and best efforts to reutilize old fairy tales.

Friedrich Karl Waechter, illustrator and writer,[30] has written and drawn numerous politicized fairy tales and fairy-tale plays for children. One of his first products, *Tishlein deck dich und Knüppel aus dem Sack* (*Table Be Covered and Stick Out of the Sack,* 1972) is a radical rendition of the Grimms' **"The Table, the Ass, and the Stick."** His story takes place in a small town named Breitenrode a long time ago. (From the pictures the time can be estimated to be the early twentieth century.) Fat Jakob Bock, who owns a large lumber mill and most of the town, exploits his workers as much as he can. When a young carpenter named Philip invents a magic table that continually spreads as much food as one can eat upon command, Bock (the name means ram in German) takes over the invention and incorporates it since it was done on company time. He promises Philip his daughter Caroline if he now invents a 'stick out of the sack'—the power Bock needs to guard his property. Philip is given the title of inventor and put to work as a white-collar worker separating him from his friends, the other carpenters, who had helped him build the magic table. At first Philip and his friends are not sure why Bock wants the stick, but an elf named Xram (an anagram for Marx spelled backwards) enlightens them. They decide to work together on this invention and to keep control over it. But, when it is finished, Bock obtains it and plants the magic table as stolen property in the house of Sebastien, a 'trouble-maker', who always wants to organize the workers around their own needs. Bock accuses Sebastien of stealing the table and asserts that he needs the stick to punish thieves like Sebastien and to protect his property. However, Philip exposes Bock as the real thief, and the greedy man is chased from the town. Then the workers celebrate as Philip announces that the magic table will be owned by everyone in the town while Xram hides the stick. The final picture shows men, women, children, dogs, cats, and other animals at a huge picnic sharing the fruits of the magic table while Bock departs.

Like the narrative itself, Waechter's drawings are intended to invert the present socialization process in West Germany. The story-line is primarily concerned with private property relations, and it begins traditionally with the master/slave relationship. The ostensible command of the tale—'obey the boss and you'll cash in on the profits'—is gradually turned into another command—'freedom and happiness can only be attained through collective action and sharing.' The narrative flow of the tale confirms this reversed command, and the reading process becomes a learning process about socialization in capitalist society. Philip experiences how the fruits of collective labor expended by himself and his friends are expropriated by Bock. With the magical help of Xram (i.e., the insights of Marx) the workers learn to take control over their own labor and to share the fruits equally among themselves. Here the master/slave relationship is concretely banished, and the new work and social relationships are based on cooperation and collective ownership of the means of production. The virtues of Philip and the workers—diligence, perseverence, imagination, honesty—are used in a struggle to overcome male domination rooted in private property relations. Socialization is seen as a struggle for self-autonomy against exploitative market and labor conditions.

In Andreas and Angela Hopf's *Der Feuerdrache Minimax* (*The Fire Dragon Minimax*, 1973), also an illustrated political fairy tale,[31] the authors use a unique process to depict the outsider position of children and strange-looking creatures and also the need for the outsider to be incorporated within the community if the community is to develop. The Hopfs superimpose red drawings of Minimax and the little girl Hilde onto etchings of medieval settings and characters.[32] The imposition and juxtaposition of red figures on black and white prints keep the reader's focus on contrast and differences. The narrative is a simple reutilization of numerous motifs which commonly appear in the Grimms' tales and associate dragons, wolves, and other animals with forces of destruction endangering the *status quo*. *The Fire Dragon Minimax* demonstrates how the *status quo* itself must be questioned and challenged. The story takes place during the Middle Ages in the walled town of Gimpelfingen. While sharpening his sword, the knight causes sparks to fly, and the town catches fire. There is massive destruction, and the dragon is immediately blamed for the fire, but Hilde, who had fled the flames, encounters Minimax, who had been bathing in the river when the fire had begun. So she knows that he could not have caused the fire. In fact, he helps extinguish part of the fire and then carries Hilde to his cave since he prefers to roast potatoes with his flames and sleep for long hours rather than burn down towns. The knight pretends to fight in the interests of the town and accuses Minimax of starting the fire and kidnapping Hilde. He darns his armor and goes in search of the dragon, but he is no contest for Minimax, who overwhelms him. The knight expects the dragon to kill him, but Minimax tells him instead to take Hilde home since her parents might be worried about her. Again the knight lies to the townspeople and tells them that he has rescued Hilde and killed the dragon. Hilde tries to convince the people that he is lying, but she is only believed by a handful of people who fortunately decide to see if Minimax is alive or dead. Upon finding him, they realize the truth and bring Minimax back to town. This causes the knight to flee in fear. Minimax is welcomed by the townspeople, and he helps them rebuild the town. Thereafter, he remains in the town, roasts potatoes for the children or takes them on rides in the sky. Hilde is his favorite, and he flies highest with her and often tells her fairy tales about dragons.

Obviously the Hopfs are concerned with racism and militarism in this tale. The dragon represents the weird-looking alien figure, who acts differently from the 'normal' people. And the Hopfs show how the strange and different creature is often used by people in power as a scapegoat to distract attention from the real enemy, namely the people in power. In contrast to the dominant master/slave relationship established in the medieval community, Hilde and the dragon form a friendship based on mutual recognition. Their relationship is opposed to the dominant power relationship of male patriarchy in the town. In terms of problems in today's late capitalist society, the tale also relates to feminism and the prevention of cruelty to animals. The activism of Hilde on behalf of the dragon sets norms of behavior for young girls, when she asserts hereself and uses her talents for the benefit of oppressed creatures in the community. As in Waechter's politicized fairy tale, the textual symbols of goal-oriented behavior are aimed at cooperation and collectivism, not domination and private control.

The publishing house which has been most outspoken in behalf of such general socialist goals in children's culture has been Basis Verlag in West Berlin. Working in a collective manner, the people in this group have produced a number of excellent studies on fairy tales and children's literature,[33] as well as a series of different types of books for young readers. Here I want to remark on just one of their fairy-tale experiments entitled *Zwei Korken für Schlienz* (*Two Corks for Schlienz,* 1972) by Johannes Merkel based on the Grimms' tale **"How Six Travelled through the World."** The reutilized fairy tale deals with housing difficulties in large cities, and the text is accompanied by amusing photos with superimposed drawings. Four young people with extraordinary powers seek to organize tenants to fight against an exploitative landlord. Ultimately, they fail, but in the process they learn, along with the readers, to recognize their mistakes. The open ending suggests that the four will resume their struggle in the near future—this time without false illusions.

Most of the tales in *Janosch erzählt Grimm's Märchen* (*Janosch Tells Grimm's Fairy Tales,* 1972) are intended to smash false illusions, too, but it is not so apparent that Janosch has a socialist goal in mind, i.e., that he envisions collective living and sharing as a means to eliminate the evils in the world.[34] He is mainly concerned with the form and contents of fifty Grimms' tales which he wants to parody to the point of bursting their seams. He retells them in a caustic manner using modern slang, idiomatic expressions, and pointed references to deplorable living conditions in affluent societies. Each tale endeavors to undo the socialization of a Grimms' tale by inverting plots and characters and adding new incidents. Such inversion does not necessarily amount to a 'happier' or more 'emancipatory' view of the world. If Janosch is liberating, it is because he is so humanely candid, often cynical, and disrespectful of conditioned and established modes of thinking and behavior. For instance, in **"The Frog Prince"** it is the frog who loses his ball and is pursued by a girl. The frog is forced by his father to accept the annoying girl in the subterranean water palace. Her pestering, however, becomes too much for him, and he suffocates her. This causes her transformation into a frog princess whereupon she marries the frog prince and explains to him how she had been captured by human beings and changed herself into an ugly girl to escape malicious treatment by humans. Her ugliness prevented other humans from marrying her and allowed her to return to her true form.

Such an inversion makes a mockery of the Grimms' tale and perhaps makes the reader aware of the potential threat which humans pose to nature and the animal world. This point can be argued. But what is clear from the story is that Janosch fractures the social framework of audience expectations, whether or not the readers are familiar with the original Grimms' tales. The numerous illustrations by Janosch are just as upsetting, and the tales derive their power by not conforming to the socialization of reading the Grimms' tales as harmless stories. His anarchistic, somewhat cynical rejection of the Grimms and the norms they represent is related to his rejection of the hypocritical values of the new rich in post-war Germany created by a so-called 'economic miracle'. For instance, in **"Puss 'n Boots,"** a marvelous cat exposes his young master Hans to the emptiness and meaninglessness of high society. When Hans experiences how rich people place more stock in objects than in the lives of other people, he decides to abandon his dreams of wealth and success and to lead a carefree life on a modest scale with the cat. This is not to say that the cat or Hans are model characters or point to models for creating a new society. They are symbols of refusal, and by depicting such refusal, Janosch seeks to defend a 'questioning spirit,' which is totally lacking in the Grimms tales and very much alive in his provocative *re-visions,* where everything depends on a critical new viewpoint.

One of Janosch's major supporters of re-visions is Hans-Joachim Gelberg, who has been one of the most important proponents for the reutilization of the Grimms' tales and the creation of more politicized and critical stories for children and adults. Gelberg edits special yearbooks, which include various types of experimental fairy tales and have received prestigious awards in West Germany,[35] for Gelberg has pointed in new directions for a children's literature that refuses to be infantile and condescending. In addition to the yearbooks, Gelberg has published a significant volume of contemporary fairy tales entitled *Neues vom Rumpelstilzchen und andere Haus-Märchen von 43 Autoren,* 1976.[36] Since there are fifty-eight different fairy tales and poems, it is difficult to present a detailed discussion of the reutilization techniques in regard to socialization in the tales. Generally speaking, the direction is the same: a wholesale rethinking and reconceptualization of traditional fairy-tale motifs to question standard reading and rearing processes. Since the title of the book features *Rumpelstiltskin,* and since the motto of the book—'No, I would rather have something living than all the treasures of the world'—is taken from his tale, I shall deal with the two versions of *Rumpelstiltskin* by Rosemarie Künzler and Irmela Brender[37] since they represent the basic critical attitude of most of the authors.

Both Künzler and Brender shorten the tale drastically and take different approaches to the main characters. Künzler begins by stressing the boastful nature of the miller who gets his daughter into a terrible fix. She is bossed around by the king and then by some little man who promises to help her by using extortion. When the little man eventually barters for her first-born child, the miller's daughter is shocked into her senses. She screams and tells the little man that he is crazy, that she will never marry the horrid king, nor would she ever give her child away. The angry little man stamps so hard that he causes the door of the room to spring open, and the miller's daughter runs out into the wide world and is saved. This version is a succinct critique of male exploitation and domination of women. The miller's daughter allows herself to be pushed around until she has an awakening. Like Janosch, Künzler projects the refusal to conform to socialization as the first step toward actual emancipation.

Brender's version is different. She questions the justice in the Grimms' tale from Rumpelstiltskin's point of view, for she has always felt that the poor fellow has been treated unfairly. After all, what he wanted most was something living, in other words, some human contact. She explains that Rumpelstiltskin did not need money since he was capable of producing gold any time he wanted it. He was also willing to work hard and save the life of the miller's daughter. Therefore, the miller's daughter could have been more understanding and compassionate. Brender does not suggest that the miller's daughter should have given away the child, but as the young queen, she could have invited Rumpelstiltskin to live with the royal family. This way Rumpelstiltskin would have found the human companionship he needed, and everyone would have been content. The way things end in the Grimms' version is for Brender totally unjust. Her technique is a play with possibilities to open up rigid social relations and concern about private possession. Through critical reflection her narrative shifts the goal of the Grimms' story from gold and power to justice and more humane relations based on mutual consideration and cooperation.

Both Künzler and Brender seek a humanization of the socialization process by transforming the tales and criticizing commodity exchange and male domination, and they incorporate a feminist perspective which is at the very basis of an entire book entitled *Märchen für tapfere Mädchen* (*Fairy Tales for Girls with Spunk,* 1978) by Doris Lerche, illustrator, and O.F. Gmelin, writer.[38] They use two fictitious girls named Trolla and Svea and a boy named Bror from the North to narrate different types of fairy tales which purposely seek to offset our conditioned notions of sexual roles and socialization. For instance, the very beginning of *Little Red Cap* indicates a markedly different perspective from the Grimms' version: 'There was once a fearless girl. . . . '[39] She is not afraid of the wolf, and, even though she is swallowed by him in her grandmother's bed, she keeps her wits about her, takes out a knife, cuts herself a hole in his stomach while he sleeps, and rescues herself and granny. In Gmelin's rendition of *Hans and Gretel,* the poor parents are not the enemies of the children, rather poverty is the source of trouble. To help the parents, the children go into the woods in search for food and eventually they become lost. Then they encounter a woman who is no longer a witch, but an outcast who has learned to live by the brutal rule of the land set by others. Hans and Gretel overcome the obstacles which she places in their quest for food, but they do not punish her. They are more concerned in re-establishing strong bonds of cooperation and love with their parents. The children return home without a treasure, and the ending leaves the future fate of the family open.

IV

The open endings of many of the reutilized fairy tales from West Germany indicate that the future for such fairy tales may also be precarious. Given the social import and the direct political tendency of the tales to contradict and criticize the dominant socialization process in West Germany, these tales are not used widely in schools, and their distribution is limited more to groups partial to the tales among the educated classes in West Germany. They have also been attacked by the conservative press because of their 'falsifications' and alleged harmfulness to children. Nevertheless, the production of such tales has not abated in recent years, and such continuous publication may reflect something about the diminishing appeal of the Grimms' tales and the needs of young and adult readers to relate to fantastic projections which are connected more to the concrete conditions of their own reality.

Folk tales and fairy tales have always been dependent on customs, rituals, and values in the particular socialization process of a social system. They have always symbolically depicted the nature of power relationships within a given society. Thus, they are strong indicators of the level of civilization, that is, the essential quality of a culture and social order. The effectiveness of emancipatory and reutilized tales has not only depended on the tales themselves but also on the manner in which they have been received, their use and distribution in society. The fact that West German writers are arguing that it is time for the Brothers Grimm to stop looking over our shoulders may augur positive changes for part of the socialization process. At the very least, they compel us to reconsider where socialization through the reading of the Grimms' tales has led us.

Notes

[1] It has always been fashionable to try to rewrite folk tales and the classical ones by the Grimms. However, the recent trend is more international in scope, not just centered in Germany, and more political in intent. For some examples see, Jay Williams, *The Practical Princess and other Liberating Fairy Tales* (London: Chatto & Windus, 1979); Astrid Lindgren, *Märchen* (Hamburg: Oetingen, 1978), which first appeared in Swedish; *The Prince and the Swineherd, Red Riding Hood, Snow White* by the Fairy Story Collective (Liverpool, 1976), three different publications by four women from the Merseyside Women's Liberation Movement. I shall

discuss this international trend in my final chapter, 'The liberating potential of the fantastic in contemporary fairy tales for children.'

[2] My focus is on the development in West Germany only. The official attitude toward fairy tales in East Germany has gone through different phases since 1949. At first they were rejected, but more recently there has been a favorable policy, so long as the tales do not question the existing state of affairs. Thus, the older fairy tales by the Grimms are accorded due recognition while reutilization of the tales in a manifest political manner critical of the state and socialization is not condoned. See Sabine Brandt. 'Ropkäppchen und der Klassenkampf,' *Der Monat,* 12 (1960), pp. 64-74.

[3] See Dieter Richter and Jochen Vogt (eds), *Die heimlichen Erzieher, Kinderbücher und politisches Lernen* (Reinbek bei Hamburg: Rowohlt, 1974) and Linda Dégh, 'Grimms' household tales and its place in the household: the social relevance of a controversial classic,' *Western Folklore,* 38 (April 1979), pp. 83-103.

[4] See Erich Kaiser, ' "Ent-Grimm-te" Märchen,' *Westermanns Pädagogische Beiträge,* 8 (1975), pp. 448-59, and Hildegard Pischke, 'Das veränderte Märchen,' *Literatur für Kinder,* ed. by Maria Lypp (Göttingen: Vandenhoeck & Ruprecht, 1977), pp. 94-113.

[5] See Heinz Rölleke's introduction and commentaries to the 1810 manuscript written by the Grimms in *Die älteste Märchensammlung der Brüder Grimm* (Cologny-Geneva: Fondation Martin Bodmer, 1975); Werner Psaar and Manfred Klein, *Wer hat Angst vor der bösen Geiss?* (Braunschweig: Westermann, 1976), pp. 9-30; Ingeborg Weber-Kellermann's introduction to *Kinder- und Hausmärchen gesammelt durch die Brüder Grimm,* Vol. I (Frankfurt and Main: Insel, 1976), pp. 9-18.

[6] Weber-Kellermann, *Kinder- und Hausmärchen gesammelt durch die Brüder Grimm,* Vol. I, p. 14.

[7] *I bid.*, pp. 23-4. This is taken from the 1819 preface by the Brothers Grimm.

[8] *Ibid.*, p. 24.

[9] Rölleke (ed.), *Die älteste Märchensammlung der Brüder Grimm*, p. 144. Unless otherwise indicated, all the translations in this chapter are my own. In most instances I have endeavored to be as literal as possible to document the historical nature of the text.

[10] *Ibid.*, p. 145.

[11] *Kinder- und Hausmärchen gesammelt durch die Brüder Grimm,* pp. 35-6.

[12] *Contes de Perrault,* ed. by Gilbert Rouger (Paris: Garnier 1967), p. 113.

[13] Brüder Grimm, *Kinder- und Hausmärchen. In der ersten Gestalt.* (Frankfurt am Main, 1962), p. 78.

[14] 'Perrault's "Little Red Riding Hood": victim of revision,' *Children's Literature,* 7 (1978), p. 68.

[15] For the best analysis of Perrault and his times, see Marc Soriano, *Les Contes de Perrault* (Paris: Gallimard, 1968).

[16] The word *sittsam* is used in the 1857 edition and carries with it a sense of chastity, virtuousness, and good behavior.

[17] *Die älteste Sammlung der Brüder Grimm,* pp. 246, 248 (op. cit., note 5).

[18] *Ibid.,* pp. 249, 251.

[19] *Ibid.,* p. 250.

[20] Psaar and Klein, *Wer hat Angst vor der bösen Geiss?* pp. 112-36.

[21] See *The Uses of Enchantment: The Meaning and Importance of Fairy Tales* (New York: Knopf, 1976). For a critique of Bettelheim's position, see James W. Heisig, 'Bruno Bettelheim and the fairy tales,' *Children's Literature,* 6 (1977). pp. 93-114, and my own criticism in the chapter, 'On the use and abuse of folk and fairy tales: Bruno Bettelheim's moralistic magic wand,' in *Breaking the Magic Spell: Radical Theories of Folk and Fairy Tales* (London: Heinemann, 1979), pp. 160-82.

[22] Helmut Fend, *Sozialisation durch Literatur* (Weinheim: Beltz, 1979), p. 30, remarks:

> 'Socialization proves itself to be a process of resubjectification of cultural objectifications. In highly complex cultures and societies this involves the learning of complex sign systems and higher forms of knowledge as well as the general comprehension of the world for dealing with natural problems and the general self-comprehension of human beings. Through the process of resubjectification of cultural objectifications, structures of consciousness, that is, subjective worlds of meaning, are constructed. Psychology views this formally as abstraction from particular contents and speaks about the construction of cognitions, about the construction of a 'cognitive map,' or a process of internalization. In a depiction of how cultural patterns are assumed in a substantive way, the matter concerns what conceptions about one's own person, which skills and patterns or interpretations, which norms and values someone takes and accepts in a certain

culture relative to a sub-sphere of a society. Generally speaking, what happens in the socialization process is what hermeneutical research defines as 'understanding'. Understanding is developed and regarded here as an interpretative appropriation of linguistically transmitted meanings which represent socio-historical forms of life. To be sure, this understanding has a differentiated level of development which is frequently bound by social class.'

[23] See Richard Hoggart, *The Uses of Literacy* (London: Chatto & Windus, 1957).

[24] Frankfurt am Main: Klostermann, 1970.

[25] Emanuel K. Schwartz, 'A psychoanalytical study of the fairy tale,' *American Journal of Psychotherapy,* 10 (1956), p. 755. See also Julius E. Heuscher, *A Psychiatric Study of Fairy Tales* (Springfield, Illinois: Thomas, 1963).

[26] The terms are from Victor Laruccia's excellent study, 'Little Red Riding Hood's metacommentary: paradoxical injunction, semiotics, and behavior,' *Modern Language Notes,* 90 (1975), pp. 517-34. Laruccia notes (p. 520) that,

> all messages have two aspects, a command and a report, the first being a message about the nature of the relationship between sender and receiver, the second the message of the content. The crucial consideration is how these two messages relate to each other. This relationship is central to all goal-directed activity in any community since all human goals necessarily involve a relation with others.

Laruccia's essay includes a discussion of the way male domination and master/slave relationships function in the Grimms' tales.

[27] See Dieter Richter (ed.), *Das politische Kinderbuch* (Darmstadt: Luchterhand, 1973). A writer such as Kurd Lasswitz began creating political fairy tales at the end of the nineteenth century. One of the first collections of political fairy tales published during the Weimar period is Ernst Friedrich (ed.), *Proletarischer Kindergarten* (Berlin: Buchverlag der Arbeiter-Kunst-Ausstellung, 1921), which contains stories and poems as well.

[28] All these writers either wrote political fairy tales or wrote about them during the 1920s and early part of the 1930s. One could add many other names to this list, such as Ernst Bloch, Bruno Schönlank, Berta Lask, Oskar Maria Graf, Kurt Held, Robert Grötzsch, and even Bertolt Brecht. The most important fact to bear in mind, aside from the unwritten history of this development, is that the present-day writers began to hark back to this era.

[29] See my article 'Down with Heidi, down with Struwwelpeter, three cheers for the revolution: towards a new children's literature in West Germany,' *Children's Literature,* 5 (1976), pp. 162-79.

[30] Waechter is one of the most gifted writers and illustrators for children in West Germany today. He is particularly known for the following books: *Der Anti-Struwwelpeter* (1973), *Wir können noch viel zusammenmachen* (1973), *Die Kronenklauer* (1975), and *Die Bauern im Brunnen* (1978).

[31] The publisher of *Der Feuerdrache Minimax* is Rowohlt in Reinbek bei Hamburg. Angela Hopf has written several interesting books which are related to political fairy tales: *Fabeljan* (1968), *Die grosse Elefanten-Olympiade* (1972), *Die Minimax-Comix* (1974), and *Der Regentropfen Pling Plang Pling* (1981).

[32] For a thorough and most perceptive analysis of this book, see Hermann Hinkel and Hans Kammler, 'Der Feuerdrache Minimax—ein Märchen?—ein Bilderbuch,' *Die Grundschule,* 3 (1975), pp. 151-60.

[33] Among the more interesting studies related to the fairy tale are: Dieter Richter and Johannes Merkel, *Märchen, Phantasie und soziales Lernen* (Berlin: Basis, 1974); Andrea Kuhn, *Tugend und Arbeit. Zur Sozialisation durch Kinder- und Jugendliteratur im 18. Jahrhundert* (Berlin: Basis, 1975); Andrea Kuhn und Johannes Merkel, *Sentimentalität und Geschäft. Zur Sozialisation durch Kinder- und Jugendliteratur im 19. Jahrhundert* (Berlin: Basis, 1977).

[34] The publisher of *Janosch erzählt Grimms Märchen* is Beltz & Gelberg in Weinheim. Janosch, whose real name is Horst Eckert, is considered one of the most inventive and provocative illustrators and writers for young people in West Germany. Among his many titles, the most important are: *Das Auto heisst Ferdinand* (1964), *Wir haben einen Hund zu Haus* (1968), *Flieg Vogel flieg* (1971), *Mein Vater ist König* (1974), *Das grosse Janosch-Buch* (1976), *Ich sag, du bist ein Bär* (1977), *Oh, wie schön ist Panama* (1978), *Die Maus hat rote Strümpfe an* (1978).

[35] A good example is *Erstes Jahrbuch der Kinderliteratur. 'Geh und spiel mit dem Riesen,'* ed. by Hans-Joachim Gelberg (Weinheim: Beltz, 1971), which won the German Youth Book Prize of 1972.

[36] Many of the tales were printed in other books edited by Gelberg, or they appeared elsewhere, indicative of the great trend to reutilize fairy tales.

[37] Translations of the tales by Brender and Künzler have been published in my book *Breaking the Magic Spell,* pp. 180-2.

[38] Gmelin, in particular, has been active in scrutinizing the value of fairy tales and has changed his position in

the course of the last eight years. See Otto Gmelin, 'Böses kommt aus märchen,' *Die Grundschule,* 3 (1975), pp. 125-32.

[39] Lerche and Gmelin, *Märchen für tapfere Mädchen* (Giessen: Schlot, 1978), p. 16.

John M. Ellis (essay date 1983)

SOURCE: "Introduction: The Problem of the Status of the Tales," in *One Fairy Story Too Many: The Brothers Grimm and Their Tales,* University of Chicago Press, 1983, pp. 1-12.

[*In the following excerpt, Ellis examines the changes the Grimm brothers made to their source material, arguing that the Grimms' nationalism motivated them to promote the tales as specifically German in origin, despite strong evidence to the contrary.*]

The Grimms' fairy tales—***Kinder- und Hausmärchen*** (***KHM***) constitute one of the best-known and most loved books in the world; translated into dozens of languages, they are read by children and adults everywhere.[1] There are perhaps two different kinds of contexts within which they are read and enjoyed: the first, that of world children's literature, the second that of the folklore and folk literature of Germany in particular and Europe in general. In both contexts, they are thought of as stories told by the simpler German people to their children, and passed on from one generation to the next in this way until recorded for all time by the brothers Grimm. But this widespread view, common to laymen and scholars alike, is in fact based on serious misconceptions, and in this book [*One Fairy Story Too Many*] I want to set out a very different view of the status of the tales.

The first step in this reexamination of the status of the ***KHM*** must be to turn our attention away from the familiar kinds of present-day context in which we think of them—those of children's books, and German folklore—and back to the context in which they arose, the cultural scene of early nineteenth-century Germany; for the stresses and strains of that original context produced distortions and misconceptions that have been at work ever since.

The first volume of the ***KHM*** appeared in 1812, in an era extraordinarily rich in the great names of German literature and of German culture generally. The age of German romanticism had followed so quickly on the heels of German classicism that the two had overlapped in large measure; in 1812 writers alive and active included Goethe, Hölderlin, Tieck, Hoffmann, Brentano, Arnim, Eichendorff, the Schlegel brothers, and the Grimms; Kleist had died only the previous year, Schiller, Novalis, and Herder a few years previously. Similarly, German philosophy and music were both at a peak. But this cultural brilliance was a very recent phenomenon, and in fact the result of a drastic transformation; only a few decades before, Germany had been suffering from a cultural poverty which was just as remarkable as the soon-to-follow richness. So sudden a transformation inevitably brought strains and distortions, and those strains are very much involved in the outlook of the Grimms and therefore in the origins of the ***KHM.***

Once before, around the year 1200, Germany had had a glorious period when half a dozen of the greatest figures in the history of German literature were active. But as those great writers died off, a long period of relative cultural poverty set in which lasted for many centuries; between the years 1200 and 1800 there is scarcely a writer who can stand with even the second rank of those who were active in these two great eras. While France, England, and Italy had long since developed brilliant literatures, the German renaissance had been almost barren. It is impossible completely to account for this strange phenomenon, but several historical circumstances clearly contributed to it. To begin with, Germany was unified very late in comparison to the other great European powers; until late in the nineteenth century, it remained a hodgepodge of small independent states. It lacked (and still lacks to this day) a single, dominant cultural center of the magnitude of Paris or London. Another important factor was linguistic: no standard language emerged until the end of the Middle Ages, and so for a long time there was no linguistic vehicle for the formation of a national literature. In fact, there was no single dialect with an unbroken literary tradition of any real length; in Old High German times, the leading literary dialect had been the dialect of the west central area close to the Rhine, but in the High Middle Ages (circa 1200) preeminence passed to the Upper German dialects of the south, and in the modern period leadership passed again to the east central district of Saxony, as a compromise standard language based on the dialect of that area slowly took hold. In each case, the tradition of former literary dialects was interrupted, and they were relegated to merely regional status. A third major factor was the repeated devastation of Germany during the Thirty Years' War (1618-48)—a crucial period in the development of modern Europe, during which cultural progress in Germany was held up. Almost every European power took part in the Thirty Years' War, but it was fought largely on German soil. The line of battle went up and down Germany and then back again, so that the same area was devastated again and again at intervals of a few years, as one side advanced and then retreated over it. These three decades might have been Germany's renaissance.

Whatever the reasons, however, Germany in the mid-eighteenth century was culturally backward compared to its neighbors, and consequently afflicted by a national cultural inferiority complex—a circumstance that was to shape and to some extent misshape the character of the great revival soon to come. Germany at this time looked enviously at the culture of its neighbors; even so great a German patriot and national hero as Frederick the Great, king of Prussia, despised the German language, spoke and wrote in French, and was so convinced of the great superiority of French literature and culture generally that even when Mozart and Goethe arrived on the scene, he thought little of them.

As the astonishing transformation began to take place between 1770 and 1780, with the appearance of Lessing, Herder, Goethe, Schiller, Haydn, Mozart, and Kant, to be followed by many more great figures in the next few decades, two paths seemed possible for German culture, and from the start there was ambivalence about the choice. The first was to look to European culture: to look, to learn, to some extent to emulate and to borrow, to come up to its standards, and in general to aim to become a worthy member of the family of European cultures. This became the predominant way of the great writers of German classicism. But there was another possibility: to stress the uniqueness of German culture, its specifically German character with its own laws and rules, its own standards and goals.

At the beginning, the resurgence of German culture had seemed to take the second path. The writers of the *Sturm und Drang* ("Storm and Stress") group, which included Herder and the young Goethe, firmly rejected the rather feeble neoclassicism which had prevailed in early eighteenth-century Germany and had advocated a literature based on Aristotle's theories as interpreted by the classic French writers. Instead, the Sturm und Drang took the position that Germany's art should be a reflection of its own culture, and express its own genius in its own unique way. Transcultural standards could not be used to judge any one culture's products; what was really important was the relationship of the whole people to those products. Such was the tenor of the 1773 manifesto of the movement, *Blätter von deutscher Art und Kunst* ("On the German way of life and German art"), to which Goethe contributed an essay on German architecture (praising the Gothic rather than classical style); Justus Möser one on German history, much concerned to argue for Germany as a nation, in spite of its weak and utterly fragmented state in 1773; and Herder essays on Shakespeare—whom he praised as an original and unique genius who broke all the narrow rules of neoclassicism (particularly French neoclassicism)—and on folk poetry, particularly Ossian as an expression of the spirit of an ancient people through its primitive poetry. In this last, it is already possible to see the setting emerge for the later activities of the brothers Grimm.

Yet the Sturm und Drang was soon over; Goethe and Schiller became the leading figures of German classicism, and the emphasis shifted to a broader concern with mankind and literature in general, rather than the narrower preoccupation with the characteristic quality of German culture. By 1795, it might have seemed that the Sturm und Drang had been largely an expression of the national cultural inferiority complex, and that a more mature and confident culture no longer needed to be so concerned to make a case for itself. But just as Germany seemed firmly to have chosen the one path over the other, there came a sudden reversal of direction: in the middle of the last decade of the century, the German romantics appeared on the scene, and the strong nationalism that predominated in this movement made that of the Sturm und Drang seem moderate by comparison. The earlier group was evidently arguing from a position of weakness the case for a culture that was then undeveloped; but the romantics appeared in the middle of a brilliant cultural scene, and their patriotism could hardly be so nervous in character. It was generally quite the reverse—exuberant and confident. To take one example: Möser's essay on German history had been a rational plea for Germany as a nation; but when the romantic Friedrich von Hardenberg wrote (under the pseudonym of Novalis) *his* essay on the history of Germany, *Die Christenheit oder Europa* ("Christendom, or Europe"), it expressed an almost mystic view of the medieval German nation of the Holy Roman Empire as a Christian utopia. Möser and his contemporaries were struggling to put a depressed Germany on the European map; but for Novalis, Germany dominated the European map. With the romantics came a sudden, heady sense of the brilliance of German culture; a nation which had been a poor relation in Europe suddenly reveled not in equality but in preeminence.

Enormously influential and long-lasting attitudes and directions in German culture and scholarship were formed at this time: many of these dominated the nineteenth century and reached into the twentieth. From this period dates the notion that Germany is *the* nation of music. Similarly, the common idea of Germany as the preeminent nation in philosophy arises from the domination of Europe by the philosophy of Hegel until the rise of the analytic movement in the twentieth century. German philological scholarship, initiated at this time, dominated European thinking on the study of language until structuralism began to make an impact toward the middle of the twentieth century. Indeed, German scholars like Jacob Grimm were the founders of the discipline of philology.

The romantics' concern with German culture led in many directions: to an interest in folksongs; to the study of Germanic legends and folklore; to a rediscovery of the national past, including particularly the glorious national literature of the Middle Ages; to the study of the national language and its place in the European family of languages; and so on. But in all of this, German nationalism was a major factor.

Jacob Grimm (1785-1863) and his brother Wilhelm (1786-1859) were very much part of this environment. Enormously active and productive scholars, they made many contributions to the study of German culture apart from their fairy tale collection: notably, a collection of German legends, their famous dictionary of the German language, and Jacob's historical work on the German language. "Grimm's law" is still a landmark in the explanation of how an Indo-European dialect developed into the Germanic group of languages. And all of this was done quite consciously in a spirit of devotion to their fatherland, as countless passages in the brothers' letters make clear.

Such, then, is the general cultural context in which the Grimms' ***Kinder- und Hausmärchen*** arose. Jacob and Wilhelm presented the ***KHM*** to their public essentially as a monument of national folklore. In so doing they were making claims about their sources and their treatment of those sources (a reasonably faithful recording of folk material, with little or no editorial contribution on their part) which . . . were fraudulent. But this was not mere idiosyncratic behavior; there were strong contemporary currents moving the Grimms in this direction, and those currents are the ultimate source of the half-truths and untruths which have accompanied the ***KHM*** from that day to this. Having said this, however, I must add an important caveat: the mood of the times did not determine this situation to the extent that the Grimms innocently followed contemporary ideas without realizing they were themselves distorting the truth; it will become clear that they consciously and deliberately misrepresented what they had done, and deceived their public.

Before it is possible to appreciate what the Grimms really did in publishing their ***KHM,*** we must first consider what at the time they seemed to be doing, and what since that time they have generally been thought to have done; from this, the central issues and principles involved in the appearance of the ***KHM*** will emerge.

At the time of the first publication of the ***KHM,*** the Grimms appeared to be breaking new ground, and that impression has always remained, regardless of changes of emphasis caused by any of the evidence which appeared later on.

Johann Karl August Musäus had published *Volksmärchen der Deutschen* ("Popular fairy tales of the Germans," 1782-87) some thirty years before the brothers Grimm published their fairy tales (1812-15), but a crucial difference between the two seemed immediately visible; while Musäus, tales are simply announced as being by Musäus, the Grimms offered theirs as ***Kinder- und Hausmärchen, Gesammelt durch die Brüder Grimm*** **("Children's and household fairytales, collected by the Brothers Grimm")**. Musäus wrote his tales, but the Grimms apparently collected theirs.

Herder's essay *Ossian und die Lieder alter Völker* ("Ossian and the songs of ancient peoples," 1773)[2] had led the way toward an interest in folk culture in Germany, and in the following decades there was much collecting of folk material: folksongs, legends, folktales, and fairy tales. But while Herder began this movement, its manifestations were not always in the spirit he had intended. His interest was in the direct and natural expression of folk literature as an antidote to the pedantry of neoclassicism, and he therefore valued its unschooled quality and its direct and unreflective language as a vehicle of genuine feeling.

The contrast between the Grimms and Musäus appeared to exemplify a deep difference between those who preserved Herder's attitude to the integrity of the folk material, and those who simply wished to use it for their own purposes. Musäus considered the tales which formed the basis for his text as mere raw material, which had to be reworked by the artist before it achieved real value. In his prefatory essay, he appeals to his reader to decide whether he, Musäus, has been successful in creating from this raw material a real work of art: "whether, then, the author in reworking this raw material has succeeded as his neighbor the sculptor does, who with skillful hand produces, from a clumsy marble cube through the work of his hammer and chisel, now a god, now a demigod or spirit, which sits resplendently in the art galleries, while previously it was only a common piece of masonry."[3] Evidently, Musäus lacked that respect for the inherent eloquence of folk material which made Herder write that "unspoiled children, women, people of good common sense, formed more by activity than by abstract philosophizing—these are, if what I was talking of is eloquence, in that case the sole and best orators of our time."[4] Musäus's use of words like "common" or "clumsy" to refer to folk material would have been unthinkable for Herder.

Achim von Arnim and Clemens Brentano published a folk-song collection—*Des Knaben Wunderhorn* ("The boy's magic horn," 1805-8)—and Brentano by himself some volumes of *Märchen,* but their attitudes were much closer to those of Musäus than of Herder. "The credentials of folk-poetry as a source of new poetic vigour lay in its authenticity," writes a recent scholar, "yet Arnim and Brentano freely adapted, polished, archaized, rewrote, and even slipped in poems of their own with faked 'sources' (all to the deep chagrin of the Grimm brothers who were simultaneously collecting German folk-tale and legend . . .)."[5]

The Grimms, indeed, appeared to reach back to Herder for their attitudes. They announced themselves, on the title page of the ***KHM,*** as collectors rather than writers, and they too wrote disparagingly of the plainness of written language when contrasted with the vigor and color of the folk storyteller's expression. Or so it seemed.

Almost immediately, something happened which was an embarrassment to the position the Grimms had claimed for the ***KHM;*** in 1819 the preface to the second edition of the ***KHM*** seemed to retreat from the position taken by those of the two first edition volumes of 1812 and 1815. And, indeed, this proved to be only the first of a long series of similar embarrassments, details of which I shall consider in later chapters. But these embarrassments had remarkably little effect, and even today their importance is not fully grasped either in popular opinion or in the scholarship on the ***KHM.*** The reason for this is obvious enough. Very soon after their publication, the ***KHM*** became one of the most loved books in the world. A standard view of the provenance of the tales emerged, which itself became a story as charming and as loved as any of the tales themselves; and, more importantly, it was just as durable, and like any fairy story just as immune to subversion by any consciousness of the facts of the real world. Here is a typical and recent formulation of that tale: the Grimms, we are told, "spent much of their time wandering about the country, gleaning from peasants and the simpler townspeople a rich harvest of legends, which they wrote down as nearly as possible in the words in which they were told."[6]

Now this is, just like the other tales, a fairy story without a word of truth in it—but one with an irresistible appeal both in popular belief and even in scholarly opinion. For what is truly remarkable here is not just that it can be shown to be quite false, but that the evidence of easily available published sources made a large part of this general view dubious more than a hundred and fifty years ago, and all of the rest of it completely untenable more than fifty years ago—long before Heinz Rölleke's republication of some of the most important of this evidence, valuable though Rölleke's editions have been in spreading an awareness that all was not well with the popular view.[7] Yet it survives though all indications have long been to the contrary; and it is possible to see at work a determination that it should survive. When, for example, scholars have come across individual facts that were inconsistent with the popular view, we shall see that they have commonly either ignored them or tried to explain them away and draw the narrowest possible conclusions from them. As a result, many opportunities for a complete reevaluation have been avoided.

There has even been a striking reluctance on the part of those who have known most about the relevant sources either to see the force of any new evidence they brought to light or, at least, to communicate any awareness of possible significance. A particularly striking demonstration of this reluctance could be seen in the years 1970-71, when no less than four full-length biographies of the brothers appeared—by Michaelis-Jena, Gerstner, Peppard, and Denecke.[8] Even at this late date, not one of these scholars offered any serious challenge to the basic outline of the popular view, though mention is made of individual pieces of evidence which should have led in that direction; and often, as we shall see, they resorted to highly implausible ideas in order to avoid the impact of the evidence. Clearly, the general mood of scholarship has been a remarkably inhibited one. Perhaps the most important consequence of this climate was that the discovery of any one discrepancy between the facts and the popular view was able to remain an isolated discovery instead of serving as a warning to scholars that others might also exist. Yet the strangest aspect of all in this situation is that the popular misconception has its origin not in faulty scholarship or careless scholars but, rather, in deception by the Grimms themselves. It is as well to be aware at the outset of some important corollaries to and extensions of the popular view which show that a good deal is at stake in its being upheld as true, or even more or less true. A number of scholars, for example—justifiably enough, if the facts indeed are as they have assumed them to be—have attributed to the ***KHM*** and to the Grimms a considerable importance in the general history of folklore studies. And, again, these views continue to be heard today, long after it should be obvious that the facts will not support them. Joseph Campbell is a typical example:

> The special distinction of the work of Jacob and Wilhelm Grimm was its scholarly regard for the sources. Earlier collectors had felt free to manipulate folk materials; the Grimms were concerned to let the speech of the people break directly into print . . . No one before the Grimms had readily acquiesced to the irregularities, the boorishness, the simplicity of the folk tale. Anthologists had arranged, restored, and tempered; poets had built new masterpieces out of the rich raw material. But an essentially ethnographical approach, no one had so much as conceived.[9]

Even as late as 1974, the well-known scholars Iona and Peter Opie concurred in this view: "The Grimms were . . . the first to write the tales down in the way ordinary people told them, and not attempt to improve them; and they were the first to realize that everything about the tales was of interest, even including the identity of the person who told the tale."[10] This leads to an important conclusion about the Grimms; they are, if all this is true, the founders of the "scientific study of folklore and folk literature."[11] Ruth Michaelis-Jena, writing recently in the journal *Folklore,* took essentially the same view, seeing the Grimms as "the true begetters of *Märchenforschung* (fairy tale research), pioneers and unique seen in the context of their time"; and she too praised the Grimms' "scientific method," and their "emphasis on the story-teller."[12] To the reader of the most recent published commentary on the Grimms, it must seem that such views are ineradicable, for even writers who have been exposed to and shaken by some of the strong contrary evidence republished during the 1970s continue almost mechanically to express them once more. Linda Dégh, for example, writing in 1979, after expressing surprise at what had recently appeared in print—though nobody who had kept up with the record of what had been in print a quarter of a century earlier should have been surprised—still goes on to tell us, as so many previous writers have done, that the Grimms "established a new discipline: the science of folklore. Their example of collecting oral literature launched general fieldwork."[13]

More indicative still of the continuing currency of this view is an article in the very latest edition of that repository of received opinion, the *Encyclopaedia Britannica.* The author of the article is Ludwig Denecke, former head of the Brothers Grimm Museum in Kassel and author of many books on the Grimms, who maintains that the ***KHM*** "became and remains a model for the collecting of folktales everywhere," and that it is still "the earliest 'scientific' collection of folktales" having aimed at "a genuine reproduction of the teller's words and ways."[14]

One consequence of the popular view, then, would be a unique importance for the Grimms as folklorists. Another consequence would be a very special status for the tales within German culture. For if it is true, as the best-selling history of German literature puts it, that the Grimms "collected them from the mouth of the common people"[15]—then it would seem also to be true that, as J. G. Robertson says, the tales reflect "the mind of the German Volk,"[16] providing a key to some of its characteristic attitudes and feelings.[17]

Historians of folklore commonly see matters in the same way; Giuseppe Cocchiara, in his *The History of Folklore in Europe,* thinks the ***KHM*** important because "it preserves the beliefs of ancient Germanic peoples."[18]

It is important to understand why the Grimms' alleged emphasis on the identity and voice of the "storyteller" is so important a part of the basis of these judgments. Many if not most fairy tales are either international in their scope or at least incorporate figures, motifs, or situations which can be found in the tales of many countries. Versions of many of the tales in the ***KHM,*** for example, can be found in the *Histoire ou Contes du temps passé avec des moralités* (1697) of Charles Perrault and *Il Pentamerone* (1634-36) of Gianbattista Basile. What is specifically *German* in the character of the ***KHM*** would have to reside precisely in the *particular* version or flavor of a given tale, and this is why the actual expression of the version told in Germany is so important; it is the specific form, more than the story outline itself, that will be of value for the study of German folklore.

There is much at stake in the popular view, therefore, and this surely gives us another reason for the reluctance of scholars to question it. Even when contrary evidence was becoming well known, and had to be dealt with, it was minimized with formulations such as that of the Opies: "They did not always adhere to the high standards they set themselves"; or Michaelis-Jena: "The brothers had taken it upon themselves to make slight, and what they considered justified, changes."[19] Gerstner brushed the troublesome facts aside with evident impatience. The Grimms, he said, did not want "to change anything essential, or to falsify anything"; nevertheless, "they did not want a slavish reproduction of what they had heard from this or that woman."[20] To question the Grimms' procedure was, for him, simply unreasonable quibbling. To be sure, the odd lapse here or there, or fairly unimportant stylistic changes, need not undermine the general validity of the popular view; we might even, with Kurt Schmidt, excuse it by reminding ourselves of the great difference between modern ethnographic standards and those of the early nineteenth century: "Present-day thinking about the recording of folk traditions is stricter, and it could see the Grimms' conception (actually Wilhelm's) almost as falsification. For the Grimms' era, however, it meant a significant step forwards in the conceptual framework of the discipline."[21] Gerstner developed this point further: "For those born later, it would have been an easy thing to capture the story-telling in shorthand or on tape."[22] If we accept this reassurance, we can go back to enjoying our fairy tale.

Yet the evidence is of far more radical import than this would imply; . . . the changes introduced by the Grimms were far more than mere stylistic matters, and . . . the facts of their editorial procedure, taken together with the evidence as to their sources, are sufficient completely to undermine any notion that the Grimms' fairy tales are of folk, or peasant, or even German origin. And the facts also show the Grimms' attempts to foster these illusions. . . .

Notes

[1] *Kinder- und Hausmärchen, Gesammelt durch die Brüder Grimm*, 2 vols. (Berlin, 1812 and 1815). The six subsequent editions of the Grimms' collection supervised by them were published in 1819, 1837, 1840, 1843, 1850 and 1857 respectively. The second and third editions (1819 and 1837) contained a third volume in addition to the two volumes of all the other

editions; this third volume contains notes to the tales and the dates of these volumes are 1822 (second edition) and 1856 (third edition) respectively. In the first edition, much briefer notes had been included at the end of each of the two volumes. Because of the long delay in the issue of the third edition's third volume, it became virtually a part of the seventh edition. In the course of this study, I cite the text of the first edition of the *KHM* as reprinted in *Die Kinder- und Hausmärchen der Brüder Grimm. Vollständige Ausgage in der Urfassung*, edited by Friedrich Panzer (Wiesbaden, 1953), itself virtually a reprint of his earlier edition in two volumes (Munich, 1913), apart from new material in the introduction. A thorough and detailed analysis of the differences in the gross contents of the various editions (stories added or subtracted; different prefaces, etc.) can be found in Crane 1917.

[2] Johann Gottfried Herder, "Auszug aus einem Briefwechsel über Ossian und die Lieder alter Völker," in Herder 1773. I cite this essay in the edition by Heinz Kindermann, in the series *Deutsche Literatur: Reihe Irrationalismus*, 6 (Darmstadt, 1968), 149-89.

[3] I cite Musäus's *Volksmärchen der Deutschen* in the edition of the Winkler-Verlag (Munich, 1961), here p. 13. This edition erroneously gives the dates of Musäus's *Volksmärchen* as 1782-86, probably because Musäus published the tales in five volumes at the rate of one a year, and that would seem to indicate 1782-86 as the correct dates. However, Musäus missed a year (1785); the dates of the five volumes were 1782, 1783, 1784, 1786 and 1787.

[4] "Über Ossian," Herder 1773, p. 168.

[5] Reed 1972, p. 520.

[6] From the anonymous preface of the *Grimm's Fairy Tales* (Anon. 1968).

[7] Rölleke 1975b. See also Rölleke 1977. See chapters 3 and 4 of the present work for discussion of this material.

[8] Michaelis-Jena 1970; Gerstner 1970; Peppard 1971; Denecke 1971. The justification for the summary statements on these works and others made in this introductory chapter will emerge during the rest of my study.

[9] Campbell 1944, pp. 834-35. In her original translator's preface to the 1901 edition, Margaret Hunt had written that "they wrote down every story exactly as they heard it."

[10] Opie and Opie 1974, p. 26.

[11] Ibid., p. 27.

[12] Michaelis-Jena 1971, pp. 265, 268.

[13] Dégh 1979, p. 87.

[14] Ludwig Denecke, "Grimm Brothers," in *the New Encyclopaedia Britannica*, 15th ed., *Macropaedia* 8 (1980): 427-29.

[15] Martini 1955, p. 322.

[16] Robertson 1953, p. 457.

[17] Louis L. Snyder (1951) proceeded to investigate their significance, given this assumption. He found in them "many sentiments typical of German nationalism . . . which . . . existed among the old peasants, nurses, and workers from whom the Grimms obtained their material" (p. 216). This conclusion, too, is based on misconception; in chapter 6 I consider the conclusions Snyder draws from his analysis of the *KHM.*

[18] Cocchiara 1981, p. 231.

[19] Opie and Opie 1974, p. 26; Michaelis-Jena 1971, p. 166. See also Michaelis-Jena 1970, p. 52: "They wrote down the stories as close to the original as possible, including peculiarities of the teller's turn of phrase and speech."

[20] Gerstner 1970, p. 92.

[21] Schmidt 1931, p. 81. For a similar view, see Panzer 1953, p. 50. Also Michaelis-Jena 1970, p. 52; they were "purely scientific within the limits of their time."

[22] Gerstner 1970, p. 92. . . .

Maria M. Tatar (essay date 1986)

SOURCE: "Born Yesterday: Heroes in the Grimms' Fairy Tales," in *Fairy Tales and Society: Illusion, Allusion, and Paradigm,* edited by Ruth B. Bottigheimer, University of Pennsylvania Press, 1986, pp. 95-114.

[*In the following essay, Tatar examines both heroes and heroines in* Grimm's Fairy Tales, *arguing that, contrary to "conventional wisdom," the protagonists (males in particular) are neither strong nor clever but rather "simple," "silly," "foolish," and "useless."*]

> There comes an old man with his three sons—
> I could match this beginning with an old tale.
>
> —Shakespeare, *As You Like It*

Identifying fairy tale heroes by name is no mean feat. In the Grimms' collection, only one in every ten actually has a name. But it is also no secret that the most celebrated characters in fairy tales are female. Cinderella, Snow White, Little Red Riding Hood, and Sleeping Beauty: these are the names that have left so vivid an imprint on childhood memories. With the exception of Hansel, who shares top billing with his sister, male protagonists are exceptionally unmemorable in name, if not in deed. Lacking the colorful descriptive sobriquets that accord their female counterparts a distinctive identity, these figures are presented as types and defined by their parentage (the miller's son), by their station in life (the prince), by their relationship to siblings (the youngest brother), by their level of intelligence (the simpleton), or by physical deformities ("Thumbling").[1]

Most people may be at a loss when it comes to naming fairy tale heroes, but few have trouble characterizing them. "In song and story," writes Simone de Beauvoir, "the young man is seen departing adventurously in search of woman; he slays the dragon, he battles giants." And what are this young man's attributes? One commentator on the Grimms' collection describes him as "active, competitive, handsome, industrious, cunning, acquisitive." That list sums up the conventional wisdom on the dragon-slayers and giant-killers of fairy tale lore.[2]

That conventional wisdom proves, however, to be a fairy tale so far as German folklore is concerned. A reading of the first edition of the ***Nursery and Household Tales*** reveals that there are exactly two dragon-slayers and only one giant-killer in the entire collection of more than 150 tales.[3] One of those stories, **"Johannes-Wassersprung and Caspar-Wassersprung"** rehearses the classic story of the slaying of a seven-headed dragon and the liberation of a princess, but (for unknown reasons) that tale never did make it to the second edition of the ***Nursery and Household Tales.*** The other dragon-slaying hero bears the distinctly unheroic name **"Stupid Hans"** (**"Dummhans"**), and the contest in which he dispatches three dragons, each with a different number of heads, is less than gripping. As for the one giant-killer, he succeeds in decapitating three giants, but only because the proper sword is placed directly in his path. if there is any attribute that these heroes share, it is naiveté. Like so many other heroes in the Grimms' collection, they are decidedly unworldly figures. "Innocent," "silly," "useless," "foolish," "simple," and "guileless": these are the actual adjectives applied again and again to fairy tale heroes in the Grimms' collection.

Among folklorists, it is the fashion to divide heroes into two separate and distinct classes. There are active heroes and passive heroes, "formal heroes" and "ideal heroes," dragon-slayers and male Cinderellas, tricksters and simpletons.[4] In theory, the oppositions active/passive, seeker/victim, and naive/cunning seem to serve as useful guides for classifying fairy tale heroes. But in practice it is not always easy to determine whether a hero relies on his own resources or depends on helpers. Does he have a zest for danger or does he simply weather the various adventures that befall him? Just what is his level of intelligence? What at first blush appear to be perfectly straight-forward choices are in the end fraught with complexities. The happy-go-lucky simpleton who appears to succeed without trying is, for example, not always as doltish as his name or his reputation in the village would lead us to believe, and the roguish trickster does not always live up to his reputation for shrewd reasoning.

There is a further complication. Despite their seeming artlessness, fairy tales are not without occasional ironic touches that subvert surface meanings. In particular, the epithets and predicates reserved for their protagonists can highlight utterly uncharacteristic traits. The eponymous heroine of **"Clever Else"** ranks high on the list of dull-witted characters; the tale **"Hans in Luck"** charts a steady decline in its hero's fortunes; and the courageous tailor in the tale of that title displays more bravado than bravery.[5] In the world of fairy tales, a simpleton can easily slip into the role of the cunning trickster; a humble miller's son can become a king; and a cowardly fool can emerge as a stout-hearted hero. Character traits display an astonishing lack of stability, shifting almost imperceptibly into their opposites as the tale unfolds. Bearing this in mind, let us take the measure of male protagonists in the Grimms' collection to determine what character traits they share and to assess the extent to which the plots of their adventures possess a degree of predictability.

If the female protagonists of fairy tales are often as good as they are beautiful, their male counterparts generally appear to be as young and naive as they are stupid. Snow White's stepmother may be enraged by her stepdaughter's superior beauty, but the fathers of male heroes are eternally exasperated by the unrivaled obtuseness of their sons. To the question, Who is the stupidest of them all? most fairy-tale fathers would reply: my youngest son. Yet that son is also the chosen son, the son who ultimately outdoes his older and wiser siblings. In an almost perverse fashion, fairy tales featuring male protagonists chart the success story of adolescents who do not even have the good sense to heed the instructions of the many helpers and donors who rush to their aid in an attempt to avert catastrophes and to ensure a happy ending. "You don't really deserve my help," declares one such helper in frustration after his sage advice has been disregarded on no less than three occasions.[6]

In fairy tales the world over, the least likely to succeed paradoxically becomes the most likely to succeed. Merit rarely counts; luck seems to be everything. Aladdin, the prototype of the undeserving hero who succeeds in living happily ever after, begins his rise to wealth and power under less than auspicious circumstances. The introductory paragraphs of his tale give the lie to the view that classical fairy tales reward virtue and punish evil. "Once upon a time," so the story of "Aladdin and the Enchanted Lamp" begins, "there lived in a certain city of China an impoverished tailor who had a son called Aladdin. From his earliest years this Aladdin was a headstrong and incorrigible good-for-nothing." When he grows older, he refuses to learn a trade and persists in his idle ways until his father, "grieving over the perverseness of his son," falls ill and dies. Yet this same Aladdin, who becomes ever more wayward after sending his father to the grave, ultimately inherits a sultan's throne. As one critic correctly points out, the story of Aladdin and his enchanted lamp exalts and glorifies a figure who stands as "one of the most undeserving characters imaginable." It is telling that Aladdin could make his way easily from the pages of German translations of the *Thousand and One Nights* into the oral narratives of one region in Germany. Once his exotic name was changed to "Dummhans," he was quickly assimilated into Pomeranian folklore—so much so that it was difficult to distinguish him from native sons.[7]

The heroes of the ***Nursery and Household Tales*** may, for the most part, be unlikely to win prizes for intelligence and good behavior, but they are even less likely to earn awards for courage. Their stories chronicle perilous adventures, but they themselves often remain both cowardly and passive. When summoned to discharge the first in a series of three tasks, the simpleton in the tale known as **"The Queen Bee"** simply sits down and has a good cry. In **"The Three Feathers,"** the hero sits down and "feels sad" instead of rising to the challenges posed by his father. Fairy tale heroines have never stood as models of an enterprising spirit, but it is also not rare for fairy tale heroes to suffer silently and to endure hardships in a hopelessly passive fashion.

For all their shortcomings, the simpletons in the Grimms' fairy tales do possess one character trait that sets them apart from their fraternal rivals: compassion. That compassion is typically reserved for the natural allies and benefactors of fairy tale heroes: the animals that inhabit the earth, the waters, and the sky.[8] Even before the simpleton embarks on a journey to foreign kingdoms or undertakes various tasks to liberate a princess, he must prove himself worthy of assistance from nature or from supernatural powers by displaying compassion. Of the various tests, tasks, and trials imposed on the hero, this first test figures as the most important, for it establishes the privileged status of the young simpleton. Once he exhibits the virtue of compassion—with its logical concomitant of humility—he can do virtually no wrong, even when he violates interdictions, disregards warnings, and ignores instructions. This preliminary test, a test of the hero's character, comes to serve the dual function of singling out the hero from his brothers and of furnishing him with potential helpers for the tasks that lie ahead.

Two fairy tales from the Grimms' collection illustrate the extent to which compassion is rewarded. In **"The Queen Bee,"** the youngest of three sons defends an ant hill, a bevy of ducks, and a beehive from the assaults of his mischievous brothers. "Leave the animals alone," he admonishes his elders on three occasions. Compassion pays off in the end, for this youngest of three sons is also the only one to escape being turned to stone—a punishment that perfectly suits the crimes of his callous siblings. With the help of his newly won allies, the simpleton of the family discharges three "impossible" tasks spelled out for him on a stone slab. He gathers a thousand pearls that lie strewn about the forest; he fetches a bedroom key from the sea's depths; and he succeeds in identifying the youngest of three "completely identical" sisters. Or, to be more precise, the ants gather the pearls, the ducks fetch the key, and the bees identify the youngest sister. Yet the simpleton is credited with disenchanting the palace in which the trio of princesses resides, and he thereby wins the hand of the youngest and earns the right to give the two other sisters in marriage to his brothers.

The hero of **"The White Snake,"** like the simpleton of **"The Queen Bee,"** hardly lifts a finger to win his bride. Once he displays compassion for wildlife by coming to the rescue of three fish, a colony of ants, and three ravens, he joins the ranks of the "chosen" heroes who receive assistance from helpers as soon as they are charged with carrying out tasks. Although male fairy tale figures have customarily been celebrated for their heroic exploits and feats, their greatest achievement actually rests on the successful passing of a character test. By enshrining compassion and humility, which—unlike intelligence and brute strength—are acquired characteristics rather than innate traits, the Grimms' tales make it clear to their implied audience (which gradually came to be adolescents) that even the least talented of youths is equipped with the potential to rise to the top.[9]

Once the hero has succeeded in passing the preliminary character test, he is braced for the tasks that lie ahead. The grateful beneficiaries of his compassionate acts and humble deeds are quick to even out the balance sheets. As soon as the hero finds himself faced with an impossible task—emptying a lake with a perforated spoon, building and furnishing a castle overnight, devouring a mountain of bread in twenty-four hours—help is at hand. For every task that requires wisdom, courage, endurance, strength, or simply an appetite and thirst of gargantuan proportions, there is a helper—or a group of helpers—possessing the requisite attributes. And ultimately the achievements of the helper redound to the hero, for he is credited with having drained the lake, built the castle, and consumed the bread.

Passing the preliminary test and carrying out the basic tasks are in themselves sufficient to secure a princess' and her kingdom. Nonetheless, a number of fairy tales mount a third act in keeping with the ternary principle governing their plots.[10] This final trial which the hero must endure is motivated by the reappearance of the fraternal rivals who vexed the hero in his earlier, preheroic days. The brothers seize the earliest opportunity to pilfer the hero's riches, alienate him from his beloved, malign his good name, or banish him from the land. Yet they are no match for the hero, who deftly succeeds in outwitting them and in surviving their murderous assaults. Although the hero is rarely instrumental in carrying out the tasks imposed on him, in the end he acquires the attributes of his helpers and possesses the strength, courage, and wit needed to defeat his rivals.

Just as the humble male protagonist matures and is elevated to a higher station in life, so his antagonists are demeaned and demoted in the final, optional segment of the tale. If the hero distinguishes himself from the start by showing mercy and compassion for animals, he remains singularly uncharitable when it comes to dealing with human rivals. "Off with everyone's head but my own," proclaims the hero of **"The King of the Golden Mountain."** And he makes good on that threat. Even brothers and brides are dispatched by fairy tale heroes without a moment's hesitation once their deceit comes to light. Treachery is punished as swiftly and as predictably as compassion is rewarded. This third phase of the hero's career endows his story with a kind of symmetry and balance for which all tales strive. Like the first two acts, the final act stages a contest between a youth and his two older but morally inferior brothers. Both dramatic conflicts culminate in the rewarding of good will and the punishment of treachery; the last act simply intensifies the reward (a princess and a kingdom) and the punishment (death). In doing so, it gives not only added moral resonance but also a measure of finality to the tale. The hero has not only attained the highest office in the land but also eliminated his every competitor. For that office, he was singled out in the tale's first episode, made singular in the tale's second part, and celebrated as the sole and single heir to the throne in the tale's coda.

The trajectory of the hero's path leads him to the goal shared by all fairy tales, whether they chart the fortunes of downtrodden male or downtrodden female protagonists. In keeping with the fundamental law requiring the reversal of all conditions prevailing in its introductory paragraphs, the fairy tale ends by enthroning the humble and enriching the impoverished. The male heroes of fairy tales are humble in at least one, and often in both, senses of the term. More often than not they are low men on the totem pole in families of common origins. But whether born to the crown or raised on a farm, they are also humble in character: without this special quality they would fail to qualify for the munificence of helpers and donors. Humility therefore seems to be the badge of the fairy tale hero. And since humbleness, in one of its shades of meaning, can inhere in members of any social class, both princes and peasants are eligible to assume the role of hero in fairy tales.

Humility may be an innate characteristic of fairy tale heroes, but it also comes to color the psychological makeup of fairy tale heroines. Female protagonists are by nature just as humble as their male counterparts, but they display that virtue in a strikingly different fashion. Fairy tales often highlight psychological characteristics by translating them into elements of plot, and with female heroines, this proves especially true. Daughters of millers and daughters of kings alike are not merely designated as humble; they are actually humbled in the course of their stories. In fact, "humbled" is perhaps too mild a term to use for the many humiliations to which female protagonists must submit.

Since most fairy tales end with marriage, it seems logical to assume that a single tale suffices to illustrate the contrasting fates of male and female protagonists. Yet though there is often a happy couple at the end of a fairy tale, the fate of only one single, central character is at stake as the tale unfolds. That pivotal figure stands so firmly rooted at the center of events that all other characters are defined solely by their relationship to him or her and thereby lack an autonomous sphere of action. Note that in **"Cinderella,"** for instance, even the bridegroom, for all the dashing chivalry attributed to him by Walt Disney and others, remains a colorless figure. The tale tells us nothing more about him than that he is the son of a king. Lacking a history, a story, and even a name, he is reduced to the mere function of prince-rescuer waiting in the wings for his cue. The brides in stories of male heroes fare little better. Relegated to subordinate roles, they too fail to command our attention and to engage our interest. Still, there are exceptions to every rule, and the Grimms' collection provides one noteworthy exception to the rule that only one character can occupy center stage in fairy tales. **"The Goose Girl at the Spring"** weaves together the fates of both partners in the marriage with which it concludes. To be sure, there are signs that the tale is not of one piece, that at some historical juncture it occurred to one teller of tales to fuse two separate and distinct plots.[11] Nonetheless those two plots conveniently dovetail to create a single narrative. The story of the humble count and of the humbled princess who marries him offers an exemplary study in contrasts between the lot of males and females in fairy tales culminating in marriage ceremonies.

"The Goose Girl at the Spring" commences with an account of the heroine's future bridegroom. Although this young man is handsome, rich, and noble, he must—like the most lowly fairy tale heroes—prove his mettle by displaying the virtues of compassion and humility. Without these twin virtues, his otherwise impeccable credentials would prove utterly worthless. And indeed, we learn not only that the young count is able to "feel compassion" but also that he is, despite his noble station in life, not too proud to translate compassion into action. Once he demonstrates his humility by easing the burdens of a feeble old hag, shunned by everyone but him, he earns himself a passport to luck and success. Like his many artlessly benevolent folkloric kinsmen, the count becomes the recipient of a gift that accords him a privileged status among potential suitors of a princess. The emerald etui he receives from the old hag ultimately leads him to his bride, a princess masquerading as a shepherdess.

Neither the count nor his rustic bride can boast humble origins. The unsightly girl tending geese at the beginning of the tale is not at all what she seems. At the well, she peels off her rural costume along with her rough skin to reveal that she must be a princess. Despite her aristocratic origins, she too can in the end ascend to a higher position, for her fairy tale days are spent in the most modest of circumstances. Unlike her groom, however, she was pressed into assuming a humble position when her own father exiled her from the household. Like countless folkloric heroines, she suffers a humiliating fall that reduces her from a princess to a peasant, from a privileged daughter to an impoverished menial. Fairy tale heroes receive gifts and assistance once they actively prove their compassion and humility; heroines, by contrast, become the beneficiaries of helpers and rescuers only after they have been abased and forced to learn humility.

There are many well-known tales of victimized female heroines who rise to or return to the ranks of royalty once they have been humbled and humiliated.[12] But no tales spell out more explicitly that humiliation figures as a prerequisite for a happy ending than **"King Thrushbeard," "The Mongoose,"** and **"The Six Servants."** The bride of King Thrushbeard furnishes the classic example of the heroine who earns a king and a crown as soon as straitened circumstances break her arrogance and pride. It is not enough that she curses the false pride that led to her downfall; her husband must also solemnly state: "All of this was done to crush your pride and to punish you for the haughty way in which you treated me." When King Thrushbeard generously offers to reinstate her to a royal position, she feels so deeply mortified that she declares herself unworthy to become his bride. The princess in the tale known as **"The Mongoose"** also finds herself humbled by her prospective husband. Nonetheless, she takes the defeat in stride and declares to herself with more than a touch of satisfaction: "He is cleverer than you!" The princess-heroine of **"The Six Servants"** is also cheerfully repentant and resigned to her fate by the end of her story. Reduced to tending swine with her husband (a prince who has duped her into believing that he is a peasant), she is prepared to accept her lot: "I've only got what I deserved for being so haughty and proud." After revealing his true station in life, her husband justifies the deception by declaring: "I suffered so much for you, it was only right that you should suffer for me."

As the tale **"The Six Servants"** makes clear, young men "suffer" by taking the credit for tasks carried out by animal helpers, human servants, or supernatural assistants. Women suffer by being forced into a lowly social position. Male heroes demonstrate from the start a meekness and humility that qualify them for an ascent to wealth, the exercise of power, and happiness crowned by wedded bliss; their female counterparts undergo a process of humiliation and defeat that ends with a rapid rise in social status through marriage, but that also signals a loss of pride and the abdication of power.

Before we move on to another category of heroes, a quick review of our first class is in order. The naive hero in tales of three sons lacks the brains and brawn conventionally associated with heroic figures; he must rely on helpers with superhuman or supernatural powers to carry out every task demanded by a king in return for the hand of a princess. Instead of slaying dragons, he offers to louse them; instead of killing giants, he befriends them and makes himself at home in their dwellings. His demonstrations of compassion set the stage for the reversal of fortunes characteristic of fairy tale plots. Only from a position of humility can he be elevated to the loftiest office in the land. Just as this hero works his way up the social ladder by climbing down it, so too he acquires intelligence and power by putting obtuseness and vulnerability on display. Although it is never explicitly stated that he becomes smart and strong in the end, most fairy tales imply that their heroes have acquired the attributes of royalty right along with the office of king.

The youngest of three sons makes his way through magical kingdoms where an ant might plead for a favor, an enchanted princess could call on his services, or a dwarf might suddenly demand a crust of bread. But a second group of heroes in the Grimms' tales moves in what appears to be a more realistic setting: villages and the roads connecting them. The cast of characters in tales with those heroes includes kings and princesses. But the tales themselves lack the supernatural dimension of fairy tales and tend to be more down-to-earth in tone and more earthy in humor. The heroes are often far enough along in life to have a profession: many are apprentices, but some are tailors, foresters, tradesmen, or mercenaries. Many are "men" and not "boys." (One is so old that he finds himself obliged to choose the eldest of twelve princesses when a king offers him one of his daughters in marriage.) Still, these heroes do not seem equipped with much more intelligence, strength, or valor than the young simpletons of fairy tales. They may not be village idiots, but in accordance with the general tendency of German folklore to avoid endowing male protagonists with heroic traits, their strengths are rarely spelled out.

Naiveté also appears to be the principal hallmark of village boys and men. But what appears to be a character defect is in fact turned to good account once the protagonist determines to seek his fortunes in the world. Nietzsche once observed that fear is an index of intelligence, thus confirming the old saw that fools rush in where wise men fear to tread.[13] The more naive the hero, the more foolhardy and fearless he is, and the more likely he is to rise to the challenges of various tasks devised to foil the suitors of a princess. Naiveté implies fearlessness, which in turn can take on the character of courage.

In much the same way that naiveté can shade into courage, it can also translate into cunning. A hero's stupidity can take such extreme forms that it utterly disarms his antagonists. A young man who starts out handicapped by his boundless naiveté may in the end triumph over his adversaries by outwitting them. The protagonist unwise to the ways of the world can therefore be in the best possible position to exhibit heroic qualities by the close of his story.

Heroic feats performed by figures with clear character defects—lack of wisdom and wit—can, however, end by producing comic effects. "Blockhead," "Numbskull," or "Simpleton" rush into one hazardous situation after another, simply because they are too naive to know better; they get the upper hand by putting their dimwittedness on display, taking every word of advice that they hear literally; but they also escape harm because they are so naive that they confound their opponents. It may be true that they succeed in accomplishing the tasks laid out for them, but there is more than a touch of vaudeville to their every move.

The burlesque effect produced by tales chronicling the deeds of fearless heroes is perhaps most pronounced in **"The Fairy Tale of One Who Went Forth to Learn Fear."** The hero of that tale tries in vain to learn to be afraid, or more precisely, to shudder. Through one hair-raising episode after another he preserves his equanimity and coolly turns the tables on his would-be terrorizers. In one last desperate attempt to discover what it is to feel fear, he spends three nights warding off and ultimately exorcising the demons haunting a castle. His reward is the hand of a princess, but still he feels no fear. Only in his marriage bed does he finally learn to shudder, when his resourceful wife pulls off his covers and pours a bucket of live minnows on him. Bruno Bettelheim is surely right to read psycho-sexual implications into this final act of the fairy tale, particularly since the art of shuddering rather than the actual experience of fear constitutes the overt tale value. But the hero's inability to feel fear ought not to be construed as a negative trait: Bettelheim asserts that "the hero of this story could not shudder due to repression of all sexual feelings."[14] It is precisely the absence of the capacity to fear that enables the sprightly hero to withstand the horrors of a haunted castle and consequently to win the hand of his bride. Indeed, the ability to fear comes so close to courage in this tale that the protagonist begins to take on, for all his unflinching artlessness, heroic attributes. Unlike his humble and helpless kinsmen in classical fairy tales of three sons, he breezily accomplishes one task after another without resorting to aid from friendly foreign agents. Were it not for the comic overtones to the adventures of this fairy tale hero, it would seem entirely appropriate to place him in the class of heroes who live by their courage and wits..

If naiveté and courage are virtually synonyms in the folkloric lexicon, naiveté and cunning are also not far apart in meaning.[15] Indeed the more hopelessly naive and obtuse the hero of a tale, the more likely it is that he will triumph over his adversaries and that his adventures will be crowned with success. **"The Courageous Tailor,"** who decorates himself for having dispatched seven flies with one blow, seems to stand as the very incarnation of fatuous vanity. Yet his bravado endows him with the power to outwit giants, to accomplish the tasks posed by his bride's belligerent father, and to subdue a blue-blooded wife who is repelled by the thought of a marriage below her own social station. In this tale, the line dividing naiveté from shrewdness and bravado from bravery has been effaced. The naive hero without fear and brains is virtually indistinguishable from the trickster.

By now it should be clear that the humble and naive youngest of three sons is a not so distant cousin of the fearless and naive hero. In fact, the hero of the Grimms' **"Crystall Ball"** combines the attributes of humble heroes and fearless fools: he possesses the simplicity and humility that go hand-in-hand with his familial status as the youngest of three sons, and he is also said to have "a heart without fear." It is above all his foolishly dauntless spirit that gives him the audacity to line up as the twenty-fourth suitor to seek out a princess imprisoned in the **"Castle of the Golden Sun"** and to undertake her liberation. And it is solely his slow-wittedness that provides him with the means for arriving in the kingdom inhabited by the princess. He "forgets" to return a magical hat to two giants and thereby receives just the right means for transporting himself to that kingdom. In fairy tales, brashness can clearly accomplish as much as bravery; naiveté is as effective as craft. The manifest lack of a virtue often translates into its possession. Just as Cinderella proves to be the fairest and the noblest of them all despite her shabby attire and her station at the hearth, so the simpleton of the family ultimately prevails over his older and wiser antagonists.

As noted, the rigors of a fairy tale hero's life endow him in the end with the attributes commonly associated with royalty. Even if the humble simpleton never lifts a sword and is incapable of answering a single question, let alone a riddle, he becomes a prince in more than just name. The feats of every woodland helper become his own deeds and accomplishments, and he becomes a figure with all the heroic qualities of dragon-slayers and giant-killers. Since our other class of tales, those featuring the comic adventures of heroes without fear, generally dispenses with tests of compassion, it also does away with the helpers who are responsible for elevating humble protagonists to heroic stature. Fear-less heroes must instead rely wholly on their own mental and physical resources—however modest they may be. It is those resources that are put to the test in the opening paragraphs of the tale, where brashness achieves more than bravery and artlessness proves more effective than artifice.

Since the hero without fear displays a greater measure of self-reliance than his humble kinsmen, the plot of his adventures contains the potential for greater realism. Gone are encounters with talking animals, supernatural counselors, and other exotic agents. Instead the hero meets hunters, locksmiths, sextons, innkeepers, and other such folk. He may not marry a peasant's daughter, but the castle in which he finally takes up residence has the distinct odor of the barnyard. Again, we are in the village rather than in an enchanted forest. Yet it would be misleading to label these tales realistic. They do not strive to hold a mirror up to the social conditions of the age or culture in which they were told. These are tall tales, stories that take advantage of exaggeration, punning, parody, and literalism to produce comic effects.

The many realistic touches in these folktales, in tandem with their farcical aspect, point to their basic affinity with tales of tricksters, where professional fools, tradesmen, retired soldiers, and youths of various other callings conspire to thwart their masters, creditors, or any of the other overprivileged. Through ingenious disingenuousness they succeed in coming out on top. An open-ended episodic principle organizes the plot of both tall tales featuring heroes without fear and trickster stories. One absurd skirmish follows another, with no distinctive growth, development, or maturity after one episode or another. By contrast, the humble hero's adventures take the form of a three-act drama, with a test in the first act, tasks in the second, and a final trial crowned by success in the third. The goal may be the same for both types of heroes, but the paths bear little resemblance to each other.[16]

Fairy tales charting the adventures of male protagonists posit from the start one dominant character trait that establishes a well-defined identity for the hero even as it proclaims his membership in the class of heroic figures. The verbal tag attached to the character ("Dummy," "the youngest of three sons," "Blockhead") ensures that he is recognized as the central character of the narrative. But in the course of the hero's odyssey, his dominant character trait begins to shade into its opposite through a process that can be termed inversion. The humble hero weds a woman of royal blood; the brazen fool proves his mettle; and the naive simpleton outwits just about anyone. In fairy tales, the youth lacking a good pedigree, a stout heart, and a sharp wit is precisely the one who wins himself a princess and a kingdom.

Inversion of character traits is a common occurrence in fairy tales. A reversal of the conditions prevailing at the start is, after all, manifestly the goal of every tale. The folktale in general, as Max Lüthi has observed, has "a liking for all extremes, extreme contrasts in particular." Its characters, he further notes, are either beautiful or ugly, good or bad, poor or rich, industrious or lazy, and humble or noble.[17] Yet much as readers and critics insist on the fairy tale's low tolerance for ambiguity and stress the inflexibility of the attributes assigned to heroes and villains, the frequency with which inversion appears suggests that they overstate their case. Just as "Beast" can be at once savage and civilized, so the youngest of three sons can be both a simpleton and a sage, a humble lad and a prince, a coward and a hero. Both character attributes and social conditions rapidly shift from one extreme to the other in fairy tales.

That character traits are not as standardized or programmed as would appear becomes evident if we analyze the fate of one character who does not figure prominently in the pantheon of fairy tale heroes. The eponymous protagonist of **"Hans in Luck"** might, in fact, well be called an antihero. In the course of his travels, he outwits no one—instead he becomes the victim of numerous transparently fraudulent transactions. His fortunes, rather than rising, steadily decline. And at the end of his journey, he seems no wiser and is decidedly less prosperous than he was at its beginning. Still, Hans is said to be lucky, and he feels himself to be among the happiest men on earth. The steps of Hans's journey to felicity are easy enough to retrace. After serving his master loyally and diligently for a period of seven years, Hans winds his way home with a weighty emolument: a chunk of gold the size of his head. Hans happily barters this monetary burden for a horse that will speed him on his way home. In the further course of his journey, he exchanges the horse for a cow, the cow for a pig, the pig for a goose, and the goose for a grindstone and rock. Even after these two worthless rocks land at the bottom of a well leaving him nothing to show for his labors of seven years, Hans remains undaunted. He literally jumps for joy and praises God for liberating him from the burdens that slowed his journey homeward. Unencumbered by earthly possessions and with a light heart, Hans heads for his mother's home.

Conventional wisdom has it that the happy-go-lucky hero of this tale stands as the archetypal benighted fool. The very title of the tale, **"Hans in Luck,"** is charged with irony: only a fool would delight in parting with the hefty wages Hans receives from his master. Yet on closer inspection, it becomes clear that the story of lucky Hans may also celebrate freedom from the burden of labor. On the last leg of his journey, Hans jettisons grindstone and rock—the tools of the trade that was to secure for him a steady flow of cash; at the outset of his journey, he rids himself of the gold with which his labor was compensated. In a stunning reversal of the value system espoused in fairy tales, Hans's story not only substitutes rags for riches but also supplants marriage to a princess in a foreign land with a return home to mother. In short, it ends where most tales begin. Instead of charting the course of an odyssey toward wealth and marriage, it depicts the stations of a journey toward poverty and dependence. But in remaining wholly indifferent to the wages of labor and freeing himself from its drudgery, Hans displays a kind of wisdom that invalidates ironic readings of his tale's title. Bereft of material possessions yet rich in spirit, he turns his back on the world of commerce to embrace his mother.[18]

The story of lucky Hans dramatically demonstrates the impossibility of establishing a fixed set of character traits shared by male heroes. Like Hans, who is both foolish and wise, poor and rich, lucky and unfortunate, the heroes of numerous fairy tales possess attributes that imperceptibly shift into their opposites. All the same, it is clear that certain oppositions (humble/noble, naive/cunning, timid/courageous, compassionate/ruthless) are encoded on virtually every fairy tale with a male hero. It is, then, difficult to draw up an inventory of immutable character traits largely because a single figure within a tale can—and usually does—have one character trait and its opposite. But it is also equally difficult, if for different reasons, to establish precise models for the plots of tales featuring male heroes. For every score of heroes who wed princesses and inherit kingdoms, there is one who returns home as an impoverished bachelor. For ten heroes who receive assistance and magical gifts by demonstrating compassion, there is one who acquires aid and magical objects through an act of violence. For every animal bridegroom who is released from a curse through the love and devotion of a woman, there is one who is disenchanted by the callous treatment he receives at the hands of his bride. To be sure, there is a measure of predictability in these plots, but only if we bear in mind that every narrative norm established can be violated by its opposite. Thus the preliminary test of good character at the start of tales with a ternary plot structure can be replaced by a demonstration of the hero's ruthlessness. The story of a hero dependent on magical helpers in carrying out appointed tasks can exist side by side with the tale of a hero who acts autonomously and takes on the characteristics of helpers.[19].

Recognizing and appreciating the fairy tale's instability—its penchant for moving from one extreme to another—is vital for understanding its characters, plots, and thematic orientation. Fairy tale figures have few fixed traits; they are totally re-formed once they reach the goals of their journeys, when they become endowed with the very qualities in which they were once found wanting. Male protagonists may adhere slavishly to the ground rules of heroic decorum, or they may break every rule in the book; either way, their stories end with the accession to a throne. And finally, the conditions prevailing at the start of tales are utterly reversed by the end. The fairy tale, in sum, knows no stable middle ground. Inversion of character traits, violation of narrative norms, and reversal of initial conditions are just a few of the ways in which it overturns notions of immutability and creates a fictional world in which the one constant value is change.

In this context, it is worth emphasizing once again some of the disparities between folkloric fantasies and social realities. The radical reversals that lift fairy tale heroes from humble circumstances to a royal station in life were virtually unknown during the age in which fairy tales developed and flourished, but they undeniably correspond to childhood fantasies of past ages and of our own day. If in real life the youngest of three sons rarely had the wherewithall to succeed in life or to transcend his station in life, fairy tales held out the promise that humility and other virtues might well outweigh the benefits of an inheritance. But beyond offering consolation to underprivileged sons who lived in an era when primogeniture was custom or law, fairy tales more generally respond to the insecurities of every child. Even the eldest child is likely to perceive himself as the least gifted or least favored among his siblings and can thereby readily identify with simpleton heroes. Fundamental psychological truths, rather than specific social realities, appear to have given rise to the general plot structure of those tales.

A stable plot still leaves room for much variation. Skillful raconteurs can take the same story line and give it unique twists and turns. The tone may vary from one tale to the next, and the hero may also be presented in different lights. As Robert Darnton has shown, comparing different national versions of a single tale type can be a revealing exercise. Reading through various tellings of "Jack the Giant Killer," one can register the changes from "English fantasy to French cunning and Italian burlesque." More important, there are subtle shifts in the character of the protagonist as he slips from one culture into another. Darnton has observed that the trickster figure is especially prevalent in French folklore and literature.[20] By contrast, as we have seen, the simpleton (or to put it in more flattering terms) the guileless youth figures prominently in the Grimms' collection. These differences between the folkloric heroes of the two cultures may, however, be more apparent than real, for the roguish Gallic trickster and his naive Teutonic counterpart have more in common than one would suspect. Even the names most frequently bestowed in the ***Nursery and Household Tales*** on the types ("Dummling" for the simpleton and "Daumerling" for the trickster) suggest that they are kindred spirits. Both the simpleton and the trickster ultimately make good by outwitting or out-doing their seemingly superior adversaries. Still, the shift in emphasis from cunning to naiveté as one moves across the Rhine is telling, suggesting as it does that the French celebrate cleverness and audacity while the Germans enshrine the virtues of naiveté and guilelessness.

If we take a closer look at German literary traditions—both oral and written—it becomes clear that the naive hero is by no means a folkloristic aberration. He fits squarely into a long line of such figures. Wolfram von Eschenbach's Parzival, who comes to incarnate the highest chivalric ideals, is described as "der tumme" ("the young and inexperienced one"). Dressed by his mother in the costume of a fool, he mounts a wretched nag to seek his fortune in the world. Although there are hints that he is something of a dragon-slayer (he arrives at Munsalvæsche at Michaelmas, the Feast of St. Michael, the vanquisher of Satan as dragon), the only dragons he slays are emblazoned on his opponent's helmet. But like folkloric heroes, Parzival knows no fear and consequently displays valor on the battlefield. Although he fails the initial test of compassion put to him, in the course of his adventures he learns humility and demonstrates compassion.

Remaining in the same poetic climate but moving to another era, we find that Richard Wagner's Siegfried also launches his heroic career as a naive youth without fear. The resemblances between his story and the **"Fairy Tale of One Who Went Forth to Learn Fear"** are unmistakable. To his cantankerous guardian, Mime, Siegfried confides that he wishes to learn what it is to fear—to which Mime responds that the wise learn fear quickly, the stupid have a harder time of it.[21] Siegfried clearly belongs in the latter category. Like the "one who went forth to learn fear," he discovers that emotion in the experience of love. As he sets eyes on the sleeping Brünnhilde, he feels a mystifying quickening of emotions:

> How cowardly I feel.
> Is this what they call fear?
> Oh mother! mother!
> Your fearless child!
> A woman lies in sleep:
> She has taught him to be afraid!
>
> (*Siegfried,* Act III)

No one was more surprised by the resemblances between the Grimms' fairy tale character and the heroic Siegfried than Richard Wagner. In a letter to his friend Theodor Uhlig, he wrote: "Haven't I ever told you this amusing story? It's the tale of the lad who ventures forth to learn what fear is and who is so dumb that he just can't do it. Imagine my amazement when I suddenly realized that that lad is no one else but—young Siegfried."[22]

It would not be a difficult task to identify countless other guileless fools and lads without fear in German literature. From the Baroque era through the Romantic period up to the present, naiveté is the signature of many a literary hero. The protagonist of Grimmelshausen's *Simplicius Simplicissimus* may be a clever rogue, but his name is telling. Like Parzival, he moves from foolish innocence to an understanding of the ways of the world, though his story ends in disillusion. Goethe's *Wilhelm Meister's Apprenticeship,* perhaps the finest exemplar of the *Bildungsroman*—that most hallowed of German literary traditions—gives us a naive innocent who happens to be fortunate enough to stumble into the right circles. We do not have to look far in the Romantic era for heroes pure in heart and innocent in spirit. Every one of them—from Novalis's Heinrich von Ofterdingen to Josef von Eichendorff's Florio—begins the first leg of his journey into the wild blue yonder as a charmingly naive young man wholly untutored in worldly matters.

In an introduction to the *Magic Mountain,* Thomas Mann made a point of bowing in the direction of Hans Castorp's literary antecedents. Mystified by the way in which the weight of literary tradition had—without his knowing it—determined his protagonist's character, he was also flattered by the company in which his hero was placed. Both Parzival and Wilhelm Meister, he noted, belong to the class of "guileless fools," and his Hans Castorp is no different. His "simplicity and artlessness" make him a legitimate literary cousin of those two quester figures. Yet Hans Castorp can also display all the wisdom of an innocent: when he wants something, he can be "clever," "crafty," and "shrewd." That

Mann further emphasized resemblances "here and there" between Hans Castorp's story and fairy tales comes as no surprise.[23]

It may seem to be stretching a point to suggest that fairy tales can tell us something about what French historians call "mentalités." Yet storytellers have, throughout the ages, embroidered the narratives passed on to them with the cultural values as well as with the facts of their own contemporary milieu. Every subtle change can be significant, so long as it takes place on a large scale and does not simply represent one idiosyncratic telling of a tale. What the Grimms' collection tells us about fairy tales does not deviate fundamentally from what other German folkloric and literary sources declare. Naiveté has a special charm and magic of its own.

Notes

[1] Max Lüthi asserts that the disproportionately large number of female heroines in fairy tales can be traced to the prominent role played by women in shaping the plots. See "The Fairy-Tale Hero," in *Once upon a Time: On the Nature of Fairy Tales,* trans. Lee Chadeayne and Paul Gottwald (Bloomington: Indiana University Press, 1976), pp. 135-46. By contrast Ralph S. Boggs asserts that 80 percent of German tales have a hero, and that only 20 percent have a heroine ("The Hero in the Folk Tales of Spain, Germany and Russia," *Journal of American Folklore* 44 [1931]: 27-42). Neither Lüthi nor Boggs identifies his statistical sample.

[2] Simone de Beauvoir's characterization appears in *The Second Sex,* trans. H. M. Parshley (New York: Bantam, 1952), pp. 271-72. For the list of heroic attributes, see Jack Zipes, *Fairy Tales and the Art of Subversion: The Classical Genre for Children and the Process of Civilization* (New York: Wildman Press, 1983), p. 57.

[3] The first edition is reprinted in *Die Kinder- und Hausmärchen der Brüder Grimm: Vollständige Ausgabe in der Urfassung,* ed. Friedrich Panzer (Wiesbaden: Emil Vollmer, 1953).

[4] On the various types of heroes, see Katalin Horn, *Der aktive und der passive Märchenheld* (Basel: Schweizerische Gesellschaft für Volkskunde, 1983); August von Löwis of Menar, *Der Held im deutschen und russischen Märchen* (Jena: Eugen Diederichs, 1912); Ralph S. Boggs, "The Hero in the Folk Tales of Spain, Germany and Russia," pp. 27-42; Vincent Brun, "The German Fairy Tale," *Menorah Journal* 27 (1939): 147-55; and Louis L. Snyder, "Cultural Nationalism: The Grimm Brothers' Fairy Tales," in *Roots of German Nationalism* (Bloomington: Indiana University Press, 1978), pp. 35-54.

[5] Constance Spender makes this point. See "Grimms' Fairy Tales," *The Contemporary Review* 102 (1912): 673-79.

[6] These are the words of the fox in the Grimms' version of "The Golden Bird."

[7] *Tales from the Thousand and One Nights,* trans. N. J. Dawood (Harmondsworth: Penguin, 1973), p. 165. Robert Crossley makes the point about Aladdin's lack of merit ("Pure and Applied Fantasy; or, From Faerie to Utopia," in *The Aesthetics of Fantasy Literature and Art,* ed. Roger C. Schlobin [Notre Dame, Ind.: University of Notre Dame Press, 1982], pp. 176-91). On Aladdin's fortunes in Germany, see Erich Sielaff, "Bemerkungen zur kritischen Aneignung der deutschen Volksmärchen," *Wissenschaftliche Zeitschrift der Universität Rostock* 2 (1952/53): 241-301.

[8] On the ethnographic significance of animals in fairy tales, see Lutz Röhrich, "Mensch und Tier im Märchen," *Schweizerisches Archiv für Volkskunde* 49 (1953): 165-93.

[9] Eugen Weber finds that the celebration of compassion in fairy tales reflects the rareness of that virtue during the age in which the tales flourished: "Kindness, selflessness is the greatest virtue (perhaps because there is so little to give, perhaps precisely because it is so rare)." See "Fairies and Hard Facts: The Reality of Folktales," *Journal of the History of Ideas* 42 (1981): 93-113.

[10] On the three phases of action in classical fairy tales, see E. Meletinsky, S. Nekludov, E. Novik, and D. Segal, "Problems of the Structural Analysis of Fairytales," in *Soviet Structural Folkloristics,* ed. P. Maranda (The Hague: Mouton, 1974), pp. 73-139. The authors divide the action of fairy tales into a preliminary test, a basic test, and an additional final test.

[11] Note the use in the tale of such heavy-handed transitions as "But now I must tell more about the king and the queen, who had left with the count." On the presence of only one single sharply defined plot in classical fairy tales, see Max Lüthi, *The European Folktale: Form and Nature,* trans. John D. Niles (Philadelphia: Institute for the Study of Human Issues, 1982), p. 34. Lüthi uses the term *Einsträngigkeit* (single-strandedness) to designate the absence of digressive plot lines in fairy tales. *Einsträngigkeit* is the term that Walter A. Berendsohn also uses to characterize the fairy tale's single-track plot structure in *Grundformen volkstümlicher Erzählkunst in den Kinder- und Hausmärchen der Brüder Grimm: Ein stilkritischer Versuch* (Hamburg: W. Gente, 1921), p. 33. The term has its origins in Axel Olrik's essay of 1919, which has been translated and printed as "Epic Laws of Folk Narrative," in *The Study of Folklore,* ed. Alan Dundes (Englewood Cliffs, NJ: Prentice-Hall, 1965), pp. 129-41.

[12] On abasement as "a prelude to and precondition of *affiliation*" in "Cinderella," see Madonna Kolbenschlag, *Kiss Sleeping Beauty Good-Bye: Breaking the Spell of Feminine Myths and Models* (New York: Doubleday, 1979), p. 72.

[13] Friedrich Nietzsche, "Morgenröte," 4:241, in *Friedrich Nietzsche: Werke in drei Bänden,* ed. Karl Schlechta (Munich: Hanser, 1954), 3:1172.

[14] Bruno Bettelheim, *The Uses of Enchantment: The Meaning and Importance of Fairy Tales* (New York: Random House, Vintage Books, 1977), p. 281.

[15] Stith Thompson emphasizes the ambiguous nature of the trickster's intellect: "The adventures of the Trickster, even when considered by themselves, are inconsistent. Part are the result of his stupidity, and about an equal number show him overcoming his enemies through cleverness." See *The Folktale* (1946; repr. Berkeley: University of California Press, 1977), p. 319. In *World Folktales: A Scribner Resource Collection* (New York: Charles Scribner's Sons, 1980), Atelia Clarkson and Gilbert B. Cross confirm the ambiguity when they point out that "the most incongruous feature of the American Indian trickster is his tendency to become a dupe or play the buffoon even though he was the wily, clever trickster in a story told the day before" (p. 285).

[16] Variants of the tale of the courageous tailor demonstrate that a single core theme can lend itself to two different types of narratives: a biographical tale that focuses on the life of the hero and on his attempt to win the hand of a princess and an episodic tale that focuses on the various pranks played by a trickster. See the seven variants of "Das tapfere Schneiderlein," in Leander Petzoldt, *Volksmärchen mit Materialien* (Stuttgart: Ernst Klett, 1982), pp. 42-72.

[17] Max Lüthi, *The European Folktale,* pp. 34-35.

[18] For a reading of the story along similar lines, see Roderick McGillis, "Criticism in the Woods: Fairy Tales as Poetry," *Children's Literature Association Quarterly* 7 (1982): 2-8.

[19] As Vladimir Propp put it, "when a helper is absent from a tale, this quality is transferred to the hero." See *Morphology of the Folktale,* trans. Laurence Scott (Austin: University of Texas Press, 1968), p. 83.

[20] Robert Darnton, "Peasants Tell Tales: The Meaning of Mother Goose," in his *The Great Cat Massacre and Other Episodes in French Cultural History* (New York: Basic Books, 1984), pp. 9-72. The quoted phrase appears on p. 44.

[21] The retort is in Wagner's first version of *Siegfried* (Richard Wagner, *Skizzen und Entwürfe zur Ring-Dichtung,* ed. Otto Strobel [Munich: F. Bruckmann, 1930], p. 113).

[22] The letter, dated 10 May 1851, appears in Richard Wagner, *Sämtliche Briefe,* ed. Gertrud Strobel and Werner Wolf (Leipzig: VEB Deutscher Verlag für Musik, 1979), 4:42-44. Heinz Rölleke discusses Wagner's dependence on the Grimms' fairy tale in "Märchen von einem, der auszog, das Fürchten zu lernen: Zu Überlieferung und Bedeutung des *KHM* 4," *Fabula* 20 (1979): 193-204.

[23] Thomas Mann, *The Magic Mountain,* trans. H. T. Lowe-Porter (New York: Alfred A. Knopf. 1964), pp. 719-29. Castorp is described, in German, as a "Schalk"; he is "verschmitzt" and "verschlagen." Mann's remarks on the fairy tale quality of Castorp's story appear on p. v. Unfortunately Lowe-Porter translated Mann's term *Märchen* (fairy tale) as "legend."

Christa Kamenetsky (essay date 1992)

SOURCE: "*Marchenkritik* in the Context of European Romanticism," in *The Brothers Grimm and Their Critics: Folktales and the Quest for Meaning,* Ohio University Press, 1992, pp. 181-214.

[*In the following chapter from her book* The Brothers Grimm and Their Critics, *Kamenetsky considers the response to the tales in the context of the Romantic movement and the Grimms' broader interest in folklore, including the folklore of other nations.*]

Folklore and the Middle Ages

During the Romantic movement, the critical reception of the ***Kinder- und Hausmärchen*** in Germany and abroad coincided with a new appreciation of nature, myths, and the medieval past. Being inspired by Rousseau, Johann Gottfried Herder had prepared the ground for this trend by urging all nations to search out their native folklore and traditions. In folk songs, folktales, myths, and legends, one believed to see remnants of a Golden Age in which people had still lived in harmony with God and nature. It was this quest for native *Naturpoesie* (folk or nature poetry) that motivated Clemens Brentano and Achim von Arnim to publish a German folk-song collection, titled *Des Knaben Wunderhorn* (*The Boy's Wunderhorn*) in 1805. Brentano then too urged his friends, among whom were poets, painters, scholars, and writers, to make a further search for legends and tales among the common folk. His call also reached the Brothers Grimm, who contributed more than their due share to his collection.[1]

Only a few decades earlier, the German philosopher Immanuel Kant still had regarded the Middle Ages as an aberration of the human mind, yet since Herder's days the trend had swung in the opposite direction. In Germany as well as in the British Isles, the growing preconcern with native "roots" drew particular attention to the Nordic and Celtic traditions rather than to those of classical Greece and Rome. The storm clouds of Macpherson's *Ossian* seemed to correspond more closely to the mood of Herder and Goethe at that time, who even learned Celtic to grasp the full meaning of what they believed to be a genuine epic. Inspired by Herder's essays, one also began to feel closer to "the wild genius" of Shakespeare, discovering in his writings the spirit of the "Nordic" homeland. A book review editor of the *Edinburgh Review* noted in 1827: "Of all literatures, accordingly, the German has the best as well as the most translations; men like Goethe, Wieland, Schlegel, Tieck have not disdained this task. Of Shakespeare three entire versions are admitted to be good, and we know not how many partial or considered as bad."[2] August Wilhelm Schlegel's Shakespeare translation at that time expressed the same love of *Naturpoesie* as did Brentano's and Arnim's folk-song collection. A similar spirit moved Sir Walter Scott to search for folk ballads in the border countries of Southern Scotland[3] and Wilhelm Grimm to translate Sir Walter Scott's ballads along with others from Denmark.

When, in 1806, Heinrich von der Hagen published a new edition of the *Nibelungenlied* (*Song of the Nibelung*), August Wilhelm Schlegel and Ludwig Tieck hailed it as evidence of national poetry, as proof of *Naturpoesie* belonging to the "folk soul" of the nation. Jacob Grimm enthusiastically compared it to the epics of Homer. Following a similar motivation, both Jacob and Wilhelm Grimm had prepared a translation of the *Elder Edda* and the *Nibelungenlied,* although they abandoned the latter project after the first volume upon discovering that Hagen's edition had reached the market before they had time to finish their work.[4]

It is often overlooked that the Romantics needed courage and perseverance to publish *Naturpoesie,* as they were swimming against the tide of a literary establishment. All too fresh in their memories were the harsh words that King Frederick the Great had spoken against the *Nibelungenlied,* calling the great Austrian epic "nothing but plunder—not worth a shot of gun powder."[5] A number of critics still continued to feel that way as they attacked the Romantics from the rigid standpoints of the neoclassical tradition. Even as they gradually began to appreciate medieval epics, they still considered folklore as subliterary material not worthy of the printer's ink. The transition toward a new conception of literature and language was not a smooth one that merely happened without a struggle. It turned out to be a particularly rough road for the Brothers Grimm, who came to defend not only epic literature but also the simple folktale as a living tradition of the vernacular. The general Romantic quest for *Naturpoesie* favored their folktale publication,[6] yet they still had to defend their endeavors against different conceptions of folktales held by a number of their colleagues, not just by a critical opposition.

Only gradually did an awakening interest in epic poetry make room for the legitimate use of the German vernacular and dialects in literary publications. In the preceding decades many German poets had still preferred to write in French, Latin, Italian, or Greek, although Hamann and Herder had already paved the way for a new appreciation of the old languages in their epic vitality. As the Romantics rediscovered the native folk spirit of the past in the language of the simple peasant and of the child, they also began to see a link between the language of medieval poetry and the traditional folk song, in all of which they recognized the vivid, concrete, and spontaneous expression of another, more wholesome age. The Brothers Grimm went one step further by searching for that naive spirit also in the prose of traditional legends and folktales, which up until that time had not been taken too seriously. Knowing that their friends were still preoccupied with the collection of poetry rather than with prose, Jacob wrote prophetically in 1807: "In our time a great love of folk songs has developed, and it will also draw attention to the legends and folktales that still circulate among the peasants and that have been preserved for us in forgotten places."[7]

The revived interest in the Middle Ages gradually drew the Romantic poets' attention from the *Minnelieder* (medieval love songs) and the old folk songs to the more zesty and humorous works of Hans Sachs and the German folk-book tradition. In 1807 Joseph Görres published *Die teutschen Volkbücher* (*The German Folk Books*),[8] which became a literary as well as a popular success. The *Volksbücher* (also called chap-books) included such popular medieval legends as "Dr. Faustus," "The Horned Siegfried," and "Beautiful Magelone," as well as humorous anecdotes, proverbs, and swanks. Their language was often crude and not meant for children, yet it closely resembled the spoken speech of earlier days, and as such, it appealed to the Romantics so much more than the tired prose of more-pretentious literary works. What formerly had been treated with contempt now arose as a new wellspring for the poetic imagination. The folk books were not just literature by the people and for the people, but they were living evidence of the "folk soul" of the past. To many Romantic writers they promised an inspiration of their own work in regard to both theme and style, a true revival from the source of folkdom.

The Brothers Grimm were fascinated by the folk books, for poetic as well as for scholarly reasons. In the language of these medieval tales they discovered traces of the old folkways, quaint expressions and dialects that resembled those of the vernacular language and the oral folk tradition of their own time. Many themes and character traits, too, seemed to correspond with those that occurred in the folktales that they recorded from storytellers. Thus, the folk books also provided them with valuable resource material for a comparative study of folktale variants, of which they later made use in their notes to the ***Kinder- und Hausmärchen.***

To the German Romantics, tradition was not a rigid or dead subject that had been transmitted mechanically from one generation to the next. Rather, it was alive and demanded to be kept alive by a creative mind open to the ancient folk imagination. It was in this spirit that Wilhelm published the ***Altdänische Heldenlieder, Balladen und Märchen*** (***Old Danish Hero Songs, Ballads, and Folktales***) in 1811. Believing in the vigor of the old languages, he selected among the folk ballads only the oldest ones, and among these only those that appeared to have been preserved most loyally since the thirteenth century. In translating the ballads and tales, he made his primary concern to bring alive again what had almost been forgotten. Even though he took some liberties in the word choice, he managed to recreate the essential imagery, mood, and rhythm in a masterly fashion. Especially because he avoided clinging pedantically to every single word, he came very close to the original feeling and spirit of the songs, so that even today scholars compliment him on the art of his translation. Wilhelm's skill in translation and his feeling for language were talents that seemed to predetermine his later success with what has come to be known as his folktale style. He wrote in his introduction to this work: "The poetry of these folktales touch upon everyone's heart and soul. In these tales there is a sense of magic that can also be found here (in Germany) and conveyed to children: in secret forests, in subterranean caverns, and in the depth of the sea."[9] Wilhelm expressed similar thoughts about the poetic effect of folktales in his introduction to the first edition of the ***Kinder- und Hausmärchen.***

Jacob and Wilhelm Grimm published the ***Kinder- und Hausmärchen*** in 1812. Their previous collection activities and the general Romantic interest in *Naturpoesie* were encouraging factors in this endeavor. Still, it needed courage on their part to concern themselves with stories that in their time were still somewhat contemptuously called "nursery tales." Their friends had primarily focused attention on folk songs, ballads, and epics, while considering folktales as subliterary material that belonged nowhere except in the nursery. The *Volksbücher,* too, had contained some tales, but generally these seemed to belong to a greater degree to grown-ups, not to children. The Grimms titled their collection of folktales ***Kinder- und Hausmärchen*** (***Children's and Household Stories***), so as to indicate that these tales were not merely of interest to children but to the entire household, be it parents, grandparents, or servants. To play it safe, Wilhelm added a long preface to the first edition of the work, explaining and justifying their endeavor. In this preface as well as in later ones and related essays, he and Jacob contemplated the age and nature of the tales and their relation to myths and medieval epics of older times, as well as their universal human significance.[10]

Volksmärchen versus Kunstmärchen

The hallmark of the ***Kinder- und Hausmärchen*** was its supposed loyalty to tradition. "In this sense," wrote Wilhelm in his preface to the 1812 edition, "there exists in Germany not a single collection."[11] The method with which the Grimms collected the tales differed from that of their predecessors. Herder, for example, had still composed ballads in imitation of the folk ballads, in a similar way as Scott, who followed his trail; Brentano, too, had felt no qualms about inventing his own "fairy tales" while mingling folktale motifs with his own story elements. Like Heinrich Wackenroder and Novalis (Friedrich von Hardenberg), he concerned himself to a greater degree with the *Kunstmärchen,* or literary fairy tale, as an art form. In and by themselves, *Kunstmärchen* were a highly respected form of imaginative writing,[12] yet they had little bearing on the search for genuine folk traditions. The Grimms were concerned with the *Volksmärchen,* or folktale, not with the literary fairy tale. Both genres were related and in some cases overlapped, yet as scholars of linguistics and medieval literature, the Grimms were embarking on a comparative study of *Naturpoesie*[13] in which only the folktale could be considered suitable for research. Substantial changes in folktales would have presented a serious obstacle to their goal. Even though Jacob and Wilhelm at times differed in their views regarding the question to what extent a collector was permitted to change a ballad, song, or tale without becoming disloyal to tradition, they both agreed on one essential point, namely that *Naturpoesie* should be preserved in loyalty to the style and substance of medieval epics.

Well known among the "fairy tale" collections prior to the ***Kinder- und Hausmärchen*** had been the tales of *Pentamerone* by Giambattista Basile (originally called *La cunto di la cunti* or *The Tale of Tales,* 1634-36), the *Contes de ma mère l'Oye* (*Tales of My Mother Goose,* 1697) by Charles Perrault, the *Contes des fées* (*Fairy Tales,* 1697-98) by Madame d'Aulnoy, and the collection by Musäus, titled *Volksmährchen der Deutschen* [*sic*] (*Folktales of the Germans,* 5 vols., 1782-87). All of these and others were commonly called *"Märchen"* or *"Mährchen,"*[14] (a term derived from the word *Mare* or *Märe*), meaning tales, news, tidings, or "fairy tales," which made it difficult for the Grimms to defend their own tales as "different." What distinguished the Grimms' folktale collection from the other collections may be partially explained by the general distinction between the *Volksmärchen* (folktales) and *Kunstmärchen* (literary fairy tale or fantasies), for it was only the first that belonged to the inherited oral folk tradition. In their essays and correspondence, the Grimms used the terms *Volksmärchen* and *Kindermärchen* (children's tales) synonymously, while setting them off against the *Kunstmärchen* or *Wundermärchen* (tales of wonder) as something that had to be treated with a similar reverence as medieval manuscripts.

How sensitive the Grimms were to a confusion of folktales with literary fairy tales or tales of wonder we may gather from Jacob Grimm's letter addressed to Sir Walter Scott in 1815. Jacob had initially inquired about a possible exchange of medieval manuscripts with Scott. In the course of his correspondence he mentioned his own and Wilhelm's work on *Tristem,* his research on Nordic languages and dialects, as well as their recent publication of the ***Kinder- und Hausmärchen,*** to which he referred here simply as *Kindermärchen.* In return, Scott had sent to the Grimms some of the requested materials, replying, among other things, that he had not seen the Berlin edition of this work yet and that he should like to possess it. He remembered having read with delight the *Volksmärchen* of Musäus, recognizing in these the story of "The Mountain Spirit of Rammelsberg" and other tales in which he perceived similarities with Scottish tales, in fact the very ". . . outline of the stories of our nurseries and schools." Scott continued, "I have also a curious and miscellaneous collection of books in German containing the *Gehörnte Siegfried* and other romantic tales,"[15] Even though Jacob's return letter indicates that he was happy about Scott's kind response, it also showed that he was unwilling to accept Scott's basic misunderstanding regarding the true nature of the ***Kinder- und Hausmärchen.*** After thanking him for the manuscripts, he tried to convey to him that their *Kindermärchen* were not exactly what he perceived them to be:

> The tales of Musäus are generally touching, yet this quality may be ascribed to their unexplainable substance, not to their manneristic style that, while not without spirit, is but modern and often French in its satirical aspects. Therefore, it has been one of my most pronounced efforts to be as different as possible in style from Musäus. What I have gained or lost in this process you may be better able to judge for yourself after you have seen the book.[16]

Jacob evidently felt embarrassed that Scott had not understood the scholarly or poetic reasons behind their collection. Perhaps Jacob expected too much of Scott at that time, for after all, Scott had not seen the work and consequently also did not know Wilhelm's elaborate defense of the uniqueness of their collection. It turned out that later Scott became one of the Grimm's most ardent supporters in the British Isles.

The aspect to which the Grimms objected most in Musäus's collection was his stylistic embellishment of folktales. By imposing upon traditional tales his own fantasy and a satiric style, Musäus came close to the mannerism of Charles Perrault and Madame d'Aulnoy, thus removing himself substantially from the tone and language of the old storytellers. The Grimms, on the other hand, used every means of research available to them in medieval studies and linguistics to come as close as possible to the original folktale language. The style that especially Wilhelm Grimm created in rewriting the collected tales is generally known and revered today as the "folktale style." It is self-evident that Wilhelm, too, changed the language to some degree in this process, but he never did so arbitrarily. The issue of his loyalty to tradition still needs closer attention in a later chapter.

It was not only Scott who at first did not quite grasp the Grimms' original intentions. Clemens Brentano, for example, who initially had motivated them to collect folk songs as well as folktales, also did not quite understand the significance of the folktales' epic connection, or else he did not care enough about the subject to continue his endeavor. It had been a generous gesture on Brentano's part that he handed over his own collected folktales to the Brothers Grimm in 1811, yet by misplacing the Grimms' final manuscript during the same year, he almost destroyed their project.[17] It was fortunate that in anticipation of Brentano's unpredictable attitudes Wilhelm had prepared a copy of more than thirty folktales which they had mailed to his Berlin address, a precaution that saved these tales for inclusion in the ***Kinder- und Hausmärchen.*** Wilhelm had also indicated to Jacob at that time that he was afraid Clemens might change the tales too much before submitting them to the printer.[18] The entire incident shows that Brentano did not share the Grimms' fascination with the historical and poetic value of folktales but rather preferred to use them as a springboard for his own imagination.

For different reasons also the Grimms' friends August Wilhelm and Friedrich Schlegel did not quite understand the value of their endeavors on behalf of the folktale collection. Whereas Brentano had moved toward writing *Kunstmärchen,* the Schlegels swayed in the opposite direction of medieval scholarship. Being actively involved in editing their literary journal, *Das Athenaeum,* and in writing scholarly essays on mythology, philosophy, and *Naturpoesie,* they failed to understand how intelligent men like the Brothers Grimm should have wasted so much time on children's stories. Thus Friedrich Schlegel wrote somewhat cynically in 1815:

> As far as *Ammenmärchen* (nursery tales) are concerned, we do not wish to underestimate their value too much, but we believe that excellent qualities are just as rare in this genre of literature as in all other ones. Every good nurse shall entertain children, or at least calm them down and put them to sleep. If she manages to accomplish this through her stories, we can't expect more of her. Yet to clean out the entire attic stuffed with well-intended nonsense while insisting that every piece of junk be honored in the name of an age-old legend, this is indeed asking too much of an educated person.[19]

Personally, Friedrich Schlegel enjoyed folktales, and the Brothers Grimm knew it, but he thought it below his dignity to take them all too seriously. In this case, too, the misunderstanding was based on a superficial association of the Grimms' ***Kindermärchen*** with other collections known at that time. There was Ludwig Tieck's *Ritter Blaubart* (*Knight Bluebeard*) of 1797, for example, which bore the ironic subtitle *Ein Ammenmärchen* (*A Nurse's Tale*), although in its psychological complexity it was no children's tale at all but rather a refined *Kunstmärchen* with literary merits in its own right. Johann Gustav Büsching's publication of *Volks-Sagen, Märchen und Legenden* (*Folk Sagas, Folktales, and Legends*) which he published only three months prior to the ***Kinder- und Hausmärchen,***[20] may further have added to the confusion of terms. This work contained some local legends collected orally but also tales gleaned from the works of Musäus and others who had no connection with Grimm. Possibly the greatest confusion arose on account of a rival publication of folktales by Albert Ludwig Grimm, which had appeared in 1808 under the title of *Kindermährchen* (sic.) (*Children's Tales*). Wilhelm Grimm noted explicitly in his introduction to the 1812 edition of the ***Kinder- und Hausmärchen*** that their collection had absolutely nothing in common with that of a certain Mr. A. L. Grimm who accidentally shared their name.[21] In his turn, A. L. Grimm emphatically disassociated himself from the Brothers Grimm by criticizing the "all-inclusive" nature of their tales that exposed children prematurely to cruel characters and events.[22]

Märchen at Home and Abroad

In spite of such misunderstandings and confusions, however, the critical reception of the ***Kinder- und Hausmärchen*** was overwhelmingly positive, and so was the popular response shortly after its publication. How much support the Grimms received from their friends and colleagues in the Romantic age may well be perceived by the returns of his folklore questionnaire, the *Circular wegen Auffassung der Volkspoesie* (*Round-Letter on Behalf of Collecting Folk Poetry*)[23] that Jacob mailed to his friends and acquaintances in 1815. Over a period of a little more than a year, he counted 360 responses from all regions of Germany, as well as from Bohemia, Austria, and the Netherlands. In accordance with his instructions, these friends not only sent him folktales but also nursery rhymes, children's songs, children's games, ballads, legends, proverbs, folk superstitions, and even some "quaint" colloquial expressions that seemed to belong to an older age. All of these they recorded in loyalty to those versions that they had heard in their own environment. In his instructions, Jacob had reminded his friends that they should look out for variants in the songs and tales they heard, because these would undoubtedly provide valuable insights into the living folk tradition. From the questionnaire returns, the Grimms then collected a number of variants, on the basis of which they undertook comparative folktale studies. The Grimms later incorporated some of these responses in their notes, which they published in the third volume of the second edition of the ***Kinder- und Hausmärchen*** in 1819.[24] It is regrettable that they did not make a concise analysis of the questionnaire returns, as it might have provided folklorists today with more evidence regarding the exact origins of some variants and the circumstances under which they had been recorded. Alone the data pertaining to the informants would have made invaluable research material for a modern scientific analysis. One copy of the questionnaire itself, however, was found among the Grimm papers. Jacob had scribbled into its margins the numbers of the returns and the respective dates when he had received them. Still, it was the first large-scale research of its kind, and it fully served the purpose that the Grimms had in mind.

In itself the questionnaire provides valuable evidence not only of Jacob's inquiring mind and systematic approach to folklore research but also of the wide support that he received from his acquaintances and friends who shared his love of *Naturpoesie*. As Brentano had inspired the Grimms to set out in search of the oral tradition, so the Grimms, in turn, inspired others to do the same. The ***Kinder- und Hausmärchen*** provided the living example of the results of such a search, yet the questionnaire provided clear-cut instructions for the methods to be used in fieldwork collections. As such, it was equally encouraging for others to collect folktales on their own.

From the perspective of children's literature, the ***Kinder- und Hausmärchen*** was an instant success in Germany and abroad. Especially because the language of the tale followed so closely the oral tradition of the common folk, the work appealed to children as well as to adults. Here was storytelling at its very best: the colloquial language flowed smoothly, rhythmically, and with ease while plots and themes spoke of human endeavors, be they within the context of adventure, reality, or the realm of the imagination. Both the language and the themes spoke directly to the heart and soul of the people.

The warm popular response to the ***Kinder- und Hausmärchen*** is well reflected in its publishing history. Even though the editions were not large and the sales were relatively modest, every edition had an increasing number of tales, with the exception of the ***Kleine Ausgabe*** (***Short Edition***) of 1825 that was especially designed for children. In all, seven editions were published between 1812 and 1857, and already in the 1820s numerous translations of the work spoke for its success. A sure sign of the work's influence were the many collections that were directly or indirectly inspired by the ***Kinder- und Hausmärchen.*** In his introduction to the third volume of the work in 1822, Wilhelm Grimm humbly observed: "The loyal perception of tradition, the natural expression, and, if it does not sound presumptuous, the richness and variety of the work have evoked a continuous interest in and recognition of the work at home and abroad."[25]

Wilhelm Grimm himself carefully took stock of the influence that their collection had exercised at home and abroad. An annotated bibliography that he attached to the sixth edition of the ***Kinder- und Hausmärchen*** (1850) encompassed numerous translations of their work in European countries. Among these were also Edgar Taylor's first English translation, the *German Popular Stories* (1823), which Wilhelm praised on account of its completeness and accuracy. His comments on this translation also betray his acquaintance with Cohen's complimentary review of their work in the English *Quarterly Review.* He further mentioned another English translation by Richard Doyle and John Edward Taylor, entitled *Fairy Ring: A New Collection of Popular Tales* (London, 1846), illustrated by Otto Spekter in 1847. He further listed with a note of satisfaction a Dutch translation by Hegermann and Lindencrone (1820), several Danish translations by Lindencrone, Öhlenschlager, and Molbeck (1835-1842), a Swedish translation by Reutendahl (1832), and some French translations (1834-1838), of which the first had been a single story, "The Juniper Tree," which appeared in the *Journal de débats* in Paris.[26]

To the sixth edition of the ***Kinder- und Hausmärchen*** Wilhelm also added a still longer supplementary list of folktale publications in Germany and abroad. Among the German-language works, he mentioned in his introduction collections from Austria, Bohemia, Prussia, Saxony, and Westphalia, and among individual works, he singled out the collections of W. Bechstein and W. Panzer. He also listed Hans Christian Andersen's *Eventyr fortalis for horn* (*Fairy Tales*), which had been published in Copenhagen in 1840.[27] Through Jessen's German translation he was familiar with this work, but since he also knew Danish, he may have read the original version as well. It is peculiar that he did include this work, as it is only partially based on the Danish folk tradition and generally would be classified as a volume of literary fairy tales rather than folktales. Yet, since Wilhelm included no other *Kunstmärchen* except for these, we may deduce that he considered Andersen's tales much closer to the folk tradition than the rest.[28]

Wilhelm's review of folktale publications also concerned collections of Scotland, Norway, and Sweden, although it was by no means restricted to the sphere of the Nordic Germanic traditions. It encompassed folktale collections of Ireland, Brittany, Finland, Livland, Kurland, Estland, Walachia, Hungary, Poland, Russia, the "Slavonic peoples," and Greece. Even the tales of the North American Indians won his attention with one of the longest reviews of the entire essay. Particular mention must be made of Wilhelm's appraisal regarding Thomas Crofton Croker's *Fairy Legends of the South of Ireland* (London, 1823), which had been the first work in the British Isles to follow the Romantic folklore revival and specifically the model of the Grimms' ***Kinder- und Hausmärchen.*** Having read the Grimms' tales as a young lad, Croker wandered across the countryside of Southern Ireland for three years, collecting songs and tales from the Irish peasants, shepherds, and miners.[29] Wilhelm was so thoroughly charmed by the spirit of these old Celtic traditions that he translated the work during the same year it appeared, publishing it under the title of ***Irische Elfenmärchen.*** Croker, in his turn, translated Wilhelm's long introduction **"Über die Elfen"** (**"About the Fairies"**) into English. He attached it to the second edition of his work, along with a "Dedicatory Letter" to the Brothers Grimm.[30]

The warm enthusiasm with which Wilhelm embraced the folktale collections of many lands unmistakenly bears the stamp of Herder's international orientation. His extensive comments (spanning more than seventy pages) testify to his genuine interest in other folk cultures and traditions, not just his own. Like Herder, he first of all perceived in the folktale collection of each culture the unique spirit and language of its own folk heritage, and then some universal elements reflecting the spirit of humanity shared by all.[31] This world-open attitude on the part of both Brothers Grimm has not yet received the attention it deserves. Partially because of mistranslations or misinterpretations and partially because of political distortions, a number of critics during the last century and ours did portray the Grimms one-sidedly as German nationalists with little or no concern for other cultures and traditions.

The positive critical responses to the Grimms' ***Kinder- und Hausmärchen*** came from two quarters: namely from those concerned with a revival of the medieval past and from those who believed in the merits of imaginative literature for children. Many critics during the early and mid-nineteenth century, in both Germany and the British Isles, still considered folk literature and children's literature on separate planes and were not ready for the Grimms' revolutionary idea that both were essentially related. Consequently, those who supported the cultivation of folklore used a different set of arguments than those who supported folklore as literature for children. The Grimms themselves were quite aware of the fact that their work had a two-fold appeal. On the one hand, it had attracted scholars who, by following their example, had made folktales the basis of philological and comparative studies while on the other hand, it had caught the attention of those who wished to free children from the narrow confines of a moralistic and didactic approach to education. Jacob Grimm consciously referred to this duality in the reception of their ***Kindermärchen*** in his preface to Anton Dietrich's *Russische Volksmärchen* (*Russian Folktales*) in 1831.[32] Folktales had recently become a two-fold center of interest, he observed, namely for students of medieval literature as well as for children. One had also begun to discover an important link between the language and ethics of folktales and those of medieval poetry. He reminded medieval scholars that they should not neglect to consult both folktales and epics mutually, for only an understanding of both could help in establishing their deeper meaning. He left no doubt that this meaning lay embedded in their mythical symbols, their childlike naivete, and their very language.[33]

The Grimms' Response to the Fearful

The great appeal that folktales had for children proved that children needed food for the imagination, Jacob wrote. Folktales were so much richer in substance and language than those rationally constructed tales written especially for them. To be honest, hadn't children long grown weary of barren tales that had nothing to offer to them except, as Jacob put it, "the thin suds of an empty morality"? By contrast, folktales were endowed with a poetic spirit that provided children with a much more nutritious diet. At last, children could be happy that one had returned to them what rightfully belonged to their domain, namely "the full taste of the still undiminished source of the old fantasy" (*"den unversiegten Quell der alten Fantasie"*).[34] Jacob implied that the native tradition in every land poured forth a never-ending stream of songs and tales that were sparkling and alive with the old folk imagination. As the spiritual history of the nation's past, and as the very essence of poetry, they appealed to all ages and needed neither embellishments nor added moralities to make them especially suitable for children.[35] In reflecting the humanity of man, the language of folktales was easily understood by all: It was naive yet vivid and concrete, and as it mirrored the childhood of mankind, so it appealed to the heart of the child.

Among Jacob Grimm's correspondences with Reimer, his publisher, exists an often-quoted letter stating explicitly that their folktale collection was not at all intended for children but that he was glad it appealed to them.[36] Does this letter represent a contradiction to his assertion that folktales belonged to children? Did he perhaps change his mind, as some critics suggested, or, what may be worse, did he live with the contradictions without bothering to resolve them in his mind? Was he ambiguous in regard to the question whether or not folktales were suitable for children, or did he have a definite theory of their value for young readers?

If we consider the Grimms' theory of the folktales' epic context,[37] this question may be resolved. What appears to be a dilemma in reality is nothing but a respect for the dual appeal of the vivid epic language that was an integral part of the folktale world. To the Grimms there was no clear-cut "either-or" solution to this question, for they thought that folktales were rich enough in themselves to appeal to adults and children alike. As they did not recognize a sharp line of division between folktales and epics, they considered both simultaneously as resource material for medieval and linguistic studies and as food for the child's imagination. They saw no reason why children should be artificially separated from the "old fantasy" that had existed in the childhood of mankind. Folktales were as much the domain of children as they were the domain of scholars.[38]

The dual nature and appeal of folktales, as the Grimms perceived it, was not evident to those among their contemporaries who were used to considering simple "nursery tales" and epic literature in two entirely different compartments. Achim von Arnim, for example, strongly advised them to change some tales in the ***Kinder- und Hausmärchen*** so as to make them more digestible for children. Unlike Friedrich Schlegel, who did not wish to spend much time thinking about the nature of folktales at all, Arnim did value the folktales' poetic appeal to children but thought they should be adapted to their taste and age. Why should some selections not be altered or omitted, so as to render the work as a whole more suitable for young readers? He never quite understood why at that time the Grimms insisted that children should read the folktales as they read the Bible, without adornments, abridgements, or alterations regarding their epic substance.

On January 28, 1813, Jacob responded in a letter to Arnim that he did not think that folktales were meant for children alone. Children were as imaginatively receptive to folktales as were older folks, he observed, and he saw no reason why the tales should be tailored for them in a special way.

> I believe that, in God's name, all children should read the entire folktale collection and be left to themselves in this process. What is the difference if there are some incomprehensible elements in the language and narrative of the folktales, such as in the Low German tales? One can always skip those things and even be glad if something is left for the

> future. Anyhow, you won't ever be able to give a book to children that is perfectly comprehensible to them, for there will always be some aspects of composition or syntax that, while clear to us, will be unclear to them. Yet, it's always pleasant to guess a little, which usually brings out some new aspects . . . My old principle, that I have already defended earlier, has always been that one shall write to please oneself rather than to give in to external pressures. Therefore, this book of folktales has not been written for children at all, but it makes me very glad that they do like it. I would not have worked on it with such a pleasure if I had not believed that with respect to poetry, mythology, and history it would have appeared just as important to the more serious and older adults as it has to me.[39]

Jacob stated that parents and educators expected too much of children too early, and altogether the wrong things from literature. Literature should not be used to teach children or to preach to them. The true "lessons" of literature emerged from a certain wisdom in the stories themselves that ignited and illuminated what the child already knew and possessed. Neither parents, nor teachers, nor books could bring wisdom to children from the "outside" "as if it were a bundle of firewood." Children had to be ready for a given tale to respond to it in a meaningful way. Jacob's remarks on reading readiness have a rather modern ring, but even more so his comments on the need for a nondidactic approach to folktales.

In his introduction to the second edition of the ***Kinder- und Hausmärchen*** (1819) Wilhelm Grimm, too, reacted to the criticism voiced by Arnim and others. It appears from his comments that a number of concerned parents and educators, too, had voiced the question of whether the tales were indeed suitable reading material for children. Were not some of the stories too harsh and cruel for young and sensitive minds? Wilhelm argued that in depicting good and evil forces in the world, folktales reflected the natural balance of life and an age-old human experience. Why should children be protected from what was natural? By using an analogy of nature, he explained that as the sunlight was unthinkable without the shadow, and as day would be incomplete without night, so evil in folktales was the foil for all that was good. For every sadness there was joy, for every fear there was consolation. Together, good and evil made up the substance of life and were true symbols of humanity. It would be a mistake to shield children from what they had a right to know and from what they wanted to know.

He still used another analogy in which he compared children to young plants in need of sunlight and the fresh air outdoors:

> Rain and dew fall on everything that exists on earth, as a blessing to all. Whoever does not dare to place his plants outside under the weather, fearing that they might be too sensitive and suffer damage, certainly will not demand that the rain and the dew should stay away because of it. Yet everything can grow under natural conditions, and this is what we shall keep in mind. By the way, we do not know of a healthy and strong book created by the people to which such objections would not apply to an ever greater degree. The Bible would have to be ranked at the top of such a list.[40]

Wilhelm's very choice of words betrays his Romantic belief that children should be raised naturally, without the artificial constraints that overprotective parents placed on them. In this case being "outside under the weather" meant to expose children to folktales without fear that they might catch a cold or suffer emotional damage. We recognize in such parables some educational theories of John Locke,[41] but more so those of Jean Jacques Rousseau, who permitted Emile to roam around freely under all weather conditions in the natural environment of the countryside, without having to fit himself into a tight schedule and, more importantly, without having to listen to moralistic lectures.[42] The contrast that Wilhelm Grimm creates here between the stuffy indoors and the fresh outdoors indicates his acceptance of the new Romantic trends in education. Romantic also is his association of the concepts of organic growth, health, and nature. He perceived the same reflection of vigor, purity, and wholeness in nature as in children and the age-old folktale. Confirming his Romantic faith in the innocence, health, and wisdom of both, he referred to the old proverb that the truth lay in the eye of the beholder. Those who wished to see evil certainly would find it, he wrote, yet to the pure everything was pure. Wilhelm wrote, "Children point without fear toward the stars, yet others who are steeped in folk superstitions are afraid they might offend an angel by doing so."[43] These "others" were exactly those who objected to unabridged folktales for children: parents and educators to whom he responded in this introduction. To grasp the deeper meaning of folktales, he advised them, one should read them with the naive mind of the child, not with the fears and phobias of an adult. While admitting that in this edition he had excised from the text of the tales some crude and offensive expressions, he insisted that in principle he would not consent to change the epic substance of the tales to the extent that they would alter the traditional concepts of good and evil.

The English Quest for Nordic Roots

In the British Isles, the earliest critics of the ***Kinder- und Hausmärchen*** at first did not bother too much about children as a potential audience of the tales but rather saw the tales' greatest significance as a valuable resource for medieval scholarship. Mr. Francis Cohen, who in 1819 first called attention to the merits of this work in the *Quarterly Review,* devoted nearly the entire length of his essay to the "northern antiquities" that the Brothers Grimm had discovered in these quaint old tales. Although Cohen's book review was indexed under the title of "Antiquities of Nursery Literature," the reviewer seemed to ignore the fact that the book was also intended for children. Being primarily impressed by the new potential that the Grimms' comparative approach offered to a study of other cultures and traditions, and especially his own, he wrote:

> Under the title of ***Kinder- und Hausmärchen*** they [the Brothers Grimm] have published a collection of German popular stories, singular in its kind, both for extent and variety, and from which we have acquired much information. In this collection we recognize a host of English and French and Italian stories of the same genre and species and extent in printed books, but the greatest part of the German popular nursery stories are stated by the editors to be traditionary [*sic*], some local, others widely known; and MM. Grimm say that they are confident that all those which they have so gathered from the oral tradition, with the exception indeed of Puss in Boots, are pure German and not borrowed from the stranger.[44]

What impressed him most was that the Grimms had taken considerable pains to show the relationship between folktales and Norse mythology, which the Grimms had emphasized in various essays and introductions. While ignoring the Grimms' argument, however, that precisely because of this epic relationship, folktales were suitable for children, he insisted that the tales were mainly material for interested scholars and only for "children of larger growth." Nevertheless, he commented enthusiastically on the Grimms' own analysis, indicating that the tales held many old folk beliefs that had almost been forgotten:

> *Thornrosa,* who is set a sleeping in consequence of the wounds inflicted by her spindle, is *Brynhilda* cast into slumber by the *Sleep Thorn* of Odin. The manner in which Loke hangs to the giant-eagle is better understood after a perusal of the story of **"The Golden Goose,"** to which the lads and lasses who touch it, adhere inseparably. In the stories of the **"Wicked Goldsmith,"** the **"Speaking Fish,"** and the **"Eating of the Bird's Heart,"** who does not recognize the fable of Sigurd?[45]

Over several pages at length, he then continued to draw upon other parallels in "Teutonic" folk traditions that the famous Dr. John Leyden had already observed in relation to German and Scottish ballads and folktales. There was the tale of "Frog-Lover," for example, which in every part of Germany, and also in the Grimms' collection, was known under the name of **"King of the Frogs."** In citing a similar passage in each, he called the readers' attention to the fact that "the rhythmical address of the aquatic lover, who is, of course, an enchanted prince, corresponds in the two languages":[46]

> "The Frog Lover"
> Open the door, my hinny, my heart,
> Open the door mine ain wee thing.
> And mind the words that you and I spak
> Down in the Meadow at the well spring.
>
> **"Der Froschkönig"** (**"King of the Frogs"**)
>
> Königstochter, Jüngste,
> Mach mir auf.
> Weisst du nicht was gestern
> Du zu mir gesagt
> Bei dem kühlen Brunnenwasser?
> Königstochter, Jüngste,
> mach mir auf.[47]
>
> (Princess, youngest,
> Open the door.
> Don't you remember what you told me
> yesterday
> At the cool well water?
> Princess, youngest,
> Open the door.)[48]

He concluded that such similarities spoke of the common "Teutonic stock" of all folktales in the Nordic countries, which proved that also English folktales were older than epics and romances.

The reviewer ascribed such similarities in folktales to the common origin of all popular fictions in the Nordic countries. Especially in England and in the Scottish Lowlands one might discover "offsets and grafts from the Teutonic stock,"[49] so much more as possibly most of the English folktales were of Nordic origin. As far as the age of folktales was concerned, he speculated that they were older than the epics and romances. In that sense, he disagreed with Dr. Leyden (and also with the Brothers Grimm), who had ascribed an older age to the epic tradition. At this point it is also essential to note that the Grimms had not made a claim to the purely German nor to the purely Nordic origin of German, English, or Scottish folktales. Ironically, it was Cohen, not the Grimms, who confined his comparisons to examples in folktales belonging to the northern or Teutonic sphere of influence. The Grimms themselves had also included in their study of variants the broader context of world mythology and epics. A case in point was the reviewer's limited analysis of comparable sound patterns in three tales: the voice of a bird in the Grimms' **"The Juniper Tree"** (**"Der Machandelbaum"**), the mewing of a cat in a Scottish tale, and the song of a troll in a Danish story.[50] Regardless of the basic themes underlying all three tales, he focused only on similar-sounding folk rhymes. This method of comparing variants differed substantially from that used by Wilhelm Grimm in his notes to the same tale of **"The Juniper Tree."** First, he singled out a basic motif, the bones collected and buried by the little girl, and then the main theme of the tale: death and resurrection. From here he would draw upon parallel bone motifs in relation to the death and recollection theme in the Egyptian myth of "Osiris," the Norse myth of "Thor and his Goat," and a comparable scene in the English *Perceval* (on which Jacob had written a long essay).[51] In all three of these examples in the discussion, he never left out of sight the great epic themes in folktales, thus never permitting the sound to take over the sense or meaning of their epic substance. This does not mean that Wilhelm was insensitive to comparable sound patterns. While referring in his notes to Dr. Leyden's study of this folktale, for example, he compared the "Kyvitt! Kyvitt!" of **"The Juniper Tree"** verse to the Scottish verse "Pew, wew, pew, wew (Pipi, wiwi), my minny me slew,"[52] yet in this case, too, the selection called attention to comparable themes, not just to similar sounds. It appears, then, that the reviewer learned only a part of the Grimms' comparative method without grasping its essential epic and thematic approach.

If at times the reviewer ventured beyond the realm of the Nordic sphere into other regions of the world, he did so in an exaggerated and arbitrary manner that bordered on the ridiculous. Thus, he interpreted the occurrence of frog motifs in German and Scottish folktales to their common origin in crocodiles that might be traced to the Calmuck Tartars. Yet even more of a pseudo-scientific "Giantology" was apparent in his suggestions that Tom Thumb might trace his noble ancestry to Anglo-Saxon kings, that Tom Hickathrift was related to the hammer-throwing Thor, the Norse god of thunder, and that Jack's famous beanstalk was a descendent of Yggdrasil, the mythical Nordic World Ash. What he omitted was the needed epic and linguistic documentation based on a close comparative study of language and major themes. Such exaggerations were bound to introduce some misunderstandings regarding the Grimms' methodology of comparative folktale studies. Ironically, Cohen reaped nothing but praise for his review of the book, but the review itself contributed to some of the first myths about the Grimms regarding the nature, method, and meaning of the ***Kinder- und Hausmärchen.***

The Plea for Imagination: Taylor and Scott

Edgar Taylor, a lawyer and former student of medieval and comparative literature, was so fascinated with the essay on the Grimms' collection in the *Quarterly Review* that he invited Francis Cohen to translate the work together with him into English. Under the title of *German Popular Stories,* the Grimms' folktales entered the English-speaking world in 1823. The volume consisted only of a selection of tales and a few additional ones from other sources, but it was well-written and achieved popular success, partially because Taylor had consciously used a simple folk style in which the purely English elements were predominant. In this effort he sacrificed some accuracy in the translation, but the work read well and helped to disseminate the German traditions in England. Taylor had also omitted the notes accompanying the German edition and rather apologetically wrote to the Grimms: "I am afraid you will still think I am sacrificing too much to the public taste, but in truth, I began the work less as antiquarian Man [than] as one who meant to amuse."[53]

Judging by the Grimms' earlier negative reaction to Arnim's proposal of adjusting the tales to children's needs, one might have expected a similar response to Taylor's translation, but the opposite was the case. As a matter of fact, Wilhelm found the translation "accurate" precisely because Taylor had remained loyal to the epic spirit and substance of the tales, which had also been his own objective throughout. In this context, it did not matter to them that he had taken a few liberties in the translation. The Grimms thanked Taylor for the copy of the work that he had sent them, congratulating him on a job well done.[54] Soon thereafter, Wilhelm began to warm up to the idea of bringing out a shorter German edition of the ***Kinder- und Hausmärchen,*** also without the scholarly notes. To his publisher, Reimer, he wrote in 1824:

> In London a translation of the ***Kindermärchen*** has appeared under the title of ***German Popular Stories.*** . . . It has found such a popular response that already now, after only three quarters of a year has passed since its publication, they are preparing a second edition of the work. Now I, too, wish we could bring out a *small German edition* [kleine deutsche Ausgabe] which, like the English edition, would contain only a selection of stories in a *single volume.*[55]

Not only the Grimms themselves but also their friend Professor George Benecke of Göttingen commented enthusiastically about Taylor's translation in a letter addressed to Wilhelm Grimm on March 1, 1826, in which he wrote: "These tales please me even more in translation than in the German edition. They sound more childlike, more naive, and more spirited." In this connection he still complimented Wilhelm on his own folktale style by adding that the editor of the *Fairy Legends* and especially Mr. Steward might learn much from him.[56] It was implied that Taylor had come much closer to Wilhelm's folktale style than either Thomas Crofton Croker or William Grant Stewart. Such judgments on the part of both the Brothers Grimm and Benecke are important ones to observe, especially in view of our analysis of the Grimms' concept of loyalty to tradition and the nature of Wilhelm's folktale style.

Such a short edition that Wilhelm had mentioned was indeed published at Christmastime in 1825, subtitled

Kleine Ausgabe (***Small Edition***), and its publishing success in Germany may well be ascribed to Taylor's inspiration. In this small volume Wilhelm not only made the tale selections for younger children but he also included seven illustrations of his brother, Ludwig Grimm, inspired by the copper engravings of George Cruikshank, that had first appeared in the English translation. Even though some of his language modifications are more evident in this edition than in the previous ones, Wilhelm did not follow Arnim's proposal of altering the tales substantially so as to please young children.[57]

Viewed from the perspective of the history of children's literature, Taylor's preface to the ***German Popular Stories*** represents a milestone in the direction of imaginative folk literature for children. Like Jacob and Wilhelm Grimm, he clearly perceived that children needed food for the imagination, not just lessons in manners and morals. He wrote that he had compiled this work because his young friends to whom he had told the tales had induced him to it by their "eager relish."[58] This indicates that he had actually told the stories to children before he published them in translation. Such an experience in storytelling may have helped him in developing a prose that resembled the oral style, but it must also have made him more aware of children's needs for the "old fantasy," as Jacob Grimm used to call it.

Taylor's interest in the child as a potential reading audience of folktales is particularly evident in the objections he raised against the severe restrictions that adults placed on children's reading choices at his time:

> Much might be urged against that too rigid and philosophic (we may rather say unphilosophic) exclusion of works of fancy and fiction from the libraries of children, which is advocated by some. Our imagination is surely as susceptible to improvement by exercise as our judgment or our memory; and so long as such fictions only are presented to the young mind as do not interfere with the important department of moral education, there can surely be no objection to their pleasurable employment of a faculty in which so much of our happiness in every period of life consists.[59]

His plea for imagination in children's literature sounds like an apology, and yet, against the background of didactic tales at his time, an explanation on his part was needed to overcome prevailing didactic trends. Sir Walter Scott made a similar point in a letter addressed to Taylor on January 16, 1823, which Taylor attached to a later edition of the ***German Popular Stories:***

> There is also a sort of wild fairy interest in them, which makes me think them fully better adapted to awaken the imagination and soften the heart of childhood than the good-boy stories which have been in later years composed for them. In the latter case, their minds are as if they were put into the stocks, like their feet at the dancing-school, and the moral always consists in good moral conduct being crowned with temporal success. Truth is, I would not give one tear shed over Little Red Riding Hood, for all the benefit to be derived from a hundred histories of Jemmy Goodchild. . . . In a word, I think the selfish tendencies will be soon enough acquired in this arithmetical age; and that, to make a higher class of character, our wild fictions—like our own wild music—will have more effect in awakening the fancy and elevating the disposition than the cooler and more elaborate compositions of modern authors and composers.[60]

Scott claimed that contrary to what most parents believed, not only the folktales were unsuitable for children but also dozens of stories that had been especially written for them. The tales of Marie Edgeworth represented an exception to the rule, but the rest of what was called "children's literature" missed out on life and literature altogether by being too obsessed with the element of rational instruction.

Judging by the support that the ***German Popular Stories*** received from the Grimms themselves, their friend Benecke, and Scott, Taylor indeed deserves credit for his translation. On the other hand, he, too, contributed some myths to the Grimms' supposed intent of the work and their method of collecting the tales, which have persisted up to the present. In the first place, since he omitted the Grimms' notes, his words in the preface were taken at their face value. Potentially they might have been corrected when Margaret Hunt brought out another complete translation with the notes later in the nineteenth century,[61] but these still did not place the notes within the context of the Grimms' epic theories, and the original works were difficult to obtain. First, Taylor repeated Cohen's mistaken notion that all of the tales were of "the highest Northern antiquity," including the tale **"Tom Thumb,"** even though he admitted that there existed variants of this tale in the Russian, Celtic, and Scandinavian folk tradition. Secondly, he introduced the mistaken notion that the Grimms' tales were based solely on the oral tradition, and thirdly, that most of them were derived from peasants: "The collection from which the following Tales are mainly taken is one of great extent, obtained for the most part by M. M. Grimm from the mouths of German peasants."[62]

Even though at the beginning of his preface Taylor acknowledged that the Grimms had "so admirably edited" the tales, his expression "by word of mouth" was the phrase that many critics after his time mistook for the Grimms' sole method of recording the tales. They simply assumed that the Grimms had committed them to print "exactly as they heard them." When twentieth-century researchers established as a fact that the Grimms had recorded the tales not only from peasants but also from townsfolk and educated persons, that they had changed the style and also individual motifs in the tales (although never the epic tale substance) from one edition to the next, and that, finally, they had also included tales from "printed sources" (folk books, chronicles, etc.), they assumed that the Grimms had not lived up to their promises. It has been particularly disconcerting to modern critics to discover that some of the Grimms' informants had been of French Huguenot descent, which seemed to contradict their claim that these were German popular stories. Yet, did the Grimms make such a claim? It was Taylor who changed the title of the ***Kinder- und Hausmärchen*** into ***German Popular Stories,*** and it was he (together with Cohen) who claimed that these stories were of purely German and Nordic descent. It remains to be examined in a later chapter to what degree both Cohen and Taylor misrepresented the Grimms' methods and intent. Although initially such misunderstandings were barely noticed, they snowballed at a later age when more distortions were added to them. In our time, they even culminated in a character assassination of the Grimms in Ellis's book *One Fairy Story Too Many, The Brothers Grimm and Their Tales.*[63]

How such myths took their course may well be observed in an 1824 review of the Grimms' ***German Popular Stories*** in the *Emperial Magazine.* While focusing solely on their "purely German and Nordic origin," the reviewer altogether ignored the Grimms' comparative view of international variants within the context of myth and epic. In taking over some notions of Cohen and Taylor, he further embellished these with his own fantasies. Simultaneously, he also ignored the folk tales' appeal to the childlike imagination. Instead, he merely referred to them as "quaint nursery stories" that really were not suitable for children of a younger age, as it was their main purpose to show "the antiquity of many of our nursery tales, and their evident Saxon and Germanic origin."[64] Evidently, he had mistaken a portion of Taylor's interpretation for the Grimms' own views on that subject, without consulting the original source.

Later in the century, Taylor's plea for imaginative children's stories fortunately dominated over the didactic voices raised against folktales. At least they motivated John Ruskin to call to his readers' attention that children needed folktales as they needed food for the imagination. In the best spirit of Taylor and Scott, he urged them to use folktales with children while doing away with the tiresome new tales whose sole purpose it was to teach a moral lesson. "Lost in the new tales is a simplicity of their conception of love and beauty, as they emphasize too much deliberate wisdom," he wrote. Children should not be told explicity in stories how to choose between right or wrong but rather should be allowed the freedom of making their own judgments by following the course of the story plot. Being given such a freedom of interpretation, they would undoubtedly develop what he called a self command. "Children so trained," he explained, "have no need of moral fairy tales. The effect of the endeavor to make stories moral upon the literary merit of the work itself is as harmful as the motive of the effort is false, for every fairy tale worth recording at all is the remnant of a tradition possessing true historical value."[65]

Ruskin's words once more focused attention on the need for fairy tales without a purpose, tales that were to be enjoyed for their own imaginative contents and also for their traditional value. Yet he did not speak the last word on the subject. Didactic writers preceding him did a thorough job in spreading their gospel against "fairy tales" in general and the Grimms' collection in particular. Their arguments against the reading of folktales may be worth a closer examination, especially in view of the question of how and to what extent they resemble or differ from those that, for one reason or another, are still voiced in the twentieth century.

The Irish Connection

The Grimms' relationship with Thomas Crofton Croker is of significance for our understanding of the ***Kinder- und Hausmärchen*** for several reasons. One of these relates to the influence of this work on fieldwork collections as well as comparative folktale studies in Ireland. Another reason is that it reveals the Grimms' attitude toward the concept of loyalty to tradition, perhaps even more clearly than do Wilhelm's various prefaces to the work. In itself, the story of mutual respect and translations attests to the Grimms' persistent efforts toward a better understanding of folk cultures other than their own.

In 1815 Jacob and Wilhelm Grimm received a gift from a friend who had just purchased it during a trip to London: a newly published work by an anonymous author, entitled *Fairy Legends and Traditions of the South of Ireland.* As the Grimms recognized his style from an earlier publication, *Researches of the South of Ireland,* they assumed that the author was Thomas Crofton Croker of Cork, Ireland. An inquiry placed with the London publisher of the work soon proved that they were correct. In less than a year the Grimms translated the work and published it under the title of *Irische Elfernmärchen* (*Irish Fairy Tales*), to which Wilhelm added a sixty-two page essay **"Uber die Elfen" ("About the Fairies")**. What caught their interest in this work was Croker's claim that he had loyally collected these tales from the mouths of the Irish peasants, hoping to capture the flavor of the Irish language, customs, folk beliefs, and ways of thinking.[66]

As a boy, Thomas Crofton Croker had read the Grimms' ***Kinder- und Hausmärchen,*** and the idea of fieldwork research so much inspired him that at the age of fourteen he set out with an older friend to wander for two years across Southern Ireland, collecting and recording the tales of the common folk. To these tales he later added tales from Scotland and Wales, as well as from England.

An accident happened shortly before the manuscript went to the printer, which had some serious implications: Croker lost the manuscript. After an unsuccessful search, he tried to reconstruct the tales, turning in this process to the help of some of his friends who had formerly supplied him with tales for the work. Croker then published the work anonymously, hoping in this way to acknowledge the help of others. Unfortunately, one of his friends later took advantage of this humble gesture by claiming the copyright of these stories and discrediting their authenticity.

The Grimms' translation of the work revealed their deep respect for folktales and legends of Ireland and promoted a broader interest in Celtic tradition. The long comparative essay that Wilhelm attached to the translation, titled **"Über die Elfen,"** was the first of its kind by attempting a systematic comparison of fairy lore and folk beliefs in Ireland, Scotland, England, and Wales. Wilhelm's system of numbering the titles and subtitles of his essay gives the appearance of an encyclopedic essay, which in fact it is, judging by its objective to classify the fairy lore of the British Isles. Such a format lent an air of scientific objectivity to the essay, setting the stage for numerous other comparative works of fairy lore later in the century and in our time, such as Katherine Briggs's *Dictionary of the Fairies.* Wilhelm drew upon examples and comparisons contained in Croker's *Fairy Legends,* but he broadened the scope of comparison by relating examples from Danish, Swedish, Norwegian, Icelandic, German, and Serbian folklore.

Far from being dry and schematic, however, the essay remained lively and poetic throughout. Characteristic of Wilhelm's style is his fine perception of the old *Naturpoesie,* enhanced by the descriptive quality of the text. The poetic tone of his narrative reminds one of his famous introductions to the ***Kinder- und Hausmärchen.***

> The Elves, which in their true share are but a few inches high, have an airy, almost transparent body so delicate in their form, that a dew drop, when they dance on it, trembles indeed but never breaks. Both sexes are of extraordinary beauty and mortal beings cannot be compared with them. They do not live alone or in pairs but always in large societies. They are invisible to us, particularly in the day-time . . . [67]

As it was his main objective to describe and analyze yet not to embellish and entertain his audience, his style had little to do with fantasy writing, even though its tone and use of imagery contributed substantially to the poetic nature of its subject.

Systematic and modern in his approach was that he analyzed the topic first of all from a typological perspective, considering separately the fairies, the cluricauns, the banshee, the phooka, along with dwarfs, mermaids, brownies, witches, and other creatures. Within each category he proceeded like an anthropologist, giving close attention to their respective habitat, dress, food, age, social life, magic powers, and interactions with humans. Thus, he informed the reader about the various group gatherings of the elves, for example, their fondness of secrecy, dancing, singing, playing ball—and occasionally, of throwing small pebbles at humans. He explained their light side in terms of their helpfulness, kindness, and cooperation and their dark and evil side in terms of their mean tricks, obnoxious behavior, and vengeful actions.

While trying to maintain a clear distinction among various fairy creatures along national and cultural lines, Wilhelm also pointed out cross-cultural correspondences and striking similarities. Further, he would draw upon comparisons with fairy superstitions reflected in folk songs, ballads, legends, epic literature, customs, laws, and folk beliefs in such countries as Denmark, Norway, Sweden, Germany, Iceland, France, and Serbia. Among these, he gave special attention to stories about elves and dwarfs from the *Elder Edda* and the *Younger Edda,* discussing in conclusion how even the well-meaning "light elves" of Norse mythology over time had assumed darker and meaner features because of the impact of Christianity. Like Jacob in the ***Deutsche Mythologie,*** Wilhelm blamed it largely on missionaries and priests that the folk belief in fairy lore around the world was gradually vanishing. In an attempt to destroy "evil pagan superstitions," they had blackened the pagan folk beliefs in the minds of the people while absorbing others into church customs and rituals. Over the centuries, angels had assumed some features of the fairies. This could be observed in designs of the eighth century, which still showed them as men in long white robes, whereas paintings of the twelfth century already depicted them like fairies: as women or fragile young children with long, flowing hair.[68]

When, in 1826, the Grimms sent to Croker a copy of the newly published translation, titled *Irische Elfenmärchen,* he was delighted about it and even more so about Wilhelm's essay. In the preface to the second edition of *Fairy Legends* (1828), he wrote that normally an author had little reason to plume himself if his work appeared in French or German, as the exchange of ideas among European nations had become a common thing. This case was different, he said, as the work had been translated by no lesser persons than the eminent Brothers Grimm, whose friendship and valuable correspondence it had also procured him. He called their translation "faithful and spirited," announcing that they had prefixed to it a most learned and valuable introduction respecting fairy superstition in general. With pride he quoted Wilhelm Grimm: "Whoever has a relish for innocent and simple poetry will feel attracted by these tales. They possess a peculiar flavour, which is not without its charm."[69] They came from a country, wrote Wilhelm, with whom Germany had only had few relations, and those few had not even been pleasant ones, but whose people could trace back their history to ancient roots and still spoke their own language. Perhaps more so than elsewhere, the language of the Irish folktales and legends bore traces of this ancient past, and so did Irish folk beliefs and superstitions.

Croker dedicated the second edition of *Fairy Legends* to Wilhelm Grimm with the words: "To Dr. Wilhelm Grimm, Secretary of the Prince's Library, Member of the Royal Scientific Society of Göttingen etc., etc., etc., At Cassel in Hesse." The greatest compliment that Croker paid Wilhelm was that, in his turn, he had translated his essay "About the Fairies" from German into English, attaching it to the same edition as an introduction. He stated that he had given this essay without note or comment of his own, because he perfectly agreed with him in every point regarding a scientific analysis of fairy lore.

Croker commented favorably about Wilhelm's scientific method of supplying comparative notes to the tales. He fully appreciated what he called "a clear and firm view of the subject" rather than "a poetic amplification." It might be argued that Croker's own style in the *The Fairy Legends* did reflect some "poetic amplification,"[70] yet his comments show that he was quite conscious of the dangers of taking too many liberties in rendering folktales by turning them into fantasies.

At first, Croker reaped due applause for his contributions to Irish folktales, also in England and Scotland. *Frazer's Magazine* introduced him as "The King of All Fairies," who had appointed himself "the historiographer to King Oberon and all his Cluricauns." In an illustration it introduced the "Fairy King," mentioning that this famous author, who was only the size of a leprechaun, standing only four and a half feet high, had won many national and international honors.[71] An article in the *Quarterly Review* of 1825 praised Croker for having captured in his tales "the very smoke flavor of the turf in simple pleasant huts."[72] The German translation of his work still further enhanced his fame. It was through this translation that Sir Walter Scott first became acquainted with the book in Abbotsford. Like Thomas Moore and Henry Crabbe, Scott had admired Croker's earlier publications, among them his collection of early Irish folk poetry, the "keens" of Ireland (traditional funeral songs), as well as his *Researches of the South of Ireland,* which included travel descriptions along with legends and local superstitions. Being especially impressed with the *Fairy Legends,* he wrote to him in a letter: "You are our—I speak of the Celtic Nation—great authority now on Fairy Superstitions and have made Fairy Land your Kingdom. . . . I have been reading the German translation of your tales," he added as an explanation, "and the Grimms' very elaborate introduction."[73]

Scott sensed in many Irish fairy tales some tales of his own country. Both hinted at the Gaelic-Celtic connection in folklore, which he had long pursued in language and history. "The extreme similarities of your fictions to ours is striking," he wrote to Croker. "The Cluricaune (which is the admirable subject for a pantomime) is not known here. The beautiful superstition of the Banshee seems in a great measure peculiar to Ireland, . . . but I think I could match all of your other tales with something similar."[74] He related to him a number of additional tales of the Highlanders that, in his view, resembled those of the Irish.

Croker's reputation began to suffer severely after Thomas Keightley published in 1828 a comparative folklore study, titled *Fairy Mythology,* in which he confessed that he and his friends had merely played a joke on him by telling him their own fantasies instead of geniune Irish folktales. Gleefully, he pointed to "The Soul Cages," a tale which he claimed as his invention, even though he admitted that two persons whom he met occasionally were, for unknown reasons, quite familiar with the story. Taking advantage of the first anonymous edition of Croker's *Fairy Legends,* Keightley then replenished those tales that he claimed to have contributed to the work, without giving credit to Croker for having first recorded them prior to losing the manuscript. Without betraying that his "assistance" to the work had in reality consisted only of reconstructing four tales, he vainly claimed to have supplied him with "the bulk" of them.[75]

It is unlikely that Croker would have printed "The Soul Cages" if he had not heard and recorded it himself previously. The fact that Keightley reprinted the tale himself in his *Fairy Mythology* further attests to the fact that he considered it a genuine folktale after all. That his academic honesty left something to be desired is also evident in that he failed to acknowledge in his work Wilhelm Grimm's essay "About the Fairies," whose method he adopted throughout in his comparative study of fairy lore. He did mention the Brothers Grimm in his notes, but only in very general terms and without reference to this essay.

In the second edition of *Fairy Legends* Croker did take a stand on Keightley's accusation, affirming the loyalty of his approach to the folk tradition: "Deeply as I lament that such delusions should exist," he wrote, "these facts will sufficiently prove that I have not (as has been insinuated) conjured up forgotten tales, or attempted to perpetuate the creed which has disappeared."[76]

The Grimms were convinced that Croker had generally caught the tone of the geniune Celtic fairy tales and, more significantly, that his tales did justice to the Irish oral tradition. Wilhelm Grimm warmly reviewed the work in ***Göttingische Gelehrte Anzeigen*** in 1826, in which he especially praised the choice of language in which Croker had rendered the tales.

> The anonymous author has captured the traditions of the place with an obvious loyalty, and he has spent an unusual care in rendering them. . . . The Irishmen themselves will have a special pleasure in recognizing in these tales scenes reflecting their own character, proverbial expressions, native jokes and analogues, and untranslateable idioms; but foreigners, too, have a feeling for these things and value them.[77]

Wilhelm considered Croker's tales loyal to the "spirit of tradition." These words are of significance in relation to his own proclamation of loyalty in the 1812 preface to the ***Kinder- und Hausmärchen,*** as he in neither case said anything about a requirement regarding a "word-by-word" accuracy. Instead, he commented favorably on Croker's skillful use of proverbs, "and other little things of this kind that add a lively touch to his presentation—all of which cannot be learned through books."[78] In the rhythm of proverbial speech patterns, he felt the very breath of the folk tradition or, as he put it, "the very smoke flavor of the turf in simple peasant huts." He liked Croker's use of the natural colloquial style. He fully realized that Croker had "translated" these tales from the original Gaelic, just as he and Jacob had translated many of the contributions to the ***Kinder- und Hausmärchen*** from various German dialects. Jacob was more exacting in his critique of the *Fairy Legends,* as far as the concept of loyalty to tradition was concerned. He had the advantage over Wilhelm of knowing Gaelic as well as English and thus used the judgment of a linguist in criticizing some of the liberties Croker had taken in rendering the tales:

> The content of this collection is genuine, and in a skillful way the tales are interwoven with strange, daring, but lively turns of speech, with images and proverbs of the common folk, all of which contribute to its realism. It is regrettable, however, that the narrative leans a little to the taste of the time, still more so than one might wish for, especially when he makes use of irony. This easily creates the impression that the fairy tale elements are only the products of an excited imagination—an impression that is detrimental to the deeper significance of the work.[79]

Overall, however, Jacob's evaluation of *The Fairy Legends* was positive, for otherwise he would not have cooperated with Wilhelm in translating the work into German. Given his knowledge of Celtic and Gaelic folklore and his acquaintance with the Gaelic language, it is not likely that he would have become the victim of another *Ossian* delusion. In his ***Deutsche Mythologie,*** in which he used a similar comparative method that Wilhelm had introduced in his essay **"About the Fairies,"** he made substantial use of Croker's work, also in connection with comparisons based on a linguistic analysis. It must be noted, however, that Jacob, too, failed to give credit to Wilhelm for his pioneer work in comparative fairy-lore studies, although he recognized the contributions of Croker and Keightley in corresponding footnotes. In his chapter "Wights and Elves," he stated:

> Celtic tradition, which runs particularly rich on this subject, I draw from the following works: *Fairy Legends and Traditions of the South of Ireland,* by Crofton Croker, Lond. 1825; 2nd ed., parts 1,2,2, Lond. 1828. The *Fairy Mythology,* by Th. Keightley, vols. 1,2, Lond. 1828.[80]

Jacob did not mention the controversy, yet his critical comments on Croker's style betray that Keightley's derogatory comments had not escaped him. This is further evident from the fact that neither he nor Keightley included in their translated work *Über die Elfen* the most controversial story, "The Soul Cages," thus giving Keightley the benefit of the doubt.

A British reviewer caught up with the controversy and spared no words to express his contempt for Keightley. Praising Croker's efforts in capturing the genuine flavor of the Irish folktale, he wrote: "It's like the peat taste of whiskey which touches the Irish origin of liquor, and it is liked and appreciated for its peculiar flavor." Yet, chiding Keightley, he added "And since he has had so much intercourse with the 'good people,' we would have him consider how severely they punish those witless mortals who approach them with presumption and selfishness. Even the legend of the peasant has its moral."[81]

It is possible that the high esteem that especially Wilhelm Grimm and Sir Walter Scott had for Croker did influence the reviewer's opinion at that time, yet also Croker's other folkloristic and historical contributions attest to his loyalty to the spirit of tradition. The poet Harry Crabbe praised him highly for rendering "the sense of the original keens" with great skill and loyalty. Croker's biographical work on Joseph Holt, General of the Irish Rebels, also received high praise regarding its respect for historical details. There is no question that Croker added his own flavor to the tales, but he did not embellish the tales as some of the fairy-tale writers of the *Cabinet des fées* had done before him.

The Grimms' tolerance of the occasional intrusion of Croker's personal style illustrates well that they were not dogmatic about the concept of loyalty, as long as it reflected the spirit of the native folk tradition. Overall, they ranked his loyalty to the folk tradition much higher than that of Musäus, Albert Ludwig Grimm, and other German folktale collectors at the time.

Additional unpublished translations of nine Irish fairy legends by Wilhelm Grimm were discovered among the Grimms' manuscripts in the Hessian State Archives of Marburg in 1985 that attest to Wilhelm's fondness for the Irish folk tradition. With support from the European Folktale Society (Europäische Märchengesellschaft), Werner Moritz and Charlotte Oberfeld edited and published these under the title of *Irische Land- und Seenmärchen* (*Irish Folktales of Land and Sea*) in 1986, giving reference to Thomas Crofton Croker as the original collector of the tales and Wilhelm Grimm as the translator.[82] This work provides new testimony to Wilhelm's sustained interest in Irish folklore within the context of international folktale collections.

Notes

[1] Heinz Rölleke, *Die Märchen der Brüder Grimm*. Series: *Artemis Einführungen*, vol. 18 (Munich: Artemis Verlag, 1985), pp. 70-85. See also T. F. Crane, "The External History of the Kinder- und Hausmärchen of the Brothers Grimm," *Modern Philology* 14, 10, 1917, pp. 577-611. Rölleke substantially revised the critical perception of the role of the Grimms' informants while also calling attention to the need for investigating the folktales from a comparative rather than a strictly national perspective.

[2] Herder established his name as a humanist not only through his writings on the philosophy of the history of mankind and his international folk song collection *Stimme der Völker in Liedern: Volkslieder* (1778-79) but also by his essays on Homer, Ossian, and Shakespeare. He defined his concept of *Naturpoesie* in his essay "Auszug aus einem Briefwechsel über Ossian und die Lieder alter Völker" ("Excerpt from a Correspondence about Ossian and Songs of the Old Nations"). Herder's approach to *Naturpoesie* differed from that of the Brothers Grimm not only because he included it in the poetry of "poetic geniuses" but also in that he used such poetry as an inspiration to write his own "folk ballads." Johann Gottfried Herder, *Sämmtliche Werke 5* (Berlin: Weidmannsche Verlagsbuchhandlung, 1894), Bernard Suphan, ed.

[3] "The State of German Literature," *Edinburgh Review* 24 (June-Oct., 1927), p. 304.

[4] Sir Walter Scott, *Minstrelsy of the Scottish Border Countries: Consisting of Historical and Romantic Ballads Collected in the Southern Countries of Scotland* (Edinburgh: Ballantyne, 1802-03). See Preface of the 1830 edition.

[5] Hans Kohn, *Prelude to Nation-States: The French-German Experience, 1781-1815* (Princeton, N.J.: Princeton University Press, 1964), p. 127.

[6] Richard Benz, *Die deutsche Romantik: Geschichte einer geistlichen Bewegung* (Stuttgart: Klett, 1956), pp. 239-45. Also H. G. Schenk, *The Mind of the European Romantics: An Essay on Cultural History* (London: Constable, 1966), with a preface by Isaiah Berlin. See in particular Chapter 5, "Forebodings and Nostalgia for the Past," pp. 32-46.

[7] Jacob Grimm, *"Alte und neue Sagen und Wahrsagungen,"* in *Zeitung für Einsiedler* (*Trosteinsamkeit*), 1804, cited by Kohn, p. 178.

[8] Joseph Görres, *Die teutschen Volksbücher* (Heidelberg: Mohr und Zimmer, 1807). Goethe, too, had concerned himself with the *Volksbücher*. Next to the tale of Melusine (which he reworked into a *Kunstmärchen*), he used the folk book story of Dr. Johannes Faustus as a model for his *Urfaust* und *Faust*. The Brothers Grimm recognized certain "stock characters" of folktales in the folk book characters of the Schildbürger and others, which convinced them of the close connection between these words and German folktales.

[9] Wilhelm Grimm, *Altdänische Heldenlieder, Balladen und Märchen* (Heidelberg: Mohr und Zimmer, 1811). See also Maria Greverius, *"Wege zu Wilhelm Grimm's 'Altdänischen Heldenliedern,' "* in *Brüder Grimm Gedenken* 1, Ludwig Denecke, ed. (Marburg: Elvert Verlag, 1963), pp. 469-88. Unlike Herder and Scott, Wilhelm Grimm did not compose his own "folk ballads."

[10] Jacob and Wilhelm Grimm, *Kinder- und Hausmärchen* (Berlin: Reimer, 1812).

[11] Ibid., Introduction, p. iv.

[12] Marianne Thalmann, *The Romantic Fairy Tale: Seeds of Surrealism* (Ann Arbor: University of Michigan Press, 1970), pp. 4-24. Thalmann predominantly discusses the *Kunstmärchen*. For a thorough discussion of the *Volksmärchen* see Stith Thompson, *The Folktale* (Bloomington: Indiana University Press, 1963); Max Lüthi, *Once Upon a Time: On the Nature of Fairy Tales* (Bloomington: Indiana University Press, 1970); and Max Lüthi, *Volksmärchen und Volkssage: Zwei Grundformen erzählender Dichtung* (Bern: Franke Verlag, 1961).

[13] At first, the major motivation for a correspondence between Jacob Grimm and Sir Walter Scott was an exchange of medieval manuscripts on which both of them had been working independently, yet Jacob also expressed his hope that he would motivate Scott to aid him in an international folktale collection project. Walter Schoof and Jörn Göres, eds., *Unbekannte Briefe der Brüder Grimm. Unter Ausnutzung des Grimmschen Nachlasses* (Bonn: Althenäum, 1960). Of particular relevance is Jacob Grimm's letter to Sir Walter Scott on June 9, 1814.

[14] Joseph Prestel, *Handbuch zur Jugendliteratur. Geschichte der deutschen Jugendschriften* (Freiburg, Brsg.: Herder Verlag, 1933). Consult the chapter on folk literature for youth.

[15] H. J. G. Grierson, David Cook and W. M. Parker, eds., *The Letters of Sir Walter Scott 1811-1814* vol. 3 (London: Constable & Company, 1933) (Centenary edition), pp. 285-89.

[16] Ibid.

[17] Joseph Lefftz, ed., *Märchen der Brüder Grimm: Urfassung im der Original-handschrift der Abtei Oelenberg im Elsass.* Series: *Wissenschaftliche Reihe der Lothring. Wissenschaftl. Gesellschaft.* Series C, vol. 1 (Straßbourg: Wissenschaftliche Gesellschaft zu Straßburg, 1927). Already in 1924 Franz Schulz published the manuscript of the tales with the Bibliophile-Society in Frankfurt am Main. See Friedrich Panzer, ed., *Die Kinder- und Hausmärchen der Brüder Grimm. Vollständige Ausgabe in der Urfassung* (Wiesbaden: Emil Vollmer Verlag, n.d., about 1955), p. 42n. The rediscovered manuscript is usually referred to as the *Oelenberg-Handschrift.* See also Hermann Gerstner, *Die Brüder Grimm: Biographie mit 48 Bildern* (Gerabonn: Hohenloher Verlag, 1971), pp. 85-98; and Gabriele Seitz, *Die Brüder Grimm: Leben, Werk, Zeit* (Munich: Winkler Verlag, 1984), pp. 90-122.

[18] Gerstner, p. 108.

[19] Prestel, p. 258.

[20] Johann Gustav Büsching, ed., *Volks-Sagen, Märchen und Legenden* (Leipzig: Carl Heinrich Reclam, 1812).

[21] Wilhelm Grimm, *Kinder- und Hausmärchen* (Berlin: Reimer, 1812), Introduction.

[22] Albert Ludwig Grimm, *Kindermärchen* (Heidelberg: Mohr and Zimmer, 1809) and Peter Leberecht (Ludwig Tieck's pseudonym), *Ritter Blaubart: Ein Ammenmärchen (in vier Akten)* (Leipzig: Karl August Nicolai, 1797). See also Ludwick Tieck, *Werke* 4 vols., Marianne Thalmann, ed. (Munich: Winkler Verlag, 1964).

[23] Jacob Grimm, *Circular wegen Aufsammlung der Volkspoesie,* Ludwig Denecke, ed., with an introduction by Kurt Ranke (Kassel: Bärenreiter Verlag, 1965). Jacob actually did send out this questionnaire of 360 copies. See Chapter 7.

[24] Jacob and Wilhelm Grimm, *Kinder- und Hausmärchen,* 2d ed., Vol. 3 (Berlin: Reimer, 1822). Vol. 1 contained Wilhelm's essay about the nature of folktales.

[25] *Kinder- und Hausmärchen,* 7th ed., 3 vols. (Göttingen: Diederichs, 1856/57). Like the third, fourth, fifth, and sixth editions, this work was subtitled *Grosse Ausgabe* (Large Edition). Grimms' notes to the folktales were published separately in its first volume of 1856, and the two expanded folktale volumes followed in 1857. The seventh edition has become popularly known as the *Grosse Ausgabe,* even though its two folktale volumes alone had less pages than the sixth edition.

[26] Johannes Bolte and Georg Polivka, *Anmerkungen zu den Kinder- und Hausmärchen der Brüder Grimm* (Leipzig: Diederich'sche Verlagsbuchhandlung 1913-1918). Vol. 5 contains an analysis of the Grimms' international influences on folktale collections around the world.

[27] *Kinder- und Hausmärchen* 6th ed. (Göttingen: Verlag der Dieterich'schen Buchhandlung, 1850), Introduction, pp. i-lxxvi.

[28] Gerstner, pp. 168-85. In his autobiography Andersen himself comments on this meeting with Jacob Grimm in Berlin and Copenhagen. See Hans Christian Andersen. *Das Märchen meines Lebens: Briefe und Tagebücher,* trans. from the Danish with an afterword by Erling Nielsen (Munich: Winkler Verlag, 1967), pp. 349-53.

[29] See also Christa Kamenetsky, "The Irish Fairy Legends and the Brothers Grimm," *Proceedings of the Ninth Annual Children's Literature Association in Gainesville, Florida, 1981* (Ann Arbor, Mi.: Malloy Lith. and the Children's Literature Association, 1983), pp. 77-87.

[30] *Irische Elfenmärchen,* trans. Wilhelm and Jacob Grimm (Leipzig: Friedrich Fleischer, 1826). Walzel, pp. 3-73.

[31] Christa Kamenetsky, "Herder und der Mythos des Nordens," *Revue de littérature comparée* 47, 1 (Jan.-Mar. 1973), pp. 23-41.

[32] Jacob Grimm, "Vorwort" (Introduction) in *Russische Volksmärchen in den Urschriften gesammelt und ins Deutsche übersetzt,* trans. and ed. Anton Dietrich (Jena: Diederichs, 1931).

[33] Jacob Grimm, ibid.

[34] Ibid.

[35] Walter Schoof, *Die Entstehungsgeschichte der Kinder- und Hausmärchen* (Hamburg: Hauswedell, 1959), pp. 10-15.

[36] Prestel, p. 235.

[37] Bolte and Polivka, Vol. 5, pp. 533-49.

[38] Panzer, Introduction, p. 37. See also Ulrike Bastian, *Die Kinder- und Hausmärchen der Brüder Grimm in der literaturpädagogischen Diskussion des 19. und 20. Jahrhunderts* (Frankfurt am Main: M. Haag und Herchen, 1986).

[39] Reinhold, Steig, *Achim von Arnim und Jacob und Wilhelm Grimm* (Stuttgart: Cotta Verlag), p. 269.

[40] *Kinder- und Hausmärchen,* 2d ed. (Berlin: Reimer, 1819). Introduction.

[41] John Locke, "Dialogues Concerning Education" (London, 1745) in John Locke, *The Educational Writing of John Locke,* James L. Axtell, ed. (Cambridge: Harvard University Press, 1970), pp. 270-74. See also Samuel F. Pickering, Jr., *John Locke and Children's Books in Eighteenth Century England* (Knoxville: University of Tennessee Press, 1981). Also Bettina Hürlimann, *Three Centuries of Children's Books in Europe* (Cleveland: World Publishing Company, 1968), Chapters 3 and 4.

[42] Jean Jacques Rousseau, *Emile,* trans. B. Foxley (London: J. M. Dent & Sons, 1911). For Rousseau's influence on the history of children's literature, consult John Rowe Townsend, *Written for Children: An Outline of English Language Children's Literature,* 2d ed. (Boston: The Horn Book and Lippincott Company, 1975), Part 3.

[43] *Kinder- und Hausmärchen,* 2d ed. (1819), Introduction.

[44] "Fairy Tales of the Lilliputian Cabinet, Containing Twenty-Five Choice Pieces of Fancy and Fiction, collected by Benjamin Tabart" *Quarterly Review* 21 (1819), pp. 91-114. The review was anonymous, but Taylor made reference to Mr. Francis Cohen as its author, who was also the (unnamed) co-translator of the *German Popular Tales* in 1823. See also Ruth Michaelis Jena and Ludwig Denecke, "Edgar and John Edward Taylor, die ersten englischen Übersetzer der Kinder- und Hausmärchen" in *Brüder Grimm Gedenken,* vol. 2, pp. 190-95.

[45] Ibid. The reviewer took this quote out of context from Wilhelm Grimm's folktale analysis of the 1819 edition of the *Kinder- und Hausmärchen* (see introduction). Both Brothers Grimm followed the Indo-Germanic myth theory of Rask, but simultaneously they also made room for other theories. A subsequent review article on the *Kinder- und Hausmärchen* in the *Emperial Magazine* 5 (1824) followed the simplistic interpretation of the Grimms' ideas in the *Quarterly Review,* without reexamining the Grimms' own views on the subject on the basis of original research.

[46] *Quarterly Review.*

[47] Ibid.

[48] Ibid.

[49] Ibid.

[50] Compare Wilhelm's notes on "The Juniper Tree" in *Kinder- und Hausmärchen,* 2d ed., Vol. 2.

[51] Ibid.

[52] Ibid.

[53] Otto Hartwig, "Zur ersten englischen Übersetzung der Kinder- und Hausmärchen der Brüder Grimm," *Zentralblatt für Bibliothekswesen* (Jan.-Fb. 1898), pp. 6-7.

[54] Ibid.

[55] Wilhelm Grimm's letter to Georg Reimer, dated August 16, 1823. Hans Gürtler and Albert Leitzmann, eds. *Briefe der Brüder Grimm* (Jena: Verlag der Fromannschen Buchhandlung, 1823), p. 127.

[56] Wilhelm Grimm's letter to Professor Georg Benecke, dated March 1, 1826. Hartwig, pp. 20-28. Wilhelm's references to William Grant Stewart show his familiarity with Stewart's work *The Popular Superstitions and Festive Amusements of the Highlanders of Scotland* (Edinburgh, 1823) that discussed the powers and traits of fairies, ghosts, witches, and brownies. See also Richard Dorson. *The British Folklorists: A History* (Chicago: University of Chicago Press, 1968), pp. 156-57. It is possible that Stewart's work in some ways inspired Wilhelm to compose his comparative essay "About the Fairies" that he attached to the German translation of Croker's work. In turn, Wilhelm's almost anthropological survey of leprechauns and related fairy spirits may have inspired Katherine Briggs and other folklorists in this century to compile dictionaries of the fairies.

[57] *Kinder- und Hausmärchen. Kleine Ausgabe* (Berlin: Reimer, 1825). This short edition was the most popular one with children and exceeded all other editions in terms of sales. Still in his introduction to the 1850 edition of the *Kinder- und Hausmärchen* Wilhelm

commented favorably about the illustrations by George Cruikshank, as well as those of Richard Doyle and Otto Specter in later English editions of the work (1846 and 1847), mentioning that Specter's illustrations were attached to individual tales published separately in London.

[58] Edgar Taylor, "Introduction" in *German Popular Stories,* trans. Edgar Taylor (London: Murray, 1823).

[59] John Ruskin, "Preface," in *Grimm's Household Tales* 3d ed., Margaret Hunt, trans. and ed. (London: George Bell & Sons, 1910).

[60] Letter of Sir Walter Scott to John Taylor, Abbotsford, January 16, 1823. Taylor attached this letter to *German Popular Tales* 2d ed., 1826.

[61] Ruskin.

[62] Taylor, "Introduction."

[63] John M. Ellis, *One Fairy Story Too Many. The Brothers Grimm and Their Tales* (Chicago: University of Chicago Press, 1983). The author of this work prematurely draws his conclusions without having investigated Grimms' own notes on the subject (for example, Vol. 3 of the 1819 edition or the Grimms' volume of notes published in 1856) and without comprehending Grimms' concept of "loyalty" to tradition within the context of their research on epic literature. He uncritically disseminates some misinformation initiated by Taylor and other early critics regarding the supposed "purely Nordic," "purely German" peasant origin of the Grimms' folktales. He is also mistaken in his notion that Jacob Grimm's *Circular-Brief,* the first European folk questionnaire, supposedly remained only a plan that was never carried out (see note 23).

[64] "Popular Tales and Romances of Northern Nations" *Emperial Magazine* VI (1824): 192-96.

[65] Ruskin.

[66] (London: Murray, 1925). Croker first published this work anonymously. See also Wilhelm Grimm, "Über die Elfen" ("About the Fairies") in *Irische Elfenmärchen.* This more than sixty-page essay that already contained the comparative framework of Jacob Grimm's *Deutsche Mythologie.* For a related analysis see Kamenetsky, "The Irish Fairy Legends and the Brothers Grimm."

[67] Thomas Crofton Croker, "Preface," *Fairy Legends,* 2d ed. (London: Murray, 1828).

[68] Wilhelm Grimm, "About the Fairies," Ibid. Wilhelm commented in general terms about the *Edda* as a vital source of Norse mythology, meaning the *Elder Edda* (about 800 A.D.) as well as the *Younger Edda* or *Snorri Edda* (about 1250 A.D.).

[69] Croker, "Preface," *Fairy Legends,* 2d ed.

[70] Ibid.

[71] Thomas Wright, "The National Fairy Mythology of England," *Frazer's Magazine* (July 1834), pp. 51-67.

[72] "Fairy Legends and Traditions of the South of Ireland" (review) *Quarterly Review* (June/Oct. 1825), pp. 197-210.

[73] "Sir Walter Scott and Mr. Crofton Croker," *Gentlemen's Magazine* (October 1854), pp. 453-56.

[74] Ibid.

[75] See John Hennig, "The Brothers Grimm and T. C. Croker" *Modern Language Review* 41 (1946), pp. 44-54.

[76] Croker, "Introduction," *Fairy Legends,* 2d ed.

[77] Wilhelm Grimm (untitled review of *Fairy Legends of the South of Ireland*) *Göttingische Gelehrte Anzeigen* (Ja. 12, 1826), in *Kleinere Schriften von Wilhelm Grimm* vol. 2 (Berlin: Dümmler, 1881).

[78] Henning, pp. 52-53.

[79] Bolte and Polivka, vol. 1, pp. 551-52.

[80] Jacob Grimm, *Teutonic Mythology* vol. 1 (New York: Dover, 1975).

[81] Wright, p. 51.

[82] *Irische Land- und Seenmärchen,* collected by Thomas Crofton Croker, trans. Wilhelm Grimm, eds. Werner Moritz and Charlotte Oberfeld, in cooperation with Siegfried Heyer (Marburg: N. G. Elwert Verlag, 1986).

Donald Haase (essay date 1993)

SOURCE: "Response and Responsibility in Reading Grimms' Fairy Tales," in *The Reception of Grimms' Fairy Tales: Responses, Reactions, Revisions,* edited by Donald Haase, Wayne State University Press, 1993, pp. 230-49.

[*In the following essay, Haase discusses the importance of each individual reader's response to* Grimms' Fairy Tales, *suggesting that "the recipient and context of reception are as much a determinant of meaning as the text itself."*]

The Engraver Responsible for the title page of the nineteenth-century American edition of Grimms' tales translated by Edgar Taylor evidently was given the original German text to work from. And he evidently had some trouble deciphering the German typeface he encountered. Little did he know it was the ***Kinder-und Hausmärchen*** he had before him and not—as we read on the American title page—the *Rinder und Hans Märchen* (Alderson n2). Fortunately, the error did no lasting damage, and the Grimms' ***Children's and Household Tales*** did not become known to Americans as the *Cattle and Hans Tales.* But the error is worth noting, not simply for its humor but also for what it suggests about responsibility in reading Grimms' fairy tales. The engraver responsible was in one sense not responsible enough. Without the necessary information, experience, and context, he understandably took the Fraktur *K* for an *R,* and the *u* for an *n.* Irresponsible? Well, yes, in that this constitutes an inappropriate response to the foreign lettering. But certainly he had no reason to assume the letters were any others than those he perceived them to be. In fact, he made sense of an otherwise unintelligible language in the best way he could—by responding to the individual letters as shapes resembling those he knew. Responding to the text, he distorted it in one sense; yet in another sense he gave what might have seemed to him a distorted text shape and meaning.

Our engraver is not so different from Katy in Grimms' tale of **"Freddy and Katy"** (No. 59). Unable to make sense of her husband's idiomatic and metaphoric language except on a literal level, she carries out his instructions in ways that seem bizarre and irresponsible to him but appear perfectly sensible and logical to her. If we were to level charges of irresponsibility at the engraver—or the reader—who responds to a text without the requisite context, then we might expect a reply echoing Katy's: "I didn't know that. You should have told me" (***Complete Fairy Tales*** 226).

This is precisely what contemporary Grimm scholars have undertaken to do: to tell the uninformed what it is they need to know in order to respond responsibly to the ***Kinder- und Hausmärchen.*** Weary of psychotherapists, spiritualists, astrologers, and other assorted interpreters reading Grimms' tales with the same blind spot as our nineteenth-century engraver, informed Grimm scholars have begun a process of reeducation by defining what a responsible reading is and what a reader needs to know to arrive at one. Here I want to review this critical reception of the Grimms' tales and explore the implications for reading, understanding, and responding to them.

Heinz Rölleke has led the way in laying out the ground rules for an informed understanding of the ***Kinder- und Hausmärchen.*** His meticulous philological-historical studies and text-editions have illuminated the genesis, development, and nature of the Grimms' collection; and he has persuasively argued that a responsible interpretation of any single tale must be based on a thorough philological and text-historical analysis.[1] His point is lucidly made in a discussion of **"Brier Rose"** (No. 50) in his 1985 introduction to the Grimms' tales:

> One would hope that philological-literary and folkloric research would offer in the future a more solid foundation for fairy-tale interpretation, which is running wild everywhere. The make up of texts and appropriate textual understanding should become indispensable prerequisites for every fairy-tale interpretation; otherwise the way is open for sheer caprice. Only when the textual history of Grimms' tale of **"Brier Rose"** [for example] has been illuminated as much as possible, when the historical and cultural, as well as the generic prerequisites are generally recognized, can a sound interpretation be generated by any of the variously emphasized positions of those disciplines that have in the meantime turned their attention to the fairy tale—whether the text is analyzed from theological, mythological, psychoanalytic, anthroposophic, pedagogical, or literary perspectives. (*Die Märchen* 97)

Rölleke has no sympathy for interpretations that have not considered a specific tale's textual ancestry. While he allows that fairy tales are "rich enough . . . to permit" private and undisciplined readings, he insists that "serious" scholary commentary must take into account facts surrounding the origin and development of the texts (*Die wahren Märchen* 315). Not only the Grimms' editorial revisions must be taken into account, including those in both the seven Large Editions and the ten Small Editions of the ***Kinder- und Hausmärchen,*** but also the identity of their informants and/or the written sources, insofar as these can be established. Such "filters"[2] have all shaped the content, style, and meaning of the text in some way, so that any more or less definitive statements about the text's significance must be based on an accurate recognition and understanding of these. For example, Rölleke has repeatedly corrected Helmut Brackert's claim to see sociohistorical significance in **"Hansel and Gretel"** (No. 15), particularly in the tale's introductory reference to "a great famine." This "große Teuerung," Rölleke cautions, could not be taken as evidence that the tale reflects "social conditions and problems of earliest times" if readers like Brackert knew that the motif was first inserted into the story by Wilhelm Grimm in 1843, when he borrowed it from a version of the tale published by August Stöber in 1842.[3]

But the actual extent and implications of Rölleke's well-founded scholarly position on responsibility become most evident in his contention that before we can make any interpretive claims about the nature and significance of the ***Kinder- und Hausmärchen*** as a whole, we need "some 240 individual studies" of the tales the Grimms published in, deleted from, or used to compile and annotate their collection throughout its publishing history:

> For each text, one would need to describe its history before the Grimms; to uncover the form in which the Grimms became familiar with the tale, through hearing or reading it; and to document and interpret the changes made, whether as a result of a misunderstanding, for reasons of stylistic improvement, motivation, embellishment, or abridgement, or above all as the result of manifold contamination. And this must be done not only for the first edition of 1812-15, but for all seventeen editions of the collection, . . . taking into account, of course, the manuscript material in the form of inscribed notations and textual changes. ("New Results" 101-2)

Only after putting all these pieces of an enormous jigsaw puzzle together can we begin to understand and interpret the Grimms' stories and their collection responsibly. Until then, Rölleke warns, "all wholesale judgments . . . must remain unprovable" (102). In fact, from this perspective, responsible—let alone definitive—interpretation appears to be indefinitely deferred. Given the likely impossibility of fully reconstructing the complete heritage of every Grimm text and pre-text, as well as the fact that "one does not find, either, in direct testimony or statements by the Grimm brothers or their contributors, so much as a hint that would render permissible such deductive conclusions," we might well ask whether responsible interpretation and understanding are possible at all under the circumstances Rölleke describes.

Rölleke's formidable view of the reader's responsibility is clearly informed by his philological orientation and expertise. The American folklorist Alan Dundes, on the other hand, offers an equally demanding prescription for responsible fairy-tale interpretation that reflects his specific folkloric interests and expertise. Dundes has emphasized the inadequacy both of folkloristic investigations that collect variants of a tale type without interpretive effort and literary interpretations that fail to consider a tale's "full panoply of oral texts" (41). Literary critics who privilege a specific text—and it is normally the Grimm version of a tale—too quickly deduce its meaning and make interpretive or cultural generalizations on the basis of this single variant alone. Only when the full stock of variants is considered and understood as manifestations of a single *tale type* can a reader responsibly propose an interpretation and draw broader conclusions.

Like Rölleke, Dundes insists on a textual reconstruction undertaken by viewing the tale in a context of multiple texts. But unlike Rölleke, Dundes, as a folklorist, seeks not to reconstruct the textual history of a tale philologically and to use earlier texts to understand a specific Grimm tale or even the collection as a whole; rather, he uses variants—which may be philologically unrelated—to reconstruct a generally representative and hypothetical text that implicitly becomes the object of interpretation.

Dundes's position raises significant questions about the ontology of the interpreted fairy-tale text that go beyond the scope of my arguments here. More pertinent is the notion that responsible readings of Grimms' tales involve more than the reader and the specific Grimm texts, and even more than their immediate contexts. In fact, Dundes's responsible interpretation emerges from multiple readings of multiple texts and is, in the final analysis, a reading of a hypothetical composite text that transcends the actual, individual texts considered. "There is no one single text in folklore," writes Dundes, "there are only texts" (16). In this interpretive scenario, responsibility is not dictated by the reader's response to a text, buy by his or her attention to a full (but necessarily incomplete) complement of international variants.

From a sociohistorical perspective, Jack Zipes articulates yet another view of the fairy tale that places specific demands on the reader to adopt a multidimensional view of any text. Eschewing a one-dimensional view, Zipes emphasizes the multiple layers of sociohistorical references and values that inform Grimms' tales—strata of significance that reflect the perspectives of the various tellers who have helped give any specific tale its current shape (*The Brothers Grimm* 43-61, 135-46). These are basically the filters of which Rölleke writes. But Zipes goes a step beyond Rölleke and speculates not only about the Grimms' contributions to a tale, about the traces of their informants and sources, but also about the unspecified yet inevitably present tellers of the tale from even further back in history and the chain of storytellers. In any given Grimm text we might find the voice of the Grimms' informant, the voice of either Jacob or Wilhelm himself, the voice of the tale's "submerged creator," and the voices of the "intervening tale tellers who pass on the narrative from author to listeners and future tellers" (50). So Zipes is more likely to attribute certain motifs in **"Cinderella"** (No. 21) to storytellers from a past and unspecified matriarchal society than is Rölleke, whose philological orientation is not conducive to such speculation, and who would thus focus only on what he knows about the identifiable sources and informants (137-38; Rölleke, "Die Frau").

Furthermore, because fairy tales consist of multiple layers of often contradictory values, Zipes recommends that readers begin "exploring historical paths" in the tales (*The Brothers Grimm* 43-61). In other words, the reader's responsibility is to tease apart the layers of socio-historical evidence in the tales so as to understand better each story's historical development and reception, and to understand our own responses to the meanings and values discovered in the tales (46). This procedure becomes crucial if we are to comprehend the often contradictory values that fairy tales seem to contain and the contradictory reception they receive. And it is crucial if we are to grasp both the hazardous and liberating potential of fairy tales as agents of socialization (27).

All these positions usefully clarify the problem of critical responsibility in fairy-tale interpretation. The parade of filters, variants, and voices makes one thing evident: the Grimm fairy tale is not necessarily an integrated symbolic gesture with an inherent, immutable, and clearly defined meaning. I contest Maria Tatar's assertion that "the symbolic codes woven into fairy tales are relatively easy to decipher" (92). Rather, I would make two arguments: (1) fairy tales consist of chaotic symbolic codes that have become highly ambiguous and invite quite diverse responses; and (2) these responses will reflect a recipient's experience, perspective, or predisposition.

Despite the various methodological stipulations that seek to reconstruct a tale's "actual" meaning and to control the outcome of fairy-tale interpretation, there is a growing consensus that the significance of a fairy-tale text frequently remains elusive. Gerhard Haas's remarks are representative of this consensus:

> What fairy tales originally and actually meant can hardly ever be determined with any certainty. . . . The European folktales that have been fixed in literary form were, over centuries, composed of so many narrative layers, different perspectives, experiences, and forms of sensibility that it is just inconceivable that these texts could have preserved a unified—as is generally presumed—statement about the nature of human beings. Any other assumption is pure wishful thinking.[4]

There is compelling evidence for the ambiguous nature of fairy tales and the limitations of responsible fairy-tale interpretation. In the first place, the longevity of the fairy tale—its reception by diverse societies in diverse contexts—attests to its broad interpretive potential and its apparent flexibility (Dégh 76-77). Grimms' tales have served the needs of the Nazis, Freudian psychoanalysts, theologians, feminists, and the Waldorf schools—to name just a few of the diverse groups who have utilized them—and this wide applicability implies that instability in the tales' symbolic associations and core values accounts for their stability in the world-wide canon.

Similarly, the diversity of critical fairy-tale interpretations encourages sober consideration of the genre's remarkable potential for meaning. With similar ideological premises, some feminists berate Grimms' **"Cinderella"** and tales of its type for the heroine's passivity and dependency, while others praise the story for its positive depiction of female independence.[5] In the case of **"Little Red Riding Hood"** (No. 26), Erich Fromm inteprets the tale as the product of men-hating women, while Jack Zipes, discussing the *Trials and Tribulations of Little Red Riding Hood,* sees the story as a projection of misogynous males. For Bruno Bettelheim the tale focuses on adolescence and genital obsessions (166-83), while for Alan Dundes it revolves around orality and infantile fantasies (43).

How is it that so many reasonable people reach so many diverse and often contradictory conclusions about the same texts? One answer, of course, is that many readers have been operating irresponsibly—like the engraver of the "Cattle and Hans Tales." Bruno Bettelheim, for example, can make universal psychotherapeutic claims for Grimms' tales because he is almost thoroughly uninformed. He ignores diverse variants of the tales; he falsely assumes that the stories accurately reflect ancient oral narratives; and he neglects the sociohistorical setting in which they were revised and edited. Beyond such scholarly irresponsibility, however, the motley history of fairy-tale interpretation finds an explanation in the scholarly rediscovery of the complex editorial history surrounding Grimms' tales. Over the last fifteen years, Grimm scholarship has been dominated by Heinz Rölleke's philological investigation of Grimms' informants and variants, and by the search for multiple historical voices speaking simultaneously in the tales. These complementary research projects, which identify diverse narrators and layers of sociohistorical reality, have exposed the palimpsest-like nature of Grimms' texts and undercut the idea of one-dimensional meaning.

The feminist critic Karen Rowe, for example, uses the bifocal vision of a fairy tale's significance to explain how contradictory interpretations are equally legitimate. Noting the coexistence of repressive, misogynistic elements and an overall message of rebirth, coming of age, or liberation, she discerns two voices in the classical fairy tales: a patriarchal voice speaking to and for a male-dominated society, and a submerged female voice speaking a code of liberation. As she puts it, a fairy tale is "speaking at one level to a total culture, but at another to a sisterhood of readers who will understand the hidden language, the secret revelations of the tale" (15). Rowe's notion of a hidden language speaking to a sisterhood of readers suggests not only the double potential in responding to fairy tales, but also the potential problems in undertaking a responsible reading of fairy tales, in particular the difficulty for male readers who may be deaf to the sister's voice.[6] In this case we could ask whether responses and responsibility to fairy tales differ by gender.

Wolfgang Mieder puts a more general twist on this double potential of the fairy tale and the reader's response when he comments on the role of the reader's perspective in contemporary fairy-tale reception: "The moment one ceases to look at a fairy tale as a symbolic expression of the idea and belief that everything will work out in the end, the cathartic nature of the tale vanishes. Rather than enjoying the final happy state of the fairy tale heroes and heroines at the very end of the fairy tale, modern adults tend to concentrate on the specific problems of the fairy tales, since they reflect today's social reality in a striking fashion" (6). In other words, focusing macroscopically on the utopian plot of fairy tales gives us one view of its significance, while attending microscopically to the details of specific characters and motifs—such as the passivity of classic heroines—gives us a quite different understanding and evokes a different response. So the reader's focus or perspective determines his or her understanding of a tale.

But why should the reader's own perspective override that of the tale itself? Ostensibly a product of "low" or popular culture, the fairy tale, with its simple structures and language, might be thought more singly denotative and resistant to such caprice and ambiguity. Richly connotative structures and discourse, after all, are traditionally characteristic of "high" or literary culture. The Grimm fairy tale, however, is—despite its apparent simplicity—an institutionalized literary genre. And while its language is apparently simple, it is one-dimensional and denotative only in terms of the fictional and generically determined world it represents. The absence of an identifiable narrator (indeed the presence of multiple, incomplete, and conflicting narrative voices) gives little direction as the reader fills out the details of the story. In this way, the reader—like the storyteller who retells a fairy tale—is invited into the re-creative process and made responsible for concretizing the characterizations, settings, motivations, and valuations that the text itself has not specified. So, the reader's understanding of the text and response to it are potentially wide open, making the structures and language of the fairy tale richly multivalent and dependent on the reader's own projections. Whether those projections reflect an institutionalized understanding of the fairy tale or an idiosyncratic response depends on the experience of the reader and the circumstances of reception.

In dealing with the Grimms' tales we have ambiguous texts that belong to both the classical canon and the popular canon. Because of their surface simplicity, Grimms' tales are not only fully accessible to but also produced and marketed for a "lay" audience outside the interpretive institutions. Accordingly, the recipients of fairy tales are overwhelmingly not scholars. Instead, the fairy-tale audience comprises a wide spectrum of readers and auditors, but in particular children. And there is "a necessary difference" between these recipients and the "licensed practitioners" of institutional interpretation (Kermode 73). Lacking a sense of critical responsibility, these recipients possess a response-ability—an ability to respond that will not wait for and could not use the 240 dissertations that scholars need to understand Grimms' collection definitively.

The responses of popular fairy-tale recipients occur not only in ignorance of scholarly data and in reaction to ambiguous texts; they also occur to some extent outside the constraints imposed by a public context. While traditional storytelling was a public event that to some degree controlled the individual response, the printing of texts has increasingly privatized fairy-tale reception (Schenda 85), which increases individual control over the text. Kay Stone has argued that "told stories have more possibilities for openness than do those in printed and filmed media," but she ultimately acknowledges the freedom of the individual recipient to respond outside the interpretive limits imposed by each medium ("Three Transformations" 54). Moreover, because some traditional folkloric symbols have lost their original significance for new generations or foreign cultures, they are now "empty" and are no longer interpreted by readers but used to conform to the individual's own frame of reference. The fairy-tale recipient, in the words of Hermann Bausinger, is limited by an individual "horizon of symbolic understanding" ("Aschenputtel" 147-50). Irresponsible readings may ensue, but they nonetheless reflect the actual conditions of most fairy-tale reception.

Try as we will, and should, to stress responsible historical readings, to publicize the facts of Grimms' fairy tales and the complexities of fairy-tale interpretation, we cannot ignore the recipients and their irresponsible responses. By attending to their responses, we can learn a great deal about how fairy tales generate meaning and function in contemporary society. As an illustration, allow me a personal and admittedly anecdotal example. Once, when reading **"Rumpelstiltskin"** (No. 55) to my six-year-old daughter for what I believe was the first time, I casually experimented to gauge whether she had already developed a sense of common fairy-tale vocabulary, motifs, and style. While reading (from Zipes's translation *The Complete Fairy Tales of the Brothers Grimm*), I would pause at certain points and ask her to guess the next word. Generally, the results were predictable. For example, "Once upon a———there was a miller who was poor, but he had a beautiful———" elicited correctly from her the words "time" and "daughter" (209). The most interesting responses, however, were the following concerning the trials of the miller's daughter. In the first trial, the king locks the maiden in a room with the straw and commands, "Now get to work! If you don't spin this straw into gold by morning, then you must———." "Die" was my daughter's correct response. The second trial also involves the threat of death. In the third trial, there is a shift. Here the king offers not a threat but a reward. When the king states, "You must spin all this into gold tonight. If you succeed, you shall become my———," my daughter hesitated and came forth not with the actual word "wife" (211), but instead with a word revealing her own interpretation of the events: "slave."

This response illuminates the story's "meaning"—its potential for reception. While opposing critical camps may argue whether the tale is misogynistic or not, whether it depicts a woman's oppression by men or her ultimate achievement of autonomy and power over men, this naive response cuts to the core of the issue and vividly displays not only the tale's potential significance, but also precisely how fairy tales appear to function in the socialization process. The child's choice of the word "slave" for the text's own use of "wife" reveals the tale's ability literally to define social roles. The response effectively exposes the tale's equation of domestic exploitation—that is, slavery—with the concept of marriage. It is thus not only a legitimate response that can be confirmed by more scholarly analysis, but it is also and more importantly a response that illuminates the meaningful operation of fairy tales in a contemporary social context. It opens a window on the generation of meaning in fairy tales and on the significance of fairy-tale language in a communicative context. In other words, the study of response productively shifts the emphasis from *what* fairy tales mean or meant historically to the question of *how* fairy tales mean in a given context.

For all the debate and controversy over the meaning of Grimms' tales in society, there have been in fact few studies of a practical or experimental nature that attempt to determine how fairy tales are actually received in diverse contexts. The focus of research on Grimm reception has been for the most part on more or less conventional literary-historical questions of influence, adaptation, and what used to be called in comparative literary scholarship "fortune studies." While such studies do elucidate important forms of public response, other equally significant manifestations of private response are only begining to receive attention. The problem, of course, is in part one of accessibility. While the documentation and analysis of editions, translations, adaptations, and other published responses to Grimms' tales are relatively easy to undertake, the reliable documentation of individual subjective responses is much more difficult. As a consequence, most of the scholarship on the reception of Grimms' tales by children, for example, does not actually examine children's responses. Instead, like Bruno Bettelheim's influential work, it interprets tales abstractly according to a specific theory of reception. Unlike Jack Zipes, who also proposes a theory of fairy-tale reception, few in the debate over the Grimms have actually recognized that the reader's response to a fairy tale is "difficult to interpret, since the reception of an individual tale varies according to the background and experience of the reader" (*Fairy Tales and the Art of Subversion* 174).

The relatively few studies that have attempted to understand individual responses to Grimms' tales have approached the problem with varying perspectives and diverse methods. While psychologists such as Anne-Marie Tausch have experimentally studied responses to Grimms' tales in order to gauge their emotional and ethical effects on children, Rudolf Messner has interviewed children more informally to try to understand what makes fairy tales appropriate or inappropriate at different times. Pedagogues, on the other hand, have been concerned with what children's responses to fairy tales can tell us about the effects of reading in a didactic context. Michael Sahr's experiments with children's responses to Grimms' **"Old Sultan"** (No. 48), for example, were devised to determine the long- and short-term effects of hearing a fairy tale on children's attitudes and to discern the pedagogical implications of various media adaptations ("Zur experimentellen Erschließung"; "Zur Wirkung"). Similarly concerned with the process of reading and the effects of media on understanding, Helge Weinrebe has studied children's responses to investigate how verbal texts and illustrations influence personal responses to fairy tales.

While these studies reach general conclusions about the operation of specific texts and the effects of their content or form, others have asked how particular groups of recipients respond to Grimms' stories. Jessica Schmitz and Renate Meyer zur Capellen have collaborated to study the responses of kindergartners from five different German schools, including the children of foreign workers and affluent German families. Schmitz's transcripts of discussions with the children about **"The Wolf and the Seven Young Kids"** (No. 5) have been analyzed from a psychoanalytic perspective by Meyer zur Capellen against the socioeconomic background of each group. Focusing on another class of readers entirely—sick children—Gisela Haas has examined the fairy-tale drawings of hospitalized children and concluded that their diverse responses are shaped by the unique problems and desires of the individual.

The few studies that intentionally set out to examine the responses of children as individuals have been done by parents using their own children as subjects, much like early studies of childhood language acquisition conducted by linguists. That can be both an advantage and disadvantage depending on the methods employed. Ben Rubenstein's study of his daughter's responses to **"Cinderella"** is not so much a study of a child's response as it is his own Freudian reading of the tale and of his daughter's relationship to himself. Eugen Mahler's informal reports on conversations with his two children about Andersen's **"The Ugly Duckling"** and Grimm Nos. 4 and 6 are openly characterized as the "observations and thoughts of a father." Unfortunately, his observations remain ultimately inconclusive and do not give us a useful model for eliciting responses. Nina Mikkelsen, on the other hand, attempts a somewhat more methodical study of her daughter's responses to versions of **"Snow White"** (No. 53) during her third and fourth years. Especially interested in how preliterate children "read" and create meaning, Mikkelsen provides an illuminating analysis of her daughter's changing responses to the different Snow White texts over time.

Despite the diverse perspectives, experimental rigor, and methods of these studies, some conclusions indicate how the study of response illuminates significant issues in fairy-tale scholarship. Three examples are particularly revealing. The first involves two psychological experiments that have tested Bettelheim's assertion that fairy tales have therapeutic effects on children. While psychological testing of children by William C. Crain et al. appears to support Bettelheim's contention that children find fairy tales meaningful and thought-provoking, there is only speculation about how this might be the case. When Patricia Guérin Thomas studied the responses of kindergarten and third-grade pupils to **"Brother and Sister"** (No. 11) and **"The Queen Bee"** (No. 62), she found that their responses do depend on the children's developmentally determined inner conflicts and cognitive understanding of moral themes. Neither study, however, found evidence in the children's responses that would confirm Bettelheim's thesis that fairy tales actually help children resolve psychological conflicts.

The study of response has also shed light on the question of sexism in Grimms' tales. Like Bettelheim's assertions about the therapeutic role of fairy tales, discussions of sexism and its effect on readers rarely rely on the responses of real people. Instead, pronouncements about the influence of fairy tales on perceptions of gender roles normally revolve around a critic's own interpretation and the theoretical effects of fairy tales on recipients. Recognizing that scholars often presume to speak for readers, Kay Stone has undertaken to restore the reader's voice and to "describe actual rather than theoretical connections between fairy tales and their readers" ("Misuses of Enchantment" 126). She has done this by conducting formal interviews about the Cinderella story and analyzing "the reactions of readers of various ages and backgrounds, both male and female" (130). Stone's study of readers' reactions to **"Cinderella"** leads to two important conclusions. First, because the story elicits diverse responses among readers, she concludes that there is no single truth about the meaning and impact of fairy tales, especially when it comes to the question of sexism. Second, despite the diversity of responses, Stone identifies patterns that indicate women read and respond to tales differently from men. Women in particular may continue to perceive the female models found in fairy tales as problematic, and may interpret and reinterpret them as they struggle with their own identity. So by turning to the reactions of actual readers, Stone cuts through the unresolved theoretical speculation and delivers concrete insights into the tale's actual reception. In doing so she clarifies the issue of sexist content in fairy tales, the genre's impact on readers' perceptions of gender, and the role of gender itself in reading the tales.

A final example of how the study of readers' reactions can illuminate larger issues is provided by Kristin Wardetzky. Like Stone, Wardetzky advocates an empirical investigation to bring credibility to the abstract theoretical debates about the effects of fairy tales on children. Whereas Stone used interviews with North American subjects of diverse ages, Wardetzky (as part of a larger study) asked 1,577 children between eight and ten years of age in former East Germany to invent fairy tales stimulated by given story openers. Wardetzky's discovery that the children's tales differ in significant ways from the Grimms' leads her to reject the conventional wisdom that Grimms' stories exert a paradigmatic influence on children's understanding of fairy tales. In fact, Wardetzy's study suggests that far from being controlled by traditional fairy tales and preoccupied through them with social or moral issues, children may adapt tales to serve their own imaginative needs for heroic status (172). Like the experimental studies of psychologists testing Bettelheim's therapeutic theories and like Stone's investigation of sexism in fairy tales, Wardetzky's empirical study of children's fairy tales represents a serious challenge to conventional theories about the psychosocial function of Grimms' tales.

Despite my focus on subjective responses to Grimms' fairy tales, it should be clear that I am not arguing that we abandon responsible readings of the kind prescribed in the first part of this essay. Nor am I proposing that we discontinue reeducating readers about the facts of Grimms' fairy tales and the implications of these facts for an understanding of the texts. After all, analyses informed by the important data resulting from the work of Heinz Rölleke, for example, demystify the genre and correct the pseudoscholarly interpretations that make unjustifiable historical claims or implications. But I am suggesting that private readings of fairy tales can be equally illuminating, even if the responses are irresponsible from a scholarly point of view. Both the private and public reception of fairy tales demand our attention because they tell us something about the living meaning of fairy tales and their role in society. As the history of fairy-tale interpretation and fairy-tale exploitation has shown, the recipient and context of reception are as much a determinant of meaning as the text itself. So I am arguing as well that there is as much danger in institutionalizing response as there is in institutionalizing the genre.

If, as Christa Bürger has claimed, the emancipatory potential of the fairy tale resides not in its content but in its reception (103), then institutionalizing interpretation betrays the genre's liberating function. When the Grimms appropriated the folktale in the nineteenth century for scientific purposes, they institutionalized the genre and gave scholars considerable authority over it. Scholars, along with editors and publishers, not only determined which tales would be privileged in print, which variants would be standardized and canonized, and what shape the published text would ultimately take; they also legitimized the text's interpretation. The chilling extent of that authority is evident when Bruno Jöckel, in a 1939 study written in fascist Germany, refers to "official fairy-tale research" (5), an expression that finds its ironic echo in 1980 when Hermann Bausinger knowingly refers to "Verwalter des Märchenerbes," or "custodians of the fairy-tale inheritance" ("Anmerkungen" 45). To insist too strongly on the scholar's custodial role denies the individual reader's power over fairy tales (Haase). The role of the scholar is not to be a ventriloquist for the reader. The scholar's burden of responsibility lies in reconstructing the meaning of a fairy tale not only by attending to the voices that speak through it, but also by acknowledging the diverse voices that speak in response to it.

"The Golden Key"—the last of Grimms' two hundred tales—is conventionally interpreted as a parable about the inexhaustible meaning of fairy tales.[7] For me, however, the story goes even further and tells us that significance lies in reception. The Grimms—perhaps denying or camouflaging their own appropriation of the stories they edited—want us to believe that it is not scholars who hold the key to fairy tales, but a solitary child who accidentally finds one in the snow. The focus of the story is not on what the child finds, but on his process of discovery. Finding a key, he posits the existence of a lock. Finding a locked casket, he searches for a keyhole. Finding a keyhole, he inserts the key and begins turning it. The discovery of what lies in the casket, however, remains under his—not our—control, for "we must wait until he unlocks the casket and completely lifts the cover. That's when we'll learn what wonderful things he found" (***Complete Fairy Tales*** 631). The "things" themselves remain undefined and indeterminate, not simply because fairy tales have an endless potential for meaning, but because they are the child's discovery, not ours. We cannot dictate what the child—or any other reader—will find; we must wait for him (or her) to show us what can be found. And so it is in recognizing the recipient's control over the text's meaning that we also recognize the central place of reader response in studying Grimms' fairy tales.

Notes

[1] Rölleke's important essays are collected in *"Nebeninschriften"* and *"Wo das Wünschen noch geholfen hat."*

[2] Rölleke, *Die Märchen* 84. See also Dollerup, Reventlow, and Hansen.

[3] Rölleke chides Brackert in "August Stöbers Einfluß" 86; "Die Stellung" 128; "New Results" 108; and "Homo oeconomicus" 37-38.

[4] Gerhard Haas 15. See also Bausinger, "Aschenputtel"; Holbek; Lange 84-85; Röhrich; Simonsen; Wolfersdorf 9. While all these writers question whether the ultimate, original, or inherent significance of the fairy tale can be discerned, they do so with varying degrees of skepticism and from different points of view. Folklorist Holbek, for example, does not doubt "that tales do possess inherent cores of meaning," but he admits the possibility that these meanings "may . . . forever remain elusive" (27).

[5] See, for example, Bernikow; Kavablum; Kolbenschlag 61-99; Lieberman 192-94; Lüthi 61; and Yolen. See also Vera Dika on Ericka Beckman's feminist revision of the Cinderella tale in her 1986 film.

[6] See Jeannine Blackwell's description of the subversive female narrative voice speaking to daughters in fairy tales as told by nineteenth-century German women. The double voice of women narrators, albeit in a different cultural context, is also taken up by Bar-Itzhak and Shenhar in *Jewish Moroccan Folk Narratives from Israel.*

[7] See Rölleke's commentary in Grimm, *Kinder- und Hausmärchen: 1837* 1265; and *Kinder- und Hausmärchen: Ausgabe letzter Hand* 3: 516.

Works Cited

Alderson, Brian. *Grimm Tales in English.* British Library exhibition notes. London: British Library, 1985. N. pag.

Bar-Itzhak, Haya, and Aliza Shenhar, eds. and trans. *Jewish Moroccan Folk Narratives from Israel.* Detroit: Wayne State UP, 1993.

Bausinger, Hermann. "Anmerkungen zu Schneewittchen." Brackert, *Und wenn sie nicht gestorben sind* 39-70.

———. "Aschenputtel: Zum Problem der Märchensymbolik." *Zeitschrift für Volkskunde* 52 (1955): 144-55.

Bernikow, Louise. "Cinderella: Saturday Afternoon at the Movies." *Among Women.* New York: Harmony Books, 1980. 17-38, 271-72.

Bettelheim, Bruno. *The Uses of Enchantment: The Meaning and Importance of Fairy Tales.* New York: Knopf, 1976.

Blackwell, Jeannine. "Fractured Fairy Tales: German Women Authors and the Grimm Tradition." *Germanic Review* 62 (1987): 162-74.

Bottigheimer, Ruth B., ed. *Fairy Tales and Society: Illusion, Allusion, and Paradigm.* Philadelphia: U of Pennsylvania P, 1986.

Brackert, Helmut. "Hänsel und Gretel oder Möglichkeiten und Grenzen literaturwissenschaftlicher Märchen-Interpretation." Brackert, *Und wenn sie nicht gestorben sind* 9-38.

———, ed. *Und wenn sie nicht gestorben sind . . . . Perspektiven auf das Märchen.* Frankfurt a.M.: Suhrkamp, 1980.

Bürger, Christa. "Zur ideologischen Betrachtung von Sagen und Märchen." *Phantasie und Realität in der Kinderliteratur.* Ed. Karl E. Maier. Bad Heilbrunn: Klinkhardt, 1976, 102-7.

Crain, William C., et al. "The Impact of Hearing a Fairy Tale on Children's Immediate Behavior." *Journal of Genetic Psychology* 143 (1983): 9-17.

Déga, Linda. "What Did the Grimm Brothers Give to and Take from the Folk?" McGlathery 66-90.

Dika, Vera. "A Feminist Fairy Tale." *Art in America* 75 (April 1987): 31-33.

Dollerup, Cay, Iven Reventlow, and Carsten Rosenberg Hansen. "A Case Study of Editorial Filters in Folktales: A Discussion of the *Allerleirauh* Tales in Grimm." *Fabula* 27 (1986): 12-30.

Dundes, Alan. "Interpreting Little Red Riding Hood Psychoanalytically." McGlathery 16-51.

Fromm, Erich. *The Forgotten Language: An Introduction to the Understanding of Dreams, Fairy Tales and Myths.* New York: Rinehart, 1951. 235-41.

Garlichs, Ariane, ed. *Kinder leben mit Märchen.* Kassel: Röth, 1988.

Grimm, Brothers. *The Complete Fairy Tales of the Brothers Grimm.* Trans. Jack Zipes. New York: Bantam, 1987.

———. *Kinder- und Hausmärchen: Ausgabe letzter Hand mit den Originalanmerkungen der Brüder Grimm.* Ed. Heinz Rölleke. 3 vols. Stuttgart: Reclam, 1980.

———. *Kinder- und Hausmärchen gesammelt durch die Brüder Grimm: Vollständige Ausgabe auf der Grundlage der dritten Auflage (1837).* Ed. Heinz Rölleke. Frankfurt a.M.: Deutscher Klassiker Verlag, 1985.

Haas, Gerhard. "Die 'Logik' der Märchen: Überlegungen zur zeitgenössischen Märcheninterpretation und Märchendidaktik." *Märchen in Erziehung und Unterricht.* Ed. Ottilie Dinges, Monika Born, and Jürgen Janning. Kassel: Röth, 1986.

Haas, Gisela. "Kranke Kinder malen Märchen." Garlichs 36-54.

Haase, Donald. "Yours, Mine, or Ours? Perrault, the Brothers Grimm, and the Ownership of Fairy Tales." *Once upon a Folktale: Capturing the Folklore Process with Children.* Ed. Gloria Blatt. New York: Teachers College Press, 1993. 63-77.

Holbek, Bengt. "The Many Abodes of Fata Morgana or the Quest for Meaning in Fairy Tales." *Journal of Folklore Research* 22 (1985): 19-28.

Jöckel, Bruno. *Der Weg zum Märchen.* Berlin-Steglitz: Dion, 1939.

Kavablum, Lea. *Cinderella: Radical Feminist, Alchemist.* N.p.: privately printed, 1973.

Kermode, Frank. "Institutional Control of Interpretation." *Salmagundi* 43 (1979): 72-86.

Kolbenschlag, Madonna. *Kiss Sleeping Beauty Good-Bye: Breaking the Spell of Feminine Myths and Models.* 1979. New York: Bantam, 1981.

Lange, Günter. "Grimms' Märchen aus der Sicht eines Religionspädagogen." *Hanau 1985-1986: 200 Jahre Brüder Grimm.* Ed. Stadt Hanau/Hauptamt. Hanau: Stadt Hanau, 1986. 73-90.

Lieberman, Marcia. " 'Some Day My Prince Will Come': Female Acculturation through the Fairy Tale." *College English* 34 (1972): 383-95. Rpt. in *Don't Bet on the Prince: Contemporary Feminist Fairy Tales in North America and England.* Ed. Jack Zipes. New York: Methuen, 1986. 185-200.

Lüthi, Max. *Once upon a Time: On the Nature of Fairy Tales.* Trans. Lee Chadeayne and Paul Gottwald. Bloomington: Indiana UP, 1976.

Mahler, Eugen. "Gespräche über Märchen: Beobachtungen und Gedanken eines Vaters." Garlichs 55-70, 110-11.

McGlathery, James M., ed. *The Brothers Grimm and Folktale.* Urbana: U of Illinois P, 1988.

Messner, Rudolf. "Kinder und Märchen—was sie verbindet und was sie trennt." Garlichs 106-9.

Meyer zur Capellen, Renate. "Kinder hören ein Märchen, fürchten sich und wehren sich." Brackert, *Und wenn sie nicht gestorben sind* 210-22.

Mieder, Wolfgang. "Grimm Variations: From Fairy Tales to Modern Anti-Fairy Tales." *Tradition and Innovation in Folk Literature.* Hanover: UP of New England, 1987. 1-44.

Mikkelsen, Nina. "Sendak, *Snow White,* and the Child as Literary Critic." *Language Arts* 62 (1985): 362-73.

Röhrich, Lutz. "The Quest of Meaning in Folk Narrative Research." McGlathery 1-15.

Rölleke, Heinz. "August Stöbers Einfluß auf die *Kinder- und Hausmärchen* der Brüder Grimm." *Fabula* 24 (1983): 11-20. Rpt. in Rölleke, *"Wo das Wünschen noch geholfen hat"* 75-87.

———. "Die Frau in den Märchen der Brüder Grimm." *Die Frau im Märchen.* Ed. Sigrid Früh and Rainer Wehse. Kassel: Röth, 1985. 72-88.

———. "Der Homo oeconomicus im Märchen." *Der literarische Homo oeconomicus: Vom Märchenhelden zum Manager: Beiträge zum Ökonomieverständnis in der Literatur.* Ed. Werner Wunderlich. Bern: Haupt, 1989. 23-40.

———. *Die Märchen der Brüder Grimm: Eine Einführung.* Munich: Artemis, 1985.

———. *"Nebeninschriften": Brüder Grimm-Arnim und Brentano—Droste-Hülshoff: Literarhistorische Studien.* Bonn: Bouvier, 1980.

———. "New Results of Research on *Grimms' Fairy Tales.*" McGlathery 101-11. (Trans. of "Neue Ergebnisse zu den 'Kinder- und Hausmärchen' der Brüder Grimm." *Jacob und Wilhelm Grimm: Vorträge und Ansprachen.* Göttingen: Vandenhoeck & Ruprecht, 1986. 39-48.)

———. "Die Stellung des Dornröschenmärchens zum Mythos und zur Heldensage." *Antiker Mythos in unseren Märchen.* Ed. Wolfdietrich Siegmund. Kassel: Röth, 1984. 125-37, 197-98.

———, ed. *Die wahren Märchen der Brüder Grimm.* Frankfurt a.M.: Fischer, 1989.

———. *"Wo das Wünschen noch geholfen hat": Gesammelte Aufsätze zu den 'Kinder- und Hausmärchen' der Brüder Grimm.* Bonn: Bouvier, 1985.

Rowe, Karen. "To Spin a Yarn: The Female Voice in Folklore and Fairy Tale." Bottigheimer 53-74.

Rubenstein, Ben. "The Meaning of the Cinderella Story in the Development of a Little Girl." *American Imago* 12 (1955): 197-205. Rpt. in *Cinderella: A Casebook.* Ed. Alan Dundes. 1982. New York: Wildman: 1983. 219-28.

Sahr, Michael. "Zur experimentellen Erschließung von Lesewirkungen: Eine empirische Studie zum Märchen 'Der alte Sultan.' " *Zeitschrift für Pädagogik* 26 (1980): 365-81.

———. "Zur Wirkung von Märchen: Eine medienvergleichende Betrachtung zum Grimmschen Märchen: Der alte Sultan." *Das gute Jugendbuch* 27 (1977): 67-75. Rpt. in *Kinderliteratur und Rezeption: Beiträge der Kinder- literaturforschung zur literaturwissenschaftlichen Pragmatik.* Ed. Bettina Hurrelmann. Baltmannsweiler: Schneider, 1980. 351-65.

Schenda, Rudolf. "Telling Tales—Spreading Tales: Changes in the Communicative Form of a Popular Genre." Bottigheimer 74-94.

Schmitz, Jessica. "Erfahrungen beim Erzählen eines Märchens im Kindergarten am Beispiel *Der Wolf und die sieben jungen Geißlein.*" Brackert, *Und wenn sie nicht gestorben sind* 193-210.

Simonsen, Michèle. "Do Fairy Tales Make Sense?" *Journal of Folklore Research* 22 (1985): 29-36.

Stone, Kay F. "The Misuses of Enchantment: Controversies on the Significance of Fairy Tales." *Women's Folklore, Women's Culture.* Ed. Rosan A. Jordan and Susan J. Kalcik. Philadelphia: U of Philadelphia P, 1985. 125-45. (Rev. and trans. of "Mißbrauchte Verzauberung: Aschenputtel als Weiblichkeitsideal in Nordamerika." *Über Märchen für Kinder von heute: Essays zu ihrem Wandel und ihrer Funktion.* Ed. Klaus Doderer. Weinheim: Beltz, 1983. 78-93.)

———. "Three Transformations of Snow White." McGlathery 52-65.

Tatar, Maria. *The Hard Facts of the Grimms' Fairy Tales.* Princeton: Princeton UP, 1987.

Tausch, Anne-Marie. "Einige Auswirkungen von Märcheninhalten." *Psychologische Rundschau* 18 (1967): 104-16.

Thomas, Patricia Guérin. "Children's Responses to Fairy Tales: A Developmental Perspective." Diss. Adelphi U, 1983.

Wardetzky, Kristin. "The Structure and Interpretation of Fairy Tales Composed by Children." *Journal of American Folklore* 103 (1990): 157-76.

Weinrebe, Helge M. A. *Märchen, Bilder, Wirkungen: Zur Wirkung und Rezeptionsgeschichte von illustrierten Märchen der Brüder Grimm nach 1945.* Frankfurt a.M.: Lang, 1987.

Wolfersdorf, Peter. *Märchen und Sage in Forschung, Schule und Jugendpflege.* Braunschweig: Waisenhaus, 1958.

Yolen, Jane. "America's Cinderella." *Children's Literature in Education* 8 (1977): 21-29.

Zipes, Jack. *The Brothers Grimm: From Enchanted Forests to the Modern World.* New York: Routledge, 1988

———. *Fairy Tales and the Art of Subversion: The Classical Genre for Children and the Process of Civilization.* New York: Wildman, 1983.

———. *The Trials and Tribulations of Little Red Riding Hood: Versions of the Tale in Sociocultural Context.* South Hadley, MA: Bergin & Garvey, 1983. 1-65.

FURTHER READING

Biography

Michaelis-Jena, Ruth. *The Brothers Grimm.* London: Routledge and Kegan Paul, 1970, 212 p.

Traces the lives of the Grimms from the perspective of their accomplishments as leaders in the study of Germanic literature and language.

Criticism

Bottigheimer, Ruth B. *Grimms' Bad Girls and Bold Boys: The Moral and Social Vision of the Tales.* New Haven, Conn.: Yale University Press, 1987, 211 p.

With a special attention to gender, examines motifs that appear frequently in the tales to determine the social and moral beliefs they reflect.

Carsch, Henry. "Witchcraft and Spirit Possession in Grimm's Fairy Tales." *Journal of Popular Culture* 2, No. 4 (Spring 1969): 627-48.

Takes an anthropological approach to the tales to demonstrate how certain recurring figures—primarily witches—function in the service of social control.

Kamenetsky, Christa. "The Sources of the Collection." In *The Brothers Grimm and Their Critics,* pp. 113-50. Athens: Ohio University Press, 1992.

Details both the sources of the tales and the influences on the Grimms' editing style.

McGlathery, James M. *Grimms' Fairy Tales: A History of Criticism on a Popular Classic.* Columbia, S.C.: Camden House, 1993, 135 p.

Surveys criticism and scholarship on the tales in a format suitable for readers with little or no background in either literary or folkloric studies.

McGlathery, James M., Larry W. Danielson, Ruth E. Lorbe, and Selma K. Richardson, eds. *The Brothers Grimm and Folktale.* Urbana: University of Illinois Press, 1988, 258 p.

Collection of essays by prominent folktale scholars, including Jack Zipes, Heinz Rölleke, Kay Stone, Maria M. Tatar, and Ruth B. Bottigheimer.

Mieder, Wolfgang. "Grim Variations: From Modern Fairy Tales to Modern Anti-Fairy Tales." *The Germanic Review* 62, No. 2 (Spring 1987): 90-102.

Argues that modern adult interpretations focusing on the negative or violent aspects of the tales overlook the symbolic import of their essentially optimistic conclusions.

Tatar, Maria. *The Hard Facts of the Grimms' Fairy Tales.* Princeton, N.J.: Princeton University Press, 1987, 277 p.

Suggests that the emphasis on violence, cruelty, and other ugly facts of life in the tales resonates with the "psychic realities" of the imagination and unconscious.

Zipes, Jack. *The Brothers Grimm: From Enchanted Forests to the Modern World.* New York: Routledge, 1988, 205 p.

Examines the tales from a socio-historical perspective, studying in particular the Grimms' modes of production and the factors of reception that led to the institutionalization of the genre.

———. "The Enchanted Forest of the Brothers Grimm: New Modes of Approaching the Grimms' Fairy Tales." *The Germanic Review* 62, No. 2 (Spring 1987): 66-74.

Looks at specific social types—such as the soldier, the hunter, the miller, or the tailor—and argues that the forest represents for these characters a place belonging to the common people, free from social constraints.

Additional coverage of the lives and works of the Grimms can be found in the following sources published by Gale: *Dictionary of Literary Biography,* Vol. 90; *Major Authors and Illustrators for Children and Young Adults;* and *Something about the Author,* Vol. 22.

Dante Gabriel Rossetti

1828-1882

(Born Gabriel Charles Dante Rossetti) English poet, translator, and short story writer.

The following entry contains late twentieth-century criticism of Rossetti's works. For a chronological survey of earlier criticism, see *NCLC*, Volume 4.

INTRODUCTION

Equally renowned as a painter and poet, Rossetti was the leader of the Pre-Raphaelite Brotherhood, a group of artists and writers who sought to emulate the purity and simplicity of the Italian Proto-Renaissance school of art. A successful painter, Rossetti filled his canvases with richly colored expressions of human beauty, frequently characterized by elements of the supernatural. His poetry likewise features rich and sensuous imagery, vivid detail, and an aura of mysticism. Although the subjects of his verse are typically considered narrow, Rossetti is acknowledged as a master of the ballad and sonnet forms. "The Blessed Damozel," "Sister Helen," and the sonnet sequence "The House of Life" are often noted among his finest poetic achievements.

Biographical Information

An exiled Italian patriot, Rossetti's father came to England four years before Rossetti's birth in 1828. Rossetti received his early education at home and was particularly influenced by Thomas Percy's *Reliques*, the works of Sir Walter Scott, and the medieval romances. Rossetti later attended King's College School and studied art at the Royal Academy. Displeased with the conventional methods of painting taught at the Academy, Rossetti left in 1848 to study with the English painter Ford Madox Brown. After a short time, however, he joined painters John Everett Millais and William Holman Hunt in founding the Pre-Raphaelite Brotherhood. Rossetti quickly became the leader of the group and later inspired English poet and artist William Morris, painter Edward Burne-Jones, and poet Algernon Charles Swinburne to become members. In 1850, Rossetti published his first poem, "The Blessed Damozel" in the Pre-Raphaelite journal *The Germ*; other early verses also appeared in *The Germ*, as did his only complete short story, "Hand and Soul."

In 1860, after a nine-year engagement, Rossetti married Elizabeth Siddal, the subject of many of his paintings and sketches. By the time of their wedding, however, she was obviously consumptive, and after two unhappy years of marriage, she died from an overdose of laudunum, a form of opium, which she had been taking regularly for her illness. In a fit of remorse and guilt, Rossetti buried the only manuscript of his poems with his wife. At the urging of friends, he finally allowed the manuscript to be exhumed in 1869. The following year, Rossetti published a collection entitled *Poems*. This volume, which contains much of his finest work, established Rossetti's reputation as a leading poet. Despite eliciting considerable praise from various sources, including his admiring associates Morris and Swinburne, the publication of *Poems* prompted the venomous attack of Robert Buchanan in his 1871 essay "The Fleshly School of Poetry." Devastated by Buchanan's criticism, Rossetti became convinced that he was the object of an undeserved and insidious campaign. Although he continued his work as a translator and poet, Rossetti's subsequent dependence on whiskey and the sedative drug chloral to alleviate his anxiety and insomnia precipitated a gradual decline in health that ended with his death in 1882 at the age of fifty-four.

Major Works

Rossetti's early romantic ballad "The Blessed Damozel" is characteristic of much of his later poetry, with its sensuous detail and theme of lovers parted by death who long for reunion. The 1870 volume *Poems* includes the verses "Eden Bower," "The Stream's Secret," and "Sister Helen," the last of which is regarded as one of the finest nineteenth-century literary ballads. This work also contains versions of "Jenny," which centers on a young and thoughtless prostitute, and "The Burden of Ninevah," an acutely pessimistic poem aimed at the enduring faults of civilization. The influence of Rossetti's painting is felt throughout *Poems*. Just as his literary background prompted his choice of mythological, allegorical, and literary subjects for his paintings, his love of detail, color, and mysticism shaped much of his poetry. Rossetti's second collection, entitled *Ballads and Sonnets* (1881), contains the completed version of "The House of Life," a sonnet sequence primarily devoted to themes of love, which many critics praise as evidence of Rossetti's mastery of the sonnet form. *Ballads and Sonnets* also includes the passionate, melancholy poems of Rossetti's last years and the historical ballad "The King's Tragedy," a blend of romantic and literary themes reminiscent of his earlier "Dante at Verona." Among Rossetti's few prose works, "Hand and Soul" is an allegorical tale set in thirteenth-century Italy. In it, Rossetti describes the appearance of a mysterious woman who asks Chiaro dell'Erma to paint her beautiful form, which she suggests will reflect the painter's own soul.

Critical Reception

Most of the positive criticism of Rossetti's poetry during his own lifetime was subsequently overshadowed by Robert Buchanan's essay "The Fleshly School of Poetry," in which he claimed that Rossetti's only artistic aim was "to extol fleshliness as the distinct and supreme end of poetic and pictorial art; to aver that poetic expression is greater than poetic thought, and by inference that the body is greater than the soul, and sound superior to sense." After his death, Rossetti's works suffered from critical neglect: Until relatively recently, few critical studies of his poetry were published. However, with the renewed interest in Pre-Raphaelitism, numerous new assessments have appeared. By the latter half of the twentieth century, critics had begun to focus on the cultural and ideological components of Rossetti's verse, particularly on the implications of the erotic, sensuous, and feminine elements in his writing. Modern critics have also recognized Rossetti as a distinguished artist and verbal craftsman whose work greatly influenced such notable contemporaries as Morris and Swinburne, as well as the Aesthetes and Decadents of the later nineteenth century.

PRINCIPAL WORKS

"Hand and Soul" (short story) published in the journal *The Germ*, 1850
The Early Italian Poets from Ciullo to Dante Alighieri (1100-1200-1300) in the Original Metres, Together with Dante's "Vita Nuova" [translator; also published as *Dante and His Circle*] (poetry) 1861
Poems (poetry) 1870
Ballads and Sonnets (poetry) 1881
The Complete Poetical Works of Dante Gabriel Rossetti (poetry) 1903

CRITICISM

Ronnalie Roper Howard (essay date 1967)

SOURCE: "Rossetti's *A Last Confession:* A Dramatic Monologue," in *Victorian Poetry,* Vol. V, No. 1, Spring, 1967, pp. 21-9.

[*In the following essay, Howard evaluates "A Last Confession" as a skillfully-crafted dramatic monologue.*]

Critics have often suggested that Dante Gabriel Rossetti's poetic failures are connected with (or dependent on) his metaphysical problems, that there is no intellectual or emotional conviction behind his religious and supernatural symbols, which are then mere ornamentation, or behind his expressions of mystic union, which are then mere wishful thinking. Most recently and persuasively Harold L. Weatherby has analyzed Rossetti's failure as an inability to establish the proper relationship between form and content, as the poetic use of a spiritual and supernatural reality in which he did not believe.[1] Weatherby finds Rossetti intellectually conditioned by the scientific scepticism of his age but emotionally compelled to follow out his strong predilections for both the supernatural and the flesh.

In at least one poem, however, Rossetti resolves his intellectual-emotional dichotomy, and is enabled to do so precisely because he chooses an objective, critical form which allows him his supernatural trappings without his having to be committed to them. **"A Last Confession"** is usually felt to be uncharacteristic of Rossetti, a pallid imitation of the Browningesque character study. But the main reason it has not been treated with more respect, I think, is that it has not been given the kind of painstaking attention paid to (and required by) a Browning monologue. A careful examination of the poem proves that Rossetti understood not only the external features of the dramatic monologue but also its essential nature, that he used it without giving up his characteristic sensuous detail or his predilection for the religious and supernatural, that in fact he made his personal predilections functional within the whole, objectifying and thus transcending them. Although Rossetti's failures have long been of greater critical interest than his successes, an estimate of his poetry must finally include both. If there are many poems in which his mysticism fails to convince, in which his religious symbolism seems to belie a basic scepticism, there are others in which he sees his materials steadily and sees them whole. The prevalent critical misunderstanding of **"A Last Confession"** is perhaps indicative of a general tendency to ignore in Rossetti's poetry most of what is detached and ironic.

The dramatic monologue, as described by Robert Langbaum, is identifiable by more than its external characteristics—a speaker other than the poet, a listener, a specific occasion, and an interplay between the speaker and the listener. More importantly the form involves a tension on the part of the reader between sympathy and moral judgment, disequilibrium between what the speaker reveals and what we understand, a strategic significance of the monologue in the present tense of the poem's occasion. That is, the speaker is a pole for the reader's sympathy precisely because he *is* the poem (there is no vision of the facts except his; there are no facts presented outside of his vision) and because, as Langbaum says, he is "so much particularized, because his characterization through contradictory qualities renders inapplicable the publicly recognized categories of character . . . since it is between the categories that we find the counterpart of our own life."[2] Nevertheless, his contradictory qualities—villain and aesthete, criminal because he loves, etc.—also give rise to our moral judgment, a judgment conditioned by the discrepancy between what the speaker reveals and our perception of the limitations and distortions of his vision, and by our awareness of his strategy, his concern with the particular effect of his speech at the moment rather than with its truth. It is because it has these intrinsic qualities that **"A Last Confession"** is a true dramatic monologue.

The poem, Rossetti's longest work in blank verse, is a deathbed confession to a Catholic priest by an Italian wounded in the Italian resistance to Austria, 1848. The narrator tells of his adopting a little girl abandoned by her parents during the Austrian occupation, of his raising her and falling passionately in love with her when she was fourteen, of her gradually changing, growing away from him, and of his killing her at Iglio when she spurned his love. The framework of the poem is one of war and violence (both his original meeting with the girl and his approaching death are a result of the Austrian invasion), and the interrupted narrative flow reflects the disruption of Italian life during the occupation and the narrator's sense of guilt, his fear, his fever and hallucinations. Externally the narrative, loosely chronological but filled with apparently irrelevant flashbacks and digressions, is held together by the time sequence, climaxed by the account of the murder, and by leitmotifs signifying his sense of guilt—the knife, the sands of Iglio, the woman's scornful laugh. Internally the movement of the poem is determined by the narrator's strategy, his desire in the face of death to lessen the magnitude of his crime, to secure relief from the torments of his conscience, to obtain pardon, or at least sympathy, from the priest.

The dramatic monologue typically involves enough suspension of the reader's judgment that he can read himself temporarily into the narrator's point of view. Certainly the narrator of **"A Last Confession"** gains our sympathy, not only because he is a dying man with the torments of hell (as he believes) ahead of him, but also because the intensity of his nature draws us in. Even on his deathbed he can curse the enemy (ll. 184-185, 407-411) and be proud of having spent his adult life defending Italy, the "weeping desolate mother" (l. 254). His devotion to the girl, as it emerges in the poem, has been equal to his commitment to his country, and, paradoxically, he has murdered her out of love. The passionateness of his nature is oddly juxtaposed with the poetic, even ethereal, propensity of his imagination, as evidenced by his giving the little girl a glass figurine of Cupid and by his bright dream of heaven and a pleasant doomsday. He is thus particularized by intensity and contradictoriness. And, of course, there is no vision except his by which to test the sincerity of his confession, no other side of the story from the point of view of the dead girl, no judgment on the part of the priest to prompt us to judgment. Critics have long been sympathetically involved enough to arrest their judgments so completely as to lose the peculiar effect of the dramatic monologue, the tension between sympathy and judgment.

The monologue itself, however, prompts us to judgment from within. With no word from the priest we feel his presence: he is part of the immediate occasion for the monologue, the source of the irony of situation encompassing the poem, the reason for the particular strategy the narrator adopts. For the monologue is the confession of a murder of passion to a celibate, and the strategy involves gaining sympathy for a physical love resulting in murder from a man sworn to chastity in a spiritual cause. This is not to say that the narrator is himself fully aware of his strategy, his distortions, or even his original motivations. Rather, it seems as though the monologue is an attempt to justify the murder as much to himself as to the priest before he can finally confess it.

The first verse paragraph introduces one leitmotif (the knife), the narrator's sense of guilt, and the first key to the tenor of the whole poem. About the ominous gift he explains matter-of-factly that Lombard girls carry daggers, "for they know / That they might hate another girl to death / Or meet a German lover" (ll. 2-4). But since he knew when he bought the knife that it might be a "parting gift" (l. 25), the instrument represents a desire, perhaps subconscious, to kill her. And the motive of jealousy (which becomes clearer later in the poem) is hinted in his suggestion that a Lombard girl might "meet a German lover." Thus part of his strategy involves from the beginning the concealment (or, at the very best, ignorance) of the true nature of his motivation.

Paragraph two represents a second facet of his strategy, the attempt to draw the priest sympathetically into his narrative—"O Father, if you knew all this / You cannot know, then you would know too, Father, / And only then, if God can pardon me" (ll. 17-19)—while at the same time he is aware that there is little common to both their experiences which would provide a basis for understanding. Too, there is the slightest implication in this first direct address to the priest that to know, to understand, would be to forgive.

His strategy in the next three paragraphs picks up the hint from the second of the great change in the girl (ll. 10-13) and directs attention, not to the murder, but to her attitude at Iglio, her proud posture—"Her neck unbent not, neither did her eyes / Move, nor her foot left beating of the sand"—and her scorn—"Only she put it by from her and laughed" (ll. 43-45). The laugh has become symbolic to him of the scene of parting, of her change toward him, of her scorn, and, as he finally tells it, of her degradation. It haunts him throughout the poem and is one means by which he seeks to justify the murder: "Father, you hear my speech and not her laugh; / But God heard that. Will God remember all?" (ll. 46-47)—implying that the provocation would serve to justify the crime, in part at least, to God.

The narrator stresses his point about the change in the girl by switching from his memory of her scornful laugh to his memory of her childish one and the story of how he first adopted her. There is no reason to doubt that his taking her in was motivated by the highest humanitarian sympathy, but his insistence here on his courage, patriotism, and piety seems strained, designed to put himself in the best possible light and to demonstrate to the priest his spirituality: "With that, God took my mother's voice and spoke . . . / And so I took her with me" (ll. 91, 94). Keeping her, he says, "doubled my own danger: but I knew / That God would help me" (ll. 99-102).

Though he excuses himself for the apparent irrelevancy of some parts of his narrative (ll. 103-105), he goes on with another digression about his last night's dream, a lovely wish-fulfillment dream in which the laughter that haunts him is transformed into the happy laughter of heavenly maidens. There are, however, no real irrelevancies in his narrative, which compulsively follows out its own logic, directed on the one hand by his strategy and on the other by his irrepressible fear and sense of guilt. The description of the dream ends with the first mention of his hallucinations (both dream and hallucination are expressions of his fear of hell fire), and by implication the contrast of the blessed maidens and the girl casts the girl with the demonic (part of his strategy).

The incidents from his past life with the girl which he now relates are those most significant to him and those which would best serve to justify him. From them we learn incidentally the overpowering strength of his physical passion for her and the motive for his crime. The story of the "earliest gift" he gave her, a glass image of Love (ironically the last is an instrument of death), is intended to show the priest the depth of their early mutual attachment. It suggests much more. How much his memory and his subconscious desire have distorted the actual incident we have no way of knowing, but as he tells it the story has strong overtones of sexual initiation and emphasizes the sensuality of his love. He makes it explicit that the image represented Cupid (Eros) and recalls how he told her about Cupid's ruling the loves of human beings, initiated her, in other words, into the knowledge of the strength of passion in human life. His words to her on discovering that Love's dart had pierced her hand—"'That I should be the first to make you bleed, / Who love and love and love you!'" (ll. 174-175)—suggest sexual initiation even more explicitly. And his recollection of her response is of a love speech: she sobs "'not for the pain at all, / . . . but for the Love, the poor good Love / You gave me'" (ll. 177-179). The significance for him of her words is underscored when he repeats them later (ll. 487-489) with "Love" in lower case.

As the narrative progresses and the dying man describes the growth of his love for the girl, the not yet extinguished sensuality of his nature becomes more and more apparent, and his passion for his country becomes intertwined with his passion for the girl. Thus paragraph fourteen (ll. 180-200) contains both his cursing of Metternich and his account of how the girl first aroused him physically: "She was still / A child; and yet that kiss was on my lips / So hot all day where the smoke shut us in" (ll. 198-200). But although in this and the next paragraph he seems to be talking to himself more than to the priest, dwelling on his memory of her womanly attractiveness, he is at least fitfully aware of his listener, enough to return to his strategy and to play down the underlying sensuality of his love, and subtly equate it with the spirit:

For now, being always with her, the first
  love
I had—the father's, brother's love—was
  changed,
I think, in somewise; like a holy thought
Which is a prayer before one knows of it.

(ll. 201-204)

His preface rings strangely false in juxtaposition with the following description of her "breasts half globed / Like folded lilies deepset in the stream" (ll. 225-226), her mouth "Made to bring death to life,—the under-lip / Sucked in, as if it strove to kiss itself" (ll. 230-231), and her "great eyes, / That sometimes turned half dizzily beneath / The passionate lids" (ll. 244-246). When the strategy begins to break down, as here, we begin to perceive the truth. Even as the narrator describes his love for his country (ll. 253-264) his remarks suggest sublimated sexual energy, for he speaks of his fight for Italy as "a love to clasp, . . . / All things together that a man / Needs for his blood to ripen" (ll. 261-263).

Thus, because he does indeed have a strategy, because he is perhaps himself confused about his motives and his nature, the reliability of the narrator is called into doubt. Significantly, the girl's actions as he relates them are sufficiently ambiguous to allow more than one interpretation. We have, of course, only his to go on. When he describes how once he almost chided her for leaping about and laughing, her song in answer is ambiguous in its intent; both it and her actions, as he relates them (ll. 337-341), suggest flirtatiousness. Yet her ostensible point is stated clearly in her question to him: "'Weeping or laughing, which was best?'" At any rate, we see in the narrator's complete memory of the song and in his tears (ll. 272-278) that he has interpreted it as a love song.

In the next incident we again have only his interpretation of her ambiguous action. She is now a woman, as he emphasized more than once, and he feels "some impenetrable restlessness / Growing in her to make her changed and cold" (ll. 370-371). When in the Duomo she prays before "Some new Madonna gaily decked, / Tinselled and gewgawed, a slight German toy" (ll. 385-386) rather than the one "wrought / In marble by some great Italian hand" (ll. 354-355), he is shaken, and "sharply" questions her of "her transferred devotion" (ll. 388-389). His interpretation is at odds with the fact that in Roman Catholicism one's devotion is not to the statue but to Mary, of whom the image serves as the visual reminder, but it is characteristic of him that his vision of the incident involves a confusion of patriotism, religion, and love. What he fears, what he sees symbolically in her praying before the "slight German toy" (echo of the "German lover") is the transference of her affection for him to someone else. He makes the fear of loss explicit when he describes their going out again into the square:

. . . and the face
Which long had made a day in my life's night
Was night in day to me; as all men's eyes
Turned on her beauty, and she seemed to
  tread
Beyond my heart to the world made for her.

(ll. 399-403)

At this point, with renewed fear of damnation and perhaps a sense of confessing too much, of drawing too dangerously close to the real motive for the murder, he bursts out that if the priest mistakes his words and so absolves him, the blessing will burn his soul. He repeats:

If you mistake my words
And so absolve me, Father, the great sin
Is yours, not mine: mark this: your soul shall
  burn
With mine for it.

(ll. 418-421)

Though he asks not to be absolved, the strategy is apparent. He has of course tacitly asked for absolution throughout his confession; he wants the priest to take over part of the responsibility for his soul. At the least he desires understanding, a human forgiveness:

Father, Father,
How shall I make you know? You have not
  known
The dreadful soul of woman, who one day
Forgets the old and takes the new to heart.

(ll. 448-451)

To be understood and forgiven he becomes almost Machiavellian; to make the priest know the "dreadful soul of woman" he impassionedly and at length equates his loss with an imaginary situation in which the priest loses heaven after one year in it (ll. 460-474):

Even so I stood the day her empty heart
Left her place empty in our home, while yet
I knew not where she went nor why she went
Nor how to reach her: so I stood the day
When to my prayers at last one sight of her
Was granted, and I looked on heaven made
  pale
With scorn, and heard heaven mock me in
  that laugh.

(ll. 475-481)

—spiritual metaphor to describe earthly (even earthy) loss.

His passion for her (even now that she has been some time dead)—more sensual, more powerful, more jealous than he admits—at last betrays him into blasphemy as he momentarily forgets both strategy and confession in addressing her: "Ah! be it even in flame, / We may have sweetness yet" (ll. 485-486). His confusion is apparent when he asks her to say, "As once in childish sorrow" (l. 487), what amounts to a declaration of love. What he seems to want is the child's devotion to a father—but from an adult, fully ripened woman. There is no evidence in his narrative (in fact it is noticeably absent) that she ever considered him as a lover or as anything but a father, which is perhaps why he, having nothing else, so emphasizes her child's love for him.

Nor are the ambiguities surrounding the girl resolved by the murder scene. In the village as he hides from the spies he hears the harlot's laugh, and three hours later the girl's laugh reminds him of it:

> She had not left me long;
> But all she might have changed to, or might change to,
> (I know nought since—she never speaks a word—)
> Seemed in that laugh.
>
> (ll. 523-526)

To take this motive for the killing at face value—as critics have long done[3]—is to judge the speaker as he wishes to be judged, to ignore his strategy, to lose, in other words, the effect of tension between sympathy and judgment. In actuality we must judge him precisely because the motive as he gives it is false. The facts do not force us to conclude that the girl is either depraved or in danger of depravity; we have only his judgment to go on, and the soundness of that judgment is questionable. Because of the ambiguity of her actions, her guilt or innocence remains problematic. His very language as he confesses the motive—what she might have changed to, or might change to, seemed in her laugh—suggests his own uncertainty about her guilt, his unwillingness to commit himself unequivocally to a judgment distorted by his intense passion for her, his fear that she may take a lover, his frenzy at being rejected. It is not to save her soul that he kills her; it is to prevent her from taking "a German lover," from going "Beyond [his] heart to the world made for her." It is the strategy which demands that he spiritualize his motive.

Besides being incapable, finally, of confessing frankly to a crime of passion, he describes the murder as though it were an act devoid of volition, talking of fire and blood and of knowing that he had stabbed her when he found her "laid against [his] feet" (l. 538). At the very last, however, the strategy again breaks down, and the poem ends in hallucination and fear, a plea for the priest to tell him what hope there is, and the premonition—"but I shall hear her laugh / Soon, when she shows the crimson steel to God" (ll. 558-559). The final irony is that for all of the fearful and desperate manipulation of fact and emotion in his confession, the magnitude of his crime stands bare in the sight of God. And he knows it.

The poem is not only a skillful and subtle dramatic monologue; it is also characteristic of Rossetti in its details: Rossetti's penchant for the abstraction upper case "Love" becomes a means of objectively exploring the relationship between the narrator and the girl; his characteristic sensuous detail becomes in context an indication of the narrator's intense physicality; his predilection for the religious, transformed into the narrator's beliefs, provides the occasion for the poem, the reason and direction for the monologue's present tense strategy, the rationalization for the murder; his fascination with the supernatural and the demonic creates the hallucinatory apparition of the girl, symbol of guilt and fear. The success of the poem is perhaps a result of the fact that because of the dramatic monologue form, the poet is committed to none of these materials, but stays outside of his poem directing our judgment by demonstrating the distortions of the narrator's vision through the workings of his strategy. A form based on disequilibrium seems peculiarly appropriate for a poet of whom it has so often been protested that he does not believe in the symbols and trappings of his poems. It is a way out of the problem of belief and value while still allowing him the materials which appeal to his aesthetic sense, a legitimate artistic means of feeling one way and thinking another.

Notes

[1] "Problems of Form and Content in the Poetry of Dante Gabriel Rossetti," *VP,* II (Winter, 1964), 11-19.

[2] *The Poetry of Experience* (New York, 1957), p. 204.

[3] For example, Lafcadio Hearn in *Pre-Raphaelite and Other Poets,* ed. John Erskine (New York, 1922), p. 75, says that the narrator "has reason to suspect unchastity" of his beloved and kills her on the instant; Arthur C. Benson, *Rossetti* (London, 1916), p. 123, asserts that he kills her half in mad passion and half to save her from degradation; and—further off than all—Garnet Smith writes in "Dante Gabriel Rossetti," *Contemporary Review,* CXXXIII (1928), 629: "That he might save her soul, the penitent has slain his love."

D. M. R. Bentley (essay date 1979)

SOURCE: "Political Themes in the Work of Dante Gabriel Rossetti," in *Victorian Poetry,* Vol. 17, No. 3, Autumn, 1979, pp. 159-79.

[*In the following essay, Bentley studies the theme of modern indifference to God in Rossetti's political poetry.*]

Max Beerbohm's well-known caricature of the young Dante Gabriel Rossetti "precociously manifesting . . . that queer indifference to politics which marked him in his prime and in his decline"[1] embodies a basic untruth. For despite Beerbohm's and, indeed, Rossetti's own assertions to the contrary,[2] Rossetti was far from indifferent to politics, either in his youth, in his "prime," or in his "decline." From almost the beginning to almost the end of his poetic and artistic career he manifested a sporadic but nevertheless keen and satirical interest in contemporary English and European affairs. In the following pages I will examine a number of poems by Rossetti which either deal directly with political subjects or contain references and overtones of a political and, as is often the case, of a socio- or religio-political nature. A brief examination of Rossetti's early essays into political satire and of his shorter political poems of the late forties will establish the background against which to view **"The Burden of Nineveh,"** the longest and most important of the poet-painter's meditations on contemporary political, social, and, ultimately, religious problems.

The earliest artistic manifestation of Rossetti's satirical bent came in the early forties when he designed (c.1840-41) and had lithographed (c.1845)[3] a set of comic or punning "Playing-Cards" which, for the most part, are devoted to political satire. Since these cards were produced when Rossetti had barely entered his teens it would clearly be a mistake to place too great an emphasis on them. Yet they do provide evidence of a precocious interest in politics and related matters. The various satirical references to Prince Albert (the Knave of Diamonds) and to Sir Robert Peel (the Knave of Spades) in the pack suggest that the young Rossetti—perhaps reflecting the opinions of his politically radical father—viewed with dismay the conservative tendencies which were ushered in with the Queen's accession in 1837 and with Peel's second Ministry (1841-46). This would certainly accord with W. M. Rossetti's estimate of his brother as a liberal in ideals, though something of a conservative in practice.[4] However, the depiction of the Prince Consort as a very Germanic Knave with a female personification of British Art impaled on his bayonet suggests a more specific target for Rossetti's early satire. In 1841 Peel appointed the Prince Consort as Chairman of the Royal Commission which was set up in that year with the general aim of promoting the arts in England.[5] The Commission's most immediate task was to select the artists to decorate the new Houses of Parliament, which were then approaching completion. Although Rossetti enthusiastically approved most of the designs submitted for this purpose when they went on exhibit at Westminster in July, 1843—feeling that they gave "the lie to the vile snarling assertion that British Art is slowly but surely falling, never more to rise"[6]—his earlier cartoon suggests that in 1841 he had distinct misgivings about the possible effects of Prince Albert's Germanic influence on British art.[7] Even in his early teens, then, at the time when he was enjoying a reputation among his fellow art students as a "sketcher of chivalric and satiric subjects,"[8] Rossetti was sensitive to political issues, especially insofar as they affected the arts in England.

Something of the same use of cards as a vehicle for political satire is carried over from the "Playing-Cards" into **"The English Revolution of 1848"** *(No connection with over the way)*. In this, his first directly satirical poem, Rossetti pokes fun at the last flickers of Chartism, which, as his brother recalls, "formed a transitory alarm to Londoners in the early months of 1848."[9] Two stanzas of **"The English Revolution of 1848"** convey the overall tone of the piece (notice the use of cards in the first to denote the levelling tendencies of the Chartists):

Ho cock your eyes, my gallant pals, and swing your heavy staves:
Remember—Kings and Queens being out, the great cards will be Knaves.
And when the pack is ours—oh then at what a slapping pace
Shall the tens be trodden down to five, and the fives kicked down to ace!

It was but yesterday the *Times* and *Post* and *Telegraph*
Told how from France King Louy-Phil was shaken out like chaff;
To-morrow, boys, the *National*, the *Siècle*, and the *Débats*,
Shall have to tell the self-same tale of "La Reine Victoria."

(***Works***, pp. 261-262)

The imaginary Chartist from whose incendiary speech this is taken is finally *"nailed by a policeman"* when he incites his followers to burn down the "Exchange, or Parliament" or one of the fashionable "Squares" or Royal "Palaces" near "Trafalgar Square." The poem closes as he is led away pleading "Oh please sir, don't! It isn't me. It's him. Oh don't, sir, please!" **"The English Revolution of 1848"** is full of a certain cockney vitality and humor. Despite its conspicuous lack of political and poetic *gravitas* it nevertheless reveals that Rossetti was conversant with the personalities (he mentions several Chartist leaders by name) and the issues which were at stake in 1848, the year of widespread revolution in Europe. Since Rossetti himself clearly did not take **"The English Revolution"** at all seriously we may speculate that his poem was written, at least in part, to badger his new friends Millais and Hunt, who are known to have been sympathetic spectators at the great Chartist demonstration in April, 1848. Indeed, some of Rossetti's information on the Chartists may have been gleaned from these two artists, and more from the poet Ebenezer Jones, who, when Rossetti met him in 1848, "would hardly talk on any subject but Chartism" (***Works,*** p. 614).

Rossetti's attitude toward the political events of 1848 was by no means as flippant or detached as **"The English Revolution of 1848"** might suggest. As amused as he was by the efforts of the Chartists in England, he took a more serious view of the revolutions *"over the way."* The European events of 1848-49 must have held much the same significance for Rossetti as did those which began in France in June and July of 1789 for young poets such as Coleridge and Blake. Certainly, in the three sonnets which will now be considered, Rossetti is, generally speaking, within the conventions of liberal Romanticism both in his optimistic attitude toward revolution and in his pessimistic interpretation of the post-revolutionary tendency towards restoration, retribution, and repression. But even in **"At the Sun-Rise in 1848,"** a sonnet which shows that he to some extent "shared the aspirations and exultations of the year of vast European upheavals,"[10] Rossetti is cautious in his endorsement of liberty at the expense of authority. In marked contrast to his brother William Michael's "unqualified support of revolutionary and democratic, national liberation movements,"[11] there is something of the Mill of the essay on Alfred de Vigny in Rossetti's clear-sighted ability to see both sides of the revolutionary coin, to appreciate that what is gain to the peasant is loss to the king. Towards the end of the sonnet he cautions "Man, in [his] just pride" against the destructive aspect of revolution, urging him to remember that he was not made by God merely to destroy the authority of Churches ("priests") and monarchs (a "king . . . and yet another king") and to ensure that his "sons' sons shall ask / What the word *king* may mean in their day's task" (***Works,*** p. 171). To stress the positive aspect of revolution implied by the metaphorical dawn of his title, Rossetti both begins and ends his sonnet with an allusion to the birth of light in Genesis 1.3. For Rossetti the revolutionary **"Sun-Rise in 1848"** is creative only insofar as it partakes of God's initial impulse to create a better order out of chaos: "if light [there] is," the sonnet concludes, "It is because God said, Let there be light." Rossetti's use of the Biblical account of the Creation in this context implies an acceptance, not just of God's primacy over man, but of an order—albeit an order of opposites ("If it is day with us, with them 'tis night")—through which the "round world keeps its balancing." It is indicative of Rossetti's fundamentally Christian consciousness of history that he places and judges contemporary revolutions in what may literally be termed the light of God. In Rossetti's early political poems, then—and this applies as much to **"The Burden of Nineveh"** as to **"At the Sun-Rise in 1848"**—light must be regarded (the imperative is Rossetti's own) as the symbol of God's continuing presence in the world.

The year 1849, which saw the collapse of the revolutions of 1848 and the re-establishment of the status quo in Europe, furnished the setting for two sonnets which are pessimistic and prophetic in character. Although the first of these, **"Vox Ecclesiae, Vox Christi,"** deals generally with the brutal suppression of the revolutions of 1848, its primary target is "Christ's Church" (***Works,*** p. 175), which used its altars to bless the weapons and to absolve the soldiers of the counter-revolutionary armies. In order to satirize the "Christian habit of using the 'not peace, but a sword' text to sanctify militarism"[12] Rossetti draws a somewhat Blakean contrast in the sonnet between the teaching of the Church ("Vox Ecclesiae") and that of Christ ("Vox Christi"). The epigraph of the sonnet, from Revelation 6.9-10, a plea to the Lord to "judge and avenge" those who "were slain for the word of God, and for the testimony that they held," serves, once again, to refer contemporary events to a religious and, in this case, apocalyptic framework. According to Rossetti's analysis, the support given by the (Catholic) Church to the counter-revolutionary forces, particularly in Hungary,[13] was a grotesque perversion of "Christ's law," a perversion made all the more reprehensible for being motivated by a "hate of truth" and for being perpetrated on "fierce youth" by "evil age." By making the seeds of good bear "fruit in wrong" the elders of the Church have so perverted Christ's teaching as to enact a Black Mass of bloodshed in which the "wine-cup at the altar is / As Christ's own blood indeed." (Of course there is a reference here to the Catholic belief in the Real Presence.) For Rossetti the blood of those who died "'neath the altar" (this phrase echoes Revelation 6.9 in the epigraph) is "as the blood of Christ's elect, at divers seasons spilt / On the altar-stone." Moreover, this blood has so tainted the Church as to make the altar itself a "stone of stumbling" (here the reference is to Isaiah 8.14) that must be "rent up ere the true Church be built." The implication is that the revolutionaries who were killed by "weapons blessed for carnage" by the established Church are, in fact, the martyrs of the "true Church." The quotation from Revelation which heads the sonnet thus becomes a direct appeal to the Christian God to recognize these martyrs of the "true Church" and to avenge their "blood on them that dwell on the earth."

"Vox Ecclesiae, Vox Christi" is a richer and more subtle sonnet than W. M. Rossetti's "The Evil under the Sun"[14] (earlier called "How long O Lord" and later entitled "Democracy Downtrodden"), which was also inspired by the Austrian suppression of Hungary in 1849. Indeed, in its very richness and subtlety, as well as in its subject matter and form, Rossetti's poem recalls and invites comparison with Milton's sonnet "On the Late Massacre in Piemont" which opens with the cry "Avenge, O Lord, thy slaughter'd Saints."[15] **"Vox Ecclesiae, Vox Christi"** is finally remarkable, not just as a powerful indictment of the Church's role in the political events of 1848-49, but as the first example of Rossetti's tendency to draw upon the language and imagery of the Old and New Testament Prophets to give resonance to his condemnation of contemporary injustices.

The second of Rossetti's political sonnets of 1849, **"On Refusal of Aid between Nations,"** was also occasioned by Austria's brutalization of Hungary and Italy in that year. As a statement about international apathy and non-intervention this sonnet has almost universal application. In 1869 Rossetti considered re-titling it "On the Refusal of Aid to Hungary 1849, to Poland 1861, to Crete 1867" (***Letters,*** II, 721); and on March 21, 1940, it was reprinted in the *Times*[16] as a comment on Russia's entry into Finland in that year.

"On Refusal of Aid between Nations" is particularly interesting within the corpus of Rossetti's political poems because, in its pessimistic and apocalyptic view of civilization on the brink of disaster, it bridges the gap between the guarded optimism of **"At the Sun-Rise in 1848"** and the unmitigated pessimism of **"The Burden of Nineveh"** (1850). The octave of the sonnet explores the perception that the "earth is changing," that the "seasons totter in their walk," and that the God who presides over both "nations" and "kings" is a Judge of the Last Day who, with just wrath, weighs "the rod / . . . in [His] hand to smite [the] world" (***Works,*** p. 175). For Rossetti the realization that "Man is parcelled out in men," that mankind is no longer a unified body but a collection of individuals who excuse their lack of concern for the plight of others by pleading "'He is he, I am I'," is a sure and telling sign that the "earth falls asunder, being old." Rossetti's sonnet "On the Field of Waterloo" (1849) also closes on the perception that "the earth is old" (***Works,*** p. 186). Moreover, several other poems that were either wholly or partly written in 1849 partake of this pessimistic sense of living in the last days. In **"A Last Confession,"** for instance, the protagonist, who, it should be remembered, is an Italian *maqui* with a bitter hatred for "old Metternich" (***Works,*** p. 47), also experiences a feeling of impending apocalypse. "In my dream," he tells the priest, "I thought our world was setting, and the sun / Flared, a spent taper" (***Works,*** p. 46). An equivalent sense of an ending occurs at the conclusion of **"The Bride's Prelude"** where the priest assures the heroine that "The world's soul, for its sins, was sped / And the sun's courses numberèd" (***Works,*** p. 34). In all these poems Rossetti equates the disintegration of moral values, whether at the political or personal level, with the irreversible running down of the sun; and in none of them does he give us any cause to think that the course of history offers any other, more optimistic possibility. If account is also taken of the fact that the lines from **"The Bride's Prelude"** just quoted were not written until 1869 and that **"A Last Confession"** is set in an Italy struggling against Metternich's reference to itself as a "geographical expression," it does not seem unfair to deduce that Rossetti's sense of an imminent, apocalyptic ending for the world arose directly from the awareness of political and social disintegration expressed so powerfully and concisely in **"On Refusal of Aid between Nations."**

It is worth taking a moment to view the political sonnets of 1848-49, the sonnets which comprise what might be called Rossetti's "revolutionary series," as a unit. This slight shift in perspective makes it clear that Rossetti sees political events as occurring within the Biblical scale of time that begins with the Creation in Genesis and ends with the Last Judgment in Revelation. The central symbol of this continuum is the sun, which, by Rossetti's analysis of contemporary socio-political events, is in 1849 well past its peak of energy. In none of the three sonnets in the "revolutionary series" does Rossetti question either the Christian conception of time or the moral and spiritual values that it implies. Rather, his criticism and, ultimately, his pessimism stem from a recognition of man's failure to take full account of the teleology and eschatology of Christianity. Although Rossetti's guardedly optimistic endorsement of revolution in 1848 probably owes a debt to his early reading of Shelley and Blake, both of whom proclaim the birth of a new world and the death of the old, his pessimism in face of the events of 1849 draws more on the Prophetic Books of the Old and New Testaments. Moreover, with **"On Refusal of Aid between Nations"** there emerges a concern for mankind as a whole that runs counter to the Romantic emphasis on individual liberty which, it has been suggested, contributed to Rossetti's earlier championship of revolution against the established political and religious orders. Without wholly endorsing H. N. Fairchild's somewhat simplistic analysis of nineteenth-century Catholic poetry, with its de-emphasis of individuality, as a "force opposed to Romanticism" (IV, 243), it is nevertheless true to say that Rossetti's lament over the breakup of mankind as a unified body suggests a vision that might well be classified as less Romantic than Catholic. Needless to say, this need not imply that Rossetti approved of the Catholic Church's role in the struggles of the late forties. **"Vox Ecclesiae, Vox Christi"** proves that he emphatically did not. However, if Pope Pius IX had condemned the principle of non-intervention soon after he acceded to the Papacy in 1846, and not waited until the *Syllabus* of 1864 to do so, he would unquestionably have had the support of the author of **"On Refusal of Aid between Nations."**[17]

Even with Rossetti's political poems of 1848 and 1849 firmly in mind, it is still astonishing to remember that he wrote **"The Burden of Nineveh,"** his series of "reflexions humoristiques sur la chute des civilisations et des empires,"[18] within only a few months of completing *Ecce Ancilla Domini!* (1849-50). When we move from the painting to the poem, we move from a world inspired by the gilt aureoles and white robes of early Christian art to a world dominated by the colossal form of an Assyrian "Bull-god" seen in the grey, contemporary setting of the British Museum:

> Now, thou poor god, within this hall
> Where the blank windows blind the wall
> From pedestal to pedestal,
> The kind of light shall on thee fall
> Which London takes the day to be:
> While school-foundations in the act
> Of holiday, three files compact,
> Shall learn to view thee as a fact.

(***Works,*** p. 56)

Although **"The Burden of Nineveh"** was originally written and published (in the *Oxford and Cambridge Magazine* for August, 1856) in a humorously satirical vein that recalls **"The English Revolution of 1848,"** the version of the poem that appeared in ***Poems*** (1870)—from which the above is quoted—is more serious and, hence, more reminiscent of the political sonnets of 1848 and 1849. Oswald Doughty goes some way towards explaining the transition from *Ecce Ancilla Domini!* to **"The Burden of Nineveh"** when he remarks that the poem was written in the "anticlimax of recent humiliations," by which he means "the failure of *The Germ* and the [Pre-Raphaelite] Brotherhood, [and] the perpetual embarrassment of poverty."[19] Doughty's explanation of Rossetti's state of mind at the time of writing **"The Burden of Nineveh"** would be more inclusive and accurate if it took into account both the disastrous exhibition of *Ecce Ancilla Domini!* in 1850 and—since the poem is at base about "la chute des civilisations"—Rossetti's general pessimism in regard to the state of European civilization in 1849.

It was propitious both psychologically and imaginatively for Rossetti that, at the time when he was acutely disillusioned by a combination of political, professional, and personal circumstances, he was confronted with an image, part man and part beast, which exactly suited his feeling of having been brutalized by a brutal society:

> I have no taste for polyglot:
> At the Museum 'twas my lot,
> Just once, to jot and blot and rot
> In Babel for I know not what.
> I went at two, I left at three.
> Round those still floors I tramp'd, to win
> By the great porch the dirt and din;
> And as I made the last door spin
> And issued, they were hoisting in
> A wingèd beast from Nineveh.[20]

Rossetti's direct inspiration for **"The Burden of Nineveh"** could have been any one of the seven colossal figures which arrived at the British Museum between the end of 1850 and the beginning of 1852 "fresh from 'Layard's Nineveh'."[21] However, Rossetti's description of the figure as a "Bull-god" with a "human face" later in the poem, coupled with his brother's recollection that the poem had its genesis in the "autumn of 1850" ("Notes," p. 649), provides good reason for associating its inspiration with one particular figure. Of the seven Assyrian colossi held by the British Museum only three are human-headed winged bulls (the remaining four have the bodies of lions), and of these three, two did not arrive at the Museum until towards the end of 1851.[22] The remaining colossal winged bull arrived in London "at the end of September, 1850" (Gadd, pp. 58, 126) and, moreover, it was the only one which arrived at the Museum in one piece (the later ones were cut into segments to facilitate transportation).[23] It thus seems certain that the "wingèd beast from Nineveh" which "they are hoisting in" through the entrance of the British Museum in the "autumn of 1850" was the human-headed winged bull (No. 118872) which to the present day is exhibited in the Nimrud Central Saloon on the ground floor of the Museum.

Rossetti's detailed description of the "wingèd beast" in the second stanza of **"The Burden of Nineveh"** agrees very well with the first of the human-headed winged bulls to arrive at the British Museum:

> A human face the creature wore,
> And hoofs behind and hoofs before,
> And flanks with dark runes fretted o'er
> 'Twas bull, 'twas mitred Minotaur,
> A dead disbowelled mystery:
> The mummy of a buried faith
> Stark from the charnel without scathe,
> Its wings stood for the light to bathe,—
> Such fossil cerements as might swathe
> The very corpse of Nineveh.

(***Works,*** p. 55)

There is, however, more to this stanza than meets the eye: we should not be deceived into thinking that it is *merely* a description of the "Bull-god." The fact that Rossetti uses some poetic license in comparing the human-headed winged bull with the Greek Minotaur—

a creature which is usually represented with a bull's *head* and human *body*—was possibly intended to alert us to the symbolic overtones of the description. Not only does Rossetti compare the "Bull-god" with a "Minotaur" but he goes on to liken it to an Egyptian "mummy" and, perhaps more importantly, he (aptly enough) describes its head-gear as a "mitre." Taken together, these metaphorical aspects of the description suggest that Rossetti is using the Assyrian figure as a summary image for the extravagances of faiths, both buried and unburied. It is surely not fortuitous that the "mitred" head of the "Bull-god" has reminded several critics of a Roman Catholic prelate.[24] Later in the poem, in stanza 8, Rossetti connects the "Bull-god" with "that zealous tract: / 'ROME'" (***Works,*** p. 56). This is perhaps an allusion, by way of two puns—"Tract" / Tractarianism and "bull" / Papal Bull—to the religio-political controversies surrounding Tractarianism and Roman Catholicism which reached a peak in 1850 with the Gorham Case (Baptismal Regeneration) and the so-called "papal aggression" (the reestablishment of the Roman Catholic hierarchy in England and Wales). Significantly, "ROME" is the only upper-case word that appears in the poem, and it is perhaps capitalized in stanza 8 to differentiate it from the lower-case "Rome" that is linked with "Greece" and "Egypt" in the succeeding stanza. In view of Rossetti's attitude toward the Catholic Church as expressed in **"Vox Ecclesiae, Vox Christi"** it is neither inconsistent nor surprising that he should implicate "ROME" in his condemnation of the pride and vanity of earthly empires in **"The Burden of Nineveh."** Indeed, it would be more surprising if he did not. Rossetti, it appears, shared with many Victorians, including the Ruskin of *Notes on the Construction of Sheepfolds* (1851) and the Hunt of *Our English Coasts, 1852,*[25] a distrust, which was partly political, of the spiritual imperialism of the Catholic Church.

Although **"The Burden of Nineveh"** was directly inspired by the arrival of the "Bull-god" "fresh from 'Layard's Nineveh'," and many details in the poem seem to have been drawn from Layard's account of his excavations in *Nineveh and Its Remains* (1849),[26] it was to the Prophetic Books of the Old Testament, particularly the books of Nahum and Jonah, that Rossetti went to vitalize his satirical portrait of a contemporary world whoring after false gods. That Rossetti intended **"The Burden of Nineveh"** to be an ominous comment on the state of England, filled with vague but familiar parallels with religions and empires past and present, is, it has been suggested, evident even in his metaphorical description of the "Bull-god" in the second stanza of the poem. The very title of the poem is in fact a direct transcription of the opening words of Nahum, the book that deals specifically with the fall of Nineveh. In the *Oxford and Cambridge Magazine* Rossetti appended a note to the title quoting a *"Dictionary"* definition of *"Burden* [as a] 'Heavy calamity; the chorus of a song'" (p. 514). This note serves not only to suggest the implicit *gravitas* of the poem but to direct the reader to its varying refrain (the last line of each stanza) where the parallel between Nineveh and London is developed with a weighty inevitability that, as R. L. Megroz suggests, makes each of the stanzas sound like "separate foot-steps of that gigantic bull."[27]

For Rossetti, the chief cause of Nineveh's (and London's) fall is her proud and sinful indifference to the Christian God. To vitalize this perception he alludes several times to the attempts of Nahum and Jonah to warn the city of impending destruction. The description of Nineveh as a "Delicate harlot" in stanza 15, for instance, recalls the "whoredoms of [Nineveh] the well-favoured harlot" of Nahum 3.4. Like Blake before him, Rossetti connects social with sexual corruption; and he prepares the way for the condemnation of Nineveh as a "harlot" by alluding first to "Sardanapalus," whose epitaph "eat, drink and lust; the rest is nothing" is quoted by Layard, and then to "pale Semiramis," the queen who, again according to Layard, introduced the worship of Venus-Astarte to Nineveh.[28] In stanzas 6, 12, and 15 the allusions to Jonah's futile attempt to bear "abroad / To Nineveh the voice of God" (***Works,*** p. 57)—the "brackish lake [that] lay in his road" and the "gourd" which God sent to shelter him from the sun by the walls of Nineveh—are all drawn from the Prophet's own account in the four chapters of Jonah. Towards the end of his meditation on the destruction of Nineveh, Rossetti invokes Christ's temptation by Satan ("Pride's lord and Man's"), not only to suggest that it was pride that led to Nineveh's downfall, but to prepare the way for the suggestion, toward the end of the poem, that London in her pride and idolatry will be destroyed by a wrathful God as surely as was Nineveh.

In **"The Burden of Nineveh"** the eroding element of the wind, often in Rossetti's work a symbol for the passage of time, is the destructive agent of the omnipresent and omnipotent Christian God. The very same "callous wind" that whipped up "burial clouds of sand" around the "Bull-god" until "another land" covered "his eyes" and "blinded him with destiny" blows through the "dirt and din" of London and seems to sweep up the "shadow from the ground." The "Bull-god" in its mound of sand seemed immune to "Time [which] passed, of like import / With the wild Arab boys at sport." But its supposed immunity is merely relative, for all the while "older grew / By ages the old earth and sea" (***Works,*** pp. 55-56). In the final analysis it is only the Christian God "before whose countenance / The years recede, the years advance" (***Works,*** p. 57) who is immune to the ravages of time. Thus, although Rossetti is unquestionably pessimistic in his analysis of civilizations past and passing, he does not, as Harold L.

Weatherby asserts, question "the very rudiments of religious thought"[29] in **"The Burden of Nineveh."** Nor is there a "thoroughly sceptical sort of idea" (Weatherby, p. 17) at the heart of the poem. As in his political sonnets of 1848 and 1849, Rossetti's aim in **"The Burden of Nineveh"** is to point out, with the pessimism of a Spengler rather than the skepticism of a Hardy, the apocalyptic consequences of the contemporary failure to regard the message of Christianity. That is why, in the penultimate stanza of the poem, Rossetti describes the cuneiform inscription on the "Bull-god's" side, not as "runes," but as "those scriptured flanks it cannot see" (***Works,*** p. 58). It is the set, forward-looking visage of the colossus which prevents it from seeing either the message behind it or the sky above it. And it is this horizontal gaze, indifferent to scripture and light alike, that makes the "Bull-god" of Nineveh with its wings "which do not fly" and its feet "planted . . . [on] the sod," an appropriate symbol for the false gods of a progressive and materialistic[30] London.

The central irony of **"The Burden of Nineveh,"** then, is that the "Bull-god" with its horizontal gaze and flightless wings is enjoying a second coming as the god of London. This irony, which perhaps brings with it the suggestion that the discovery of the "winged beast" in some measure fulfills the reign of the Anti-Christ prophesied by the coming of the beast in Revelation 13, is given a final, knife-like twist in the last three stanzas of the poem. First Rossetti looks ahead to the day when "ships of unknown sail and prow," the ships perhaps of "some tribe of the Australian plough," will carry the "Bull-god" from the "desert place" where England's capital once stood as a "relic . . . / Of London, not of Nineveh" (***Works,*** p. 58). On finding the "Bull-god" in the ruins of London, he conjectures, these possibly antepodean people of the distant future "when / Man's age is hoary among men" might justifiably assume that the English "race / . . . walked not in Christ's lowly ways, / But bowed its pride and vowed its praise / Unto the God of Nineveh." The last stanza of the poem makes it clear that what initially arose as a fanciful comparison between Nineveh and London ("the smile rose first,—anon drew nigh / The thought") has now become so frighteningly real that the "Bull-god" seems all the time to have been the god of London rather than of Nineveh. The final twist of the knife occurs in the last two lines of the poem where Rossetti asks: "O Nineveh, was this thy God,—/ Thine also, mighty Nineveh?" By the conclusion of the poem the "burden of Nineveh" has indeed, in Oliver Elton's words, become "the burden of London."[31]

Only once more in his life did Rossetti use the arrival of an ancient monument in London as the occasion for a satirical poem. In 1878 Cleopatra's Needle was erected on the Thames embankment[32] and three years later Rossetti used the historical associations both of Cleopatra and of the word "needle" itself to inveigh against what he saw as England's indifference to the "sweet speech" (***Works,*** p. 233) of its finest poets. In **"Tiber, Nile, and Thames"** (1881) he makes an extraordinary connection between the Egyptian "obelisk" and the "chill stone" of London's streets that "with poison froze the god-fired breath" of Keats, Coleridge, and Chatterton. The basic link in this connection is forged in the octave of the sonnet where Rossetti builds up the associations of Cleopatra's Needle by recounting the legend that "Fulvia, Mark Anthony's shameless wife" used "her sharp needle" to pierce the "god-like tongue" of the "murdered Cicero." Perhaps because the restrictions of the sonnet form allowed Rossetti to present only the bare essentials of the connection between Fulvia's needle and Cleopatra's, between the grisly fate of Cicero and the Romantic poets whom he mentions, **"Tiber, Nile, and Thames"** does not rise much above the level of the "grim anecdote" (***Letters,*** IV, 1838) embodied in its octave. It is impossible to say, and hence futile to ask, what the poem would have been like if Rossetti had developed its central metaphor—as he doubtless could have—with the ominous and pessimistic intensity of **"The Burden of Nineveh."**

Late in 1852, Rossetti took time off from his Marian and Dantean paintings then in progress to write what, in a burlesque, cockney spirit, he called "summat on the Dook" (***Letters,*** I, 116). The funeral of the Duke of Wellington took place on November 18, 1852, and the "public frenzy" surrounding it, he told Thomas Woolner a few months later, was sufficient to wring "something *de rigeur*" from even the "most apathetic" (***Letters,*** I, 133) of its spectators—Rossetti himself. In view of Rossetti's inability, laconically expressed in **"On the Field of Waterloo"** (1849), to respond either positively ("I believe one should have thrilled") or negatively ("Am I to weep?" [***Works,*** p. 186]) to the great victory and massive carnage of the Duke's most famous battle, it is indeed surprising that he should have written a poem thirteen stanzas long on **"Wellington's Funeral."** Of course Rossetti was writing as a contemporary of Tennyson, who was made poet laureate less than two years earlier; and it is of the "Ode on the Death of the Duke of Wellington" that we will be immediately reminded by **"Wellington's Funeral."** But it was not an "ode" that Rossetti intended to write. Characteristically, he uses the "duteous mourning" and "reverent mood" (***Works,*** p. 196) surrounding the state funeral as the occasion for a meditation, not on Wellington's military victories, but on the "solemn mirth" that accompanies a soul's "new birth" into Heaven. "If our eyes were opened," he asks—perhaps echoing Blake's "If the doors of perception were cleansed"—would the "escort [that] floats / Here" not appear as "Fiery horses, chariots / Fire-footed?" For Rossetti this particular "soul's labour shall be scann'd / And found good" by God because of the "peace which this man wrought / Passing well" in Europe. In the central stanzas of the poem Rossetti supplies the corrective to the Church's abuse of the "not peace, but a sword" text which he had so bitterly condemned in **"Vox Ecclesiae, Vox Christi."** The only valid reason for resorting to "bloodshed Christ abhorr'd," he maintains in **"Wellington's Funeral,"** is to bring about peace:

> "'Twas thus in His decrees
> Who Himself, the Prince of Peace,
> For His harvest's high increase
> Sent a sword."
>
> (*Works,* p. 196)

Rossetti brings **"Wellington's Funeral"** to a close—after saluting the "Veterans" of the Napoleonic Wars and using the French Coup d'État of December 2, 1851, to suggest the vanity of Napoleon's imperialistic hopes—by returning, once more, to Wellington, the man, whose "long tale of conquering strife / Shows no triumph like his life / Lost and won" (*Works,* p. 197).

Despite such memorable touches as the oxymoron "solemn mirth," there are several unsatisfactory images and metaphors in **"Wellington's Funeral."** The "banshee-strain" with which the dead at Waterloo are credited is only marginally less inappropriate than the comparison between Wellington's achievements and the "All Hail!'" with which Gabriel greeted the Blessed Virgin at the Annunciation. The impression left by the poem is that, as a poet, Rossetti is trying to participate in and comment on the pompous solemnity of Wellington's funeral but that his mind cannot entirely escape from the preoccupations of the Marian work with which he was engaged as a painter. However, although certain touches in the poem are regrettable it is difficult to deny the sincerity of Rossetti's hope that, with Wellington's "great work" in establishing the basis for European peace, "Michael's sword" (*Works,* p. 196), "once lent for human lack," will at last be "rendered back" to God.

History, of course, has not confirmed Rossetti's hope for a lasting peace in Europe. Two of his later sonnets, **"After the French Liberation of Italy"** (1859) and **"After the German Subjugation of France, 1871,"** were occasioned by breaches of the peace which occurred in his own lifetime. The connection between a corrupt society and a whore, which occurs not only in **"The Burden of Nineveh"** but also in **"Dante at Verona"** (1848-50)—where Rossetti puns on the word Republic ("RESPUBLICA—a public thing: / A shameful shameless prostitute") to describe Florence who "takes by turn . . . / A night with each" (*Works,* p. 13) of her rulers—forms the central metaphor of both these later political sonnets. Although, as his brother records, Rossetti approved of the "French Liberation of Italy" in 1859, or, more strictly speaking, Napoleon III's expulsion of Austria from Lombardy in that year, "he objected to . . . other features of [Napoleon III's] Italian policy" ("Notes," p. 667). Having observed Rossetti's pessimism develop out of the "revolutionary series" of sonnets into **"The Burden of Nineveh"** it is not surprising to learn that he wrote **"After the French Liberation of Italy"** "to commemorate his forecast of bad times for Europe generally" ("Notes," p. 667). In the octave of the sonnet the encounter between Europe, the "loveless whore," and Napoleon III's France is described with explicit and memorable pungency:

> with a single kiss
> At length, and with one laugh of satiate bliss,
> The wearied man a minute rests above
> The wearied woman, no more urged to move
> In those long throes of longing.
>
> (*Works,* p. 205)

The "forecast of bad times" comes in the sestet of the sonnet in the form of the "harlot's child," conceived in Europe's "bought body . . . to scourge her for her sin."

This "harlot's child" finally makes its presence felt in **"After the German Subjugation of France, 1871,"** which is a subtler and more complex sonnet than **"After the French Liberation of Italy."** Here, after a gestation period of "years for months," the whore's "babe new-born; / Out of the womb's rank furnace" is present at her "wedding feast" (*Works,* p. 217). Parodying the "gospel-tongues of flame" (*Works,* p. 179) which he had sensed in the **"Place de la Bastille"**—that symbol of liberation from repression—in 1849, Rossetti says that it is the "fiery tongues [of] . . . / Hell's Pentecost," coupled with a chorus of "scoffs" from such Biblical traitors as Absalom and Shimei, which provide the "tumultuous sound" to "hail this birth" of the "harlot's child." The poem closes on the terrible and apocalyptic image of the "closing teeth of Hell" ripping the flesh of the whore's "Lord of yesterday" (Napoleon III's France) to the accompaniment of the "vanished world's last yell." In the description of the whore's womb as a "rank furnace" there is perhaps something of Milton's Hell, which is also described as a *"Furnace"* in *Paradise Lost* I.62. But it is finally Blake's "London," where the "Harlot's curse . . . blights with plagues the Marriage hearse," that is most insistently recalled by **"After the German Subjugation of France, 1871."** Indeed there is something of the fiercely satirical connection between social and sexual evil in Blake's poem translated to the sphere of international politics in Rossetti's two sonnets of 1859 and 1871.

With only one exception, a sonnet on the assassination of **"Czar Alexander the Second (13th of March 1881),"** Rossetti wrote no poems on contemporary political events in the last decade of his life. This does not mean, however, that he abandoned completely the themes of his political poems of the late forties and early fifties. Rather, he transferred the central, overriding theme of all his political poems—the paramount importance of God over Man—to the realm of his two historical ballads—**"The White Ship"** (1878-80) and **"The King's Tragedy"** (1881). It is permissible to speculate that it was Rossetti's profound and increasing pessimism over political events in Europe between the late forties and the early seventies that led him, towards the end of his life, to express his religio-political ideas in an historical rather than a contemporary context. A brief examination of **"Czar Alexander the Second"** will show, not only that Rossetti maintained a consistent political position from 1848 to 1881, but also that his political thinking is central to the two historical ballads of 1878-81.

Rossetti's conviction that the assassination of Czar Alexander the Second "bears witness of his people's woe" (***Works,*** p. 233) to God is reminiscent of the warnings against regicide, delivered from the same religious platform, in **"At the Sun-Rise in 1848."** Rossetti makes it clear that his sympathy for the murdered Czar arose from the fact that "Alexander the Liberator,"[33] as Swinburne sarcastically called him, had granted the Russian serfs "rich freedom, lifelong land, whereon to sheave / Their country's harvest." Rossetti clearly did not share Swinburne's estimation of Czar Alexander II as an "hypocritical oppressor" who, above all, was "guilty of monarchy" (*Swinburne Letters,* IV, 260, 203). To Rossetti the Czar's murderers are "the first / Of Russia's traitors." They are guilty, not only of regicide, but of using, and provoking the serfs to use on them, the very "torment"—the "knout's red-ravening fangs"—that the Czar's "edicts disallow'd." Here can be seen emerging clearly for the first time Rossetti's championship of a liberal monarch. It is surely no coincidence that in the same year that he wrote **"Czar Alexander the Second"** he chose as the subject of **"The King's Tragedy"** a monarch whom he also conceived to have been a liberal—King James I of Scotland. W. M. Rossetti, who in 1881 was encouraged by his brother to write his sequence of overtly political *Democratic Sonnets* (and then, for mainly practical reasons, discouraged by his brother from publishing them until 1907[34]), tells us that it was not merely James I's "interesting combination of poetry and kingship" which attracted Rossetti but, perhaps more important, his "virtues . . . in vindicating the common people against oppression" ("Notes," p. 660). By Rossetti's conception of him, James I is the "King whom poor men bless for their King" (***Works,*** p. 149) because:

he . . . tamed the nobles' lust
And curbed their power and pride,
And reached out an arm to right the poor
Through Scotland far and wide.

(***Works,*** p. 147)

Clearly Rossetti, as a liberal Royalist, saw King James I and Czar Alexander II in a similar light. To him both were just, humanitarian rulers whose liberal reforms in favor of the common people resulted in their murders by men who were traitors, not just to their respective countries and people, but to God. Moreover, Rossetti's James I is a Christ-like figure who calmly resigns himself to the "will" of the God "Who has one same death for a hind / And one same death for a King" (***Works,*** p. 149) and, at the end of the poem, goes to his death neither as a "King" nor as a "Knight" but as a "Man" (***Works,*** p. 158). In the last analysis, it is the perception that all men, be they humanist rulers or humble peasants, are, in death, subordinate to the will of God that lies at the core of all Rossetti's political poems, be they contemporary or historical. Rossetti's most explicit statement of this fundamentally Christian view of existence is to be found in **"The White Ship."** Here "poor Berold" the "butcher of Rouen" (***Works,*** p. 138) uses the drowning of King Henry I's son to exemplify the perception, expressed chorically at the beginning, middle, and end of the poem, that though *"Lands are swayed by a King on a throne. . . . The sea hath no King but God alone"* (***Works,*** pp. 138, 141, and 144). It is this assertion of the omnipotence of a Christian God in the face of the evil, corruption, and death of the world that rescues Rossetti's political poems and historical ballads, pessimistic as they unquestionably are, from skepticism.

As a pessimist Rossetti may perhaps underestimate man's ability to choose right over wrong, to avoid the dreadful consequences of his own mistakes, but this does not preclude him from deferring final judgment to the just, wrathful, and omnipresent God who watches and waits to judge the world in the background of all Rossetti's serious religio-political poems. It is possible to ignore the many-sided sympathy and the compassionate sense of justice, that made Rossetti, in youth, cautious of the destructive aspect of revolution and, in maturity, the champion of liberal monarchs. It is possible to deplore the absurdities of his imagination when they occur in the wrong place, such as when Gabriel is brought in to give an "All Hail!" to the Duke of Wellington or when sex is used, perhaps a little too graphically, as a political metaphor in the sonnets of 1859 and 1871. But it is difficult either to ignore or to deplore the judiciousness and sincerity with which he examines and inveighs against what he saw as a contemporary failure to regard the teachings of Christ. In contrast to Tennyson and to Kipling—whose "Recessional" would furnish an interesting comparison with

"The Burden of Nineveh"—Rossetti was chiefly a poet-painter rather than a poet-prophet. Perhaps because of the hostile reception of *Ecce Ancilla Domini!* in 1850 he could not feel any deep sense of identity with the reading public to which his warnings were directed. But like many politically and socially conscious men of his time Rossetti felt a sense of impending doom as Austria, France, and Germany spread their tentacles across Europe and as the brutal materialism and colossal bestiality of his own society took it away from the teachings of true Christianity. Living in a proud, pompous, and militaristic time Rossetti envisioned the world on the brink of the Apocalypse: he could find the solutions to contemporary problems only in the eschatology of Christianity. It was in the context of the ultimate and terrible consequences of man's indifferences to God that Rossetti viewed the battle between authority and liberty, between monarchy and democracy, between the institutional Church and the "true Church," between mankind and man, a debate which is as old as what, to him, was an aging world.

Notes

[1] *Rossetti and His Circle* (London, 1922), caption to frontispiece.

[2] See, for instance, Rossetti's letter of 1880, quoted in T. Hall Caine, *Recollections of Dante Gabriel Rossetti* (Boston, 1883), pp. 200-201, in which he writes, not without irony: "My friends . . . consider me exceptionally averse to politics; and I suppose I must be, for I never read a parliamentary debate in my life! At the same time I will add that, among those whose opinions I most value, some think me not altogether wrong when I venture to speak of the momentary momentousness and eternal futility of many noisiest questions. However, you must simply view me as a nonentity in any practical relation to such matters." The present essay bears out Caine's own comment, *Recollections,* pp. 270-271, that "it would, nevertheless, be wrong to say that [Rossetti] was wholly indifferent to important political issues, of which he took often a very judicial view."

[3] See Virginia Surtees, *The Paintings and Drawings of Dante Gabriel Rossetti (1828-1882): A Catalogue Raisonné* (Oxford Univ. Press, 1971), I, No. 4. Although none of the cards is illustrated by Surtees, two are reproduced in H. C. Marillier, *Dante Gabriel Rossetti: An Illustrated Memorial of His Life and Art* (London, 1899), pp. 214-215 and several in *The Bookman* (London), 40 (June, 1911), 130-131. . . .

[4] See *Dante Gabriel Rossetti as Designer and Writer* (London, 1889), pp. 135-136. It is notable that Rossetti's Knave of Spades (Peel) contains references to Free Trade, Catholic Emancipation, and the Irish Problem.

[5] The Commission's statement of purpose is quoted in John Steegman, *Victorian Taste: A Study of the Arts and Architecture from 1830-1870* (London, 1970), p. 130.

[6] *Letters of Dante Gabriel Rossetti,* ed. Oswald Doughty and John Robert Wahl (Oxford Univ. Press, 1965), I, 16. Hereafter cited as *Letters.*

[7] Rossetti's Knave of Diamonds is inscribed "OVERBECK PINXIT" in probable reference to the fact (see John Nicoll, *The Pre-Raphaelites* [London, 1970], p. 19) that "it was initially proposed" (doubtless with the approval of Prince Albert) that "Overbeck . . . should be asked" to decorate the new Houses with frescoes.

[8] F. G. Stephens, cited by William M. Rossetti, ed., *Dante Gabriel Rossetti: His Family Letters, with a Memoir* (London, 1895), I, 96-97.

[9] William M. Rossetti, "Notes," in *The Works of Dante Gabriel Rossetti* (London, 1911), p. 673. Hereafter cited as *Works.*

[10] William M. Rossetti, "Notes," in *Works,* p. 663.

[11] Leonid M. Arinshtein with William E. Fredeman, "William Michael Rossetti's Democratic Sonnets," *VS,* 14 (1971), 266.

[12] H. N. Fairchild, "Dante Gabriel Rossetti," in *Christianity and Romanticism in the Victorian Era,* Vol. IV of *Religious Trends in English Poetry* (Columbia Univ. Press, 1957), 391.

[13] See William M. Rossetti, "Notes," in *Works,* p. 664.

[14] The sonnet on which the last issue of *The Germ* closes. See Arinshtein and Fredeman, p. 242n.

[15] See John Milton, *Complete Poems and Major Prose,* ed. Merritt Y. Hughes (New York, 1957), pp. 167-168.

[16] Kerrison Preston points this out in *Blake and Rossetti* (London, 1944), p. 67.

[17] [J. C. Earle], "Rossetti's Poems," *Catholic World,* 19 (May, 1874), 271, sees "On Refusal of Aid between Nations" as an "exquisite vindication of one of the least popular of the condemnations in the *Syllabus*—that of non-intervention." It is worth noting that in August, 1847 (i.e. within a year of the accession of Pius IX) Rossetti expressed delight over the new Pope's attempts to take the lead in the struggle to achieve Italian unity and independence. Writing to his mother about the Austrians' forced retreat from Ferrara in Northern Italy at that time, he says gleefully: "The papers . . . affirm . . . that the Pope has said that, if the unjustifiable interference is continued, he shall first

make a protest to all the Sovereigns of Europe against Austria; that, in case this should fail, he will excommunicate both Emperor and people; and that, when driven to the last extremity, he will himself ride in the van of his own army with the sword and the Cross" (*Letters,* I, 32). Of course, when Pius IX refused to make war on the Austrians in 1848, the liberal hopes which had been pinned on him were dashed, and not long after this the Pope himself largely abandoned his politically liberal ideas.

[18] Gabriel Sarrazin, *Poetes modernes de L'Angleterre* (Paris, 1884), p. 238.

[19] *A Victorian Romantic: Dante Gabriel Rossetti* (London, 1949), p. 104.

[20] This is the first stanza of "The Burden of Nineveh" as it appears in the *Oxford and Cambridge Magazine,* August, 1856, p. 512. The justification for quoting it here, in preference to the first stanza of the *Poems* (1870) version of the poem, is that it perhaps conveys more truly Rossetti's mood when he first confronted the "Bull-god" in 1850. The narrator of the later version of "The Burden of Nineveh" is a more serious student of ancient art who has spent several hours "rejoicing" over the art of "Dead Greece" (*Works,* p. 55)—perhaps the Elgin Marbles.

[21] This phrase occurs only in the *Oxford and Cambridge Magazine,* August, 1856, p. 514.

[22] The details of the transportation and the dates of arrival of these colossi are given in C. J. Gadd, *The Stones of Assyria* (London, 1936), pp. 124-127 and 159-160.

[23] See Gadd, p. 160; and see also the *Illustrated London News,* February 28, 1852, p. 184 for a picture of one of the human-headed winged lions being hauled up the front steps of the British Museum . . . .

[24] See for example *Victorian and Later English Poets,* ed. James Stephens, Edwin L. Beck, and Royall H. Snow (New York, 1949), p. 1239.

[25] See Leslie Parris, *Landscape in Britain, c. 1750-1850* (London, 1973), pp. 127-128 for a discussion of the relationship between Ruskin's *Notes* and Hunt's painting. It is worth noting that Rossetti was not the only one amongst his family and artistic associates who was interested in Nineveh. In a letter from Brighton dated August 14, 1850—only weeks before the composition of "The Burden of Nineveh"—Christina Rossetti tells William Michael that she has borrowed "the first volume of Layard's *Nineveh*" (*The Family Letters of Christina Georgina Rossetti, with Some Supplementary Letters and Appendices,* ed. William Michael Rossetti [London, 1908], p. 14). And Hunt tells us that sometime earlier than this he had applied unsuccessfully for the post of draftsman on Layard's second expedition to Nineveh (see *Pre-Raphaelitism and the Pre-Raphaelite Brotherhood* [London, 1905-06], I. 346). Moreover, in a letter to his brother of August 30, 1851 Rossetti compares the rusticated complexions of Hunt and Millais with the "'sun-dried bricks' of Nineveh" (*Letters,* I. 103)—a phrase that occurs continually throughout Layard's *Nineveh*—thus raising the possibility that a majority of the Pre-Raphaelite brothers were conversant with the book. Nor is it fortuitous that, in the version of "The Burden of Nineveh" that appeared and fascinated Ruskin (see "Notes," *Works,* p. 649) in the *Oxford and Cambridge Magazine,* Rossetti pointedly alludes to the controversy over "Whether the great R. A.'s a bunch / Of gods or dogs, and whether Punch / Is right about the P.R.B."

[26] It is likely that the illustrations of the disinterment and transportation of the colossal winged bull which serve as frontispieces to both volumes of Austen Henry Layard, *Nineveh and its Remains* (London and New York, 1849) were a secondary source of inspiration for Rossetti's poem. Moreover, Rossetti's source for the image of the London crowds going past "as marshalled to the strut / Of ranks of gypsum quaintly cut" (*Works,* p. 58), an image which forms a striking visual parallel between the people of London and Nineveh, is almost certainly the numerous illustrations of tablets depicting processions of one sort or another in Layard's *Nineveh.* Similarly the description, towards the beginning of the poem, of the "carven warriors" with their bows, "cymbals," and "chariots" (*Works,* p. 55) which, Rossetti imagines, must have seemed to come alive when the "sculptured" courts of Nineveh were unearthed, is strongly reminiscent of tablets depicting war and hunting parties that are illustrated in Layard, II, 66. The suggestion in stanza 3 of the 1870 version of "The Burden of Nineveh" that the "Bull-god" was moulded ("rush-wrapping, / Wound'ere it dried, still ribbed the thing") is less accurate than the original lines: "some colour'd Arab straw matting. / Half ripp'd, was still upon the thing." For Layard's description of the matting woven by Arab women (Rossetti's "brown maidens [who] sing / From purple mouths" while moving "languidly") for the transportation of the colossus, see Layard, II, 67. Layard frequently describes his excitement at unearthing various Assyrian artifacts, alluded to by Rossetti in stanzas 4, 11, and 12: see Layard, I, 73 (the bull): I, 299, II, 14-16 and 206 (the "ivory tablets" of stanza 12): and II, 71-72. Many other details in the poem are taken from Layard's spirited account of the life of the expeditionary party. For the Christians kneeling in the shadow of the "Bull-god" (st. 8), see Layard, II, 293-294 and also I, 234 and 243; and for Layard's comments on Nineveh as Egypt's "antiquity" (st. 11), see II, 21-23. The "winged teraphim" of stanza 12 are

probably the images of Baal described in Layard, II, 341. Many of the Biblical accounts of Nineveh's destruction used by Rossetti are also quoted in *Nineveh and Its Remains;* see, for instance, II, 192 and 338.

[27] *Dante Gabriel Rossetti, Painter-Poet of Heaven in Earth* (London, 1928), p. 304.

[28] See Layard, II, 360-361 and II, 345 and 362n.

[29] "Problems of Form and Content in the Poetry of Dante Gabriel Rossetti," *VP.* 2 (1964), 17.

[30] Rossetti's Queen of Hearts in his "Playing-Cards" is a gold sovereign engraved with the head of Queen Victoria to show the "real reigning . . . sovereign" of Victorian England; see *The Bookman* (London), 40 (June, 1911), 130-131.

[31] *A Survey of English Literature, 1830-1880* (London, 1920), II, 5.

[32] For an account of the shipment and installation of the Needle, by the man who financed it, see Erasmus Wilson, *Our Egyptian Obelisk: Cleopatra's Needle* (London, 1877).

[33] *The Swinburne Letters,* ed. Cecil Y. Lang (Yale Univ. Press, 1961), IV, 119 and 128.

[34] See Arinshtein and Fredeman, pp. 242-246.

D. M. R. Bentley (essay date 1982)

SOURCE: "'The Blessed Damozel'": A Young Man's Fantasy," in *Victorian Poetry,* Vol. 20, Nos. 3-4, Autumn-Winter, 1982, pp. 31-43.

[*In the following essay, Bentley interprets "The Blessed Damozel" as a poem celebratory of "medieval-Catholic awareness."*]

Early in 1848, Dante Gabriel Rossetti submitted several poems to Leigh Hunt for approval. Evidently the young poet did not find the older man's comments, though obviously "flattering,"[1] particularly perspicacious. In a letter to his aunt Charlotte Polidori written a short time later he says, "Where Hunt, in his kind letter, speaks of my 'Dantesque heavens,' he refers to one or two of the poems the scenes of which are laid in the celestial regions, and which are written in a kind of Gothic manner which I suppose he is pleased to think belongs to the school of Dante" (***Letters,*** 34). There can be little doubt that one of the poems to which Hunt was referring is **"The Blessed Damozel"** (the other is probably **"Mater Pulchrae Delectionis,"** an early version of **"Ave"**). In a sense, Hunt's informal comments on **"The Blessed Damozel"** establish the precedent for most of the criticism on the poem published in the first half of this century. Critics have been "pleased to think" that **"The Blessed Damozel"** is indebted, not just to Dante and the other poets of his circle, but to a small galaxy of Romantic and Victorian writers, including Coleridge, Keats, Goethe, Musset, Blake, Shelley, Tennyson, and the Bailey of *Festus.* More frequently mentioned than applied is T. Hall Caine's dubious reminiscence that Rossetti himself gave Poe's "The Raven" as the direct inspiration and point of departure for his poem (p. 284).[2] There is no need to rehearse here the various literary echoes that have been found singing together in **"The Blessed Damozel"** since Paull Franklin Baum has already done this in his lengthy introduction to *The Blessed Damozel. The Unpublished Manuscript, Text and Collation* which, though published over forty years ago, remains the "standard and only really useful edition of the poem" (WEF, 23.32). The point may be made, however, that the inspiration for **"The Blessed Damozel"** was pictorial as well as literary, and almost certainly includes such favorites of the young Rossetti as Filippo Pistrucci's *Iconologia* (with its "coloured allegorical designs" [*Memoir,* p. 85][3] of female figures with emblematic adjuncts), Richard Hurst's translation of Gombauld's *Endimion,* and the Aldine edition of Colonna's *Hypnerotomachia Poliphili* (both of which contain striking illustrations of scenes where a female lover is depicted in "the celestial regions").[4] Unquestionably there also lie in the background of the poem the medieval paintings "with two levels, a heavenly and an earthly one"[5] to which Rossetti's later painting of *The Blessed Damozel* in the form of a diptych makes formal "reference."[6] But a Lowesian journey along the road and across the bridge to **"The Blessed Damozel"** is not the aim of the present discussion; rather, the aim is to explore the dynamics and meanings of the poem with a view to elucidating the significance of the damozel herself for the male speaker and of the poem itself for the young Rossetti. The initial question in dealing with **"The Blessed Damozel"** thus comes to the fore: in this "young man's fantasy" (the phrase is John Masefield's)[7] is it possible to differentiate fully and finally between the narrator and the author?

This question is complicated by the fact that between the first appearance of the poem in *The Germ* in 1850 and its publication in ***Ballads and Sonnets*** in 1881 Rossetti made a number of changes to it which to a large extent justify Kenneth L. Knickerbocker's argument that though **"The Blessed Damozel"** "had its inception as a form of poetic exercise" by 1869—which is to say, seven years after the death of Elizabeth Siddal Rossetti—it had "become freighted with biographical details."[8] Although it is doubtful whether all the details added, and in some cases subtracted, in the course of Rossetti's creative career are as biographical as Knickerbocker maintains, it is difficult to doubt that in the years after his wife's death in 1862, **"The Blessed**

Damozel" came to have an increasingly personal meaning for the poet-painter, that—to use Husserl's term as applied by E. D. Hirsh, Jr.[9]—the "horizon" of intention in the poem expanded to encompass its author's "fantasy" of joining his own lost love in a heaven of endless unity. To get an idea of how the meaning of **"The Blessed Damozel"** changed for Rossetti down the years, the evolution of one, particularly telling, stanza may be briefly rehearsed.[10] In *The Germ,* the first four lines of stanza eight, a description of the pious activities of the new arrivals in Heaven, read as follows:

Heard hardly, some of her new friends,
Playing at holy games,
Spake gentle-mouthed among themselves
Their virginal chaste names.

Apart from the revision of the first line to read "She scarcely heard her sweet new friends" in the *Oxford and Cambridge Magazine,* this stanza remained substantially the same in 1856 as it had been in 1850. In the Trial Books of 1869 and in ***Poems*** (1870), however, the blessed Damozel's "new friends" are no longer engaged in "Playing at holy games" but are now depicted "Amid their loving games," and by 1881 the four lines have been completely recast to read:

Around her, lovers newly met
'Mid deathless love's acclaims,
Spoke evermore among themselves
Their heart-remembered names.

A slight variation of this, the final, version of the stanza is inscribed at the center of Rossetti's 1876 drawing for the background of *The Blessed Damozel* (S. 244G)[11] which, like the finished painting, depicts several pairs of "lovers, newly met" embracing fervently amidst the lush greenery of Heaven. While they do not tell the whole story, the changes, first from "holy games" to "loving games" in 1869 and then from "virginal chaste names" to "heart-remembered names" in 1881, are, to a degree, symptomatic of how Rossetti's attitude toward **"The Blessed Damozel"** changed through the years, of how, increasingly, it partook of his urge to secularize his early poems and, moreover, assumed the burden of his wish-fulfillment fantasies.

The fact that Rossetti himself, a man for whom life imitated art, apparently came increasingly to share the sensual fantasies of the speaker of **"The Blessed Damozel"** provides the post-1870 poem with a context that justifies Jerome J. McGann's reading of it as a transvaluation of the "Christian idea of . . . Divine Love" through a replacement of "Love as agape with love as Eros" (48-52). A related, though different (because less personal), context of significance for the latter-day **"Blessed Damozel"** was provided for the last Romantics by the later habits and consequent myth of Rossetti as an unstable and obsessive visionary, as a figure preoccupied by an ethereal yet sensual ideal of woman, bent on both recapturing the vanished past in all its physical details and on projecting an earthly love into an eternity beyond death. "Yet now, and in this place, / Surely she leaned o'er me—her hair / Fell all about my face . . . / Nothing: the autumn fall of leaves. . . . " These lines, given by Rossetti to the parenthetical speaker in all the published versions of **"The Blessed Damozel,"** contain a combination of fantasy, sensuality, and longing in the midst of decay which, together with the emphasis on "hair" and, of course, on the glorified lady herself in the poem, draws attention to how easily the poem supports the romantic image of the "Pre-Raphaelite" poet. It is not an image of the implied poet that the relatively ascetic and religious Rossetti of the early Pre-Raphaelite period, of the years just before and after the publication of *The Germ* (January-May, 1850), would necessarily have countenanced; to accept it as a valid significance for the poem as originally conceived is, therefore, to accede to an inverted historicism which can only obscure the true significance of **"The Blessed Damozel"** as related to the context provided by its first publication in February, 1850, in the organ of the Pre-Raphaelite Brotherhood.

The critical difficulties posed by the biographical and historical accretions that adhere to **"The Blessed Damozel"** are formidable but at least partly soluble. For while it is a moot and metaphysical point whether once alerted to a textual interpretation, however superadded or projective, a reader can regain his innocence, a choice can be made in the matter of text which holds out the promise of at least a gestural return to a pre-lapsarian state. A decision to focus on *The Germ* version of **"The Blessed Damozel"** may not guarantee a pure response to it but, on the most basic bibliographical grounds, it provides the firmest foundation for a discussion of the poem in relation to Rossetti's program of the Pre-Raphaelite period when, it must be noted, he was as far from being obsessed by his dead wife as not having met her allowed and almost as far distant from the recluse whose behavior fuelled the inferences of the last Romantics. The decision to focus here on *The Germ* version of **"The Blessed Damozel"** is not made in ignorance of the fact that in the aesthetics of texts there are both unfortunate and fortunate falls; however, the advantages to be gained for the present discussion by examining **"The Blessed Damozel"** in the form that can be assumed to reflect Rossetti's intentions in the days of the P.R.B. seem to outweigh the benefits of considering it in any of the later versions, where the aesthetic improvements are themselves an aspect of the poet's revisionist view of his own past. Like the Auden of "In Memory of W. B. Yeats" and, indeed, the Yeats of such a poem as "Leda and the Swan," the Rossetti of **"The Blessed Damozel"** (as well as of other significantly revised poems such as **"My Sister's Sleep"**) calls into question the axiom that the last authorized text is for all intents and purposes definitive.

With all this in mind, it is worth returning to ponder Rossetti's description of **"The Blessed Damozel"** in his letter to Charlotte Polidori as a poem "written in a kind of Gothic manner," for herein resides a valuable clue to its initial conception and general character. The word "Gothic" points to the medieval dimension of the poem which Rossetti attempted to recreate through several means. There is, first of all, the title, which links the resonantly Catholic adjective "Blessed" with the Anglo-Norman word "Damozel," thus serving notice, like the Gothic script in which the title is printed in *The Germ,* of the antiquarian nature of what is to follow. Also "Gothic" in character is the stanza form of the poem, an extension of the common ballad quatrain to a sestet ($a_4b_3c_4b_3d_4b_3$), of which Joseph F. Vogel remarks: "It appears that [Rossetti] thought of the verse of **'The Blessed Damozel'** as basically a ballad verse (the stanza itself he probably derived from ballads)"[12]—and, perhaps, intended as a formalistic allusion to the Middle Ages. Further, and more obvious, embodiments of the Gothic mise-en-scène of **"The Blessed Damozel"** are found in the archaic diction of the poem ("ungirt," "Herseemed," "Circlewise," and so on),[13] in its dramatis personae ("Cecily, Gertrude, Magdalen, / Margaret, and Rosalys"), and in its stage furniture ("citherns and citoles"). To an ungentle reader it might seem that in **"The Blessed Damozel"** Rossetti has merely pieced together some stunning words from old romaunts to create a poetry with a vaguely exotic flavor. Yet the "Gothic" manner of the poem, its stylistic idiom and vocal coloring, is the signpost that points to one of its fundamental raisons d'être: the imaginative recreation of the young Rossetti's conception of a medieval "consciousness"[14] and awareness. Richard L. Stein's astute observation that for Rossetti "the most important belief of the Middle Ages was the identification of flesh and spirit" and, moreover, an important "medieval theme" for him was "love" (pp. 127-128), suggests that the notoriously physical rendition of the spiritual Damozel and, indeed, the central love interest of the poem are key aspects of his attempt in this early "poetic exercise" to give form to his conception of the "nature of Gothic" which, as Stein argues, differs markedly from that of Ruskin.

A recognition of the fact that **"The Blessed Damozel"** was, at the outset, intended (perhaps argumentatively) as the re-creation of a medieval awareness throws into clear relief the relation between Rossetti and his narrator, or, better, between the implied poet and the historical percipient in the poem—an omniscient and speculative figure whose style and assumptions characterize him as the representative of the medieval-Catholic awareness that the reader is invited to enter. The function of the percipient of **"The Blessed Damozel"** is complex; like the implied poet of Rossetti's **"Sonnets for Pictures"** his task is to present a "picture" (in this case the "diptych" composed of the blessed Damozel and her earthbound lover) and to imagine the words and feelings of its personae (again, the damozel and her lover). Through his re-creation of a spatial and emotional relationship that is radically alien to the "modern" mind, the percipient inducts the reader-spectator into the medieval-Catholic awareness that he was designed by Rossetti to embody. In effect, he forces the reader-spectator to relinquish the demand for a fixed point of view from which to perceive the external world and asks him to accept (by the willing suspension of disbelief that is the artistic equivalent of an act of faith) a medieval-Catholic awareness in which Heaven and Earth are simultaneously knowable, spirit and flesh are identified, and so on. When William Michael Rossetti claimed that the title *Songs of the Art Catholic,* under which his brother sent a number of early poems to William Bell Scott in 1847, suggests that "the poems embodied conceptions and a point of view related to pictorial art [and] also that this art was, in sentiment though not necessarily in dogma, Catholic—medieval and unmodern" (***Works,*** p. 661), he might have been thinking in particular of the function of the percipient in **"The Blessed Damozel."** And Rossetti's own later remark, regarding **"Ave,"** that "the emotional influence . . . employed demands above all an inner standing-point" (***Works,*** p. 661), could well stand as a gloss on the sympathetic response to the percipient's medieval-Catholic awareness that is demanded of the reader of **"The Blessed Damozel."**

Before proceeding to examine the poem itself, the point needs to be made that the role of the percipient in **"The Blessed Damozel,"** like those of the parenthetical speaker and the damozel herself, is a dramatic and progressive one. Not only does he present and elaborate the scenario of the poem, but he reacts to it, moving from a clear perception, through a purposeful retention and a sensual apprehension, to a final loss of the bright vision of the heavenly damozel; indeed his reactions to what he envisages constitute both an important means of entering his awareness and an important element—a delicate subplot—in the mental drama of the poem. Neither the implied poet nor the assumed reader can be said or asked wholly to suspend judgment of the, by turns, fantastic and despairing responses of the parenthetical speaker. While the same may hold true for some of the speculative utterances of the percipient, it would be difficult and illegitimate either to claim that Rossetti, with his Pre-Raphaelite and Early Christian aims and ideals, does not endorse the essentials of the awareness that the percipient represents or to argue that **"The Blessed Damozel"** is other than a celebration of certain things: the ideals represented by and in the materialization of the Damozel herself, the intensity of the parenthetical speaker's love for her, and the devotion of the one for the other which, like the relationship between Dante and Beatrice, transcends death itself. No large ironies separate the percipient from Rossetti as they frequently do the speaker from the author of, say, a dramatic monologue. The very mention of dramatic monologue calls to mind "**A Last Confession,**" the Browningesque poem of the Italian *maqui* that Rossetti apparently wrote shortly after **"The Blessed Damozel,"** and might suggest that the depictions of mind(s) in action in the earlier poem are merely the feeble anticipations of the method that is more fully developed under the influence of Browning in the later one. If tenable, the foregoing discussion of the nature and function of the percipient in **"The Blessed Damozel"** indicates, however, that Rossetti's primary concern in that poem was not to make his historically distant narrator a fully rounded character as in a Browning monologue but to recreate a mental awareness which he admired to the extent that he felt it worth reexperiencing by his fellow Victorians.

In the opening stanza of **"The Blessed Damozel"** the reader is presented by the percipient with a vivid picture of the Damozel which is at once realistic and emblematic in the "Gothic manner":

> The blessed Damozel leaned out
> From the gold bar of Heaven:
> Her blue eyes were deeper much
> Than a deep water, even.
> She had three lilies in her hand,
> And the stars in her hair were seven.
>
> Her robe, ungirt from clasp to hem,
> No wrought flowers did adorn,
> But a white rose of Mary's gift
> On the neck meetly worn;
> And her hair, lying down her back,
> Was yellow like ripe corn.

Thomas H. Brown is quite right in remarking that these two stanzas function as a "still-life within the framework of the poem" (p. 273). The Damozel is initially envisaged for the reader and by the speaker in a static posture and a physical form that is not only insistently pictorial but, in its emphasis on emblematic rather than sensual detail, entirely orthodox within Rossetti's intuitive yet knowledgeable conception of the Catholic Middle Ages. Just as Dante on the first anniversary of the death of Beatrice drew the resemblance of an angel (S. 42), so the percipient, on the tenth anniversary, it transpires, of the death of the Damozel, boldly envisages the dead woman as fit company for the Blessed Virgin. The explicitly and implicitly Marian tenor of the description emphasizes the virtue and purity of the angelic Damozel: her title of "blessed" indicates her saintliness and her affinity with the Virgin; her floral adjuncts, the "three lilies in her hand" and the "white rose of Mary's gift" are emblematic of her innocence;[15] her eyes are blue, a color associated with the Virgin Mary; her unadorned robe, with its "clasp," is indicative of her purity;[16] and even her yellow hair accords with traditional representations of the Blessed Virgin.[17] It is little wonder that the Rev. Alfred Gurney, who was for many years the incumbent of the prominent Anglo-Catholic church of St. Barnabas, Pimlico, read **"The Blessed Damozel"** as "an exposition of the spiritual significance of Mary" and saw the Damozel herself as a representation of that "Beauty [which] is one with Purity [and] one with Charity" (Baum, p. liii). Several details of the description serve to consolidate the reader's awareness that the blessed Damozel is, indeed, in the "celestial regions": the seven stars in her hair (perhaps those of Amos 5.8 and Revelation 1.16 and 20) recall the starry crown of the Queen of Heaven in Revelation 12.1 (Baum, p. xxxiii); the white rose on her robe suggests the rose of Dante's Empyrean; and, perhaps, the lilies in her hand remember Pistrucci's depiction of "Celestial Beauty" as a female figure with lilies for an adjunct.[18] As if to diminish the distance between Heaven and earth, as well as to emphasize the physicality of the Damozel, the percipient includes two comparisons with things in nature in the poem: the Damozel's eyes, he says, are "deeper . . . / Than deep water . . ." and her hair, he says, is "yellow like ripe corn." Now of course it is both inevitable and conventional that the heavenly be described in terms of the earthly, but in this instance the tropes of the percipient represent clear choices through which the reader understands his awareness to be naturalistic (for Rossetti a medieval characteristic) and, moreover, attuned to the physicality of the Damozel (though not as yet, to the sensual possibilities of that physicality).

Following the opening description of the Blessed Damozel, the percipient proceeds by means of a tension-building contrast between time conceived as an eternal day in Heaven and time on earth, "ten years" of which have passed since the Damozel's death, to an introduction of her emotional, earth-bound lover.

> (To *one* it is ten years of years:
> . . . Yet now, here in this place
> Surely she leaned o'er me,—her hair
> Fell all about my face. . . .
> Nothing: the Autumn-fall of leaves.
> The whole year sets apace.)

The parentheses enclosing this stanza serve two purposes: they isolate the earth-bound lover in a typographical equivalent of a predella and, within that paratactic frame, they present the thoughts of the troubled and fantastic mind of the lover as separate from yet accessible to the percipient, as part of the awareness into which the reader enters. The painful intensity of the lover's devotion to the Damozel and his evident desire to renew contact with her, besides being a central node of feeling in the poem, serve a rhetorical function in that they provide the causal referents for the percipient's ensuing assertions that the damozel does indeed exist in a physical heaven ("It was the terrace of God's house / That she was standing on . . .") and that she, too, shares the desire to be united with her lover, albeit, necessarily, after this death. Such assertions, which take the form of the percipient's ever more detailed (and, therefore, reassuring and convincing) descriptions of the Damozel's Heaven, are the means by which the reader-spectator comes to share in the medieval-Catholic's vision, not only of Heaven (its location and components), but also of the soul's journey there (in the likeness of "thin flames").[19]

In the several stanzas following the intrusion of the parenthetical speaker, the percipient gives what, in essence, is the verbal equivalent of a "Gothic" painting of Heaven. Of these stanzas, the cumulative effect of which is to locate and, as it were, flesh out, a Heaven that is, at once, inconceivably distant and readily envisaged, quietistically spiritual and tangibly physical (indeed, palatial), the most controversial is the one containing the percipient's second description of the blessed Damozel:

> And still she bowed herself, and stooped
> Into the vast waste calm;
> Till her bosom's pressure must have made
> The bar she leaned on warm,
> And the lilies lay as if asleep
> Along her bended arm.

The last four lines of this delightful stanza are sometimes adduced to prove the depiction of Heaven in **"The Blessed Damozel"** to be excessively physical and sensual. It is crucial to realize that, as in the earlier, naturalistic comparison of the Damozel's hair with "ripe corn," the charmingly sensual and tenderly maternal components of the passage are the speculative and fanciful additions of the percipient: "her bosom's pressure *must have* made / The bar she leaned on warm . . ."; "the lilies lay *as if* asleep / Along her bended arm." The shift from the relative detachment of the opening stanzas to the sensitive empathy of the later description is interesting. It reveals a shift in the putative psychology of the percipient who, after prolonged exposure to the vision of the damozel and, perhaps also, in sympathy with the parenthetical speaker whose thoughts are a part of his own consciousness, is now preparing to enter more fully into the intense emotional life, the transcendent love, of the damozel and her lover. Needless to say, the percipient's ability to assume the damozel's point of view, and the resultant account of her speech that occupies the greater part of the remainder of the poem, provide a further means by which the reader-spectator enters into the awareness of a medieval-Catholic.

The Damozel's speech, in which she looks forward longingly to her lover's arrival in Heaven, demands that the reader-spectator adopt a point of view related to pictorial art and envisage the stages of the lover's initiation—his purification and purgation, the approach of the pair to "the dear Mother," and the intercession of the Mediatrix with Christ on behalf of their love—as a series of medieval paintings or panels. As in the opening stanzas of the poem, it is the stanza form itself which in the Damozel's speech exhibits a paratactic quality, framing within its regular contours the episodes of the solemnly imagined events:

> When round his head the aureole clings,
> And he is clothed in white,
> I'll take his hand, and go with him
> To the deep wells of light,
> And we will step down as to a stream
> And bathe there in God's sight.
>
> . . . . .
>
> Herself shall bring us, hand in hand,
> To Him round whom all souls
> Kneel—the unnumbered solemn heads
> Bowed with their aureoles:
> And angels, meeting us, shall sing
> To their citherns and citoles.

In highly pictorial lines such as these the spirit of Early Christian art is captured. But while their technique is carefully pictorial, these and other lines in the Damozel's speech draw for imagery and resonance on literary sources, particularly the *Divine Comedy* and the Book of Revelation—the "deep wells of light" that are likened to "a stream," for instance, recalling both the "lume in forma di riviera" in the *Paradiso,* XXX and the "pure river of water of life" in Revelation 22.1.

At almost the exact center of the Damozel's orderly and stylized speech are two parenthetical stanzas given over to the earthly lover's doubts about his own worthiness to enter Heaven. It is easy to miss the fact that the first of these is a reflexive comment on the mentality of the Damozel and, by extension, on the awareness of the percipient:

> (Alas! to *her* wise simple mind
> These things were all but known
> Before: they trembled on her sense,—
> Her voice had caught their tone.
> Alas for lonely Heaven! Alas
> For life wrung out alone!

The function of these lines, and of the following stanza, is not just to provide an explicit gloss on the "wise simple mind" of the believing medieval-Catholic that is being presented and celebrated in **"The Blessed Damozel"** but also, through the interjected sorrows, anxieties, and questions of the earthly lover, to explore the form that doubt might take in a sceptical mind of the Middle Ages and, by so doing, to provide the passive or unbelieving reader of the Victorian period with a mimesis of his own mental processes:

Alas, and though the end were reached. . . .
Was *thy* part understood
Or borne in trust? And for her sake
Shall this too be found good?—
May the close lips that knew not prayer
Praise ever, though they would?)

Although, ostensibly, this is a dialogue of one within the mind of the earthly lover, it also functions in a dialogic manner within the "inner standing-point" of the poem as a whole, posing rhetorical questions of the reader-spectator and forcing him to recognize whatever gap exists between his own mentality and the "wise simple" awareness embodied in the damozel and the percipient. If tenable, this possibility suggests that the earthly lover, no less than the damozel and the percipient, is a rhetorical device employed by the implied poet of **"The Blessed Damozel"** to argue the reader-spectator towards an appreciation and acceptance of the "Catholic—medieval and unmodern" "conceptions and . . . point of view" which the poem embodies.

The final lines of **"The Blessed Damozel,"** where the Damozel has "mildly" concluded her speech and is hopefully awaiting the arrival of her lover in Heaven, also serve a distinctly rhetorical purpose:

She ceased;
The light thrilled past her, filled
With Angels, in strong level lapse.
Her eyes prayed, and she smiled.

(I saw her smile.) But soon their flight
Was vague 'mid the poised spheres,
And then she cast her arms along
The golden barriers.
And laid her face between her hands,
And wept. (I heard her tears.)

The "barriers" of this final stanza achieve special force when compared with the "golden bar" across which the Damozel leans at the beginning and middle of the poem. That "the . . . bar" has now become "The . . . barriers" indicates the percipient's recognition (which is also the damozel's) that between the quick and the dead there can only be visionary communication. Thus the Damozel's sorrow that her lover's soul is not amongst those being carried to Heaven by the Angels (whose flight does mediate between earth and Heaven) is bracketed by the simple affirmations of the parenthetical speaker who is, literally, given the last words in the poem. If the way the poem ends bequeaths a final validity on the transcendent love of the earthbound speaker, it does not at all negate those aspects of **"The Blessed Damozel"** which make the poem an unmistakable celebration, not merely of intense emotion, but of the Damozel herself, her meticulously pictorial Heaven, and, above all, of the wise, simple, and visionary consciousness of the percipient through whose eyes, ears, sympathies, and speculations the reader-spectator comes to participate in an awareness of the Catholic Middle Ages.

It should now be clear that, whatever significance **"The Blessed Damozel"** came to have for the later Rossetti or for later generations, the poem, at the time of its publication in *The Germ,* partook of the Pre-Raphaelite program to recover a mode of awareness that they associated with the Catholic Middle Ages and to make it accessible to their Victorian contemporaries. If the poem offers a Kantean answer to such conventional, empirical questions as "who is speaking?" and "what is real?" it does so as part of its strategy of demanding that the reader adopt an "inner standing-point" in order to reexperience its emotional influence. But if the percipient of **"The Blessed Damozel"** was designed by Rossetti as a window into Gothic consciousness, he also offers glimpses of the implied poet and the real poet-painter of the Pre-Raphaelite period. So celebratory is the poem of a medieval-Catholic awareness that, when read beside *The Germ* version of **"My Sister's Sleep"** for instance, it justifies Swinburne's conception of the implied poet of the Pre-Raphaelite period as a "Christian" (Lang, II, 105). Yet the articulation, through the meditations of the earthbound lover, of deep self-questionings and all-questioning points to a Rossetti of the Pre-Raphaelite period who knew about religious doubt as well as medieval faith, about personal misgiving as well as idealistic vision, about despair as well as hope. A hundred years after his death the mercurial amalgam that can be sensed behind **"The Blessed Damozel"** continues to intrigue.

Notes

[1] The text of Hunt's letter of March 31, 1848, which is indeed flattering (he hails Rossetti as an "unquestionable poet") is printed in *Memoir,* pp. 122-123; DGR's letter to Hunt is in W. H. Arnold's *Ventures in Book Collecting* (New York, 1923), pp. 211-215.

[2] Caine quotes the now well-known statement, supposedly by Rossetti, that in "The Blessed Damozel" he had "determined to reverse the conditions" of "The Raven"; in his revised edition (1928) Caine omitted the statement (p. 186).

[3] Rossetti was interested in the *Iconologia* (1821, 1824), a work devoted, in the words of its subtitle, to the "art of representing by allegorical figures the various abstract conceptions of the mind." Hereafter cited as *Iconologia.*

[4] These were among the "libro sommamente mistico" ("supremely mystical books") in his father's library which, as William Michael recalls (*Memoir,* p. 62), the young Rossetti "inspected from time to time, with some gusto not unmingled with awe."

[5] Ronnalie Roper Howard, *The Dark Glass: Vision and Technique in the Poetry of Dante Gabriel Rossetti* (Ohio Univ. Press, 1972), p. 44.

[6] Richard L. Stein, *The Ritual of Interpretation* (Harvard Univ. Press, 1975), p. 153.

[7] *Thanks Before Going* (London, 1946), p. 50.

[8] "Rossetti's 'The Blessed Damozel'," *SP,* 29 (1932), 500.

[9] See *Validity in Interpretation* (Yale Univ. Press, 1967).

[10] See also P. F. Baum, "Introduction," *The Blessed Damozel. The Unpublished Manuscript, Text, and Collection* (Univ. of North Carolina Press, 1937). Quotations from *The Germ* version of "The Blessed Damozel" are taken from Baum's edition.

[11] Another study (S. 244M) for the painting depicts several figures playing cymbals, in a possible reference to Psalm 150.

[12] *Dante Gabriel Rossetti's Versecraft* (Univ. of Florida Press, 1971), p. 100.

[13] Although J. A. Sanford, "The Morgan Manuscript of Rossetti's 'The Blessed Damozel'," *SP,* 35 (1938), 471-486 casts doubt on the authenticity of the supposed 1847 manuscript of the poem, it is worth noting that such period words as "Damozel" and "Circle-wise" appear in *The Germ* where the MS has "damsel" and "circle" since it was late in 1849 that Rossetti spent "several days" at the British Museum "reading up all manner of old romaunts, to pitch upon stunning words of poetry" (DW 43). One of the works that Rossetti may have encountered at this time is *The Old English Versions of the Gesta Romanorum,* edited for the Roxburgh Club by Sir Frederick Madden, which contains details subsumed into "The Staff and Scrip" as well as a picturesque, Anglo-Norman vocabulary of words such as "demeselle."

[14] See Thomas H. Brown, "The Quest of Dante Gabriel Rossetti in 'The Blessed Damozel'," *VP,* 10 (1972), 274-275 for the argument that the "entire drama" of the poem is "enacted within the single consciousness of the earthbound lover." In addition to Howard, pp. 43f. and Stein, pp. 147f., Paul Lauter, "The Narrator of 'The Blessed Damozel'," *MLN,* 73 (1958), 344-348 and W. Stacy Johnson, "D. G. Rossetti as Painter and Poet," *VP,* 3 (1965), 9-18 offer discussions of the narrative problem in "The Blessed Damozel."

[15] See *Works,* p. 173 for the lily as emblem of "Innocence." The "three lilies" in the Damozel's hand bring to mind the "Threefold Plant" (*Works,* p. 662) of "Mater Pulchrae Delectionis," *The Girlhood of Mary Virgin* and *Ecce Ancilla Domini!*

[16] The garments of Rossetti's more earthly women—Ophelia, Guenevere, the prostitute in *Found* and the bride of "The Bride's Prelude"—have ornate dresses while the Virgin in *Girlhood* and *Ecce Ancilla Domini!* is plainly attired. The clasp (or cognate "loin-belt") appears as an emblem of virginity in "The Bride's Prelude" and *Hesterna Rosa.*

[17] See Lucien Pissarro, *Rossetti* (London, n.d.), S. 44, and Mrs. [Anne] Jameson, *Legends of the Madonna, as Represented in the Fine Arts* (London, 1852), p. liv for Rossetti's breach of a "rule of the Brotherhood" in altering the color of the model's hair in *Ecce Ancilla Domini!* to accord with the traditional representation of the Virgin with yellow hair.

[18] *Iconologia,* No. 35. Pistrucci depicts "Astrology," No. 27, as a female figure with stars in her hair.

[19] In the painting of *The Blessed Damozel* (1875-1878) three angelic figures clothed in flames carry palm branches—Rossetti's emblem for the soul's victory over death and triumph in Heaven.

John P. McGowan (essay date 1982)

SOURCE: "'The Bitterness of Things Occult': D. G. Rossetti's Search for the Real," in *Critical Essays on Dante Gabriel Rossetti,* edited by David G. Reide, Twayne, 1992, pp. 113-27.

[*In the following essay, originally published in* Victorian Poetry *in 1982, McGowan probes Rossetti's attempts to reconcile art and reality in his poetry.*]

In his *Autobiography,* Yeats claims that Dante Rossetti, "though his dull brother did once persuade him that he was agnostic," was a "devout Christian."[1] This description is wildly inaccurate, yet it indicates one way to read Rossetti's poetry. Rossetti accepts the traditional Christian notion that man confronts a created world which contains within it certain universal meanings. The artist's task is to uncover those meanings and to present them to an audience, a task which involves a certain amount of interpretation. Rossetti's problem is that he cannot get the world to speak to him; its meanings continually elude him, so that his poetry is unable to present the real fashioned in such a way as to make its true meaning evident. His poetry keeps falling away from the real and the universal toward the poet's personal experiences. This failure to find an adequate poetic subject might be attributed to Rossetti's lack of talent or lack of faith, but his struggles also suggest the predicament of the post-Romantic Victorian poets who found that the sources of Romantic poetry were no longer fruitful. The result is a poetry (which includes some excellent poems) constructed out of a recognition of its own failure, a poetry which undermines its own validity in face of the reality it has failed to express. Despite all the poet's efforts, reality keeps secret from him its hidden meanings.[2]

An early sonnet, **"St. Luke the Painter"** (later incorporated into ***The House of Life*** LXXV), describes a Christian aesthetic, one in which art "rends the mist / Of devious symbols," finding in "sky-breadth and field-silence" the way to God. Rossetti aligns himself with this art which acts to make apparent the meaning of experience, and accepts the priestly role given to the artist. Lamenting the fact that modern art "has turned in vain / To soulless self-reflections of man's skill," the poet piously hopes that art will return to that time when it was "God's priest." Art must learn to "pray again."

Two consequences of this Christian aesthetic should be noted. First, a thing is never its appearance merely: there is always something beyond or beneath what is present to the senses, and the artist searches out this deeper significance. William Rossetti characterized "the intimate intertexture of a spiritual sense with a material form" as "one of the influences which guided the [Pre-Raphaelite] movement."[3] Holman Hunt would certainly have agreed with this statement, as well as with the aesthetic of **"St. Luke the Painter."** Hunt thought that the advantage of faithfulness to nature in pictorial representation was that such accuracy would make the symbolic import of the represented image more apparent.[4]

The inability to identify meaning simply as appearance, the need to represent the thing so that qualities not on the surface are manifested, leads to the second important feature of a Christian art: the identification of art with prayer. Luke is honored because he "first taught Art to fold her hands and pray" and the poet's hope is that art will learn to "pray again." The artist prays that hidden meanings might be revealed to him.

Resistance to Yeats's characterization of Rossetti as a Christian is based on Rossetti's having abandoned, after the early poems and paintings, specifically Christian themes or any adherence to Christian dogma. But Yeats's comment is true to Rossetti's retention, throughout his career, of his conviction in significances beyond sense and the need for "prayerful" poems. The problem becomes how to gain access to those hidden meanings. Hunt's belief that attention to physical detail reveals spiritual significance is, of course, derived from Ruskin, but this theory works only in the context of religious faith. Rossetti lacks Hunt's faith, if not the desires faith can satisfy, and his art strives to develop satisfactory means of access other than faith to the spiritual. Long after his art has been stripped of any Christian trappings, the poem as prayer remains one of Rossetti's stocks in trade.

> What thing unto mine ear
> Wouldst thou convey,—what secret thing,
> O wandering water ever whispering?
> Surely thy speech shall be of her.
> Thou water, O thou whispering wanderer,
> What message dost thou bring?
>
> (ll. 1-6)

"The Stream's Secret" (from which this stanza is taken) presents Rossetti at his most listless. The poet's passive stance is broken only by the voicing of his plea, but even that action is languidly performed, and continually announces its imminent end. The poet hopes his own words will spur the stream to talk, to divulge its secret. He waits anxiously for his own voice to be replaced by the stream's. But in vain. "Still silent? Can no art / Of Love's then move thy pity? Nay" (ll. 199-200). The stream retains its secret, and the discouraged poet stops speaking to cry, adding his tears to the stream's "cold" water. This poem is hardly Rossetti at his best or most attractive, but it embodies that despair which gave rise to charges of morbidity. The poet, immersed in Dante and the Romantics, goes to nature to find an intimation (a symbol) of the larger significances which give experience meaning, and only finds dead material things which resist his prayer, remain silent, and refuse incorporation into art.

"The Woodspurge" is a famous example of how nature is dead for Rossetti in a way that it was not for Dante or the Romantics.[5] The woodspurge's "cup of three" reminds the reader of the Christian synthesis which did unite the individual to the world around him, but the point of the poem is that this union no longer exists. The poet remains totally isolated in his grief, just as the individuality of the woodspurge remains inviolate despite the speaker's investigation. The poem might almost be read as a repudiation of the Ruskinian aesthetic adopted by Hunt. The poet has gone to nature and looked with care at the particular thing, and the result is neither an awakening of faith nor a feeling of greater participation in some unity which includes both poet and flower.

In **"Jenny"** it is not the natural world, but another person, who faces the speaker as an alien reality which he cannot get to speak. The speaker stops several times to inquire of the sleeping prostitute: "Whose person or whose purse may be / The lodestar of your reverie?" (ll. 20-21); "I wonder what you're thinking of" (l. 58).

Jenny, asleep, is unable to answer, and so the speaker supplies the answers himself, offering what he imagines her thoughts must be.

Nothing could more completely distinguish Rossetti from the Romanticism of Wordsworth than this failure to find a voice beyond himself. The speaker of **"Jenny"** is a scholar or writer who has hidden from the world in his "room . . . full of books" (ll. 22-23). On this night he has escaped from his study to confront "life" and cull a lesson from the confrontation, much as Wordsworth does from his meeting with the leech gatherer. But Rossetti's speaker, far from gaining new insights from his encounter, spends the night only with his own thoughts. His habit of self-involved meditation results in Jenny's playing the same role as a book to him. "You know not what a book you seem, / Half-read by lightning in a dream!" (ll. 51-52). Of course, the leech gatherer only fosters an intensely personal meditation in Wordsworth as well, but the difference is that Wordsworth finds in the encounter a way to transcend himself, to change the current of his thoughts. Rossetti's speaker achieves no such transcendence. Jenny is subsumed entirely into him, another manifestation of his thoughts.[6]

The futility of his thoughts, their emptiness and unreality, overcomes the speaker at various times in the poem: " . . . my thoughts run on like this / With wasteful whims more than enough" (ll. 56-57); "Let the thoughts pass, an empty cloud!" (l. 155). The reality of Jenny lies before the speaker, but he is painfully aware that her "truth" has escaped him.

Come, come, what use in thoughts like this?
Poor little Jenny, good to kiss,—
You'd not believe by what strange roads
Thought travels, when your beauty goads
A man tonight to think of toads!
Jenny, wake up . . . Why there's the dawn!

(ll. 298-302)

"Thought," travelling by "strange roads," strays from the real. Everything returns the speaker to the prison of self. The absence of sexual union in the poem points toward the absence of any corresponding spiritual union. Many of the sexual puns which would describe the situation also adequately describe the speaker's failure to effect a union between thought and reality, self and other. This meeting has been sterile; the speaker has not penetrated this incomprehensible other being whose thoughts remain completely unknown to him. These parallels between the physical and epistemological planes are suggested by the ending of the poem.

And must I mock you to the last,
Ashamed of my own shame,—aghast
Because some thoughts not born amiss
Rose at a poor fair face like this?
Well, of such thoughts, so much I know:
In my life, as in hers, they show,
By a far gleam which I may near,
A dark path I can strive to clear.

(ll. 383-390)

This passage is difficult because the reference of "thoughts" is ambiguous. Two readings are possible, each of which illuminates certain important features of Rossetti's poetry. The first possibility is that the "thought" which "shames" the speaker is lust, and he mocks Jenny because she has fostered that emotion in him. Much of the poem has focused, in no flattering terms, on "man's changeless sum / Of lust" (ll. 278-279). The last lines suggest, then, that the speaker (in Wordsworthian fashion) has formed a new resolution. The experience of lust has intimated to him (the "far gleam") the existence of love, a state which he might attain by "clearing" the "dark path" of base desires. (The path's darkness also indicates his ignorance and inexperience.) The speaker leaves Jenny to go seek love. We might call this the "Wordsworthian" or "optimistic" reading. Although union with this particular woman is impossible, the speaker has recognized that physical love is an analogue of spiritual love, and that through physical love he can move toward the realm of spiritual love. Love can be the solution to the radical split between self and other. The dead world can be brought to life by love, and much of Rossetti's later poetry explores both how physical love either symbolizes or leads to spiritual love, and how love serves to connect self to the world.

This "optimistic" reading must be qualified, however, since the poem does not exhibit a Wordsworthian confidence that any substantial contact with Jenny has been made. The second possible reference of "thoughts" (l. 385) is to the meditations contained in the poem. The speaker's shame is his chagrined awareness that, characteristically, his night with the prostitute was spent in "thought," not in bed. He recovers his self-pride by asserting his difference from Jenny, an assertion cemented by his placing the coins in her hair. Both the speaker and Jenny are thinking beings whose thoughts "show" the "far gleam" of a purity beyond this world's degradation, but the speaker sticks to his image of Jenny as "thoughtless" (l. 7) to suggest that only he will follow the "gleam" and clear the "dark path." The speaker leaves Jenny and her physical world behind to retreat into the realm of pure thought. The poem reveals a strong disgust with the bestial in man, so the final choice of purity by the speaker, even when seen as partly a defensive reaction to his inability to participate in Jenny's world, is not a total surprise.

While the reader's ironic understanding of the speaker's limits is deliberately set up by Rossetti, the tensions explored in the poem are Rossetti's as well as the protagonist's. At times able to find in the physical an analogue for the spiritual, at other times Rossetti can only see the physical and the spiritual as complete opposites. The speaker's attitude toward Jenny, with its strange mixture of sympathy and contempt, accurately reflects Rossetti's own confusions over the exact relations of thought to life. He longs for the correspondences between thought and world found by the Romantics. But those correspondences elude him, and the world constructed by thought seems far superior to the dead world discovered by the senses.[7] However, Rossetti is rarely able to effect a retreat into pure thought with a clear conscience. He still believes in a reality which exists independent of thought, and which is also stronger than thought. If Rossetti's difficulty in finding a home in nature distinguishes him from the Romantics, his uneasiness with residence in the halls built by imagination equally demonstrates his separation from the moderns.

Poem after poem places the speaker in a position of readiness from which he strains to catch the message he is persuaded the world must hold. In **"Love-Lily"** the speaker's "life grows faint to hear" the approach of a "spirit" who "on my mouth his finger lays" and "shows" the silenced poet the "Eden of Love." **"The Sea-Limits"** is another listening poem, with "secret continuance sublime" identified as the sea's song. The poet here exhorts his readers to listen not only to the sea but also to a shell "which echo[es] . . . the whole sea's speech." When he emphasizes listening to the world, Rossetti's conception of poetry can be likened to this shell. Poetry should "echo" the voice of the world, not introducing personal or solipsistic reveries, but presenting the meanings of a world all men live in. The word "echo," which appears in many Rossetti poems, suggests a perfect harmony, a faithful reproduction of something given to the poet.[8] Yet an echo is secondary and weaker than the original sound. Rossetti seems determined to find meaning in the external world rather than in a world created by imagination, even when it means accepting a secondary and passive voice for the poet. However, his voice is weakest, not when he echoes truths present in nature, but when he laments that the secret of life's meanings is being kept from him. "The bitterness of things occult" remains the greatest burden he must bear.[9]

That thoughts exist separate from the actual significance of reality afflicts Rossetti's notion of art. Far from being an "aestheticist" in the sense that he wishes art to have no relation to life, Rossetti continually bemoans art's failed attempts to embody the real. His poetry points the way toward modern "aestheticism" only insofar as it contemplates art's difficulties in reaching beyond itself and becoming real. In **"Jenny"** the speaker tries to imagine how Jenny's "true nature" might be portrayed by an artist. How would "Raffael" or "Leonardo" have painted the prostitute? The beautiful women painted by these masters showed to "men's souls" what "God can do" (ll. 238-240), but the artist who would portray Jenny must show a beautiful face which reveals the evil men have done while still showing that God cherishes the fallen woman. Such a portrait, the speaker concludes, could not be painted, for reasons which seem archetypally Victorian: religious doubt and the audience's prudery. How could an artist portray God's love for the sinner when he has "no sign" that such love exists. "All dark. No sign on earth / What measure of God's rest endows / The many mansions of his house" (ll. 247-249). This failure to see a way to paint Jenny is followed by the lament: "If but a woman's heart might see / Such erring heart unerringly / For once! But that can never be" (ll. 250-252). The flat despair of the second sentence falls limply after the soaring hope of the first. Even where reality could be made to speak, the cherished respectability of the Victorian audience would insure that the revealed meanings would never be heeded.

The relation of art to the real is complicated further when, continuing his lament that no Victorian audience would allow itself to contemplate the reality of Jenny, the speaker describes her as

> a rose shut in a book
> In which pure women may not look,
> For its base pages claim control
> To crush the flower within the soul.
>
> (ll. 253-256)

This passage, on one level, links Victorian prudery to the horror of Jenny's existence. Society condemns Jenny to a particular life and death by turning on her, and yet this same society is hypocritical enough to claim that the book which would present Jenny faithfully will corrupt "pure" women.[10]

More interesting in terms of the argument presented here is how this passage develops the relationship between art and life. The metaphor of the rose which is killed when it is pressed into a book suggests that the artist kills reality when he transforms it into art. Has the poet not taken the "rose," Jenny, and shut her into his own book? Making Jenny the subject of a poem is an extension of the process by which the speaker has attributed all his own thoughts to the sleeping prostitute. Art is substituted for reality just as the speaker's thoughts were substituted for Jenny's. Everything—God's silence, society's fragmentation and prudery, the speaker's solipsism, and the poet's imposition of form and interpretation—conspires to leave life's secrets inviolate and to identify art as merely the domain of personal reveries.

Both poems entitled **"The Portrait"** consider how the artist, through his art, appropriates reality and controls the meanings it reveals.[11] In the sonnet, the poet-painter glories in his ownership of the real.

> Let all men note
> That in all years (O Love, thy gift is this!)
> They that would look on her must come to
> me.

The form the portrait painter has given to his love is how she will exist for others from this point on. The earlier poem is more troubled by the hubris implied by the artist setting up his art as the sole point of access to a particular reality. The poem opens by establishing that where art is, reality is no longer. "This is her picture as she was." And the reader learns that "only this, of love's whole prize / Remains." The painting is so lifelike that the poet can cry, "'Tis she!," but he quickly qualifies this ecstasy: "though of herself, alas! / Less than her shadow on the grass / Or than her image in the stream." The limitation of Art is that while it may faithfully represent the real, it always remains only a representation of the object represented. The portrait is what remains of the poet-painter's love, but these remains are incomplete since the painting has not captured "what is secret and unknown, / Below the earth, above the skies." Not only does the loved one's life elude the artist's attempt to capture it, but the portrait also fails to convey some "mystery" about the loved one which "takes counsel with my soul alone." Because the material image is not the living woman, the essential, spiritual truth about her is not conveyed.

It might seem a long way from the "living woman" of this poem to the "dead, thoughtless" prostitute of **"Jenny."** But these two ways of characterizing the other are linked for Rossetti. Jenny is dead insofar as the artist must enliven her to make her suitable material for poetry. The speaker has interpreted her, created an image of her in his thoughts, tried to imagine her reality. But, in doing all this, he worries that he has crushed the "rose" of the actual Jenny. The mystery which transcends the painted image of the woman in **"The Portrait"** addresses the same fear that the woman presented in art is only the artist's recreation of the real in terms of his art. Even where it means belittling his art, Rossetti needs to assert the existence of a reality which is other than the artist and his imagination.

In fact, **"The Portrait"** implies that life and art are inimical, that the living thing is never art, that art only holds images of the dead. The poem narrates how the two lovers first exchanged vows of love. The "next day" the poet-painter remembers his ecstasy and decides he "must make them all [his] own / And paint this picture." He begins the task immediately.

> And as I wrought, while all above
> And all around was fragrant air,
> In the sick burthen of my love
> It seemed each sun-thrilled blossom there
> Beat like a heart among the leaves.
> O heart that never beats nor heaves,
> In that one darkness lying still,
> What now to thee my love's great will
> Or that fine web that sunshine weaves?

The speaker's feeling that all nature is alive as he paints is juxtaposed with the fact of the loved one's death. The "sick burthen" of his love is the need to make the previous day's perfection all his "own" by freezing it in a painting. The cause of the woman's death is never given, but the poet-painter's attempt to capture her in art results in his having exchanged her for the portrait with which he is left. The poem implies a choice between life and art. Where one is, the other is not. And since for Rossetti life comes first, the work of art becomes merely a surrogate for the reality which inspires it.

The last four stanzas continue this opposition between art and life, but the poet wavers as to which is most desirable. Reality is associated with "day" and "light," art with "darkness" and "night." Only in art can the speaker retain his memory of that once perfect love.

> For now doth daylight disavow
> Those days,—nought left to see or hear.
> Only in solemn whispers now
> At night-time these things reach mine ear.

Art, existing in the realm of dream, memory and night-time, remains a repository for contents which the harsh light of reality disavows. The speaker, preferring night-time, "delay[s] his sleep till dawn." But he cannot live entirely in the night world; the dawn is inevitable.

> And as I stood there suddenly
> All wan with traversing the night,
> Upon the desolate verge of light
> Yearned loud the iron-bosomed sea.

Implacable ("iron-bosomed") and desolate, reality returns, usurping the speaker's reveries and memories. The better world the poet establishes in art, the more satisfying realm of night in which desires are fulfilled in dream and imagination, must yield to the cold light of day. Reality both gives birth to the need to imagine something better than the real *and* acts to deny that imagined world's validity. The very fact that reality raises the question of meaning and then refuses to answer it makes the poet retreat to an artistic world full of significance. At the same time, the poet begins to suspect that the answer to the question of meaning is that reality is inimical to human desires.[12] Rossetti's acceptance that there exists a reality independent of the self and its desires, and that art should depict that reality, necessitated his submission to the "bitterness of things occult."

The poet's goal in ***The House of Life*** is to ground personal experience in reality by finding in emotion and the loved woman symbols of general truths about Love, Life, Hope, and those other personified abstractions which occupy these sonnets alongside the detailed descriptions of individual things. Of ***The House of Life*** Rossetti wrote; "To speak in the first person is often to speak most vividly; but these emotional poems are in no sense 'occasional.' The 'life' involved is life representative, as associated with love and death, with aspiration and foreboding, or with ideal art and beauty. Whether the recorded moment exists in the region of fact or thought is a question indifferent to the Muse, so long only as her touch can quicken it" (Doughty, p. 379). Rossetti knew very well that he had trouble effecting this movement from the particular to the general, and we must take this statement as one of desire not of achievement, but there can be little doubt that the sonnets address this concern directly.

The importance of love for Rossetti lies in its seeming ability to elevate personal experience into the realm of the archetypal. The loved woman embodies all life and all truth. In **"Heart's Hope"** (V) the poet tells his readers that "one loving heart" can "signify" to "all hearts all things," that the present spring can represent "other Springs gone by." The poet dedicates himself to the task of symbolizing absent things and meanings in these given particulars; the woman serves as the symbol for which the religious poet has been seeking. The way in which the symbols work is left vague, but the poet claims to have experienced moments of "instantaneous penetrating sense." Dawn, birth, and imagery of spring dominate this sonnet, as they do many of Rossetti's happier love poems when he feels that love is granting him an insight into and union with a world beyond himself. The meaning of things dawns on the poet as he perceives the loved one: he is born into a new world which now makes sense to him. And this insight validates his art. The sonnet begins by asking, "what word's power" will allow the poet to realize and embody his new-found knowledge. However, **"Heart's Hope,"** it should be noted, is set almost entirely in the subjunctive mood and stands as a statement of the poet's projects and hopes, not of what he has already accomplished.

There is no need to doubt that love (be it for Lizzie Siddal, Janey Morris, or any other woman) granted Rossetti a sense of being at home in a world in which the bitterness of hidden meanings was, at least temporarily, assuaged. But the success of much of the love poetry need not blind the reader to the problems the poet encounters in trying to make his love experiences "signify all things."[13] The woman in these poems is often enough a shadowy figure, and she is almost always as silent as Jenny. (In fact, the emphasis on physical description turns the woman into a virtual icon, to remind the reader of Rossetti's other career as a painter.) Often the woman becomes a mystery herself, rather than a transparency through which all meanings are revealed, and the poet is reduced to contemplating a reality which excludes him, which he cannot know. Of **"True Woman"** (LVI) he writes:

How strange a thing to be what Man can know
But as a sacred secret! Heaven's own screen
Hides her soul's purest depth and loveliest glow.

More than any individual poem, however, the structure of ***The House of Life*** as a whole reveals Rossetti's uneasiness with immersion in personal experience. The poems move from the personal to the non-personal, from happy moments with the loved one to memories of her and meditations on the general significance of love after death.[14] Most readers will agree that the sonnets of Part I, "Youth and Change," are better than those of Part II, "Change and Fate," but what is interesting is Rossetti's compulsion to relinquish his celebration of an individual love experience to write the more general poems of the second part. Rossetti is uneasy with the personal unless he can attach general significance to it, and so he consciously designs his sonnet sequence to move from the particular to the general.

Even in the first part, "Youth and Change," the harsh realities of change and death break in to show the youth that something beyond him exists. The beauty of a poem like **"Silent Noon"** (XIX) depends not only on its evocation of a perfect moment, but also on its suggestion of that moment's fragility. The lovers have succeeded in escaping for a brief instant (while the sun stops overhead) a reality which is indifferent to their needs.[15] ***The House of Life*** as a whole sequence denies the possibility of resting in the particular or in the moment, pleasant as such resting might be. Reality always crashes in and reestablishes a less satisfactory, but more real, world.

The sonnets often isolate intense moments but then work to reincorporate such moments into the general continuity of time.[16] Rossetti's sonnet on the sonnet describes his attempt to capture moments of "instantaneous penetrating sense."

A Sonnet is a moment's monument,—
Memorial from the Soul's eternity
To one dead deathless hour.

The moment is both "dead" and "deathless" because it is past, lost forever, and yet the significance it offers, taken from the "eternal" realm which is the soul's domain, is timeless, always true. Art can "memorialize" that eternal significance. Here, then, is one solution to "the bitterness of things occult." Moments of revelation illuminate the true meaning of things in the world, and art can record these momentary insights.[17]

Twentieth-century readers are familiar enough with the consequences of an aesthetics of the moment. Inevitably, emphasis on the moment leads to a discontinuity between moments of revelation and the uniformative daily life of "habit" and "oblivion" (to use Proust's terms). Often enough, this aesthetic leads to a celebration of art's superiority to life, since art affords these glorious moments. Certainly some of Rossetti's sonnets find in the moment the only pleasures life offers. In **"Severed Selves"** (XL) the lovers look forward to the hour of reunion, "an hour slow to come, how quickly past, / Which blooms, fades, and only leaves at last / Faint as shed flowers, the attenuated dream." In this poem, life itself seems a dream when compared to passion's intense hour. Rossetti is close at times to Pater's advocation of concentrated moments of intense feeling, and to identifying those moments as the most real things ever encountered, with the resultant acceptance of art, which captures and sustains those moments, as more real than life.

But Rossetti exists on the Victorian side of Pater and it is the tension between art and life, along with the conviction that life is more real, which constitutes Rossetti's poetry. While the moment is an end in itself for Pater, and turns life into art for Proust, it exists for Rossetti as an exception, a wonderful but somewhat unreal escape from the boredom and pain of the everyday. A poet whose experience of radical discontinuities generates in him a desire for continuity, Rossetti will only be satisfied when the particular touches on the general. He strives to make the personal a fit subject for the public, art express the nature of the real, and the moment take its place in a temporal sequence. Whenever the particular cannot be linked to these larger frameworks, Rossetti suspects that these smaller entities do not partake of the real, and are only figments of the imagination.

Many of Rossetti's poems yield these figments, sponsored by desire, in the face of a reality which overwhelms the poet's aspirations. The poet who has been unable to get reality to speak when he pleads for it to do so discovers the voice of reality when it denies him what he wants. Recognizing reality in this resistance to his desires, the poet submissively yields.[18] The **"Willowwood Sonnets"** (XLIX-LII) provide one example. The poet sits with "Love" by a well, listening for the "certain secret thing" Love has to tell. Turning Love's lute-playing into the "passionate voice" of his dead beloved, the poet is granted a vision of the lady in the water of the well. Now that the poet is absorbed in this vision, Love begins to sing, yet the message is a despairing one: "Your last hope lost, who so in vain invite / Your lips to that their unforgotten food." Love's advice is to forget the past since memory only causes the poet to feed longings which can never be satisfied. With the end of Love's song, the face seen in the well falls "back drowned," and the poet is alone once more. The reality which disperses his vision is a reality incompatible with the human desire for permanence.

It seems odd that when, uncharacteristically, Rossetti succeeds in getting a voice outside the self to speak, the message is so often dismal. The poet has begged life, reality, to reveal itself and its deepest meanings to him, and on the few occasions his request bears fruit, the lesson is that life's laws and man's hopes inevitably conflict.

> There came an image in Life's retinue
>   That had Love's wings and bore his gonfalon:
>   Fair was the web, and nobly wrought thereon,
> O soul-sequestered face, thy form and hue!
> Bewildering sounds, such as Spring wakens to,
>   Shook in its folds; and through my heart its power
>   Sped trackless as the immemorable hour
> When birth's dark portal groaned and all was new.
>
> But a veiled woman followed, and she caught
>   The banner round its staff, to furl and cling,—
>   Then plucked a feather from the bearer's wing,
> And held it to his lips that stirred it not,
> And said to me, "Behold, there is no breath:
> I and this Love are one, and I am Death."

In the octave of **"Death and Love"** (XLVIII), the "image" from "Life's retinue" possesses the poet utterly, granting him a "power" which he likens to being present at the mysterious origin of all life, the primal Spring. That origin is an "immemorable hour," its fundamental reality seemingly guaranteed by its transcending any incorporation into human memory or speech. Even when granted an insight into reality far beyond what he has enjoyed before, the poet can only distinguish "bewildering sounds." The mysteries here strain the poet's ability to articulate them.

In the sestet, the full consequences of this revelation become apparent. Even to have penetrated this far into "Life's retinue" is to have gone beyond the limits of the human, to have moved toward death. "Death" might be read metaphorically here. The poet could be saying that union with another in love, which results in the birth of new life (a child, his poetry), also involves a death to self which makes the new life possible. Tied as it is to birth, death here might even take on its Elizabethan, sexual meaning, with the "power" which possesses the poet being sexual passion. But the brutal and bare statement, "Behold, there is no breath," denies all metaphorical readings. The creative union the poet has hoped to find in love, a union beyond self with the real, is declared as identical to death: "I and this Love are one, and I am Death." Denied any experience of union in life, Rossetti comes to believe union can only be found in death.

Such a conclusion would seem preposterous if it were not for the evidence of the poems. The sonnets were written over a period of years, so they are not consistently gloomy. But a poem like **"Michelangelo's Kiss"** (XCIV) states clearly Rosstti's conviction that no satisfactory union will be experienced in this life: " . . . even thus the Soul, / Touching at length some sorely-chastened goal, / Earns oftenest but a little." After such failure, the only question remains: "What holds for her Death's garner? And for thee?" At times, Rossetti welcomes the bitterest message of reality—the necessity of death with its annihilation of all hopes for this life—because at least this action to end life proves that the reality he seeks is out there. Determined to prove reality exists and is meaningful, Rossetti can find in the forces that thwart him a confirmation that something exists beyond self. Rossetti's need to yield his own desires and his imaginative art to a transcendent reality explains the presence of death, even the worship of and wish for it, in his poems. At times he even identifies himself with this overwhelming force. In **"The Monochord"** (LXXIX) he considers how "Life's self," imagined as the "sky's vast vault or ocean's sound," "draws my life from me," pulling his small self back into a larger, universal self. And the poet's ambiguous response to this dissolution is expressed by his experiencing "regenerate rapture" at the very moment he perceives the "devious coverts of dismay." In death, the poet's isolation, his sojourn in what one poem calls the "cloud's confines," will end, and he will participate in the reality he never quite penetrated during his lifetime. With death will come complete knowledge of the meaning of things occult: "Strange to think by the way, / Whatever there is to know, / That we shall know one day" **("The Cloud Confines")**. In **"The Portrait"** that demystifying death is imagined as a birth into union and knowledge.

How shall my soul stand rapt and awed,
When, by the new birth born abroad
  Throughout the music of the suns,
  It enters in her soul at once
And knows the silence there for God!

A longing for death because it will rectify the painful ignorance of life would seem proof enough of a poet's failure to fashion through his art some sustaining meaning. But Rossetti's failure is both more complete—and more poignant. He cannot even affirm death wholeheartedly, because he does not know if it will satisfy the desire for union. Along with the poems which call on death as the solution are those poems which wonder if death, too, might cheat his hopes. **"Cloud and Wind"** (XLIV) contemplates the horrible possibility that death only reveals "that all is vain / And that Hope sows what Love shall never reap." Death might only be a "sleep" which "Ne'er notes" the very things the poet hopes to witness. Ignorant even here, Rossetti is forced back to prayer, pleading:

That when the peace is garnered in from
    strife,
  The work retrieved, the will regenerate,
  This soul may see thy face, O lord of death!

(LXVI)[19]

Notes

[1] (New York, 1953), pp. 188-189.

[2] The word "secret" recurs throughout Rossetti's poetry, revealing the poet's belief that some truth or meaning exists, which is being kept from him.

[3] Quoted from John Dixon Hunt, *The Pre-Raphaelite Imagination 1848-1900* (London, 1968), p. 129.

[4] Carol Christ (*The Finer Optic* [Yale Univ. Press, 1975], pp. 56-62) discusses in detail how the Pre-Raphaelites, especially Hunt, understood the interconnection between "truth to Nature" and the functioning of individual objects as symbols.

[5] McGann uses "The Woodspurge" as one example of his thesis that "Rossetti does not want us to symbolize," and he deliberately divests objects of meanings beyond themselves so that the reader is "restored to a kind of innocence" of immediate response (p. 233). Obviously, McGann's understanding of Rossetti directly contradicts the interpretation being offered here, which sees the resistance of natural objects to a symbolic reading as an indication of the poet's desire to find such meanings, a desire which is often not satisfied. For another discussion of this particular poem and the "resistance" of details to interpretation, see *The Finer Optic,* pp. 40-44.

[6] Writing on "Jenny," both James Paul Seigel ("'Jenny': The Divided Sensibility of a Young and Thoughtful Man of the World," *SEL,* 9 [1969], 677-694) and James G. Nelson, ("The Rejected Harlot: A Reading of Rossetti's 'A Last Confession' and 'Jenny,'" *VP,* 10 [1972], 123-130) discuss the speaker's distance from

the woman, and the irony (set up by Rossetti) of his failure to make any significant contact with her.

[7] The fullest description of Rossetti's separation of himself from the everyday world of Victorian England is Jerome Buckley's "Pre-Raphaelite Past and Present: The Poetry of the Rossettis" in *Victorian Poetry,* Stratford-upon-Avon Studies No. 15 (London, 1972), pp. 123-138.

[8] Some poems which use the image of the "echo" are "Plighted Promise," "Farewell to the Glen" (LXXXIV), "A Day of Love" (XVI), "Stillborn Love" (LV), "Adieu," and "The Cloud Confines."

[9] The lines quoted are from the sonnet written for the painting "Our Lady of the Rocks" by Leonardo da Vinci. Florence Saunders Boos (*The Poetry of D. G. Rossetti* [The Hague, 1976], pp. 224-228) offers a detailed reading of this interesting poem.

[10] That "Jenny" would find a place within "a book in which pure woman may not look" reads like an anticipation of the "fleshly poet" controversy. See Seigel (pp. 677-680) for Rossetti's apprehensions about the reception this poem would receive.

[11] The longer poem "The Portrait" is one of Rossetti's earliest poems; written in 1847, it was heavily revised for *Poems* (1870). The sonnet "The Portrait" is number X of *The House of Life.*

[12] Edward Said, in chapter 4 of *Beginnings* (New York, 1975), discusses nineteenth-century literature in terms of an oscillation between "authority" and "molestation." Writers of the period were searching for an "authority" beyond self to justify their artistic visions, and are concerned about the "author" who sets himself up as creator of a world. Said finds in the novels of the period characters, such as Lydgate in *Middlemarch* and Ahab in *Moby Dick,* who try to create worlds out of themselves and who are finally "molested" by a reality which is larger than their individual visions. These characters embody urges found in the authors themselves, and nineteenth-century writers usually work to assure that their visions are "authorized" by the very nature of things; in other words, the authors align themselves with the forces that "molest" the character's desires. The suggestion here is that Rossetti's poetry reveals a similar need to "molest" the poet's more extravagant desires, and for reasons similar to those outlined by Said.

[13] The fullest description of love's place in Rossetti's poetry is Stephen Spector's excellent essay "Love, Unity and Desire in the Poetry of Dante Gabriel Rossetti," *ELH,* (1971), 432-448. Spector sees love as one expression of Rossetti's overwhelming need "to bridge the gap between the subjective and objective worlds" (p. 432), but he concludes that love does not afford such unity and that Rossetti's poems are about "the desire for unity," not the "experience of unity" (p. 443). If McGann is the critic whose understanding of Rossetti is most distant from that presented here, Spector's views are the most similar.

[14] There has been a series of studies of the structure of *The House of Life* over the past fifteen years. The quick outline presented here is drawn from Robert D. Hume's "Inorganic Structure in *The House of Life,*" *PLL,* 5 (1969), 282-295, and especially Houston A. Baker, "The Poet's Progress: Rossetti's *The House of Life,*" *VP,* 8 (1970), 1-14.

[15] Spector (pp. 445-446) offers a wonderful evaluation of these moments of escape in Rossetti's love poems and how they generally combine light and dark, suggesting that the peace of escape is also a retreat from the world into death.

[16] George P. Landow, "'Life touching lips with Immortality': Rossetti's Typological Structures," *SR,* 17 [1978], 247-265) argues at length (see esp. pp. 258-261) for the view presented here that isolated moments in Rossetti are always finally related to a larger temporal framework.

[17] John Dixon Hunt ("A Moment's Monument: Reflections on Pre-Raphaelite Vision in Poetry and Painting" [in Sambrook, pp. 243-264]) offers an excellent discussion of the adherence to an aesthetics of the moment by various writers and artists associated with the Pre-Raphaelite movement. The argument here, of course, is that Rossetti does not find the moment all sufficient. For another discussion of the functioning of the moment, specifically limited to a consideration of Rossetti's poetry, see Stanley M. Holberg, "Rossetti and the Trance," *VP,* 8 (1970), 299-314.

[18] Apart from the Willowwood sonnets and "Death and Love" (discussed here), only six other poems in *The House of Life* introduce a transcendent voice: "Love's Bauble" (XXII), "The Morrow's Message" (XXXVIII), "Love's Fatality" (LIV), "Love's Last Gift" (LIX), "The Love-Moon" (XXXVII), and "The Sun's Shame" (XCIII). Of these, only "Love's Bauble" and "Love's Last Gift" could be considered "positive" in any way.

[19] This essay was first written as part of an NEH Summer Seminar on Victorian and Modern Poetics directed by Carol Christ at the University of California at Berkeley. Thanks are due to the Endowment, and to Professor Christ and members of the seminar who read and helped in the revision of an early draft.

Daniel A. Harris (essay date 1984)

SOURCE: "D. G. Rossetti's 'Jenny': Sex, Money, and the Interior Monologue," in *Victorian Poetry,* Vol. 22, No. 2, Summer, 1984, pp. 197-215.

[*In the following essay, Harris focuses on Rossetti's critique of Victorian culture through a poetic representation of silence, sexuality, and economic exchange in "Jenny."*]

Rossetti's indictment of prostitution and male attitudes toward sexual exploitation in Victorian England is also the first interior monologue in English literary tradition unrecognized as such;[1] the poem (1848-1870) breaks the ground for Eliot's "The Love Song of J. Alfred Prufrock," Molly's effusions in *Ulysses,* and Bernard's concluding monologue in Woolf's *The Waves.* Rossetti's protagonist names his discourse an interior monologue as he imagines addressing Jenny directly: "Suppose I were to think aloud,—/ What if to her all this were said?" (ll. 156-157). This unsounded self-questioning transforms his preceding language into silent thought and interiorizes what follows. Rossetti thus marks the speaker's ethical crisis—is a whore a person?—by a problem in language-use. Simultaneously, he alters the form of the poem from its earlier drafts and thereby changes the history of dramatic monologue. The protagonist of the first draft *is* a conventional "speaker"; he asks, "Nay, wherefor [sic] should such things be said?" (l. 58)—and his question, pointing his exterior speech, subverts the interior form Rossetti ultimately achieves.[2] In the final version, instead of censoring an utterance, the silent protagonist thinks to breach his soundless discourse by direct conversational address—and retreats into silence. Rossetti, instead of representing a silencing of sound that renders the suppressed thought inaudible, toys with the protagonist's potential communication; tempting him to speak, he questions the kinds of social interchange that a purchaser can have with a whore. The participants in this deathly still life cannot or do not engage each other, linguistically or sexually. The prostitute sleeps; the protagonist keeps silence. Only money links them. When the protagonist gives Jenny "These golden coins," imagining her as "A Danaë for a moment"—and himself as a self-mocking Zeus (ll. 342, 379)—he uses his linguistic skills in mythologizing to make his coin a surrogate for sexual potency. The triangulation of language with sex and money, the enmeshing of silence and speech within dehumanizing systems of sexual and economic exchange, the treatment of all three categories along the same axis of giving and withholding, is the major ideological pattern in the poem; it transcends both the protagonist's moral ambivalence and his impulses to aestheticize his experience, problems Rossetti's commentators have already explored.[3] The triangulation—even more than the subject, prostitution—is what makes **"Jenny"** radical, a cultural criticism of depersonation that treats the protagonist's modes of discourse as inseparable from his sexual, psychological, and economic quandaries. This essay will show, first, how Rossetti converts dramatic monologue into silent discourse and uses the tension between speech and silence to expose the lineaments of Victorian censorship. Then, it will examine the very different silences of Jenny and the protagonist: Rossetti deploys the interior monologue itself to reveal cultural values in the poem.

Rossetti's capacity to interiorize the dramatic monologue he inherited from Tennyson and Browning derives from Coleridge, whose "conversation poems" shape the modern history of dramatic monologue. Rossetti remembers "Frost at Midnight" in his first draft; the "exceeding silentness" of Jenny's chamber (l. 51) recalls the "extreme silentness" of Coleridge's cottage (l. 10).[4] Rossetti, understanding the generic invitation in dramatic monologue that the interior auditor's formal silence become a psychological response to the monologist's utterance, intuits Coleridge's interest in an auditor whose silence is physiological as well as formal and psychological: like Coleridge's sleeping son Hartley, Jenny sleeps throughout the protagonist's discourse, leaving him in a soundless vacuum. As Rossetti eliminates Jenny's possible response, he develops (what Coleridge anticipates) a new poetic imagery that elicits the nuances of silence as they surround various potentialities of speech. The monologist encounters a speech situation that bars him from communication: the "auditor" is unconscious. He is thus liberated to create his world—indeed, his auditor—at will. Whether his freedom manifests itself as a generous bestowal (Coleridge) or a narcissistic self-indulgence (Rossetti) that terrifies the protagonist with his unrestrained imaginings, it requires the prevention of the auditor's response. But silent discourse and spoken utterance, each in the presence of an unresponsive auditor, differ. While silent discourse, no less than spoken utterance, can embody interpersonal relationships, it postulates an alienation of protagonist from auditor, a closure of speech possibility that is not demanded by the genre but poetically designed as a distinctively new element in its history. This is the possibility—beyond the enforced silence of the sleeper—that Rossetti elicits from "Frost at Midnight." Coleridge does not indicate whether his monologist's "meditation" (l. 9) is spoken, thought, or written; the poem tranquilly accepts the ambiguous status of its language. Rossetti, enacting the Victorian concern to designate linguistic status, reads Coleridge's poem as a silent discourse. When he considers how Hartley's "gentle breathings" fill the "momentary pauses of the thought" (ll. 45, 47), he construes "thought" as silent, envisages a subtle tension between the child's non-linguistic breathings and the father's language-filled silence, and creates a rhythmic correspondence between exterior silences that emblematizes the reciprocity between father and son. With such a silent protagonist, Rossetti can—by demarcating silent discourse as such, as in the final version of **"Jenny"**—make formally explicit, as a new advantage to dramatic monologue, the choice of speech underlying every poem in the genre.

"Jenny" shows Rossetti's understanding that writing, if it normally represents speech, can also represent silent thought. With a fine mimetic propriety, he knows that writing which imitates unspoken discourse can move toward speech far more easily than writing which represents speech can imitate its own cancellation: the "spoken" first draft of **"Jenny"** can embody silence only by erasing its own text. With a writing that represents silent discourse, moreover, Rossetti can characterize speaking itself as a decisive and momentous act, by withholding, in a powerful suspension of linguistically filled silence, utterance that threatens to break formal boundaries. The possibility of that suppressed speech continually points to the rich linguistic activity that occurs in silence. For interior monologue, particularly when conducted in the presence of an auditor, offers a double vision of silence: to the auditor, silence is an absence of sound that cannot signify; to the reader, it is the environment of cognition and language formation. **"Jenny"** demonstrates—with the acuity of nineteenth-century empiricism—the fallacy of the currently fashionable opposition between silence and speech. What differentiates silence from speech is hardly the presence of linguistic activity in the second and not the first, but rather the social aspects of each. Silence normally precludes the making of a speech-community (save in cases of ritual); speech is a social contract, a denial of alienation from communal relations. In **"Jenny"** the protagonist's dilemma is whether to treat the whore as a human being by addressing her "aloud." Observe Rossetti's mimetic trade-off in writing interior monologue: he sacrifices the outward representation of social relations permitted by conventional dramatic monologue (the auditor remains visible through the monologist's discourse) for an inner representation of the protagonist's mind. This sacrifice is consistent with the situation: the whore, having no valid social existence, need not be represented poetically save as a figure (trope, icon) in the man's imagination.

Rossetti's political satire in excluding Jenny from the exterior representation allowed typical auditors (e.g., Menoeceus in Tennyson's "Tiresias") permits him to develop a total privacy in which the protagonist can unfold his mind entirely. As he reviews the design of **"Jenny"** while dismissing Buchanan's charges in "The Fleshly School of Poetry," he rejects his earlier drafts:

> Nor did I omit to consider how far a treatment from without might here [with the subject of prostitution] be possible. But the motive powers of art reverse the requirement of science, and demand first of all an *inner* standing-point. . . . The beauty and pity, the self-questionings and all-questionings which ["such a mystery"] brings with it, can come with full force only from the mouth of one alive to its whole appeal, such as the speaker put forward in the poem,—that is, of a young and thoughtful man of the world. (***Collected Works,*** I, 484-485)

Compared with Rossetti's standard dramatic monologues, **"A Portrait"** and **"A Last Confession," "Jenny"** offers more than a "subjective point of view"; its interiority secludes linguistic activity itself: the poem is so subjective that its language is inaudible. Such fugitive silence—whether used for sexual fantasy or social analysis—contrasts radically with the outspokenness of **"Jenny"** the poetic artifact, and that "*inner* standing-point" is part of Rossetti's polemic. Despite an increased public discussion of prostitution, the subject was still largely interdicted when Rossetti wrote **"Jenny."**[5] When he revised his drafts to make speaking about the topic "aloud" a major psychological issue, he found the precise formal means by which to imitate the public's general refusal to acknowledge the problem: the protagonist's silence satirically mimics public hypocrisies in blinking the issue. Further, having the protagonist worry about speaking "aloud," Rossetti accentuates his struggle to wrest free from a powerful public censorship so internalized that he cannot readily discover his own attitudes. Indeed, the protagonist's effort to breach that cultural taboo is so dangerously fraught that it leads him back to his most reactionary excoriation of Jenny in the discourse (ll. 158-170); his revulsion against speaking "aloud" is as pathetic and contemptible as his temptation to seek a relationship by speaking appears daringly humane.

The social repressions behind the protagonist's failure to speak underscore Rossetti's own forthright breaking of taboo to scrutinize prostitution and men's responses to it. He presents the very impulse to treat the topic as part of the political statement of the poem; he thus rejects the blandishments of a genre that characteristically, as in Browning, lets the writer evade responsibility for his utterance. Rossetti further points his violation of public silence through writing by raising the parallel issue of reading. Because the scholarly protagonist compares Jenny to a book (ll. 51-52, 125-129, 158-162, 253-266), Rossetti likens the reader's act of reading the poem **"Jenny"** to the protagonist's figurative "reading" of Jenny the auditor. The doubling here implicates the reader in the same dilemmas that beset the protagonist. Finding the courage to commit a prohibited and dangerous act—reading the poem, attempting to confront Jenny the prostitute without bigotry—are comparable rejections of censorship demanding integrity and self-knowledge; satirically, "pure women may not look" in Jenny's book (l. 254), associated as it is with the female genitals (ll. 158-162, 264-266). As the protagonist defensively substitutes a "reading" of Jenny for sexual activity, his literary approach to his subject—and with it, the reader's—becomes confused with sexual desire.[6] The equation between the cognitive act of reading and the sexualized contemplation of a whore shows how, in a repressive society, reading is magnified into its sexual "equivalent" in a manner that erases all distinctions between mental and physical acts. The equation also questions the reader's motives for reading **"Jenny"**: when does desire for aesthetic pleasure or intellectual knowledge turn into self-titillation, a fascination with pornography like the protagonist's?

Emphasizing by his form the difficulty of thinking freely against censorship, Rossetti simultaneously liberates his protagonist from psychic restraints: he silences Jenny entirely, puts her to sleep.[7] By making Jenny unconscious, Rossetti neutralizes her as a source of censorship. While the protagonist's capacity to impute attributes to Jenny remains unimpaired, Jenny cannot respond: the inequity, typical of all monologues, particularly suits a poem about the imbalances of sexual power.[8] If the protagonist actually spoke to Jenny awake, he would have to accept her responsive speech; her possible replies (dramatic monologue invites the reader to imagine the auditor's response) suggest the pressures the protagonist experiences so uneasily. If, indeed, "to her all this were said" (l. 157), her answer—whether grateful or hostile—would create precisely the linguistic, and thus human, bond the protagonist fears. First, Jenny might thank the protagonist for his understanding, welcome his sexual restraint, and tell him the pathetic history he barely intuits. This conventional response, palatable to a conservative ideology, would maintain the status quo of prostitution, male domination, and the use of sympathy in place of social reform. But the protagonist's response to his own thought of speaking "aloud"—vindictively comparing Jenny's mind to a sewer or vagina contaminated by sexual disease (ll. 165-169)—suggests that he anticipates an explosive and hostile reply. Here, she is critical, businesslike; she spurns his sympathy as liberal sentimentality; she exposes his hypocrisy—and perhaps his sexual anxieties—in coming to a whore for sex and using her, instead, for linguistic fantasies.[9] She accuses him of arrogance in thinking he can envisage her work; she refuses further chatter. To conceive either the protagonist's outrage or his apologetic bafflement in being thus answered is to appreciate both the safety he finds in Jenny's silence and Rossetti's keen strategy in rendering Jenny unconscious. While this scenario does not characterize all the protagonist's reasons for contemplating speech, it helps explain why Jenny's silence cancels the protagonist's fear of censorship.

Jenny's silence, however, has attributes separate from the protagonist's needs. Except for Tennyson's "Tithonus," no poem in the genre so queries the ontological status of the auditor's consciousness. Jenny's unconsciousness renders her an object having a merely animal or natural existence; deprived of speech both by sleep and by generic function, she has, like the female culture she represents, "no voice"; her bodily passivity precludes even the gestural language usually given to auditors in place of speech.[10] Rossetti shrewdly makes her body exhibit formally her oppression as a woman and as a whore: she is—as the "wild unchildish elf" jeers—an unconscious "thing" (ll. 77, 79) that signifies the dehumanization of prostitution and (the protagonist learns) marriage (ll. 207-213). The obvious problem with the notion of the whore as object, however, is that it scants Rossetti's intellectual strength in representing Jenny as an object even when, asleep, she is not enacting her function as whore. A less acute poet would have represented sleep as an escape from objecthood, but Rossetti likens Jenny the sexual commodity (a thing to be bought) with Jenny the woman (a natural phenomenon lacking consciousness): objects both. Further, Rossetti implies that Jenny chooses to sleep: if she is her customer's commodity, she can choose another kind of objectification in refusing sex for money. Compared with Hartley's sleep in "Frost at Midnight," Jenny's is less a gaining of innocence than a sloughing off of social, moral, and economic roles. In the protagonist's conservative reading of this escape (ll. 67-69, 166, 343), as in Greg's influential accounts of prostitutes' lives, Jenny chooses oblivion from pain and self-hatred.[11] More radically, and more consistently with Rossetti's incipient feminism, Jenny, choosing sleep, simultaneously rejects language use and the sale of her sexuality in an economic system that metonymizes her into the sole marketable part of her body. As she closes her mouth in silence, she also closes her other pouches: what the protagonist calls her "magic purse" (l. 344) and thus her genitals. This initiating action, shaping the protagonist's discourse, is the primary image by which Rossetti collocates language, sex, and money. Jenny is a whore who, during business, decides not to work; she thus abrogates the equations between time and money, sex and money, and regains her personhood. She frees herself from the linguistic naming that—as in the opening rhyme of **"Jenny"** with "guinea"—imprisons her in a code that equates selfhood with monetary value as established by sexual labor. This rebellious action, however, by which Jenny ironically deploys the male capitalist's power to choose when to sell, is costly. Jenny gains freedom from the objecthood designated by male culture only by accepting a self-objectification that magically replaces men's: her natural sleep spurns the humankind in which she has no personal identity. The pathos of this liberty is that it entails loss of self and will; unlike the protagonist in his silence, Jenny must choose a silence so extreme (sleep) that she must sacrifice the powers of self-creation he enjoys. The freedom Jenny finds in sleep cannot, because inactive, have positive value.

The protagonist misses this self-negating paradox in Jenny's freedom; he sees only an unconventional—nearly outrageous—denial of his presence and his demands. Her sleep affronts his male power, makes him a "thing" comparable to the prostitute. As his role as her temporary owner is threatened, he cannot understand her new status: she becomes a "riddle that one shrinks / To challenge" (ll. 280-281). Is a whore who sleeps a whore? The protagonist's anxiety in being cancelled is intense: he resorts to familiar intellectual images of books (ll. 23-24); he employs the passive voice to escape the scene (l. 29), refers to Jenny's subordinate pose (ll. 66, 93-94); seeking safe, conventional roles, he attempts to rouse her (ll. 89, 96, 303) so that he can evade the problems of interpretation her sleep presents; and he names her twenty-six times, as if to touch linguistically a figure who has already eluded him. His flippant query, "Whose person or whose purse may be / The lodestar of your reverie?" (ll. 20-21), temporarily conceals his discomfiture; but four paragraphs later he cautiously reaffirms his identity by naming himself the subject of her dreams: "If of myself you think at all, / What is the thought?" (ll. 59-60; see also ll. 336-339). Male power is thus hollow, fragile: the protagonist, to exist to himself, needs to be perceived.

Since Jenny cannot acknowledge his sexual and monetary power, he resorts to his compensatory imagination to validate his roles: the protagonist's silent discourse is a response to Jenny's virtual disappearance. Structurally—and psychologically—it occurs instead of sexual intercourse; indeed, in one manuscript the protagonist complains, "I meant a woman good to kiss / Tonight should yield me something more / Than bloodless perking metaphor."[12] Language assumes a specifically sexual character and loses its identity as a general means of signifying; in linguistic fantasy, he gains the sexual power Jenny denies him. But because Jenny is a prostitute as well as a woman, his language use is simultaneously monetized: Jenny the person (the agent of sexual gratification) is the commodity (the economic unit he purchases); when he names Jenny a whore, he designates her sexuality a commodity having a specific value. When the protagonist gives Jenny money for sexual services not performed, his "golden coins" substitute for the ejaculation he does not have, as the Zeus/Danaë allusion indicates. The alignment of his unwilling continence with the silence of his discourse, collocating semen and language, is paralleled by the correspondence between money and language that emerges when, at the end, the protagonist makes his coins metonyms of his silent discourse. With linguistic functions promiscuously fused with other modes of valuation in an incestuous vacuum, the problem arises of releasing language from a self-reflexiveness of contingent and duplicative meanings that bars analysis and true perception. The protagonist confronts this situation because his initial intent to (re)place Jenny in her proper role and satisfy himself imaginatively gradually becomes a desire to understand sympathetically the person he initially discards so cavalierly; these contradictory aims, dividing him between the reactionary male jealous of his power and the compassionate liberal seeking social justice, render his language use ambivalent. But the conflict ends inconclusively, as it must, because the progressive side of the debate, as well as the reactionary, is contaminated by a language triangulated with the very categories of sex and money whose confusion accounts for Jenny's oppression.

The filiation of language with sex, and then money, is immediately evident in the first verse paragraph. As a "thoughtless queen" (l. 7), Jenny's unconsciousness grants the protagonist license to fill her mind with his own conceptions; nor can he perceive his imputations as such. When he conceives her as roses that should "unclose" "Their purfled buds" (l. 117) and then thinks of her brain "as a volume seldom read" whose pages might "Be parted" by his thoughts (ll. 158, 160-161), the fusion of image patterns makes the sexuality of his compensatory imagination obvious. His discourse is a linguistic fondling, no less abrasive and presumptuous because silent, in which he commercializes the sleeping prostitute by designating her values. He assigns her an extraordinary variety of poses. Caught in his self-pleasing alliteration, "Lazy laughing languid Jenny" (l.1) is not so much observed as stereotyped; the "queen / Of kisses (ll. 7-8) becomes a series of flowers in natural metaphors (ll. 12, 14, 16) that effectively blink urban prostitution; when the protagonist names her "Poor shameful Jenny, full of grace" (l. 18), he wittily combines the Queen of Heaven and Mary Magdalen in an outrageous parody that demonstrates his linguistic power to change the object of his imagination at will.[13] Like the hapless model in Christina Rossetti's "In an Artist's Studio," who becomes the guises in which the painter dresses her, Jenny is the victim of an insistent linguistic fecundity that trumpets the sexual prowess the protagonist is literally denied. Jenny of course does not exist in this catalogue; as sacred and secular myths intermix self-referentially, excluding the person they are meant to signify, the language of sexuality achieves a radical self-enclosure in which reality barely intervenes. As the protagonist self-critically observes at a later point,

> Yet, Jenny, looking long at you,
> The woman almost fades from view.
> A cipher of man's changeless sum
> Of lust, past, present, and to come,
> Is left.
>
> (ll. 276-280)

Rossetti's diction shows how the protagonist's fantasies have cancelled Jenny. She becomes a "cipher," "A person who fills a place, but is of no importance or worth" *(OED)*. She is, next, a sign, not a person; her signifying refers not to herself but to male desire, the "lust" that negates her. As she objectifies male desire, she is reified as that destructive, "changeless sum" of lust that, like Keats's nightingale, remains immutable in human experience despite changes in its exemplars. Hideously, the cipher of lust is then animalized as a toad that covers her sexually, like a palimpsest (l. 282);[14] the image, pointing to men's power to mold women to their imaginations, underscores the ugly sexuality men fear in themselves and thus project upon women. Perhaps most importantly, Rossetti's image interweaves the signifying modes of language, sex, and money in a closed system that compromises the open referentiality of language. Like the other monetary puns ("change," l. 186; "discounted," l. 359), "changeless" absorbs modes of perception and behavior that should be exempt from a merely economic valuation but, in Victorian England, are not. As a monetary sign distorts Jenny's body, sexual possessiveness and monetary acquisitiveness erase her literal reality. Looking at Jenny transmuted, a man sees the symbol of his own material desire, the self-confining reflection of his mind.

Because the assignation of monetary value changes everything into commodities, the linguistic disguises the protagonist gives Jenny are economic as well as sexual. Naming—as the protagonist names Nell a "prize" (l. 192)—alters personal character into economic worth and betrays language to a system in which the value of a commodity refers only to the price of other commodities; as with paper money that theoretically signifies a certain quantity of gold, the actual referent is lost. Rossetti brilliantly illustrates this process of cancelling a person as the protagonist criticizes the disguising of women in Western pictorial art:

> Fair shines the gilded aureole
> In which our highest painters place
> Some living woman's simple face.
> (ll. 230-232)

In the "preachings" of painting (l. 240), as with language, the mimetic process (evolved by men) conceals an ideology of male domination that conspires with organized religion to negate women while pretending to idealize them. But the idealization deceives—not only because it falsifies the "living woman's" true condition or because it offers the image of female purity as a sop to women's cancellation. The idealization is fraudulent because, while supposedly an icon of religious beauty, it actually emblematizes men's monetary desire and their habitual translation of the world into economic terms: worshipping the Virgin, they actually adore earthly treasures. For the aureole is a gold coin that monetizes the female model and the spiritual life alike; derived from Donne's "The Canonization" (l. 7), the image changes the woman's "real" into her minted, "stamped face." Ironically rhymed with "soul" (l. 229), the aureole visually separates the head from the body; the dismemberment, recalling Jenny's distortion into a "cipher," bespeaks the brutality couched in the idealizing stereotypes purveyed by art and the Church; to the protagonist, the representing of the woman's "stilled features" (l. 233) seems a killing. The metamorphosis of the woman's face into a coin parallels the transformation of the female genitals into the "magic purse" (l. 344). In both instances her body is wrenched into an economic emblem of male desire; both changes reflect a world in which "golden sun and silver moon"—the natural forces of the cosmos—are "Counted for life-coins" (ll. 224, 226).[15] Falsely spiritualized, women are sacrificed to men's deceptive devotion to a spiritual salvation that conceals an unregenerate quest for material wealth; the condition of women in the iconography of the Church, the protagonist's language suggests, is that of women on the streets. In such a monetized universe, no wonder that the protagonist's agonized question about Christian redemption—"Shall soul not somehow pay for soul?" (l. 229)—fails to transcend its literal meaning: spiritual salvation is a matter of economic exchange in which no one (including the protagonist at the end) gives "charity" for nothing.

The passage exemplifies the protagonist's gradual increase in critical understanding: he perceives the violent hostility in men's presumably aesthetic imaging of a woman's "*stilled* features." This murderous hatred characterizes language as he presents it generally. Language, the tool of false categorizations, misnamings, and fraudulent valuations, is the medium of sexual hatred, not only between the sexes, but among women and among men. Linguistic hostility (companioned by fear) even permeates the animal world: the image of "some sheep that jog / Bleating before a barking dog" (ll. 305-306) shows the natural order made noisily frantic by capitalist trade. Compared with the protagonist's silence or the "lullaby" he only imagines (ll. 245-247), the language-world of the poem is a "din" (l. 70). Jenny is assaulted by "envy's voice at virtue's pitch" (l. 71): the virtuous matron, masking her jealousy in the language of moral rectitude, resents Jenny's economic independence from men and thus reveals how a male power-system incites hatred among women. In a culture where the premium placed on virginity inverts the economic advantages of selling one's sexuality, the "pale girl's dumb rebuke" (l. 73) springs from similar motives: her "dumb" anger (suppressed; foolish) reiterates as self-hatred and jealousy the unspoken male injunction to remain chaste, powerless. When the "wise unchildish elf" designates Jenny a "thing" to the young "schoolmate lesser than himself" (ll. 77-78), deanimates life by instituting irrational categories, he shows how language, transmitting stereotypes, perpetuates social injustice; by proving his burgeoning sexuality in naming Jenny his potential purchase, he triumphs sexually over the younger male child. In this competition between men where women are pawns, the protagonist recognizes a sexual hostility that originates with men and then ramifies outwards. This difficult, important recognition sparks his sharpest condemnation of male speech and his most explicit effort to dissociate himself from male culture: "the hatefulness of man, / . . . / Whose acts are ill and his speech ill" (ll. 83-85) comprehends not only men's hatred of women but the vileness of men themselves.[16] An ineradicable disease in the male mind contaminates everyone its language touches: male children who mimic their elders to gain power; women who, like the matron, unconsciously repeat male language as their own; prostitutes who must escape it by sleep or drink. Whatever its form, this linguistic barbarism is far more immune to healing than the "desecrated mind, / Where all contagious currents meet" (ll. 164-165) that the protagonist, imagining the mind syphilitic, attributes to Jenny. The pathos and repugnancy is that men cannot "hear" their own corruption. No wonder: their emblem is the toad Lust, seated "within a stone" (l. 282), "deaf" (l. 291), obsessively trapped in its alienated silence.

As the episode of the "gilded aureole" indicates, male language is deceptive as well as hostile. The protagonist shares Rossetti's negative Romantic suspicion that authentic speech is an illusion. This suspicion resounds most clearly at the end, when, self-mocking, he protests that his expression of love, not counterfeit, "rang true" (l. 380). But duplicitous speech emerges everywhere. Well-intentioned adults may have told the rural Jenny "a child's tale" of London's "broil and bale" (ll. 133-134) and thus hastened her doom.[17] In London, a corrupted "child can tell the tale there, how / Some things which are not yet enroll'd / In market-lists are bought and sold" (ll. 136-138). The lists deceive by omitting mention of people bought and sold for sex; because the official male ideology maintains that human beings are not commodities, whores are not named. Rossetti's brilliant diction, like his carefully truncated epigraph (*The Merry Wives of Windsor,* IV.i),[18] shows how Jenny's humanity is disputed linguistically as well as socially. Similar duplicities pervade the image of Jenny "Like a rose shut in a book," crushed (l. 253): with "each dead rose-leaf . . . , / Pale as transparent Psyche-wings" superimposed upon "the vile text" (ll. 257-259), one reads, as with a palimpsest, a language doubled and made morally contradictory and obscure. These are some of the deceptions in language, spoken, written, or implied, that lead the protagonist to distrust male linguistic culture.

The very silence of the protagonist's interior monologue thus reflects his revulsion with deceptive male speech. Other motives notwithstanding, keeping silent means escaping a hostile world where naming brutally curtails free thought; a refuge from the "din" of common life, silence rebels against male behavior and "ill" speech. Not to speak when all language use seems corrosive appears the only ethical means, if socially self-destructive, of preserving one's integrity. Rossetti considers the protagonist's attempt to elude male culture a positive sign of a willingness to change. Even the freedom to engage silently in fantasy, however sexist, becomes a way of self-discovery; by contrast, the matron, the pale girl, and the schoolboy all speak publicly the codified languages in which they have been indoctrinated. Spoken language reflects the instinct to establish fixed categories that exclude each other, boundaries that obscure perception and analysis. But the "dumb" protagonist finds freedom in silence. What he sees, uncensored, distresses and confuses him, but his vision is real: he sees that Jenny in her silence is "Just as another woman sleeps!" (l. 177). Courageously, he imagines "another woman" in the figure of his "cousin Nell," his possible bride (ll. 185-219): he silently dares to think of his wife and a whore simultaneously. His radical conjunction attacks, morally and socially, the roots of Western sexism.[19] Temporarily, it renders language and thought chaotic: the protagonist, his previous conceptions thrown "in heaps / Of doubt and horror," does not know "what to say / Or think" (ll. 178-180). As he sees the natural kinship between Jenny and Nell, Jenny becomes a person for whom he can have affections. Conventional distinctions between corruption and purity dissolve. A whore is not naturally evil, nor can he distinguish evil from good; the resemblance between Jenny and Nell "makes a goblin of the sun" (l. 206), turns all conventional moralities topsy-turvy, and mocks the patriarchal principle itself. He recognizes the central role of money and class in shaping individual histories: while Nell may use marriage to save herself from the economic necessities that compel Jenny to sell herself, the family of her "fair tree" may need economic assistance from Jenny's grandchildren (ll. 211-213); married women without other professions may not have the "moral" luxury to refuse the "tainted" money for which men indifferently strive. Even more outrageously, Nell's husband may at the Last Judgment confront his bastard daughter by the prostitute, a daughter "lost" (l. 218) in her mother's profession. Will the husband/customer/father name his bastard "whore" or "daughter"? Here, in this oblique autobiographical speculation, the protagonist confronts Nell's imagined husband with the same dilemmas in naming that he himself does. The blurring of categories in this intense moral self-confrontation forces a creative reexamination of existing codes of perception; in this explosion of the pieties of Victorian family life, the blurring has its being through a silence that eludes predetermined mental patterns.

The protagonist thus correlates silence with the possibilities of discovering truth or thinking clearly; utterance—including its artifactual forms as paintings or texts—means falsehood and deception. Rossetti's design implies a profoundly negative view of outward speech: if the linkage of speech and truth is structured to seem rare or impossible, if it is silence that is normatively associated with honesty and purity, then humankind's capacities for significant communication are severely limited. But these equations do not hold absolutely; both at the crisis of utterance ("What if to her all this were said?") and at the closure, Rossetti breaks them to assay a coincidence between speech and truth. These calculated near breaches of the silence stipulated by interior monologue warrant attention.

When the protagonist contemplates speaking "aloud," he risks self-exposure to attempt honesty, clarity in self-expression. His possible speech act reflects a need for catharsis derived directly from recognitions he cannot suppress: knowledge of human commodities (ll. 135-144), the vacant wastage of the whore's aging into disease (ll. 148-150), his own vision of the Chelsea Embankment as a "fiery serpent" (l. 154; see Numbers 21.4-9), an image of England's shamefully hypocritical infection by an evil it can purge only through an uncensored understanding. To voice such a knowledge would violate the social and personal taboos surrounding prostitution, name England's responsibility, and appraise honestly his own ambivalence as both a user of women and a potential reformer without a plan. With such a sounded publishing of unwanted truths, he would attempt to circumvent his education long enough to discover his own perceptions. Escaping from "ill" male speech, brutal and deceptive, he would seek a new language, desexualized and demonetized, liberated from the constraints against its power to shape rather than obey cultural laws; speaking out to Jenny, he would dismiss their traditional roles as buyer and seller to acknowledge Jenny's realness. While one may sentimentalize the protagonist's motives for speech—forget his constant lapses into stereotypical thinking, his prurience, his callow toying with Jenny as his property—his basic striving for some kind of honesty remains plain. But as Rossetti harshly demonstrates, the protagonist's courage to speak flags as it surfaces; the passive self-erasure in "What if to her all this were said" attests his uneasiness in criticizing a cultural system in which he, together with other men, enjoys dominance. He immediately retreats into a virulent attack against Jenny; his failure to speak "aloud," to break the form of interior monologue, constitutes a profoundly political balking at any alteration in the imbalances of sexual and economic power. He swallows his "true" speech back into an outward silence that resembles that of Lust, "deaf, blind, alone."

In the speech climax of **"Jenny,"** personal reformation is thwarted by an inveterate sexism and the protagonist's inability to breach his interior monologue with a "true" outward language free from male prejudices. By comparison, the closing attempts at utterance are more ambiguous. Here, self-conscious in his language use, increasingly critical of "ill" speech, he is nevertheless intermittently obtuse about the connotations of his discourse; yet he simultaneously displays a rare wit whose self-satire suggests a new capacity for analytic thought. The protagonist's linguistic behavior in the closure encapsulates the major themes and ambivalences of the poem; that he reaches no satisfactory resolution reflects Rossetti's pragmatic—and pessimistic—understanding that the revising of one's psyche cannot come instantaneously.

The protagonist makes two surrogate efforts to "speak" his feelings; both make sounds—a kiss, the "tinkling" of coin—that breach the silence of interior monologue without gaining the semantic content of spoken language. The first—"only one kiss" (l. 391)—is Rossetti's mordant comment on the form of his poem: the protagonist finally moves his mouth to demonstrate the interiority of his monologue. But this surrogate signifies poorly: if the kiss expresses affection, he also uses his mouth, not to speak, but to validate his masculinity by getting some sex for his money; his previous (illusory?) self-ennoblement in behaving chastely here yields to conventional desire. This intermixing of motives indicates that gesture itself cannot signify accurately; it requires speech to mean clearly. This problem recurs in the protagonist's other attempt to project his emotions outwards: is the money he leaves Jenny a gift or a payment? As another speech surrogate, coin tells less than gesture; it lacks the intrinsic affection of a kiss. What does this act mean? how is it related to sex and language use? how does the protagonist construe it?

First, the protagonist's giving money is a sexual act. As he carefully places his coins in Jenny's hair (l. 340) and then alludes to himself as Zeus showering Danaë's lap with his fertility, Rossetti again points to the protagonist's confusion of Jenny's head with her genitals.[20] Using money to enact a sexual event that never occurred, he reestablishes objectified relations between buyer and seller and bonds himself with other men in an approved male behavior. The implicit equation of semen with coin—as when the protagonist names sun and moon "life-coins" (l. 226)—sterilizes life forces. Thus monetized, the sexual instinct is reduced to its most universal and least kindred denominator, its market value. As with the Virgin's face in the "gilded aureole," sexual desire masks avarice: the "spending" of "coin" can never exhaust the "changeless sum" of lust (l. 278); this "money" moves from one hoard to another, from the male genitals to Jenny's "magic purse" (l. 344). Even if giving money is a charitable gesture, its value is defined by conventional sexual and monetary behavior. Giving charity instead of payment replaces contemporary Victorian values with a Christian behavior visible but barely actualized in the poem; here, the protagonist again rejects male culture by using money to express personal value, personal affection. Thus engaging in paradox—using a universal equivalent to embody particularities of tenderness—he seeks quixotically to change the "language" of money into a mode of signification it can never achieve. Money can only become a language, and not merely a contextual gesture, when it is enmeshed in a real language that states the emotions the coin represents.

The protagonist's gift/payment is also a specific linguistic act. Not only does he use money in place of spoken utterance, coins instead of words. With money he purchases time for new linguistic activity. Money sparks his fantasies of what Jenny will do with it; having bought Jenny's physical body, he also purchases license to imagine (and control?) her sexual future. Money, permitting his fantasy, also shapes its form: what he imputes to Jenny—dreams of power, economic independence, well-being (ll. 346-364)—are imaginings that all return to their point of economic enablement instead of transcending it. Similarly, religious worship is subliminally hostage to mercantile self-interest; like the beauty of religious icons, the elegance of these linguistic fantasies disguises the dehumanized labor of prostitution and "confers / New magic on the magic purse," by providing an attractive metaphor for the "Grim web . . . clogged with shrivelled flies!" (ll. 343-345). If the protagonist criticizes his trope for concealing economic realities, he pursues his linguistic decorations anyway; for all his easy wish that Jenny—given the proper clothes, carriage, economic freedom to maneuver—may marry and thus escape prostitution, he remains fundamentally more allured by the niceties of his own silent arabesques than by her history.

This predilection for linguistic self-seduction is particularly evident as he describes Jenny's transition from prostitute to wife:

> For even the Paphian Venus seems
> A goddess o'er the realms of love,
> When silver-shrined in shadowy grove:
> Aye, or let offerings nicely plac'd
> But hide Priapus to the waist,
> And whoso looks on him shall see
> An eligible deity.
>
> (ll. 365-371)

To remember that this crucial passage connects prostitution and marriage is to see how much the protagonist, prettifying his language, takes a self-conscious literary pleasure in removing the topic from Victorian England. As he subsumes Jenny's dreams to classical allusion, as the cash-rich Venus of ritual prostitution pimps for Jenny, an elegant linguistic surface disguises an analysis that the protagonist makes trenchant almost despite himself. The allusive language misnames the phenomenon, "covers for" corrupt and monetized sex. Ritual prostitution, acceptable to classical religion, is foreign to contemporary England: the Keatsian chiaroscuro, peaceably erasing ugliness, belies London prostitution as contemplated earlier. Such a glozing imagination is not purchased cheap; this one costs an Oxford education or its like. In this desperately arch view of prostitution, even the gods can be bribed to go straight. The tacit attack on religions for acquiescing in women's prostitution shows a "silver-shrined" goddess illumined by a moon denatured into coin; encased in the precious metal—like Priapus, like Lust—she is paralyzed by her mercantile identity. This conversion of sexual desire into avarice recurs in the pun that takes the "shadowy grove" genitally, enshrines it in coin, and fills it much as Jenny's "magic purse" is filled. The same meanings inform the image of Priapus, whose genitals are concealed by coin in hilarious modesty that accurately values his denatured sexuality.[21] Note the hypocrises: Priapus' monetary dress, as obscene as his sexual lust, does not offend Victorian pruderies; women marrying for money apparently love a chaste god but also seek the sexuality hidden behind the monetary disguise. Both Venus and Priapus are hoards to their respective lovers; the money they represent compensates for their grotesque sexual passions.

The verse paragraph is whimsically serious; its tone and diction evade the realities it embodies. When, mock-heroically, the protagonist casts himself and Jenny as Zeus and Danaë (ll. 376-379), he once again deploys ancient mythology to mask a situation he thinks shameful (ll. 92, 384). No matter that irony laces both passages, that Jenny as Danaë "for a moment" undercuts his mythologizing to show the tawdry melodrama of his imagination. At issue is the honesty of the protagonist's self-awareness: does he understand what his language implies? In all the images that beautify prostitution, his language remains thoroughly monetized; the core of economic transaction is irreducibly present, like the "changeless sum" of lust. Even when the protagonist expresses a genuine emotion, he cannot escape the monetized language by which he has treated all relations thus far. Yet he protests extravagantly:

> Jenny, my love rang true! for still
> Love at first sight is vague, until
> That tinkling makes him audible.
>
> (ll. 380-382)

In this discrimination between true and counterfeit coin (or feeling), his language of emotion is reified and quantified, made such by Victorian culture: human experiences are interpretable solely in monetary terms. As the protagonist renames his discourse "coinage," he levels the medium of communication to a universal equivalency that, because it can designate a value for all things, it cannot distinguish between particulars. Emotion, mind thought have no reality without material tokens.

This dark conclusion pertains directly to Rossetti's form and the protagonist's attitude toward his silent discourse: language has no being, silence cannot signify in a social context without physical signs as indicators; the personification Love has no credible existence until his grotesquely inappropriate attribute, the "tinkling" of coin, makes him physically "audible." The sound of money substitutes for sounded speech. As the protagonist worries about the disappearance of his interior monologue—the fact that it is nonexistent because not heard—he imagines that "These golden coins" can make Jenny realize his presence. This final maneuver substitutes money for both his imagined discourse and the speaking aloud he has refused. But coin mediates between silent monologue and the outer world in destructive ways. Money, cancelling genuine sex or emotion, also cancels the protagonist's discourse; Rossetti deploys this final mediation to stress the reality of that interior monologue. As the sole token of the protagonist's presence, money excludes all reference to speech or its possibility; what Jenny, waking, will see is neither the person who left it nor his thoughts; as Rossetti compares what Jenny sees with what the reader sees, he affirms the richness of silent discourse. Money may symbolize the discourse but, for all its "tinkling," cannot "speak" it. Static, fixed in its valuations, money negates variety, struggle, and all the protagonist's vacillations. The metonymic disguising of the monologue as a few coins, coming after such a tumultuous and sometimes courageous meditation, constitutes a brazenly false metaphor. But Rossetti's ultimate irony is that coin cancels the protagonist along with his discourse. Having chosen the "wrong" means of becoming "audible," he will be known only by his money; to Jenny, he will have reduced himself and his feelings to shiny metallic things. He becomes, like the prostitute, an object. With this final turn in the relations between silence and false speech, Rossetti's skill in shaping his form to his themes emerges afresh. The protagonist's silencing of his own discourse—not by keeping silent but by leaving money—is a censorship no less insidious than the censorship of public silence, for it pretends to have revealed and made open what in fact has been suppressed. Next to this negation of interior monologue, the artifactual reality of Rossetti's poem and its audacity in speaking out seem all the more impressive.

Notes

[1] Only Jan B. Gordon, "A Portrait of 'Jenny': Rossetti's Aesthetics of Communion," *HSL,* 1 (1969), 90, correctly names the poem an interior monologue; he follows the hint of William Clyde De Vane, "The Harlot and the Thoughtful Young Man: A Study of the Relation between Rossetti's *Jenny* and Browning's *Fifine at the Fair,*" *SP,* 29 (1932), 469, who writes of "the speaker of the poem, or rather the thinker of it." By contrast, Jules Paul Seigel, "*Jenny:* The Divided Sensibility of a Young and Thoughtful Man of the World," *SEL,* 9 (1969), 685, misses the interiority of the poem by calling it a spoken "dialogue of the mind with itself" in which "it makes little difference to the young man whether [Jenny] hears." Robert Buchanan ["Thomas Maitland"], "The Fleshly School of Poetry: Mr. D. G. Rossetti," *Contemporary Review,* 18 (1871), 344, calls the poem a "soliloquy"; so does R. G. Howarth, "On Rossetti's 'Jenny'," *N&Q,* 173 (1937), 20. Lise Rodgers, "The Book and the Flower: Rationality and Sensuality in Dante Gabriel Rossetti's *Jenny,*" *JNT,* 10 (1980), 159, thinks the poem a "dramatic monologue"; so also G. L. Hersey, "Rossetti's 'Jenny': A Realistic Altarpiece," *YR,* 69 (1979), 17. Ronnalie Roper Howard, *The Dark Glass: Vision and Technique in the Poetry of Dante Gabriel Rossetti* (Ohio Univ. Press, 1972), p. 100, calls it a "dramatic reflective poem"; Rosalie Glynn Grylls, "Rossetti and Browning," *PULC,* 33 (1972), 239, unaccountably claims that the poem is in "narrative form."

[2] Paull F. Baum, "The Bancroft Manuscripts of Dante Gabriel Rossetti," *MP,* 39 (1941), 50.

[3] For the protagonist's tendency to aestheticize his experience, see Gordon, passim; for his self-division, see in particular Seigel, passim. Rossetti's radical perspective in this poem derives partly from his engagement in revolutionary issues at the time of the first draft, 1848; his reformist interest in prostitution is reflected in his friendship with Josephine Butler, the crusader for prostitutes' rights (see Glen Petrie, *A Singular Iniquity: The Campaigns of Josephine Butler* [New York, 1971], p. 35). Rossetti owned Henry Mayhew's *London Labour and the London Poor* (1861), with Bracebridge Hemyng's long article on prostitution (see Helen Simpson Culler, "Studies in Rossetti's Reading," Diss. Yale Univ. 1943, p. 314). Nevertheless, Florence Saunders Boos, *The Poetry of Dante G. Rossetti: A Critical Reading and Source Study* (The Hague, 1976), p. 158, writes that "it does not occur to [the protagonist] that acts which the prostitute commits may be . . . the result of economic coercion rather than choice."

[4] Baum, p. 50. Nicholas Shrimpton, "Rossetti's Pornography," *EIC,* 29 (1979), 331, rightly observes that the poem derives from Coleridge's "conversation poems"; but he sees the conversation poem as "reflective" (p. 333) rather than dialogic and claims that "if 'Jenny' is a dramatic monologue it is not a very good one" (p. 325). In Dante Gabriel Rossetti, *Collected Works,* ed. William Michael Rossetti (London, 1897), I, xxvi, W. M. Rossetti remarks that "In the long run [Rossetti] perhaps enjoyed and revered Coleridge beyond any other modern poet whatsoever."

[5] Among the treatments of prostitution contemporaneous with "Jenny" are William Bell Scott, "Rosabell" (1837); Elizabeth Gaskell, *Mary Barton* (1848); William Holman Hunt, "The Shepherd Hireling" (1852) and "The Awakened Conscience" (1854); J. B. Talbot, *The Miseries of Prostitution* (London, 1844); William Acton, *Prostitution. Considered in its Moral, Social and Sanitary Aspects* (London, 1857); [W. R. Greg,]

Prostitution, The Westminster Review, 53 (1850), 448-506; and Henry Mayhew's various letters to *The Morning Chronicle* (1849). Buchanan, p. 343, typifies writers who would have preferred that prostitution remain undiscussed; De Vane, p. 472, minimizes the daring of "Jenny" in 1870.

[6] Compare Rodgers, p. 157, who equates the "book" with "rationality," as opposed to sensuality. Robert N. Keane, "Rossetti's 'Jenny': Moral Ambiguity and the '*Inner* Standing Point,'" *PLL,* 9 (1973), 276, observes more subtly that the protagonist's "own occupation as a writer [gives] him a strength that allows him to feel superior to Jenny."

[7] To the protagonist, Jenny falls asleep gradually. But the standard irony of dramatic monologue, that the monologist knows less than he might, suggests that Jenny sleeps throughout; the protagonist indifferently fails to notice.

[8] Rossetti's commentators, misunderstanding the dynamics of imputation in dramatic monologue, have taken the protagonist's subjectivity as objective truth. To Boos, p. 156, "Jenny is a weak, trivial person, attracted solely to money, personal finery, and gaudy luxuries"; for D. M. R. Bentley, "'Ah, Poor Jenny's Case': Rossetti and the Fallen Woman/Flower," *UTQ,* 50 (1980-81), 192, thinks that the protagonist sees Jenny "as she really is—a prostitute with the dreams of a prostitute." Compare Stephen J. Spector, "Love, Unity, and Desire in the Poetry of Dante Gabriel Rossetti," *ELH,* 38 (1971), 435: ironically, "the speaker has no knowledge at all of Jenny's mind, even though he pretends to read her thoughts."

[9] Compare Keane, p. 276, who accepts the protagonist's notion that Jenny's "mind is sluggish and corrupted"; Rodgers, pp. 161-162, argues of this passage that "He no longer assumes that her thoughts are designing, but simply that *she has none.*" Both readings miss the dynamics of recoil in this section.

[10] Her pose, derived from Sara Coleridge's in "The Eolian Harp" and the speaker's in Browning's "Porphyria's Lover," suggests her submissiveness; but Shrimpton, p. 336, argues that Jenny's position paralyzes the protagonist.

[11] Greg, p. 452 n. 2, cites a prostitute's "Verses for My Tombstone, If Ever I Should Have One" thus: *"My thoughts were racked in striving not to think";* See also p. 454: "If we did not drink, we could not stand the memory of what we have been, and the thought of what we are, for a day."

[12] "Jenny" (1858-59), MS, p. 11, in the Fairfax Murray Library, Fitzwilliam Museum, University of Cambridge; in a later ms in the Fitzwilliam Museum, p. 31, the protagonist blames himself for talking so much. Quoted by the kind permission of Mrs. Imogen Rossetti Dennis and the Syndics of the Fitzwilliam Museum, Cambridge.

[13] Compare Harold L. Weatherby, "Problems of Form and Content in the Poetry of Dante Gabriel Rossetti," *VP,* 2 (1964), 17: "'Jenny' does not commit [Rossetti] to the specific use of any sort of spiritual machinery"; Rossetti in fact pinions Jenny between specific Christian types to show how they compromise personal identity.

[14] Compare Rossetti's more callous first draft, whose syntax runs, "Like a toad within a stone . . . So art thou in this world, *ma belle*" (ll. 84, 99; Baum, pp. 50-51). Commentators have ignored the palimpsest of Rossetti's final version; Jenny herself has been incorrectly viewed as the symbol of lust. See, e.g., Rodgers, p. 164; Bentley, p. 179, 191; Gordon, p. 101; Seigel, p. 687.

[15] Commentators have avoided the monetary content of this image: see, e.g., Rodgers, p. 163; Gordon, pp. 98-99, both of whom explain the image away; Bentley, p. 190, calls the "gilded aureole" simply a "sign of sanctity."

[16] Rossetti revised this central line many times: "Whose acts are foul and his speech hard" (Bancroft MS, line 35; Baum, p. 49); "Whose nets are foul and his speech hard" (Fairfax Murray MS, p. 3). He did not reach the final text until the so-called Exhumation Proofs for *Poems* (1870), first proofs (second issue), after October 14, 1869 (Firestone Library, Princeton University).

[17] Rossetti conceived Jenny as a temporary, socially mobile prostitute, not caught for life; she exemplifies the kind described by Judith Walkowitz, "The Making of an Outcast Group," in Martha Vicinus, ed., *A Widening Sphere: Changing Roles of Victorian Women* (Indiana Univ. Press, 1977), pp. 72-79, particularly those who move to the city rather than face rural impoverishment.

[18] As Hersey, p. 18, observes, Rossetti deliberately omits Mistress Quickly's concluding clause, "if she be a whore." He thus has her cancel Jenny entirely, in a censorship that leaves no room for the ambiguity—the "if"—of Jenny's situation; the irony of Mistress Quickly posing as staunch moralist is delicious. Compare Bentley, p. 185; Keane, p. 273.

[19]Bentley, p. 189, strangely suggests that this passage "could be dismissed as a simple error of taste"; but Rodgers, p. 162, rightly identifies it as the moral climax of the poem.

[20]Shrimpton, p. 325, takes the giving of money only as "an act of charity"; so also Rodgers, p. 165.

[21]Compare Gordon, p. 102, who argues that Jenny herself becomes "an eligible deity," whereas it is the god Priapus himself who grossly lures the ladies.

Jean Wasko (essay date 1987)

SOURCE: "The Web of Eroticism in Rossetti's 'Troy Town,' 'Eden Bower,' and 'Rose Mary,'" in *Papers on Language and Literature,* Vol. 23, No. 3, Summer, 1987, pp. 333-44.

[*In the following essay, Wasko explores Rossetti's alignment of eroticism with themes of death, destruction, and deceit in three ballads written between 1869 and 1871.*]

In the introductory sonnet to ***The House of Life*** Dante Gabriel Rossetti suggests that the sonnet pays "tribute" or addresses itself to a threefold theme—life, love, and death, a focus which his ballads share.[1] Several of his early ballads, written between 1848 and 1854 when he was also busy translating the *Vita Nuova,* offer variations on a Dantesque vision of love as the creative, dynamic force in this triune complex. Thus love, as a source of heavenly salvation in **"The Staff and Scrip,"** triumphs over death in a setting characterized by ornate medievalism. In the more earthy **"Stratton Water,"** love—this time physical rather than spiritual—is a natural, vital force, a prime mover in the cycle of life. And **"The Bride's Prelude,"** a third ballad from this early period, shows that life has no force, no vivifying movement, without the saving power of love. But in mid-life, no longer content with the vision of the *Vita Nuova,* Rossetti added a new dimension to his old theme, focusing in the ballads from this period on the destructive potential of love in its relationship to life and death. In **"Troy Town," "Eden Bower,"** and **"Rose Mary,"** written between 1869 and 1871, the medievalism that Rossetti found useful in presenting the spiritual quality of creative love gives way to a new metaphor—emphatic eroticism.

Many critics have written about the erotic qualities of Rossetti's art, but his own comments prove most telling. In response to Robert Buchanan's charge of "fleshliness," Rossetti defended the sensual elements in his poetry. Admitting that the sonnet now called **"Nuptial Sleep"** embodies a "beauty of universal function" (482), Rossetti argued that the spirituality of the greater part of ***The House of Life*** outweighs the sensuality of this one stanza: "here all the passionate and just delights of the body are declared—somewhat figuratively, it is true, but unmistakably—to be naught if not ennobled by the concurrence of the soul at all times" (482). Further, he notes:

> That I may nevertheless take a wider view than some poets or critics of how much, in the material conditions absolutely given to man to deal with as distinct from his spiritual aspirations, is admissible within the limits of Art,—this I say, is possible enough; nor do I wish to shrink from such responsibility. But to state that I do so to the ignoring or overshadowing of spiritual beauty, is an absolute falsehood. . . . [485-86]

When Rossetti speaks of "material conditions" in relation to love, he speaks of physical passion, the concrete manifestation of an always more important spiritual relationship. This particular argument presents none of the irreconcilable tension that certain scholars find between themes associated with **"Body's Beauty"** and **"Soul's Beauty"** in Rossetti's works.[2] It gives credence instead to Yeats's view of the morally satisfying aesthetic synthesis that Rossetti creates: "He listens to the cry of the flesh till it becomes proud and passes beyond the world where some immense desire that the intellect cannot understand mixes with the desire for a body's warmth and softness." Thus physical passion becomes rarified, but as Bowra notes, never "so rarified that it seems to have no relation to any familiar world." For, he concludes, "Rossetti knew that there is one beauty of the flesh and another beauty of the spirit," which "in the end . . . are united in a single harmony," so that ideally, "each fulfills and glorifies the other."[3] Although Rossetti, as a painter and poet, is often accused of sensual excesses, three of his most sensuous poems, **"Troy Town," "Eden Bower,"** and **"Rose Mary,"** show a moral perspective which condemns sensuality that is unalloyed with a more powerful spirituality, even as Rossetti seems, finally, to question the redemptive power of spiritual love.

"Troy Town" and **"Eden Bower"** are each designed to illustrate an upset in the ideal balance between the worship of beauty of the spirit and beauty of the flesh, a dichotomy drawn in the sonnets written to accompany two paintings. These sonnets, **"Soul's Beauty"** and **"Body's Beauty,"** clarify the stories behind the beautiful women in *Sibylla Palmifera* and *Lilith.* In *Sibylla Palmifera* Rossetti intended "to embody the . . . Principle of Beauty which draws all high-toned men to itself, whether with the aim of embodying it in art or attaining it in life."[4] The worship of the lady in **"Soul's Beauty"** has an uplifting effect on her "bondsman" since following ideal beauty gives form to his life. On the other hand, the Lilith figure, in the painting for which the sonnet **"Body's Beauty"** was written, uses her beauty to destroy. She "draws men to watch the bright web she can weave / Till hearts and body and life are in its hold" (216). When the spiritual component in the quest for beauty is absent, the impulse toward that beauty becomes erotic rather than uplifting, and the outcome, according to Rossetti's essentially moral perspective, is destruction and death.

In **"Troy Town"** Rossetti presents the two faces of beauty and shows the destruction which results when beauty elicits a purely erotic response. Although the poem is a ballad, its narrative action is limited by Rossetti's focus on the moment of pause between two well-known stories. Prior to the Trojan War Helen, in the temple of Venus, offers the goddess a cup in the shape of her breast. In return for her gift, she asks for the love of Paris, to whom Venus owes a debt. Venus, with a smug awareness of future catastrophe, grants the wish, and Cupid's arrows strike the ill-fated pair. In the final stanza, Paris, caught in a web of desire, longs "to clasp" Helen's "golden head!" (307). Helen's reminder to Venus of her debt to Paris recalls the story which precedes the poem. The echoing refrain forecasts the fall of Troy, the story to come when Helen's beauty is rewarded as she wishes. The refrain—*"O Troy Town! . . . O Troy's down, / Tall Troy's on fire!"*—and other repetitive devices do more than merely add to the suspense and the sense of inevitability. As Ronnalie Roper Howard comments: "The refrain has its own kind of music, a harsh clanging which suggests catastrophe . . . the refrain is the poem's comment on the destructiveness of eroticism and briefly sums up the whole theme of the poem in every stanza."[5] The refrain functions as the warp of a fabric having alternating strands of eroticism and death.

The first stanza of **"Troy Town,"** which establishes the thematic tension between "soul's beauty" and "body's beauty," is formally split by the alternating refrain lines. Helen is both "Heavenborn" and the earthly queen of Sparta. Her "two breasts" are "the sun and moon of the heart's desire," suggesting opposing forces (305).[6] "Love's lordship" lies between the two poles of beauty and may by drawn in either direction. The refrain, which divides the stanza and focuses on the fall of Troy, serves to emphasize the destruction which results when eroticism, the attractive force of body's beauty, is out of control. The images of beauty in the stanza contrast sharply with the images of destruction in the refrain which laments the fall of Troy, *"O Troy Town!,"* and suggests spent passion through phallic and fire images, *"O Troy's down, / Tall Troy's on fire!"*

In addition to developing the idea of duality, the refrain links death with eroticism in the texture of **"Troy Town."** Those critical statements that have not been kind to this refrain seem based on a misunderstanding of Rossetti's intention. Friedman, who views the poem only as it relates to the ballad tradition, writes: "When Helen in the early passages is negotiating her translation to Troy, the burden . . . stimulates lively forebodings; in the later stanzas, it contributes nothing." But he does not see the refrain in terms of a sustained pattern of eroticism and death. Robert Cooper calls the refrain "monotonous." Waugh, who finds the poem effective when read aloud, notes that the refrain exercises "a hypnotic effect on the hearer, drawing him into the poem."[7] This, it seems, is the effect Rossetti wished to create, in order to show, through the form of the poem, the seductive power of eroticism which ensnares "the hearts and body and life" (216) of those who are enthralled by body's beauty.

Rossetti uses repetition, another ballad device, to weave the stanzaic web more tightly. Howard names "repetition, sexual suggestion, and sexual symbolism" as the major poetic devices, noting that "repetition emphasizes physical passion, suggesting obsessive force."[8] Further, these devices serve to enhance the already tight stanzaic structure. Each seven-line stanza has only three rhymes. Two of these are repeated in all fourteen stanzas, and, in addition to the refrain, every fourth line ends in "heart's desire." The prominent beat of the trochaic tetrameter lines alternates with the shorter, heavily stressed refrain. And the tetrameter lines often begin and end with stressed syllables in order to heighten the beat. This tight, almost metronomic, stanzaic pattern is augmented by repetitions which tend to group at points of erotic intensity. The conclusion of the poem, for example, is replete with repetition and added internal rhyme:

Paris turned upon his bed,
(O Troy Town!)
Turned upon his bed and said,
Dead at heart with heart's desire—
"Oh to clasp her golden head!"
(O Troy's down,
Tall Troy's on fire!)

[307]

With the rhyme of "bed," "dead," and "head," Rossetti knots the strands of eroticism and death woven throughout the poem.

At another point of erotic intensity the imagery works with the repetition and internal rhyme to draw diverse elements in the narrative together. Specifically, the image of the apple unites the stories that precede and follow the incident narrated in the poem. Helen reminds Venus that "Once an apple stirred the beat / Of thy heart with heart's desire" (306). As Venus had coveted an apple to reward her beauty, Helen covets Paris, the ill-fated Trojan prince, as a reward for her own. The lines also suggest the biblical story in which, traditionally, an apple leads to sexual passion and another fall. Further, Helen relates the image of the apple to the earlier image of her breasts in a purely sensual stanza:

"Mine are apples grown to the south,
(O Troy Town!)
Grown to taste in the days of drouth,
Taste and waste to the heart's desire:
Mine are apples meet for his mouth."
(O Troy's down,
Tall Troy's on fire!)

[306]

The erotic nature of the relationship Helen seeks is clear. With the link between the apple, sexual passion, the garden of Eden, and the fall established, the web is complete. In the subsequent stanzas, with the prominent ballad rhythm suggesting inevitability, Venus and Cupid do their work, and when Paris falls victim to body's beauty, Troy falls with him.

In **"Eden Bower,"** like **"Troy Town"** in its use of eroticism, Rossetti focuses directly on the Adamic myth. Lilith, a snake given woman's form for Adam's pleasure, has been cast outside the garden upon the creation of Eve, his human wife.[9] In a long, seductive monologue culminating with her description of the Fall, Lilith tries to persuade the snake, her former mate, to exchange his shape for hers so that she can tempt Eve. Motivated by hatred and the desire for revenge, Lilith uses her sexuality as her strength, and the power of eroticism is once again the focus of the poem.

While **"Troy Town"** focuses on the fatal attraction of eroticism, Lilith's passion is repulsive or "grotesque."[10] It is not simply body's beauty that ensnares in **"Eden Bower."** In its portrayal of the potentially destructive side of love, **"Eden Bower"** shows love's power to deceive. The central problem the poem presents is our inability to distinguish erotic attraction from love's spiritually uplifting passion. Here deceit leads man into the erotic death trap.

The element of deceit begins in the title of the poem, which plays upon the double significance of "Bower." In its relation to Eden the word suggests prelapsarian shelter, but it also evokes the connotation of a lady's bedroom, particularly to those familiar with Rossetti's **"Song of the Bower."** Thus, the drama of the poem takes place in a setting which combines innocence and experience. The changeable figure of Lilith introduces a further element of deception, for although "Not a drop of her blood was human, / . . . she was made like a soft sweet woman" (308). The form that eroticism takes, then, is problematic because passion so closely resembles love. Yet as the next stanza suggests, the consequences of mistaking the two are grave:

> Lilith stood on the skirts of Eden;
> *(Alas the hour!))*
> She was the first that thence was driven;
> With her was hell and with Eve was heaven.
>
> [308]

Following Eve leads to salvation while the worship of Lilith results in damnation.[11]

Throughout the poem the refrain relates the theme of deceit to the consequences of eroticism. The refrain line, *"Sing Eden Bower!"* is a final condensation of two earlier versions, *"Sing the bower in flower,"* and *"Eden Bower's in flower."*[12] Although Rossetti came to see that the longer lines would interrupt the movement of the poem, the spirit of the original lines, which suggest that Eden is fruitful, happy, and safe, is retained. The alternate lines, *"Alas the hour!"* revised from *"And it's O the day and the hour!"* emphasize the deception in the first lines by hinting at the impending fall. Thus Eden, like Lilith, seems to change its shape from stanza to stanza.

Rossetti adapts the incremental repetition techniques of the traditional ballad in order to create a pattern of duplicity and deceit. The ninth stanza, for example, which begins "O thou God, the Lord God of Eden!" echoes blasphemously in the tenth stanza, "O thou Snake, the King-snake of Eden!" as Lilith worships good and evil with the same words (309). Repetition draws a similar parallel in another pair of stanzas in which Lilith addresses the snake as "O my love, thou Love-snake of Eden!" and then "O bright Snake, the Death-worm of Adam!" (312). Much has been made of these lines as the link between eroticism and death, but they are also a part of the pattern of deception.[13] The love that leads to hell often takes the same form as the love that leads to heaven. Further, the incremental series beginning "Lend thy shape for the love of Lilith!" and continuing, "for the hate of Adam . . . for the shame of Eden!" suggests a confusion of motivating emotions (310). The repetitive line "Lo God's grace, by the grace of Lilith!" (313) is far-reaching in its duplicity. The concept of grace figures prominently in several ballads that develop variations on the love theme. Death in **"The Staff and Scrip,"** for example, becomes the lady's "gift and grace" (80) because dying for true love leads to salvation. In **"Troy's Town"** Venus laughs at Helen and taunts, "Thy gift hath grace" (307), suggesting that Helen will be rewarded with the love she requests, a grace that will lead, ironically, to destruction. **"Eden Bower"** draws upon both uses of "grace," emphasizing the duplicity in a relationship that can lead to eternal happiness or eternal damnation.

The biblical story in **"Eden Bower"** is, after all, a story of deceit. The serpent in the garden, whether it be the devil or Lilith, deceives Eve, who deceives Adam, who, in turn, tries to deceive God. But as Lilith points out in an imagined taunt to Eve, God will not be fooled although Adam will try to blame Eve who will accuse the snake. Both are cast out of Eden into a new life, but the pattern of duplicity continues. Eve will be both "bride" and "mother" (313); the pair will produce "two babes" who will be both "travail and treasure." Part of the tragedy of the poem's conclusion is the ambiguity regarding the nature of love that remains both a blessing and a curse.,

In **"Rose Mary,"** written in 1871, Rossetti reworks the theme of deceit and attempts to resolve the problem left open at the end of **"Eden Bower."** This poem is staged once again in a medieval setting. Traditional gothic trappings—a crystal from the exotic East, a secret shrine full of symbols, a seer, and an atmosphere of mystery—adorn this poem as the elements of medieval romance decorate **"The Staff and Scrip"** and **"The Bride's Prelude."** Rose Mary, at her mother's urging, looks into the beryl stone to see if danger lurks on the path that her lover James will follow on his way to make shrift before their wedding day. Only a virgin, according to the tradition that Rossetti draws upon, can see into the beryl.[14] Because Rose Mary is not a virgin, the vision that the beryl allows her is false. She sees an ambush in the valley where James's sworn foe, the Wardin of Holycleugh, waits. Advised to take the high road to avoid him, James is killed in an ambush on a misty hill. Evil spirits had entered the beryl stone and deceived the sinful seer. Watching over the dead knight's body, Rose Mary's mother finds a letter in his pocket wrapped in a lock of golden hair, not one of her daughter's dark tresses. The hair, she discovers, belongs to Jocelind, sister of the Wardin of Holycleugh, whom James intended to marry. Rose Mary, unaware of James's treachery, enters the shrine of the beryl. Conscious of the evil in the stone, she cleaves it with a sword, knowing that the act of destroying the stone will bring her death. Because she has remained faithful, she is transported to heaven while James is consigned to hell.

In keeping with the ballad tradition, **"Rose Mary"** begins with dialogue which is employed at intervals throughout. At times, particularly when the narrative advances, the language is beautifully and appropriately simple in the best ballad style:

> Daughter, once more I bid you read;
> But now let it be for your own need:
> Because to-morrow, at break of day,
> To Holy Cross he rides on his way
> Your knight Sir James of Heronhaye."
>
> [103]

The stanza, with the tetrameter rhythm of the traditional ballad, is once again Rossetti's own five-line variation. Vogel notes that the alternation of couplets and triplets and the limited enjambment produce the effect of a refrain ballad, which he describes as "a kind of inexorableness—a feeling of advancing steadily through the tale's ominous events to its final catastrophe."[15] Rossetti avoids the abrupt transitions that are characteristic of the ballad only by introducing the Beryl Songs to link the sections.

Although **"Rose Mary"** has much in common with the traditional ballad both in form and in narrative development, like Rossetti's other ballads it is not simply a poem that tells a story. Although the unifying force of the erotic metaphor in the earlier ballads is absent in **"Rose Mary,"** the same human passions concern Rossetti. The idea of love as a deceiver, developed in **"Eden Bower,"** is broadened in **"Rose Mary"** where life itself becomes a mystery to be read and interpreted. After Rose Mary has been deceived by the beryl, her mother's words sum up the theme of the poem:

> "Ah! would to God I clearly told
> How strong those powers, accurst old:
> Their heart is the ruined house of lies;
> O girl, they can seal the sinful eyes,
> Or show the truth by contraries."
>
> [117]

It has been said that Rossetti's ***The House of Life*** might more appropriately be called *The House of Love;* here in keeping with the theme of deceit, the same human sphere becomes a "house of lies." Howard describes this poem as "Rossetti's largest treatment of the essential opacity of the universe and human life," an opacity which, it would seem, becomes actively malevolent at times.[16]

The difference between appearance and reality lies, as Howard suggests, at the center of this poem, where each section presents a central deceit.[17] In the first section, the mother believes that her daughter is pure so she encourages her to read the beryl. The girl's very name testifies to her purity.[18] The mother's ironic words "A bride you'll be, as a maid you are" (104) capsulize the element of deceit and forecast the tragic conclusion, for Rose Mary is not a maid, nor will she be a bride. Toward the conclusion of this section Rose Mary expresses relief: "Thank God, thank God, thank God I saw" (117). But she has not seen the truth. In the second section, where the mother knows of her daughter's sin, James's betrayal becomes the central deceit, again underscored by an ironic remark: "Be sure as he loved you, so will I!" (117). But James did not love Rose Mary, and love, like sight, cannot be trusted. In the third section the mother learns of James's betrayal, but Rose Mary never does. Her last words reveal her delusion:

> "One were our hearts in joy and pain,
> And our souls e'en now grow one again.
> And O my love, if our souls are three,
> O thine and mine shall the third soul be,—
> One threefold love eternally."
>
> [132]

She cleaves the beryl and dies for the sake of a spiritualized, idealized love, but love has deceived her.

The beryl lies at the center of the theme of deceit, for as soon as the stone is introduced, the pattern of narrative simplicity breaks down. Descriptive similes, images of cloud and shadow, and an element of mystery accompany the beryl stone. The mother's words as she addresses the beryl, in sharp contrast with the earlier simplicity in her dialogue, take on the tone of incantation and share the opaque quality of the beryl:

"Ill fare" (she said) "with a fiend's faring:
But Moslem blood poured forth like wine
Can hallow Hell, 'neath the Sacred Sign:
And my lord brought this from Palestine."

[105]

The descriptive passages relating to the secret shrine of the beryl are intricate, symbolic and gothic:

To the north, a fountain glittered free;
To the south, there glowed a red fruit-tree;
To the east, a lamp flames high and fair;
To the west, a crystal casket rare
Held fast a cloud of fields of air.

[128]

Although the beryl songs have met with much adverse criticism, including, finally, Rossetti's own condemnation, they fit into the pattern of confusion that surrounds that stone.

For Rossetti, the beryl represented a microcosm of the world. To his old friend Dr. Thomas Gordon Hake, Rossetti wrote: "Many thanks for your information about the Beryl. I had no idea what the stone was really like, but perceive that for my purpose the elements must be somehow mystically condensed in it as a sort of mimic world."[19] In the poem itself the description of the beryl evokes the idea that the stone reflects the world:

Shaped it was to a shadowy sphere,—
World of our world, the sun's compeer,
That bears and buries the toiling year.

[104]

The world that the beryl reflects is the world of half-truths, of shadows, and of mists. Rose Mary, who hides her own sin, fears that the pastoral vision may hide a terrible reality:

"Ah! vainly I searched from side to side:—
Woe's me! and where do the foemen hide?
Woe's me! and perchance I pass them by,
And under the new dawn's blood-red sky
Even where I gaze the dead shall lie."

[107]

The fear that sin will obscure her vision is justified; the sins of the flesh prevent her from seeing the truth, which for Rossetti is spiritual love.[20]

The problem of reading the signs in a confused opaque world is developed further through the images of sight and blindness. When Rose Mary saw the vision of death, she "shrank blindfold in her fallen hair" (108). The significance of hair in relation to the image pattern of sight is particularly evocative. In **"Body's Beauty," "Eden Bower,"** and **"Troy Town,"** hair has been associated with eroticism; here too James's betrayal is discovered through a telltale lock of hair. It is fitting, then, that Rose Mary's blindness, the result of her sin, is evoked with the image of hair. Ironically, the mother advises her daughter to "Fear no trap you cannot see" (110), and Rose Mary, reassured, expresses her relief: "thank God I saw!" (112). But she has been deceived by appearances.

The vision of salvation through love in **"Rose Mary"** lacks the conviction behind a similar salvation in **"The Staff and Scrip."** The lines regarding heavenly reunion, resonant with religiosity—"And our souls e'en now grow one again . . . One threefold love eternally" (132)—must be read ironically. The erotic vision of love's dark deceitful side developed in **"Troy Town"** and **"Eden Bower"** ultimately foils Rossetti's attempt to return to the Dantesque ideal. As a synthesis of spirituality and eroticism, "Rose Mary" fails because the happy ending is undercut by irony.

Thus these three ballads show the process through which Rossetti's early Dantesque faith in love evolves into a more complex vision. **"Troy Town"** suggests that the saving power of love, prominent in the early ballads, is balanced by an equally powerful destructive impulse, embodied in the metaphor of eroticism. In **"Eden Bower"** our inability to distinguish between spiritual love and erotic attraction defies resolution. In **"Rose Mary"** the power of the erotic vision and the dilemma that it presents undercut the salvation offered by love. Rossetti's exposure, in the erotic ballads, of love as a two-faced deceiver prohibits our faith in its gift of grace.

Notes

[1] Dante Gabriel Rossetti, *The Collected Works of Dante Gabriel Rossetti,* ed. William Michael Rossetti (London: Ellis and Elvey, 1887) 1: 176. All future references to Rossetti's poetry are to this edition and will be cited parenthetically in the text.

[2] See Philip McM. Pittman, "The Strumpet and the Snake: Rossetti's Treatment of Sex as Original Sin," *Victorian Poetry* 12 (1974): 46-47; David Sonstroem, *Rossetti and the Fair Lady* (Middletown, CT: Wesleyan UP, 1970) 16; and Masao Miyoshi, *The Divided*

Self: A Perspective on the Literature of the Victorians (New York: New York UP, 1969) 252.

[3] W. B. Yeats, "The Happiest of the Poets," *Essays and Introductions* (New York: Collier, 1973) 53; Cecil Bowra, *The Romantic Imagination* (1949; New York: Oxford UP, 1961) 211-12.

[4] Rossetti cited by Oswald Doughty, *A Victorian Romantic: Dante Gabriel Rossetti* (1949; London: Oxford UP, 1960) 347.

[5] Ronnalie Roper Howard, *The Dark Glass: Vision and Technique in the Poetry of Dante Gabriel Rossetti* (Athens, OH: Ohio UP, 1972) 142.

[6] To note just a few examples, the sonnet "Passion and Worship" in the concluding sestet associates the sun with passion and the moon with worship. The two sonnets "Silent Noon" and "Gracious Moonlight" seem to contrast physical with spiritual love.

[7] Albert B. Friedman, *The Ballad Revival: Studies in the Influences of Popular on Sophisticated Poetry* (Chicago: U of Chicago P, 1961) 323; Robert Cooper, *Lost on Both Sides: Dante Gabriel Rossetti: Critic and Poet* (Athens, OH: Ohio UP, 1970) 202; Evelyn Waugh, *Rossetti: His Life and Works* (New York: Dodd, 1928) 157.

[8] Howard 141.

[9] Pittman notes the sources for the Lilith legend as Jewish folklore and Talmudic legend (47).

[10] Howard 144; Pittman 52.

[11] Barbara Charlesworth Gelpi, in "The Feminization of D. G. Rossetti," *The Victorian Experience: The Poets,* ed. Richard A. Levine (Athens, OH: Ohio UP, 1982) writes about Rossetti's "ambivalence" toward women: "The goddess of one painting turns siren or betrayer in another—or . . . a combination of the two" (102).

[12] Paull Franklin Baum, ed., *Dante Gabriel Rossetti: Poems and Ballads and Sonnets: Selections from the Posthumous Poems and Hand and Soul* (Garden City: Doubleday, 1937) 55.

[13] Howard 148.

[14] Clyde K. Hyder, "Rossetti's 'Rose Mary': A study in the Occult," *Victorian Poetry* 1 (1963): 205. Hyder discusses crystal-gazing and legendary sources associated with it.

[15] Joseph F. Vogel, *Dante Gabriel Rossetti's Versecraft,* U of Florida Humanities Monograph 34 (Gainsville: U of Florida P, 1971) 57.

[16] Howard 155.

[17] Howard 153-54.

[18] For comment on Rossetti's use of the name Rose Mary, see Doughty 447; Howard 153; Hyder 199; and Sonstroem 101.

[19] Rossetti, *Letters of Dante Gabriel Rossetti,* ed. Oswald Doughty and John Robert Wahl (London: Clarendon, 1965) 3: 1010.

[20] For quite a different reading, which presents this poem as Rossetti's triumph over Victorian morality that would condemn Rose Mary for her sexual sin, see David G. Riede, *Dante Gabriel Rossetti and the Limits of Victorian Vision* (Ithaca, NY: Cornell UP, 1983) 171-78.

Jerome McGann (essay date 1988)

SOURCE: "Dante Gabriel Rossetti and the Betrayal of Truth," in *Victorian Poetry,* Vol. 26, No. 4, Winter, 1988, pp. 339-61.

[*In the following essay, McGann traces Rossetti's career-spanning concern with disillusionment and the betrayal of artistic ideals.*]

Rossetti has a notebook entry dating from the early 1870s in which he speaks of certain "Days when the characters of men came out as strongly as secret writing exposed to fire."[1] What is illuminating and complex in this figure centers in the pun on the word "characters," where both people and writing are imagined as encrypted forms—indeed, as encrypted transforms of each other. Their respective truths appear only when the false innocence of the surface is removed.

As with Blake, when he spoke of a similar process in *The Marriage of Heaven and Hell,* the agent of revelation here is fire, and a fire associated, as in Blake, with hell. But in Blake there is nothing sinister in such fire, which is seen as a "divine" agency (that is to say, as part of the human process of engraving). In Rossetti, however, the fire threatens because the "characters" are sinister and threatening. Lurking below Rossetti's metaphor are suggestions of torture and even damnation, of a world in which "the characters of men" practice concealment and deceit.

This is not an image which Rossetti would have produced when he began to test his imaginative resources in the 1840s. But it has arrived at the heart of his work, and it can help to guide us should we choose to approach him from more customary angles—for example, down the avenues of his early prose works like **"Hand and Soul"** or the fragmentary **"St. Agnes of**

Intercession." These tales seem typically Rossettian in their treatment of the relation between love and art; but their extreme deceptiveness, their preoccupation with false appearances, is equally central to what they are doing, and equally a Rossettian trademark.

Like its companion tale **"Hand and Soul," "St. Agnes of Intercession"** anatomizes the character and situation of a young painter whose "impulse towards art" was "a vital passion" (1:400).[2] When he falls in love with a young woman of comfortable means—as he puts it, "of more ease than my own" (1:402)—he is driven to seek "such a position as would secure me from reproaching myself with any sacrifice made for her sake." That is the young man's painfully delicate way of saying that he set about trying to become a commercially successful painter, which meant, in practical terms, submitting his work for exhibition. To this end he "laboured constantly and unweariedly" for many days and nights on a work whose "principal female figure" was his betrothed, Miss Mary Arden.

In these initial details we glimpse the characteristic tension which will dominate Rossetti's story: between an exalted ideal of art, on one hand, and certain quotidian practical exigencies on the other. The young man's reflections on the opening day of the exhibition make these contradictions very explicit:

> My picture, I knew, had been accepted, but I was ignorant of a matter perhaps still more important,—its situation on the walls. On that now depended its success. . . . That is not the least curious feature of life as evolved in society,— . . . when a man, having endured labour, gives its fruits into the hands of other men, that they may do their work between him and mankind: confiding it to them, unknown, without seeking knowledge of them . . . without appeal to the sympathy of kindred experience: submitting to them his naked soul, himself, blind and unseen. (1:403)

Centrally at issue here is the public and commercial "success" of the work, as opposed to its "artistic achievement" or "intrinsic value." Or rather, the passage shows how the sensibility of a man who is committed to the "intrinsic values" of art suffers a crucifixion of the imagination when he feels compelled to operate in and through the mediations "evolved in society." His initial anxiety about whether his picture will even be accepted for exhibition succeeds to a whole train of others which crystallize in one immediate concern: whether the painting will be prominently displayed—in the jargon of the day, whether it will be "on the line"—or whether it will be relegated to some less prestigious, or even less visible, position.

These misgivings surface as soon as he begins to make a tour of the exhibition with another man, also unnamed in the story, whom the painter accidentally encounters. This man, a poet and an art critic, gives a further turn of the screw to the young painter's anxieties. Rossetti's painter fears and respects his companion's power in the culture-industry of their world, but he has only contempt for the man's artistic taste and poetic skills. He is able to conceal his actual views and feelings until the poet-critic pauses in their tour of the exhibition, pulls out a sheaf of his poems, and asks the painter for his opinion. After reading them hurriedly the young man manages an answer. It is a nice moment:

> "I think," I coolly replied, "that when a poet strikes out for himself a new path in style, he should first be quite convinced that it possesses sufficient advantages to counterbalance the contempt which the swarm of his imitators will bring upon poetry."
>
> My ambiguity was successful. I could see him take the compliment to himself, and inhale it like a scent, while a slow broad smile covered his face. It was much as if, at some meeting, on a speech being made complimentary to the chairman, one of the waiters should elbow that personage aside, plant his knuckles on the table, and proceed to return thanks. (1:407)

This passage dramatizes the deep connections joining the painter's artistic fastidiousness and "idealism" to his tortured duplicity and servile cowardice. "Successful" is just the right word, in this context, to describe his wary but contemptuous reply to the other man's fatuous request for praise. If he wants to be "successful" as an artist, he cannot afford to offend this man. Indeed, he even has to cultivate him to some extent. So the young painter stays with him throughout the exhibition, suffering his absurd displays of self-importance. Through it all, however, the young painter keeps his distance from the man—inwardly, spiritually, in secret. He practices a fraud on his companion when he equivocates about the man's bad verse. That false representation is his way of preserving his sense of integrity and his commitment to true art. The moment is troubled and troubling, however, because it sets those key Rossettian values quite literally on a false ground.

The entire scene from **"St. Agnes of Intercession,"** written in 1848-50 (but revised in 1870),[3] is thus an emblem of Rossetti's career as an artist and poet. Later I will return to deal with the matter of Miss Mary Arden—that is to say, with Rossetti's habit of linking his artistic ideals and imaginative practices to the women whose images dominated his life. For now I wish to concentrate on the problem of the material conditions of artistic production as Rossetti experienced them in his age. Unlike Blake's and Byron's, Rossetti's work does not foreground the artistic opportunities which are offered when an artist seeks to utilize the physical and institutional structures within which all such work is necessarily carried out. Rossetti is as self-conscious as they are about those media, but to him the structures more often rose up as obstacles to be overcome rather than adventures to be risked. **"St. Agnes of Intercession,"** in the scene I have been recapitulating, pays greatest attention to the difficulties raised by the institutions of imagination: most particularly, those means of production which establish the possibility, or the terms, on which a painter or a poet is able to encounter an audience.

If Rossetti's feeling for those difficulties makes him a less innocent poet than either Blake or Byron, it also set him in a position where he could explore, far more profoundly than any English poet had previously done, the significance of imaginative work in an age of mechanical reproduction, in an age where "the best that has been known and thought in the world" is seen to be quite literally a *product,* the output of what we now call the "culture" or the "consciousness industries." Like Baudelaire in France, Rossetti was the first poet in England to see this very clearly; and, again like Baudelaire, he recoiled from it, and tried to imagine ways for evading those institutional powers, and for recovering an ideal of artistic and poetic transcendence. But like Baudelaire once again, what he accomplished was far otherwise and far more important. What he accomplished was a critical definition of the symbolistic imagination when its work has been forced by circumstance to be carried out within a marketing and commercial frame of reference.

II

In that context, Rossetti is constantly driven to work by indirection. This happens because he operates in the belief—the ideology—that life is one thing, art another. Art for Rossetti appeared to him—as in Chiaro's vision in **"Hand and Soul"**—as life in its finer tone, the one certain means by which human beings can soar beyond the confusions of a mortal and veiled existence. His ideology of the sacred character of the poetic life made him an acute observer of the illusions of the quotidian world—in this he is like his sister Christina. But whereas, for her, sacramentalism—the ritually practiced religious life—was the one fundamental necessity, for Dante Gabriel that necessity was located in the practice of art.

This point of view established the basic contradiction within which Rossetti's work was to develop. The practical dimension of the contradiction can be expressed as follows: how does one paint or write poetry when the world of getting and spending constantly impinges, transforming the fair illusion of a pure pursuit of Beauty into other, darker forms—at worst unworthy, at best distracting, but in any case equally illusionistic? This is the great contradiction raised by poetry in the age of Victorian commercial imperialism, and first given profound expression in Tennyson's 1832 *Poems.* Rossetti would not find a solution to that problem, any more than anyone else would. In fact the problem has no solution, because its importance as a problem lies not in any realities it consciously questions but in the illusions it unwittingly exposes. It is a problem without a solution because it is a problem framed within its own rooted misunderstanding about the nature of art and imagination: that these are transcendental forms standing free of the sublunary orders of human things.

One face of the illusion appears as the idea that "effort and expectation and desire," or striving, seeking and finding, will eventually produce a solution. Rossetti is the first Victorian poet to show clearly the falseness of such convictions. The important secondary illusion is that the sublunary world and the world of art differ from each other in every important respect—as the material world is thought to differ in all important respects from the world of spirit. This illusion Rossetti will also discredit, at first with excitement and confidence, in his explorations of erotic experience, but finally in fear and trembling, as the full import of his erotic explorations slowly dawns upon him. In the end Rossetti's poetry (and his art as well, though I shall not be concentrating on that aspect of his work)[4] will repeat Dante's journey in the opposite direction, descending from various illusory heavens through a purgatory of unveilings to the nightmares and hells of his greatest work, the unwilled revelations arrived at in ***The House of Life.***

It is important to realize that Rossetti did not set out to discredit that ideology. **"Hand and Soul,"** for example, tells a story of the triumph of art and the artistic life over base circumstances. The problem is that the story doubts the truth of its own apparent theme. It is a hoaxing tale in more ways than one. It is a hoax, formally speaking, in that it consciously imitates the hoaxes of Edgar Allan Poe—those tales like "Von Kempelen and his Discovery" which present themselves to the reader as nonfictions. Rossetti's work is written to secure a real belief in its fictional representations. Written in the form of a personal essay, it deceived "more than one admirer . . . who made enquiry in Florence and Dresden after the pictures of Chiaro" (2:524).

Like Poe and Baudelaire, Rossetti catches the reader out by feeding him the illusions he wants to believe. The ultimate effect of such a story is to expose the structure of those illusions. But, unlike Poe and Baudelaire, Rossetti himself more than half believed in the illusions he was calling out. For Rossetti, then, the story is not initially conceived as a hoax at all but as a serious conjuring trick. R. L. Megroz was acute to see that "in his imaginative adventures, Rossetti was always casting the horoscope of his life."[5] **"Hand and Soul"** is in this respect, at least initially, a serious act of magic, an effort to put into writing a story that might prove to be the actual plot of Rossetti's own life. If the story could be imagined to be true, in the second half of the nineteenth century in England (either as a piece of "past" history or as the sketch of the true "future"), then art could be said to transcend circumstance. And Rossetti was not the only one who sought to turn the fictions of that story into truths.

The greatness, as well as the horror, of Rossetti's career can be traced to his insistence upon interrogating that cherished belief in the mission of art to unveil, or achieve, transcendence. To discover the truth of that belief Rossetti made an experiment of his life and his life's work, where his deepest convictions were put to a series of empirical tests. Rossetti's work is an effort to confirm empirically those narrative imaginings he had initially set forth in **"St. Agnes of Intercession"** and **"Hand and Soul."**

The experiment led Rossetti to complete the curve of the demonic imagination outlined half a century before by Blake when he showed that "he who will not defend Truth may be compelled to / Defend a Lie, that he may be snared & caught & taken" (*Milton* 8:47). For the truths Rossetti discovered did not confirm the story he was committed to. In the first place, the artist's life Rossetti came to know in those years had none of the mythic purity of Chiaro's tale. Rossetti had to scramble for success, seek out commissions, constantly resupply himself with the money he loved to call "tin" (thereby dismissing it from the serious concerns he kept imagining for himself). The more he made his way as an artist, the more difficult he found the demands that such a life placed upon him. These were not the grandiose spiritual difficulties laid upon the high-minded Chiaro; they were crass and quotidian demands, nightmarishly worse even than those glimpsed in **"St. Agnes of Intercession."**

Rossetti had various tricks by which he held off the enormity of this experimental life that he was pursuing. He paraded his refusals to exhibit in the ordinary professional ways, and nurtured the myth, both for himself and for others, of bohemian genius. But while Millais, Brown, and Edward Jones were making their way by more conventional means, Rossetti was nonetheless making his way—in certain respects, not least of all monetary, even more successfully. But it was a way that left only ashes in his mouth.

Nothing shows his situation so well as his relations with the people whose commissions he was seeking. It began with the earliest of them, Francis McCracken for instance, in the early fifties. Perceiving McCracken as "an absolute Guy—worse than Patmore" (*L* 1:185),[6] Rossetti manipulated him into buying things at grossly inflated prices, and then ridiculed him to his friends—for example in his contemptuous parody of Tennyson's "The Kraken" which Rossetti called "MacCraken."[7] Throughout the fifties and sixties Rossetti cosseted and condescended to his buyers. They seemed, most of them, altogether too easy marks: eager, relatively ignorant, contemptible in the end. To Ford Madox Ford, for example, he remarked, "I'll forebear from springing at the unaccustomed throat of Trist, if possible; but really a man shouldn't buy pictures without nerving himself beforehand against commercial garotte" (*L* 2:520). This sort of thing is a refrain in his letters. Yet his own idealization of the practice of art turned his behavior into a kind of self-immolation. If Trist and the other buyers were suffering executions in their pocketbooks, Rossetti's "commercial garotte" was strangling his own soul.

By 1865-66 Rossetti had become a very successful painter indeed, measured both in terms of his celebrity and his income. At the same time it had become apparent to himself, in any case, that his experiment with his life and his ideals had not gone well. The course of his commercial career had its parallel in the course of his devotional life—by which I mean his love life. Elizabeth's suicide in 1862 was no more than the exponent and capstone of his disastrous quests for the Beatrice which his experiment required. Their life together had not been an "ideal" in any sense, either before or after the marriage, though his initial imagination of her meaning for him was—just that, that she was to be deeply meaningful. Then too there were his infidelities, we do not know exactly how many. In a sense they were not infidelities to Elizabeth at all, since his attachment to her was never personal. What he worshiped was her image, and that he had himself created, first in his imagination, and then later, in the series of incredible drawings and paintings which he devoted to that image. His were infidelities, therefore, to his own soul, to his idea of himself, to the vision which had come to Chiaro in the late 1840s.

The extent of those infidelities were defined for him in the death of his wife and unborn child. The most celebrated act of his life—burying his volume of largely unpublished poems in the coffin with Elizabeth—was a form of expiation, of course, but its full significance has to be understood in the context of his artistic and poetic careers. His steady success as a painter became for Rossetti an index of how he was betraying his mission as an artist. The greater his success in securing commissions, the more erratic his output as a painter became. His cynical attitude toward his various patrons was matched only by his scandalous failure to meet obligations even after he had been paid. Through it all, however, he began to imagine that what he was betraying as a painter he was preserving as a poet. His paintings were hopelessly entangled with commercial affairs, but his poetry, it seemed to him, had been nurtured apart from worldly concerns. When in the fall of 1860 he sent a manuscript book of his original poetry to William Allingham for comments and criticism, his accompanying remarks are revealing:

> When I think how old most of these things are, it seems like a sort of mania to keep thinking of them still, but I suppose one's leaning still to them depends mainly on their having no trade associations, and being still a sort of thing of one's own. I have no definite ideas as to doing anything with them, but should like, even if they lie at rest, to make them as good as I can. (*L* 1:377)

After he published, successfully, his 1861 ***The Early Italian Poets,*** a volume of his original work, ***Dante at Verona and Other Poems,*** was advertised. But Elizabeth's death intervened, along with the accompanying sense that his unfaithfulness was not simply, or even fundamentally, marital. The gift of his book of poems to Elizabeth's corpse was a gesture asserting that his artistic soul was still alive, and that he still had the integrity to preserve its life. He sent his poems out of the world.

But this left him more painfully in the world than ever, and the years 1862-68 are a record of what Oswald Doughty once labelled "Disillusion" and "Success."[8] For Rossetti these were two faces of the same reality. Doughty's terms apply to Rossetti's artistic career, but they carry ironical overtones because, so far as Rossetti was concerned, his very success as a painter only multiplied his sense of moral disillusion. In this connection, though we must be very clear about the commercialism of the paintings, we are precisely *not* to judge the significance of those paintings through Rossetti's contradicted Victorian ideology. He despised the commercial face he saw in his work, but we must read and judge that work in another light.

If the paintings were commercial to a degree—and they were—they triumph in and through that commercialism. Like the poems, they are deceptions, sometimes even self-deceptions. Formally considered, they often appear to us as genre paintings; but the appearance is fraudulent. Rossetti's paintings come forth showing different kinds of representational faces. In every case the representational surface is distorted or disfigured, however, and those disruptions signal the truth about his work which Rossetti was concealing, partly from himself, and wholly from his contemporary audience. For his oils are not at all representational, they are abstract experiments in the use of color and (most importantly) the conventions of painterly space. Critics have never seriously faulted Rossetti's composition and his use of color, of course, but many have complained about his draughtsmanship. It is the drawing, however, which most graphically reveals the experimental character of his work, for it is the drawing which tilts his pictures out of their conventional structures. These paintings seduce and then abandon the corrupted eye of the conventional viewer, and in the process they contrive to deliver a secret meaning through the surface of betrayed appearances.

In this way Rossetti experienced an overthrow of certain traditional ideas about success and failure in art, illusion and disillusion in life. His success and disillusion are both real. But in his work we observe success being measured by disillusion, and disillusion being founded on success.

This pattern is recurrent and graphically displayed in the case of his poetical work as well. In 1868-69, finding it impossible to paint at all, he began writing poetry again. After much urging by relatives and friends, he published sixteen of these new sonnets in the *Fortnightly Review* (March 1869), and in the succeeding months he continued to write. Eventually he began to articulate the possibility of exhuming the book he had buried with Elizabeth, as part of a project to print "some old and new poems . . . for private circulation" (*L* 2:716). Rossetti's tentative moves toward returning his poetry to the world were given a crucial impetus when he read an anonymous article on his verse in *Tinsley's Magazine* in August 1869, at the very time he was working on the proofs for his "Trial Book" of poems. Once again he clearly describes the dialectic which is driving his new writing:

> So after twenty years one stranger does seem to have discovered one's existence. However I have no cause to complain, since I have all I need of an essential kind, and have taken little trouble about it,—except always in the nature of my work,—the poetry especially in which I have done no pot-boiling at any rate. So I am grateful to that art, and nourish against the other that base grudge which we bear those whom we have treated shabbily. (*L* 2:729)

It is an astonishing passage for a man who, in 1869, had the kind of celebrity and success which Rossetti enjoyed. That H. Buxton Forman—the young author of the *Tinsley's* piece—would write an essay on Rossetti's poetry, when so little had appeared in print, and most of that in relatively inaccessible places, testifies to the kind of attention which his name commanded. Yet to Rossetti it seemed that his very existence had only just then been discovered, after twenty years of—what, invisibility? Yes, this was the way he saw it: the blankness which his commercial work as a painter had left where the image of his soul had once appeared.

III

Late in 1869, therefore, Rossetti began putting together a book of poetry which was to recoup those losses and betrayals he had been accumulating since the early fifties. He was full of anxiety about every detail of this project. Between mid-August 1869 and March 1, 1870, he received for correction and revision at least three sets of initial proofs (August 20-September 21), two so-called Trial Books (October 3-November 25), and a final complete proof of the first edition. The changes made in these proofs and Trial Books were massive: many poems were added and some were removed; large additions were written into the proof materials at all six major stages; titles were changed, and numerous local corrections and alterations were made; and finally, not least significant, the ordering of the poems underwent important and radical transformations. In the next two months, April and May, Rossetti continued to harass his publishers with extensive revisions and large-scale alterations of every kind. Nor was the physical appearance of the book a matter of small moment: the paper, the binding, the cloth, the color, the kind of dies to be struck for the embossed cover designs, and so forth—all these matters engrossed his attention. Rossetti's ***Poems*** of 1870 were bringing the whole soul of the man into activity.[9]

To Rossetti's imagination, that soul was the one he had almost lost through his life of betrayal—through his worldliness. But in objective truth it was another, more demonic soul to which his life's work had been devoted, and entirely faithful. Rossetti's concern that his book make a good appearance, in every sense, reflects his desire that it be a perfect image of beauty, of finishedness, of his commitment to perfection. His notorious efforts to control as completely as possible the immediate critical reception of the book must be understood as part of this obsession with the appearance of his work, the impression it would create. By 1870 he had a large network of friends and friendly acquaintances who were well-connected in the periodical press. All were enlisted to launch the book into the world—in pre-publication reviews wherever possible—not simply to a chorus of praise, but in terms that were to represent Rossetti's ***Poems*** as a work of the greatest artistic moment—indeed, as the very exponent and symbol of what "a work of art" means.[10]

In this sense, Rossetti's ***Poems*** (1870)—even more than Swinburne's *Poems and Ballads* (1866), which had created such a sensation four years earlier—is a manifesto for what Pater would call "Aesthetic Poetry." Comprised in that event, however, as Walter Benjamin so acutely observed in his great work on Baudelaire, is the understanding that the "work of art" has now identified itself with, and as, the commodity.[11] The work was to be so carefully prepared, so thoroughly worked and polished, so packaged and promoted that it would ravish its audience and establish Rossetti's fame. The book was meant to "succeed" in the same way, only far more absolutely, that the painter, in **"St. Agnes of Intercession,"** set out to succeed. Consumed for months with his corrections and revisions, Rossetti was perhaps able to blink the commercial forms and "trade associations" that were concealed in this attention to his craft, but the commodity-status of his work emerges very clearly in those other investments: his obsession with the physical appearance of his book, on one hand, and—crucially—his campaign to manage the reviews, on the other.

But if Rossetti's ***Poems*** (1870) return and re-establish the contradictions he had begun to explore in the late forties and early fifties, the intervening years had made an enormous difference in his work. In those years a happy liberal view might look for, and might even discover, signs of a "growing artistic maturity," of a "development" toward some "greater self-consciousness" in his work which could suggest that he had "transcended" in some measure the network of initial contradictions.[12] But in fact Rossetti's "development," if one can call it that, is in the opposite direction—toward a more complete immersion within the contradictions, indeed, toward an enslavement to them. In twenty years Rossetti had moved from the margin to the very heart of his culture: as Blake would have said, "he became what he beheld." In tracing that movement, ***Poems*** (1870) achieved its greatness. The analogy to *Les Fleurs du Mal* is quite exact, so that what Benjamin said of the latter can be applied, pari passu, to Rossetti: "Baudelaire was a secret agent—an agent of the secret discontent of his class with its own rule."[13] In Rossetti's case as well, therefore, "the point of departure is the object riddled with error" (Benjamin, p. 103). And in the nineteenth century there are few English books of poetry more secretly discontented, more riddled with error, than this book of Rossetti's.

We may begin to unriddle that error by a critical retracing of the history of the book. In his reply to Buchanan's "The Fleshly School of Poetry," Rossetti defended his dramatic monologue **"Jenny"** by a general argument about the nature of art. When he first wrote the poem "some thirteen years ago," he says, he understood that the subject-matter—a young man's visit to a prostitute—might have called for "a treatment from without." Such an objective treatment would have set a critical distance between the poem and its problematic subject. Rossetti rejected the option because "the motive powers of art reverse the requirement of science, and demand first of all an *inner* standing-point such as the speaker put forward in the poem,—that is, of a young and thoughtful man of the world" (2:484-485). This is more than the classic defense, that poems are not to be read as "personal expressions." Rossetti is rather speaking as a student of Browning, whose work with the dramatic monologue Rossetti so much admired. In that form an effort is made to confine subjectivity to the core of what Coleridge once called the "dramatic truth of such . . . situations, supposing them real."[14]

The dramatic monologue moves to take the "lyrical" out of the "ballad." Rossetti's "*inner* standing-point" is thus a Victorian explanation of what Keats called "negative capability," or the process by which the author's conscious separation from his subject—the typical structure of a poem by, say, Rochester or Pope—is canceled in a process of deep sympathetic engagement. In Rossetti's case, however, as in Browning's, the chameleonic turn involves a transfer of sympathy from the poet to some figure or character who is concretely imagined in the poem. The so-called "poetry of experience" becomes, in Victorian hands, a form for introducing modes of subjectivity into historically removed materials, or into contemporary materials which might be, for various reasons, problematic.

In the Victorian dramatic monologue, this transfer of sympathy cancels the traditional structure on which the identity of the poet, formally speaking, depends. Browning was not especially interested in, or perhaps even aware of, the crisis (and therefore the opportunity) which was emerging for poetry in this dismantling of the conventions of sincerity. But Rossetti was. Browning's spy will succeed to the absent gods of Flaubert and later Joyce, who stand apart from their creations, paring their fingernails. This is the theory, or rather the ideology, in which Rossetti too has taken his stand.

But as with Baudelaire's *flaneur,* Rossetti's disengagement becomes an exponent of social alienation, as is quite clear in **"Jenny"** itself. The sympathy of Rossetti's "young and thoughtful man of the world" is for a sleeping figure, a prostitute who never responds and who in the poem cannot respond. Her condition merely replicates the incompetent thought and limited sympathies of the young man, however. He does not understand her, or her "case," because she exists for him in an aesthetic condition alone, that state where sympathy appears as the indifference of appreciation. In the end, both prostitute and young man are figures of the latent structures of alienation of poetry itself as these structures have descended into Rossetti's hands. In fact, he here reveals the image of that "thoughtful" young man's soul as self-contradicted, an image with the face of a prostitute superimposed on the face of his sister.

In **"Jenny,"** the frame erected by the dramatic monologue works to reveal alienation rather than establish sympathy, and to suggest—ultimately—that the dramatic monologue is a construction of chinese boxes. More than recording a failed quest for sympathetic engagement, the poem judges this to be the failure of poetry (or art) itself. This judgment is an extremely critical one, in the nineteenth century, because poetry and art were then generally regarded as the ultimate depositories, and even the creators, of spiritual and human values. In calling that ideology into question, Rossetti's work has contrived to imagine the experience of being distanced altogether from experience. It is to have fashioned a vehicle for conveying, quite literally, the feeling of the absence of feeling.[15]

Nowhere is this experience more clearly visible than in ***The House of Life,*** which must be the most alienated, and probably the most horrifying, major poem in the language. This culminant achievement is so integrated with his whole life's work, and in particular with the project that became ***Poems*** (1870), that the connections have to be sketched. ***Poems*** (1870), we may recall, is separated into three parts. The initial section is composed principally of a series of longer pieces—dramatic monologues, stories, ballads, and a few translations. Here the deployment of Rossetti's "*inner* standing-point" is most clearly shown—not simply in monologues like **"A Last Confession"** and **"Jenny,"** but in all the literary ballads (**"Troy Town," "Stratton Water," "Sister Helen,"** and so forth), where the use of the ballad convention historicizes the style and voicing as well the narrative materials. The point of view in **"Dante at Verona,"** similarly antiqued, is much closer to Dante's age than to Rossetti's. Likewise, Rossetti employs translation, here and elsewhere, as yet another depersonalizing convention. The third section of ***Poems*** (1870), which follows ***The House of Life,*** is largely devoted to a variant type of Rossettian translation: "Sonnets for Pictures," so-called.

Paradoxically, Rossetti's use of these nonsubjective verse forms intensifies the aura of poetic self-consciousness. He turns away from his own age and self, but in doing so the contemporaneous relevance of his acts of historical displacement is only heightened. **"Dante at Verona"** is in this respect a clear allegory, but an allegory which deconstructs itself. Dante's alienation has its contemporary (Rossettian) analogy in the speaker of the poem, who celebrates Dante's critique of luxurious society. But whereas the Dante of Rossetti's poem speaks out openly and plainly against the world of Can Grande, there is no plain speaking at the contemporary level, merely gestures and vague allusions.

Yet **"Dante at Verona"** does not exemplify what is best and most innovative in Rossetti's poetry. To see that, in the nonpersonal and antiqued material, we have to look at some other things—for example, the excellent **"An Old Song Ended,"** which begins by quoting the last stanza of an antique ballad and then "ends" it with four more stanzas. The story, rendered in the convention of a dialogue between a dying lady—a Mariana figure—and an unnamed interlocutor, lets us know that she will die before her lover returns. The poem finishes with the lady's last reply to the final question put to her:

"Can you say to me some word
I shall say to him?"
"Say I'm looking in his eyes
Though my eyes are dim."

This is quintessential Rossetti, an ambiguous icon constructed from a play on the phrase "looking in." Henceforth the lady will be haunting her absent lover, in the same way that Rossetti is haunted by the old song. (That connection between lady and old song, in fact, makes the absent lover an obvious figura of Rossetti and the contemporary poet.) Henceforth an "external" presence who will be looking into his eyes as he observes the external world, she becomes as well an internal ghost who, though dead, is destined to live on in the way he looks at his world.

This haunted and self-conscious figure is at the heart of all Rossetti's poems and paintings. We rightly see a poem like **"The Blessed Damozel"** as typical work for just that reason. Of all the verse printed in the first section of ***Poems*** (1870), **"The Stream's Secret"** is closest to ***The House of Life.*** But **"The Blessed Damozel"** is more relevant for understanding the sonnet sequence because its antiqued character highlights how the "*inner* standing-point" works in those sonnets. Rossetti disjoins himself from the first-person speaker in **"The Blessed Damozel"** by invoking the formalities of the ballad convention; but because he does not historicize his materials as clearly and resolutely as he does, for example, in **"Stratton Water"** or his other old tales, the scenes in the poem appear to float in a kind of abstraction, outside space and time. That ambiguous condition, where one feels unmoored and alienated even as one seems to live a determinate and eventual existence, defines what we know as ***The House of Life.***

IV

The House of Life is more than a mere presentation, or case history, of personality dismemberment. It is that, of course, but it is also part of a project—an execution—of such dismemberment, an active agent in the destructive project it is unfolding. This complicity is what makes the work, and the whole volume which it epitomizes, so fearful and so magnificent. The sonnets record a history by which "changes" associated with a period of "Youth"—these are figured principally as the changing experiences of love—are finally transfixed in (and as) the immobilized forms of "Fate." The history unfolds through a set of losses and disintegrations which culminate as the loss of identity.[16]

At the outset of the sequence, the notorious **"Nuptial Sleep"** appears far removed from the terrible images which emerge in the concluding six sonnets:

At length their long kiss severed with sweet smart:
And as the last slow sudden drops are shed
From sparkling eaves when all the storm has fled,
So singly flagged the pulses of each heart.
Their bosoms sundered, with the opening start
Of married flowers to either side outspread
From the knit stem; yet still their mouths, burnt red,
Fawned on each other where they lay apart.

Sleep sank them lower than the tide of dreams,
And their dreams watched them sink, and slid away.
Slowly their souls swam up again, through gleams
Of watered light and dull drowned waifs of day;
Till from some wonder of new woods and streams
He woke, and wondered more: for there she lay.

(6a/5)[17]

Here is the supreme imagination of triumph in the work. One might not appreciate this fact because the previous sonnet, **"The Kiss,"** represents an actual experience of erotic consummation. It is, moreover, an experience recorded for us in the first person:

I was a child beneath her touch,—a man
When breast to breast we clung, even I and she,—
A spirit when her spirit looked through me,—
A god when all our life-breath met to fan
Our life-blood, till love's emulous ardours ran,
Fire within fire, desire in deity.

(6/4, ll. 9-14)

After those lines, the movement to the third person in **"Nuptial Sleep,"** a modulation from major to minor, comes as a shock, since it conveys the impression of incredible detachment on the part of the speaker, whom we associate with the lover. That shock is the rhetorical equivalent of the "wonder" recorded at the end of the sonnet, where—following an experience of ecstatic physical union—the beloved appears to the eyes of the lover as a unique identity, wholly individuated despite the previous moments of mutual absorption. The lover's (actual) "wonder" is thus reduplicated, or realized, in the rhetoric of the speaker, who is spellbound before his imagination of the separate lovers. **"Nuptial Sleep"** argues, in other words, that the heart of the "poignant thirst / And exquisite hunger" (**"Bridal Birth,"** 2/1) of this work is an ecstasy which culminates not in the extinction but in the establishment of individual identities through love. This argument is clinched by the tense shift executed between the sonnets, which transfers to identity and self-consciousness the values associated, both traditionally and in the previous sonnet(s), with intense feeling: immediateness, and spontaneity.

But the achievement in the sonnet is tenuous and fragile, and finally self-conflicted. Lover observes beloved much as the young man in **"Jenny"** observes, lovingly, the sleeping prostitute; and the perspective is here explicitly revealed as the perspective of art and poetry. This "wonder" matches passivities to passivities, and thus contradicts the developing energetic impulses of the poem itself. Furthermore, although the watery medium of sleep and dreams does not here directly threaten the ideal of self-identity in the sonnet, those forms prefigure the conditions of loss later realized in **"Willowwood."**

As in **"Hand and Soul,"** then, the apparitions here are images of the artist's "soul," or that to which he is ultimately committed. That is to say, the sonnet raises up an imagining of self-identity achieved through artistic practice. As ***The House of Life*** gradually delineates the features of that soul, however, a hollowed-out figure emerges from the expectant shadows of Beauty. For the story told by the sequence is that the images are insubstantial: literally, that the supreme moment of **"Nuptial Sleep"** was a supreme fiction only. In this respect ***The House of Life*** is the story of betrayed hopes; and if that were all it had to tell us, it would scarcely deserve to hold more than our minimal interest. As we shall see, however, what Rossetti's work ultimately reveals are not its betrayals but its self-betrayals.

The instabilities we glimpse in **"Nuptial Sleep"** initiate the sequence of illusions that forms the ground of the conclusive nightmares of the work. These will culminate in the terror of **"He and I"** (98/47), the definitive representation of identity-loss in the sequence. The sonnet operates through the simple contradiction of first- and third-person pronouns, both of which are "identified with" the poet. They are the residua of the first- and third-person narrators whose careers in ***The House of Life*** we initially traced in **"The Kiss"** and **"Nuptial Sleep."** Here they emerge as the obverse and reverse of a single self-conflicted figure, the schizoid form of a disintegrated identity which has lost itself in a house of mirrors.[18]

Pronouns, those ultimate shifters, figure largely in Rossetti's sonnet sequence. The iconographical status of **"He and I,"** however, contrasts with the more fluid pronominal ambiguities which play themselves out in most of the earlier sonnets. This happens because Rossetti depicts first the process and then the achievement, first "Change" and then "Fate." **"He and I"** is the "Fate" that awaits Rossettian "Change," an entropic nightmare immortalized in one dead deathless sonnet.

"Life-in-Love" is very different, a not untypical instance of Rossettian deconstruction observed in a "changing" phase.

> Not in thy body is thy life at all,
> But in this lady's lips and hands and eyes;
> Through these she yields thee life that vivifies
> What else were sorrow's servant and death's thrall.
> Look on thyself without her, and recall
> The waste remembrance and forlorn surmise
> That lived but in a dead-drawn breath of sighs
> O'er vanished hours and hours eventual.
> Even so much life hath the poor tress of hair
> Which, stored apart, is all love hath to show
> For heart-beats and for fire-heats long ago;
> Even so much life endures unknown, even where,
> 'Mid change the changeless night environeth,
> Lies all that golden hair undimmed in death.
>
> (36/16)

The second person pronoun here slides from ambiguity to ambiguity. Isolated thus, in solitary quotation, we register the simple alternative that it may be taken to refer either to "the poet" (a.k.a. D. G. Rossetti) or to the "old love" (a.k.a. Elizabeth Siddal Rossetti), with "this lady" standing as the "new love" (a.k.a. Jane Morris).[12] The "meaning" in each case is that both "poet" and "old love" are resurrected in the experience of "new love," which revivifies and redeems what would otherwise be encorpsed forever.

Were we to restore the sonnet to its larger (1881) context in the sequence, we would observe a further fall into ambiguity; for it is impossible to read **"Life-in-Love"** after the preceding sonnet, **"The Lamp's Shrine,"** and not respond to the inertia of the latter's second person pronouns, which all refer to the allegorical figure "Lord Love." Finally, because Rossetti rhymes this sonnet with the soon to follow **"Death-in-Love,"** yet another nominal presence comes to fill the shifting pronoun, and even names itself: "I am Death."

In this case, the fact that **"The Lamp's Shrine"** was only added to ***The House of Life*** in 1881 reduces by one the number of substantive options in the 1870 sequence, but its addition also calls attention to the unstable and shifting form of the work as a whole. In Rossetti's lifetime ***The House of Life*** appeared in no less than four relatively coherent forms: as a sequence of 16 sonnets; as a sequence of 50 sonnets and 11 songs; as a sequence of 25 sonnets and 5 songs; and as a sequence of 101 sonnets. Rossetti treated that last as the finished sequence even though it lacked the crucial sonnet **"Nuptial Sleep."**[20] Today, as for many years, most readers enter the work through the 102 sonnet version, where **"Nuptial Sleep,"** sequenced with the appropriately unstable number 6a/5, is restored.

And indeed this ambiguous presence of **"Nuptial Sleep"** in ***The House of Life*** is singularly appropriate, for only in that sonnet is the ultimate ideal of the work, self-identity through love, defined. That Rossetti repeatedly unsettled the forms of the sequence emphasizes the overall lack of resolution of the work, but that he should have removed **"Nuptial Sleep"** from his last imagination of the work is a truly remarkable revelation of his loss of faith in the identity he set out to fashion and represent. Needless to say, this surrender of faith, this betrayal, is the ambiguous sign under which the work will triumph.

V

Poems (1870) is the first chapter in Rossetti's history of ultimate dissolution/disillusion. But the book is more than the record of a personal and psychic catastrophe, it is the portrait of an age. We glimpse this most clearly, if also most simply, when we recall that the book is full of various social and political poems with distinct, if obliquely presented, points of contemporary reference. **"The Burden of Nineveh,"** an unusually direct work, involves an ironic meditation on England's imperial imagination. This fact is glossed in the multiple pun of the title. At the proof stage Rossetti set an explanatory headnote under that title to emphasize his word play: "BURDEN. Heavy calamity; the chorus of a song.—*Dictionary.*"[21] Rossetti directs us to read the poem as a "burden" in the Old Testament prophetic sense, with a relevance for England emphasized by the storied names (Thebes, Rome, Babylon, Greece, Egypt) called in the roll of the poem. Finally, that Nineveh is also "a burden to" England, an example of the self-destructive imperialism under which she currently labors, is made all but explicit at the conclusion of the poem. It is particularly apt, in Rossetti's book, that the focus in the poem on decadence should be the British Museum, the repository of the nation's cultural treasures. Rossetti's poem reflects the excitement of cultural imperialism with a special force because the British Museum, at that time, was relatively small, so that recent acquisitions of Near Eastern treasure were peculiarly visible and celebrated occurrences. **"The Burden of Nineveh"** draws out the implications of what Byron, sixty years earlier, had already sketched in *The Curse of Minerva.*

But this is a unique poem in a book which generally proceeds by careful, not to stay stealthy, indirection. **"Troy Town"** generates an entire network of references to that fabled history of a civilization which, according to the myth, found destruction through indulgence and illicit love. This Troy theme plays a key role in linking ***The House of Life*** poems to the less personal material, as Rossetti must have realized: through all the proof stages **"Troy Town"** was the opening poem. In that position it would have emphasized more strongly the social dimensions of the book. But at the last minute Rossetti replaced it with **"The Blessed Damozel."**

Changes of that and other kinds are the hallmark of Rossetti's discontented book. This is why, from a social point of view, the steps that Rossetti takes to marginalize his "social themes" are in the end more important, more significant, than the themes themselves. They remind us that works like **"Troy Town"** are in themselves even more obliquely mediated, as pieces of social commentary, than *The Idylls of the King.* What we should attend to, here and throughout ***Poems*** (1870), are not any of the "ideas" but what the book is doing and being made to do, how carefully its materials are managed, packaged, and polished. Unlike Swinburne in his deliberately outrageous *Poems and Ballads,* Rossetti does everything in his power to make sure his book will behave.

This manic sense of decorum makes the book not more "crafted" but more "crafty." It is a monument to its own shame, a kind of whited sepulchre. We can see how this comes about if we trace the structure of change in Rossetti's book. We begin by reflecting once again on those disintegrative mechanisms we observed earlier. One notes for instance that they are heavily "languaged," so to speak, and that the extreme level of the verbal artifice is a mode that holds off, brackets out, "reality." All is arranged so that what occurs seems to occur at the level of the signs alone, as a play of signifiers and signifieds. No names are given, no definite events are alluded to, no places, no times, no "referential" concretions of any kind—other than the (1870) book in which ***The House of Life*** is printed. Many of the works in that book have points of reference, as we have seen, but not ***The House of Life*** poems, which occupy the abstract space first clearly delineated in **"The Blessed Damozel."** Yet, paradoxically, these sonnets and songs constitute the most "personal" work in the entire volume.

The book itself, in other words, provides the key referential point which alone really clarifies what is happening in ***The House of Life.*** Critics have often observed the claustrophobia and abstraction of the sonnets, but if we consider the sequence wholly in itself, we would have to see it simply as an event in language. By printing and publishing the work when and how he did, Rossetti provided the local habitation which could give social and ethical names—rather than merely technical ones—to the sonnets.

In simplest terms—they are critical for Rossetti—the act of printing and publishing establishes the "trade associations" of his work. These associations are, however, what he wants to avoid or cancel out, in order to "prove" that art occupies a transcendental order. Rossetti wants to establish what the Romantics called "the truth of imagination," but ***Poems*** (1870) ends by showing instead how that "truth" is rather "an imagination" of imagination—and an imagining which, when carried out in the world, can have disastrous consequences. The most prominent sign of disaster in the book is psychic disintegration, but the social significances of that sign are never far to seek. Perhaps the greatest "moral" of Rossetti's book, for instance, could be expressed as follows: that active moves to escape "trade associations"—to evade or avoid them rather than to oppose, in concrete and positive ways, the compromised "world" they represent—inevitably involve a complicity with that world. It was a truth Rossetti glimpsed early in **"St. Agnes,"** but in ***Poems*** (1870) it is fully exposed. Indeed, it is executed. In the horrors of his book Rossetti carried out the (concealed) truth of imagination for his age: that it has a truth, that it serves the world even in fleeing the world, that the truth is both a dream and a nightmare, and that it destroys the individual.

The marvel of Rossetti's work is that he chose to follow his own "*inner* standing-point" in declaring those contradictory truths, that he submitted to their "execution." We therefore trace the choices made by his work even in what must seem (for Rossetti) the least likely of places, the early reviews. One observes initially that they mirror the contradictions exposed in Rossetti's book. Whether written by friends or enemies, accomplices or neutral observers, two lines of understanding are repeated. ***Poems*** (1870) is a celebration of art, on one hand, or of love on the other; and to the degree that a mediation of the two is carried out, the book is said to be devoted to Beauty. But the mediating concept of Beauty merely resituates the contradictory registrations elsewhere. Thus, we can alternately see the book as a manifesto of "fleshliness" and eroticism, or of "mysticism" and spirituality. The contradictions are multiplied: what many find labored and obscure others see as crafted and sharply defined; and so the descriptive terms proliferate: abstract, ornate, pictorial, self-conscious, impersonal, and so forth.

These varied responses are the integrals of Rossetti's differential achievements. So much finish at the surface, so much apparent control—in a work that is also, plainly, nervous and highly unstable. Rossetti's perpetual acts of revision at every level, in the months immediately preceding publication, are but a dramatic instance of the consummate lack of resolution in the book. The book shifts and changes as it seeks its ideal of articulation, that monochord of which audience approval is the tonic, reciprocity the dominant. It is a mad, an inhuman ideal—what Marx ironically called "the soul of the commodity": a form crafted so as to be universally irresistible. It is the nineteenth-century's revenant of Dante's summum bonum, the encorpsed form of what was once alive.

Rossetti was more deeply complicit with his immediate institutions of reception than appears even from his attempt to manage the reviews. This became most obvious when the voices of negation began to be heard, the critical notices which culminate in Buchanan's famous review. Its date of publication—well over a year after the initial appearance of ***Poems*** (1870)—is quite important, because it tells us how far Rossetti identified himself with Buchanan. **"The Stealthy School of Criticism"** shouts back at the champion of late Victorian moral and poetic order, but it does not challenge that order, or argue that Rossetti's book challenged it. Furthermore, the poem particularly singled out by Buchanan for denunciation, **"Nuptial Sleep,"** which was also the key sonnet of ***The House of Life,*** was removed from the sequence by Rossetti when he published his new and (otherwise augmented) version of the work in 1881. Like the young painter in **"St. Agnes,"** Rossetti despised and sneered at the "poet-critic" who attacked his work, but Rossetti too, in the end, deferred.

It is an illuminating act of bad faith and betrayal, reminding us of the fear and trembling in which Rossetti worked out his damnation. We might wish that he would have done otherwise, that he would have braved it and defied his critics. But in fact he took the better part, for the shame of that betrayal is an eloquent sign of the ambiguous situation Rossetti's book has exposed. Buchanan is what Shelley would have called "The Phantasm of Rossetti" in a play where Prometheus does not appear as a character. What is Promethean in ***Poems*** (1870) is not "Rossetti" but what Rossetti has done. Assuming the inner standing point throughout, the book dramatizes Rossetti's enslavement to the commercial culture he despises. That culture thereby grows again in Rossetti's book, like some terrible virus in a laboratory dish. ***Poems*** (1870) is a coin "whose face reveals / The soul—its converse, to what Power 'tis due."

Rossetti's work set out to prove the Victorian theory of cultural touchstones which Arnold was developing elsewhere in his ideological prose: to prove that Ideal Beauty was transcendent. His achievement was to have shown that the theory was a confidence trick which Victorian society played on itself. Thus, the clear path to fulfillment sketched in **"Hand and Soul"** becomes, in the empirical testing of that prediction which Rossetti's work carried out, a field of endless wandering—in Rossetti's recurrent figuration, a maze.[22] Similarly, the Beatricean vision which was to mediate the quest for perfection continually shifted out of focus, or turned into nightmare forms.

The characteristic experience here is to be found in various pictures which Rossetti, obsessively over-painting, turned into palimpsests and cryptic surfaces. Somewhere beneath the face of Alexa Wilding hovered the unseen head of Fanny Cornforth, or Elizabeth Siddal would float about the canvas occupied by the face of Jane Morris. Rossetti fled his haunted and haunting canvasses and sought relief in poetry, which for a brief time seemed open to pure forms, transparent expressions. But the hope turned to illusion as his poetry delivered up its secret and invisible texts to the fire of his art. In the 1870s, as he plunged deeper into that abyss of Beauty, neither poetry nor painting offered any sustaining fantasies of escape.

"An untruth was never yet the husk of a truth," Rossetti argues at the conclusion to **"The Stealthy School of Criticism"** (I.488) as he makes a final dismissal of the various deceits of Robert Buchanan. Perhaps that relation of truth to untruth never held before, but the observation—the metaphor—is wonderfully apt for Rossetti's work, which tells the truth of false appearances, the truth that is in the husks of beauty and truth. Rossetti's poetry crucifies itself on its own infernal machineries. These always want to appear otherwise, as benevolences, but for the sake of truth Rossetti chose an unusual and lonely path: to will a suspension of disbelief in those inherited lies of art. Thence the nightmares of paradise appear in his work in their many forms, the most critical being called, commonly, Love and Art. They are dangerous and deceitful names, like the realities they denote, and in Rossetti's work none—neither names nor realities—are ever just what they seem.

This is an art difficult to practice, the index of a world not easy to survive. Rossetti allegorized both in a dramatic figure which became familiar to us only much later. It appears in another of Rossetti's notebooks, an entry of uncertain date, though it was clearly written a few years later than the passage I quoted at the outset. This time Rossetti copies a passage from Petronius and then translates it to his own verse.

> I saw the Sibyl at Cumae
> (One said) with my own eye
> She hung in a cage to read her runes
> To all the passers-by
> Said the boys "What wouldst thou Sibyl?"
> She answered "I would die"![23]

That scene of cultural desperation Eliot later made famous as the epigraph to a poem about another wasted world. To find it written almost fifty years before in a Rossetti notebook will surprise us only if we read as twentieth-century literary historians, that is to say, if we continue to misunderstand what Rossetti's poetry is actually about.

Notes

[1] This is from one of the notebooks in the British Library (Ashley 1410; Notebook I, 4r), much of whose material remains unpublished, though W. M. Rossetti reproduced large portions of it in his 1911 edition of the works of his brother; see below n.2.

[2] My texts for Rossetti's work will be taken from *The Collected Works of Dante Gabriel Rossetti* (London, 1886), 2 vols. For texts not available in this edition I have used *The Works of Dante Gabriel Rossetti* (London, 1911). Both collected editions were edited by W. M. Rossetti. Where necessary, page numbers are given in the text.

[3] According to W. M. Rossetti (*Works* 1:525-526).

[4] See David Riede, *Dante Gabriel Rossetti and the Limits of Victorian Vision* (Ithaca, 1983) for an excellent handling of the parallel forms of Rossetti's imaginative work.

[5] Rodolphe L. Megroz, *Dante Gabriel Rossetti, Painter Poet of Heaven and Earth* (London, 1928), p. 185.

[6] References to Rossetti's letters are from *Letters of Dante Gabriel Rossetti,* ed. Oswald Doughty and John Robert Wahl, 4 vols. (Oxford, 1965), cited in the text as *L* followed by volume and page number.

[7] The poem is printed in *L* 1:164.

[8] These are the titles of Chapters I and II in Book III in Doughty's biography *Dante Gabriel Rossetti: A Victorian Romantic* (London, 1949).

[9] The best account of the Trial Books and the publication history of the 1870 volume is Janet Camp Troxell's "The 'Trial Books' of Dante Gabriel Rossetti," reprinted from *The Colophon,* New Series III, no. 2 (1938) in *The Princeton University Library Chronicle* 33 (1972): 177-192; but see also Robert N. Keane, "D. G. Rossetti's *Poems,* 1870: A Study in Craftsmanship," *Princeton University Library Chronicle* 33:193-209.

[10] See Doughty, *Dante Gabriel Rossetti,* pp. 439-453 for a good account of Rossetti's campaign to control the reviews.

[11] See Walter Benjamin, *Charles Baudelaire: A Lyric Poet in the Era of High Capitalism,* trans. Harry Zohn (London, 1973).

[12] In a sense, of course, Rossetti's work does make an advance from the relative unselfconscious and even innocent work of the early years. What I mean to indicate here is the inadequacy of the commonplace idea that Rossetti's poetry, as it develops, gains some kind of wisdom or imitable moral depth. Indeed, it seems to me that the climax of his career was "penultimate" in the sense that, after completing the work for the 1870 volume and the associated *House of Life* poetry, Rossetti's poetry experienced a sharp falling-off, a collapse that parallels the curve of his last years.

[13] Benjamin, p. 104n. The quotation immediately following is from p. 103.

[14] See *Biographia Literaria,* ed. James Engell and W. J. Bate (Princeton, 1983) 2:6.

[15] Rossetti's paintings—and Burne-Jones's, for that matter—are similarly charged.

[16] Joan Rees has an excellent general comment on Rossetti's significance as a poet: "A slight shift of position, and what has been taken as an emblem of salvation becomes a mark of damnation. This is the central moral insight of Rossetti's work" (Joan Rees, *The Poetry of Dante Gabriel Rossetti: Modes of Self-Expression* [Cambridge, 1981], p. 101).

[17] In identifying the sonnets I always give two numbers: the second being the number in the 1870 volume, the first the number in 1881. The one exception is for this sonnet, the so-called 6a (a number which indicates that Rossetti removed it from the sequence printed in 1881, though later editors, perceiving its centrality, have always restored it).

[18] See Henry Treffry Dunn, *Recollections of Dante Gabriel Rossetti and His Circle, or Cheyne Walk Life,* ed. Rosalie Mander (Westerham, 1984), p. 14: "Mirrors and looking-glasses of all shapes, sizes and design lined the walls. Whichever way I looked I saw myself gazing at myself."

[19] I refer here to the traditional "biographical" level of exegesis, which plots the poem as a story of Rossetti's relations with Elizabeth Siddal (the Old Love) and Jane Morris (the New Love). The fullest treatment of this subject is in Doughty, but the best discussion of the subject in terms of the formal structure of the sonnet sequence is William E. Fredeman's "Rossetti's 'In Memoriam': An Elegiac Reading of *The House of Life,*" *Bulletin of the John Rylands Library* 47 (1965): 298-341.

[20] The twenty-five sonnet, five-song version is the MS Rossetti made of the poems he wrote in 1870-71. He made a gift of it to Jane Morris, the person who had inspired most of the work. The MS (Bodleian Library) was printed (most of it) in *The Kelmscott Love Sonnets of Dante Gabriel Rossetti,* ed. John Robert Wahl (Capetown, 1954).

[21] The following discussion depends heavily upon a study of the MS and proof material in the Ashley Library (British Museum) and the Fitzwilliam Museum.

[22] The central "maze" poem by Rossetti is "Troy Town," whose title means (at one level) a labyrinth (see OED).

[23] W. M. Rossetti printed these lines in 1911; his text differs slightly from the Notebook's (II.12v).

Andrew Leng (essay date 1990)

SOURCE: "Behind 'Golden Barriers': Framing and Taming the Blessed Damozel," in *The Victorian Newsletter,* No. 77, Spring, 1990, pp. 13-16.

[*In the following essay, Leng investigates narrative technique and its relation to gender themes in "The Blessed Damozel."*]

Some time after 1866 Dante Gabriel Rossetti formulated this eroticized theory of *ut pictura poesis:*

> Picture and poem bear the same relation to each other as beauty does in man and woman: the point of meeting where the two are most identical is the supreme perfection. (***Works*** 606)[1]

Most discussions of Rossetti and the sister arts mention this quotation: Richard Stein sees Rossetti's statement as a "fragment" which "seems to outline and analogy between an intellectualized concept of love and his composite art" (196-97); and Maryann Ainsworth believes it is particularly applicable to "the most successful instances of the picture-poem idea" which "came to him during his last ten years," that is, between 1872 and 1882 (6-7).

Perhaps the fullest and most perceptive analysis of Rossetti's formulation of *ut pictura poesis* has been made by Ian Fletcher, who suggests that

> The "beauty" of the picture is reciprocated by the "identical"—if superficially dissimilar—beauty of the poem resulting in an indivisible ideal unity, comparable only to the state of love. In Rossetti's sonnets for pictures of women, the metaphor is actualized as an encounter between observer-poet and portrait-beloved. (28-29)

Certainly Rossetti's emphasis on a reciprocal, identical beauty indicates that his hypothetical point of "supreme perfection" occurs at a moment of higher, aesthetic synthesis. That is, a kind of vicarious, erotic union occurs between male artist-spectator and female art-object, an aesthetically creative rather than a procreative dialectic.

The fictional artist's desire for reconciliation and identity with the female subject of his art—his anima—is, as Barbara Charlesworth Gelpi has shown, a central Rossettian topos. Rossetti's anima first appeared in the selection of poems he sent to William Bell Scott for his perusal in November 1847 under the title "Songs of the Art Catholic," in her guises as the speaker's sister, Margaret, in **"My Sister's Sleep,"** as the Virgin Mary in **"Mater Pulchrae Delectionis,"** and as the eponymous heroine of **"The Blessed Damozel."** Gelpi argues convincingly that in the poems which feature versions of his anima Rossetti was striving to achieve "union of the self by uniting masculine and feminine principles within the self," claiming that this "internal drama" (1) lends psychological coherence to his work.

Gelpi feels that while it may be coherent **"The Blessed Damozel"** is problematic. She points out that if the anima "becomes an end in herself, the imaginative symbol of all that the conscious self desires, then she is dangerous," and concludes that the poem "ends not with a union of self achieved but with such a union still hoped for, and in that obsessive, unfulfilled wish for union lies the danger" (4). However, I shall be arguing that although the union of male and female fails to occur in **"The Blessed Damozel"** the "danger" of the anima's domination of the male is averted because of two factors not considered by Gelpi: firstly, because the poem's "two" male speakers, the omniscient and the parenthetical narrators, eventually unite to form a single voice, a dominant male discourse; and secondly, because as the male position consolidates, the once vociferous and dominant Damozel is neutralized, eventually losing her voice and weeping.

The nature, unity and function of the narrative voices in **"The Blessed Damozel"** have been the subject of continued debate among Rossetti critics. In his analysis of the first published version of the poem, which appeared in the second number of *The Germ* (80-83) in February 1850, D. M. R. Bentley claims that the poem was intended as an almost polemical exercise in "the re-creation of a medieval awareness" which throws into relief the relationship between "the impiled poet and the historical percipient in the poem." Bentley defines this "historical percipient" as

> an omniscient and speculative figure whose style and assumptions characterize him as the representative of the medieval-Catholic awareness that the reader is invited to enter. The function of the percipient in **"The Blessed Damozel"** is complex: like the implied poet of Rossetti's **"Sonnets for Pictures"** his task is to present a "picture" (in some case the "diptych" composed of the blessed Damozel and her earthbound lover) and to imagine the world and feelings of its personae. . . . Through his re-creation of a spatial and emotional relationship that is radically alien to the "modern" mind, the percipient inducts the reader-spectator into the medieval-Catholic awareness that he was designed by Rossetti to embody. (6)

This ingenious critical construction of a poem equipped with an implied poet, percipient narrator, parenthetical speaker and Damozel, fails to take sufficient account of the fact that as one of Bentley's own footnotes concedes, many commentators see the "entire drama" of the poem as being "enacted within the single consciousness of the earthbound lover," the parenthetical speaker. In part our perception of the whole poem as a product of the parenthetical speaker's schizophrenic consciousness may be a response to Rossetti's failure completely to control point of view in **"The Blessed Damozel."** This lack of control is sufficient reason to regard Bentley's view that there are four levels of narration as being somewhat optimistic; a more convincing case has been made by Paul Lauter and Thomas Brown for the earthbound, parenthetical-print speaker being the presiding consciousness, the former arguing that the poem's vision "can be regarded entirely as the grieving . . . lover's projection" (346).

With her "blue grave eyes," "three white lilies" and "white rose of Mary's gift" (ll. 3, 5, 9), the Damozel is evidently a Marian anima figure. What the narrator does in an attempt to unite himself with his anima is to activate the simultaneous processes of aesthetic and erotic unification which bring the poem and picture and man and woman into Rossetti's reciprocal state of ideal conjunction. Thus as the poem begins poetry and painting become nearly identical, as the top part of the Rossettian "diptych," the initial description of the Damozel, is presented as a monumental tableau. But this vision is not totally static: the lady's "still look" (l. 16) is, paradoxically, still full of "wonder" (l. 15), a characteristically Rossettian attribution of psychological animation to a static, pictorialized figure. The Damozel's powerful gaze strives to penetrate and thus to overcome the "steep gulph" of time and space which separates her from her beloved.

Consequently she leans out from "the gold bar of heaven" (l. 2) in an effort to escape the confines of pictorial stasis which the frame-like heavenly barrier imposes. Realizing that she is consigned to remain perpetually silent and still within her golden frame the Damozel immediately challenges the limitations of her condition by leaning and gazing outward, and warming her pictorial barrier with the pressure of her bosom. Eventually and inevitably, after ten stanzas, the Damozel breaks her pictorial vow of silence with a petulant outburst:

"I wish that he were come to me,
 For he will come," she said.
"Have I not prayed in solemn heaven?
 On earth has he not prayed?
Are not two prayers a perfect strength?
 And shall I feel afraid?"

(ll. 61-6)

The Damozel's prayers have been reciprocated and, significantly, anticipated by her earthly lover, who is encased, as Bentley points out, in parentheses which are the "typographical equivalent of a predella" (39). The parenthetical typography of **"The Blessed Damozel"** is the most striking example of Rossetti's literary pictorialism, a device which complements the pictorial image of the "gold bar," and appears virtually to have dictated the bipartite form of Rossetti's Early Renaissance style depiction of *The Blessed Damozel* (1875-8).[2]

Bentley claims that the "fantastic mind of the lover" is "separate from yet accessible to the percipient" narrator, but if anything the reverse is true: the parenthetical speaker, who becomes the reclining figure in the painting's predella, has access to the scene described by the seemingly omniscient narrator. He adds an important coda to the initial description, emphatically qualifying it in terms of immediate first-person, present tense experience:

 to them she left, her day
Had counted as ten years.

(To one it is ten years of years:
 . . . Yet now, here in this place
Surely she leaned o'er me,—her hair
 Fell all about my face . . .
Nothing: the Autumn-fall of leaves.
 The whole year sets apace.)

(ll. 17-24)

The bland omniscience of the first voice which explains that a day for the Damozel counts as ten years for those left behind is abruptly corrected by "one" who apparently knows better, the hyperbolical lover for whom the Damozel's "day" is "ten years of years." Because the main narrative and the parenthetical one substantially overlap there is a sense of reciprocity, and a point of intersection and interaction is thereby established.

Momentarily her lover is convinced that the Damozel has been in contact with him and he fantasizes that it is her hair—the yellow hair of a corn goddess—which fell about his face. In **"Body's Beauty"** "one strangling golden hair" ensnares Lilith's victims but here the Damozel's hair is a reassuringly tangible token of her reality. Rapunzel-like it links heaven and earth almost as if it would draw the man heavenward, and like the gold bar of heaven the yellow hair defines the world of its two inhabitants, not as a barrier but as an inclusive and natural frame, embracing both lovers. As this fantasy dissolves it is replaced by a natural correlative for the falling hair, falling leaves, which are an ironic earthly equivalent of the corn image, signifying decay instead of fertility. Both the "hair, lying down" (l. 11) the Damozel's back and the dead leaves of the parenthetical speaker's world are featured in the appropriate heavenly and earthbound sections of Rossetti's painting, reinforcing the reader-spectator's sense of a close correspondence between bipartite poem and painting.

Although he says relatively little directly the parenthetical narrator in fact controls the movement of **"The Blessed Damozel."** Rather like the sestet in a sonnet the parenthetical speaker's comments initiate a volta, changing our point of view and perception of the Damozel by meditating upon particular aspects of her existence. Subsequently this speaker interrupts the Damozel as she anticipates teaching him in heaven, and again it is evident that he hears or knows what is said in the main body of the poem because he comments directly upon it:

"And I myself will teach him—
 I myself lying so,—
The songs I sing here; which his mouth
 Shall pause in hushed and slow,
Finding some knowledge at each pause
 And some thing new to know."

(Alas! to *her* wise simple mind
 These things were all but known
Before: they trembled on her sense,—
 Her voice had caught their tone.
Alas for lonely Heaven! Alas
 For life wrung out alone!

Alas, and though the end were reached . . .
 Was *thy* part understood
Or borne in trust? And for her sake
 Shall this too be found good?—
May the close lips that knew not prayer
 Praise ever thought they would?)

(ll. 85-102)

The lady's certainty that her lover's mouth shall "'pause in'" between her songs "'finding some new knowledge at each pause'" is clearly a cue to the earthly lover to rehearse his lines for heaven. He duly responds with a lament which reveals an interesting aspect of their former relationship: with "*her* wise simple mind" the Damozel had had intuitive foreknowledge of heaven's songs, whereas he had been doubtful. Therefore in the second stanza of his second speech the lover engages in an intense self-interrogation, asking himself: "was *thy* part understood?" "May the close lips that knew not prayer / Praise ever, though they would?" Evidently the earthly lover remains as yet unable to make the leap of faith necessary to re-unite him with the Damozel, and we therefore return to the speaker who knows her part.

When Rossetti published **"The Blessed Damozel"** in the 1870 edition of ***Poems*** these parenthetical stanzas were revised, condensed, and I think, clarified:

(Alas! We two, we two, thou say'st
Yea, one wast thou with me
That once of old. But shall God lift
To endless unity
The soul whose likeness with thy soul
Was but its love for thee?)

(ll. 97-102)

In this stanza the prospect of endless unity with the Damozel's soul seems even more unlikely to her lover because his sense of inferiority has been intensified, and in the oil painting the male's inferiority is graphically established by the small scale of his figure in comparison with the Damozel's above him: his head is about the same size as one of her lilies.

The problem which the poem tries to resolve, but which the static painting does not and cannot deal with, is how to subordinate the confident decisive Damozel to a weak, passive male. In *The Germ* version of the poem this problem is particularly acute because it is evident that *"her"* mind is decidedly more wise than simple, while his wallows in repeated lamentation. Rossetti's revisions of *The Germ* text go some way towards eliminating the repetitive histrionic quality from his voice but in both versions of the poem the male is dominated by the female, and both texts reverse this situation in almost identical concluding stanzas:

She gazed and listened and then said,
Less sad of speech than mild:
"All this is when he comes." She ceased;
The light thrilled past her, filled
With Angels, in strong level lapse.
Her eyes prayed, and she smiled.

(I saw her smile.) But soon their flight
Was vague 'mid the poised spheres.
And then she cast her arms along
The golden barriers,
And laid her face between her hands
And wept. (I heard her tears.)

(ll. 139-50)[3]

Given the final words in **"The Blessed Damozel"** the parenthetical speaker is uncharacteristically assertive, and because his statements are affirmations of the percipient's descriptions they read like parenthetical asides by him. Thus the juxtaposition of the impersonal, "Her eyes prayed, and she smiled" with, "I saw her smile," constitutes a significant convergence of "objective" and "subjective" points of view.

The ultimate integration of the twin aspects of the male psychology represented by Rossetti's main and parenthetical speakers is predicated upon a decisive shift in the latter's perception of the Damozel. Previously she had been vastly superior and therefore dominant inducing in her earthly lover a sense of inadequacy which results in his identity crisis. Objectively he recognizes her manifest superiority, but subjectively and parenthetically he is disturbed by this perception, at first rejecting the existence of his vision as "nothing." However, having heard the Damozel speak he is forced to admit her existence and question his worthiness of her.

The strategy finally adopted for reconciling the male to his anima is not to elevate him but to neutralize her. The Damozel's "gold bar" of the first stanza becomes the imprisoning "golden barriers" of the final one behind which she now retreats, becoming "mild" of speech, and regresses into the passive mode of Mariana, waiting for him to come. She becomes silent and therefore meek and benign, praying with her eyes and smiling and although the smile pleases the earthly lover his final triumph occurs when the Damozel cries. Seeing the smile and hearing the tears the earthly lover gains complete control of his vision and her mind. She ceases to be wise and becomes simple, crying for her beloved instead of threatening to teach him.

For the observer-poet of **"The Blessed Damozel"** the moment of "supreme" perfection occurs only when he is in complete harmony with himself, when his two voices virtually match, and when his anima is entirely subordinated to him. In a more covert fashion **"The Blessed Damoze!"** makes a similar point to Browning's "My Last Duchess": total male power resides in the complete control of a female art-object. The Duke is only happy when "all smiles" have stopped and Rossetti's earthly lover is happiest when the Damozel smiles contentedly but cries helplessly.

Notes

[1] The 1974 edition of the *Princeton Encyclopedia of Poetry and Poetics* translates Horace's dictum *ut pictura poesis* thus: "as is painting so is poetry"; and it gives a brief history of the topos.

[2] This version is in the Fogg Museum of Art, Harvard University, and is reproduced by Surtees no. 244.

[3] There are a few minor changes in punctuation in the 1870 version of "The Blessed Damozel." In addition; "the light thrilled past her" becomes "the light thrilled towards her," the angels are in "strong level flight" instead of "lapse," and "their path was vague in distant spheres," instead of "vague 'mid the poised spheres."

Works Cited

Ainsworth, Maryann Wynn. "Dante Gabriel Rossetti and the Double Work of Art." *Dante Gabriel Rossetti and the Double Work of Art.* Ed. Ainsworth. New Haven: Yale University Art Gallery, 1976. 6-7.

Bentley, D. M. R. "'The Blessed Damozel': A Young Man's Fantasy." *Victorian Poetry* 20 (Autumn-Winter 1982): 31-43.

Brown, Thomas. "The Quest of Dante Gabriel Rossetti in 'The Blessed Damozel.'" *Victorian Poetry* 10 (Autumn 1972): 273-77.

Fletcher, Ian. *Swinburne.* London: Longman, 1973.

Gelpi, Barbara Charlesworth. "The Image of the Anima in the Work of Dante Gabriel Rossetti." *Victorian Newsletter* No. 45 (Spring 1974): 1-7.

The Germ: A Facsimile Reprint of the Literary Organ of the Pre-Raphaelite Brotherhood, Published in 1850. Ed. William Michael Rossetti. London: Elliot Stock, 1901.

Lauter, Paul and Thomas Brown. "The Narrator of 'The Blessed Damozel.'" *Modern Language Notes* 73 (1958): 344-48.

Rossetti, Dante Gabriel. *The Works of Dante Gabriel Rossetti.* Ed William Michael Rossetti. London: Ellis, 1911.

Stein, Richard. *The Ritual of Interpretation.* Cambridge: Harvard UP, 1975.

Surtees, Virginia. *The Paintings and Drawings of Dante Gabriel Rossetti: A Catalogue Raissonné.* 2 vols. Oxford: Clarendon, 1971.

Antony H. Harrison (essay date 1990)

SOURCE: "Dante Rossetti: Parody and Ideology," in *Victorian Poets and Romantic Poems: Intertextuality and Ideology,* University Press of Virginia, 1990, pp. 90-107.

[*In the following essay, Harrison discusses the parodic nature and self-consciously aesthetic ideology of Rossetti's poetry.*]

In a recent essay, Claus Uhlig comes to the problematic conclusion that many literary works, because of their deliberate intertextuality, concern themselves preeminently with their own histories or genealogies. "It is doubtlessly true, and all the more so since the Romantic era," he insists, "that the aging of poetic forms and genres constantly increases their self-consciousness as knowledge of their own historicity. Through this progressive self-reflection, whose sphere is intertextuality, literature is in the end transformed into metaliterature, mere references to its own history."[1] For Uhlig views of history and of the self in relation to history—especially our creations or works in relation to past works—are deeply ideological.[2] As has often been observed, it was during the nineteenth century that "the modern discipline of history first came fully into its own as a truly rigorous inquiry into the past."[3] Ultimately, however, because of "the very success of scientific history at reconstituting the past," the powerful awareness of the past itself became "burdensome and intimidating . . . revealing—in Tennyson's metaphor—all the models that could not be remodeled." In fact, the apocalyptic aims of the Romantic poets early in the century begin to reflect "the idea that history, simply by existing, exhausts possibilities, leaving its readers with a despairing sense of their own belatedness and impotence. And this despair in turn leads to anxious quests for novelty, to a hectic avant-gardism, and in the end to an inescapable fin de siècle ennui."[4]

As self-appointed heirs of the Romantics, the Pre-Raphaelite poets—Dante Rossetti foremost among them—display in their works an extraordinary degree of historical self-consciousness, as would seem appropriate to their concept of themselves as a transitional, literary avant-garde.[5] Once observed, the powerful effects of Rossetti's own historical self-consciousness upon his poetry compel us to look at his work in new ways. Many of his poems are deliberate intertexts, works that manipulate palimpsests parodically in order both to resist the social actuality which obsessed his contemporaries and to open up new tracks for future writers. This is a fundamentally Romantic, specifically Wordsworthian project.[6] There is a crucial difference, however, between Rossetti's project and that of Wordsworth—or Blake, Shelley, and Keats, for that matter. Whereas these historically hyperconscious Romantics were visibly dedicated to supplanting the ideologies of their literary precursors with their own literary and political ideologies, Rossetti attempts uniquely to employ the intertextual dimensions of his work to create the illusion of altogether eliding and superseding ideology, as it is commonly conceived. Moving beyond even Uhlig's formulation of the metaliterary implications of intertextuality, Rossetti appears virtually to embrace intertextuality *as* a coherent and self-sufficient ideology. The intertextual dimensions of his poetry enable him seemingly to marginalize "those modes of feeling, valuing, perceiving and believing which have some kind of relation to the maintenance and reproduction of social power,"[7] by refocusing all such modes of experience on the structure, history, and intrinsic qualities of literary textuality itself, propounding as a supreme value the creation and deciphering of texts that are highly ornamental, artistically complex, and layered. Since no text is autonomous, all texts being derivative (as are all creators of texts), this dialectical activity becomes for Rossetti the preeminent mode of self-definition, intellectual inquiry, social understanding, and spiritual self-generation.

In a brief preface to his translations of the early Italian poets (1861), Rossetti laments the deteriorating form in which thirteenth-century Italian poems have become available to nineteenth-century readers because of "clumsy transcription and pedantic superstructure." He insists that, "At this stage the task of talking much more about them in any language is hardly to be entered upon; and a translation . . . remains perhaps the most direct form of commentary."[8] Here Rossetti quite properly implies that a translation *is* an interpretation, but one which most closely echoes or contains an originary text. These remarks may, in fact, be seen as Rossetti's first comments in print to broach matters of literary appropriation, transvaluation, and intertextuality. That his first published volume consists entirely of translations suggests a useful starting place for any study of Rossetti's own poetic works, whose sources in the poetry of Dante, Petrarch, Milton, Poe, Keats, Shelley, and even the Gothic novelists have been thoroughly discussed by critics, but without helping us to grapple in genuinely productive ways with the unique difficulties presented by Rossetti's verse.

The more often we read certain poems by Rossetti, the more puzzling, uncertain, and ambiguous their tone, their purpose, and of course, therefore, their meaning seems to become. Such is the case with works that we sense are to some extent derivative, referring to earlier texts formally, imagistically, or ideologically. Some of Rossetti's most important poems, these works are often pervasively self-reflexive, and their original versions date from the late 1840s and early 1850s when, as David Riede has made clear, Rossetti was still intensively searching for "an idea of the world." During this period, "gradually, Rossetti was beginning to distill a personal style and voice from the multitudinous mass of literary and artistic precedents and from his own mixed ethnic heritage, but despite his uneasy balancing of traditions, he remained uncertain about his artistic direction and purpose. For this reason, in both his writing and his painting, his best works of the late 1840s and early 1850s are all attempts to explore or expound the relation of the artist to his art, to nature, to society."[9] A short list of these works would include the **"Old and New Art"** sonnets, **"The Portrait," "Ave," "The Staff and the Scrip," "Sister Helen," "The Bride's Prelude,"** numerous other sonnets from ***The House of Life,*** **"Jenny," "The Burden of Nineveh,"** and **"The Blessed Damozel."** In these poems, as in the bulk of Rossetti's paintings, stylistic mannerisms, tonal ambiguities, and echoes of form and conventions from certain of his literary precursors—Keats, Browning, Milton, and Dante especially—so obtrude that the intertextual effects upon the reader are disorienting and for some readers distracting. That is to say that the poem's ostensible subject matter and purpose seem to be subsumed and overpowered by such an extreme degree of artistic self-consciousness that the poetic project itself is surrounded by uncertainty.

We finish the last stanza of **"The Portrait,"** for instance, trying to unravel a constellation of interactive images and elaborate conceits that invite symbolic or even allegorical interpretation and that vaguely echo Poe, Browning, and Petrarchan tradition. By the poem's conclusion the speaker has fully demonstrated the depth of his passion for his dead beloved. He has done so while contemplating the portrait he had painted of her when alive and remembering the circumstances that led to its creation:

Here with her face doth memory sit
Meanwhile, and wait the day's decline,
Till other eyes shall look from it,
Eyes of the spirit's Palestine,
Even than the old gaze tenderer:
While hopes and aims long lost with her
Stand round her image side by side
Like tombs of pilgrims that have died
About the Holy Sepulchre.[10]

Once we have deciphered this stanza and the poem that it concludes, attention has shifted altogether from the ostensible subject of the poem (the prospect of salvation through the haunting memories of a dead beloved)—to the hermeneutic project itself. The problems of reading, interpreting, making sense of the elaborate ornamental surfaces of the poem have thrust themselves so far forward and required such "fundamental brainwork" of us, that we become finally more interested in surfaces, in techniques and their employment, than in the subject matter being presented. Issues of aesthetics—symbolism, form, style, tone, etc.—fully displace and supersede matters of substance—theme or philosophy or ideology. Rather than a "willing suspension of disbelief," Rossetti seems bent at every turn on enforcing disbelief and distraction upon the reader in ways that remind us of the new generation of radically self-conscious parodic novelists—Fowles, Barth, Borges, or Eco, for instance.

One simple explanation of the purpose and effect of Rossetti's deliberate destabilization and subversion of his own texts might fall properly into line with Jerome McGann's insistence (some twenty years ago) that Rossetti's procedures serve to reinforce his central aestheticism: literature's last gift, like love's, is merely literature itself.[11] Art and artistry must, therefore, like a beautiful woman, draw attention to themselves—their elaborate, complex, ornamental surfaces—in order to enthrall or seduce us. This explanation, however, does not finally do justice to the complex of responses that Rossetti's best poems evoke. The frequent reader of these texts finds them not only ornate and beautiful but also rich and deep in their allusiveness to other texts and to the entire literary enterprise. He finds them simultaneously sincere and parodic; derivative yet original; fraught with ineffable philosophic weight yet somehow hollow; ambiguous; ironic—and finally, elusive.

A general approach to Rossetti's poems that proves more adequate in explaining their complex operations than those of the past—biographical, new critical, or aestheticist—derives from recent expansions of our modes of critical thinking that have emerged from the concern among semioticians, deconstructionists, and new historical critics with all matters related to intertextuality and self-reflexiveness in literature. Rossetti's best known poem, **"The Blessed Damozel,"** serves as an illuminating exemplary text.

As all readers of this inverted elegy know, it dramatizes the craving for reunion felt by two lovers separated by death. The central dialogue is between the full-bosomed Damozel—lamenting her separation while leaning earthward from the gold bar of heaven—and her distant beloved who thinks about her from below. The poem's pathos derives, for some readers, from the fact that for the Damozel the distance between the two is finally insuperable; however, her lover, whose voice and perspective gradually merge with that of the narrator, ironically claims to hear her voice, her words, her tears, but their communication is one-sided, and the Damozel remains a victim of Heaven's exquisite torture of separation, as her languorous suffering is exacerbated by witnessing the pairs of joyous lovers reuniting around her. As all readers of the poem also know, the lovers' dialogue is embedded in an elaborate setting and is at various levels fantastical: the narrator's cosmic vision seems so portentous, and at once detailed yet ambiguous, as to be fantastic; each lover fantasizes about the present circumstances of the other; and the Damozel fantasizes about the pair's future together after reunion in heaven.[12]

The reader of this poem is likely to scrutinize it with special attention, because a number of its features strike us as curious—hyperconscious, oddly derivative, even self-mocking. The more we contemplate the poem's possible purpose and meaning, the more unsettling and disorienting we find the work. As almost every commentator on the poem has noted, we are puzzled, for instance, from the very first stanzas by the unorthodox combination of the spiritual and the sensual or erotic. The former elements include an array of traditional religious symbols and an insistence upon medieval numerology, while the latter elements are introduced into the poem with images of the Damozel's gown "ungirt from clasp to hem," her hair "yellow like ripe corn," and her "bosom" pressing against the bar of heaven (***Poetical Works,*** p. I). Further, the attempt at cosmological mapping early in the poem is accomplished in such deliberately vague terms that it seems disorienting rather than helpful. That the "rampart of God's house" looks downward over absolute Space toward the solar system is clear enough from stanza 5. That Rossetti insistently refines upon this scheme in stanza 6, using redefinitions even more abstract than their originals (Space becomes a "flood of ether"), along with mixed metaphors, seems altogether to undercut the project of mapping the cosmos, however. We are no wiser afterwards than we were before. The language of stanza 7 is so trite and hyperbolic—invoking such phrases as "deathless love" and "heart-remembered names"—that it verges on the ironic, especially as the associations of spirituality that such terminology elicits are abruptly truncated in the next stanza's notorious description of the Damozel's palpably "warm" bosom. Such startling pseudoeroticism, seemingly determined to explode all former theological concepts of heaven, culminates in mid poem when the Damozel describes the rebaptism of their love at the anticipated moment of reunion: "As unto a stream we will step down. / And bathe there in God's sight."

Unsettling descriptions and events punctuate the last third of the poem as well. How are we to respond to the moment at which the earth-bound lover, for the first time with certainty, perceives the sound of the Damozel's voice in a continuation of what is presumably "that bird's song" of stanza II: "We two, we two, thou says't?" he says. Somehow the source of this light chirrup seems incommensurate with the lover's insistence (in an allusion to II Corinthians 6:14) upon the eternal union of his and the Damozel's souls. The presentation of the heavenly court in the next stanza also seems overly literal. Indeed, the depiction of Mary and her five handmaidens sitting round to pass judgment on the cases of lovers is deflated by the scene's evocation of the historical courts of love presided over by Eleanor of Acquitaine in late twelfth-century France. This association is reinforced by the image of an audience of angels playing citherns and citholes, as well as the poem's pervasive archaisms, including its title. The penultimate demystification of the poem's issues comes with the damozel's plea "Only to live as once on earth / With Love"—surely a radical literalization of Keats's antitraditional notion of enjoying "ourselves here after by having what we call happiness on Earth repeated in a finer tone."[13] And the poem's final perplexing move—drawing our attention away from its substance to the problem of narrative form—is the last stanza's perspectival sleight of hand, in which the identity of the omniscient narrator merges with that of the aggrieved lover. This formal trick for some readers makes the conclusion seem as equivocal or hollow or contrived as it is full of pathos.

How then does the reader deal with this curious poem whose tone seems to exist in some unexplored grey area—some void of linguistic ether—between sincerity on the one hand and parody, as it is traditionally understood, on the other? He may go so far as to conclude that **"The Blessed Damozel"** is, in some rare and complex fashion, a hoax; that it was written with tongue partially in cheek; or that it awkwardly presents itself as at once serious and mocking and thus a novel kind of parody for the mid-nineteenth century, a work that is self-reflexive and self-parodic while densely allusive—echoing, imitating, or parodying a number of originary or enabling texts and traditions. That is to say, it is pervasively, complexly intertextual and dialogic. Given the extent to which tonal ambiguities, dialogism, and intertextuality are striking features of other major poems by Rossetti as well as **"The Blessed Damozel,"** it is worth investigating, in theoretical as well as practical terms, the full implications of the parodic horizons in Rossetti's verse.

Some especially useful theoretical discussion of parody has appeared in recent years in the writing of Barthes, Genette, Riffaterre, and Bakhtin. But these theorists have done work that serves, finally, to marginalize, bracket, or in other ways delimit and deflate parody both as a literary genre (or subgenre) and as a medium for self-conscious ideological discourse. Linda Hutcheon's recent book, *A Theory of Parody*, however, largely succeeds in rehabilitating parody by cogently redefining it as a specific mode of discourse and by enlarging our notions of what constitutes parody and what literary parody can accomplish.[14] In doing so, she forcefully demonstrates the interrelations between parody and some central issues that emerge in recent semiotic, formalist, and new historical approaches to literature and literary theory.

According to Hutcheon, in her own appropriation and reification of recent theorists, "a parodic text [is] defined as a formal synthesis, an incorporation of a backgrounded text into itself. But the textual doubling of parody (unlike pastiche, allusion, quotation, and so on) functions to mark difference. . . . on a pragmatic level parody [is] not limited to producing a ridiculous effect (*para* as 'counter' or 'against'), but . . . the equally strong suggestion of complicity and accord (*para* as 'beside') allow[s] for an opening up of the range of parody."[15] Thus, there exist "both comic and serious types of parody." Indeed, as Hutcheon points out, "even in the nineteenth century, when the ridiculing definition of parody was most current . . . reverence was often perceived as underlying the intention of parody."[16] Further, parody "is never a mode of parasitic symbiosis. On the formal level, it is always a paradoxical structure of contrasting synthesis, a kind of differential dependence of one text upon another." Parody, moreover, can involve a whole ethos or set of conventions rather than a single text: paradoxically, "parody's transgressions [or transvaluations of a text or a set of conventions] ultimately [are] authorized by the very norm it seeks to subvert. . . . In formal terms, it inscribes the mocked conventions onto itself thereby guaranteeing their continued existence." But, of course, "this paradox of legalized though unofficial subversion . . . posits, as a prerequisite to its very existence, a certain aesthetic institutionalization which entails the acknowledgment of recognizable, stable forms and conventions."[17] But the texts, conventions, traditions, or institutions encoded by an author in a parodic text require a sophisticated reader to recognize them and to decode the text, that is, to perceive the work at hand as parodic and dialogic, as transcontextual and transvaluative. Most works thus understood are also perceived finally as avant-garde. They engage in a form of what Barthes termed "double-directed" discourse, often "rework[ing] those discourses whose weight has become tyrannical." (For Rossetti, these would include the traditions of Dante and Milton.)

I would argue that these descriptions of parody powerfully illuminate the operations of many poems by Rossetti that clearly present themselves *as* avant-garde works. The dominant traditions with which they are in dialogue and which they attempt to transvalue are those of Petrarchism, Christianity, and Romanticism—especially in its exotic or supernatural and its medievalist guises.

In the case of **"The Blessed Damozel"** a unique equilibrium between preservation and subversion of originary texts, their conventions and values, is achieved. As I have already suggested, formally Rossetti's poem inverts the traditional conventions of the pastoral elegy; here it is primarily the dead beloved who grieves volubly for her lover who remains alive. The expected natural details of the genre's setting are also displaced: that is, they are either thoroughly etherealized or replaced with deliberately artificial props, such as the gold bar of heaven and its fountains of light. Symbolism full of potentially Christian meaning—such as the seven stars in the Damozel's hair and the three lilies in her hand—are drained of all such meaning and become merely ornamental.[18] Courtly and Petrarchan conventions, like the poem's pseudo-Dantean cosmology with its heavenly vistas, are thrust upon us with such literalness that they become at best disorienting and at worst absurd. The bizarre deployment of the supernatural here, too, displaces our usual conceptions of God, Heaven, angels, and the rituals conventionally associated with them. This heaven of lovers is a nontraditional fantasy, a bricolage of previous religious and literary conventions, images, values, and beliefs here appropriated and reformulated to authorize a new romantic ideology. This ideology is entirely aesthetic and insists that internalized sensory responses to experience alone constitute the spiritual. But such responses require a sense of loss or separation as a catalyst for their generation and thus seem to become wholly solipsistic and self-reflexive, as does the art which undertakes to represent them. In the world(s) of this poem, fantasy finally subsumes experience, and the most powerful fantasies emerge as much from previous art and literature as from experience itself. **"The Blessed Damozel"** read in this way must be seen finally as *seriously* parodic of its pretexts. The poem presents various dialogues—with medieval, Miltonic, Romantic, and Gothic precursors; with the traditional elegy; with the lovers who are themselves in dialogue. Finally, however, the poem appears to be in inconclusive dialogue with its own tentative values, images, and aspirations which emerge from its self-conscious reworkings of past artworks and their ideologies. Rather than asserting explicit positions on the amatory, religious, and philosophical questions it raises, the poem elides such questions in favor of emphasizing through its self-reflexivity the purely literary and aesthetic ones which emerge from its complexly dialogical operations.

Such inconclusiveness, equivocation, and ambiguity are common qualities of Rossetti's poems drafted early in his career, as might be seen from analysis of other important works. **"The Burden of Nineveh,"** for instance, is an interior monologue triggered by archaeological events. The speaker contemplates their meaning upon leaving the British Museum, where he has just viewed the Elgin Marbles, "the prize / Dead Greece vouchsafes to living eyes." As he makes "the swing-door spin" and issues from the building, workers are "hoisting in / A winged beast from Nineveh." By the end of the poem the speaker's thoughts have led him to an epiphanic historical vision:

> . . . on my sight . . . burst
> That future of the best or worst
> When some may question which was first,
> Of London or Nineveh.

In the course of the poem other questions of historicity and ideology are contemplated explicitly, alongside implicit questions about parody and self-referentiality as qualities that inevitably inhere in every religious artifact and, indeed, every work of art. Ultimately, according to this poem that invokes and argues against Ruskin, art is only an illusory index of the culture which produced it. Art defiantly rejects its originary historical contexts and transgresses—by transcending and eliding—the ideological values of the culture from which it emerges.

Paradoxically, this activity can take place only by means of parodic procedures, which precisely define the texts—as well as their historical positions and their ideologies—that Rossetti's poem presents itself as supplanting. This set of simultaneous moves within the poem draws attention to the phenomenology of the text itself as layered artifact. Just as the "meaning" of the Assyrian Bull-god (and every artwork) depends upon the contexts, the historical and ideological vantage points from which it is read or observed, so the sequence of parodic strategies within the poem draws attention to the phenomenology of *this* text as an accretive fabrication: its "meaning" can be construed only by deciphering the text as palimpsest. The speaker concludes that,

> . . . it may chance indeed that when
> Man's age is hoary among men,—
> His centuries threescore and ten,—
> His furthest childhood shall seem then
> More clear than later times may be:
> Who, finding in this desert place
> This form, shall hold us for some race
> That walked not in Christ's lowly ways,
> But bowed its pride and vowed its praise
> Unto the god of Nineveh.
>
> The smile rose first,—anon drew nigh
> The thought: . . . Those heavy wings spread high,
> So sure of flight, which do not fly;
> That set gaze never on the sky;
> Those scriptured flanks it cannot see;
> Its crown, a brow-contracting load;
> Its planted feet which trust the sod: . . .
> (So grew the image as I trod:)
> O Nineveh, was this thy God,—
> Thine also, mighty Nineveh?

Like the phenomenon of the Bull-god, Rossetti's poem reconstitutes hermeneutics as a branch of archaeology. But also like the Assyrian artifact, this poem, which subsumes all of its pre-texts, appears self-sufficient and elusive: "From their dead Past thou livs't alone; / And still thy shadow is thine own." The Bull-god as text provides a commentary not only upon its progenitors and successors along with their respective contexts but also upon itself as an accommodation of all possible historical and ideological contexts. It is a "dead disbowelled mystery" with "human face," with "hoofs behind and hoofs before," and "flanks with dark runes fretted o'er."

The parodied texts that Rossetti appropriates—the "fretted runes" Rossetti frets over—in his speaker's questions to the Bull-god include works by Shelley and Keats, who are echoed here, but also (and more generally) works by Ruskin and biblical books. By the time Rossetti began reshaping **"The Burden of**

Nineveh" in 1856, Ruskin's absolutist and evangelical view that art is a clear embodiment of the historically specific spiritual and moral values of the culture which produced it had been fully elaborated in *The Stones of Venice.* Against that general position, Rossetti here argues a historically relativistic case. Similarly, references to the book of Jonah and Christ's temptations by Satan (p. 27) serve—especially in light of the poem's conclusion—as an ironic commentary on the myopic absolutism and the ahistoricism of Christian "orthodoxy." They also serve, however, to insist on the much greater longevity of Christian texts (its art) than the historically limited spiritual beliefs that inspired them. These texts, again in a general way, are parodied here in the mock-prophetic tone and substance of the last three stanzas.

Rossetti's appropriations of Shelley's "Ozymandias" and Keats's "Ode on a Grecian Urn" are more direct and specific. His procedure with respect to these texts is deliberately self-parodic, as well: the author in his relation to these pre-texts behaves as the English have behaved in appropriating and assimilating into their own gigantic cultural monument (the British Museum) the works of art from many great civilizations that preceded the British Empire:

And now,—they and their gods and thou
All relics here together,—now
Whose profit? whether bull or cow,
Isis or Ibis, who or how,
Whether of Thebes of Nineveh?

At the same time Rossetti's use of Shelley and Keats is parodic in the sense of working with and extending the conventions as well as the apparent insights of their poems.

Near the end of **"The Burden of Nineveh"** Rossetti invokes the central image of "Ozymandias": the half-buried monument to the pharaoh, around which "the lone and level sands stretch far away." Rossetti's speaker retrospectively envisions "the burial-clouds of sand" which, centuries past, "Rose o'er" the Bull-god's eyes "And blinded him with destiny" (p. 29). Rossetti is in a position, however, to update Shelley's historically limited view of the "collossal Wreck" that is Ozymandias's monument. This artifact, too, or portions of it, might well be plundered and given new life as a historical "fact / Connected with [a] zealous tract" in the British collection, as Rossetti gives new life to Shelley's poem and enriches its central irony.

In stanza 3 of **"The Burden of Nineveh"** Rossetti similarly parodies Keats's "Ode on a Grecian Urn," appropriating a Romantic text that also concerns itself with the transcontextualization of an artifact from an ancient civilization and the hermeneutical problems that result. Rossetti borrows Keats's strategy of asking questions of the artifact and answering them in a way that only proliferates questions. At the same time Rossetti heightens the historical self-consciousness of this project by introducing into his stanzas parodic echoes of Keats's "Ode to Psyche" as well. Rossetti's historical questions—

What song did the brown maidens sing,
From purple mouths alternating,
When that [rush-wrapping] was woven
languidly?
What vows, what rites, what prayers preferr'd,
What songs has the strange image heard?

—echo not only the concluding questions of stanza I in "Ode on a Grecian Urn," but also Keats's catalogue of rituals and service belatedly needed for the proper worship of Psyche, who has no temple,

Nor altar heap'd with flowers;
Nor virgin-choir to make delicious
moan
Upon the midnight hours;
No voice, no lute, no pipe, no incense
sweet
From chain-swung censer teeming;
No shrine, no grove, no oracle, no heat
Of pale-mouth'd prophet dreaming.[19]

The questions both poets ask can be answered only with precise and extensive historical knowledge which both poets refuse to supply, insisting that the present artifact supersedes such concerns, as well as all cultural works and rituals that have enabled its production. This text annuls and supplants such absences (to which it paradoxically draws attention) by its exclusive presence.

With its parodies of the Bible, Shelley, and Keats, the "burden" of Rossetti's **"Nineveh"** thus becomes a weight of critical and self-critical meaning that elides traditional ideologies; it is also a refrain, as an inevitable and recontextualized reenactment of historically layered creative moments and *their* patterns of meaning. This poem tells us not only of the burdens of the past as they are appropriated by the present but of the fact that all parodies as artistic reenactments are burdensome: weighted with critical commentary on all historical eras, all relevant works of art, all ideologies of all writers and readers, including the present ones.

In such poems as **"The Blessed Damozel"** and **"The Burden of Nineveh,"** begun early in his career, Rossetti was searching not only for an "idea of the world," as David Riede has argued, and a coherent system of aesthetic values; he was also searching with extreme caution for a secure idea of a discrete self, as well as an idea of the self in relation to others.[20] The latter part of this quest, in the early versions of his poems, focuses almost exclusively upon explorations of the amatory self and the artistic self, that is, the self in its highest or quintessential synchronic relations with society individualized in the form of a lover; and the self in its supreme, because creative, diachronic relations with the great creative selves of the past. While the quest for love reveals psychological compulsion, the quest for position displays a willed ambition to demonstrate unique talent.

In the 1848 sonnets included among the three "Old and New Art" poems of the ***House of Life,*** **"Not as These"** grapples with the young artist's yearning to distinguish himself from contemporaries and precursors alike. It insists in the end, however, that artistic greatness in the future can be achieved, not by looking to one's contemporaries, but by confronting the "great Past":

Unto the lights of the great Past, new-lit
Fair for the Future's track, look thou
instead,—
Say thou instead, "I am not as *these* are."

The implication here is unmistakable: the track to the future is in every sense *over* that of the past. In order to *become* the future the prospective artist must reillumine the works of his great precursors; that is, he must appropriate, transvalue, and transcontextualize them. The same point is made, albeit abstractly, in the final sonnet of this subsequence, **"The Husbandman."** Here the possibility is raised of regenerating in oneself those whom God "Called . . . labour in his vineyard first." For,

Which of ye knoweth *he* is not that last
Who may be first by faith and will?—yea, his
The hand which after the appointed days
And hours shall give a Future to their
Past?

These poems suggest what Rossetti's translations in 1861 and other early works such as **"The Blessed Damozel"** and **"The Burden of Nineveh"** confirm: that as early as 1848 Rossetti had formulated at least the outlines of an avant-garde program to achieve success and importance as an artist. And that program was deeply intertextual and dialogic, requiring parodic reworkings of those earlier poets and poetic ethos he reverenced most. This program is visible even in a poem as ostensibly self-referential, ahistorical, and nonideological as **"The Portrait."**

In this poem Browning's "My Last Duchess" is the pre-text being simultaneously displaced and admired. On a grander scale, however, Rossetti's work sets out obliquely to destabilize and subvert the entire Dantean ethos, especially the orthodox Christian conventions of belief associated with Dante, Petrarch, and their imitators. In form, theme, and characterization, Rossetti's poem presents itself as a sequel to Browning's, which it deliberately echoes from the first stanza. A monologic meditation rather than a dramatic monologue, **"The Portrait"** presents a speaker whose character is the obverse of the duke of Ferrara's: rather than merely an admirer of art, he is an artist for whom the portrait serves as a potential mode of communion with his dead beloved, not her replacement and a controllable improvement upon the original. Before her death the artist's beloved herself constituted the ideal, while her portrait is "Less than her shadow on the grass / Or than her image in the stream." This speaker is, moreover, a genuine lover rather than one concerned with wives as "objects," symbols of wealth, power, and social station. While Browning's duke is a thoroughgoing materialist, Rossetti's artist-lover is obsessed with the ephemeral and spiritual dimensions of his relationship: having "shrined" his beloved's face "Mid mystic trees," he anticipates the day when his soul shall

. . . stand rapt and awed,
When, by the new birth borne abroad
Throughout the music of the suns,
It enters in her soul at once
And knows the silence there for God!

Ultimately, Browning's duke is concerned with marriage vows as a means to increased wealth and power, while for Rossetti's painter the twice-spoken words of love—"whose silence wastes and kills"—though "disavowed" by fate, are merely precursors to permanent, visually communicated vows.

In these ways, then, Rossetti's poem responds directly to Browning's, presenting the positive amatory *and* aesthetic values absent from "My Last Duchess." Like all true parodies, Rossetti's is thus authorized by and dependent upon its pre-text, but it also supersedes it. At the same time, **"The Portrait"** appropriates and supersedes the Petrarchan and Dantean conventions of love's spiritualizing influence which inform the value system of the poem and to which it adheres. That is, after unquestionably accepting both the Dantean language and situation that serve to apotheosize a dead beloved as an agent of salvation, Rossetti displaces them from their originary Christian contexts by presenting the moment of the speaker's own apotheosis and reunion with her in a parodic sexual image of penetration. The "knowledge" of God that he hopes to attain in uniting with his beloved's soul is *transcendently* carnal. Yet, such parodic qualities upon which the full "meaning" of Rossetti's poem depends are ambiguously encoded and require decoding by a sophisticated reader. They are embedded in variously vague, abstract, or merely generalized language and metaphors that allow "innocent" readings of the text, thus appearing to elide ideological commitment.

From such a perspective the parodic qualities of Rossetti's early poems, including **"The Portrait," "The Blessed Damozel,"** and **"The Burden of Nineveh,"** seem to be largely self-protective. Through their reliance upon great and familiar literary precursors, his poems accrue authority. Through their self-reflexivity and circularity they preempt any judgment that might easily be passed on matters of ideology. Moreover, through their transvaluation and transcontextualization of the forms, conventions, imagery, and typological structures of originary texts, Rossetti's poems locate their existence at the boundaries of the avant-garde and of ideological commitment. They simultaneously assert and elide values which might, presented differently, be seen to confront and displace the fundamental values embodied in the historically specific texts and traditions Rossetti parodies. Such a visible subversion of the ideological dispositions of his pre-texts, however, would make Rossetti's poem, like those of his precursors, subject to imprisonment by history. To elude such a fate Rossetti employs intertextual strategies to generate poems that present themselves as avant-garde intertexts, whose deep consciousness of historicity itself is deployed to defuse any delimiting ideological or historical critique.

But despite initial appearances, Rossetti's poems do embody a historically specific ideology. As I have suggested, the tentative and oblique repudiation, subversion, and devaluation of conventional ideological statement in Rossetti's work lead to a reconstitution of ideology in exclusively aesthetic terms. Through the processes of allusion, parody, and self-parody by which "new art" is generated, Rossetti's poems individually exalt purely aesthetic valuation above political or social or religious valuation. Art is represented as the unique source of fulfillment, permanence, and transcendence in life. Thus, as a unified body of work, Rossetti's productions do bear a definable "relation to the maintenance and reproduction of social power." They actively participate in the competitive, historically localized phenomenon of poetic supersessions. In doing so they reinforce the aesthetic ideology they inscribe and (revising Shelley and Wordsworth) relocate the structures of immutable worldly and spiritual power in the exclusive habitations of the artist's studio and the poet's study.

Notes

[1] Claus Uhlig, "Literature as Textual Palingenesis: On Some Principles of Literary History," *New Literary History* 16 (1985): 503.

[2] On this topic see, for instance, the recent work of Jerome J. McGann and Hayden White, as well as that of Marilyn Butler, Terry Eagleton, Frederick Jameson, and Jane Tompkins.

[3] Elliot Gilbert, "The Female King: Tennyson's Arthurian Apocalypse," *PMLA* 48 (1983): 866. Also see A. Dwight Culler, *The Victorian Mirror of History* (New Haven: Yale Univ. Press, 1985), and Peter Allen Dale, *The Victorian Critic and the Idea of History: Carlyle, Arnold, Pater* (Cambridge, Mass.: Harvard Univ. Press, 1977).

[4] Gilbert, "The Female King," p. 866.

[5] See Herbert Sussman, "The Pre-Raphaelite Brotherhood and Their Circle: The Formation of the Victorian Avant-Garde," *The Victorian Newsletter* 57 (1980): 7-9, and, by the same author, *Fact into Figure: Typology in Carlyle, Ruskin, and the Pre-Raphaelite Brotherhood* (Columbus: Ohio State University Press, 1979), pp. 44-45, 55.

[6] In *Michael,* for instance, Wordsworth dedicates his work expressly to "youthful Poets, who . . . / Will be my second self when I am gone." *Wordsworth: Poetical Works,* ed. Thomas Hutchinson, rev. Ernest de Selincourt (Oxford: Oxford Univ. Press, 1969), p. 104.

[7] Terry Eagleton, *Literary Theory: An Introduction* (Minneapolis: Univ. of Minnesota Press, 1983), p. 15.

[8] Dante G. Rossetti, *The Early Italian Poets,* ed. Sally Purcell (Berkeley: Univ. of California Press, 1981), p. 1.

[9] David Riede, *Dante Gabriel Rossetti and the Limits of Victorian Vision* (Ithaca, N.Y.: Cornell Univ. Press, 1983), pp. 34-35.

[10] *The Complete Poetical Works of Dante Gabriel Rossetti,* ed. William Michael Rossetti (Boston: Roberts Brothers, 1887), pp. 132-33. Hereafter all poems by Rossetti will be cited parenthetically in the text to page numbers from this edition.

[11] Jerome J. McGann, "Rossetti's Significant Details," *Victorian Poetry* 7 (1969): 41-54; reprinted in *Pre-Raphaelitism: A Collection of Critical Essays,* ed. David Sambrook (Chicago: Univ. of Chicago Press, 1974).

[12] An essay which also concerns itself with matters of fantasy and one which takes a view of "The Blessed Damozel" opposed to my own is D. M. R. Bentley's "'The Blessed Damozel': A Young Man's Fantasy," *Victorian Poetry* 20 (1982): 31-43.

[13] Keats to Benjamin Bailey, Nov. 17, 1817, in *The Letters of John Keats,* ed. Hyder E. Rollins, 2 vols. (Cambridge: Harvard Univ. Press, 1958), 1:185.

[14] Linda Hutcheon, *A Theory of Parody* (London: Methuen, 1985).

[15] Ibid., p. 54.

[16] Ibid., p. 57.

[17] Ibid., p. 75.

[18] See McGann, "Rossetti's Significant Details."

[19] *The Poems of John Keats,* ed. Jack Stillinger (Cambridge: Harvard Univ. Press, 1978), p. 365.

[20] See Riede, *Dante Gabriel Rossetti,* p. 273.

J. Hillis Miller (essay date 1991)

SOURCE: "The Mirror's Secret: Dante Gabriel Rossetti's Double Work of Art," in *Victorian Poetry,* Vol. 29, No. 4, Winter, 1991, pp. 333-49.

[*In the following essay, Miller offers an analysis of "the double mirroring structure" of Rossetti's poetry.*]

> And still she sits, young while the earth is old,
> And, subtly of her self contemplative,
> Draws men to watch the bright web she can weave,
> Till heart and body and life are in its hold.[1]

If Rossetti's Lilith looks only, speculatively, at her own image in the mirror, she also looks self-consciously aware of the looks of all those men whom she draws by her indifference into her fatal net. Rossetti's source here is that text from Goethe which he translated:

> Hold thou thy heart against her shining hair,
> If, by thy fate, she spread it once for thee;
> For, when she nets a young man in that snare,
> So twines she him he never may be free.
>
> ("Lilith—from Göthe," ***W,*** p. 541)

Lilith's mirroring of herself and our fatal mirroring of ourselves in the painting are doubled by the mirror imaged on the canvas. Moreover, the painting mirrors a Victorian Pre-Raphaelite boudoir, and also Rossetti's feelings about Fanny Cornforth. The painting, in addition, mirrors the poem, **"Body's Beauty,"** Sonnet 78 of ***The House of Life,*** of which it is an "illustration." Or is it the other way around, the poem a "caption" for the painting? Ultimately, both poem and painting are mirrors of, mirrored by, other works, echoing before and after, works in painting and in poetry by Rossetti himself, and multitudinous works in a complex tradition—graphic, literary, and philosophical—going back to the Bible and to the Greeks, in one direction, and forward, to our day, for example to John Hollander's admirable *The Head of the Bed.* In this tangled network of relations, "Mirror on mirror mirrored is all the show."[2]

These mirrorings are all, however, in one way or another odd, ambiguous, subversive, irrational. The mirrored image undoes what seeks its image there. Each mirrored image is somehow different from the exact reflection which tells the truth unequivocally, as when I look at my face in the mirror in the morning. There I am, as I am. "I am that I am." The mirror tells me so. I suffice to myself, like God. Or do I?

Far from producing an emblem of such fullness and completion, image matching image, Lilith's subtle contemplation of herself weaves a net, and behind the net there is a gulf. Into this abyss the men she fascinates will fall. This gulf is that "orchard pit" which was Rossetti's constant dream, that ugly ditch beside the apple tree with the Lilith or Siren figure in the crotch of its branches, offering a fatal apple and a fatal kiss. Why is it that when we men contemplate not ourselves in the mirror but our incongruous other self, a desirable woman contemplating herself, our own integrity is mutilated, destroyed?

> Men tell me that sleep has many dreams; but all my life I have dreamt one dream alone.
>
> I see a glen whose sides slope upward from the deep bed of a dried-up stream, and either slope is covered with wild apple-trees. In the largest tree, within the fork whence the limbs divide, a fair, golden-haired woman stands and sings, with one white arm stretched along a branch of the tree, and with the other holding forth a bright red apple, as if to some one coming down the slope. Below her feet the trees grow more and more tangled, and stretch from both sides across the deep pit below: and the pit is full of the bodies of men.
>
> They lie in heaps beneath the screen of boughs, with her apples bitten in their hands; and some are no more than ancient bones now, and some seem dead but yesterday. She stands over them in the glen, and sings for ever, and offers her apple still. (**"The Orchard Pit,"** ***W,*** pp. 607-608)

If *Lady Lilith* mirrors Fanny Cornforth and a certain kind of Victorian decor (its furniture, costume, and psychosocial structures, its domestic economy), this mimetism is peculiar, since this Victorian boudoir, with its mirror, double candlestick, cosmetic bottle, chest, and settee, seems to be out of doors. What is mirrored in the mirror on the wall is not an interior but an exterior woodland scene, a scene of branches going from left to right matching in reverse Lilith's tresses, which spread from right to left. The branches duplicate themselves in smaller and smaller repetitions out to invisibility in a *mise en abîme.* The scene in the mirror is in fact the orchard pit. Or is the mirror a window? No, it cannot be so, since the roses and the candles are reflected there. How odd, however, that the Lady Lilith should be combing her hair outdoors, surrounded by all those bedroom appurtenances and by roses and poppies which might be either inside or out. In Eden there was no inside or out, but this scene is the diabolical mirror image of Eden, as Lilith is of Eve.

The confusion of interior and exterior, mirror and window, is characteristic of all that art Walter Pater called "aesthetic." In such art, nature has been made over into the images of art, and those images made over once more, at a double remove. As Pater puts it in a splendid formulation:

> Greek poetry, medieval or modern poetry, projects, above the realities of its time, a world in which the forms of things are transfigured. Of that transfigured world this new poetry takes possession, and sublimates beyond it another still fainter and more spectral, which is literally an artificial or "earthly paradise." It is a finer ideal, extracted from what in relation to any actual world is already an ideal. Like some strange second flowering after date, it renews on a more delicate type the poetry of a past age, but must not be confounded with it. The secret of the enjoyment of it is that inversion of home-sickness known to some, that incurable thirst for the sense of escape, which no actual form of life satisfies, no poetry even, if it be merely simple and spontaneous.[3]

In "aesthetic" poetry and painting even the most meticulously naturalistic scene, in what Pater calls, apropos of Rossetti, an "insanity of realism" (p. 209), is emblematic. Such a scene is absorbed into a spiritualized human interior, inside and outside at once, since the distinction, uneasily, no longer exists, just as the distinction between the spiritual and material no longer exists. To go outside is not to be outside but to remain claustrophobically enclosed, and the interior is no safe enclosure. It is exposed to the dangers of a fatal encounter. The orchard pit is within and without at once, just as the window in Sir John Everett Millais' *Mariana* (an illustration of Tennyson's "Mariana") is also a mirror of her state, and just as the same ambiguity functions in the mirror of Tennyson's "The Lady of Shalott," in this case illustrated by Holman Hunt. Pater, with his characteristic genius as a critic, has once more provided a definitive formulation of this aspect of Rossetti's work:

> With him indeed, as in some revival of the old mythopoeic age, common things—dawn, noon, night—are full of human or personal expression, full of sentiment. The lovely little sceneries scattered up and down his poems, glimpses of a landscape, not indeed of broad open-air effects, but rather that of a painter concentrated upon the picturesque effect of one or two selected objects at a time—the "hollow brimmed with mist," or the "ruined weir," as he sees it from one of the windows, or reflected in one of the mirrors of his "house of life" (the vignettes for instance seen by Rose Mary in the magic beryl) attest, by their very freshness and simplicity, to a pictorial or descriptive power in dealing with the inanimate world, which is certainly also one half of the charm, in that other, more remote and mystic, use of it. For with Rossetti this sense of lifeless nature, after all, is translated to a higher service, in which it does but incorporate itself with some phase of strong emotion. Every one understands how this may happen at critical moments of life; what a weirdly expressive soul may have crept, even in full noonday, into "the white-flower'd elder-thicket," when Godiva saw it "gleam through the Gothic archways in the wall," at the end of her terrible ride [Tennyson, "Godiva"]. To Rossetti it is so always, because to him life is a crisis at every moment (pp. 532-533).

What that "crisis" is, cutting off before from after, and dividing the moment too within itself, and what feeling every moment as a crisis has to do with this particular version of the pathetic fallacy, remains to be identified. Window or mirror, as Pater has seen, are means to the same vision. What is seen there is natural, human, and spiritual, all at once. The framed image is always, as Pater's brilliantly chosen quotations from Rossetti indicate, some version of the orchard pit, the "hollow brimmed with mist," the "ruined weir," or that maelstrom into which the lovers are swept in the poetic fragment of **"The Orchard-Pit":**

> My love I call her, and she loves me well:
> But I love her as in the maelstrom's cup
> The whirled stone loves the leaf inseparable
> That clings to it round all the circling swell,
> And that the same last eddy swallows up.
> (*W*, p. 240)

In "Lady Lilith" the mirroring of a boudoir which turns out to be an abyssal wood of storm-tossed branches also mirrors the reflection of Lilith in her hand-held mirror. Though the back of that mirror is turned toward the spectator, the image in the mirror on the wall tells him what chasm is no doubt pictured there behind the screen of reflected hair. This chasm is imaged over and over throughout Rossetti's work by way of displaced figures in the "outside" framed in a window or in a mirror.

The other mirrorings are equally alogical. The relation between Rossetti's painting and his poetry is asymmetrical, skewed. This is true not in the sense that one overtly contradicts the other, but in the sense that each exceeds the other, however deliberately they may be matched, as in the case of *Lady Lilith* and **"Body's Beauty."** Each says more or less than the other, and says it differently, in ways which have only in part to do with the differences of medium. Either may be taken as the "original" of which the other is the "illustration" or the explanatory poetic "superscription," writing on top of another graphic form. This relation does not depend, of course, on the chronology of Rossetti's actual creation of the two works in question. In each case, however, the secondary version in the other medium is always in one way or another a travesty, a misinterpretation, a distorted image in the mirror of the other art.

The relation to "the tradition" of the double, self-subversive work of art is, once more, a false mirroring. Whether one takes the more immediate context of Rossetti's other work or, as does John Dixon Hunt in *The Pre-Raphaelite Imagination,* the wider context of Pre-Raphaelite work generally, or Rossetti's relation to his immediate predecessors, Shelley and Tennyson, or the relation of his work to the whole Western tradition, this relation of work to context, as the passage from Pater quoted above suggests, is not a straightforward copying, continuation, or reflection. It is a strange second flowering after date, a sublimation or rarefaction which is also a swerving, a distortion.

Nonetheless, this subversive mirroring is already part of the tradition, traditional even in Plato or Milton, however much that deconstructive mirroring may have been apparently suppressed. "Aesthetic" poetry was already a part, though sometimes a secret part, of "ancient" and "modern" poetry. Pater's chronology of the development of Western poetry in fact describes a synchronic tension within it among patterns which may not be reconciled in any synthesis, dialectic, or historical movement. Rossetti's false mirroring of the tradition does but tell a secret which is already there, everywhere within that "tradition," but often hidden.

What is the secret that the distorting mirror always tells and keeps? Loss. All Rossetti's work is haunted by an experience of devastating loss. That loss has always already occurred or is about to occur or is occurring, in memory or in anticipation within the divided moment. It occurs proleptically, antileptically, metaleptically, the feared future standing for the already irrevocable past, and vice versa, in a constant far-fetching reversal of late and early. The longed-for future may not be. The poet of **"The Stream's Secret"** knows or is told by the mirroring stream that it may not be. The past was disastrous, even if it held moments of joy. Those moments have passed, their joy turned into the desolation of their loss. "What whisper'st thou?" the poet asks that moving and murmuring, mirroring stream:

Nay, why
Name the dead hours? I mind them well:
Their ghosts in many darkened doorways dwell
With desolate eyes to know them by.

(**"The Stream's Secret,"** *W,* p. 114)

The loss in question is experienced perpetually in that everlasting moment of crisis (in the etymological sense of division) in which the mind dwells. Of that division the mind makes an emblem in those natural scenes glimpsed through a window or reflected in a mirror. These scenes in turn become human figures which then become those personified abstractions, Life, Death, Time, and so on, which populate, as Pater observed, Rossetti's work. These personifications constitute in their humanized particularity the "insanity of realism" in Rossetti. "And this delight in concrete definition," says Pater, "is allied with another of his conformities to Dante, the really imaginative vividness, namely, of his personifications—his hold upon them, or rather their hold upon him, with the force of a Frankenstein, when once they have taken life from him. Not Death only and Sleep, for instance, and the winged spirit of Love, but certain particular aspects of them, a whole 'populace' of special hours and places, 'the hour' even 'which might have been, yet might not be,' are living creatures, with hands and eyes and articulate voices" (Pater, "Dante Gabriel Rossetti," p. 531).

These personifications result from a process miming the progressive sublimation of aesthetic poetry. They are a further refinement of what is already a transfigured or humanized nature. Their meaning is always some aspect of that absolute loss which is exacerbated, always, by having almost been its opposite, like a swimmer who almost makes the shore and then is swept away:

Look in my face; my name is Might-have-been;
I am also called No-more, Too-late, Farewell;
Unto thine ear I hold the dead-sea shell
Cast up thy Life's foam-fretted feet between;
Unto thine eyes the glass where that is seen
Which had Life's form and Love's, but by my spell
Is now a shaken shadow intolerable,
Of ultimate things unuttered the frail screen.

(**"A Superscription,"** *W,* p. 107)

The figure in the glass, "Might-have-been," is one's own face, just as Pater's metonymic "mistake" in naming the monster with the name of its creator catches accurately the relation between Doctor Frankenstein and his creature, the made making and unmaking the maker. Rossetti's personifications keep their hold upon him because they are figures for himself. All those persons, personifications, and scenes—the orchard pit, the ruined weir, the stormy branches—are one's own face in the mirror, caught in the eternal moment of crisis as the confrontation of a perpetual loss.

Loss of what? Loss as such, total and irrevocable. Absence. To name this loss one's own death or (fear of) castration, or the confrontation with the woman who has (or who does not have) the phallus (Lilith as snake), or the death of the beloved, or that betrayal by the beloved which is always the story of love for Rossetti, is only to conjure one more shadow in the glass, one more frail screen, like all the other images in Rossetti, for "ultimate things unuttered," and, in any literal way, unutterable. It is as if I looked in the mirror and saw nothing there, or were to see an image which is not myself but a figure of my absence or of my incompletion.

Precisely this happens in a little poem, **"The Mirror."** Here the poet's failure to find a reciprocating feeling in the lady he loves is imaged as the unsettling experience of seeing what he thinks is his own image in a distant mirror and then finding it is not himself, so that he is for the moment imageless:

> She knew it not:—most perfect pain
> To learn: this too she knew not. Strife
> For me, calm hers, as from the first.
> 'Twas but another bubble burst
> Upon the curdling draught of life,—
> My silent patience mine again.
> As who, of forms that crowd unknown
> Within a distant mirror's shade,
> Deems such an one himself, and makes
> Some sign; but when the image shakes
> No whit, he finds his thought betray'd,
> And must seek elsewhere for his own.

(**"The Mirror,"** *W*, p. 194)

"For his own": the phrase has a straightforward enough grammatical ellipsis and yet, dangling uncompleted in the open as it does at the end of the poem, possessive adjective without a noun, it shimmers with alternative possibilities. He must seek elsewhere for his own image, and the missing noun mimes the absence of what the speaker seeks. As the logic of the figurative relation between first and second stanzas affirms, however, his missing image is a trope for the female counterpart who would complete him. Her absence or indifference, her failure to match feeling with his feeling, is in turn a figure for something missing in himself. It is as if for Rossetti "the mirror stage" were not the discovery of one's self (the *Ideal-Ich*) in the mirror but the discovery of a vacancy there, an empty glass.

The structure of **"The Mirror"** is "the same" as that in **"Body's Beauty."** In fact, all Rossetti's work consists of two intersubjective patterns, a desired one "which might have been, yet might not be," and its asymmetrical mirror image, which always and irrevocably exists. This double intersubjective structure is, like all such models, with difficulty distinguished, if it may be distinguished at all, from a solipsistic relation of the self to itself. The Other, however totally other, is still experienced as part of myself or as something I wish were part of myself. In **"Willowwood,"** the four-sonnet sequence within ***The House of Life,*** Love grants the Narcissus-like poet the privilege of kissing his beloved's lips. These rise to meet his lips at the surface of a "woodside well": "her own lips rising there / Bubbled with brimming kisses at my mouth" (***W,*** p. 91). It is a phantom kiss, though, and of course he kisses his own imaged lips.

The desired side of this mismatched pair of patterns is expressed in **"The Stream's Secret."** It is a wish for future joy, the Might-still-be which stands as a future anterior for Might-have-been. This Might-still-be remains always Not-quite-yet. The mirror, which has been vacant of any images but hollow shadows of unfulfilled desire, will (or will never) become suddenly full, the reflection of a double, completed image. The lovers, in this impossible imaginary encounter, will view their joint image in the stream's mirror and then, no longer needing the mediation of any mirror, will look only in one another's eyes:

> So, in that hour of sighs
> Assuaged, shall we beside this stone
> Yield thanks for grace; while in thy mirror shown
> The twofold image softly lies,
> Until we kiss, and each in other's eyes
> Is imaged all alone.
>
> Still silent? Can no art
> Of Love's then move thy pity?

(**"The Stream's Secret,"** *W*, p. 117)

The stream is still silent and does not tell Love's secret, since there is no secret to tell. The mirror's secret is that there is no secret. "Love's Hour," the hour when "she and I shall meet . . . stands . . . not by the door" (p. 117), however much the poet strains to believe that it does. The ultimate things unuttered are here and now, on the surface of the stream's mirror, not at the bottom of some abysmal depth. The stream will always remain vacant of any twofold image. Instead there is always, as the present without presence of crisis, the contrary image there. This image is the incongruous double of the desired one. It is the pattern, in fact, of **"Willowwood,"** or, altered, of **"Body's Beauty,"** or, in a different form, of **"The Mirror,"** or, in a different form again, of **"The Portrait,"** or, different still, of **"Love's Nocturn."** In this antithetical system, I look in the mirror and see not my own image but that of my female counterpart who looks not at me but at herself, subtly of herself contemplative, or, as in **"The Portrait,"** I see her image still remaining after her death. This death is experienced, uncannily, as if my own image should remain in the mirror when I was no longer standing before it:

This is her picture as she was:
  It seems a thing to wonder on,
As though mine image in the glass
  Should tarry when myself am gone.

(**"The Portrait,"** *W*, p. 169)

In **"Love's Nocturn,"** the counterstructure takes the form of the poet's imagining that he meets his own image "face to face," as he is "groping in the windy stair" leading down to the place where all dreams are.[4] That image he would send to his lady's sleep, but he fears another image already usurps his place. His image must return then to the dream-fosse, having enjoyed one kiss not of the lady's lips but of their reflection in her mirror:

Like a vapour wan and mute,
  Like a flame, so let it pass;
One low sigh across her lute,
  One dull breath against her glass;
  And to my sad soul, alas!
      One salute
Cold as when Death's foot shall pass.

(**"Love's Nocturn,"** *W*, p. 72)

I have emphasized the differences among all these versions of the counter-pattern not only to confirm what I said earlier about the relation of incongruity between any work and the context it "mirrors," even the immediate context of other work by the same maker, but also to suggest that this counter-pattern always manifests itself differently. More precisely, each of its exemplars must be aberrant and none must be governed by an archetype. This pattern denies the existence of any archetype or model, the exact repetition of which might turn loss into completion. Ultimately, this structure may never be fixed in a definitive version, any more than Rossetti's personified beings, Love, Death, Sleep, and so on, may be systematized into a coherent counter-theology. Against this perpetually wandering structure is always set the primary structure of lover and beloved meeting face to face in a perfect match.

"Structure" here is a misleading term, not only because of its currently fashionable resonances, and not only because it does not cover all that is in question here, but because, like any possible term, it begs the questions it should keep open. It reinstates the metaphysical or "logocentric" assumptions that this "double triangle" dismantles. This "structure," "system," or "figure," this "emblem," "hieroglyph," "polygram," or "multigraph," is a complexity that cannot be unified. It remains incoherent or heterogeneous, always doubled and redoubled in repetitions that subvert rather than reinforce. Its heterogeneity lies not only in its resistance to conceptual unification or logical interpretation, but in its combining in an uneasy mélange: concept ("speculation"); figures of speech (the mirror image as image for image); figures, in the sense of persons in their relations (those reflected in the mirror); graphic or representational elements (the mirror itself, the Pre-Raphaelite woman, her landscape); and narrative material (the story of disastrous love Rossetti always tells). How can one name this except reductively, or in a figure that refigures the problem?

Perhaps Rossetti's own final figure for a sonnet, combining as it does graphic and verbal elements, might do best. Having called the sonnet a "moment's monument," carved "in ivory or in ebony," with "flowering crest impearled and orient," like some ornate coat of arms, picture and words combined, he defines the sonnet, in the sestet of his sonnet about the sonnet, as a coin. The obverse and converse of this coin combine a double, simultaneous orientation toward the experiences of the self or "soul" and toward that unnameable power, or absence of power, "Life," "Love," "Death," that governs the Soul. It is the coin itself, the double work of art—not the soul which one side of it reveals—which is, in all senses of the idiom, "due to" the Power. If the coin's face "reveals / The Soul," the "Power" is that unutterable thing of which the coin's converse is the revelation. At the same time, the converse acts as a frail screen protecting the Soul from that revelation. Or perhaps one might better say that it is the dumb silver of metal between which keeps obverse and converse, Soul and Power, apart, both for good and for ill:

A Sonnet is a coin: its face reveals
  The Soul,—its converse, to what Power 'tis
    due:—
Whether for tribute to the august appeals
  Of Life, or dower in Love's high retinue,
It serve; or, 'mid the dark wharf's cavernous
  breath,
In Charon's palm it pay the toll to Death.

(**"Introductory Sonnet,"** *W*, p. 74)

A final, concentrated "example" of this double-faced coin is **"Memorial Thresholds."** This poem substitutes doorway for window or mirror and proposes two possibilities: that the threshold remain permanently vacant, or that it be filled once more, in the memorial reduplication of a déjà vu, with the form of the beloved. Here, she is imagined as having once actually stood in the same doorway somewhere, of which the new threshold is a repetition:

City, of thine a single simple door,
  By some new Power reduplicate, must be
  Even yet my life-porch in eternity,

Even with one presence filled, as once of yore:
Or mocking winds whirl round a chaff-strown floor
Thee and thy years and these my words and me.

(**"Memorial Thresholds,"** *W,* p. 101)

Why is it that the doorway, in Rossetti's numismatics of art, remains always empty? What is the meaning of the discovery that the mirror's secret is its vacancy? A placing of Rossetti's double-pattern of presence mirrored by absence in relation to the long tradition of such doublings may help to unriddle the secret of this secret. My discussion must be brief and incomplete because there would be no end to the labyrinthine wanderings of the critic who attempted the absurd task of a topographical mapping of all the "ways and days" intricately interwoven in this *topos* of the memorial threshold, window, or glass.

The places within this place would include: the glasses of the Apostle Paul in First and Second Corinthians, with their echo of Genesis, a passage in 1 James (1.21-25); the paradigm of the mirror in Book 10 of *The Republic* and the mirror in *The Sophist* (239d); the speech of Aristophanes in *The Symposium;* the Narcissus story in Ovid's *Metamorphoses;* the great passage on "Speculation" in the interchange between Ulysses and Achilles in Shakespeare's *Troilus and Cressida;* Eve's admiration of her own image in Book 4 of *Paradise Lost;* passages in Rossetti's more imediate predecessors, such as Shelley's "Alastor" and "Epipsychidion"; the Fuseli of so many nightmarish doors, windows, and mirrors; Tennyson's "Mariana" and "The Lady of Shalott." Finally, among Rossetti's contemporaries or successors, there would be: George Meredith, who recapitulates and reinterprets the interplay between Ovid and Milton, Narcissus and Adam, in *The Egoist;* Baudelaire's Dandy who *"doit vivre et dormir devant un miroir";*[5] Whistler's *The Little White Girl* and Swinburne's poem on this painting, "Before the Mirror"; Mallarmé's *Herodiade;* a splendid passage at the beginning of Thomas Hardy's *Far From the Madding Crowd;* Wilde's *The Picture of Dorian Gray;* Yeats's "Ribh Denounces Patrick"; all those mirrors in Picasso; the eerily uncanny moment in Freud's *"Das Unheimliche"* when he sees his own image in a mirror but does not recognize it as his own, and detests it (the reverse of the pattern in Rossetti's **"The Mirror,"** where the image is not his own); Benjamin's essay on the photograph and the loss of aura in Baudelaire;[6] Beardsley's illustrations for Belinda's toilet in *The Rape of the Lock;* and lastly all those paradigmatic mirrors of our own day, in Jacques Lacan's "The Mirror Stage," or in Luce Irigaray's *Speculum of the other woman,* an investigation in part of the whole tradition of the mirror-structure from Plato to Freud as it bears on the question of the male interpretation of sexual difference.[7]

This seemingly diverse and miscellaneous set of references, discontinuous points in the sky of Western culture, are in fact rigorously organized into a repeated constellation, or rather a double constellation, a Gestaltist duck-rabbit, like that big dipper which is either Charles's wain or the great bear, depending on how one looks at it. In all these texts, a complex asymmetrical structure is present in one form or another, in one degree or another of completion of explicit expression. Indeed, this structure is "fundamental" in all Western "thought" and "literature," in the sense that it both affirms and endangers any fundament or ground. The structure involves a pair which becomes potentially subverted by a triangular relation among three persons or images, though it remains precariously balanced. This stable triangle is then incongruously mirrored in another triangle which parodies it and so undermines its stability.

This complex structure is the speculative as such, the reflective or the theoretical, the positing, hypothetically, as an image, of what may be seen and known, in a movement of thinking and seeing which is also a working or making. This movement goes out from itself in order to strive to return to itself in a confirmation of itself by way of an other which is or should be the perfect image of itself, not really other than itself. Even God, it seems, cannot know himself until he has gone outside himself and so can see himself outside himself.[8] Speculation (from *speculum,* mirror), theory (*theoria,* seeing, as in "theatrical"), art or poetry (*poesis,* making), and imitation (*mimesis,* miming, as in the great mirror/doorway scene in the Marx brothers' *Duck Soup*)—all come together in the crisscross of reflections in the mirror of this double paradigm.

The pattern of completion within this paradigm is the perfect mirroring of one male figure by another, by its own image in the glass. To the speculative, the theoretical, the poetic, and the mimetic can be added the self-generating, self-sustaining, and constantly self-transcending relation of the dialectical as another name for this system of reflections. The image of the mirrored and mirroring pair, in the tradition of this motif, oscillates between being the mirroring of male by male, in perfect match, Narcissus completing his own image is the pool, and being the mirroring of male by female, in another form of perfect matching, concave matching convex, as in the androgynous couple in Aristophanes' speech in *The Symposium.*

My focus here will be on a version of this paradigm which in one way or another adds a third figure, Echo in the Narcissus story, the fascinated male watching the woman who is subtly of herself contemplative in Rossetti's poem, or, as in a novel by a male author with a female protagonist, the intimate relation of indirect discourse in which a male narrator follows the thoughts and feelings of the heroine as she thinks about herself, as in the chapter of "Clara's Meditations" in Meredith's *The Egoist.*

Such a triangle remains stable, a sure support for ontological ground, only so long as it is all male or only so long as the female is defined as the adequate "image" of the male, a case of good rather than bad mimesis. An example of the all-male triangle is the Trinity: Father, Son, and Holy Ghost; the One, his filial image, and the relation between them; or God, his perfect image, the Son, and that creation fabricated by God in the image of the Son, so that the world as a whole and every part of it separately has the countenance of God and is signed with his genuine signature. An example of the second would be the definition of Eve in *Paradise Lost* as created in the image of Adam, who is in turn created in the image of God: "He for God only. She for God in him."

The female as third, however, or, more dangerously yet, as the doubled pair watched by a male spectator, the woman as two out of three, always introduces the possibility of a mismatching, a deflection of the closed circuit of reflections. The female, according to a sexist tradition going back to Plato and Aristotle, is an imperfect male, missing one member. The female introduces the deconstructing absence, the perpetual too little or too much that makes it impossible for the balance to come right and so keeps the story going, whether it is the story of an unassuaged desire which Rossetti always tells, or whether it is the story of thought which that love story tropologically represents. Theoretically, the woman opens up the triangle beyond any hope of closing it again or of filling the gap. This gap is the echoing cavern where false images are, that place of shades and shadows, for example, in Rossetti's **"Love's Nocturn"** which doubles the real bodies of men, "as echoes of man's speech / Far in secret clefts are made" (*W,* p. 71).

It should be clear now, as clear as one's own face in the glass, what this double triangle of mirrored images in Rossetti "means." Or is it? The double triangle records the moment of confrontation with the loss of the *Logos*—head sense or patron of meaning, caption. Its meaning is the absence of meaning, decapitation, decollation. God in speculation looks at himself in the mirror of the world, having engendered his material counterpart, the creation, by way of his mirror image, the Son. Man, too, along with the rest of the world, is "in the image of God created," as Lilith says sardonically in Rossetti's **"Eden Bower"** (*W,* p. 110). Man, then, in imitation of God, as God's mimic or mime, looks in the mirror and sees a sister-image there that does not fit him. Or, in the version of this that has been my interest here, the male writer or artist takes an interest in the situation of the female who looks in the mirror and discovers her lack, the missing man, as when Tennyson's Mariana says, finally, "He will not come." This interest in what is more than or different from himself becomes, for such a male artist, fascination. It is fascination by a plus-value which in the end leads to the loss of all in spend-thrift speculation.

The prolonged instant of specular fascination, drawing the male spectator into the abyss, is a version of what I call "the linguistic moment." This is the moment when signs are cut off from any extralinguistic grounding and become fascinating in themselves, in their self-sustaining and self-annihilating interplay. The momentum of this moment may make it an eternal instant. It becomes the prolonged, persisting time of poise or lack in a present which is no present. It has no presence, since it engages the signs of something missing, that is, signs as such. The sign by definition is the presence of an absence. There is nothing beyond such a moment. It cannot be gone beyond in any dialectical or speculative *Aufhebung.* It remains balanced interminably in sterile repetition, in a horrible parody of the self-engendering and self-mirroring of God.

The specular encounter, when the male looks in the mirror and does not find his image there, does not even find the answering look of his female counterpart, but sees a woman seeing herself, is the linguistic moment. In this moment occurs the dismantling of that male speculative system which ought to lead to absolute knowledge of the self by itself. Possession becomes dispossession; appropriation, expropriation. The male is entangled in the web of Lady Lilith's hair, drawn by the Siren in the tree into the Orchard Pit, put into a perpetual state of Might-have-been or Might-yet-be. What he writes or paints thereafter is constructed over the abyss of his loss, as Rossetti rescued the manuscript of ***The House of Life*** from his self-slain wife's coffin. He had put the manuscript just between her cheek and her hair. Such writing is without ground, like the words whirled by the mocking wind round a chaff-strewn floor in **"Memorial Thresholds,"** in a repetition of the failure of poetic language at the end of Shelley's "Epipsychidion." As in the case of the imagined long love embrace in **"The Stream's Secret,"** the linguistic moment suspends things over the gulf of their absence, as a matter of Might-have-been and Might-yet-be but never Is-now. The Now is an empty mirror, a stream that tells no secrets.

The speculative moment of fullness and its subversive counterpart are necessary to one another. Each implies the other and is surreptitiously present in any of its expressions. Nevertheless, they may not be combined or reconciled in any way, dialectically or otherwise. Rather, they set up in their relation an ungovernable oscillation that inhibits thought from proceeding, short-circuiting it in a feedback phenomenon. One finds oneself in a double blind-alley of thinking and feeling in which one cannot decide which corridor to take, since each corridor leads, manifestly, to a blank wall. Aesthetic art, the art of Rossetti and the Pre-Raphaelites generally, is, as Pater says, an art which satisfies that strange inversion of homesickness known to some, the desire to get as far away from home, from the "real world," as possible. Home, for Rossetti, figures death, the Orchard Pit. Therefore anyone would wish to escape from it into a world of shadows or of signs referring to prior signs, for example, into that poetry about poetry or strange second flowering after date Pater describes. The world of shadows or of signs, however, lies in the pit. Lilith and her counterparts in Rossetti's work draw men, precisely, into a realm of shadows. Either way, you have had it. The Medusa face of Rossetti's woman, since she draws her power from the annihilating energy of signs, is equally fatal in face-to-face or in mirrored encounter.

To mention Medusa is to remember Freud's "Medusa's Head" and "The Taboo of Virginity."[9] According to Freud, the male fears equally that the female will or will not possess the phallus. For Lacan, the phallus is not the penis, but what the penis stands for, the head or source of meaning, and therefore the grounding of the interplay among signs. The double horror of the phallic female makes up an essential part of the mirror structure I am discussing here. It is present, for example, in Herodias' image of herself as a reptile, in Mallarmé's poem, and in the terror that her own hair inspires in her. It is present as one moment in John Hollander's splendid version of the Lilith story in Canto 7 of *The Head of the Bed:*

> He dared not move
> Toward her one leg, toward her covered places
> Lest he be lost at once, staring at where
> Lay, bared in the hardened moonlight, a stump
> Pearly and smooth, a tuft of forest grass.[10]

The emblem of the girl with the penis is present in Rossetti, too, in the Lilith of **"Eden Bower,"** who whispers to the snake: "To thee I come when the rest is over; / A snake was I when thou wast my lover. / I was the fairest snake in Eden" (***W,*** p. 109), or in the monumental figure of *Mnemosyne.* In Rossetti's painting, the shape and position of Mnemosyne's lamp mime an erect phallus. Rossetti's caption for the painting calls attention to the winged mobility of this oddly shaped lamp: "Thou fill'st from the winged chalice of the soul / Thy lamp, O Memory, fire-winged to its goal" (***W,*** p. 229). The doubleness here is the doubleness of the two-faced coin: the soul, on the one hand, and the source of energy for the activity of memory, on the other hand. The relation between soul and memory is that coming and going, toward the past, toward the future, in a perpetual interchange moving toward a "goal" it never reaches, by way of a recollection of the permanent "Might-have-been yet might not be."

In Rossetti's version of the game of "Phallus, Phallus, who's got the Phallus?," the balance among a set of alternating possibilities never comes right. There is always one too many or one too few, not enough to go around, or one left over. This always leaves an Old Maid, or a Wild Card that governs the game but remains outside it, always somewhere else, neither King nor Queen, but Jack of Displacement. If the woman does not have the phallus, there is no ground. If she has it, she must have it as phantasm, as shadow, as that which is never where it is, hence there is no ground. If she has none, then I do, or do I? If she has one, then I must, mustn't I? If she does, then I don't. She's got it. If she doesn't, then I don't, or fear I may not. Either way, I've had it, or haven't had it, in a constant oscillation of possession and dispossession which can never be stilled into a stable, motionless system.

The Medusa solidifies me, turns me to stone, and so, as Freud says, I have no loss to fear. On the other hand, as he also says, my petrifaction is my horror at my confrontation of an absence, and so I fall into the Orchard Pit. On the one hand, art may be the result of the Medusa's effect, a fixed thing in language or in graphic form of what can then safely be confronted in mirror images or in the shadows of art. This submission to the Medusa is both good and bad, both true and false art, undecidably. On the other hand, art may itself be the Medusa's head that petrifies and makes permanent the flowing and the soft, so that *Mnemosyne* stands there permanently for the beholder safely to see, as though she were reflected in a mirror. This in its turn is both good and bad, both submission to the Lilith figure and triumph over her.

The uncanniness of the double mirroring structure lies in this permanent undecidability. Does the art of poetry which presents this system induce a loss? Does it force me as spectator to submit to Lilith's snare? Or does it ward off this loss apotropaically? Does it serve as a frail screen keeping me from unutterable things? Does it save me by mirroring the Medusa or the Lilith figure, freezing her in the double mirror of an art which moves back and forth from painting to poetry in a play of reflections which does not stay still long enough to be caught? There is no way to tell. It is always both and neither. The mirror keeps its secret to the end.

Medusa, it happens, is present as such in Rossetti's work, present as a double work of art in which picture and verse give form once more to all that double system, the two-faced coin of the mirror motif in Rossetti. This double work of art expresses once more the double attitude toward that double system I have tried to catch. With the final ambiguous admonition of "Aspecta Medusa"—against seeing, against theory, and in praise of mirror images—I shall end:

Andromeda, by Perseus saved and wed,
Hankered each day to see the Gorgon's head:
Till o'er a fount he held it, bade her lean,
And mirrored in the wave was safely seen
That death she lived by.
Let not thine eyes know
Any forbidden thing itself, although
It once should save as well as kill: but be
Its shadow upon life enough for thee.

(*W*, p. 209)

Notes

[1] Dante Gabriel Rossetti, "Body's Beauty," ll. 5-8, Sonnet 78, *The House of Life* in *Works*, ed. William M. Rossetti (London, 1911), p. 100. Further citations will be from this edition, identified as *W*, followed by the page number.

[2] William Butler Yeats, "The Statues," l. 22, *Collected Poems* (London, 1950), p. 323.

[3] Walter Pater, "Aesthetic Poetry," in *Walter Pater: Three Major Texts*, ed. William E. Buckler (New York, 1986), p. 520.

[4] See A. Dwight Culler's excellent discussion of Rossetti's motifs of the windy and winding stair: "The Windy Stair: An Aspect of Rossetti's Poetic Symbolism," *Ventures Magazine* 9, no. 2 (1969): 65-75.

[5] Charles Baudelaire, *Oeuvres Complètes* (Paris, 1961), p. 1273.

[6] Walter Benjamin, *"Über einige Motive bei Baudelaire,"* in *Illuminationem* (Frankfurt am Main, 1969), pp. 201-245; trans. Harry Zohn, "On Some Motifs in Baudelaire," in *Illuminations* (New York, 1969), pp. 155-200.

[7] See Luce Irigaray, *Speculum of the other woman*, trans. Gillian C. Gill (Ithaca, 1985); and Jacques Lacan, "The mirror stage as formative of the function of the 'I,'" in *Écrits*, trans. Alan Sheridan (New York, 1977), pp. 1-7.

[8] For the Hegelian recapitulation of this movement of speculation and the word-play it involves, see Jean-Luc Nancy, *La remarque spéculative* (Paris, 1973).

[9] Sigmund Freud, "Medusa's Head," trans. James Strachey, *International Journal of Psycho-Analysis* 22 (1941): 69-70; and "The Taboo of Virginity," trans. James Strachey, in *The Standard Edition of the Complete Psychological Works of Sigmund Freud* (London, 1957), 9:191-208.

[10] John Hollander, *The Head of the Bed* (Boston, 1974), p. 11.

Ernest Fontana (essay date 1992)

SOURCE: "Rossetti's 'On the Field of Waterloo': An Intertextual Reading," in *Victorian Poetry*, Vol. 30, No. 2, Summer, 1992, pp. 179-82.

[*In the following essay, Fontana examines Rossetti's "On the Field of Waterloo" in relation to William Wordsworth's earlier poem on the same subject.*]

As many of his critics have demonstrated, most recently Antony H. Harrison, 3 forms of intertextuality constitute a central feature of Dante Gabriel Rossetti's poetry.[1] For Harrison, many of Rossetti's poems, such as **"A Portrait"** (whose chief pre-text is in his view Browning's "My Last Duchess"), are "deliberate intertexts, works which manipulate palimpsests parodically in order both to resist the social actuality which obsessed his contemporaries and to open up new 'tracks' for future writers." For Harrison, what is distinct about Rossetti's use of intertextuality is its "tentative and oblique repudiation, subversion, and devaluation of conventional ideological statement" and its "reconstitution of ideology in purely aesthetic terms."[2]

One poem that demonstrates some of the intertextual patterns described by Harrison, but which he ignores, is Rossetti's sonnet **"On the Field of Waterloo."** Unpublished in Rossetti's lifetime, the sonnet is part of a sequence of verse and prose epistolary travel Notes, written for his brother William Michael, in late September and October of 1849 during his trip to France and Belgium with Holman Hunt, "the longest and most extensive continental wandering" of his life.[3]

So then, the name which travels side by side
With English life from childhood—Waterloo—
Means this. The sun is setting. "Their strife grew
Till the sunset, and ended," says our guide.
It lacked the "chord" by stage-use sanctified,
Yet I believe one should have thrilled. For me,
I grinned not, and 'twas something;—certainly
These held their point, and did not turn but died:

So much is very well. "Under each span
Of these ploughed fields" ('tis the guide still) "there rot
Three nations' slain, a thousand-thousandfold."
Am I to weep? Good sirs, the earth is old:
Of the whole earth there is no single spot
But hath among its dust the dust of man.[4]

The most salient pre-text for this sonnet is Wordsworth's sonnet "After Visiting the Field of Waterloo," which appears, as does Rossetti's later poem, in a sequence of travel-inspired verse—in Wordsworth's case *Memorials of A Tour on the Continent 1820* (1822). Rossetti's sonnet does not, however, merely reconstitute the ideology of Wordsworth's earlier sonnet "in purely aesthetic terms," but actively questions its universalized humanitarianism.

Significantly, Wordsworth's sonnet is a reflection on feelings after the event, whereas Rossetti's dramatizes in the present tense the feelings of the speaker as he visits the storied field. In the octet of Wordsworth's sonnet the speaker imagines the conventional iconographic personification Victory, "a winged Goddess—clothed in vesture wrought / Of rainbow colours"[5] hovering, diaphanously, over the battlefield and, suddenly, vanishing:

She vanished; leaving prospect blank and cold
Of wind-swept corn that wide around us rolled
In dreary billows, wood, and meagre cot,
And monuments that soon must disappear.
(ll. 6-9)

The ephemerality and evanescence of the English victory, symbolized by the vanished personification and the "monuments that soon must disappear," are counterposed against images of enduring, but drearily monotonous and repetitive, natural processes that survive the symbols of human ambition, glory, and power. These are the images, not the imagined personification of Victory, that the Wordsworthian speaker encounters directly at Waterloo.

With the coordinate conjunction "Yet," the Italian sonnet turns, belatedly, in meaning in line 10:

Yet a dread local recompense we found;
While glory seemed betrayed, while patriot-zeal
Sank in our hearts, we felt as men *should* feel
With such vast hoards of hidden carnage near,
And horror breathing from the silent ground!

(ll. 10-14)

Although the English speaker does not perceive the "glory" or "patriot-zeal" he anticipated, he feels something more ethical and universally human, "as men *should* feel." The concluding lines move from the distancing visual imagery of the extended octet to more immediate auditory and kinesthetic imagery. The silence of the field and the buried dead becomes an audible murmur of wasted human life. Instead of the glory of English victory, the speaker feels and hears the horror of human carnage.

For Rossetti's speaker as for Wordsworth's, Waterloo is storied ground; for the later Victorian, a name resonant with associations from childhood. Rossetti's speaker observes his response to both the battlefield and his theatrical guide, who seeks to elicit from the speaker a response of Wordsworthian sublimity. As the sun sets the guide refers to the strife which "grew till sunset." Yet the speaker who "should have thrilled" does not, though he recognizes—with considerable understatement—"'twas something" that the English "held their point, and did not turn but died." In the octet, the speaker fails to respond to the Wordsworthian imperative of sublime, universal human feeling.[6] If Wordsworth's speaker and companion "felt as men should feel," Rossetti's speaker fails to thrill as "one should have thrilled"; if Wordsworth italicizes and thereby foregrounds his auxiliary of obligation, Rossetti, in his failure to oblige, does not.

In the sestet of Rossetti's narrative sonnet, the guide continues his attempt to elicit from the Rossettian speaker the appropriate universal, sublime "should" feelings by remarking that the dead of three nations, "a thousand-thousand fold," rot at Waterloo. Once again the speaker does not respond appropriately nor does he know how to respond: "Am I to weep?" He appears to lack the normative human feeling that the Wordsworthian speaker refers to as "what men *should* feel." The empirical, skeptical Rossettian speaker knows too much to feel as the Wordsworthian speaker, who himself had felt too deeply to respond merely as a conventional and insularly patriotic English visitor. Rossetti's speaker dismisses the Wordsworthian sublime by observing the scientific fact that Waterloo, despite its storied associations, is not unique; the whole earth, not merely Waterloo, is a burial ground: "of the whole earth there is no single spot / But hath among its dust the dust of man."

Rossetti's self-regarding speaker rejects the humanitarian sublimity of Wordsworth's earlier sonnet, which itself had rejected a parochial patriotism, for the sake of a skeptical, anti-ideological empiricism. The fact that the entire earth is a burial ground, and that the visitor who knows this cannot respond to Waterloo as he should—as a dramatic special case—subverts and devalues the ambitious, universalized humanitarianism of Wordsworth's "After Visiting the Field of Waterloo," substituting for it a dogged empiricism of observation and feeling. Rossetti's reevaluation here is not overtly "aesthetic" as Harrison argues are many of Rossetti's post-texts, but empirical to the point of extreme skepticism. **"On the Field of Waterloo"** "creates the illusion of altogether eliding and superseding ideology," not for the sake of textual "self-reflexivity and circularity" (Harrison, pp. 746, 759), but for the sake of fidelity to both emotional and scientific fact. For Rossetti, Wordsworth was "good, but unbearable" (***Letters,*** 1:361), and it is against this "unbearable" and overbearing universalizing of humanitarian feeling, Wordsworth's emphasis on what man "*should* feel," that Rossetti's sonnet reacts.[7]

In the prose section of his letter to his brother (October 18, 1849) that includes this sonnet, Rossetti confesses "Between you and me, William, Waterloo is simply a bore" (***Letters,*** 1:81). This confidence, this "secret," Rossetti dramatizes and extrapolates, through intertextuality, into an accomplished sonnet utterance. Although sympathetic to the progressive movements of 1848, both to Chartism in England and republicanism in France (Doughty, pp. 71-72), Rossetti's insistence on fidelity to his own inner emotional life rendered him skeptical of political abstractions and the universalizing moral-political discourses of a previous generation, the generation not only of Wordsworth but of his father, a liberal political exile from the post-Napoleonic Naples of Ferdinand IV.[8] This skepticism is enacted pointedly in **"On the Field of Waterloo."**

Notes

[1] The most complete discussion of sources and influences on Rossetti's poetry is to be found in Florence S. Boos, *The Poetry of Dante G. Rossetti: A Critical Reading and Source Study* (The Hague, 1976), pp. 259-286.

[2] Antony H. Harrison, "Dante Gabriel Rossetti: Parody and Ideology," *SEL* 29 (1989): 746, 760. See also his *Victorian Poets and Romantic Poems* (Charlottesville, 1989).

[3] Oswald Doughty, *Dante Gabriel Rossetti, A Victorian Romantic,* 2nd ed. (London, 1960), p. 86.

[4] *The Letters of Dante Gabriel Rossetti,* ed. Oswald Doughty and John Robert Wahl (Oxford, 1965), 1:80-81. The sonnet was not published in either the 1870 or 1881 editions of Rossetti's poems, nor included in William Michael's 1886 edition of *The Collected Works.* It first appears in William Michael's edition of *The Family Letters* (London, 1895), 2:78-79, and has since been reprinted in Doughty's edition of *The Letters* and as part of the entire verse sequence entitled "A Trip to Paris and Belgium," in *The Essential Rossetti,* ed. John Hollander (New York, 1990), pp. 112-133.

[5] *William Wordsworth: The Poems,* ed. John O. Hayden (New Haven, 1981), 2:411.

[6] David G. Riede has noted "a necessary diminishment from the bardic Wordsworthian stance" in Rossetti's poetry (*Dante Gabriel Rossetti and the Limits of Victorian Vision* [Ithaca, 1983], p. 117).

[7] A similar rejection of seer-like generalization can be seen in "The Woodspurge," which David Riede designates a "poetry of nonstatement" (p. 57), "a kind of minimalist poetry" in which "meaning cannot be focused beyond the reach of the senses" (p.58). Riede in his chapter "Diminished Romanticism," from *Dante Gabriel Rossetti,* argues that in Rossetti's poetry "the more manageable province" of male-female love comes to replace the ambitious Wordsworthian themes of the "'vast empire' of nature and the universal" (p. 121).

[8] For an account of Gabriele Rossetti's somewhat operatic political career in Naples, see Doughty, pp. 20-21, pp. 28-29.

FURTHER READING

Anderson, Amanda S. "D. G. Rossetti's 'Jenny': Agency, Intersubjectivity, and the Prostitute." *Genders* 4 (March 1989): 103-21.

Reading of Rossetti's poem "Jenny" that explores the ways in which the figure of the fallen woman operates in Victorian literature.

Boos, Florence Saunders. *The Poetry of Dante G. Rossetti: A Critical Reading and Source Study.* The Hague: Mouton, 1976, 297 p.

In-depth study of Rossetti's "The House of Life," narrative ballads, and lyrical poetry preceded by a survey of critical reaction to his work.

Brown, Thomas H. "The Quest of Dante Gabriel Rossetti in 'The Blessed Damozel.'" *Victorian Poetry* 10, No. 3 (Autumn 1972): 273-77.

Contends that "The Blessed Damozel" contains "three distinct voices or speakers" and that in the poem Rossetti endeavors to fuse naturalism and supernaturalism.

Gelpi, Barbara Charlesworth. "The Feminization of D. G. Rossetti." In *The Victorian Experience: The Poets,* edited by Richard A. Levine, pp. 94-114. Athens: Ohio University Press, 1982.

Analyzes several of Rossetti's poems in light of his close relationship with his mother.

Hardesty, William H., III. "Rossetti's Lusty Women." *Cimarron Review* 35 (April 1976): 20-24.

Examines the theme of frustrated feminine desire in "The Blessed Damozel," "Troy Town," and "Jenny."

McGann, Jerome J. "Rossetti's Significant Details." *Victorian Poetry* 7, No. 1 (Spring 1969): 41-54.

Probes Rossetti's unconventional use of Christian imagery to pursue the theme of human love.

Pfordresher, John. "Dante Gabriel Rossetti's 'Hand and Soul': Sources and Significance." *Studies in Short Fiction* 19, No. 2 (Spring 1982): 103-32.

Investigates the origins of Rossetti's tale "Hand and Soul" and its relation to the development of the Victorian short story.

Rees, Joan. *The Poetry of Dante Gabriel Rossetti: Modes of Self-Expression.* Cambridge: Cambridge University Press, 1981, 204 p.

Details the development of Rossetti's poetry, examining the poet's sources, influences, imagery, themes, and style.

Spatt, Hartley S. "Dante Gabriel Rossetti and the Pull of Silence." *The Victorian Newsletter*, No. 63 (Spring 1983): 7-12.

Studies Rossetti's unusual perspective as both a poet and a painter, which allowed him to create thematic paradoxes of silence and speech in his works.

Zweig, Robert. "'Death-In-Love': Rossetti and the Victorian Journey Back to Dante." In *Sex and Death in Victorian Literature*, edited by Regina Barreca, pp. 178-93. London: Macmillan, 1990.

Examines and evaluates the considerable influence of Dante Alighieri's works on Rossetti's poetry.

Additional coverage of Rossetti's life and career is contained in the following sources published by the Gale Group: *Concise Dictionary of British Literary Biography*, 1832-1890; *Dictionary of Literary Biography*, Vol. 35; *DISCovering Authors*; and *World Literature Criticism.*

Nineteenth-Century Literature Criticism

Cumulative Indexes
Volumes 1-77

How to Use This Index

The main references

Calvino, Italo
1923–1985 .... **CLC 5, 8, 11, 22, 33, 39, 73; SSC 3**

list all author entries in the following Gale Literary Criticism series:

BLC = *Black Literature Criticism*
CLC = *Contemporary Literary Criticism*
CLR = *Children's Literature Review*
CMLC = *Classical and Medieval Literature Criticism*
DA = *DISCovering Authors*
DAB = *DISCovering Authors: British*
DAC = *DISCovering Authors: Canadian*
DAM = *DISCovering Authors: Modules*
DRAM: *Dramatists Module;* ***MST***: *Most-Studied Authors Module;*
MULT: *Multicultural Authors Module;* ***NOV***: *Novelists Module;*
POET: *Poets Module;* ***POP***: *Popular Fiction and Genre Authors Module*
DC = *Drama Criticism*
HLC = *Hispanic Literature Criticism*
LC = *Literature Criticism from 1400 to 1800*
NCLC = *Nineteenth-Century Literature Criticism*
PC = *Poetry Criticism*
SSC = *Short Story Criticism*
TCLC = *Twentieth-Century Literary Criticism*
WLC = *World Literature Criticism, 1500 to the Present*

The cross-references

See also CANR 23; CA 85-88;
obituary CA116

list all author entries in the following Gale biographical and literary sources:

AAYA = *Authors & Artists for Young Adults*
AITN = *Authors in the News*
BEST = *Bestsellers*
BW = *Black Writers*
CA = *Contemporary Authors*
CAAS = *Contemporary Authors Autobiography Series*
CABS = *Contemporary Authors Bibliographical Series*
CANR = *Contemporary Authors New Revision Series*
CAP = *Contemporary Authors Permanent Series*
CDALB = *Concise Dictionary of American Literary Biography*
CDBLB = *Concise Dictionary of British Literary Biography*
DLB = *Dictionary of Literary Biography*
DLBD = *Dictionary of Literary Biography Documentary Series*
DLBY = *Dictionary of Literary Biography Yearbook*
HW = *Hispanic Writers*
JRDA = *Junior DISCovering Authors*
MAICYA = *Major Authors and Illustrators for Children and Young Adults*
MTCW = *Major 20th-Century Writers*
NNAL = *Native North American Literature*
SAAS = *Something about the Author Autobiography Series*
SATA = *Something about the Author*
YABC = *Yesterday's Authors of Books for Children*

Literary Criticism Series Cumulative Author Index

20/1631
See Upward, Allen
A/C Cross
See Lawrence, T(homas) E(dward)
Abasiyanik, Sait Faik 1906-1954
See Sait Faik
See also CA 123
Abbey, Edward 1927-1989 **CLC 36, 59**
See also CA 45-48; 128; CANR 2, 41; MTCW 2
Abbott, Lee K(ittredge) 1947- **CLC 48**
See also CA 124; CANR 51; DLB 130
Abe, Kobo 1924-1993**CLC 8, 22, 53, 81; DAM NOV**
See also CA 65-68; 140; CANR 24, 60; DLB 182; MTCW 1, 2
Abelard, Peter c. 1079-c. 1142 **CMLC 11**
See also DLB 115, 208
Abell, Kjeld 1901-1961 **CLC 15**
See also CA 111
Abish, Walter 1931- **CLC 22**
See also CA 101; CANR 37; DLB 130
Abrahams, Peter (Henry) 1919- **CLC 4**
See also BW 1; CA 57-60; CANR 26; DLB 117; MTCW 1, 2
Abrams, M(eyer) H(oward) 1912- **CLC 24**
See also CA 57-60; CANR 13, 33; DLB 67
Abse, Dannie 1923- **CLC 7, 29; DAB; DAM POET**
See also CA 53-56; CAAS 1; CANR 4, 46, 74; DLB 27; MTCW 1
Achebe, (Albert) Chinua(lumogu) 1930-**C L C 1, 3, 5, 7, 11, 26, 51, 75; BLC 1; DA; DAB; DAC; DAM MST, MULT, NOV; WLC**
See also AAYA 15; BW 2, 3; CA 1-4R; CANR 6, 26, 47; CLR 20; DLB 117; MAICYA; MTCW 1, 2; SATA 38, 40; SATA-Brief 38
Acker, Kathy 1948-1997 **CLC 45, 111**
See also CA 117; 122; 162; CANR 55
Ackroyd, Peter 1949- **CLC 34, 52**
See also CA 123; 127; CANR 51, 74; DLB 155; INT 127; MTCW 1
Acorn, Milton 1923- **CLC 15; DAC**
See also CA 103; DLB 53; INT 103
Adamov, Arthur 1908-1970 **CLC 4, 25; DAM DRAM**
See also CA 17-18; 25-28R; CAP 2; MTCW 1
Adams, Alice (Boyd) 1926-**CLC 6, 13, 46; SSC 24**
See also CA 81-84; CANR 26, 53, 75; DLBY 86; INT CANR-26; MTCW 1, 2
Adams, Andy 1859-1935 **TCLC 56**
See also YABC 1
Adams, Brooks 1848-1927 **TCLC 80**
See also CA 123; DLB 47
Adams, Douglas (Noel) 1952- **CLC 27, 60; DAM POP**
See also AAYA 4; BEST 89:3; CA 106; CANR 34, 64; DLBY 83; JRDA; MTCW 1
Adams, Francis 1862-1893 **NCLC 33**
Adams, Henry (Brooks) 1838-1918 **TCLC 4, 52; DA; DAB; DAC; DAM MST**
See also CA 104; 133; CANR 77; DLB 12, 47, 189; MTCW 1
Adams, Richard (George) 1920-**CLC 4, 5, 18; DAM NOV**
See also AAYA 16; AITN 1, 2; CA 49-52; CANR 3, 35; CLR 20; JRDA; MAICYA; MTCW 1, 2; SATA 7, 69
Adamson, Joy(-Friederike Victoria) 1910-1980 **CLC 17**
See also CA 69-72; 93-96; CANR 22; MTCW 1; SATA 11; SATA-Obit 22
Adcock, Fleur 1934- **CLC 41**
See also CA 25-28R; CAAS 23; CANR 11, 34, 69; DLB 40
Addams, Charles (Samuel) 1912-1988**CLC 30**
See also CA 61-64; 126; CANR 12, 79
Addams, Jane 1860-1945 **TCLC 76**
Addison, Joseph 1672-1719 **LC 18**
See also CDBLB 1660-1789; DLB 101
Adler, Alfred (F.) 1870-1937 **TCLC 61**
See also CA 119; 159
Adler, C(arole) S(chwerdtfeger) 1932-**CLC 35**
See also AAYA 4; CA 89-92; CANR 19, 40; JRDA; MAICYA; SAAS 15; SATA 26, 63, 102
Adler, Renata 1938- **CLC 8, 31**
See also CA 49-52; CANR 5, 22, 52; MTCW 1
Ady, Endre 1877-1919 **TCLC 11**
See also CA 107
A.E. 1867-1935 **TCLC 3, 10**
See also Russell, George William
Aeschylus 525B.C.-456B.C. **CMLC 11; DA; DAB; DAC; DAM DRAM, MST; DC 8; WLCS**
See also DLB 176
Aesop 620(?)B.C.-564(?)B.C. **CMLC 24**
See also CLR 14; MAICYA; SATA 64
Affable Hawk
See MacCarthy, Sir(Charles Otto) Desmond
Africa, Ben
See Bosman, Herman Charles
Afton, Effie
See Harper, Frances Ellen Watkins
Agapida, Fray Antonio
See Irving, Washington
Agee, James (Rufus) 1909-1955 **TCLC 1, 19; DAM NOV**
See also AITN 1; CA 108; 148; CDALB 1941-1968; DLB 2, 26, 152; MTCW 1
Aghill, Gordon
See Silverberg, Robert
Agnon, S(hmuel) Y(osef Halevi) 1888-1970 **CLC 4, 8, 14; SSC 30**
See also CA 17-18; 25-28R; CANR 60; CAP 2; MTCW 1, 2
Agrippa von Nettesheim, Henry Cornelius 1486-1535 **LC 27**
Aherne, Owen
See Cassill, R(onald) V(erlin)
Ai 1947- **CLC 4, 14, 69**
See also CA 85-88; CAAS 13; CANR 70; DLB 120
Aickman, Robert (Fordyce) 1914-1981 **C L C 57**
See also CA 5-8R; CANR 3, 72
Aiken, Conrad (Potter) 1889-1973**CLC 1, 3, 5, 10, 52; DAM NOV, POET; PC 26; SSC 9**
See also CA 5-8R; 45-48; CANR 4, 60; CDALB 1929-1941; DLB 9, 45, 102; MTCW 1, 2; SATA 3, 30
Aiken, Joan (Delano) 1924- **CLC 35**
See also AAYA 1, 25; CA 9-12R; CANR 4, 23, 34, 64; CLR 1, 19; DLB 161; JRDA; MAICYA; MTCW 1; SAAS 1; SATA 2, 30, 73
Ainsworth, William Harrison 1805-1882 **NCLC 13**
See also DLB 21; SATA 24
Aitmatov, Chingiz (Torekulovich) 1928- **C L C 71**
See also CA 103; CANR 38; MTCW 1; SATA 56
Akers, Floyd
See Baum, L(yman) Frank
Akhmadulina, Bella Akhatovna 1937- **C L C 53; DAM POET**
See also CA 65-68
Akhmatova, Anna 1888-1966**CLC 11, 25, 64; DAM POET; PC 2**
See also CA 19-20; 25-28R; CANR 35; CAP 1; MTCW 1, 2
Aksakov, Sergei Timofeyvich 1791-1859 **NCLC 2**
See also DLB 198
Aksenov, Vassily
See Aksyonov, Vassily (Pavlovich)
Akst, Daniel 1956- **CLC 109**
See also CA 161
<indexbo**Aksyonov, Vassily (Pavlovich)** 1932- **CLC 22, 37, 101**
See also CA 53-56; CANR 12, 48, 77
Akutagawa, Ryunosuke 1892-1927 **TCLC 16**
See also CA 117; 154
Alain 1868-1951 **TCLC 41**
See also CA 163
Alain-Fournier **TCLC 6**
See also Fournier, Henri Alban
See also DLB 65
Alarcon, Pedro Antonio de 1833-1891**NCLC 1**
Alas (y Urena), Leopoldo (Enrique Garcia) 1852-1901 **TCLC 29**
See also CA 113; 131; HW 1
Albee, Edward (Franklin III) 1928-**CLC 1, 2, 3, 5, 9, 11, 13, 25, 53, 86, 113; DA; DAB; DAC; DAM DRAM, MST; DC 11; WLC**
See also AITN 1; CA 5-8R; CABS 3; CANR 8, 54, 74; CDALB 1941-1968; DLB 7; INT CANR-8; MTCW 1, 2
Alberti, Rafael 1902- **CLC 7**
See also CA 85-88; DLB 108; HW 2
Albert the Great 1200(?)-1280 **CMLC 16**
See also DLB 115
Alcala-Galiano, Juan Valera y
See Valera y Alcala-Galiano, Juan

Andreas-Salome, Lou 1861-1937 **TCLC 56**
See also DLB 66
Andress, Lesley
See Sanders, Lawrence
Andrewes, Lancelot 1555-1626 **LC 5**
See also DLB 151, 172
Andrews, Cicily Fairfield
See West, Rebecca
Andrews, Elton V.
See Pohl, Frederik
Andreyev, Leonid (Nikolaevich) 1871-1919 **TCLC 3**
See also CA 104
Andric, Ivo 1892-1975 **CLC 8**
See also CA 81-84; 57-60; CANR 43, 60; DLB 147; MTCW 1
<indexbo**Androvar**
See Prado (Calvo), Pedro
Angelique, Pierre
See Bataille, Georges
Angell, Roger 1920- **CLC 26**
See also CA 57-60; CANR 13, 44, 70; DLB 171, 185
Angelou, Maya 1928-**CLC 12, 35, 64, 77; BLC 1; DA; DAB; DAC; DAM MST, MULT, POET, POP; WLCS**
See also AAYA 7, 20; BW 2, 3; CA 65-68; CANR 19, 42, 65; CDALBS; CLR 53; DLB 38; MTCW 1, 2; SATA 49
Anna Comnena 1083-1153 **CMLC 25**
Annensky, Innokenty (Fyodorovich) 1856-1909 **TCLC 14**
See also CA 110; 155
Annunzio, Gabriele d'
See D'Annunzio, Gabriele
Anodos
See Coleridge, Mary E(lizabeth)
Anon, Charles Robert
See Pessoa, Fernando (Antonio Nogueira)
Anouilh, Jean (Marie Lucien Pierre) 1910-1987 **CLC 1, 3, 8, 13, 40, 50; DAM DRAM; DC 8**
See also CA 17-20R; 123; CANR 32; MTCW 1, 2
Anthony, Florence
See Ai
Anthony, John
See Ciardi, John (Anthony)
Anthony, Peter
See Shaffer, Anthony (Joshua); Shaffer, Peter (Levin)
Anthony, Piers 1934- **CLC 35; DAM POP**
See also AAYA 11; CA 21-24R; CANR 28, 56, 73; DLB 8; MTCW 1, 2; SAAS 22; SATA 84
Anthony, Susan B(rownell) 1916-1991 **TCLC 84**
See also CA 89-92; 134
Antoine, Marc
See Proust, (Valentin-Louis-George-Eugene-) Marcel
Antoninus, Brother
See Everson, William (Oliver)
Antonioni, Michelangelo 1912- **CLC 20**
See also CA 73-76; CANR 45, 77
Antschel, Paul 1920-1970
See Celan, Paul
See also CA 85-88; CANR 33, 61; MTCW 1
Anwar, Chairil 1922-1949 **TCLC 22**
See also CA 121
Apess, William 1798-1839(?)**NCLC 73; DAM MULT**
See also DLB 175; NNAL
Apollinaire, Guillaume 1880-1918**TCLC 3, 8, 51; DAM POET; PC 7**
See also Kostrowitzki, Wilhelm Apollinaris de
See also CA 152; MTCW 1
Appelfeld, Aharon 1932- **CLC 23, 47**
See also CA 112; 133
Apple, Max (Isaac) 1941- **CLC 9, 33**
See also CA 81-84; CANR 19, 54; DLB 130
Appleman, Philip (Dean) 1926- **CLC 51**
See also CA 13-16R; CAAS 18; CANR 6, 29, 56
Appleton, Lawrence
See Lovecraft, H(oward) P(hillips)
Apteryx
See Eliot, T(homas) S(tearns)
Apuleius, (Lucius Madaurensis) 125(?)-175(?) **CMLC 1**
See also DLB 211
Aquin, Hubert 1929-1977 **CLC 15**
See also CA 105; DLB 53
Aquinas, Thomas 1224(?)-1274 **CMLC 33**
See also DLB 115
Aragon, Louis 1897-1982 **CLC 3, 22; DAM NOV, POET**
See also CA 69-72; 108; CANR 28, 71; DLB 72; MTCW 1, 2
Arany, Janos 1817-1882 **NCLC 34**
Aranyos, Kakay
See Mikszath, Kalman
Arbuthnot, John 1667-1735 **LC 1**
See also DLB 101
Archer, Herbert Winslow
See Mencken, H(enry) L(ouis)
Archer, Jeffrey (Howard) 1940- **CLC 28; DAM POP**
See also AAYA 16; BEST 89:3; CA 77-80; CANR 22, 52; INT CANR-22
Archer, Jules 1915- **CLC 12**
See also CA 9-12R; CANR 6, 69; SAAS 5; SATA 4, 85
Archer, Lee
See Ellison, Harlan (Jay)
Arden, John 1930-**CLC 6, 13, 15; DAM DRAM**
See also CA 13-16R; CAAS 4; CANR 31, 65, 67; DLB 13; MTCW 1
Arenas, Reinaldo 1943-1990 **CLC 41; DAM MULT; HLC**
See also CA 124; 128; 133; CANR 73; DLB 145; HW 1; MTCW 1
Arendt, Hannah 1906-1975 **CLC 66, 98**
See also CA 17-20R; 61-64; CANR 26, 60; MTCW 1, 2
Aretino, Pietro 1492-1556 **LC 12**
Arghezi, Tudor 1880-1967 **CLC 80**
See also Theodorescu, Ion N.
See also CA 167
Arguedas, Jose Maria 1911-1969**CLC 10, 18; HLCS 1**
See also CA 89-92; CANR 73; DLB 113; HW 1
Argueta, Manlio 1936- **CLC 31**
See also CA 131; CANR 73; DLB 145; HW 1
Ariosto, Ludovico 1474-1533 **LC 6**
Aristides
See Epstein, Joseph
Aristophanes 450B.C.-385B.C.**CMLC 4; DA; DAB; DAC; DAM DRAM, MST; DC 2; WLCS**
See also DLB 176
Aristotle 384B.C.-322B.C. **CMLC 31; DA; DAB; DAC; DAM MST; WLCS**
See also DLB 176
Arlt, Roberto (Godofredo Christophersen) 1900-1942**TCLC 29; DAM MULT; HLC**
See also CA 123; 131; CANR 67; HW 1, 2
Armah, Ayi Kwei 1939- **CLC 5, 33; BLC 1; DAM MULT, POET**
See also BW 1; CA 61-64; CANR 21, 64; DLB 117; MTCW 1
Armatrading, Joan 1950- **CLC 17**
See also CA 114
Arnette, Robert
See Silverberg, Robert
Arnim, Achim von (Ludwig Joachim von Arnim) 1781-1831 **NCLC 5; SSC 29**
See also DLB 90
<indexbod**Arnim, Bettina von** 1785-1859 **NCLC 38**
See also DLB 90
Arnold, Matthew 1822-1888**NCLC 6, 29; DA; DAB; DAC; DAM MST, POET; PC 5; WLC**
See also CDBLB 1832-1890; DLB 32, 57
Arnold, Thomas 1795-1842 **NCLC 18**
See also DLB 55
Arnow, Harriette (Louisa) Simpson 1908-1986 **CLC 2, 7, 18**
See also CA 9-12R; 118; CANR 14; DLB 6; MTCW 1, 2; SATA 42; SATA-Obit 47
Arouet, Francois-Marie
See Voltaire
Arp, Hans
See Arp, Jean
Arp, Jean 1887-1966 **CLC 5**
See also CA 81-84; 25-28R; CANR 42, 77
Arrabal
See Arrabal, Fernando
<indexbody>**Arrabal, Fernando** 1932-**CLC 2, 9, 18, 58**
See also CA 9-12R; CANR 15
Arrick, Fran **CLC 30**
See also Gaberman, Judie Angell
Artaud, Antonin (Marie Joseph) 1896-1948 **TCLC 3, 36; DAM DRAM**
See also CA 104; 149; MTCW 1
Arthur, Ruth M(abel) 1905-1979 **CLC 12**
See also CA 9-12R; 85-88; CANR 4; SATA 7, 26
Artsybashev, Mikhail (Petrovich) 1878-1927 **TCLC 31**
See also CA 170
Arundel, Honor (Morfydd) 1919-1973**CLC 17**
See also CA 21-22; 41-44R; CAP 2; CLR 35; SATA 4; SATA-Obit 24
Arzner, Dorothy 1897-1979 **CLC 98**
Asch, Sholem 1880-1957 **TCLC 3**
See also CA 105
Ash, Shalom
See Asch, Sholem
Ashbery, John (Lawrence) 1927-**CLC 2, 3, 4, 6, 9, 13, 15, 25, 41, 77; DAM POET; PC 26**
See also CA 5-8R; CANR 9, 37, 66; DLB 5, 165; DLBY 81; INT CANR-9; MTCW 1, 2
Ashdown, Clifford
See Freeman, R(ichard) Austin
Ashe, Gordon
See Creasey, John
Ashton-Warner, Sylvia (Constance) 1908-1984 **CLC 19**
See also CA 69-72; 112; CANR 29; MTCW 1, 2
Asimov, Isaac 1920-1992 **CLC 1, 3, 9, 19, 26, 76, 92; DAM POP**
See also AAYA 13; BEST 90:2; CA 1-4R; 137; CANR 2, 19, 36, 60; CLR 12; DLB 8; DLBY 92; INT CANR-19; JRDA; MAICYA; MTCW 1, 2; SATA 1, 26, 74
Assis, Joaquim Maria Machado de

See Baum, L(yman) Frank
Banim, John 1798-1842 **NCLC 13**
See also DLB 116, 158, 159
Banim, Michael 1796-1874 **NCLC 13**
See also DLB 158, 159
Banjo, The
See Paterson, A(ndrew) B(arton)
Banks, Iain
See Banks, Iain M(enzies)
Banks, Iain M(enzies) 1954- **CLC 34**
See also CA 123; 128; CANR 61; DLB 194; INT 128
Banks, Lynne Reid **CLC 23**
See also Reid Banks, Lynne
See also AAYA 6
Banks, Russell 1940- **CLC 37, 72**
See also CA 65-68; CAAS 15; CANR 19, 52, 73; DLB 130
Banville, John 1945- **CLC 46, 118**
See also CA 117; 128; DLB 14; INT 128
Banville, Theodore (Faullain) de 1832-1891 **NCLC 9**
Baraka, Amiri 1934-**CLC 1, 2, 3, 5, 10, 14, 33, 115; BLC 1; DA; DAC; DAM MST, MULT, POET, POP; DC 6; PC 4; WLCS**
See also Jones, LeRoi
See also BW 2, 3; CA 21-24R; CABS 3; CANR 27, 38, 61; CDALB 1941-1968; DLB 5, 7, 16, 38; DLBD 8; MTCW 1, 2
Barbauld, Anna Laetitia 1743-1825**NCLC 50**
See also DLB 107, 109, 142, 158
Barbellion, W. N. P. **TCLC 24**
See also Cummings, Bruce F(rederick)
Barbera, Jack (Vincent) 1945- **CLC 44**
See also CA 110; CANR 45
Barbey d'Aurevilly, Jules Amedee 1808-1889 **NCLC 1; SSC 17**
See also DLB 119
Barbour, John c. 1316-1395 **CMLC 33**
See also DLB 146
Barbusse, Henri 1873-1935 **TCLC 5**
See also CA 105; 154; DLB 65
Barclay, Bill
See Moorcock, Michael (John)
Barclay, William Ewert
See Moorcock, Michael (John)
Barea, Arturo 1897-1957 **TCLC 14**
See also CA 111
Barfoot, Joan 1946- **CLC 18**
See also CA 105
Barham, Richard Harris 1788-1845**NCLC 77**
See also DLB 159
Baring, Maurice 1874-1945 **TCLC 8**
See also CA 105; 168; DLB 34
Baring-Gould, Sabine 1834-1924 **TCLC 88**
See also DLB 156, 190
<index**Barker, Clive** 1952- **CLC 52; DAM POP**
See also AAYA 10; BEST 90:3; CA 121; 129; CANR 71; INT 129; MTCW 1, 2
Barker, George Granville 1913-1991 **CLC 8, 48; DAM POET**
See also CA 9-12R; 135; CANR 7, 38; DLB 20; MTCW 1
Barker, Harley Granville
See Granville-Barker, Harley
See also DLB 10
Barker, Howard 1946- **CLC 37**
See also CA 102; DLB 13
Barker, Jane 1652-1732 **LC 42**
Barker, Pat(ricia) 1943- **CLC 32, 94**
See also CA 117; 122; CANR 50; INT 122
Barlach, Ernst 1870-1938 **TCLC 84**
See also DLB 56, 118
Barlow, Joel 1754-1812 **NCLC 23**
See also DLB 37
Barnard, Mary (Ethel) 1909- **CLC 48**
See also CA 21-22; CAP 2
Barnes, Djuna 1892-1982**CLC 3, 4, 8, 11, 29; SSC 3**
See also CA 9-12R; 107; CANR 16, 55; DLB 4, 9, 45; MTCW 1, 2
Barnes, Julian (Patrick) 1946- **CLC 42; DAB**
See also CA 102; CANR 19, 54; DLB 194; DLBY 93; MTCW 1
Barnes, Peter 1931- **CLC 5, 56**
See also CA 65-68; CAAS 12; CANR 33, 34, 64; DLB 13; MTCW 1
Barnes, William 1801-1886 **NCLC 75**
See also DLB 32
Baroja (y Nessi), Pio 1872-1956**TCLC 8; HLC**
See also CA 104
Baron, David
See Pinter, Harold
Baron Corvo
See Rolfe, Frederick (William Serafino Austin Lewis Mary)
Barondess, Sue K(aufman) 1926-1977 **CLC 8**
See also Kaufman, Sue
See also CA 1-4R; 69-72; CANR 1
Baron de Teive
See Pessoa, Fernando (Antonio Nogueira)
Baroness Von S.
See Zangwill, Israel
Barres, (Auguste-) Maurice 1862-1923**TCLC 47**
See also CA 164; DLB 123
Barreto, Afonso Henrique de Lima
See Lima Barreto, Afonso Henrique de
Barrett, (Roger) Syd 1946- **CLC 35**
Barrett, William (Christopher) 1913-1992 **CLC 27**
See also CA 13-16R; 139; CANR 11, 67; INT CANR-11
Barrie, J(ames) M(atthew) 1860-1937 **TCLC 2; DAB; DAM DRAM**
See also CA 104; 136; CANR 77; CDBLB 1890-1914; CLR 16; DLB 10, 141, 156; MAICYA; MTCW 1; SATA 100; YABC 1
Barrington, Michael
See Moorcock, Michael (John)
Barrol, Grady
See Bograd, Larry
Barry, Mike
See Malzberg, Barry N(athaniel)
Barry, Philip 1896-1949 **TCLC 11**
See also CA 109; DLB 7
Bart, Andre Schwarz
See Schwarz-Bart, Andre
Barth, John (Simmons) 1930-**CLC 1, 2, 3, 5, 7, 9, 10, 14, 27, 51, 89; DAM NOV; SSC 10**
See also AITN 1, 2; CA 1-4R; CABS 1; CANR 5, 23, 49, 64; DLB 2; MTCW 1
Barthelme, Donald 1931-1989**CLC 1, 2, 3, 5, 6, 8, 13, 23, 46, 59, 115; DAM NOV; SSC 2**
See also CA 21-24R; 129; CANR 20, 58; DLB 2; DLBY 80, 89; MTCW 1, 2; SATA 7; SATA-Obit 62
Barthelme, Frederick 1943- **CLC 36, 117**
See also CA 114; 122; CANR 77; DLBY 85; INT 122
Barthes, Roland (Gerard) 1915-1980**CLC 24, 83**
See also CA 130; 97-100; CANR 66; MTCW 1, 2
Barzun, Jacques (Martin) 1907- **CLC 51**
See also CA 61-64; CANR 22
Bashevis, Isaac
See Singer, Isaac Bashevis
Bashkirtseff, Marie 1859-1884 **NCLC 27**
Basho
See Matsuo Basho
Bass, Kingsley B., Jr.
See Bullins, Ed
Bass, Rick 1958- **CLC 79**
See also CA 126; CANR 53; DLB 212
Bassani, Giorgio 1916- **CLC 9**
See also CA 65-68; CANR 33; DLB 128, 177; MTCW 1
Bastos, Augusto (Antonio) Roa
See Roa Bastos, Augusto (Antonio)
Bataille, Georges 1897-1962 **CLC 29**
See also CA 101; 89-92
Bates, H(erbert) E(rnest) 1905-1974**CLC 46; DAB; DAM POP; SSC 10**
See also CA 93-96; 45-48; CANR 34; DLB 162, 191; MTCW 1, 2
Bauchart
See Camus, Albert
Baudelaire, Charles 1821-1867 **NCLC 6, 29, 55; DA; DAB; DAC; DAM MST, POET; PC 1; SSC 18; WLC**
Baudrillard, Jean 1929- **CLC 60**
Baum, L(yman) Frank 1856-1919 **TCLC 7**
See also CA 108; 133; CLR 15; DLB 22; JRDA; MAICYA; MTCW 1, 2; SATA 18, 100
Baum, Louis F.
See Baum, L(yman) Frank
Baumbach, Jonathan 1933- **CLC 6, 23**
See also CA 13-16R; CAAS 5; CANR 12, 66; DLBY 80; INT CANR-12; MTCW 1
Bausch, Richard (Carl) 1945- **CLC 51**
See also CA 101; CAAS 14; CANR 43, 61; DLB 130
Baxter, Charles (Morley) 1947- **CLC 45, 78; DAM POP**
See also CA 57-60; CANR 40, 64; DLB 130; MTCW 2
Baxter, George Owen
See Faust, Frederick (Schiller)
Baxter, James K(eir) 1926-1972 **CLC 14**
See also CA 77-80
Baxter, John
See Hunt, E(verette) Howard, (Jr.)
Bayer, Sylvia
See Glassco, John
Baynton, Barbara 1857-1929 **TCLC 57**
Beagle, Peter S(oyer) 1939- **CLC 7, 104**
See also CA 9-12R; CANR 4, 51, 73; DLBY 80; INT CANR-4; MTCW 1; SATA 60
Bean, Normal
See Burroughs, Edgar Rice
Beard, Charles A(ustin) 1874-1948 **TCLC 15**
See also CA 115; DLB 17; SATA 18
Beardsley, Aubrey 1872-1898 **NCLC 6**
Beattie, Ann 1947-**CLC 8, 13, 18, 40, 63; DAM NOV, POP; SSC 11**
See also BEST 90:2; CA 81-84; CANR 53, 73; DLBY 82; MTCW 1, 2
Beattie, James 1735-1803 **NCLC 25**
See also DLB 109
Beauchamp, Kathleen Mansfield 1888-1923
See Mansfield, Katherine
See also CA 104; 134; DA; DAC; DAM MST; MTCW 2
Beaumarchais, Pierre-Augustin Caron de 1732-1799 **DC 4**
See also DAM DRAM
Beaumont, Francis 1584(?)-1616**LC 33; DC 6**

See also CDBLB Before 1660; DLB 58, 121

Beauvoir, Simone (Lucie Ernestine Marie Bertrand) de 1908-1986**CLC 1, 2, 4, 8, 14, 31, 44, 50, 71; DA; DAB; DAC; DAM MST, NOV; WLC**
See also CA 9-12R; 118; CANR 28, 61; DLB 72; DLBY 86; MTCW 1, 2

Becker, Carl (Lotus) 1873-1945 **TCLC 63**
See also CA 157; DLB 17

Becker, Jurek 1937-1997 **CLC 7, 19**
See also CA 85-88; 157; CANR 60; DLB 75

Becker, Walter 1950- **CLC 26**

Beckett, Samuel (Barclay) 1906-1989 **CLC 1, 2, 3, 4, 6, 9, 10, 11, 14, 18, 29, 57, 59, 83; DA; DAB; DAC; DAM DRAM, MST, NOV; SSC 16; WLC**
See also CA 5-8R; 130; CANR 33, 61; CDBLB 1945-1960; DLB 13, 15; DLBY 90; MTCW 1, 2

Beckford, William 1760-1844 **NCLC 16**
See also DLB 39

Beckman, Gunnel 1910- **CLC 26**
See also CA 33-36R; CANR 15; CLR 25; MAICYA; SAAS 9; SATA 6

Becque, Henri 1837-1899 **NCLC 3**
See also DLB 192

Beddoes, Thomas Lovell 1803-1849 **NCLC 3**
See also DLB 96

Bede c. 673-735 **CMLC 20**
See also DLB 146

Bedford, Donald F.
See Fearing, Kenneth (Flexner)

Beecher, Catharine Esther 1800-1878 **NCLC 30**
See also DLB 1

Beecher, John 1904-1980 **CLC 6**
See also AITN 1; CA 5-8R; 105; CANR 8

Beer, Johann 1655-1700 **LC 5**
See also DLB 168

Beer, Patricia 1924- **CLC 58**
See also CA 61-64; CANR 13, 46; DLB 40

Beerbohm, Max
See Beerbohm, (Henry) Max(imilian)

Beerbohm, (Henry) Max(imilian) 1872-1956 **TCLC 1, 24**
See also CA 104; 154; CANR 79; DLB 34, 100

Beer-Hofmann, Richard 1866-1945**TCLC 60**
See also CA 160; DLB 81

Begiebing, Robert J(ohn) 1946- **CLC 70**
See also CA 122; CANR 40

Behan, Brendan 1923-1964 **CLC 1, 8, 11, 15, 79; DAM DRAM**
See also CA 73-76; CANR 33; CDBLB 1945-1960; DLB 13; MTCW 1, 2

Behn, Aphra 1640(?)-1689 **LC 1, 30, 42; DA; DAB; DAC; DAM DRAM, MST, NOV, POET; DC 4; PC 13; WLC**
See also DLB 39, 80, 131

Behrman, S(amuel) N(athaniel) 1893-1973 **CLC 40**
See also CA 13-16; 45-48; CAP 1; DLB 7, 44

Belasco, David 1853-1931 **TCLC 3**
See also CA 104; 168; DLB 7

Belcheva, Elisaveta 1893- **CLC 10**
See also Bagryana, Elisaveta

Beldone, Phil "Cheech"
See Ellison, Harlan (Jay)

Beleno
See Azuela, Mariano

Belinski, Vissarion Grigoryevich 1811-1848 **NCLC 5**
See also DLB 198

Belitt, Ben 1911- **CLC 22**
See also CA 13-16R; CAAS 4; CANR 7, 77; DLB 5

Bell, Gertrude (Margaret Lowthian) 1868-1926 **TCLC 67**
See also CA 167; DLB 174

Bell, J. Freeman
See Zangwill, Israel

Bell, James Madison 1826-1902 **TCLC 43; BLC 1; DAM MULT**
See also BW 1; CA 122; 124; DLB 50

Bell, Madison Smartt 1957- **CLC 41, 102**
See also CA 111; CANR 28, 54, 73; MTCW 1

Bell, Marvin (Hartley) 1937-**CLC 8, 31; DAM POET**
See also CA 21-24R; CAAS 14; CANR 59; DLB 5; MTCW 1

Bell, W. L. D.
See Mencken, H(enry) L(ouis)

Bellamy, Atwood C.
See Mencken, H(enry) L(ouis)

Bellamy, Edward 1850-1898 **NCLC 4**
See also DLB 12

Bellin, Edward J.
See Kuttner, Henry

Belloc, (Joseph) Hilaire (Pierre Sebastien Rene Swanton) 1870-1953 **TCLC 7, 18; DAM POET; PC 24**
See also CA 106; 152; DLB 19, 100, 141, 174; MTCW 1; YABC 1

Belloc, Joseph Peter Rene Hilaire
See Belloc, (Joseph) Hilaire (Pierre Sebastien Rene Swanton)

Belloc, Joseph Pierre Hilaire
See Belloc, (Joseph) Hilaire (Pierre Sebastien Rene Swanton)

Belloc, M. A.
See Lowndes, Marie Adelaide (Belloc)

Bellow, Saul 1915-**CLC 1, 2, 3, 6, 8, 10, 13, 15, 25, 33, 34, 63, 79; DA; DAB; DAC; DAM MST, NOV, POP; SSC 14; WLC**
See also AITN 2; BEST 89:3; CA 5-8R; CABS 1; CANR 29, 53; CDALB 1941-1968; DLB 2, 28; DLBD 3; DLBY 82; MTCW 1, 2

Belser, Reimond Karel Maria de 1929-
See Ruyslinck, Ward
See also CA 152

Bely, Andrey **TCLC 7; PC 11**
See also Bugayev, Boris Nikolayevich
See also MTCW 1

Belyi, Andrei
See Bugayev, Boris Nikolayevich

Benary, Margot
See Benary-Isbert, Margot

Benary-Isbert, Margot 1889-1979 **CLC 12**
See also CA 5-8R; 89-92; CANR 4, 72; CLR 12; MAICYA; SATA 2; SATA-Obit 21

Benavente (y Martinez), Jacinto 1866-1954 **TCLC 3; DAM DRAM, MULT; HLCS 1**
See also CA 106; 131; HW 1, 2; MTCW 1, 2

Benchley, Peter (Bradford) 1940- **CLC 4, 8; DAM NOV, POP**
See also AAYA 14; AITN 2; CA 17-20R; CANR 12, 35, 66; MTCW 1, 2; SATA 3, 89

Benchley, Robert (Charles) 1889-1945**TCLC 1, 55**
See also CA 105; 153; DLB 11

Benda, Julien 1867-1956 **TCLC 60**
See also CA 120; 154

Benedict, Ruth (Fulton) 1887-1948 **TCLC 60**
See also CA 158

Benedict, Saint c. 480-c. 547 **CMLC 29**

Benedikt, Michael 1935- **CLC 4, 14**
See also CA 13-16R; CANR 7; DLB 5

Benet, Juan 1927- **CLC 28**
See also CA 143

<indexb**Benet, Stephen Vincent** 1898-1943 **TCLC 7; DAM POET; SSC 10**
See also CA 104; 152; DLB 4, 48, 102; DLBY 97; MTCW 1; YABC 1

Benet, William Rose 1886-1950 **TCLC 28; DAM POET**
See also CA 118; 152; DLB 45

Benford, Gregory (Albert) 1941- **CLC 52**
See also CA 69-72, 175; CAAE 175; CAAS 27; CANR 12, 24, 49; DLBY 82

Bengtsson, Frans (Gunnar) 1894-1954**TCLC 48**
See also CA 170

Benjamin, David
See Slavitt, David R(ytman)

Benjamin, Lois
See Gould, Lois

Benjamin, Walter 1892-1940 **TCLC 39**
See also CA 164

Benn, Gottfried 1886-1956 **TCLC 3**
See also CA 106; 153; DLB 56

Bennett, Alan 1934-**CLC 45, 77; DAB; DAM MST**
See also CA 103; CANR 35, 55; MTCW 1, 2

Bennett, (Enoch) Arnold 1867-1931 **TCLC 5, 20**
See also CA 106; 155; CDBLB 1890-1914; DLB 10, 34, 98, 135; MTCW 2

Bennett, Elizabeth
See Mitchell, Margaret (Munnerlyn)

Bennett, George Harold 1930-
See Bennett, Hal
See also BW 1; CA 97-100

Bennett, Hal **CLC 5**
See also Bennett, George Harold
See also DLB 33

Bennett, Jay 1912- **CLC 35**
See also AAYA 10; CA 69-72; CANR 11, 42, 79; JRDA; SAAS 4; SATA 41, 87; SATA-Brief 27

Bennett, Louise (Simone) 1919-**CLC 28; BLC 1; DAM MULT**
See also BW 2, 3; CA 151; DLB 117

Benson, E(dward) F(rederic) 1867-1940 **TCLC 27**
See also CA 114; 157; DLB 135, 153

Benson, Jackson J. 1930- **CLC 34**
See also CA 25-28R; DLB 111

Benson, Sally 1900-1972 **CLC 17**
See also CA 19-20; 37-40R; CAP 1; SATA 1, 35; SATA-Obit 27

Benson, Stella 1892-1933 **TCLC 17**
See also CA 117; 155; DLB 36, 162

Bentham, Jeremy 1748-1832 **NCLC 38**
See also DLB 107, 158

Bentley, E(dmund) C(lerihew) 1875-1956 **TCLC 12**
See also CA 108; DLB 70

Bentley, Eric (Russell) 1916- **CLC 24**
See also CA 5-8R; CANR 6, 67; INT CANR-6

<in**Beranger, Pierre Jean de** 1780-1857 **NCLC 34**

Berdyaev, Nicolas
See Berdyaev, Nikolai (Aleksandrovich)

Berdyaev, Nikolai (Aleksandrovich) 1874-1948 **TCLC 67**
See also CA 120; 157

Berdyayev, Nikolai (Aleksandrovich)
See Berdyaev, Nikolai (Aleksandrovich)

Berendt, John (Lawrence) 1939- **CLC 86**
See also CA 146; CANR 75; MTCW 1

See also CA 1-4R; CANR 1, 33; DLB 14, 207; MTCW 1, 2
Bradbury, Ray (Douglas) 1920-**CLC 1, 3, 10, 15, 42, 98; DA; DAB; DAC; DAM MST, NOV, POP; SSC 29; WLC**
See also AAYA 15; AITN 1, 2; CA 1-4R; CANR 2, 30, 75; CDALB 1968-1988; DLB 2, 8; MTCW 1, 2; SATA 11, 64
Bradford, Gamaliel 1863-1932 **TCLC 36**
See also CA 160; DLB 17
Bradley, David (Henry), Jr. 1950- **CLC 23, 118; BLC 1; DAM MULT**
See also BW 1, 3; CA 104; CANR 26; DLB 33
Bradley, John Ed(mund, Jr.) 1958- **CLC 55**
See also CA 139
Bradley, Marion Zimmer 1930-**CLC 30; DAM POP**
See also AAYA 9; CA 57-60; CAAS 10; CANR 7, 31, 51, 75; DLB 8; MTCW 1, 2; SATA 90
Bradstreet, Anne 1612(?)-1672**LC 4, 30; DA; DAC; DAM MST, POET; PC 10**
See also CDALB 1640-1865; DLB 24
Brady, Joan 1939- **CLC 86**
See also CA 141
Bragg, Melvyn 1939- **CLC 10**
See also BEST 89:3; CA 57-60; CANR 10, 48; DLB 14
Brahe, Tycho 1546-1601 **LC 45**
Braine, John (Gerard) 1922-1986**CLC 1, 3, 41**
See also CA 1-4R; 120; CANR 1, 33; CDBLB 1945-1960; DLB 15; DLBY 86; MTCW 1
Bramah, Ernest 1868-1942 **TCLC 72**
See also CA 156; DLB 70
Brammer, William 1930(?)-1978 **CLC 31**
See also CA 77-80
Brancati, Vitaliano 1907-1954 **TCLC 12**
See also CA 109
Brancato, Robin F(idler) 1936- **CLC 35**
See also AAYA 9; CA 69-72; CANR 11, 45; CLR 32; JRDA; SAAS 9; SATA 97
Brand, Max
See Faust, Frederick (Schiller)
Brand, Millen 1906-1980 **CLC 7**
See also CA 21-24R; 97-100; CANR 72
Branden, Barbara **CLC 44**
See also CA 148
Brandes, Georg (Morris Cohen) 1842-1927 **TCLC 10**
See also CA 105
Brandys, Kazimierz 1916- **CLC 62**
Branley, Franklyn M(ansfield) 1915-**CLC 21**
See also CA 33-36R; CANR 14, 39; CLR 13; MAICYA; SAAS 16; SATA 4, 68
Brathwaite, Edward (Kamau) 1930-**CLC 11; BLCS; DAM POET**
See also BW 2, 3; CA 25-28R; CANR 11, 26, 47; DLB 125
Brautigan, Richard (Gary) 1935-1984**CLC 1, 3, 5, 9, 12, 34, 42; DAM NOV**
See also CA 53-56; 113; CANR 34; DLB 2, 5, 206; DLBY 80, 84; MTCW 1; SATA 56
Brave Bird, Mary 1953-
See Crow Dog, Mary (Ellen)
See also NNAL
Braverman, Kate 1950- **CLC 67**
See also CA 89-92
Brecht, (Eugen) Bertolt (Friedrich) 1898-1956 **TCLC 1, 6, 13, 35; DA; DAB; DAC; DAM DRAM, MST; DC 3; WLC**
See also CA 104; 133; CANR 62; DLB 56, 124; MTCW 1, 2
Brecht, Eugen Berthold Friedrich
See Brecht, (Eugen) Bertolt (Friedrich)
Bremer, Fredrika 1801-1865 **NCLC 11**
Brennan, Christopher John 1870-1932**TCLC 17**
See also CA 117
Brennan, Maeve 1917-1993 **CLC 5**
See also CA 81-84; CANR 72
Brent, Linda
See Jacobs, Harriet A(nn)
Brentano, Clemens (Maria) 1778-1842**NCLC 1**
See also DLB 90
Brent of Bin Bin
See Franklin, (Stella Maria Sarah) Miles (Lampe)
Brenton, Howard 1942- **CLC 31**
See also CA 69-72; CANR 33, 67; DLB 13; MTCW 1
Breslin, James 1930-1996
See Breslin, Jimmy
See also CA 73-76; CANR 31, 75; DAM NOV; MTCW 1, 2
Breslin, Jimmy **CLC 4, 43**
See also Breslin, James
See also AITN 1; DLB 185; MTCW 2
Bresson, Robert 1901- **CLC 16**
See also CA 110; CANR 49
Breton, Andre 1896-1966**CLC 2, 9, 15, 54; PC 15**
See also CA 19-20; 25-28R; CANR 40, 60; CAP 2; DLB 65; MTCW 1, 2
Breytenbach, Breyten 1939(?)- **CLC 23, 37; DAM POET**
See also CA 113; 129; CANR 61
Bridgers, Sue Ellen 1942- **CLC 26**
See also AAYA 8; CA 65-68; CANR 11, 36; CLR 18; DLB 52; JRDA; MAICYA; SAAS 1; SATA 22, 90
Bridges, Robert (Seymour) 1844-1930 **TCLC 1; DAM POET**
See also CA 104; 152; CDBLB 1890-1914; DLB 19, 98
Bridie, James **TCLC 3**
See also Mavor, Osborne Henry
See also DLB 10
Brin, David 1950- **CLC 34**
See also AAYA 21; CA 102; CANR 24, 70; INT CANR-24; SATA 65
Brink, Andre (Philippus) 1935- **CLC 18, 36, 106**
See also CA 104; CANR 39, 62; INT 103; MTCW 1, 2
Brinsmead, H(esba) F(ay) 1922- **CLC 21**
See also CA 21-24R; CANR 10; CLR 47; MAICYA; SAAS 5; SATA 18, 78
Brittain, Vera (Mary) 1893(?)-1970 **CLC 23**
See also CA 13-16; 25-28R; CANR 58; CAP 1; DLB 191; MTCW 1, 2
Broch, Hermann 1886-1951 **TCLC 20**
See also CA 117; DLB 85, 124
Brock, Rose
See Hansen, Joseph
Brodkey, Harold (Roy) 1930-1996 **CLC 56**
See also CA 111; 151; CANR 71; DLB 130
Brodskii, Iosif
See Brodsky, Joseph
Brodsky, Iosif Alexandrovich 1940-1996
See Brodsky, Joseph
See also AITN 1; CA 41-44R; 151; CANR 37; DAM POET; MTCW 1, 2
Brodsky, Joseph 1940-1996 **CLC 4, 6, 13, 36, 100; PC 9**
See also Brodskii, Iosif; Brodsky, Iosif Alexandrovich
See also MTCW 1
Brodsky, Michael (Mark) 1948- **CLC 19**
See also CA 102; CANR 18, 41, 58
Bromell, Henry 1947- **CLC 5**
See also CA 53-56; CANR 9
Bromfield, Louis (Brucker) 1896-1956**TCLC 11**
See also CA 107; 155; DLB 4, 9, 86
Broner, E(sther) M(asserman) 1930- **CLC 19**
See also CA 17-20R; CANR 8, 25, 72; DLB 28
Bronk, William (M.) 1918-1999 **CLC 10**
See also CA 89-92; CANR 23; DLB 165
Bronstein, Lev Davidovich
See Trotsky, Leon
Bronte, Anne 1820-1849 **NCLC 71**
See also DLB 21, 199
Bronte, Charlotte 1816-1855 **NCLC 3, 8, 33, 58; DA; DAB; DAC; DAM MST, NOV; WLC**
See also AAYA 17; CDBLB 1832-1890; DLB 21, 159, 199
Bronte, Emily (Jane) 1818-1848**NCLC 16, 35; DA; DAB; DAC; DAM MST, NOV, POET; PC 8; WLC**
See also AAYA 17; CDBLB 1832-1890; DLB 21, 32, 199
Brooke, Frances 1724-1789 **LC 6, 48**
See also DLB 39, 99
Brooke, Henry 1703(?)-1783 **LC 1**
See also DLB 39
Brooke, Rupert (Chawner) 1887-1915 **TCLC 2, 7; DA; DAB; DAC; DAM MST, POET; PC 24; WLC**
See also CA 104; 132; CANR 61; CDBLB 1914-1945; DLB 19; MTCW 1, 2
Brooke-Haven, P.
See Wodehouse, P(elham) G(renville)
Brooke-Rose, Christine 1926(?)- **CLC 40**
See also CA 13-16R; CANR 58; DLB 14
Brookner, Anita 1928- **CLC 32, 34, 51; DAB; DAM POP**
See also CA 114; 120; CANR 37, 56; DLB 194; DLBY 87; MTCW 1, 2
Brooks, Cleanth 1906-1994 **CLC 24, 86, 110**
See also CA 17-20R; 145; CANR 33, 35; DLB 63; DLBY 94; INT CANR-35; MTCW 1, 2
Brooks, George
See Baum, L(yman) Frank
Brooks, Gwendolyn 1917- **CLC 1, 2, 4, 5, 15, 49; BLC 1; DA; DAC; DAM MST, MULT, POET; PC 7; WLC**
See also AAYA 20; AITN 1; BW 2, 3; CA 1-4R; CANR 1, 27, 52, 75; CDALB 1941-1968; CLR 27; DLB 5, 76, 165; MTCW 1, 2; SATA 6
Brooks, Mel **CLC 12**
See also Kaminsky, Melvin
See also AAYA 13; DLB 26
Brooks, Peter 1938- **CLC 34**
See also CA 45-48; CANR 1
Brooks, Van Wyck 1886-1963 **CLC 29**
See also CA 1-4R; CANR 6; DLB 45, 63, 103
Brophy, Brigid (Antonia) 1929-1995 **CLC 6, 11, 29, 105**
See also CA 5-8R; 149; CAAS 4; CANR 25, 53; DLB 14; MTCW 1, 2
Brosman, Catharine Savage 1934- **CLC 9**
See also CA 61-64; CANR 21, 46
Brossard, Nicole 1943- **CLC 115**
See also CA 122; CAAS 16; DLB 53
Brother Antoninus
See Everson, William (Oliver)
The Brothers Quay

See also CA 33-36R; CAAS 1; CANR 45, 73; DLB 6

Bush, Ronald 1946- **CLC 34**
See also CA 136

Bustos, F(rancisco)
See Borges, Jorge Luis

Bustos Domecq, H(onorio)
See Bioy Casares, Adolfo; Borges, Jorge Luis

Butler, Octavia E(stelle) 1947-**CLC 38; BLCS; DAM MULT, POP**
See also AAYA 18; BW 2, 3; CA 73-76; CANR 12, 24, 38, 73; DLB 33; MTCW 1, 2; SATA 84

Butler, Robert Olen (Jr.) 1945-**CLC 81; DAM POP**
See also CA 112; CANR 66; DLB 173; INT 112; MTCW 1

Butler, Samuel 1612-1680 **LC 16, 43**
See also DLB 101, 126

Butler, Samuel 1835-1902 **TCLC 1, 33; DA; DAB; DAC; DAM MST, NOV; WLC**
See also CA 143; CDBLB 1890-1914; DLB 18, 57, 174

Butler, Walter C.
See Faust, Frederick (Schiller)

Butor, Michel (Marie Francois) 1926-**CLC 1, 3, 8, 11, 15**
See also CA 9-12R; CANR 33, 66; DLB 83; MTCW 1, 2

Butts, Mary 1892(?)-1937 **TCLC 77**
See also CA 148

Buzo, Alexander (John) 1944- **CLC 61**
See also CA 97-100; CANR 17, 39, 69

Buzzati, Dino 1906-1972 **CLC 36**
See also CA 160; 33-36R; DLB 177

Byars, Betsy (Cromer) 1928- **CLC 35**
See also AAYA 19; CA 33-36R; CANR 18, 36, 57; CLR 1, 16; DLB 52; INT CANR-18; JRDA; MAICYA; MTCW 1; SAAS 1; SATA 4, 46, 80

Byatt, A(ntonia) S(usan Drabble) 1936- **CLC 19, 65; DAM NOV, POP**
See also CA 13-16R; CANR 13, 33, 50, 75; DLB 14, 194; MTCW 1, 2

Byrne, David 1952- **CLC 26**
See also CA 127

Byrne, John Keyes 1926-
See Leonard, Hugh
See also CA 102; CANR 78; INT 102

Byron, George Gordon (Noel) 1788-1824 **NCLC 2, 12; DA; DAB; DAC; DAM MST, POET; PC 16; WLC**
See also CDBLB 1789-1832; DLB 96, 110

Byron, Robert 1905-1941 **TCLC 67**
See also CA 160; DLB 195

C. 3. 3.
See Wilde, Oscar

Caballero, Fernan 1796-1877 **NCLC 10**

Cabell, Branch
See Cabell, James Branch

Cabell, James Branch 1879-1958 **TCLC 6**
See also CA 105; 152; DLB 9, 78; MTCW 1

Cable, George Washington 1844-1925 **TCLC 4; SSC 4**
See also CA 104; 155; DLB 12, 74; DLBD 13

Cabral de Melo Neto, Joao 1920- **CLC 76; DAM MULT**
See also CA 151

Cabrera Infante, G(uillermo) 1929-**CLC 5, 25, 45, 120; DAM MULT; HLC**
See also CA 85-88; CANR 29, 65; DLB 113; HW 1, 2; MTCW 1, 2

Cade, Toni
See Bambara, Toni Cade

Cadmus and Harmonia
See Buchan, John

Caedmon fl. 658-680 **CMLC 7**
See also DLB 146

Caeiro, Alberto
See Pessoa, Fernando (Antonio Nogueira)

Cage, John (Milton, Jr.) 1912-1992 **CLC 41**
See also CA 13-16R; 169; CANR 9, 78; DLB 193; INT CANR-9

Cahan, Abraham 1860-1951 **TCLC 71**
See also CA 108; 154; DLB 9, 25, 28

Cain, G.
See Cabrera Infante, G(uillermo)

Cain, Guillermo
See Cabrera Infante, G(uillermo)

Cain, James M(allahan) 1892-1977**CLC 3, 11, 28**
See also AITN 1; CA 17-20R; 73-76; CANR 8, 34, 61; MTCW 1

Caine, Mark
See Raphael, Frederic (Michael)

Calasso, Roberto 1941- **CLC 81**
See also CA 143

Calderon de la Barca, Pedro 1600-1681 **LC 23; DC 3; HLCS 1**

Caldwell, Erskine (Preston) 1903-1987**CLC 1, 8, 14, 50, 60; DAM NOV; SSC 19**
See also AITN 1; CA 1-4R; 121; CAAS 1; CANR 2, 33; DLB 9, 86; MTCW 1, 2

Caldwell, (Janet Miriam) Taylor (Holland) 1900-1985**CLC 2, 28, 39; DAM NOV, POP**
See also CA 5-8R; 116; CANR 5; DLBD 17

Calhoun, John Caldwell 1782-1850**NCLC 15**
See also DLB 3

Calisher, Hortense 1911-**CLC 2, 4, 8, 38; DAM NOV; SSC 15**
See also CA 1-4R; CANR 1, 22, 67; DLB 2; INT CANR-22; MTCW 1, 2

Callaghan, Morley Edward 1903-1990**CLC 3, 14, 41, 65; DAC; DAM MST**
See also CA 9-12R; 132; CANR 33, 73; DLB 68; MTCW 1, 2

Callimachus c. 305B.C.-c. 240B.C. **CMLC 18**
See also DLB 176

Calvin, John 1509-1564 **LC 37**

Calvino, Italo 1923-1985**CLC 5, 8, 11, 22, 33, 39, 73; DAM NOV; SSC 3**
See also CA 85-88; 116; CANR 23, 61; DLB 196; MTCW 1, 2

Cameron, Carey 1952- **CLC 59**
See also CA 135

Cameron, Peter 1959- **CLC 44**
See also CA 125; CANR 50

Campana, Dino 1885-1932 **TCLC 20**
See also CA 117; DLB 114

Campanella, Tommaso 1568-1639 **LC 32**

Campbell, John W(ood, Jr.) 1910-1971 **CLC 32**
See also CA 21-22; 29-32R; CANR 34; CAP 2; DLB 8; MTCW 1

Campbell, Joseph 1904-1987 **CLC 69**
See also AAYA 3; BEST 89:2; CA 1-4R; 124; CANR 3, 28, 61; MTCW 1, 2

Campbell, Maria 1940- **CLC 85; DAC**
See also CA 102; CANR 54; NNAL

Campbell, (John) Ramsey 1946-**CLC 42; SSC 19**
See also CA 57-60; CANR 7; INT CANR-7

Campbell, (Ignatius) Roy (Dunnachie) 1901-1957 **TCLC 5**
See also CA 104; 155; DLB 20; MTCW 2

Campbell, Thomas 1777-1844 **NCLC 19**
See also DLB 93; 144

Campbell, Wilfred **TCLC 9**
See also Campbell, William

Campbell, William 1858(?)-1918
See Campbell, Wilfred
See also CA 106; DLB 92

Campion, Jane **CLC 95**
See also CA 138

Campos, Alvaro de
See Pessoa, Fernando (Antonio Nogueira)

Camus, Albert 1913-1960**CLC 1, 2, 4, 9, 11, 14, 32, 63, 69; DA; DAB; DAC; DAM DRAM, MST, NOV; DC 2; SSC 9; WLC**
<indeSee also CA 89-92; DLB 72; MTCW 1, 2

Canby, Vincent 1924- **CLC 13**
See also CA 81-84

Cancale
See Desnos, Robert

Canetti, Elias 1905-1994**CLC 3, 14, 25, 75, 86**
See also CA 21-24R; 146; CANR 23, 61, 79; DLB 85, 124; MTCW 1, 2

Canfield, Dorothea F.
See Fisher, Dorothy (Frances) Canfield

Canfield, Dorothea Frances
See Fisher, Dorothy (Frances) Canfield

Canfield, Dorothy
See Fisher, Dorothy (Frances) Canfield

Canin, Ethan 1960- **CLC 55**
See also CA 131; 135

Cannon, Curt
See Hunter, Evan

Cao, Lan 1961- **CLC 109**
See also CA 165

Cape, Judith
See Page, P(atricia) K(athleen)

Capek, Karel 1890-1938 **TCLC 6, 37; DA; DAB; DAC; DAM DRAM, MST, NOV; DC 1; WLC**
See also CA 104; 140; MTCW 1

Capote, Truman 1924-1984**CLC 1, 3, 8, 13, 19, 34, 38, 58; DA; DAB; DAC; DAM MST, NOV, POP; SSC 2; WLC**
See also CA 5-8R; 113; CANR 18, 62; CDALB 1941-1968; DLB 2, 185; DLBY 80, 84; MTCW 1, 2; SATA 91

Capra, Frank 1897-1991 **CLC 16**
See also CA 61-64; 135

Caputo, Philip 1941- **CLC 32**
See also CA 73-76; CANR 40

Caragiale, Ion Luca 1852-1912 **TCLC 76**
See also CA 157

Card, Orson Scott 1951-**CLC 44, 47, 50; DAM POP**
See also AAYA 11; CA 102; CANR 27, 47, 73; INT CANR-27; MTCW 1, 2; SATA 83

Cardenal, Ernesto 1925- **CLC 31; DAM MULT, POET; HLC; PC 22**
See also CA 49-52; CANR 2, 32, 66; HW 1, 2; MTCW 1, 2

Cardozo, Benjamin N(athan) 1870-1938 **TCLC 65**
See also CA 117; 164

Carducci, Giosue (Alessandro Giuseppe) 1835-1907 **TCLC 32**
See also CA 163

Carew, Thomas 1595(?)-1640 **LC 13**
See also DLB 126

Carey, Ernestine Gilbreth 1908- **CLC 17**
See also CA 5-8R; CANR 71; SATA 2

Carey, Peter 1943- **CLC 40, 55, 96**
See also CA 123; 127; CANR 53, 76; INT 127; MTCW 1, 2; SATA 94

Carleton, William 1794-1869 **NCLC 3**

See also DLB 159
Carlisle, Henry (Coffin) 1926- **CLC 33**
See also CA 13-16R; CANR 15
Carlsen, Chris
See Holdstock, Robert P.
Carlson, Ron(ald F.) 1947- **CLC 54**
See also CA 105; CANR 27
Carlyle, Thomas 1795-1881 **NCLC 70; DA; DAB; DAC; DAM MST**
See also CDBLB 1789-1832; DLB 55; 144
Carman, (William) Bliss 1861-1929 **TCLC 7; DAC**
See also CA 104; 152; DLB 92
Carnegie, Dale 1888-1955 **TCLC 53**
Carossa, Hans 1878-1956 **TCLC 48**
See also CA 170; DLB 66
Carpenter, Don(ald Richard) 1931-1995 **CLC 41**
See also CA 45-48; 149; CANR 1, 71
Carpenter, Edward 1844-1929 **TCLC 88**
See also CA 163
Carpentier (y Valmont), Alejo 1904-1980 **CLC 8, 11, 38, 110; DAM MULT; HLC**
See also CA 65-68; 97-100; CANR 11, 70; DLB 113; HW 1, 2
Carr, Caleb 1955(?)- **CLC 86**
See also CA 147; CANR 73
Carr, Emily 1871-1945 **TCLC 32**
See also CA 159; DLB 68
Carr, John Dickson 1906-1977 **CLC 3**
See also Fairbairn, Roger
See also CA 49-52; 69-72; CANR 3, 33, 60; MTCW 1, 2
Carr, Philippa
See Hibbert, Eleanor Alice Burford
Carr, Virginia Spencer 1929- **CLC 34**
See also CA 61-64; DLB 111
Carrere, Emmanuel 1957- **CLC 89**
Carrier, Roch 1937- **CLC 13, 78; DAC; DAM MST**
See also CA 130; CANR 61; DLB 53; SATA 105
Carroll, James P. 1943(?)- **CLC 38**
See also CA 81-84; CANR 73; MTCW 1
Carroll, Jim 1951- **CLC 35**
See also AAYA 17; CA 45-48; CANR 42
Carroll, Lewis **NCLC 2, 53; PC 18; WLC**
See also Dodgson, Charles Lutwidge
See also CDBLB 1832-1890; CLR 2, 18; DLB 18, 163, 178; DLBY 98; JRDA
Carroll, Paul Vincent 1900-1968 **CLC 10**
See also CA 9-12R; 25-28R; DLB 10
Carruth, Hayden 1921- **CLC 4, 7, 10, 18, 84; PC 10**
See also CA 9-12R; CANR 4, 38, 59; DLB 5, 165; INT CANR-4; MTCW 1, 2; SATA 47
Carson, Rachel Louise 1907-1964 **CLC 71; DAM POP**
See also CA 77-80; CANR 35; MTCW 1, 2; SATA 23
Carter, Angela (Olive) 1940-1992 **CLC 5, 41, 76; SSC 13**
See also CA 53-56; 136; CANR 12, 36, 61; DLB 14, 207; MTCW 1, 2; SATA 66; SATA-Obit 70
Carter, Nick
See Smith, Martin Cruz
Carver, Raymond 1938-1988 **CLC 22, 36, 53, 55; DAM NOV; SSC 8**
See also CA 33-36R; 126; CANR 17, 34, 61; DLB 130; DLBY 84, 88; MTCW 1, 2
Cary, Elizabeth, Lady Falkland 1585-1639 **LC 30**
Cary, (Arthur) Joyce (Lunel) 1888-1957 **TCLC 1, 29**
See also CA 104; 164; CDBLB 1914-1945; DLB 15, 100; MTCW 2
Casanova de Seingalt, Giovanni Jacopo 1725-1798 **LC 13**
Casares, Adolfo Bioy
See Bioy Casares, Adolfo
Casely-Hayford, J(oseph) E(phraim) 1866-1930 **TCLC 24; BLC 1; DAM MULT**
See also BW 2; CA 123; 152
Casey, John (Dudley) 1939- **CLC 59**
See also BEST 90:2; CA 69-72; CANR 23
Casey, Michael 1947- **CLC 2**
See also CA 65-68; DLB 5
Casey, Patrick
See Thurman, Wallace (Henry)
Casey, Warren (Peter) 1935-1988 **CLC 12**
See also CA 101; 127; INT 101
Casona, Alejandro **CLC 49**
See also Alvarez, Alejandro Rodriguez
Cassavetes, John 1929-1989 **CLC 20**
See also CA 85-88; 127
Cassian, Nina 1924- **PC 17**
Cassill, R(onald) V(erlin) 1919- **CLC 4, 23**
See also CA 9-12R; CAAS 1; CANR 7, 45; DLB 6
Cassirer, Ernst 1874-1945 **TCLC 61**
See also CA 157
Cassity, (Allen) Turner 1929- **CLC 6, 42**
See also CA 17-20R; CAAS 8; CANR 11; DLB 105
Castaneda, Carlos (Cesar Aranha) 1931(?)-1998 **CLC 12, 119**
See also CA 25-28R; CANR 32, 66; HW 1; MTCW 1
Castedo, Elena 1937- **CLC 65**
See also CA 132
Castedo-Ellerman, Elena
See Castedo, Elena
Castellanos, Rosario 1925-1974 **CLC 66; DAM MULT; HLC**
See also CA 131; 53-56; CANR 58; DLB 113; HW 1; MTCW 1
Castelvetro, Lodovico 1505-1571 **LC 12**
Castiglione, Baldassare 1478-1529 **LC 12**
Castle, Robert
See Hamilton, Edmond
Castro, Guillen de 1569-1631 **LC 19**
Castro, Rosalia de 1837-1885 **NCLC 3; DAM MULT**
Cather, Willa
See Cather, Willa Sibert
Cather, Willa Sibert 1873-1947 **TCLC 1, 11, 31; DA; DAB; DAC; DAM MST, NOV; SSC 2; WLC**
See also AAYA 24; CA 104; 128; CDALB 1865-1917; DLB 9, 54, 78; DLBD 1; MTCW 1, 2; SATA 30
Catherine, Saint 1347-1380 **CMLC 27**
Cato, Marcus Porcius 234B.C.-149B.C. **CMLC 21**
See also DLB 211
Catton, (Charles) Bruce 1899-1978 **CLC 35**
See also AITN 1; CA 5-8R; 81-84; CANR 7, 74; DLB 17; SATA 2; SATA-Obit 24
Catullus c. 84B.C.-c. 54B.C. **CMLC 18**
See also DLB 211
Cauldwell, Frank
See King, Francis (Henry)
Caunitz, William J. 1933-1996 **CLC 34**
See also BEST 89:3; CA 125; 130; 152; CANR 73; INT 130
Causley, Charles (Stanley) 1917- **CLC 7**
See also CA 9-12R; CANR 5, 35; CLR 30; DLB 27; MTCW 1; SATA 3, 66
Caute, (John) David 1936- **CLC 29; DAM NOV**
<iSee also CA 1-4R; CAAS 4; CANR 1, 33, 64; DLB 14
Cavafy, C(onstantine) P(eter) 1863-1933 **TCLC 2, 7; DAM POET**
See also Kavafis, Konstantinos Petrou
See also CA 148; MTCW 1
Cavallo, Evelyn
See Spark, Muriel (Sarah)
Cavanna, Betty **CLC 12**
See also Harrison, Elizabeth Cavanna
See also JRDA; MAICYA; SAAS 4; SATA 1, 30
Cavendish, Margaret Lucas 1623-1673 **LC 30**
See also DLB 131
Caxton, William 1421(?)-1491(?) **LC 17**
See also DLB 170
Cayer, D. M.
See Duffy, Maureen
Cayrol, Jean 1911- **CLC 11**
See also CA 89-92; DLB 83
Cela, Camilo Jose 1916- **CLC 4, 13, 59; DAM MULT; HLC**
See also BEST 90:2; CA 21-24R; CAAS 10; CANR 21, 32, 76; DLBY 89; HW 1; MTCW 1, 2
Celan, Paul **CLC 10, 19, 53, 82; PC 10**
See also Antschel, Paul
See also DLB 69
Celine, Louis-Ferdinand **CLC 1, 3, 4, 7, 9, 15, 47**
See also Destouches, Louis-Ferdinand
See also DLB 72
Cellini, Benvenuto 1500-1571 **LC 7**
Cendrars, Blaise 1887-1961 **CLC 18, 106**
See also Sauser-Hall, Frederic
Cernuda (y Bidon), Luis 1902-1963 **CLC 54; DAM POET**
See also CA 131; 89-92; DLB 134; HW 1
Cervantes (Saavedra), Miguel de 1547-1616 **LC 6, 23; DA; DAB; DAC; DAM MST, NOV; SSC 12; WLC**
Cesaire, Aime (Fernand) 1913- **CLC 19, 32, 112; BLC 1; DAM MULT, POET; PC 25**
See also BW 2, 3; CA 65-68; CANR 24, 43; MTCW 1, 2
Chabon, Michael 1963- **CLC 55**
See also CA 139; CANR 57
Chabrol, Claude 1930- **CLC 16**
See also CA 110
Challans, Mary 1905-1983
See Renault, Mary
See also CA 81-84; 111; CANR 74; MTCW 2; SATA 23; SATA-Obit 36
Challis, George
See Faust, Frederick (Schiller)
Chambers, Aidan 1934- **CLC 35**
See also AAYA 27; CA 25-28R; CANR 12, 31, 58; JRDA; MAICYA; SAAS 12; SATA 1, 69
Chambers, James 1948-
See Cliff, Jimmy
<See also CA 124
Chambers, Jessie
See Lawrence, D(avid) H(erbert Richards)
Chambers, Robert W(illiam) 1865-1933 **TCLC 41**
See also CA 165; DLB 202; SATA 107
Chandler, Raymond (Thornton) 1888-1959 **TCLC 1, 7; SSC 23**

See also AAYA 25; CA 104; 129; CANR 60; CDALB 1929-1941; DLBD 6; MTCW 1, 2
Chang, Eileen 1920-1995 **SSC 28**
See also CA 166
Chang, Jung 1952- **CLC 71**
See also CA 142
Chang Ai-Ling
See Chang, Eileen
Channing, William Ellery 1780-1842 **NCLC 17**
See also DLB 1, 59
Chao, Patricia 1955- **CLC 119**
<indexSee also CA 163
Chaplin, Charles Spencer 1889-1977 **CLC 16**
See also Chaplin, Charlie
See also CA 81-84; 73-76
Chaplin, Charlie
See Chaplin, Charles Spencer
See also DLB 44
Chapman, George 1559(?)-1634**LC 22; DAM DRAM**
See also DLB 62, 121
Chapman, Graham 1941-1989 **CLC 21**
See also Monty Python
See also CA 116; 129; CANR 35
Chapman, John Jay 1862-1933 **TCLC 7**
See also CA 104
Chapman, Lee
See Bradley, Marion Zimmer
Chapman, Walker
See Silverberg, Robert
Chappell, Fred (Davis) 1936- **CLC 40, 78**
See also CA 5-8R; CAAS 4; CANR 8, 33, 67; DLB 6, 105
Char, Rene(-Emile) 1907-1988**CLC 9, 11, 14, 55; DAM POET**
See also CA 13-16R; 124; CANR 32; MTCW 1, 2
Charby, Jay
See Ellison, Harlan (Jay)
Chardin, Pierre Teilhard de
See Teilhard de Chardin, (Marie Joseph) Pierre
Charles I 1600-1649 **LC 13**
Charriere, Isabelle de 1740-1805 **NCLC 66**
Charyn, Jerome 1937- **CLC 5, 8, 18**
See also CA 5-8R; CAAS 1; CANR 7, 61; DLBY 83; MTCW 1
Chase, Mary (Coyle) 1907-1981 **DC 1**
See also CA 77-80; 105; SATA 17; SATA-Obit 29
Chase, Mary Ellen 1887-1973 **CLC 2**
See also CA 13-16; 41-44R; CAP 1; SATA 10
Chase, Nicholas
See Hyde, Anthony
Chateaubriand, Francois Rene de 1768-1848 **NCLC 3**
See also DLB 119
Chatterje, Sarat Chandra 1876-1936(?)
See Chatterji, Saratchandra
See also CA 109
Chatterji, Bankim Chandra 1838-1894**NCLC 19**
Chatterji, Saratchandra **TCLC 13**
See also Chatterje, Sarat Chandra
Chatterton, Thomas 1752-1770 **LC 3; DAM POET**
See also DLB 109
Chatwin, (Charles) Bruce 1940-1989**CLC 28, 57, 59; DAM POP**
See also AAYA 4; BEST 90:1; CA 85-88; 127; DLB 194, 204
Chaucer, Daniel
See Ford, Ford Madox
Chaucer, Geoffrey 1340(?)-1400 **LC 17; DA; DAB; DAC; DAM MST, POET; PC 19; WLCS**
See also CDBLB Before 1660; DLB 146
Chaviaras, Strates 1935-
See Haviaras, Stratis
See also CA 105
Chayefsky, Paddy **CLC 23**
See also Chayefsky, Sidney
See also DLB 7, 44; DLBY 81
Chayefsky, Sidney 1923-1981
See Chayefsky, Paddy
See also CA 9-12R; 104; CANR 18; DAM DRAM
Chedid, Andree 1920- **CLC 47**
See also CA 145
Cheever, John 1912-1982 **CLC 3, 7, 8, 11, 15, 25, 64; DA; DAB; DAC; DAM MST, NOV, POP; SSC 1; WLC**
See also CA 5-8R; 106; CABS 1; CANR 5, 27, 76; CDALB 1941-1968; DLB 2, 102; DLBY 80, 82; INT CANR-5; MTCW 1, 2
Cheever, Susan 1943- **CLC 18, 48**
See also CA 103; CANR 27, 51; DLBY 82; INT CANR-27
Chekhonte, Antosha
See Chekhov, Anton (Pavlovich)
Chekhov, Anton (Pavlovich) 1860-1904**TCLC 3, 10, 31, 55; DA; DAB; DAC; DAM DRAM, MST; DC 9; SSC 2, 28; WLC**
See also CA 104; 124; SATA 90
Chernyshevsky, Nikolay Gavrilovich 1828-1889 **NCLC 1**
Cherry, Carolyn Janice 1942-
See Cherryh, C. J.
See also CA 65-68; CANR 10
Cherryh, C. J. **CLC 35**
See also Cherry, Carolyn Janice
See also AAYA 24; DLBY 80; SATA 93
Chesnutt, Charles W(addell) 1858-1932 **TCLC 5, 39; BLC 1; DAM MULT; SSC 7**
See also BW 1, 3; CA 106; 125; CANR 76; DLB 12, 50, 78; MTCW 1, 2
Chester, Alfred 1929(?)-1971 **CLC 49**
See also CA 33-36R; DLB 130
Chesterton, G(ilbert) K(eith) 1874-1936 **TCLC 1, 6, 64; DAM NOV, POET; SSC 1**
See also CA 104; 132; CANR 73; CDBLB 1914-1945; DLB 10, 19, 34, 70, 98, 149, 178; MTCW 1, 2; SATA 27
Chiang, Pin-chin 1904-1986
See Ding Ling
See also CA 118
Ch'ien Chung-shu 1910- **CLC 22**
See also CA 130; CANR 73; MTCW 1, 2
Child, L. Maria
See Child, Lydia Maria
Child, Lydia Maria 1802-1880 **NCLC 6, 73**
See also DLB 1, 74; SATA 67
Child, Mrs.
<indexSee Child, Lydia Maria
Child, Philip 1898-1978 **CLC 19, 68**
See also CA 13-14; CAP 1; SATA 47
Childers, (Robert) Erskine 1870-1922 **TCLC 65**
See also CA 113; 153; DLB 70
Childress, Alice 1920-1994**CLC 12, 15, 86, 96; BLC 1; DAM DRAM, MULT, NOV; DC 4**
See also AAYA 8; BW 2, 3; CA 45-48; 146; CANR 3, 27, 50, 74; CLR 14; DLB 7, 38; JRDA; MAICYA; MTCW 1, 2; SATA 7, 48, 81
Chin, Frank (Chew, Jr.) 1940- **DC 7**
See also CA 33-36R; CANR 71; DAM MULT; DLB 206
Chislett, (Margaret) Anne 1943- **CLC 34**
See also CA 151
Chitty, Thomas Willes 1926- **CLC 11**
See also Hinde, Thomas
See also CA 5-8R
<inde**Chivers, Thomas Holley** 1809-1858 **NCLC 49**
See also DLB 3
Choi, Susan **CLC 119**
Chomette, Rene Lucien 1898-1981
See Clair, Rene
See also CA 103
Chopin, Kate **TCLC 5, 14; DA; DAB; SSC 8; WLCS**
See also Chopin, Katherine
See also CDALB 1865-1917; DLB 12, 78
Chopin, Katherine 1851-1904
See Chopin, Kate
See also CA 104; 122; DAC; DAM MST, NOV
Chretien de Troyes c. 12th cent. - **CMLC 10**
See also DLB 208
Christie
See Ichikawa, Kon
Christie, Agatha (Mary Clarissa) 1890-1976 **CLC 1, 6, 8, 12, 39, 48, 110; DAB; DAC; DAM NOV**
<inSee also AAYA 9; AITN 1, 2; CA 17-20R; 61-64; CANR 10, 37; CDBLB 1914-1945; DLB 13, 77; MTCW 1, 2; SATA 36
Christie, (Ann) Philippa
See Pearce, Philippa
See also CA 5-8R; CANR 4
Christine de Pizan 1365(?)-1431(?) **LC 9**
See also DLB 208
Chubb, Elmer
See Masters, Edgar Lee
Chulkov, Mikhail Dmitrievich 1743-1792**LC 2**
See also DLB 150
Churchill, Caryl 1938- **CLC 31, 55; DC 5**
See also CA 102; CANR 22, 46; DLB 13; MTCW 1
Churchill, Charles 1731-1764 **LC 3**
See also DLB 109
Chute, Carolyn 1947- **CLC 39**
See also CA 123
Ciardi, John (Anthony) 1916-1986 **CLC 10, 40, 44; DAM POET**
See also CA 5-8R; 118; CAAS 2; CANR 5, 33; CLR 19; DLB 5; DLBY 86; INT CANR-5; MAICYA; MTCW 1, 2; SAAS 26; SATA 1, 65; SATA-Obit 46
Cicero, Marcus Tullius 106B.C.-43B.C. **CMLC 3**
See also DLB 211
Cimino, Michael 1943- **CLC 16**
See also CA 105
Cioran, E(mil) M. 1911-1995 **CLC 64**
See also CA 25-28R; 149
Cisneros, Sandra 1954- **CLC 69, 118; DAM MULT; HLC; SSC 32**
See also AAYA 9; CA 131; CANR 64; DLB 122, 152; HW 1, 2; MTCW 2
Cixous, Helene 1937- **CLC 92**
See also CA 126; CANR 55; DLB 83; MTCW 1, 2
Clair, Rene **CLC 20**
See also Chomette, Rene Lucien
<in**Clampitt, Amy** 1920-1994 **CLC 32; PC 19**
See also CA 110; 146; CANR 29, 79; DLB 105
Clancy, Thomas L., Jr. 1947-

See also CA 73-76; 33-36R; CANR 35; CLR 36; MAICYA; MTCW 1; SATA 15

Colvin, James
See Moorcock, Michael (John)

Colwin, Laurie (E.) 1944-1992**CLC 5, 13, 23, 84**
See also CA 89-92; 139; CANR 20, 46; DLBY 80; MTCW 1

Comfort, Alex(ander) 1920-**CLC 7; DAM POP**
See also CA 1-4R; CANR 1, 45; MTCW 1

Comfort, Montgomery
See Campbell, (John) Ramsey

Compton-Burnett, I(vy) 1884(?)-1969**CLC 1, 3, 10, 15, 34; DAM NOV**
See also CA 1-4R; 25-28R; CANR 4; DLB 36; MTCW 1

Comstock, Anthony 1844-1915 **TCLC 13**
See also CA 110; 169

Comte, Auguste 1798-1857 **NCLC 54**

Conan Doyle, Arthur
See Doyle, Arthur Conan

Conde, Maryse 1937- **CLC 52, 92; BLCS; DAM MULT**
See also Boucolon, Maryse
See also BW 2; MTCW 1

Condillac, Etienne Bonnot de 1714-1780 **L C 26**

Condon, Richard (Thomas) 1915-1996**CLC 4, 6, 8, 10, 45, 100; DAM NOV**
See also BEST 90:3; CA 1-4R; 151; CAAS 1; CANR 2, 23; INT CANR-23; MTCW 1, 2

Confucius 551B.C.-479B.C. **CMLC 19; DA; DAB; DAC; DAM MST; WLCS**

Congreve, William 1670-1729 **LC 5, 21; DA; DAB; DAC; DAM DRAM, MST, POET; DC 2; WLC**
See also CDBLB 1660-1789; DLB 39, 84

Connell, Evan S(helby), Jr. 1924-**CLC 4, 6, 45; DAM NOV**
See also AAYA 7; CA 1-4R; CAAS 2; CANR 2, 39, 76; DLB 2; DLBY 81; MTCW 1, 2

Connelly, Marc(us Cook) 1890-1980 **CLC 7**
See also CA 85-88; 102; CANR 30; DLB 7; DLBY 80; SATA-Obit 25

Connor, Ralph **TCLC 31**
See also Gordon, Charles William
See also DLB 92

Conrad, Joseph 1857-1924**TCLC 1, 6, 13, 25, 43, 57; DA; DAB; DAC; DAM MST, NOV; SSC 9; WLC**
See also AAYA 26; CA 104; 131; CANR 60; CDBLB 1890-1914; DLB 10, 34, 98, 156; MTCW 1, 2; SATA 27

Conrad, Robert Arnold
See Hart, Moss

Conroy, Pat
See Conroy, (Donald) Pat(rick)
See also MTCW 2

Conroy, (Donald) Pat(rick) 1945-**CLC 30, 74; DAM NOV, POP**
See also Conroy, Pat
See also AAYA 8; AITN 1; CA 85-88; CANR 24, 53; DLB 6; MTCW 1

Constant (de Rebecque), (Henri) Benjamin 1767-1830 **NCLC 6**
See also DLB 119

Conybeare, Charles Augustus
See Eliot, T(homas) S(tearns)

Cook, Michael 1933- **CLC 58**
See also CA 93-96; CANR 68; DLB 53

Cook, Robin 1940- **CLC 14; DAM POP**
See also BEST 90:2; CA 108; 111; CANR 41; INT 111

Cook, Roy
See Silverberg, Robert

Cooke, Elizabeth 1948- **CLC 55**
See also CA 129

Cooke, John Esten 1830-1886 **NCLC 5**
See also DLB 3

Cooke, John Estes
See Baum, L(yman) Frank

Cooke, M. E.
See Creasey, John
<inde**Cooke, Margaret**
See Creasey, John

Cook-Lynn, Elizabeth 1930- **CLC 93; DAM MULT**
See also CA 133; DLB 175; NNAL

Cooney, Ray **CLC 62**

Cooper, Douglas 1960- **CLC 86**

Cooper, Henry St. John
See Creasey, John

Cooper, J(oan) California (?)-**CLC 56; DAM MULT**
See also AAYA 12; BW 1; CA 125; CANR 55; DLB 212

Cooper, James Fenimore 1789-1851**NCLC 1, 27, 54**
See also AAYA 22; CDALB 1640-1865; DLB 3; SATA 19

Coover, Robert (Lowell) 1932- **CLC 3, 7, 15, 32, 46, 87; DAM NOV; SSC 15**
See also CA 45-48; CANR 3, 37, 58; DLB 2; DLBY 81; MTCW 1, 2
<indexb**Copeland, Stewart (Armstrong)** 1952- **CLC 26**

Copernicus, Nicolaus 1473-1543 **LC 45**

Coppard, A(lfred) E(dgar) 1878-1957 **TCLC 5; SSC 21**
See also CA 114; 167; DLB 162; YABC 1

Coppee, Francois 1842-1908 **TCLC 25**
See also CA 170

Coppola, Francis Ford 1939- **CLC 16**
See also CA 77-80; CANR 40, 78; DLB 44

Corbiere, Tristan 1845-1875 **NCLC 43**

Corcoran, Barbara 1911- **CLC 17**
See also AAYA 14; CA 21-24R; CAAS 2; CANR 11, 28, 48; CLR 50; DLB 52; JRDA; SAAS 20; SATA 3, 77

Cordelier, Maurice
See Giraudoux, (Hippolyte) Jean

Corelli, Marie 1855-1924 **TCLC 51**
See also Mackay, Mary
See also DLB 34, 156

Corman, Cid 1924- **CLC 9**
See also Corman, Sidney
See also CAAS 2; DLB 5, 193

Corman, Sidney 1924-
See Corman, Cid
See also CA 85-88; CANR 44; DAM POET

Cormier, Robert (Edmund) 1925-**CLC 12, 30; DA; DAB; DAC; DAM MST, NOV**
See also AAYA 3, 19; CA 1-4R; CANR 5, 23, 76; CDALB 1968-1988; CLR 12, 55; DLB 52; INT CANR-23; JRDA; MAICYA; MTCW 1, 2; SATA 10, 45, 83

Corn, Alfred (DeWitt III) 1943- **CLC 33**
See also CA 104; CAAS 25; CANR 44; DLB 120; DLBY 80

Corneille, Pierre 1606-1684 **LC 28; DAB; DAM MST**

Cornwell, David (John Moore) 1931- **CLC 9, 15; DAM POP**
See also le Carre, John
See also CA 5-8R; CANR 13, 33, 59; MTCW 1, 2

Corso, (Nunzio) Gregory 1930- **CLC 1, 11**
See also CA 5-8R; CANR 41, 76; DLB 5, 16; MTCW 1, 2

Cortazar, Julio 1914-1984**CLC 2, 3, 5, 10, 13, 15, 33, 34, 92; DAM MULT, NOV; HLC; SSC 7**
See also CA 21-24R; CANR 12, 32; DLB 113; HW 1, 2; MTCW 1, 2

CORTES, HERNAN 1484-1547 **LC 31**

Corvinus, Jakob
See Raabe, Wilhelm (Karl)

Corwin, Cecil
See Kornbluth, C(yril) M.

Cosic, Dobrica 1921- **CLC 14**
See also CA 122; 138; DLB 181

Costain, Thomas B(ertram) 1885-1965 **C L C 30**
See also CA 5-8R; 25-28R; DLB 9

Costantini, Humberto 1924(?)-1987 **CLC 49**
See also CA 131; 122; HW 1

Costello, Elvis 1955- **CLC 21**

Costenoble, Philostene
See Ghelderode, Michel de

Cotes, Cecil V.
See Duncan, Sara Jeannette

Cotter, Joseph Seamon Sr. 1861-1949 **T C L C 28; BLC 1; DAM MULT**
See also BW 1; CA 124; DLB 50

Couch, Arthur Thomas Quiller
See Quiller-Couch, SirArthur (Thomas)

Coulton, James
See Hansen, Joseph

Couperus, Louis (Marie Anne) 1863-1923 **TCLC 15**
See also CA 115

Coupland, Douglas 1961-**CLC 85; DAC; DAM POP**
See also CA 142; CANR 57

Court, Wesli
See Turco, Lewis (Putnam)

Courtenay, Bryce 1933- **CLC 59**
See also CA 138

Courtney, Robert
See Ellison, Harlan (Jay)

Cousteau, Jacques-Yves 1910-1997 **CLC 30**
See also CA 65-68; 159; CANR 15, 67; MTCW 1; SATA 38, 98

Coventry, Francis 1725-1754 **LC 46**

Cowan, Peter (Walkinshaw) 1914- **SSC 28**
See also CA 21-24R; CANR 9, 25, 50

Coward, Noel (Peirce) 1899-1973**CLC 1, 9, 29, 51; DAM DRAM**
See also AITN 1; CA 17-18; 41-44R; CANR 35; CAP 2; CDBLB 1914-1945; DLB 10; MTCW 1, 2

Cowley, Abraham 1618-1667 **LC 43**
See also DLB 131, 151

Cowley, Malcolm 1898-1989 **CLC 39**
See also CA 5-8R; 128; CANR 3, 55; DLB 4, 48; DLBY 81, 89; MTCW 1, 2

Cowper, William 1731-1800 **NCLC 8; DAM POET**
See also DLB 104, 109

Cox, William Trevor 1928- **CLC 9, 14, 71; DAM NOV**
See also Trevor, William
See also CA 9-12R; CANR 4, 37, 55, 76; DLB 14; INT CANR-37; MTCW 1, 2

Coyne, P. J.
See Masters, Hilary

Cozzens, James Gould 1903-1978**CLC 1, 4, 11, 92**
See also CA 9-12R; 81-84; CANR 19; CDALB

Danticat, Edwidge 1969- **CLC 94**
See also AAYA 29; CA 152; CANR 73; MTCW 1

Danvers, Dennis 1947- **CLC 70**

Danziger, Paula 1944- **CLC 21**
See also AAYA 4; CA 112; 115; CANR 37; CLR 20; JRDA; MAICYA; SATA 36, 63, 102; SATA-Brief 30

Da Ponte, Lorenzo 1749-1838 **NCLC 50**

Dario, Ruben 1867-1916 **TCLC 4; DAM MULT; HLC; PC 15**
See also CA 131; HW 1, 2; MTCW 1, 2

Darley, George 1795-1846 **NCLC 2**
See also DLB 96

Darrow, Clarence (Seward) 1857-1938 **TCLC 81**
See also CA 164

Darwin, Charles 1809-1882 **NCLC 57**
See also DLB 57, 166

Daryush, Elizabeth 1887-1977 **CLC 6, 19**
See also CA 49-52; CANR 3; DLB 20

Dasgupta, Surendranath 1887-1952 **TCLC 81**
See also CA 157

Dashwood, Edmee Elizabeth Monica de la Pasture 1890-1943
See Delafield, E. M.
See also CA 119; 154

Daudet, (Louis Marie) Alphonse 1840-1897 **NCLC 1**
See also DLB 123

Daumal, Rene 1908-1944 **TCLC 14**
See also CA 114

Davenant, William 1606-1668 **LC 13**
See also DLB 58, 126

Davenport, Guy (Mattison, Jr.) 1927- **CLC 6, 14, 38; SSC 16**
See also CA 33-36R; CANR 23, 73; DLB 130

Davidson, Avram (James) 1923-1993
See Queen, Ellery
See also CA 101; 171; CANR 26; DLB 8

Davidson, Donald (Grady) 1893-1968 **CLC 2, 13, 19**
See also CA 5-8R; 25-28R; CANR 4; DLB 45

Davidson, Hugh
See Hamilton, Edmond

Davidson, John 1857-1909 **TCLC 24**
See also CA 118; DLB 19

Davidson, Sara 1943- **CLC 9**
See also CA 81-84; CANR 44, 68; DLB 185

Davie, Donald (Alfred) 1922-1995 **CLC 5, 8, 10, 31**
See also CA 1-4R; 149; CAAS 3; CANR 1, 44; DLB 27; MTCW 1

Davies, Ray(mond Douglas) 1944- **CLC 21**
See also CA 116; 146

Davies, Rhys 1901-1978 **CLC 23**
See also CA 9-12R; 81-84; CANR 4; DLB 139, 191

Davies, (William) Robertson 1913-1995 **CLC 2, 7, 13, 25, 42, 75, 91; DA; DAB; DAC; DAM MST, NOV, POP; WLC**
See also BEST 89:2; CA 33-36R; 150; CANR 17, 42; DLB 68; INT CANR-17; MTCW 1, 2

Davies, W(illiam) H(enry) 1871-1940 **TCLC 5**
See also CA 104; DLB 19, 174

Davies, Walter C.
See Kornbluth, C(yril) M.

Davis, Angela (Yvonne) 1944- **CLC 77; DAM MULT**
See also BW 2, 3; CA 57-60; CANR 10

Davis, B. Lynch
See Bioy Casares, Adolfo; Borges, Jorge Luis

Davis, Harold Lenoir 1894-1960 **CLC 49**
See also CA 89-92; DLB 9, 206

Davis, Rebecca (Blaine) Harding 1831-1910 **TCLC 6**
See also CA 104; DLB 74

Davis, Richard Harding 1864-1916 **TCLC 24**
See also CA 114; DLB 12, 23, 78, 79, 189; DLBD 13

Davison, Frank Dalby 1893-1970 **CLC 15**
See also CA 116

Davison, Lawrence H.
See Lawrence, D(avid) H(erbert Richards)

Davison, Peter (Hubert) 1928- **CLC 28**
See also CA 9-12R; CAAS 4; CANR 3, 43; DLB 5

Davys, Mary 1674-1732 **LC 1, 46**
See also DLB 39

Dawson, Fielding 1930- **CLC 6**
See also CA 85-88; DLB 130

Dawson, Peter
See Faust, Frederick (Schiller)

Day, Clarence (Shepard, Jr.) 1874-1935 **TCLC 25**
See also CA 108; DLB 11

Day, Thomas 1748-1789 **LC 1**
See also DLB 39; YABC 1

Day Lewis, C(ecil) 1904-1972 **CLC 1, 6, 10; DAM POET; PC 11**
See also Blake, Nicholas
See also CA 13-16; 33-36R; CANR 34; CAP 1; DLB 15, 20; MTCW 1, 2

Dazai Osamu 1909-1948 **TCLC 11**
See also Tsushima, Shuji
See also CA 164; DLB 182

de Andrade, Carlos Drummond 1892-1945
See Drummond de Andrade, Carlos

Deane, Norman
See Creasey, John

de Beauvoir, Simone (Lucie Ernestine Marie Bertrand)
See Beauvoir, Simone (Lucie Ernestine Marie Bertrand) de

de Beer, P.
See Bosman, Herman Charles

de Brissac, Malcolm
See Dickinson, Peter (Malcolm)

de Chardin, Pierre Teilhard
See Teilhard de Chardin, (Marie Joseph) Pierre

Dee, John 1527-1608 **LC 20**

Deer, Sandra 1940- **CLC 45**

De Ferrari, Gabriella 1941- **CLC 65**
See also CA 146

Defoe, Daniel 1660(?)-1731 **LC 1, 42; DA; DAB; DAC; DAM MST, NOV; WLC**
See also AAYA 27; CDBLB 1660-1789; DLB 39, 95, 101; JRDA; MAICYA; SATA 22

de Gourmont, Remy(-Marie-Charles)
See Gourmont, Remy (-Marie-Charles) de

de Hartog, Jan 1914- **CLC 19**
See also CA 1-4R; CANR 1

de Hostos, E. M.
See Hostos (y Bonilla), Eugenio Maria de

de Hostos, Eugenio M.
See Hostos (y Bonilla), Eugenio Maria de

Deighton, Len **CLC 4, 7, 22, 46**
See also Deighton, Leonard Cyril
<iSee also AAYA 6; BEST 89:2; CDBLB 1960 to Present; DLB 87

Deighton, Leonard Cyril 1929-
See Deighton, Len
See also CA 9-12R; CANR 19, 33, 68; DAM NOV, POP; MTCW 1, 2

Dekker, Thomas 1572(?)-1632 **LC 22; DAM DRAM**
See also CDBLB Before 1660; DLB 62, 172

Delafield, E. M. 1890-1943 **TCLC 61**
See also Dashwood, Edmee Elizabeth Monica de la Pasture
See also DLB 34

de la Mare, Walter (John) 1873-1956 **TCLC 4, 53; DAB; DAC; DAM MST, POET; SSC 14; WLC**
See also CA 163; CDBLB 1914-1945; CLR 23; DLB 162; MTCW 1; SATA 16

Delaney, Franey
See O'Hara, John (Henry)

Delaney, Shelagh 1939- **CLC 29; DAM DRAM**
See also CA 17-20R; CANR 30, 67; CDBLB 1960 to Present; DLB 13; MTCW 1

Delany, Mary (Granville Pendarves) 1700-1788 **LC 12**

Delany, Samuel R(ay, Jr.) 1942- **CLC 8, 14, 38; BLC 1; DAM MULT**
See also AAYA 24; BW 2, 3; CA 81-84; CANR 27, 43; DLB 8, 33; MTCW 1, 2

De La Ramee, (Marie) Louise 1839-1908
See Ouida
See also SATA 20

de la Roche, Mazo 1879-1961 **CLC 14**
See also CA 85-88; CANR 30; DLB 68; SATA 64

De La Salle, Innocent
See Hartmann, Sadakichi

Delbanco, Nicholas (Franklin) 1942- **CLC 6, 13**
See also CA 17-20R; CAAS 2; CANR 29, 55; DLB 6

del Castillo, Michel 1933- **CLC 38**
See also CA 109; CANR 77

<in**Deledda, Grazia (Cosima)** 1875(?)-1936 **TCLC 23**
See also CA 123

Delibes, Miguel **CLC 8, 18**
See also Delibes Setien, Miguel

Delibes Setien, Miguel 1920-
See Delibes, Miguel
See also CA 45-48; CANR 1, 32; HW 1; MTCW 1

DeLillo, Don 1936- **CLC 8, 10, 13, 27, 39, 54, 76; DAM NOV, POP**
See also BEST 89:1; CA 81-84; CANR 21, 76; DLB 6, 173; MTCW 1, 2

de Lisser, H. G.
See De Lisser, H(erbert) G(eorge)
See also DLB 117

De Lisser, H(erbert) G(eorge) 1878-1944 **TCLC 12**
See also de Lisser, H. G.
See also BW 2; CA 109; 152

Deloney, Thomas 1560(?)-1600 **LC 41**
<indeSee also DLB 167

Deloria, Vine (Victor), Jr. 1933- **CLC 21; DAM MULT**
See also CA 53-56; CANR 5, 20, 48; DLB 175; MTCW 1; NNAL; SATA 21

Del Vecchio, John M(ichael) 1947- **CLC 29**
See also CA 110; DLBD 9

de Man, Paul (Adolph Michel) 1919-1983 **CLC 55**
See also CA 128; 111; CANR 61; DLB 67; MTCW 1, 2

De Marinis, Rick 1934- **CLC 54**
See also CA 57-60; CAAS 24; CANR 9, 25, 50

Dembry, R. Emmet
See Murfree, Mary Noailles

Demby, William 1922- **CLC 53; BLC 1; DAM**

See also CA 89-92; CANR 13, 55; INT CANR-13
Donleavy, J(ames) P(atrick) 1926-**CLC 1, 4, 6, 10, 45**
See also AITN 2; CA 9-12R; CANR 24, 49, 62, 80; DLB 6, 173; INT CANR-24; MTCW 1, 2
Donne, John 1572-1631**LC 10, 24; DA; DAB; DAC; DAM MST, POET; PC 1; WLC**
See also CDBLB Before 1660; DLB 121, 151
Donnell, David 1939(?)- **CLC 34**
Donoghue, P. S.
See Hunt, E(verette) Howard, (Jr.)
Donoso (Yanez), Jose 1924-1996**CLC 4, 8, 11, 32, 99; DAM MULT; HLC; SSC 34**
See also CA 81-84; 155; CANR 32, 73; DLB 113; HW 1, 2; MTCW 1, 2
Donovan, John 1928-1992 **CLC 35**
See also AAYA 20; CA 97-100; 137; CLR 3; MAICYA; SATA 72; SATA-Brief 29
Don Roberto
See Cunninghame Graham, R(obert) B(ontine)
Doolittle, Hilda 1886-1961**CLC 3, 8, 14, 31, 34, 73; DA; DAC; DAM MST, POET; PC 5; WLC**
See also H. D.
<See also CA 97-100; CANR 35; DLB 4, 45; MTCW 1, 2
Dorfman, Ariel 1942- **CLC 48, 77; DAM MULT; HLC**
See also CA 124; 130; CANR 67, 70; HW 1, 2; INT 130
Dorn, Edward (Merton) 1929- **CLC 10, 18**
See also CA 93-96; CANR 42, 79; DLB 5; INT 93-96
Dorris, Michael (Anthony) 1945-1997 **CLC 109; DAM MULT, NOV**
See also AAYA 20; BEST 90:1; CA 102; 157; CANR 19, 46, 75; DLB 175; MTCW 2; NNAL; SATA 75; SATA-Obit 94
Dorris, Michael A.
See Dorris, Michael (Anthony)
Dorsan, Luc
See Simenon, Georges (Jacques Christian)
Dorsange, Jean
See Simenon, Georges (Jacques Christian)
Dos Passos, John (Roderigo) 1896-1970 **CLC 1, 4, 8, 11, 15, 25, 34, 82; DA; DAB; DAC; DAM MST, NOV; WLC**
See also CA 1-4R; 29-32R; CANR 3; CDALB 1929-1941; DLB 4, 9; DLBD 1, 15; DLBY 96; MTCW 1, 2
Dossage, Jean
See Simenon, Georges (Jacques Christian)
Dostoevsky, Fedor Mikhailovich 1821-1881 **NCLC 2, 7, 21, 33, 43; DA; DAB; DAC; DAM MST, NOV; SSC 2, 33; WLC**
Doughty, Charles M(ontagu) 1843-1926 **TCLC 27**
See also CA 115; DLB 19, 57, 174
Douglas, Ellen **CLC 73**
See also Haxton, Josephine Ayres; Williamson, Ellen Douglas
Douglas, Gavin 1475(?)-1522 **LC 20**
See also DLB 132
Douglas, George
See Brown, George Douglas
Douglas, Keith (Castellain) 1920-1944 **TCLC 40**
See also CA 160; DLB 27
Douglas, Leonard
See Bradbury, Ray (Douglas)
Douglas, Michael
See Crichton, (John) Michael
Douglas, (George) Norman 1868-1952 **TCLC 68**
See also CA 119; 157; DLB 34, 195
Douglas, William
See Brown, George Douglas
Douglass, Frederick 1817(?)-1895**NCLC 7, 55; BLC 1; DA; DAC; DAM MST, MULT; WLC**
See also CDALB 1640-1865; DLB 1, 43, 50, 79; SATA 29
Dourado, (Waldomiro Freitas) Autran 1926- **CLC 23, 60**
See also CA 25-28R; CANR 34; DLB 145; HW 2
Dourado, Waldomiro Autran
See Dourado, (Waldomiro Freitas) Autran
Dove, Rita (Frances) 1952-**CLC 50, 81; BLCS; DAM MULT, POET; PC 6**
See also BW 2; CA 109; CAAS 19; CANR 27, 42, 68, 76; CDALBS; DLB 120; MTCW 1
Doveglion
See Villa, Jose Garcia
Dowell, Coleman 1925-1985 **CLC 60**
See also CA 25-28R; 117; CANR 10; DLB 130
Dowson, Ernest (Christopher) 1867-1900 **TCLC 4**
See also CA 105; 150; DLB 19, 135
Doyle, A. Conan
See Doyle, Arthur Conan
Doyle, Arthur Conan 1859-1930**TCLC 7; DA; DAB; DAC; DAM MST, NOV; SSC 12; WLC**
See also AAYA 14; CA 104; 122; CDBLB 1890-1914; DLB 18, 70, 156, 178; MTCW 1, 2; SATA 24
Doyle, Conan
See Doyle, Arthur Conan
Doyle, John
See Graves, Robert (von Ranke)
Doyle, Roddy 1958(?)- **CLC 81**
See also AAYA 14; CA 143; CANR 73; DLB 194
Doyle, Sir A. Conan
See Doyle, Arthur Conan
Doyle, Sir Arthur Conan
See Doyle, Arthur Conan
Dr. A
See Asimov, Isaac; Silverstein, Alvin
Drabble, Margaret 1939-**CLC 2, 3, 5, 8, 10, 22, 53; DAB; DAC; DAM MST, NOV, POP**
See also CA 13-16R; CANR 18, 35, 63; CDBLB 1960 to Present; DLB 14, 155; MTCW 1, 2; SATA 48
Drapier, M. B.
See Swift, Jonathan
Drayham, James
See Mencken, H(enry) L(ouis)
Drayton, Michael 1563-1631 **LC 8; DAM POET**
See also DLB 121
Dreadstone, Carl
See Campbell, (John) Ramsey
Dreiser, Theodore (Herman Albert) 1871-1945 **TCLC 10, 18, 35, 83; DA; DAC; DAM MST, NOV; SSC 30; WLC**
See also CA 106; 132; CDALB 1865-1917; DLB 9, 12, 102, 137; DLBD 1; MTCW 1, 2
Drexler, Rosalyn 1926- **CLC 2, 6**
See also CA 81-84; CANR 68
Dreyer, Carl Theodor 1889-1968 **CLC 16**
See also CA 116
Drieu la Rochelle, Pierre(-Eugene) 1893-1945 **TCLC 21**
See also CA 117; DLB 72
Drinkwater, John 1882-1937 **TCLC 57**
See also CA 109; 149; DLB 10, 19, 149
Drop Shot
See Cable, George Washington
Droste-Hulshoff, Annette Freiin von 1797-1848 **NCLC 3**
See also DLB 133
Drummond, Walter
See Silverberg, Robert
Drummond, William Henry 1854-1907**TCLC 25**
See also CA 160; DLB 92
Drummond de Andrade, Carlos 1902-1987 **CLC 18**
See also Andrade, Carlos Drummond de
See also CA 132; 123
Drury, Allen (Stuart) 1918-1998 **CLC 37**
See also CA 57-60; 170; CANR 18, 52; INT CANR-18
Dryden, John 1631-1700**LC 3, 21; DA; DAB; DAC; DAM DRAM, MST, POET; DC 3; PC 25; WLC**
See also CDBLB 1660-1789; DLB 80, 101, 131
Duberman, Martin (Bauml) 1930- **CLC 8**
See also CA 1-4R; CANR 2, 63
Dubie, Norman (Evans) 1945- **CLC 36**
See also CA 69-72; CANR 12; DLB 120
Du Bois, W(illiam) E(dward) B(urghardt) 1868-1963 **CLC 1, 2, 13, 64, 96; BLC 1; DA; DAC; DAM MST, MULT, NOV; WLC**
See also BW 1, 3; CA 85-88; CANR 34; CDALB 1865-1917; DLB 47, 50, 91; MTCW 1, 2; SATA 42
Dubus, Andre 1936- **CLC 13, 36, 97; SSC 15**
See also CA 21-24R; CANR 17; DLB 130; INT CANR-17
Duca Minimo
See D'Annunzio, Gabriele
Ducharme, Rejean 1941- **CLC 74**
See also CA 165; DLB 60
Duclos, Charles Pinot 1704-1772 **LC 1**
Dudek, Louis 1918- **CLC 11, 19**
See also CA 45-48; CAAS 14; CANR 1; DLB 88
Duerrenmatt, Friedrich 1921-1990 **CLC 1, 4, 8, 11, 15, 43, 102; DAM DRAM**
See also CA 17-20R; CANR 33; DLB 69, 124; MTCW 1, 2
Duffy, Bruce 1953(?)- **CLC 50**
See also CA 172
Duffy, Maureen 1933- **CLC 37**
See also CA 25-28R; CANR 33, 68; DLB 14; MTCW 1
Dugan, Alan 1923- **CLC 2, 6**
See also CA 81-84; DLB 5
du Gard, Roger Martin
See Martin du Gard, Roger
Duhamel, Georges 1884-1966 **CLC 8**
See also CA 81-84; 25-28R; CANR 35; DLB 65; MTCW 1
Dujardin, Edouard (Emile Louis) 1861-1949 **TCLC 13**
See also CA 109; DLB 123
Dulles, John Foster 1888-1959 **TCLC 72**
See also CA 115; 149
Dumas, Alexandre (pere)
See Dumas, Alexandre (Davy de la Pailleterie)
Dumas, Alexandre (Davy de la Pailleterie) 1802-1870 **NCLC 11; DA; DAB; DAC; DAM MST, NOV; WLC**
See also DLB 119, 192; SATA 18

4; BLC 1; DAM MULT
See also BW 2, 3; CA 29-32R; CANR 18, 42, 74; DLB 117; MTCW 1, 2; SATA 66
Elaine **TCLC 18**
See also Leverson, Ada
El Crummo
See Crumb, R(obert)
Elder, Lonne III 1931-1996 **DC 8**
See also BLC 1; BW 1, 3; CA 81-84; 152; CANR 25; DAM MULT; DLB 7, 38, 44
Elia
See Lamb, Charles
Eliade, Mircea 1907-1986 **CLC 19**
See also CA 65-68; 119; CANR 30, 62; MTCW 1
Eliot, A. D.
See Jewett, (Theodora) Sarah Orne
Eliot, Alice
See Jewett, (Theodora) Sarah Orne
Eliot, Dan
See Silverberg, Robert
Eliot, George 1819-1880 **NCLC 4, 13, 23, 41, 49; DA; DAB; DAC; DAM MST, NOV; PC 20; WLC**
See also CDBLB 1832-1890; DLB 21, 35, 55
Eliot, John 1604-1690 **LC 5**
See also DLB 24
<indexb**Eliot, T(homas) S(tearns)** 1888-1965 **CLC 1, 2, 3, 6, 9, 10, 13, 15, 24, 34, 41, 55, 57, 113; DA; DAB; DAC; DAM DRAM, MST, POET; PC 5; WLC**
See also AAYA 28; CA 5-8R; 25-28R; CANR 41; CDALB 1929-1941; DLB 7, 10, 45, 63; DLBY 88; MTCW 1, 2
Elizabeth 1866-1941 **TCLC 41**
Elkin, Stanley L(awrence) 1930-1995 **CLC 4, 6, 9, 14, 27, 51, 91; DAM NOV, POP; SSC 12**
See also GA 9-12R; 148; CANR 8, 46; DLB 2, 28; DLBY 80; INT CANR-8; MTCW 1, 2
Elledge, Scott **CLC 34**
Elliot, Don
See Silverberg, Robert
Elliott, Don
See Silverberg, Robert
Elliott, George P(aul) 1918-1980 **CLC 2**
See also CA 1-4R; 97-100; CANR 2
Elliott, Janice 1931- **CLC 47**
See also CA 13-16R; CANR 8, 29; DLB 14
Elliott, Sumner Locke 1917-1991 **CLC 38**
See also CA 5-8R; 134; CANR 2, 21
Elliott, William
See Bradbury, Ray (Douglas)
Ellis, A. E. **CLC 7**
Ellis, Alice Thomas **CLC 40**
See also Haycraft, Anna
See also DLB 194; MTCW 1
Ellis, Bret Easton 1964-**CLC 39, 71, 117; DAM POP**
See also AAYA 2; CA 118; 123; CANR 51, 74; INT 123; MTCW 1
Ellis, (Henry) Havelock 1859-1939 **TCLC 14**
See also CA 109; 169; DLB 190
Ellis, Landon
See Ellison, Harlan (Jay)
Ellis, Trey 1962- **CLC 55**
See also CA 146
Ellison, Harlan (Jay) 1934- **CLC 1, 13, 42; DAM POP; SSC 14**
See also AAYA 29; CA 5-8R; CANR 5, 46; DLB 8; INT CANR-5; MTCW 1, 2
Ellison, Ralph (Waldo) 1914-1994 **CLC 1, 3, 11, 54, 86, 114; BLC 1; DA; DAB; DAC; DAM MST, MULT, NOV; SSC 26; WLC**
See also AAYA 19; BW 1, 3; CA 9-12R; 145; CANR 24, 53; CDALB 1941-1968; DLB 2, 76; DLBY 94; MTCW 1, 2
Ellmann, Lucy (Elizabeth) 1956- **CLC 61**
See also CA 128
Ellmann, Richard (David) 1918-1987**CLC 50**
See also BEST 89:2; CA 1-4R; 122; CANR 2, 28, 61; DLB 103; DLBY 87; MTCW 1, 2
Elman, Richard (Martin) 1934-1997 **CLC 19**
See also CA 17-20R; 163; CAAS 3; CANR 47
Elron
See Hubbard, L(afayette) Ron(ald)
Eluard, Paul **TCLC 7, 41**
See also Grindel, Eugene
Elyot, Sir Thomas 1490(?)-1546 **LC 11**
Elytis, Odysseus 1911-1996 **CLC 15, 49, 100; DAM POET; PC 21**
See also CA 102; 151; MTCW 1, 2
Emecheta, (Florence Onye) Buchi 1944-**C L C 14, 48; BLC 2; DAM MULT**
See also BW 2, 3; CA 81-84; CANR 27; DLB 117; MTCW 1, 2; SATA 66
Emerson, Mary Moody 1774-1863 **NCLC 66**
Emerson, Ralph Waldo 1803-1882 **NCLC 1, 38; DA; DAB; DAC; DAM MST, POET; PC 18; WLC**
See also CDALB 1640-1865; DLB 1, 59, 73
Eminescu, Mihail 1850-1889 **NCLC 33**
Empson, William 1906-1984**CLC 3, 8, 19, 33, 34**
See also CA 17-20R; 112; CANR 31, 61; DLB 20; MTCW 1, 2
Enchi, Fumiko (Ueda) 1905-1986 **CLC 31**
See also CA 129; 121; DLB 182
Ende, Michael (Andreas Helmuth) 1929-1995 **CLC 31**
See also CA 118; 124; 149; CANR 36; CLR 14; DLB 75; MAICYA; SATA 61; SATA-Brief 42; SATA-Obit 86
Endo, Shusaku 1923-1996 **CLC 7, 14, 19, 54, 99; DAM NOV**
See also CA 29-32R; 153; CANR 21, 54; DLB 182; MTCW 1, 2
Engel, Marian 1933-1985 **CLC 36**
See also CA 25-28R; CANR 12; DLB 53; INT CANR-12
Engelhardt, Frederick
See Hubbard, L(afayette) Ron(ald)
Enright, D(ennis) J(oseph) 1920-**CLC 4, 8, 31**
See also CA 1-4R; CANR 1, 42; DLB 27; SATA 25
Enzensberger, Hans Magnus 1929- **CLC 43**
See also CA 116; 119
Ephron, Nora 1941- **CLC 17, 31**
See also AITN 2; CA 65-68; CANR 12, 39
Epicurus 341B.C.-270B.C. **CMLC 21**
See also DLB 176
Epsilon
See Betjeman, John
Epstein, Daniel Mark 1948- **CLC 7**
See also CA 49-52; CANR 2, 53
Epstein, Jacob 1956- **CLC 19**
See also CA 114
Epstein, Jean 1897-1953 **TCLC 92**
Epstein, Joseph 1937- **CLC 39**
See also CA 112; 119; CANR 50, 65
Epstein, Leslie 1938- **CLC 27**
See also CA 73-76; CAAS 12; CANR 23, 69
Equiano, Olaudah 1745(?)-1797 **LC 16; BLC 2; DAM MULT**
See also DLB 37, 50
ER **TCLC 33**
See also CA 160; DLB 85
Erasmus, Desiderius 1469(?)-1536 **LC 16**
Erdman, Paul E(mil) 1932- **CLC 25**
See also AITN 1; CA 61-64; CANR 13, 43
Erdrich, Louise 1954-**CLC 39, 54, 120; DAM MULT, NOV, POP**
See also AAYA 10; BEST 89:1; CA 114; CANR 41, 62; CDALBS; DLB 152, 175, 206; MTCW 1; NNAL; SATA 94
Erenburg, Ilya (Grigoryevich)
See Ehrenburg, Ilya (Grigoryevich)
Erickson, Stephen Michael 1950-
See Erickson, Steve
See also CA 129
Erickson, Steve 1950- **CLC 64**
See also Erickson, Stephen Michael
See also CANR 60, 68
Ericson, Walter
See Fast, Howard (Melvin)
Eriksson, Buntel
See Bergman, (Ernst) Ingmar
Ernaux, Annie 1940- **CLC 88**
See also CA 147
Erskine, John 1879-1951 **TCLC 84**
See also CA 112; 159; DLB 9, 102
Eschenbach, Wolfram von
See Wolfram von Eschenbach
Eseki, Bruno
See Mphahlele, Ezekiel
Esenin, Sergei (Alexandrovich) 1895-1925 **TCLC 4**
See also CA 104
<indexbo**Eshleman, Clayton** 1935- **CLC 7**
See also CA 33-36R; CAAS 6; DLB 5
Espriella, Don Manuel Alvarez
See Southey, Robert
Espriu, Salvador 1913-1985 **CLC 9**
See also CA 154; 115; DLB 134
Espronceda, Jose de 1808-1842 **NCLC 39**
Esse, James
See Stephens, James
Esterbrook, Tom
See Hubbard, L(afayette) Ron(ald)
Estleman, Loren D. 1952-**CLC 48; DAM NOV, POP**
See also AAYA 27; CA 85-88; CANR 27, 74; INT CANR-27; MTCW 1, 2
Euclid 306B.C.-283B.C. **CMLC 25**
Eugenides, Jeffrey 1960(?)- **CLC 81**
See also CA 144
Euripides c. 485B.C.-406B.C.**CMLC 23; DA; DAB; DAC; DAM DRAM, MST; DC 4; WLCS**
See also DLB 176
Evan, Evin
See Faust, Frederick (Schiller)
Evans, Caradoc 1878-1945 **TCLC 85**
Evans, Evan
See Faust, Frederick (Schiller)
Evans, Marian
See Eliot, George
Evans, Mary Ann
See Eliot, George
Evarts, Esther
See Benson, Sally
Everett, Percival L. 1956- **CLC 57**
See also BW 2; CA 129
Everson, R(onald) G(ilmour) 1903- **CLC 27**
See also CA 17-20R; DLB 88
Everson, William (Oliver) 1912-1994 **CLC 1, 5, 14**
See also CA 9-12R; 145; CANR 20; DLB 212; MTCW 1

Evtushenko, Evgenii Aleksandrovich
See Yevtushenko, Yevgeny (Alexandrovich)
Ewart, Gavin (Buchanan) 1916-1995**CLC 13, 46**
See also CA 89-92; 150; CANR 17, 46; DLB 40; MTCW 1
Ewers, Hanns Heinz 1871-1943 **TCLC 12**
See also CA 109; 149
Ewing, Frederick R.
See Sturgeon, Theodore (Hamilton)
Exley, Frederick (Earl) 1929-1992 **CLC 6, 11**
See also AITN 2; CA 81-84; 138; DLB 143; DLBY 81
Eynhardt, Guillermo
See Quiroga, Horacio (Sylvestre)
Ezekiel, Nissim 1924- **CLC 61**
See also CA 61-64
Ezekiel, Tish O'Dowd 1943- **CLC 34**
See also CA 129
Fadeyev, A.
See Bulgya, Alexander Alexandrovich
Fadeyev, Alexander **TCLC 53**
See also Bulgya, Alexander Alexandrovich
Fagen, Donald 1948- **CLC 26**
Fainzilberg, Ilya Arnoldovich 1897-1937
See Ilf, Ilya
See also CA 120; 165
Fair, Ronald L. 1932- **CLC 18**
See also BW 1; CA 69-72; CANR 25; DLB 33
Fairbairn, Roger
See Carr, John Dickson
Fairbairns, Zoe (Ann) 1948- **CLC 32**
See also CA 103; CANR 21
Falco, Gian
See Papini, Giovanni
Falconer, James
See Kirkup, James
Falconer, Kenneth
See Kornbluth, C(yril) M.
Falkland, Samuel
See Heijermans, Herman
Fallaci, Oriana 1930- **CLC 11, 110**
See also CA 77-80; CANR 15, 58; MTCW 1
Faludy, George 1913- **CLC 42**
See also CA 21-24R
Faludy, Gyoergy
See Faludy, George
Fanon, Frantz 1925-1961 **CLC 74; BLC 2; DAM MULT**
See also BW 1; CA 116; 89-92
Fanshawe, Ann 1625-1680 **LC 11**
Fante, John (Thomas) 1911-1983 **CLC 60**
See also CA 69-72; 109; CANR 23; DLB 130; DLBY 83
Farah, Nuruddin 1945-**CLC 53; BLC 2; DAM MULT**
See also BW 2, 3; CA 106; DLB 125
Fargue, Leon-Paul 1876(?)-1947 **TCLC 11**
See also CA 109
Farigoule, Louis
See Romains, Jules
Farina, Richard 1936(?)-1966 **CLC 9**
See also CA 81-84; 25-28R
Farley, Walter (Lorimer) 1915-1989 **CLC 17**
See also CA 17-20R; CANR 8, 29; DLB 22; JRDA; MAICYA; SATA 2, 43
Farmer, Philip Jose 1918- **CLC 1, 19**
See also AAYA 28; CA 1-4R; CANR 4, 35; DLB 8; MTCW 1; SATA 93
Farquhar, George 1677-1707 **LC 21; DAM DRAM**
See also DLB 84
Farrell, J(ames) G(ordon) 1935-1979 **CLC 6**
See also CA 73-76; 89-92; CANR 36; DLB 14; MTCW 1
Farrell, James T(homas) 1904-1979**CLC 1, 4, 8, 11, 66; SSC 28**
See also CA 5-8R; 89-92; CANR 9, 61; DLB 4, 9, 86; DLBD 2; MTCW 1, 2
Farren, Richard J.
See Betjeman, John
Farren, Richard M.
See Betjeman, John
Fassbinder, Rainer Werner 1946-1982**CLC 20**
See also CA 93-96; 106; CANR 31
Fast, Howard (Melvin) 1914- **CLC 23; DAM NOV**
See also AAYA 16; CA 1-4R; CAAS 18; CANR 1, 33, 54, 75; DLB 9; INT CANR-33; MTCW 1; SATA 7; SATA-Essay 107
Faulcon, Robert
See Holdstock, Robert P.
Faulkner, William (Cuthbert) 1897-1962**CLC 1, 3, 6, 8, 9, 11, 14, 18, 28, 52, 68; DA; DAB; DAC; DAM MST, NOV; SSC 1; WLC**
<inSee also AAYA 7; CA 81-84; CANR 33; CDALB 1929-1941; DLB 9, 11, 44, 102; DLBD 2; DLBY 86, 97; MTCW 1, 2
Fauset, Jessie Redmon 1884(?)-1961 **CLC 19, 54; BLC 2; DAM MULT**
See also BW 1; CA 109; DLB 51
Faust, Frederick (Schiller) 1892-1944(?) **TCLC 49; DAM POP**
See also CA 108; 152
Faust, Irvin 1924- **CLC 8**
See also CA 33-36R; CANR 28, 67; DLB 2, 28; DLBY 80
Fawkes, Guy
See Benchley, Robert (Charles)
Fearing, Kenneth (Flexner) 1902-1961 **CLC 51**
See also CA 93-96; CANR 59; DLB 9
Fecamps, Elise
See Creasey, John
Federman, Raymond 1928- **CLC 6, 47**
See also CA 17-20R; CAAS 8; CANR 10, 43; DLBY 80
Federspiel, J(uerg) F. 1931- **CLC 42**
See also CA 146
Feiffer, Jules (Ralph) 1929- **CLC 2, 8, 64; DAM DRAM**
See also AAYA 3; CA 17-20R; CANR 30, 59; DLB 7, 44; INT CANR-30; MTCW 1; SATA 8, 61
Feige, Hermann Albert Otto Maximilian
See Traven, B.
Feinberg, David B. 1956-1994 **CLC 59**
See also CA 135; 147
Feinstein, Elaine 1930- **CLC 36**
See also CA 69-72; CAAS 1; CANR 31, 68; DLB 14, 40; MTCW 1
Feldman, Irving (Mordecai) 1928- **CLC 7**
See also CA 1-4R; CANR 1; DLB 169
Felix-Tchicaya, Gerald
See Tchicaya, Gerald Felix
Fellini, Federico 1920-1993 **CLC 16, 85**
See also CA 65-68; 143; CANR 33
Felsen, Henry Gregor 1916- **CLC 17**
See also CA 1-4R; CANR 1; SAAS 2; SATA 1
Fenno, Jack
See Calisher, Hortense
Fenollosa, Ernest (Francisco) 1853-1908 **TCLC 91**
Fenton, James Martin 1949- **CLC 32**
See also CA 102; DLB 40
Ferber, Edna 1887-1968 **CLC 18, 93**
See also AITN 1; CA 5-8R; 25-28R; CANR 68; DLB 9, 28, 86; MTCW 1, 2; SATA 7
Ferguson, Helen
See Kavan, Anna
Ferguson, Samuel 1810-1886 **NCLC 33**
See also DLB 32
Fergusson, Robert 1750-1774 **LC 29**
See also DLB 109
<inde**Ferling, Lawrence**
See Ferlinghetti, Lawrence (Monsanto)
Ferlinghetti, Lawrence (Monsanto) 1919(?)- **CLC 2, 6, 10, 27, 111; DAM POET; PC 1**
See also CA 5-8R; CANR 3, 41, 73; CDALB 1941-1968; DLB 5, 16; MTCW 1, 2
Fernandez, Vicente Garcia Huidobro
See Huidobro Fernandez, Vicente Garcia
Ferrer, Gabriel (Francisco Victor) Miro
See Miro (Ferrer), Gabriel (Francisco Victor)
Ferrier, Susan (Edmonstone) 1782-1854 **NCLC 8**
See also DLB 116
Ferrigno, Robert 1948(?)- **CLC 65**
See also CA 140
Ferron, Jacques 1921-1985 **CLC 94; DAC**
See also CA 117; 129; DLB 60
Feuchtwanger, Lion 1884-1958 **TCLC 3**
See also CA 104; DLB 66
Feuillet, Octave 1821-1890 **NCLC 45**
See also DLB 192
Feydeau, Georges (Leon Jules Marie) 1862-1921 **TCLC 22; DAM DRAM**
See also CA 113; 152; DLB 192
Fichte, Johann Gottlieb 1762-1814 **NCLC 62**
See also DLB 90
Ficino, Marsilio 1433-1499 **LC 12**
Fiedeler, Hans
See Doeblin, Alfred
Fiedler, Leslie A(aron) 1917- **CLC 4, 13, 24**
See also CA 9-12R; CANR 7, 63; DLB 28, 67; MTCW 1, 2
Field, Andrew 1938- **CLC 44**
See also CA 97-100; CANR 25
Field, Eugene 1850-1895 **NCLC 3**
See also DLB 23, 42, 140; DLBD 13; MAICYA; SATA 16
Field, Gans T.
See Wellman, Manly Wade
Field, Michael 1915-1971 **TCLC 43**
See also CA 29-32R
Field, Peter
See Hobson, Laura Z(ametkin)
Fielding, Henry 1707-1754 **LC 1, 46; DA; DAB; DAC; DAM DRAM, MST, NOV; WLC**
See also CDBLB 1660-1789; DLB 39, 84, 101
Fielding, Sarah 1710-1768 **LC 1, 44**
See also DLB 39
Fields, W. C. 1880-1946 **TCLC 80**
See also DLB 44
Fierstein, Harvey (Forbes) 1954- **CLC 33; DAM DRAM, POP**
See also CA 123; 129
Figes, Eva 1932- **CLC 31**
See also CA 53-56; CANR 4, 44; DLB 14
Finch, Anne 1661-1720 **LC 3; PC 21**
See also DLB 95
Finch, Robert (Duer Claydon) 1900- **CLC 18**
See also CA 57-60; CANR 9, 24, 49; DLB 88
Findley, Timothy 1930- **CLC 27, 102; DAC; DAM MST**
See also CA 25-28R; CANR 12, 42, 69; DLB 53
Fink, William

MULT, POET; DC 2; HLC; PC 3; WLC
See also CA 104; 131; DLB 108; HW 1, 2; MTCW 1, 2

Garcia Marquez, Gabriel (Jose) 1928-**CLC 2, 3, 8, 10, 15, 27, 47, 55, 68; DA; DAB; DAC; DAM MST, MULT, NOV, POP; HLC; SSC 8; WLC**
See also AAYA 3; BEST 89:1, 90:4; CA 33-36R; CANR 10, 28, 50, 75; DLB 113; HW 1, 2; MTCW 1, 2

Gard, Janice
See Latham, Jean Lee

Gard, Roger Martin du
See Martin du Gard, Roger

Gardam, Jane 1928- **CLC 43**
See also CA 49-52; CANR 2, 18, 33, 54; CLR 12; DLB 14, 161; MAICYA; MTCW 1; SAAS 9; SATA 39, 76; SATA-Brief 28

Gardner, Herb(ert) 1934- **CLC 44**
See also CA 149

Gardner, John (Champlin), Jr. 1933-1982 **CLC 2, 3, 5, 7, 8, 10, 18, 28, 34; DAM NOV, POP; SSC 7**
See also AITN 1; CA 65-68; 107; CANR 33, 73; CDALBS; DLB 2; DLBY 82; MTCW 1; SATA 40; SATA-Obit 31

Gardner, John (Edmund) 1926-**CLC 30; DAM POP**
See also CA 103; CANR 15, 69; MTCW 1

Gardner, Miriam
See Bradley, Marion Zimmer

Gardner, Noel
See Kuttner, Henry

Gardons, S. S.
See Snodgrass, W(illiam) D(e Witt)

Garfield, Leon 1921-1996 **CLC 12**
See also AAYA 8; CA 17-20R; 152; CANR 38, 41, 78; CLR 21; DLB 161; JRDA; MAICYA; SATA 1, 32, 76; SATA-Obit 90

Garland, (Hannibal) Hamlin 1860-1940 **TCLC 3; SSC 18**
See also CA 104; DLB 12, 71, 78, 186

Garneau, (Hector de) Saint-Denys 1912-1943 **TCLC 13**
See also CA 111; DLB 88

Garner, Alan 1934-**CLC 17; DAB; DAM POP**
See also AAYA 18; CA 73-76; CANR 15, 64; CLR 20; DLB 161; MAICYA; MTCW 1, 2; SATA 18, 69

Garner, Hugh 1913-1979 **CLC 13**
See also CA 69-72; CANR 31; DLB 68

Garnett, David 1892-1981 **CLC 3**
See also CA 5-8R; 103; CANR 17, 79; DLB 34; MTCW 2

Garos, Stephanie
See Katz, Steve

Garrett, George (Palmer) 1929-**CLC 3, 11, 51; SSC 30**
See also CA 1-4R; CAAS 5; CANR 1, 42, 67; DLB 2, 5, 130, 152; DLBY 83

Garrick, David 1717-1779 **LC 15; DAM DRAM**
See also DLB 84

Garrigue, Jean 1914-1972 **CLC 2, 8**
See also CA 5-8R; 37-40R; CANR 20

Garrison, Frederick
See Sinclair, Upton (Beall)

Garth, Will
See Hamilton, Edmond; Kuttner, Henry

Garvey, Marcus (Moziah, Jr.) 1887-1940 **TCLC 41; BLC 2; DAM MULT**
See also BW 1; CA 120; 124; CANR 79

Gary, Romain **CLC 25**
See also Kacew, Romain
See also DLB 83

Gascar, Pierre **CLC 11**
See also Fournier, Pierre

Gascoyne, David (Emery) 1916- **CLC 45**
See also CA 65-68; CANR 10, 28, 54; DLB 20; MTCW 1

Gaskell, Elizabeth Cleghorn 1810-1865**NCLC 70; DAB; DAM MST; SSC 25**
<indexSee also CDBLB 1832-1890; DLB 21, 144, 159

Gass, William H(oward) 1924-**CLC 1, 2, 8, 11, 15, 39; SSC 12**
See also CA 17-20R; CANR 30, 71; DLB 2; MTCW 1, 2

Gasset, Jose Ortega y
See Ortega y Gasset, Jose

Gates, Henry Louis, Jr. 1950-**CLC 65; BLCS; DAM MULT**
See also BW 2, 3; CA 109; CANR 25, 53, 75; DLB 67; MTCW 1

Gautier, Theophile 1811-1872 **NCLC 1, 59; DAM POET; PC 18; SSC 20**
See also DLB 119

Gawsworth, John
See Bates, H(erbert) E(rnest)

Gay, John 1685-1732 **LC 49; DAM DRAM**
See also DLB 84, 95

Gay, Oliver
See Gogarty, Oliver St. John

Gaye, Marvin (Penze) 1939-1984 **CLC 26**
See also CA 112

Gebler, Carlo (Ernest) 1954- **CLC 39**
See also CA 119; 133

Gee, Maggie (Mary) 1948- **CLC 57**
See also CA 130; DLB 207

Gee, Maurice (Gough) 1931- **CLC 29**
See also CA 97-100; CANR 67; CLR 56; SATA 46, 101

Gelbart, Larry (Simon) 1923- **CLC 21, 61**
See also CA 73-76; CANR 45

Gelber, Jack 1932- **CLC 1, 6, 14, 79**
See also CA 1-4R; CANR 2; DLB 7

Gellhorn, Martha (Ellis) 1908-1998 **CLC 14, 60**
See also CA 77-80; 164; CANR 44; DLBY 82, 98

Genet, Jean 1910-1986**CLC 1, 2, 5, 10, 14, 44, 46; DAM DRAM**
<indSee also CA 13-16R; CANR 18; DLB 72; DLBY 86; MTCW 1, 2

Gent, Peter 1942- **CLC 29**
See also AITN 1; CA 89-92; DLBY 82

Gentlewoman in New England, A
See Bradstreet, Anne

Gentlewoman in Those Parts, A
See Bradstreet, Anne

George, Jean Craighead 1919- **CLC 35**
See also AAYA 8; CA 5-8R; CANR 25; CLR 1; DLB 52; JRDA; MAICYA; SATA 2, 68

George, Stefan (Anton) 1868-1933**TCLC 2, 14**
See also CA 104

Georges, Georges Martin
See Simenon, Georges (Jacques Christian)

Gerhardi, William Alexander
See Gerhardie, William Alexander

Gerhardie, William Alexander 1895-1977 **CLC 5**
<See also CA 25-28R; 73-76; CANR 18; DLB 36

Gerstler, Amy 1956- **CLC 70**
See also CA 146

Gertler, T. **CLC 34**
See also CA 116; 121; INT 121

Ghalib **NCLC 39**
See also Ghalib, Hsadullah Khan

Ghalib, Hsadullah Khan 1797-1869
See Ghalib
See also DAM POET

Ghelderode, Michel de 1898-1962**CLC 6, 11; DAM DRAM**
See also CA 85-88; CANR 40, 77

Ghiselin, Brewster 1903- **CLC 23**
See also CA 13-16R; CAAS 10; CANR 13

Ghose, Aurabinda 1872-1950 **TCLC 63**
See also CA 163

Ghose, Zulfikar 1935- **CLC 42**
See also CA 65-68; CANR 67

Ghosh, Amitav 1956- **CLC 44**
See also CA 147; CANR 80

Giacosa, Giuseppe 1847-1906 **TCLC 7**
See also CA 104

Gibb, Lee
See Waterhouse, Keith (Spencer)

Gibbon, Lewis Grassic **TCLC 4**
See also Mitchell, James Leslie

Gibbons, Kaye 1960-**CLC 50, 88; DAM POP**
See also CA 151; CANR 75; MTCW 1

Gibran, Kahlil 1883-1931 **TCLC 1, 9; DAM POET, POP; PC 9**
See also CA 104; 150; MTCW 2

Gibran, Khalil
See Gibran, Kahlil

Gibson, William 1914- **CLC 23; DA; DAB; DAC; DAM DRAM, MST**
See also CA 9-12R; CANR 9, 42, 75; DLB 7; MTCW 1; SATA 66

Gibson, William (Ford) 1948- **CLC 39, 63; DAM POP**
See also AAYA 12; CA 126; 133; CANR 52; MTCW 1

Gide, Andre (Paul Guillaume) 1869-1951 **TCLC 5, 12, 36; DA; DAB; DAC; DAM MST, NOV; SSC 13; WLC**
See also CA 104; 124; DLB 65; MTCW 1, 2

Gifford, Barry (Colby) 1946- **CLC 34**
See also CA 65-68; CANR 9, 30, 40

Gilbert, Frank
See De Voto, Bernard (Augustine)

Gilbert, W(illiam) S(chwenck) 1836-1911 **TCLC 3; DAM DRAM, POET**
See also CA 104; 173; SATA 36

Gilbreth, Frank B., Jr. 1911- **CLC 17**
See also CA 9-12R; SATA 2

Gilchrist, Ellen 1935-**CLC 34, 48; DAM POP; SSC 14**
See also CA 113; 116; CANR 41, 61; DLB 130; MTCW 1, 2

Giles, Molly 1942- **CLC 39**
See also CA 126

Gill, Eric 1882-1940 **TCLC 85**

Gill, Patrick
See Creasey, John

Gilliam, Terry (Vance) 1940- **CLC 21**
See also Monty Python
See also AAYA 19; CA 108; 113; CANR 35; INT 113

Gillian, Jerry
See Gilliam, Terry (Vance)

Gilliatt, Penelope (Ann Douglass) 1932-1993 **CLC 2, 10, 13, 53**
See also AITN 2; CA 13-16R; 141; CANR 49; DLB 14

Gilman, Charlotte (Anna) Perkins (Stetson) 1860-1935 **TCLC 9, 37; SSC 13**
See also CA 106; 150; MTCW 1

Gilmour, David 1949- **CLC 35**

See Hope, Anthony
Hawthorne, Julian 1846-1934 **TCLC 25**
See also CA 165
Hawthorne, Nathaniel 1804-1864 **NCLC 39; DA; DAB; DAC; DAM MST, NOV; SSC 3, 29; WLC**
See also AAYA 18; CDALB 1640-1865; DLB 1, 74; YABC 2
Haxton, Josephine Ayres 1921-
See Douglas, Ellen
See also CA 115; CANR 41
Hayaseca y Eizaguirre, Jorge
See Echegaray (y Eizaguirre), Jose (Maria Waldo)
Hayashi, Fumiko 1904-1951 **TCLC 27**
See also CA 161; DLB 180
Haycraft, Anna
See Ellis, Alice Thomas
See also CA 122; MTCW 2
Hayden, Robert E(arl) 1913-1980 **CLC 5, 9, 14, 37; BLC 2; DA; DAC; DAM MST, MULT, POET; PC 6**
See also BW 1, 3; CA 69-72; 97-100; CABS 2; CANR 24, 75; CDALB 1941-1968; DLB 5, 76; MTCW 1, 2; SATA 19; SATA-Obit 26
Hayford, J(oseph) E(phraim) Casely
See Casely-Hayford, J(oseph) E(phraim)
Hayman, Ronald 1932- **CLC 44**
See also CA 25-28R; CANR 18, 50; DLB 155
Haywood, Eliza (Fowler) 1693(?)-1756 **LC 1, 44**
See also DLB 39
Hazlitt, William 1778-1830 **NCLC 29**
See also DLB 110, 158
Hazzard, Shirley 1931- **CLC 18**
See also CA 9-12R; CANR 4, 70; DLBY 82; MTCW 1
Head, Bessie 1937-1986 **CLC 25, 67; BLC 2; DAM MULT**
See also BW 2, 3; CA 29-32R; 119; CANR 25; DLB 117; MTCW 1, 2
Headon, (Nicky) Topper 1956(?)- **CLC 30**
Heaney, Seamus (Justin) 1939- **CLC 5, 7, 14, 25, 37, 74, 91; DAB; DAM POET; PC 18; WLCS**
See also CA 85-88; CANR 25, 48, 75; CDBLB 1960 to Present; DLB 40; DLBY 95; MTCW 1, 2
Hearn, (Patricio) Lafcadio (Tessima Carlos) 1850-1904 **TCLC 9**
See also CA 105; 166; DLB 12, 78, 189
Hearne, Vicki 1946- **CLC 56**
See also CA 139
Hearon, Shelby 1931- **CLC 63**
See also AITN 2; CA 25-28R; CANR 18, 48
Heat-Moon, William Least **CLC 29**
See also Trogdon, William (Lewis)
See also AAYA 9
Hebbel, Friedrich 1813-1863**NCLC 43; DAM DRAM**
See also DLB 129
Hebert, Anne 1916-**CLC 4, 13, 29; DAC; DAM MST, POET**
See also CA 85-88; CANR 69; DLB 68; MTCW 1, 2
Hecht, Anthony (Evan) 1923- **CLC 8, 13, 19; DAM POET**
See also CA 9-12R; CANR 6; DLB 5, 169
Hecht, Ben 1894-1964 **CLC 8**
See also CA 85-88; DLB 7, 9, 25, 26, 28, 86
Hedayat, Sadeq 1903-1951 **TCLC 21**
See also CA 120
Hegel, Georg Wilhelm Friedrich 1770-1831 **NCLC 46**
See also DLB 90
Heidegger, Martin 1889-1976 **CLC 24**
See also CA 81-84; 65-68; CANR 34; MTCW 1, 2
Heidenstam, (Carl Gustaf) Verner von 1859-1940 **TCLC 5**
See also CA 104
Heifner, Jack 1946- **CLC 11**
See also CA 105; CANR 47
Heijermans, Herman 1864-1924 **TCLC 24**
See also CA 123
Heilbrun, Carolyn G(old) 1926- **CLC 25**
See also CA 45-48; CANR 1, 28, 58
Heine, Heinrich 1797-1856**NCLC 4, 54; PC 25**
See also DLB 90
Heinemann, Larry (Curtiss) 1944- **CLC 50**
See also CA 110; CAAS 21; CANR 31; DLBD 9; INT CANR-31
Heiney, Donald (William) 1921-1993
See Harris, MacDonald
<inSee also CA 1-4R; 142; CANR 3, 58
Heinlein, Robert A(nson) 1907-1988**CLC 1, 3, 8, 14, 26, 55; DAM POP**
See also AAYA 17; CA 1-4R; 125; CANR 1, 20, 53; DLB 8; JRDA; MAICYA; MTCW 1, 2; SATA 9, 69; SATA-Obit 56
Helforth, John
See Doolittle, Hilda
Hellenhofferu, Vojtech Kapristian z
See Hasek, Jaroslav (Matej Frantisek)
Heller, Joseph 1923-**CLC 1, 3, 5, 8, 11, 36, 63; DA; DAB; DAC; DAM MST, NOV, POP; WLC**
See also AAYA 24; AITN 1; CA 5-8R; CABS 1; CANR 8, 42, 66; DLB 2, 28; DLBY 80; INT CANR-8; MTCW 1, 2
Hellman, Lillian (Florence) 1906-1984**CLC 2, 4, 8, 14, 18, 34, 44, 52; DAM DRAM; DC 1**
See also AITN 1, 2; CA 13-16R; 112; CANR 33; DLB 7; DLBY 84; MTCW 1, 2
Helprin, Mark 1947-**CLC 7, 10, 22, 32; DAM NOV, POP**
See also CA 81-84; CANR 47, 64; CDALBS; DLBY 85; MTCW 1, 2
Helvetius, Claude-Adrien 1715-1771 **LC 26**
Helyar, Jane Penelope Josephine 1933-
See Poole, Josephine
See also CA 21-24R; CANR 10, 26; SATA 82
Hemans, Felicia 1793-1835 **NCLC 71**
See also DLB 96
Hemingway, Ernest (Miller) 1899-1961 **CLC 1, 3, 6, 8, 10, 13, 19, 30, 34, 39, 41, 44, 50, 61, 80; DA; DAB; DAC; DAM MST, NOV; SSC 1, 25; WLC**
See also AAYA 19; CA 77-80; CANR 34; CDALB 1917-1929; DLB 4, 9, 102, 210; DLBD 1, 15, 16; DLBY 81, 87, 96, 98; MTCW 1, 2
Hempel, Amy 1951- **CLC 39**
See also CA 118; 137; CANR 70; MTCW 2
<ind**Henderson, F. C.**
See Mencken, H(enry) L(ouis)
Henderson, Sylvia
See Ashton-Warner, Sylvia (Constance)
Henderson, Zenna (Chlarson) 1917-1983**SSC 29**
See also CA 1-4R; 133; CANR 1; DLB 8; SATA 5
Henkin, Joshua **CLC 119**
See also CA 161
Henley, Beth **CLC 23; DC 6**
See also Henley, Elizabeth Becker
See also CABS 3; DLBY 86
Henley, Elizabeth Becker 1952-
See Henley, Beth
See also CA 107; CANR 32, 73; DAM DRAM, MST; MTCW 1, 2
Henley, William Ernest 1849-1903 **TCLC 8**
See also CA 105; DLB 19
Hennissart, Martha
See Lathen, Emma
See also CA 85-88; CANR 64
Henry, O. **TCLC 1, 19; SSC 5; WLC**
See also Porter, William Sydney
Henry, Patrick 1736-1799 **LC 25**
Henryson, Robert 1430(?)-1506(?) **LC 20**
See also DLB 146
Henry VIII 1491-1547 **LC 10**
See also DLB 132
Henschke, Alfred
See Klabund
Hentoff, Nat(han Irving) 1925- **CLC 26**
See also AAYA 4; CA 1-4R; CAAS 6; CANR 5, 25, 77; CLR 1, 52; INT CANR-25; JRDA; MAICYA; SATA 42, 69; SATA-Brief 27
Heppenstall, (John) Rayner 1911-1981 **CLC 10**
See also CA 1-4R; 103; CANR 29
Heraclitus c. 540B.C.-c. 450B.C. **CMLC 22**
See also DLB 176
Herbert, Frank (Patrick) 1920-1986 **CLC 12, 23, 35, 44, 85; DAM POP**
See also AAYA 21; CA 53-56; 118; CANR 5, 43; CDALBS; DLB 8; INT CANR-5; MTCW 1, 2; SATA 9, 37; SATA-Obit 47
Herbert, George 1593-1633 **LC 24; DAB; DAM POET; PC 4**
See also CDBLB Before 1660; DLB 126
Herbert, Zbigniew 1924-1998 **CLC 9, 43; DAM POET**
See also CA 89-92; 169; CANR 36, 74; MTCW 1
Herbst, Josephine (Frey) 1897-1969 **CLC 34**
See also CA 5-8R; 25-28R; DLB 9
Hergesheimer, Joseph 1880-1954 **TCLC 11**
See also CA 109; DLB 102, 9
Herlihy, James Leo 1927-1993 **CLC 6**
See also CA 1-4R; 143; CANR 2
Hermogenes fl. c. 175- **CMLC 6**
Hernandez, Jose 1834-1886 **NCLC 17**
Herodotus c. 484B.C.-429B.C. **CMLC 17**
See also DLB 176
Herrick, Robert 1591-1674**LC 13; DA; DAB; DAC; DAM MST, POP; PC 9**
See also DLB 126
Herring, Guilles
See Somerville, Edith
Herriot, James 1916-1995**CLC 12; DAM POP**
See also Wight, James Alfred
See also AAYA 1; CA 148; CANR 40; MTCW 2; SATA 86
Herrmann, Dorothy 1941- **CLC 44**
See also CA 107
Herrmann, Taffy
See Herrmann, Dorothy
Hersey, John (Richard) 1914-1993**CLC 1, 2, 7, 9, 40, 81, 97; DAM POP**
See also AAYA 29; CA 17-20R; 140; CANR 33; CDALBS; DLB 6, 185; MTCW 1, 2; SATA 25; SATA-Obit 76
Herzen, Aleksandr Ivanovich 1812-1870 **NCLC 10, 61**
Herzl, Theodor 1860-1904 **TCLC 36**
See also CA 168
Herzog, Werner 1942- **CLC 16**

See also CA 9-12R; 125; CANR 4; DLB 16
Holmes, Oliver Wendell, Jr. 1841-1935 **TCLC 77**
See also CA 114
Holmes, Oliver Wendell 1809-1894 **NCLC 14**
See also CDALB 1640-1865; DLB 1, 189; SATA 34
Holmes, Raymond
See Souster, (Holmes) Raymond
Holt, Victoria
See Hibbert, Eleanor Alice Burford
Holub, Miroslav 1923-1998 **CLC 4**
See also CA 21-24R; 169; CANR 10
Homer c. 8th cent. B.C.- **CMLC 1, 16; DA; DAB; DAC; DAM MST, POET; PC 23; WLCS**
See also DLB 176
Hongo, Garrett Kaoru 1951- **PC 23**
See also CA 133; CAAS 22; DLB 120
Honig, Edwin 1919- **CLC 33**
See also CA 5-8R; CAAS 8; CANR 4, 45; DLB 5
Hood, Hugh (John Blagdon) 1928- **CLC 15, 28**
See also CA 49-52; CAAS 17; CANR 1, 33; DLB 53
Hood, Thomas 1799-1845 **NCLC 16**
See also DLB 96
Hooker, (Peter) Jeremy 1941- **CLC 43**
See also CA 77-80; CANR 22; DLB 40
hooks, bell **CLC 94; BLCS**
See also Watkins, Gloria
See also MTCW 2
Hope, A(lec) D(erwent) 1907- **CLC 3, 51**
See also CA 21-24R; CANR 33, 74; MTCW 1, 2
Hope, Anthony 1863-1933 **TCLC 83**
See also CA 157; DLB 153, 156
Hope, Brian
See Creasey, John
Hope, Christopher (David Tully) 1944- **CLC 52**
See also CA 106; CANR 47; SATA 62
Hopkins, Gerard Manley 1844-1889 **NCLC 17; DA; DAB; DAC; DAM MST, POET; PC 15; WLC**
See also CDBLB 1890-1914; DLB 35, 57
Hopkins, John (Richard) 1931-1998 **CLC 4**
See also CA 85-88; 169
Hopkins, Pauline Elizabeth 1859-1930 **TCLC 28; BLC 2; DAM MULT**
See also BW 2, 3; CA 141; DLB 50
Hopkinson, Francis 1737-1791 **LC 25**
See also DLB 31
Hopley-Woolrich, Cornell George 1903-1968
See Woolrich, Cornell
See also CA 13-14; CANR 58; CAP 1; MTCW 2
Horatio
See Proust, (Valentin-Louis-George-Eugene-) Marcel
Horgan, Paul (George Vincent O'Shaughnessy) 1903-1995 **CLC 9, 53; DAM NOV**
See also CA 13-16R; 147; CANR 9, 35; DLB 212; DLBY 85; INT CANR-9; MTCW 1, 2; SATA 13; SATA-Obit 84
Horn, Peter
See Kuttner, Henry
Hornem, Horace Esq.
See Byron, George Gordon (Noel)
Horney, Karen (Clementine Theodore Danielsen) 1885-1952 **TCLC 71**
See also CA 114; 165
Hornung, E(rnest) W(illiam) 1866-1921 **TCLC 59**
See also CA 108; 160; DLB 70
Horovitz, Israel (Arthur) 1939- **CLC 56; DAM DRAM**
See also CA 33-36R; CANR 46, 59; DLB 7
Horvath, Odon von
See Horvath, Oedoen von
See also DLB 85, 124
Horvath, Oedoen von 1901-1938 **TCLC 45**
See also Horvath, Odon von
See also CA 118
Horwitz, Julius 1920-1986 **CLC 14**
See also CA 9-12R; 119; CANR 12
Hospital, Janette Turner 1942- **CLC 42**
See also CA 108; CANR 48
Hostos, E. M. de
See Hostos (y Bonilla), Eugenio Maria de
Hostos, Eugenio M. de
See Hostos (y Bonilla), Eugenio Maria de
Hostos, Eugenio Maria
See Hostos (y Bonilla), Eugenio Maria de
Hostos (y Bonilla), Eugenio Maria de 1839-1903 **TCLC 24**
See also CA 123; 131; HW 1
Houdini
See Lovecraft, H(oward) P(hillips)
Hougan, Carolyn 1943- **CLC 34**
See also CA 139
Household, Geoffrey (Edward West) 1900-1988 **CLC 11**
See also CA 77-80; 126; CANR 58; DLB 87; SATA 14; SATA-Obit 59
Housman, A(lfred) E(dward) 1859-1936 **TCLC 1, 10; DA; DAB; DAC; DAM MST, POET; PC 2; WLCS**
See also CA 104; 125; DLB 19; MTCW 1, 2
Housman, Laurence 1865-1959 **TCLC 7**
See also CA 106; 155; DLB 10; SATA 25
Howard, Elizabeth Jane 1923- **CLC 7, 29**
See also CA 5-8R; CANR 8, 62
Howard, Maureen 1930- **CLC 5, 14, 46**
See also CA 53-56; CANR 31, 75; DLBY 83; INT CANR-31; MTCW 1, 2
Howard, Richard 1929- **CLC 7, 10, 47**
See also AITN 1; CA 85-88; CANR 25, 80; DLB 5; INT CANR-25
Howard, Robert E(rvin) 1906-1936 **TCLC 8**
See also CA 105; 157
Howard, Warren F.
See Pohl, Frederik
Howe, Fanny (Quincy) 1940- **CLC 47**
See also CA 117; CAAS 27; CANR 70; SATA-Brief 52
Howe, Irving 1920-1993 **CLC 85**
See also CA 9-12R; 141; CANR 21, 50; DLB 67; MTCW 1, 2
Howe, Julia Ward 1819-1910 **TCLC 21**
See also CA 117; DLB 1, 189
Howe, Susan 1937- **CLC 72**
See also CA 160; DLB 120
Howe, Tina 1937- **CLC 48**
See also CA 109
Howell, James 1594(?)-1666 **LC 13**
See also DLB 151
Howells, W. D.
See Howells, William Dean
Howells, William D.
See Howells, William Dean
Howells, William Dean 1837-1920 **TCLC 7, 17, 41**
See also CA 104; 134; CDALB 1865-1917; DLB 12, 64, 74, 79, 189; MTCW 2
Howes, Barbara 1914-1996 **CLC 15**
See also CA 9-12R; 151; CAAS 3; CANR 53; SATA 5
Hrabal, Bohumil 1914-1997 **CLC 13, 67**
See also CA 106; 156; CAAS 12; CANR 57
Hroswitha of Gandersheim c. 935-c. 1002 **CMLC 29**
See also DLB 148
Hsun, Lu
See Lu Hsun
Hubbard, L(afayette) Ron(ald) 1911-1986 **CLC 43; DAM POP**
See also CA 77-80; 118; CANR 52; MTCW 2
Huch, Ricarda (Octavia) 1864-1947 **TCLC 13**
See also CA 111; DLB 66
Huddle, David 1942- **CLC 49**
See also CA 57-60; CAAS 20; DLB 130
Hudson, Jeffrey
See Crichton, (John) Michael
Hudson, W(illiam) H(enry) 1841-1922 **TCLC 29**
See also CA 115; DLB 98, 153, 174; SATA 35
Hueffer, Ford Madox
See Ford, Ford Madox
Hughart, Barry 1934- **CLC 39**
See also CA 137
Hughes, Colin
See Creasey, John
Hughes, David (John) 1930- **CLC 48**
See also CA 116; 129; DLB 14
Hughes, Edward James
See Hughes, Ted
See also DAM MST, POET
Hughes, (James) Langston 1902-1967 **CLC 1, 5, 10, 15, 35, 44, 108; BLC 2; DA; DAB; DAC; DAM DRAM, MST, MULT, POET; DC 3; PC 1; SSC 6; WLC**
See also AAYA 12; BW 1, 3; CA 1-4R; 25-28R; CANR 1, 34; CDALB 1929-1941; CLR 17; DLB 4, 7, 48, 51, 86; JRDA; MAICYA; MTCW 1, 2; SATA 4, 33
Hughes, Richard (Arthur Warren) 1900-1976 **CLC 1, 11; DAM NOV**
See also CA 5-8R; 65-68; CANR 4; DLB 15, 161; MTCW 1; SATA 8; SATA-Obit 25
Hughes, Ted 1930-1998 **CLC 2, 4, 9, 14, 37, 119; DAB; DAC; PC 7**
See also Hughes, Edward James
See also CA 1-4R; 171; CANR 1, 33, 66; CLR 3; DLB 40, 161; MAICYA; MTCW 1, 2; SATA 49; SATA-Brief 27; SATA-Obit 107
Hugo, Richard F(ranklin) 1923-1982 **CLC 6, 18, 32; DAM POET**
See also CA 49-52; 108; CANR 3; DLB 5, 206
Hugo, Victor (Marie) 1802-1885 **NCLC 3, 10, 21; DA; DAB; DAC; DAM DRAM, MST, NOV, POET; PC 17; WLC**
See also AAYA 28; DLB 119, 192; SATA 47
Huidobro, Vicente
See Huidobro Fernandez, Vicente Garcia
Huidobro Fernandez, Vicente Garcia 1893-1948 **TCLC 31**
See also CA 131; HW 1
Hulme, Keri 1947- **CLC 39**
See also CA 125; CANR 69; INT 125
Hulme, T(homas) E(rnest) 1883-1917 **TCLC 21**
See also CA 117; DLB 19
Hume, David 1711-1776 **LC 7**
See also DLB 104
Humphrey, William 1924-1997 **CLC 45**
See also CA 77-80; 160; CANR 68; DLB 212
Humphreys, Emyr Owen 1919- **CLC 47**
See also CA 5-8R; CANR 3, 24; DLB 15

66; DLBY 83; INT CANR-10; MTCW 1, 2; SATA 62
James, Andrew
See Kirkup, James
James, C(yril) L(ionel) R(obert) 1901-1989 **CLC 33; BLCS**
See also BW 2; CA 117; 125; 128; CANR 62; DLB 125; MTCW 1
James, Daniel (Lewis) 1911-1988
See Santiago, Danny
See also CA 174; 125
James, Dynely
See Mayne, William (James Carter)
James, Henry Sr. 1811-1882 **NCLC 53**
James, Henry 1843-1916 **TCLC 2, 11, 24, 40, 47, 64; DA; DAB; DAC; DAM MST, NOV; SSC 8, 32; WLC**
See also CA 104; 132; CDALB 1865-1917; DLB 12, 71, 74, 189; DLBD 13; MTCW 1, 2
James, M. R.
See James, Montague (Rhodes)
See also DLB 156
James, Montague (Rhodes) 1862-1936 **TCLC 6; SSC 16**
See also CA 104; DLB 201
James, P. D. 1920- **CLC 18, 46**
See also White, Phyllis Dorothy James
See also BEST 90:2; CDBLB 1960 to Present; DLB 87; DLBD 17
James, Philip
See Moorcock, Michael (John)
James, William 1842-1910 **TCLC 15, 32**
See also CA 109
James I 1394-1437 **LC 20**
Jameson, Anna 1794-1860 **NCLC 43**
See also DLB 99, 166
Jami, Nur al-Din 'Abd al-Rahman 1414-1492 **LC 9**
Jammes, Francis 1868-1938 **TCLC 75**
Jandl, Ernst 1925- **CLC 34**
Janowitz, Tama 1957- **CLC 43; DAM POP**
See also CA 106; CANR 52
Japrisot, Sebastien 1931- **CLC 90**
Jarrell, Randall 1914-1965 **CLC 1, 2, 6, 9, 13, 49; DAM POET**
See also CA 5-8R; 25-28R; CABS 2; CANR 6, 34; CDALB 1941-1968; CLR 6; DLB 48, 52; MAICYA; MTCW 1, 2; SATA 7
Jarry, Alfred 1873-1907 **TCLC 2, 14; DAM DRAM; SSC 20**
<See also CA 104; 153; DLB 192
Jarvis, E. K.
See Bloch, Robert (Albert); Ellison, Harlan (Jay); Silverberg, Robert
Jeake, Samuel, Jr.
See Aiken, Conrad (Potter)
Jean Paul 1763-1825 **NCLC 7**
Jefferies, (John) Richard 1848-1887 **NCLC 47**
See also DLB 98, 141; SATA 16
Jeffers, (John) Robinson 1887-1962 **CLC 2, 3, 11, 15, 54; DA; DAC; DAM MST, POET; PC 17; WLC**
See also CA 85-88; CANR 35; CDALB 1917-1929; DLB 45, 212; MTCW 1, 2
Jefferson, Janet
See Mencken, H(enry) L(ouis)
Jefferson, Thomas 1743-1826 **NCLC 11**
See also CDALB 1640-1865; DLB 31
Jeffrey, Francis 1773-1850 **NCLC 33**
See also DLB 107
Jelakowitch, Ivan
See Heijermans, Herman
Jellicoe, (Patricia) Ann 1927- **CLC 27**
See also CA 85-88; DLB 13
Jen, Gish **CLC 70**
See also Jen, Lillian
Jen, Lillian 1956(?)-
See Jen, Gish
See also CA 135
Jenkins, (John) Robin 1912- **CLC 52**
See also CA 1-4R; CANR 1; DLB 14
Jennings, Elizabeth (Joan) 1926- **CLC 5, 14**
See also CA 61-64; CAAS 5; CANR 8, 39, 66; DLB 27; MTCW 1; SATA 66
Jennings, Waylon 1937- **CLC 21**
Jensen, Johannes V. 1873-1950 **TCLC 41**
See also CA 170
Jensen, Laura (Linnea) 1948- **CLC 37**
See also CA 103
Jerome, Jerome K(lapka) 1859-1927 **TCLC 23**
See also CA 119; DLB 10, 34, 135
Jerrold, Douglas William 1803-1857 **NCLC 2**
See also DLB 158, 159
Jewett, (Theodora) Sarah Orne 1849-1909 **TCLC 1, 22; SSC 6**
See also CA 108; 127; CANR 71; DLB 12, 74; SATA 15
Jewsbury, Geraldine (Endsor) 1812-1880 **NCLC 22**
See also DLB 21
Jhabvala, Ruth Prawer 1927- **CLC 4, 8, 29, 94; DAB; DAM NOV**
See also CA 1-4R; CANR 2; 29, 51, 74; DLB 139, 194; INT CANR-29; MTCW 1, 2
Jibran, Kahlil
See Gibran, Kahlil
Jibran, Khalil
See Gibran, Kahlil
Jiles, Paulette 1943- **CLC 13, 58**
See also CA 101; CANR 70
Jimenez (Mantecon), Juan Ramon 1881-1958 **TCLC 4; DAM MULT, POET; HLC; PC 7**
See also CA 104; 131; CANR 74; DLB 134; HW 1; MTCW 1, 2
Jimenez, Ramon
See Jimenez (Mantecon), Juan Ramon
Jimenez Mantecon, Juan
See Jimenez (Mantecon), Juan Ramon
Jin, Ha 1956- **CLC 109**
See also CA 152
Joel, Billy **CLC 26**
See also Joel, William Martin
Joel, William Martin 1949-
See Joel, Billy
See also CA 108
John, Saint 7th cent. - **CMLC 27**
John of the Cross, St. 1542-1591 **LC 18**
Johnson, B(ryan) S(tanley William) 1933-1973 **CLC 6, 9**
See also CA 9-12R; 53-56; CANR 9; DLB 14, 40
Johnson, Benj. F. of Boo
See Riley, James Whitcomb
Johnson, Benjamin F. of Boo
See Riley, James Whitcomb
Johnson, Charles (Richard) 1948- **CLC 7, 51, 65; BLC 2; DAM MULT**
See also BW 2, 3; CA 116; CAAS 18; CANR 42, 66; DLB 33; MTCW 2
Johnson, Denis 1949- **CLC 52**
See also CA 117; 121; CANR 71; DLB 120
Johnson, Diane 1934- **CLC 5, 13, 48**
See also CA 41-44R; CANR 17, 40, 62; DLBY 80; INT CANR-17; MTCW 1
Johnson, Eyvind (Olof Verner) 1900-1976 **CLC 14**
See also CA 73-76; 69-72; CANR 34
Johnson, J. R.
See James, C(yril) L(ionel) R(obert)
Johnson, James Weldon 1871-1938 **TCLC 3, 19; BLC 2; DAM MULT, POET; PC 24**
See also BW 1, 3; CA 104; 125; CDALB 1917-1929; CLR 32; DLB 51; MTCW 1, 2; SATA 31
Johnson, Joyce 1935- **CLC 58**
See also CA 125; 129
Johnson, Judith (Emlyn) 1936- **CLC 7, 15**
See also CA 25-28R, 153; CANR 34
Johnson, Lionel (Pigot) 1867-1902 **TCLC 19**
See also CA 117; DLB 19
Johnson, Marguerite (Annie)
See Angelou, Maya
Johnson, Mel
See Malzberg, Barry N(athaniel)
<indexbody>**Johnson, Pamela Hansford** 1912-1981 **CLC 1, 7, 27**
See also CA 1-4R; 104; CANR 2, 28; DLB 15; MTCW 1, 2
Johnson, Robert 1911(?)-1938 **TCLC 69**
See also BW 3; CA 174
Johnson, Samuel 1709-1784 **LC 15; DA; DAB; DAC; DAM MST; WLC**
See also CDBLB 1660-1789; DLB 39, 95, 104, 142
Johnson, Uwe 1934-1984 **CLC 5, 10, 15, 40**
See also CA 1-4R; 112; CANR 1, 39; DLB 75; MTCW 1
Johnston, George (Benson) 1913- **CLC 51**
See also CA 1-4R; CANR 5, 20; DLB 88
Johnston, Jennifer 1930- **CLC 7**
See also CA 85-88; DLB 14
Jolley, (Monica) Elizabeth 1923- **CLC 46; SSC 19**
See also CA 127; CAAS 13; CANR 59
Jones, Arthur Llewellyn 1863-1947
See Machen, Arthur
See also CA 104
Jones, D(ouglas) G(ordon) 1929- **CLC 10**
See also CA 29-32R; CANR 13; DLB 53
Jones, David (Michael) 1895-1974 **CLC 2, 4, 7, 13, 42**
See also CA 9-12R; 53-56; CANR 28; CDBLB 1945-1960; DLB 20, 100; MTCW 1
Jones, David Robert 1947-
See Bowie, David
See also CA 103
Jones, Diana Wynne 1934- **CLC 26**
See also AAYA 12; CA 49-52; CANR 4, 26, 56; CLR 23; DLB 161; JRDA; MAICYA; SAAS 7; SATA 9, 70
Jones, Edward P. 1950- **CLC 76**
See also BW 2, 3; CA 142; CANR 79
Jones, Gayl 1949- **CLC 6, 9; BLC 2; DAM MULT**
<inSee also BW 2, 3; CA 77-80; CANR 27, 66; DLB 33; MTCW 1, 2
Jones, James 1921-1977 **CLC 1, 3, 10, 39**
See also AITN 1, 2; CA 1-4R; 69-72; CANR 6; DLB 2, 143; DLBD 17; DLBY 98; MTCW 1
Jones, John J.
See Lovecraft, H(oward) P(hillips)
Jones, LeRoi **CLC 1, 2, 3, 5, 10, 14**
See also Baraka, Amiri
See also MTCW 2
Jones, Louis B. 1953- **CLC 65**
See also CA 141; CANR 73
Jones, Madison (Percy, Jr.) 1925- **CLC 4**

See also CA 13-16R; CAAS 11; CANR 7, 54; DLB 152
Jones, Mervyn 1922- **CLC 10, 52**
See also CA 45-48; CAAS 5; CANR 1; MTCW 1
Jones, Mick 1956(?)- **CLC 30**
Jones, Nettie (Pearl) 1941- **CLC 34**
See also BW 2; CA 137; CAAS 20
Jones, Preston 1936-1979 **CLC 10**
See also CA 73-76; 89-92; DLB 7
Jones, Robert F(rancis) 1934- **CLC 7**
See also CA 49-52; CANR 2, 61
Jones, Rod 1953- **CLC 50**
See also CA 128
Jones, Terence Graham Parry 1942- **CLC 21**
See also Jones, Terry; Monty Python
See also CA 112; 116; CANR 35; INT 116
Jones, Terry
See Jones, Terence Graham Parry
See also SATA 67; SATA-Brief 51
Jones, Thom 1945(?)- **CLC 81**
See also CA 157
Jong, Erica 1942- **CLC 4, 6, 8, 18, 83; DAM NOV, POP**
See also AITN 1; BEST 90:2; CA 73-76; CANR 26, 52, 75; DLB 2, 5, 28, 152; INT CANR-26; MTCW 1, 2
Jonson, Ben(jamin) 1572(?)-1637 **LC 6, 33; DA; DAB; DAC; DAM DRAM, MST, POET; DC 4; PC 17; WLC**
See also CDBLB Before 1660; DLB 62, 121
Jordan, June 1936-**CLC 5, 11, 23, 114; BLCS; DAM MULT, POET**
See also AAYA 2; BW 2, 3; CA 33-36R; CANR 25, 70; CLR 10; DLB 38; MAICYA; MTCW 1; SATA 4
Jordan, Neil (Patrick) 1950- **CLC 110**
See also CA 124; 130; CANR 54; INT 130
Jordan, Pat(rick M.) 1941- **CLC 37**
See also CA 33-36R
Jorgensen, Ivar
See Ellison, Harlan (Jay)
Jorgenson, Ivar
See Silverberg, Robert
Josephus, Flavius c. 37-100 **CMLC 13**
Josipovici, Gabriel 1940- **CLC 6, 43**
See also CA 37-40R; CAAS 8; CANR 47; DLB 14
Joubert, Joseph 1754-1824 **NCLC 9**
Jouve, Pierre Jean 1887-1976 **CLC 47**
See also CA 65-68
Jovine, Francesco 1902-1950 **TCLC 79**
Joyce, James (Augustine Aloysius) 1882-1941 **TCLC 3, 8, 16, 35, 52; DA; DAB; DAC; DAM MST, NOV, POET; PC 22; SSC 3, 26; WLC**
See also CA 104; 126; CDBLB 1914-1945; DLB 10, 19, 36, 162; MTCW 1, 2
Jozsef, Attila 1905-1937 **TCLC 22**
See also CA 116
Juana Ines de la Cruz 1651(?)-1695 **LC 5; HLCS 1; PC 24**
<indexbo**Judd, Cyril**
See Kornbluth, C(yril) M.; Pohl, Frederik
Julian of Norwich 1342(?)-1416(?) **LC 6**
See also DLB 146
Junger, Sebastian 1962- **CLC 109**
See also AAYA 28; CA 165
Juniper, Alex
See Hospital, Janette Turner
Junius
See Luxemburg, Rosa
Just, Ward (Swift) 1935- **CLC 4, 27**
See also CA 25-28R; CANR 32; INT CANR-32
Justice, Donald (Rodney) 1925- **CLC 6, 19, 102; DAM POET**
See also CA 5-8R; CANR 26, 54, 74; DLBY 83; INT CANR-26; MTCW 2
Juvenal c. 60-c. 13 **CMLC 8**
See also Juvenalis, Decimus Junius
See also DLB 211
<index**Juvenalis, Decimus Junius** 55(?)-c. 127(?)
See Juvenal
Juvenis
See Bourne, Randolph S(illiman)
Kacew, Romain 1914-1980
See Gary, Romain
See also CA 108; 102
Kadare, Ismail 1936- **CLC 52**
See also CA 161
Kadohata, Cynthia **CLC 59**
See also CA 140
Kafka, Franz 1883-1924**TCLC 2, 6, 13, 29, 47, 53; DA; DAB; DAC; DAM MST, NOV; SSC 5, 29; WLC**
See also CA 105; 126; DLB 81; MTCW 1, 2
Kahanovitsch, Pinkhes
See Der Nister
Kahn, Roger 1927- **CLC 30**
See also CA 25-28R; CANR 44, 69; DLB 171; SATA 37
Kain, Saul
See Sassoon, Siegfried (Lorraine)
Kaiser, Georg 1878-1945 **TCLC 9**
See also CA 106; DLB 124
Kaletski, Alexander 1946- **CLC 39**
See also CA 118; 143
Kalidasa fl. c. 400- **CMLC 9; PC 22**
Kallman, Chester (Simon) 1921-1975 **CLC 2**
See also CA 45-48; 53-56; CANR 3
Kaminsky, Melvin 1926-
See Brooks, Mel
See also CA 65-68; CANR 16
Kaminsky, Stuart M(elvin) 1934- **CLC 59**
See also CA 73-76; CANR 29, 53
Kandinsky, Wassily 1866-1944 **TCLC 92**
See also CA 118; 155
Kane, Francis
See Robbins, Harold
Kane, Paul
See Simon, Paul (Frederick)
Kane, Wilson
See Bloch, Robert (Albert)
Kanin, Garson 1912- **CLC 22**
See also AITN 1; CA 5-8R; CANR 7, 78; DLB 7
Kaniuk, Yoram 1930- **CLC 19**
See also CA 134
Kant, Immanuel 1724-1804 **NCLC 27, 67**
See also DLB 94
Kantor, MacKinlay 1904-1977 **CLC 7**
See also CA 61-64; 73-76; CANR 60, 63; DLB 9, 102; MTCW 2
Kaplan, David Michael 1946- **CLC 50**
Kaplan, James 1951- **CLC 59**
See also CA 135
Karageorge, Michael
See Anderson, Poul (William)
Karamzin, Nikolai Mikhailovich 1766-1826 **NCLC 3**
See also DLB 150
Karapanou, Margarita 1946- **CLC 13**
See also CA 101
Karinthy, Frigyes 1887-1938 **TCLC 47**
See also CA 170
Karl, Frederick R(obert) 1927- **CLC 34**
See also CA 5-8R; CANR 3, 44
Kastel, Warren
See Silverberg, Robert
Kataev, Evgeny Petrovich 1903-1942
See Petrov, Evgeny
See also CA 120
Kataphusin
See Ruskin, John
Katz, Steve 1935- **CLC 47**
See also CA 25-28R; CAAS 14, 64; CANR 12; DLBY 83
Kauffman, Janet 1945- **CLC 42**
See also CA 117; CANR 43; DLBY 86
<in**Kaufman, Bob (Garnell)** 1925-1986 **CLC 49**
See also BW 1; CA 41-44R; 118; CANR 22; DLB 16, 41
Kaufman, George S. 1889-1961**CLC 38; DAM DRAM**
See also CA 108; 93-96; DLB 7; INT 108; MTCW 2
Kaufman, Sue **CLC 3, 8**
See also Barondess, Sue K(aufman)
Kavafis, Konstantinos Petrou 1863-1933
See Cavafy, C(onstantine) P(eter)
See also CA 104
Kavan, Anna 1901-1968 **CLC 5, 13, 82**
See also CA 5-8R; CANR 6, 57; MTCW 1
Kavanagh, Dan
See Barnes, Julian (Patrick)
Kavanagh, Julie 1952- **CLC 119**
See also CA 163
Kavanagh, Patrick (Joseph) 1904-1967 **CLC 22**
See also CA 123; 25-28R; DLB 15, 20; MTCW 1
Kawabata, Yasunari 1899-1972 **CLC 2, 5, 9, 18, 107; DAM MULT; SSC 17**
See also CA 93-96; 33-36R; DLB 180; MTCW 2
Kaye, M(ary) M(argaret) 1909- **CLC 28**
See also CA 89-92; CANR 24, 60; MTCW 1, 2; SATA 62
Kaye, Mollie
See Kaye, M(ary) M(argaret)
Kaye-Smith, Sheila 1887-1956 **TCLC 20**
See also CA 118; DLB 36
Kaymor, Patrice Maguilene
See Senghor, Leopold Sedar
Kazan, Elia 1909- **CLC 6, 16, 63**
See also CA 21-24R; CANR 32, 78
Kazantzakis, Nikos 1883(?)-1957 **TCLC 2, 5, 33**
See also CA 105; 132; MTCW 1, 2
Kazin, Alfred 1915-1998 **CLC 34, 38, 119**
See also CA 1-4R; CAAS 7; CANR 1, 45, 79; DLB 67
Keane, Mary Nesta (Skrine) 1904-1996
See Keane, Molly
See also CA 108; 114; 151
Keane, Molly **CLC 31**
See also Keane, Mary Nesta (Skrine)
See also INT 114
Keates, Jonathan 1946(?)- **CLC 34**
See also CA 163
Keaton, Buster 1895-1966 **CLC 20**
Keats, John 1795-1821**NCLC 8, 73; DA; DAB; DAC; DAM MST, POET; PC 1; WLC**
See also CDBLB 1789-1832; DLB 96, 110
Keene, Donald 1922- **CLC 34**
See also CA 1-4R; CANR 5

Kivi, Aleksis 1834-1872 **NCLC 30**
Kizer, Carolyn (Ashley) 1925-**CLC 15, 39, 80; DAM POET**
See also CA 65-68; CAAS 5; CANR 24, 70; DLB 5, 169; MTCW 2
Klabund 1890-1928 **TCLC 44**
See also CA 162; DLB 66
Klappert, Peter 1942- **CLC 57**
See also CA 33-36R; DLB 5
Klein, A(braham) M(oses) 1909-1972**CLC 19; DAB; DAC; DAM MST**
See also CA 101; 37-40R; DLB 68
Klein, Norma 1938-1989 **CLC 30**
See also AAYA 2; CA 41-44R; 128; CANR 15, 37; CLR 2, 19; INT CANR-15; JRDA; MAICYA; SAAS 1; SATA 7, 57
Klein, T(heodore) E(ibon) D(onald) 1947- **CLC 34**
See also CA 119; CANR 44, 75
Kleist, Heinrich von 1777-1811 **NCLC 2, 37; DAM DRAM; SSC 22**
See also DLB 90
Klima, Ivan 1931- **CLC 56; DAM NOV**
See also CA 25-28R; CANR 17, 50
Klimentov, Andrei Platonovich 1899-1951
See Platonov, Andrei
See also CA 108
Klinger, Friedrich Maximilian von 1752-1831 **NCLC 1**
See also DLB 94
Klingsor the Magician
See Hartmann, Sadakichi
Klopstock, Friedrich Gottlieb 1724-1803 **NCLC 11**
See also DLB 97
Knapp, Caroline 1959- **CLC 99**
See also CA 154
Knebel, Fletcher 1911-1993 **CLC 14**
<indexSee also AITN 1; CA 1-4R; 140; CAAS 3; CANR 1, 36; SATA 36; SATA-Obit 75
Knickerbocker, Diedrich
See Irving, Washington
Knight, Etheridge 1931-1991**CLC 40; BLC 2; DAM POET; PC 14**
See also BW 1, 3; CA 21-24R; 133; CANR 23; DLB 41; MTCW 2
Knight, Sarah Kemble 1666-1727 **LC 7**
See also DLB 24, 200
Knister, Raymond 1899-1932 **TCLC 56**
See also DLB 68
Knowles, John 1926- **CLC 1, 4, 10, 26; DA; DAC; DAM MST, NOV**
See also AAYA 10; CA 17-20R; CANR 40, 74, 76; CDALB 1968-1988; DLB 6; MTCW 1, 2; SATA 8, 89
Knox, Calvin M.
See Silverberg, Robert
Knox, John c. 1505-1572 **LC 37**
See also DLB 132
<Knye, Cassandra
See Disch, Thomas M(ichael)
Koch, C(hristopher) J(ohn) 1932- **CLC 42**
See also CA 127
Koch, Christopher
See Koch, C(hristopher) J(ohn)
Koch, Kenneth 1925- **CLC 5, 8, 44; DAM POET**
See also CA 1-4R; CANR 6, 36, 57; DLB 5; INT CANR-36; MTCW 2; SATA 65
Kochanowski, Jan 1530-1584 **LC 10**
Kock, Charles Paul de 1794-1871 **NCLC 16**
Koda Shigeyuki 1867-1947
See Rohan, Koda
See also CA 121
Koestler, Arthur 1905-1983**CLC 1, 3, 6, 8, 15, 33**
See also CA 1-4R; 109; CANR 1, 33; CDBLB 1945-1960; DLBY 83; MTCW 1, 2
Kogawa, Joy Nozomi 1935- **CLC 78; DAC; DAM MST, MULT**
See also CA 101; CANR 19, 62; MTCW 2; SATA 99
Kohout, Pavel 1928- **CLC 13**
See also CA 45-48; CANR 3
Koizumi, Yakumo
See Hearn, (Patricio) Lafcadio (Tessima Carlos)
Kolmar, Gertrud 1894-1943 **TCLC 40**
See also CA 167
Komunyakaa, Yusef 1947-**CLC 86, 94; BLCS**
See also CA 147; DLB 120
Konrad, George
See Konrad, Gyoergy
Konrad, Gyoergy 1933- **CLC 4, 10, 73**
See also CA 85-88
Konwicki, Tadeusz 1926- **CLC 8, 28, 54, 117**
See also CA 101; CAAS 9; CANR 39, 59; MTCW 1
Koontz, Dean R(ay) 1945- **CLC 78; DAM NOV, POP**
See also AAYA 9; BEST 89:3, 90:2; CA 108; CANR 19, 36, 52; MTCW 1; SATA 92
Kopernik, Mikolaj
See Copernicus, Nicolaus
Kopit, Arthur (Lee) 1937-**CLC 1, 18, 33; DAM DRAM**
See also AITN 1; CA 81-84; CABS 3; DLB 7; MTCW 1
Kops, Bernard 1926- **CLC 4**
See also CA 5-8R; DLB 13
Kornbluth, C(yril) M. 1923-1958 **TCLC 8**
See also CA 105; 160; DLB 8
Korolenko, V. G.
See Korolenko, Vladimir Galaktionovich
Korolenko, Vladimir
See Korolenko, Vladimir Galaktionovich
Korolenko, Vladimir G.
See Korolenko, Vladimir Galaktionovich
Korolenko, Vladimir Galaktionovich 1853-1921 **TCLC 22**
See also CA 121
Korzybski, Alfred (Habdank Skarbek) 1879-1950 **TCLC 61**
See also CA 123; 160
Kosinski, Jerzy (Nikodem) 1933-1991**CLC 1, 2, 3, 6, 10, 15, 53, 70; DAM NOV**
See also CA 17-20R; 134; CANR 9, 46; DLB 2; DLBY 82; MTCW 1, 2
Kostelanetz, Richard (Cory) 1940- **CLC 28**
See also CA 13-16R; CAAS 8; CANR 38, 77
Kostrowitzki, Wilhelm Apollinaris de 1880-1918
See Apollinaire, Guillaume
See also CA 104
Kotlowitz, Robert 1924- **CLC 4**
See also CA 33-36R; CANR 36
Kotzebue, August (Friedrich Ferdinand) von 1761-1819 **NCLC 25**
See also DLB 94
<in**Kotzwinkle, William** 1938-**CLC 5, 14, 35**
See also CA 45-48; CANR 3, 44; CLR 6; DLB 173; MAICYA; SATA 24, 70
Kowna, Stancy
See Szymborska, Wislawa
Kozol, Jonathan 1936- **CLC 17**
See also CA 61-64; CANR 16, 45
Kozoll, Michael 1940(?)- **CLC 35**
Kramer, Kathryn 19(?)- **CLC 34**
Kramer, Larry 1935-**CLC 42; DAM POP; DC 8**
See also CA 124; 126; CANR 60
Krasicki, Ignacy 1735-1801 **NCLC 8**
Krasinski, Zygmunt 1812-1859 **NCLC 4**
Kraus, Karl 1874-1936 **TCLC 5**
See also CA 104; DLB 118
Kreve (Mickevicius), Vincas 1882-1954**TCLC 27**
See also CA 170
Kristeva, Julia 1941- **CLC 77**
See also CA 154
Kristofferson, Kris 1936- **CLC 26**
See also CA 104
Krizanc, John 1956- **CLC 57**
Krleza, Miroslav 1893-1981 **CLC 8, 114**
See also CA 97-100; 105; CANR 50; DLB 147
Kroetsch, Robert 1927- **CLC 5, 23, 57; DAC; DAM POET**
See also CA 17-20R; CANR 8, 38; DLB 53; MTCW 1
Kroetz, Franz
See Kroetz, Franz Xaver
Kroetz, Franz Xaver 1946- **CLC 41**
See also CA 130
Kroker, Arthur (W.) 1945- **CLC 77**
<See also CA 161
Kropotkin, Peter (Aleksieevich) 1842-1921 **TCLC 36**
See also CA 119
Krotkov, Yuri 1917- **CLC 19**
See also CA 102
Krumb
See Crumb, R(obert)
Krumgold, Joseph (Quincy) 1908-1980 **CLC 12**
See also CA 9-12R; 101; CANR 7; MAICYA; SATA 1, 48; SATA-Obit 23
Krumwitz
See Crumb, R(obert)
Krutch, Joseph Wood 1893-1970 **CLC 24**
See also CA 1-4R; 25-28R; CANR 4; DLB 63, 206
Krutzch, Gus
See Eliot, T(homas) S(tearns)
Krylov, Ivan Andreevich 1768(?)-1844**NCLC 1**
See also DLB 150
Kubin, Alfred (Leopold Isidor) 1877-1959 **TCLC 23**
See also CA 112; 149; DLB 81
Kubrick, Stanley 1928- **CLC 16**
See also AAYA 30; CA 81-84; CANR 33; DLB 26
Kumin, Maxine (Winokur) 1925- **CLC 5, 13, 28; DAM POET; PC 15**
See also AITN 2; CA 1-4R; CAAS 8; CANR 1, 21, 69; DLB 5; MTCW 1, 2; SATA 12
Kundera, Milan 1929- **CLC 4, 9, 19, 32, 68, 115; DAM NOV; SSC 24**
See also AAYA 2; CA 85-88; CANR 19, 52, 74; MTCW 1, 2
Kunene, Mazisi (Raymond) 1930- **CLC 85**
See also BW 1, 3; CA 125; DLB 117
Kunitz, Stanley (Jasspon) 1905-**CLC 6, 11, 14; PC 19**
See also CA 41-44R; CANR 26, 57; DLB 48; INT CANR-26; MTCW 1, 2
Kunze, Reiner 1933- **CLC 10**
See also CA 93-96; DLB 75
Kuprin, Aleksandr Ivanovich 1870-1938 **TCLC 5**

DLB 10, 19, 36, 98, 162, 195; MTCW 1, 2
Lawrence, T(homas) E(dward) 1888-1935 **TCLC 18**
See also Dale, Colin
See also CA 115; 167; DLB 195
Lawrence of Arabia
See Lawrence, T(homas) E(dward)
Lawson, Henry (Archibald Hertzberg) 1867-1922 **TCLC 27; SSC 18**
See also CA 120
Lawton, Dennis
See Faust, Frederick (Schiller)
Laxness, Halldor **CLC 25**
See also Gudjonsson, Halldor Kiljan
Layamon fl. c. 1200- **CMLC 10**
See also DLB 146
Laye, Camara 1928-1980 **CLC 4, 38; BLC 2; DAM MULT**
See also BW 1; CA 85-88; 97-100; CANR 25; MTCW 1, 2
Layton, Irving (Peter) 1912-**CLC 2, 15; DAC; DAM MST, POET**
See also CA 1-4R; CANR 2, 33, 43, 66; DLB 88; MTCW 1, 2
Lazarus, Emma 1849-1887 **NCLC 8**
Lazarus, Felix
See Cable, George Washington
Lazarus, Henry
See Slavitt, David R(ytman)
Lea, Joan
See Neufeld, John (Arthur)
Leacock, Stephen (Butler) 1869-1944**TCLC 2; DAC; DAM MST**
See also CA 104; 141; CANR 80; DLB 92; MTCW 2
Lear, Edward 1812-1888 **NCLC 3**
See also CLR 1; DLB 32, 163, 166; MAICYA; SATA 18, 100
Lear, Norman (Milton) 1922- **CLC 12**
See also CA 73-76
Leautaud, Paul 1872-1956 **TCLC 83**
See also DLB 65
Leavis, F(rank) R(aymond) 1895-1978**CLC 24**
See also CA 21-24R; 77-80; CANR 44; MTCW 1, 2
Leavitt, David 1961- **CLC 34; DAM POP**
See also CA 116; 122; CANR 50, 62; DLB 130; INT 122; MTCW 2
Leblanc, Maurice (Marie Emile) 1864-1941 **TCLC 49**
See also CA 110
Lebowitz, Fran(ces Ann) 1951(?)-**CLC 11, 36**
See also CA 81-84; CANR 14, 60, 70; INT CANR-14; MTCW 1
Lebrecht, Peter
See Tieck, (Johann) Ludwig
le Carre, John **CLC 3, 5, 9, 15, 28**
See also Cornwell, David (John Moore)
See also BEST 89:4; CDBLB 1960 to Present; DLB 87; MTCW 2
Le Clezio, J(ean) M(arie) G(ustave) 1940- **CLC 31**
See also CA 116; 128; DLB 83
Leconte de Lisle, Charles-Marie-Rene 1818-1894 **NCLC 29**
Le Coq, Monsieur
See Simenon, Georges (Jacques Christian)
Leduc, Violette 1907-1972 **CLC 22**
See also CA 13-14; 33-36R; CANR 69; CAP 1
Ledwidge, Francis 1887(?)-1917 **TCLC 23**
See also CA 123; DLB 20
Lee, Andrea 1953- **CLC 36; BLC 2; DAM MULT**
See also BW 1, 3; CA 125
Lee, Andrew
See Auchincloss, Louis (Stanton)
Lee, Chang-rae 1965- **CLC 91**
See also CA 148
Lee, Don L. **CLC 2**
See also Madhubuti, Haki R.
Lee, George W(ashington) 1894-1976**CLC 52; BLC 2; DAM MULT**
See also BW 1; CA 125; DLB 51
Lee, (Nelle) Harper 1926- **CLC 12, 60; DA; DAB; DAC; DAM MST, NOV; WLC**
See also AAYA 13; CA 13-16R; CANR 51; CDALB 1941-1968; DLB 6; MTCW 1, 2; SATA 11
Lee, Helen Elaine 1959(?)- **CLC 86**
See also CA 148
<ind**Lee, Julian**
See Latham, Jean Lee
Lee, Larry
See Lee, Lawrence
Lee, Laurie 1914-1997 **CLC 90; DAB; DAM POP**
See also CA 77-80; 158; CANR 33, 73; DLB 27; MTCW 1
Lee, Lawrence 1941-1990 **CLC 34**
See also CA 131; CANR 43
Lee, Li-Young 1957- **PC 24**
See also CA 153; DLB 165
Lee, Manfred B(ennington) 1905-1971**CLC 11**
See also Queen, Ellery
See also CA 1-4R; 29-32R; CANR 2; DLB 137
Lee, Shelton Jackson 1957(?)- **CLC 105; BLCS; DAM MULT**
See also Lee, Spike
See also BW 2, 3; CA 125; CANR 42
Lee, Spike
See Lee, Shelton Jackson
<indexhaSee also AAYA 4, 29
Lee, Stan 1922- **CLC 17**
See also AAYA 5; CA 108; 111; INT 111
Lee, Tanith 1947- **CLC 46**
See also AAYA 15; CA 37-40R; CANR 53; SATA 8, 88
Lee, Vernon **TCLC 5; SSC 33**
See also Paget, Violet
See also DLB 57, 153, 156, 174, 178
Lee, William
See Burroughs, William S(eward)
Lee, Willy
See Burroughs, William S(eward)
Lee-Hamilton, Eugene (Jacob) 1845-1907 **TCLC 22**
See also CA 117
Leet, Judith 1935- **CLC 11**
Le Fanu, Joseph Sheridan 1814-1873**NCLC 9, 58; DAM POP; SSC 14**
See also DLB 21, 70, 159, 178
<indexbody>**Leffland, Ella** 1931- **CLC 19**
See also CA 29-32R; CANR 35, 78; DLBY 84; INT CANR-35; SATA 65
Leger, Alexis
See Leger, (Marie-Rene Auguste) Alexis Saint-Leger
Leger, (Marie-Rene Auguste) Alexis Saint-Leger 1887-1975 **CLC 4, 11, 46; DAM POET; PC 23**
See also CA 13-16R; 61-64; CANR 43; MTCW 1
Leger, Saintleger
See Leger, (Marie-Rene Auguste) Alexis Saint-Leger
Le Guin, Ursula K(roeber) 1929- **CLC 8, 13, 22, 45, 71; DAB; DAC; DAM MST, POP; SSC 12**
See also AAYA 9, 27; AITN 1; CA 21-24R; CANR 9, 32, 52, 74; CDALB 1968-1988; CLR 3, 28; DLB 8, 52; INT CANR-32; JRDA; MAICYA; MTCW 1, 2; SATA 4, 52, 99
Lehmann, Rosamond (Nina) 1901-1990**CLC 5**
See also CA 77-80; 131; CANR 8, 73; DLB 15; MTCW 2
Leiber, Fritz (Reuter, Jr.) 1910-1992 **CLC 25**
See also CA 45-48; 139; CANR 2, 40; DLB 8; MTCW 1, 2; SATA 45; SATA-Obit 73
Leibniz, Gottfried Wilhelm von 1646-1716**LC 35**
See also DLB 168
Leimbach, Martha 1963-
See Leimbach, Marti
See also CA 130
Leimbach, Marti **CLC 65**
See also Leimbach, Martha
Leino, Eino **TCLC 24**
See also Loennbohm, Armas Eino Leopold
Leiris, Michel (Julien) 1901-1990 **CLC 61**
See also CA 119; 128; 132
Leithauser, Brad 1953- **CLC 27**
See also CA 107; CANR 27; DLB 120
Lelchuk, Alan 1938- **CLC 5**
See also CA 45-48; CAAS 20; CANR 1, 70
Lem, Stanislaw 1921- **CLC 8, 15, 40**
See also CA 105; CAAS 1; CANR 32; MTCW 1
Lemann, Nancy 1956- **CLC 39**
See also CA 118; 136
Lemonnier, (Antoine Louis) Camille 1844-1913 **TCLC 22**
See also CA 121
Lenau, Nikolaus 1802-1850 **NCLC 16**
L'Engle, Madeleine (Camp Franklin) 1918- **CLC 12; DAM POP**
See also AAYA 28; AITN 2; CA 1-4R; CANR 3, 21, 39, 66; CLR 1, 14, 57; DLB 52; JRDA; MAICYA; MTCW 1, 2; SAAS 15; SATA 1, 27, 75
Lengyel, Jozsef 1896-1975 **CLC 7**
See also CA 85-88; 57-60; CANR 71
Lenin 1870-1924
See Lenin, V. I.
See also CA 121; 168
Lenin, V. I. **TCLC 67**
See also Lenin
Lennon, John (Ono) 1940-1980 **CLC 12, 35**
See also CA 102
Lennox, Charlotte Ramsay 1729(?)-1804 **NCLC 23**
See also DLB 39
Lentricchia, Frank (Jr.) 1940- **CLC 34**
See also CA 25-28R; CANR 19
Lenz, Siegfried 1926- **CLC 27; SSC 33**
See also CA 89-92; CANR 80; DLB 75
Leonard, Elmore (John, Jr.) 1925-**CLC 28, 34, 71, 120; DAM POP**
See also AAYA 22; AITN 1; BEST 89:1, 90:4; CA 81-84; CANR 12, 28, 53, 76; DLB 173; INT CANR-28; MTCW 1, 2
Leonard, Hugh **CLC 19**
See also Byrne, John Keyes
See also DLB 13
Leonov, Leonid (Maximovich) 1899-1994 **CLC 92; DAM NOV**
See also CA 129; CANR 74, 76; MTCW 1, 2
Leopardi, (Conte) Giacomo 1798-1837**NCLC 22**

Maas, Peter 1929- **CLC 29**
See also CA 93-96; INT 93-96; MTCW 2
Macaulay, Rose 1881-1958 **TCLC 7, 44**
See also CA 104; DLB 36
Macaulay, Thomas Babington 1800-1859 **NCLC 42**
See also CDBLB 1832-1890; DLB 32, 55
MacBeth, George (Mann) 1932-1992**CLC 2, 5, 9**
See also CA 25-28R; 136; CANR 61, 66; DLB 40; MTCW 1; SATA 4; SATA-Obit 70
MacCaig, Norman (Alexander) 1910-**CLC 36; DAB; DAM POET**
See also CA 9-12R; CANR 3, 34; DLB 27
MacCarthy, Sir(Charles Otto) Desmond 1877-1952 **TCLC 36**
See also CA 167
MacDiarmid, HughCLC 2, 4, 11, 19, 63; PC 9
See also Grieve, C(hristopher) M(urray)
See also CDBLB 1945-1960; DLB 20
MacDonald, Anson
See Heinlein, Robert A(nson)
Macdonald, Cynthia 1928- **CLC 13, 19**
See also CA 49-52; CANR 4, 44; DLB 105
MacDonald, George 1824-1905 **TCLC 9**
See also CA 106; 137; CANR 80; DLB 18, 163, 178; MAICYA; SATA 33, 100
Macdonald, John
See Millar, Kenneth
MacDonald, John D(ann) 1916-1986 **CLC 3, 27, 44; DAM NOV, POP**
See also CA 1-4R; 121; CANR 1, 19, 60; DLB 8; DLBY 86; MTCW 1, 2
Macdonald, John Ross
See Millar, Kenneth
Macdonald, Ross **CLC 1, 2, 3, 14, 34, 41**
See also Millar, Kenneth
See also DLBD 6
MacDougal, John
See Blish, James (Benjamin)
MacEwen, Gwendolyn (Margaret) 1941-1987 **CLC 13, 55**
See also CA 9-12R; 124; CANR 7, 22; DLB 53; SATA 50; SATA-Obit 55
Macha, Karel Hynek 1810-1846 **NCLC 46**
Machado (y Ruiz), Antonio 1875-1939**TCLC 3**
See also CA 104; 174; DLB 108; HW 2
Machado de Assis, Joaquim Maria 1839-1908 **TCLC 10; BLC 2; HLCS 1; SSC 24**
See also CA 107; 153
Machen, Arthur **TCLC 4; SSC 20**
See also Jones, Arthur Llewellyn
See also DLB 36, 156, 178
Machiavelli, Niccolo 1469-1527**LC 8, 36; DA; DAB; DAC; DAM MST; WLCS**
MacInnes, Colin 1914-1976 **CLC 4, 23**
See also CA 69-72; 65-68; CANR 21; DLB 14; MTCW 1, 2
MacInnes, Helen (Clark) 1907-1985 **CLC 27, 39; DAM POP**
See also CA 1-4R; 117; CANR 1, 28, 58; DLB 87; MTCW 1, 2; SATA 22; SATA-Obit 44
Mackay, Mary 1855-1924
See Corelli, Marie
See also CA 118
Mackenzie, Compton (Edward Montague) 1883-1972 **CLC 18**
See also CA 21-22; 37-40R; CAP 2; DLB 34, 100
Mackenzie, Henry 1745-1831 **NCLC 41**
See also DLB 39
Mackintosh, Elizabeth 1896(?)-1952
See Tey, Josephine
See also CA 110
MacLaren, James
See Grieve, C(hristopher) M(urray)
Mac Laverty, Bernard 1942- **CLC 31**
See also CA 116; 118; CANR 43; INT 118
MacLean, Alistair (Stuart) 1922(?)-1987**CLC 3, 13, 50, 63; DAM POP**
See also CA 57-60; 121; CANR 28, 61; MTCW 1; SATA 23; SATA-Obit 50
Maclean, Norman (Fitzroy) 1902-1990 **CLC 78; DAM POP; SSC 13**
See also CA 102; 132; CANR 49; DLB 206
MacLeish, Archibald 1892-1982**CLC 3, 8, 14, 68; DAM POET**
See also CA 9-12R; 106; CANR 33, 63; CDALBS; DLB 4, 7, 45; DLBY 82; MTCW 1, 2
MacLennan, (John) Hugh 1907-1990 **CLC 2, 14, 92; DAC; DAM MST**
See also CA 5-8R; 142; CANR 33; DLB 68; MTCW 1, 2
MacLeod, Alistair 1936-**CLC 56; DAC; DAM MST**
See also CA 123; DLB 60; MTCW 2
Macleod, Fiona
See Sharp, William
MacNeice, (Frederick) Louis 1907-1963 **CLC 1, 4, 10, 53; DAB; DAM POET**
See also CA 85-88; CANR 61; DLB 10, 20; MTCW 1, 2
MacNeill, Dand
See Fraser, George MacDonald
Macpherson, James 1736-1796 **LC 29**
See also Ossian
See also DLB 109
Macpherson, (Jean) Jay 1931- **CLC 14**
See also CA 5-8R; DLB 53
MacShane, Frank 1927- **CLC 39**
See also CA 9-12R; CANR 3, 33; DLB 111
Macumber, Mari
See Sandoz, Mari(e Susette)
Madach, Imre 1823-1864 **NCLC 19**
Madden, (Jerry) David 1933- **CLC 5, 15**
See also CA 1-4R; CAAS 3; CANR 4, 45; DLB 6; MTCW 1
Maddern, Al(an)
See Ellison, Harlan (Jay)
Madhubuti, Haki R. 1942-**CLC 6, 73; BLC 2; DAM MULT, POET; PC 5**
See also Lee, Don L.
See also BW 2, 3; CA 73-76; CANR 24, 51, 73; DLB 5, 41; DLBD 8; MTCW 2
Maepenn, Hugh
See Kuttner, Henry
Maepenn, K. H.
See Kuttner, Henry
Maeterlinck, Maurice 1862-1949 **TCLC 3; DAM DRAM**
See also CA 104; 136; CANR 80; DLB 192; SATA 66
Maginn, William 1794-1842 **NCLC 8**
See also DLB 110, 159
Mahapatra, Jayanta 1928- **CLC 33; DAM MULT**
See also CA 73-76; CAAS 9; CANR 15, 33, 66
Mahfouz, Naguib (Abdel Aziz Al-Sabilgi) 1911(?)-
See Mahfuz, Najib
See also BEST 89:2; CA 128; CANR 55; DAM NOV; MTCW 1, 2
Mahfuz, Najib **CLC 52, 55**
See also Mahfouz, Naguib (Abdel Aziz Al-Sabilgi)
See also DLBY 88
Mahon, Derek 1941- **CLC 27**
See also CA 113; 128; DLB 40
Mailer, Norman 1923-**CLC 1, 2, 3, 4, 5, 8, 11, 14, 28, 39, 74, 111; DA; DAB; DAC; DAM MST, NOV, POP**
See also AITN 2; CA 9-12R; CABS 1; CANR 28, 74, 77; CDALB 1968-1988; DLB 2, 16, 28, 185; DLBD 3; DLBY 80, 83; MTCW 1, 2
Maillet, Antonine 1929- **CLC 54, 118; DAC**
See also CA 115; 120; CANR 46, 74, 77; DLB 60; INT 120; MTCW 2
Mais, Roger 1905-1955 **TCLC 8**
See also BW 1, 3; CA 105; 124; DLB 125; MTCW 1
Maistre, Joseph de 1753-1821 **NCLC 37**
Maitland, Frederic 1850-1906 **TCLC 65**
Maitland, Sara (Louise) 1950- **CLC 49**
See also CA 69-72; CANR 13, 59
Major, Clarence 1936-**CLC 3, 19, 48; BLC 2; DAM MULT**
See also BW 2, 3; CA 21-24R; CAAS 6; CANR 13, 25, 53; DLB 33
Major, Kevin (Gerald) 1949- **CLC 26; DAC**
See also AAYA 16; CA 97-100; CANR 21, 38; CLR 11; DLB 60; INT CANR-21; JRDA; MAICYA; SATA 32, 82
Maki, James
See Ozu, Yasujiro
Malabaila, Damiano
See Levi, Primo
Malamud, Bernard 1914-1986**CLC 1, 2, 3, 5, 8, 9, 11, 18, 27, 44, 78, 85; DA; DAB; DAC; DAM MST, NOV, POP; SSC 15; WLC**
See also AAYA 16; CA 5-8R; 118; CABS 1; CANR 28, 62; CDALB 1941-1968; DLB 2, 28, 152; DLBY 80, 86; MTCW 1, 2
Malan, Herman
See Bosman, Herman Charles; Bosman, Herman Charles
Malaparte, Curzio 1898-1957 **TCLC 52**
Malcolm, Dan
See Silverberg, Robert
Malcolm X **CLC 82, 117; BLC 2; WLCS**
<See also Little, Malcolm
Malherbe, Francois de 1555-1628 **LC 5**
Mallarme, Stephane 1842-1898 **NCLC 4, 41; DAM POET; PC 4**
Mallet-Joris, Francoise 1930- **CLC 11**
See also CA 65-68; CANR 17; DLB 83
Malley, Ern
See McAuley, James Phillip
Mallowan, Agatha Christie
See Christie, Agatha (Mary Clarissa)
Maloff, Saul 1922- **CLC 5**
See also CA 33-36R
Malone, Louis
See MacNeice, (Frederick) Louis
Malone, Michael (Christopher) 1942-**CLC 43**
See also CA 77-80; CANR 14, 32, 57
Malory, (Sir) Thomas 1410(?)-1471(?)**LC 11; DA; DAB; DAC; DAM MST; WLCS**
See also CDBLB Before 1660; DLB 146; SATA 59; SATA-Brief 33
Malouf, (George Joseph) David 1934-**CLC 28, 86**
See also CA 124; CANR 50, 76; MTCW 2
Malraux, (Georges-)Andre 1901-1976**CLC 1, 4, 9, 13, 15, 57; DAM NOV**
See also CA 21-22; 69-72; CANR 34, 58; CAP 2; DLB 72; MTCW 1, 2

See also CA 25-28R; CANR 61; DLB 14, 207
McIlwraith, Maureen Mollie Hunter
See Hunter, Mollie
See also SATA 2
McInerney, Jay 1955-**CLC 34, 112; DAM POP**
See also AAYA 18; CA 116; 123; CANR 45, 68; INT 123; MTCW 2
McIntyre, Vonda N(eel) 1948- **CLC 18**
See also CA 81-84; CANR 17, 34, 69; MTCW 1
McKay, ClaudeTCLC 7, 41; BLC 3; DAB; PC 2
See also McKay, Festus Claudius
See also DLB 4, 45, 51, 117
McKay, Festus Claudius 1889-1948
See McKay, Claude
See also BW 1, 3; CA 104; 124; CANR 73; DA; DAC; DAM MST, MULT, NOV, POET; MTCW 1, 2; WLC
McKuen, Rod 1933- **CLC 1, 3**
See also AITN 1; CA 41-44R; CANR 40
McLoughlin, R. B.
See Mencken, H(enry) L(ouis)
McLuhan, (Herbert) Marshall 1911-1980 **CLC 37, 83**
See also CA 9-12R; 102; CANR 12, 34, 61; DLB 88; INT CANR-12; MTCW 1, 2
McMillan, Terry (L.) 1951- **CLC 50, 61, 112; BLCS; DAM MULT, NOV, POP**
See also AAYA 21; BW 2, 3; CA 140; CANR 60; MTCW 2
McMurtry, Larry (Jeff) 1936-**CLC 2, 3, 7, 11, 27, 44; DAM NOV, POP**
See also AAYA 15; AITN 2; BEST 89:2; CA 5-8R; CANR 19, 43, 64; CDALB 1968-1988; DLB 2, 143; DLBY 80, 87; MTCW 1, 2
McNally, T. M. 1961- **CLC 82**
McNally, Terrence 1939- **CLC 4, 7, 41, 91; DAM DRAM**
See also CA 45-48; CANR 2, 56; DLB 7; MTCW 2
McNamer, Deirdre 1950- **CLC 70**
McNeal, Tom **CLC 119**
McNeile, Herman Cyril 1888-1937
See Sapper
See also DLB 77
McNickle, (William) D'Arcy 1904-1977 **C L C 89; DAM MULT**
See also CA 9-12R; 85-88; CANR 5, 45; DLB 175, 212; NNAL; SATA-Obit 22
McPhee, John (Angus) 1931- **CLC 36**
See also BEST 90:1; CA 65-68; CANR 20, 46, 64, 69; DLB 185; MTCW 1, 2
McPherson, James Alan 1943- **CLC 19, 77; BLCS**
See also BW 1, 3; CA 25-28R; CAAS 17; CANR 24, 74; DLB 38; MTCW 1, 2
McPherson, William (Alexander) 1933- **C L C 34**
See also CA 69-72; CANR 28; INT CANR-28
Mead, George Herbert 1873-1958 **TCLC 89**
Mead, Margaret 1901-1978 **CLC 37**
See also AITN 1; CA 1-4R; 81-84; CANR 4; MTCW 1, 2; SATA-Obit 20
Meaker, Marijane (Agnes) 1927-
See Kerr, M. E.
See also CA 107; CANR 37, 63; INT 107; JRDA; MAICYA; MTCW 1; SATA 20, 61, 99
Medoff, Mark (Howard) 1940- **CLC 6, 23; DAM DRAM**
See also AITN 1; CA 53-56; CANR 5; DLB 7; INT CANR-5
Medvedev, P. N.
See Bakhtin, Mikhail Mikhailovich
Meged, Aharon
See Megged, Aharon
Meged, Aron
See Megged, Aharon
Megged, Aharon 1920- **CLC 9**
See also CA 49-52; CAAS 13; CANR 1
Mehta, Ved (Parkash) 1934- **CLC 37**
See also CA 1-4R; CANR 2, 23, 69; MTCW 1
Melanter
See Blackmore, R(ichard) D(oddridge)
Melies, Georges 1861-1938 **TCLC 81**
Melikow, Loris
See Hofmannsthal, Hugo von
Melmoth, Sebastian
See Wilde, Oscar
Meltzer, Milton 1915- **CLC 26**
See also AAYA 8; CA 13-16R; CANR 38; CLR 13; DLB 61; JRDA; MAICYA; SAAS 1; SATA 1, 50, 80
Melville, Herman 1819-1891 **NCLC 3, 12, 29, 45, 49; DA; DAB; DAC; DAM MST, NOV; SSC 1, 17; WLC**
See also AAYA 25; CDALB 1640-1865; DLB 3, 74; SATA 59
Menander c. 342B.C.-c. 292B.C. **CMLC 9; DAM DRAM; DC 3**
See also DLB 176
Mencken, H(enry) L(ouis) 1880-1956 **T C L C 13**
See also CA 105; 125; CDALB 1917-1929; DLB 11, 29, 63, 137; MTCW 1, 2
Mendelsohn, Jane 1965(?)- **CLC 99**
See also CA 154
Mercer, David 1928-1980**CLC 5; DAM DRAM**
See also CA 9-12R; 102; CANR 23; DLB 13; MTCW 1
Merchant, Paul
See Ellison, Harlan (Jay)
Meredith, George 1828-1909 **TCLC 17, 43; DAM POET**
See also CA 117; 153; CANR 80; CDBLB 1832-1890; DLB 18, 35, 57, 159
Meredith, William (Morris) 1919-**CLC 4, 13, 22, 55; DAM POET**
See also CA 9-12R; CAAS 14; CANR 6, 40; DLB 5
Merezhkovsky, Dmitry Sergeyevich 1865-1941 **TCLC 29**
See also CA 169
Merimee, Prosper 1803-1870**NCLC 6, 65; SSC 7**
See also DLB 119, 192
Merkin, Daphne 1954- **CLC 44**
See also CA 123
Merlin, Arthur
See Blish, James (Benjamin)
Merrill, James (Ingram) 1926-1995**CLC 2, 3, 6, 8, 13, 18, 34, 91; DAM POET**
See also CA 13-16R; 147; CANR 10, 49, 63; DLB 5, 165; DLBY 85; INT CANR-10; MTCW 1, 2
Merriman, Alex
See Silverberg, Robert
Merriman, Brian 1747-1805 **NCLC 70**
Merritt, E. B.
See Waddington, Miriam
Merton, Thomas 1915-1968 **CLC 1, 3, 11, 34, 83; PC 10**
See also CA 5-8R; 25-28R; CANR 22, 53; DLB 48; DLBY 81; MTCW 1, 2
Merwin, W(illiam) S(tanley) 1927- **CLC 1, 2, 3, 5, 8, 13, 18, 45, 88; DAM POET**
See also CA 13-16R; CANR 15, 51; DLB 5, 169; INT CANR-15; MTCW 1, 2
Metcalf, John 1938- **CLC 37**
See also CA 113; DLB 60
Metcalf, Suzanne
See Baum, L(yman) Frank
Mew, Charlotte (Mary) 1870-1928 **TCLC 8**
See also CA 105; DLB 19, 135
Mewshaw, Michael 1943- **CLC 9**
See also CA 53-56; CANR 7, 47; DLBY 80
Meyer, June
See Jordan, June
Meyer, Lynn
See Slavitt, David R(ytman)
Meyer-Meyrink, Gustav 1868-1932
See Meyrink, Gustav
See also CA 117
Meyers, Jeffrey 1939- **CLC 39**
See also CA 73-76; CANR 54; DLB 111
Meynell, Alice (Christina Gertrude Thompson) 1847-1922 **TCLC 6**
See also CA 104; DLB 19, 98
Meyrink, Gustav **TCLC 21**
See also Meyer-Meyrink, Gustav
See also DLB 81
Michaels, Leonard 1933- **CLC 6, 25; SSC 16**
See also CA 61-64; CANR 21, 62; DLB 130; MTCW 1
Michaux, Henri 1899-1984 **CLC 8, 19**
See also CA 85-88; 114
Micheaux, Oscar (Devereaux) 1884-1951 **TCLC 76**
See also BW 3; CA 174; DLB 50
Michelangelo 1475-1564 **LC 12**
Michelet, Jules 1798-1874 **NCLC 31**
Michels, Robert 1876-1936 **TCLC 88**
Michener, James A(lbert) 1907(?)-1997 **C L C 1, 5, 11, 29, 60, 109; DAM NOV, POP**
See also AAYA 27; AITN 1; BEST 90:1; CA 5-8R; 161; CANR 21, 45, 68; DLB 6; MTCW 1, 2
Mickiewicz, Adam 1798-1855 **NCLC 3**
Middleton, Christopher 1926- **CLC 13**
See also CA 13-16R; CANR 29, 54; DLB 40
Middleton, Richard (Barham) 1882-1911 **TCLC 56**
See also DLB 156
Middleton, Stanley 1919- **CLC 7, 38**
See also CA 25-28R; CAAS 23; CANR 21, 46; DLB 14
Middleton, Thomas 1580-1627 **LC 33; DAM DRAM, MST; DC 5**
See also DLB 58
Migueis, Jose Rodrigues 1901- **CLC 10**
Mikszath, Kalman 1847-1910 **TCLC 31**
See also CA 170
Miles, Jack **CLC 100**
Miles, Josephine (Louise) 1911-1985**CLC 1, 2, 14, 34, 39; DAM POET**
See also CA 1-4R; 116; CANR 2, 55; DLB 48
Militant
See Sandburg, Carl (August)
Mill, John Stuart 1806-1873 **NCLC 11, 58**
See also CDBLB 1832-1890; DLB 55, 190
Millar, Kenneth 1915-1983 **CLC 14; DAM POP**
See also Macdonald, Ross
See also CA 9-12R; 110; CANR 16, 63; DLB 2; DLBD 6; DLBY 83; MTCW 1, 2
Millay, E. Vincent
See Millay, Edna St. Vincent
Millay, Edna St. Vincent 1892-1950 **TCLC 4,**

49; DA; DAB; DAC; DAM MST, POET; PC 6; WLCS
See also CA 104; 130; CDALB 1917-1929; DLB 45; MTCW 1, 2

Miller, Arthur 1915-**CLC 1, 2, 6, 10, 15, 26, 47, 78; DA; DAB; DAC; DAM DRAM, MST; DC 1; WLC**
See also AAYA 15; AITN 1; CA 1-4R; CABS 3; CANR 2, 30, 54, 76; CDALB 1941-1968; DLB 7; MTCW 1, 2

Miller, Henry (Valentine) 1891-1980**CLC 1, 2, 4, 9, 14, 43, 84; DA; DAB; DAC; DAM MST, NOV; WLC**
See also CA 9-12R; 97-100; CANR 33, 64; CDALB 1929-1941; DLB 4, 9; DLBY 80; MTCW 1, 2

Miller, Jason 1939(?)- **CLC 2**
See also AITN 1; CA 73-76; DLB 7

Miller, Sue 1943- **CLC 44; DAM POP**
See also BEST 90:3; CA 139; CANR 59; DLB 143

Miller, Walter M(ichael, Jr.) 1923-**CLC 4, 30**
See also CA 85-88; DLB 8

Millett, Kate 1934- **CLC 67**
See also AITN 1; CA 73-76; CANR 32, 53, 76; MTCW 1, 2

Millhauser, Steven (Lewis) 1943-**CLC 21, 54, 109**
See also CA 110; 111; CANR 63; DLB 2; INT 111; MTCW 2

Millin, Sarah Gertrude 1889-1968 **CLC 49**
See also CA 102; 93-96

Milne, A(lan) A(lexander) 1882-1956**TCLC 6, 88; DAB; DAC; DAM MST**
See also CA 104; 133; CLR 1, 26; DLB 10, 77, 100, 160; MAICYA; MTCW 1, 2; SATA 100; YABC 1

Milner, Ron(ald) 1938-**CLC 56; BLC 3; DAM MULT**
See also AITN 1; BW 1; CA 73-76; CANR 24; DLB 38; MTCW 1

Milnes, Richard Monckton 1809-1885 **NCLC 61**
See also DLB 32, 184

Milosz, Czeslaw 1911- **CLC 5, 11, 22, 31, 56, 82; DAM MST, POET; PC 8; WLCS**
See also CA 81-84; CANR 23, 51; MTCW 1, 2

Milton, John 1608-1674 **LC 9, 43; DA; DAB; DAC; DAM MST, POET; PC 19; WLC**
See also CDBLB 1660-1789; DLB 131, 151

Min, Anchee 1957- **CLC 86**
See also CA 146

Minehaha, Cornelius
See Wedekind, (Benjamin) Frank(lin)

Miner, Valerie 1947- **CLC 40**
See also CA 97-100; CANR 59

Minimo, Duca
See D'Annunzio, Gabriele

Minot, Susan 1956- **CLC 44**
See also CA 134

Minus, Ed 1938- **CLC 39**

Miranda, Javier
See Bioy Casares, Adolfo

Mirbeau, Octave 1848-1917 **TCLC 55**
See also DLB 123, 192

Miro (Ferrer), Gabriel (Francisco Victor) 1879-1930 **TCLC 5**
See also CA 104

Mishima, Yukio 1925-1970**CLC 2, 4, 6, 9, 27; DC 1; SSC 4**
See also Hiraoka, Kimitake
See also DLB 182; MTCW 2

Mistral, Frederic 1830-1914 **TCLC 51**
See also CA 122

Mistral, Gabriela **TCLC 2; HLC**
See also Godoy Alcayaga, Lucila
See also MTCW 2

Mistry, Rohinton 1952- **CLC 71; DAC**
See also CA 141

Mitchell, Clyde
See Ellison, Harlan (Jay); Silverberg, Robert

Mitchell, James Leslie 1901-1935
See Gibbon, Lewis Grassic
See also CA 104; DLB 15

Mitchell, Joni 1943- **CLC 12**
See also CA 112

Mitchell, Joseph (Quincy) 1908-1996**CLC 98**
See also CA 77-80; 152; CANR 69; DLB 185; DLBY 96

Mitchell, Margaret (Munnerlyn) 1900-1949 **TCLC 11; DAM NOV, POP**
See also AAYA 23; CA 109; 125; CANR 55; CDALBS; DLB 9; MTCW 1, 2

Mitchell, Peggy
See Mitchell, Margaret (Munnerlyn)

Mitchell, S(ilas) Weir 1829-1914 **TCLC 36**
See also CA 165; DLB 202

Mitchell, W(illiam) O(rmond) 1914-1998**CLC 25; DAC; DAM MST**
See also CA 77-80; 165; CANR 15, 43; DLB 88

Mitchell, William 1879-1936 **TCLC 81**

Mitford, Mary Russell 1787-1855 **NCLC 4**
See also DLB 110, 116

Mitford, Nancy 1904-1973 **CLC 44**
See also CA 9-12R; DLB 191

Miyamoto, (Chujo) Yuriko 1899-1951 **TCLC 37**
See also CA 170, 174; DLB 180

Miyazawa, Kenji 1896-1933 **TCLC 76**
See also CA 157

Mizoguchi, Kenji 1898-1956 **TCLC 72**
See also CA 167

Mo, Timothy (Peter) 1950(?)- **CLC 46**
See also CA 117; DLB 194; MTCW 1

Modarressi, Taghi (M.) 1931- **CLC 44**
See also CA 121; 134; INT 134

Modiano, Patrick (Jean) 1945- **CLC 18**
See also CA 85-88; CANR 17, 40; DLB 83

Moerck, Paal
See Roelvaag, O(le) E(dvart)

Mofolo, Thomas (Mokopu) 1875(?)-1948 **TCLC 22; BLC 3; DAM MULT**
See also CA 121; 153; MTCW 2

Mohr, Nicholasa 1938-**CLC 12; DAM MULT; HLC**
See also AAYA 8; CA 49-52; CANR 1, 32, 64; CLR 22; DLB 145; HW 1, 2; JRDA; SAAS 8; SATA 8, 97

Mojtabai, A(nn) G(race) 1938- **CLC 5, 9, 15, 29**
See also CA 85-88

Moliere 1622-1673**LC 10, 28; DA; DAB; DAC; DAM DRAM, MST; WLC**

Molin, Charles
See Mayne, William (James Carter)

Molnar, Ferenc 1878-1952 **TCLC 20; DAM DRAM**
See also CA 109; 153

Momaday, N(avarre) Scott 1934- **CLC 2, 19, 85, 95; DA; DAB; DAC; DAM MST, MULT, NOV, POP; PC 25; WLCS**
See also AAYA 11; CA 25-28R; CANR 14, 34, 68; CDALBS; DLB 143, 175; INT CANR-14; MTCW 1, 2; NNAL; SATA 48; SATA-Brief 30

Monette, Paul 1945-1995 **CLC 82**
See also CA 139; 147

Monroe, Harriet 1860-1936 **TCLC 12**
See also CA 109; DLB 54, 91

Monroe, Lyle
See Heinlein, Robert A(nson)

Montagu, Elizabeth 1720-1800 **NCLC 7**

Montagu, Mary (Pierrepont) Wortley 1689-1762 **LC 9; PC 16**
See also DLB 95, 101

Montagu, W. H.
See Coleridge, Samuel Taylor

Montague, John (Patrick) 1929- **CLC 13, 46**
See also CA 9-12R; CANR 9, 69; DLB 40; MTCW 1

Montaigne, Michel (Eyquem) de 1533-1592 **LC 8; DA; DAB; DAC; DAM MST; WLC**

Montale, Eugenio 1896-1981**CLC 7, 9, 18; PC 13**
See also CA 17-20R; 104; CANR 30; DLB 114; MTCW 1

Montesquieu, Charles-Louis de Secondat 1689-1755 **LC 7**

Montgomery, (Robert) Bruce 1921-1978
See Crispin, Edmund
See also CA 104

Montgomery, L(ucy) M(aud) 1874-1942 **TCLC 51; DAC; DAM MST**
See also AAYA 12; CA 108; 137; CLR 8; DLB 92; DLBD 14; JRDA; MAICYA; MTCW 2; SATA 100; YABC 1

Montgomery, Marion H., Jr. 1925- **CLC 7**
See also AITN 1; CA 1-4R; CANR 3, 48; DLB 6

Montgomery, Max
See Davenport, Guy (Mattison, Jr.)

Montherlant, Henry (Milon) de 1896-1972 **CLC 8, 19; DAM DRAM**
See also CA 85-88; 37-40R; DLB 72; MTCW 1

Monty Python
See Chapman, Graham; Cleese, John (Marwood); Gilliam, Terry (Vance); Idle, Eric; Jones, Terence Graham Parry; Palin, Michael (Edward)
See also AAYA 7

Moodie, Susanna (Strickland) 1803-1885 **NCLC 14**
See also DLB 99

Mooney, Edward 1951-
See Mooney, Ted
See also CA 130

Mooney, Ted **CLC 25**
See also Mooney, Edward

Moorcock, Michael (John) 1939-**CLC 5, 27, 58**
See also Bradbury, Edward P.
See also AAYA 26; CA 45-48; CAAS 5; CANR 2, 17, 38, 64; DLB 14; MTCW 1, 2; SATA 93

Moore, Brian 1921-1999**CLC 1, 3, 5, 7, 8, 19, 32, 90; DAB; DAC; DAM MST**
See also CA 1-4R; 174; CANR 1, 25, 42, 63; MTCW 1, 2

Moore, Edward
See Muir, Edwin

Moore, G. E. 1873-1958 **TCLC 89**

Moore, George Augustus 1852-1933**TCLC 7; SSC 19**
See also CA 104; DLB 10, 18, 57, 135

Moore, Lorrie **CLC 39, 45, 68**
See also Moore, Marie Lorena

Moore, Marianne (Craig) 1887-1972**CLC 1, 2, 4, 8, 10, 13, 19, 47; DA; DAB; DAC; DAM**

See also CA 118; DLB 149
Musgrave, Susan 1951- **CLC 13, 54**
See also CA 69-72; CANR 45
Musil, Robert (Edler von) 1880-1942 **TCLC 12, 68; SSC 18**
See also CA 109; CANR 55; DLB 81, 124; MTCW 2
Muske, Carol 1945- **CLC 90**
See also Muske-Dukes, Carol (Anne)
<indexbody>**Muske-Dukes, Carol (Anne)** 1945-
See Muske, Carol
See also CA 65-68; CANR 32, 70
Musset, (Louis Charles) Alfred de 1810-1857 **NCLC 7**
See also DLB 192
My Brother's Brother
See Chekhov, Anton (Pavlovich)
Myers, L(eopold) H(amilton) 1881-1944 **TCLC 59**
See also CA 157; DLB 15
Myers, Walter Dean 1937- **CLC 35; BLC 3; DAM MULT, NOV**
See also AAYA 4, 23; BW 2, 3; CA 33-36R; CANR 20, 42, 67; CLR 4, 16, 35; DLB 33; INT CANR-20; JRDA; MAICYA; MTCW 2; SAAS 2; SATA 41, 71; SATA-Brief 27
Myers, Walter M.
See Myers, Walter Dean
Myles, Symon
See Follett, Ken(neth Martin)
Nabokov, Vladimir (Vladimirovich) 1899-1977 **CLC 1, 2, 3, 6, 8, 11, 15, 23, 44, 46, 64; DA; DAB; DAC; DAM MST, NOV; SSC 11; WLC**
See also CA 5-8R; 69-72; CANR 20; CDALB 1941-1968; DLB 2; DLBD 3; DLBY 80, 91; MTCW 1, 2
Nagai Kafu 1879-1959 **TCLC 51**
See also Nagai Sokichi
See also DLB 180
Nagai Sokichi 1879-1959
See Nagai Kafu
See also CA 117
Nagy, Laszlo 1925-1978 **CLC 7**
See also CA 129; 112
Naidu, Sarojini 1879-1943 **TCLC 80**
Naipaul, Shiva(dhar Srinivasa) 1945-1985 **CLC 32, 39; DAM NOV**
See also CA 110; 112; 116; CANR 33; DLB 157; DLBY 85; MTCW 1, 2
Naipaul, V(idiadhar) S(urajprasad) 1932- **CLC 4, 7, 9, 13, 18, 37, 105; DAB; DAC; DAM MST, NOV**
See also CA 1-4R; CANR 1, 33, 51; CDBLB 1960 to Present; DLB 125, 204, 206; DLBY 85; MTCW 1, 2
Nakos, Lilika 1899(?)- **CLC 29**
Narayan, R(asipuram) K(rishnaswami) 1906- **CLC 7, 28, 47; DAM NOV; SSC 25**
See also CA 81-84; CANR 33, 61; MTCW 1, 2; SATA 62
Nash, (Frediric) Ogden 1902-1971 **CLC 23; DAM POET; PC 21**
See also CA 13-14; 29-32R; CANR 34, 61; CAP 1; DLB 11; MAICYA; MTCW 1, 2; SATA 2, 46
Nashe, Thomas 1567-1601(?) **LC 41**
See also DLB 167
Nashe, Thomas 1567-1601 **LC 41**
Nathan, Daniel
See Dannay, Frederic
Nathan, George Jean 1882-1958 **TCLC 18**
See also Hatteras, Owen
See also CA 114; 169; DLB 137
Natsume, Kinnosuke 1867-1916
See Natsume, Soseki
See also CA 104
Natsume, Soseki 1867-1916 **TCLC 2, 10**
See also Natsume, Kinnosuke
See also DLB 180
Natti, (Mary) Lee 1919-
See Kingman, Lee
See also CA 5-8R; CANR 2
Naylor, Gloria 1950-**CLC 28, 52; BLC 3; DA; DAC; DAM MST, MULT, NOV, POP; WLCS**
See also AAYA 6; BW 2, 3; CA 107; CANR 27, 51, 74; DLB 173; MTCW 1, 2
Neihardt, John Gneisenau 1881-1973**CLC 32**
See also CA 13-14; CANR 65; CAP 1; DLB 9, 54
Nekrasov, Nikolai Alekseevich 1821-1878 **NCLC 11**
Nelligan, Emile 1879-1941 **TCLC 14**
See also CA 114; DLB 92
Nelson, Willie 1933- **CLC 17**
See also CA 107
Nemerov, Howard (Stanley) 1920-1991**CLC 2, 6, 9, 36; DAM POET; PC 24**
See also CA 1-4R; 134; CABS 2; CANR 1, 27, 53; DLB 5, 6; DLBY 83; INT CANR-27; MTCW 1, 2
Neruda, Pablo 1904-1973**CLC 1, 2, 5, 7, 9, 28, 62; DA; DAB; DAC; DAM MST, MULT, POET; HLC; PC 4; WLC**
See also CA 19-20; 45-48; CAP 2; HW 1; MTCW 1, 2
Nerval, Gerard de 1808-1855**NCLC 1, 67; PC 13; SSC 18**
Nervo, (Jose) Amado (Ruiz de) 1870-1919 **TCLC 11; HLCS 1**
See also CA 109; 131; HW 1
Nessi, Pio Baroja y
See Baroja (y Nessi), Pio
Nestroy, Johann 1801-1862 **NCLC 42**
See also DLB 133
Netterville, Luke
See O'Grady, Standish (James)
Neufeld, John (Arthur) 1938- **CLC 17**
See also AAYA 11; CA 25-28R; CANR 11, 37, 56; CLR 52; MAICYA; SAAS 3; SATA 6, 81
Neville, Emily Cheney 1919- **CLC 12**
See also CA 5-8R; CANR 3, 37; JRDA; MAICYA; SAAS 2; SATA 1
Newbound, Bernard Slade 1930-
See Slade, Bernard
See also CA 81-84; CANR 49; DAM DRAM
Newby, P(ercy) H(oward) 1918-1997 **CLC 2, 13; DAM NOV**
See also CA 5-8R; 161; CANR 32, 67; DLB 15; MTCW 1
Newlove, Donald 1928- **CLC 6**
See also CA 29-32R; CANR 25
<indexb**Newlove, John (Herbert)** 1938- **CLC 14**
See also CA 21-24R; CANR 9, 25
Newman, Charles 1938- **CLC 2, 8**
See also CA 21-24R
Newman, Edwin (Harold) 1919- **CLC 14**
See also AITN 1; CA 69-72; CANR 5
Newman, John Henry 1801-1890 **NCLC 38**
See also DLB 18, 32, 55
Newton, (Sir)Isaac 1642-1727 **LC 35**
Newton, Suzanne 1936- **CLC 35**
See also CA 41-44R; CANR 14; JRDA; SATA 5, 77
Nexo, Martin Andersen 1869-1954 **TCLC 43**
Nezval, Vitezslav 1900-1958 **TCLC 44**
See also CA 123
Ng, Fae Myenne 1957(?)- **CLC 81**
See also CA 146
Ngema, Mbongeni 1955- **CLC 57**
See also BW 2; CA 143
Ngugi, James T(hiong'o) **CLC 3, 7, 13**
See also Ngugi wa Thiong'o
Ngugi wa Thiong'o 1938- **CLC 36; BLC 3; DAM MULT, NOV**
See also Ngugi, James T(hiong'o)
See also BW 2; CA 81-84; CANR 27, 58; DLB 125; MTCW 1, 2
Nichol, B(arrie) P(hillip) 1944-1988 **CLC 18**
See also CA 53-56; DLB 53; SATA 66
Nichols, John (Treadwell) 1940- **CLC 38**
See also CA 9-12R; CAAS 2; CANR 6, 70; DLBY 82
Nichols, Leigh
See Koontz, Dean R(ay)
Nichols, Peter (Richard) 1927- **CLC 5, 36, 65**
See also CA 104; CANR 33; DLB 13; MTCW 1
Nicolas, F. R. E.
See Freeling, Nicolas
Niedecker, Lorine 1903-1970 **CLC 10, 42; DAM POET**
See also CA 25-28; CAP 2; DLB 48
Nietzsche, Friedrich (Wilhelm) 1844-1900 **TCLC 10, 18, 55**
See also CA 107; 121; DLB 129
Nievo, Ippolito 1831-1861 **NCLC 22**
Nightingale, Anne Redmon 1943-
See Redmon, Anne
See also CA 103
Nightingale, Florence 1820-1910 **TCLC 85**
See also DLB 166
Nik. T. O.
See Annensky, Innokenty (Fyodorovich)
Nin, Anais 1903-1977 **CLC 1, 4, 8, 11, 14, 60; DAM NOV, POP; SSC 10**
See also AITN 2; CA 13-16R; 69-72; CANR 22, 53; DLB 2, 4, 152; MTCW 1, 2
Nishida, Kitaro 1870-1945 **TCLC 83**
Nishiwaki, Junzaburo 1894-1982 **PC 15**
See also CA 107
Nissenson, Hugh 1933- **CLC 4, 9**
See also CA 17-20R; CANR 27; DLB 28
Niven, Larry **CLC 8**
See also Niven, Laurence Van Cott
See also AAYA 27; DLB 8
Niven, Laurence Van Cott 1938-
See Niven, Larry
See also CA 21-24R; CAAS 12; CANR 14, 44, 66; DAM POP; MTCW 1, 2; SATA 95
Nixon, Agnes Eckhardt 1927- **CLC 21**
See also CA 110
Nizan, Paul 1905-1940 **TCLC 40**
See also CA 161; DLB 72
Nkosi, Lewis 1936- **CLC 45; BLC 3; DAM MULT**
See also BW 1, 3; CA 65-68; CANR 27; DLB 157
Nodier, (Jean) Charles (Emmanuel) 1780-1844 **NCLC 19**
See also DLB 119
Noguchi, Yone 1875-1947 **TCLC 80**
Nolan, Christopher 1965- **CLC 58**
See also CA 111
Noon, Jeff 1957- **CLC 91**

See also CA 148
Norden, Charles
See Durrell, Lawrence (George)
Nordhoff, Charles (Bernard) 1887-1947 **TCLC 23**
See also CA 108; DLB 9; SATA 23
Norfolk, Lawrence 1963- **CLC 76**
See also CA 144
Norman, Marsha 1947-**CLC 28; DAM DRAM; DC 8**
See also CA 105; CABS 3; CANR 41; DLBY 84
Normyx
See Douglas, (George) Norman
Norris, Frank 1870-1902 **SSC 28**
See also Norris, (Benjamin) Frank(lin, Jr.)
See also CDALB 1865-1917; DLB 12, 71, 186
Norris, (Benjamin) Frank(lin, Jr.) 1870-1902 **TCLC 24**
See also Norris, Frank
See also CA 110; 160
Norris, Leslie 1921- **CLC 14**
See also CA 11-12; CANR 14; CAP 1; DLB 27
North, Andrew
See Norton, Andre
North, Anthony
See Koontz, Dean R(ay)
North, Captain George
See Stevenson, Robert Louis (Balfour)
North, Milou
See Erdrich, Louise
Northrup, B. A.
See Hubbard, L(afayette) Ron(ald)
North Staffs
See Hulme, T(homas) E(rnest)
Norton, Alice Mary
See Norton, Andre
See also MAICYA; SATA 1, 43
Norton, Andre 1912- **CLC 12**
See also Norton, Alice Mary
See also AAYA 14; CA 1-4R; CANR 68; CLR 50; DLB 8, 52; JRDA; MTCW 1; SATA 91
Norton, Caroline 1808-1877 **NCLC 47**
See also DLB 21, 159, 199
Norway, Nevil Shute 1899-1960
See Shute, Nevil
See also CA 102; 93-96; MTCW 2
Norwid, Cyprian Kamil 1821-1883 **NCLC 17**
Nosille, Nabrah
See Ellison, Harlan (Jay)
Nossack, Hans Erich 1901-1978 **CLC 6**
<indexhSee also CA 93-96; 85-88; DLB 69
Nostradamus 1503-1566 **LC 27**
Nosu, Chuji
See Ozu, Yasujiro
Notenburg, Eleanora (Genrikhovna) von
See Guro, Elena
Nova, Craig 1945- **CLC 7, 31**
See also CA 45-48; CANR 2, 53
Novak, Joseph
See Kosinski, Jerzy (Nikodem)
Novalis 1772-1801 **NCLC 13**
See also DLB 90
Novis, Emile
See Weil, Simone (Adolphine)
Nowlan, Alden (Albert) 1933-1983 **CLC 15; DAC; DAM MST**
See also CA 9-12R; CANR 5; DLB 53
Noyes, Alfred 1880-1958 **TCLC 7**
See also CA 104; DLB 20
Nunn, Kem **CLC 34**
See also CA 159
Nye, Robert 1939- **CLC 13, 42; DAM NOV**
See also CA 33-36R; CANR 29, 67; DLB 14; MTCW 1; SATA 6
Nyro, Laura 1947- **CLC 17**
Oates, Joyce Carol 1938-**CLC 1, 2, 3, 6, 9, 11, 15, 19, 33, 52, 108; DA; DAB; DAC; DAM MST, NOV, POP; SSC 6; WLC**
See also AAYA 15; AITN 1; BEST 89:2; CA 5-8R; CANR 25, 45, 74; CDALB 1968-1988; DLB 2, 5, 130; DLBY 81; INT CANR-25; MTCW 1, 2
O'Brien, Darcy 1939-1998 **CLC 11**
See also CA 21-24R; 167; CANR 8, 59
O'Brien, E. G.
See Clarke, Arthur C(harles)
O'Brien, Edna 1936- **CLC 3, 5, 8, 13, 36, 65, 116; DAM NOV; SSC 10**
See also CA 1-4R; CANR 6, 41, 65; CDBLB 1960 to Present; DLB 14; MTCW 1, 2
O'Brien, Fitz-James 1828-1862 **NCLC 21**
See also DLB 74
O'Brien, Flann **CLC 1, 4, 5, 7, 10, 47**
See also O Nuallain, Brian
O'Brien, Richard 1942- **CLC 17**
See also CA 124
O'Brien, (William) Tim(othy) 1946- **CLC 7, 19, 40, 103; DAM POP**
See also AAYA 16; CA 85-88; CANR 40, 58; CDALBS; DLB 152; DLBD 9; DLBY 80; MTCW 2
Obstfelder, Sigbjoern 1866-1900 **TCLC 23**
See also CA 123
O'Casey, Sean 1880-1964 **CLC 1, 5, 9, 11, 15, 88; DAB; DAC; DAM DRAM, MST; WLCS**
See also CA 89-92; CANR 62; CDBLB 1914-1945; DLB 10; MTCW 1, 2
O'Cathasaigh, Sean
See O'Casey, Sean
Ochs, Phil 1940-1976 **CLC 17**
See also CA 65-68
O'Connor, Edwin (Greene) 1918-1968 **CLC 14**
See also CA 93-96; 25-28R
O'Connor, (Mary) Flannery 1925-1964 **CLC 1, 2, 3, 6, 10, 13, 15, 21, 66, 104; DA; DAB; DAC; DAM MST, NOV; SSC 1, 23; WLC**
See also AAYA 7; CA 1-4R; CANR 3, 41; CDALB 1941-1968; DLB 2, 152; DLBD 12; DLBY 80; MTCW 1, 2
O'Connor, Frank **CLC 23; SSC 5**
See also O'Donovan, Michael John
See also DLB 162
O'Dell, Scott 1898-1989 **CLC 30**
See also AAYA 3; CA 61-64; 129; CANR 12, 30; CLR 1, 16; DLB 52; JRDA; MAICYA; SATA 12, 60
Odets, Clifford 1906-1963 **CLC 2, 28, 98; DAM DRAM; DC 6**
See also CA 85-88; CANR 62; DLB 7, 26; MTCW 1, 2
O'Doherty, Brian 1934- **CLC 76**
See also CA 105
O'Donnell, K. M.
See Malzberg, Barry N(athaniel)
O'Donnell, Lawrence
See Kuttner, Henry
O'Donovan, Michael John 1903-1966 **CLC 14**
See also O'Connor, Frank
See also CA 93-96
Oe, Kenzaburo 1935- **CLC 10, 36, 86; DAM NOV; SSC 20**
See also CA 97-100; CANR 36, 50, 74; DLB 182; DLBY 94; MTCW 1, 2
O'Faolain, Julia 1932- **CLC 6, 19, 47, 108**
See also CA 81-84; CAAS 2; CANR 12, 61; DLB 14; MTCW 1
O'Faolain, Sean 1900-1991 **CLC 1, 7, 14, 32, 70; SSC 13**
See also CA 61-64; 134; CANR 12, 66; DLB 15, 162; MTCW 1, 2
O'Flaherty, Liam 1896-1984 **CLC 5, 34; SSC 6**
See also CA 101; 113; CANR 35; DLB 36, 162; DLBY 84; MTCW 1, 2
Ogilvy, Gavin
See Barrie, J(ames) M(atthew)
O'Grady, Standish (James) 1846-1928 **TCLC 5**
See also CA 104; 157
O'Grady, Timothy 1951- **CLC 59**
See also CA 138
O'Hara, Frank 1926-1966 **CLC 2, 5, 13, 78; DAM POET**
See also CA 9-12R; 25-28R; CANR 33; DLB 5, 16, 193; MTCW 1, 2
O'Hara, John (Henry) 1905-1970 **CLC 1, 2, 3, 6, 11, 42; DAM NOV; SSC 15**
See also CA 5-8R; 25-28R; CANR 31, 60; CDALB 1929-1941; DLB 9, 86; DLBD 2; MTCW 1, 2
O Hehir, Diana 1922- **CLC 41**
See also CA 93-96
Okigbo, Christopher (Ifenayichukwu) 1932-1967 **CLC 25, 84; BLC 3; DAM MULT, POET; PC 7**
See also BW 1, 3; CA 77-80; CANR 74; DLB 125; MTCW 1, 2
Okri, Ben 1959- **CLC 87**
See also BW 2, 3; CA 130; 138; CANR 65; DLB 157; INT 138; MTCW 2
Olds, Sharon 1942- **CLC 32, 39, 85; DAM POET; PC 22**
See also CA 101; CANR 18, 41, 66; DLB 120; MTCW 2
Oldstyle, Jonathan
See Irving, Washington
Olesha, Yuri (Karlovich) 1899-1960 **CLC 8**
See also CA 85-88
Oliphant, Laurence 1829(?)-1888 **NCLC 47**
See also DLB 18, 166
Oliphant, Margaret (Oliphant Wilson) 1828-1897 **NCLC 11, 61; SSC 25**
See also DLB 18, 159, 190
Oliver, Mary 1935- **CLC 19, 34, 98**
See also CA 21-24R; CANR 9, 43; DLB 5, 193
Olivier, Laurence (Kerr) 1907-1989 **CLC 20**
See also CA 111; 150; 129
Olsen, Tillie 1912-**CLC 4, 13, 114; DA; DAB; DAC; DAM MST; SSC 11**
See also CA 1-4R; CANR 1, 43, 74; CDALBS; DLB 28, 206; DLBY 80; MTCW 1, 2
Olson, Charles (John) 1910-1970 **CLC 1, 2, 5, 6, 9, 11, 29; DAM POET; PC 19**
See also CA 13-16; 25-28R; CABS 2; CANR 35, 61; CAP 1; DLB 5, 16, 193; MTCW 1, 2
Olson, Toby 1937- **CLC 28**
See also CA 65-68; CANR 9, 31
Olyesha, Yuri
See Olesha, Yuri (Karlovich)
Ondaatje, (Philip) Michael 1943-**CLC 14, 29, 51, 76; DAB; DAC; DAM MST**
See also CA 77-80; CANR 42, 74; DLB 60; MTCW 2
Oneal, Elizabeth 1934-
See Oneal, Zibby
See also CA 106; CANR 28; MAICYA; SATA 30, 82
Oneal, Zibby **CLC 30**

See Kingsley, Charles
Partridge, Anthony
See Oppenheim, E(dward) Phillips
Pascal, Blaise 1623-1662 **LC 35**
Pascoli, Giovanni 1855-1912 **TCLC 45**
See also CA 170
Pasolini, Pier Paolo 1922-1975 **CLC 20, 37, 106; PC 17**
See also CA 93-96; 61-64; CANR 63; DLB 128, 177; MTCW 1
Pasquini
See Silone, Ignazio
Pastan, Linda (Olenik) 1932- **CLC 27; DAM POET**
See also CA 61-64; CANR 18, 40, 61; DLB 5
Pasternak, Boris (Leonidovich) 1890-1960 **CLC 7, 10, 18, 63; DA; DAB; DAC; DAM MST, NOV, POET; PC 6; SSC 31; WLC**
See also CA 127; 116; MTCW 1, 2
Patchen, Kenneth 1911-1972 **CLC 1, 2, 18; DAM POET**
See also CA 1-4R; 33-36R; CANR 3, 35; DLB 16, 48; MTCW 1
Pater, Walter (Horatio) 1839-1894 **NCLC 7**
See also CDBLB 1832-1890; DLB 57, 156
Paterson, A(ndrew) B(arton) 1864-1941 **TCLC 32**
See also CA 155; SATA 97
Paterson, Katherine (Womeldorf) 1932- **CLC 12, 30**
See also AAYA 1; CA 21-24R; CANR 28, 59; CLR 7, 50; DLB 52; JRDA; MAICYA; MTCW 1; SATA 13, 53, 92
Patmore, Coventry Kersey Dighton 1823-1896 **NCLC 9**
See also DLB 35, 98
Paton, Alan (Stewart) 1903-1988 **CLC 4, 10, 25, 55, 106; DA; DAB; DAC; DAM MST, NOV; WLC**
See also AAYA 26; CA 13-16; 125; CANR 22; CAP 1; DLBD 17; MTCW 1, 2; SATA 11; SATA-Obit 56
Paton Walsh, Gillian 1937-
See Walsh, Jill Paton
See also CANR 38; JRDA; MAICYA; SAAS 3; SATA 4, 72
Patton, George S. 1885-1945 **TCLC 79**
Paulding, James Kirke 1778-1860 **NCLC 2**
See also DLB 3, 59, 74
Paulin, Thomas Neilson 1949-
See Paulin, Tom
See also CA 123; 128
Paulin, Tom **CLC 37**
See also Paulin, Thomas Neilson
See also DLB 40
Paustovsky, Konstantin (Georgievich) 1892-1968 **CLC 40**
See also CA 93-96; 25-28R
Pavese, Cesare 1908-1950 **TCLC 3; PC 13; SSC 19**
See also CA 104; 169; DLB 128, 177
Pavic, Milorad 1929- **CLC 60**
See also CA 136; DLB 181
Pavlov, Ivan Petrovich 1849-1936 **TCLC 91**
See also CA 118
Payne, Alan
See Jakes, John (William)
Paz, Gil
See Lugones, Leopoldo
Paz, Octavio 1914-1998 **CLC 3, 4, 6, 10, 19, 51, 65, 119; DA; DAB; DAC; DAM MST, MULT, POET; HLC; PC 1; WLC**
See also CA 73-76; 165; CANR 32, 65; DLBY 90, 98; HW 1, 2; MTCW 1, 2
p'Bitek, Okot 1931-1982 **CLC 96; BLC 3; DAM MULT**
See also BW 2, 3; CA 124; 107; DLB 125; MTCW 1, 2
Peacock, Molly 1947- **CLC 60**
See also CA 103; CAAS 21; CANR 52; DLB 120
Peacock, Thomas Love 1785-1866 **NCLC 22**
See also DLB 96, 116
Peake, Mervyn 1911-1968 **CLC 7, 54**
See also CA 5-8R; 25-28R; CANR 3; DLB 15, 160; MTCW 1; SATA 23
Pearce, Philippa **CLC 21**
See also Christie, (Ann) Philippa
<indexhaSee also CLR 9; DLB 161; MAICYA; SATA 1, 67
Pearl, Eric
See Elman, Richard (Martin)
Pearson, T(homas) R(eid) 1956- **CLC 39**
See also CA 120; 130; INT 130
Peck, Dale 1967- **CLC 81**
See also CA 146; CANR 72
Peck, John 1941- **CLC 3**
See also CA 49-52; CANR 3
Peck, Richard (Wayne) 1934- **CLC 21**
See also AAYA 1, 24; CA 85-88; CANR 19, 38; CLR 15; INT CANR-19; JRDA; MAICYA; SAAS 2; SATA 18, 55, 97
Peck, Robert Newton 1928- **CLC 17; DA; DAC; DAM MST**
See also AAYA 3; CA 81-84; CANR 31, 63; CLR 45; JRDA; MAICYA; SAAS 1; SATA 21, 62
Peckinpah, (David) Sam(uel) 1925-1984 **CLC 20**
See also CA 109; 114
Pedersen, Knut 1859-1952
See Hamsun, Knut
See also CA 104; 119; CANR 63; MTCW 1, 2
Peeslake, Gaffer
See Durrell, Lawrence (George)
Peguy, Charles Pierre 1873-1914 **TCLC 10**
See also CA 107
Peirce, Charles Sanders 1839-1914 **TCLC 81**
Pena, Ramon del Valle y
See Valle-Inclan, Ramon (Maria) del
Pendennis, Arthur Esquir
See Thackeray, William Makepeace
Penn, William 1644-1718 **LC 25**
See also DLB 24
PEPECE
See Prado (Calvo), Pedro
Pepys, Samuel 1633-1703 **LC 11; DA; DAB; DAC; DAM MST; WLC**
See also CDBLB 1660-1789; DLB 101
Percy, Walker 1916-1990 **CLC 2, 3, 6, 8, 14, 18, 47, 65; DAM NOV, POP**
See also CA 1-4R; 131; CANR 1, 23, 64; DLB 2; DLBY 80, 90; MTCW 1, 2
Percy, William Alexander 1885-1942 **TCLC 84**
See also CA 163; MTCW 2
Perec, Georges 1936-1982 **CLC 56, 116**
See also CA 141; DLB 83
Pereda (y Sanchez de Porrua), Jose Maria de 1833-1906 **TCLC 16**
See also CA 117
Pereda y Porrua, Jose Maria de
See Pereda (y Sanchez de Porrua), Jose Maria de
Peregoy, George Weems
See Mencken, H(enry) L(ouis)
Perelman, S(idney) J(oseph) 1904-1979 **CLC 3, 5, 9, 15, 23, 44, 49; DAM DRAM; SSC 32**
See also AITN 1, 2; CA 73-76; 89-92; CANR 18; DLB 11, 44; MTCW 1, 2
Peret, Benjamin 1899-1959 **TCLC 20**
See also CA 117
Peretz, Isaac Loeb 1851(?)-1915 **TCLC 16; SSC 26**
See also CA 109
Peretz, Yitzkhok Leibush
See Peretz, Isaac Loeb
Perez Galdos, Benito 1843-1920 **TCLC 27; HLCS 1**
See also CA 125; 153; HW 1
Perrault, Charles 1628-1703 **LC 2**
See also MAICYA; SATA 25
Perry, Brighton
See Sherwood, Robert E(mmet)
Perse, St.-John
See Leger, (Marie-Rene Auguste) Alexis Saint-Leger
Perutz, Leo(pold) 1882-1957 **TCLC 60**
See also CA 147; DLB 81
Peseenz, Tulio F.
See Lopez y Fuentes, Gregorio
Pesetsky, Bette 1932- **CLC 28**
See also CA 133; DLB 130
Peshkov, Alexei Maximovich 1868-1936
See Gorky, Maxim
See also CA 105; 141; DA; DAC; DAM DRAM, MST, NOV; MTCW 2
Pessoa, Fernando (Antonio Nogueira) 1888-1935 **TCLC 27; DAM MULT; HLC; PC 20**
See also CA 125
Peterkin, Julia Mood 1880-1961 **CLC 31**
See also CA 102; DLB 9
Peters, Joan K(aren) 1945- **CLC 39**
See also CA 158
Peters, Robert L(ouis) 1924- **CLC 7**
See also CA 13-16R; CAAS 8; DLB 105
Petofi, Sandor 1823-1849 **NCLC 21**
Petrakis, Harry Mark 1923- **CLC 3**
See also CA 9-12R; CANR 4, 30
Petrarch 1304-1374 **CMLC 20; DAM POET; PC 8**
Petrov, Evgeny **TCLC 21**
See also Kataev, Evgeny Petrovich
Petry, Ann (Lane) 1908-1997 **CLC 1, 7, 18**
See also BW 1, 3; CA 5-8R; 157; CAAS 6; CANR 4, 46; CLR 12; DLB 76; JRDA; MAICYA; MTCW 1; SATA 5; SATA-Obit 94
Petursson, Halligrimur 1614-1674 **LC 8**
Peychinovich
See Vazov, Ivan (Minchov)
Phaedrus c. 18B.C.-c. 50 **CMLC 25**
See also DLB 211
Philips, Katherine 1632-1664 **LC 30**
See also DLB 131
<indexbo**Philipson, Morris H.** 1926- **CLC 53**
See also CA 1-4R; CANR 4
Phillips, Caryl 1958- **CLC 96; BLCS; DAM MULT**
See also BW 2; CA 141; CANR 63; DLB 157; MTCW 2
Phillips, David Graham 1867-1911 **TCLC 44**
See also CA 108; DLB 9, 12
Phillips, Jack
See Sandburg, Carl (August)
Phillips, Jayne Anne 1952- **CLC 15, 33; SSC 16**
See also CA 101; CANR 24, 50; DLBY 80; INT CANR-24; MTCW 1, 2
Phillips, Richard
See Dick, Philip K(indred)

Reznikoff, Charles 1894-1976 **CLC 9**
See also CA 33-36; 61-64; CAP 2; DLB 28, 45
Rezzori (d'Arezzo), Gregor von 1914-1998 **CLC 25**
See also CA 122; 136; 167
Rhine, Richard
See Silverstein, Alvin
Rhodes, Eugene Manlove 1869-1934**TCLC 53**
Rhodius, Apollonius c. 3rd cent. B.C.- **CMLC 28**
See also DLB 176
R'hoone
See Balzac, Honore de
Rhys, Jean 1890(?)-1979 **CLC 2, 4, 6, 14, 19, 51; DAM NOV; SSC 21**
See also CA 25-28R; 85-88; CANR 35, 62; CDBLB 1945-1960; DLB 36, 117, 162; MTCW 1, 2
Ribeiro, Darcy 1922-1997 **CLC 34**
See also CA 33-36R; 156
Ribeiro, Joao Ubaldo (Osorio Pimentel) 1941- **CLC 10, 67**
See also CA 81-84
Ribman, Ronald (Burt) 1932- **CLC 7**
See also CA 21-24R; CANR 46, 80
Ricci, Nino 1959- **CLC 70**
See also CA 137
Rice, Anne 1941- **CLC 41; DAM POP**
<iSee also AAYA 9; BEST 89:2; CA 65-68; CANR 12, 36, 53, 74; MTCW 2
Rice, Elmer (Leopold) 1892-1967 **CLC 7, 49; DAM DRAM**
See also CA 21-22; 25-28R; CAP 2; DLB 4, 7; MTCW 1, 2
Rice, Tim(othy Miles Bindon) 1944- **CLC 21**
See also CA 103; CANR 46
Rich, Adrienne (Cecile) 1929-**CLC 3, 6, 7, 11, 18, 36, 73, 76; DAM POET; PC 5**
See also CA 9-12R; CANR 20, 53, 74; CDALBS; DLB 5, 67; MTCW 1, 2
Rich, Barbara
See Graves, Robert (von Ranke)
Rich, Robert
See Trumbo, Dalton
Richard, Keith **CLC 17**
See also Richards, Keith
Richards, David Adams 1950- **CLC 59; DAC**
See also CA 93-96; CANR 60; DLB 53
Richards, I(vor) A(rmstrong) 1893-1979**CLC 14, 24**
See also CA 41-44R; 89-92; CANR 34, 74; DLB 27; MTCW 2
Richards, Keith 1943-
See Richard, Keith
See also CA 107; CANR 77
Richardson, Anne
See Roiphe, Anne (Richardson)
Richardson, Dorothy Miller 1873-1957**TCLC 3**
See also CA 104; DLB 36
Richardson, Ethel Florence (Lindesay) 1870-1946
See Richardson, Henry Handel
See also CA 105
Richardson, Henry Handel **TCLC 4**
See also Richardson, Ethel Florence (Lindesay)
See also DLB 197
Richardson, John 1796-1852 **NCLC 55; DAC**
See also DLB 99
Richardson, Samuel 1689-1761**LC 1, 44; DA; DAB; DAC; DAM MST, NOV; WLC**
See also CDBLB 1660-1789; DLB 39
Richler, Mordecai 1931-**CLC 3, 5, 9, 13, 18, 46, 70; DAC; DAM MST, NOV**
See also AITN 1; CA 65-68; CANR 31, 62; CLR 17; DLB 53; MAICYA; MTCW 1, 2; SATA 44, 98; SATA-Brief 27
Richter, Conrad (Michael) 1890-1968**CLC 30**
See also AAYA 21; CA 5-8R; 25-28R; CANR 23; DLB 9, 212; MTCW 1, 2; SATA 3
Ricostranza, Tom
See Ellis, Trey
Riddell, Charlotte 1832-1906 **TCLC 40**
See also CA 165; DLB 156
Ridgway, Keith 1965- **CLC 119**
See also CA 172
Riding, Laura **CLC 3, 7**
<indexhanSee also Jackson, Laura (Riding)
Riefenstahl, Berta Helene Amalia 1902-
See Riefenstahl, Leni
See also CA 108
Riefenstahl, Leni **CLC 16**
See also Riefenstahl, Berta Helene Amalia
Riffe, Ernest
See Bergman, (Ernst) Ingmar
Riggs, (Rolla) Lynn 1899-1954 **TCLC 56; DAM MULT**
See also CA 144; DLB 175; NNAL
Riis, Jacob A(ugust) 1849-1914 **TCLC 80**
See also CA 113; 168; DLB 23
Riley, James Whitcomb 1849-1916**TCLC 51; DAM POET**
See also CA 118; 137; MAICYA; SATA 17
Riley, Tex
See Creasey, John
Rilke, Rainer Maria 1875-1926**TCLC 1, 6, 19; DAM POET; PC 2**
See also CA 104; 132; CANR 62; DLB 81; MTCW 1, 2
Rimbaud, (Jean Nicolas) Arthur 1854-1891 **NCLC 4, 35; DA; DAB; DAC; DAM MST, POET; PC 3; WLC**
Rinehart, Mary Roberts 1876-1958**TCLC 52**
See also CA 108; 166
Ringmaster, The
See Mencken, H(enry) L(ouis)
Ringwood, Gwen(dolyn Margaret) Pharis 1910-1984 **CLC 48**
See also CA 148; 112; DLB 88
Rio, Michel 19(?)- **CLC 43**
Ritsos, Giannes
See Ritsos, Yannis
Ritsos, Yannis 1909-1990 **CLC 6, 13, 31**
See also CA 77-80; 133; CANR 39, 61; MTCW 1
Ritter, Erika 1948(?)- **CLC 52**
Rivera, Jose Eustasio 1889-1928 **TCLC 35**
See also CA 162; HW 1, 2
Rivers, Conrad Kent 1933-1968 **CLC 1**
See also BW 1; CA 85-88; DLB 41
Rivers, Elfrida
See Bradley, Marion Zimmer
Riverside, John
See Heinlein, Robert A(nson)
Rizal, Jose 1861-1896 **NCLC 27**
Roa Bastos, Augusto (Antonio) 1917-**CLC 45; DAM MULT; HLC**
See also CA 131; DLB 113; HW 1
Robbe-Grillet, Alain 1922-**CLC 1, 2, 4, 6, 8, 10, 14, 43**
See also CA 9-12R; CANR 33, 65; DLB 83; MTCW 1, 2
Robbins, Harold 1916-1997 **CLC 5; DAM NOV**
See also CA 73-76; 162; CANR 26, 54; MTCW 1, 2
Robbins, Thomas Eugene 1936-
See Robbins, Tom
See also CA 81-84; CANR 29, 59; DAM NOV, POP; MTCW 1, 2
Robbins, Tom **CLC 9, 32, 64**
See also Robbins, Thomas Eugene
See also BEST 90:3; DLBY 80; MTCW 2
Robbins, Trina 1938- **CLC 21**
See also CA 128
Roberts, Charles G(eorge) D(ouglas) 1860-1943 **TCLC 8**
See also CA 105; CLR 33; DLB 92; SATA 88; SATA-Brief 29
Roberts, Elizabeth Madox 1886-1941 **TCLC 68**
See also CA 111; 166; DLB 9, 54, 102; SATA 33; SATA-Brief 27
Roberts, Kate 1891-1985 **CLC 15**
See also CA 107; 116
Roberts, Keith (John Kingston) 1935-**CLC 14**
See also CA 25-28R; CANR 46
Roberts, Kenneth (Lewis) 1885-1957**TCLC 23**
See also CA 109; DLB 9
Roberts, Michele (B.) 1949- **CLC 48**
See also CA 115; CANR 58
Robertson, Ellis
See Ellison, Harlan (Jay); Silverberg, Robert
Robertson, Thomas William 1829-1871**NCLC 35; DAM DRAM**
Robeson, Kenneth
See Dent, Lester
Robinson, Edwin Arlington 1869-1935**TCLC 5; DA; DAC; DAM MST, POET; PC 1**
See also CA 104; 133; CDALB 1865-1917; DLB 54; MTCW 1, 2
Robinson, Henry Crabb 1775-1867**NCLC 15**
See also DLB 107
Robinson, Jill 1936- **CLC 10**
See also CA 102; INT 102
Robinson, Kim Stanley 1952- **CLC 34**
See also AAYA 26; CA 126
Robinson, Lloyd
See Silverberg, Robert
Robinson, Marilynne 1944- **CLC 25**
See also CA 116; CANR 80; DLB 206
Robinson, Smokey **CLC 21**
See also Robinson, William, Jr.
Robinson, William, Jr. 1940-
See Robinson, Smokey
See also CA 116
Robison, Mary 1949- **CLC 42, 98**
See also CA 113; 116; DLB 130; INT 116
Rod, Edouard 1857-1910 **TCLC 52**
Roddenberry, Eugene Wesley 1921-1991
See Roddenberry, Gene
See also CA 110; 135; CANR 37; SATA 45; SATA-Obit 69
Roddenberry, Gene **CLC 17**
See also Roddenberry, Eugene Wesley
See also AAYA 5; SATA-Obit 69
Rodgers, Mary 1931- **CLC 12**
See also CA 49-52; CANR 8, 55; CLR 20; INT CANR-8; JRDA; MAICYA; SATA 8
Rodgers, W(illiam) R(obert) 1909-1969**CLC 7**
See also CA 85-88; DLB 20
Rodman, Eric
See Silverberg, Robert
Rodman, Howard 1920(?)-1985 **CLC 65**
See also CA 118
Rodman, Maia
See Wojciechowska, Maia (Teresa)
Rodriguez, Claudio 1934- **CLC 10**
See also DLB 134

191; DLBD 18; MTCW 1, 2
Satterfield, Charles
See Pohl, Frederik
Saul, John (W. III) 1942-**CLC 46; DAM NOV, POP**
See also AAYA 10; BEST 90:4; CA 81-84; CANR 16, 40; SATA 98
Saunders, Caleb
See Heinlein, Robert A(nson)
Saura (Atares), Carlos 1932- **CLC 20**
See also CA 114; 131; CANR 79; HW 1
Sauser-Hall, Frederic 1887-1961 **CLC 18**
See also Cendrars, Blaise
See also CA 102; 93-96; CANR 36, 62; MTCW 1
Saussure, Ferdinand de 1857-1913 **TCLC 49**
Savage, Catharine
See Brosman, Catharine Savage
Savage, Thomas 1915- **CLC 40**
See also CA 126; 132; CAAS 15; INT 132
Savan, Glenn 19(?)- **CLC 50**
Sayers, Dorothy L(eigh) 1893-1957 **TCLC 2, 15; DAM POP**
See also CA 104; 119; CANR 60; CDBLB 1914-1945; DLB 10, 36, 77, 100; MTCW 1, 2
Sayers, Valerie 1952- **CLC 50**
See also CA 134; CANR 61
Sayles, John (Thomas) 1950- **CLC 7, 10, 14**
See also CA 57-60; CANR 41; DLB 44
Scammell, Michael 1935- **CLC 34**
See also CA 156
Scannell, Vernon 1922- **CLC 49**
See also CA 5-8R; CANR 8, 24, 57; DLB 27; SATA 59
Scarlett, Susan
See Streatfeild, (Mary) Noel
Scarron
See Mikszath, Kalman
Schaeffer, Susan Fromberg 1941- **CLC 6, 11, 22**
See also CA 49-52; CANR 18, 65; DLB 28; MTCW 1, 2; SATA 22
Schary, Jill
See Robinson, Jill
Schell, Jonathan 1943- **CLC 35**
<indexSee also CA 73-76; CANR 12
Schelling, Friedrich Wilhelm Joseph von 1775-1854 **NCLC 30**
See also DLB 90
Schendel, Arthur van 1874-1946 **TCLC 56**
Scherer, Jean-Marie Maurice 1920-
See Rohmer, Eric
See also CA 110
Schevill, James (Erwin) 1920- **CLC 7**
See also CA 5-8R; CAAS 12
Schiller, Friedrich 1759-1805 **NCLC 39, 69; DAM DRAM**
See also DLB 94
Schisgal, Murray (Joseph) 1926- **CLC 6**
See also CA 21-24R; CANR 48
Schlee, Ann 1934- **CLC 35**
See also CA 101; CANR 29; SATA 44; SATA-Brief 36
Schlegel, August Wilhelm von 1767-1845 **NCLC 15**
See also DLB 94
Schlegel, Friedrich 1772-1829 **NCLC 45**
See also DLB 90
Schlegel, Johann Elias (von) 1719(?)-1749**L C 5**
Schlesinger, Arthur M(eier), Jr. 1917-**CLC 84**
See also AITN 1; CA 1-4R; CANR 1, 28, 58; DLB 17; INT CANR-28; MTCW 1, 2; SATA 61
Schmidt, Arno (Otto) 1914-1979 **CLC 56**
See also CA 128; 109; DLB 69
Schmitz, Aron Hector 1861-1928
See Svevo, Italo
See also CA 104; 122; MTCW 1
Schnackenberg, Gjertrud 1953- **CLC 40**
See also CA 116; DLB 120
Schneider, Leonard Alfred 1925-1966
See Bruce, Lenny
See also CA 89-92
Schnitzler, Arthur 1862-1931**TCLC 4; SSC 15**
See also CA 104; DLB 81, 118
Schoenberg, Arnold 1874-1951 **TCLC 75**
See also CA 109
Schonberg, Arnold
See Schoenberg, Arnold
Schopenhauer, Arthur 1788-1860 **NCLC 51**
See also DLB 90
Schor, Sandra (M.) 1932(?)-1990 **CLC 65**
See also CA 132
Schorer, Mark 1908-1977 **CLC 9**
See also CA 5-8R; 73-76; CANR 7; DLB 103
Schrader, Paul (Joseph) 1946- **CLC 26**
See also CA 37-40R; CANR 41; DLB 44
Schreiner, Olive (Emilie Albertina) 1855-1920 **TCLC 9**
See also CA 105; 154; DLB 18, 156, 190
Schulberg, Budd (Wilson) 1914- **CLC 7, 48**
See also CA 25-28R; CANR 19; DLB 6, 26, 28; DLBY 81
Schulz, Bruno 1892-1942**TCLC 5, 51; SSC 13**
See also CA 115; 123; MTCW 2
Schulz, Charles M(onroe) 1922- **CLC 12**
See also CA 9-12R; CANR 6; INT CANR-6; SATA 10
Schumacher, E(rnst) F(riedrich) 1911-1977 **CLC 80**
See also CA 81-84; 73-76; CANR 34
Schuyler, James Marcus 1923-1991**CLC 5, 23; DAM POET**
See also CA 101; 134; DLB 5, 169; INT 101
Schwartz, Delmore (David) 1913-1966**CLC 2, 4, 10, 45, 87; PC 8**
See also CA 17-18; 25-28R; CANR 35; CAP 2; DLB 28, 48; MTCW 1, 2
Schwartz, Ernst
See Ozu, Yasujiro
Schwartz, John Burnham 1965- **CLC 59**
See also CA 132
Schwartz, Lynne Sharon 1939- **CLC 31**
See also CA 103; CANR 44; MTCW 2
Schwartz, Muriel A.
See Eliot, T(homas) S(tearns)
Schwarz-Bart, Andre 1928- **CLC 2, 4**
See also CA 89-92
Schwarz-Bart, Simone 1938- **CLC 7; BLCS**
See also BW 2; CA 97-100
Schwob, Marcel (Mayer Andre) 1867-1905 **TCLC 20**
See also CA 117; 168; DLB 123
Sciascia, Leonardo 1921-1989 **CLC 8, 9, 41**
See also CA 85-88; 130; CANR 35; DLB 177; MTCW 1
Scoppettone, Sandra 1936- **CLC 26**
See also AAYA 11; CA 5-8R; CANR 41, 73; SATA 9, 92
Scorsese, Martin 1942- **CLC 20, 89**
See also CA 110; 114; CANR 46
Scotland, Jay
See Jakes, John (William)
Scott, Duncan Campbell 1862-1947 **TCLC 6; DAC**
See also CA 104; 153; DLB 92
Scott, Evelyn 1893-1963 **CLC 43**
See also CA 104; 112; CANR 64; DLB 9, 48
Scott, F(rancis) R(eginald) 1899-1985**CLC 22**
See also CA 101; 114; DLB 88; INT 101
Scott, Frank
See Scott, F(rancis) R(eginald)
Scott, Joanna 1960- **CLC 50**
See also CA 126; CANR 53
Scott, Paul (Mark) 1920-1978 **CLC 9, 60**
See also CA 81-84; 77-80; CANR 33; DLB 14, 207; MTCW 1
Scott, Sarah 1723-1795 **LC 44**
See also DLB 39
Scott, Walter 1771-1832 **NCLC 15, 69; DA; DAB; DAC; DAM MST, NOV, POET; PC 13; SSC 32; WLC**
See also AAYA 22; CDBLB 1789-1832; DLB 93, 107, 116, 144, 159; YABC 2
Scribe, (Augustin) Eugene 1791-1861 **NCLC 16; DAM DRAM; DC 5**
See also DLB 192
Scrum, R.
See Crumb, R(obert)
Scudery, Madeleine de 1607-1701 **LC 2**
Scum
See Crumb, R(obert)
Scumbag, Little Bobby
See Crumb, R(obert)
Seabrook, John
See Hubbard, L(afayette) Ron(ald)
Sealy, I. Allan 1951- **CLC 55**
Search, Alexander
See Pessoa, Fernando (Antonio Nogueira)
Sebastian, Lee
See Silverberg, Robert
Sebastian Owl
See Thompson, Hunter S(tockton)
Sebestyen, Ouida 1924- **CLC 30**
See also AAYA 8; CA 107; CANR 40; CLR 17; JRDA; MAICYA; SAAS 10; SATA 39
Secundus, H. Scriblerus
See Fielding, Henry
Sedges, John
See Buck, Pearl S(ydenstricker)
Sedgwick, Catharine Maria 1789-1867**NCLC 19**
See also DLB 1, 74
Seelye, John (Douglas) 1931- **CLC 7**
See also CA 97-100; CANR 70; INT 97-100
Seferiades, Giorgos Stylianou 1900-1971
See Seferis, George
See also CA 5-8R; 33-36R; CANR 5, 36; MTCW 1
Seferis, George **CLC 5, 11**
See also Seferiades, Giorgos Stylianou
Segal, Erich (Wolf) 1937- **CLC 3, 10; DAM POP**
See also BEST 89:1; CA 25-28R; CANR 20, 36, 65; DLBY 86; INT CANR-20; MTCW 1
Seger, Bob 1945- **CLC 35**
Seghers, Anna **CLC 7**
See also Radvanyi, Netty
See also DLB 69
Seidel, Frederick (Lewis) 1936- **CLC 18**
See also CA 13-16R; CANR 8; DLBY 84
Seifert, Jaroslav 1901-1986 **CLC 34, 44, 93**
See also CA 127; MTCW 1, 2
Sei Shonagon c. 966-1017(?) **CMLC 6**
Sejour, Victor 1817-1874 **DC 10**
See also DLB 50
Sejour Marcou et Ferrand, Juan Victor
See Sejour, Victor

Smith, Adam 1723-1790 **LC 36**
See also DLB 104
Smith, Alexander 1829-1867 **NCLC 59**
See also DLB 32, 55
Smith, Anna Deavere 1950- **CLC 86**
See also CA 133
Smith, Betty (Wehner) 1896-1972 **CLC 19**
See also CA 5-8R; 33-36R; DLBY 82; SATA 6
Smith, Charlotte (Turner) 1749-1806 **NCLC 23**
See also DLB 39, 109
Smith, Clark Ashton 1893-1961 **CLC 43**
See also CA 143; MTCW 2
Smith, Dave **CLC 22, 42**
See also Smith, David (Jeddie)
See also CAAS 7; DLB 5
Smith, David (Jeddie) 1942-
See Smith, Dave
See also CA 49-52; CANR 1, 59; DAM POET
Smith, Florence Margaret 1902-1971
See Smith, Stevie
See also CA 17-18; 29-32R; CANR 35; CAP 2; DAM POET; MTCW 1, 2
Smith, Iain Crichton 1928-1998 **CLC 64**
See also CA 21-24R; 171; DLB 40, 139
Smith, John 1580(?)-1631 **LC 9**
See also DLB 24, 30
Smith, Johnston
See Crane, Stephen (Townley)
Smith, Joseph, Jr. 1805-1844 **NCLC 53**
Smith, Lee 1944- **CLC 25, 73**
See also CA 114; 119; CANR 46; DLB 143; DLBY 83; INT 119
Smith, Martin
See Smith, Martin Cruz
Smith, Martin Cruz 1942- **CLC 25; DAM MULT, POP**
See also BEST 89:4; CA 85-88; CANR 6, 23, 43, 65; INT CANR-23; MTCW 2; NNAL
Smith, Mary-Ann Tirone 1944- **CLC 39**
See also CA 118; 136
Smith, Patti 1946- **CLC 12**
See also CA 93-96; CANR 63
Smith, Pauline (Urmson) 1882-1959 **TCLC 25**
Smith, Rosamond
See Oates, Joyce Carol
Smith, Sheila Kaye
See Kaye-Smith, Sheila
Smith, Stevie **CLC 3, 8, 25, 44; PC 12**
See also Smith, Florence Margaret
See also DLB 20; MTCW 2
Smith, Wilbur (Addison) 1933- **CLC 33**
See also CA 13-16R; CANR 7, 46, 66; MTCW 1, 2
Smith, William Jay 1918- **CLC 6**
See also CA 5-8R; CANR 44; DLB 5; MAICYA; SAAS 22; SATA 2, 68
Smith, Woodrow Wilson
See Kuttner, Henry
Smolenskin, Peretz 1842-1885 **NCLC 30**
Smollett, Tobias (George) 1721-1771 **LC 2, 46**
See also CDBLB 1660-1789; DLB 39, 104
Snodgrass, W(illiam) D(e Witt) 1926- **CLC 2, 6, 10, 18, 68; DAM POET**
See also CA 1-4R; CANR 6, 36, 65; DLB 5; MTCW 1, 2
Snow, C(harles) P(ercy) 1905-1980 **CLC 1, 4, 6, 9, 13, 19; DAM NOV**
See also CA 5-8R; 101; CANR 28; CDBLB 1945-1960; DLB 15, 77; DLBD 17; MTCW 1, 2
Snow, Frances Compton
See Adams, Henry (Brooks)
Snyder, Gary (Sherman) 1930- **CLC 1, 2, 5, 9, 32, 120; DAM POET; PC 21**
See also CA 17-20R; CANR 30, 60; DLB 5, 16, 165, 212; MTCW 2
Snyder, Zilpha Keatley 1927- **CLC 17**
See also AAYA 15; CA 9-12R; CANR 38; CLR 31; JRDA; MAICYA; SAAS 2; SATA 1, 28, 75
Soares, Bernardo
See Pessoa, Fernando (Antonio Nogueira)
Sobh, A.
See Shamlu, Ahmad
Sobol, Joshua **CLC 60**
Socrates 469B.C.-399B.C. **CMLC 27**
Soderberg, Hjalmar 1869-1941 **TCLC 39**
Sodergran, Edith (Irene)
See Soedergran, Edith (Irene)
Soedergran, Edith (Irene) 1892-1923 **TCLC 31**
Softly, Edgar
See Lovecraft, H(oward) P(hillips)
Softly, Edward
See Lovecraft, H(oward) P(hillips)
Sokolov, Raymond 1941- **CLC 7**
See also CA 85-88
Solo, Jay
See Ellison, Harlan (Jay)
Sologub, Fyodor **TCLC 9**
See also Teternikov, Fyodor Kuzmich
Solomons, Ikey Esquir
See Thackeray, William Makepeace
Solomos, Dionysios 1798-1857 **NCLC 15**
Solwoska, Mara
See French, Marilyn
Solzhenitsyn, Aleksandr I(sayevich) 1918- **CLC 1, 2, 4, 7, 9, 10, 18, 26, 34, 78; DA; DAB; DAC; DAM MST, NOV; SSC 32; WLC**
See also AITN 1; CA 69-72; CANR 40, 65; MTCW 1, 2
Somers, Jane
See Lessing, Doris (May)
Somerville, Edith 1858-1949 **TCLC 51**
See also DLB 135
Somerville & Ross
See Martin, Violet Florence; Somerville, Edith
Sommer, Scott 1951- **CLC 25**
See also CA 106
Sondheim, Stephen (Joshua) 1930- **CLC 30, 39; DAM DRAM**
See also AAYA 11; CA 103; CANR 47, 68
Song, Cathy 1955- **PC 21**
See also CA 154; DLB 169
Sontag, Susan 1933- **CLC 1, 2, 10, 13, 31, 105; DAM POP**
See also CA 17-20R; CANR 25, 51, 74; DLB 2, 67; MTCW 1, 2
Sophocles 496(?)B.C.-406(?)B.C. **CMLC 2; DA; DAB; DAC; DAM DRAM, MST; DC 1; WLCS**
See also DLB 176
Sordello 1189-1269 **CMLC 15**
Sorel, Georges 1847-1922 **TCLC 91**
See also CA 118
Sorel, Julia
See Drexler, Rosalyn
Sorrentino, Gilbert 1929- **CLC 3, 7, 14, 22, 40**
See also CA 77-80; CANR 14, 33; DLB 5, 173; DLBY 80; INT CANR-14
Soto, Gary 1952- **CLC 32, 80; DAM MULT; HLC**
See also AAYA 10; CA 119; 125; CANR 50, 74; CLR 38; DLB 82; HW 1, 2; INT 125; JRDA; MTCW 2; SATA 80
Soupault, Philippe 1897-1990 **CLC 68**
See also CA 116; 147; 131
Souster, (Holmes) Raymond 1921- **CLC 5, 14; DAC; DAM POET**
See also CA 13-16R; CAAS 14; CANR 13, 29, 53; DLB 88; SATA 63
Southern, Terry 1924(?)-1995 **CLC 7**
See also CA 1-4R; 150; CANR 1, 55; DLB 2
Southey, Robert 1774-1843 **NCLC 8**
See also DLB 93, 107, 142; SATA 54
Southworth, Emma Dorothy Eliza Nevitte 1819-1899 **NCLC 26**
Souza, Ernest
See Scott, Evelyn
Soyinka, Wole 1934- **CLC 3, 5, 14, 36, 44; BLC 3; DA; DAB; DAC; DAM DRAM, MST, MULT; DC 2; WLC**
See also BW 2, 3; CA 13-16R; CANR 27, 39; DLB 125; MTCW 1, 2
Spackman, W(illiam) M(ode) 1905-1990 **CLC 46**
See also CA 81-84; 132
Spacks, Barry (Bernard) 1931- **CLC 14**
See also CA 154; CANR 33; DLB 105
Spanidou, Irini 1946- **CLC 44**
Spark, Muriel (Sarah) 1918- **CLC 2, 3, 5, 8, 13, 18, 40, 94; DAB; DAC; DAM MST, NOV; SSC 10**
See also CA 5-8R; CANR 12, 36, 76; CDBLB 1945-1960; DLB 15, 139; INT CANR-12; MTCW 1, 2
Spaulding, Douglas
See Bradbury, Ray (Douglas)
Spaulding, Leonard
See Bradbury, Ray (Douglas)
Spence, J. A. D.
See Eliot, T(homas) S(tearns)
Spencer, Elizabeth 1921- **CLC 22**
See also CA 13-16R; CANR 32, 65; DLB 6; MTCW 1; SATA 14
Spencer, Leonard G.
See Silverberg, Robert
Spencer, Scott 1945- **CLC 30**
See also CA 113; CANR 51; DLBY 86
Spender, Stephen (Harold) 1909-1995 **CLC 1, 2, 5, 10, 41, 91; DAM POET**
See also CA 9-12R; 149; CANR 31, 54; CDBLB 1945-1960; DLB 20; MTCW 1, 2
Spengler, Oswald (Arnold Gottfried) 1880-1936 **TCLC 25**
See also CA 118
Spenser, Edmund 1552(?)-1599 **LC 5, 39; DA; DAB; DAC; DAM MST, POET; PC 8; WLC**
See also CDBLB Before 1660; DLB 167
Spicer, Jack 1925-1965 **CLC 8, 18, 72; DAM POET**
See also CA 85-88; DLB 5, 16, 193
Spiegelman, Art 1948- **CLC 76**
See also AAYA 10; CA 125; CANR 41, 55, 74; MTCW 2
Spielberg, Peter 1929- **CLC 6**
See also CA 5-8R; CANR 4, 48; DLBY 81
Spielberg, Steven 1947- **CLC 20**
See also AAYA 8, 24; CA 77-80; CANR 32; SATA 32
Spillane, Frank Morrison 1918-
See Spillane, Mickey
See also CA 25-28R; CANR 28, 63; MTCW 1, 2; SATA 66
Spillane, Mickey **CLC 3, 13**
See also Spillane, Frank Morrison

See also MTCW 2
Spinoza, Benedictus de 1632-1677 **LC 9**
Spinrad, Norman (Richard) 1940- **CLC 46**
See also CA 37-40R; CAAS 19; CANR 20; DLB 8; INT CANR-20
Spitteler, Carl (Friedrich Georg) 1845-1924 **TCLC 12**
See also CA 109; DLB 129
Spivack, Kathleen (Romola Drucker) 1938- **CLC 6**
See also CA 49-52
Spoto, Donald 1941- **CLC 39**
See also CA 65-68; CANR 11, 57
Springsteen, Bruce (F.) 1949- **CLC 17**
See also CA 111
Spurling, Hilary 1940- **CLC 34**
See also CA 104; CANR 25, 52
Spyker, John Howland
See Elman, Richard (Martin)
Squires, (James) Radcliffe 1917-1993**CLC 51**
See also CA 1-4R; 140; CANR 6, 21
Srivastava, Dhanpat Rai 1880(?)-1936
See Premchand
See also CA 118
Stacy, Donald
See Pohl, Frederik
Stael, Germaine de 1766-1817
See Stael-Holstein, Anne Louise Germaine Necker Baronn
See also DLB 119
Stael-Holstein, Anne Louise Germaine Necker Baronn 1766-1817 **NCLC 3**
See also Stael, Germaine de
See also DLB 192
Stafford, Jean 1915-1979**CLC 4, 7, 19, 68; SSC 26**
See also CA 1-4R; 85-88; CANR 3, 65; DLB 2, 173; MTCW 1, 2; SATA-Obit 22
Stafford, William (Edgar) 1914-1993 **CLC 4, 7, 29; DAM POET**
See also CA 5-8R; 142; CAAS 3; CANR 5, 22; DLB 5, 206; INT CANR-22
Stagnelius, Eric Johan 1793-1823 **NCLC 61**
Staines, Trevor
See Brunner, John (Kilian Houston)
Stairs, Gordon
See Austin, Mary (Hunter)
Stalin, Joseph 1879-1953 **TCLC 92**
Stannard, Martin 1947- **CLC 44**
See also CA 142; DLB 155
Stanton, Elizabeth Cady 1815-1902**TCLC 73**
See also CA 171; DLB 79
Stanton, Maura 1946- **CLC 9**
See also CA 89-92; CANR 15; DLB 120
Stanton, Schuyler
See Baum, L(yman) Frank
Stapledon, (William) Olaf 1886-1950 **TCLC 22**
See also CA 111; 162; DLB 15
Starbuck, George (Edwin) 1931-1996**CLC 53; DAM POET**
See also CA 21-24R; 153; CANR 23
Stark, Richard
See Westlake, Donald E(dwin)
Staunton, Schuyler
See Baum, L(yman) Frank
Stead, Christina (Ellen) 1902-1983 **CLC 2, 5, 8, 32, 80**
See also CA 13-16R; 109; CANR 33, 40; MTCW 1, 2
Stead, William Thomas 1849-1912 **TCLC 48**
See also CA 167
Steele, Richard 1672-1729 **LC 18**
See also CDBLB 1660-1789; DLB 84, 101
Steele, Timothy (Reid) 1948- **CLC 45**
See also CA 93-96; CANR 16, 50; DLB 120
Steffens, (Joseph) Lincoln 1866-1936 **TCLC 20**
See also CA 117
Stegner, Wallace (Earle) 1909-1993**CLC 9, 49, 81; DAM NOV; SSC 27**
See also AITN 1; BEST 90:3; CA 1-4R; 141; CAAS 9; CANR 1, 21, 46; DLB 9, 206; DLBY 93; MTCW 1, 2
Stein, Gertrude 1874-1946**TCLC 1, 6, 28, 48; DA; DAB; DAC; DAM MST, NOV, POET; PC 18; WLC**
See also CA 104; 132; CDALB 1917-1929; DLB 4, 54, 86; DLBD 15; MTCW 1, 2
Steinbeck, John (Ernst) 1902-1968**CLC 1, 5, 9, 13, 21, 34, 45, 75; DA; DAB; DAC; DAM DRAM, MST, NOV; SSC 11; WLC**
See also AAYA 12; CA 1-4R; 25-28R; CANR 1, 35; CDALB 1929-1941; DLB 7, 9, 212; DLBD 2; MTCW 1, 2; SATA 9
Steinem, Gloria 1934- **CLC 63**
See also CA 53-56; CANR 28, 51; MTCW 1, 2
Steiner, George 1929- **CLC 24; DAM NOV**
See also CA 73-76; CANR 31, 67; DLB 67; MTCW 1, 2; SATA 62
Steiner, K. Leslie
See Delany, Samuel R(ay, Jr.)
Steiner, Rudolf 1861-1925 **TCLC 13**
See also CA 107
Stendhal 1783-1842**NCLC 23, 46; DA; DAB; DAC; DAM MST, NOV; SSC 27; WLC**
See also DLB 119
Stephen, Adeline Virginia
See Woolf, (Adeline) Virginia
Stephen, SirLeslie 1832-1904 **TCLC 23**
See also CA 123; DLB 57, 144, 190
Stephen, Sir Leslie
See Stephen, SirLeslie
Stephen, Virginia
See Woolf, (Adeline) Virginia
Stephens, James 1882(?)-1950 **TCLC 4**
See also CA 104; DLB 19, 153, 162
Stephens, Reed
See Donaldson, Stephen R.
Steptoe, Lydia
See Barnes, Djuna
Sterchi, Beat 1949- **CLC 65**
Sterling, Brett
See Bradbury, Ray (Douglas); Hamilton, Edmond
Sterling, Bruce 1954- **CLC 72**
See also CA 119; CANR 44
Sterling, George 1869-1926 **TCLC 20**
See also CA 117; 165; DLB 54
Stern, Gerald 1925- **CLC 40, 100**
See also CA 81-84; CANR 28; DLB 105
Stern, Richard (Gustave) 1928- **CLC 4, 39**
See also CA 1-4R; CANR 1, 25, 52; DLBY 87; INT CANR-25
Sternberg, Josef von 1894-1969 **CLC 20**
See also CA 81-84
Sterne, Laurence 1713-1768 **LC 2, 48; DA; DAB; DAC; DAM MST, NOV; WLC**
See also CDBLB 1660-1789; DLB 39
Sternheim, (William Adolf) Carl 1878-1942 **TCLC 8**
See also CA 105; DLB 56, 118
Stevens, Mark 1951- **CLC 34**
See also CA 122
Stevens, Wallace 1879-1955 **TCLC 3, 12, 45; DA; DAB; DAC; DAM MST, POET; PC 6; WLC**
See also CA 104; 124; CDALB 1929-1941; DLB 54; MTCW 1, 2
Stevenson, Anne (Katharine) 1933-**CLC 7, 33**
See also CA 17-20R; CAAS 9; CANR 9, 33; DLB 40; MTCW 1
Stevenson, Robert Louis (Balfour) 1850-1894 **NCLC 5, 14, 63; DA; DAB; DAC; DAM MST, NOV; SSC 11; WLC**
See also AAYA 24; CDBLB 1890-1914; CLR 10, 11; DLB 18, 57, 141, 156, 174; DLBD 13; JRDA; MAICYA; SATA 100; YABC 2
Stewart, J(ohn) I(nnes) M(ackintosh) 1906-1994 **CLC 7, 14, 32**
See also CA 85-88; 147; CAAS 3; CANR 47; MTCW 1, 2
Stewart, Mary (Florence Elinor) 1916-**CLC 7, 35, 117; DAB**
See also AAYA 29; CA 1-4R; CANR 1, 59; SATA 12
Stewart, Mary Rainbow
See Stewart, Mary (Florence Elinor)
Stifle, June
See Campbell, Maria
Stifter, Adalbert 1805-1868**NCLC 41; SSC 28**
See also DLB 133
Still, James 1906- **CLC 49**
See also CA 65-68; CAAS 17; CANR 10, 26; DLB 9; SATA 29
Sting 1951-
See Sumner, Gordon Matthew
See also CA 167
Stirling, Arthur
See Sinclair, Upton (Beall)
Stitt, Milan 1941- **CLC 29**
See also CA 69-72
Stockton, Francis Richard 1834-1902
See Stockton, Frank R.
See also CA 108; 137; MAICYA; SATA 44
Stockton, Frank R. **TCLC 47**
See also Stockton, Francis Richard
See also DLB 42, 74; DLBD 13; SATA-Brief 32
Stoddard, Charles
See Kuttner, Henry
Stoker, Abraham 1847-1912
See Stoker, Bram
See also CA 105; 150; DA; DAC; DAM MST, NOV; SATA 29
Stoker, Bram 1847-1912**TCLC 8; DAB; WLC**
See also Stoker, Abraham
See also AAYA 23; CDBLB 1890-1914; DLB 36, 70, 178
Stolz, Mary (Slattery) 1920- **CLC 12**
See also AAYA 8; AITN 1; CA 5-8R; CANR 13, 41; JRDA; MAICYA; SAAS 3; SATA 10, 71
Stone, Irving 1903-1989 **CLC 7; DAM POP**
See also AITN 1; CA 1-4R; 129; CAAS 3; CANR 1, 23; INT CANR-23; MTCW 1, 2; SATA 3; SATA-Obit 64
Stone, Oliver (William) 1946- **CLC 73**
See also AAYA 15; CA 110; CANR 55
Stone, Robert (Anthony) 1937-**CLC 5, 23, 42**
See also CA 85-88; CANR 23, 66; DLB 152; INT CANR-23; MTCW 1
Stone, Zachary
See Follett, Ken(neth Martin)
Stoppard, Tom 1937-**CLC 1, 3, 4, 5, 8, 15, 29, 34, 63, 91; DA; DAB; DAC; DAM DRAM, MST; DC 6; WLC**
See also CA 81-84; CANR 39, 67; CDBLB 1960 to Present; DLB 13; DLBY 85; MTCW

1, 2
Storey, David (Malcolm) 1933-**CLC 2, 4, 5, 8; DAM DRAM**
See also CA 81-84; CANR 36; DLB 13, 14, 207; MTCW 1
Storm, Hyemeyohsts 1935- **CLC 3; DAM MULT**
See also CA 81-84; CANR 45; NNAL
Storm, Theodor 1817-1888 **SSC 27**
Storm, (Hans) Theodor (Woldsen) 1817-1888 **NCLC 1; SSC 27**
See also DLB 129
Storni, Alfonsina 1892-1938 **TCLC 5; DAM MULT; HLC**
See also CA 104; 131; HW 1
Stoughton, William 1631-1701 **LC 38**
See also DLB 24
Stout, Rex (Todhunter) 1886-1975 **CLC 3**
See also AITN 2; CA 61-64; CANR 71
Stow, (Julian) Randolph 1935- **CLC 23, 48**
See also CA 13-16R; CANR 33; MTCW 1
Stowe, Harriet (Elizabeth) Beecher 1811-1896 **NCLC 3, 50; DA; DAB; DAC; DAM MST, NOV; WLC**
See also CDALB 1865-1917; DLB 1, 12, 42, 74, 189; JRDA; MAICYA; YABC 1
Strachey, (Giles) Lytton 1880-1932 **TCLC 12**
See also CA 110; DLB 149; DLBD 10; MTCW 2
Strand, Mark 1934- **CLC 6, 18, 41, 71; DAM POET**
See also CA 21-24R; CANR 40, 65; DLB 5; SATA 41
Straub, Peter (Francis) 1943- **CLC 28, 107; DAM POP**
See also BEST 89:1; CA 85-88; CANR 28, 65; DLBY 84; MTCW 1, 2
Strauss, Botho 1944- **CLC 22**
<indexSee also CA 157; DLB 124
Streatfeild, (Mary) Noel 1895(?)-1986**CLC 21**
See also CA 81-84; 120; CANR 31; CLR 17; DLB 160; MAICYA; SATA 20; SATA-Obit 48
Stribling, T(homas) S(igismund) 1881-1965 **CLC 23**
See also CA 107; DLB 9
Strindberg, (Johan) August 1849-1912**TCLC 1, 8, 21, 47; DA; DAB; DAC; DAM DRAM, MST; WLC**
See also CA 104; 135; MTCW 2
Stringer, Arthur 1874-1950 **TCLC 37**
See also CA 161; DLB 92
Stringer, David
See Roberts, Keith (John Kingston)
Stroheim, Erich von 1885-1957 **TCLC 71**
Strugatskii, Arkadii (Natanovich) 1925-1991 **CLC 27**
See also CA 106; 135
Strugatskii, Boris (Natanovich) 1933-**CLC 27**
See also CA 106
Strummer, Joe 1953(?)- **CLC 30**
Strunk, William, Jr. 1869-1946 **TCLC 92**
See also CA 118; 164
Stuart, Don A.
See Campbell, John W(ood, Jr.)
Stuart, Ian
See MacLean, Alistair (Stuart)
Stuart, Jesse (Hilton) 1906-1984**CLC 1, 8, 11, 14, 34; SSC 31**
See also CA 5-8R; 112; CANR 31; DLB 9, 48, 102; DLBY 84; SATA 2; SATA-Obit 36
Sturgeon, Theodore (Hamilton) 1918-1985 **CLC 22, 39**
See also Queen, Ellery
See also CA 81-84; 116; CANR 32; DLB 8; DLBY 85; MTCW 1, 2
Sturges, Preston 1898-1959 **TCLC 48**
See also CA 114; 149; DLB 26
Styron, William 1925-**CLC 1, 3, 5, 11, 15, 60; DAM NOV, POP; SSC 25**
See also BEST 90:4; CA 5-8R; CANR 6, 33, 74; CDALB 1968-1988; DLB 2, 143; DLBY 80; INT CANR-6; MTCW 1, 2
Su, Chien 1884-1918
See Su Man-shu
See also CA 123
Suarez Lynch, B.
See Bioy Casares, Adolfo; Borges, Jorge Luis
Suckow, Ruth 1892-1960 **SSC 18**
See also CA 113; DLB 9, 102
Sudermann, Hermann 1857-1928 **TCLC 15**
See also CA 107; DLB 118
Sue, Eugene 1804-1857 **NCLC 1**
See also DLB 119
Sueskind, Patrick 1949- **CLC 44**
See also Suskind, Patrick
Sukenick, Ronald 1932- **CLC 3, 4, 6, 48**
See also CA 25-28R; CAAS 8; CANR 32; DLB 173; DLBY 81
Suknaski, Andrew 1942- **CLC 19**
See also CA 101; DLB 53
Sullivan, Vernon
See Vian, Boris
Sully Prudhomme 1839-1907 **TCLC 31**
Su Man-shu **TCLC 24**
See also Su, Chien
Summerforest, Ivy B.
See Kirkup, James
Summers, Andrew James 1942- **CLC 26**
Summers, Andy
See Summers, Andrew James
Summers, Hollis (Spurgeon, Jr.) 1916-**CLC 10**
See also CA 5-8R; CANR 3; DLB 6
Summers, (Alphonsus Joseph-Mary Augustus) Montague 1880-1948 **TCLC 16**
See also CA 118; 163
Sumner, Gordon Matthew **CLC 26**
See also Sting
Surtees, Robert Smith 1803-1864 **NCLC 14**
See also DLB 21
Susann, Jacqueline 1921-1974 **CLC 3**
See also AITN 1; CA 65-68; 53-56; MTCW 1, 2
Su Shih 1036-1101 **CMLC 15**
Suskind, Patrick
See Sueskind, Patrick
See also CA 145
Sutcliff, Rosemary 1920-1992 **CLC 26; DAB; DAC; DAM MST, POP**
See also AAYA 10; CA 5-8R; 139; CANR 37; CLR 1, 37; JRDA; MAICYA; SATA 6, 44, 78; SATA-Obit 73
Sutro, Alfred 1863-1933 **TCLC 6**
See also CA 105; DLB 10
Sutton, Henry
See Slavitt, David R(ytman)
Svevo, Italo 1861-1928 **TCLC 2, 35; SSC 25**
See also Schmitz, Aron Hector
Swados, Elizabeth (A.) 1951- **CLC 12**
See also CA 97-100; CANR 49; INT 97-100
Swados, Harvey 1920-1972 **CLC 5**
See also CA 5-8R; 37-40R; CANR 6; DLB 2
Swan, Gladys 1934- **CLC 69**
See also CA 101; CANR 17, 39
Swarthout, Glendon (Fred) 1918-1992**CLC 35**
See also CA 1-4R; 139; CANR 1, 47; SATA 26
Sweet, Sarah C.
See Jewett, (Theodora) Sarah Orne
Swenson, May 1919-1989**CLC 4, 14, 61, 106; DA; DAB; DAC; DAM MST, POET; PC 14**
See also CA 5-8R; 130; CANR 36, 61; DLB 5; MTCW 1, 2; SATA 15
Swift, Augustus
See Lovecraft, H(oward) P(hillips)
Swift, Graham (Colin) 1949- **CLC 41, 88**
See also CA 117; 122; CANR 46, 71; DLB 194; MTCW 2
Swift, Jonathan 1667-1745 **LC 1, 42; DA; DAB; DAC; DAM MST, NOV, POET; PC 9; WLC**
See also CDBLB 1660-1789; CLR 53; DLB 39, 95, 101; SATA 19
Swinburne, Algernon Charles 1837-1909 **TCLC 8, 36; DA; DAB; DAC; DAM MST, POET; PC 24; WLC**
See also CA 105; 140; CDBLB 1832-1890; DLB 35, 57
Swinfen, Ann **CLC 34**
Swinnerton, Frank Arthur 1884-1982**CLC 31**
See also CA 108; DLB 34
Swithen, John
See King, Stephen (Edwin)
Sylvia
See Ashton-Warner, Sylvia (Constance)
Symmes, Robert Edward
See Duncan, Robert (Edward)
Symonds, John Addington 1840-1893 **NCLC 34**
See also DLB 57, 144
Symons, Arthur 1865-1945 **TCLC 11**
See also CA 107; DLB 19, 57, 149
Symons, Julian (Gustave) 1912-1994 **CLC 2, 14, 32**
See also CA 49-52; 147; CAAS 3; CANR 3, 33, 59; DLB 87, 155; DLBY 92; MTCW 1
Synge, (Edmund) J(ohn) M(illington) 1871-1909 **TCLC 6, 37; DAM DRAM; DC 2**
See also CA 104; 141; CDBLB 1890-1914; DLB 10, 19
Syruc, J.
<indSee Milosz, Czeslaw
Szirtes, George 1948- **CLC 46**
See also CA 109; CANR 27, 61
Szymborska, Wislawa 1923- **CLC 99**
See also CA 154; DLBY 96; MTCW 2
T. O., Nik
See Annensky, Innokenty (Fyodorovich)
Tabori, George 1914- **CLC 19**
See also CA 49-52; CANR 4, 69
Tagore, Rabindranath 1861-1941**TCLC 3, 53; DAM DRAM, POET; PC 8**
See also CA 104; 120; MTCW 1, 2
Taine, Hippolyte Adolphe 1828-1893 **NCLC 15**
Talese, Gay 1932- **CLC 37**
See also AITN 1; CA 1-4R; CANR 9, 58; DLB 185; INT CANR-9; MTCW 1, 2
Tallent, Elizabeth (Ann) 1954- **CLC 45**
See also CA 117; CANR 72; DLB 130
Tally, Ted 1952- **CLC 42**
See also CA 120; 124; INT 124
Talvik, Heiti 1904-1947 **TCLC 87**
Tamayo y Baus, Manuel 1829-1898 **NCLC 1**
Tammsaare, A(nton) H(ansen) 1878-1940 **TCLC 27**
See also CA 164
Tam'si, Tchicaya U
See Tchicaya, Gerald Felix

Tan, Amy (Ruth) 1952- **CLC 59, 120; DAM MULT, NOV, POP**
See also AAYA 9; BEST 89:3; CA 136; CANR 54; CDALBS; DLB 173; MTCW 2; SATA 75

Tandem, Felix
See Spitteler, Carl (Friedrich Georg)

Tanizaki, Jun'ichiro 1886-1965**CLC 8, 14, 28; SSC 21**
See also CA 93-96; 25-28R; DLB 180; MTCW 2

Tanner, William
See Amis, Kingsley (William)

Tao Lao
See Storni, Alfonsina

Tarassoff, Lev
See Troyat, Henri

Tarbell, Ida M(inerva) 1857-1944 **TCLC 40**
See also CA 122; DLB 47

Tarkington, (Newton) Booth 1869-1946**TCLC 9**
See also CA 110; 143; DLB 9, 102; MTCW 2; SATA 17

Tarkovsky, Andrei (Arsenyevich) 1932-1986 **CLC 75**
See also CA 127

Tartt, Donna 1964(?)- **CLC 76**
See also CA 142

Tasso, Torquato 1544-1595 **LC 5**

Tate, (John Orley) Allen 1899-1979**CLC 2, 4, 6, 9, 11, 14, 24**
See also CA 5-8R; 85-88; CANR 32; DLB 4, 45, 63; DLBD 17; MTCW 1, 2

Tate, Ellalice
See Hibbert, Eleanor Alice Burford

Tate, James (Vincent) 1943- **CLC 2, 6, 25**
See also CA 21-24R; CANR 29, 57; DLB 5, 169

Tavel, Ronald 1940- **CLC 6**
See also CA 21-24R; CANR 33

Taylor, C(ecil) P(hilip) 1929-1981 **CLC 27**
See also CA 25-28R; 105; CANR 47

Taylor, Edward 1642(?)-1729 **LC 11; DA; DAB; DAC; DAM MST, POET**
See also DLB 24

Taylor, Eleanor Ross 1920- **CLC 5**
See also CA 81-84; CANR 70

Taylor, Elizabeth 1912-1975 **CLC 2, 4, 29**
See also CA 13-16R; CANR 9, 70; DLB 139; MTCW 1; SATA 13

Taylor, Frederick Winslow 1856-1915 **TCLC 76**

Taylor, Henry (Splawn) 1942- **CLC 44**
See also CA 33-36R; CAAS 7; CANR 31; DLB 5

Taylor, Kamala (Purnaiya) 1924-
See Markandaya, Kamala
See also CA 77-80

Taylor, Mildred D. **CLC 21**
See also AAYA 10; BW 1; CA 85-88; CANR 25; CLR 9, 58; DLB 52; JRDA; MAICYA; SAAS 5; SATA 15, 70

Taylor, Peter (Hillsman) 1917-1994**CLC 1, 4, 18, 37, 44, 50, 71; SSC 10**
See also CA 13-16R; 147; CANR 9, 50; DLBY 81, 94; INT CANR-9; MTCW 1, 2

Taylor, Robert Lewis 1912-1998 **CLC 14**
See also CA 1-4R; 170; CANR 3, 64; SATA 10

Tchekhov, Anton
See Chekhov, Anton (Pavlovich)

Tchicaya, Gerald Felix 1931-1988 **CLC 101**
See also CA 129; 125

Tchicaya U Tam'si
See Tchicaya, Gerald Felix

Teasdale, Sara 1884-1933 **TCLC 4**
See also CA 104; 163; DLB 45; SATA 32

Tegner, Esaias 1782-1846 **NCLC 2**

Teilhard de Chardin, (Marie Joseph) Pierre 1881-1955 **TCLC 9**
See also CA 105

Temple, Ann
See Mortimer, Penelope (Ruth)

Tennant, Emma (Christina) 1937-**CLC 13, 52**
See also CA 65-68; CAAS 9; CANR 10, 38, 59; DLB 14

Tenneshaw, S. M.
See Silverberg, Robert

Tennyson, Alfred 1809-1892 **NCLC 30, 65; DA; DAB; DAC; DAM MST, POET; PC 6; WLC**
See also CDBLB 1832-1890; DLB 32

Teran, Lisa St. Aubin de **CLC 36**
See also St. Aubin de Teran, Lisa

Terence c. 184B.C.-c. 159B.C.**CMLC 14; DC 7**
See also DLB 211

Teresa de Jesus, St. 1515-1582 **LC 18**

Terkel, Louis 1912-
See Terkel, Studs
See also CA 57-60; CANR 18, 45, 67; MTCW 1, 2

Terkel, Studs **CLC 38**
See also Terkel, Louis
See also AITN 1; MTCW 2

Terry, C. V.
See Slaughter, Frank G(ill)

Terry, Megan 1932- **CLC 19**
See also CA 77-80; CABS 3; CANR 43; DLB 7

Tertullian c. 155-c. 245 **CMLC 29**

Tertz, Abram
See Sinyavsky, Andrei (Donatevich)

Tesich, Steve 1943(?)-1996 **CLC 40, 69**
See also CA 105; 152; DLBY 83

Tesla, Nikola 1856-1943 **TCLC 88**

Teternikov, Fyodor Kuzmich 1863-1927
See Sologub, Fyodor
See also CA 104

Tevis, Walter 1928-1984 **CLC 42**
See also CA 113

Tey, Josephine **TCLC 14**
See also Mackintosh, Elizabeth
See also DLB 77

Thackeray, William Makepeace 1811-1863 **NCLC 5, 14, 22, 43; DA; DAB; DAC; DAM MST, NOV; WLC**
See also CDBLB 1832-1890; DLB 21, 55, 159, 163; SATA 23

Thakura, Ravindranatha
See Tagore, Rabindranath

Tharoor, Shashi 1956- **CLC 70**
See also CA 141

Thelwell, Michael Miles 1939- **CLC 22**
See also BW 2; CA 101

Theobald, Lewis, Jr.
See Lovecraft, H(oward) P(hillips)

Theodorescu, Ion N. 1880-1967
See Arghezi, Tudor
See also CA 116

Theriault, Yves 1915-1983 **CLC 79; DAC; DAM MST**
See also CA 102; DLB 88

Theroux, Alexander (Louis) 1939- **CLC 2, 25**
See also CA 85-88; CANR 20, 63

Theroux, Paul (Edward) 1941- **CLC 5, 8, 11, 15, 28, 46; DAM POP**
See also AAYA 28; BEST 89:4; CA 33-36R; CANR 20, 45, 74; CDALBS; DLB 2; MTCW 1, 2; SATA 44

Thesen, Sharon 1946- **CLC 56**
See also CA 163

Thevenin, Denis
See Duhamel, Georges

Thibault, Jacques Anatole Francois 1844-1924
See France, Anatole
See also CA 106; 127; DAM NOV; MTCW 1, 2

Thiele, Colin (Milton) 1920- **CLC 17**
See also CA 29-32R; CANR 12, 28, 53; CLR 27; MAICYA; SAAS 2; SATA 14, 72

Thomas, Audrey (Callahan) 1935-**CLC 7, 13, 37, 107; SSC 20**
See also AITN 2; CA 21-24R; CAAS 19; CANR 36, 58; DLB 60; MTCW 1

Thomas, D(onald) M(ichael) 1935- **CLC 13, 22, 31**
See also CA 61-64; CAAS 11; CANR 17, 45, 75; CDBLB 1960 to Present; DLB 40, 207; INT CANR-17; MTCW 1, 2

Thomas, Dylan (Marlais) 1914-1953**TCLC 1, 8, 45; DA; DAB; DAC; DAM DRAM, MST, POET; PC 2; SSC 3; WLC**
See also CA 104; 120; CANR 65; CDBLB 1945-1960; DLB 13, 20, 139; MTCW 1, 2; SATA 60

Thomas, (Philip) Edward 1878-1917 **TCLC 10; DAM POET**
See also CA 106; 153; DLB 98

Thomas, Joyce Carol 1938- **CLC 35**
See also AAYA 12; BW 2, 3; CA 113; 116; CANR 48; CLR 19; DLB 33; INT 116; JRDA; MAICYA; MTCW 1, 2; SAAS 7; SATA 40, 78

Thomas, Lewis 1913-1993 **CLC 35**
See also CA 85-88; 143; CANR 38, 60; MTCW 1, 2

Thomas, M. Carey 1857-1935 **TCLC 89**

Thomas, Paul
See Mann, (Paul) Thomas

Thomas, Piri 1928- **CLC 17; HLCS 1**
See also CA 73-76; HW 1

Thomas, R(onald) S(tuart) 1913- **CLC 6, 13, 48; DAB; DAM POET**
See also CA 89-92; CAAS 4; CANR 30; CDBLB 1960 to Present; DLB 27; MTCW 1

Thomas, Ross (Elmore) 1926-1995 **CLC 39**
See also CA 33-36R; 150; CANR 22, 63

Thompson, Francis Clegg
See Mencken, H(enry) L(ouis)

Thompson, Francis Joseph 1859-1907**TCLC 4**
See also CA 104; CDBLB 1890-1914; DLB 19

Thompson, Hunter S(tockton) 1939- **CLC 9, 17, 40, 104; DAM POP**
See also BEST 89:1; CA 17-20R; CANR 23, 46, 74, 77; DLB 185; MTCW 1, 2

Thompson, James Myers
See Thompson, Jim (Myers)

Thompson, Jim (Myers) 1906-1977(?)**CLC 69**
See also CA 140

Thompson, Judith **CLC 39**

Thomson, James 1700-1748 **LC 16, 29, 40; DAM POET**
See also DLB 95

Thomson, James 1834-1882 **NCLC 18; DAM POET**
See also DLB 35

Thoreau, Henry David 1817-1862**NCLC 7, 21, 61; DA; DAB; DAC; DAM MST; WLC**
See also CDALB 1640-1865; DLB 1

Thornton, Hall
See Silverberg, Robert

Thucydides c. 455B.C.-399B.C. **CMLC 17**
See also DLB 176
Thurber, James (Grover) 1894-1961 **CLC 5, 11, 25; DA; DAB; DAC; DAM DRAM, MST, NOV; SSC 1**
See also CA 73-76; CANR 17, 39; CDALB 1929-1941; DLB 4, 11, 22, 102; MAICYA; MTCW 1, 2; SATA 13
Thurman, Wallace (Henry) 1902-1934**TCLC 6; BLC 3; DAM MULT**
See also BW 1, 3; CA 104; 124; DLB 51
Ticheburn, Cheviot
See Ainsworth, William Harrison
Tieck, (Johann) Ludwig 1773-1853 **NCLC 5, 46; SSC 31**
See also DLB 90
Tiger, Derry
See Ellison, Harlan (Jay)
Tilghman, Christopher 1948(?)- **CLC 65**
See also CA 159
Tillinghast, Richard (Williford) 1940-**CLC 29**
See also CA 29-32R; CAAS 23; CANR 26, 51
Timrod, Henry 1828-1867 **NCLC 25**
See also DLB 3
Tindall, Gillian (Elizabeth) 1938- **CLC 7**
See also CA 21-24R; CANR 11, 65
Tiptree, James, Jr. **CLC 48, 50**
See also Sheldon, Alice Hastings Bradley
See also DLB 8
Titmarsh, Michael Angelo
See Thackeray, William Makepeace
Tocqueville, Alexis (Charles Henri Maurice Clerel, Comte) de 1805-1859**NCLC 7, 63**
Tolkien, J(ohn) R(onald) R(euel) 1892-1973 **CLC 1, 2, 3, 8, 12, 38; DA; DAB; DAC; DAM MST, NOV, POP; WLC**
See also AAYA 10; AITN 1; CA 17-18; 45-48; CANR 36; CAP 2; CDBLB 1914-1945; CLR 56; DLB 15, 160; JRDA; MAICYA; MTCW 1, 2; SATA 2, 32, 100; SATA-Obit 24
Toller, Ernst 1893-1939 **TCLC 10**
See also CA 107; DLB 124
Tolson, M. B.
See Tolson, Melvin B(eaunorus)
Tolson, Melvin B(eaunorus) 1898(?)-1966 **CLC 36, 105; BLC 3; DAM MULT, POET**
See also BW 1, 3; CA 124; 89-92; CANR 80; DLB 48, 76
Tolstoi, Aleksei Nikolaevich
See Tolstoy, Alexey Nikolaevich
Tolstoy, Alexey Nikolaevich 1882-1945**TCLC 18**
See also CA 107; 158
Tolstoy, Count Leo
See Tolstoy, Leo (Nikolaevich)
Tolstoy, Leo (Nikolaevich) 1828-1910**TCLC 4, 11, 17, 28, 44, 79; DA; DAB; DAC; DAM MST, NOV; SSC 9, 30; WLC**
See also CA 104; 123; SATA 26
Tomasi di Lampedusa, Giuseppe 1896-1957
See Lampedusa, Giuseppe (Tomasi) di
See also CA 111
Tomlin, Lily **CLC 17**
See also Tomlin, Mary Jean
Tomlin, Mary Jean 1939(?)-
See Tomlin, Lily
See also CA 117
Tomlinson, (Alfred) Charles 1927-**CLC 2, 4, 6, 13, 45; DAM POET; PC 17**
See also CA 5-8R; CANR 33; DLB 40
Tomlinson, H(enry) M(ajor) 1873-1958**TCLC 71**
See also CA 118; 161; DLB 36, 100, 195
Tonson, Jacob
See Bennett, (Enoch) Arnold
Toole, John Kennedy 1937-1969 **CLC 19, 64**
See also CA 104; DLBY 81; MTCW 2
Toomer, Jean 1894-1967**CLC 1, 4, 13, 22; BLC 3; DAM MULT; PC 7; SSC 1; WLCS**
See also BW 1; CA 85-88; CDALB 1917-1929; DLB 45, 51; MTCW 1, 2
Torley, Luke
<indexhanSee Blish, James (Benjamin)
Tornimparte, Alessandra
See Ginzburg, Natalia
Torre, Raoul della
See Mencken, H(enry) L(ouis)
Torrey, E(dwin) Fuller 1937- **CLC 34**
See also CA 119; CANR 71
Torsvan, Ben Traven
See Traven, B.
Torsvan, Benno Traven
See Traven, B.
Torsvan, Berick Traven
See Traven, B.
Torsvan, Berwick Traven
See Traven, B.
Torsvan, Bruno Traven
See Traven, B.
Torsvan, Traven
See Traven, B.
Tournier, Michel (Edouard) 1924-**CLC 6, 23, 36, 95**
See also CA 49-52; CANR 3, 36, 74; DLB 83; MTCW 1, 2; SATA 23
Tournimparte, Alessandra
See Ginzburg, Natalia
Towers, Ivar
See Kornbluth, C(yril) M.
Towne, Robert (Burton) 1936(?)- **CLC 87**
See also CA 108; DLB 44
Townsend, Sue **CLC 61**
See also Townsend, Susan Elaine
See also AAYA 28; SATA 55, 93; SATA-Brief 48
Townsend, Susan Elaine 1946-
See Townsend, Sue
See also CA 119; 127; CANR 65; DAB; DAC; DAM MST
Townshend, Peter (Dennis Blandford) 1945- **CLC 17, 42**
See also CA 107
Tozzi, Federigo 1883-1920 **TCLC 31**
See also CA 160
Traill, Catharine Parr 1802-1899 **NCLC 31**
See also DLB 99
Trakl, Georg 1887-1914 **TCLC 5; PC 20**
See also CA 104; 165; MTCW 2
Transtroemer, Tomas (Goesta) 1931-**CLC 52, 65; DAM POET**
See also CA 117; 129; CAAS 17
Transtromer, Tomas Gosta
See Transtroemer, Tomas (Goesta)
Traven, B. (?)-1969 **CLC 8, 11**
See also CA 19-20; 25-28R; CAP 2; DLB 9, 56; MTCW 1
Treitel, Jonathan 1959- **CLC 70**
Tremain, Rose 1943- **CLC 42**
See also CA 97-100; CANR 44; DLB 14
Tremblay, Michel 1942- **CLC 29, 102; DAC; DAM MST**
See also CA 116; 128; DLB 60; MTCW 1, 2
Trevanian **CLC 29**
See also Whitaker, Rod(ney)
Trevor, Glen
See Hilton, James
Trevor, William 1928-**CLC 7, 9, 14, 25, 71, 116; SSC 21**
See also Cox, William Trevor
See also DLB 14, 139; MTCW 2
Trifonov, Yuri (Valentinovich) 1925-1981 **CLC 45**
See also CA 126; 103; MTCW 1
Trilling, Lionel 1905-1975 **CLC 9, 11, 24**
See also CA 9-12R; 61-64; CANR 10; DLB 28, 63; INT CANR-10; MTCW 1, 2
Trimball, W. H.
See Mencken, H(enry) L(ouis)
Tristan
See Gomez de la Serna, Ramon
Tristram
See Housman, A(lfred) E(dward)
Trogdon, William (Lewis) 1939-
See Heat-Moon, William Least
See also CA 115; 119; CANR 47; INT 119
Trollope, Anthony 1815-1882**NCLC 6, 33; DA; DAB; DAC; DAM MST, NOV; SSC 28; WLC**
See also CDBLB 1832-1890; DLB 21, 57, 159; SATA 22
Trollope, Frances 1779-1863 **NCLC 30**
See also DLB 21, 166
Trotsky, Leon 1879-1940 **TCLC 22**
See also CA 118; 167
Trotter (Cockburn), Catharine 1679-1749**LC 8**
See also DLB 84
Trout, Kilgore
See Farmer, Philip Jose
Trow, George W. S. 1943- **CLC 52**
See also CA 126
Troyat, Henri 1911- **CLC 23**
See also CA 45-48; CANR 2, 33, 67; MTCW 1
Trudeau, G(arretson) B(eekman) 1948-
<inSee Trudeau, Garry B.
See also CA 81-84; CANR 31; SATA 35
Trudeau, Garry B. **CLC 12**
See also Trudeau, G(arretson) B(eekman)
See also AAYA 10; AITN 2
Truffaut, Francois 1932-1984 **CLC 20, 101**
See also CA 81-84; 113; CANR 34
Trumbo, Dalton 1905-1976 **CLC 19**
See also CA 21-24R; 69-72; CANR 10; DLB 26
Trumbull, John 1750-1831 **NCLC 30**
See also DLB 31
Trundlett, Helen B.
See Eliot, T(homas) S(tearns)
Tryon, Thomas 1926-1991 **CLC 3, 11; DAM POP**
See also AITN 1; CA 29-32R; 135; CANR 32, 77; MTCW 1
Tryon, Tom
See Tryon, Thomas
Ts'ao Hsueh-ch'in 1715(?)-1763 **LC 1**
Tsushima, Shuji 1909-1948
See Dazai Osamu
See also CA 107
Tsvetaeva (Efron), Marina (Ivanovna) 1892-1941 **TCLC 7, 35; PC 14**
See also CA 104; 128; CANR 73; MTCW 1, 2
Tuck, Lily 1938- **CLC 70**
See also CA 139
Tu Fu 712-770 **PC 9**
See also DAM MULT
Tunis, John R(oberts) 1889-1975 **CLC 12**
See also CA 61-64; CANR 62; DLB 22, 171; JRDA; MAICYA; SATA 37; SATA-Brief 30
Tuohy, Frank **CLC 37**

See Mencken, H(enry) L(ouis)
Verdu, Matilde
See Cela, Camilo Jose
Verga, Giovanni (Carmelo) 1840-1922 **TCLC 3; SSC 21**
See also CA 104; 123
Vergil 70B.C.-19B.C. **CMLC 9; DA; DAB; DAC; DAM MST, POET; PC 12; WLCS**
See also Virgil
Verhaeren, Emile (Adolphe Gustave) 1855-1916 **TCLC 12**
See also CA 109
Verlaine, Paul (Marie) 1844-1896 **NCLC 2, 51; DAM POET; PC 2**
Verne, Jules (Gabriel) 1828-1905 **TCLC 6, 52**
See also AAYA 16; CA 110; 131; DLB 123; JRDA; MAICYA; SATA 21
Very, Jones 1813-1880 **NCLC 9**
See also DLB 1
Vesaas, Tarjei 1897-1970 **CLC 48**
See also CA 29-32R
Vialis, Gaston
See Simenon, Georges (Jacques Christian)
Vian, Boris 1920-1959 **TCLC 9**
See also CA 106; 164; DLB 72; MTCW 2
Viaud, (Louis Marie) Julien 1850-1923
See Loti, Pierre
See also CA 107
Vicar, Henry
See Felsen, Henry Gregor
Vicker, Angus
See Felsen, Henry Gregor
Vidal, Gore 1925- **CLC 2, 4, 6, 8, 10, 22, 33, 72; DAM NOV, POP**
See also AITN 1; BEST 90:2; CA 5-8R; CANR 13, 45, 65; CDALBS; DLB 6, 152; INT CANR-13; MTCW 1, 2
Viereck, Peter (Robert Edwin) 1916- **CLC 4**
<indexhanSee also CA 1-4R; CANR 1, 47; DLB 5
Vigny, Alfred (Victor) de 1797-1863 **NCLC 7; DAM POET; PC 26**
See also DLB 119, 192
Vilakazi, Benedict Wallet 1906-1947 **TCLC 37**
See also CA 168
Villa, Jose Garcia 1904-1997 **PC 22**
See also CA 25-28R; CANR 12
Villaurrutia, Xavier 1903-1950 **TCLC 80**
See also HW 1
Villiers de l'Isle Adam, Jean Marie Mathias Philippe Auguste, Comte de 1838-1889 **NCLC 3; SSC 14**
See also DLB 123
Villon, Francois 1431-1463(?) **PC 13**
See also DLB 208
Vinci, Leonardo da 1452-1519 **LC 12**
Vine, Barbara **CLC 50**
See also Rendell, Ruth (Barbara)
See also BEST 90:4
Vinge, Joan (Carol) D(ennison) 1948- **CLC 30; SSC 24**
See also CA 93-96; CANR 72; SATA 36
Violis, G.
See Simenon, Georges (Jacques Christian)
Virgil 70B.C.-19B.C.
See Vergil
See also DLB 211
Visconti, Luchino 1906-1976 **CLC 16**
See also CA 81-84; 65-68; CANR 39
Vittorini, Elio 1908-1966 **CLC 6, 9, 14**
See also CA 133; 25-28R
Vivekananda, Swami 1863-1902 **TCLC 88**
Vizenor, Gerald Robert 1934- **CLC 103; DAM MULT**
See also CA 13-16R; CAAS 22; CANR 5, 21, 44, 67; DLB 175; MTCW 2; NNAL
Vizinczey, Stephen 1933- **CLC 40**
See also CA 128; INT 128
Vliet, R(ussell) G(ordon) 1929-1984 **CLC 22**
See also CA 37-40R; 112; CANR 18
Vogau, Boris Andreyevich 1894-1937(?)
See Pilnyak, Boris
See also CA 123
Vogel, Paula A(nne) 1951- **CLC 76**
See also CA 108
Voigt, Cynthia 1942- **CLC 30**
See also AAYA 3, 30; CA 106; CANR 18, 37, 40; CLR 13, 48; INT CANR-18; JRDA; MAICYA; SATA 48, 79; SATA-Brief 33
Voigt, Ellen Bryant 1943- **CLC 54**
See also CA 69-72; CANR 11, 29, 55; DLB 120
Voinovich, Vladimir (Nikolaevich) 1932- **CLC 10, 49**
See also CA 81-84; CAAS 12; CANR 33, 67; MTCW 1
Vollmann, William T. 1959- **CLC 89; DAM NOV, POP**
See also CA 134; CANR 67; MTCW 2
Voloshinov, V. N.
See Bakhtin, Mikhail Mikhailovich
Voltaire 1694-1778 **LC 14; DA; DAB; DAC; DAM DRAM, MST; SSC 12; WLC**
von Aschendrof, BaronIgnatz
See Ford, Ford Madox
von Daeniken, Erich 1935- **CLC 30**
See also AITN 1; CA 37-40R; CANR 17, 44
von Daniken, Erich
See von Daeniken, Erich
von Heidenstam, (Carl Gustaf) Verner
See Heidenstam, (Carl Gustaf) Verner von
von Heyse, Paul (Johann Ludwig)
See Heyse, Paul (Johann Ludwig von)
von Hofmannsthal, Hugo
See Hofmannsthal, Hugo von
von Horvath, Odon
See Horvath, Oedoen von
von Horvath, Oedoen
See Horvath, Oedoen von
von Liliencron, (Friedrich Adolf Axel) Detlev
See Liliencron, (Friedrich Adolf Axel) Detlev von
Vonnegut, Kurt, Jr. 1922- **CLC 1, 2, 3, 4, 5, 8, 12, 22, 40, 60, 111; DA; DAB; DAC; DAM MST, NOV, POP; SSC 8; WLC**
See also AAYA 6; AITN 1; BEST 90:4; CA 1-4R; CANR 1, 25, 49, 75; CDALB 1968-1988; DLB 2, 8, 152; DLBD 3; DLBY 80; MTCW 1, 2
Von Rachen, Kurt
See Hubbard, L(afayette) Ron(ald)
von Rezzori (d'Arezzo), Gregor
See Rezzori (d'Arezzo), Gregor von
von Sternberg, Josef
See Sternberg, Josef von
Vorster, Gordon 1924- **CLC 34**
See also CA 133
Vosce, Trudie
See Ozick, Cynthia
Voznesensky, Andrei (Andreievich) 1933- **CLC 1, 15, 57; DAM POET**
See also CA 89-92; CANR 37; MTCW 1
Waddington, Miriam 1917- **CLC 28**
See also CA 21-24R; CANR 12, 30; DLB 68
Wagman, Fredrica 1937- **CLC 7**
See also CA 97-100; INT 97-100
Wagner, Linda W.
See Wagner-Martin, Linda (C.)
Wagner, Linda Welshimer
See Wagner-Martin, Linda (C.)
Wagner, Richard 1813-1883 **NCLC 9**
See also DLB 129
Wagner-Martin, Linda (C.) 1936- **CLC 50**
See also CA 159
Wagoner, David (Russell) 1926- **CLC 3, 5, 15**
See also CA 1-4R; CAAS 3; CANR 2, 71; DLB 5; SATA 14
Wah, Fred(erick James) 1939- **CLC 44**
See also CA 107; 141; DLB 60
Wahloo, Per 1926-1975 **CLC 7**
See also CA 61-64; CANR 73
Wahloo, Peter
See Wahloo, Per
Wain, John (Barrington) 1925-1994 **CLC 2, 11, 15, 46**
See also CA 5-8R; 145; CAAS 4; CANR 23, 54; CDBLB 1960 to Present; DLB 15, 27, 139, 155; MTCW 1, 2
Wajda, Andrzej 1926- **CLC 16**
See also CA 102
Wakefield, Dan 1932- **CLC 7**
See also CA 21-24R; CAAS 7
Wakoski, Diane 1937- **CLC 2, 4, 7, 9, 11, 40; DAM POET; PC 15**
See also CA 13-16R; CAAS 1; CANR 9, 60; DLB 5; INT CANR-9; MTCW 2
Wakoski-Sherbell, Diane
See Wakoski, Diane
Walcott, Derek (Alton) 1930- **CLC 2, 4, 9, 14, 25, 42, 67, 76; BLC 3; DAB; DAC; DAM MST, MULT, POET; DC 7**
See also BW 2; CA 89-92; CANR 26, 47, 75, 80; DLB 117; DLBY 81; MTCW 1, 2
Waldman, Anne (Lesley) 1945- **CLC 7**
See also CA 37-40R; CAAS 17; CANR 34, 69; DLB 16
Waldo, E. Hunter
See Sturgeon, Theodore (Hamilton)
Waldo, Edward Hamilton
See Sturgeon, Theodore (Hamilton)
Walker, Alice (Malsenior) 1944- **CLC 5, 6, 9, 19, 27, 46, 58, 103; BLC 3; DA; DAB; DAC; DAM MST, MULT, NOV, POET, POP; SSC 5; WLCS**
See also AAYA 3; BEST 89:4; BW 2, 3; CA 37-40R; CANR 9, 27, 49, 66; CDALB 1968-1988; DLB 6, 33, 143; INT CANR-27; MTCW 1, 2; SATA 31
Walker, David Harry 1911-1992 **CLC 14**
See also CA 1-4R; 137; CANR 1; SATA 8; SATA-Obit 71
Walker, Edward Joseph 1934-
See Walker, Ted
See also CA 21-24R; CANR 12, 28, 53
Walker, George F. 1947- **CLC 44, 61; DAB; DAC; DAM MST**
See also CA 103; CANR 21, 43, 59; DLB 60
Walker, Joseph A. 1935- **CLC 19; DAM DRAM, MST**
See also BW 1, 3; CA 89-92; CANR 26; DLB 38
Walker, Margaret (Abigail) 1915-1998 **CLC 1, 6; BLC; DAM MULT; PC 20**
See also BW 2, 3; CA 73-76; 172; CANR 26, 54, 76; DLB 76, 152; MTCW 1, 2
Walker, Ted **CLC 13**
See also Walker, Edward Joseph
See also DLB 40
Wallace, David Foster 1962- **CLC 50, 114**
See also CA 132; CANR 59; MTCW 2
Wallace, Dexter

See Masters, Edgar Lee
Wallace, (Richard Horatio) Edgar 1875-1932 **TCLC 57**
See also CA 115; DLB 70
Wallace, Irving 1916-1990 **CLC 7, 13; DAM NOV, POP**
See also AITN 1; CA 1-4R; 132; CAAS 1; CANR 1, 27; INT CANR-27; MTCW 1, 2
Wallant, Edward Lewis 1926-1962**CLC 5, 10**
See also CA 1-4R; CANR 22; DLB 2, 28, 143; MTCW 1, 2
Wallas, Graham 1858-1932 **TCLC 91**
Walley, Byron
See Card, Orson Scott
Walpole, Horace 1717-1797 **LC 49**
See also DLB 39, 104
Walpole, Hugh (Seymour) 1884-1941**TCLC 5**
See also CA 104; 165; DLB 34; MTCW 2
Walser, Martin 1927- **CLC 27**
See also CA 57-60; CANR 8, 46; DLB 75, 124
Walser, Robert 1878-1956 **TCLC 18; SSC 20**
See also CA 118; 165; DLB 66
Walsh, Jill Paton **CLC 35**
See also Paton Walsh, Gillian
See also AAYA 11; CLR 2; DLB 161; SAAS 3
Walter, Villiam Christian
See Andersen, Hans Christian
Wambaugh, Joseph (Aloysius, Jr.) 1937-**CLC 3, 18; DAM NOV, POP**
See also AITN 1; BEST 89:3; CA 33-36R; CANR 42, 65; DLB 6; DLBY 83; MTCW 1, 2
Wang Wei 699(?)-761(?) **PC 18**
Ward, Arthur Henry Sarsfield 1883-1959
See Rohmer, Sax
See also CA 108; 173
Ward, Douglas Turner 1930- **CLC 19**
See also BW 1; CA 81-84; CANR 27; DLB 7, 38
Ward, Mary Augusta
See Ward, Mrs. Humphry
Ward, Mrs. Humphry 1851-1920 **TCLC 55**
See also DLB 18
Ward, Peter
See Faust, Frederick (Schiller)
Warhol, Andy 1928(?)-1987 **CLC 20**
See also AAYA 12; BEST 89:4; CA 89-92; 121; CANR 34
Warner, Francis (Robert le Plastrier) 1937- **CLC 14**
See also CA 53-56; CANR 11
Warner, Marina 1946- **CLC 59**
See also CA 65-68; CANR 21, 55; DLB 194
Warner, Rex (Ernest) 1905-1986 **CLC 45**
See also CA 89-92; 119; DLB 15
Warner, Susan (Bogert) 1819-1885 **NCLC 31**
See also DLB 3, 42
Warner, Sylvia (Constance) Ashton
See Ashton-Warner, Sylvia (Constance)
Warner, Sylvia Townsend 1893-1978 **CLC 7, 19; SSC 23**
See also CA 61-64; 77-80; CANR 16, 60; DLB 34, 139; MTCW 1, 2
Warren, Mercy Otis 1728-1814 **NCLC 13**
See also DLB 31, 200
Warren, Robert Penn 1905-1989**CLC 1, 4, 6, 8, 10, 13, 18, 39, 53, 59; DA; DAB; DAC; DAM MST, NOV, POET; SSC 4; WLC**
See also AITN 1; CA 13-16R; 129; CANR 10, 47; CDALB 1968-1988; DLB 2, 48, 152; DLBY 80, 89; INT CANR-10; MTCW 1, 2; SATA 46; SATA-Obit 63
Warshofsky, Isaac
See Singer, Isaac Bashevis
Warton, Thomas 1728-1790 **LC 15; DAM POET**
See also DLB 104, 109
Waruk, Kona
See Harris, (Theodore) Wilson
Warung, Price 1855-1911 **TCLC 45**
Warwick, Jarvis
See Garner, Hugh
Washington, Alex
See Harris, Mark
Washington, Booker T(aliaferro) 1856-1915 **TCLC 10; BLC 3; DAM MULT**
See also BW 1; CA 114; 125; SATA 28
Washington, George 1732-1799 **LC 25**
See also DLB 31
Wassermann, (Karl) Jakob 1873-1934 **TCLC 6**
See also CA 104; 163; DLB 66
Wasserstein, Wendy 1950- **CLC 32, 59, 90; DAM DRAM; DC 4**
See also CA 121; 129; CABS 3; CANR 53, 75; INT 129; MTCW 2; SATA 94
Waterhouse, Keith (Spencer) 1929- **CLC 47**
See also CA 5-8R; CANR 38, 67; DLB 13, 15; MTCW 1, 2
Waters, Frank (Joseph) 1902-1995 **CLC 88**
See also CA 5-8R; 149; CAAS 13; CANR 3, 18, 63; DLB 212; DLBY 86
Waters, Roger 1944- **CLC 35**
Watkins, Frances Ellen
See Harper, Frances Ellen Watkins
Watkins, Gerrold
See Malzberg, Barry N(athaniel)
Watkins, Gloria 1955(?)-
<indexhang>See hooks, bell
See also BW 2; CA 143; MTCW 2
Watkins, Paul 1964- **CLC 55**
See also CA 132; CANR 62
Watkins, Vernon Phillips 1906-1967 **CLC 43**
See also CA 9-10; 25-28R; CAP 1; DLB 20
Watson, Irving S.
See Mencken, H(enry) L(ouis)
Watson, John H.
See Farmer, Philip Jose
Watson, Richard F.
See Silverberg, Robert
Waugh, Auberon (Alexander) 1939- **CLC 7**
See also CA 45-48; CANR 6, 22; DLB 14, 194
Waugh, Evelyn (Arthur St. John) 1903-1966 **CLC 1, 3, 8, 13, 19, 27, 44, 107; DA; DAB; DAC; DAM MST, NOV, POP; WLC**
See also CA 85-88; 25-28R; CANR 22; CDBLB 1914-1945; DLB 15, 162, 195; MTCW 1, 2
Waugh, Harriet 1944- **CLC 6**
See also CA 85-88; CANR 22
Ways, C. R.
See Blount, Roy (Alton), Jr.
Waystaff, Simon
See Swift, Jonathan
Webb, (Martha) Beatrice (Potter) 1858-1943 **TCLC 22**
See also Potter, (Helen) Beatrix
See also CA 117; DLB 190
Webb, Charles (Richard) 1939- **CLC 7**
See also CA 25-28R
Webb, James H(enry), Jr. 1946- **CLC 22**
See also CA 81-84
Webb, Mary (Gladys Meredith) 1881-1927 **TCLC 24**
See also CA 123; DLB 34
Webb, Mrs. Sidney
See Webb, (Martha) Beatrice (Potter)
Webb, Phyllis 1927- **CLC 18**
See also CA 104; CANR 23; DLB 53
Webb, Sidney (James) 1859-1947 **TCLC 22**
See also CA 117; 163; DLB 190
Webber, Andrew Lloyd **CLC 21**
See also Lloyd Webber, Andrew
Weber, Lenora Mattingly 1895-1971 **CLC 12**
See also CA 19-20; 29-32R; CAP 1; SATA 2; SATA-Obit 26
Weber, Max 1864-1920 **TCLC 69**
See also CA 109
Webster, John 1579(?)-1634(?) **LC 33; DA; DAB; DAC; DAM DRAM, MST; DC 2; WLC**
See also CDBLB Before 1660; DLB 58
Webster, Noah 1758-1843 **NCLC 30**
See also DLB 1, 37, 42, 43, 73
Wedekind, (Benjamin) Frank(lin) 1864-1918 **TCLC 7; DAM DRAM**
See also CA 104; 153; DLB 118
Weidman, Jerome 1913-1998 **CLC 7**
See also AITN 2; CA 1-4R; 171; CANR 1; DLB 28
Weil, Simone (Adolphine) 1909-1943**TCLC 23**
See also CA 117; 159; MTCW 2
Weininger, Otto 1880-1903 **TCLC 84**
Weinstein, Nathan
See West, Nathanael
Weinstein, Nathan von Wallenstein
See West, Nathanael
Weir, Peter (Lindsay) 1944- **CLC 20**
See also CA 113; 123
Weiss, Peter (Ulrich) 1916-1982**CLC 3, 15, 51; DAM DRAM**
See also CA 45-48; 106; CANR 3; DLB 69, 124
Weiss, Theodore (Russell) 1916-**CLC 3, 8, 14**
See also CA 9-12R; CAAS 2; CANR 46; DLB 5
Welch, (Maurice) Denton 1915-1948**TCLC 22**
See also CA 121; 148
Welch, James 1940- **CLC 6, 14, 52; DAM MULT, POP**
See also CA 85-88; CANR 42, 66; DLB 175; NNAL
Weldon, Fay 1931- **CLC 6, 9, 11, 19, 36, 59; DAM POP**
See also CA 21-24R; CANR 16, 46, 63; CDBLB 1960 to Present; DLB 14, 194; INT CANR-16; MTCW 1, 2
Wellek, Rene 1903-1995 **CLC 28**
See also CA 5-8R; 150; CAAS 7; CANR 8; DLB 63; INT CANR-8
Weller, Michael 1942- **CLC 10, 53**
See also CA 85-88
Weller, Paul 1958- **CLC 26**
Wellershoff, Dieter 1925- **CLC 46**
See also CA 89-92; CANR 16, 37
Welles, (George) Orson 1915-1985**CLC 20, 80**
See also CA 93-96; 117
Wellman, John McDowell 1945-
See Wellman, Mac
See also CA 166
Wellman, Mac 1945- **CLC 65**
See also Wellman, John McDowell; Wellman, John McDowell
Wellman, Manly Wade 1903-1986 **CLC 49**
See also CA 1-4R; 118; CANR 6, 16, 44; SATA 6; SATA-Obit 47
Wells, Carolyn 1869(?)-1942 **TCLC 35**
See also CA 113; DLB 11
Wells, H(erbert) G(eorge) 1866-1946**TCLC 6, 12, 19; DA; DAB; DAC; DAM MST, NOV; SSC 6; WLC**

See also AAYA 18; CA 110; 121; CDBLB 1914-1945; DLB 34, 70, 156, 178; MTCW 1, 2; SATA 20

Wells, Rosemary 1943- **CLC 12**
See also AAYA 13; CA 85-88; CANR 48; CLR 16; MAICYA; SAAS 1; SATA 18, 69

Welty, Eudora 1909- **CLC 1, 2, 5, 14, 22, 33, 105; DA; DAB; DAC; DAM MST, NOV; SSC 1, 27; WLC**
See also CA 9-12R; CABS 1; CANR 32, 65; CDALB 1941-1968; DLB 2, 102, 143; DLBD 12; DLBY 87; MTCW 1, 2

Wen I-to 1899-1946 **TCLC 28**

Wentworth, Robert
See Hamilton, Edmond

Werfel, Franz (Viktor) 1890-1945 **TCLC 8**
See also CA 104; 161; DLB 81, 124

Wergeland, Henrik Arnold 1808-1845 **NCLC 5**

Wersba, Barbara 1932- **CLC 30**
See also AAYA 2, 30; CA 29-32R; CANR 16, 38; CLR 3; DLB 52; JRDA; MAICYA; SAAS 2; SATA 1, 58; SATA-Essay 103

Wertmueller, Lina 1928- **CLC 16**
See also CA 97-100; CANR 39, 78

Wescott, Glenway 1901-1987 **CLC 13**
See also CA 13-16R; 121; CANR 23, 70; DLB 4, 9, 102

Wesker, Arnold 1932- **CLC 3, 5, 42; DAB; DAM DRAM**
See also CA 1-4R; CAAS 7; CANR 1, 33; CDBLB 1960 to Present; DLB 13; MTCW 1

Wesley, Richard (Errol) 1945- **CLC 7**
See also BW 1; CA 57-60; CANR 27; DLB 38

Wessel, Johan Herman 1742-1785 **LC 7**

West, Anthony (Panther) 1914-1987 **CLC 50**
See also CA 45-48; 124; CANR 3, 19; DLB 15

West, C. P.
See Wodehouse, P(elham) G(renville)

West, (Mary) Jessamyn 1902-1984 **CLC 7, 17**
See also CA 9-12R; 112; CANR 27; DLB 6; DLBY 84; MTCW 1, 2; SATA-Obit 37

West, Morris L(anglo) 1916- **CLC 6, 33**
See also CA 5-8R; CANR 24, 49, 64; MTCW 1, 2

West, Nathanael 1903-1940 **TCLC 1, 14, 44; SSC 16**
See also CA 104; 125; CDALB 1929-1941; DLB 4, 9, 28; MTCW 1, 2

West, Owen
See Koontz, Dean R(ay)

West, Paul 1930- **CLC 7, 14, 96**
See also CA 13-16R; CAAS 7; CANR 22, 53, 76; DLB 14; INT CANR-22; MTCW 2

West, Rebecca 1892-1983 **CLC 7, 9, 31, 50**
See also CA 5-8R; 109; CANR 19; DLB 36; DLBY 83; MTCW 1, 2

Westall, Robert (Atkinson) 1929-1993 **CLC 17**
See also AAYA 12; CA 69-72; 141; CANR 18, 68; CLR 13; JRDA; MAICYA; SAAS 2; SATA 23, 69; SATA-Obit 75

Westermarck, Edward 1862-1939 **TCLC 87**

Westlake, Donald E(dwin) 1933- **CLC 7, 33; DAM POP**
See also CA 17-20R; CAAS 13; CANR 16, 44, 65; INT CANR-16; MTCW 2

Westmacott, Mary
See Christie, Agatha (Mary Clarissa)

Weston, Allen
See Norton, Andre

Wetcheek, J. L.
See Feuchtwanger, Lion

Wetering, Janwillem van de
See van de Wetering, Janwillem

Wetherald, Agnes Ethelwyn 1857-1940 **TCLC 81**
See also DLB 99

Wetherell, Elizabeth
See Warner, Susan (Bogert)

Whale, James 1889-1957 **TCLC 63**

Whalen, Philip 1923- **CLC 6, 29**
See also CA 9-12R; CANR 5, 39; DLB 16

Wharton, Edith (Newbold Jones) 1862-1937 **TCLC 3, 9, 27, 53; DA; DAB; DAC; DAM MST, NOV; SSC 6; WLC**
See also AAYA 25; CA 104; 132; CDALB 1865-1917; DLB 4, 9, 12, 78, 189; DLBD 13; MTCW 1, 2

Wharton, James
See Mencken, H(enry) L(ouis)

Wharton, William (a pseudonym) CLC 18, 37
See also CA 93-96; DLBY 80; INT 93-96

Wheatley (Peters), Phillis 1754(?)-1784 **LC 3, 50; BLC 3; DA; DAC; DAM MST, MULT, POET; PC 3; WLC**
See also CDALB 1640-1865; DLB 31, 50

Wheelock, John Hall 1886-1978 **CLC 14**
<See also CA 13-16R; 77-80; CANR 14; DLB 45

White, E(lwyn) B(rooks) 1899-1985 **CLC 10, 34, 39; DAM POP**
See also AITN 2; CA 13-16R; 116; CANR 16, 37; CDALBS; CLR 1, 21; DLB 11, 22; MAICYA; MTCW 1, 2; SATA 2, 29, 100; SATA-Obit 44

White, Edmund (Valentine III) 1940- **CLC 27, 110; DAM POP**
See also AAYA 7; CA 45-48; CANR 3, 19, 36, 62; MTCW 1, 2

White, Patrick (Victor Martindale) 1912-1990 **CLC 3, 4, 5, 7, 9, 18, 65, 69**
See also CA 81-84; 132; CANR 43; MTCW 1

White, Phyllis Dorothy James 1920-
See James, P. D.
See also CA 21-24R; CANR 17, 43, 65; DAM POP; MTCW 1, 2

White, T(erence) H(anbury) 1906-1964 **CLC 30**
See also AAYA 22; CA 73-76; CANR 37; DLB 160; JRDA; MAICYA; SATA 12

<inde**White, Terence de Vere** 1912-1994 **CLC 49**
See also CA 49-52; 145; CANR 3

White, Walter
See White, Walter F(rancis)
See also BLC; DAM MULT

White, Walter F(rancis) 1893-1955 **TCLC 15**
See also White, Walter
See also BW 1; CA 115; 124; DLB 51

White, William Hale 1831-1913
See Rutherford, Mark
See also CA 121

Whitehead, E(dward) A(nthony) 1933- **CLC 5**
See also CA 65-68; CANR 58

Whitemore, Hugh (John) 1936- **CLC 37**
See also CA 132; CANR 77; INT 132

Whitman, Sarah Helen (Power) 1803-1878 **NCLC 19**
See also DLB 1

Whitman, Walt(er) 1819-1892 **NCLC 4, 31; DA; DAB; DAC; DAM MST, POET; PC 3; WLC**
See also CDALB 1640-1865; DLB 3, 64; SATA 20

Whitney, Phyllis A(yame) 1903- **CLC 42; DAM POP**
See also AITN 2; BEST 90:3; CA 1-4R; CANR 3, 25, 38, 60; CLR 58; JRDA; MAICYA; MTCW 2; SATA 1, 30

Whittemore, (Edward) Reed (Jr.) 1919- **CLC 4**
See also CA 9-12R; CAAS 8; CANR 4; DLB 5

Whittier, John Greenleaf 1807-1892 **NCLC 8, 59**
See also DLB 1

Whittlebot, Hernia
See Coward, Noel (Peirce)

Wicker, Thomas Grey 1926-
See Wicker, Tom
See also CA 65-68; CANR 21, 46

Wicker, Tom **CLC 7**
See also Wicker, Thomas Grey

Wideman, John Edgar 1941- **CLC 5, 34, 36, 67; BLC 3; DAM MULT**
See also BW 2, 3; CA 85-88; CANR 14, 42, 67; DLB 33, 143; MTCW 2

Wiebe, Rudy (Henry) 1934- **CLC 6, 11, 14; DAC; DAM MST**
See also CA 37-40R; CANR 42, 67; DLB 60

Wieland, Christoph Martin 1733-1813 **NCLC 17**
See also DLB 97

Wiene, Robert 1881-1938 **TCLC 56**

Wieners, John 1934- **CLC 7**
See also CA 13-16R; DLB 16

Wiesel, Elie(zer) 1928- **CLC 3, 5, 11, 37; DA; DAB; DAC; DAM MST, NOV; WLCS**
See also AAYA 7; AITN 1; CA 5-8R; CAAS 4; CANR 8, 40, 65; CDALBS; DLB 83; DLBY 87; INT CANR-8; MTCW 1, 2; SATA 56

Wiggins, Marianne 1947- **CLC 57**
<indexSee also BEST 89:3; CA 130; CANR 60

Wight, James Alfred 1916-1995
See Herriot, James
See also CA 77-80; SATA 55; SATA-Brief 44

Wilbur, Richard (Purdy) 1921- **CLC 3, 6, 9, 14, 53, 110; DA; DAB; DAC; DAM MST, POET**
See also CA 1-4R; CABS 2; CANR 2, 29, 76; CDALBS; DLB 5, 169; INT CANR-29; MTCW 1, 2; SATA 9

Wild, Peter 1940- **CLC 14**
See also CA 37-40R; DLB 5

Wilde, Oscar 1854(?)-1900 **TCLC 1, 8, 23, 41; DA; DAB; DAC; DAM DRAM, MST, NOV; SSC 11; WLC**
See also CA 104; 119; CDBLB 1890-1914; DLB 10, 19, 34, 57, 141, 156, 190; SATA 24

Wilder, Billy **CLC 20**
See also Wilder, Samuel
See also DLB 26

Wilder, Samuel 1906-
See Wilder, Billy
See also CA 89-92

Wilder, Thornton (Niven) 1897-1975 **CLC 1, 5, 6, 10, 15, 35, 82; DA; DAB; DAC; DAM DRAM, MST, NOV; DC 1; WLC**
See also AAYA 29; AITN 2; CA 13-16R; 61-64; CANR 40; CDALBS; DLB 4, 7, 9; DLBY 97; MTCW 1, 2

Wilding, Michael 1942- **CLC 73**
See also CA 104; CANR 24, 49

Wiley, Richard 1944- **CLC 44**
See also CA 121; 129; CANR 71

Wilhelm, Kate **CLC 7**
See also Wilhelm, Katie Gertrude
See also AAYA 20; CAAS 5; DLB 8; INT CANR-17

Wilhelm, Katie Gertrude 1928-
See Wilhelm, Kate
See also CA 37-40R; CANR 17, 36, 60; MTCW

1
Wilkins, Mary
See Freeman, Mary Eleanor Wilkins
Willard, Nancy 1936- **CLC 7, 37**
See also CA 89-92; CANR 10, 39, 68; CLR 5; DLB 5, 52; MAICYA; MTCW 1; SATA 37, 71; SATA-Brief 30
William of Ockham 1285-1347 **CMLC 32**
Williams, Ben Ames 1889-1953 **TCLC 89**
See also DLB 102
Williams, C(harles) K(enneth) 1936-**CLC 33, 56; DAM POET**
See also CA 37-40R; CAAS 26; CANR 57; DLB 5
Williams, Charles
See Collier, James L(incoln)
Williams, Charles (Walter Stansby) 1886-1945 **TCLC 1, 11**
See also CA 104; 163; DLB 100, 153
Williams, (George) Emlyn 1905-1987**CLC 15; DAM DRAM**
See also CA 104; 123; CANR 36; DLB 10, 77; MTCW 1
<i**Williams, Hank** 1923-1953 **TCLC 81**
Williams, Hugo 1942- **CLC 42**
See also CA 17-20R; CANR 45; DLB 40
Williams, J. Walker
See Wodehouse, P(elham) G(renville)
Williams, John A(lfred) 1925-**CLC 5, 13; BLC 3; DAM MULT**
See also BW 2, 3; CA 53-56; CAAS 3; CANR 6, 26, 51; DLB 2, 33; INT CANR-6
Williams, Jonathan (Chamberlain) 1929- **CLC 13**
See also CA 9-12R; CAAS 12; CANR 8; DLB 5
Williams, Joy 1944- **CLC 31**
See also CA 41-44R; CANR 22, 48
Williams, Norman 1952- **CLC 39**
See also CA 118
Williams, Sherley Anne 1944-**CLC 89; BLC 3; DAM MULT, POET**
See also BW 2, 3; CA 73-76; CANR 25; DLB 41; INT CANR-25; SATA 78
Williams, Shirley
See Williams, Sherley Anne
Williams, Tennessee 1911-1983**CLC 1, 2, 5, 7, 8, 11, 15, 19, 30, 39, 45, 71, 111; DA; DAB; DAC; DAM DRAM, MST; DC 4; WLC**
See also AITN 1, 2; CA 5-8R; 108; CABS 3; CANR 31; CDALB 1941-1968; DLB 7; DLBD 4; DLBY 83; MTCW 1, 2
Williams, Thomas (Alonzo) 1926-1990**CLC 14**
See also CA 1-4R; 132; CANR 2
Williams, William C.
See Williams, William Carlos
Williams, William Carlos 1883-1963**CLC 1, 2, 5, 9, 13, 22, 42, 67; DA; DAB; DAC; DAM MST, POET; PC 7; SSC 31**
See also CA 89-92; CANR 34; CDALB 1917-1929; DLB 4, 16, 54, 86; MTCW 1, 2
Williamson, David (Keith) 1942- **CLC 56**
See also CA 103; CANR 41
Williamson, Ellen Douglas 1905-1984
See Douglas, Ellen
See also CA 17-20R; 114; CANR 39
Williamson, Jack **CLC 29**
See also Williamson, John Stewart
See also CAAS 8; DLB 8
Williamson, John Stewart 1908-
See Williamson, Jack
See also CA 17-20R; CANR 23, 70
Willie, Frederick
See Lovecraft, H(oward) P(hillips)
Willingham, Calder (Baynard, Jr.) 1922-1995 **CLC 5, 51**
See also CA 5-8R; 147; CANR 3; DLB 2, 44; MTCW 1
Willis, Charles
See Clarke, Arthur C(harles)
Willis, Fingal O'Flahertie
See Wilde, Oscar
Willy
See Colette, (Sidonie-Gabrielle)
Willy, Colette
See Colette, (Sidonie-Gabrielle)
Wilson, A(ndrew) N(orman) 1950- **CLC 33**
See also CA 112; 122; DLB 14, 155, 194; MTCW 2
Wilson, Angus (Frank Johnstone) 1913-1991 **CLC 2, 3, 5, 25, 34; SSC 21**
See also CA 5-8R; 134; CANR 21; DLB 15, 139, 155; MTCW 1, 2
Wilson, August 1945- **CLC 39, 50, 63, 118; BLC 3; DA; DAB; DAC; DAM DRAM, MST, MULT; DC 2; WLCS**
See also AAYA 16; BW 2, 3; CA 115; 122; CANR 42, 54, 76; MTCW 1, 2
Wilson, Brian 1942- **CLC 12**
Wilson, Colin 1931- **CLC 3, 14**
See also CA 1-4R; CAAS 5; CANR 1, 22, 33, 77; DLB 14, 194; MTCW 1
<indexbo**Wilson, Dirk**
See Pohl, Frederik
Wilson, Edmund 1895-1972**CLC 1, 2, 3, 8, 24**
See also CA 1-4R; 37-40R; CANR 1, 46; DLB 63; MTCW 1, 2
Wilson, Ethel Davis (Bryant) 1888(?)-1980 **CLC 13; DAC; DAM POET**
See also CA 102; DLB 68; MTCW 1
Wilson, John 1785-1854 **NCLC 5**
Wilson, John (Anthony) Burgess 1917-1993
See Burgess, Anthony
See also CA 1-4R; 143; CANR 2, 46; DAC; DAM NOV; MTCW 1, 2
Wilson, Lanford 1937- **CLC 7, 14, 36; DAM DRAM**
See also CA 17-20R; CABS 3; CANR 45; DLB 7
Wilson, Robert M. 1944- **CLC 7, 9**
See also CA 49-52; CANR 2, 41; MTCW 1
Wilson, Robert McLiam 1964- **CLC 59**
See also CA 132
Wilson, Sloan 1920- **CLC 32**
See also CA 1-4R; CANR 1, 44
Wilson, Snoo 1948- **CLC 33**
See also CA 69-72
Wilson, William S(mith) 1932- **CLC 49**
See also CA 81-84
Wilson, (Thomas) Woodrow 1856-1924**TCLC 79**
See also CA 166; DLB 47
Winchilsea, Anne (Kingsmill) Finch Counte 1661-1720
See Finch, Anne
Windham, Basil
See Wodehouse, P(elham) G(renville)
Wingrove, David (John) 1954- **CLC 68**
See also CA 133
Wintergreen, Jane
See Duncan, Sara Jeannette
Winters, Janet Lewis **CLC 41**
See also Lewis, Janet
See also DLBY 87
Winters, (Arthur) Yvor 1900-1968 **CLC 4, 8, 32**
See also CA 11-12; 25-28R; CAP 1; DLB 48; MTCW 1
Winterson, Jeanette 1959-**CLC 64; DAM POP**
See also CA 136; CANR 58; DLB 207; MTCW 2
Winthrop, John 1588-1649 **LC 31**
See also DLB 24, 30
Wirth, Louis 1897-1952 **TCLC 92**
Wiseman, Frederick 1930- **CLC 20**
See also CA 159
Wister, Owen 1860-1938 **TCLC 21**
See also CA 108; 162; DLB 9, 78, 186; SATA 62
Witkacy
See Witkiewicz, Stanislaw Ignacy
Witkiewicz, Stanislaw Ignacy 1885-1939 **TCLC 8**
See also CA 105; 162
Wittgenstein, Ludwig (Josef Johann) 1889-1951 **TCLC 59**
See also CA 113; 164; MTCW 2
Wittig, Monique 1935(?)- **CLC 22**
See also CA 116; 135; DLB 83
Wittlin, Jozef 1896-1976 **CLC 25**
See also CA 49-52; 65-68; CANR 3
Wodehouse, P(elham) G(renville) 1881-1975 **CLC 1, 2, 5, 10, 22; DAB; DAC; DAM NOV; SSC 2**
See also AITN 2; CA 45-48; 57-60; CANR 3, 33; CDBLB 1914-1945; DLB 34, 162; MTCW 1, 2; SATA 22
Woiwode, L.
See Woiwode, Larry (Alfred)
Woiwode, Larry (Alfred) 1941- **CLC 6, 10**
See also CA 73-76; CANR 16; DLB 6; INT CANR-16
Wojciechowska, Maia (Teresa) 1927-**CLC 26**
See also AAYA 8; CA 9-12R; CANR 4, 41; CLR 1; JRDA; MAICYA; SAAS 1; SATA 1, 28, 83; SATA-Essay 104
Wolf, Christa 1929- **CLC 14, 29, 58**
See also CA 85-88; CANR 45; DLB 75; MTCW 1
Wolfe, Gene (Rodman) 1931- **CLC 25; DAM POP**
See also CA 57-60; CAAS 9; CANR 6, 32, 60; DLB 8; MTCW 2
Wolfe, George C. 1954- **CLC 49; BLCS**
See also CA 149
Wolfe, Thomas (Clayton) 1900-1938**TCLC 4, 13, 29, 61; DA; DAB; DAC; DAM MST, NOV; SSC 33; WLC**
See also CA 104; 132; CDALB 1929-1941; DLB 9, 102; DLBD 2, 16; DLBY 85, 97; MTCW 1, 2
Wolfe, Thomas Kennerly, Jr. 1930-
See Wolfe, Tom
See also CA 13-16R; CANR 9, 33, 70; DAM POP; DLB 185; INT CANR-9; MTCW 1, 2
Wolfe, Tom **CLC 1, 2, 9, 15, 35, 51**
See also Wolfe, Thomas Kennerly, Jr.
See also AAYA 8; AITN 2; BEST 89:1; DLB 152
Wolff, Geoffrey (Ansell) 1937- **CLC 41**
See also CA 29-32R; CANR 29, 43, 78
Wolff, Sonia
See Levitin, Sonia (Wolff)
Wolff, Tobias (Jonathan Ansell) 1945- **CLC 39, 64**
See also AAYA 16; BEST 90:2; CA 114; 117; CAAS 22; CANR 54, 76; DLB 130; INT 117; MTCW 2
Wolfram von Eschenbach c. 1170-c. 1220

Literary Criticism Series Cumulative Topic Index

This index lists all topic entries in Gale's *Classical and Medieval Literature Criticism, Contemporary Literary Criticism, Literature Criticism from 1400 to 1800, Nineteenth-Century Literature Criticism,* and *Twentieth-Century Literary Criticism.*

NCLC Cumulative Nationality Index

CZECH
Macha, Karel Hynek **46**

DANISH
Andersen, Hans Christian **7**
Grundtvig, Nicolai Frederik Severin **1**
Jacobsen, Jens Peter **34**
Kierkegaard, Soren **34**

ENGLISH
Ainsworth, William Harrison **13**
Arnold, Matthew **6, 29**
Arnold, Thomas **18**
Austen, Jane **1, 13, 19, 33, 51**
Bagehot, Walter **10**
Barbauld, Anna Laetitia **50**
Barham, Richard Harris **77**
Barnes, William **75**
Beardsley, Aubrey **6**
Beckford, William **16**
Beddoes, Thomas Lovell **3**
Bentham, Jeremy **38**
Blake, William **13, 37, 57**
Borrow, George (Henry) **9**
Bronte, Anne **4, 71**
Bronte, Charlotte **3, 8, 33, 58**
Bronte, (Jane) Emily **16, 35**
Browning, Elizabeth Barrett **1, 16, 66**
Browning, Robert **19**
Bulwer-Lytton, Edward (George Earle Lytton) **1, 45**
Burney, Fanny **12, 54**
Burton, Richard F. **42**
Byron, George Gordon (Noel) **2, 12**
Carlyle, Thomas **22**
Carroll, Lewis **2, 53**
Clare, John **9**
Clough, Arthur Hugh **27**
Cobbett, William **49**
Coleridge, Samuel Taylor **9, 54**
Coleridge, Sara **31**
Collins, (William) Wilkie **1, 18**
Cowper, William **8**
Crabbe, George **26**
Craik, Dinah Maria (Mulock) **38**
Darwin, Charles **57**
De Quincey, Thomas **4**
Dickens, Charles (John Huffam) **3, 8, 18, 26, 37, 50**
Disraeli, Benjamin **2, 39**
Dobell, Sydney Thompson **43**
Eden, Emily **10**
Eliot, George **4, 13, 23, 41, 49**
FitzGerald, Edward **9**
Forster, John **11**
Froude, James Anthony **43**
Gaskell, Elizabeth Cleghorn **5, 70**
Gilpin, William **30**
Godwin, William **14**
Gore, Catherine **65**
Hazlitt, William **29**
Hemans, Felicia **29, 71**
Hood, Thomas **16**
Hopkins, Gerard Manley **17**
Hunt (James Henry) Leigh **1, 70**
Huxley, T. H. **67**
Inchbald, Elizabeth **62**
Ingelow, Jean **39**
Jefferies, (John) Richard **47**
Jerrold, Douglas William **2**
Jewsbury, Geraldine (Endsor) **22**
Keats, John **8, 73**
Kemble, Fanny **18**
Kingsley, Charles **35**
Lamb, Charles **10**
Lamb, Lady Caroline **38**
Landon, Letitia Elizabeth **15**
Landor, Walter Savage **14**
Lear, Edward **3**
Lennox, Charlotte Ramsay **23**
Lewes, George Henry **25**
Lewis, Matthew Gregory **11, 62**
Linton, Eliza Lynn **41**
Macaulay, Thomas Babington **42**
Marryat, Frederick **3**
Martineau, Harriet **26**
Mayhew, Henry **31**
Mill, John Stuart **11, 58**
Mitford, Mary Russell **4**
Montagu, Elizabeth **7**
More, Hannah **27**
Morris, William **4**
Newman, John Henry **38**
Norton, Caroline **47**
Oliphant, Laurence **47**
Opie, Amelia **65**
Paine, Thomas **62**
Pater, Walter (Horatio) **7**
Patmore, Coventry **9**
Peacock, Thomas Love **22**
Piozzi, Hester **57**
Planche, James Robinson **42**
Polidori, John Willam **51**
Radcliffe, Ann (Ward) **6, 55**
Reade, Charles **2, 74**
Reeve, Clara **19**
Robertson, Thomas William **35**
Robinson, Henry Crabb **15**
Rogers, Samuel **69**
Rossetti, Christina (Georgina) **2, 50, 66**
Rossetti, Dante Gabriel **4, 77**
Sala, George Augustus **46**
Shelley, Mary Wollstonecraft (Godwin) **14**
Shelley, Percy Bysshe **18**
Smith, Charlotte (Turner) **23**
Southey, Robert **8**
Surtees, Robert Smith **14**
Symonds, John Addington **34**
Tennyson, Alfred **30, 65**
Thackeray, William Makepeace **5, 14, 22, 43**
Trollope, Anthony **6, 33**
Trollope, Frances **30**
Wordsworth, Dorothy **25**
Wordsworth, William **12, 38**

FILIPINO
Rizal, Jose **27**

FINNISH
Kivi, Aleksis **30**
Lonnrot, Elias **53**
Runeberg, Johan **41**

FRENCH
Augier, Emile **31**
Balzac, Honore de **5, 35, 53**
Banville, Theodore (Faullain) de **9**
Barbey d'Aurevilly, Jules Amedee **1**
Baudelaire, Charles **6, 29, 55**
Becque, Henri **3**
Beranger, Pierre Jean de **34**
Bertrand, Aloysius **31**
Borel, Petrus **41**
Chateaubriand, Francois Rene de **3**
Comte, Auguste **54**
Constant (de Rebecque), (Henri) Benjamin **6**
Corbiere, Tristan **43**
Daudet, (Louis Marie) Alphonse **1**
Dumas, Alexandre **9**
Dumas, Alexandre (Davy de la Pailleterie) **11, 71**
Feuillet, Octave **45**
Flaubert, Gustave **2, 10, 19, 62, 66**
Fourier, Charles **51**
Fromentin, Eugene (Samuel Auguste) **10**
Gaboriau, Emile **14**
Gautier, Theophile **1**
Gobineau, Joseph Arthur (Comte) de **17**
Goncourt, Edmond (Louis Antoine Huot) de **7**
Goncourt, Jules (Alfred Huot) de **7**
Hugo, Victor (Marie) **3, 10, 21**
Joubert, Joseph **9**
Kock, Charles Paul de **16**
Laclos, Pierre Ambroise Francois Choderlos de **4**
Laforgue, Jules **5, 53**
Lamartine, Alphonse (Marie Louis Prat) de **11**
Lautreamont, Comte de **12**
Leconte de Lisle, Charles-Marie-Rene **29**
Maistre, Joseph de **37**
Mallarme, Stephane **4, 41**
Maupassant, (Henri Rene Albert) Guy de **1, 42**
Merimee, Prosper **6, 65**
Michelet, Jules **31**
Musset, (Louis Charles) Alfred de **7**
Nerval, Gerard de **1, 67**
Nodier, (Jean) Charles (Emmanuel) **19**
Pixerecourt, Guilbert de **39**
Renan, Joseph Ernest **26**
Rimbaud, (Jean Nicolas) Arthur **4, 35**
Sade, Donatien Alphonse Francois **3**
Sainte-Beuve, Charles Augustin **5**
Sand, George **2, 42, 57**
Scribe, (Augustin) Eugene **16**
Senancour, Etienne Pivert de **16**
Stael-Holstein, Anne Louise Germaine Necker **3**
Stendhal **23, 46**
Sue, Eugene **1**
Taine, Hippolyte Adolphe **15**
Tocqueville, Alexis (Charles Henri Maurice Clerel) **7, 63**
Valles, Jules **71**
Verlaine, Paul (Marie) **2, 51**
Vigny, Alfred (Victor) de **7**
Villiers de l'Isle Adam, Jean Marie Mathias Philippe Auguste **3**

GERMAN
Arnim, Achim von (Ludwig Joachim von Arnim) **5**
Arnim, Bettina von **38**
Bonaventura **35**
Buchner, (Karl) Georg **26**
Claudius, Matthias **75**
Droste-Hulshoff, Annette Freiin von **3**
Eichendorff, Joseph Freiherr von **8**
Fichte, Johann Gottlieb **62**
Fontane, Theodor **26**
Fouque, Friedrich (Heinrich Karl) de la Motte **2**
Goethe, Johann Wolfgang von **4, 22, 34**
Grabbe, Christian Dietrich **2**
Grimm, Jacob Ludwig Karl **3, 77**
Grimm, Wilhelm Karl **3, 77**
Hebbel, Friedrich **43**
Hegel, Georg Wilhelm Friedrich **46**
Heine, Heinrich **4, 54**
Hoffmann, E(rnst) T(heodor) A(madeus) **2**
Holderlin, (Johann Christian) Friedrich **16**
Immerman, Karl (Lebrecht) **4, 49**
Jean Paul **7**
Kant, Immanuel **27, 67**

NCLC-77 Title Index

Title Index

ISBN 0-7876-1671-0

90000

9 780787 616717